POSTCARDS

IRELAND

for a stroll on the Dingle Peninsula. See chapter 9. © Nik Wheeler Photography.

Hailed as one of Ireland's natural wonders, the 760-foot Cliffs of Moher stretch for more than 5 miles along County Clare's Atlantic coast and offer panoramic views, especially from the 19th-century O'Brien's Tower at the northern end. See chapter 10. © Tom Till Photography.

Drombeg stone circle in County Cork has been dated to sometime between 153 B.C. *A.D. 127. It is one of the finest examples of a stone circle in Ireland, but little is kn* *bout its ritual purpose. See chapter 8. © Greg Gawlowski/Photo 20-20.*

When should I travel to get the best airfare?
Where do I go for answers to my travel questions?
What's the best and easiest way to plan and book my trip?

frommers.travelocity.com

Frommer's, the travel guide leader, has teamed up with **Travelocity.com**, the leader in online travel, to bring you an in-depth, easy-to-use resource designed to help you plan and book your trip online.

At **frommers.travelocity.com**, you'll find free online updates about your destination from the experts at Frommer's plus the outstanding travel planning and purchasing features of Travelocity.com. Travelocity.com provides reservations capabilities for 95 percent of all airline seats sold, more than 47,000 hotels, and over 50 car rental companies. In addition, Travelocity.com offers more than 2,000 exciting vacation and cruise packages. Travelocity.com puts you in complete control of your travel planning with these and other great features:

> **Expert travel guidance from Frommer's** - over 150 writers reporting from around the world!
>
> **Best Fare Finder** - an interactive calendar tells you when to travel to get the best airfare
>
> **Fare Watcher** - we'll track airfare changes to your favorite destinations
>
> **Dream Maps** - a mapping feature that suggests travel opportunities based on your budget
>
> **Shop Safe Guarantee** - 24 hours a day / 7 days a week live customer service, and more!

Whether traveling on a tight budget, looking for a quick weekend getaway, or planning the trip of a lifetime, Frommer's guides and Travelocity.com will make your travel dreams a reality. You've bought the book, now book the trip!

Other Great Guides for Your Trip:

Frommer's Portable Dublin

Frommer's Ireland from $50 a Day

Frommer's Ireland's Best-Loved Driving Tours

Here's what the critics say about Frommer's:

"Amazingly easy to use. Very portable, very complete."
—*Booklist*

♦

"The only mainstream guide to list specific prices. The Walter Cronkite of guidebooks—with all that implies."
—*Travel & Leisure*

♦

"Complete, concise, and filled with useful information."
—*New York Daily News*

♦

"Hotel information is close to encyclopedic."
—*Des Moines Sunday Register*

♦

"Detailed, accurate and easy-to-read information for all price ranges."
—*Glamour Magazine*

Ireland

2001

by Robert Emmet Meagher

with Mark Meagher
& Elizabeth Neave

IDG Books Worldwide, Inc.
An International Data Group Company
Foster City, CA • Chicago, IL • Indianapolis, IN • New York, NY

ABOUT THE AUTHORS

Robert Emmet Meagher, a dual citizen of Ireland and the United States, is Professor of Humanities at Hampshire College in Amherst, Massachusetts. The author of more than a dozen books, plays, and translations, he has lived and worked in Ireland, twice holding visiting professorships at Trinity College Dublin.

Mark Meagher, an avid naturalist as well as a competitive cyclist and kayaker, has lived and studied in Ireland and is currently completing graduate studies in architecture at Harvard University.

Elizabeth Neave, after studying and teaching in Dublin, pursued her graduate studies in education at Smith College and currently teaches elementary school in the Connecticut public schools.

IDG BOOKS WORLDWIDE, INC.

An International Data Group Company
909 Third Ave.
New York, NY 10022

Find us online at **www.frommers.com**

ISBN 0-7645-6135-9
ISSN 1080-9104

Editor: Lisa Renaud/Dog-Eared Pages
Production Editor: Tammy Ahrens
Photo Editor: Richard Fox
Design by Michele Laseau
Cartographer: Roberta Stockwell
Production by IDG Books Indianapolis Production Department

SPECIAL SALES

For general information on IDG Books Worldwide's books in the U.S., please call our Consumer Customer Service department at 1-800-762-2974. For reseller information, including discounts, bulk sales, customized editions, and premium sales, please call our Reseller Customer Service department at 1-800-434-3422.

Manufactured in the United States of America

5 4 3 2 1

Contents

List of Maps

This book is dedicated to Ireland's peacemakers, north and south.

ACKNOWLEDGMENTS

A book, like a barn, must be raised by many hands. In this case, the hands are too many to count or to name. Fortunately, the hospitality of the Irish is a legend that need not be retold in detail here. We have been welcomed, aided, and abetted every step of the way, and our deep thanks go out to everyone who helped us. A few special friends of this book, however, deserve special notice. So, to a book full of lists, we will add one more: the Irish Tourist Board and the Northern Ireland Tourist Board; Debbie, postmaster of the East Hartland Post Office; Laura Duffy of Dublin Tourism and John Brady of Clonmel Tourism; Pam, Howard, and Nancy of Trombley Sydney Travel; and, as ever, Matt Hannafin, our genial and generous bodhisattva. Finally, special gratitude is due Lisa Renaud, who has skillfully piloted this work into print with remarkable grace and good humor.

AN INVITATION TO THE READER

There are so many more of you than there are of us that this book can only be informed and enhanced when you share your experiences with us. We welcome your letters. Let us know when we've led you straight and when astray—and let us in on your secret finds, provided that you're willing to have them shared with other readers in future editions. Anticipating your letters, thanks in advance for your contributions. Please send correspondence to:

Frommer's Ireland 2001
IDG Books Worldwide, Inc.
909 Third Ave.
New York, NY 10022

AN ADDITIONAL NOTE

Please be advised that travel information is subject to change at any time—and this is especially true of prices. We therefore suggest that you write or call ahead for confirmation when making your travel plans. The authors, editors, and publisher cannot be held responsible for the experiences of readers while traveling. Your safety is important to us, however, so we encourage you to stay alert and be aware of your surroundings. Keep a close eye on cameras, purses, and wallets, all favorite targets of thieves and pickpockets.

WHAT THE SYMBOLS MEAN

✪ **Frommer's Favorites**

Our favorite places and experiences—outstanding for quality, value, or both.

The following abbreviations are used for credit cards:

AE	American Express	DISC	Discover
CB	Carte Blanche	MC	MasterCard
DC	Diners Club	V	Visa

FIND FROMMER'S ONLINE

www.frommers.com offers up-to-the-minute listings on almost 200 cities around the globe—including the latest bargains and candid, personal articles updated daily by Arthur Frommer himself. No other Web site offers such comprehensive and timely coverage of the world of travel.

The Best of Ireland

"The modern American tourist," wrote historian Daniel J. Boorstin, "has come to expect both more strangeness and more familiarity than the world naturally offers." That said, Ireland continues to offer more than its share of both.

When I first traveled to Ireland more than 25 years ago, I was not expecting a foreign country. Born and raised in an Irish-American enclave in Chicago, I was taught by Irish nuns, and baptized and chastised by Irish priests. I went off to Ireland anticipating pretty much what I had known as a child, only with more green. I imagined that I had already had "the Irish experience" in Chicago, over the counter, as it were, and that now, in the motherland, I would have the same experience in prescription strength. I was wrong about that.

At first glance, Ireland presents a familiar face to American visitors. The language is the same, only "hillier," the faces are familiar, the food recognizable, the stout legendary. Many visitors, notably Irish Americans, experience their arrival as a kind of homecoming. It takes a while for this experience to wear off. When it does, the other face of Ireland shows itself, and this is when the country becomes truly exciting.

Ireland is a place of profound contradiction and complexity. For one thing, it is at the same time both ancient and adolescent. It's as young as it is old.

Ireland's age is obvious to anyone with a car. Within a half day's drive of downtown Dublin lie Neolithic tombs, Bronze Age forts, early Christian monastic sites, Viking walls, Norman castles, Georgian estates—enough antiquity to make your head spin, all in plain sight, and as commonplace as Wal-Mart in the United States. The Irish past doesn't exist just in books; it's in the backyard. A shovel, digging for peat or potatoes, may well strike a 5,000-year-old grave. Thousands of unexcavated ancient sites litter the countryside. Any visitor to Ireland who ventures beyond its shops and pubs will soon be struck by how the country reeks of age.

What is less obvious is how new Ireland is, as a nation. The Republic of Ireland, with its own constitution and currency, is barely 50 years old. Mary McAleese, the current president of Ireland, is only the eighth person to hold that office. In political age, Ireland, for all its antiquity, is a mere adolescent. Like any adolescent, it's doing many things for the first time, and at least a few of its contradictions make sense when you keep that fact in mind. Compounding Ireland's youth

Ireland

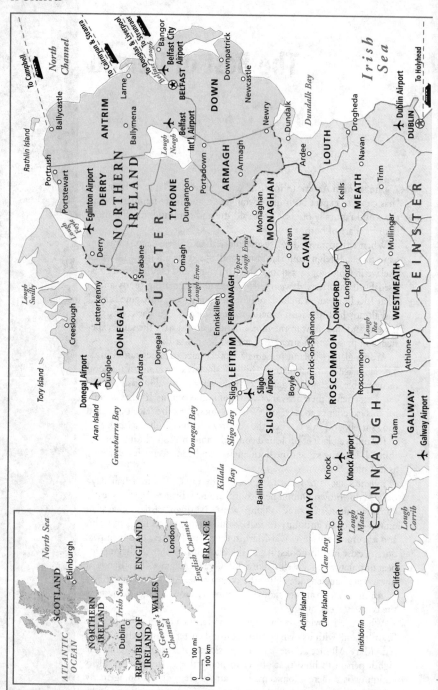

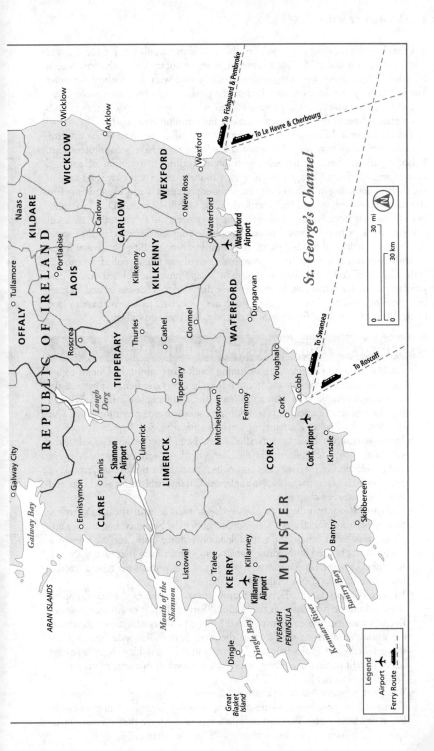

as a nation is the youth of its people. Roughly half of the population is under 25, and nearly a quarter is under 15. This means that, in many homes, those who once fought for Irish independence are living under the same roof with those who have never known anything else. In these same homes, the gap between generations is often seismic. It is indeed curious that in a country where what happened 1,000 years ago reads like yesterday's news, it is common to feel old and outnumbered at 30.

The quality that defines a people derives not from what they wear or eat or drive, but from what they have been through, and the Irish people have been through a lot. Ireland's past has been remarkably tumultuous, inspiring a tradition of courage, humor, and creativity. Change is nothing new to the island, yet the rate and scale of the changes occurring in Ireland today are without precedent. Recalling again my first trip to Ireland—with my family, to settle there for a while—I was in Dun Laoghaire, just off the boat from Wales. I had been trying to place a call to the real-estate agent who had the keys to our home, but one pay phone after another had failed to work. As I held a fourth dead handset to my ear, I heard someone calling out to me. It was an Irish motorist, a stranger to me, who had noticed my plight, pulled over to the curb, and rolled down his window. "You're in Ireland now," he pointed out, "where you'll sooner see the statues movin' than a phone that works." That was Ireland 25 years ago, more boastful of its magic than its machines. In Ireland today, you have to look harder for the magic than for a phone that works, but both are still there.

1 The Best Picture-Postcard Small Towns

- **Dalkey** (County Dublin): This charming south-coast suburb of Dublin enjoys both easy access to the city and freedom from its snarls and frenzy. It has a castle, an island, a mountaintop folly, and a few parks, all in ample miniature. With all the fine and simple restaurants and pubs and shops anyone needs for a brief visit or a long stay, Dalkey is a tempting town to settle into. See chapter 4.
- **Inistioge** (County Kilkenny): Nestled in the Nore River Valley, cupped in the soft palm of rounded hills, this idyllic riverfront village with two spacious greens and a collection of pleasant cafes and pubs is among the most photographed of Irish towns. It also attracts hosts of anglers, as fish invariably show good taste and love this place. See chapter 6.
- **Kilkenny** (County Kilkenny): Slightly larger than a small town but terribly picture-postcard nonetheless, Kilkenny may offer the best surviving Irish example of a medieval town. Its walls, the splendidly restored castle, and the renowned design center housed in the castle stables draw visitors from Ireland and abroad. Kilkenny, however, is no museum. Many regard it as perhaps the most attractive large town in Ireland. See chapter 6.
- **Kinsale** (County Cork): Kinsale's narrow streets all lead to the sea, dropping steeply from the hills that rim the beautiful harbor. This is undoubtedly one of Ireland's most picturesque towns, and the myriad visitors who crowd the streets every summer attest to the fact that the secret is out. The walk from Kinsale through Scilly to Charles Fort and Frower Point is breathtaking. Kinsale has the added benefit of possessing the greatest concentration of fine restaurants outside Dublin. See chapter 8.
- **Westport** (County Mayo): It's never a surprise in Ireland when someone says Westport is his favorite town—it's small and bursting. Someday it might explode into a city, but for now Westport remains a hyperactive town that somehow manages to be as friendly and welcoming as a village. See chapter 10.

2 The Best Natural Wonders

- **The Slieve Bloom Mountains** (County Laois): Slieve Bloom, Ireland's largest and most unspoiled blanket bog, has been described as a "scenic bulge" rising gently above the midland's peat fields. Its beauty—gentle slopes, glens, rivers, waterfalls, and boglands—is subtle rather than dramatic, but it is comparatively untouched. You can have it more or less to yourself, apart from its deer, foxes, and badgers, and an occasional marten or otter. See chapter 5.

- **MacGillycuddy's Reeks** (County Kerry): One of several mountain ranges on the Iveragh Peninsula, MacGillycuddy's Reeks boasts the highest mountain in Ireland, Carrantuohill (3,404 ft.). Whether gazed at from afar or explored up close on foot, the Reeks are among Ireland's greatest spectacles. See chapter 9.

- **The Burren** (County Clare): The Burren—from the Irish *Boireann,* meaning "a rocky place"—is one of the strangest landscapes you're ever likely to see: a vast limestone grassland, spread with a quilt of wildflowers from as far afield as the Mediterranean, the Alps, and the Arctic. Its inhabitants include the pine marten and nearly every species of butterfly found in Ireland. See chapter 10.

- **Cliffs of Moher** (County Clare): Rising from Hag's Head to the south, these magnificent sea cliffs reach their full height of 760 feet just north of O'Brien's Tower. The views of the open sea, of the distant Aran Islands, and of the Twelve Bens of Connemara (see below) are spectacular. A walk south along the cliff edge at sunset makes a perfect end to any day. See chapter 10.

- **Croagh Patrick** (County Mayo): Rising steeply 2,500 feet above the coast, Croagh Patrick is Ireland's holiest mountain, to which the saint is said to have retreated in penance. The place is biblically imposing. Traditionally, barefoot pilgrims climb it on the last Sunday of July, but in recent years hundreds of Nike-shod tourists have been making the ascent daily. The view from above can be breathtaking or nonexistent—the summit is often wrapped in clouds, adding to its mystery. See chapter 10.

- **The Twelve Bens** (County Galway): Amid Connemara's central mountains, bogs, and lakes rises a rugged range known as the Twelve Bens, crowning a landscape that is among the most spectacular in Ireland. Some of the peaks are bare and rocky, others clothed in peat. The loftiest, Benbaun, in the Connemara National Park, reaches a height of 2,395 feet. See chapter 12.

- **Slieve League** (County Donegal): The Slieve League peninsula stretches for 30 miles (48km) into the Atlantic and is 12 miles (19km) across at its widest point. Its wonderfully pigmented bluffs are the highest sea cliffs in Europe, and can be gazed at from Carrigan Head or walked along, if you dare. From below or from above, Slieve League serves up some of the most dazzling sights in Ireland. See chapter 13.

- **The Giant's Causeway** (County Antrim): In case you lose count, roughly 40,000 tightly packed, mostly hexagonal basalt columns form the giant Finn McCool's path from the Antrim headland into the sea toward the Scottish island of Staffa. This volcanic wonder, formed 60 million years ago, can be marveled at from a distance or negotiated cautiously on foot. See chapter 15.

3 The Best Castles

- **Trim Castle** (County Meath): Trim, also called King John's Castle, newly restored as a "preserved ruin," is the most massive and important Anglo-Norman castle in Ireland. It proved all but impregnable for over 4 centuries (late 12th

. . . we are a very perverse, complex people. It's what makes us lovable. We're banking heavily that God has a sense of humor.

—Jim Murray, *Los Angeles Times,* 1976

mid-17th), suffering only one siege during that entire period. In fact, until it collapsed sometime in the 17th century, it never underwent any significant alteration. For anyone with imagination, Trim is a virtual gateway into medieval Ireland. See chapter 5.

- **Cahir Castle** (County Tipperary): One of the largest of Ireland's medieval fortresses, this castle is in an extraordinary state of preservation. Tours explain some fascinating features of the military architecture, and then you're free to roam through a maze of tiny chambers, spiral staircases, and vertiginous battlements. See chapter 6.
- **Kilkenny Castle** (County Kilkenny): Although parts of the castle date from the 13th century, the existing structure has the feel of an 18th-century palace. There have been many modifications since medieval times, including the addition of beautiful landscaping around the castle. See chapter 6.
- **Blarney Castle** (County Cork): Despite the mobs of tourists who besiege the castle daily, this majestic tower house is worth a visit. While you're there, check out the Badger Cave and dungeons at the tower's base, as well as the serpentine paths that wind through the castle gardens, in a picturesque rocky glen. Need we mention the Stone? You sidle in under the upper wall with your head hanging over a 10-story drop. You kiss it. It's a thing people do. See chapter 7.
- **Charles Fort** (County Cork): On a promontory in stunning Kinsale Harbor, the fort's massive walls enclose a complex array of buildings in varying states of repair. At the entrance you're handed a map and left on your own to explore, discover, and almost certainly get lost in the maze of courtyards, passages, walls, and barracks. See chapter 8.
- **Bunratty Castle** (County Clare): The castle has been restored and filled with a curious assortment of medieval furnishings, giving the modern-day visitor a glimpse into the life of its past inhabitants. This is the first stop for many arrivals from Shannon, so expect crowds. See chapter 10.
- **Carrickfergus Castle** (County Antrim): This fortress on the bank of Belfast Lough is the best-preserved Norman castle in Ireland. It consists of an imposing tower house and a high wall punctuated by corner towers. See chapter 15.
- **Dunluce Castle** (County Antrim): The castle ruins surmount a razor-sharp promontory jutting into the sea. This was no doubt a highly defensible setting, and the castle wasn't abandoned until a large section collapsed and fell into the breakers one day in 1639. See chapter 15.

4 The Best of Ancient Ireland

- **Newgrange** (County Meath): Poised atop a low hill north of the River Boyne, Newgrange is the centerpiece of a dramatic megalithic cemetery dating from more than 5,000 years ago. The massive, heart-shaped mound and passage tomb were constructed, it seems, as a communal vault to house cremated remains. The tomb's passage is so perfectly aligned with the equinoctial sunrise that the central chamber, deep within the mound, is marvelously illuminated at the winter solstice. See chapter 5.

- **Hill of Tara** (County Meath): Of ritual significance from the Stone Age to the Christian period, Tara has seen it all and kept it all a secret. This was the traditional center and seat of Ireland's high kings, who could look out from here and survey their realm. Although the Tara hill is only 512 feet above sea level, from here you can see each of Ireland's four Celtic provinces on a clear day. The site is mostly unexcavated, and tells its story in whispers. It's a place to be walked slowly, with an imagination steeped in Ireland's past. See chapter 5.
- **Loughcrew** (County Meath): At this little-known site, not far from Newgrange, a series of cruciform passage tombs crown two hills. On the east hill, a guide unlocks the door to one of the domed tombs, answering your questions with a personal touch not possible at the larger, more popular sites. More rewarding, however, is a hike up the west hill to a second, more solitary series of tombs where the connections to be made between ruin and imaginative reconstruction are your own. See chapter 5.
- **Lough Gur** (County Limerick): This lakefront site will convince you that the Neolithic farmers of Ireland had an estimable sense of real estate. Inhabited for more than 4,000 years, the ancient farming settlement offers a number of prehistoric remains. The most impressive of these is the largest surviving stone circle in Ireland, made up of 113 stones. See chapter 10.
- **Dún Aengus** (County Galway): No one knows who built this massive stone fort, or when. The eminent archaeologist George Petrie called Dún Aengus "the most magnificent barbaric monument in Europe." Facing the sea, where its three stone rings meet steep 200-foot cliffs, Dún Aengus stands guard today as ever over the southern coast of the island of Inishmore, the largest of the Arans. See chapter 11.
- **Carrowmore and Carrowkeel** (County Sligo): These two megalithic cities of the dead (Europe's largest) on the Coolera Peninsula may have once contained more than 200 passage tombs. The two together—one in the valley and the other atop a nearby mountain—convey an unequaled sense of the scale and wonder of the ancient megalithic peoples' reverence for the dead. Carrowmore is well presented and interpreted, while Carrowkeel is left to itself and to those who seek it out. See chapter 13.
- **Navan Fort** (County Antrim): There is now little to see of this place's past greatness, though it was once the ritual and royal seat of Ulster. Thankfully, the interpretive center here is nothing short of remarkable, and it offers a great introduction to the myth and archaeology of the fort, known in Irish as Emain Macha. See chapter 15.

5 Remnants of the Golden Age: The Best Early Christian Ruins

- **Glendalough** (County Wicklow): Nestled in "the glen of the two lakes," this important monastic settlement was founded in the 6th century by St. Kevin, who was looking for tranquil seclusion. Its setting is disarmingly scenic, exactly the opposite of the harsh environment you'd expect ascetic medieval monks to have sought out. Although quite remote, Glendalough suffered numerous assaults from the Vikings and the English, and eventually dwindled into insignificance. Today its picturesque ruins collude with the countryside to create one of the loveliest spots in Ireland. See chapter 5.
- **Jerpoint Abbey** (County Kilkenny): Jerpoint is perhaps the finest representative of the many Cistercian abbeys whose ruins dot the Irish landscape. What draw visitors are the splendid cloister, the most richly carved in Ireland, and

impressive tomb sculptures. The abbey's tower is the tallest of its kind in Ireland. See chapter 6.

- **The Rock of Cashel** (County Tipperary): In name and appearance, "the Rock" suggests a citadel, a place more familiar with power than with prayer. In fact, Cashel (or *Caiseal*) means "fortress," and so it was. The rock is a huge outcropping—or rather *up*cropping—of limestone topped with some of the most spectacular ruins in Ireland, including what was formerly the country's finest Romanesque chapel. This was the seat of clerics and kings, a center to rival Tara. Now, however, the two sites vie only for tourists. See chapter 6.
- **Skellig Michael** (County Kerry): Eight miles (13km) offshore of the Iveragh Peninsula, rising sharply 714 feet out of the Atlantic, is a stunning crag of rock dedicated to the Archangel Michael. In flight from the world, early Irish monks in pursuit of "white martyrdom" chose this spot to build their austere hermitage. Today, the journey to Skellig, across choppy seas, and the arduous climb to its summit are challenging and unforgettable. See chapter 9.
- **Inishmurray** (County Sligo): This uninhabited island nearly 4 miles (6.5km) off the Sligo coast is home to a most striking monastic complex, surrounded by what appear to be the walls of an even more ancient stone fort. Despite its remoteness, the Vikings sought out this outpost of peace-seeking monks for destruction in 802. Today its circular ruins and the surrounding sea present a stunning sight, well worth the effort required to reach the shores. See chapter 13.
- **Clonmacnois** (County Offaly): This was once one of Ireland's most important religious, artistic, and literary centers, a place of pilgrimage and high culture. Founded in the mid–5th century at the axis of the River Shannon and the medieval east-west thoroughfare known as the Eiscir Riada, Clonmacnois thrived for centuries until its prime riverfront location nearly proved its undoing. In the 830s, Vikings sailed up the Shannon from Limerick and brought havoc that returned many times in the ensuing centuries. Even in ruins, Clonmacnois remains a place of peculiar beauty and serenity. See chapter 14.

6 The Best Literary Spots

- **Glasnevin Cemetery** (County Dublin): Besides being the setting for part of the sixth episode of *Ulysses,* this is the resting place of James Joyce's parents and several other members of his family. The English-born poet Gerard Manley Hopkins is buried here, in the Jesuit plot. Maud Gonne, the Irish nationalist and longtime Dublin resident who is said to have inspired Yeats's play *Cathleen ní Houlihan,* is buried in the Republican plot. See chapter 4.
- **Newman House** (County Dublin): Cardinal John Henry Newman was the first rector of the Catholic University in Dublin, which was housed in two buildings on St. Stephen's Green in the center of the city's south side. He worked in that capacity from 1852 until his retirement in 1859. The Catholic University later became University College Dublin, where Gerard Manley Hopkins was sent in 1884, as a professor of Greek; after 5 years of teaching here, Hopkins died at the age of 44. James Joyce studied here from 1899 to 1902. See chapter 4.
- **North Dublin:** The streets north of the Liffey are home to many of the characters in James Joyce's stories and novels; Joyce lived in this part of Dublin and had a special affinity for it. Much has changed since his time, and Bloom's house at 7 Eccles St. has been replaced by a new wing of the Mater Private Hospital. Still, many mementos of the city as it was in 1904 survive. Tours of the area begin at the James Joyce Centre. See chapter 4.

- **St. Patrick's Cathedral** (County Dublin): Jonathan Swift was born in Dublin in 1667, and entered Trinity College in his 15th year. He later became dean of St. Patrick's Cathedral, and is buried alongside Hester Johnson (Stella) in the cathedral's south aisle. See chapter 4.
- **The Aran Islands:** John Millington Synge set his play *Riders to the Sea* on Inishmaan, and wrote an account of life on the islands, titled simply *The Aran Islands.* Liam O'Flaherty, known for his novel *Famine,* is from the island of Inishmore. See chapters 11 and 12.
- **County Sligo:** It seems at times that every hill, house, and lake in the county is signposted in recognition of some relation to W. B. Yeats. The poet's writing was informed by the landscape, mythology, and people of this region. Many of Sligo's natural and historic monuments—including Lough Gill, Glencar Lake, Ben Bulben Mountain, and Maeve's tomb atop Knocknarea Mountain—appear in Yeats's poetry. There are also several museums housing first editions, photographs, and other memorabilia, and Yeats's grave is in Drumcliff. See chapter 13.

7 The Best Gardens

- **Powerscourt Gardens** (County Wicklow): One of the most grandiose of Irish gardens, set amid the natural splendor of the northern Wicklow Hills. Only 12 miles (19km) from Dublin, the gardens and nearby waterfall make a great day's outing, and a welcome respite from the noise and congestion of the city. See chapter 5.
- **Japanese Gardens** (County Kildare): On the grounds of the National Stud, this is considered the only authentic Japanese garden in Ireland, and one of the finest in Europe. A Japanese specialist planned the structure and symbolism, and most of the plants and even the stones were imported from Japan. See chapter 5.
- **Creagh Gardens** (County Cork): Meandering paths lead the visitor past a sequence of exquisite vistas, with many hidden corners to explore. The garden is on a beautiful estuary. See chapter 8.
- **Ilnacullin** (County Cork): A ferry conveys visitors from a lovely, rhododendron-rimmed bay in the town of Glengarriff to Garinish Island, the unlikely site of a fine Italianate garden. The formal garden, with the Casita at its center, is linked to a "wild garden" that showcases a collection of rhododendrons, azaleas, and rare trees. See chapter 8.
- **Glenveagh National Park** (County Donegal): The gardens and castle are located in a barren, beautiful valley high in the hills of Donegal, along the banks of Lough Veagh. The park contains a statuary garden, a walled garden, and a rhododendron-lined path that leads to a stunning vista overlooking castle and lake. See chapter 13.
- **Mount Stewart Gardens** (County Down): Built upon an elaborate plan, Mount Stewart contains several small gardens of distinctive character. The Ards Peninsula provides a climate conducive to cultivating many subtropical species. The statuary, topiary, and planting designs reflect a touch of whimsy. See chapter 15.

8 The Best Attractions for the Whole Family

- **The Ark: A Cultural Centre for Children** (Dublin): A unique chance for kids to have hands-on exposure to art, music, and theater in workshop sessions with artists. There are also excellent theater productions for families. See chapter 4.

- **Dublin's Viking Adventure** (Dublin): This is a fun learning experience. Kids travel back in time to be part of Viking life with "real Vikings" working and interacting in a model Norse town. It's on the site where the Vikings made their home in Dublin. See chapter 4.
- **Dublin Zoo in the Phoenix Park** (Dublin): Kids love this 30-acre zoo, with its array of creatures, animal-petting corner, and train ride. The surrounding park has room to run, picnic, and explore for hours (or days!). See chapter 4.
- **Irish National Heritage Park** (County Wexford): Nearly 9,000 years of Irish history come alive here in ways that will fascinate visitors of all ages. The whole family will be captivated by the story of ancient Ireland, from its first inhabitants to its Norman conquerors. See chapter 6.
- **Muckross House, Gardens, and Traditional Farms** (Killarney, County Kerry): This stunning Victorian mansion with its exquisite gardens is also home to skilled artisans at work. Nearby are a series of reconstructed traditional farms, with animals and docents, providing a gateway to rural Ireland as it was for centuries. See chapter 9.
- **Bunratty Castle and Folk Park** (County Clare): Kids are enthralled by this great restored medieval castle and re-created 19th-century village. It's complete with a school and loaded with active craftspeople. See chapter 10.
- **Marble Arch Caves** (Marlbank, County Fermanagh): Adventurous families are guided by boat through well-lit underground waterways to explore caves and view amazing stone formations. See chapter 15.

9 Greens Amid the Green: The Best Golf

- **Portmarnock Golf Club** (County Dublin): These links are on a peninsula 10 miles (16km) north of Dublin, where the rapidly changing winds add to the challenge. Founded in 1894, Portmarnock is thought by some to offer Ireland's most difficult golf. See chapter 4.
- **Old Head Golf Links** (County Cork): You would have to hallucinate to imagine a more spectacular setting than this. The youngest of Ireland's world-class golf courses, opened in 1997, is already on its way to becoming a legend. See chapter 8.
- **Ballybunion Golf Club** (County Kerry): This seaside club offers two 18-hole courses; the Old Course is often ranked among the world's finest. See chapter 9.
- **Waterville Golf Links** (County Kerry): This course, on a treeless plain overlooking the Atlantic breakers, is one of Ireland's most stunningly scenic golf venues. See chapter 9.
- **County Sligo Golf Club** (County Sligo): Also known as "Rosses Point," the championship course lies between the sea and a ridge of majestically imposing hills. See chapter 13.
- **Royal County Down** (County Down): One of the treasures of Northern Ireland. *Golf Magazine* referred to this club as one of the world's best little-known courses in 1993. See chapter 15.

10 The Best Active Vacations

- **Sailing Ireland's West Coast:** Spectacular coastal scenery, interesting harbor towns, and an abundance of islands make the West Coast a delight for cruising sailors. Yacht charter is available in Kilrush, County Clare. See chapter 3.

- **Horseback Riding in the Galty Mountains:** The gentle contours of Tipperary's Galty Mountains offer the perfect scenic backdrop for trail riding. You'll be provided with all you need for a horse-riding holiday at Bansha House, a commodious B&B with access to an excellent nearby equestrian program. See chapter 6.
- **Sea Kayaking in West Cork:** The many bays, headlands, and islands of this wild, rocky coast offer innumerable opportunities for exploration by kayak. A great base is Maria's Schoolhouse, where you'll find comfortable and friendly accommodations and an outstanding sea-kayaking program run by Jim Kennedy. See chapter 8.
- **Bicycling in the Southwest:** The peninsulas and islands of Cork and Kerry are perfect for cycling, with light traffic and an abundance of beautiful places to visit. Roycroft's Stores in Skibbereen, County Cork, rent bikes that are a notch above the usual rental equipment. See chapters 8 and 9.
- **Walking the Donegal Coast:** The cliff-rimmed headlands of Donegal are the most spectacular in Ireland, and the best way to explore them is on foot. Among the finest walks are Slieve League, Glen Head, and Horn Head. See chapter 13.

11 The Best Bird Watching

- **Shannon Callows** (counties Galway, Tipperary, and Offaly): The low-lying meadows along the Shannon and Little Brosna Rivers flood in the winter, creating a massive temporary lake that is the wintering grounds for many species of wildfowl. In the summer, the meadows are home to one of Ireland's few remaining corncrake populations. See chapter 3.
- **Great Saltee Island** (County Wexford): A barren, seemingly lifeless rock during much of the year, this island becomes an avian paradise during the summer, when it fills to overflow capacity with nesting seabirds. See chapter 6.
- **North Slob** (County Wexford): The north side of Wexford Harbor is the site of the Wexford Wildfowl Reserve, home to thousands of geese from October to April. The interpretive center is open year-round and has exhibits about the geese, other avian visitors to the Slob, and nearby areas of ornithological interest. See chapter 6.
- **Cape Clear** (County Cork): A bird observatory and resident warden are on this island at the country's southernmost extremity, where many important discoveries regarding patterns of migration have been made. Boat tours for birders are available from North Harbour. See chapter 8.
- **Loop Head** (County Clare): Remote Loop Head and the nearby Bridges of Ross are known as great sea-watching sites from late summer to early fall. See chapter 10.
- **Strangford Lough** (County Down): The shores of Strangford Lough mark one of the premier bird-watching sites in the world. Although best known for the thousands of pale-bellied brent geese that can be seen there every fall, it offers wonders year-round, and contains the family-friendly wildlife reserve Castle Espie. See chapter 15.

12 The Best Luxury Accommodations

- **The Shelbourne** (Dublin; ☎ **800/225-5843** from the U.S., or 01/676-6471): The Shelbourne, built in 1824 on the north side of Stephen's Green, may be the most distinguished visitor's address in Dublin. In 1921 the Irish Constitution was drafted in room 112, and the guest register is a partial "who's who" of the past century and a half. The Shelbourne epitomizes old Dublin charm and elegance. See chapter 4.

- **Marlfield House** (County Wexford; ☎ 800/323-5463 from the U.S., or 055/21124): This grand 1820 house, amid mature gardens and woods, is one of Ireland's most elegant and comfortable guest mansions. Equally renowned is the cuisine, served in the dining room or the conservatory. Amenities abound. See chapter 6.

- **Waterford Castle** (County Waterford; ☎ 051/878203): An oasis of elegance and tranquillity circled by the River Suir, this island retreat offers both grandeur and informality, along with shoreline walks, a championship golf course, exquisite cuisine, and warm genuine hospitality. See chapter 6.

- **Ashford Castle** (County Mayo; ☎ 800/346-7007 from the U.S., or 092/46003): *Accommodation* is an understatement for the degree of luxury and elegance you'll find at this castle on the north shore of Lough Corrib. Its magnificent grounds comprise 350 acres of park and woods and a golf course. Its two restaurants, the Connaught Room and the George V Room, will likely leave you unmotivated to leave the grounds. See chapter 10.

- **Delphi Lodge** (County Galway; ☎ 095/42222): This was once the country hideaway for the Marquis of Sligo, and now it can be yours, too. Inside, the emphasis is on clean, bright simplicity in perfect taste; the grounds and environs are among the most beautiful in Ireland. Tranquillity, comfort, and fishing are the operative words here. You will want to stay longer than you'd planned—and by renting one of the cottages for a week or more, you can make the indulgence more affordable. See chapter 12.

13 The Best Moderately Priced Accommodations

- **Lorum Old Rectory** (County Carlow; ☎ 0503/75282): Hospitality is one of those intangibles that no one is able to define in advance but which everyone knows when they've found it. A venerably warm and gracious home, exquisite meals, a lovely setting, and a style that puts its guests in rare form and humor make this place among Ireland's best. See chapter 5.

- **Foxmount Farm** (County Waterford; ☎ 051/874308): The Kents are tremendous hosts, and their elegant 18th-century home is a perfect place to base yourself for exploring the southeast. Kids will enjoy the family farm, and there's a great pub just down the lane. See chapter 6.

- **Maria's Schoolhouse** (County Cork; ☎ 028/33002): This 1883 stone schoolhouse has been creatively restored as a hostel and guesthouse. Breakfast and dinner are served in the lofty dining room, and a small kitchen is available for those who prefer to do their own cooking. The place has the added attraction of being the base for an excellent sea-kayaking program. See chapter 8.

- **Bruckless House** (County Donegal; ☎ 073/37071): This mid-18th-century farmhouse, restored with impeccable taste, has many charms, including award-winning gardens and a stable of Connemara ponies. Spacious, welcoming, and comfortable, Bruckless House feels like home (or better) after only a very short time. See chapter 13.

- **Rhu-Gorse** (County Donegal; ☎ 073/21685): The views of Lough Eske from this eminently comfortable modern guesthouse are not to be believed. If you have the makings of a convert to Donegal, it will happen here. See chapter 13.

- **Glencarne House** (County Leitrim; ☎ 079/67013): This attentively restored late-Georgian house on a 100-acre working farm offers a rare quality of hospitality and charm to midland lake region visitors. Lovely, spacious rooms, chiropractic beds, gracious hosts, and award-winning breakfasts are yours for surprisingly affordable rates. Dinners are the high point, so there's no need to venture out once you've settled in. See chapter 14.
- **Ross Castle** (County Cavan; ☎ 049/854-0237): A tower room in a centrally heated haunted castle—with the longest bathtub I've ever seen—awaits you at Ross Castle. It won't take too big a bite out of your wallet, either. This might not be elegance, but it is unquestionably memorable. Warm, comfortable Ross Castle and nearby Ross House are great places to relax beside Lough Sheelin, a noteworthy source of trout and pike. See chapter 14.
- **Slieve Croob Inn** (County Down; ☎ 028/4377-1412): Whether you want to drop anchor and set up a home away from home in a self-catering cottage or just spend a night in a magically stunning landscape, it doesn't get much better than this perfectly tasteful hideaway in the magical Mournes. See chapter 15.
- **The Saddlers House and Old Rectory** (County Derry; ☎ 028/7126-9691 for Saddlers House, 028/7126-4223 for Old Rectory): Compared to the Old Rectory, the Saddlers House is modest. Its rooms are clean and spare, decorated with the simplicity that its merchant origins seem to demand. The Rectory rooms are more lavish—high ceilings and plaster roses evoke its elegant Georgian origins. Both houses, run by the inimitable Joan Pyne, are a brief stroll from the center of Derry. See chapter 15.

14 The Best Restaurants

- **Restaurant Patrick Guilbaud** (Dublin; ☎ 01/676-4192): The only thing modest and unassuming about this exquisite Dublin home of French nouvelle cuisine is its location. Head chef Guillaume Le Brun combines the finest Irish ingredients and French artistry to create consistently lauded specialties of the house. They include wild Irish salmon, Connemara lobster, and fillet of lamb. See chapter 4.
- **The Motte** (County Kilkenny; ☎ 056/58655): Slow delectation is the requirement at the Motte. Everything demands it—from the dimly glowing dining room to the thoughtful staff and the exquisitely prepared food. Chef Alan Walton's concoctions of cream and fresh herbs and rich dark chocolate desserts defy speed, making a delicious, lingering evening the only real possibility. See chapter 6.
- **Ballymaloe House** (County Cork; ☎ 800/323-5463 from the U.S., or 021/465-2531): Ballymaloe, which includes a school, a restaurant, and gardens, has become synonymous with Irish cooking raised to the highest level. Committed to the adage that well begun is half done, Ballymaloe focuses on the finest and freshest local ingredients, requiring only art and not alchemy to produce arguably the finest Irish fare on the island. See chapter 8.
- **Blair's Cove House** (County Cork; ☎ 027/61127): It may be true that you can't eat the scenery, but the scenery can surely whet the appetite, as it does here. Blair's Cove House is one of the most idyllic and romantic spots in Ireland to enjoy an unforgettable meal. You can also spend a week, if you can't pull yourselves away. This is one of the finest restaurants on the isle, in a part of Ireland to which you're all too likely to become attached. See chapter 8.
- **Lettercollum House** (County Cork; ☎ 023/46251): The emphasis here is on fresh, local, organic ingredients; a walled garden provides the vegetables, and pigs

are raised on the premises. With these fine materials, chef Con McLoughlin concocts dishes of pure delight, simple yet surprising. There is always a vegetarian entree. See chapter 8.

- **Moran's Oyster Cottage** (County Galway; ☎ 091/796113): A short drive from Galway center, this seafood mecca is worth a drive from Dublin. For six generations, the Morans have focused on what they know and do best—seafood and nothing but, all day every day. You may not find better oysters and wild salmon anywhere, and surely not at this price. See chapter 11.

- **Cromleach Lodge** (County Sligo; ☎ 071/65155): In this lovely country house with panoramic views of Lough Arrow and environs, Christy and Moira Tighe have created a culinary destination with few peers. The menu, Irish in focus, changes daily and never fails to delight. The eight-course gourmet menu is the ultimate indulgence. See chapter 13.

- **The Corncrake** (County Donegal; ☎ 077/74534): Such a judicious blend of fresh ingredients and culinary imagination is a rare treat. The nettle soup, roast lamb, and desserts of Noreen Lynch and Brid McCartney warrant a detour to the town of Carndonagh, where the living room of a small row house has been transformed into an extraordinary restaurant. See chapter 13.

15 The Best Pubs

- **The Abbey Tavern** (County Dublin): A short distance from Dublin center, the Abbey Tavern is the perfect place to recover and refuel after exploring Howth Head, Ireland's Eye, and the attractive fishing and yachting village of Howth on the northern tip of Dublin Bay. The Abbey is known far and wide for its ballads as well as its brew. See chapter 4.

- **The Brazen Head** (County Dublin): Nearly qualifying as one of Ireland's ancient sites, the Brazen Head, commissioned by Charles II, is more than 300 years old, and its stout is as fresh as it comes. Among its illustrious alumni are Wolfe Tone, Daniel O'Connell, and Robert Emmet, who planned the Dublin rising of 1803 under the Head's low timbers. In fact, he was hanged not far from here when everything went wrong. See chapter 4.

- **An Bodhran** (County Cork): A hangout for University College Cork students serious about their traditional music and stout, An Bodhran has a lot of old-style character, which recent renovations have only enhanced. See chapter 7.

- **The Blue Haven** (County Cork): Everything the Blue Haven offers is first-rate: food, drink, lodging, and a cozy bar with an open fire. This particular haven is also in the center of one of Ireland's most appealing seaside towns. You'll soon measure everyone else's traditional Irish lamb stew by the one you found here. See chapter 8.

- **Gus O'Connor's** (County Clare): Doolin, a dot of a town on the Clare Coast, is a hot spot for traditional Irish music, and Gus O'Connor's has been at the center of the action for more than 150 years. Great music and distinguished seafood make this otherwise-ordinary spot worth a major detour. See chapter 10.

- **Moran's Oyster Cottage** (County Galway): Famed for its seafood, this centuries-old thatched-cottage pub on the weir also draws a perfect pint. This may well be the oyster capital of Ireland. It's 12 miles (19km) out of Galway and well worth the drive—or the walk, for that matter. See chapter 11.

- **Smugglers Creek** (County Donegal): This place would be worth a stop if only for its spectacular cliff-top views of Donegal Bay. Stone walls, beamed ceilings, open fires, excellent fare, and the brew that's true are among the charms proprietor Conor Britton has on tap. See chapter 13.
- **The Crown Liquor Saloon** (County Antrim): This National Trust pub, across from the Grand Opera House in Belfast, is a Victorian gem. Your mouth will drop open at its antique publican splendor even before you lift your first pint. See chapter 15.

2 Planning Your Trip: The Basics

It may be well to begin with a caution, offered in this case by John Steinbeck in *Travels with Charley:* "A journey is like a marriage. The certain way to be wrong is to think you control it." Fair enough. A trip too tightly packed and planned, with no room for the spontaneous and unexpected, is often not worth the effort. And yet, when you are so poorly prepared that surprise runs riot, you might wish you'd stayed home. In travel, as in Buddhism, the middle ground is recommended. Lay down your plans like pavement, and then romp on the grass at will. Our aim in this chapter is to help you prepare the way.

1 The Lay of the Land

The island of Ireland lies well over 2,000 miles (3,228km) due east of Newfoundland and, on a clear day, can be glimpsed from the northern Welsh coast. The capital city of the Republic shares nearly the same latitude as Edmonton, Alberta, and Bremen, Germany, but distinguishes itself by its palm trees and bougainvillea. The Gulf Stream is responsible for Ireland's mild disposition, originating in the Caribbean and sending its warm currents and tropical sea life northward to Ireland's grateful shores. On occasion, as part of the bargain, it sends a hurricane, as in 1987, when tropical storm Charlie tore into the east coast of Ireland and brought Caribbean havoc to the resort town of Bray. We were living at the time in Killiney, on the coast just north of Bray. Our house leaked like a ship going down, and with each blast, we expected to see the prow of a ship come smashing through our bedroom window. The Irish Sea has a notorious temper— something worth remembering when you're planning to cross it—but needs inspiration from the tropics to throw a truly dangerous fit.

With a landmass of approximately 32,600 square miles, Ireland is roughly the same size as the state of Maine, though shaped somewhat differently. In rounded figures, it is at most 300 miles (484km) north to south, and 170 miles (274km) east to west. No point in Ireland is farther than 70 miles (113km) from one of its encircling waters: the Atlantic Ocean, the Irish Sea, and the St. George and North channels. It may seem strange, but in the past, the Irish rarely saw their offshore waters as a resource. Traditionally, the Irish disliked fish and avoided learning to swim. The sea was to be feared. It was perilous to cross, and, worse, its waves brought invaders, one after another.

The country's topography is unusual. Instead of its shores sloping to the sea and its interior rising to mountain peaks, the reverse is the case. Shaped like a saucer, Ireland's twisted, 2,000-mile (3,228km) coastline is, with a few notable exceptions, a breachless bulwark of mountains, cliffs, and highlands. Its interior is generally flat, a broad limestone plain made up of fertile farmland and raised bogs, graced with the occasional lake and wetland. Some would say that Ireland has only hills—its highest peak, Carantuohill in County Kerry, reaches to only about 3,400 feet. All would agree that Ireland has few crags. Most of its heights, whether mountains or hills, were rounded off and smoothed into graceful slopes tens of thousands of years ago by receding glaciers. Ireland's longest and greatest river is the Shannon, flowing 230 miles (371km) south and west across the midlands from its source in the Cuileagh Mountains of County Cavan to its estuary in County Limerick. The island's largest lake, Lough Neagh, occupies 153 square miles of counties Antrim and Armagh in the north.

One of Europe's least densely populated countries (third behind Finland and Sweden), Ireland is commonly described as unspoiled, even "untouched." Not so. Lovely as it is, the Irish landscape is no wilderness, and is certainly not untouched. For example, only about 1% of the hardwood forests have survived 6,000 years of deforestation. In fact, Ireland, once a rich source of timber for the British fleet, has imported virtually all of its wood for more than 200 years. The recent planting of pine forests around the island is only another, though more positive, instance of human intervention.

On the bright side, the predominance of small-scale mixed agriculture has long contributed to the preservation of an unusually wide range of flora and fauna in the Irish countryside, with the notable and famous exception of snakes and other reptiles. As it happens, Mother Nature, not St. Patrick, deserves credit for Ireland's "snakelessness"—all she gave to the island, herpetologically speaking, is one lonely type of common lizard, featured several years ago on a 32p postage stamp.

In recent years, Ireland has gone increasingly "green" in its policies. It has created a number of national parks for the sake of both enjoying and protecting the island's natural beauty. Four are open to the public: Connemara National Park in County Galway, Glenveagh National Park in County Donegal, Killarney National Park in County Kerry, and Wicklow Mountains National Park in County Wicklow. Others are planned, including Burren National Park in County Clare, which is currently under development.

2 The Regions in Brief

Ireland is a land divided many different ways, all of which are significant in finding your course through its history, along its roads, and amid its people.

The first and most recent division is between **"the South"** (the Republic of Ireland, Éire, or the "Free State") and **"the North"** (Northern Ireland, commonly and confusingly referred to as "Ulster"). The South is a sovereign, independent nation made up of 26 counties, while the North, with 6 counties, remains part of Great Britain. The line partitioning the land and people of Ireland into two political entities was drawn in the Anglo-Irish Treaty of 1921 and remains a matter of dispute. In simplest practical terms, for the tourist, the line between north and south represents a national border.

Still very much alive on the maps and in the minds of the Irish, however, is another, much older, **Gaelic set of divisions** corresponding to the four points of the compass. In this early scheme of things, Ulster is north, Leinster is east,

Munster is south, Connaught is west, and the traditional center of Ireland is the hill of Uisneach in County Westmeath.

Next, there are the **counties,** in terms of which the Irish and their visitors mostly orient themselves. These are the "states" of Ireland, from which individuals and families hail, and in terms of which mail is routed. They are signposts one needs to know. Each of the counties has its boasts and its reputation. One county is frequently the butt of another's jokes, and they all tangle in fierce athletic contests as they pursue annual national titles in Gaelic football and hurling. The island's 32 counties, grouped under the four traditional provinces of Ireland cited above, are listed here:

> **In Ulster** (to the north): Cavan, Donegal, and Monaghan in the Republic; Antrim, Armagh, Derry, Down, Fermanagh, and Tyrone in Northern Ireland.
> **In Munster** (to the south): Clare, Cork, Kerry, Limerick, Tipperary, and Waterford.
> **In Leinster** (to the east): Dublin, Carlow, Kildare, Kilkenny, Laois, Longford, Louth, Meath, Offaly, Westmeath, Wexford, and Wicklow.
> **In Connaught** (to the west): Sligo, Mayo, Galway, Roscommon, and Leitrim.

Lastly, in more immediately practical terms for the tourist, Ireland may be divided into **regions:** the southeast, the southwest, the west, the northwest, the midlands, and Northern Ireland. These, with several specific cities and their environs—Dublin, Cork, and Galway—make up the principal areas of interest for Ireland's visitors and serve to structure the information in this guide.

DUBLIN & ENVIRONS   Dublin is ground zero for the profound, high-speed changes transforming Ireland into a prosperous, venturesome European country. What was old and venerable in the city remains so, though it now shares space with an all-out 20- and 30-something Irish renaissance. There's something here for everyone. Within an hour or slightly more north and south of Dublin—by car or public transportation—lie a handful of engaging coastal towns, the barren beauty of the Dublin Mountains, some of the most important prehistoric and early Christian ruins of Europe, Kildare thoroughbred country, the beaches and lush gardens of County Wicklow, and the new Wicklow Mountains National Park.

THE SOUTHEAST   Boasting the best (warmest and least wet) weather in Ireland, the southeast coast is, on most days, one alternative to a pub for getting out of the rain. Besides its weather, the southeast offers sandy beaches, **Waterford**'s city walls and crystal works, Kilkenny and Cahir castles, the Rock of Cashel, the Irish National Heritage Park at Ferrycarig, and Ireland's largest bird sanctuary, on the Saltee Islands.

CORK & ENVIRONS   Cork, Ireland's second city in size, is Dublin's rival in sport and stout but little else. It does provide a congenial gateway to the south and west of Ireland, which many consider Ireland's Oz, the ultimate destination. Within arm's reach of Cork are the truly impressive Blarney Castle (with its less impressive stone), the culinary and scenic delights of Kinsale, the Drombeg Stone Circle, Sherkin and Clear Islands, and Mizen Head. Also in this region are the spectacular expanses of West Cork, one of my very favorite landscapes.

THE SOUTHWEST   The mountains and seascapes of the southwest, the wettest corner of Ireland, make the same point as Seattle: There are more important things in life than staying dry. The once-remote splendors of County Kerry are no longer a secret, so at least during high season, visitors must be prepared to share the view. Some highlights of this region are the Dingle Peninsula, the Skellig and the Blaskett Islands, Staigue Fort, Tralee and its annual international and folk festivals, and dazzling views of sea, shore, and mountains—a new one, it seems, at every bend in the road. Killarney is a destination not for itself, but for what lies nearby—its famed lakes, its mountain peaks (the tallest in Ireland), and the ever-present sea. The "Ring of Kerry" is less glamorously known as N70 and N71, a 110-mile (178km) circuit of the Iveragh Peninsula. Next to the Book of Kells, it's the most visited attraction in Ireland, which is both a recommendation and a warning. Nearby, Killarney National Park—25,000 acres of mountains, woodlands, waterfalls, and wildlife—provides a carless, dramatic haven from tour buses and from the din of massed camera shutters clicking away.

THE WEST   The west of Ireland, once a land of last resort, today offers a first and hardly disappointing taste of Ireland's beauty and diversity for those who fly into Shannon Airport. County Clare's natural offerings, the 700-foot Cliffs of Moher and the limestone grasslands of the Burren, are unforgettable. Counties Limerick and Clare also contain a number of historic sites, from the Stone Age center at Lough Gur to an array of impressive castles. They include Knappogue, Bunratty, King John's, Ashrod, and (just over the county line in Galway) Dunguaire. Farther to the north of Galway lies County Mayo, whose most charming artificial effort may be the town of Westport on Clew Bay. Nearby, 2,500 feet up stands Croagh Patrick, a place of pilgrimage for centuries. Another, more recent pilgrimage site is the shrine of Knock, with its massive basilica. Also nearby, off the Connemara and southern Mayo coasts, is a string of islands—including Inishbofin, Inishturk, and Clare—which are well worth the crossing. Achill Island, Ireland's largest, is a favored vacation spot and is accessible by car.

GALWAY & ENVIRONS   Galway, on the threshold of Connemara, one of the more desolate habitable landscapes in the world, is like an exile's last fling. That is, it defies what lies just around the corner. It's a prospering port and university city, sought out by foreign tourists and Irish youth. There's nothing sleepy about Galway.

Just beyond the city stretches Connemara, boasting (besides the greatest number of rocks you'll ever see in one place) the Twelve Bens, Kylemore Abbey, a nearly 4,000-acre national park, and its charming "capital," the town of Clifden. Meanwhile, offshore lie the legendary Aran Islands—Inishmore, Inishmaan, and Inisheer—further studies in irresistible desolation.

THE NORTHWEST   One becomes convinced that bleak is beautiful in Ireland, and the northwest surely matches the rest of Ireland in beauty. This is especially true of Donegal, with its 200 miles (323km) of drenched, jagged coastline that, for the cold-blooded, offers some of the finest surfing in the world. Inland, the Deeryveagh Mountains and Glenveagh National Park offer as much wilderness as can be found anywhere in Ireland. County Sligo contains the greatest concentration of megalithic sites in Ireland: the stone circles, passage tombs, dolmens, and cairns of, most notably, Carrowmore, Knocknarea, and Carrowkeel. Also among the county's timeless monuments is the poetry of Yeats, who might be called the poet laureate of Sligo. Nearby Leitrim's unspoiled lakes are a favorite retreat, particularly for people carrying fishing poles.

THE MIDLANDS   The thought of midlands, any midlands, is likely to bring yawns, until you get there. The lush center of Ireland, bisected by the mighty but lazy Shannon, is no exception. This is a land of pastures, rivers, lakes, woods, and gentle mountain slopes, an antidote to the barren beauty of Connemara and a retreat, in high season, from the throngs of tourists who crowd the coasts. The midlands have no cities, and their towns are not their attractions; the shores and waters of the Shannon and Lough Derg and of their many lesser cousins provide much of the lure. Outdoor pursuits—cycling, boating, fishing, trekking, and hunting—are the heart of the matter here. The midlands also offer visits to some remarkable sites, such as Birr Castle and its splendid gardens, and Clonmacnois, now the stunning ruins of a famous Irish monastic center.

NORTHERN IRELAND   Across the border, in a corner of both Ireland and the United Kingdom, Northern Ireland's six counties are well worth exploring. The stunning Antrim coast (particularly between Ballycastle and Cushendum), the 37,000 black basalt columns of the Giant's Causeway, and the luring nine Glens of Antrim are perhaps the greatest draw for sightseers. Written in a minor key is the loveliness of the Fermanagh Lake District to the south, while County Down with its Mourne Mountains marks the sunniest and driest spot in the North. The city walls of Derry, Carrickfergus Castle, Belfast's "Golden Mile," and Navan Fort (or Emain Macha, the royal center of Ulster for 800 years) are only some of the sights, ancient and current, the North has to offer.

3 Visitor Information

To get your planning under way, contact the following offices of the Irish Tourist Board and the Northern Ireland Tourist Board. They are eager to answer your questions, and have bags of genuinely helpful information, mostly free of charge.

After you've perused the brochures, surf the Net to scoop up even more information. See "Planning Your Trip: An Online Directory," on p. 000, for our roundup of the best sites.

IN THE UNITED STATES

- **Irish Tourist Board,** 345 Park Ave., New York, NY 10154 (☎ **800/ 223-6470** from the U.S., or 212/418-0800; fax 212/371-9052).
- **Northern Ireland Tourist Board,** 551 Fifth Ave., Suite 701, New York, NY 10176 (☎ **800/326-0036** from the U.S., or 212/922-0101; fax 212/922-0099).

IN CANADA

- **Irish Tourist Board,** 160 Bloor St. E., Suite 1150, Toronto, ON M4W 1B9 (☎ **416/929-2777;** fax 416/929-6783).
- **Northern Ireland Tourist Board,** 2 Bloor St. W., Suite 1501, Toronto, ON M4W 3E2 (☎ **800/576-8174** or 416/925-6368; fax 416/925-6033).

IN THE UNITED KINGDOM

- **Irish Tourist Board/Bord Fáilte,** 150 New Bond St., London W1Y 0AQ (☎ **020/7493-3201;** fax 020/7493-9065).
- **Northern Ireland Tourist Board,** 11 Berkeley St., London W1X 5AD (☎ **020/7766-9920;** fax 020/7766-9929).

IN AUSTRALIA

- **Irish Tourist Board,** 36 Carrington St., 5th Level, Sydney, NSW 2000 (☎ **02/9299-6177;** fax 02/9299-6323).

IN NEW ZEALAND

- **Irish Tourist Board,** Dingwall Building, 2nd Floor, 87 Queen St., Auckland (☎ **0064-9-379-8720;** fax 0064-9-302-2420).

IN IRELAND

- **Irish Tourist Board/Bord Fáilte,** Baggot Street Bridge, Dublin 2 (☎ **01/602-4000;** fax 01/602-4100; www.ireland.travel.ie).
- **Northern Ireland Tourist Board,** 16 Nassau St., Dublin 2 (☎ **01/679-1977;** fax 01/679-1863).

IN NORTHERN IRELAND

- **Irish Tourist Board,** 53 Castle St., Belfast BT1 1GH (☎ **028/9032-7888;** fax 028/9024-0201).
- **Northern Ireland Tourist Board,** St. Anne's Court, 59 North St., Belfast BT1 1NB (☎ **028/9024-6609;** fax **028/9031-2424;** www.ni-tourism.com).

4 Entry Requirements & Customs

ENTRY REQUIREMENTS

For citizens of the United States, Canada, Australia, and New Zealand entering the Republic of Ireland for a stay of up to 3 months, no visa is necessary, but a valid passport is required.

Citizens of the United Kingdom, when traveling on flights originating in Britain, do not need to show documentation to enter Ireland. Nationals of the United Kingdom and colonies who were not born in Great Britain or Northern Ireland must have a valid passport or national identity document.

For entry into Northern Ireland, the same conditions apply.

CUSTOMS
WHAT YOU CAN BRING TO IRELAND

Since the European Union's (EU) introduction of a single market on January 1, 1993, goods brought into Ireland and Northern Ireland fall into two categories: (1) goods bought duty-paid and value-added-tax–paid (VAT-paid) in other EU countries and (2) goods bought under duty-free and VAT-free allowances at duty-free shops.

Regarding the first category, if the goods are for personal use, no further duty or VAT needs to be paid. The limits for goods in this category are 800 cigarettes, 10 liters of spirits, 45 liters of wine, and 55 liters of beer. This category normally applies to Irish citizens, visitors from Britain, and travelers from other EU countries.

Impressions

There are over 30 words in the Irish language which are equivalent to the Spanish mañana. But somehow none of them conveys the same sense of urge
—Patrick Kavanagh (1

The second category pertains primarily to overseas visitors, such as U.S. and Canadian citizens. The following duty-free and VAT-free items may be brought into the country for personal use: 200 cigarettes, 1 liter of liquor, 2 liters of wine, and other goods (including beer) not exceeding the value of £34 ($56.10) per adult. There are no restrictions on bringing currency into Ireland.

The Irish and Northern Irish Customs systems operate on a Green, Red, and Blue Channel format. The first two are for passengers coming from the United States and non-EU countries. The Green Channel is for anyone not exceeding the duty-free allowances, and the Red Channel is for anyone with extra goods to declare. If you are like most visitors, bringing in only your own clothes and personal effects, choose the Green Channel. The Blue Channel is exclusively for use by passengers entering Ireland from another EU country.

In addition to your luggage, you may bring in sports equipment for your own recreational use or electronic equipment for your own business or professional use while in Ireland. Prohibited goods include firearms, ammunition, and explosives; narcotics; meat, poultry, plants, and their byproducts; and domestic animals from outside the United Kingdom.

WHAT YOU CAN BRING HOME

Returning **U.S. citizens** who have been away for 48 hours or more are allowed to bring back, once every 30 days, $400 worth of merchandise duty-free. You'll be charged a flat rate of 10% duty on the next $1,000 worth of purchases. Be sure to have your receipts handy. On gifts, the duty-free limit is $100. You cannot bring fresh foodstuffs into the United States; tinned foods are allowed. For more information, contact the **U.S. Customs Service,** 1301 Constitution Ave. (P.O. Box 7407), Washington, DC 20044 (☎ **202/ 927-6724**), and request the free pamphlet *Know Before You Go.* It's also available on the Web at www.customs.ustreas.gov/travel/kbygo.htm.

Citizens of the U.K. who are returning from a European Community (EC) country will go through a separate Customs Exit (the Blue Channel) for EC travelers. In essence, there is no limit on what you can bring back from an EC country, as long as the items are for personal use (this includes gifts) and you have already paid the necessary duty and tax. However, Customs law sets out guidance levels. If you bring in more than these levels, you may be asked to prove that the goods are for your own use. Guidance levels on goods bought in the EC for your own use are 800 cigarettes, 200 cigars, 1kg smoking tobacco, 10 liters of spirits, 90 liters of wine (of which not more than 60 liters can be sparkling wine), and 110 liters of beer. For more information, contact **HM Customs & Excise,** Passenger Enquiry Point, 2nd Floor Wayfarer House, Great South West Road, Feltham, Middlesex TW14 8NP (☎ **020/ 8910-3744,** from outside the U.K. 44/181-910-3744; www.hmce.gov.uk).

Canadians should check the booklet *I Declare,* which you can download or order from Revenue Canada (☎ **613/993-0534; www.ccra-adrc.gc.ca**). **Australians** can contact the Australian Customs Service (☎ **1-300/363-263** within Australia, 61-2/6275-6666 from outside Australia; www.customs. gov.au/). **New Zealand** citizens should contact New Zealand Customs (☎ **09/359-6655;** www.customs.govt.nz/).

5 Money

CASH/CURRENCY

The Republic of Ireland, unlike the United Kingdom, lies within the new "Eurozone." As of January 1999, Ireland has adopted the single European currency known as the **"euro."** Although the euro will not appear as hard currency until 2002, it is already the medium of exchange in the Republic. The **punt,** or Irish pound, no longer trades as an independent currency. Its value is permanently fixed at 1.27 euros. Consequently, the fluctuating value of the euro is of concern to you as a visitor, because the punt remains a fixed multiple of that value. In shops and elsewhere, prices already appear in both punts and euros; before we know it, punts will disappear from both signs and pockets. But that day is not yet upon us, so in this guide prices in the Republic are still given in punts. In converting prices in punts to U.S. dollars, we used the rate IR£1 = $1.40.

So far, the United Kingdom has resisted the euro and retained its traditional currency, the **pound sterling,** which continues to trade independently on the world currency market. Northern Ireland, as part of the UK, uses the British pound. The British pound is not legal tender in the Republic, and the Irish pound is not legal tender in the North. In converting prices for this guide, we used the rate £1 = $1.65.

In this volume, the £ sign symbolizes both the Irish and the British pound. The Irish pound is officially designated by the £ sign preceded by IR: IR£. Each unit of paper currency is called a "note." The pound notes, which are printed in denominations of £5, £10, £20, £50, and £100, come in different sizes and colors (the larger the size, the greater the value). There are still some £1 notes in circulation, although these are being phased out in favor of the £1 coin. (The old £1 note is a work of art, so try to find one before they disappear altogether.) Since 1971, the Irish monetary system has been on the decimal system. The pound is divided into 100 pence ("p"); coins come in denominations of £1, 50p, 20p, 10p, 5p, and 1p.

The British currency used in Northern Ireland, identified by engravings of British royalty, follows pretty much the same pattern as that of the Republic, with notes in denominations of £5, £10, £20, £50, and £100. Coins are issued in £1, 50p, 20p, 10p, 5p, 2p, and 1p denominations.

Note: The value of both the Irish and the British pound fluctuates daily, so it is best to begin checking exchange rates well in advance of your visit to gain a sense of their recent range. Deciding when and where to convert and how much is always a gamble. Shop around and avoid exchanging in airports and train stations. Banks are best, and on any given day one bank will offer a better rate than another. Any purchase on a U.S. credit card offers an exchange rate far more favorable than anything an individual is likely to negotiate, so I make a point of converting as little currency as possible and using my credit card to the max. Whatever you do, don't convert small amounts daily. The fees alone will impoverish you. Rates of exchange are available daily in most newspapers, and on the Net (try **www.xe.net/currency/** or **www.x-rates.com**).

CREDIT CARDS

Leading international credit cards such as American Express, Carte Blanche, Diners Club, MasterCard (also known as Access or Eurocard), and Visa (also known as Visa/Barclay) are readily accepted throughout all 32 counties. Most establishments display on their windows or shop fronts the symbols or logos of the credit cards they accept. MasterCard and Visa are the most widely accepted, with American Express an often-distant third. However, note that many banks (including Citibank) are beginning to add a service charge to every transaction made in a foreign currency; check with your card's issuer before you leave to avoid a nasty surprise when you get your bill.

ATMS

Any town large enough to have a bank branch (all but the smallest villages) will have an ATM, most likely linked to a network that includes your home bank. **Cirrus** (☎ **800/424-7787;** www.mastercard.com/atm) and **Plus** (☎ **800/843-7587;** www.visa.com/atms) are the two most popular networks. Use the toll-free numbers to locate ATMs in your destination.

Check with your bank to make sure the PINs on your bank cards and credit cards will work in Ireland.

TRAVELER'S CHECKS

Traveler's checks are something of an anachronism from the days before the ATM (automated teller machine) made cash accessible at any time, but some travelers still prefer the security they provide. You can get them at almost any bank, for a small service charge. American Express traveler's checks are also available over the phone by calling ☎ **800/221-7282** or 800/721-9768, or you can purchase checks online at **www.americanexpress.com**. AmEx gold or platinum cardholders can avoid paying the fee by ordering over the telephone; platinum cardholders can also purchase checks fee-free in person at AmEx Travel Service locations. American Automobile Association members can obtain checks with no fee at most AAA offices.

6 When to Go

CLIMATE

You have to be part psychic to even begin making bets on Irish weather, but don't bet too heavily. The only thing consistent about Irish weather is its changeability; often, the best of times and the worst of times may be only hours, or minutes, apart.

With that disclaimer solidly in place, it's safe to offer a few useful observations. If you think east equals dry and west equals wet, you'll be right except when you're wrong, which will be less than half the time. The driest and sunniest parts of Ireland are the northeast and the southeast—which is not to say that they are reliably either dry or sunny.

In Ireland, the thermometers, gratefully, are a lot less busy than the barometers. Temperatures are mild and fluctuate within what any New Englander would call "spring." The generally coldest months, January and February, bring frosts but seldom snow, and the warmest months, July and August, rarely become hot. Remember, in Ireland any temperature over 70°F is "hot," and 32°F is truly "freezing." Both are unusual. For a complete guide to Irish weather on the Net, including year-round averages and daily updates, consult **www.ireland.com/weather**.

When you're packing, *layers* is the word to remember, at any time of year. And don't forget wool—the Irish attraction to it is no accident. *One other tip:* The Irish are becoming more and more casual in their dress, so you can think Oregon rather than Manhattan.

Impressions

Ireland has one of the world's heaviest rainfalls. If you see an Irishman with a tan, it's rust.

—Dave Allen (b. 1936)

In sum, the weather is neither the reason for coming to Ireland nor a reason for staying away, unless you're looking for the beaches of Mexico or Greece, which remain in Mexico and Greece.

Average Monthly Temperatures in Dublin

	Jan	Feb	Mar	Apr	May	June	July	Aug	Sept	Oct	Nov	Dec
Temp (°F)	36–46	37–48	37–49	38–52	42–57	46–62	51–66	50–65	48–62	44–56	39–49	38–47
Temp (°C)	2–8	3–9	3–9	3–11	6–14	8–17	11–19	10–18	9–17	7–13	4–9	3–8

HIGH & LOW SEASONS

Apart from the mercurial sphere of climatic considerations, there's the matter of cost and crowds. These, too, go up and down in the course of the year.

The precise difference between high and low season, however, varies greatly from one locale to another. At one extreme, there's Dublin, which really doesn't have a low season. It's always crowded, and prices there never truly plummet. At the other extreme, there are places like Inishowen or Cape Clear, where tourism has no appreciable dimmer switch.

A few generalizations, however, might be helpful. Transatlantic airfares often drop significantly in the winter months, which makes a trip to Ireland that much more affordable; and, if your destination is Dublin, the weather is not likely a defining factor, as so much of Dublin's lure dwells indoors. Elsewhere in Ireland, the more off-season you are, the more negotiable will be your lodging. In many cases you can practically ignore any stated prices and simply ask for the innkeeper's best offer. The lowest prices that hotels are willing to tolerate in print are often appreciably higher than the lowest prices they're willing to accept on a given day when rooms might go empty.

It's often the hedge months—April, May, and October—when you can get simultaneously lucky with weather, crowds, and prices, especially in the Southeast, which often enjoys an early spring and yet whose tourist season tends to be highly concentrated.

HOLIDAYS

The Republic observes the following national holidays: New Year's Day (Jan 1), St. Patrick's Day (Mar 17), Easter Monday (lunar/variable), May Day (May 1), first Monday in June and August (Summer Bank Holidays), last Monday in October (Autumn Bank Holiday), Christmas (Dec 25), and St. Stephen's Day (Dec 26). Good Friday (the Fri before Easter) is mostly observed, but not statutory.

In the North, the schedule of holidays is the same as in the Republic, with some exceptions: the North's Bank Holidays fall on the last Monday of May and August; the Battle of the Boyne is celebrated on Orangeman's Day (July 12); and Boxing Day (Dec 26), not St. Stephen's Day, follows Christmas.

Ireland Calendar of Events

This sampling of events is drawn from 2000 schedules. Be sure to consult the calendars available from the tourist boards of Ireland and of Northern Ireland for 2001; they're usually released in January. The most up-to-date listings of events can be found at **www.ireland.travel.ie** and **www.entertainmentireland.ie** (for Ireland), **www.eventguide.ie** and **www.visitdublin.com** (for Dublin).

January

- **Funderland.** Simmonscourt RDS, Dublin 4. The silver celebration of this annual indoor Christmas fair. Contact Don Bird (☎ **01/283-8188;** e-mail: bird@iol.ie). December 26 to January 16.
- **Connemara Four Seasons Walking Festival.** Connemara and the Western Islands. Contact Michael Gibbons, Connemara Walking Centre (☎ **095/21379;** fax 095/21845; www.walkingireland.com). December 27 to January 3.
- **Dublin International Theatre Symposium.** An annual event at the Samuel Beckett Centre, Trinity College, Dublin 2. Contact Mary O'Donovan (☎ **01/280-0544;** fax 01/239-0918; e-mail: panpan@iol.ie). Early January.
- **A.I.G. Europe Championship Hurdle Race.** Leopardstown Racetrack. County Dublin. Call (☎ **01/835-1965**). January 23.

February

- **Rugby International, Ireland v. Italy.** Lansdowne Road, Ballsbridge, County Dublin. Contact Irish Rugby Football Union, 62 Lansdowne Rd., Dublin 4 (☎ **01/668-4601;** fax 01/660-5640). February 4.
- **Hennessey Cognac Gold Cup.** Leopardstown Racetrack. County Dublin. February 6. Call (☎ **01/835-1965**).
- **All Ireland Dancing Championships.** West County Hotel, Ennis, County Clare. Contact Maire Ni Chorbaid (☎ **01/475-2220;** fax 01/475-1053; e-mail:cirg@tinet.ie). February 6 to 12.
- **Newtownabbey Arts Festival 2000.** A millennial celebration of the arts. Ballyearl Arts Centre, Newtownabbey, Co. Antrim. Call (☎ **028/9335-2681**). February 15 to 28.

March

- **Opera Week.** Ulster's Castlward Opera Company presents Rossini's *Barber of Seville.* Grand Opera House, Belfast. Call (☎ **028/9024-1919**). February 28 to March 4.
- **Irish Student National Surfing Championships.** Surf's up, and Ireland's finest are here. Bundoran, County Donegal. Contact Zoe Lally (☎ **096/49428;** fax 096/49020). March 11 and 12.
- **Celtic Spring Festival.** A cultural feast whose menu includes a drama festival and a celebration of the Irish language. Derry City. Call (☎ **028/7126-7234**). March 14 to 21.
- ✪ **The National St. Patrick's Day Festival.** Street theater, sports, music, and other festivities culminating in Ireland's grandest parade, with marching bands, drill teams, floats, and delegations from around the world. Dublin. Contact Festival Office, St. Stephen's Green House, Earlsfort Terrace, Dublin 2 (☎ **01/676-3205;** fax 01/676-3208; e-mail: info@paddyfest.ie; www.stpatricksday.ie). March 16 to 19.
- **St. Patrick's Day.** Parades and festivities in celebration of Ireland's patron saint. All over Ireland, North and South. March 17.
- **Limerick International Band Festival.** University of Limerick and O'Connell Street, Limerick. For 30 years, marching bands, concert bands, and drill teams worldwide have converged on Limerick for this rousing bandfest. Contact Caroline Nolan-Diffley (☎ **061/315-634;** www.shannon-dev.ie/bandfest). March 18 and 19.
- **Inishowen Traditional Singers Circle—11th Annual International Folk Song and Ballad Seminar.** Ballyliffen, Clonmany, County Donegal. Contact Jimmy McBride (☎ **077/61210**). March 26 to 29.

- **Rugby International, Ireland v. Wales.** Lansdowne Road, Ballsbridge, County Dublin. Contact Irish Rugby Football Union, 62 Lansdowne Rd., Dublin 4 (☎ **01/668-4601;** fax 01/660-5640).
- **Dublin Film Festival.** The best in Irish and international cinema. More than 100 films are featured, with screenings of the best in Irish and world cinema, plus seminars and lectures on filmmaking. Cinemas throughout Dublin. Contact Aine O'Halloran (☎ **01/679-2937;** fax 01/679-2929; www.iol.ie/dff/). April 6 to 16.
- **World Irish Dancing Championships.** Waterfront Hall, Belfast. The premier international competition in Irish dancing, with more than 4,000 contenders from as far as New Zealand. Contact Maire Ni Chorbaid (☎ **01/475-2220;** fax 01/475-1053; e-mail:cirg@tinet.ie). April 21 to 27.
- **Samhlaíocht Chiarrai/Kerry Arts Festival.** A spring festival of music, drama, film, dance, literature, craft, and visual art. Contact Maggie Fitsimmons, director (☎ **066/712-9934;** fax 066/712-0934). April 22 to 24.
- **Cork International Choral Festival.** Ireland's premier choral event, featuring competitive and noncompetitive performances by adult choirs of international standing, as well as performances by Irish and foreign dance groups. Multiple venues in Cork. Contact John Fitzpatrick (☎ **021/ 308308;** fax 021/308309; www.musweb.com/corkchoral.htm). April 26 to 30.

May

- **Belfast Marathon and Fun Runs.** An epic race of 4,500 international runners through the city. Start and finish at Maysfield, Belfast. Call (☎ **028/9027-0466**). May 1.
- **County Wicklow Gardens Festival.** Heritage properties and gardens, as well as many private grounds, open their gates to visitors on selected dates throughout County Wicklow and surrounding areas. Contact Wicklow County Tourism (☎ **0404/20100;** fax 0404/67792). May 5 to July 28.
- **Volta 2001.** The Galway Early Music Festival. An international celebration of the music, dance, and dress of the 12th to the 17th centuries. Musicians from near and afar take to the streets of the medieval city of Galway, providing a blast from the past. Events include concerts, workshops, street music, dance, and historical reenactment. Contact Justina McElligott (☎ **091/528-266;** www.wombat.ie/pages/early-music).
- **Sligo Arts Festival.** A burst of music, street events, and exhibitions spread across 30 sites in renascent Sligo town. Contact Danny Kirrane (☎ **0471/69802**). May 26 to 28.

June

- **Edenderry Three-Day Canal Angling Festival.** A festival organized by the Edenderry Coarse Angling Club to promote fishing in the area. Tourists are welcome to take part, provided that they book in advance. Canals around Edenderry, County Offaly. Contact Pauric Kelly (☎ **0405/ 32071**). June 5 to 9.
- **AIB Music Festival in Great Irish Houses.** This is a 10-day festival of classical music performed by leading Irish and international artists in some of the Dublin area's great Georgian buildings and mansions. Various venues throughout Dublin and neighboring counties Wicklow and

Kildare. Contact Crawford Tipping, Blackrock Post Office, County Dublin (☎ **01/278-1528;** fax 01/278-1529). June 8 to 17.

- **Dunlavin Festival of Arts.** Dunlavin, County Wicklow. This normally sleepy town wakes to 3 days of arts, crafts, music, parades, and street entertainment. Contact Margaret Lynott (☎ **045/401-459**). June 16 to 18.

✪ **Bloomsday.** Dublin's unique day of festivity commemorates 24 hours in the life of Leopold Bloom, the central character of James Joyce's *Ulysses.* Every aspect of the city, including the menus at restaurants and pubs, seeks to duplicate the aromas, sights, sounds, and tastes of Dublin on June 16, 1904. Special ceremonies are held at the James Joyce Tower and Museum, and there are guided walks of Joycean sights. The streets of Dublin and various venues. Contact the James Joyce Centre, 35 N. Great George's St., Dublin 1 (☎ **01/878-8547;** fax 01/878-8488; www. jamesjoyce.ie). June 16.

- **Galway Hookers Regatta.** This is the 15th annual regatta in Portaferry featuring a fleet of traditional Irish craft, including some venerable "hookers" from Galway Bay. Call (☎ **028/9182-4000**).

July

- **Summer Schools.** Study sessions meeting in Dublin include the Irish Theatre Summer School in conjunction with the Gaiety School of Acting at Trinity College, the Synge Summer School in County Wicklow, the James Joyce Summer School at Newman House, and the International Summer Schools in Irish Studies at Trinity College and the National University of Ireland. Contact the Irish Tourist Board. July and August.

✪ **Murphy's Irish Open Golf Championship.** This is Ireland's premier international golf event, televised to more than 90 countries and featuring the world's top players. Ballybunion Golf Club, Ballybunion, County Kerry. For details, contact the Golfing Union of Ireland (☎ **01/ 269-4111;** fax 01/269-5368; www.gui.ie). June 29 to July 2.

✪ **Budweiser Irish Derby.** One of the richest horse races in Europe, and widely accepted as the definitive European middle-distance classic. This is Ireland's version of the Kentucky Derby or Royal Ascot. It's a fashionable gathering of racing fans from all over Ireland and abroad. Curragh, County Kildare. For information, contact the Curragh Racecourse Office, the Curragh, County Kildare (☎ **045/441205;** fax 054/ 441442). *Note:* An Irish Racing Calendar for each year is also available from the Irish Tourist Board. July 2.

- **Battle of the Boyne Commemoration.** This annual event, sometimes called Orangeman's Day, recalls the historic battle between two 17th-century kings. It's a national day of parades and celebration all over Northern Ireland. Belfast and 18 other centers. Contact the House of Orange, 65 Dublin Rd., Belfast BT2 7HE (☎ **028/9032-2801**). July 12.

✪ **Galway Arts Festival and Races.** A 2-week feast in the streets of Galway, featuring international theater, big-top concerts, literary evenings, street shows, arts, parades, music, and more. Five days of racing and more merriment, music, and song follow. Galway City and Racecourse. Contact Fergal McGrath (☎ **091/509705/6;** fax 091/562655; www. galwayartsfestival.ie). July 19 to 30.

- **Lughnasa Fair.** A spectacular revival in a 12th-century Norman castle. Costumed magicians, entertainment, and crafts. Carrickfergus Castle, County Antrim. Call (☎ **028/4336 6455**). July 29.

✪ **Kerrygold Dublin Horse Show.** This is the principal sporting and social event on the Irish national calendar, attracting visitors from all parts of the world. More than 2,000 horses, the cream of Irish bloodstock, are entered, with dressage, jumping competitions each day, and more. Highlights include a fashionable ladies' day (don't forget your hat!), formal hunt balls each evening, and the awarding of the Aga Khan Trophy and the Nation's Cup by the president of Ireland. RDS Showgrounds, Ballsbridge. Contact Niamh Kelly, RDS, Merrion Road, Ballsbridge, Dublin 4 (☎ 01/668-0866; fax 01/660-4014; www.rds.ie). August 9 to 13.

• **Puck Fair.** Each year the residents of this tiny Ring of Kerry town carry on an ancient tradition by capturing a wild goat and enthroning it as "king" over 2 days of unrestricted merrymaking. Killorglin, County Kerry. Contact Brid Moriarty (☎ 066/976-2366; fax 066/976-2059; www.puckfair.ie). August 10 to 12.

✪ **Kilkenny Arts Festival.** This 1-week festival features a broad spectrum of the arts, from classical and traditional music to plays, one-person shows, readings, films, poetry, and visual arts exhibitions. Kilkenny. Contact Maureen Kennelly (☎ 056/63663; fax 056/51704). August 11 to 20.

• **Summer Music Festival, Dublin.** St. Stephen's Green is the setting for this series of free lunchtime band concerts of popular and Irish traditional music, as well as afternoon open-air performances of Shakespearean plays, sponsored by the Office of Public Works. Last 2 weeks of August.

✪ **Rose of Tralee International Festival.** A carnival-like atmosphere prevails at this 5-day event, with a full program of concerts, street entertainment, horse races, and a beauty and talent pageant leading up to the selection of the "Rose of Tralee." Tralee, County Kerry. Contact Noreen Cassidy, Rose of Tralee Festival Office, Ashe Memorial Hall, Denny Street, Tralee, County Kerry (☎ 066/712-1322; fax 066/22654; www.roseoftralee.ie). August 18 to 22.

✪ **Fleadh Cheoil na hEireann.** This is Ireland's major summer festival of traditional music, with competitions held to select the all-Ireland champions in all categories of instruments and singing. The venue changes each year; as of this writing, next year's location had not been announced, but you can check the Web site at www.fleadhcheoil.com. Contact Comhaltas Ceoltoiri Éireann (☎ 01/280-0295; fax 01/280-3759). August 21 to 27.

• **Oul' Lammas Fair.** Ballycastle, County Antrim. Chartered in 1606, this is Ireland's oldest continuous fair, featuring horse and sheep sales and hundreds of street stalls. Contact Ballycastle Tourist Information (☎ 028/2076-2024). August 28 and 29.

September

• **Ireland's Matchmaking Festival.** Come and see how the pros do it. Lisdoonvarna, County Clare. Contact James White (☎ 065/74005; fax 065/74406). September 1 to October 6.

• **Cape Clear Island International Storytelling Festival.** Performances and workshops on a magically beautiful island that inspires stories of its own. Cape Clear Island, County Cork. Contact Chuck Kruger (☎ and fax 028/39157; http://indigo.ie/~ckstory/story.htm). September 1 to 15.

✪ **All-Ireland Hurling and Football Final.** Tickets must be obtained months in advance for these two national amateur sporting events, the equivalent of the Super Bowl for Irish national sports. Croke Park, Dublin 3. Contact the Gaelic Athletic Association (☎ 01/836-3222; fax 01/836-6420). Two weekends in September.

- **Searching for the Elusive Irish Ancestor Family History Conference.** Belfast and Dublin. An annual conference focused on family history and on practical research in the country's main genealogical archives. Includes lectures, tours, and entertainment. Contact Shane McAteer (☎ 048/ 332288; www.uhf.org.uk). September 19 to 27.

✪ **Galway International Oyster Festival.** First held in 1954, this event attracts oyster aficionados from all over the globe. Highlights include the World Oyster-Opening Championship, a golf tournament, a yacht race, an art exhibition, a gala banquet, traditional music and song, and lots of oyster eating. Galway and environs. Contact Ann Flanagan (☎ 091/ 522066; fax 091/527282; www.galwayoysterfest.com). September 23 to 26.

- **Irish Antique Dealers' Fair.** Annual show sponsored jointly by the RDS and the Irish Antique Dealers' Association. This is Ireland's premier annual antiques fair. RDS Showgrounds, Ballsbridge, County Dublin. Contact Louis O'Sullivan (☎ 01/285-9294). September 27 to October 1.

October

✪ **Dublin Theatre Festival.** A world-class theater festival showcasing new plays by Irish authors and presenting a range of productions from abroad. Theaters throughout Dublin. Call ☎ 01/677-8439; fax 01/679-7709; www.iftn.ie/dublinfestival). October 2 to 14.

- **Derry City Two Cathedrals Festival.** Derry City. 2000 marks the 9th year of this extraordinary celebration of harmony and counterpoint between Derry's Catholic and Protestant cathedrals. The combined Festival Chorus is joined by international musical luminaries in a 2-week world-class concert series. Contact Dermot Carlin (☎ 028/7126-8335). Mid-October each year.

- **Cork International Film Festival.** At theatrical venues across the city, this world-renowned film festival offers screenings of features, documentaries, short films, and special programs. Contact Michael Hanniganm (☎ 021/271711; fax 021/275945; www.corkfilmfest.org). October 8 to 15.

✪ **Wexford International Festival Opera.** For more than 40 years, this event, held in Wexford's Theatre Royal, has been highly acclaimed for its productions of 18th- and 19th-century operatic masterpieces, plus classical music concerts, recitals, and more. Contact Jerome Hynes (☎ 053/22400; fax 053/424289; www.wexfordopera.com). October 19 to November 5.

- **Guinness Cork Jazz Festival.** Ireland's no. 2 city stages a first-rate festival of jazz. (Meanwhile, not to be outdone, nearby Kinsale plays host to its own fringe jazz festival.) Cork City (and Kinsale). Contact Ray Fitzgerald (☎ 021/278979; fax 021/270463). October 27 to 30.

✪ **Dublin City Marathon.** More than 3,000 runners from both sides of the Atlantic and the Irish Sea participate in this popular run through the streets of Dublin City. Dublin city center. For entry forms and information, contact Carol McCabe at ☎ 01/626-3746, or point your browser to www.dublincitymarathon.ie. October 30.

- **Banks of the Folye Halloween Festival.** A colorful riverside carnival of clowns, buskers, and street theater, with a spectacular fireworks display on the 31st. Derry City. Call (☎ 028/7126-7284). October 30 and 31.

- **Belfast Festival at Queens.** Ulster's best-known arts festival, this annual event attracts a huge following for drama, opera, music, and film events in and around Queens University. Queens University, Belfast. Contact Festival House, 25 College Gardens, Belfast BT9 6BS (☎ 028/9066-7687; fax 028/9066-5577). Concurrent with the main festival there's also a fringe festival in the Cathedral Quarter (☎ 028/9027-0466 for info). October 29 to November 14.

December

- **Dublin Grand Opera.** An operatic fling, with great works presented by the Dublin Grand Opera Society. Gaiety Theatre, South King Street, Dublin 2 (☎ 01/677-1717). Early December.
- **Woodford Mummers Feile.** A festival of traditional music, song, dance, and mime performed by mummers in traditional costume. Woodford, County Galway. Contact Marie McMahon (☎ 0509/49248). December 26 to 27.
- **Christmas Horse Racing Festival.** Three days of winter racing for thoroughbreds. Leopardstown Racetrack. County Dublin. Call (☎ 01/835-1965). December 26 to 29.

7 Health & Insurance

STAYING HEALTHY

As a rule, no health documents are required to enter Ireland or Northern Ireland from the United States, Canada, the United Kingdom, Australia, New Zealand, or most other countries. If, in the previous 14 days, a traveler has visited areas where a contagious disease is prevalent, proof of immunization for such disease may be required.

If you have a condition that could require emergency care but might not be readily recognizable, consider joining **Medic Alert** (☎ 800/432-5378; www.medicalert.org). It provides ID tags, cards, and a 24-hour emergency information hotline. If you are diabetic, you can call the **American Diabetes Association** (☎ 800/342-2383; www.diabetes.org/ada/c60e.asp) for a Diabetes Travel Kit and other information for traveling with diabetes.

If you require the services of a physician, dentist, or other health professional during your stay in Ireland, your accommodations host may be in the best position to recommend someone local. Otherwise, you can call the **Irish Medical Council,** Lynn House, Portabello Court, Lower Rathmines Road, Dublin 6 (☎ 01/496-5588) for a referral.

INSURANCE

When you're planning a trip, it is wise to consider insurance coverage for the various risk aspects of travel: health and accident, cancellation or disruption of services, and lost or stolen luggage. Travel insurance makes especially good sense if you're purchasing nonrefundable airline tickets or a package tour that requires you to pay up front.

Before buying any new coverage, check your own insurance policies (automobile, medical, and homeowner) to see if they cover the elements of travel abroad. Also check the membership contracts of automobile and travel clubs, and the benefits extended by credit-card companies.

If you decide you need further coverage, consider one of the following companies, which specialize in short-term policies for travelers: **M.H. Ross Insurance Brokers** (☎ 800/423-3632; e-mail: rosswiteby@aol.com); **Travel**

Guard International (☎ 877/216-4885; www.travel-guard.com); or **Travel Insurance International,** Travelers Insurance Co. (☎ 800/243-3174), whose policies make them particularly attractive for senior citizens or anyone with a preexisting medical condition.

8 Tips for Travelers with Special Needs

FOR TRAVELERS WITH DISABILITIES

A disability shouldn't stop anyone from traveling. There are more resources out there than ever before. **The Moss Rehab Hospital** (☎ 215/456-5995; www.mossresorcenet.org) has been providing friendly and helpful phone advice and referrals for years through its Travel Information Service. You'll find links to a number of travel agents who specialize in planning trips for travelers with disabilities here and through **Access-Able Travel Source (www.access-able.com)**, another excellent online source.

You can join the **Society for the Advancement of Travel for the Handicapped** (SATH; ☎ 212/447-7284; fax 212/725-8253; www.sath.org) to gain access to their vast network of connections in the travel industry. Membership requires a tax-deductible contribution of $45 annually for adults, $30 for seniors and students.

Travelers with vision impairments should contact the **American Foundation for the Blind** (☎ 800/232-5463) for information on traveling with Seeing-Eye dogs.

For the past 30 years, the **National Rehabilitation Board of Ireland,** 24/25 Clyde Rd., Ballsbridge, Dublin 4 (☎ 01/608-0400), has encouraged facilities to accommodate people with disabilities. Consequently, more and more hotels and public buildings now have ramps or graded entrances and rooms specially fitted for wheelchair access. Unfortunately, many of the older hotels, guesthouses, and landmark buildings still have steep steps both outside and within. For a list of the properties that cater to the needs of patrons with disabilities, contact the National Rehabilitation Board in advance.

The **Irish Wheelchair Association,** 24 Blackheath Dr., Clontarf, Dublin 3 (☎ 01/833-8241), loans free wheelchairs for travelers in Ireland. A donation is appreciated. Branch offices are at Parnell Street, Kilkenny (☎ 056/62775); White Street, Cork (☎ 021/966354); Henry Street, Limerick (☎ 061/313691); and Dominick Street, Galway (☎ 091/771550), as well as in a range of other towns less frequently visited by tourists.

If you plan to travel by rail in Ireland, be sure to check out Iarnrod Eireann's Web site (**www.irishrail.ie**), which includes services for travelers with disabilities.

For advice on travel to Northern Ireland, contact **Disability Action,** Portside Business Park, 189 Airport Rd. West, Belfast BT3 9ED (☎ 028/9079-1900). The Northern Ireland Tourist Board also publishes a helpful annual *Information Guide to Accessible Accommodation,* available from any of its offices worldwide.

FOR SENIORS

One of the benefits of age is that travel often costs less. Always bring an ID card, especially if you've kept your youthful glow. Also mention the fact that you're a senior when you first make your travel reservations, since many airlines and hotels offer discount programs for senior travelers.

Members of the **American Association of Retired Persons** (AARP; ☎ 800/424-3410; www.aarp.org) get discounts on hotels, airfares, and car rentals. The AARP offers members a wide range of benefits, including *Modern Maturity* magazine and a monthly newsletter.

Seniors, known in Ireland and Northern Ireland as OAPs (old age pensioners), enjoy a variety of discounts and privileges. Native OAPs ride the public transport system free of charge, but the privilege does not extend to tourists. Visiting seniors can avail themselves of other discounts, however, particularly on admission to attractions and theaters. Always ask about a senior discount if special rates are not posted; the discount is usually 10%.

The Irish Tourist Board publishes a list of reduced-rate hotel packages for seniors, **Golden Holidays/For the Over 55s.** These packages are usually available from March to June and September to November.

Some tour operators in the United States, such as **CIE Tours International** (☎ **800/243-8687** or 973/292-3438; www.cietours.com), which operates in Ireland and Northern Ireland, give travelers over age 55 cash discounts on selected departures of regular tour programs throughout the year. In addition, **SAGA Tours** (☎ **800/343-0273** or 617/262-2262) operates tours to Ireland specifically geared to seniors or anyone over 50. **Elderhostel** (☎ **877/ 426-8056;** www.elderhostel.org) offers a range of educational travel programs for seniors.

FOR STUDENTS, TEACHERS & YOUTH

With almost half its population under age 25, Ireland is geared to students, whether you're planning to study or are just passing through.

Two excellent source books can help you explore the opportunities for study in Ireland: *The Transitions Abroad Alternative Travel Directory,* an annual guide to living, learning, and working overseas, published by *Transitions Abroad,* **www.transitionsabroad.com**; and *Work, Study, Travel Abroad: The Whole World Handbook,* compiled by the Council on International Educational Exchange (CIEE). Both are available in bookstores.

Ireland in general is extremely student-friendly. Most attractions have a reduced student-rate admission charge, with the presentation of a valid student ID card. A range of travel discounts are available to students, teachers (at any grade level, kindergarten through university), and youth (anyone under 25). For further information on international student, teacher, and youth identity cards and fares, call the national office of **Council Travel** (☎ **800/ 226-8624;** www.counciltravel.com). The staff can make your reservations or refer you to the Council Travel office nearest you. Council Travel operates more than 40 offices in the United States and works through a network of world affiliates. (Even if you're not eligible for Council's student, teacher, and youth discounts, it offers full travel services, with the advantage of a growing network of local offices and overseas affiliates.)

In Canada, **Travel CUTS,** 200 Ronson St., Suite 320, Toronto, ON M9W 5Z9 (☎ **800/667-2887** or 416/614-2887; www.travelcuts.com), offers similar services. **USIT/Campus Travel,** 52 Grosvenor Gardens, London SW1W 0AG (☎ **087/0240-1010,** www.usitcampus.co.uk), opposite Victoria Station, is Britain's leading specialist in student and youth travel.

In Ireland, Council Travel's affiliate is **USIT, the Irish Student Travel Service,** 19 Aston Quay, Dublin 2 (☎ **01/679-8833;** www.usitnow.ie). In Northern Ireland, contact USIT in the Sountain Centre, College Street, Belfast BT1 6ET (☎ **028/9032-4073**), or at Queens University Travel, Student Union Building, University Road, Belfast BT7 1PE (☎ **028/ 9024-1830**). In the United States, USIT is at 891 Amsterdam Ave., New York, NY 10025 (☎ **212/663-5435**). (For the hopelessly curious among you,

USIT is the acronym for the organization's original name, "Union of Students of Ireland Travel," but as the man told me when I asked, "It doesn't stand for anything anymore. It's just USIT.")

U.S. firms offering educational programs to Ireland include **Academic Travel Abroad** (☎ **800/556-7896** or 202/785-9000), **Cultural Heritage Alliance** (☎ **800/323-4466** or 215/923-7060), and **Irish American Cultural Institute** (☎ **800/232-3746** or 973/605-1991).

FOR FAMILIES

Instead of hotels or B&Bs, families might consider a farm stay or a vacation rental home, where children are likely to have the opportunity to meet and make friends with local children. The information provided below on farmhouse accommodations and self-catering will be helpful in pursuing such options.

En route, if given 24-hour advance notice, airlines can arrange for a special child menu and can warm any baby food you bring with you. On arrival, car-rental companies can have children's car seats on hand if you've requested them ahead of time. Throughout the island, entrance fees and tickets on public transportation are often reduced by at least half for children. Family rates for parents with children may be available. In this guide, a "family" rate, unless otherwise stated, is for two adults with two children. Additional increments are often charged for larger families. Aside from all too familiar fast-food fare, many hotels and restaurants offer children's menus. Some hotels, guesthouses, and B&Bs provide baby-sitting, and others can arrange it. See the "Fast Facts" feature for each major city for listings of drugstores and other crucial health information. An especially helpful general source for planning an overseas family trip is *Take Your Kids to Europe* (3rd edition), published by Globe Pequot Press, available at bookstores for $17.95.

FOR GAY & LESBIAN TRAVELERS

Gay Ireland has rapidly come out of the closet since homosexuality became legal in the North in 1982 and in the Republic in July 1993. Although the gay and lesbian community has received increasing support over the past several years, much of Ireland continues to discourage its gay population. In cities such as Dublin, Cork, and Galway, however, gay and lesbian visitors can find more formal support and an open, if small, gay community.

Two essential publications for the gay or lesbian visitor to Ireland are the *Gay Community News* and *In Dublin* magazine. *Gay Community News* is a free newspaper of comprehensive Irish gay-related information published on the last Friday of each month and widely available in the city center. You can always find a copy at the **National Lesbian and Gay Federation** (see below), where it is published and where you can get advice on gay-related legal issues. The *Gay Community News* is also distributed by Books Upstairs, 36 College Green, across from Trinity College; Waterstone's on Dawson Street, also near Trinity; the Well Fed Cafe on Crow Street in Temple Bar; the George on South Great George's Street off Dame Street; and other progressive haunts.

The most comprehensive Web site for gay organizations, events, issues, and information throughout Ireland can be found on "Ireland's Pink Pages," **http://indigo.ie/~outhouse**.

In Dublin, which comes out twice a month and is for sale at news agents and bookstores throughout the city, has a page that lists gay events, current club information, AIDS and health information resources, accommodations options, and helpful organizations.

The following organizations and help lines are staffed by knowledgeable and friendly people:

- **National Lesbian and Gay Federation** (**NLGF**), 6 S. William St., Dublin 2 (☎ **01/670-6377;** fax 01/679-1603; http://homepage. tinet.ie/~nlgf), available Monday to Friday noon to 6pm.
- **Gay Switchboard Dublin,** Carmichael House, North Brunswick Street, Dublin 7 (☎ **01/872-1055;** fax 01/873-5737; gsd@iol.ie), Sunday to Friday 8 to 10pm and Saturday 3:30 to 6pm.
- **Lesbian Line Dublin** (☎ **01/872-9911**), Thursday 7 to 9pm.
- **LOT** (**Lesbians Organizing Together**), the umbrella group of the lesbian community, 5 Capel St., Dublin 1 (☎ and fax **01/872-7770**), accommodates drop-ins Fridays 10am to 4pm. LOT also sponsors LEA/Lesbian Education Awareness (☎ and fax **01/872-0460;** e-mail: leanow@indigo.ie).
- The **Gay and Lesbian AA Group** meets in Outhouse, 6 S. William St., Dublin 2, on Friday evenings at 8pm.
- **AIDS Helpline Dublin** (☎ **01/872-4277**), run Monday to Friday 7 to 9pm and Saturday 3 to 5pm, offers assistance with HIV/AIDS prevention, testing, and treatment.

Gay and lesbian travelers seeking information and assistance on travel abroad might want to consult the **International Gay and Lesbian Travel Association** (**IGLTA**), 4331 North Federal Hwy., Suite 304, Fort Lauderdale, FL 33308 (☎ **800/448-8550** or 954/776-2626; fax 954-776-3303; www.iglta.org). General gay and lesbian travel agencies include **Family Abroad** (☎ **800/999-5500** or 212/459-1800) for gays and lesbians, and **Above and Beyond Tours** (☎ **800/397-2681;** www.abovebeyondtours.com), mainly for gays. Additional helpful resources include the Ferrari Guides, whose titles include *Gay Travel A–Z, Men's Travel in Your Pocket, Women's Travel in Your Pocket,* and *Inn Places.* All four are published by Ferrari Publications, P.O. Box 37887, Phoenix, AZ 85069 (www.q-net.com). *Women Going Places* is available from Inland Book Company, P.O. Box 12061, East Haven, CT 06512. Also, **Council Travel** (☎ **888/COUNCIL** for an office near you) can supply a free pamphlet called *AIDS and International Travel* that includes information on hotlines, HIV testing, blood transfusions, and traveling with AIDS overseas.

9 Getting There

BY PLANE

About half of all visitors from North America arrive in Ireland on direct transatlantic flights to Dublin Airport, Shannon Airport, or Belfast International Airport. (Since March 27, 1994, transatlantic flights to the Republic are no longer required to stop in Shannon.) The other half fly first into Britain or Europe, then "backtrack" into Ireland by air or sea. In the Republic, there are seven smaller regional airports, all of which (except Knock) offer service to Dublin and several of which receive some EC international traffic. They are Cork, Donegal, Galway, Kerry, Knock, Sligo, and Waterford. In Northern Ireland, the secondary airports are Belfast City Airport and Derry City Airport. Services and schedules are always subject to change, so be sure to consult your preferred airline or travel agent as soon as you begin to sketch your itinerary. The routes and carriers listed below are provided to suggest the range of possibilities for air travel to Ireland.

Planning Basics

Backtracking to Ireland

Many travelers opt to fly to Britain and backtrack into Dublin (see "From London to Dublin," below). Carriers serving Britain from the United States include **American Airlines** (☎ 800/433-7300; www.aa.com), **British Airways** (☎ 800/247-9297; www.british-airways.com), **Continental Airlines** (☎ 800/231-0856; www.continental.com), **Delta Airlines** (☎ 800/241-4141; www.delta.com), **Northwest Airlines** (☎ 800/447-4747; www.nwa.com), **TWA** (☎ 800/892-4141; www.twa.com), **United** (☎ 800/241-6522; www.ual.com), and **Virgin Atlantic Airways** (☎ 800/862-8621; www.fly.virgin.com).

FROM THE U.S.

The Irish national carrier, **Aer Lingus** (☎ 800/474-7424; www.aerlingus.ie) is the traditional leader in providing transatlantic flights to Ireland. Aer Lingus offers scheduled flights from Boston, Chicago, Los Angeles, Newark, and New York JFK to Dublin, Shannon, and Belfast International Airports, with connecting flights to Ireland's regional airports.

Note: Aer Lingus offers educational discounts to full-time students, which can be booked through CIEE/Council Travel (see above). It also sells an attractively priced Eurosaver Green Pass for those who want to combine an Aer Lingus round-trip transatlantic flight to Ireland with a side trip to Britain or the Continent, or a domestic flight within Ireland, including the North.

Excellent transatlantic service is also provided by **Delta Airlines** (☎ 800/241-4141; www.delta-air.com). It offers scheduled daily flights from Atlanta and New York JFK to both Dublin and Shannon, with feed-in connections from Delta's network of gateways throughout the United States.

Also offering daily transatlantic service to Ireland is **Continental Airlines** (☎ 800/231-0856; www.continental.com), with two flights a day from their Newark hub, one to Shannon and one to Dublin. In addition, limited scheduled service from Chicago, Miami, Mexico City, and Washington, D.C., to Shannon is offered by **Aeroflot** (☎ 888/340-6400). **Royal Jordanian Airlines** (☎ 800/223-0474) flies twice a week, Mondays and Thursdays, to Shannon from Chicago.

FROM LONDON TO DUBLIN

The following carriers operate air service from London to Dublin: **Aer Lingus** (☎ 800/474-7424 from the U.S., or 020/8899-4747 in Britain); **British Airways** (☎ 0345/222111) offered by **City Flyer Express** (☎ 800/247-9297 from the U.S. or 0345/222111 in Britain); **British Midland** (☎ 800/788-0555 from the U.S., or 0870/607-0555 in Britain; www.iflybritishmidland.com); **CityJet** (☎ 0345/445588 in Britain); and **Ryanair** (☎ 0541/569569 in Britain; www.ryanair.com). In addition to the London-Dublin routes, there are direct flights from London to Cork, Kerry, Knock, Shannon, and Waterford, as well as flights from more than 20 other British cities to Ireland's airports.

Direct flights into **Belfast International Airport** (www.bial.co.uk) include flights by **British Airways** (☎ 0345/222111; www.british-airways.com) from Birmingham, Edinburgh, and London/Heathrow; and by **Virgin Express** (☎ 800/891199; www.fly.virgin.com) from London/Heathrow. In addition, there is service into **Belfast City Airport** (☎ 01232/457745; www.belfastcityairport.com) by a range of carriers, including **British Airways** flights from Edinburgh, Glasgow, Leeds, Liverpool, and Manchester, and by

Jersey European (☎ 0990/676676) from Birmingham, Bristol, Exeter, London Stansted, and London Gatwick. Service to **Derry City Eglinton Airport** is provided by **British Airways** from Glasgow and Manchester, and by **Ryanair** (☎ 0541/569569 in Britain) from London Stansted.

FROM THE CONTINENT

Major direct flights into Dublin from the continent include service from Amsterdam on **KLM** (☎ 800/374-7747 from the U.S.); Barcelona on **Iberia** (☎ 800/772-4642 in the U.S.); Brussels on **Sabena** (☎ 800/952-2000 in the U.S.); Copenhagen on **Aer Lingus** and **SAS** (☎ 800/221-2350 in the U.S.); Frankfurt on **Aer Lingus** and **Lufthansa** (☎ 800/645-3880 in the U.S.); Paris on **Aer Lingus** and **Air France** (☎ 800/237-2747 in the U.S.); Prague on CSA **Czech Airlines** (☎ 212/765-6588 in the U.S.); and Rome on **Aer Lingus.** Quite recently, **Cork Airport** (www.cork-airport.com) has passed Shannon and become the number two airport in Ireland, though it offers no nonstop transatlantic service. **Aer Lingus, British Airways, KLM,** and **Ryanair** are among the airlines flying into Cork and providing a rapidly growing network of connections with Great Britain and the Continent (see above for their contact info). Direct service to Shannon from the Continent includes **Aer Lingus** from Düsseldorf, Frankfurt, Paris, and Zurich; **Aeroflot** from Moscow; and **Virgin Express** from Brussels.

FLY FOR LESS: TIPS FOR GETTING THE BEST AIRFARES

- **Take advantage of APEX fares.** Advance-purchase booking is often the key to getting the lowest fare. You generally must be willing to make your plans and buy your tickets as far ahead as possible. Be sure you understand cancellation and refund policies before you buy.
- **Consolidators,** also known as bucket shops, are a good place to find low fares, often below even the airlines' discounted rates. There's nothing shady about the reliable ones—basically, they're just big travel agents that get discounts for buying in bulk and pass some of the savings on to you. Some of the most reliable consolidators include **Cheap Tickets** (☎ **800/377-1000;** www.cheaptickets.com), **Council Travel** (☎ **800/226-8624;** www.counciltravel.com), **STA Travel** (☎ **800/781-4040;** www.sta.travel.com), **Lowestfare.com** (☎ **888/278-8830;** www.lowestfare.com), **Cheap Seats** (☎ **800/451-7200;** www.cheapseatstravel.com), and **1-800-FLY-CHEAP** (www.flycheap.com).
- Search the **Internet** for cheap fares—though it's still best to compare your findings with the research of a dedicated travel agent. Two of the better-respected virtual travel agents are **Travelocity (www.travelocity.com)** and **Microsoft Expedia (www.expedia.com)**. See "Planning Your Trip: An Online Directory," on p. 63, for further discussion on this topic and other recommendable sites.
- Consider a **charter flight.** They're often a good value, though they offer fewer frills, and their tickets are ordinarily nonrefundable. From the United States, **Sceptre Charters** (☎ **800/221-0924** or 718/738-9400) operates the largest and most reliable charter program to Ireland. It flies to Shannon from Boston, Philadelphia, Chicago, and Los Angeles. Several companies in Canada operate charter flights from Toronto to Ireland, including **Signature Vacations** (☎ **800/268-7063** in Canada or 800/268-1105 from the U.S.), **Air Transat Holidays** (☎ **800/587-2672** in Canada, or 514/987-1550), and **Regent Holidays** (☎ **800/387-4860** in Canada, or 905/673-3343).

BY FERRY

If you're traveling to Ireland from Britain or the Continent, especially if you're behind the wheel of a car, ferries can get you there. The Irish Sea has a reputation, however, so it's always a good idea to consider an over-the-counter pill or patch to guard against seasickness. (Be sure to take any pills *before* you set out; once you're under way, it's generally too late.)

Several car and passenger ferries offer reasonably comfortable furnishings, cabin berths (for longer crossings), restaurants, duty-free shopping, and lounges.

Prices fluctuate seasonally and depend on your route, your time of travel, and whether you are on foot or in a car. It's best to check with your travel agent for up-to-date details, but just to give you an idea, the lowest one-way adult fare in high season on the cruise ferry from Holyhead to Dublin is £20 (that's British pounds, or $33). Add your car, and the grand total will be £149 (again, in pounds sterling, or $245.85). The Web sites given below have regularly updated schedules and prices.

FROM BRITAIN

Irish Ferries (www.irishferries.ie) operates from Holyhead, Wales, to Dublin, and from Pembroke, Wales, to Rosslare, County Wexford. For reservations, call Scots-American Travel (☎ **561/563-2856** in the U.S. or 01/638-3333 in Ireland). **Stena Line** (☎ **888/274-8724** in the U.S. or 01233/647022 in Britain; www2.stenaline.com) sails from Holyhead to Dun Laoghaire, 8 miles (13km) south of Dublin; from Fishguard, Wales, to Rosslare; and from Stranraer, Scotland, to Belfast, Northern Ireland. **Swansea/Cork Ferries** (☎ **011792/456116** in Britain; www.swansea-cork.ie) links Swansea, Wales, to Cork. **P&O European Ferries** operates from Cairnryan, Scotland, to Larne, Northern Ireland. For reservations, call Scots-American Travel (☎ **561/563-2856** in the U.S., or 01/638-3333 in Ireland; www.poef.com). **Norse Irish Ferries** (☎ **0151/9441010** in Britain; www.norse-irish-ferries. co.uk) sails between Liverpool and Belfast. **Seacat Scotland Ltd.** (☎ **800/ 551743** in Britain or 01/874-1231 in Ireland; www.team-packet.com) operates ferries from Liverpool, England, and Douglas, Isle of Man, to Dublin; from Stranraer, Heysham, and Troon, Scotland, to Belfast; and from Campbeltown, Scotland, to Ballycastle, Co. Antrim.

FROM CONTINENTAL EUROPE

Irish Ferries sails from Roscoff and Cherbourg, France, to Rosslare. For reservations, call Scots-American Travel (☎ **561/563-2856** in the U.S. or 01/ 638-3333 in Ireland). **Brittany Ferries** (☎ **021/277801** in Cork; www. brittany-ferries.com) connects Roscoff, France, to Cork.

Note: Because the Irish Ferries company is a member of the Eurail system, you can travel free on the ferries between Rosslare and Roscoff or Cherbourg if you hold a valid Eurail Pass.

10 Getting Around

BY PLANE

Because Ireland is such a small country, it's unlikely you'll be flying from place to place. If you do require an air transfer, however, **Aer Lingus** (☎ 01/ 705-3333; www.aerlingus.com) operates daily scheduled flights linking Dublin with Cork, Galway, Kerry, Knock, Shannon, and Sligo.

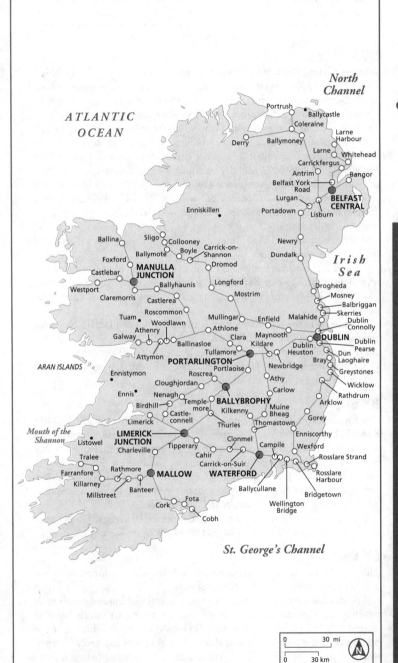

ATLANTIC OCEAN

North Channel

Portrush
Ballycastle
Coleraine
Derry   Ballymoney
Larne Harbour
Larne   Whitehead
Carrickfergus
Antrim   Bangor
Belfast York Road
Lurgan   **BELFAST CENTRAL**
Portadown   Lisburn

Enniskillen

Newry   *Irish Sea*
Dundalk

Ballina
Sligo   Collooney
Ballymote   Boyle   Carrick-on-Shannon
Foxford   Dromod
Castlebar   **MANULLA JUNCTION**   Ballyhaunis
Westport   Longford
Claremorris   Castlerea   Mostrim
Roscommon
Tuam   Woodlawn   Mullingar   Enfield   Drogheda
Athenry   Athlone   Maynooth   Mosney
Galway   Ballinasloe   Clara   Balbriggan
Attymon   Tullamore   Kildare   Skerries
PORTARLINGTON   Dublin Connolly
Portlaoise   Newbridge   **DUBLIN**
Dublin Heuston   Dublin Pearse
ARAN ISLANDS   Roscrea   Athy   Bray
Ennistymon   Cloughjordan   Carlow   Dun Laoghaire
Ennis   **BALLYBROPHY**   Greystones
Nenagh   Temple-more   Muine Bheag   Wicklow
Birdhill   Kilkenny   Rathdrum
Castle-connell   Thurles   Thomastown   Gorey
Mouth of the Shannon   **LIMERICK JUNCTION**   Clonmel   Arklow
Listowel   Limerick   Tipperary   Enniscorthy
Tralee   Charleville   Cahir   Campile   Wexford
Farranfore   Rathmore   Carrick-on-Suir   **WATERFORD**   Rosslare Strand
Killarney   **MALLOW**   Rosslare Harbour
Millstreet   Banteer   Ballycullane   Bridgetown
Cork   Fota   Wellington Bridge
Cobh

St. George's Channel

0   30 mi
0   30 km

Transport fares—air, ferry, train—are either "single" (one-way) or "return" (round-trip).

BY TRAIN

Iarnrod Eireann/Irish Rail Travel Centre, 35 Lower Abbey St., Dublin 1 (☎ **01/703-1839**), operates a network of train services throughout Ireland. With the exception of flying, train travel is the fastest way to get around the country. Most lines radiate from Dublin to other principal cities and towns. From Dublin, the journey time to Cork is 3 hours; to Belfast, 2 hours; to Galway, 3 hours; to Limerick, 2¼ hours; to Killarney, 4 hours; to Sligo, 3¼ hours; and to Waterford, 2¾ hours. For train departure times and fares, call (in Dublin) ☎ **01/836-6222** Monday to Saturday 8:30am to 6pm, Sunday 9am to 6pm. Outside of regular business hours, call ☎ **01/703-1842/1843.** For rail inquiries anywhere in Ireland, call toll-free ☎ **1850/366222.** Iarnrod Eireann has an excellent interactive Web site (**www.irishrail.ie**) where you can map out and schedule all your comings and goings in Ireland. You'll find updated timetables for DART, Intercity, and Suburban lines, as well as useful links to other travel services.

Iarnrod Eireann/Irish Rail also offers an enticing array of weekend to week-long holiday packages or **RailBreaks** to practically every corner of Ireland, North as well as South. For details, contact the Irish Rail Travel Centre (see above).

In addition to the Irish Rail service between Dublin and Belfast, **Northern Ireland Railways** (☎ **888/BRITRAIL** or 028/9089-9411; www.raileurope. com) operates three main routes from its hub in Belfast. They run north and west from Belfast to Derry via Ballymena; east to Bangor, tracing the shores of Belfast Lough; and south to Dublin via Newry.

BY BUS

Bus Eireann, with its hub at Busaras/Central Bus Station, Dublin 1 (☎ **01/ 836-6111;** www.buseireann.ie), operates an extensive system of express bus service, as well as local service to nearly every town in Ireland. Express routes include Dublin to Donegal (4¼ hr.), Killarney to Limerick (2½ hr.), Limerick to Galway (2 hr.), and Limerick to Cork (2 hr.). The Bus Eireann Web site provides the latest timetables and fares for bus service throughout Ireland. Bus travel is usually affordable, reliable, and comfortable.

For bus travel within Northern Ireland, contact **Ulsterbus,** Europa Buscentre, 10 Glengall St., Belfast (☎ **028/9033-3000;** www.translink.co.uk).

BY CAR

Although Ireland offers an extensive network of public transportation, the advantages of having your own car are obvious.

The disadvantages begin with the cost of rental and continue with each refueling. In high season, weekly rental rates on a compact vehicle begin at around $250 (if you've shopped around) and ascend steeply—but it's at the pump that you're likely to go into shock. Irish gas prices can easily be triple what you pay in the United States. The sole consolation is that Ireland is comparatively small, so distances are comparatively short.

Another fact of life on the road in Ireland is that space is limited. Most Irish roads and highways are surprisingly narrow, made to order for what many

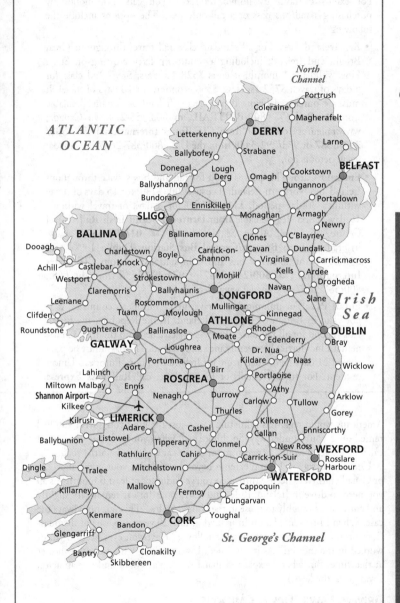

North Channel

ATLANTIC OCEAN

Irish Sea

St. George's Channel

Portrush
Coleraine
Magherafelt
Letterkenny
DERRY
Larne
Ballybofey
Strabane
BELFAST
Donegal
Lough Derg
Omagh
Cookstown
Dungannon
Ballyshannon
Portadown
Bundoran
Enniskillen
Monaghan
Armagh
SLIGO
Newry
BALLINA
Ballinamore
Clones
C'Blayney
Dooagh
Charlestown
Carrick-on-Shannon
Cavan
Dundalk
Achill
Castlebar
Knock
Boyle
Virginia
Carrickmacross
Westport
Strokestown
Kells
Ardee
Claremorris
Ballyhaunis
Mohill
Navan
Drogheda
Leenane
Roscommon
LONGFORD
Slane
Clifden
Tuam
Moylough
Mullingar
Kinnegad
Roundstone
Oughterard
Ballinasloe
ATHLONE
Rhode
DUBLIN
GALWAY
Loughrea
Moate
Edenderry
Bray
Portumna
Dr. Nua
Gort
Birr
Kildare
Naas
Wicklow
Lahinch
ROSCREA
Portlaoise
Miltown Malbay
Ennis
Nenagh
Durrow
Athy
Arklow
Shannon Airport
Thurles
Carlow
Tullow
Gorey
Kilkee
Cashel
Kilkenny
Enniscorthy
Kilrush
LIMERICK
Adare
Callan
Ballybunion
Listowel
Tipperary
Clonmel
New Ross
WEXFORD
Dingle
Rathluirc
Cahir
Carrick-on-Suir
Rosslare Harbour
Tralee
Mitchelstown
WATERFORD
Killarney
Mallow
Fermoy
Cappoquin
Kenmare
Dungarvan
Glengarriff
Bandon
CORK
Youghal
Bantry
Clonakilty
Skibbereen

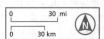

0   30 mi
0   30 km

Money-Saving Rail & Bus Passes

For extensive travel by public transport, you can save money by purchasing a rail/bus pass or a rail-only pass. The options include the following:

- **Brit/Ireland Pass:** For all standard-class rail travel throughout Great Britain and Ireland, including a round-trip ferry crossing on Stena Line. Valid for 1 month, it costs $528 1st class, $396 2nd class for 5 days of travel; $752 1st class, $566 economy for 10 days of travel. It must be purchased before departure for Ireland or Britain. Available from **BritRail** (☎ **800/BRITRAIL,** or 800/555-2748 in Canada; www.raileurope.com), or from **CIE Tours International** (☎ **800/243-8687** or 973/292-3438 from the U.S., 800/387-2667 in Canada; www.cietours.co).

- **Emerald Card:** This pass is good for rail and bus service throughout Ireland and Northern Ireland. It costs £200 ($280) for 15 days of travel within a 30-day period, £115 ($161) for 8 days of travel within a 15-day period. It's available from **Iarnrod Eireann/Irish Rail,** Travel Centre, 35 Lower Abbey St., Dublin 1 (☎ **01/703-1839;** www.irishrail.ie); from **Busaras/Central Bus Station,** Dublin 1 (☎ **01/836-6111**), at all major bus and train stations; or from **CIE Tours International** (☎ **800/243-8687** or 973/292-3438 from the U.S., 800/387-2667 in Canada; www.cietours.co).

- **Eurail Pass:** For unlimited rail travel in 17 European countries. It is not valid in Britain or Northern Ireland. In the Republic, the Eurail Pass is good for all rail travel, Expressway coaches, and the Irish Continental Lines ferries between France and Ireland. The pass must be purchased 21 days before departure for Ireland by a non–European Union resident. For further details or for purchase, call **Rail Pass Express**

Americans would regard as miniature cars—just the kind you'll wish you had rented once you're under way. So think small when you pick out your rental car. The choice is yours: between room in the car and room on the road.

Unless your stay in Ireland extends beyond 6 months, your own valid U.S. or Canadian driver's license (provided you've had it for at least 6 months) is all you need to drive in Ireland. Rules and restrictions for car rental vary slightly and correspond roughly to those in the United States. (This was not always the case. When I first rented a car in Ireland, nearly 20 years ago, one of the questions on the rental agreement read as follows: "Have you ever been in jail or worked in the theater?" As it happened, I was working with a Dublin theater at that time. But when I explained that I was a playwright and not an actor, I was given the keys.)

DRIVING LAWS, TIPS & CAUTIONS

Highway safety, or the lack thereof, has reached the level of a national crisis in Ireland during the past several years. The number of highway fatalities is shocking, and has caused Ireland to be ranked as the second-most-dangerous country in Europe in which to drive (second only to Greece and twice as dangerous as its next "competitor").

(☎ 800/722-7151; www.eurail.com). Also available from Council Travel and other travel agents.

- **Freedom of Northern Ireland:** Seven days unlimited travel on bus and train in the North for £37 ($61.05), 5 days for £25 ($41.25), or 1 day for £10 ($16.50). It's available from **Northern Ireland Railways,** Central Station, East Bridge Street, Belfast (☎ 028/9089-9411); and **Ulsterbus,** Europa Buscentre, 10 Glengall St., Belfast (☎ 028/9033-3000; www.translink.co.uk); as well as all major bus and train stations in Northern Ireland.

- **Irish Explorer:** For use in the Republic of Ireland, this pass is good for either 8 days of combined rail and bus services for £100 ($140) or 5 days of rail for only £83 ($116.20). It's available from **Iarnrod Eireann/Irish Rail Travel Centre,** 35 Lower Abbey St., Dublin 1 (☎ 01/703-1839; www.irishrail.ie); and **Busaras/Central Bus Station,** Dublin 1 (☎ 01/836-6111); as well as all major bus and train stations.

- **Irish Rover:** For use in the Republic of Ireland and the North, this pass entitles you to 5 days of rail travel for £83 ($116.20). It's available from **Iarnrod Eireann/Irish Rail Travel Centre,** 35 Lower Abbey St., Dublin 1 (☎ 01/703-1839; www.irishrail.ie), and all major train stations.

Note: Three-day passes are good for any 3 days in an 8-day period; 5-day passes for any 5 days in a 15-day period; 8-day passes for any 8 days in a 15-day period; and 15-day passes for any 15 days in a 30-day period. The Emerald Card, the Irish Explorer, and the Irish Rover passes can be purchased in Ireland at most mainline rail stations and Bus Eireann ticket offices. In the United States, they're available from **CIE Tours International** (☎ 800/243-8687).

In light of Ireland's unfortunate highway statistics, every possible precaution is in order. Try to avoid driving late at night, after dark and as the pubs close; get off the road when driving conditions are compromised by rain, fog, or excessive holiday traffic; and don't drive alone. Getting used to left-side driving, stick shift (almost all rental cars have standard transmissions), and a new landscape are enough for the driver to manage, without having to find his or her way. Every novice driver in Ireland needs a hawk-eyed navigator to point the way. With this in mind, I would strongly recommend driving only an hour or two on the day you arrive, just far enough to get to a nearby hotel or bed-and-breakfast. Finally, it goes without saying that driving either intoxicated or exhausted, or both (which is often the state of tourists disembarking from an overnight transatlantic flight), is only asking for notice in the next day's *Irish Times.*

While the excessive speed of many Irish drivers can be a fierce annoyance on the open road, the snail's pace of traffic in Dublin provides its own form of frustration. There is simply no point in renting a car for your time in Dublin. The pace of traffic in the capital's city center is now officially down to 8kmph (about 5mph), as against an average of 15kmph in most other European capitals. You may not have clocked yourself lately, but it's likely that you're nearly better off on foot. Especially when you consider parking!

A common concern for would-be motorists from abroad is the fact that the Irish, in both the North and South, drive on the left. The thought of this whitens some knuckles even before they touch the wheel. In my own experience, and from what I know more widely, it really isn't a matter for dread. The sight of oncoming vehicles in one's accustomed lane is instantly instructive, even persuasive.

"Roundabouts" admittedly take a little getting used to. Just remember always to turn left into a roundabout and to *yield* to vehicles on the right. If you're going to slip up and forget momentarily where you belong, it's more likely to happen after you return home, when your guard is down and before you realize you've formed a strange habit overseas. Seriously, be careful in the first days and weeks after you return home, especially when making sharp left turns.

One signal that could be particularly misleading to U.S. drivers is a flashing yellow light at a pedestrian traffic light. This means yield to pedestrians, and proceed only if the crossing is clear.

There are relatively few major (extended, limited access, divided) highways to speak of in the Republic—only national (N), regional (R), and rural or unclassified roads. N50 and higher are primary roads; numbers lower than 50 indicate secondary roads. Regional roads usually have a name, not a number. In the North, there are two Major Motorways (M), equivalent to interstates, as well as a network of lesser A- and B-level roads. Speed limits are posted. In general, the limit for urban areas is 46kmph (29 mph), for open but nondivided highways 95kmph (59 mph), and for major motorways 110kmph (68 mph).

The enforcement of speed limits is becoming increasingly stringent, and Irish roads have some built-in enforcers. Roads are often slick, with many bends and rises, any one of which can present a sheep or other four-legged pedestrian on very short notice. The low density of traffic on some of Ireland's roads can promote the deadly fantasy that you have the road to yourself. Don't wait to be contradicted.

Both the North and the South have appropriately severe laws on the books against drunk driving, and they will gladly throw them at you. Irish hospitality has its limits. Both also enforce the mandatory use of seat belts in the front seat, and the North extends that to rear-seat passengers. Additionally, it is against the law in the Republic for any child under 12 to sit in the front seat.

RENTALS

Major international car-rental firms are represented at airports and cities throughout Ireland and Northern Ireland. They include **Alamo-Treaty** (☎ 800/522-9696 from the U.S.; www.goalamo.com), **Auto-Europe** (☎ 800/223-5555 from the U.S.; www.autoeurope.com), **Avis** (☎ 800/331-1084 from the U.S.; www.avis.com), **Budget** (☎ 800/472-3325 from the U.S.; www.budgetrentacar.com), **Hertz** (☎ 800/838-0826 from the U.S.; www.hertz.com), **Murrays Europcar** (☎ 800/800-6000 from the U.S.), **National** (☎ 800/227-7368 from the U.S.; www.nationalcar.com), and **Payless/Bunratty** (☎ 800/729-5377 from the U.S.; www.paylesscar.com). It's best to shop around, because it is difficult to say who will be offering the best rate at any given moment, although Budget seems consistently quite competitive and tries hard to accommodate special circumstances and needs.

I strongly urge you to make car-rental arrangements well in advance of your departure. Leaving such arrangements until the last minute—or, worse, until your arrival in Ireland—can mean you wind up either walking or wishing you were. Ireland is a small country, and in high season, it can completely run out of rental cars—but before it does, it runs out of *affordable* rental cars. Discounts are common in the off-season, of course, but it's also possible to negotiate a decent deal for July and August, if you put in enough time and effort.

In my experience, **Auto Europe** (☎ **800/223-5555;** fax 207/828-1177; www.autoeurope.com) offers superior rates and service on overseas rentals and long-term leases. Their agreements are clear, straightforward, and all-inclusive. Better yet, they can beat any bona fide offer from another company; ask for the "Beat Rate Desk." Another well-established firm offering long-term leases and rentals is **Europe by Car** (☎ **800/223-1516**).

In addition, a variety of Irish-based companies have desks at the major airports and full-service offices in city or town locations. The leader among the Irish-based firms is **Dan Dooley/Kenning Rent-a-Car** (☎ **800/331-9301** from the U.S.; www.dan-dooley.ie).

The car-rental rates quoted by many companies do not include the inevitable 12.5% government tax (VAT), nor do they include CDW (collision damage waiver) or insurance against theft of the rental vehicle. If you have your own auto insurance, you may be covered; check your existing policy before you pay for additional coverage you may not need. If you do not have your own auto insurance, and you rent with a credit card that provides free protection, be sure to call your card's customer service line to make certain there are no invisible or whispered restrictions on that coverage. Tell the company exactly where you are going, for how long, and let the staff assure you that all is well. (Note that while many cards offer collision protection, they do not cover you for liability.) One common hitch is that the complimentary CDW may be invalid beyond 30 consecutive days, which means you must return the car within 30 days and take out a second rental to extend the coverage beyond the 30-day limit. In 1999, Visa eliminated all coverage on rental cars in Ireland, and MasterCard limited its coverage. Be certain that your information is current. Always confirm the details of your coverage when you charge your car rental to your credit card. Make certain that the distinction between Ireland and Northern Ireland is clear both to you and to those with whom you are negotiating.

If you are renting a car in the Republic and taking it into the North (or vice versa), be sure to ask the car-rental firm if the rental insurance the company provides covers cross-border transport. If not, you may be required to buy extra insurance. If you rent a car in the Republic, it is best to return it to the Republic, and if you rent it in the North, return it in the North (some firms charge extra for cross-border drop-offs).

PARKING

Some small cities and most towns have free street parking, but larger cities confine parking to metered spaces or parking garages and lots. "Disc-parking" is also in effect in many places. Under this system, you buy a paper disc and display it for the time you are parked in a certain area. Discs in Dublin currently cost 40p to 80p (56¢ to $1.12) per hour of use; they're sold in most shops, hotels, and tourist offices. Some towns also follow the "pay and display" system, which is similar to the disc system: You buy a parking voucher (usually for 20p/28¢ to 40p/56¢ per hour) from a machine at the site and display the voucher for the time you are parked. Remember not to park on double yellow lines.

Dublin, in particular, has recently taken the gloves off in an effort to crack down on parking violations—so be extra vigilant there. The city is poised to hike the current fine of £15 ($21) to £65 ($91), which will likely be the slap you'll feel by the time this edition hits the stands.

In Belfast and other large cities in the North, certain security measures are in place. Control zone signs indicate that no unattended vehicle can be left there at any time. That means if you are a single traveler, you cannot leave your car; if you are a twosome, one person must remain in the car while it's parked. Also, unlocked cars anywhere in the North are subject to a fine, for security reasons.

BY TAXI & HACKNEY

Taxis and hackneys look very much alike. Both drive you where you ask them to, and the drivers collect a fee at the end and are quite likely to entertain you with stories. There are some significant differences, however. Hackneys are not allowed to wait at taxi "ranks" or display a sign atop their cars; they don't use meters; and they are not regulated by any municipal or state agency. In other words, they are private individuals doing business as drivers for hire. They agree with you on a fare, which could be more or less than the regulated fee a taxi would charge. Both taxis and hackneys advertise in the classifieds or "Golden Pages."

DRIVING SERVICES

There is still another way of getting around Ireland by car. If cost is no concern, or if you can't shake the fear of the left lane, you might want to consider being chauffeured in style. The fleets of such services usually begin at ground level with a basic Mercedes sedan and stretch from there. If you're interested, contact **Carey Limousine International** (☎ **800/336-4646;** www. careyint.com), whose 8-hour daily rate is currently around $450. In Ireland, with offices in Dublin and Shannon, we recommend Bord Fáilte–approved **Dave Sullivan Chauffeur Drive Limited** (☎ **01/820-1076;** fax 01/ 820-6333; www.chauffeur.ie). A typical 8-hour bottom line for two people in and around Dublin will run about $350. For larger parties, Chrysler Voyagers are available.

BY FERRY

The coast of Ireland is not so razor-straight as, say, the borders of Kansas. A number of passenger and car ferries cut across the wider gaps, shaving hours off point-to-point driving times. These routes operate between Tarbert, County Kerry, and Killimer, County Clare; Passage East, County Waterford, and Ballyhack, County Wexford; and Glenbrook, east of Cork City, and Carrigaloe, outside of Cobh. For details, see chapter 10, "The West" (particularly the section on County Clare); chapter 6, "The Southeast"; and chapter 7, "Cork City."

Additionally, because Ireland includes a number of must-see islands, getting around includes getting on a boat now and then. Some boats, including all major ferries, have official licenses and offer regular scheduled service. Sometimes, however, making a crossing is a matter of staring out across a body of water to where you want to be and asking someone with a boat to take you there. Both methods work. To supplement the boat listings in this guide, you might want to request a copy of Information Sheet 50C—*Island Boat/ Air Services*—from the Irish Tourist Board.

11 From Cottages to Castles: Putting a Roof over Your Head

In Ireland, a man's (or woman's) home is often quite literally a castle, and some castles are homes away from home for visitors. In fact, Ireland offers a remarkable array of roofs, some quite affordable and others outrageously lavish. There is something for everyone, from families on a budget to lovers on the splurge of a lifetime. Here's a sketch of what's out there.

BED & BREAKFASTS

Throughout Ireland, in the cities and in the sticks, private homes are often open to lodgers, by the night or longer. A warm bed and a solid, hot breakfast can be expected, and other meals are negotiable. While most B&Bs are regulated and inspected by Tourism Quality Services (look for the shamrock seal of approval), approximately 12,000 premises are under no external supervision. Regulated or not, they are all different, as are your hosts. (*Note:* Establishments without governmental supervision or approval are not necessarily inferior to those stamped with the green shamrock. Approval involves an annual fee, as well as specific restrictions that some proprietors prefer not to embrace.)

For a modest fee, the Irish Tourist Board will send a detailed listing of roughly 2,000 approved B&Bs, complete with a color photo of each. Or, better yet, you can follow the recommendations in this book. Needless to say, you receive the personal touch when you stay in someone's home, and more often than not, this is a real bonus. For those on the move (spending only a night or two in each location) and on a budget, this choice is often hard to beat.

Make your reservation at least 24 hours in advance (48 hr. in high season); your room will ordinarily be held until 6pm. The cost for a room with private bath is roughly $25 to $40 per person, per night. *Note:* More and more B&Bs accept credit cards, but some still do not.

In the North, the Northern Ireland Tourist Board inspects each of its recommended bed-and-breakfasts annually. In 1998, it issued the first edition of its *Information Guide to Bed & Breakfast,* which is available free from the NITB. The NITB also sells a useful comprehensive annual listing titled *Where to Stay in Northern Ireland.*

HOTELS & GUESTHOUSES

Be Our Guest, a full guide to the hotels and inns of Ireland, is distributed by the Irish Hotel Federation and is available from the Irish Tourist Board. It's also online at **ireland.iol.ie/be-our-guest/**. Hotels and guesthouses, depending on their size and scope, offer a good deal more than a bed and a meal—everything from nightclubs to golf courses. Some were castles in a former life, others have been elegant hotels from birth, and many are nondescript.

Spa Vacations

If healing, renewal, and healthful relaxation are a central goal of your vacation, you might consider one of the centers, spas, or retreats approved by the **Health Farms of Ireland Association,** Rinville, Oranmore, County Galway. For an inviting brochure detailing the association's offerings, contact Margaret McNulty (☎ **091/790606;** fax 091/790837; www.galwaybayhealthfarm.ie).

The governments of the Republic and of the North inspect and rate all approved hotels and guesthouses. In the Republic, hotels can aspire to five stars, but guesthouses can reach no higher than four. In the North, hotels receive one to four stars, and guesthouses are either grade A or grade B. The least expensive options might cost no more than a home-style bed-and-breakfast, and the most expensive can be over 10 times that. See "Accommodations" sections throughout this book for reviews of my top choices.

FARMHOUSE ACCOMMODATIONS

The vast majority of Irish farms—more than 150,000 in all—are relatively small and remain family-owned and -operated. In recent years, many of these farms have opened their doors to visitors. They offer an attractive alternative to hotels, guesthouses, and more standard B&B homes, particularly for families. The **Irish Farm Holidays Association** produces an annual book that lists farmhouse accommodations throughout the country. It is available from the Irish Tourist Board.

Farm holidays can take various forms, from one-night-at-a-time bed-and-breakfasts to extended self-catering rentals. Many of the farmhouse accommodations, in addition to breakfast, offer high tea, a full dinner, or both. Some are everything you could dream of—full working family farms in untouched, often spectacular surroundings—while others stretch the meaning of *farm* to include country houses with a garden and a dog nearby, or guesthouses that are more "lodging with greenery" than "farm with lodging."

One of the newest developments on the Irish tourism scene is Irish Country Holidays, a program that invites visitors to share everyday life with the Irish in communities that are usually off the tourist track. Visitors are put up in homes, farms, self-catering cottages, or hotels, and they're given the opportunity to take part in turf cutting, bread baking, cheese making, butter churning, salmon smoking, wood turning, and pottery making. Leisure activities such as fishing, canoeing, rock climbing, hill walking, cycling, and horse riding are also available. At night there are traditional Irish music, song, dance, and amateur drama productions. Each package is custom planned. For more information, contact Martina O'Brien, **Irish Country Holidays,** Discovery Centre, Rearcross, County Tipperary (☎ **062/79330;** fax 062/79331).

THE HIDDEN IRELAND

The Hidden Ireland offers still another alternative to hotels, guesthouses, and B&Bs. This is an organization of homeowners whose homes, often some of Ireland's oldest and grandest, are of particular architectural merit and character—in other words, they're the houses you drive past that make you wonder how you could talk your way in, just to have a look around. The good news and the bad news about the Hidden Ireland is that there are *people* living in these houses—who take visitors into their family, eat their meals with them, and share the evening with them. This can mean "big house, close quarters," or it can mean something delightfully unforgettable, depending on the personalities involved (both yours and theirs). To explore this option, contact the Hidden Ireland, 37 Lower Baggot St., Dublin 2 (☎ **01/662-7166,** or 800/688-0299 from the U.S.; fax 01/662-7144; www.hidden-ireland.com).

SELF-CATERING

If you want to stay a while and establish a base, you might want to consider renting an apartment, town house, cottage, or castle. Self-catering is a huge trend in Ireland, and the range of available accommodations is startling. The

ECEAT, the European Centre for Eco Agro Tourism, was established in 1993 to foster and support small-scale, sustainable green tourism throughout Europe. Their guides currently offer 1,200 select sites—farms, natural campsites, guesthouses, and small hotels in 21 countries—committed to the preservation of natural and cultural landscapes. Look for a copy of *The Green Holiday Guides: Great Britain and Ireland* in bookstores, or contact the Ireland coordinator, Margaret Hedge, Triskel Flower Farm, Cloonagh, Beltra, Co. Sligo (☎ **071/66714**).

minimum rental period is usually 1 week, although shorter periods are sometimes negotiable off-season. For families or small groups, this is definitely a bargain way to go.

In high season, in both the Republic and the North, a cottage sleeping seven could cost anywhere from $250 to more than $1,000 per week. While this guide does not focus on self-catering, you will find a scattering of specific recommendations in the chapters that follow. Both the Irish Tourist Board and the Northern Ireland Tourist Board prepare helpful annual guides to self-catering.

If you are the nesting type, are planning a family reunion, or just want to settle into one bit of Irish turf for a week or more, we can recommend highly several self-catering companies. They offer especially attractive accommodations throughout Ireland, mostly along the coasts. One is **Trident Holiday Homes,** 15 Irishtown Rd., Irishtown, Dublin 4 (☎ **01/668-3534;** fax 01/660-6465; www.thh.ie). If you want a real splurge, contact **Elegant Ireland,** 15 Harcourt St., Dublin 2 (☎ **01/475-1632;** fax 01/475-1012; www. elegant.ie), which can situate you in anything from a castle to a fine Georgian manor house. Elegant Ireland also offers customized tours, catering to personal interests such as architecture, gardens, and golf. For alluring seaside properties in County Kerry, you will be surprised by what's on offer from **Cashelfean Holiday Houses,** Durrus, County Cork (☎ **027/62000;** fax 027/62012; www.cashelfean.com). In the west of Ireland, from Kerry to Connemara, a selection of traditional Irish cottages, fully equipped to meet modern expectations, is offered by **Rent an Irish Cottage plc.,** 85 O'Connell St., Limerick, County Limerick (☎ **061/411109;** fax 061/314821; www. rentacottage.ie).

Finally, for self-catering in any of the North's areas of outstanding natural beauty, there is one sure-shot recommendation: **Rural Cottage Holidays Ltd.,** St. Anne's Ct., 59 North St., Belfast BT1 1NB (☎ **028/9024-1100;** fax 028/9024-1100). Founded in 1994 by the Northern Irish Tourist Board, Rural Cottage Holidays has restored and refurbished more than 30 traditional homes of character and charm, and done so with remarkable care and style. Each of these gems is in an area of special beauty and interest and is hosted by a nearby local family.

YOUTH HOSTELS

Ordinarily, youth hostels fall beyond the scope of what we recommend in this book. You should be aware, however, that some Irish hostels are broadening their scope and redesigning their accommodations to welcome travelers of all ages, as well as families. Some of these, although they cost a fraction of even a modest bed-and-breakfast, provide remarkably appealing accommodations. In fact, with sufficient notice, the Irish Youth Hostel Association is able to rent some entire hostels to clubs or groups at remarkably reasonable rates.

An Óige, the Irish Youth Hostel Association, 61 Mountjoy St., Dublin 7 (☎ **01/830-4555;** fax 01/830-5808; www.irelandyha.org), is the place to begin your planning. At one time, anyone showing up at an Irish Youth Hostel in a car was turned away. But that was then. The net has widened considerably. These places are sometimes hard to get to and very hard to leave. Most often located in drop-dead-beautiful spots and housed in former residences of real character, several hostels in particular offer private rooms for couples and families, some with private bathrooms. Before you dismiss this option, explore the Web site and see if you can believe the views and the prices.

The corresponding organization in the North, whose hostels are maintained to a very high standard, is **YHANI** (Northern Ireland's Youth Hostels Association), 22–32 Donegall Rd., Belfast BT12 5JN (☎ **028/9032-4733;** fax 028/90439699; www.hini.org). When you come across related references to **HINI** (Hostelling International Northern Ireland), don't be confused. It's another name for the same organization.

PRACTICAL MATTERS

RATES Room charges quoted in this guide include 12.5% government tax (VAT) in the Republic of Ireland and 17.5% VAT in Northern Ireland. They do not (unless otherwise noted) include service charges, which are usually between 10% and 15% (most places add 12.5%). Most hotels and guesthouses automatically add the service charge onto your final bill, although in recent years many family-run or limited-service places have begun the practice of not charging for service, leaving it as an option for the guest. Home-style B&Bs do not ordinarily charge for service.

The price categories used throughout this guide indicate the cost of a double room for two per night, including tax but not service charges.

Very Expensive	£175 ($245) and up
Expensive	£135–£175 ($189–$245)
Moderate	£70–£135 ($98–$189)
Inexpensive	Under £70 ($98)

Note: Many accommodations span more than one of these categories, and in those cases, we've done our best to assign each to the category that best represents its characteristic rates in high season.

Ordinarily, the Irish cite the per-person price of a double room—a policy not followed in this guide, which for the sake of uniform comparison assumes double occupancy. Most accommodations make adjustments for children. Children accompanying their parents are often assessed on an ad hoc sliding scale. In other words, a smallish, angelic child may well incur only a nominal fee, if any, but a hellion may pay full price. So it pays to have your children put their best, most silent feet forward when you enter a hotel or guesthouse. If you're traveling on your own, there is most often a supplemental charge for single occupancy of a double room.

If you have a talent for it, room prices in hotels—especially privately owned hotels in the off-season—are negotiable. I have it on the best of authority (the experienced manager of a revered old hotel) that a polite entry into such negotiations is to ask, "Is that your best rate?" or "Can you do a little bit better?" The same hotelier described to me an occasion when a big-booted Texan slammed a fistful of bills down on the reception desk and bellowed, "Fifty bucks, take it or leave it." This approach to negotiation is not recommended.

TERMINOLOGY The Irish use the phrase "en suite" to indicate a room with private bathroom. A "double" has a double bed, and a "twin" has two single beds. An "orthopedic" bed has an extra-firm mattress. Queen- and king-size beds are not common except in large, deluxe hotels.

RESERVATIONS   Many hotels can be booked through toll-free numbers in the United States; better yet, the prices offered can be appreciably (as much as 40%) lower than those offered at the door. For those properties that do not have a U.S. reservation number, the fastest way to reserve is by telephone, fax, or e-mail. Fax and e-mail are advisable, because they give you a written confirmation. You can then follow up by sending a deposit check (usually the equivalent of one night's room rate) or by giving your credit-card number.

If you arrive in Ireland without a reservation, the staff members at the tourist offices throughout the Republic and Northern Ireland will gladly find you a room using a computerized reservation service known as **Gulliver.** You can also call the Gulliver line directly (☎ **00800/668-668-66**). This is a nationwide and cross-border "freephone" facility for credit-card bookings, operated daily 8am to 11pm. Gulliver is also accessible from the United States (☎ **011800/668-668-66**).

QUALITY & VALUE   Despite the various systems of approval, regulation, and rating, accommodations in Ireland are quite uneven in quality and cost. A budget hostel might be cleaner and more accommodating than a guesthouse or hotel and cost only a third as much. Tourism in Ireland is a boom industry, and there is a general rush to be a part of it. Understandably and regrettably, the gatekeepers are not as rigorous as their reputation, so it is always wise to consult a fellow traveler or a reliable guidebook in booking your lodgings (which, of course, is what you're doing).

If possible, always ask to see your room before committing yourself to a stay. In any given lodging, the size and quality of the rooms can vary considerably, often without any corresponding variation in cost. This is particularly true of single rooms, which can approach boarding-house standards even in a semi-luxurious hotel. Don't be discouraged by this, but be alert so you're not disappointed. If you have complaints, state them at once and unambiguously, which will likely bring an immediate resolution. Saving up your disappointments to file them all at once, like your taxes, seldom gets you anywhere.

Note: Many lodgings close for a few days or more on and around Christmas, even when they announce that they are open year-round. If you plan to visit Ireland during the Christmas holidays, double-check that the hotels, restaurants, and attractions you're counting on will be open. In this guide, what is true on Sundays is nearly always true on bank holidays. And be aware that only the most expensive hotels have air-conditioning—and there are only a handful of days a year when you would want it.

12 Tips on Restaurants & Pubs

RESTAURANTS

Ireland has an admirable range of restaurants in all price categories. The settings range from old-world hotel dining rooms, country mansions, and castles to skylit terraces, shop-front bistros, riverside cottages, thatched-roof pubs, and converted chapels. Best of all, the food is fresh, varied, and delicious (see the appendix, "Ireland in Depth.").

Before you book a table, here are a few things you should know:

RESERVATIONS   Except for self-service eateries, informal cafes, and some popular seafood spots, most restaurants encourage reservations. The more expensive restaurants absolutely require reservations because there is little turnover—once a table is booked, it is yours for the whole lunch period or for the evening until closing. Seatings for Friday and Saturday nights (and Sun lunch) are often booked a week or more in advance at some places, so have a few options in mind if you're booking at the last minute.

Here's a tip for those who don't mind dining early: if you stop into or phone a restaurant and find that it is booked from 8 or 8:30pm onward, ask if you can dine early (at 6:30 or 7pm), with a promise to leave by 8pm. You will sometimes get a table. Quite a few restaurants are experimenting with lower-priced early-bird and pretheater menus to attract people for early evening seating.

TABLE D'HÔTE OR À LA CARTE Most restaurants offer two menus: *table d'hôte*, a fixed-price three- or four-course lunch or dinner with a variety of choices; and *à la carte*, a menu offering a wide choice of individually priced appetizers (starters), soups, main courses, salads or vegetables, and desserts (sweets).

With the former, you pay the set price whether you take each course or not. If you do take each course, the total price offers very good value. With the latter, you choose what you want and pay accordingly. If you are a salad-and-entree person, then à la carte will probably work out to be less expensive; if you want all the courses and the trimmings, stick with the table d'hôte.

Finer restaurants push the table d'hôte menu at lunchtime, particularly for business clientele. In the evening, both menus are readily available. In the less expensive restaurants, coffee shops, and cafes, you can usually order à la carte at any time.

Here's a tip for those on a budget: If you want to try a top-rated restaurant but can't afford dinner, have your main meal there in the middle of the day by trying the table d'hôte set lunch menu. You'll experience the same great cuisine at half the price of a nighttime meal.

PRICES Meal prices at restaurants include a 12.5% VAT in the Republic of Ireland and a 17.5% VAT in Northern Ireland, but the service charge is extra. In perhaps half of all restaurants, a set service charge is added automatically; it can range from 10% to 15%. In the remaining restaurants, it is now the custom not to add any service charge, leaving the amount of the tip up to you. This can be confusing for a visitor, but each restaurant normally prints its policy on the menu. If it is not clear, ask.

When no service charge is added, tip as you normally would in the United States, up to 15% depending on the quality of the service. If 10% to 12.5% has already been added to your bill, leave an appropriate amount that will total 15% if service has been satisfactory.

The price categories used in this book are based on the price of a complete dinner (or lunch, if dinner is not served) for one person, including tax and tip, but not wine or alcoholic beverages:

Very Expensive	£43 ($60) and up
Expensive	£27–£43 ($38–$60)
Moderate	£13–£27 ($18–$38)
Inexpensive	Under £13 ($18)

DINING TIPS If you are fond of a cocktail or beer before or during your meal, be sure to check in advance if a restaurant has a full license—some restaurants are licensed to sell only wine.

Don't be surprised if you are not ushered to your table as soon as you arrive at a restaurant. This is not a delaying tactic—many of the better dining rooms

Some restaurants offer a fixed-price three-course tourist menu during certain hours and days. These menus offer limited choices, but are usually lower in price than the restaurant's regular table d'hôte menu. Look for a tourist menu with a green Irish chef symbol in the window, listing the choices and the hours when the prices are in effect.

carry on the old custom of seating you in a lounge or bar area while you sip an apéritif and peruse the menu. Your waiter then comes to discuss the choices and to take your order. You are not called to the table until the first course is about to be served.

PUBS

The mainstay of Irish social life, day and night, is unquestionably the pub. With more than 10,000 specimens throughout the country, there are pubs in every city, town, and hamlet, on every street and at every turn.

The origin of pubs reaches back several centuries to a time when, for lack of trendy coffee bars or health clubs, neighbors would gather in a kitchen to talk and maybe sample some home brew. As a certain spot grew popular, word spread and people came from all directions, always assured of a warm welcome. Such places gradually became known as public houses—"pubs," for short. In time, the name of the person who tended a public house was mounted over the doorway, and many pubs still bear a family or proprietor's name, such as Davy Byrnes, Doheny and Nesbitt, or W. Ryan. Many, in fact, have been in the same family for generations. Although they might have added televisions, pool tables, and dartboards, their primary purpose is still to be a stage for conversation and a warm spot to down a pint or pack in an inexpensive lunch of pub grub. Pub grub is often a lot better than its name suggests; in recent years, many pubs have converted or expanded into restaurants, serving excellent unpretentious meals at prices to which you can lift a pint.

PUB HOURS In the Republic of Ireland, hours in May to September are 10:30am to 11:30pm Monday to Saturday. October to April hours are 10:30am to 11pm. On Sunday year-round, bars are open from 12:30 to 2pm and from 4 to 11pm. Nightclubs and discos close at 2am. If the pub does not appear to be closing when the appointed hour arrives, it's because the official closing times are often not the actual closing times. Some laws, it seems, are made to be broken.

In the North, pubs are open year-round from 11:30am to 11pm Monday to Saturday, 12:30 to 2pm and 7 to 10pm on Sunday.

13 Tips on Sightseeing & Shopping

SIGHTSEEING DISCOUNTS

Sightseeing on a budget? Ireland offers several ways to cut costs and stretch a dollar (or a pound). Here are a few ways to save on admission charges at major attractions.

A **Heritage Card** entitles you to unlimited admission to the more than 100 attractions all over Ireland operated by Dúchas, the Heritage Service. These include castles, stately homes, historic monuments, national parks, and more. The card, which costs £15 ($21) for adults, £10 ($14) for seniors, £6 ($8.40) for children and students, and £36 ($50.40) for a family, is available from participating attractions or by credit card at ☎ **01/647-2461**. Further information is available on the Web at **www.heritageireland.ie**. If you plan to do serious sightseeing, this is a wise purchase. It's far more pleasant to pick up one of these cards the first time you visit a Heritage site than to realize a week later how much you would have saved if you had.

Detailed information about National Trust attractions in Northern Ireland is available from the Northern Ireland Tourist Board.

VAT REFUNDS

When shopping in the Republic of Ireland and Northern Ireland, bear in mind that the price of most goods, excluding books and children's clothing and footwear, already includes valued-added tax (VAT), a government tax of 17.36%. VAT is a hidden tax—it is already included on the price tags and in prices quoted to you.

As a visitor, you can avoid paying this tax, *if* you follow a few simple procedures. *Note:* EU residents are not entitled to a VAT refund on goods purchased. As of July 1, 1999, EU residents are not entitled to duty-free shopping in airports and other transit terminals.

The easiest way to make a VAT-free purchase is to arrange for a store to ship the goods directly abroad to your home; such a shipment is not subject to VAT. However, you do have to pay for shipping, so you might not save that much in the end.

If you want to take your goods with you, you must pay the full amount for each item, including all VAT charges (unless you are shopping at a store that offers tax-free purchases to non-EU visitors). However, you can have that tax refunded to you in a number of ways. Here are the main choices:

For a store refund, get a full receipt at the time of purchase that shows the name, address, and VAT paid. (Customs does not accept cash-register tally slips.) Save your receipts until you're ready to depart Ireland; go to the Customs Office at the airport or ferry port to have your receipts stamped and your goods inspected. A passport and other forms of identification (a driver's license, for example) may be required. Stamped receipts should then be sent to the store where you made the purchase, which will then issue a VAT refund check to you by mail to your home address. Most stores deduct a small handling fee for this service.

Global Refund (☎ 800/566-9828) is one of several private companies offering a cash refund on purchases made at thousands of shops that display a variety of stickers, such as "Tax Back," "Cash Refund," and "Tax Saver." Refunds can be collected in the currency of your choice as you depart from Dublin or Shannon Airport. The nominal fee for this service is calculated on the amount of money you spend in each store. These booths are open year-round (except Dec 25 and 26) in the arrivals halls of Dublin Airport and Shannon Airport.

To get a refund, do the following:

1. Make purchases from stores displaying an appropriate sticker, and be sure to get VAT-refund vouchers from these participating shops each time you make a purchase.
2. Fill out each form with your name, address, passport number, and other required details.
3. When departing Ireland, have any vouchers with a value of over £200 ($280) stamped and validated by a Customs official.

4. Go to the VAT-refund booth corresponding to your vouchers at Dublin Airport (Departures Hall) or Shannon Airport (Arrivals Hall), turn in your stamped forms, and receive cash payments in U.S. or Canadian dollars, British pounds sterling, or Irish punts.

If you are departing from Ireland through a ferry port, or if you don't have time to get to the ETS booth before you leave, you can send your stamped vouchers to the appropriate VAT refund company and receive a refund by mail, or have your refund applied to your credit-card account.

14 Tracing Your Irish Roots

Whether your name is Kelly or Klein, you might have some ancestral ties with Ireland—about 40 million Americans do. If you are planning to visit Ireland to trace your roots, you'll enjoy the greatest success if you do some planning. The more information you can gather about your family before your visit, the easier it will be to find your ancestral home or even a distant cousin once you arrive.

For the personal pursuit of Irish kin, *Tracing Your Ancestors in Ireland,* published by the Irish Tourist Board, provides many points of departure. It outlines the range of resources for genealogical research in Dublin, as well as throughout the island, and helps you get started. It's free of charge at any Irish Tourist Board office.

In Ireland, you can do the research and footwork yourself, or you can use the services of a commercial agency. One of the best firms is **Hibernian Research Co.,** P.O. Box 2097, Dublin 6 (☎ **01/496-6522;** fax 01/ 497-3011). The researchers, all trained by the Chief Herald of Ireland, have a combined total of more than 100 years' professional experience in working on all aspects of family histories. Among the cases that Hibernian Research handled were U.S. President Ronald Reagan, Canadian Prime Minister Brian Mulrooney, and Ireland's own President Mary Robinson.

You may also wish to consult **ENECLANN,** a Trinity College Dublin Campus Company, at the Innovation Centre, O'Reilly Institute, Trinity College, Dublin 2 (☎ **01/608-2391;** fax 01/671-0281; www.eneclann.tcd.ie). A full description of their highly qualified and touted genealogical services and their fees are available on their Web site.

If you prefer to do the digging yourself, Dublin City is the location for all the Republic of Ireland's centralized genealogical records, and Belfast is the place to go for Ulster ancestral hunts. Here are the major sources of information:

The National Library, Kildare Street, Dublin 2 (☎ **01/603-0200**), has resources that include an extensive collection of pre-1880 Catholic records of baptisms, births, and marriages. Its other genealogical material includes trade directories, journals of historical and archaeological societies, local histories, and most newspapers. In addition, the library has a comprehensive indexing system that enables you to identify the material you need to consult.

The Genealogical Office, 2 Kildare St., Dublin (☎ **01/661-8811;** fax 01/662-1062), attached to the National Library, incorporates the office of the

---

Impressions

A man travels the world over in search of what he needs and returns home to find it.

—George Moore (1852–1933): *Brook Kerith*

Chief Herald and operates a specialist consultation service on how to trace your ancestry. In-house searches by the office researcher are billed at the rate of £35 ($49) per hour.

The Office of the Registrar General, Joyce House, 8/11 Lombard St. E., Dublin 2 (☎ **01/671-1000**), is the central repository for records relating to births, deaths, and marriages in the Republic (Catholic marriages from Jan 1, 1864; all other marriages from Apr 1, 1845). This office does not engage in genealogical research. Full birth, death, or marriage certificates each cost £5.50 ($7.70). General searches cost £12 ($16.80). The office is open weekdays from 9:30am to 12:30pm and 2:15 to 4:30pm.

The National Archives, Bishop Street, Dublin 8 (☎ **01/407-2300;** fax 01/407-2333; www.nationalarchives.ie), was previously known as the Public Record Office. A fire severely damaged this facility in the early 1920s, and many valuable source documents were lost. However, numerous records rich in genealogical interest are still available. They include *Griffith's Primary Valuation of Ireland, 1848–63,* which records the names of all those owning or occupying land or property in Ireland at the time; the complete national census of 1901 to 1911; and tithe listings, indexes to wills, administrations, licenses, and marriage bonds. In addition, there is also an ever-expanding collection of Church of Ireland Parish Registers on microfilm. You'll also find partial surviving census returns for the 19th century, reports and records relating to the period of the 1798 rebellion, crime and convict records, and details of those sentenced to transportation to Australia. There is no fee for conducting personal searches for family history and genealogy in the archives, and an instruction booklet is provided to get you started. There is a fee for photocopies. The National Archives reading room is open Monday to Friday, 10am to 5pm.

The Registry of Deeds, Kings Inns, Henrietta Street, Dublin 1 (☎ **01/ 670-7500;** fax 01/804-8406; www.irlgov.ie/landreg), has records that date from 1708 and relate to all the usual transactions affecting property—notably leases, mortgages, and settlements—and some wills. The fee of £10 ($14) per day includes instructions on how to handle the indexes.

The Public Record Office of Northern Ireland, 66 Balmoral Ave., Belfast BT9 6NY (☎ **028/9025-1318;** fax 028/9025-5999; www.proni.nics.gov.uk), has the surviving official records of Northern Ireland. They include tithe and valuation records from the 1820s and 1830s, copies of wills from 1858 for Ulster, the records of many landed estates in Ulster, and copies of most pre-1900 registers of baptisms, marriages, and burial papers for all denominations in Ulster. The office is open weekdays 9:15am to 4:45pm (until 8:45pm on Thurs, closed for 2 weeks in late Nov).

If you know the county or town that your ancestors came from, you can also consult the local genealogical centers, parish records, and libraries throughout Ireland and Northern Ireland. Or you can begin your search by visiting a couple of especially helpful sites on the Web: **www.genealogy.ie** and **www. familysearch.com**.

15 Suggested Itineraries

To make the rounds of Ireland, North and South, you'll need at least 2 weeks—or, better, 3 weeks. With even a week, however, you can convince yourself and others you've been there.

Here are a few recommended itineraries, with the number of days suggested for each city or touring center indicated in parentheses. Each tour starts or finishes near Shannon or Dublin, the two main arrival and departure points. You can ask your travel agent to design a trip based on your interests or on the amount of time you can spend.

1 Week—Southern Coast: Shannon area (1), Kerry (2), Cork (2), Wexford (1), Dublin (1).

1 Week—Main Highlights: Shannon area (1), Kerry (1), Cork (1), Waterford (1), Dublin (2), Galway (1).

1 Week—East Coast: Dublin (3), Dundalk (1), Kilkenny (1), Waterford (1), Wexford (1).

1 Week—West Coast: Kerry (2), Galway and Connemara (2), Sligo (2), Shannon area (1).

1 Week—The Northwest: Shannon area (1), Sligo (2), Donegal (3), Shannon (1).

1 Week—The North: Newcastle (1), Belfast (2), Antrim Coast (2), Derry (1), Enniskillen (1).

2 Weeks: The Coastal Circuit: Shannon (1); Kerry (2); Cork (1); Dublin (2); Belfast (2); Sligo (1); Donegal (2); Galway, Mayo, and Connemara (2); Shannon (1).

3 Weeks—The Complete Tour: Shannon (1), Kerry (2), Cork (1), Kilkenny (1), Waterford or Wexford (1), Dublin (3), Belfast (2), Portrush (1), Derry or Enniskillen (2), Sligo (1), Donegal (2), Mayo (1), Galway and Connemara (2), Shannon (1).

All of the above itineraries describe circles, which are not for everyone. When time is scarce, some people, like me, prefer to settle into one place for a week and reach out from there. This is the "hub" plan, surely a viable alternative to the 7-day dash. If it's your first time in Ireland, Dublin and Galway make great hubs. Whether you decide to tour or to stay put might depend on whether you're primarily in search of sights or stories. You'll see more sights while moving around, but you'll likely hear more stories if you stay around for them.

Fast Facts: Ireland

American Express The only American Express offices in Ireland are in Dublin, Galway, and Killarney. There are no longer offices in the North. In an emergency, traveler's checks can be reported lost or stolen by dialing collect ☎ **1-44-1-273-571-600.**

Business Hours **Banks** are open Monday to Wednesday and on Friday from 10am to 12:30pm and from 1:30 to 3pm, on Thursday from 10am to 12:30pm and from 1:30 to 5pm. Some banks are beginning to stay open through the lunch hour. Most **business offices** are open from 9am to 5pm, Monday to Friday. **Stores and shops** are open from 9am to 5:30pm Monday to Wednesday and Friday to Saturday, and from 9am to 8pm on Thursday. Some bookshops and tourist-oriented stores also are open on Sunday from 11am or noon until 4 or 5pm. During the peak season (May to Sept), many gift and souvenir shops post Sunday hours. Some country towns have an early closing day when shops close at 1pm. For more exact regional shopping hours, see individual chapters.

Climate See "When to Go," earlier in this chapter.

Closing Times   It is often the case with "Attractions" that new visitors will not be admitted 30 minutes prior to the stated closing time; so, for example, don't expect to slip into a museum or castle at 4:35 when it officially closes at 5pm.

Currency   See "Money," earlier in this chapter.

Currency Exchange   Currency-exchange services, signposted as BUREAU DE CHANGE, are in all banks and at many branches of the Irish post-office system, known as **An Post.** A bureau de change operates daily during flight arrival and departure times at Dublin airport; a foreign currency note-exchanger machine is also available on a 24-hour basis in the main arrivals hall. Many hotels and travel agencies offer bureau de change services, although the best rate of exchange is usually given at banks or, better yet, when you use your credit card for purchases or expenses.

Customs   See "Entry Requirements & Customs," earlier in this chapter.

Dentists   For listings, look under "Dental Surgeons" in the Golden Pages (yellow pages) of the Irish telephone book or in the Yellow Pages of the Northern Ireland telephone book—or better yet, ask your innkeeper for advice. Expect to pay up front.

Doctors   If you need to see a physician, most hotels and guesthouses will contact a house doctor for you. (You will also find referral services for the greater Dublin area listed in "Fast Facts: Dublin," in chapter 4.) Otherwise, consult the Golden Pages of the Irish telephone book or the Yellow Pages of the Northern Ireland telephone book. As with dentists, expect to pay for treatment up front and be reimbursed after the fact by your insurance company.

Driving Rules   See "Getting Around," earlier in this chapter.

Drugs & Firearms   The laws against the importation of illegal drugs and firearms are quite severe and will be enforced. Consult the nearest Irish or Northern Ireland consulate before presuming to bring any firearm into Ireland.

Drugstores   Drugstores are usually called "chemist shops" or "pharmacies." Look under "Chemists—Pharmaceutical" in the Golden Pages of the Irish telephone book or "Chemists—Dispensing" in the Yellow Pages of the Northern Ireland telephone book.

Electricity   The standard electrical current is 220 volts AC in the Republic of Ireland, 240 volts in Northern Ireland. Most hotels have 110-volt shaver points for use in bathrooms, but other 110-volt equipment (such as hair dryers) will not work without a transformer and a plug adapter. Computers and sensitive electronic equipment may require more than the standard over-the-counter voltage converter. Some laptops have built-in converters. Consult the manufacturer of your computer for specifics. In any event, you will always need a plug adapter.

Embassies/Consulates   The **American Embassy** is at 42 Elgin Rd., Ballsbridge, Dublin 4 (☎ **01/668-8777**); the **Canadian Embassy** at 65/68 St. Stephen's Green, Dublin 2 (☎ **01/678-1988**); the **British Embassy** at 33 Merrion Rd., Dublin 4 (☎ **01/205-3700**); and the **Australian Embassy** at Fitzwilton House, Wilton Terrace, Dublin 2 (☎ **01/676-1517**). In addition, there is an **American Consulate** at 14 Queen St., Belfast BT1 6EQ (☎ **028/9032-8239**).

Emergencies   For the **Garda** (police), fire, or other emergencies, dial
☎ **999.**

Etiquette   The Irish still observe a range of traditional courtesies, such
as males holding doors for females, and the young and strong giving up
a seat on a bus for senior citizens and pregnant women. Contrary to their
media image, the Irish are generally neither loud nor assertive in public.
If you prefer not to be spotted as a tourist, mind your decibels and your
stride. Even when we whisper, it's our gait that gives us away. Try not
looking at your fellow pedestrians as members of the other team, "inter-
ference" as it were, and you'll blend in.

   I always try to remember that we are the strangers, the outsiders, when
we travel abroad. In an embarrassing moment, when what's going on
makes no sense, chances are the joke is on us. You can react in two ways:
belligerently or with humor. Try the latter.

   One deep breach in hospitality that many travelers from the United
States will note is the obliviousness and insensitivity of many Irish
smokers to the discomfort they bring to nonsmokers. Smokers still pretty
much have the wheel in Ireland. In public places, smokers often light up
without hesitation directly under "no smoking" signs. For some pubs I'd
recommend gas masks, were they feasible. When a hotel or restaurant or
pub makes significant provision for nonsmokers, we try to note it in this
book. Unless otherwise indicated, nonsmokers will have to fend for
themselves. On a more promising note, in February of 2000, the new
Irish Health Minister, Micheál Martin "declared war" on smoking in
Ireland and said that it was his aim to create "a tobacco-free society." His
declaration rallied something less than a standing army of militant nonsmokers, but it's likely that the seed of a revolution has been planted.

Internet Access   Public access terminals are no longer hard to find in
Ireland; they're now in shopping malls, hotels, and even hostels, especially in the larger towns and more tourist-centered areas. Additionally,
there are an increasing number of Internet cafes sprouting up across the
island. We've done our best to locate and list many of these in the chapters that follow.

Language   See the "Language" section in the appendix, "Ireland in
Depth."

Liquor Laws   Individuals must be age 18 or over to be served alcoholic
beverages in Ireland. For pub hours, see "Tips on Restaurants & Pubs,"
earlier in this chapter. Restaurants with liquor licenses are permitted to
serve alcohol during the hours when meals are served. Hotels and guesthouses with licenses can serve during normal hours to the public;
overnight guests, referred to as "residents," can be served after closing
hours. Alcoholic beverages by the bottle can be purchased at liquor
stores, at pubs displaying "off-license" signs, and at most supermarkets.

   Ireland has very severe laws and penalties regarding driving while
intoxicated, so don't even think about it.

Mail   In Ireland, mailboxes are painted green with the word POST on
top. In Northern Ireland, they are painted red with a royal coat of arms
symbol. From the Republic, an airmail letter or postcard to the United
States or Canada, not exceeding 25 grams, costs 45p (63¢) and takes 5
to 7 days to arrive. Prestamped aerogrammes or air letters are 45p (63¢).
From Northern Ireland to the United States or Canada, airmail letters

Telephone Dialing Info at a Glance

- **To place a call from your home country to Ireland,** dial the international access code (011 in the U.S., 0011 in Australia, 0170 in New Zealand, 00 in the U.K.), plus the country code (**353** for the Republic, **44** for the North), and finally the number, remembering to omit the initial 0, which is for use only within Ireland (for example, to call the County Kerry number 066/00000 from the United States, you'd dial 011-353-66/00000).

- **To place a direct international call from Ireland,** dial the international access code (**00**) plus the country code (U.S. and Canada 1, the U.K. 44, Australia 61, New Zealand 64), the area or city code, and the number (for example, to call the U.S. number 212/000-0000 you'd dial 00-1-212/000-0000). Several widely used toll-free international access codes are **AT&T** ☎ 1-800/550-000, **Sprint** ☎ 1/800-552-001, and **MCI** ☎ 1-800/55-1001. *Note:* To dial direct to Northern Ireland from the Republic, simply replace the 028 prefix with 048.

- **To place a collect call to the United States from Ireland,** dial ☎ 1-800/550-000 for USA Direct service.

- **To reach directory assistance,** dial ☎ **1190** within Ireland. From the United States, the (toll) number to call is ☎ **00353-91-770220.**

cost 39p (64¢) and postcards 34p (56¢). Delivery takes about 5 days to a week.

Newspapers/Magazines   The national daily newspapers in the Republic of Ireland are the *Irish Times, Irish Independent,* the *Irish Examiner,* the *Herald,* the *Star,* and the *Evening Echo.* The national Sunday editions are the *Sunday Independent, Sunday Press, Sunday Tribune, Sunday World,* and the Irish-language *Anola.* Prime dailies in the North are the *Belfast Newsletter,* the *Irish News,* and the *Belfast Telegraph.* For up-to-date listings of events throughout Ireland, the biweekly *Event Guide* is free and widely available.

Police   In the Republic of Ireland, a law enforcement officer is called a **Garda,** a member of the *Garda Siochana* (guardian of the peace); in the plural, it's *Gardai* (pronounced *gar*-dee) or simply "the Guards." Dial ☎ 999 to reach the Gardai in an emergency. Except for special detachments, Irish police are unarmed and wear dark blue uniforms. In Northern Ireland, you can reach the police by dialing ☎ **999.**

Radio/TV   In the Republic of Ireland, RTÉ (Radio Telefis Éireann) is the national broadcasting authority. There are two nationwide TV channels, RTÉ 1 and Network 2; a new Irish-language channel, TnaG (Teilifís na Gaeilge); and six nationwide VHF radio stations, Radio 1, 2FM, Radió na Gaeltachta (in Irish and English), FM3 (offering classical music), Today F.M., and RTÉ Cork. Smaller local stations serve specific regions. In North America, RTÉ radio is available through the Galaxy 5 satellite and at www.rte.ie. RTÉ, jointly with Telecom Éireann, owns and operates Cablelink Ltd., which provides a range of cable and satellite channels from Britain and farther abroad.

The latest addition to the Irish airwaves is TV3, Ireland's first independent and wholly commercial station.

In the North, there are Ulster Television, BBC-TV (British Broadcasting Corporation), and ITN-TV (Independent), plus BBC Radio 1, 2, and 3. Satellite programs via CNN, SKY News, and other international operators are also received.

Rest Rooms   Public rest rooms are usually simply called "toilets," or are marked with international symbols. In the Republic of Ireland, some of the older ones still carry the Gaelic words *Fir* (Men) and *Mna* (Women). The newest and best-kept rest rooms are found at shopping complexes and at multistory car parks. Some cost 10p (14¢) to enter. Free rest rooms are available to customers of sightseeing attractions, museums, hotels, restaurants, pubs, shops, theaters, and department stores. Gas stations normally do not have public toilets.

Safety   The Republic of Ireland has enjoyed a traditionally low crime rate, particularly when it comes to violent crime. Those days are not entirely over, but they do regrettably seem to be passing, especially in the cities. By U.S. standards, Ireland is still very safe, but not safe enough to warrant carelessness. Travelers should take normal precautions to protect their belongings from theft and themselves from harm.

In recent years, the larger cities have been prey to pickpockets, purse-snatchers, car thieves, and drug traffickers. To alert visitors to potential dangers, the Garda Siochana publishes a small leaflet, *A Short Guide to Tourist Security,* which is available at tourist offices and other public places. The booklet advises you not to carry large amounts of money or important documents like your passport or airline tickets when strolling around. Leave them in a safe-deposit box at your hotel. Do not leave cars unlocked or cameras, binoculars, or other expensive equipment unattended. Be alert and aware of your surroundings, and do not wander in lonely areas alone at night. Ask at your hotel about which areas are safe and which are not, and when.

In the north of Ireland, safety is a somewhat greater concern because of the political unrest that has prevailed there for the past 30 years. Before traveling to Northern Ireland, contact the U.S. State Department and the Northern Ireland Tourist Board to obtain the latest safety recommendations. The **U.S. Department of State 24-hour hotline (☎ 202/647-5225)** provides travel warnings and security recommendations, as well as emergency assistance.

Taxes   As in many European countries, sales tax is called VAT (value-added tax) and is often already included in the price quoted to you or shown on price tags. In the Republic, VAT rates vary—for hotels, restaurants, and car rentals, it is 12.5%; for souvenirs and gifts, it is 17.36%. In Northern Ireland, the VAT is 17.5% across the board. VAT charged on services such as hotel stays, meals, car rentals, and entertainment cannot be refunded to visitors, but the VAT on products such as souvenirs is refundable. For full details on VAT refunds for purchases, see "VAT Refunds," under "Tips on Sightseeing & Shopping," earlier in this chapter.

Telephone   In the Republic, the telephone system is known as Telecom Éireann; in Northern Ireland, it's British Telecom. Phone numbers in Ireland are currently in flux, as digits are added to accommodate expanded service. Every effort has been made to ensure that the numbers and information in this guide are accurate at the time of writing. If you have difficulty reaching a party, the Irish toll-free number for directory assistance is ☎ **1190.** From the United States, the (toll) number to call is ☎ **00353-91-770220.**

Local calls from a phone booth cost 20p (28¢) within the Republic of Ireland, and 20p (33¢) in the North for the first minute. The most efficient way to make calls from public phones is to use a Callcard (in the Republic) or Phonecard (in the North). Both are prepaid computerized cards that you insert into the phone instead of coins. They can be purchased in a range of denominations at phone company offices, post offices, and many retail outlets (such as newsstands). There's a local and international phone center at the General Post Office on O'Connell Street.

Overseas calls from Ireland can be quite costly, whether you use a local phonecard or your own calling card. If you think you will want to call home regularly while in Ireland, you may want to open an account with **Swiftcall** (toll-free in Ireland ☎ **0800-794-381;** www.swiftcall.com). Its rates represent a considerable savings, not only from Ireland to the United States but vice versa (handy for planning your trip as well as keeping in touch afterward). **Premiere WORLDLINK** (☎ **800/432-6169**) offers an array of additional services for overseas travelers—such as toll-free voice-mail boxes, fax mail, and news services—which can be crucial for keeping in touch when you don't know where or when you can be reached.

Time   Ireland follows Greenwich Mean Time (1 hr. earlier than Central European Time) from November to March, and British Standard Time (the same as Central European Time) from April to October. Ireland is five time zones earlier than the eastern United States (when it's noon in New York, it's 5pm in Ireland).

Ireland's latitude makes for longer days and shorter nights in the summer, and the reverse in the winter. In June, there is bright sun until 11pm, but in December, it is truly dark at 4pm.

Tipping   Most hotels and guesthouses add a service charge to the bill, usually 12.5% to 15%, although some smaller places add only 10% or nothing at all. Always check to see what amount, if any, has been added to your bill. If it is 12.5% to 15%, and you feel this is sufficient, then there is no need for more gratuities. However, if a smaller amount has been added or if staff members have provided exceptional service, it is appropriate to give additional cash gratuities. For porters or bellhops, tip 50p (70¢) to £1 ($1.40) per piece of luggage. For taxi drivers, hairdressers, and other providers of service, tip as you would at home, an average of 10% to 15%.

For restaurants, the policy is usually printed on the menu—either a gratuity of 10% to 15% is added to your bill or no service charge is added, leaving it up to you. Always ask if you are in doubt. As a rule, staff members at bars do not expect a tip, except when table service is provided.

Water   Tap water throughout the island of Ireland is generally safe to drink, though contamination of ground water and private wells is an increasing problem. If you prefer bottled water, it is readily available at all hotels, guesthouses, restaurants, and pubs.

Yellow Pages   The classified section of telephone books in the Republic of Ireland is called the Golden Pages. In the North, it's the Yellow Pages.

Planning Your Trip: An Online Directory

Frommer's Online Directory will help you take better advantage of the travel-planning information available online. Section 1 lists general Internet resources that can make any trip easier, such as sites for obtaining the best possible prices on airline tickets. In section 2 you'll find some top sites specifically for Ireland.

This is not a comprehensive list, but a discriminating selection to get you started. Recognition is given to sites based on their content value and ease of use. Inclusion here is not paid for—unlike some Web-site rankings, which are based on payment. Finally, remember that this is a press-time snapshot of leading Web sites; some undoubtedly will have evolved, changed, or moved by the time you read this.

1 The Top Travel-Planning Web Sites

By Lynne Bairstow

Lynne Bairstow is the co-author of *Frommer's Mexico,* and the editorial director of *e-com* magazine.

WHY BOOK ONLINE?

Online agencies have come a long way over the past few years, now providing tips for finding the best fare, and giving you suggested dates or times to travel that yield the lowest price if your plans are at all flexible. Other sites even allow you to establish the price you're willing to pay, and they check the airlines' willingness to accept it. However, in some cases, these sites may not always yield the best price. Unlike a travel agent, for example, they may not have access to charter flights offered by wholesalers.

Online booking sites aren't the only places to reserve airline tickets—all major airlines have their own Web sites and often offer incentives (bonus frequent-flyer miles or net-only discounts, for example) when you buy online or buy an e-ticket.

The new trend is toward conglomerated booking sites. By June 2001, a consortium of major U.S. airlines is planning to launch a Web site called **Orbitz.com**, which will offer fares lower than those available through travel agents. American, United, Delta, Northwest, and Continental have initiated this effort, based on their success at selling airline seats on their own sites.

Check Out Frommer's Site

We highly recommend **Arthur Frommer's Budget Travel Online** (**www.frommers.com**) as an excellent travel-planning resource. Of course, we're a little biased, but you'll find indispensable travel tips, reviews, monthly vacation giveaways, and online booking. Among the most popular features of this site are the regular "Ask the Expert" bulletin boards, which feature Frommer's authors answering your questions via online postings.

Subscribe to Arthur Frommer's Daily Newsletter (**www.frommers.com/newsletters**) to receive the latest travel bargains and inside travel secrets in your e-mailbox every day. You'll read daily headlines and articles from the dean of travel himself, highlighting last-minute deals on airfares, accommodations, cruises, and package vacations.

Search our Destinations archive (**www.frommers.com/destinations**) of more than 200 domestic and international destinations for great places to stay and dine, and tips on sightseeing. Once you've researched your trip, the online reservation system (**www.frommers.com/booktravelnow**) takes you to Frommer's favorite sites for booking your vacation at affordable prices.

The best of the travel-planning sites are now highly personalized; they store your seating preferences, meal preferences, tentative itineraries, and credit-card information, allowing you to quickly plan trips or check agendas.

In many cases, booking your trip online can be better than working with a travel agent. It gives you the widest variety of choices, control, and the 24-hour convenience of planning your trip when you choose. All you need is some time—and often a little patience—and you're likely to find that the fun of online travel research will greatly enhance your trip.

WHO SHOULD BOOK ONLINE?

Online booking is best for travelers who want to know as much as possible about their travel options, for those who have flexibility in their travel dates, and for bargain hunters.

One of the biggest successes in online travel for both passengers and airlines is the offer of last-minute specials, such as American Airlines' weekend deals or other Internet-only fares that must be purchased online. Another advantage is that you can cash in on incentives for booking online, such as rebates or bonus frequent-flyer miles.

Business and other frequent travelers also have found numerous benefits in online booking, as the advances in mobile technology provide them with the ability to check flight status, change plans, or get specific directions from handheld computing devices, mobile phones, and pagers. Some sites will even e-mail or page a passenger if their flight is delayed.

Online booking is increasingly able to accommodate complex itineraries, even for international travel. The pace of evolution on the Net is rapid, so you'll probably find additional features and advancements by the time you visit these sites. The future holds ever-increasing personalization and customization for online travelers.

TRAVEL-PLANNING & BOOKING SITES

Below are listings for sites for planning and booking travel. The following sites offer domestic and international flight, hotel, and rental-car bookings, plus news, destination information, and deals on cruises and vacation packages. Free (one-time) registration is required for booking.

Travelocity (incorporates Preview Travel). www.travelocity.com; www. previewtravel.com; www.frommers.travelocity.com

Travelocity is Frommer's online travel-planning and booking partner. Travelocity uses the SABRE system to offer reservations and tickets for more than 400 airlines, plus reservations and purchase capabilities for more than 45,000 hotels and 50 car-rental companies. An exclusive feature of the SABRE system is its **Low Fare Search Engine,** which automatically searches for the three lowest-priced itineraries based on a traveler's criteria. Last-minute deals and consolidator fares are included in the search. If you book with Travelocity, you can select specific seats for your flights with online seat maps, and also view diagrams of the most popular commercial aircraft. Its hotel finder provides street-level location maps and photos of selected hotels. With the **Fare Watcher** e-mail feature, you can select up to five routes and receive e-mail notices when the fare changes by $25 or more.

Travelocity's **Destination Guide** includes updated information on some 260 destinations worldwide—supplied by Frommer's.

Note to AOL Users: You can book flights, hotels, rental cars, and cruises on AOL at keyword: Travel. The booking software is provided by Travelocity/ Preview Travel and is similar to the Internet site. Use the AOL "Travelers Advantage" program to earn a 5% rebate on flights, hotel rooms, and car rentals.

Expedia. expedia.com

Expedia is Travelocity's major competitor. It offers several ways of obtaining the best possible fares: **Flight Price Matcher** service allows your preferred airline to match an available fare with a competitor; a comprehensive **Fare Compare** area shows the differences in fare categories and airlines; and **Fare Calendar** helps you plan your trip around the best possible fares. Its main limitation is that, like many online databases, Expedia focuses on the major airlines and hotel chains, so don't expect to find too many budget airlines or one-of-a-kind B&Bs here.

TRIP.com. www.trip.com

TRIP.com began as a site geared toward business travelers, but its innovative features and highly personalized approach have broadened its appeal to leisure travelers as well. It is the leading travel site for those using mobile devices to access Internet travel information.

TRIP.com includes a trip-planning function that provides the average and lowest fare for the route requested, in addition to the current available fare. An on-site "newsstand" features breaking news on airfare sales and other travel specials. Among its most popular features are Flight TRACKER and intelli-TRIP. **Flight TRACKER** allows users to track any commercial flight en route to its destination anywhere in the U.S., while accessing real-time FAA-based flight monitoring data. **intelliTRIP** is a travel search tool that allows users to identify the best airline, hotel, and rental-car rates in less than 90 seconds.

In addition, the site offers e-mail notification of flight delays, plus city resource guides, currency converters, and a weekly e-mail newsletter of fare updates, travel tips, and traveler forums.

Online Directory

More people still look online than book online, partly due to fear of putting their credit-card numbers out on the Net. Secure encryption, and increasing experienced buying online, has removed this fear for most travelers. In some cases, however, it's simply easier to buy from a local travel agent who can deliver your tickets to your door (especially if your travel is last-minute or if you have special requests). You can find a flight online and then book it by calling a toll-free number or contacting your travel agent, though this is somewhat less efficient. To be sure you're in secure mode when you book online, look for a little icon of a padlock at the bottom of your Web browser.

Yahoo! Travel. www.travel.yahoo.com
Yahoo! is currently the most popular of the Internet information portals, and its travel site is a comprehensive mix of online booking, daily travel news, and destination information. The **Best Fares** area delivers on what it promises, plus provides feedback on refining your search if you have flexibility in travel dates or times. There is also an active section of Message Boards for discussions on travel in general and specific destinations.

LAST-MINUTE DEALS & OTHER ONLINE BARGAINS

There's nothing airlines hate more than flying with lots of empty seats. The Net has enabled airlines to offer last-minute bargains to entice travelers to fill those seats. Most of these are announced on Tuesday or Wednesday and are valid for travel the following weekend, but some can be booked weeks or months in advance. You can sign up for weekly e-mail alerts at the airlines' own sites or check sites that compile lists of these bargains, such as **Smarter Living** or **WebFlyer** (see below). To make it easier, visit a site that will round up all the deals and send them in one convenient weekly e-mail.

Important Note: See "Getting There," in chapter 2, for the Web addresses of airlines serving Ireland. These sites offer schedules and flight booking, and most have pages where you can sign up for e-mail alerts for weekend deals and other late-breaking bargains.

Cheap Tickets. www.cheaptickets.com
Cheap Tickets has exclusive deals that aren't available through more mainstream channels. One caveat about the Cheap Tickets site is that it will offer fare quotes for a route, and later show that this fare is not valid for your dates of travel—most other Web sites, such as Expedia, consider your dates of travel before showing what fares are available. Despite its problems, Cheap Tickets can be worth the effort because its fares can be lower than those offered by its competitors.

✪ **1travel.com. www.1travel.com**
Here you'll find deals on domestic and international flights and hotels. 1travel.com's **Saving Alert** compiles last-minute air deals so you don't have to scroll through multiple e-mail alerts. A feature called "Drive a little using low-fare airlines" helps map out strategies for using alternative airports to find lower fares. And **Farebeater** searches a database that includes published fares, consolidator bargains, and special deals exclusive to 1travel.com. *Note:* The travel agencies listed by 1travel.com have paid for placement.

Bid for Travel. www.bidfortravel.com
Bid for Travel is another of the travel auction sites, similar to Priceline (see below), which are growing in popularity. In addition to airfares, Internet users can place a bid for vacation packages and hotels.

LastMinuteTravel.com. www.lastminutetravel.com
Suppliers with excess inventory come to this online agency to distribute unsold airline seats, hotel rooms, cruises, and vacation packages. It's got great deals, but an excess of advertisements and slow-loading graphics.

Moment's Notice. www.moments-notice.com
As the name suggests, Moment's Notice specializes in last-minute vacation deals. You can browse free, but if you want to purchase a trip you have to join Moment's Notice, which costs $25.

✪ Priceline.com. travel.priceline.com
Priceline lets you "name your price" for domestic and international airline tickets and hotel rooms. You select a route and dates, guarantee with a credit card, and make a bid for what you're willing to pay. If one of the airlines in Priceline's database has a fare lower than your bid, your credit card will automatically be charged for a ticket.

But you can't say when you want to fly—you have to accept any flight leaving between 6am and 10pm on the dates you selected, and you may have to make a stopover. No frequent-flyer miles are awarded, and tickets are nonrefundable and can't be exchanged for another flight. So if your plans change, you're out of luck. Priceline can be good for travelers who have to take off on short notice (and who are thus unable to qualify for advance purchase discounts). But be sure to shop around first, because if you overbid, you'll be required to purchase the ticket—and Priceline will pocket the difference between what it paid for the ticket and what you bid.

Priceline says that over 35% of all reasonable offers for domestic flights are being filled on the first try, with much higher fill rates on popular routes (New York to San Francisco, for example). They define "reasonable" as not more than 30% below the lowest generally available advance-purchase fare for the same route.

Smarter Living. www.smarterliving.com
Best known for its e-mail dispatch of weekend deals on 20 airlines, Smarter Living also keeps you posted about last-minute bargains.

SkyAuction.com. www.skyauction.com
An auction site with categories for airfare, travel deals, hotels, and much more.

Travelzoo.com. www.travelzoo.com
At this Internet portal, more than 150 travel companies post special deals. It features a Top 20 list of the best deals on the site, selected by its editorial staff each Wednesday night. This list is also available via an e-mailing list, free to those who sign up.

WebFlyer. www.webflyer.com
WebFlyer is a comprehensive online resource for frequent flyers and also has an excellent listing of last-minute air deals. Click on "Deal Watch" for a roundup of weekend deals on flights, hotels, and rental cars from domestic and international suppliers.

ONLINE TRAVELER'S TOOLBOX

Exchange Rates. www.x-rates.com
See what your dollar is worth in pounds.

✪ Mapquest. www.mapquest.com
The best of the mapping sites that let you choose a specific address or destination; in seconds, it will return a map and detailed directions. It really is easier

Check Your E-mail While You're on the Road

You don't have to be out of touch just because you don't carry a laptop while you travel. Web browser–based free e-mail programs make it much easier to stay in e-touch.

With public Internet access available in all of the principal cities and an increasing number of small towns, it shouldn't be difficult for you to log on regularly during your travels in Ireland. In a few simple steps you can set yourself up to receive messages while overseas from each of your e-mail accounts.

The first step to uninterrupted e-mail access is to set up an account with a freemail provider, if you don't have one already: **hotmail.com** is one among scores of companies offering this service. The advantage of freemail is that all you need in order to check your mail from anywhere in the world is a terminal with Internet access; since most Internet cafe computers aren't set up to retrieve POP mail, this is the best option. Most freemail providers will allow you to configure your account to retrieve mail from multiple POP mail accounts, or you can arrange with your home ISP to have your mail forwarded to the freemail account.

Once in Ireland, you can use this book to find Internet cafes in Ireland's cities and principal towns; we've listed many in the chapters that follow. In areas where Internet cafes haven't yet appeared, we've often been able to find Internet access in the local public library, and you'll find several Internet-savvy libraries listed in the guide. Many hostels now provide Internet access for residents, as do an increasing number of hotels. If you travel with a laptop, you'll be glad to find that not only hotels but quite a few guesthouses provide a telephone jack in all rooms for dial-up access; many Internet cafes also provide an Ethernet hook-up for travelers who want to surf the Internet from their laptop.

There are also some helpful online resources for finding Internet cafes in Ireland. The best general guide for finding the nearest Internet cafe is **http://netcafeguide.com/ireland.htm**. For a limited listing of Internet cafes in Irish cities, visit **home.netcom.com/~pohallor/ireland/isp1.htm**; for cities in Northern Ireland, try **www.thenisite.com/internet.htm**.

than calling, asking, and writing down directions. The site also links to special travel deals and helpful sites.

U.S. Customs Service Traveler Information.
www.customs.ustreas.gov/travel/index.htm

HM Customs & Excise Passenger Enquiries. www.open.gov.uk

Canada Customs and Revenue Agency. www.ccra-adrc.gc.ca

Australian Customs. www.dfat.gov.au

New Zealand Customs Service. www.customs.govt.nz
Planning a shopping spree and wondering what you're allowed to bring home? Check the latest regulations at these thorough sites.

Visa ATM Locator. www.visa.com/pd/atm/

MasterCard ATM Locator. www.mastercard.com/atm
Find ATMs in hundreds of cities around the world. Both sites include maps for some locations, and both list airport ATM locations, some with maps.

The Weather Channel. **www.weather.com**
Weather forecasts for cities around the world.

2 The Top Web Sites for Ireland

by Mark Meagher

Also check the Web sites listed on the individual hotel and attractions listings throughout this book.

COUNTRY GUIDES

D-Tour: A Visitor's Guide to Ireland for People with Disabilities. http:// ireland.iol.ie/infograf/dtour
This site offers various resources for those with disabilities who are traveling in Ireland, including extensive listings of wheelchair-accessible accommodations.

Go Ireland. www.goireland.com
Similar in scope to the Irish Tourist Board site listed below, GoIreland.com is a well-organized guide to lodging, dining, pubs, getting around, entertainment, sightseeing, and car rentals. Click on "Itineraries" to get ideas for sample tours through various regions. You can even trace your Irish roots on this site.

Heritage of Ireland. www.heritageireland.ie
Though this site is hindered somewhat by awkward use of frames, it's quite a lovely tour of Ireland's historic attractions. From the home page, click on "Historic Sites" to see images and descriptions of attractions by region and town. Other sections cover maps, tours, and an "A–Z" guide to the country.

Interactive Ireland. www.iol.ie/~discover/
An excellent compilation of Irish links. The site includes a gazetteer of Irish towns with brief descriptions of attractions, accommodations, and restaurants; abundant links provide further information. Be sure to scroll through the long, eclectic list of links on the home page; it's a fascinating assortment of information on all things Irish.

Ireland.com. www.ireland.com
Presented by the *Irish Times,* this site includes late-breaking news and per-spectives from Dublin's major newspaper. A section called Dublin Live includes advice on lodging, entertainment, attractions, food and drink, sport, and weather. You can see live views of Dublin's O'Connell Bridge, and find tips on getting around, such as the following warning about trying to get any-where quickly during the commute hour: "The greatest ever work of fiction produced in Dublin is the bus timetable."

Ireland for Visitors. http://goireland.about.com
This compendium of Web sites from About.com includes dozens of categories, from Dining to Package Tours to Travelogues. While this site is composed pri-marily of links to other Web sites, you'll also find some short feature stories about Ireland.

Irelandseye.com. www.irelandseye.com
This whimsical site isn't focused solely on travel—you can seek out the super-natural on the "ghost watch" webcam or generate random Irish proverbs ("If you lie down with dogs, you'll rise with fleas"). Beyond proverbs, you'll find excepts from numerous guides to Ireland for sale at the site, including lodging listings, magazine-style features, history, and suggested tours.

Online Directory

✪ **Irish Tourist Board (Bord Failte). www.ireland.travel.ie**
The most comprehensive online guide to travel in the Republic of Ireland, the official site of the Irish Tourist Board (Bord Fáilte) provides information for most tourism facilities. You'll find an exhaustive events calendar, the latest tourism news, and access to Gulliver, an online accommodations booking service. There are also links to several Web sites devoted to specific regions within Ireland: click on "Associated Sites," then "Regions of Ireland."

✪ **Island Ireland. http://islandireland.com/**
This is the best place to begin your search on any topic related to Irish culture, the arts, genealogy, or the outdoors. There aren't many broken links, and each site is screened for the quality of its content. Especially fascinating is the list of "good sites from around the country," an eclectic collection of online information from each of Ireland's counties.

Northern Ireland Tourist Board. www.ni-tourism.com
Other than the flamboyant introductory page, this site offers a no-nonsense interface and abundant pages packed with all the information you'll need to get started planning your travels in Northern Ireland. For exploration in depth, however, you'll have to look elsewhere—text descriptions are brief and images often absent, an inconvenience when you're trying to assess a particular B&B, restaurant, or pub.

LODGING SITES FOR IRELAND

Many of the sites in the section above include accommodation listings. The sites below are devoted exclusively to lodgings in Ireland. In addition to the sites below, you can go to worldwide hotel directories (such as All Hotels, www.all-hotels.com) and search the Ireland listings.

✪ **Accommodations in Ireland. www.lodgings-ireland.com/**
A helpful compendium of the best marketing groups for specialty accommodations in Ireland. Included you'll find "Hidden Ireland," a collection of privately owned castles and country manor houses (plus a few elegant townhouses); "Ireland's Blue Book," a selection of upscale hotels, manor houses, and B&Bs across the country; "The Great Fishing Houses of Ireland"; and "Irish Farmhouse Holidays," a list of tourist board–approved B&Bs on working farms.

An Oige: Irish Youth Hostel Association. www.irelandyha.org
An Oige operates 34 youth hostels around Ireland, most of them in beautiful rural locations and many in buildings of historical interest. The site provides photos, locator maps, bus and rail info, contact numbers, and Internet booking.

Be Our Guest. www.beourguest.ie
The official site of the Irish Hotels Federation, this is a comprehensive list of hotels that you can search by location or desired amenities. Most listings include pictures of the properties, rates, number of rooms, facilities, and contact information.

Elegant Ireland. www.elegant.ie
If you're eager to rent a 14-bedroom medieval castle with professional staff, then look no further. There are some humbler houses for rent as well, though the selection of properties is decidedly upscale. For each house you'll find photos, description, prices, and amenities.

Hotels and Travel: Ireland. www.hotelstravel.com/ireland.html
A nice selection of lodging choices, well organized by county and city. Some of the listings (which include prices, amenities, and descriptions) link to the

hotels' own Web pages, where you can explore images of the hotels and rooms, and, in some cases, availability.

Irish Accommodations. www.transatlan.com/ireland/
Whether you're looking for a B&B, hotel, or guesthouse, this site has extensive listings, including prices, brief descriptions, pictures, e-mail (if available), and, for some properties, reviews.

Town and Country Homes. www.townandcountry.ie
The most comprehensive list of B&Bs in Ireland, this site includes every B&B approved by the Irish Tourist Board (Bord Failte). You'll find images of the properties, prices, number of rooms, and nearest town.

FOOD & DRINK

Guinness. www.guinness.ie
A very slick site, showcasing the remarkable flair for advertising that has been a trademark of Guinness since its beginnings. Check out the animated screensavers, read a history of Guinness, or get tips on brewing your own.

Pub Reviews from the Virtual Irish Pub. www.visunet.ie/vip/pubguide/
A collection of reviews for pubs throughout Ireland submitted by visitors to the site.

Sheridans Cheesemongers. www.irishcheese.com
Numerous local cheese makers throughout Ireland have perfected their products in recent decades, resulting in nothing short of an Irish cheese renaissance. Sheridans, with shops in Dublin and Galway, is one of best resources for exploring Ireland's cheese heritage. The best feature of this no-frills site is a (partial) gazetteer of Irish cheeses with photographs and descriptions. You can also order the cheeses and have them delivered to your door (within the European Union).

A Taste of Ireland. www.thecia.ie/tasteofireland
A guide to member restaurants of Euro-Toques, an association of chefs and restaurant owners devoted to promoting local produce and traditional recipes throughout Europe. Most descriptions are minimal, but a few include links to restaurant Web sites with menus and photos. There's a lot more to Irish cuisine these days than boiled potatoes, and this site helps you find the delicacies.

DUBLIN

The Event Guide. www.eventguide.ie
The online presence of Dublin's eponymous free weekly, this site chronicles the city's cultural life. You'll find current listings for Dublin's clubs, theaters, cinemas, and concert halls interspersed with interviews, profiles of performers, and some information on events outside Dublin.

Ostlan Dublin Restaurant Guide. www.ostlan.com
A searchable database of Dublin restaurant reviews. The site's official reviewers don't offer much in the way of criticism; better are the more candid opinions offered by visitors to the site. There's a concise pub guide, as well as an interesting forum for online discussion.

Sonaco City Guide to Dublin. www.sonaco.com/cityguide/Dublin/
The best thing about this site is the extensive list of Dublin attractions. The descriptions are cursory, but links are provided for attractions with their own Web site. Descriptions include hours of admission and a contact telephone number.

Temple Bar Properties. **www.temple-bar.ie**
Here you'll find abundant information on Temple Bar, Dublin's new cultural hub. The heart of the site is a calendar of events, many of them free of charge. Sophisticated graphics and a simple interface make navigating this site a pleasure.

AROUND IRELAND

Belfast: Life@Belfast. **www.belfastcity.cjb.net**
The best parts of this site are its virtual tours. Enjoy images of Belfast's legendary pubs or take a historical tour. You'll also find information on entertainment, shopping, and getting around.

Cape Clear Island. **www.oilean-chleire.ie/**
A collection of information and links for Cape Clear, Ireland's southernmost inhabited island. Be sure to visit the Cape Clear Island Bird Observatory site.

Clare Ireland. **www.clareireland.com/**
On this site featuring all things related to County Clare, you'll find visitor information, links to local news and weather, a helpful message board, and a genealogical service.

Cork-Guide. **www.cork-guide.ie/corkcity.htm**
You'll find dozens of lodging options and restaurants to choose from on this exhaustive city guide. Also listed are attractions, shops, entertainment options, nightclubs, and pubs.

Derry Visitor and Convention Bureau. **www.derryvisitor.com**
An online guide to one of Northern Ireland's principal cities, with abundant information and links.

Galway.net homepage. **www.galway.net**
The links to accommodations, restaurants, pubs, and shops are far from comprehensive. Most listings include a photo and brief descriptive text; many have links to a very schematic interactive map of the city. One of the best features of this site is a county Galway events calendar, with links provided for the major venues.

Web Guide to Sligo. **www.sligo.ie**
Includes an excellent guide to archaeological sites in county Sligo, an interesting virtual tour of Sligo Abbey, information on W.B. Yeats, and a calendar of current events. The listings of accommodations and restaurants are very basic.

OTHER WORTHWHILE SITES

AllExperts.com. **www.allexperts.com/getExpert.asp?Category=144**
This is a site where fellow travelers volunteer to answer your questions about Ireland. Pick an expert and zap that person your question via e-mail. If the Web address above is troublesome, go to allexperts.com and search for "Ireland." Some experts specialize in a city (Dublin) while others have more general interests (golf, pubs, and so on).

Ireland's Pink Pages. **http://indigo.ie/~outhouse**
A list of resources compiled by the Outhouse, Dublin's lesbian, gay, bisexual, transgendered, and transvestite community center. You can search by region for B&Bs, bars, helplines, and other information.

Another useful address is **www.gcn.ie**, the home of Gay Community News, Ireland's largest gay monthly.

Irish Architecture Online. www.archeire.com
This fascinating site illuminates Ireland's medieval castles, Georgian monuments, and modern buildings. There are links to numerous architectural sites of interest, including Architectural Dublin, the Irish Architectural Archive, the Irish Georgian Society, and several sites featuring the works of individual Irish architects.

Mad Maps. www.mad-map.ie/
Navigate your way through eight of Ireland's most popular cities using these colorful hand-drawn maps. Street names are indicated, and you can zoom in on the places that interest you. There's also a search by street name, but very few streets are currently listed.

The Megalith Map. www.megalith.ukf.net/
An interactive map providing information and links for each of Ireland and Great Britain's stone circles and stone rows.

Stones of Ireland. www.stonepages.com/ireland/ireland.html
A site documenting Ireland's archaeological heritage, including tombs, stone forts, dolmens, standing stones, and stone circles.

Unison Irish Regional Newspapers Online. www.unison.ie/allpapers.php3
A news service providing access to articles from Irish regional newspapers. Other features include world and national news, weather, and a travel advisor.

GETTING AROUND

Aer Rianta. www.aer-rianta.ie
Information for the three principal airports in the Republic of Ireland: Dublin, Shannon, and Cork. Includes arrival and departure info, daily advisories for each airport, and basic maps of the terminals.

Belfast International Airport. www.bial.co.uk
Information for Belfast's largest airport, with flights from the U.K. and a handful of cities in continental Europe.

Bus Eirean. www.buseireann.ie
Bus schedules and fares for the Republic of Ireland's national bus service.

Irish Ferries. www.irishferries.ie
Get information on ferry travel between Ireland, Britain, and France from one of Ireland's largest ferry companies.

Iarnrod Eirean. www.irishrail.ie
Timetables, fares, and general information for rail travel throughout the Republic of Ireland, including Dublin's DART and Suburban rail lines.

Northern Ireland Railways. www.nirailways.co.uk/
A guide to rail travel in Northern Ireland, with timetables and route maps.

Online Directory

3 Ireland Outdoors

To many a prospective visitor, "Ireland Outdoors" might prompt only images of rain and more rain. Well, I'm not going to deny that it rains occasionally in Ireland. What's missing from that picture is what people *do* in the rain. I wouldn't be able to count the number of times I've been told, "If we waited for the sun to blaze, we'd never do anything." And the Irish do plenty.

The truth is that the Irish are the Mediterraneans of the north. Like the Greeks and southern Italians, they love the outdoors and spend as much of their time in it as possible. The fact that Ireland doesn't enjoy a Mediterranean climate is a minor technicality. When my family lived on the shore south of Dublin, we daily watched our neighbors, both in their 70s, walk past our house to the beach in their white terry-cloth robes—in December as well as July—for a dip in the Irish Sea. For my part, I would go as far as to wade into the froth in the heat of summer, only to withdraw, shuddering.

The Irish climate doesn't stop the Irish from doing anything they want, when they want, from golfing to hiking to windsurfing to biking. And the same is becoming true of their visitors. The days are long gone when the most aerobic thing tourists did in Ireland was tracing their roots. Practically every corner of Ireland is packed with opportunities for outdoor pursuits. When it absolutely pours or when the sun sets—equally inevitable—there are always the health and leisure clubs at hundreds of hotels from Mizen Head to the North Antrim coast. Look around: The Irish are mostly trim at every age, and they don't get or stay that way huddled in front of peat fires or packed into pubs. There may not be much wilderness in Ireland, but there are some of the clearest streams and most unspoiled landscapes in all of Europe.

1 Bicycling

Bicycling is the best way to see the Irish landscape in its many forms, from barren bogland to crashing surf to inland lakes. The distances are quite manageable, and in a week or two on a bike, you can travel through several of the regions described in this guide or explore one in greater detail. Accommodation in the form of hostels, B&Bs, and hotels is abundantly available for touring cyclists who don't want to deal with the extra weight of a tent and sleeping bag.

Even if you're not game to undertake a full-fledged bike tour, day trips on two wheels can be a great way to stretch your legs after

Impressions

To know fully even one field or one lane is a lifetime's experience. In the world of poetic experience it is depth that counts and not width. A gap in a hedge, a smooth rock surfacing a narrow lane, a view of a woody meadow, the stream at the junction of four small fields—these are as much as a man can fully experience.

—Patrick Kavanagh (1904–1967)

spending too much time in the car. Rentals are available in most towns that cater in any way to tourists.

Roads in Ireland are categorized as M (Motorway), N (National), or R (Regional); some still bear the older T (Trunk) and L (Link) designations. For reasons of scenery as well as safety, you'll probably want to avoid the busier roads. The R and L roads are always suitable for cycling, as are the N roads in outlying areas where there isn't too much traffic. The disadvantage of the smallest roads in remote areas is that they are rarely signposted, so you should have a good map and compass to be sure of your way. In some areas of the west and northwest, *only* the N roads are consistently signposted.

On a serious riding tour, plan to bring your own bicycle if you're not going with an outfitter that will supply a good one for you—the ones typically available for rental are, with few exceptions, impossibly heavy and fitted with unreliable components. Ask your airline about the cost of bringing your bike; some carriers charge around $75, while others will take bikes free if they're properly packed and are taking the place of one of your allowable checked bags.

If you must rent a bike, bring a few small items. Helmets are only sporadically available, and your chances of finding one that fits are poor; so bring one if you care about your head. The panniers (saddlebags) offered for rental are often unbelievably flimsy, and may begin to fall apart shortly after departure. Bring your own unless you want to leave a trail of your stuff. If you have cycling shoes and good pedals, you can easily attach them to the rental bike and make your trip immeasurably more enjoyable. With advance notice, most rental shops can outfit a bike with such handy extras as toe clips, bar ends, and water-bottle cages; an advance booking can also improve your chances of reserving the right size bike. Many rental outfits can also arrange a one-way rental over a short distance (up to 100 miles/161km or so). The national companies, such as Raleigh Rent-A-Bike and Rent-A-Bike Ireland, are set up for one-way rentals throughout the country.

Anyone cycling in Ireland should be prepared for two inevitable obstacles to progress: wind and hills. Outside the midlands, there are hills just about everywhere, and those on the back roads can have outrageously steep grades. Road engineering is rather primitive—instead of having switchbacks on a steep slope, roads often climb by the most direct route. The prevailing winds on Ireland's west coast blow from south to north, so by traveling in the same direction you can save a lot of effort over the course of a long tour.

Cyclists have long favored the coastal roads of the southwest, west, and northwest. The quiet roads and rugged scenery of the Beara Peninsula (see chapter 8) make it perfect for a cycling tour, along with the nearby Dingle Peninsula (see chapter 9). The spectacular Iveragh Peninsula (see chapter 9) is okay for cycling if you don't mind dodging tour buses on the renowned "Ring of Kerry" road. Donegal is one of the hilliest regions, and rewards the energetic cyclist with some of the country's most spectacular coastal and mountain scenery.

Also ideal for cycling are Ireland's many islands; you can bring your bike on all passenger ferries, often for no extra charge, and discover roads with little or no traffic. Some of the best islands with accommodations are Cape Clear, County Cork (see chapter 8); Great Blasket Island, County Kerry (see chapter 9); and the Aran Islands, County Galway (see chapter 11).

BICYCLING OUTFITTERS & RESOURCES

If you want to design your own itinerary and bike independently, several rental agencies with depots nationwide permit one-way rental. They include **Raleigh Ireland** (Ireland's largest), Raleigh House, Kylemore Road, Dublin 10 (☎ **01/626-1333;** fax 01/626-1770); and **Rent-A-Bike International,** 58 Lower Gardiner St., Dublin 1 (☎ **01/872-5399;** fax 01/874-4247). Mountain and cross-country bike rental rates average £10 ($14) per day, £40 ($56) per week. The negotiable one-way drop-off fee, where available, averages £15 ($21).

If you want your cycling trip to Ireland to be orchestrated and outfitted by affable experts on the ground, you might want to consult or sign on with **Irish Cycling Safaris.** It's run by Eamon Ryan and family, who offer trips to practically every part of Ireland suitable for two wheels. They're found at Belfield House, UCD, Dublin 4 (☎ **01/260-0749;** fax 01/706-1168; www.kerna.ie/ics/).

Those of you interested in more independent cycling adventures in the southeast of Ireland can get expert help organizing and outfitting your dream from **Celtic Cycling,** Lorum Old Rectory, Bagenalstown, County Carlow (☎ **0503/75282;** fax 0503/75455; www.celticcycling.com).

Two well-regarded U.S. companies offer complete bicycle itineraries in Ireland, with bikes, gear, the services of a support van, good food, and accommodations in local inns and hotels of character included in one price. Contact **Backroads** (☎ **800/GO-ACTIVE** or 510/527-1555; www.backroads.com); or **VBT,** formerly Vermont Bicycle Tours (☎ **800/BIKE-TOUR;** www.vbt.com).

2 Walking

In recent years, much work has been done to promote hiking in Ireland, notably the creation of a network of long-distance trails. In fact, you'll find more than 25 such marked trails in Ireland today. The first to open was the **Wicklow Way,** which begins just outside Dublin and proceeds through rugged hills and serene pastures on its 82-mile (132km) course. Others include the **South Leinster Way,** the **Beara Peninsula** (see chapter 8), the **Kerry Way** (see chapter 9), the **Dingle Way** (see chapter 9), and the **Ulster Way** (see chapter 15). Most trails are routed so that meals and accommodations—whether in B&Bs, hostels, or hotels—are never more than a day's walk apart.

The long-distance routes are the best-marked trails in Ireland, although the standards for signposting will seem surprisingly inadequate to those familiar with similar trails in America. It is generally assumed in Ireland that walkers possess a map and compass and know how to use them. Markers are frequently miles apart, and often seem to be lacking at crucial crossroads. Because trees on Irish hillsides rarely impede visibility, a post or cairn on each summit usually indicates the way between two peaks. The walker is expected to be able to find his or her own way in between. A compass becomes crucial when a fog blows in and all landmarks quickly disappear. Be warned: This can happen quite unexpectedly, and the safest strategy when you can't see your way is to stay exactly where you are until the fog clears.

The walks listed in this guide are on clearly marked trails whenever possible, and if sections are without markings, that is indicated. We can't give you all the information you'll need for the walks, of course, so you should consult appropriate local sources for advice before setting out.

For inland hill walking, try the Wicklow Way (see chapter 5), the Blackstairs Mountains (see chapter 6), the Galty Mountains (see chapter 6), or Glenveagh National Park (see chapter 13). For coastal walks, the best-known kind in this island country, try the Beara Peninsula (see chapter 8), the Iveragh Peninsula (see chapter 9), the Dingle Peninsula (see chapter 9), the Maumturks in Connemara (see chapter 12), and the Donegal Bay Coast (see chapter 13).

WALKING RESOURCES

Guides with maps for most of the long-distance trails in Ireland are available from bookstores, shops, and tourist offices in the local area. Many of the relevant guides can be obtained from **An Óige,** the Irish Youth Hostel Association, 61 Mountjoy St., Dublin 1 (☎ **01/830-4555**), or in the North from **YHANI,** Northern Ireland's Youth Hostel Association, 22 Donegal Rd., Belfast BT12 5JN (☎ **028/9032-4733**).

Ordnance survey maps are available in several scales; the most helpful to the walker is the 1:50,000, or 1¼ inches to 1 mile, scale. This series is currently available for all of Northern Ireland and a limited number of locations in the Republic. The ½-inch-to-1-mile series covers the whole country in 25 maps, and local maps are available in most shops. They indicate roads, major trails, and historic monuments in some detail. Although they are on too small a scale for walkers, they are all that is available in many areas. For ordnance survey maps, contact **Ordnance Survey Service,** Phoenix Park, Dublin 8 (☎ **01/802-5300**), or **Ordnance Survey of Northern Ireland,** Colby House, Stranmillis Court, Belfast BT9 5BJ (☎ **028/9066-1244;** www.osni.gov.uk). The Irish Tourist Board's booklet *Walking Ireland* and the Northern Ireland Tourist Board's *An Information Guide to Walking* are both very helpful. Other excellent resources include *Best Irish Walks,* edited by Joss Lynam (Passport Books, 1995); and *Irish Long Distance Walks: A Guide to the Waymarked Trails,* by Michael Fewer (Gill and Macmillan, 1993).

The **Ballyknocken House B&B,** Ashford, County Wicklow (☎ **0404/44614;** fax 0404/44627), offers 2- to 7-day walking tours of the Wicklow Mountains for individuals or groups. The tours include lodging, meals (breakfast, picnic lunch, and dinner), and transport to and from the trailheads. Rates are £285 to £295 ($399 to $413) per person, double occupancy, for 1 week, and £178 to £188 ($249.20 to $263.20) per person, double occupancy, for 4 nights and 3 days. The owner of Ballyknocken House, Mary Byrne, is quite knowledgeable about the Wicklow trails, and can help guests choose a route suitable to their interests and fitness.

In the West of Ireland, you have a wide selection of guided walks in the Burren, from 1 day to a week or more. Contact **Burren Walking Holidays,** with the Carrigann Hotel (see chapter 10), Lisdoonvarna (☎ **065/7074036;** fax 065/7074567). In the southwest, contact **SouthWest Walks Ireland,** 40 Ashe St., Tralee, County Kerry (☎ **066/712-8733;** fax 066/712-8762; e-mail: swwi@iol.ie). For a full walking holiday package to County Kerry, consult **BCT Scenic Walking,** 703 Palomar Airport Rd., Suite 200, Carlsbad, CA 92009 (☎ **800/473-1210;** www.bctwalk.com).

The Northern Ireland Tourist Board's Web site (**www.ni-tourism.com**) has a walking and hiking page that lists self-guided tours, 14 short hikes along the Ulster Way, and names and addresses of organizations offering guided walks throughout the North. For walking holidays in Northern Ireland, contact **Walk Ulster,** Bleach Green Centre, Lurgan Road, Banbridge BT32 4LU (☎ **028/4066-2126**).

3 Bird Watching

Because of its small size, Ireland cannot offer a tremendous diversity of habitats to its avian inhabitants. Partially for this reason, Ireland has only two-thirds as many recorded nesting species as Great Britain. Nevertheless, the country has remained a place of great interest to birders primarily because of its position on the migration routes of many passerines and seabirds, which find the isle a convenient stopping point on their Atlantic journeys. Most of the important seabird nesting colonies are on the west coast, the westernmost promontory of Europe; exceptions are Lambey Island, near Dublin, and Great Saltee in County Wexford. Sandy beaches and tidal flats on the east and west coasts are nesting grounds for large populations of winter waders and smaller, isolated tern colonies. In the North, the largest seabird colony is on Rathlin Island, off the North Antrim coast.

Ireland's lakes and wetlands serve as a wintering ground for great numbers of wild-fowl. Every year as many as 10,000 Greenland white-fronted geese winter on the north shores of Wexford Harbor, making it a mecca for birders. In the winter, flooded fields, or "callows," provide habitats for wigeons, whooping swans, and plover; the callows of the Shannon and the Blackwater are especially popular with birders. Another spectacular avian event is the annual fall migration of brent geese. On the shores of Strangford Lough in County Down—Europe's premier brent-watching site—you might see as many as 3,000 on a single day.

Until recently, rural Ireland was home to large numbers of a small bird known as the corncrake (*Crex crex*), whose unusual cry during breeding season was a common feature of the early summer night. Sadly, the introduction of heavy machinery for cutting silage has destroyed the protective high-grass environment in which the mother corncrake lays her eggs and raises her chicks. (The period for cutting silage coincides with the corncrake breeding period.) Ireland now has only a few areas where the corncrake still breeds. One is the ✪ **Shannon Callows,** where the bird's cry can often be heard after night's quiet replaces the noises of the day.

Some of Ireland's best bird-watching sites are Great Saltee Island in early summer (see chapter 6), the Wexford Wildfowl Reserve from October to April (see chapter 6), Cape Clear Island in the summer and fall (see chapter 8), the Skellig Islands during the summer (see chapter 9), and Loop Head in the summer and fall (see chapter 10). Rathlin Island Reserve (see chapter 15), home to Northern Ireland's largest seabird colony, is best visited in May and June.

BIRD-WATCHING RESOURCES

One of the best sources of information is the **Wexford Wildfowl Reserve,** North Slob, Wexford (☎ **053/23129;** fax 053/24785; e-mail: cjwilson@esat.clear.ie). It has a visitor center with information on local bird-watching sites and a full-time warden, Chris Wilson, who can direct you to other places corresponding to your areas of interest.

Birdwatch Ireland, Ruttledge House, 8 Longford Place, Monkstown, County Dublin (☎ **01/280-4322;** www.birdwatchireland.com), is an organization devoted to bird conservation in the Republic of Ireland.

An equivalent organization in Northern Ireland is **The Royal Society for the Protection of Birds,** Belvoir Park Forest, Belfast BT8 7QT (☎ **028/9049-1547**). The umbrella organization for birding in the North is **Birdwatch Northern Ireland,** 12 Belvoir Close, Belfast BT8 7PL (☎ **028/9069-3232;** fax 028/9064-4681).

The **Altamount Gardens,** Tullow, County Wicklow (☎ **0503/59128**), offers weekend courses in ornithology. See chapter 5 for more information.

The **Irish Bird Watching Home Page** (**www.geocities.com/RainForest/2801/**) lists and links you to information on birding events, sites, and news.

On **Cape Clear Island,** there is a bird observatory at the North Harbour, with a warden in residence from March to November, and accommodations for bird-watchers. To arrange a stay, write **Kieran Grace,** 84 Dorney Court, Shankhill, County Dublin. **Ciarán O'Driscoll** (☎ 028/39153), who operates a B&B on the island, also runs boat trips for bird-watchers around the island, and has a keen eye for vagrants and rarities.

Northern Ireland has two first-class nature centers for bird enthusiasts, both ideal for families. **Castle Espie,** Ballydrain Road, Comber, County Down BT23 6EA (☎ 028/9187-4146), is home to Ireland's largest collection of ducks, geese, and swans. The **Lough Neagh Discovery Centre,** Craigavon, County Armagh (☎ 028/3832-2205), is in the outstanding Oxford Island National Nature Reserve. For all-inclusive bird-watching packages in the North, contact **Murphy's Wildlife Tours,** 12 Belvoir Close, Belfast BT8 7PL (☎ 028/9069-3232; fax 028/90644681).

4 Golf

With nearly 300 championship courses and a myriad of others of lesser repute, Ireland has devoted a greater percentage of its soil to the game of golf than has any other country in the world. The Irish landscape and climate, like those of Scotland, seem almost to have been custom-designed to offer some of the fairest fairways, the greenest greens, and the most dramatic traps you'll ever encounter. And there is never a shortage of 19th holes. In short, Ireland is for the golfer a place of pilgrimage.

Golfing in Ireland is not confined to those with an Olympian income. Membership fees do not require mortgages, and greens fees for walk-ins are often quite modest, especially on weekdays and at off-peak hours.

We've described many of the top courses in the chapters that follow.

GOLF RESOURCES

Apart from the tourist boards, which are glad to supply brochures on golfing holidays, these are the principal organizations you may want to contact for detailed information: the **Golfing Union of Ireland,** Glencar House, 81 Englington Rd., Dublin 4 (☎ 01/269-4111; www.gui.ie). **Golfing Ireland,** 18 Parnell Sq., Dublin 1 (☎ 01/872-6711; fax 01/872-6632; e-mail: golf@iol.ie), can book tee times and arrange your itinerary for 28 clubs throughout Ireland.

A host of U.S. companies offer package golf tours. Among them are **AtlanticGolf** (☎ 800/542-6224 or 203/454-1086; fax 203/454-8840); **Fore Seasons Golf Tours** (☎ 973/228-3845; fax 973/228-0647; e-mail: FSGT Tours@aol.com); **Golf International** (☎ 800/833-1389 or 212/986-9176; fax 212/986-3720); and **Wide World of Golf** (☎ 800/214-4653 or 831/626-2400; fax 831/625-9671; www.wideworldofgolf.com).

5 Horseback Riding

Ireland is a horse-loving country, and in most areas you can find a stable offering trail rides and instruction. The **Association of Irish Riding Establishments** (**AIRE**) is the regulatory body that accredits stables, ensuring adequate safety standards and instructor competence. Riding prices range from £10 ($14) to £25 ($35) per hour; expect to pay £15 ($21) on average. A list of accredited stables throughout the country is available from the Irish Tourist Board.

A great variety of riding options can be found to suit different interests and levels of experience. Pony trekking caters primarily to beginners, and you don't need experience. Trail riding over longer distances requires the ability to trot for extended periods, and can be quite exhausting for the novice. Riding establishments also commonly offer such advanced options as jumping and dressage, and some have enclosed arenas—an attractive option on rainy days. Several establishments have accommodations and offer packages that include meals, lodging, and riding. Post-to-post trail riding allows a rider to stay at different lodgings each night, riding on trails all day. Not all stables can accommodate young children, although some make a point of being open to riders of all ages.

The **Irish National Stud** and the **Curragh** in County Kildare are the centers of a region famous for horse racing, and there are many fine stables nearby (see chapter 5). The Wicklow Hills in County Wicklow (see chapter 5) have a number of fine riding establishments, as do counties Wexford and Tipperary (see chapter 6), Galway (see chapter 12), and the Northwest (see chapter 13).

RIDING RESOURCES

A number of stables and equestrian centers provide riding holiday packages. They include **Horetown House,** Foulksmills, County Wexford (☎ **051/565771**); **Dingle Horse Riding,** Ballinaboula House, Dingle (☎ **066/915-2199;** www. dinglehorseriding.com); **Glen Valley Stables,** Glencroff, Leenane, County Galway (☎ **095/42269**); and **Beech Cottage,** Dromahair, County Leitrim (☎ and fax **071/64110**).

Request a free copy of *Equestrian Holidays Ireland* from the Irish Tourist Board, or write **Equestrian Holidays Ireland,** P.O. Box 590, Limerick (www.ehi.ie).

6 Fishing

With a coastline of more than 3,472 miles (5,603km), a plethora of lakes and ponds, and countless creeks, rills, streams, and rivers, Ireland offers an abundance of prime fish habitats. The sport of catching those fish—referred to by the Irish as angling—has a cherished tradition. Many festivals and competitions celebrating the many forms of this sport are held between March and September; for dates and locations, contact the Irish Tourist Board (you'll have to sign up well in advance to participate in most of the competitions). Among the festivals are Killybegs International Fishing Festival and the Baltimore Angling Festival in July, and the Cobh Sea Angling Festival in September.

In the northwest, Killybegs (see chapter 13) is a center for sea angling. In the west, loughs Corrib, Conn, and Mask (see chapters 10 and 12) offer much to entice the freshwater angler. The Killarney area (see chapter 9) is a popular angling destination, as are the Blackwater River near Cork (see chapter 7), and Kinsale (see chapter 8) for sea angling. Also consider the Shannon River and its lakes, especially Lough Derg (see chapter 14).

Some hotels have exclusive access to lakes and ponds, and will rent boats, gear, and *ghillies* (fishing guides) to their guests. Examples include Newport House and Enniscoe House, both in Mayo (see chapter 10); Adare Manor in Limerick (see chapter 10); Gurthalougha House on the shore of Lough Derg in Tipperary (see chapter 14); and Delphi Lodge and Ballynahinch Castle, both in County Galway (see chapter 12).

FISHING RESOURCES

Fishing seasons are as follows: salmon, January 1 to September 30; brown trout, February 15 to October 12; sea trout, June 1 to September 30; course fishing and sea

Angling for Trout & Salmon

Yeats imagined his ideal fisherman "climbing up to a place / where stone is dark under froth," and vividly pictured "the down-turn of his wrist / when the flies drop in the stream." Anglers visiting Ireland are free to do so, because they don't need a license to take brown trout, and many a small stream or mountain tarn offers free fishing. Be sure to check with the local tourist office or tackle dealer before dropping your line. The trout might not be very large, but they will make a sweet dish for supper. I advise you to bring rods, reels, and waders with you, because gear rental is rarely available. Suitable flies can always be bought locally.

If your quest is for larger brown trout, head for the bigger lakes where the underlying rock is limestone rather than granite. Oughterard in County Galway, Ballinrobe in County Mayo, and Pontoon in County Mayo are good centers for Lough Carrib, Lough Mask, and Lough Conn, respectively. No permit is required, but you need to hire a boat and an experienced boatman. May and June are the best months to fish there, as they are for the great midland lakes that can easily be reached from Mullingar in County Westmeath. The lakes around Ennis in County Clare fish well in March or April. Excellent brown trout fishing can also be had in the rivers of County Cork and County Tipperary, where you usually have to apply to the local angling club for a visitor's ticket.

Many rivers and lakes hold good stocks of salmon and sea trout. Sea trout run from late June to August. There are two main salmon runs: the spring run of older, bigger fish and the "grilse" run in June and July. Opening and closing dates vary from river to river, but most waters are open from March to September.

A license (obtained locally) is required, and advance booking is a virtual necessity for the more famous locations, such as the Salmon Weir pool in Galway City and the Ridge pool in Ballina. Serious anglers reserve accommodations by the week in centers like Waterville in County Kerry and Newport in County Mayo. If you are touring by car, it is always worth inquiring locally. Day tickets are often available from hotels or angling clubs.

Two excellent books by Peter O'Reilly, *Trout and Salmon Rivers of Ireland* (3rd edition, 1995) and *Trout and Salmon Loughs of Ireland* (1987), give full coverage of the waters available.

—J. V. Luce, Royal Irish Academy and Trinity College, Dublin

Dr. Luce, an avid world-traveled angler, learned the art from his father, A. A. Luce, former chaplain and professor of philosophy at Trinity and author of a noted book on Irish angling, titled *Fishing and Thinking*.

angling, all year. A license is required for salmon and sea trout angling; the cost is £3 ($4.20) for 1 day, £10 ($14) for 8 days, £25 ($35) annually. For all private salmon and sea trout fisheries, a permit is required in addition to the license. Prices vary greatly, from £5 to £150 ($7 to $210) per rod per day, although most permits run £20 to £25 ($28 to $35).

A helpful brochure, *Angling in Ireland,* details what fish can be caught where. It is available from the **Central Fisheries Board,** Balnagowan House, Mobhi Boreen, Glasnevin, Dublin 9 (☎ 01/837-9206; fax 01/836-0060). Another helpful resource, *The Angler's Guide,* is published by the Irish Tourist Board. Permits, licenses, and specific information can be obtained from local outfitters or the Central Fisheries Board.

In Northern Ireland, you must get a rod license from the **Fisheries Conservancy Board,** 1 Mahon Rd., Portadown, Craigavon, County Armagh (☎ **028/3833-4666**), or in the Derry area from the **Foyle Fisheries Commission,** 8 Victoria Rd., Derry BT47 2AB (☎ **028/7134-2100**). A permit may also be required; information can be obtained from local outfitters or the **Department of Culture, Arts and Leisure,** Interpoint Centre, York Street, Belfast BT4 3PW (☎ **028/9052-3434;** fax 028/9052-3121). A rod license costs £10 ($14) for 8 days; permits run £9 ($12.60) a day or £45 ($63) for 8 days. You can find a wealth of information and contacts in *An Information Guide to Game Fishing,* available from any office of the Northern Ireland Tourist Board.

7 Kayaking

Known as "canoeing" in Ireland, this sport enjoys considerable popularity. The season for white water is winter, when frequent rains fill the rivers enough for good paddling. By early summer, most white-water streams are reduced to a trickle. One exception is the Liffey, which is dam-controlled and has some minor rapids upstream from Dublin that are sometimes passable during the summer months.

Sea kayaking is much better suited to the Irish landscape and climate. It can be done year-round and permits access to one of the isle's greatest treasures: its remote seacoast.

In a sea kayak, the wonders of the Irish coast can be investigated at close hand. You'll find caves and tiny inlets, out-of-the-way cliffs and reefs inhabited by abundant seabirds, colorful crustaceans, seals, and the occasional dolphin. Many islands are within easy reach of the mainland, and with experience and good conditions, a sea kayaker can reach any of Ireland's island outposts.

A number of adventure centers offer kayaking lessons, and a few schools are devoted solely to kayaking. Some of them will rent equipment as long as you can demonstrate adequate proficiency—call ahead to make arrangements if that is what you plan to do. For those new to the sport or unfamiliar with the Irish coast, a guided excursion is the best option.

The deeply indented coast of West Cork (see chapter 8) and Kerry (see chapter 9) is a sea kayaker's paradise, with clear water, cliffs rising to dizzying heights, and rocky shorelines so full of caves in some places that they seem hollow. The west of Ireland (see chapter 10) offers many tiny islands and remote spots to explore.

KAYAKING RESOURCES

A rich source for the latest information on kayaking throughout Ireland can be found on the Web, at the official Web site of the **Irish Canoe Union:** www.irishcanoeunion.ie.

Jim Kennedy, a former world champion in kayak marathon racing, offers instruction and guided excursions along the spectacularly beautiful West Cork coast. He is based at **Maria's Schoolhouse,** Union Hall, County Cork (☎ **028/33002;** see chapter 8). Kayaking vacations are also available at **Delphi Adventure Center,** Leenane, County Galway (☎ **095/42307;** fax 095/42303; see chapter 12), and **The National Adventure Center,** Ashford, County Wicklow (☎ **0404/40169;** fax 0404/40701; see chapter 5).

8 Sailing

Whether by cruising from port to port or dinghy sailing on the lakes, many regions of Ireland can best be experienced from the water. The elaborately indented coastline offers a plethora of safe havens for overnight stops—there are more than 140 between

Cork Harbor and the Dingle Peninsula alone. This region of West Cork and Kerry is the most popular coastline for cruising, and several companies offer yacht charters.

Some of the harbors in the southwest that are most popular with sailors include Cork, Kinsale, Glandore, Baltimore, and Bantry. On the ✪ **west coast,** Killary Harbour, Westport, and Sligo have sailing clubs and are in areas of great beauty. There are also several sailing clubs and yacht charter companies in the Dublin area.

SAILING RESOURCES

Sailing schools hold courses for sailors at all levels of experience, and sometimes offer day sailing as well. Ireland also has more than 120 yacht and sailing clubs along the coast and lakes. The best sources for information are the Irish Tourist Board; the **Irish Sailing Association,** 3 Park Rd., Dun Laoghaire, County Dublin (☎ **01/280-0239;** fax 01/280-7558); and the *Irish Cruising Club Sailing Directions,* which is a publication that gives information on harbors, port facilities, tides, and other topics of interest. It's available in bookshops or through Mrs. B. McGonagle, "The Tansey," Baily, County Dublin (☎ **01/322823**).

The **Glenans Sailing Club,** 28 Merrion Sq., Dublin 2 (☎ **01/661-1481;** fax 01/ 676-4249), has two locations in West Cork and one in Mayo, and offers classes at all levels (see chapter 8). Day sailing is available during the summer at the Baltimore location. Yacht charters are available from **Sail Ireland Charters,** Trident Hotel Marina, Kinsale, County Cork (☎ **021/772927;** fax 021/774170; www.sailireland.com; see chapter 8); **Sporting Tours Ireland,** 71 Main St., Kinsale, County Cork (☎ and fax **021/774727**); **Shannon Sailing Ltd.,** New Harbor, Dromineer, Nenagh, County Tipperary (☎ **067/24499**); and **Dingle Sea Ventures,** Dingle (☎ **066/915-2244;** www.charterireland.com). Hobie Cat sailing can be arranged at the **Little Killary Adventure Centre,** Salruck, Renvyle, County Galway (☎ **095/43411**).

In addition, innumerable sailing trips are offered on Ireland's coasts, rivers, and lakes. A selection of them is listed throughout this guide.

9 Diving

With visibility averaging 49 feet and occasionally reaching 98 feet, and many wrecks to explore, the west coast of Ireland is a great place for divers—in fact, it offers some of the best scuba diving in Europe.

The Irish dive season generally starts in March and ends in October, although specific dates depend on your comfort zone. Outside these months, weather and ocean conditions could make jumping into the sea unappealing for some. The PADI openwater diver certification is the minimum requirement for all dives; most schools also offer introductory dives for novices.

The rocky coast of West Cork and Kerry is great for diving, with centers in Baltimore (see chapter 8) and Dingle (see chapter 9). On the west coast there are many great locations, one of which is the deep, sheltered Killary Harbour. Northern Ireland offers many interesting dives, with more than 400 named wrecks off the coast, and many in the Irish Sea and in Belfast Lough.

DIVING RESOURCES

The **Irish Underwater Council** (CFT, or Comhairle Fo-Thuinn), 78A Patrick St., Dun Laoghaire, County Dublin (☎ **01/284-4601;** fax 01/284-4602; www.scubaireland. com), is an association of more than 70 Irish diving clubs. It operates under the aegis of the CMAS (Confederation Mondiale des Activites Subaquatiques), the world diving federation. Its Web site lists information on diving, dive centers, and dive hotels (no pun intended) throughout the Republic, and publishes the *CFT Guide to Dive Sites* and other information on exploring the Emerald Isle's emerald waters.

The **UK Diving** Web site, **www.ukdiving.co.uk/**, features information on diving in the North, including a wreck database you can access either through a conventional listing or by pinpointing on a map. Wrecks are marked as red dots, which can be clicked on to find more information.

Irish dive centers and schools include **Oceantech Adventures,** Dun Laoghaire, County Dublin (☎ **01/280-1083;** toll-free in Ireland 800/272822; www. oceantechadventure.com); **Baltimore Diving & Watersports Centre,** Baltimore, County Cork (☎ **028/20300;** fax 028/20300); **Dingle Marina Centre,** on the marina, Dingle (☎ **066/915-2422;** fax 066/915-2425; e-mail: divedingle@tinet.ie); and **Scubadive West,** Renvyle, County Galway (☎ **095/43922;** fax 095/43923; www.scubadivewest.com).

10 Windsurfing

Windsurfing has become a popular sport in Ireland, and some spots are host to vast flotillas of colorful sails and wet-suited windsurfers when conditions are good. Some of the best locations are in remote areas of the west coast, and those spots are rarely crowded. Windsurfing schools with boards for rent can be found in most regions of the country, with the greatest concentration on the southeast and southwest coasts.

In Dublin, the most popular spot is Dollymount Beach; Salthill, behind Dun Laoghaire Harbour, is another good choice. In the southeast, try Brittas Bay (County Wicklow), Cahore (County Wexford), and Rosslare (County Wexford). Dunmore East (County Waterford), Dungarvan (County Waterford), and Cobh (County Cork) are good in the south. The most challenging waves and winds are in the west, at Brandon Bay on the Dingle Peninsula, Roundstone in Galway, Achill Island in Mayo, and Magheroarty and Rossnowlagh in Donegal.

Because even skilled windsurfers spend a sizable portion of their time in the water, the water quality is surely a concern, and the news is rather heartening. In 1999, Ireland was awarded more European Union "Blue Flags" for its beaches than ever before. A record 77 Irish beaches and four marinas received Blue Flags for excellence. In 2000, however, 12 of Ireland's 82 applicant beaches were rejected, leaving the total of Irish Blue Flag beaches at 70. County Wexford lost all of its Blue Flags, while Kerry brought home 13 flags, more than any other county in Ireland. As I write, in the summer of 2000, nearly 90% of Ireland's beaches surpass EU voluntary guideline levels. Northern Ireland currently has six Blue Flag beaches and one Blue Flag marina. Keep your eyes peeled for a blue flag—bearing a circular logo and the current year to be assured of the highest standard in water quality. To find a complete listing or to check out a particular beach in advance, go to **www.blueflag.org**.

WINDSURFING RESOURCES

Equipment rental and lessons are widely available on Ireland's coasts and lakes. Try the following centers: the **Surf Dock Centre,** Grand Canal Dock Yard, Ringsend, Dublin 4 (☎ **01/668-3945;** fax 01/668-1215); the **Dunmore East Adventure Centre,** Dunmore East, County Waterford (☎ **051/383783;** fax 051/383786); **Oysterhaven Windsurfing Centre,** Oysterhaven, Kinsale, County Cork (☎ **021/770738;** fax 021/770776); **Jamie Knox Adventure Watersports,** Maharees, Castlegregory, County Kerry (☎ **066/713-9411;** www.jamieknox.com); and, in the North, the **Ardclinis Activity Center,** High Street, Cushendall, County Antrim (☎ and fax **028/2177-1340**).

Dublin 4

Dublin, like most ancient cities, lies sprawled along a river. In fact, three visible and three underground rivers converge and flow into the Irish Sea here, on the shore of Dublin Bay. The greatest of these, or perhaps just the least lazy, is the Liffey, which has divided Dublin into north and south for more than 1,000 years. Neither as romantic as the Seine nor as mighty as the Mississippi, the Liffey is just there, old and polluted, with walls to sit on or lean against when your legs give out. Still, it is and always has been the center of things here, and it does make for a pretty picture on a good day.

While the Liffey may not be a swift and rushing torrent, the city around it is a different story. Motion is always experienced and measured with reference to fixed points, so it may not be apparent to first-time visitors just how fast Dublin is moving. Native "Dubs," however, who leave and return after several years, confess they don't believe their eyes. Greater Dublin—decreed long ago by Henry II to be "within the pale"—is now by popular consensus out of sight. This is the lair of the Celtic Tiger, the O'Camelot of the fastest-growing economy in Europe.

The Celts are definitely back. Two millennia ago, no less than Julius Caesar knew that they were the ones to beat, which he more or less did. In 1998, Dublin evened the ancient score when it leapt past Rome to become the fifth-most-visited city in Europe. Already, the year before, it had surpassed Rome, Milan, Amsterdam, and even London in *Fortune* magazine's rankings as the number one European city in which to do business. Then, most recently, in January 2000, an annual survey of world cities conducted by William M. Mercer Ltd. ranked Dublin among the world's top-10 cities in which to live, placing it above New York, Boston, and Washington, D.C. The word is definitely out that, work or play, Dublin is the place to be.

I suppose it all comes down to prosperity and pride, and Dublin currently has plenty of both. Twenty years ago most visitors to Ireland either bypassed Dublin altogether or made a mad dash from the ferry to the train station, determined to spend their first night beyond the pale. Now the opposite is the case. Dublin's centripetal force attracts millions of visitors a year and holds them. In 2000, the Dublin Renaissance is in full swing. The time has passed when aspiring Irish artists owed it to themselves to emigrate. Today, they dig in. If Joyce and Beckett and Wilde could see Dublin today, they'd be back. Maybe not on Grafton Street, but they'd be here. Dublin is simply contagious, and it's not in the Guinness. (The Irish now have one of the lowest alcohol consumption rates and the highest alcohol prices in Europe.) Neither is it in the water. (The Liffey only gets darker.) It's where it's always been, in the people.

Despite all the changes, the Liffey continues to divide the town as it once divided Viking from Celt and Norman from Norse. So far, the "new Dublin" lies mostly south of the Liffey, though a dramatic transformation of the north bank is well under way. An hour's walk from the top of Grafton Street down O'Connell and into north Dublin is a walk through time and, simultaneously, a glimpse of some of the pieces that must eventually fit together.

The tourist precinct of Dublin, as in most cities, is a small, well-defined compound. It comprises a large part of Dublin 2 and a smaller fraction of Dublin 1 (the postal code for each neighborhood is listed in "The Neighborhoods in Brief," later in this chapter). Grafton Street, St. Stephen's Green, and Temple Bar are the operative terms, and they are well worth the effort to see. That said, a visit to Dublin confined to these areas is not a true visit to Dublin, the Dublin that kicked some of the greatest writers in the English language into song. Explore, get a haircut (in a barbershop, not a salon), get lost and ask directions, and you may uncover a time capsule from the Dublin of a century ago—or was it only a generation?

1 Orientation

Just for reference: Dublin is 138 miles (222km) northeast of Shannon Airport, 160 miles (258km) northeast of Cork, 104 miles (167km) south of Belfast, 192 miles (309km) northeast of Killarney, 136 miles (219km) east of Galway, 147 miles (237km) southeast of Derry, and 88 miles (142km) north of Wexford.

ARRIVING

BY PLANE   Aer Lingus, Ireland's national airline, operates regularly scheduled flights into Dublin International Airport from Chicago, Boston, Los Angeles, Newark, and New York. **Delta Airlines** flies to Dublin from Atlanta and New York; and **Continental Airlines** flies to Dublin from Newark. Charters also operate from a number of U.S. and Canadian cities. You can also fly from the United States to London or other European cities and backtrack to Dublin (see "Getting There," in chapter 2).

Dublin International Airport (☎ 01/814-1111) is 7 miles (11km) north of the city center. **Dublin Bus** (☎ 01/873-4222) provides express coach service from the airport into the city's central bus station, **Busaras,** on Store Street. Service runs daily from 7:30am until 7:45pm (8:30pm Sun), with departures every 20 to 30 minutes. One-way fare is £3.50 ($4.90) for adults and £1.25 ($1.75) for children under age 12. These services are expanded during high season, and a **local city bus (no. 41)** is also available to the city center for £1.10 ($1.55).

There is also an excellent new private bus service called **AirCoach;** it makes 60 runs a day at 15-minute intervals between 5:30am and 11:30pm. AirCoach runs direct from the airport to Dublin's south side, servicing St. Stephen's Green, Fitzwilliam Square, Merrion Square, Ballsbridge, and Donnybrook—that is, key hotel and business districts. The one-way fare is £4 ($5.60). To confirm AirCoach departures and arrivals, call ☎ **01/844-7118.**

For speed and ease, a **taxi** is the best way to get directly to your hotel or guesthouse. Depending on your destination, fares average between £15 and £20 ($21 to $28). A 10% tip is standard. Taxis are lined up at a first-come, first-served taxi stand outside the arrivals terminal.

Major international and local car-rental companies operate desks at Dublin Airport. For a list of companies, see "Getting Around," below.

BY FERRY   Passenger and car ferries from Britain arrive at the **Dublin Ferryport** (☎ 01/855-2222), on the eastern end of the North Docks, and at the **Dun Laoghaire Ferryport.** Call **Irish Ferries** (☎ 01/661-0511) for bookings and information. There is bus and taxi service from both ports.

BY TRAIN   Irish Rail (☎ 01/836-6222) operates daily train service into Dublin from Belfast, Northern Ireland, and all major cities in the Irish Republic, including Cork, Galway, Limerick, Killarney, Sligo, Wexford, and Waterford. Trains from the south, west, and southwest arrive at **Heuston Station,** Kingsbridge, off St. John's Road; from the north and northwest at **Connolly Station,** Amiens Street; and from the southeast at **Pearse Station,** Westland Row, Tara Street.

BY BUS   Bus Eireann (☎ 01/836-6111) operates daily express coach and local bus service from all major cities and towns in Ireland into Dublin's central bus station, **Busaras,** Store Street.

BY CAR   If you are arriving by car from other parts of Ireland or on a car ferry from Britain, all main roads lead into the heart of Dublin and are well signposted to An Lar (City Centre). To bypass the city center, the East Link (toll bridge 60p/84¢) and West Link are signposted, and M50 circuits the city on three sides.

VISITOR INFORMATION

Dublin Tourism operates five year-round walk-in visitor centers in greater Dublin. The principal center is at **St. Andrew's Church,** Suffolk Street, Dublin 2, open from June to August Monday to Saturday from 9am to 8:30pm, Sunday and Bank Holidays 10:30am to 2:30pm, and the rest of the year Monday to Saturday 9am to 5:30pm. The Suffolk Street office includes a currency exchange counter, a car-rental counter, an accommodation reservations service, bus and rail information desks, a gift shop, and a cafe. For accommodation reservations throughout Ireland by credit card, contact Dublin Tourism at ☎ 011 800/668-668-66 (when calling within Ireland, omit the 011), or contact them at **reservations@dublintourism.ie** or **www.visitdublin. com.** For other information, call Bord Fáilte information at ☎ 1850/230330 from within Ireland (a local call from anywhere in the country), or ☎ 066/979-2083; you can also e-mail queries to **information@dublintourism.ie.**

The other four centers are at the Arrivals Hall of **Dublin Airport;** the new ferry terminal, **Dun Laoghaire;** the **Baggot Street Bridge,** Dublin 2; and **The Square,** Tallaght, Dublin 24 (all telephone inquiries should be directed to the numbers listed above). All centers are open year-round with at least the following hours: Monday to Friday 9am to 5:30pm and Saturday 9am to 1pm.

In addition, an independent center offers details on concerts, exhibits, and other arts events in the **Temple Bar** section at 18 Eustace St., Temple Bar, Dublin 2 (☎ 01/671-5717), open year-round Monday to Friday 9:30am to 5:30pm, and Saturday 10am to 5:30pm.

At any of these centers you can pick up the free *Tourism News;* or the free *Event Guide,* a biweekly entertainment guide, online at **www.eventguide.ie.** *In Dublin,* a biweekly arts-and-entertainment magazine selling for £2.90 ($4.05), is available at most newsstands. Dublin Tourism is also online at **www.visitdublin.com.**

CITY LAYOUT

Compared with other European capitals, Dublin is a relatively small metropolis and easily traversed. The city center—identified in Irish on bus destination signs as

Dublin Orientation

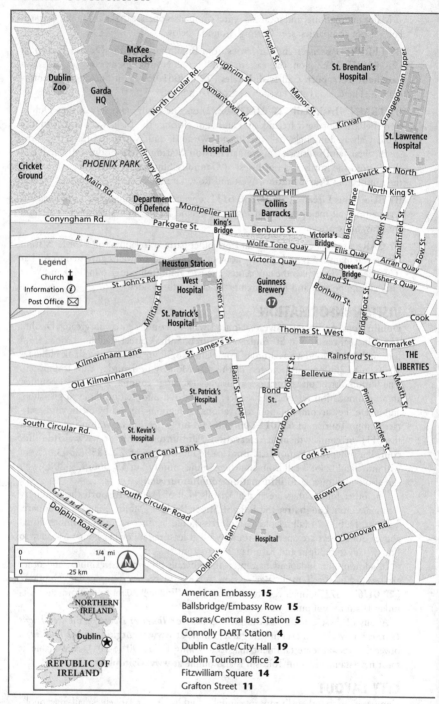

American Embassy **15**
Ballsbridge/Embassy Row **15**
Busaras/Central Bus Station **5**
Connolly DART Station **4**
Dublin Castle/City Hall **19**
Dublin Tourism Office **2**
Fitzwilliam Square **14**
Grafton Street **11**

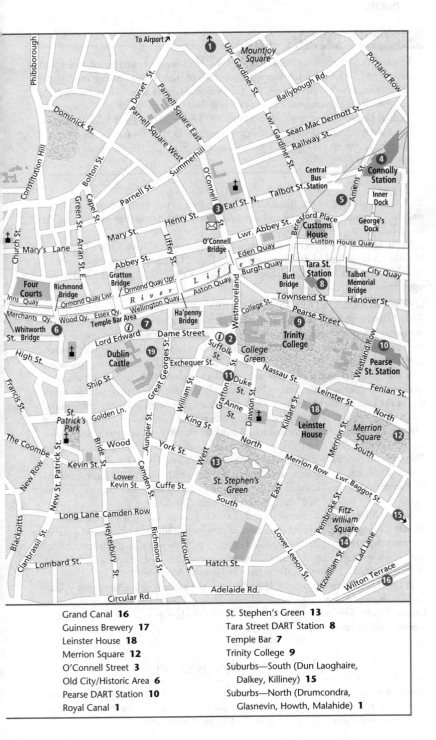

The Bird's-Eye View

To start out with the big picture and to get your bearings once and for all, make your way to the Old Jameson Distillery (see section 5 of this chapter, "Seeing the Sights") and ascend, via glass elevator, to the observation chamber atop "The Chimney." In a city without skyscrapers, this is your best 360° vantage point on Greater (and smaller) Dublin. The trip to the top costs £5 ($7) for adults, £4 ($5.60) for seniors and students, £3.50 ($4.90) for children, and £15 ($21) for a family, which comes down to under 3p (4¢) a foot. Open Monday to Saturday 10am to 6pm and Sunday 11am to 7pm.

AN LAR—is bisected by the River Liffey flowing west to east into Dublin Bay. Canals ring the city center: the Royal Canal encircles the north half, and the Grand Canal the south half.

North of the Royal Canal are the northside suburbs such as Drumcondra, Glasnevin, Howth, Clontarf, and Malahide. South of the Grand Canal are the southside suburbs of Ballsbridge, Blackrock, Dun Laoghaire, Dalkey, Killiney, Rathgar, Rathmines, and other residential areas.

MAIN ARTERIES, STREETS & SQUARES   The focal point of Dublin is the **River Liffey,** with no fewer than 15 bridges connecting its north and south banks. On the north side of the river, the main thoroughfare is **O'Connell Street,** a wide, two-way avenue that starts at the riverside quays and runs north to **Parnell Square.** Enhanced by statues, trees, and a modern fountain, the O'Connell Street of earlier days was the mainstream of the city. It is still important today, although neither as fashionable nor as safe as it used to be. Work is under way, however, to give the north side of the Liffey a mighty makeover and so to make it once again a focus of attention.

On the south side of the Liffey, **Grafton Street** is Dublin's main upscale shopping street, and it has clearly bent over backward in recent years to attract and please tourists. Narrow and restricted to pedestrians, Grafton Street sits at the center of Dublin's commercial district, surrounded by smaller and larger streets that boast a variety of shops, restaurants, and hotels. At the south end of Grafton Street is **St. Stephen's Green,** a lovely park and urban oasis ringed by rows of historic Georgian town houses, fine hotels, and restaurants.

Nassau Street starts at the north end of Grafton Street and rims the south side of **Trinity College.** The street is noted not only for its fine shops but because it leads to **Merrion Square,** another fashionable Georgian park surrounded by historic brickfront town houses. Merrion Square is also adjacent to Leinster House, the Irish House of Parliament, the National Gallery, and the National Museum.

In the older section of the city, **High Street** is the gateway to medieval and Viking Dublin, from the city's two medieval cathedrals to the old city walls and nearby Dublin Castle. The other noteworthy street in the older part of the city is **Francis Street,** Dublin's antique row.

The Neighborhoods in Brief

Trinity College Area   On the south side of the River Liffey, the Trinity College complex is a 42-acre center of academia in the heart of the city, surrounded by fine bookstores and shops. This area lies in the Dublin 2 postal code.

Temple Bar   Wedged between Trinity College and the Old City, this section has recently been spruced up and undergone massive development as the city's cultural and entertainment hub. As Dublin's self-proclaimed Left Bank, Temple Bar is the place to see and be seen. It offers a vibrant array of unique shops, art galleries, recording studios, theaters, trendy restaurants, and atmospheric pubs. This is largely the stomping ground of the young, and it's easy to feel over the hill if you're past 25. This area lies in the Dublin 2 and Dublin 8 postal codes.

Old City/Historic Area/Liberties   Dating from Viking and medieval times, the cobblestoned enclave of the historic **Old City** includes Dublin Castle, the remnants of the city's original walls, and the city's two main cathedrals, Christ Church and St. Patrick's. The adjacent **Liberties** section, just west of High Street, takes its name from the fact that the people who lived here long ago were exempt from the local jurisdiction within the city walls. Although it prospered in its early days, the Liberties fell on hard times in the 17th and 18th centuries and is only now feeling a touch of urban renewal. Highlights range from the Guinness Brewery and Royal Hospital to the original Cornmarket area. Most of this area lies in the Dublin 8 zone.

St. Stephen's Green/Grafton Street Area   A magnet for visitors, this district is home to some of the city's finest hotels, restaurants, and shops. There are some residential town houses near the Green, but this is primarily a business neighborhood. It is part of the Dublin 2 zone.

Fitzwilliam & Merrion Square   These two little square parks are surrounded by fashionable brick-faced Georgian town houses, each with a distinctive and colorful doorway. Some of Dublin's most famous citizens once resided here; today many of the houses are offices for doctors, lawyers, and other professionals. This area is part of the Dublin 2 zone.

Ballsbridge/Embassy Row   South of the Grand Canal, this is Dublin's most prestigious suburb, yet it is within walking distance of downtown. Although primarily a residential area, it is also the home of some of the city's leading hotels, restaurants, and embassies, including that of the United States. This area is part of the Dublin 4 zone.

O'Connell Street (North of the Liffey)   Once a fashionable and historic focal point, this area has lost much of its charm and importance in recent years. Shops, fast-food restaurants, and movie theaters rim the wide, sweeping thoroughfare, where you'll find a few great landmarks like the General Post Office and the Gresham Hotel. Within walking distance of O'Connell Street are four theaters, plus the Catholic Pro-Cathedral, the Moore Street open markets, the Henry Street pedestrian shopping area, the new Financial Services Centre, the ILAC Centre, the Jervis Shopping Centre, and the Central Bus Station. Regrettably, it is wise to be cautious after hours, especially after dark, in this section of the city. Most of this area lies in the Dublin 1 postal code.

Impressions

I am afraid I am more interested, Mr. Connolly, in the Dublin street names than in the riddle of the universe.

—James Joyce (1882–1941) to Cyril Connolly

2 Getting Around

Getting around Dublin is not at all daunting. Public transportation is good and getting better, taxis are plentiful and reasonably priced, and there are always your own two feet. Dublin is quite walkable. In fact, with its current traffic problems, it's a city where the foot is mightier than the wheel. If you can avoid it, don't rent a car while you're in the city. Let me repeat that: Don't rent a car while you're in the city.

BY BUS   Dublin Bus operates a fleet of green double-decker buses, single-deck buses, and minibuses (called "imps") throughout the city and its suburbs. Most buses originate on or near O'Connell Street, Abbey Street, and Eden Quay on the north side; and at Aston Quay, College Street, and Fleet Street on the south side. Bus stops are located every 2 or 3 blocks. Destinations and bus numbers are posted above the front windows; buses destined for the city center are marked with the Irish Gaelic words AN LAR.

Bus service runs daily throughout the city, starting at 6am (10am on Sun), with the last bus at 11:30pm. On Thursday, Friday, and Saturday nights, Nitelink service runs from the city center to the suburbs from midnight to 3am. Buses operate every 10 to 15 minutes for most runs; schedules are posted on revolving notice boards at each bus stop.

Inner-city fares are calculated based on distances traveled. The minimum fare is 55p (77¢); the maximum fare is £1.25 ($1.75). The Nitelink fare is a flat £2.50 ($3.50). Buy your tickets from the driver as you enter the bus; exact change is welcomed but not required. Notes of £5 or higher may not be accepted. Discounted 1-day and 4-day passes are available. A 1-day bus-only pass costs £3.30 ($4.60), and a 4-day bus and city rail pass goes for £10 ($14). With the 4-day pass, bus travel must begin after 9:45am.

For more information, contact **Dublin Bus,** 59 Upper O'Connell St., Dublin 1 (☎ **01/873-4222**).

BY DART   Although Dublin has no subway in the strict sense, there is an electrified-train rapid-transit system, known as the **DART** (Dublin Area Rapid Transit). It travels mostly at ground level or on elevated tracks, linking the city-center stations at **Tara Street, Pearse Street,** and **Amiens Street** with suburbs and seaside communities as far as Howth to the north and Bray to the south. Service operates roughly every 10 to 20 minutes Monday to Saturday from 7am to midnight and Sunday from 9:30am to 11pm. The minimum fare is 80p ($1.10). One-day, 4-day, and weekly passes, as well as family tickets, are available at reduced rates. For further information, contact **DART,** Pearse Station, Dublin 2 (☎ **01/7-3-3054**).

ON FOOT   Small and compact, Dublin is ideal for walking, as long as you remember to look left and right (in the direction opposite your instincts) for oncoming traffic, and to obey traffic signals. Each traffic light has timed "walk–don't walk" signals for pedestrians. Pedestrians have the right of way at specially marked, zebra-striped crossings; as a warning, there are usually two flashing lights at these intersections. For some walking-tour suggestions, see "Organized Tours," in section 5 of this chapter, "Seeing the Sights."

BY TAXI   Dublin taxis do not cruise the streets looking for fares; instead, they line up at ranks. Ranks are located outside all of the leading hotels, at bus and train stations, and on prime thoroughfares such as Upper O'Connell Street, College Green, and the north side of St. Stephen's Green.

Dublin Area Rapid Transit (DART) Routes

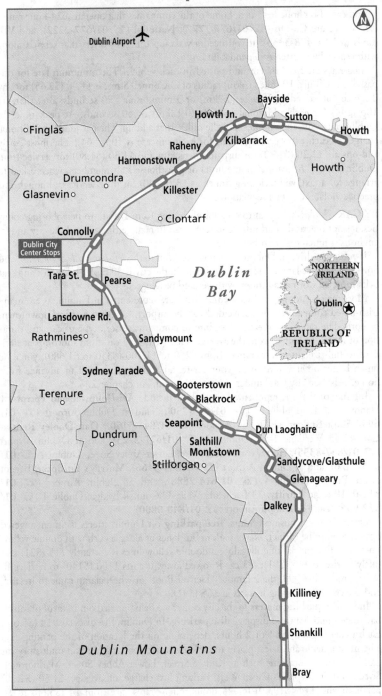

You can also phone for a taxi. Some of the companies that operate a 24-hour radio-call service are **Co-Op** (☎ **01/677-7777**), **National** (☎ **01/677-2222**), and **VIP Taxis** (☎ **01/478-3333**). If you need a wake-up call, VIP offers that service, along with especially courteous dependability.

Taxi rates are fixed by law and posted in each vehicle. The minimum fare for one passenger within a 10-mile (16km) radius of O'Connell Street is £1.90 ($2.65) for any distance not exceeding ⅝ mile (0.9km) or 3 minutes and 20 seconds; after that, it's 10p (14¢) for each additional ¹/₉ mile (0.18km) or 40 seconds. At peak times in Dublin traffic, it's the minutes, not the miles, that add up. The per-journey additional charge for each extra passenger and for each suitcase is 40p (56¢). The most costly add-ons are £1.20 ($1.70) for dispatched pickup and £1.30 ($1.80) for service from Dublin airport. *Be warned:* Some hotel or guesthouse staff members, when asked to arrange for a taxi, will tack on as much as £3 ($4.20) for their services, although this practice violates city taxi regulations.

BY CAR   Unless you plan to do a lot of driving from Dublin to neighboring counties, it's not practical or affordable to rent a car. In fact, getting around the city and its environs is much easier without a car.

If you must drive in Dublin, remember to keep to the *left-hand side of the road,* and don't drive in bus lanes. The speed limit within the city is 30 mph (46kmph), and seat belts must be worn at all times by driver and passengers.

Most major international **car-rental firms** are represented in Dublin, as are many Irish-based companies. They have desks at the airport, full-service offices downtown, or both. The rates vary greatly according to company, season, type of car, and duration of rental. In high season, the average weekly cost of a car, from subcompact standard to full-size automatic, ranges from £250 to £1,200 ($350 to $1,680); you'll be much better off if you've made your car-rental arrangements well in advance from home. (Also see "By Car" under "Getting Around," in chapter 2.)

International firms represented in Dublin include **Avis/Johnson and Perrott,** 1 Hanover St. E., Dublin 1 (☎ **01/605-7500**), and at Dublin Airport (☎ **01/605-7500**); **Budget,** at Dublin Airport (☎ **01/844-5150**); **Dan Dooley Rent-a-Car,** 42/43 Westland Row, Dublin 2 (☎ **01/677-2723**), and at Dublin Airport (☎ **01/842-8355**); **Hertz,** Irish Life Centre, Lower Abbey Street, Dublin 1 (☎ **01/676-7476**), and at Dublin Airport (☎ **01/844-5466**); **Murray's Europcar,** Baggot Street Bridge, Dublin 4 (☎ **01/614-2888**), and at Dublin Airport (☎ **01/812-0410**); and **Thrifty,** 33 Bachelors Walk, O'Connell Bridge, Dublin 1 (☎ **01/872-9366**), and at Dublin Airport (☎ **01/840-0800**).

During normal business hours, **free parking** on Dublin streets is an endangered option soon to be extinct. Never park in bus lanes or along a curb with double yellow lines. The fine for parking illegally on double yellow lines is currently £15 ($21) and likely to rise to £65 ($91); if a car is towed away, it costs £100 ($140) to retrieve it. What's more, in 1998, the infamous "Denver Boot" or wheel clamp came to Ireland, and the cost of removing it starts at £65 ($91).

Individual **parking meters** in the city center are being phased out in favor of multibay meters and "pay and display" **disc parking.** In Dublin, five discs cost £4 ($5.60). Each ticket is good for 1 or 2 hours, depending on the location of the parking site. The most reliable and safest places to park are surface parking lots and multistory car parks in central locations such as Kildare Street, Lower Abbey Street, Marlborough Street, and St. Stephen's Green West. Parking lots charge, on average, £1.50 ($2.10) per hour and £14 ($19.60) for 24 hours. Night rates vary from £4 ($5.60) to £6 ($8.40). *Note:* By the end of 2000, word has it that Dublin will introduce a 2-year experiment with personal "smart cards" whose exact rules and cost had not yet been unveiled as of this writing.

The bottom line here is that you're better off without a car in Dublin. The city is aggressively discouraging cars for commuters, much less for tourists.

BY BICYCLE   The steady flow of Dublin traffic rushing down one-way streets may be a little intimidating for most cyclists, but there are many opportunities for more relaxed pedaling in residential areas and suburbs, along the seafront, and around Phoenix Park. The Dublin Tourism office can supply you with bicycle touring information and suggested routes.

Bicycle rental averages £10 ($14) per day, £40 ($56) per week, with a £50 ($70) deposit. In the downtown area, bicycles can be rented from **Rent-a-Bike International,** 58 Lower Gardiner St., Dublin 1 (☎ 01/872-5399); and **McDonald's Cycles,** 38/39 Wexford St., Dublin 2 (☎ 01/475-2586).

Fast Facts: Dublin

For countrywide information, see "Fast Facts: Ireland," in chapter 2.

Airport   See "Orientation," earlier in this chapter.

American Express   **American Express International,** 41 Nassau St., Dublin 2 (☎ 01/679-9000), is a full-service travel agency that also offers currency exchange, traveler's checks, and (for members) mailholding. It is opposite Trinity College, just off College Green, and is open Monday to Saturday 9am to 5pm. American Express also has a desk at the **Dublin Tourism Office** on Suffolk Street (☎ 01/605-7709). In an emergency, report lost or stolen traveler's checks by dialing ☎ 1-44-1-273-571-600, collect.

Banks   Two convenient banks are the **National Irish Bank,** 66 Upper O'Connell St., open Monday to Friday 10am to 4pm (to 5pm Thurs), and the **Allied Irish Bank,** 100 Grafton St., open Monday to Friday 10am to 4pm (to 5pm Thurs). Both have ATMs that accept Cirrus network cards as well as MasterCard and Visa.

Business Hours   **Banks** are open Monday to Wednesday and on Friday from 10am to 12:30pm and from 1:30 to 3pm, on Thursday from 10am to 12:30pm and from 1:30 to 5pm. Some banks are beginning to stay open through the lunch hour. Most **business offices** are open from 9am to 5pm, Monday to Friday. **Stores and shops** are open from 9am to 5:30pm Monday to Wednesday and Friday to Saturday, and from 9am to 8pm on Thursday. Some bookshops and tourist-oriented stores also are open on Sunday from 11am or noon until 4 or 5pm. During the peak season (May to Sept), many gift and souvenir shops post Sunday hours.

Camera Supplies   For photographic equipment, supplies, and repairs, visit **Dublin Camera Exchange,** 9B Trinity St., Dublin 2 (☎ 01/679-3410); or **City Cameras,** 23A Dawson St., Dublin 2 (☎ 01/676-2891). For fast developing, try the **Camera Centre,** 56 Grafton St., Dublin 2 (☎ 01/677-5594). Or try **One Hour Photo,** 5 St. Stephen's Green, Dublin 2 (☎ 01/671-8578); 110 Grafton St., Dublin 2 (☎ 01/677-4472); at the ILAC Centre, Henry Street, Dublin 1 (☎ 01/872-8824); and 6 St. Stephen's Green, Dublin 2 (☎ 01/671-8578).

Car Rentals   See "Getting Around," above.

Currency Exchange   Currency-exchange services, signposted as BUREAU DE CHANGE, are in all banks and at many branches of the Irish post office system, known as **An Post.** A bureau de change operates daily during flight arrival and departure times at Dublin airport; a foreign currency note-exchanger machine is also available on a 24-hour basis in the main arrivals hall. Many hotels and travel agencies offer bureau de change services, although the best rate of exchange is usually given at banks or, better yet, when you use your credit card for purchases or expenses.

Dentist   For dental emergencies, contact the Eastern Health Board Head-quarters, Dr. Steevens Hospital, Dublin 8 (☎ 01/679-0700), or try **Molesworth Clinic,** 2 Molesworth Place, Dublin 2 (☎ 01/661-5544). See also "Dental Surgeons" in the Golden Pages (yellow pages) of the telephone book.

Doctor   If you need to see a physician, most hotels and guesthouses will con-tact a house doctor for you. Otherwise, you can call either the **Eastern Health Board Headquarters,** Dr. Steevens Hospital, Dublin 8 (☎ 01/679-0700); or the **Irish Medical Organization,** 10 Fitzwilliam Place, Dublin 2 (☎ 01/676-7273), 9:15am to 5:15pm for a referral.

Embassies/Consulates   **United States Embassy,** 42 Elgin Rd., Ballsbridge, Dublin 4 (☎ 01/668-8777); **Canadian Embassy,** 65/68 St. Stephen's Green, Dublin 2 (☎ 01/478/1988); **British Embassy,** 29 Merrion Rd., Dublin 4 (☎ 01/205-3700); **Australian Embassy,** Fitzwilton House, Wilton Terrace, Dublin 2 (☎ 01/676-1517).

Emergencies   For police, fire, or other emergencies, dial ☎ 999.

Eyeglasses   For 1-hour service on glasses or contact lenses, try **Specsavers,** Unit 9, GPO Arcade, Henry Street (☎ 01/872-8155), or 112 Grafton St., Dublin 2 (☎ 01/677-6980).

Gay & Lesbian Resources   Contact the **Gay Switchboard Dublin,** Carmichael House, North Brunswick Street, Dublin 7 (☎ 01/872-1055; fax 01/873-5737; e-mail gsd@iol.ie); the **National Lesbian and Gay Federation** (**NLGF**), 6 South William St., Dublin 2 (☎ 01/670-6377; fax 01/679-1603); or the **LOT/Lesbians Organizing Together,** 5 Capel St., Dublin 1 (☎ 01/872-7770). For fuller listings see "For Gay & Lesbian Travelers," in chapter 2. The most comprehensive Web site for gay organizations, events, issues, and information can be found on "Ireland's Pink Pages": **http://indigo.ie/~outhouse.**

Hairdressers/Barbers   The leading hairstyling names for women and men are Peter Mark and John Adam. **Peter Mark** has more than two dozen locations throughout Dublin and its suburbs, including 74 Grafton St., Dublin 2 (☎ 01/671-4399), and 11A Upper O'Connell St., Dublin 1 (☎ 01/874-5589). **John Adam** has shops at 13A Merrion Row, Dublin 2 (☎ 01/661-0354), and 112A Baggot St., Dublin 2 (☎ 01/661-1952).

Hospitals   For emergency care, two of the most modern are **St. Vincent's Hospital,** Elm Park (☎ 01/269-4533), on the south side of the city; and **Beau-mont Hospital,** Beaumont (☎ 01/837-7755), on the north side.

Hotlines   In Ireland, hotlines are called "helplines." For **emergencies, police, or fire,** dial 999; **Aids Helpline** (☎ 01/872-4277), Monday to Friday from 7am to 9pm and Saturday from 3 to 5pm; **Alcoholics Anonymous** (☎ 01/453-8998 and after hours 01/679-5967); **Asthma Line** (☎ 1850/445464);

Narcotics Anonymous (☎ 01/830-0944); **Rape Crisis Centre** (☎ 01/661-4911) and **FreeFone** (☎ 1800/778-888), after 5:30pm and weekends (☎ 01/661-4564); and **Samaritans** (☎ 01/872-7700 and 1850/609-090).

Information   For directory assistance, dial ☎ 1190. For visitor information offices, see section 1, "Orientation," earlier in this chapter.

Internet Access   In cyber-savvy Dublin, public access terminals are no longer hard to find, appearing in shopping malls, hotels, and hostels throughout the city center. One of the most convenient and comfortable of the many cyber cafes in town is **Betacafe,** Curve Street, Temple Bar, Dublin 2 (☎ 01/605-6800; www.betacafe.com), located above the Arthouse. Fifteen minutes online will set you back £1.50 ($2.10). It's open Monday to Saturday 10am to 10:30pm, Sunday noon to 6pm. At the **Planet Cybercafe** (☎ 01/679-0583), 23 S. Great Georges St., Dublin 2, 30 minutes online costs £2.75 ($3.85). Fast transmission rates are assured at **Cyberia Cafe,** Eustace Street, Temple Bar, Dublin 2 (☎ 01/679-7607; www.cyberiacafe.net), where 15 minutes online costs £1.50 ($2.10), or £1.25 ($1.75) for students. It's open Monday to Saturday 10am to 11pm and Sunday noon to 8pm.

Laundry/Dry Cleaning   Several centrally located do-it-yourself choices are **Suds,** 60 Upper Grand Canal St., Dublin 2 (☎ 01/668-1786); **Craft Cleaners,** 12 Upper Baggot St., Dublin 4 (☎ 01/668-8198); and **Grafton Cleaners,** 32 S. William St., Dublin 2 (☎ 01/679-4309).

Newspapers/Magazines   The three morning Irish dailies are the *Irish Times* (except Sun), *Irish Independent,* and the *Irish Examiner.* In the afternoon, the *Herald,* the *Star,* and the *Evening Echo* hit the stands. The national Sunday editions are the *Sunday Independent, Sunday Press, Sunday Tribune, Sunday World,* and the Irish-language *Anola.* Papers from other European cities can be purchased at **Eason and Son,** 40 Lower O'Connell St., Dublin 1 (☎ 01/873-3811). The leading magazines for upcoming events and happenings are *In Dublin* (£2.90/$4.05), published every 2 weeks; and the free biweekly *Event Guide* (www.eventguide.ie). The *Event Guide,* which contains up-to-date listings of events throughout Ireland, with a focus on Dublin, is widely available. *Where: Dublin,* published bimonthly, is aimed specifically at tourists and visitors and is a useful one-stop source for shopping, dining, and entertainment. It's free at most hotels.

Pharmacies   Centrally located drugstores, known locally as pharmacies or chemist shops, include **Hamilton Long and Co.,** 5 Lower O'Connell St. (☎ 01/874-8456), and **Dame Street Pharmacy,** 16 Dame St., Dublin 2 (☎ 01/670-4523). A late-night chemist shop is **Byrnes Late Night Pharmacy,** 4 Merrion Rd., Dublin 4 (☎ 01/668-3287). It closes at 9pm on weekdays, 6pm Saturday, 1pm Sunday.

Police   Dial ☎ 999 in an emergency. The metropolitan headquarters for the **Dublin Garda Siochana (Police)** is in Phoenix Park, Dublin 8 (☎ 01/677-1156).

Post Office   The **General Post Office** (GPO) is located on O'Connell Street, Dublin 1 (☎ 01/705-7000). Hours are Monday to Saturday 8am to 8pm, Sunday and holidays 10:30am to 6:30pm. Branch offices, identified by the sign OIFIG AN POST/POST OFFICE, are open Monday to Saturday only, 9am to 6pm.

Radio/TV   Apart from the Irish national stations (see "Fast Facts: Ireland," in chapter 2), there are other privately owned local stations, including Anna Livia Radio (103.8 FM) and Classic Hits Radio and Ireland Radio News (98 FM). Most receivers in the Dublin area pick up programs from Britain's BBC-TV (British Broadcasting Corporation) and ITN-TV (Independent). BBC Radio 1, 2, and 3 can also be heard. Satellite programs, on CNN, SKY News, and other international operators, are also fed into the Dublin area.

Shoe Repairs   Two reliable shops in midcity are **O'Connell's Shoe Repairs,** 3 Upper Baggot St. (☎ **01/667-2020**), and **Mister Minit,** Parnell Mall, ILAC Centre, Henry Street (☎ **01/872-3037**).

Weather   Phone ☎ **1850/241-222,** or on the Web at www.ireland.com/weather/.

Yellow Pages   The classified section of the Dublin telephone book is called the Golden Pages.

3 Accommodations

From legendary old-world landmarks to sleek high-rises, Dublin offers a great diversity of places to stay. Although prices are rising, even travelers on a moderate budget, with enough advance planning, should be able to find comfortable, attractive accommodations. Dublin is sprouting new hotels at a somewhat-alarming rate—more than 20 in the past handful of years—to meet an ever-accelerating demand. Fortunately, a concerted effort is being made to assure that the new hotels represent the economic diversity of Dublin's visitors, from Midas to Scrooge.

As in the rest of Ireland, Dublin's hotels and guesthouses are now inspected, registered, and graded by Tourism Quality Services. In 1994, the Irish Tourist Board introduced a grading system, consistent with those of other European countries and international standards, that ranks them with one to five stars. Six hotels in Dublin currently merit the five-star rating: Berkeley Court, Conrad, Jurys, Merrion, Shelbourne, and Westbury.

In general, rates for Dublin hotels do not vary as greatly with the seasons as they do in the countryside. Some hotels charge slightly higher prices during special events, such as the Dublin Horse Show. For the best deals, try to reserve a room over a weekend, and ask if there is a reduction or a weekend package in effect. Some Dublin hotels cut their rates by as much as 50% on Friday and Saturday nights, when business traffic is low. Just to complicate matters, other hotels, especially in the off-season, offer midweek specials.

For accommodation reservations throughout Ireland by credit card, contact Dublin Tourism at ☎ **011 800/668-668-66** (when calling within Ireland, omit the 011), or e-mail them at **reservations@dublintourism.ie** or **www.visitdublin.com**.

HISTORIC OLD CITY & TEMPLE BAR/TRINITY COLLEGE AREA
VERY EXPENSIVE

The Clarence. 6/8 Wellington Quay, Dublin 2. ☎ **01/670-9000.** Fax 01/670-7800. www.theclarence.ie. 50 units. MINIBAR TV TEL. £195–£210 ($273–$294) double; £450 ($630) 1-bedroom suite; £550 ($770) 2-bedroom suite. Full Irish breakfast £14 ($19.60). Rates include service charge. AE, DC, MC, V. Bus: 51B, 51C, 68, 69, or 79.

Situated between the south bank of the Liffey and Temple Bar, this Regency-style hotel belongs to an investment group that includes the rock band U2. Built in 1852, the Clarence was totally refurbished in 1996 to offer larger rooms and suites upgraded to deluxe standards. In the process it traded antique charm for bold, contemporary design. Each room or suite is unique but all rooms feature deep colors against light

Shaker-style oak furniture that includes orthopedic beds. Suites and deluxe rooms have balconies. Accommodations for nonsmokers and travelers with disabilities are available. All rooms are equipped with VCRs, PC/fax connections, private safes, and hair dryers.

Dining/Diversions: The Clarence's elegant Tea Room restaurant, in what was once the ballroom, is known for its eclectic and excellent contemporary Irish cuisine. For drinks and lighter fare there's the Octagon Bar; and after hours the Clarence is home to The Kitchen, one of Temple Bar's chic night spots.

Amenities: Room service, concierge, baby-sitter service, laundry service, and foreign-currency exchange.

EXPENSIVE

Blooms. 6 Anglesea St., Dublin 2. ☎ **800/44-UTELL** from the U.S., or 01/671-5622. Fax 01/671-5997. www.blooms.ie. 86 units. TV TEL. £138 ($193.20) double. Service charge 12.5%. AE, DC, MC, V. Parking available on street. DART: Tara St. Bus: 21A, 46A, 46B, 51B, 51C, 68, 69, or 86.

Lovers of Irish literature will feel at home at Blooms. Named after Leopold Bloom, a character in James Joyce's *Ulysses*, the hotel is in the heart of Dublin, near Trinity College and on the edge of the Temple Bar district. Guest rooms are modern and functional, with useful extras like garment presses and hair dryers.

Dining/Diversions: For formal dining, reserve a table at the Bia restaurant; for more informal fare, try the Anglesea Bar. Late-night entertainment is available in the basement-level nightclub, known simply as M.

Amenities: Room service, concierge, baby-sitting, valet and laundry/dry-cleaning service, express checkout, foreign-currency exchange.

The Central. 1–5 Exchequer St. (at the corner of Great George's St.), Dublin 2. ☎ **01/679-7302.** Fax 01/679-7303. E-mail: reservations@centralhotel.ie. 70 units. MINIBAR TV TEL. £108–£150 ($151.20–$210) double. Rates include full Irish breakfast and service charge. AE, DC, MC, V. Discounted parking in nearby public lot. Bus: 22A.

Between Trinity College and Dublin Castle, this century-old five-story hotel was renovated in 1991 and totally refurbished in 1997. The public areas retain a Victorian atmosphere, enhanced by an impressive collection of contemporary Irish art. Guest rooms, cheerfully decorated with colorful Irish-made furnishings, offer such extras as a garment press, hair dryer, and tea/coffeemaker.

Dining/Diversions: Lunch and dinner are served in the hotel's Victorian-style dining room. The tucked-away Library Bar is a quiet haven for a drink and a moment's calm.

Amenities: Room service, concierge, baby-sitting, foreign-currency exchange.

Temple Bar Hotel. Fleet St., Temple Bar, Dublin 2. ☎ **800/44-UTELL** from the U.S., or 01/677-3333. Fax 01/677-3088. www.towerhotelgroup.ie. 130 units (4 with shower only). TV TEL. £110–£190 ($154–$266). No service charge. AE, DC, MC, V. Parking available on street. DART: Tara St. Bus: 78A or 78B.

If you want to be in the heart of the action in the Temple Bar district, this is a prime place to stay. Opened in 1993, the five-story hotel was developed from a row of town houses. Great care was taken to preserve the Georgian brick-front facade and Victorian mansard roof. Guest rooms, modern with traditional furnishings and orthopedic beds, include amenities such as a garment press, towel warmer, hair dryer, and tea/coffeemaker. Rooms for nonsmokers are available.

Dining/Diversions: The hotel has a skylit garden-style restaurant, the Terrace Cafe, and an Old Dublin–theme pub, Buskers.

Amenities: Room service, concierge, baby-sitter service, foreign-currency exchange, access to a nearby health club.

Dublin Accommodations

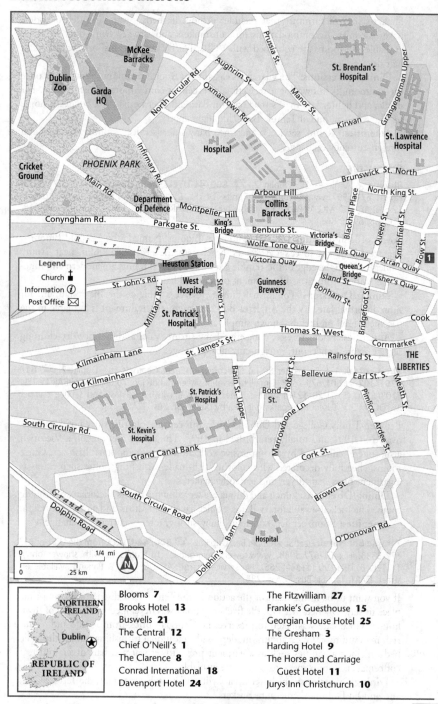

Blooms **7**
Brooks Hotel **13**
Buswells **21**
The Central **12**
Chief O'Neill's **1**
The Clarence **8**
Conrad International **18**
Davenport Hotel **24**

The Fitzwilliam **27**
Frankie's Guesthouse **15**
Georgian House Hotel **25**
The Gresham **3**
Harding Hotel **9**
The Horse and Carriage
　Guest Hotel **11**
Jurys Inn Christchurch **10**

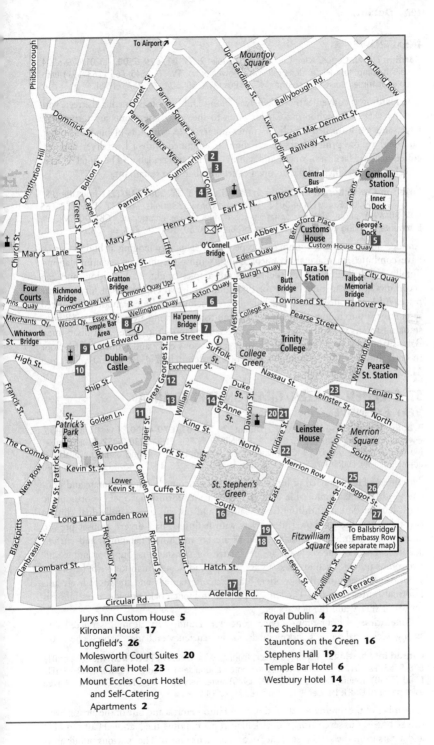

INEXPENSIVE

Harding Hotel. Copper Alley, Christchurch, Dublin 2. ☎ **01/679-6500.** Fax 01/679-6504. E-mail: harding@usit.ie. 53 units (all with shower only). TV TEL. £45–£65 ($63–$91) twin, double, or triple. No service charge. MC, V. Bus: 21A, 50, 50A, 78, 78A, or 78B.

The Harding is conveniently tucked away along Dublin's oldest medieval street, with striking views of neighboring Christchurch to the west. The rooms are surprisingly large, and are furnished simply in contemporary style, with lots of pine and bright blue and yellow print fabrics. Each room is equipped with a hair dryer and tea/coffee-making facilities. Single and family rooms are available. The hotel is fully wheelchair accessible and has an open courtyard, bar, and restaurant.

Jurys Inn Christchurch. Christ Church Place, Dublin 8. ☎ **800/44-UTELL** from the U.S., or 01/454-0000. Fax 01/454-0012. www.jurys.com. 183 units. A/C TV TEL. £62–£65 ($86.80–$91) single, double, or family room. No service charge. AE, CB, DC, MC, V. Discounted parking available at adjacent lot. Bus: 21A, 50, 50A, 78, 78A, or 78B.

An ideal location and a winning concept—to offer quality lodging at budget cost—have combined to make this one of Dublin's most sought-after accommodations. Totally refurbished in 1998, the rooms are ample, bright, and inviting, and can accommodate up to three adults or two adults and two children—all for the same price. All have coffeemakers and hair dryers. Facilities include a moderately priced restaurant, a pub lounge, and an adjacent multistory parking area. There are 38 non-smoking rooms available, and 2 rooms specially adapted for guests with disabilities. Baby-sitting can be arranged. Make your reservations early and request a fifth-floor room facing west for a memorable view of Christchurch. *Tip:* Rooms 501, 507, and 419 are especially spacious.

ST. STEPHEN'S GREEN/GRAFTON STREET AREA
VERY EXPENSIVE

Brooks Hotel. 59–62 Drury St., Dublin 2. ☎ **01/670-4000.** Fax 01/670-4455. www.iol.ie/_bizpark/s/sinnott. 75 units. A/C MINIBAR TV TEL. £180–£220 ($252–$308) double. No service charge. AE, DC, MC, V. Discounted overnight and weekend parking available at adjacent facility. DART: Tara St. or Pearse. Bus: 10, 11A, 11B, 13, 14, 15, 15A, 15B, 20B, or 46A.

The Brooks Hotel opened in June 1997 and has welcomed many corporate and holiday visitors to its comfortable quarters. The quality furnishings include orthopedic beds, handmade oak furniture from Galway, and tasteful decor. Individual climate control, three phones, powerful showers with bathtubs, hair dryers, trouser presses, and ironing boards are standard issue, as are fax machines, dataports, and current adapters. Three of the six floors are designated for nonsmokers. Superior and executive rooms provide such extras as VCRs, antique radios, and high king-size beds.

Dining/Diversions: Brooks offers Francesca's Restaurant and the more lively and informal Butter Lane Bar. The lounge, paneled in French oak, provides a restful oasis for tea or sherry and the newspaper.

Amenities: 24-hour room service, concierge, laundry/dry-cleaning service, baby-sitting, secretarial services, video rentals, foreign-currency exchange, express checkout.

Conrad International. Earlsfort Terrace, Dublin 2. ☎ **800/HILTONS** from the U.S., or 01/676-5555. Fax 01/676-5424. www.conrad-international.ie. 197 units. A/C MINIBAR TV TEL. £200 ($280) double; £410–£700 ($574–$980) suite. Service charge 15%. DC, MC, V. Free valet parking. DART: Pearse. Bus: 11A, 11B, 13, or 14A.

A member of the international subsidiary of Hilton Hotels and one of the city's newest deluxe hotels, this seven-story redbrick high-rise is opposite the National Concert Hall and across from the southeast corner of St. Stephen's Green. The spacious public areas are rich in marble, brass, contemporary art, and leafy plants. Each guest room is outfitted with contemporary furnishings, with extras such as an electronic safety lock, a writing desk, bathrobes, and three telephone lines. All beds have orthopedic mattresses. Nonsmoking floors are available.

Dining/Diversions: Choices include the Alexandra, a clubby room known for a range of gourmet Continental and Irish fare; Plurabelle, a brasserie-style restaurant; the Lobby Lounge, for traditional afternoon tea or drinks with piano background music; and Alfie Byrne's, a pub named for a former lord mayor of Dublin that serves light lunches.

Amenities: 24-hour room service, concierge, laundry/dry-cleaning, shoeshine, secretarial services, baby-sitting, express checkout, foreign-currency exchange, hairdressing salon.

✪ **The Shelbourne.** 27 St. Stephen's Green, Dublin 2. ☎ **800/225-5843** from the U.S., or 01/676-6471. Fax 01/661-6006. www.shelbourne.ie. 190 units. MINIBAR TV TEL. £390–£490 ($546–$686) double. Service charge 15%. DC, MC, V. Limited free parking. DART: Pearse. Bus: 10, 11A, 11B, 13, or 20B.

With a fanciful redbrick and white-trimmed facade, enhanced by wrought-iron railings and window boxes brimming with flowers, this grand six-story hostelry stands out on the north side of St. Stephen's Green. Built in 1824, it has played a significant role in Irish history—the new nation's constitution was signed in Room 112 in 1921. It has often been host to international leaders, stars of stage and screen, and literary giants. The public areas, replete with glowing fireplaces, Waterford chandeliers, and original art, are popular rendezvous spots for Dubliners. Guest rooms vary in size, but all offer up-to-date comforts and are furnished with antique and period pieces. The front units overlook bucolic St. Stephen's Green. In 1996, nearly $2.5 million went into refurbishing the Shelbourne's guest rooms and meeting space.

Needless to say, you don't stay here just for the beds, which represent the Irish preference for a mattress somewhere beyond soft and short of firm.

Dining/Diversions: The Dining Room offers Irish and Continental cuisine; the Horseshoe Bar and Shelbourne Bar are both ideal for a convivial drink. Locals favor the Lord Mayor's Lounge for a proper afternoon tea.

Amenities: 24-hour room service, concierge, baby-sitting, laundry/dry cleaning, video rental, safe-deposit boxes, foreign-currency exchange, beauty salon, boutiques, access to nearby health club.

Stephens Hall. 14–17 Lower Leeson St., Earlsfort Terrace, Dublin 2. ☎ **800/223-6510** from the U.S., or 01/638-1111. Fax 01/638-1122. www.premgroup.ie. 37 units. TV TEL. £160–£250 ($224–$350) double. No service charge. Full breakfast £9 ($12.60). AE, DC, MC, V. Free valet parking. DART: Pearse. Bus: 11, 11A, 11B, 13, 13A, or 13B.

With a gracious Georgian exterior and entranceway, this is Dublin's first all-suite hotel, situated on the southeast corner of St. Stephen's Green. It's ideal for visitors who plan an extended stay or who want to entertain or do their own cooking. All of the suites were redecorated in 1998. Each contains a hallway, sitting room, dining area, kitchen, bathroom, and one or two bedrooms, with orthopedic beds; other extras include fax machines, CD players, and dataports. One full floor is nonsmoking. The luxury penthouse suites, on the upper floors, offer views of the city. Ground-level town-house suites have private entrances.

Dining/Diversions: Although the idea here is for you to do your own cooking, there are a Michelin award–winning restaurant, Morels, and a bar on the premises.

Amenities: Concierge, daily maid service, baby-sitting, safe-deposit boxes, video rentals, valet parking, access to nearby health club.

Westbury Hotel. Grafton St., Dublin 2. ☎ **800/42-DOYLE** from the U.S., or 01/679-1122. Fax 01/679-7078. www.doylehotels.com. 203 units. A/C TV TEL. £230 ($322) double. Service charge 15%. AE, DC, MC, V. Free parking. DART: Tara St. or Pearse. Bus: 10, 11A, 11B, 13, or 20B.

A tasteful hybrid of modern and traditional design, this relatively new midtown hotel blends a sleek contemporary facade with a serene interior. It sits in the heart of the city's fashionable shopping district, and near all the major sights. The guest rooms, many with half-canopy or four-poster beds, are furnished with antiques, dark woods, brass trim, and floral designer fabrics. Many suites have Jacuzzis.

Dining/Diversions: Choices include the Russell Room, a French-Irish restaurant; the Sandbank, a nautical-style pub that serves fresh seafood; Charlie's Coffee Shop; and the Terrace Bar and Lounge, a favorite venue for afternoon tea or a drink, with live piano music.

Amenities: 24-hour room service, concierge, baby-sitting, laundry/dry cleaning, express checkout, hairdressing salon, 20-shop arcade, fitness room, access to Riverview Health and Fitness Club.

EXPENSIVE

Buswells. 25 Molesworth St., Dublin 2. ☎ **800/473-9527** from the U.S., or 01/614-6500. Fax 01/676-2090. E-mail: buswells@quinn-group.com. 69 units. TV TEL. £165 ($231) double. No service charge. Rates include full breakfast. AE, DC, MC, V. DART: Pearse. Bus: 10, 11A, 11B, 13, or 20B.

On a street that's oddly quiet—considering it's only 2 blocks from Trinity College and opposite the National Museum—this vintage four-story hotel has long been a meeting place for artists, poets, scholars, and politicians. Originally two 1736 Georgian town houses, it became a hotel in 1928. The public rooms contain period furniture, intricate plasterwork, Wedgwood flourishes, old prints, and memorabilia. Recent refurbishment has preserved the Georgian decor and character throughout. With a few exceptions, guest rooms are quite spacious, with bright wallpaper, mahogany beds, desks, and wardrobes, and white tiled bathrooms. All include tea/coffeemakers, hair dryers, and trouser presses.

Dining/Diversions: The hotel has an à la carte restaurant, a carvery, and two bars.

Amenities: 24-hour room service, concierge, baby-sitting, laundry, ISDN/modem facilities, foreign-currency exchange.

Georgian House Hotel. 18 Lower Baggot St., Dublin 2. ☎ **01/661-8832.** Fax 01/661-8834. E-mail: hotel@georgianhouse.ie. 70 units. TV TEL. £100–£150 ($140–$210) double. AE, CB, MC, V. Free parking. DART: Pearse. Bus: 10.

Less than 2 blocks from St. Stephen's Green, this four-story, 200-year-old brick town house sits in the heart of Georgian Dublin, within walking distance of most major attractions. Its original guest rooms were smallish, though they offered all the essentials and a colorful decor with pine furniture. The hotel has recently undergone a dramatic expansion; it now offers larger rooms and new facilities.

Dining/Diversions: The hotel has a new restaurant, specializing in shellfish and seafood, and a bar.

Amenities: Room service, concierge, baby-sitting, laundry/dry cleaning, secretarial services, leisure center with indoor pool, foreign-currency exchange.

MODERATE

Stauntons on the Green. 83 St. Stephen's Green, Dublin 2. ☎ **01/478-2300.** Fax 01/478-2263. E-mail: hotels@indigo.ie. 36 units. TV TEL. £120 ($168) double. No service charge. Rates include full breakfast. AE, DC, MC, V. Valet parking £5 ($7) per day. DART: Pearse. Bus: 14A or 62.

Opened in 1993, this beautifully restored guesthouse occupies a four-story Georgian town house on the south side of St. Stephen's Green, next door to the Irish Department of Foreign Affairs. There is no elevator, but there are rooms on the ground level. Guest rooms are decorated in traditional style, enhanced by tall windows and high ceilings; front rooms overlook the Green, and rooms at the back have views of the adjacent Iveagh Gardens. Beds are firm. Public areas include a breakfast room and a parlor with an open fireplace.

INEXPENSIVE

Frankie's Guesthouse. 8 Camden Place (off Camden St./Harcourt St.), Dublin 2. ☎ and fax **01/478-3087.** www.frankiesguesthouse.com. 12 units, 9 with private bathroom (shower only). TV. £68 ($95.20) double with private bathroom, £57 ($79.80) double with shared bathroom. Rates include breakfast. AE, MC, V. Parking available on street. Bus: 16, 16A, 16C, 19A, 22, or 22A.

Frankie has run this pleasant guest hotel for over 10 years, maintaining the small but fresh, simple white rooms to a high standard. Set on a quiet back street, the house has a Mediterranean feel, with a lovely walkway and roof garden. It welcomes mature gay, lesbian, and straight visitors alike. The double room downstairs can accommodate a traveler with disabilities. It is an easy walk to St. Stephen's Green and Grafton Street, and you can make coffee or tea in your room. I recommend that you book this place well in advance, especially for a weekend stay.

The Horse and Carriage Guest Hotel. 15 Aungier St. (at S. Great George's St.), Dublin 2. ☎ **01/478-3537.** Fax 01/478-4010. E-mail: liamtony@indigo.ie. 9 units, 3 with private bathroom. TV. £55–£70 ($77–$98) double. Rates include breakfast and unlimited use of Incognito Sauna Club facilities. AE, MC, V. Parking available at nearby lot. Bus: 14, 14A, 47, or 47A.

Set in the heart of busy Dublin center, this 3-year-old hotel warmly welcomes people of all ages and orientations, and has predominantly gay male visitors. The Incognito Sauna Club is part of the hotel complex, and the atmosphere is casual and bustling. Most rooms have soft king-size beds, and the shared bathrooms are clean and private. The three highest-priced units, the "carriage rooms," are more spacious and quieter than the others, which face a busy street. Heavily flowered wallpaper makes the rooms feel small and a bit dark, but all the accommodations are comfortable. The hotel has won awards for its remodeled turn-of-the-century facade. Hosts Liam Ledwidge and Tony Keogan are helpful and well informed on Dublin life. Aungier Street is a continuation of South Great George's Street.

SELF-CATERING

Molesworth Court Suites. Schoolhouse Lane (off Molesworth St.), Dublin 2. ☎ **01/ 676-4799.** Fax 01/676-4982. 12 units. TV TEL. £105–£220 ($147–$308) per night. £75 ($105) deposit required with booking and balance payable 4 weeks prior to arrival. AE, MC, V. DART: Pearse. Bus: 10, 11A, 11B, 13, or 20B.

In Dublin, location may not be everything, but it's close—and you can't ask for a better location than this. Tucked away behind Mansion House, Molesworth Courts is no more than 5 minutes on foot to Stephens Green and yet is country quiet. These stylish, comfortable units (one- or two-bedroom apartments, or two- or three-bedroom penthouses) offer everything you need to set up your own base in Dublin, whether for a night or a month. They're full of light and good taste and come fully furnished and equipped. They all have small balconies; and the bilevel penthouses have quite spacious verandas. The staff here goes the extra mile to be helpful. The internal phone system provides you with a private extension and your own voice mail.

If, despite the fact that you have your own kitchen, you want to let others do your cooking, you can order out from any of the roughly 25 local restaurants listed in the *Restaurant Express* menu booklet lying only an arm's reach from the couch.

FITZWILLIAM SQUARE/MERRION SQUARE AREA
VERY EXPENSIVE

Davenport Hotel. Merrion Sq., Dublin 2. ☎ **800/569-9983** from the U.S., or 01/607-3500. Fax 01/661-5663. www.ocallaghanhotels.ie. 120 units. A/C TV TEL. £145–£225 ($203–$315) double. Service charge 12.5%. AE, DC, MC, V. Free valet parking. DART: Pearse. Bus: 6, 7A, or 8.

Opened as a hotel in 1993, this building incorporates the neoclassical facade of Merrion Hall, an 1863 church. Classic Georgian windows and pillars encircle the impressive domed entranceway, with a six-story atrium lobby, marble flooring, and plaster moldings. The guest rooms, in a newly built section, have traditional furnishings, orthopedic beds, textured wall coverings, quilted floral bedspreads and matching drapes, and brass accoutrements. Each room has three telephone lines plus a computer data line, work desk, personal safe, garment press, tea and coffee welcome tray, and hair dryer. Two floors are nonsmoking. The hotel shares valet parking arrangements with its sister hotel, the Mont Clare, across the street.

Dining/Diversions: The Georgian-theme restaurant, Lanyon's, is named after a leading 19th-century Irish architect. The clubby President's Bar, decorated with framed pictures of world leaders past and present, serves drinks as well as morning coffee and afternoon tea.

Amenities: 24-hour room service, concierge, health club, laundry/dry cleaning, baby-sitting, secretarial services, express checkout.

EXPENSIVE

✪ **Longfield's.** 10 Lower Fitzwilliam St., Dublin 2. ☎ **01/676-1367.** Fax 01/676-1542. E-mail: lfields@indigo.ie. 26 units. TV TEL. £110–£160 ($154–$224) double. No service charge. Rates include full breakfast. AE, DC, MC, V. No parking available. DART: Pearse. Bus: 10.

Created from two 18th-century Georgian town houses, this small, classy hotel is named after Richard Longfield (also known as Viscount Longueville), who originally owned this site and was a member of the Irish Parliament 2 centuries ago. Totally restored and recently refurbished, it combines Georgian decor and reproduction period furnishings of dark woods and brass trim. Guest rooms offer extras such as clock radios and hair dryers. Like the eye of a storm, Longfield's is centrally located yet remarkably quiet, an elegant yet unpretentious getaway 5 minutes' walk from St. Stephen's Green.

Dining: Longfield's offers award-winning cuisine in its "No. 10" Restaurant.

Amenities: 24-hour room service, concierge, laundry/dry cleaning, baby-sitting, secretarial services, foreign-currency exchange.

Mont Clare Hotel. Merrion Sq., Dublin 2. ☎ **800/569-9983** from the U.S., or 01/607-3800. Fax 01/661-5663. www.ocallaghanhotels.ie. 74 units. A/C MINIBAR TV TEL. £110–£160 ($154–$224) double. Service charge 12.5%. AE, DC, MC, V. Free valet parking. DART: Pearse. Bus: 5, 7A, or 8.

Overlooking the northwest corner of Merrion Square, this vintage six-story brick-faced hotel recently underwent a thorough restoration. It has a typically Georgian facade, matched inside by period furnishings of dark woods and polished brass. Guest rooms were completely refurbished in 1998 and given a brighter, more contemporary feel. Each has a hair dryer, tea/coffeemaker, and garment press. Beds are orthopedic, and nonsmoking floors are available.

Dining/Diversions: The main restaurant, Goldsmith's (named for Oliver Goldsmith, one of Ireland's great writers), has a literary theme. There is also a traditional lounge bar.

Amenities: 24-hour room service, concierge, complimentary access to nearby fitness center, laundry/dry cleaning, baby-sitting, secretarial services, express checkout.

MODERATE

The Fitzwilliam. 41 Upper Fitzwilliam St., Dublin 2. ☎ **01/662-5155.** Fax 01/676-7488. 12 units. TV TEL. £70–£85 ($98–$119) double. Service charge 10%. Rates include full breakfast. AE, DC, MC, V. Limited free overnight parking. DART: Pearse. Bus: 10.

This guesthouse occupies a meticulously restored 18th-century town house on the best-preserved Georgian thoroughfare in Dublin. It's a convenient location for exploring the city. The entrance parlor has a homey atmosphere, with a carved marble fireplace and antique furnishings. The bright guest rooms have high ceilings, orthopedic beds, hair dryers, and clock radios; bathrooms are somewhat small, but impeccably clean. Tea/coffeemakers are available just outside each room. Facilities include a French restaurant in the vaulted basement.

Kilronan House. 70 Adelaide Rd., Dublin 2. ☎ **01/475-5266.** Fax 01/478-2841. www. dublinn.com. 15 units, 13 with private bathroom (shower only). TV TEL. £70–£90 ($98–$126) double. Children under 7 stay free in parents' room. Rates include full breakfast. AE, MC, V. Free private parking. Bus: 14, 15, 19, 20, or 46A.

Noel Comer is the outgoing proprietor at this comfortable guesthouse, located within 5 minutes' walk of St. Stephen's Green, just north of the Royal Canal. The sitting room on the ground floor is small and intimate, with a fire glowing through the cold months of the year. The rooms are very well kept, and those facing the front have commodious bay windows; each comes equipped with tea and coffee facilities and hair dryers. If you don't like stairs, request a room on the second floor, because there isn't an elevator. The front rooms, facing Adelaide Street, are also preferable to those in back, which face onto office buildings and a parking lot. When you book, ask about a reduction for Frommer's readers.

BALLSBRIDGE/EMBASSY ROW AREA
VERY EXPENSIVE

Berkeley Court. Lansdowne Rd., Ballsbridge, Dublin 4. ☎ **800/42-DOYLE** from the U.S., or 01/660-1711. Fax 01/661-7238. www.doyle-hotels.com. 188 units. TV TEL. £175–£220 ($245–$308) double; from £250 ($350) suite. AE, DC, MC, V. Free valet parking. DART: Lansdowne Rd. Bus: 7, 8, or 45.

The flagship of the Irish-owned Doyle Hotel group, and the first Irish member of Leading Hotels of the World, the Berkeley Court (pronounced *Bark*-lay) is nestled in a residential area near the American Embassy. The well-tended grounds were once part of the Botanic Gardens of University College. A favorite haunt of diplomats and international business leaders, the hotel is known for its posh lobby decorated with fine antiques, original paintings, mirrored columns, and Irish-made carpets and furnishings. The guest rooms, which aim to convey an air of elegance, have designer fabrics, firm half-canopy beds, dark woods, and bathrooms fitted with marble accoutrements. Suites have Jacuzzis. There are only 20 rooms for nonsmokers, so be specific when making reservations.

Dining/Diversions: Choices include the formal Berkeley Room for gourmet dining; the skylit Conservatory for casual meals; the Royal Court, a gothic-style bar; and the Court Lounge, a proper setting for afternoon tea or a relaxing drink.

Amenities: 24-hour room service, concierge, laundry service, express checkout, foreign-currency exchange, boutiques, health club.

The Burlington. Upper Leeson St., Dublin 4. ☎ **800/42-DOYLE** from the U.S., or 01/660-5222. Fax 01/660-8496. www.doylehotels.ie. 504 units. TV TEL. £164–£268 ($229.60–$375.20) double. Children under 7 stay free in parents' room. Rates include full breakfast. AE, DC, MC, V. Free parking. Bus: 10 or 18.

A favorite headquarters for conventions, meetings, conferences, and group tours, this is the largest hotel in Ireland. It's a block south of the Grand Canal, in a fashionable residential section within walking distance of St. Stephen's Green. The modern, crisply furnished seven-story property is constantly being refurbished. Guest rooms are outfitted with brass-bound oak furniture and designer fabrics. The connecting units are ideal for families.

Dining/Diversions: Choices include the Sussex, a large formal dining room; a buffet restaurant; and a coffee shop. For a real Old Dublin pub atmosphere, try Buck Mulligans, which serves a carvery-style lunch (read: lots of meat) and light evening meals as well as drinks. Annabel's is the basement-level nightclub. From May to early October, the main ballroom stages Doyle's Irish Cabaret, a 3-hour dinner show.

Amenities: 24-hour room service, concierge, valet and laundry service, foreign-currency exchange, underground and outdoor parking, gift shops, newsstand, hairdressing salons.

Jurys Hotel and Towers. Pembroke Rd., Ballsbridge, Dublin 4. ☎ **800/843-3311** from the U.S., or 01/660-5000 and 01/667-0033. Fax 01/660-5540. www.jurys.com. 394 units. AC MINIBAR TV TEL. Main hotel £195 ($273) double; Towers wing £220 ($308) double. Towers wing rates include continental breakfast. Service charge 12.5%. AE, DC, MC, V. Limited free parking. DART: Lansdowne Rd. Bus: 5, 7, 7A, or 8.

Setting a progressive tone in a city steeped in tradition, this massive hotel, which enjoyed a major refurbishment in 1999, welcomes guests to a skylit, three-story atrium lobby with a marble and teak decor. Situated opposite the American Embassy, this sprawling property is actually two interconnected hotels in one: a modern, eight-story high-rise and a 100-unit tower with its own check-in desk, separate elevators, and private entrance, as well as full access to all the main hotel's amenities. The guest rooms in the main wing have dark wood furnishings, brass trim, and designer fabrics. The Towers section is an exclusive wing of oversized concierge-style rooms with bay windows. Each unit has computer-card key access, stocked minibar, three telephone lines, well-lit work area with desk, reclining chair, tile and marble bathroom, walk-in closet, and either a king- or queen-size bed. Decor varies, from contemporary light woods with floral fabrics to dark tones with Far Eastern motifs. Towers guests also enjoy exclusive use of a private hospitality lounge with library, board room, and access to complimentary continental breakfast, daily newspapers, and coffee/tea service throughout the day.

Dining/Diversions: Choices include the Embassy Garden for Irish and Continental cuisine; the Kish for seafood; and the Coffee Dock, an around-the-clock coffee shop. This is also the home of Jurys Irish Cabaret show, Ireland's longest-running evening entertainment; the Dubliner Bar, a pub with a turn-of-the century theme; and the skylit Pavilion Lounge, overlooking the indoor/outdoor pool.

Amenities: 24-hour room service, concierge, foreign-currency exchange, valet and laundry service, safe-deposit boxes, express checkout, heated indoor/outdoor pool, therapeutic hot whirlpool, hairdressing salons, craft and clothes shops, Aer Lingus ticket office.

Ballsbridge/Embassy Row Area Accommodations

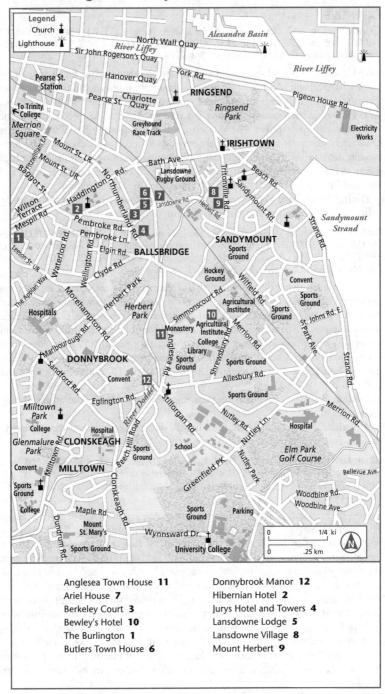

Anglesea Town House **11**
Ariel House **7**
Berkeley Court **3**
Bewley's Hotel **10**
The Burlington **1**
Butlers Town House **6**

Donnybrook Manor **12**
Hibernian Hotel **2**
Jurys Hotel and Towers **4**
Lansdowne Lodge **5**
Lansdowne Village **8**
Mount Herbert **9**

EXPENSIVE

✪ **Ariel House.** 50/52 Lansdowne Rd., Ballsbridge, Dublin 4. ☎ **01/668-5512.** Fax 01/
668-5845. 28 units. TV TEL. £136–£158 ($190.40–$221.20) double. MC, V. Closed Dec 23–
Jan 9. Free parking. DART: Lansdowne Rd. Bus: 7, 7A, 8, or 45.

Ariel House, a bastion of distinction and quality, sets the standard for Dublin guesthouses. Michael and Maurice O'Brien are warm and consummate hosts. Opened over
25 years ago by Dublin-born and San Francisco–trained hotelier Michael O'Brien,
Ariel House has been expanded and enhanced over the years. At its core is a historic
mid-19th-century mansion. The Victorian-style drawing room has Waterford glass
chandeliers, an open fireplace, and delicately carved cornices. Guest rooms are individually decorated with period furniture, fine paintings and watercolors, and crisp Irish
linens, as well as modern extras such as a hair dryer, garment press, tea/coffeemaker, and
iron and ironing board. Ariel House is 1 block from the DART station.

Dining/Diversions: The conservatory-style dining room serves breakfast, morning
coffee, and afternoon tea, and there's a wine bar.

Butlers Town House. 44 Lansdowne Rd., Ballsbridge, Dublin 4. ☎ **800/44-UTELL** from
the U.S., or 01/667-4022. Fax 01/667-3960. www.butlers-hotel.com. 19 units. A/C TV TEL.
£90–£180 ($126–$252) double. Rates include full breakfast. AE, DC, MC, V. Closed
Dec 24–27. DART: Lansdowne Rd. Bus: 7, 7A, 8, or 45.

This beautifully restored and expanded Victorian town house opened its doors to
guests in 1997. The aim is formal yet welcoming elegance, class without the starched
collar. Rooms are richly furnished with four-poster or half-tester beds, and equipped
with computer modems and individual climate control activated from a handheld
remote. It's hard to elude comfort here, and the staff is especially solicitous. One room
is equipped for travelers with disabilities. The gem here, in our opinion, is the Glendalough Room, which can be requested if you book early. The hotel offers free tea and
coffee all day.

Dining: Breakfast, afternoon tea, and high tea are served in the atrium dining
room.

Amenities: Room service (offering a limited dinner menu), baby-sitting, laundry/
dry cleaning, secretarial services.

Hibernian Hotel. Eastmoreland Place, Ballsbridge, Dublin 4. ☎ **800/525-4800** from
the U.S., or 01/668-7666. Fax 01/660-2655. www.hibernianhotel.com. 40 units. TV TEL.
£150–£170 ($210–$238) double; £185 ($259) junior suite. No service charge. AE, CB, DC,
MC, V. Free valet parking. Bus: 10.

Although the name is similar, this is not a reincarnation of the legendary Royal
Hibernian Hotel that stood on Dawson Street until the early 1980s. This handsome
four-story Victorian building was originally part of Baggot Street Hospital. After a
complete restoration, it opened as a hotel in 1993, and offers up-to-date comforts with
the charm of a country inn. In 1995, it became a member of Small Luxury Hotels of
the World, and in 1997 was named its Hotel of the Year. Antiques, graceful pillars,
and floral arrangements fill the public areas. The top floor sports a beautifully restored
dome-shaped skylight. The guest rooms, of varying size and layout, are outfitted with
orthopedic beds and individually decorated with dark woods, floral fabrics, and specially commissioned paintings of Dublin and wildlife scenes. There's one floor for
nonsmokers. In-room conveniences include a full-length mirror, garment press, hair
dryer, and tea/coffeemaker. Unlike some converted 19th-century buildings, it has an
elevator.

Dining/Diversions: On the lobby level are a cozy, parlor-like bar and a conservatory-
style restaurant.

Amenities: 24-hour room service, concierge, access to nearby health club (extra fee), laundry/dry cleaning, 24-hour butler, turndown service, baby-sitting, secretarial services, express checkout.

MODERATE

Anglesea Town House. 63 Anglesea Rd., Ballsbridge, Dublin 4. ☎ **01/668-3877.** Fax 01/668-3461. 7 units. TV TEL. £90–£100 ($126–$140) double. No service charge. Rates include full breakfast. AE, MC, V. DART: Lansdowne Rd. Bus: 10, 46A, 46B, 63, or 84.

A true bed-and-breakfast experience is the best way to describe this 1903 Edwardian-style guesthouse. Close to the Royal Dublin Showgrounds and the American Embassy, it is furnished with comfort in mind—rocking chairs, settees, a sundeck, and lots of flowering plants, as well as modern conveniences in the guest rooms. You can count on a warm welcome from hostess Helen Kirrane, and the homemade breakfast is worth getting up for.

Lansdowne Lodge. 6 Lansdowne Terrace, Shelbourne Rd., Ballsbridge, Dublin 4. ☎ **01/660-5755.** Fax 01/660-5662. www.dublinhotels.com. 12 units. TV TEL. £50–£140 ($70–$196) double. Service charge 10%. Rates include full breakfast. MC, V. Free parking. DART: Lansdowne Rd. Bus: 5, 7, or 8.

With a lovely two-story brick facade, this guesthouse enjoys a convenient location, between Lansdowne and Haddington Roads, and within a block of the DART station and major bus routes. Owner Finbarr Smyth offers a variety of individually styled rooms with armchairs and homey furnishings, including decorative bed coverings and framed paintings. All the recently renovated guest rooms have firm beds; nonsmoking rooms are available. There's a garden on the grounds.

Mount Herbert. 7 Herbert Rd., Ballsbridge, Dublin 4. ☎ **01/668-4321.** Fax 01/660-7077. www.mountherberthotel.ie. 185 units. TV TEL. £69–£99 ($96.60–$138.60) double. No service charge. AE, DC, MC, V. Free parking available only to 100 cars. DART: Lansdowne Rd. Bus: 2, 3, 5, 7, 7A, 8, 18, or 45.

Over 40 years ago, the Loughran family welcomed their first guests to what had once been the family home of Lord Robinson. The gracious residence, with its own mature floodlit gardens, now forms the core of a somewhat-sprawling complex. The Mount Herbert has expanded from 4 guest rooms to 185, and the result is a curious mix of family hospitality and large-scale uniformity. The guest rooms are bright, comfortable, and convenient to the city center, though without remarkable charm. Tea/coffee-making facilities and garment presses are standard. The property has a restaurant, a wine bar, a sauna, an indoor solarium, and a gift shop.

INEXPENSIVE

Bewley's Hotel. Merrion Rd., Ballsbridge, Dublin 4. ☎ **01/668-1111.** Fax: 01/668-1999. www.bewleyshotels.com. TV TEL. 220 units. £69 ($96.60) per room (sleeps up to 3 adults); £138 ($193.20) deluxe suite. AE, DC, MC, V. DART: Sandymount (5-min. walk). Bus: 7, 7A, 7X, 8, or 45.

The new Bewley's Hotel, located in a fashionable suburb 2 miles (3.2km) south of the city center, occupies an elegant 19th-century brick Masonic school building adjacent to the R.D.S. showgrounds and next to the British Embassy. A new wing harmonizes well with the old structure, and is indistinguishable on the interior. The hotel is an excellent value for families and groups; the only downside is its location outside the city center, a small obstacle given the frequent bus and DART service.

Public lounges and reception areas are spacious and thoughtfully restored, with mahogany wainscoting, marble paneling, and polished bronze creating a formal ambience. Rooms, too, are spacious and generously furnished—each has a writing desk, an armchair, a trouser press, tea/coffee facilities, and either a king bed or a double and a twin bed. Bathrooms are medium in size. The suites include an additional room with foldout couch, table (seats six), a tiny kitchen/bar cleverly hidden in a cabinet, and an additional bathroom (shower only). A basement restaurant (O'Connell's) is run by the Allen family of Ballymaloe fame, and offers very good food at reasonable prices; there's also an informal Bewley's tearoom.

SELF-CATERING

Donnybrook Manor. Donnybrook Manor, Donnybrook, Dublin 4. ☎ **01/676-6784.** Fax 01/676-6868. www.dubchamber.ie/brookman. 20 units. TV TEL. £650–£1,750 ($910–$2,450) per week. AE, DC, MC, V. Bus: 10, 46A, or 46B.

Donnybrook Manor, a community of tasteful redbrick town houses with stained-glass doors, is strategically situated in Donnybrook, a 25-minute walk from Grafton Street and College Green. Set well back from Donnybrook Road (N11) in its own parklands, the town houses are all but oblivious of the surrounding city. Each two-, three-, or four-bedroom unit comes complete with virtually every appliance and convenience you could want in a home-away-from-home. This is an attractive, cost-efficient alternative to a hotel or guesthouse for couples, families, or groups who will be in Dublin for 4 or more days. Rates vary depending on the size of the apartment and the season. The immediate environs are thick with exceptional gourmet shops. You can also order out or walk to a range of fine restaurants. Each town house has its own enclosed garden, complete with table and chairs. Cots, cribs, and highchairs are available.

Lansdowne Village. Newbridge Ave. (off Lansdowne Rd.), Ballsbridge, Dublin 4. ☎ **01/668-3534.** Fax 01/660-6465. 19 units. TV TEL. £400–£595 ($560–$833) per week, depending on size of apt and season. Shorter periods available at reduced rates Oct–Mar. MC, V. DART to Lansdowne Rd. Station. Bus: 2, 3, 5, 7, 7A, 8, 18, or 45.

Lansdowne Village is a modest and appealing residential development on the banks of the River Dodder, directly across from Lansdowne Stadium. Within this community, Trident Holiday Homes offers fully equipped two- and three-bedroom rental units, each with a pull-out double-bed sofa in the living room. They are bright and comfortable, well maintained so that everything really works. The location is ideal—a 5-minute walk from the DART and less than a half-hour's walk from St. Stephen's Green, but only 10 minutes from the Sandymount Strand, a favorite walking spot for Dubliners that's perfect for an after-dinner stroll. There are several shops and supermarkets nearby, so you can manage quite well without a car. The smaller units are perfect for couples, perhaps with one child; the considerably more spacious three-bedroom units are recommended for larger families or for more than one couple.

O'CONNELL STREET AREA/NORTH OF THE LIFFEY
VERY EXPENSIVE

The Gresham. 23 Upper O'Connell St., Dublin 1. ☎ **01/874-6881.** Fax 01/878-7175. E-mail: ryan@indigo.ie. 288 units. AC TV TEL. £180–£280 ($252–$392) double. Rates include service charge and full breakfast. AE, DC, MC, V. Parking £5 ($7). DART: Connolly. Bus: 40A, 40B, 40C, or 51A.

Centrally located on the city's main business thoroughfare, this Regency-style hotel is one of Ireland's oldest (established in 1817) and best-known lodgings. Although much of the tourist trade in Dublin has shifted south of the River Liffey in recent years, the Gresham is still synonymous with stylish Irish hospitality. It provides easy access to the Abbey and Gate theaters and other northside attractions. The lobby and public areas are a panorama of marble floors, molded plasterwork, and crystal chandeliers. With high ceilings and individual decor, the older guest rooms vary in size and style; all have soft lighting, tile bathrooms, and period furniture, including padded headboards and armoires. Quite recently, 100 new air-conditioned superior rooms were added in the Lavery Wing. Nonsmoking rooms are available. One-of-a-kind luxury terrace suites grace the upper front floors.

Dining/Diversions: The Aberdeen Restaurant serves formal meals; Toddy's, a trendy pub and lounge, offers light meals all day. Another bar, Magnums, attracts a late-night crowd.

Amenities: 24-hour room service, concierge, fitness center, conference rooms, well-equipped business center, ISDN/modem facilities, valet/laundry, baby-sitting, foreign-currency exchange.

EXPENSIVE

Royal Dublin. 40 Upper O'Connell St., Dublin 1. ☎ **800/528-1234** from the U.S., or 01/873-3666. Fax 01/873-3120. www.royaldublin.com. 117 units. TV TEL. £105–£154 ($147–$215.60) double. Rates include full Irish breakfast and service charge. AE, DC, MC, V. Free parking; secure car park available nearby. DART: Connolly. Bus: 36A, 40A, 40B, 40C, or 51A.

Romantically floodlit at night, this modern five-story hotel is near Parnell Square at the north end of Dublin's main thoroughfare, within walking distance of all the main theaters and northside attractions. The contemporary skylit lobby lies adjacent to lounge areas that were part of the original 1752 building. These Georgian-themed rooms are rich in high molded ceilings, ornate cornices, crystal chandeliers, gilt-edged mirrors, and open fireplaces. Guest rooms are strictly modern, with light woods, pastel fabrics, and three-sided full-length windows that extend over the busy street below. Corridors are extremely well lit, with lights at each doorway.

Dining/Diversions: The Cafe Royale Brasserie, for full meals; Raffles Bar, a clubby room with portraits of Irish literary greats, for snacks or drinks; the Georgian Lounge, for morning coffee or afternoon tea beside the open fireplace.

Amenities: 24-hour room service, concierge, laundry, foreign-currency exchange, car-rental desk, baby-sitting.

MODERATE

✪ **Chief O'Neill's.** Smithfield Village, Dublin 1. ☎ **01/817-3838.** Fax 01/817-3839. www.chiefoneills.com. 73 units. TV TEL. £125 ($175) twin or double room; £295 ($413) penthouse suites. Rates include service charge. AE, MC, V. Free parking. Bus: 25, 25A, 67, 67A, 68, 69, 79, or 90.

Chief O'Neill's is the centerpiece of Smithfield Village, a 2.5-acre "cultural urban village" newly created north of the Liffey just in from the Four Courts. The operative word throughout the village is music, traditional Irish music. This is home as well to Ceol, the Old Jameson Distillery, and The Chimney (see section 5 of this chapter, "Seeing the Sights"). There's plenty to do here; and, when you've done it all, you're only 15 minutes on foot from Temple Bar.

The rooms here quite defy description. Think primary colors, glass, light wood, chrome, Zen, and the Starship *Enterprise,* and you're part way there. Nothing scary, just a bit bold and very comfortable. There's nothing else quite like Chief O'Neill's in Dublin, and it's sure to intrigue anyone able to spend a night without a trace of anything Georgian or Victorian. Firm beds with duvets are the solid norm; coffeemakers, hair dryers, CD players, and high-speed ISDN connections are all standard. The penthouses have raised lounge areas, Jacuzzis, and rooftop balconies. One entire floor (19 rooms) is nonsmoking, and 4 rooms are specially adapted for guests with disabilities.

Chief O'Neill's Bar (featuring live Irish music most summer nights) and the Kelly and Ping Bar and Restaurant are popular destinations in themselves, as is the adjacent upscale Duck Lane shopping complex.

INEXPENSIVE

Jurys Inn Custom House. Custom House Quay, Dublin 1. ☎ **800/44-UTELL** from the U.S., or 01/607-5000. Fax 01/829-0400. www.jurys.com. 239 units. A/C TV TEL. £69 ($96.60) single, double, or family room. Rates include service charge. Full Irish breakfast £6.50 ($9.10). AE, CB, DC, MC, V. Discounted parking available at adjacent lot (£6.40/$8.96 for 24 hr.). DART: Tara Street. Bus: 27A, 27B, or 53A.

Ensconced in the grandiose new financial services district and facing the quays on which generations of Irish émigrés tore themselves from their mother soil, this the newest of the Jurys Inns looks out on both the old and the new Ireland. Following the successful Jurys formula of affordable convenience and comfort without frills, Jurys Inn Custom House provides rooms to meet most needs at one unprovocative price. Single rooms have a double bed and a pull-out sofa, while double rooms offer both a double and a twin bed. Twenty-two especially spacious rooms, if available, cost nothing extra. An ample number of nonsmoking rooms and handicapped-adapted rooms are also available. Rooms facing the quays also enjoy vistas of the Dublin hills, while those facing the financial district tend to be more quiet. All have coffeemakers, hair dryers, and modem connections. Facilities include a moderately priced restaurant, a pub lounge, and an adjacent multistory parking area. As occupancy runs at 100% from May to September and at roughly 95% for the rest of the year, be sure to book well in advance. The hotel lies a 5-minute walk from the Custom House east along Custom House Quay. Be sure to notice the painfully poignant Famine Memorial along the same quay.

Mount Eccles Court Hostel and Self-Catering Apartments. 42 N. Great George's St., Dublin 1. ☎ **01/873-0826.** Fax 01/878-3554. E-mail: info@eccleshostel.com. 10 units, 8 with private bathroom; 16 dorm units, 4 with private bathroom. £36 ($50.40) double without bathroom, £40 ($56) double with bathroom; £12.50–£15 ($17.50–$21) per person in 4-bed dorm; £10–£11 ($14–$15.40) per person in 6- to 16-bed dorm. Self-catering units £340–£440 ($476–$616) per week. MC, V. Hostel rates include continental breakfast. Bus: 1, 10A, 40B, 40C, or 41 (from the airport). 1 block east of Parnell Sq. E., at the top of O'Connell St.

If you're intrigued by the architecture of Georgian Dublin, you'll love this place. North Great George's Street comprises a short row of beautiful Georgian town houses—the splendid house that's now the James Joyce Centre is adjacent to the hostel. The massive building, constructed as a convent, has been renovated into accommodations over the past few years. The rooms in front have somewhat more appealing views than those in back, which look out on a parking lot. The first floor has a large sitting room with high ceilings, intricate plasterwork, and massive windows. Breakfast is served in a dark but atmospheric basement room with stone walls. The owners recently renovated four magnificent rooms in an adjacent town house as luxury self-catering apartments. Each has a loft sleeping area, small but well-stocked kitchen, bathroom, and hide-a-bed couch.

4 Dining

You're here. You're famished. Where do you go? A formal, old-world hotel dining room? Perhaps a casual bistro or wine bar? Ethnic cuisine, maybe? Dublin has the goods, across a wide range of price categories. Expect generally higher prices than you'd pay for comparable fare in a comparable U.S. city. (Hey, Dublin's hip—you always pay for hip.) As befits a European capital, there's plenty of Continental cuisine, with a particular leaning toward French and Italian influences. The city has a fine selection of international restaurants, with menus from Scandinavia, Russia, the Mediterranean, and China, and even exotic fare from someplace called California.

HISTORIC OLD CITY/LIBERTIES AREA
MODERATE

Lord Edward. 23 Christ Church Place, Dublin 8. ☎ **01/454-2420.** Reservations required. Main courses £9.95–£15.95 ($13.95–$22.35); fixed-price dinner £20 ($28). AE, CB, DC, MC, V. Mon–Fri noon–10:45pm; Sat 6–10:45pm. Closed Dec 24–Jan 3. Bus: 50, 54A, 56A, 65, 65A, 77, 77A, 123, or 150. SEAFOOD.

Established in 1890 and situated in the heart of the Old City opposite Christ Church Cathedral, this cozy upstairs dining room claims to be Dublin's oldest seafood restaurant. A dozen preparations of sole, including au gratin and Veronique, are served; there are many variations of prawns, from thermidor to Provençal; and fresh lobster is prepared au naturel or in sauces. Fresh fish—from salmon and sea trout to plaice and turbot—is served grilled, fried, meunière, or poached. Vegetarian dishes are also available. At lunch, light snacks and simpler fare are served in the bar.

The Mermaid Cafe. 69/70 Dame St., Dublin 2. ☎ **01/670-8236.** Reservations recommended. Dinner main courses £13.95–£18.95 ($19.55–$26.55). MC, V. Mon–Sat 12:30–2:30pm and 6–10:30pm; Sun noon–2:30pm and 6–9pm. Bus: 50, 50A, 54, 56A, 77, 77A, or 77B. IRISH/CONTINENTAL.

The Mermaid Cafe is a small place with a big reputation. Like the mild-mannered reporter for the *Daily Planet,* this could be something very ordinary. But it's not. The food here is consistently remarkable. The combination of ingredients and the blending of spices are, on paper, rather boldly inventive; and yet the resulting dishes are subtle and harmonious. As a starter, the beetroot, quail egg, and baby spinach salad offers a good launch without threatening your appetite, though the paprika smoked chicken with avocado and cilantro (especially when combined with the dangerously appealing assortment of freshly baked breads) may leave you with the will but not the room for the generous entrees soon to emerge from the kitchen. The grilled swordfish with mango relish, the roast duck breast on curried noodles, the wild salmon, and the char-grilled monkfish are all flawlessly prepared and quite memorable. After all that, we won't admit to having had dessert, but you won't be disappointed if you succumb. Complimentary caramelized pecans prove a tasty final touch. The Mermaid continues to live up to her reputation.

Old Dublin. 90/91 Francis St., Dublin 8. ☎ **01/454-2028.** Reservations recommended. Fixed-price lunch £13.50 ($18.90); fixed-price dinner £21 ($29.40). Main courses £11.50–£15.50 ($16.10–$21.70). AE, DC, MC, V. Mon–Fri 12:30–2:15pm; Mon–Sat 6–11pm. Bus: 21A, 78A, or 78B. SCANDINAVIAN/RUSSIAN.

In the heart of Dublin's antiques row, this restaurant is also on the edge of the city's medieval quarter, once settled by Vikings. It's not surprising, therefore, that many recipes reflect this background, with a long list of imaginative Scandinavian and Russian dishes. Among the best entrees are fillet of beef *Novgorod,* rare beef thinly sliced and served on sauerkraut with fried barley, mushrooms, garlic butter, sour cream, and caviar; salmon *Kulebjaka,* a pastry filled with salmon, dill herbs, rice, egg, mushrooms, and onion; and black sole *Metsa,* filled with mussels and served with prawn butter and white wine. There's a varied selection of vegetarian dishes.

Dublin Dining

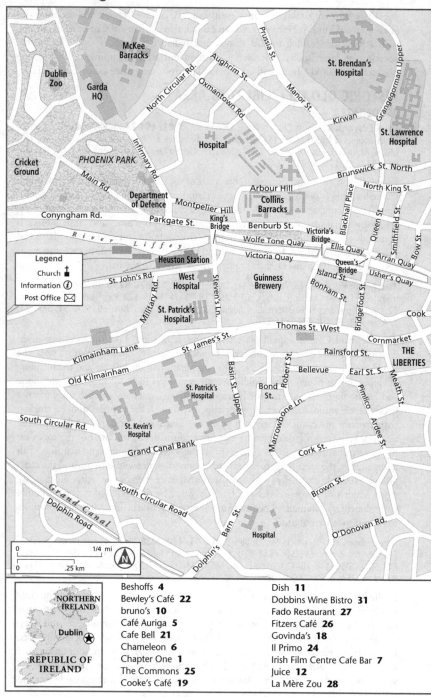

Legend
Church ✝
Information ⓘ
Post Office ✉

NORTHERN IRELAND

Dublin

REPUBLIC OF IRELAND

Beshoffs **4**
Bewley's Café **22**
bruno's **10**
Café Auriga **5**
Cafe Bell **21**
Chameleon **6**
Chapter One **1**
The Commons **25**
Cooke's Café **19**

Dish **11**
Dobbins Wine Bistro **31**
Fado Restaurant **27**
Fitzers Café **26**
Govinda's **18**
Il Primo **24**
Irish Film Centre Cafe Bar **7**
Juice **12**
La Mère Zou **28**

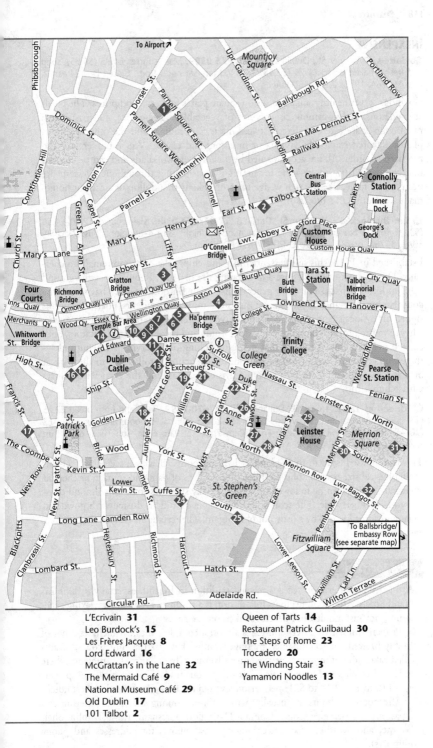

INEXPENSIVE

Govinda's. 4 Aungier St., Dublin 2. ☎ **01/475-0309.** Main courses £4.95 ($6.95); soup and freshly baked bread £1.75 ($2.45). MC, V. Mon–Sat noon–9pm. Closed Dec 24–Jan 2. Bus: 16, 16A, 19, or 22. VEGETARIAN.

Govinda's serves healthy square meals on square plates for very good prices. The meals are generous, belly-warming concoctions of vegetables, cheese, rice, and pasta. Two main courses are offered cafeteria-style. One is East Indian, and the other a simple, plainly flavored staple like lasagna or macaroni and cheese. Veggie burgers are also prepared to order. All are accompanied by a choice of two salads and can be enjoyed unaccompanied by smoke—the restaurant is nonsmoking throughout. Desserts are healthy and huge, like the rich wedge of carob cake with a dollop of cream or home-made ice cream (£1.50/$2.10).

✪ **Leo Burdock's.** 2 Werburgh St., Dublin 8. ☎ **01/454-0306.** Main courses £2.50–£4.50 ($3.50–$6.30). No credit cards. Mon–Sat noon–midnight; Sun 4–midnight. Bus: 21A, 50, 50A, 78, 78A, or 78B. FISH-AND-CHIPS/FAST FOOD.

Established in 1913, this quintessential fish-and-chips take-out shop remains a cherished Dublin institution, despite a devastating fire in 1998. Rebuilt from the ground up, Burdock's is back. For three generations, Brian Burdock's family has served the country's best fish-and-chips. Cabinet ministers, university students, poets, Americans tipped off by locals, and almost every other type in Ireland can be found in the queue. They're waiting for fish bought fresh that morning and those good Irish potatoes, both cooked in "drippings" (none of that modern cooking oil!). Service is takeout only—there's no seating, but you can sit on a nearby bench or stroll down to the park at St. Patrick's Cathedral. It's across from Christchurch, around the corner from Jurys Christchurch Inn.

✪ **Queen of Tarts.** 4 Corkhill, Dublin 2. ☎ **01/670-7499.** Soup and fresh bread £2.25 ($3.15); sandwiches and savory tarts £3–£4 ($4.20–$5.60); baked goods and cakes 50p–£3 (70¢–$4.20). No credit cards. Mon–Fri 7:30am–7pm, Sat 9am–6pm, Sun 10am–6pm. Bus: Any city-center bus. TEA SHOP.

This tearoom is David to the Goliath of Irish tearooms (Bewley's, see below), but its small physical size packs a solid pie-filled punch. Tarts of ham and spinach or cheddar cheese and chives can be followed up with the flaky sweetness of warm almond cranberry or blackberry pie. The scones here are tender and light, dusted with powdered sugar and accompanied by a little pot of fruit jam. The restaurant is small, smoke-free, and delicious.

Tea for Two

As in Britain, afternoon tea is a revered tradition in Ireland, especially in Dublin's grand hotels. Afternoon tea in its fullest form is a sit-down event and a relaxing experience, not just a quick hot beverage taken on the run.

Properly presented, afternoon tea is almost a complete meal. It includes a pot of freshly brewed tea accompanied by finger sandwiches, pastries, hot scones, cream-filled cakes, and other sweets arrayed on a silver tray. To enhance the ambience, there is often live piano or harp music. This sumptuous midafternoon pick-me-up averages £10 to £15 ($14 to $21) per person, even in the lounges of the city's best hotels.

Afternoon tea hours are usually 3 to 4:30pm. Among the hotels offering this repast are the Berkeley Court, Conrad, Davenport, Gresham, Royal Dublin, Shelbourne, and Westbury (see "Accommodations," above, for addresses and phone numbers).

You Paid What?

47,000 hotels, 700 airlines, 50 rental car companies. And a few million ways to save money.

Travelocity.com
A Sabre Company

Go Virtually Anywhere.

AOL Keyword: Travel

Will you have enough stories to tell your grandchildren?

Yahoo! Travel

Do You YAHOO!?

TEMPLE BAR/TRINITY COLLEGE AREA

EXPENSIVE

Les Frères Jacques. 74 Dame St., Dublin 2. ☎ **01/679-4555**. Reservations recommended. Fixed-price lunch £13.50 ($18.90); fixed-price dinner £21 ($29.40). AE, DC, MC, V. Mon–Fri 12:30–2:30pm; Mon–Thurs 7:15–10:30pm; Fri–Sat 7:15–11pm. Closed Dec 24–Jan 4. Bus: 50, 50A, 54, 56, or 77. FRENCH.

Well situated between Crampton Court and Sycamore Street opposite Dublin Castle, this restaurant brings a touch of haute cuisine to the lower edge of the trendy Temple Bar district. The menu offers such entrees as Daube of beef with root vegetables, rabbit lasagne with medeira sauce, and rosette of spring lamb in meat juice sabayon and tomato coulis with crispy potato straws. You might also try veal on rainbow pasta with garlic and basil sauce, and grilled lobster (from the tank) flamed in whiskey. À la carte dishes are also available.

MODERATE

bruno's. 30 E. Essex St., Dublin 2. ☎ **01/670-6767**. Reservations recommended. Dinner main courses £10.95–£13.95 ($15.35–$19.55). Service charge 10% on tables over 4. AE, CB, DC, MC, V. Mon–Fri 12:30–10:30pm; Sat 5–10:30pm. DART to Tara St. Station. Bus: 21A, 46A, 46B, 51B, 51C, 68, 69, or 86. FRENCH/MEDITERRANEAN.

This is a sure-fire spot for a flawlessly prepared, interesting lunch or dinner without serious damage to the budget. The atmosphere is light and modern, with the focus on food that is consistently excellent without flourish or pretense. The spinach and goat cheese tart; the salad of prawns with honey, lime, sesame seeds, and jalapeño peppers; and the bruscetta of chicken are all worthy of mention. The new Millennium Bridge makes bruno's all the more convenient as it crosses the Liffey at Eustace Street, which is directly opposite the restaurant.

You can now also find a bruno's at 21 Kildare St., Dublin 2 (☎ **01/662-4724**).

Café Auriga. Temple Bar Sq., Dublin 2. ☎ **01/671-8228**. Main courses £8.95–£14.95 ($12.55–$20.95); early-bird menu (5:30–7:30pm) with 3 courses for the price of the main course £8.95–£10.50 ($12.55–$14.70). AE, MC, V. Tues–Sat 5:30–11pm. Bus: Any city-center bus. CONTEMPORARY IRISH.

Café Auriga is a stylish second-floor cafe whose main dining room overlooks Temple Bar Square. Dinner is served under a ceiling of twinkling stars and is accompanied not by the sweet serenade of a lone violinist, but by the louder melodies of Dublin's top 40. The decor is stylish and simple and the crowd young, sleek, and professional. The food demonstrates the chef's facility in combining simple ingredients to create a piquant surprise for the palate. Subtly spiced, imaginative sauces accompany well-prepared fish and meat dishes, such as salmon in ginger soy sauce or breast of chicken stuffed with basil mousse. Vegetarian offerings include a succulent tagliatelle of goat cheese, cherry tomatoes, spinach, fresh herbs, and cream.

Chameleon. 1 Fownes St. Lower, Temple Bar, Dublin 2. ☎ **01/671-0362**. Set dinner menus £13.50–£21.50 ($18.90–$30.10); early-bird main courses £6.50–£7 ($9.10–$9.80). MC, V. Tues–Sat 6–11:30pm; Sun 6–10pm. Bus: Any city-center bus. INDONESIAN.

Only a dim candlelit window and an orange sign signal Chameleon, well camouflaged on a small side street off Temple Bar Square. Incense tinges the air, and rich Indonesian batiks form sumptuous backdrops for the traditional puppets and dark wood carvings that lurk in the corners. The Chameleon offers a variety of menus that feature samplings of seven different dishes and an assortment of condiments. The staff is quick to explain how to best complement chicken sate with roasted peanuts. Sambalbadjak, a red curry paste, gives rice a robust, pleasantly spicy flavor. Finally, a small morsel of pickled vegetable is also suggested as a "palate cleanser"—good advice to swallow if you want to take advantage of the abundance of delicately flavored dishes that Chameleon has to offer.

✪ **Dish.** 2 Crow St., Dublin 2. ☎ **01/671-1248.** Reservations recommended. Lunch £10.95 ($15.35); dinner main courses £7.95–£16.95 ($11.15–$23.75). Service charge 10% on tables of 6 or more. AE, DC, MC, V. Daily noon–11:30pm. DART: Tara St. Bus: 21A, 46A, 46B, 51B, 51C, 68, 69, or 86. NOUVEAU INTERNATIONAL.

With floor-to-ceiling windows, wide-beamed pine floors, light walls, and dark blue linens, Dish presents a relaxed, tasteful atmosphere. The menu is eclectic and enticing, with an emphasis on fresh grilled seafood and Mediterranean flavors, complex without being confusing. Grilled salmon with avocado, papaya and tequila-lime dressing, baked hake, and char-grilled tiger prawns were outstanding. The desserts we tried—caramelized lemon tart with cassis sauce and amaretti chocolate cheesecake—were superb. Only organic meats and the finest fresh ingredients find their way into your dish. This promises to be one of Temple Bar's finest venues, and at a modest price.

Juice. Castle House, 73 S. Great George's St., Dublin 2. ☎ **01/475-7856.** Reservations recommended Fri–Sat. Main courses £4.95–£7.25 ($6.95–$10.15); early-bird set-price dinner (Mon–Fri 5:30–7pm) £8.95 ($12.55). MC, V. Sun–Wed 9am–10:30pm; Thurs–Sat 5:30pm–4am. Bus: 50, 50A, 54, 56, or 77. VEGETARIAN.

Juice tempts carnivorous, vegan, macrobiotic, celiac, and yeast-free diners alike, using organic produce to create delicious dressings and entrees among its largely conventional but well-prepared offerings. The avocado fillet of blue cheese and broccoli wrapped in filo was superb, and I also highly recommend the spinach-and-ricotta cannelloni. The latter is included in the early-bird dinner—a great deal. Coffees, fresh-squeezed juices, organic wines, and late weekend hours add to the lure of this casual modern place, which is usually frequented by mature diners who know their food. The one anomaly here is that a restaurant so focused on health is often rather clouded in smoke.

✪ **Yamamori Noodles.** 71–2 S. Great George's St., Dublin 2. ☎ **01/475-5001.** Reservations only for parties of 4 or more persons. £3.50–£22 ($4.90–$30.80). MC, V. Sun–Wed 12:30–11pm; Thurs–Sat 12:30–11:30pm. Bus: 50, 50A, 54, 56, or 77. JAPANESE.

If you're still skeptical about Japanese cuisine, Yamamori will make you an instant believer. In a pop, casual, and exuberant atmosphere in which conversation becomes an unwarranted distraction from the fare, you may just be startled by how good the food is here. The splendid menu is a who's who of Japanese cuisine, and the prices range from budget to the big splurge. Regardless of the bottom line, however, everyone goes away feeling full and feted. It's difficult not to rave. On a raw, drizzly Dublin day, the chili chicken ramen is best summed up as a pot of bliss, while the Yamamori Yaki Soba offers, in a mound of wok-fried noodles, a well-rewarded treasure hunt for prawns, squid, chicken, and roast pork. And vegetarians will feel far from overlooked. The keywords here are freshness and perfection. The selective international wine list is well-suited to the cuisine. At 9:30pm on a Monday night, this place was jammed, not by tourists but by local Dubs, which among other things tells you that the secret is out.

INEXPENSIVE

Irish Film Centre Cafe Bar. 6 Eustace St., Temple Bar, Dublin 2. ☎ **01/677-8788.** Lunch and dinner £5–£8 ($7–$11.20). MC, V. Mon–Fri 12:30–3pm; Sat–Sun 1–3pm; daily 6–9pm. Bus: 21A, 78A, or 78B. IRISH/INTERNATIONAL.

One of the most popular drinking spots in Temple Bar, the Cafe Bar features an excellent menu that changes daily. A vegetarian and Middle Eastern menu is available for both lunch and dinner. The weekend entertainment usually includes music or comedy.

ST. STEPHEN'S GREEN/GRAFTON STREET AREA

EXPENSIVE

The Commons. 86 St. Stephen's Green, Dublin 2. ☎ **01/475-2597** or 01/478-0530. Reservations required. Fixed-price lunch £22 ($30.80); main-courses £20–£23 ($28–$32.20). AE, DC, MC, V. Mon–Fri 12:30–3pm; Mon–Sat 7:30–10:30pm. Closed 2 weeks after Christmas and first 2 weeks in Aug. DART: Pearse. Bus: 10, 11, 13, or 46A. MODERN EUROPEAN.

Nestled on the south side of St. Stephen's Green, this Michelin-starred restaurant occupies the basement level of Newman House, the historic seat of Ireland's major university. The dining-room decor blends Georgian architecture, cloister-style arches, and original contemporary artwork with Joycean influences. For a cocktail in fine weather, a "secret garden" of lush plants and trees surrounds the lovely stone courtyard terrace. The inventive menu changes daily, but you'll often see dishes such as magret of duck flavored with honey and spices, grilled shark with peppered carrot, and loin of rabbit with a stuffing of marinated prune.

EXPENSIVE/MODERATE

Cookes Café. 14 S. William St., Dublin 2. ☎ **01/679-0536.** Reservations required. Fixed-price lunch menu £14.95 ($20.95); early-bird menu 6–7:30pm £14.95 ($20.95); dinner main courses £10–£18 ($14–$25.20). Service charge 12.5%. AE, DC, MC, V. Daily 12:30–3pm; Mon–Sat 6–11pm; Sun 6–10pm. DART: Tara St. Bus: 16A, 19A, 22A, 55, or 83. CALIFORNIAN/ MEDITERRANEAN.

Named for owner and chef Johnny Cooke, this shop-front restaurant is a longtime Dublin favorite. The open kitchen and murals dominate the room; there is also an outdoor seating area with antique tables and chairs. House specialties include grilled duck with pancetta, marsala balsamic sauce, and wilted endive; sautéed brill and Dover sole with capers and croutons; and baked grouper with a ragoût of mussels, clams, artichokes, and tomatoes.

Fado Restaurant. Mansion House, Dawson St., Dublin 2. ☎ **01/676-7200.** Reservations required. Fixed-price 2-course lunch £11 ($15.40); fixed-price 3-course dinner £25 ($35); dinner main courses £11–£19.50 ($15.40–$27.30). No service charge except for larger parties. AE, MC, V. Daily 11am–10pm. DART: Pearse St. Bus: 10, 11A, 11B, 13, or 20B. CONTINENTAL.

On a bright sunny day or a balmy summer evening (they do happen in Ireland!), the spacious veranda of this eccentric Italianate venue is simply the place to be. In the nastiest of weather, too, Fado's whimsically painted vaulted Victorian dining room puts the damp far out of mind. Everything about this place suggests "occasion," so you may want to save it for such, or just conjure one on the spot. The menu is enticingly diverse. Neither rich sauces nor bistro austerities prevail. Portion sizes vary greatly in scale from one entree to another, so ask directions, as the service is excellent. We found the terrine of chicken and pistachios, the oven-baked seafood, the braised shank of Irish lamb, and the panfried fusilli with tarragon cream all to be flawless. Finishing with the fudge terrine garnished with double cream and fresh red currants proved deliciously daunting. The international wine list is judicious and contains some bright surprises, like the Stonleigh sauvignon blanc, an inspired choice from New Zealand.

La Mère Zou. 22 St. Steven's Green, Dublin 2. ☎ **01/661-6669.** Reservations recommended. Fixed-price lunch £11.50 ($16.10); early-bird dinner menu £13.50 ($18.90); dinner main courses £9.50–£17.50 ($13.30–$24.50). AE, CB, DC, MC, V. Mon–Fri 12:30–2:30pm; Mon–Thurs 6–10:30pm; Fri–Sat 6–11pm; Sun 6–9:30pm. DART: Pearse. Bus: 10, 11A, 11B, 13, or 20B. FRENCH COUNTRY.

Chef-proprietor Eric Tydgadt has created a warm, comfortable Mediterranean ambience in which to savor his fresh French country specialties. They evoke memories of superb Gallic cooking *en famille*. The emphasis is on perfectly cooked food accompanied by persuasive but "unarmed" sauces served in an unpretentious manner. Mussels are a house specialty, with an array of poultry, seafood, lamb, and game offerings. The quality of ingredients and attention to enhancing the flavor of all dishes is consistent from appetizers to dessert. The excellent wine list favors the French, but also includes several £10 ($14) house wines.

MODERATE

✪ **Fitzers Café.** 51a Dawson St., Dublin 2. ☎ **01/677-1155.** Reservations recommended. Dinner main courses £9.95–£15.95 ($13.95–$22.35). AE, DC, MC, V. Daily noon–11pm. Closed Dec 24–27 and Good Friday. DART: Pearse. Bus: 10, 11A, 11B, 13, or 20B. INTERNATIONAL.

Wedged in the middle of a busy shopping street, this bright, airy Irish-style bistro has a multiwindowed facade and modern decor. The excellent, reasonably priced food is contemporary and quickly served. Choices range from chicken breast with hot chili cream sauce or brochette of lamb tandoori with mild curry sauce to gratin of smoked cod. There are also tempting vegetarian dishes made from organic produce.

Fitzers has several other Dublin locations, including one just a few blocks away at the National Gallery, Merrion Square West (☎ **01/661-4496**); another in Ballsbridge, at 51 Dawson St. (☎ **01/677-1155**); and Fitzers Café at Temple Bar Square (☎ **01/ 679-0440**). Consistency is the operative word—count on Fitzers not to disappoint.

✪ **Il Primo.** 16 Montague St. (off Harcourt St.), Dublin 2. ☎ **01/478-3373.** Reservations required on weekends. Dinner main courses £8.90–£15.90 ($12.45–$22.25). AE, CB, DC, MC, V. Mon–Fri noon–3pm and Mon–Sat 6–11pm. MODERN ITALIAN.

Word of mouth is what brought me to Il Primo, and it's a good thing, because I doubt I would have found it myself. It's tucked away off Harcourt Street, 50 yards down from St. Stephen's Green. Once inside, you'll find some of the most distinguished, innovative Italian cuisine this side of Rome and Tuscany. Awaken your palate with a glass of sparkling Venetian prosecco; begin with a plate of Parma ham, avocado, and balsamic vinaigrette; and then go for broke with ravioli *Il Primo*—an open handkerchief of pasta over chicken, Parma ham, and mushrooms in a light tarragon cream sauce. The proprietor, Dieter Bergmann, will assist you in selecting appropriate wines, all of which he personally chooses and imports from Tuscany. Wines are available by the milliliter, not the bottle. Open any bottle and you pay for only what you drink. Il Primo is full of surprises. And if you head north, there's no need to leave Il Primo behind—Bergmann has two branches in Belfast with the same menu as the Dublin original.

Trocadero. 3 St. Andrew St., Dublin 2. ☎ **01/677-5545.** Reservations recommended. Early-bird menu (6–7:30pm) £12.50 ($17.50); main courses £11–£18 ($15.40–$25.20). AE, DC, MC, V. Mon–Sat 6pm–midnight; Sun 6–11:15pm. DART: Tara St. Bus: 16A, 19A, 22A, 55, or 83. INTERNATIONAL.

Close to the Andrews Lane and other theaters, Trocadero is a favorite gathering spot for theatergoers, performers, and press. As might be expected, the decor is theatrical, with subdued lighting, banquette seating, close-set tables, and photos of entertainers on the walls. Steaks are the specialty, but the menu also offers rack of lamb, daily fish specials, pastas, and traditional dishes such as Irish stew and corned beef and cabbage with parsley sauce. The food is not memorable, but that fails to matter here at one of Dublin's more revered auld haunts.

INEXPENSIVE

✪ **Bewley's Café.** 78/79 Grafton St., Dublin 2. ☎ **01/677-6761.** Homemade soup £2.25 ($3.15); main courses £3–£6.50 ($4.20–$9.10); lunch specials from £5 ($7); dinner main courses from £12 ($16.80). AE, DC, MC, V. Sun–Thurs 7:30am–11pm; Fri–Sat 7:30am–1am (continuous service for breakfast, hot food, and snacks). Bus: Any city-center bus. TRADITIONAL/ PASTRIES.

Bewley's, a three-story landmark founded in 1840 by a Quaker named Joshua Bewley, is a quintessential part of the Dublin experience. The interior is a subdued, mellow mix of dark wood, amber glass, and deep red velvet. Bewley's bustles with the clink of teapots and the satisfied hum of customers sated on scones, almond buns, and baked goods. Less appealing but equally filling are warm suppers of lasagne, sausages and chips, or a variety of casseroles.

Most Bewley's establishments are self-service cafeterias, but Bewley's of Grafton Street also has several full-service tearooms. Other locations are at 11 Westmoreland St., Dublin 2; 13 S. Great George's St., Dublin 2; 40 Mary St., Dublin 1 (near the ILAC shopping center north of the Liffey); shopping centers in Dundrum, Stillorgan, and Tallaght; and Dublin Airport.

Cafe Bell. St. Teresa's Courtyard, Clarendon St., Dublin 2. ☎ **01/677-7645.** All items £2–£5 ($2.80–$7). No credit cards. Mon–Sat 9am–5:30pm. Bus: 16, 16A, 19, 19A, 22A, 55, or 83. IRISH/SELF-SERVICE.

In the cobbled courtyard of early 19th-century St. Teresa's Church, this serene little place is one of a handful of dining options springing up in historic or ecclesiastical surroundings. With high ceilings and an old-world decor, Cafe Bell is a welcome contrast to the bustle of Grafton Street a block away and Powerscourt Town House Centre across the street. The menu changes daily but usually includes homemade soups, sandwiches, salads, quiches, lasagna, sausage rolls, hot scones, and other baked goods.

✪ The Steps of Rome. Chatham St., Dublin 2. ☎ **01/670-5630.** Main courses £4.50–£9 ($6.30–$12.60); pizza slices £1.60–£2 ($2.25–$2.80). No credit cards. Daily 10am–2pm and 7–11pm. ITALIAN/PIZZA.

Word is out that this restaurant just off the busy shopping thoroughfare of Grafton Street offers some of the best simple Italian fare in Dublin. Large succulent pizza slices available for takeout are one way to enjoy the wonders of this authentic Italian kitchen when the dining room is full—the seven tables huddled within this tiny restaurant

Picnic, Anyone?

The parks of Dublin offer plenty of sylvan settings for a picnic lunch; so feel free to park it on a bench, or pick a grassy patch and spread a blanket. In particular, try **St. Stephen's Green** at lunchtime (in the summer there are open-air band concerts), the **Phoenix Park,** and **Merrion Square.** You can also take a ride on the DART to the suburbs of **Dun Laoghaire, Dalkey, Killiney,** and **Bray** (to the south) or **Howth** (to the north) and picnic along a bayfront pier or promenade.

In recent years, some fine delicatessens and gourmet food shops ideal for picnic fare have sprung up. For the best selection of fixings, we recommend the following: **Gallic Kitchen,** 49 Francis St., Dublin 8 (☎ **01/454-4912**), has gourmet prepared food to go, from salmon en croûte to pastries filled with meats or vegetables, pâtés, quiches, sausage rolls, and homemade pies, breads, and cakes. **Magills Delicatessen,** 14 Clarendon St., Dublin 2 (☎ **01/671-3830**), offers Asian and Continental delicacies, meats, cheeses, spices, and salads. For a fine selection of Irish cheeses, luncheon meat, and other delicacies, seek out **Sheridan's Cheesemongers,** 11 S. Anne St., Dublin 2 (☎ **01/679-3143**), perhaps the best of Dublin's cheese emporiums, or the **Big Cheese Company,** 14/15 Trinity St. (☎ **01/671 1399**).

seem to be perennially occupied. The potato, mozzarella, and rosemary pizza, with a thick crust resembling focaccia, is unusual and exceptionally delicious. Although the pasta dishes are also quite good, it's that pizza that remains unforgettable.

FITZWILLIAM SQUARE/MERRION SQUARE AREA
VERY EXPENSIVE

☉ Restaurant Patrick Guilbaud. 21 Upper Merrion St., Dublin 2. ☎ **01/676-4192.** Reservations required. Fixed-price lunch £22 ($30.80); main courses £17–£56 ($23.80–$78.40). AE, DC, MC, V. Tues–Sat 12:30–2pm and 7:30–10:15pm. DART: Westland Row. Bus: 10, 11A, 11B, 13, or 20B. NOUVELLE FRENCH.

After being tucked away for many years on James Place, this distinguished restaurant has been transferred to elegant new quarters, and taken with it the same glowing Michelin-star reputation for fine food and artful service. The menu features such dishes as roasted West Cork turbot, veal sweetbreads with black truffles, wild sea bass with ragout of mussels, and a casserole of winter vegetables with wild mushrooms. Just to say you did, start with the open ravioli of lobster with coconut cream, and finish with the *assiette gourmande au chocolat* (five small hot and cold chocolate desserts). A private dining room is available for parties of 2 to 25.

EXPENSIVE

Dobbins Wine Bistro. 15 Stephen's Lane (off Upper Mount St.), Dublin 2. ☎ **01/676-4670.** Reservations recommended. Dinner main courses £13.50–£23 ($18.90–$32.20). AE, DC, MC, V. Mon–Fri 12:30–2:30pm; Tues–Sat 7:30–10:30pm. DART: Pearse. Bus: 5, 7A, 8, 46, or 84. IRISH/CONTINENTAL.

Almost hidden in a lane between Upper and Lower Mount Streets a block east of Merrion Square, this friendly enclave is a haven for inventive cuisine. The menu changes often, but usually includes such items as duckling with orange and port sauce; steamed paupiette of black sole with salmon, crab, and prawn filling; panfried veal kidneys in pastry; and fillet of beef topped with crispy herb bread crumbs with shallot and Madeira sauce. You'll have a choice of sitting in the bistro, with checkered tablecloths and sawdust on the floor, or on the tropical patio, with an all-weather sliding-glass roof.

☉ L'Ecrivain. 109 Lower Baggot St., Dublin 2. ☎ **01/661-1919.** Reservations recommended. Fixed-price 3-course lunch £16.50 ($23.10); fixed-price 4-course dinner £33 ($46.20); vegetarian dinner £27.50 ($38.50); main courses £19.50–£21.50 ($27.30–$30.10). Service charge 10% on food only. AE, DC, MC, V. Mon–Fri 12:30–2pm; Mon–Sat 7–11pm. Bus: 10. FRENCH/IRISH.

This is one of Dublin's truly fine restaurants, from start to finish. The atmosphere is relaxed, welcoming, and unpretentious. You can dine on the garden terrace, weather permitting, or in the newly renovated and expanded dining rooms. Each course seems to receive the same devoted attention, and most consist of traditional "best of Irish" ingredients, prepared without dense sauces. The seared sea trout with sweet potato purée and the entrecôte with caramelized onion were perfectly prepared for me, and the presentation more than competes with anything in the Museum of Modern Art. The desserts are not an afterthought, but the creations of a talented pastry chef. The crème brûlée here is the best I've tasted north of the Chunnel. The restaurant is a 5-minute walk from St. Stephen's Green. If you drive, there's ample street parking on nearby Merrion Square.

MODERATE

McGrattan's in the Lane. 76 Fitzwilliam Lane, Dublin 2. ☎ **01/661-8808.** Reservations recommended. Dinner main courses £11–£18 ($15.40–$25.20). AE, MC, V. Sun–Thurs 6pm–midnight; Fri–Sat 6pm–1am. IRISH/FRENCH.

Out of view from the general flow of traffic, this restaurant is in a lane between Baggot Street and Merrion Square. The decor ranges from a homey fireside lounge with oldies background music to a skylit, plant-filled dining room. The creative menu includes main dishes such as breast of chicken Fitzwilliam (stuffed with cheddar cheese in pastry), roast pheasant with wild mushrooms and red wine sauce, and paupiette of salmon stuffed with scallop mousse and wrapped in a pancake of puff pastry.

INEXPENSIVE

National Museum Cafe. National Museum of Ireland, Kildare St., Dublin 2. ☎ **01/662-1269.** Soup £2 ($2.80); lunch main courses under £6 ($8.40). MC, V. Tues–Sat 10am–5pm; Sun 2–5pm. Bus: 7, 7A, 8, 10, 11, or 13. CAFETERIA/TEA SHOP.

The tall windows of the National Museum Cafe look out toward the National Library across a cobbled yard; inside the cafe, an elaborate mosaic floor, enameled fireplace, marble tabletops, and chandelier lend an element of elegance to this otherwise-informal eatery. Everything is made from scratch: beef salad, chicken salad, quiche, an abundance of pastries. The soup of the day is often vegetarian, and quite good. This is a great place to step out of the rain, warm yourself, and then wander among the nation's treasures. Admission to the museum is free, so you can visit at your own pace, as often as your curiosity (and appetite) demand.

BALLSBRIDGE/EMBASSY ROW AREA

VERY EXPENSIVE

Le Coq Hardi. 35 Pembroke Rd., Ballsbridge, Dublin 4. ☎ **01/668-9070.** Reservations required. Fixed-price lunch £24.50 ($34.30); fixed-price dinner £35 ($49). Service charge 12½%. AE, CB, MC, V. Mon–Fri 12:30–2:30pm; Mon–Sat 7–10:45pm. DART: Lansdowne Rd. Bus: 18, 46, 63, or 84. FRENCH.

Decorated in radiant autumn colors, this plush 50-seat restaurant (with a new cocktail bar) draws a well-heeled local and international business clientele. Award-winning chef John Howard offers such specialties as Dover sole stuffed with prawns, *darne* (steak) of Irish wild salmon on fresh spinach leaves, fillet of hake roasted on green cabbage and bacon with Pernod butter sauce, and fillet of prime beef flamed in Irish whiskey. The 700-bin wine cellar boasts a complete collection of Château Mouton Rothschild, dating from 1945 to the present.

EXPENSIVE

Kites. 15/17 Ballsbridge Terrace, Ballsbridge, Dublin 4. ☎ **01/660-7415.** Reservations recommended. Dinner main courses £11–£20 ($15.40–$28). AE, DC, MC, V. Mon–Fri 12:30–2pm; daily 6:30–11pm. DART: Lansdowne Rd. Bus: 5, 7, 7A, 8, 46, 63, or 84. CANTONESE.

Kites is renowned in Dublin for its excellent Cantonese cuisine, a reputation focused on its seafood and hot-and-spicy dishes. The menu features the usual chow mein, curries, and sweet-and-sour dishes, as well as a host of creative entrees, such as king prawns with Chinese leaves in oyster sauce, stuffed crab claws, Singapore fried noodles, and birds' nests of fried potatoes.

Lobster Pot. 9 Ballsbridge Terrace, Ballsbridge, Dublin 4. ☎ **01/668-0025.** Reservations required. Dinner main courses £14–£19.50 ($19.60–$27.30); lobster dinner roughly £30 ($42). AE, DC, MC, V. Mon–Fri 12:30–2:30pm; Mon–Sat 6:30–10:30pm. DART: Lansdowne Rd. Bus: 5, 7, 7A, 8, 46, 63, or 84. SEAFOOD.

This upstairs restaurant is known for its lobster dishes, as you might guess from its name. The menu also regularly includes salmon, black sole, monkfish, halibut, plaice, hake, turbot, sea trout, and Dublin Bay prawns, all variously rendered. And an array of steak, lamb, and chicken dishes will tempt the landlubber's palate.

MODERATE

La Finezza. Over Kiely's, Donnybrook Rd. (N11), Donnybrook, Dublin 4. ☎ **01/283-7166.** Reservations recommended. Early-bird menu (5:30–7pm) £12.95 ($18.15); main courses £8.95–£17.50 ($12.55–$24.50). AE, MC, V. Mon–Sat 5–11pm; Sun 4–9:30pm. Bus: 10, 46A, or 46B. ITALIAN/MEDITERRANEAN.

Since its opening in the mid-1990s, La Finezza has garnered a number of awards, including restaurant of the year. Its candlelit mirrored-gallery decor is quite tasteful. The menu is imaginative and ambitious—perhaps overly so for a purist's palate. Panfried lamb cutlets and fresh pepper and black-bean mousse are simply exquisite. The presentation is delightful, and the service superb. La Finezza deserves its accolades.

✪ Roly's Bistro. 7 Ballsbridge Terrace, Dublin 4. ☎ **01/668-2611.** Reservations required. Main courses £9.50–£14.95 ($13.30–$20.95); set-price lunch £12.50 ($17.50). AE, DC, MC, V. Daily noon–3pm and 6–10pm. DART to Lansdowne Rd. Station. Bus: 5, 6, 7, 8, 18, or 45. IRISH/INTERNATIONAL.

Opened in 1992, this two-story shop-front restaurant quickly skyrocketed to success, thanks to its genial and astute host Roly Saul and its master chef Colin O'Daly. What you get is excellent and imaginatively prepared food at mostly moderate prices. The main dining rooms, with a bright and airy decor and lots of windows, can be noisy when the house is full, but the nonsmoking section has a quiet enclave of booths laid out in an Orient Express style for those who prefer a quiet tête-à-tête. Main courses include roasted venison, panfried Dublin Bay prawns, game pie with chestnuts, and wild mushroom risotto. An excellent array of international wines is offered, starting at £10.95 ($15.35) a bottle.

Señor Sassi's. 146 Upper Leeson St., Dublin 4. ☎ **01/668-4544.** Reservations recommended. Dinner main courses £8.50–£14.95 ($11.90–$20.95). AE, DC, MC, V. Mon–Thurs 12–2:30pm and 6–10:45pm; Fri 12–2:30pm and 6–11pm; Sat 7–11pm; Sun 12–4pm. Bus: 11, 11A, 11B, 13, 46A, or 46B. MEDITERRANEAN.

This innovative restaurant blends the simple and spicy flavors of Spain, Italy, southern France, and the Middle East. In a busy location, the contemporary and casual space has slate floors, marble-topped tables, and walls painted a sunny shade of yellow; seating is also available in a conservatory extension overlooking a courtyard garden. The menu includes items such as Moroccan-style couscous, tagliatelle, prawns sautéed in rum with Creole sauce, charcoal steaks, tortilla *español* (traditional omelet with potato and onions), vegetarian dishes, and warm salads. Be sure to try the unusual olive bread.

INEXPENSIVE

Da Vincenzo. 133 Upper Leeson St., Dublin 4. ☎ **01/660-9906.** Reservations recommended. Fixed-price lunch £7.95 ($11.15); dinner main courses £6.50–£12.50 ($9.10–$17.50). AE, DC, MC, V. Daily 12:30–11pm; Sun 1–10pm. Bus: 10, 11A, 11B, 46A, or 46B. ITALIAN.

Located within a block of the Burlington hotel, this informal, friendly bistro offers ground-level and upstairs seating. Glowing brick fireplaces illuminate pine walls, vases

Ballsbridge/Embassy Row Area Dining

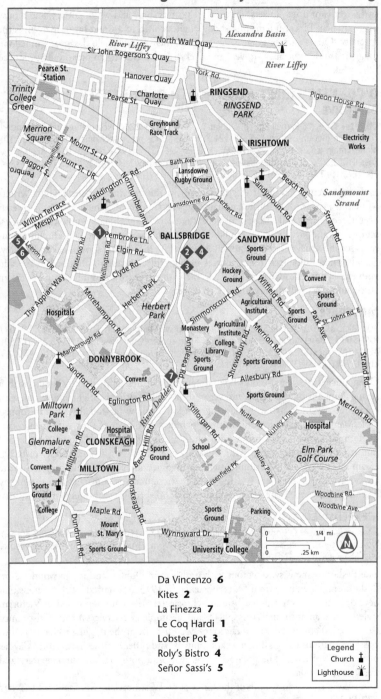

Da Vincenzo **6**
Kites **2**
La Finezza **7**
Le Coq Hardi **1**
Lobster Pot **3**
Roly's Bistro **4**
Señor Sassi's **5**

Legend
Church
Lighthouse

and wreaths of dried flowers, modern art posters, blue and white pottery, and a busy open kitchen. Pizza on light pita-style dough, cooked in a wood-burning oven, is the specialty. Other entrees range from pastas—such as tagliatelle, lasagna, cannelloni, spaghetti, and fettuccine—to veal and beef dishes, including an organically produced fillet steak.

O'CONNELL STREET AREA/NORTH OF THE LIFFEY
EXPENSIVE

Chapter One. 18 Parnell Sq. N., Dublin 1. ☎ **01/873-2266.** Reservations recommended. Fixed-price 4-course lunch £15.50 ($21.70); fixed-price pretheater dinner £16.50 ($23.10); dinner main courses £14.95–£18.95 ($20.95–$26.55). Service charge 10%. AE, MC, V. Tues–Fri 12:30–2:30pm; Tues–Sat 6–11pm. DART: Connolly. Bus: 10, 11, 11A, 11B, 12, 13, 14, 16, 16A, 19, 19A, 22, 22A, or 36. IRISH.

A literary theme prevails at this restaurant, in the basement of the Dublin Writers Museum, just north of Parnell Square and the Garden of Remembrance. It spreads over three rooms and alcoves, all accentuated by stained-glass windows, paintings, sculptures, and literary memorabilia. The staff, affiliated with the Old Dublin restaurant (see the review under "Historic Old City/Liberties Area," above), has added a few Scandinavian influences. Main courses include fillet of salmon on a bed of avocado with smoked tomato vinaigrette, black sole with citrus fruit and dill cucumber cream sauce, and roast half-duck with apricot sauce.

MODERATE

101 Talbot. 101 Talbot St. (at Talbot Lane near Marlborough St.), Dublin 1. ☎ **01/874-5011.** Reservations recommended. Main courses £8.75–£12.50 ($12.25–$17.50). AE, MC, V. Tues–Sat 5–11pm. DART: Connolly. Bus: 27A, 31A, 31B, 32A, 32B, 42B, 42C, 43, or 44A. INTERNATIONAL/VEGETARIAN.

Open since 1991, this second-floor restaurant features light, healthy foods, with a strong emphasis on vegetarian and vegan dishes. The setting is bright and casual, with contemporary Irish art on display, big windows, yellow rag-rolled walls, ash-topped tables, and newspapers to read. Entrees include seared fillet of tuna with mango cardamom salsa, roast duck breast with plum and ginger sauce, Halloumi cheese and mushroom brochette served with couscous and raita, and a blue cheese, pistachio cream sauce on pasta. The dinner menu changes weekly. Espresso and cappuccino are always available, and there is a full bar. The restaurant is convenient to the Abbey Theatre. In the works are an early-bird menu and specials for theatergoers.

INEXPENSIVE

Beshoffs. 6 Upper O'Connell St., Dublin 1. ☎ **01/872-4400.** All items £2–£5 ($2.80–$7). No credit cards. Mon–Sat 10am–9pm; Sun noon–9pm. DART: Tara St. Bus: Any city-center bus. SEAFOOD/FISH-AND-CHIPS.

The Beshoff name is synonymous with fresh fish in Dublin, and it's no wonder. Ivan Beshoff emigrated here from Odessa, Russia, in 1913 and started a fish business that developed into this top-notch fish-and-chips eatery. Recently renovated in Victorian style, it has an informal atmosphere and a simple self-service menu. Crisp chips (french fries) are served with a choice of fresh fish, from the original recipe of cod to classier variations using salmon, shark, prawns, and other local sea fare—some days as many as 20 varieties. The potatoes are grown on a 300-acre farm in Tipperary and freshly cut each day.

A second shop is just south of the Liffey at 14 Westmoreland St., Dublin 2 (☎ **01/677-8026**).

The Winding Stair. 40 Lower Ormond Quay, Dublin 1. ☎ **01/873-3292.** All items £1.50–£4 ($2.10–$5.60). AE, MC, V. Mon–Sat 10am–6pm; Sun 1–6pm. Bus: 70 or 80. IRISH.

Retreat from the bustle of the north side's busy quays at this self-service cafe and bookshop, and indulge in a light meal while browsing through some books. There are three floors—one smoke-free, and each chock-full of used books (from novels, plays, and poetry to history, art, music, and sports). A winding 18th-century staircase connects them. (A cage-style elevator serves, on request, those who are unable or prefer not to climb the stairs.) Tall, wide windows provide expansive views of the Halfpenny Bridge and River Liffey. The food is simple and healthy—sandwiches made with additive-free meats or fruits (such as banana and honey), organic salads, homemade soups, and natural juices. Evening events include poetry readings and recitals.

5 Seeing the Sights

Dublin is a city of many moods and landscapes. There are medieval churches and imposing castles, graceful Georgian squares and lantern-lit lanes, broad boulevards and crowded bridges, picturesque parks and pedestrian walkways, intriguing museums and markets, gardens and galleries, and—if you have any energy left after all that—electric nightlife. Enjoy!

THE TOP ATTRACTIONS

Áras an Uachtaráin (The Irish White House). In Phoenix Park, Dublin 7. ☎ **01/670-9155.** Free admission. Sat 9:40am–4:20pm. Closed Dec 24–26. Same-day tickets issued at Phoenix Park Visitors Centre (see below). Bus: 10, 37, or 39.

Áras an Uachtaráin (Irish for "House of the President") was once the Viceregal Lodge, the summer retreat of the British viceroy, whose ordinary digs were in Dublin Castle. From what were never humble beginnings, the original 1751 country house was expanded several times, gradually accumulating splendor. President Mary McAleese recently opened her home to visitors; guided tours originate at the Phoenix Park Visitors Centre every Saturday. After an introductory historical film, a bus brings visitors to and from Áras an Uachtaráin. The focus of the tour is the state reception rooms. The entire tour lasts 1 hour. Only 525 tickets are given out, first-come, first-served; arrive before 1:30pm, especially in summer.

Note: For security reasons, no backpacks, travel bags, strollers, buggies, cameras, or mobile phones are allowed on the tour. No smoking, eating, or drinking are permitted, and no visitor toilets are available once the tour begins.

✪ **Ceol—The Irish Traditional Music Centre.** Smithfield Village, Dublin 7. ☎ **01/817-3820.** www.ceol.ie. £5 ($7) adults, £4 ($5.60) seniors and students, £3.50 ($4.90) children, £15 ($21) family. Mon–Sat 10am–6pm; Sun 11am–6pm (last film 45 min. before closing). Bus: 25, 25A, 67, 67A, 68, 69, 79, or 90.

Ceol means "music" in Irish, and here is the place to appreciate the mighty meaning of that word. This is a must for any lover of Irish traditional music and dance, or for anyone else wondering just what all the fuss is about. No matter how much you think you know, you'll learn something more here that will deepen your appreciation of one of Ireland's most profound legacies. The beautifully designed ultra–high-tech center offers a plethora of interactive audiovisual displays and videos presenting the basic ingredients of Irish traditional music—song, dance, story, and instruments. A dazzling diversity of riches is packed into a relatively small space here. The climax of Ceol is the extraordinary film, shown in the 180° wide-screen main auditorium, titled *The Music of the People*, which is reason enough for going well out of your way to pay Ceol a visit.

Dublin Attractions

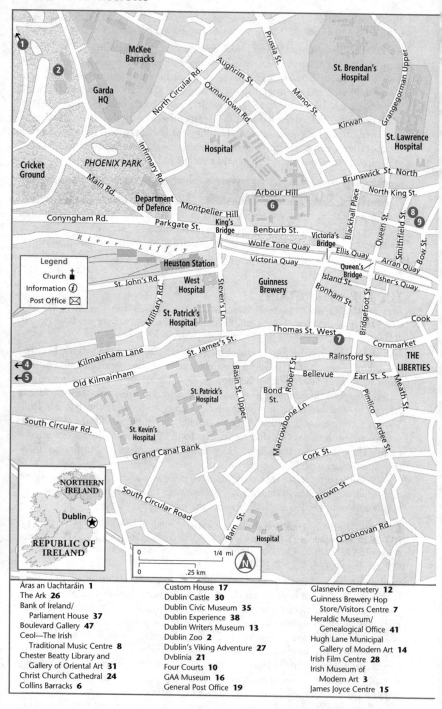

Áras an Uachtaráin **1**
The Ark **26**
Bank of Ireland/
    Parliament House **37**
Boulevard Gallery **47**
Ceol—The Irish
    Traditional Music Centre **8**
Chester Beatty Library and
    Gallery of Oriental Art **31**
Christ Church Cathedral **24**
Collins Barracks **6**

Custom House **17**
Dublin Castle **30**
Dublin Civic Museum **35**
Dublin Experience **38**
Dublin Writers Museum **13**
Dublin Zoo **2**
Dublin's Viking Adventure **27**
Dvblinia **21**
Four Courts **10**
GAA Museum **16**
General Post Office **19**

Glasnevin Cemetery **12**
Guinness Brewery Hop
    Store/Visitors Centre **7**
Heraldic Museum/
    Genealogical Office **41**
Hugh Lane Municipal
    Gallery of Modern Art **14**
Irish Film Centre **28**
Irish Museum of
    Modern Art **3**
James Joyce Centre **15**

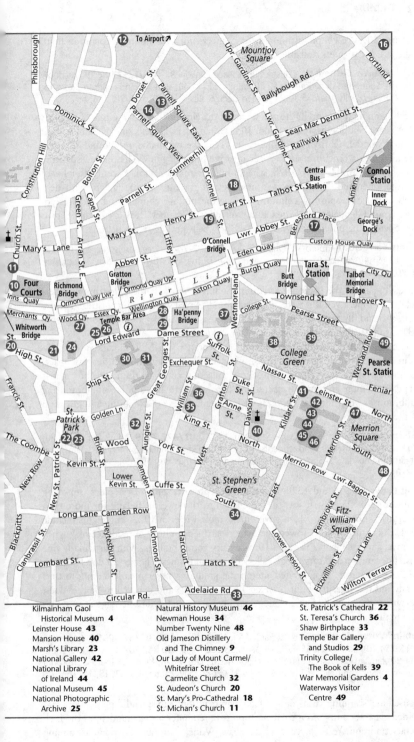

Plan on at least a couple of hours here. Some visitors, intending to spend an hour, make it a day without realizing it.

Christ Church Cathedral. Christ Church Place, Dublin 8. ☎ **01/677-8099.** cccdub@ indigo.ie. Suggested donation £2 ($2.80) adults, £1 ($1.40) students and children under 15, £5 ($7) family. Daily 10am–5:30pm. Closed Dec 26. Bus: 21A, 50, 50A, 78, 78A, or 78B.

Standing on high ground in the oldest part of the city, this cathedral is one of Dublin's finest historic buildings. It dates from 1038, when Sitric, Danish king of Dublin, built the first wooden Christ Church here. In 1171, the original simple foundation was extended into a cruciform and rebuilt in stone by Strongbow. The present structure dates mainly from 1871 to 1878, when a huge restoration took place. Highlights of the interior include magnificent stonework and graceful pointed arches, with delicately chiseled supporting columns. This is the mother church for the diocese of Dublin and Glendalough of the Church of Ireland. The new Treasury in the crypt is now open to the public, and you can hear new bells pealing in the belfry.

Collins Barracks. Benburb St., Dublin 7. ☎ **01/677-7444.** Free admission. Tours (hours vary) £1 ($1.40) adults, free for seniors and children. Tues–Sat 10am–5pm; Sun 2–5pm. Bus: 34, 70, or 80.

Officially part of the National Museum, Collins Barracks is the oldest military barracks in Europe. Even if it were empty, it would be well worth a visit for the structure itself, a splendidly restored early 18th-century masterwork by Colonel Thomas Burgh, Ireland's Chief Engineer and Surveyor General under Queen Anne.

The collection housed here focuses on the decorative arts. Most notable is the extraordinary display of Irish silver and furniture. Until the acquisition of this vast space, only a fraction of the National Museum's collection could be displayed, but that is changing, as more and more treasures find their way here. It is a prime site for touring exhibitions, so consult *The Event Guide* for details. There is also a cafe and gift shop on the premises.

Dublin Castle. Palace St. (off Dame St.), Dublin 2. ☎ **01/677-7129.** Admission £3 ($4.20) adults, £2 ($2.80) seniors and students, £1 ($1.40) children under 12. Mon–Fri 10am–5pm; Sat–Sun and holidays 2–5pm. Guided tours every 20–25 min. Bus: 50, 50A, 54, 56A, 77, 77A, or 77B.

Built between 1208 and 1220, this complex represents some of the oldest surviving architecture in the city. It was the center of British power in Ireland for more than 7 centuries, until the new Irish government took it over in 1922. Highlights include the 13th-century Record Tower; the State Apartments, once the residence of English viceroys; and the Chapel Royal, a 19th-century gothic building with particularly fine plaster decoration and carved oak gallery fronts and fittings. The newest developments are the Undercroft, an excavated site on the grounds where an early Viking fortress stood, and the Treasury, built between 1712 and 1715 and believed to be the oldest surviving office building in Ireland. Also here are a craft shop, heritage center, and restaurant.

Dublin Writers Museum. 18–19 Parnell Sq. N., Dublin 1. ☎ **01/475-0854.** Admission £3.15 ($4.40) adults, £2.65 ($3.70) seniors/students, £1.50 ($2.10) ages 3–11, £8.50 ($11.90) families (2 adults and up to 4 children). AE, DC, MC, V. Mon–Sat 10am–5pm (6pm June–Aug); Sun and holidays 11am–5pm. DART to Connolly Station. Bus: 11, 13, 16, 16A, 22, or 22A.

Housed in a stunning 18th-century Georgian mansion with splendid plasterwork and stained glass, the museum is itself an impressive reminder of the grandeur of the Irish literary tradition. Yeats, Joyce, Beckett, Shaw, Wilde, Swift, and Sheridan are among those whose lives and works are celebrated here. One of the museum's rooms is devoted to children's literature.

Dvblinia. St. Michael's Hill, Christ Church, Dublin 8. ☎ **01/679-4611.** Admission £3.95 ($5.55) adults; £2.90 ($4.05) seniors, students, and children; £10 ($14) family. AE, MC, V. Apr–Sept daily 10am–5pm; Oct–Mar Mon–Sat 11am–4pm, Sun 10am–4:30pm. Bus: 50, 78A, or 123.

What was Dublin like in medieval times? To find out, visit this historically accurate presentation of the Old City from 1170 to 1540, re-created through a series of theme exhibits, spectacles, and experiences. Highlights include an illuminated Medieval Maze, complete with visual effects, background sounds, and aromas that lead you on a journey through time from the arrival of the Anglo-Normans in 1170 to the closure of the monasteries in the 1530s. Another segment depicts everyday life in medieval Dublin with a diorama, as well as a prototype of a 13th-century quay along the banks of the Liffey. A new addition is the medieval Fayre, displaying the wares of merchants from all over Europe. You can try on a flattering new robe or, if you're feeling vulnerable, stop in at the armorer's and be fitted for chain mail and a proper helm.

Irish Film Centre. 6 Eustace St., Dublin 2. ☎ **01/679-5744,** or 01/679-3477 for cinema box office. Free admission; cinema admission £3–£4.50 ($4.20–$6.30). Centre open daily 10am–11pm; cinemas daily 2–11pm; cinema box office daily 1:30–9pm. Bus: 21A, 78A, or 78B.

Since it opened in 1991, this institute has fast become a focal point in Dublin's artsy Temple Bar district. The Irish Film Centre houses two cinemas, the Irish Film Archive, a library, a bookshop and bar, and eight film-related organizations. Free screenings of *Flashback*, a history of Irish film since 1896, start at noon Wednesday to Sunday from June to mid-September. Follow with lunch in the bar for a perfect midday outing.

Kilmainham Gaol Historical Museum. Kilmainham, Dublin 8. ☎ **01/453-5984.** Guided tour £3.50 ($4.90) adults, £2.50 ($3.50) seniors, £1.50 ($2.10) children, £8 ($11.20) family. Apr–Sept daily 9:30am–4:45pm; Oct–Mar Mon–Fri 9:30am–4pm, Sun 10am–4:45pm. Bus: 51, 51B, 78, 78A, 78B, or 79 at O'Connell Bridge.

Within these walls political prisoners were incarcerated, tortured, and killed from 1796 until 1924, when President Eamon de Valera left as its final prisoner. To walk along these corridors, through the exercise yard, or into the main compound is a moving experience that lingers hauntingly in the memory.

Note: The **War Memorial Gardens** (☎ 01/677-0236), along the banks of the Liffey, are a 5-minute walk from Kilmainham Gaol. The gardens were designed by the famous British architect Sir Edwin Lutyens (1869–1944), who completed a number of commissions for Irish houses and gardens. The gardens are fairly well maintained, and continue to present a moving testimony to Ireland's war dead. This is one of the finest small gardens in Ireland. It's open weekdays 8am to dark, Saturday 10am to dark.

✪ **National Gallery.** Merrion Sq. W., Dublin 2. ☎ **01/661-5133.** Free admission. Mon–Wed and Fri–Sat 10am–5:30pm; Thurs 10am–8:30pm; Sun 2–5pm. Guided tours Sat 3pm, Sun 2:15, 3, and 4pm. DART: Pearse. Bus: 5, 6, 7, 7A, 8, 10, 44, 47, 47B, 48A, or 62.

Established by an act of Parliament in 1854, this gallery opened in 1864, with just over 100 paintings. Today the collection of paintings, drawings, watercolors, miniatures, prints, sculpture, and objets d'art is one of Europe's finest. Every major European school of painting is represented, including an extensive assemblage of Irish work. A $14 million refurbishment of the museum was completed in 1996, and the new 44,000-square-foot Millennium Wing is scheduled to open by 2001. All public areas are wheelchair accessible. The museum has a fine gallery shop and an excellent self-service restaurant operated by Fitzers, a name synonymous with excellent, interesting cuisine at near-budget prices.

✪ **National Museum.** Kildare St. and Merrion St., Dublin 2. ☎ **01/677-7444.** Free admission. Tours (hours vary) £1 ($1.40) adults, free for seniors and children. Tues–Sat 10am–5pm; Sun 2–5pm. DART: Pearse. Bus: 7, 7A, 8, 10, 11, or 13.

Established in 1890, this museum is a reflection of Ireland's heritage from 2000 B.C. to the present. It is the home of many of the country's greatest historical finds, including the Treasury exhibit, which toured the United States and Europe in the 1970s with the Ardagh Chalice, Tara Brooch, and Cross of Cong. Other highlights range from the artifacts from the Wood Quay excavations of the Old Dublin Settlements to "Or," an extensive exhibition of Irish Bronze Age gold ornaments dating from 2200 to 700 B.C. The museum has a shop and a cafe. *Note:* The National Museum encompasses two other attractions, Collins Barracks and the Natural History Museum; see their separate listings.

The Phoenix Park. Parkgate St., Dublin 7. ☎ **01/677-0095.** Free admission. Daily 24 hr. Visitor center admission £2 ($2.80) adults, £1.50 ($2.10) seniors, £1 ($1.40) students and children, £5 ($7) family. Late Mar and Oct daily 9:30am–5pm; Apr–May daily 9:30am–5:30pm; June–Sept daily 10am–6pm; Nov to mid-Mar Sat–Sun 9:30am–4:30pm. Bus: 10, 37, or 39.

Two miles (3.2km) west of the city center, the Phoenix Park, the largest urban park in Europe, is the playground of Dublin. A network of roads and quiet pedestrian walkways traverses its 1,760 acres, which are informally landscaped with ornamental gardens and nature trails. Avenues of trees, including oak, beech, pine, chestnut, and lime, separate broad expanses of grassland. The homes of the Irish president (see below) and the U.S. ambassador are on the grounds, as is the Dublin Zoo (see "Especially for Kids," below). Livestock graze peacefully on pasturelands, deer roam the forested areas, and horses romp on polo fields. The new Phoenix Park Visitor Centre, adjacent to Ashtown Castle, offers exhibitions and an audiovisual presentation on the park's history. The cafe/restaurant is open 10am to 5pm weekdays, 10am to 6pm weekends. Free car parking is adjacent to the center. A shuttle bus runs on Saturday only from the visitor center, with stops throughout the park. One-day hop-on, hop-off service is £1 ($1.40) per person.

✪ **St. Patrick's Cathedral.** 21–50 Patrick's Close, Patrick St., Dublin 8. ☎ **01/475-4817.** www.stpatrickscathedral.ie. Admission £2.30 ($3.20) adults, £1.60 ($2.25) students and seniors, £5.50 ($7.70) family. MC, V. Mon–Fri 9am–6pm year-round; Mar–Oct Sat 9am–6pm and Sun 9–11am, 12:45–3pm, 4:15–6pm; Nov–Feb Sat 9am–5pm and Sun 10–11am, 12:45–3pm. Closed except for services Dec 24–26 and Jan 1. Bus: 65, 65B, 50, 50A, 54, 54A, 56A, or 77.

It is said that St. Patrick baptized converts on this site, and consequently a church has stood here since A.D. 450, making it the oldest Christian site in Dublin. The present cathedral dates from 1190, but because of a fire and 14th-century rebuilding, not much of the original foundation remains. It is mainly early English in style, with a square medieval tower that houses the largest ringing peal bells in Ireland, and an 18th-century spire. The 300-foot-long interior makes it the longest church in the country. St. Patrick's is closely associated with Jonathan Swift, who was dean from 1713 to 1745 and whose tomb lies in the south aisle. Others memorialized within the cathedral include Turlough O'Carolan, a blind harpist and composer and the last of the great Irish bards; Michael William Balfe, the composer; and Douglas Hyde, the first president of Ireland. St. Patrick's is the national cathedral of the Church of Ireland.

🌕 **Trinity College and The Book of Kells.** College Green, Dublin 2. ☎ **01/608-2320.** www.tcd.ie/library. Free admission to college grounds. Old Library/Book of Kells £4.50 ($6.30) adults, £4 ($5.60) seniors/students, £9 ($12.60) families, free for children under 12. Dublin Experience £3 ($4.20) adults, £2.50 ($3.50) seniors/students, £1.50 ($2.10) children, £6 ($8.40) family. Combination tickets also available. Library Mon–Sat 9:30am–5pm, Sun noon–4:30pm (opens at 9:30am June–Sept). Dublin Experience May–Sept daily 10am–5pm; closed Oct–Apr. Bus: All city center buses.

The oldest university in Ireland, Trinity was founded in 1592 by Queen Elizabeth I. It sits in the heart of the city on a beautiful 40-acre site just south of the River Liffey, with cobbled squares, gardens, a picturesque quadrangle, and buildings dating from the 17th to the 20th centuries. The college is home to the Book of Kells, an 8th-century version of the four Gospels with elaborate scripting and illumination. This famous treasure and other early Christian manuscripts are on permanent public view in the Colonnades, an exhibition area on the ground floor of the Old Library. Also housed in the Old Library is the **Dublin Experience** (see separate listing below; ☎ **01/608-1177**), an excellent multimedia introduction to the history and people of Dublin.

MORE ATTRACTIONS
ART GALLERIES & ART MUSEUMS
Boulevard Gallery. Merrion Sq. W., Dublin 2. Free admission. May–Sept Sat–Sun 10:30am–6pm. DART: Pearse. Bus: 5, 7A, 8, 46, or 62.

The fence around Merrion Square doubles as a display railing on summer weekends for an outdoor display of local art similar to those you'll find in Greenwich Village or Montmartre. Permits are given to local artists only to sell their own work, so this is a chance to meet an artist as well as to browse or buy.

Hugh Lane Municipal Gallery of Modern Art. Parnell Sq. N., Dublin 1. ☎ **01/ 874-1903.** Free admission but donations accepted. Tues–Thurs 9:30am–6pm; Fri–Sat 9:30am–5pm; Sun 11am–5pm. DART to Connolly or Tara stations. Bus: 10, 11, 11A, 11B, 13, 16, 16A, 19, 19A, 22, 22A, or 36.

Housed in a finely restored 18th-century building known as Charlemont House, this gallery is situated next to the Dublin Writers Museum. It is named after Hugh Lane, an Irish art connoisseur who was killed in the sinking of the *Lusitania* in 1915 and who willed his collection (including works by Courbet, Manet, Monet, and Corot) to be shared between the government of Ireland and the National Gallery of London. With the Lane collection as its nucleus, this gallery also contains paintings from the Impressionist and post-Impressionist traditions, sculptures by Rodin, stained glass, and works by modern Irish artists. In 1998 the museum received its most important donation since its establishment in 1908: the studio of Irish painter Francis Bacon, which will open in 2001. Bookshop open during museum hours.

Irish Museum of Modern Art (IMMA). Military Rd., Kilmainham. ☎ **01/612-9900.** www. modernart.ie. Free admission. Tues–Sat 10am–5:30pm; Sun noon–5:30pm. Bus: 79 or 90.

Housed in the splendidly restored 17th-century edifice known as the Royal Hospital, IMMA is a showcase of Irish and international art from the latter half of the 20th century. The buildings and grounds also provide a venue for theatrical and musical events, overlapping the visual and performing arts. The galleries contain the work of Irish and international artists from the small but impressive permanent collection, with numerous temporary exhibitions. There's even a drawing room, where kids and parents can record their impressions of the museum with the crayons provided. The formal gardens, an important early feature of this magnificent structure, have been

The Book of Kells

The Book of Kells is a large-format illuminated manuscript of the four Gospels in Latin, dated on comparative grounds to about A.D. 800. It's impossible to be more precise about its date because some leaves from the end of the book, where such information was normally recorded, are missing. It is the most majestic work of art to survive from the early centuries of Celtic Christianity, and has often been described as "the most beautiful book in the world." A team of talented scribes and artists working in a monastic scriptorium produced the book.

Its fascination derives from the dignified but elusive character of its main motifs, and the astonishing variety and complexity of the linear ornamentation that adorns every one of its 680 pages. Its creators managed to combine new artistic influences from Eastern Christendom with the traditional interlace patterning of Celtic metalwork to produce what Gerald of Wales, a 13th-century chronicler, called "the work not of men, but of angels." The message sometimes may not be easy to read, but everyone can admire the elegant precision of the standard script, the subtlety of the color harmonies, and the exuberant vitality of the human and animal ornamentation.

The book was certainly in the possession of the Columban monastery of Kells, a town in County Meath, during most of the Middle Ages. The Annals of Ulster record its theft from the western sacristy of the stone-built monastic church in 1007, and relate that it was recovered 2 to 3 months later from "under the sod," without the jewel-encrusted silver shrine in which such prestigious books were kept. Whether it was originally created in Kells remains an unresolved question. Some authorities think that it might have been begun, if not completed, in the great monastery founded by St. Columba himself (in about 561) on the island of Iona off the west coast of Scotland. Iona had a famous scriptorium, and remained the headquarters of the Columban monastic system until the early years of the 9th century. It then became an untenable location because of repeated Viking raids, and in 807 a remnant of the monastic community retreated to the Irish mainland to build a new headquarters at Kells. It has been suggested that the great Gospel book that we call "of Kells" may have been started on Iona, possibly to mark the bicentenary of St. Columba's death in 797, and later transferred to Kells for completion. But it is also possible to argue that the work was entirely done in Kells, and that its object was to equip the monastery with a great new book to stand on the high altar of the new foundation.

In the medieval period, the book was (wrongly) regarded as the work of St. Columba himself, and was known as the "great Gospel book of Colum Cille" (Colum of the Churches). The designation "Book of Kells" seems to have originated with the famous biblical scholar James Ussher, who made a study of its original Latin text in the 1620s. The gift shop in the Colonnades of the Old Library in Trinity College stocks a large selection of illustrative materials relating to the Book of Kells.

—J. V. Luce, Trinity College and the Royal Irish Academy

restored and are open to the public during museum hours. In 2000, a series of new galleries will be housed in the restored Deputy Master's House, in the northeast corner of the Royal Hospital site.

Temple Bar Gallery and Studios. 5–9 Temple Bar, Dublin 2. ☎ **01/671-0073.** Fax 01/ 677-7527. Free admission. Tues–Wed 11am–6pm; Thurs 11am–7pm; Sun 2–6pm. Bus: 21A, 46A, 46B, 51B, 51C, 68, 69, or 86.

Founded in 1983 in the heart of Dublin's "Left Bank," this is one of the largest studio and gallery complexes in Europe. More than 30 Irish artists work here at a variety of contemporary visual arts, including sculpture, painting, printing, and photography. Only the gallery section is open to the public; with advance notice, you can make an appointment to view individual artists at work.

BREWERIES/DISTILLERIES

Guinness Brewery Hop Store/Visitor Centre. St. James's Gate, Dublin 8. ☎ **01/ 408-4800.** www.guinness.ie. Admission £5 ($7) adults, £4 ($5.60) seniors and students, £1 ($1.40) children under 12. AE, MC, V. Apr–Sept Mon–Sat 9:30am–5pm, Sun 10:30am–4:30pm; Oct–Mar Mon–Sat 9:30am–4pm, Sun 12–4pm. Guided tours every ½ hour. Bus: 51B, 78A, or 123.

Founded in 1759, the Guinness Brewery is one of the world's largest breweries, producing the distinctive dark beer called stout, famous for its thick, creamy head. Although tours of the brewery itself are no longer allowed, visitors are welcome to explore the adjacent Guinness Hopstore, a converted 19th-century four-story building. It houses the World of Guinness Exhibition, an audiovisual presentation showing how the stout is made; the Cooperage Gallery, displaying one of the finest collections of tools in Europe; the Gilroy Gallery, dedicated to the graphic design work of John Gilroy; and last but not least a bar where visitors can sample a glass of the famous brew. By 2001 this will also be home to the largest glass of stout in the world, roughly 200 feet tall, whose head will in fact be an observatory restaurant offering spectacular views of the city.

The Old Jameson Distillery. Bow St., Smithfield Village, Dublin 7. ☎ **01/807-2355.** Admission £3.95 ($5.53) adults, £3 ($4.20) students and seniors, £1.50 ($2.10) children, £9.50 ($13.30) family. Daily 9:30am–6pm (last tour at 5pm). Chimney ascent £5 ($7) adults, £4 ($5.60) seniors and students, £3.50 ($4.90) children, £15 ($21) family. Mon–Sat 10am–6pm; Sun 11am–7pm. Bus: 67, 67A, 68, 69, 79, or 90.

This museum illustrates the history of Irish whiskey, known as *uisce beatha* (the water of life) in Irish. Housed in a former distillery warehouse, it consists of a short introductory audiovisual presentation, an exhibition area, and a whiskey-making demonstration. At the end of the tour, visitors can sample whiskey at an in-house pub, where an array of fixed-price menus (for lunch, tea, or dinner) are available. A new added attraction here at Smithfield Village is **"The Chimney,"** a ride to the top of a 185-foot brick chimney built in 1895 and converted to support an observation chamber from which you'll enjoy unparalleled views of the city.

CATHEDRALS & CHURCHES

St. Patrick's Cathedral and Christ Church Cathedral are listed above, under "The Top Attractions."

Our Lady of Mount Carmel/Whitefriar Street Carmelite Church. 56 Aungier St., Dublin 2. ☎ **01/475-8821.** Free admission. Mon and Wed–Fri 8am–6:30pm; Sat 8am–7pm; Sun 8am–7:30pm; Tues 8am–9:30pm. Bus: 16, 16A, 19, 19A, 122, 155, or 83.

One of the city's largest churches, this edifice was built between 1825 and 1827 on the site of a pre-Reformation Carmelite priory (1539) and an earlier Carmelite abbey (13th c.). It has since been extended, with a new entrance from Aungier Street. This is a favorite place of pilgrimage, especially on February 14, because the body of St. Valentine is enshrined here (Pope Gregory XVI presented it to the church in 1836). The other highlight is the 15th-century black oak Madonna, Our Lady of Dublin.

St. Audeon's Church. Cornmarket (off High St.), Dublin 8. ☎ **01/677-0088.** Admission and tour £1.50 ($2.10) adults, £1 ($1.40) seniors, 60p (84¢) children or students, £4 ($5.60) families. June–Sept daily 9:30am–5:30pm. Last admission 45 min. prior to closing. Bus: 21A, 78A, or 78B.

Situated next to the only remaining gate of the Old City walls (1214), this church is said to be the only surviving medieval parish in Dublin. Although it is partly in ruins, significant parts have survived, including the west doorway, which dates from 1190, and the 13th-century nave. In addition, the 17th-century bell tower houses three bells cast in 1423, making them the oldest in Ireland. It's a Church of Ireland property, but nearby is another St. Audeon's Church, this one Catholic and dating from 1846. It was in the latter church that Father Flash Kavanagh used to say the world's fastest mass so that his congregation was out in time for the football matches. Since 1999, entrance to the ancient church is through the new visitor center. The center's exhibition, relating the history of St. Audeons, is self-guided, while visits to the church itself are by guided tour only.

St. Mary's Pro-Cathedral. Cathedral and Marlborough sts., Dublin 1. ☎ **01/874-5441.** Free admission. Mon–Fri 8am–6pm; Sat and Sun 8am–7pm. DART: Connolly. Bus: 28, 29A, 30, 31A, 31B, 32A, 32B, or 44A.

Because Dublin's two main cathedrals (Christ Church and St. Patrick's) belong to the Protestant Church of Ireland, St. Mary's is the closest the Catholics get to having their own. Tucked into a corner of a rather-unimpressive back street, it is in the heart of the city's north side and is considered the main Catholic parish church of the city center. Built between 1815 and 1825, it is of the Greek Revival Doric style, providing a distinct contrast to the Gothic Revival look of most other churches of the period. The exterior portico is modeled on the Temple of Theseus in Athens, with six Doric columns, while the Renaissance-style interior is patterned after the Church of St. Philip de Reule of Paris. The church is noted for its Palestrina Choir, which sings a Latin Mass every Sunday at 11am.

St. Michan's Church. Church St., Dublin 7. ☎ **01/872-4154.** Free admission. Guided tour of church and vaults £2 ($2.80) adults, £1.50 ($2.10) seniors and students, 50p (70¢) children under 12. Nov–Feb Mon–Fri 12:30–2:30pm, Sat 10am–1pm; Mar–Oct Mon–Fri 10am–12:45pm and 2–4:45pm, Sat 10am–1pm. Bus: 134 (from Abbey St.).

Built on the site of an early Danish chapel (1095), this 17th-century edifice claims to be the only parish church on the north side of the Liffey surviving from a Viking foundation. Now under the Church of Ireland banner, it has some fine interior woodwork and an organ (dated 1724) on which Handel is said to have played his *Messiah.* The church was completely and beautifully restored in 1998. A unique (and, let it be noted, most macabre) feature of this church is the underground burial vault. Because of the dry atmosphere, bodies have lain for centuries without showing signs of decomposition. The church is wheelchair accessible, but the vaults are not.

St. Teresa's Church. Clarendon St., Dublin 2. ☎ **01/671-8466.** Free admission; donations welcome. Daily 8am–8pm or longer. Bus: 16, 16A, 19, 19A, 22, 22A, 55, or 83.

The foundation stone was laid in 1793, and the church was opened in 1810 by the Discalced Carmelite Fathers. After continuous enlargement, it reached its present form in 1876. This was the first post–Penal Law church to be legally and openly erected in Dublin, following the Catholic Relief Act of 1793. Among the artistic highlights are John Hogan's *Dead Christ,* a sculpture displayed beneath the altar, and Phyllis Burke's seven beautiful stained-glass windows.

WHERE THE BODIES ARE BURIED

✪ **Glasnevin Cemetery.** Finglas Rd., Dublin 11. ☎ **01/830-1133.** Free admission. Daily 8am–4pm. Free guided tours Wed and Fri 3pm from Roger Casement's grave, at the foot of the O'Connell Round Tower. Bus: 19, 19A, 40, 40A, 40B, or 40C.

Situated north of the city center, the Irish National Cemetery was founded in 1832 and covers more than 124 acres. Most people buried here were ordinary citizens, but there are also many famous names on the headstones. They range from former Irish presidents such as Eamon de Valera and Sean T. O'Kelly to other political heroes such as Michael Collins, Daniel O'Connell, Roger Casement, and Charles Stewart Parnell. Literary figures also have their place here, including poet Gerard Manley Hopkins and writers Christy Brown and Brendan Behan. Though open to all, this is primarily a Catholic burial ground, with more than the usual share of Celtic crosses. A heritage map, on sale in most bookshops, serves as a guide to who's buried where, or you can take a free 1-hour guided tour. Call the main number to book in advance.

MORE HISTORIC BUILDINGS

Although it's not open to the public, one building whose exterior is worth a look is **Mansion House,** Dawson Street, Dublin 2 (☎ **01/676-1845**). Built by Joshua Dawson, the Queen Anne–style building has been the official residence of Dublin's lord mayors since 1715. Here the first Dáil Éireann (House of Representatives) assembled, in 1919, to adopt Ireland's Declaration of Independence and ratify the Proclamation of the Irish Republic by the insurgents of 1916. Ride the DART to Pearse, or take bus no. 10, 11A, 11B, 13, or 20B.

✪ **Bank of Ireland Centre/Parliament House.** 2 College Green, Dublin 2. ☎ **01/661-5933,** ext. 2265. Free admission. Mon–Wed and Fri 10am–4pm; Thurs 10am–5pm. Guided 45-min. tours of House of Lords chamber Tues 10:30am, 11:30am, and 1:45pm (except holidays). DART: Tara St. Bus: Any city-center bus.

Although it's now a busy bank, this building was erected in 1729 to house the Irish Parliament. It became superfluous when the British and Irish Parliaments were merged in London. In fact, the Irish Parliament voted itself out of existence, becoming the only recorded parliament in history to do so. Highlights include the windowless front portico, built to avoid distractions from the outside when Parliament was in session, and the unique House of Lords chamber. The room is famed for its Irish oak wood-work, 18th-century tapestries, golden mace, and a sparkling Irish crystal chandelier of 1,233 pieces, dating from 1765.

This is also the home of the **Bank of Ireland Arts Centre,** which plays host to an impressive program of art exhibitions, concerts, and poetry readings. Entry to readings, lunchtime recitals, and exhibitions is free. Another attraction in the bank center is the **Story of Banking,** an interactive museum offering a glimpse of the history of banking and of Ireland more generally over the past 2 centuries. It's open Tuesday to Friday 10am to 4pm; admission is £1.50 ($2.10) for adults, £1 ($1.40) students.

Custom House. Custom House Quay, Dublin 1. ☎ **01/878-7760.** Admission £1 ($1.40), £3 ($4.20) family. Mid-Mar to Oct Mon–Fri 10am–12:30pm, Sat–Sun 2–5pm; Nov to mid-Mar Wed–Fri 10am–12:30pm, Sun 2–5pm. DART: Tara St.

The Custom House, which sits prominently on the Liffey's north bank, is one of Dublin's finest Georgian buildings. Designed by James Gandon and completed in 1791, it is beautifully proportioned, with a long classical facade of graceful pavilions, arcades, and columns, and a central dome topped by a 16-foot statue of Commerce. The 14 keystones over the doors and windows are known as the Riverine Heads, because they represent the Atlantic Ocean and the 13 principal rivers of Ireland.

Although burned to a shell in 1921, the building has been masterfully restored and its bright Portland stone recently cleaned. The new visitor center's exhibitions and audio-visual presentation unfold the remarkable history of the structure from its creation by James Gandon to its reconstruction after the War of Independence.

✪ **Four Courts.** Inns Quay, Dublin 8. ☎ **01/872-5555.** Free admission. Mon–Fri 11am–1pm and 2–4pm. Bus: 34, 70, or 80.

Home to the Irish law courts since 1796, this fine 18th-century building overlooks the north bank of the Liffey on Dublin's west side. With a sprawling 440-foot facade, it was designed by James Gandon and is distinguished by its graceful Corinthian columns, massive dome (64 ft. in diameter), and exterior statues of Justice, Mercy, Wisdom, and Moses (sculpted by Edward Smyth). The building was severely burned during the Irish Civil War of 1922, but has been artfully restored. The public is admitted only when court is in session, so phone in advance.

✪ **General Post Office (GPO).** O'Connell St., Dublin 1. ☎ **01/705-8833.** www.anpost.ie. Free admission. Mon–Sat 8am–8pm; Sun 10:30am–6:30pm. DART: Connolly. Bus: 25, 26, 34, 37, 38A, 39A, 39B, 66A, or 67A.

With a 200-foot-long, 56-foot-high facade of Ionic columns and Greco-Roman pilasters, this is more than a post office; it is the symbol of Irish freedom. Built between 1815 and 1818, it was the main stronghold of the Irish Volunteers in 1916. Set afire, the building was gutted and abandoned after the surrender and execution of many of the Irish rebel leaders. It reopened as a post office in 1929 after the formation of the Irish Free State. In memory of the building's dramatic role in Irish history, an impressive bronze statue of Cuchulainn, the legendary Irish hero, is on display. Look closely at the pillars outside—you can still see bullet holes from the siege.

Leinster House. Kildare St. and Merrion Sq., Dublin 2. ☎ **01/618-3000.** Free admission. By appointment only, Oct–May Mon and Fri 10am–4:30pm. DART: Pearse. Bus: 5, 7A, or 8.

Dating from 1745 and originally known as Kildare House, this building is said to have been the model for Irish-born architect James Hoban's design for the White House in Washington, D.C. It was sold in 1815 to the Royal Dublin Society, which developed it as a cultural center. The National Museum, Library, and Gallery all surround it. In 1924, however, it took on a new role when the Irish Free State government acquired it as a parliament house. Since then, it has been the meeting place for the Dáil Éireann (Irish House of Representatives) and Seanad Éireann (Irish Senate), which together constitute the Oireachtas (National Parliament). Tickets for a guided tour when the Dáil is in session (Oct to May, Tues to Thurs) must be arranged in advance from the Public Relations Office (☎ **01/618-3066**).

✪ **Newman House.** 85–86 St. Stephen's Green, Dublin 2. ☎ **01/706-7422.** Fax 01/706-7211. Guided tours £3 ($4.20) adults, £2 ($2.80) seniors, students, and children under 12. June–Aug Tues–Fri noon–5pm, Sat 2–5pm, Sun 11am–2pm. Oct–May by appointment only. Bus: 10, 11, 13, 14, 14A, 15A, or 15B.

In the heart of Dublin on the south side of St. Stephen's Green, this is the historic seat of the Catholic University of Ireland. Named for Cardinal John Henry Newman, the 19th-century writer and theologian and first rector of the university, it consists of two of the finest Georgian town houses in Dublin. They date from 1740 and are decorated with outstanding Palladian and rococo plasterwork, marble tiled floors, and wainscot paneling. No. 85 has been magnificently restored to its original splendor.

Note: Every other Sunday, Newman House hosts an antiques and collectibles fair, where dealers from throughout Ireland sell a wide range of items, including silver, rare books, paintings and prints, coins, stamps, and so forth.

Monumental Humor

Dublin boasts countless public monuments, some modest, others boldly evident. The Irish make a sport of naming them, giving their irrepressible wit and ridicule yet another outlet. A sampler:

Anna Livia, Joyce's mythical personification of the River Liffey, may be found cast in bronze on O'Connell Street across from the General Post Office. Reclining in a pool of streaming water, Anna has been renamed by locals "the floozie in the Jacuzzi."

Sweet **Molly Malone,** another figment of Irish imagination—inspiring poetry, song, and most recently sculpture—appears complete with her flower cart, all larger than life, at the intersection of Nassau and Grafton Streets, across from the Trinity College Provost's house. Ms. Malone's plunging neckline has to be a part of why she is known as "the tart with the cart."

Just around the corner from Molly on Dame Street stands another sculpture, a silent frenzy of **trumpeters** and streaming columns of water, proclaiming "You're a nation again"—popularly transliterated as "urination again."

Then there's Dublin's testimonial to arguably Ireland's greatest patriot and Dublin's most eminent native son, **Theobald Wolfe Tone.** Born at 44 Stafford St. in 1763 and graduated from Trinity College, Tone went on to spark a revolutionary fervor among the Irish. His timeless contribution to Ireland and the world is commemorated in a semicircular assemblage of rough-hewn columns on the north side of Stephen's Green—better known as "Tonehenge."

Across the Liffey, on Dublin's north side, are two theaters, the Gate and the Abbey, that have set the standard for Irish theater in this century. The Gate was founded by and flourished for decades under Michael MacLiammoir and Hilton Edwards, a respected gay couple. The Abbey, for its part, gained a reputation for stage-Irish productions served up for overseas tourists. Their stature makes them not immune from but prey to Irish irreverence—they were collectively known as "Sodom and Begorrah."

LIBRARIES

✪ **Chester Beatty Library and Gallery of Oriental Art.** Clock Tower Building. Dublin Castle, Dublin 2. ☎ **01/407-0750.** E-mail: info@cbl.ie. Free admission. Tues–Fri 10am–5pm; Sat 11am–5pm; Sun 1–5pm. Free guided tours Wed and Sat 2:30pm. DART: Sandymount. Bus: 5, 6, 6A, 7A, 8, 10, 46, 46A, 46B, or 64.

Bequeathed to the Irish nation in 1956 by Sir Alfred Chester Beatty, this extraordinary collection contains approximately 22,000 manuscripts, rare books, miniature paintings, and objects from Western, Middle Eastern, and Far Eastern cultures. There are more than 270 copies of the Koran to be found here, and the library has especially impressive biblical and early Christian manuscripts. There's a new gift shop on the premises.

Marsh's Library. St. Patrick's Close, Upper Kevin St., Dublin 8. ☎ **01/454-3511.** www.kst.dit.ie/marsh. Donation of £1 ($1.40) expected, free for children. Mon 10am–12:45pm and 2–5pm; Wed–Fri 10am–12:45pm and 2–5pm; Sat 10:30am–12:45pm. Bus: 50, 54A, or 56A.

This is Ireland's oldest public library, founded in 1701 by Narcissus Marsh, Archbishop of Dublin. It is a repository of more than 25,000 scholarly volumes, chiefly on theology, medicine, ancient history, maps, Hebrew, Syriac, Greek, Latin, and French literature.

Impressions

An author's first duty is to let down his country.
— Brendan Behan (1923–64); *Guardian* interview, April 15, 1960

In his capacity as dean of St. Patrick's Cathedral, Jonathan Swift was a governor of Marsh's Library. The interior—a magnificent example of a 17th-century scholar's library—has remained very much the same for 3 centuries. Special exhibits are designed and mounted annually.

National Library of Ireland. Kildare St., Dublin 2. ☎ **01/603-0200.** Fax 01/676-6690. Free admission. Mon–Wed 10am–9pm; Thurs–Fri 10am–5pm; Sat 10am–1pm. DART: Pearse. Bus: 10, 11A, 11B, 13, or 20B.

If you're coming to Ireland to research your roots, this library should be one of your first stops (along with the Heraldic Museum; see below). It has thousands of volumes and records that yield ancestral information. Opened at this location in 1890, this is the principal library of Irish studies. It's particularly noted for its collection of first editions and the papers of Irish writers and political figures, such as W. B. Yeats, Daniel O'Connell, and Patrick Pearse. It also has an unrivaled collection of maps of Ireland.

National Photographic Archive. Meeting House Sq., Temple Bar, Dublin 2. ☎ **01/603-0200.** E-mail: photoarchive@nli.ie. Free admission. Mon–Fri 10am–5pm. DART: Tara St. Bus: 21A, 46A, 46B, 51B, 51C, 68, 69, or 86.

The newest member of the Temple Bar cultural complex, the National Photographic Archive houses the extensive (more than 300,000 items) photo collection of the National Library, and serves as its photo exhibition space. In addition to the exhibition area, there are a library and a small gift shop. Admission to the reading room is by appointment.

LITERARY LANDMARKS

See also "Libraries," above, and the listing for the Dublin Writers Museum, under "The Top Attractions," earlier in this section. You might also be interested in the James Joyce Museum, in nearby Sandycove; it's described in section 10, "Side Trips from Dublin."

James Joyce Centre. 35 N. Great George's St., Dublin 1. ☎ **01/878-8547.** www. jamesjoyce.ie. Admission £2.75 ($3.85) adults, £2 ($2.80) seniors and students, 75p ($1.05) children, £6 ($8.40) family. Separate fees for walking tours and events. AE, MC, V. Mon–Sat 9:30am–5pm; Sun 12:30–5pm. Closed Dec 24–26. DART: Connolly. Bus: 3, 10, 11, 11A, 13, 16, 16A, 19, 19A, 22, or 22A.

Near Parnell Square and the Dublin Writers Museum, the Joyce center is in a restored 1784 Georgian town house, once the home of Denis J. Maginni, a dancing instructor who appears briefly in *Ulysses*. The Ulysses Portrait Gallery on the second floor has a fascinating collection of photographs and drawings of characters from *Ulysses* who had a life outside the novel. The recently opened Paul Leon Exhibition Room holds the table and writing table used by Joyce in Paris when he was working on *Finnegan's Wake*. The room is named after Paul Leon, an academic who aided Joyce in literary, business, and domestic affairs and salvaged many of the author's papers after Joyce and his family left Paris. There are talks and audiovisual presentations daily. Guided walking tours through the neighborhood streets of "Joyce Country" in Dublin's north inner city are offered daily.

Shaw Birthplace. 33 Synge St., Dublin 2. ☎ **01/475-0854.** Admission £2.70 ($3.80) adults, £2.20 ($3.10) seniors and students, £1.40 ($1.95) children, £7.95 ($11.15) family. Discounted combination ticket with Dublin Writers Museum and James Joyce Museum available. May–Oct Mon–Sat 10am–5pm, Sun 11am–5pm. Closed Nov–Apr. Bus: 16, 16, 19, or 22.

This simple two-story terraced house, built in 1838, was the birthplace in 1856 of George Bernard Shaw, one of Dublin's three winners of the Nobel Prize for Literature. Recently restored, it has been furnished in Victorian style to re-create the atmosphere of Shaw's early days. Rooms on view are the kitchen, the maid's room, the nursery, the drawing room, and a couple of bedrooms, including young Bernard's. The house is off South Circular Road, a 15-minute walk from St. Stephen's Green.

MORE MUSEUMS

See also "Art Galleries & Art Museums," above. The National Gallery, the National Museum, the Dublin Writers Museum, and Kilmainham Gaol Historical Museum are all listed earlier in this section, in "The Top Attractions."

Dublin Civic Museum. 58 S. William St., Dublin 2. ☎ **01/679-4260.** Free admission. Tues–Sat 10am–6pm; Sun 11am–2pm. Bus: 10, 11, or 13.

In the old City Assembly House, a fine 18th-century Georgian structure next to the Powerscourt Townhouse Centre, this museum focuses on the history of the Dublin area from medieval to modern times. In addition to old street signs, maps, and prints, you can see Viking artifacts, wooden water mains, coal covers—and even the head from the statue of Lord Nelson, which stood in O'Connell Street until it was blown up in 1965. Exhibits change three or four times a year.

GAA Museum. Croke Park, Dublin 3. ☎ **01/836-3222.** Admission £3 ($4.20) adults, £2 ($2.80) students, £1.50 ($2.10) children, £6 ($8.40) families. May–Sept daily 9:30am–5pm; Oct–Apr Tues–Sat 10am–5pm, Sun 12–5pm. Bus: 3, 11, 11A, 16, 16A, 51A, or 123.

On the grounds of Croke Park, principal stadium of the Gaelic Athletic Association, this museum dramatically presents the athletic heritage of Ireland. The Gaelic Games (Gaelic football, hurling, handball, and camogie) have long been contested on an annual basis between teams representing the various regions of Ireland. Test your skills with interactive exhibits, and peruse the extensive video archive of football finals dating back to 1931. The 12-minute film *A Sunday in September* captures admirably the hysteria of the final match. Note that the museum is open only to new stand ticket holders on match days.

✪ Heraldic Museum/Genealogical Office. 2 Kildare St., Dublin 2. ☎ **01/603-0200.** Fax 01/662-1062. Free admission. Mon–Wed 10am–8:30pm; Thurs–Fri 10am–4:30pm; Sat 10am–12:30pm. DART: Pearse. Bus: 5, 7A, 8, 9, 10, 14, or 15.

The only one of its kind in the world, this museum focuses on the uses of heraldry. Exhibits include shields, banners, coins, paintings, porcelain, and stamps depicting coats of arms. In-house searches by the office researcher are billed at the rate of £35 ($49) per hour. This is the ideal place to start researching your roots.

Natural History Museum. Merrion St., Dublin 2. ☎ **01/677-7444.** Free admission. Tues–Sat 10am–5pm; Sun 2–5pm. DART: Pearse. Bus: 7, 7A, 8, or 13A.

A division of the National Museum of Ireland, the recently renovated Natural History Museum is considered one of the finest traditional museums in the world. In addition to presenting the zoological history of Ireland, it contains examples of major animal groups from around the world, including many that are rare or extinct. The Blaschka glass models of marine animals are a big attraction.

Number Twenty Nine. 29 Lower Fitzwilliam St., Dublin 2. ☎ **01/702-6165.** Admission £2.50 ($3.50) adults, £1 ($1.40) seniors and students, free for children under 16. MC, V. Tues–Sat 10am–5pm; Sun 2–5pm. Closed 2 weeks before Christmas. DART: Pearse. Bus: 7, 8, 10, or 45.

This unique museum is in the heart of one of Dublin's fashionable Georgian streets. The restored four-story town house is designed to reflect the lifestyle of a middle-class family during the period from 1790 to 1820. The exhibition ranges from artifacts and artworks of the time to carpets, curtains, decorations, plasterwork, and bell pulls. The nursery holds dolls and toys of the era.

Waterways Visitor Centre. Grand Canal Quay, Ringsend Rd., Dublin 2. ☎ **01/677-7510.** Admission £2 ($2.80) adults, £1.50 ($2.10) seniors, £1 ($1.40) children or students, £5 ($7) families. June–Sept daily 9:30am–5:30pm; Oct–May Wed–Sun 12:30–5pm. Last admission 45 min. prior to closing. DART: Pearse (5-min. walk). Bus: 1 or 3.

Heading south from Dublin on the DART, you may have noticed the tiny Waterways Visitor Centre, a brilliant white cube floating on the Grand Canal Basin amidst massive derelict brick warehouses. This intriguing modern building is home to a fascinating exhibit describing the history of Ireland's inland waterways, a network of canals connecting Dublin westward and northward to the Shannon watershed. The center's shiny white exterior gives way inside to the subdued tones of Irish oak wall panels and a hardwood ship's floor—a series of exhibits describe aspects of canal design, and several interactive models attempt to demonstrate dynamically the daily operations of the canals. No longer used for transporting goods, the canals of Ireland are now popular with boaters and hikers, and there's some information here for those interested in these activities.

A SIGHT & SOUND SHOW

Dublin Experience. Trinity College, Davis Theatre, Dublin 2. ☎ **01/608-1688.** Admission £3 ($4.20) adults, £2.50 ($3.50) seniors, students, and children. Daily late May to early Oct, hourly shows 10am–5pm. DART: Tara St. Bus: 5, 7A, 8, 15A, 15B, 15C, 46, 55, 62, 63, 83, or 84.

An ideal orientation for first-time visitors to the Irish capital, this 45-minute multimedia sight-and-sound show traces the history of Dublin from the earliest times to the present. It takes place in the Davis Theater of Trinity College, on Nassau Street.

ESPECIALLY FOR KIDS

✪ **The Ark: A Cultural Centre for Children.** Eustace St., Temple Bar, Dublin 2. ☎ **01/670-7788.** Fax 01/670-7758. www.ark.ie. Individual activities £2–£4 ($2.80–$5.60). Daily 10am–4pm. Closed mid-Aug to mid-Sept. DART: Tara St. Bus: 51, 51B, 37, or 39.

The Ark is a unique new cultural center where an experienced staff teaches children with respect and sensitivity. The handsomely renovated building has three modern main floors that house a theater, a gallery, and a workshop for hands-on learning sessions. The wonderful semicircular theater can be configured to open onto either of the other spaces, or outdoors onto Meeting House Square. This exciting center offers organized mini-course experiences (1 to 2 hr. long) designed around themes in music, visual arts, and theater. In its debut year, the Ark offered numerous activities in photography, the concept of an Ark and animal making, music and instrument making, and the art of architecture. The workshops, performances, tours, and artist- and musician-in-residence programs are geared toward specific age groups, and the associated activities are kept small. Check the current themes and schedule, and book accordingly. The Ark enjoys huge popularity with children, families, and teachers.

✪ **Dublin Zoo.** The Phoenix Park, Dublin 8. ☎ **01/677-1425.** www.dublinzoo.ie. Admission £6.30 ($8.80) adults, £3.70 ($5.20) seniors and children 3–16, free for children under 3, £18.50–£23.50 ($25.90–$32.90) family, depending on number of children. V. Summer Mon–Sat 9:30am–6pm, Sun 10:30am–6pm. Bus: 10, 25, or 26.

Established in 1830, this is the third-oldest zoo in the world (after those in London and Paris), nestled in the city's largest playground, the Phoenix Park, about 2 miles (3.2km) west of the city center. The 30-acre zoo provides a naturally landscaped habitat for more than 235 species of wild animals and tropical birds. Highlights for youngsters include the Children's Pets' Corner and a train ride around the zoo. New additions to the zoo, part of a $24 million redevelopment, are the "Fringes of the Arctic" exhibition, the "World of Primates," the "World of Cats," and the "City Farm and Pets Corner." Current plans to double the size of the zoo focus on the creation of an "African Plains" area. The zoo also has a restaurant, coffee shop, and gift shop.

✪ **Dublin's Viking Adventure.** Temple Bar (enter from Essex St.), Dublin 8. ☎ **01/ 679-6040.** Fax 01/679-6033. Admission £4.95 ($6.95) adults, £3.95 ($5.55) seniors and students, £2.95 ($4.15) children, £13.50 ($18.90) family. AE, MC, V. Mar–Oct Tues–Sat 10am–4:30pm; Nov–Feb Tues–Sat 10am–1pm and 2–4:30pm. DART: Tara St., then no. 90 bus. Bus: 51, 51B, 79, or 90.

This popular new attraction brings you on an imaginative journey through time to an era when Dublin was a bustling Norse town. The "Vikings" who populate the village create a lively, authentic atmosphere in their period houses and detailed costumes. The townspeople engage in the activities of daily life in the Wood Quay area along the Liffey, while you watch and interact with them.

Lambert Puppet Theatre and Museum. 5 Clifden Lane, Monkstown, County Dublin. ☎ **01/280-0974.** www.lambertpuppettheatre.com. No box office; call for same-day reservations. Admission £5 ($7). Shows Sat–Sun 3:30pm. DART: Salthill. Bus: 7, 7A, or 8.

Founded by master ventriloquist Eugene Lambert, this 300-seat suburban theater presents puppet shows designed to delight audiences both young and young at heart. During intermission, you can browse in the puppet museum or look for a take-home puppet in the shop.

ORGANIZED TOURS
BUS TOURS
Dublin Bus. 59 Upper O'Connell St., Dublin 1. ☎ **01/873-4222.**

This company operates several different tours. Seats can be booked in advance at the office or at the ticket desk, Dublin Tourism, Suffolk Street. All tours depart from the office, but free pickup from many hotels is available for morning tours. Tours include the nearly 3-hour **Grand Dublin Tour** on a double-decker bus, with either an open-air or glass-enclosed upper level. It's a great vantage point for picture taking. The cost is £10 ($14) adults, £5 ($7) children under 14. It operates year-round at 10:15am and 2:15pm.

For more flexible touring, there is a guided **Dublin City Tour.** The continuous service connects 10 major points of interest, including museums, art galleries, churches and cathedrals, libraries, and historic sites. For the flat fare of £7 ($9.80) adults, £3.50 ($4.90) children under 14, £12 ($16.80) for a family of four, you can ride the bus for a full day, getting off and on as often as you wish. It operates daily from 9:30am to 6:30pm.

Dublin Bus also offers a 3-hour (North) Coast and Castle Tour, departing daily at 10am, and a nearly 4-hour South Coast Tour, departing daily at 11am and 2pm. The cost of each tour is £12 ($16.80) adults, £6 ($8.40) children under 14.

Gray Line Tours—Ireland. Gray Line Desk, Dublin Tourism Centre, Suffolk St., Dublin 2. ☎ **01/605-7705.** E-mail: grayline@tlp.ie.

A branch of the world's largest sightseeing organization, this company offers a fully guided panoramic hop-on, hop-off city tour of Dublin from March 23 to the end of November. You can join the tour at any of a number of pickup points along the route. Tours leave daily at 10am from 14 Upper O'Connell St., and at 10am from the Dublin Tourism Center on Suffolk Street, and every 20 minutes thereafter. The last

Family Favorites

There is so much for families to see and do in Dublin that it's hard to know where to begin, so we thought we'd get you started with a few child- and parent-tested favorites!

Dublin's parks give families on the go a respite from the city's ruckus. In **Merrion Square** and **St. Stephen's Green** you will find lawns for picnicking, ducks for feeding, playgrounds for swinging, and gardens for viewing. Horse-loving youngsters will especially enjoy taking a family carriage tour around the parks (see "Organized Tours," below).

West of Dublin's city center, the vast **Phoenix Park** entices visitors and locals alike (see "The Top Attractions," earlier in this section). Phoenix Park is home to the **Dublin Zoo** (see below), myriad trails, amazing trees, sports fields, playgrounds, and herds of lovely free-roaming deer. You will discover mansions, castles, and many secret gardens. Ice-cream vendors and tea houses spring up in all the right places to keep you going. Those weary of walking can take a trail ride through the park thanks to the nearby **Ashtown Riding Stables** (see section 6, "The Great Outdoors").

If a day with Vikings appeals to your family, don't miss **Dublin's Viking Adventure** (see below) or the lively **Viking Splash Tour** in a reconditioned World War II amphibious "Duck" vehicle. You'll see Dublin from land and water with a Viking tour guide who will keep the whole family dry and well entertained (see "Organized Tours," later in this section).

Interactive creative activities for families can be found in the **Temple Bar** area. **The Ark** (see above) offers unique arts classes and experiences for children. The entire family will enjoy the popular **ESB Sunday Circus** held in Meeting House Square directly behind The Ark in Temple Bar. These captivating theater, puppet, dance, music, and circus events are all free but do require that you pick up tickets for the show from 2pm on the show day at the Essex Street entrance to Meeting House Square. Performance times vary from 2 to 4pm on Sundays from May to August, and the schedule of events can be found through Temple Bar

departures are 4pm from Suffolk Street, 4:30pm from O'Connell Street. Gray Line also offers a range of full-day excursions from Dublin to such nearby sights as Glendalough, Newgrange, and Powerscourt. Grayline's Dublin city tour costs £8.50 ($11.90) adults, £7.50 ($10.50) seniors and students, £3 ($4.20) children, £20 ($28) family. Adult fares for their other tours range from $18 to $37.

HELICOPTER TOURS

This is something new to Dublin's friendly skies. **First Flight Aviation Ltd.,** Dublin, Helicopter Centre NSC, Cloghran, County Dublin (☎ **01/890-0222;** www.firstflight.ie), now offers 20-minute helicopter tours of the center city, with more distant views of Dublin Bay and the north and south coastlines. The cost is from £65 ($91) per person for the standard tour. Ask for Colm King when you call.

VIKING SPLASH TOURS

New to the Dublin scene in the summer of 2000, this is a different way to see the town, especially its Viking-related sights. Aboard a reconditioned World War II amphibious landing craft, or "duck," this tour starts on land (from Bull Alley Street

Properties, 18 Eustace St., Temple Bar, Dublin 2 (☎ 01/677-2255), or the Cultureline (☎ 01/671-5717).

Day excursions out of town are great fun, especially when there are beaches to run on and treasures to discover. North of the city is the **Malahide Castle Demesne** (see Dublin's Northern Suburbs under "Side Trips from Dublin"). This great estate features not only the beautiful **Malahide Castle** but also the fascinating **Fry Model Railway** exhibit, a display of exquisite antique dollhouses and toys at **Tara's Palace,** acres of parkland, playgrounds, and picnic areas.

The towns south of Dublin are best explored by DART light rail from the city center. You might stop in Monkstown to see a puppet show at the famous **Lambert Puppet Theatre and Museum** (see below), or, if the kids need a little seaside adventure, go on a few more stops to the charming village of Dalkey. **The Ferryman** of Coliemore Harbor (see "Dublin's Southern Suburbs" in section 10 of this chapter), just a 10-minute walk from the train, can take the family out to explore **Dalkey Island** and return you to shore. After your adventure, you can reward your daring with a creamy soft-serve ice-cream cone in the village. The park at the top of **Dalkey Hill** offers a memorable view of the town and bay beyond.

One stop after Dalkey on the DART lies the long pebbled beach of **Killiney.** This is just the place to find the perfect stone for your family collection or to take a beachcombing stroll along the strand. Farther on down the line is the seaside resort town of **Bray.** Irish water creatures, from starfish to sharks, can be found in the **National Sea Life Centre** (see chapter 5, section 1, on County Wicklow, for a full listing). Bray also sports arcades, games, and other family amusements along its boardwalk. If you get to Bray with energy and daylight to spare, the hike up **Bray Head** will give you a spectacular view of the Dublin coastline. In season, the purple heather and yellow gorse are stunning, and you might see rabbits inquiring around the bushes.

beside St. Patrick's Cathedral) and eventually splashes into the Grand Canal. Tours depart roughly every half hour Monday to Saturday 9am to 6:30pm and Sunday 11am to 6:30pm and last an hour and 15 minutes. It costs £9 ($12.60) for adults and £5 ($7) for children under 12. To contact the tour operators, call ☎ 01/296-6047 or point your browser to www.vikingsplashtours.com.

WALKING TOURS

Small and compact, Dublin lends itself to walking tours. You can grab a map and a pith helmet and set off on your own, of course, but if you want some guidance, some historical background, or just some company, you might want to consider one of the following options.

The **Dublin Tourism Office,** St. Andrew's Church, Suffolk Street, Dublin 2, has been a pioneer in the development of self-guided walking tours around Dublin. To date, four tourist trails have been mapped out and signposted throughout the city: Old City, Georgian Heritage, Cultural Heritage, and Rock 'n Stroll/Music Theme. For each trail, the tourist office has produced a handy booklet that maps out the route and provides commentary about each place along the trail.

Historical Walking Tours of Dublin. From Trinity College. ☎ **01/878-0227.** Tickets £5 ($7) adults, £4 ($5.60) seniors and students. May–Sept Mon–Fri 11am and 3pm, Sun 11am, noon, 3pm; Oct–April Fri–Sun noon.

This basic 2-hour sightseeing walk takes in Dublin's historic landmarks, from medieval walls and Viking remains around Wood Quay to Christ Church, Dublin Castle, City Hall, and Trinity College. All guides are history graduates of Trinity College, and participants are encouraged to ask questions. Tours assemble at the front gate of Trinity College; no reservations are needed. Walking tours of Trinity College are offered at Trinity's Front Square, just inside the front gate.

Jameson Literary Pub Crawl. 37 Exchequer St., Dublin 2. ☎ **01/670-5602.** Tickets £6 ($8.40) per person. Year-round. Times vary.

Walking in the footsteps of Joyce, Behan, Beckett, Shaw, Kavanagh, and other Irish literary greats, this guided tour, winner of the "Living Dublin Award," visits a number of Dublin's most famous pubs with literary connections. Actors provide appropriate performances and commentary between stops. The tour assembles at the Duke Pub on Duke Street (off Grafton Street).

Traditional Irish Musical Pub Crawl. Leaves from Oliver St. John Gogarty pub and restaurant, 57/58 Fleet St. (at Anglesea St.), Temple Bar. ☎ **01/478-0193.** Tickets £6 ($8.40) adults, £5 ($7) students and seniors. Mid-May to Oct daily 7:30pm; Nov and Feb to mid-May Fri–Sat 7:30pm. Tickets on sale at 7pm or in advance from Dublin Tourist Office.

To explore and sample the traditional music scene, meet at the Oliver St. John Gogarty pub and restaurant. The price includes a songbook. Two professional musicians, who sing as you make your way from one famous pub to another in Temple Bar, lead the tour. It lasts 2½ hours. The "crawl" better describes the way back to your hotel.

Walk Macabre. Dublin Tourism, Suffolk St., Dublin 2. ☎ **01/605-7769.** Tickets £6 ($8.40) per person. Daily 7:30pm.

The Trapeze Theatre Company offers this 90-minute walk through Dublin's Twilight Zone, revisiting local scenes of murder and intrigue. The tour includes readings and reenactments from some of the darker pages of W. B. Yeats, James Joyce, Bram Stoker, Oscar Wilde, and Sheridan LeFanu. Rated "R" for violent content, this is not for weak stomachs or light sleepers. Advance booking is essential. Tours leave from the main gates of St. Stephen's Green, opposite Planet Hollywood.

The Zosimus Experience. 28 Fitzwilliam Lane, Dublin 2. ☎ **01/661-8646.** www. zozimus.com. £6 ($8.40) per person. Daily at nightfall, by appointment.

This is the latest rage on the walking tour circuit. Its creators call it a "cocktail mix" of ghosts, murderous tales, horror stories, humor, circus, history, street theater, and whatever's left, all within the precincts of medieval Dublin. You've guessed by now that it's indescribable, and also great fun. It's essential to book in advance, when you'll receive all the specifics you need to be in the right place (outside the main gate of Dublin Castle) at the right time. Because the hour of nightfall varies, you'll learn the exact meeting time when you reserve a place. The experience lasts approximately 1½ hours.

HORSE-DRAWN CARRIAGE TOURS

Tour Dublin in style in a handsomely outfitted horse-drawn carriage with a driver who will comment on the sights as you travel the city's streets and squares. To arrange a ride, consult one of the drivers stationed with carriages at the Grafton Street side of St. Stephen's Green. Rides range from a short swing around the Green to an extensive half-hour Georgian tour or an hour-long Old City tour. Rides are available on a

Impressions

*The trees in St. Stephen's Green were fragrant of rain and the rainsodden earth gave
forth its mortal odor, a faint incense rising upward through the mould of many hearts.*
—James Joyce, *Portrait of the Artist as a Young Man,* 1916

first-come, first-served basis from approximately April to October (weather permitting), and will run you between £10 and £40 ($14 to $56) for one to four passengers, depending on duration of ride.

BICYCLE TOURS

Dublin Bike Tours. 3 Mornington Rd., Ranelagh, Dublin 6. Bookings at Dublin Tourism Centre, Suffolk St., Dublin 2. ☎ **01/679-0899** or 087/284-0799 (mobile); fax 01/679-6504. E-mail: DublinBikeTours@connect.ie. £15–£30 ($21–$42) per person, depending on tour. Daily 10am, 2pm, 6pm. "Dublin at Dawn" Sat 6am.

Riding a bike in Dublin isn't recommended. Traffic is very heavy, the streets are narrow, and pedestrians crowd every corner. For those determined to take to the streets on wheels, Dublin Bike Tours is a very good option for tours of the city and environs along mostly quieter back streets and roads at a relaxed pace. The 3-hour standard Dublin bike tour is broken by frequent stops, including one for refreshments. A range of other enticing Dublin-area tours are on offer. Or, if you want to set out on your own, you can rent bikes and all the gear, from helmets to baby seats, here as well.

6 The Great Outdoors

BEACHES   The following beaches on the outskirts of Dublin offer safe swimming and sandy strands. All can be reached by city bus: **Dollymount,** 3.5 miles (5.6km) away; **Sutton,** 7 miles (11km) away; **Howth,** 9 miles (15km) away; and **Portmarnock** and **Malahide,** each 10 miles (16km) away. In addition, the southern suburb of **Dun Laoghaire,** 7 miles (11km) away, offers a beach (at Sandycove) and a long bayfront promenade that's ideal for strolling in the sea air. For more details, inquire at the Dublin Tourism Office.

BIRD WATCHING   The estuaries, salt marshes, sand flats, and islands near Dublin Bay provide a varied habitat for a number of species. **Rockabill Island,** off the coast at Skerries, is home to an important colony of roseate terns; there is no public access to the island, but the birds can be seen from the shore. **Rogerstown and Malahide estuaries,** on the north side of Dublin, are wintering grounds for large numbers of brent geese, ducks, and waders. The **North Bull** is a spit of sand just north of Dublin Harbor, with salt marsh and extensive intertidal flats on the side facing the mainland; 198 species in all have been recorded here. **Sandymount Strand** on Dublin's south side has a vast intertidal zone; around dusk in July and August you can often see large numbers of terns, including visiting roseate terns from Rockabill Island.

DIVING   **Oceantech Adventures** in Dun Laoghaire (☎ 01/280-1083; toll-free within Ireland 800/272822; www.oceantechadventure.com) offers a five-star PADI diving school and arranges dive vacations on the west coast. Also check out the **National Diving School,** 8 St. James Terrace, Malahide, County Dublin (☎ 01/845-2000).

FISHING   The greater Dublin area offers a wide range of opportunities for freshwater angling on local rivers, reservoirs, and fisheries. A day's catch might include perch, rudd, pike, salmon, sea trout, brown trout, or freshwater eel. The **Dublin**

Angling Initiative, Balnagowan, Mobhi Boreen, Glasnevin, Dublin 9 (☎ 01/837-9209), offers a guide—the *Dublin Freshwater Angling Guide,* available for £1 ($1.40)—to tell you everything you'll need to know about local fishing.

GOLF   Dublin is one of the world's great golfing capitals. A quarter of Ireland's courses—including 5 of the top 10—lie within an hour's drive of the city. Visitors are welcome, but be sure to phone ahead and make a reservation. The following four are among the leading 18-hole courses in the Dublin area.

The **Elm Park Golf Club,** Nutley Lane, Dublin 4 (☎ 01/269-3438), is on the south side of Dublin. The inland par-69 course is very popular with visitors because it is within 3.5 miles (5.6km) of the city center and close to the Jurys, Berkeley Court, and Burlington hotels. Greens fees are £40 ($56) on weekdays, £50 ($70) on weekends.

✪ **Portmarnock Golf Club,** Portmarnock, County Dublin (☎ 01/846-2968), is 10 miles (16km) from the city center on Dublin's north side, on a spit of land between the Irish Sea and a tidal inlet. Opened in 1894, the par-72 championship course has been the scene of leading tournaments, including the Dunlop Masters (1959, 1965), Canada Cup (1960), Alcan (1970), St. Andrews Trophy (1968), and many an Irish Open. Many experts consider Portmarnock the benchmark of Irish golf. Greens fees are £75 ($105) on weekdays, £95 ($133) on weekends.

✪ **Royal Dublin Golf Club,** Bull Island, Dollymount, Dublin 3 (☎ 01/833-6346), is often compared to St. Andrews. The century-old par-73 championship seaside links is on an island in Dublin Bay, 3 miles (4.8km) northeast of the city center. Like Portmarnock, it has been rated among the world's top courses and has played host to several Irish Opens. The home base of Ireland's legendary champion Christy O'Connor, Sr., the Royal Dublin is well known for its fine bunkers, close lies, and subtle trappings. Greens fees are £65 ($91) on weekdays, £80 ($112) on weekends.

St. Margaret's Golf Club, Skephubble, St. Margaret's, County Dublin (☎ 01/864-0400), one of Dublin's newest championship golf venues, is a par-72 parkland course 3 miles (4.8km) west of Dublin Airport. In 1995, St. Margaret's was host to the Irish Open. Greens fees are £40 ($56) on weekdays, £50 ($70) on weekends.

HORSEBACK RIDING   For equestrian enthusiasts of any experience level, almost a dozen riding stables are within easy reach. Prices average about £15 ($21) an hour, with or without instruction. Many stables offer guided trail riding, as well as courses in show jumping, dressage, prehunting, eventing, and cross-country riding. For trail riding through the Phoenix Park, **Ashtown Riding Stables** (☎ 01/838-3807) are ideal. They're located in the village of Ashtown, adjoining the park and only 10 minutes by car or bus (nos. 37, 38, 39, or 70) from the city center. Among the other riding centers close to the downtown are **Calliaghstown Riding Centre,** Calliaghstown, Rathcoole, County Dublin (☎ 01/458-9236); and **Carrickmines Equestrian Centre,** Glenamuck Road, Foxrock, Dublin 18 (☎ 01/295-5990).

WALKING   The walk from Bray to Greystones along the rocky promontory of **Bray Head** is a great excursion, with beautiful views back toward Killiney Bay, Dalkey Island, and Bray, the southern terminus of the DART line. It's readily accessible from Dublin. Follow the beachside promenade south through town; at the outskirts of town the promenade turns left and up, beginning the ascent of Bray Head. Shortly after the ascent begins, a trail branches to the left—this is the cliffside walk, which continues another 3½ miles (5.6km) along the coast to Greystones. From the center of Greystones, a train will take you back to Bray. This is an easy walk, about 2 hours one way.

Dalkey Hill and **Killiney Hill** drop steeply into the sea, and command great views of Killiney Bay, Bray Head, and Sugarloaf Mountain. To get there, go south on Dalkey Avenue from the center of Dalkey (in front of the post office), a short distance from

TIMBUKTU   KALAMAZOO

AT&T Direct® Service

The easy way to call home from anywhere.

Global | **AT&T**
connection | direct
with the AT&T | service
Network |

For the easy way to call home, take the attached wallet guide.

the Dalkey DART station. About half a mile from the post office, you'll pass a road ascending through fields on your left—this is the entrance to the Dalkey Hill Park. From the parking lot, climb a series of steps to the top of Dalkey Hill; from here you can see the expanse of the bay, the Wicklow Hills in the distance, and the obelisk topping nearby Killiney Hill. If you continue on to the obelisk, there is a trail leading from there down on the seaward side to Vico Road, another lovely place for a seaside walk. It's about half a mile from the parking lot to Killiney Hill.

WINDSURFING   Certified level-one and level-two instruction and equipment rental for three water sports—kayaking, sailing, and windsurfing—are available at the **Surfdock Centre,** Grand Canal Dock Yard, Ringsend, Dublin 4 (☎ **01/668-3945;** fax 01/668-1215). The center has 42 acres of enclosed fresh water for its courses. It's open from June to September, and the rest of the year on demand.

7 Spectator Sports

GAELIC SPORTS   If your schedule permits, try to get to a **Gaelic football** game, which vaguely resembles soccer but allows use of the hands in punching the ball, or a **hurling** match, a game in which 30 men wielding heavy sticks rush around thrashing at a hard leather ball called a *sliotar*. The amateur sports are played every weekend throughout the summer at various local fields, culminating in September with the **All-Ireland Finals,** an Irish version of the Super Bowl. For schedules and admission charges, phone the **Gaelic Athletic Association,** Croke Park, Jones Road, Dublin 3 (☎ **01/836-3222**).

GREYHOUND RACING   Watching these lean, swift canines is one of the leading spectator sports in the Dublin area. Races are held throughout the year at **Shelbourne Park Greyhound Stadium,** Southlotts Road, Dublin 4 (☎ **01/668-3502**), and **Harold's Cross Stadium,** 151 Harold's Cross Rd., Dublin 6 (☎ **01/497-1081**). For a complete schedule and details for races throughout Ireland, contact **Bord na gCon** (the Greyhound Board), Limerick (☎ **061/315788**).

HORSE RACING   Dublin's racing fans gather at **Leopardstown Race Course,** off the Stillorgan road (N11), Foxrock, Dublin 18 (☎ **01/289-3607**). Six miles (9.7km) south of the city center, this is a modern facility with all-weather glass-enclosed spectator stands. Races are scheduled throughout the year, two or three times a month.

POLO   With the Dublin Mountains as a backdrop, polo is played from May to mid-September on the green fields of the Phoenix Park, on Dublin's west side. Matches take place on Wednesday evenings and Saturday and Sunday afternoons. Admission is free. For full details, contact the **All Ireland Polo Club,** the Phoenix Park, Dublin 8 (☎ **01/677-6248**), or check the sports pages of the newspapers.

8 Shopping

Known the world over for its handmade products and fine craftsmanship, Ireland offers many unique shopping opportunities. Dublin, as Ireland's commercial center, is a one-stop source for the country's best wares. Also, due to Ireland's wholehearted membership in the European Union, Irish shops are brimming with imported goods from the Continent.

Grafton Street, although only several blocks long, is Dublin's answer to Chicago's "Magnificent Mile," with a parade of fine boutiques, fashionable department stores, and specialty shops. Because it's limited to pedestrian traffic, Grafton Street often attracts street performers and sidewalk artists, giving it a festive atmosphere. The smaller streets radiating out from Grafton—Duke, Dawson, Nassau, and Wicklow—are also lined with fine small book, handcraft, and souvenir shops.

Nearby is **Temple Bar,** the hub of Dublin's Left Bank artsy district and the setting for art and music shops, secondhand clothing stores, and a host of other increasingly fine and interesting boutiques.

On the north side of the Liffey, the **O'Connell Street** area is the main inner-city shopping nucleus, along with its nearby offshoots—Abbey Street for crafts, Moore Street for its open-air market, and Henry Street, a pedestrian-only strip of department stores and indoor malls. Close at hand, west of O'Connell, are both the ILAC Centre and the new Jervis Shopping Centre.

Generally, Dublin shops are open from 9am to 5:30 or 6pm Monday to Saturday, Thursday until 8pm. There are exceptions, particularly during tourist season (May to Sept or Oct), when many shops also have Sunday hours, usually midmorning to 4pm or 5pm. Throughout the year, many bookshops are open on Sundays.

Major department stores include **Arnotts,** 12 Henry St., Dublin 1, and 112 Grafton St., Dublin 2 (☎ **01/872-1111**); **Brown Thomas,** 15–20 Grafton St., Dublin 2 (☎ **01/679-5666**); and **Clerys,** Lower O'Connell Street, Dublin 1 (☎ **01/878-6000**).

Dublin also has several clusters of shops in **multistory malls** or ground-level arcades, ideal for indoor shopping on rainy days. These include the **ILAC Centre,** Henry Street, Dublin 1; the **Jervis Shopping Centre,** Mary Street, Dublin 1; **Royal Hibernian Way,** 49/50 Dawson St., Dublin 2; and **St. Stephen's Green Shopping Complex,** St. Stephen's Green, Dublin 2.

ART

Combridge Fine Arts. 17 S. William St., Dublin 2. ☎ **01/677-4652.** DART: Pearse. Bus: 15A, 15B, 15C, 55, or 83.

In business for more than 100 years, this shop features works by modern Irish artists as well as quality reproductions of classic Irish art.

Davis Gallery. 11 Capel St., Dublin 1. ☎ **01/872-6969.** Bus: 34, 70, or 80.

One block north of the Liffey, this shop offers a wide selection of Irish watercolors and oil paintings, with emphasis on Dublin scenes, wildlife, and flora.

M. Kennedy and Sons Ltd. 12 Harcourt St., Dublin 2. ☎ **01/475-1749.** Bus: 62.

If you are looking for a souvenir that reflects Irish art, try this interesting shop, established more than 100 years ago. It's a treasure trove of books on Irish artists and works, and it stocks a lovely selection of fine-art greeting cards, postcards, and bookmarks. There are all types of artists' supplies as well, and an excellent art gallery on the upstairs level.

BOOKS

✪ **Eason and Son Ltd.** 40–42 Lower O'Connell St., Dublin 1. ☎ **01/873-3811.** www.eason.ie/. DART: Connolly. Bus: 25, 34, 37, 38A, 39A, 39B, 66A, or 67A.

For more than a century, Eason's—at this central location and at many branches throughout Ireland—has been synonymous with books. This branch offers a comprehensive selection of books and maps about Dublin and Ireland. Open Monday, Tuesday, Wednesday, and Saturday 8:30am to 6:45pm, Thursday until 8:45pm, Friday until 7:45pm, Sunday 1 to 5:45pm.

Eason/Hanna's Bookshop. 1 Dawson St., Dublin 2. ☎ **01/677-1255.** www.hannas.ie. DART: Pearse. Bus: 5, 7A, 8, or 62.

Located across from Trinity College, the newly merged Hanna's Eason or Eason Hanna's bookshop combines the scholarly bent of the old Fred Hanna's bookshop with the lighter, more populist appeal of Eason's, where you can expect to find everything from pulp fiction to paper clips.

✪ **Greene's Bookshop Ltd.** 16 Clare St., Dublin 2. ☎ **01/676-2554.** DART: Pearse. Bus: 5, 7A, 8, or 62.

Established in 1843, this shop near Trinity College is one of Dublin's treasures for bibliophiles. It's chock-full of new and secondhand books on every topic from religion to the modern novel. The catalog of Irish-interest books is issued five to six times a year. Open weekdays 9am to 5:30pm, Saturday 9am to 5pm.

✪ **Hodges Figgis.** 57 Dawson St., Dublin 2. ☎ **01/677-4754.** www.hodgesfiggis.ie. DART: Pearse. Bus: 10, 11A, 11B, 13, or 20B.

This three-story landmark store has great charm and browse appeal. Although it has everything, the sections on Irish literature, Celtic studies, folklore, and maps of Ireland are particularly good. The recently opened Hodges Figgis Cafe on the first floor seats 60 and serves wine and light meals. Open weekdays 9am to 7pm, Saturday until 6pm, Sunday noon to 6pm.

Waterstone's. 7 Dawson St., Dublin 2. ☎ **01/679-1415.** DART: Pearse. Bus: 10, 11A, 11B, 13, or 20B.

Less than a block south of Trinity College, this literary emporium has extensive sections on Irish interests, as well as crime, gay literature, health, New Age, sports, women's studies, the arts, and wine.

CERAMICS

Louis Mulcahey. 51c Dawson St., Dublin 2. ☎ **01/670-9311.** DART: Pearse. Bus: 10, 11A, 11B, 13, or 20B.

The ceramic creations of Louis Mulcahey are internationally renowned. For years he has been exporting his work throughout Ireland and the rest of the world from his studio on the Dingle Peninsula. This modest new shop across from the Shelbourne Hotel gives him a base in Dublin. In addition to pottery, he designs furniture, lighting, and hand-painted silk and cotton lamp shades.

CHINA & CRYSTAL

China & Crystal The China Showrooms. 32/33 Abbey St., Dublin 1. ☎ **01/878-6211.** www.chinashowrooms.ie. DART: Connolly. Bus: 27B or 53A.

Established in 1939, this is Ireland's oldest china and crystal shop in continuous operation. It's a one-stop source for fine china such as Belleek, Aynsley, Royal Doulton, and Rosenthal; hand-cut crystal from Waterford, Tipperary, and Tyrone; and handmade Irish pottery. Worldwide shipping is available.

✪ **Dublin Crystal Glass Company.** Brookfield Terrace, Carysfort Ave., Blackrock, County Dublin. ☎ **01/288-7932.** www.dublincrystal.ie. DART: Blackrock. Bus: 114.

This is Dublin's own distinctive hand-cut crystal business, founded in 1764 and revived in 1968. Visitors are welcome to browse in the factory shop and see the glass being made and engraved.

CRAFTS COMPLEXES

✪ **DESIGNyard.** 12 E. Essex St., Temple Bar, Dublin 2. ☎ **01/677-8453.** DART: Tara St. Bus: 21A, 46A, 46B, 51B, 51C, 68, 69, or 86.

The first thing you'll notice about DESIGNyard is its design. The Victorian warehouse, gorgeously converted into a chic contemporary applied-arts center, has a commissioned set of four wrought-iron gates—abstracts of the city plans of Dublin,

Madrid, New York, and Vienna. The ground-floor Jewellery Gallery exhibits and sells contemporary Irish and European jewelry. The first-floor Crafts Council Gallery displays and sells Irish contemporary crafts, including furniture, ceramics, glass, lighting, and textiles. All exhibited pieces are for sale. You may also make an appointment to commission an original work of Irish applied art and design. Whether you see it as a shop or a museum, DESIGNyard is well worth a visit. Open Monday and Wednesday to Saturday 10:30am to 5:30pm, Tuesday 11am to 5:30pm.

Powerscourt Townhouse Centre. 59 S. William St., Dublin 2. ☎ **01/679-4144.** Bus: 10, 11A, 11B, 13, 16A, 19A, 20B, 22A, 55, or 83.

Housed in a restored 1774 town house, this four-story complex consists of a central skylit courtyard and more than 60 boutiques, crafts shops, art galleries, snack bars, wine bars, and restaurants. The wares include all kinds of crafts, antiques, paintings, prints, ceramics, leather work, jewelry, clothing, hand-dipped chocolates, and farmhouse cheeses.

Tower Design Centre. Pearse St. (off Grand Canal Quay), Dublin 2. ☎ **01/677-5655.** Limited free parking. DART: Pearse. Bus: 2 or 3.

Along the banks of the Grand Canal, this 1862 sugar refinery was beautifully restored in 1983. In the nest of crafts workshops, you can watch the artisans at work. The merchandise ranges from fine-art greeting cards and hand-marbled stationery to pewter, ceramics, pottery, knitwear, hand-painted silks, copper-plate etchings, all-wool wall hangings, silver and gold Celtic jewelry, and heraldic gifts. Open Monday to Friday from 9am to 5:30pm.

FASHION
See also "Knitwear," below.

MEN'S
F.X. Kelly. 48 Grafton St., Dublin 2. ☎ **01/677-8142.** DART: Pearse. Bus: 10, 11A, 11B, 13, or 20B.

A long-established ready-to-wear shop, this place blends old-fashioned charm with modern design. It offers a handsome selection of styles, with emphasis on conventional clothing as well as items such as creased linen suits, painted ties, and designer sportswear. Closed Tuesday.

✪ **Kevin & Howlin.** 31 Nassau St., Dublin 2. ☎ **01/677-0257.** DART: Pearse. Bus: 7, 8, 10, 11, or 46A.

Opposite Trinity College, this shop has specialized in men's tweed garments for more than 50 years. The selection includes hand-woven Donegal tweed suits, overcoats, and jackets. In addition, there is a wide selection of scarves, vests, Patch caps, and Gatsby, Sherlock Holmes, and Paddy hats.

Louis Copeland and Sons. 39–41 Capel St., Dublin 1. ☎ **01/872-1600.** Bus: 34, 70, or 80.

With a distinctive old-world shop front, this store stands out on the north side of the River Liffey. It is known for high-quality work in made-to-measure and ready-to-wear men's suits, coats, and shirts. There are branches at 30 Pembroke St., Dublin 2 (☎ **01/661-0110**), and 18 Wicklow St., Dublin 2 (☎ **01/677-7038**).

WOMEN'S
✪ **Cleo.** 18 Kildare St., Dublin 2. ☎ **01/676-1421.** www.netsolutions.ie/cleo. DART: Pearse. Bus: 10, 11A, 11B, 13, or 20B.

For more than 50 years, the Joyce family has created designer ready-to-wear clothing in a rainbow of vibrant tweed colors—elegant ponchos, capes, peasant skirts, coat-sweaters, decorative crios belts, and brimmed hats. A new line of hand-knit sweaters incorporates 4,000- to 5,000-year-old designs from carved cairn stones found at Newgrange.

Pat Crowley. 3 Molesworth Place, Dublin 2. ☎ **01/661-5580.** Fax 01/661-2476. DART: Pearse. Bus: 10, 11A, 11B, 13, or 20B.

This designer emphasizes individuality in her exclusive line of tweeds and couture evening wear.

Sybil Connolly. 71 Merrion Sq., Dublin 2. ☎ **01/676-7281.** DART: Pearse. Bus: 5, 7A, or 8.

Irish high fashion is synonymous with this world-renowned made-to-measure designer. Evening wear and Irish linen creations are her specialties.

GIFTS & KNICKKNACKS

House of Ireland. 37–38 Nassau St., Dublin 2. ☎ **01/677-7473.** www.hoi.ie. DART: Pearse. Bus: 5, 7A, 15A, 15B, 46, 55, 62, 63, 83, or 84.

This shop opposite Trinity College is a happy blend of European and Irish products, from Waterford and Belleek to Wedgwood and Lladró. It also carries tweeds, linens, knitwear, Celtic jewelry, mohair capes, shawls, kilts, blankets, and dolls. Ask about the 10% gift offer for mentioning this guide!

The Kilkenny Shop. 6–10 Nassau St., Dublin 2. ☎ **01/677-7066.** DART: Pearse. Bus: 5, 7A, 15A, 15B, 46, 55, 62, 63, 83, or 84.

A sister operation of the Blarney Woollen Mills (see below), this modern multilevel shop is a showplace for original Irish designs and quality products, including pottery, glass, candles, woolens, pipes, knitwear, jewelry, books, and prints. The pleasant cafe is ideal for coffee and pastries or a light lunch.

Weir and Sons. 96 Grafton St., Dublin 2. ☎ **01/677-9678.** DART: Pearse. Bus: 10, 11A, 11B, 13, or 20B.

Established in 1869, this is the granddaddy of Dublin's fine jewelry shops. It sells new and antique jewelry as well as silver, china, and glass items. There is a second branch at the ILAC Centre, Henry Street (☎ **01/872-9588**).

HERALDRY

Heraldic Artists. 3 Nassau St., Dublin 2. ☎ **01/679-7020.** www.roots.ie. DART: Pearse. Bus: 5, 7A, 8, 15A, 15B, 46, 55, 62, 63, 83, or 84.

For more than 20 years, this shop has been known for helping visitors locate their family roots. In addition to tracing surnames, it sells all the usual heraldic items, from family crest parchments, scrolls, and mahogany wall plaques to books on researching ancestry.

House of Names. 26 Nassau St., Dublin 2. ☎ **01/679-7287.** DART: Pearse. Bus: 5, 7A, 8, 15A, 15B, 46, 55, 62, 63, 83, or 84.

As its name implies, this company offers a wide selection of Irish, British, and European family names affixed—along with their attendant crests and mottoes—to plaques, shields, parchments, jewelry, glassware, and sweaters.

JEWELRY

The Steensons. 16 S. Frederick St., Dublin 2. ☎ and fax **01/672-7007.** DART: Pearse. Bus: 5, 7A, 15A, 15B, 46, 55, 62, 63, or 84.

Bill and Christina Steenson, based in the North, have long been two of the most celebrated goldsmiths in Ireland. This, their first shop in the Republic, opened in

November 1999 and was an immediate success. No wonder, as their workmanship and design are exquisite. The focus here is on contemporary Irish design, though roughly 20% of their inventory comes from other European sources, especially Germany.

KNITWEAR

Blarney Woollen Mills. 21–23 Nassau St., Dublin 2. ☎ **01/671-0068.** DART: Pearse. Bus: 5, 7A, 8, 15A, 15B, 46, 55, 62, 63, 83, or 84.

A branch of the highly successful Cork-based enterprise of the same name, this shop is opposite the south side of Trinity College. Known for its competitive prices, it stocks a wide range of woolen knitwear made at the home base in Blarney, as well as crystal, china, pottery, and souvenirs.

Dublin Woollen Mills. 41–42 Lower Ormond Quay, Dublin 1. ☎ **01/677-0301.** Bus: 70 or 80.

Since 1888, this shop has been a leading source of Aran hand-knit sweaters, vests, hats, jackets, and scarves, as well as lambswool sweaters, kilts, ponchos, and tweeds at competitive prices. It's on the north side of the River Liffey next to the Halfpenny Bridge. The shop offers a 5% discount for those with current international student cards.

✪ **Monaghan's.** 15/17 Grafton Arcade, Grafton St., Dublin 2. ☎ **01/677-0823.** DART: Pearse. Bus: 10, 11A, 11B, 13, or 20B.

Established in 1960 and operated by two generations of the Monaghan family, this store is a prime source of cashmere sweaters for men and women. It boasts the best selection of colors, sizes, and styles anywhere in Ireland. Other items include traditional Aran knits, lambswool, crochet, and Shetland wool products. There's another store at 4/5 Royal Hibernian Way, off Dawson Street (☎ **01/679-4451**).

MARKETS

Blackrock Market. 19a Main St., Blackrock. ☎ **01/283-3522.** DART: Blackrock. Bus: 5, 7, 7A, 8, 17, 45, or 114.

More than 60 vendors run stalls that offer everything from gourmet cheese to vintage clothing at great prices in an indoor/outdoor setting. Open Saturday 11am to 5:30pm, Sunday noon to 5:30pm, including public holidays.

Moore Street Market. Moore St., Dublin 1. No phone. DART: Connolly. Bus: 25, 34, 37, 38A, 66A, or 67A.

For a walk into the past, don't miss the Moore Street Market, full of streetside barrow vendors plus plenty of local color and chatter. It's the city's principal open-air fruit, flower, fish, and vegetable market.

✪ **Mother Red Caps Market.** Back Lane (off High St.), Dublin 8. ☎ **01/453-8306.** Bus: 21A, 78A, or 78B.

In the heart of Old Dublin, this enclosed market, which calls itself the "mother of all markets," is surely one of Dublin's best. The stalls offer a trove of hidden treasures (some more in hiding than others), including antiques, used books and coins, silver, handcrafts, leather products, knitwear, music tapes, and furniture. There's even a fortune-teller! It's worth a trip here just to sample the wares at the Ryefield Foods stall (farm-made cheeses, baked goods, marmalades, and jams). Open Friday to Sunday 10am to 5:30pm.

MUSIC

The Celtic Note. 14–15 Nassau St., Dublin 2. ☎ **01/670-4157.** www.celticnote.ie. DART: Pearse. Bus: 5, 7A, 15A, 15B, 46, 55, 62, 63, 83, or 84.

Despite its modest size, this is perhaps the finest single source of recorded Irish music in Dublin. At the least, it's a fine place to start your search for the Irish artist or tune you can't do without. The staff is experienced and helpful, and you can listen to a CD before purchasing it. You'll pay full price here, but you're likely to find what you're looking for.

9 Dublin After Dark

A more appropriate title for this section might be "Dublin Almost Dark," because during high season, Dublin's nightlife takes place mostly in daylight. Situated roughly 53° north of the equator, Dublin in June gets really dark only as the pubs are closing. Night, then, is just a state of mind.

One general fact to keep in mind concerning Dublin's nightlife is that there are very few fixed points. Apart from a handful of established institutions, venues come and go, change character, open their doors to ballet one night and cabaret the next. *In Dublin* and The *Event Guide* offer the most thorough and up-to-date listings. They can be found on almost any magazine stand.

The award-winning Web site of the *Irish Times* (**www.ireland.com**) offers a "what's on" daily guide to cinema, theater, music, and whatever else you're up for. *Time Out* now covers Dublin as well; check their Web site at **www.timeout.com/Dublin**.

Advance bookings for most large concerts, plays, and so forth can be made through **Ticketmaster Ireland** (☎ **01/677-9409;** www.ticketmaster.ie), with ticket centers in most HMV stores, as well as at the Dublin Tourism Centre, Suffolk Street, Dublin 2.

THE PUB SCENE

The mainstay of Dublin social life, by night and by day, is unquestionably the pub. More than 1,000 specimens spread throughout the city, on every street, at every turn. In *Ulysses,* James Joyce referred to the puzzle of trying to cross Dublin without passing a pub; his characters quickly abandoned the quest as fruitless, preferring to sample a few in their path. Most visitors should follow in their footsteps and drop in on a few pubs.

You will need no assistance finding a pub, but here are a few suggestions of some of the city's most distinctive.

PUBS FOR CONVERSATION & ATMOSPHERE

✪ **Brazen Head.** 20 Lower Bridge St., Dublin 8. ☎ **01/679-5186.**

This brass-filled, lantern-lit pub claims to be the city's oldest, and it might very well be, considering that it was licensed in 1661 and occupies the site of an even earlier tavern dating from 1198. Nestled on the south bank of the River Liffey, it is at the end of a cobblestone courtyard and was once the meeting place of Irish freedom fighters such as Robert Emmet and Wolfe Tone. A full à la carte menu is offered.

The Castle Inn. Christchurch Place, Dublin 8. ☎ **01/475-1122.**

Situated between Dublin Castle and Christ Church Cathedral, this recently rejuvenated bilevel pub exudes an "old city" atmosphere. It has stone walls, flagstone steps, suits of armor, big stone fireplaces, beamed ceilings, and lots of early Dublin memorabilia. From May to September, it is also the setting for an Irish Ceili (traditional music and dance session) and Banquet.

Davy Byrnes. 21 Duke St. (off Grafton St.), Dublin 2. ☎ **01/677-5217.**

Referred to as a "moral pub" by James Joyce in *Ulysses,* this imbibers' landmark has drawn poets, writers, and literature lovers ever since. It dates from 1873, when Davy

Byrnes first opened the doors. He presided for more than 50 years, and visitors can still see his likeness on one of the turn-of-the-century murals hanging over the bar.

Doheny and Nesbitt. 5 Lower Baggot St., Dublin 2. ☎ **01/676-2945.**

The locals call this Victorian-style pub simply "Nesbitt's." The place houses two fine old "snugs"—small rooms with trap doors where women were served drinks in days of old—and a restaurant.

Flannery's Temple Bar. 47/48 Temple Bar. ☎ **01/497-4766.**

In the heart of the trendy Temple Bar district on the corner of Temple Lane, this small three-room pub was established in 1840. The decor is an interesting mix of crackling fireplaces, globe ceiling lights, old pictures on the walls, and shelves filled with local memorabilia. There's live Irish music daily.

J. W. Ryan. 28 Parkgate St., Dublin 7. ☎ **01/677-6097.**

A Victorian gem with a fine gourmet restaurant. You'll see some of Dublin's best traditional pub features, including a metal ceiling, a domed skylight, beveled mirrors, etched glass, brass lamp holders, a mahogany bar, and four old-style snugs. It's on the north side of the Liffey, near the Phoenix Park.

The Long Hall. 51 S. Great George's St., Dublin 2. ☎ **01/475-1590.**

Tucked into a busy commercial street, this is one of the city's most photographed pubs, with a beautiful Victorian decor of filigree-edged mirrors, polished dark woods, and traditional snugs. The hand-carved bar is said to be the longest counter in the city.

Neary's. 1 Chatham St., Dublin 2. ☎ **01/677-7371.**

Adjacent to the back door of the Gaiety Theatre, this celebrated enclave is a favorite with stage folk and theatergoers. Its trademarks are the pink-and-gray marble bar and the brass hands that support the globe lanterns adorning the entrance.

Palace Bar. 21 Fleet St., Dublin 2. ☎ **01/677-9290.**

This old charmer is decorated with local memorabilia, cartoons, and paintings that tell the story of Dublin through the years.

✪ **Stag's Head.** 1 Dame Court (off Dame St.), Dublin 2. ☎ **01/679-3701.**

Mounted stags' heads and eight stag-themed stained-glass windows dominate the decor, and there are wrought-iron chandeliers, polished Aberdeen granite, old barrels, skylights, and ceiling-high mirrors. Look for the stag sign inlaid into the sidewalk. This place is a classic.

PUBS WITH TRADITIONAL & FOLK MUSIC

✪ **Kitty O'Shea's.** 23–25 Upper Grand Canal St., Dublin 4. ☎ **01/660-9965.** No cover.

Just south of the Grand Canal, this popular pub is named after the sweetheart of 19th-century Irish statesman Charles Stewart Parnell. The decor reflects the Parnell era, with ornate oak paneling, stained-glass windows, old political posters, cozy alcoves, and brass railings. Traditional Irish music is on tap most every night.

Mother Red Caps Tavern. Back Lane, Dublin 8. ☎ **01/454-4655.** No cover except for concerts.

A former shoe factory in the heart of the Liberties section of the city, this large two-story pub exudes Old Dublin atmosphere. It has eclectic mahogany and stripped pine furnishings, antiques and curios on the shelves, and walls lined with old paintings and 19th-century newspaper clippings. On Sundays, there is usually a midday session of traditional Irish music; everyone is invited to bring an instrument and join in. On many nights, there is traditional music on an informal basis or in a concert setting upstairs.

O'Donoghue's. 15 Merrion Row, Dublin 2. ☎ **01/661-4303.** No cover for music.

Tucked between St. Stephen's Green and Merrion Street, this smoke-filled enclave is widely heralded as the granddaddy of traditional music pubs. A spontaneous session is likely to erupt at almost any time of the day or night.

Oliver St. John Gogarty. 57/58 Fleet St. ☎ **01/671-1822.**

Situated in the heart of Temple Bar and named for one of Ireland's literary greats, this pub has an inviting old-world atmosphere, with shelves of empty bottles, stacks of dusty books, a horseshoe-shaped bar, and old barrels for seats. There are traditional music sessions most every night from 9 to 11pm, as well as Saturday at 4:30pm, and Sunday from noon to 2pm.

LATE-NIGHT PUBS

If you're still going strong when the pubs shut down (11pm in winter, 11:30pm in summer), you might want to crawl to a "late-night pub"—one with a loophole allowing it to remain open after hours. Late-nighters for the 18-to-25 set include **Hogans,** 35 S. Great George's St., Dublin 2 (☎ **01/677-5904**), and the **Club mono** (see "More Music," below). After-hours pubs that attract the young and hip but are still congenial for those over 25 include **Whelans,** 25 Wexford St., Dublin 2 (☎ **01/ 478-0766**), and the second-oldest pub in Dublin, the **Bleeding Horse,** 24–25 Camden St., Dublin 2 (☎ **01/475-2705**). For the over-30 late crowd, these will fill the bill and the glass: **Break for the Border,** Lower Steven's Street, Dublin 2 (☎ **01/ 478-0300**); **Bad Bob's Backstage Bar,** East Essex Street, Dublin 2 (☎ **01/ 677-5482**); **Major Tom's,** South King Street, Dublin 2 (☎ **01/478-3266**); and **Sinnotts,** South King Street, Dublin 2 (☎ **01/478-4698**).

THE CLUB & MUSIC SCENE

Dublin's club and music scene is confoundingly complex and volatile. Jazz, blues, folk, country, traditional, rock, and comedy move from venue to venue, night by night. The same club could be a gay fetish scene one night and a traditional music hotspot the next, so you have to stay on your toes to find what you want. The first rule is to get the very latest listings and see what's on and where (see the introduction to "Dublin After Dark" for a couple of suggested resources). Keeping all this in mind, a few low-risk generalizations might prove helpful to give you a sense of what to expect.

One fact unlikely to change is that the night scene in Dublin is definitively young, with a retirement age of about 25. The only exceptions are some hotel venues that are outside the city center, very costly, or both. If you're over 25, your club choices are limited unless you happen to be a recognizable celebrity. In fact, even if you are or can pass for under 25, you may find yourself excluded unless you can present just the right image—a composite of outfit, hair, attitude, and natural endowment. Many of the most sizzling spots in Dublin (we'll call them trendy from here on) have a "strict" or "unfriendly" door policy, admitting only those who look and feel right for the scene within. The sought-after "look" might be unkindly described as "geek-chic" or, more neutrally, "retro."

Most trendy clubs have DJs and live music, and the genre of current choice is something called "rave," which I won't try to put into words. Another occasional ingredient of the trendy club scene in Dublin is "E" or "Ecstasy," the drug of choice among even the youngest clubgoers. Clubbers on "E" don't drink anything but water, which they must consume in great quantities. Though it may seem commonplace in this milieu, Ecstasy is both illegal and potentially lethal, and definitely not a wise vacation experience.

Cover charges tend to fluctuate not only from place to place, but from night to night and from person to person (some people can't buy their way in, while others glide in gratis). Average cover charges range from nominal to £10 ($14).

HIPPER THAN THOU

If you think you might pass muster, several of the more established cutting-edge clubs (with reputedly strict door policies) are the following:

The Kitchen. 6/8 Wellington Quay, Dublin 2. ☎ **01/677-6635.** Wed–Sun 11pm–2am.

In the basement of the Clarence Hotel in the heart of the Temple Bar district, this is one of Dublin's hottest, hippest nightclubs, partly owned by the rock group U2.

Lillie's Bordello. 45 Nassau St., Dublin 2. ☎ **01/679-9204.** Daily 10pm–1am or later.

This private three-story nightclub with two bars is open to members and nonmembers every night. The place has a stylish, self-consciously decadent ambience, with a mix of music every night.

POD. 35 Harcourt St., Dublin 2. ☎ **01/478-0166.** www.pod.ie. Wed–Sat 11pm–2am or later.

POD stands for "Place of Dance." Operated by John Reynolds (nephew of the former prime minister of Ireland, Albert Reynolds) the POD—a "European nightclub of the year"—has also won a European design award for its colorful Barcelona-inspired decor. It's as loud as it is dazzling to behold.

Republica. Earl of Kildare Hotel, Kildare St., Dublin 2. ☎ **01/679-4388.**

This is a new club to keep your eye on. When it opened in 1998, it was touted as the new benchmark in hip, with a really young scene. The fire didn't catch, however, and it changed management within a couple of months. Since then it has been widening its scene and finding its way.

Rí-Rá. 1 Exchequer St., Dublin 2. ☎ **01/677-4835.** Nightly 11:30pm–4am or later.

Though trendy, Rí-Rá has a friendlier door policy than most of its competition, so this may be the place to try first.

KINDER & GENTLER CLUBS

These established clubs, while they attract young singles and couples, have friendly door policies and are places where people of almost any age and ilk are likely to feel comfortable.

Annabel's. Burlington hotel, Upper Leeson St., Dublin 4. ☎ **01/660-5222.** Tues–Sat 10pm–2am.

Just south of the Lower Leeson Street nightclub strip, this club is one of the longest lasting in town. It welcomes a mix of tourists and locals of all ages with a disco party atmosphere.

Club M. Anglesea St., Dublin 2. ☎ **01/671-5622.** Tues–Sun 11pm–2am. Admission £5 ($7) Sun–Thurs, £7 ($9.80) Fri, £8 ($11.20) Sat.

In the basement of Blooms hotel, in the trendy Temple Bar district close to Trinity College, this club boasts Ireland's largest laser lighting system. It offers DJ-driven dance or live music for the over-23 age bracket.

Late-Night Bites

Although Dublin is keeping later and later hours, it is still nearly impossible to find anything approaching 24-hour dining. One place that comes close is the **Coffee Dock at Jurys Hotel,** Ballsbridge, Dublin 4 (☎ **01/660-5000**). It is open Monday 7am to 4:30am, Tuesday to Saturday 6am to 4:30am, Sunday 6am to 10:30pm. **Bewley's,** 78/79 Grafton St., Dublin 2 (☎ **01/677-6761**), is open until 1am on Friday and Saturday. **Juice,** 73–83 S. Great George's St., Dublin 2 (☎ **01/ 475-7856**), serves a limited menu Friday and Saturday until 4am.

YET MORE CLUBS

A few more places to try include **Court,** in the Harcourt Hotel, Harcourt Street, Dublin 2 (☎ **01/478-3677**); **Rumours,** in the Gresham Hotel, O'Connell Street, Dublin 1 (☎ **01/872-2850**); the **Vatican,** Harcourt Street, Dublin 2 (no phone— did you really expect to ring the Vatican?); and **Zanzibar,** Lower Ormond Quay, Dublin 1 (on the north side of the Liffey near Halfpenny Bridge; ☎ **01/ 878-7212**).

MORE MUSIC

For live music, there are several top choices. On a given night, you can find almost anything—jazz, blues, rock, traditional Irish, country, or folk. Rock was dominant in the 1980s—in the wake of U2's success—when Dublin spawned new bands weekly, but it is no longer in the front seat. Instead, there's a real mix, so again, check the listings. The principal live music venues include **Whelans,** 25 Wexford St., Dublin 2 (☎ **01/478-0766**); **Eamon Doran's** (mostly an under-25 crowd), 3A Crown Alley, Temple Bar, Dublin 2 (☎ **01/679-9114**); the **Club mono,** 26 Wexford St., Dublin 2 (☎ **01/475-8555**); and a real favorite, **Midnight at the Olympia,** 74 Dame St., Dublin 2 (☎ **01/677-7744**).

COMEDY CLUBS

The Irish comedy circuit is relatively new and quite popular. The timing, wit, and twist of mind required for comedy seems to me so native to the Irish that I find it difficult to draw a sharp line between those who practice comedy for a living and those who practice it as a way of life. You'll find both in the flourishing Dublin comedy clubs. Here are some of our favorites. Again, this is a mobile scene, so check the latest listing for details. Admission prices range from £4 ($5.60) to £15 ($21) depending on the night and the performer.

Comedy Improv/Comedy Cellar. International Bar, 23 Wicklow St., Dublin 2. ☎ **01/ 677-9250.**

A very small, packed venue, full of enthusiastic exchange. This is up-close, in-your-face improv, with nowhere to hide, so stake out your turf early.

Ha'Penny Bridge Inn. Beside Merchant's Arch, Wellington Quay, Dublin 2. ☎ **01/ 677-0616.**

Home to the Ha'Penny Laugh Improv Comedy Club and the Battle of the Axe. The former plays host to some of Ireland's funniest people, many of whom are on stage. The latter is a weekly show in which comedians, singers, songwriters, musicians, actors, and whoever storm the open mike in pursuit of the Lucky Duck Award.

Murphy's Laughter Lounge. O'Connell Bridge, Dublin 1. ☎ **1-800-COMEDY.**

This new 400-seat comedy venue is the current prime-time king of the Irish comedy circuit. It attracts the most popular stand-ups on the Irish scene—the O'Seinfelds, as it were—as well as international acts.

DINNER SHOWS & TRADITIONAL IRISH ENTERTAINMENT

Most of these shows are aimed at tourists, although locals also attend and enjoy them.

✪ **Abbey Tavern.** Abbey Rd., Howth, County Dublin. ☎ **01/839-0307.** Box office Mon–Sat 9am–5pm. Dinner 7pm, show 9pm; nightly in the summer months and 3 or 4 nights a week during the off-season, depending on demand. From Nov to Feb it's best to call ahead to find out on which nights shows will be offered.

After you've ordered an à la carte dinner, the show—authentic Irish ballad music, with its blend of fiddles, pipes, tin whistles, and spoons—costs an extra £3.50 ($4.90). The price of a full dinner and show averages £30 to £35 ($42–$49).

✪ **Culturlann Na hÉireann.** 32 Belgrave Sq., Monkstown, County Dublin. ☎ **01/280-0295.** www.comhaltas.com. Ceili dances Fri 9pm–midnight; informal music Fri–Sat 9:30–11:30pm; stage show mid-June to early Sept Mon–Thurs 9–10:30pm. Tickets for ceilis £5 ($7); informal music £1.50 ($2.10); stage show £6 ($8.40). DART: Monkstown. Bus: 7, 7A, or 8.

This is the home of Comhaltas Ceoltoiri Éireann, an Irish cultural organization that has been the prime mover in encouraging a renewed appreciation of and interest in Irish traditional music. The year-round entertainment programs include old-fashioned ceili dances and informal music sessions. In the summer, there's an authentic fully costumed show featuring traditional music, song, and dance. No reservations are necessary for any of the events.

Jurys Irish Cabaret. In Jurys Hotel and Towers, Pembroke Rd., Ballsbridge, Dublin 4. ☎ **01/660-5000.** May–Oct Tues–Sun dinner 7:15pm, show 8pm. Tickets £39 ($54.60). AE, DC, MC, V. Free parking. DART: Lansdowne Rd. Bus: 5, 7, 7A, or 8.

Ireland's longest-running show (more than 30 years) offers a unique mix. You'll see and hear traditional Irish and international music, rousing ballads and Broadway classics, toe-tapping set dancing and graceful ballet, humorous monologues and telling recitations, plus audience participation.

THE GAY & LESBIAN SCENE

New gay and lesbian bars, clubs, and venues appear monthly, it seems, and many clubs and organizations, such as the Irish Film Centre, have special gay events or evenings once a week to once a month. The social scene ranges from quiet pub conversation and dancing to fetish nights and hilarious contests. Cover charges range from £3 to £10 ($4.20 to $14), depending on the club or venue, with discounts for students and seniors.

Check the *Gay Community News, In Dublin, The Event Guide,* or "Dublin's Pink Pages" (http://indigo.ie/~outhouse/) for the latest listings. Folks on the help lines, **Lesbians Organizing Together** (☎ 01/872-7770) and **Gay Switchboard Dublin** (☎ 01/872-1055), are also extremely helpful in directing you to activities of particular interest. (See "Tips for Travelers with Special Needs," in chapter 2, for details on many of these resources.)

The George Bar and Night Club. 89 S. Great George's St., Dublin 2. ☎ **01/478-2983.** Admission £3–£7 ($4.20–$9.80). Daily 12:30–11pm; Wed–Sun 12:30pm–2:30am. DART: Tara St. Bus: 22A.

The George was the first gay bar in Dublin. It now houses two bars—one quiet and the other trendy, with dance music—and an after-hours nightclub, the Block, upstairs. It is a comfortable mixed-age venue. The nightclub hours are daily (except Tues and Wed) 9:30pm to 2am. Theme nights include "Carwash," a 1970s disco night every Thursday and bingo in the bar Sundays at 5pm.

Out on the Liffey. 27 Upper Ormond Quay, Dublin 1. ☎ **01/872-2480.** DART: Tara St. Walk up the Liffey and cross at Parliament Bridge. Bus: 34, 70, or 80.

A 1996 addition to the gay and lesbian scene, this relaxed, friendly pub caters to a balance of men and women and serves up pub food with good conversation. In 1998, "Out" expanded to include a happening late-night venue, Oscar's, where you can dance (or drink) until you drop.

Stonewallz. Molloy's Bar, High Street (beside Christchurch), Dublin 8. ☎ **01/872-7770.** Admission £4 ($5.60). No credit cards. Fri 10:30pm–2am. Bus: 21A, 50, 50A, 78, 78A, or 78B.

Stonewallz, one of Dublin's most popular women-only clubs, has moved to a new, more central, and expanded venue, offering three floors of music, each with its own style.

THE PERFORMING ARTS
THEATER
Dublin has a venerable and vital theatrical tradition, in which imagination and talent have consistently outstripped funding. Apart from some mammoth shows at the Point, production budgets and ticket prices remain modest, even minuscule, compared with those in New York or any other major U.S. city. With the exception of a handful of houses that offer a more or less uninterrupted flow of productions, most theaters mount shows only as they find the funds and opportunity to do so. A few venerable (or at least well-established) theaters offer serious drama more or less regularly.

In addition to the major theaters listed below, other venues present fewer, although on occasion quite impressive, productions. They also book music and dance performances. They include the **Focus Theatre,** 6 Pembroke Place, off Pembroke Street, Dublin 2 (☎ **01/676-3071**); the **Gaiety Theatre,** South King Street, Dublin 2 (☎ **01/677-1717**); the **Olympia,** 72 Dame St., Dublin 2 (☎ **01/677-7744**); the **Players,** Trinity College, Dublin 2 (☎ **01/677-3370,** ext. 1239); the **Project@The Mint,** Henry Place, off Henry Street, Dublin 1 (☎ **1850-260027**); and the **Tivoli,** 135–138 Francis St., opposite Iveagh Market, Dublin 8 (☎ **01/454-4472**).

✪ **Abbey Theatre.** Lower Abbey St., Dublin 1. ☎ **01/878-7222.** www.abbeytheatre.ie. Box office Mon–Sat 10:30am–7pm; shows Mon–Sat 8pm, Sat 2:30pm. Tickets £8–£16 ($11.20–$22.40). Senior, student, and children's discounts available Mon–Thurs evening and Sat matinee.

For more than 90 years, the Abbey has been the national theater of Ireland. The original theater, destroyed by fire in 1951, was replaced in 1966 by the current functional, although uninspired, 600-seat house. The Abbey's artistic reputation in Ireland has risen and fallen many times and is at present reasonably strong.

Andrews Lane Theatre. 9–17 St. Andrews Lane, Dublin 2. ☎ **01/679-5720.** Box office Mon–Sat 10:30am–7pm; shows Mon–Sat 8pm in theater, 8:15pm in studio. Tickets £8–£12 ($11.20–$16.80).

This relatively new venue has an ascending reputation for fine theater. It consists of a 220-seat main theater where contemporary work from home and abroad is presented, and a 76-seat studio geared for experimental productions.

The City Arts Centre. 23–25 Moss St., at City Quay. ☎ **01/677-0643.**

The City Arts Centre is an affiliate of Trans Europe Halles, the European network of independent arts centers. It presents a varied program, from dramatic productions, theatrical discussions, and readings by local writers to shows by touring companies from abroad. In May 2000, it was home to the World Stories Festival. Average ticket prices range from £5 to £7 ($7 to $9.80).

The Gate. 1 Cavendish Row, Dublin 1. ☎ **01/874-4368.** Box office Mon–Sat 10am–7pm; shows Mon–Sat 8pm. Tickets £13–£15 ($18.20–$21) or £10 ($14) for previews. AE, DC, MC, V.

Just north of O'Connell Street off Parnell Square, this recently restored 370-seat theater was founded in 1928 by Hilton Edwards and Michael MacLiammoir to provide a venue for a broad range of plays. That policy prevails today, with a program that includes a blend of modern works and the classics. Although less known by visitors, the Gate is easily as distinguished as the Abbey.

The Peacock. Lower Abbey St., Dublin 1. ☎ **01/878-7222.** www.abbeytheatre.ie. Box office Mon–Sat 10:30am–7pm; shows Mon–Sat 8:15pm, Sat 2:45pm. Tickets £5–£12 ($7–$16.80).

In the same building as the Abbey, this 150-seat theater features contemporary plays and experimental works. It books poetry readings and one-person shows, as well as plays in the Irish language.

CONCERTS

Music and dance concerts take place in a range of Dublin venues—theaters, churches, clubs, museums, sports stadiums, castles, parks, and universities—all of which can be found in local listings. The three institutions listed below stand out as venues where most world-class performances take place.

National Concert Hall. Earlsfort Terrace, Dublin 2. ☎ **01/475-1572.** www.nch.ie. Box office Mon–Sat 11am–7pm, Sun (on performance days) from 7pm. Tickets £8–£25 ($11.20–$35). Lunchtime concerts £4 ($5.60). DC, MC, V.

This magnificent 1,200-seat hall is home to the National Symphony Orchestra and Concert Orchestra, and host to an array of international orchestras and performing artists. In addition to classical music, there are evenings of Gilbert and Sullivan, opera, jazz, and recitals. The box office is open Monday to Friday from 10am to 3pm and from 6pm to close of concert. Open weekends 1 hour before concerts. Parking is available on the street.

The Point. East Link Bridge, North Wall Quay. ☎ **01/836-3633.** Tickets £10–£50 ($14–$70). AE, DC, MC, V.

With a seating capacity of 3,000, The Point is Ireland's newest large theater/concert venue, attracting top Broadway-caliber shows and international stars. The box office is open Monday to Saturday 10am to 6pm. Parking is £3 ($4.20) per car.

Royal Dublin Society (RDS). Merrion Rd., Ballsbridge, Dublin 2. ☎ **01/668-0645.** www.rds.ie. Box office hours vary according to events; shows 8pm. Most tickets £10–£30 ($14–$42).

Although best known as the venue for the Dublin Horse Show, this huge show-jumping arena is also the setting for major music concerts. It holds seating and standing room for more than 6,000 people.

10 Side Trips from Dublin

Fanning out a little over 12 miles (19km) in each direction, Dublin's southern and northern suburbs offer a variety of interesting sights and experiences. All are easy to reach by public transportation or rental car.

DUBLIN'S SOUTHERN SUBURBS

Stretching southward from Ballsbridge, Dublin's prime southern suburbs, **Dun Laoghaire,** ✪ **Dalkey,** and **Killiney,** are on the edge of Dublin Bay. They all offer lovely seaside views and walks. Dun Laoghaire has a long promenade and a bucolic park, Killiney has a stunning expanse of beach, and Dalkey has something for just about everyone.

Thanks to DART service, these towns are easily accessible from downtown Dublin. They offer a good selection of restaurants and fine places to stay. A hillside overlooking Dublin Bay outside the village of Killiney is the setting for the Dublin area's only authentic deluxe castle hotel, Fitzpatrick Castle (see "Accommodations," below).

If you're traveling to Ireland by ferry from Holyhead, Wales, your first glimpse of Ireland will be the port of Dun Laoghaire. Many people decide to base themselves here and commute into downtown Dublin each day. As a base, it is less expensive than Dalkey, but less attractive too.

ATTRACTIONS

Dalkey Castle and Heritage Centre. Castle St., Dalkey, County Dublin. ☎ **01/ 285-8366.** Admission £2.50 ($3.50) adults, £2 ($2.80) seniors and students, £1.50 ($2.10) children, £8 ($11.20) family. Apr–Oct Mon–Fri 9:30am–5pm, Sat–Sun 11am–5pm; Nov–Mar Sat–Sun 11am–5pm DART: Dalkey. Bus: 8.

The lovely seaside village of Dalkey, on the southern edge of the ancient Pale, makes a memorable outing, whether for several hours or for an entire day. However long your stay, Dalkey's Heritage Centre, housed in a 16th-century tower house, is the place to begin. Its fascinating exhibitions unfold this venerable town's remarkable history. Then, from the center's battlements, you can put it all in place as well as enjoy vistas of the Dublin area coastline. Adjoining the center is a medieval graveyard and the Church of St. Begnet, Dalkey's patron saint, whose foundations may be traced to Ireland's Early Christian period. Booklets sketching the history of the town, the church, and the graveyard are available at the Heritage Centre. You'll see and appreciate more of this landmark town if you purchase these and take them next door to the Queens Bar for a pint and quick scan. "Those who are patient," wrote the playwright Hugh Leonard, "and will sit, wait and listen or will linger along the tree-shaded roads running down to the sea, can hear the centuries pass."

The Ferryman. Coliemore Rd. (at stone wharf, adjacent to a seaside apartment complex). ☎ **01/283-4298.** Island ferry round-trip £5 ($7) adults, £3 ($4.20) children; rowboat rental £8 ($11.20)/hr. June–Aug, weather permitting.

Young Aidan Fennel heads the third generation of Fennels to ferry visitors to nearby Dalkey Island, whose only current inhabitants are a small herd of wild goats and the occasional seal. Aidan is a boat builder, and his brightly painted fleet is mostly from his hand. The island, settled about 6000 B.C., offers three modest ruins: a church that's over 1,000 years old, ramparts dating from the 15th century, and a martello tower constructed in 1804 to make Napoleon think twice. Now the island is little more than a lovely picnic spot. If you want to build up an appetite and delight your children or sweetheart, row out in one of Aidan's handmade boats.

Impressions

The Torca Shoulder of Dalkey Hill, the Telegraph Hill overlooking the two bays from Dalkey Island northward to Howth and southward to Bray, is not surpassed in its view of mountain, sea and sky . . . anywhere I have been. It is the beauty of Ireland that has made us what we are. I am the product of Dalkey's outlook.

—George Bernard Shaw (1856–1950)

James Joyce Museum. Sandycove, County Dublin. ☎ **01/280-9265.** Admission £2.70 ($3.80) adults, £2.20 ($3.10) seniors and students, £1.40 ($1.95) children, £7.95 ($11.15) family. Apr–Oct Mon–Sat 10am–1pm and 2–5pm; Sun 2–6pm. Closed Nov–Mar. DART: Sandycove. Bus: 8.

Sitting on the edge of Dublin Bay about 6 miles (9.7km) south of the city center, this 40-foot granite monument is one of a series of martello towers built in 1804 to withstand an invasion threatened by Napoleon. The tower's great claim to fame is that James Joyce lived here in 1904. He was the guest of Oliver Gogarty, who had rented the tower from the Army for an annual fee of £8 ($11.20). Joyce, in turn, made the tower the setting for the first chapter of *Ulysses,* and it has been known as Joyce's Tower ever since. Its collection of Joycean memorabilia includes letters, documents, first and rare editions, personal possessions, and photographs.

ACCOMMODATIONS
Expensive
✪ **Fitzpatrick Castle Hotel.** Killiney Hill Rd., Killiney, County Dublin. ☎ **01/284-0700.** Fax 01/285-0207. www.fitzpatrickhotels.com. 113 units. TV TEL. £149–£178 ($208.60–$249.20) double. No service charge. Breakfast £10.50 ($14.70). AE, DC, MC, V. DART: Dalkey. Bus: 59.

With a fanciful Victorian facade of turrets, towers, and battlements, this restored 1741 gem is an ideal choice for those who want to live like royalty. A 15-minute drive from the center of the city, it is between the villages of Dalkey and Killiney, on 9 acres of gardens and hilltop grounds with romantic vistas of Dublin Bay. Two generations of the Fitzpatrick family pamper guests with 20th-century comforts in a regal setting of medieval suits of armor, Louis XIV–style furnishings, Irish antiques, original oil paintings, and specially woven shamrock-pattern green carpets. Most of the guest rooms have four-poster or canopy not-so-firm beds, and many have balconies with sweeping views of Dublin and the surrounding countryside. Nonsmoking rooms are available. In spite of its size and exacting standards, the castle never fails to exude a friendly, family-run atmosphere.

Dining/Diversions: Choices include a Victorian-style French and Irish restaurant, Truffles; the Castle Grill for informal meals; the posh Cocktail Bar; and the Dungeon, a pub and nightclub.

Amenities: 24-hour room service, concierge, laundry service, courtesy minibus service to downtown and the airport, indoor swimming pool, gym, saunas, squash and tennis courts, hairdressing salon, guest privileges at nearby 18-hole golf course.

Royal Marine. Marine Rd., Dun Laoghaire, County Dublin. ☎ **800/44-UTELL** from the U.S., or 01/280-1911. Fax 01/280-1089. www.ryan-hotels.com. 103 units. TV TEL. £90–£220 ($126–$308) double. Rates include full breakfast and service charge. AE, DC, MC, V. DART: Dun Laoghaire. Bus: 7, 7A, or 8.

A tradition along the seafront since 1870, this four- and five-story landmark sits on a hill overlooking the harbor, 7 miles (11km) south of Dublin City. It's a good place to

Side Trips from Dublin

Balbriggan

Bernagearagh Bay

R127

7

Skerries

8 9 10

St. Patrick's Island

Shenick's Island

N1

R127

R128

R108

R126

11 Donabate

Lambay Island

Swords

12

R106

Malahide

13 14

Irish Sea

R106

R122

N1

Dublin Airport ✈

M1

6

Portmarnock

Ireland's Eye

R107

Sutton   Howth

16 17 18

N2 **3 4**

R104

2 R103 **5**

15

▲ Ben of Howth

R105

N3

Clontarf

North Bull Island

N4 ★ DUBLIN

Dublin Bay

Liffey

N7

Royal Canal

R119

N11

R117

R112

Dun Laoghaire

19 20 21 22

23 24 25

Sandycove

26 Dalkey Island

Dalkey

R113

Dalkey Hill ▲
Killiney Hill ▲

27 28 29 30

31

To Shankill ↓

Killiney

32

0   2 1/2 mi
0   2.5 km

NORTHERN IRELAND

Dublin ★

REPUBLIC OF IRELAND

Attractions ●
Ardgillan Castle **7**
Casino Marino **5**
Dalkey Castle Heritage
    Centre **30**
Ferryman **26**
Fry Model Railway **13**
Howth Castle Gardens **15**
James Joyce Museum **23**
Malahide Castle **14**
National Botanic Gardens **2**
Newbridge House
    & Park **11**
Skerries Mills **8**

Accommodations ■
The Court **32**
Doyle Skylon **1**
Egan's House **3**
Fitzpatrick's Castle **31**
Forte Travelodge **12**
Iona House **4**
Posthouse **6**
Redbank Guesthouse & Lodge **9**
Royal Marine **19**
Tudor House **25**

Dining ◆
Abbey Tavern **16**
Brasserie na Mara **21**
Caviston's **22**
Dee Gee's Wine & Steak Bar **17**
De Selby's **20**
Guinea Pig **27**
King Sitric **18**
Munkberrys **29**
P.D.'s Woodhouse **24**
Redbank Restaurant **10**
The Queens Bar & Restaurant **28**

stay for ready access to the ferry across the Irish Sea to and from Wales. Basically a Georgian building with a wing of modern rooms, the Royal Marine has public areas that have been beautifully restored and recently refurbished, with original molded ceilings and elaborate cornices, crystal chandeliers, marble-mantled fireplaces, and antique furnishings. The rooms, many of which offer wide-windowed views of the bay, carry through the Georgian theme, with dark woods, traditional floral fabrics, and four-poster or canopy beds. Some newer rooms have light woods and pastel tones. All units have up-to-date facilities, including hair dryers and garment presses.

Dining/Diversions: The dining room has a panoramic view of the bay, and there's a lounge bar.

Amenities: 24-hour room service, concierge, laundry service.

Moderate

The Court Hotel. Killiney Bay Rd., Killiney, County Dublin. ☎ **800/221-2222** from the U.S. Fax 01/285-2085. www.killineycourt.ie. 86 units. TV TEL. £89–£134 ($124.60–$187.60) double. Rates include full Irish breakfast and service charge. AE, DC, MC, V. DART: Killiney. Bus: 59.

Situated on 4 acres of gardens and lawns, this three-story Victorian hotel enjoys a splendid location overlooking Killiney Bay and convenient access to Dublin (the DART station is nearby). The hotel's multiple lounges and popular restaurants were recently refurbished and are bright and welcoming. The guest rooms, many of which have views of the bay, are adequate but unremarkable. There's a concierge, and room service and laundry service are available. The real draw of this hotel is its lovely setting, which is convenient for excursions to Dublin as well as evening strolls on one of the most beautiful beaches on Ireland's east coast.

Note: The Court will give up to a 20% discount to guests carrying this guide.

Tudor House. Dalkey (off Castle St. between the church and Archbolds Castle), County Dublin. ☎ **01/285-1528.** Fax 01/284-8133. www.iol.ie/tudor. 6 units (all with shower only). TV TEL. £70–£90 ($98–$126) double. Rates include full breakfast and service charge. MC, V. DART: Dalkey, then 7-min. walk.

This handsome Gothic Revival Victorian manor house, built in 1848, has been lovingly restored to its original elegance by Katie and Peter Haydon. Set back from the town center, nestled behind a church, Tudor House rises to give all the guest rooms a pleasing view of Dublin Bay over the roof and treetops of Dalkey. The decor is tasteful and serene, enhanced by antiques and fresh flowers. The blue Wedgwood Room is particularly spacious and offers a firm double bed beneath a glittering chandelier; down the hall, the cozy corner room is bright and comfortable, with twin beds. The nearby DART commuter rail cannot be seen but may be heard by a light sleeper; the Dun Laoghaire ferry port is 1¾ miles (2.8km) away. Business and touring guests alike appreciate the splendid breakfast and helpful attention of the knowledgeable hosts. The Haydons can arrange baby-sitting, laundry, dry cleaning, fax, and Internet services.

DINING

Expensive

Brasserie na Mara. Harbour, Dun Laoghaire, County Dublin. ☎ **01/280-6767.** Reservations required. 4-course table d'hôte lunch £12.95 ($18.15); 4-course fixed-price dinner £20.95 ($29.35); main courses £10–£16 ($14–$22.40). Mon–Fri 12:30–2:30pm; Mon–Sat 6:30–10pm. DART: Dun Laoghaire. Bus: 7, 7A, 8, or 46A. SEAFOOD/CONTEMPORARY IRISH.

Award-winning chef Adrian Spelman keeps this fine seafood restaurant high on the charts, even in ever-steepening competition. Set squarely in the bustle of Dun Laoghaire's busy seafront, this elegant restaurant has been a benchmark for South Dublin cuisine since 1971. In addition to the house specialty, seafood, you can count on an array of poultry and meat dishes, from guinea fowl to Irish beef, as well as vegetarian options. Flaming desserts—another specialty—provide both high drama and suitable closure.

Guinea Pig. 17 Railway Rd., Dalkey, County Dublin. ☎ **01/285-9055.** Reservations required. 5-course table d'hôte £28.50 ($39.90); special-value menu Sun–Fri 6–8pm, Sat 6–7pm £14.50 ($20.20). AE, DC, MC, V. Sun 5–9:30pm; Mon–Sat 5:30–11:30pm. DART: Dalkey. Bus: 8. SEAFOOD/FRENCH.

The Guinea Pig, like its namesake, is small and easily overlooked, but to do so would be a loss—it's a fine restaurant with a well-deserved following. The menu emphasizes whatever is freshest and in season. It often includes a signature dish called *symphony de la mer* (a potpourri of fish and crustaceans), wild salmon with coriander sauce, fillets of lemon sole with cockle and mussel sauce, and rack of lamb. While offering a worthy wine list, the Guinea Pig also offers a surprisingly adequate house white and red for a fraction of the price of their rack-mates. The culinary domain of chef-owner Mervyn Stewart, a former mayor of Dalkey, the restaurant is decorated in Irish country style with Victorian touches.

Moderate

Caviston's Seafood Restaurant. 59 Glasthule Rd., Dun Laoghaire, County Dublin. ☎ **01/ 280-2715.** Reservations recommended. Main courses £7.50–£15 ($10.50–$21). DC, MC, V. Tues–Sat 3 sittings: noon, 1:30pm, 3pm. SEAFOOD.

Fresh, fresh fish is the hallmark of this tiny restaurant in Dun Laoghaire. It's run by the Caviston family, whose neighboring delicatessen and fish shop is legendary. There's no doubt that such expertise in scales and fins transfers to the preparation of fish in the restaurant itself: fish dishes are simply prepared, depending on one or two well-chosen ingredients to enhance delicate flavors. Unfortunately, the pleasure of lunch here dissipates quickly under the impatient influence of a waitstaff who rush diners in order to accommodate three lunchtime sittings.

De Selby's. 17/18 Patrick St. (off George's St.), Dun Laoghaire, County Dublin. ☎ **01/ 284-1761.** Reservations recommended. Dinner main courses £6.95–£13.95 ($9.75–$19.55). AE, CB, DC, MC, V. Mon–Thurs noon–2:30pm and 5–10pm; Fri–Sat noon–2:30pm and 5–11pm; Sun noon–10pm. DART: Dun Laoghaire. Bus: 7, 7A, 8, or 46A. INTERNATIONAL.

Named after a self-styled Dun Laoghaire philosopher in a Flann O'Brien book, this restaurant is in the center of the town. Its partially restored brick walls and fresh decor are accompanied by a new menu, which features more fresh fish entrees. There's also an outdoor eating area. The menu includes traditional Irish stew, Dublin Bay scampi, salmon en croûte, grilled lamb cutlets, steaks, and burgers. It's a busy spot, especially on weekends, patronized by those enjoying a day's outing at the seaport.

Munkberrys. Castle St., Dalkey, County Dublin. ☎ **01/284-7185.** Reservations recommended. 4-course fixed-price dinner £21.95 ($30.75). Main courses £8.50–£15.50 ($11.90–$21.70). Early-bird fixed-price dinner (Mon–Sat 5:30–7pm) £14.95 ($20.95). AE, DC, MC, V. Mon–Fri noon–2:30pm; Mon–Fri 5:30–10pm; Sat 5:30–10:30pm; Sun noon–6pm. DART: Dalkey. CONTINENTAL.

Crisp linens, candlelit glass, and tasteful contemporary art lend an immediate calm to this intimate street-front restaurant. The excitement here lies in the food, provoking at once both the eye and the palate. The crostini of goats cheese with fresh figs and spicy tomato chutney arrived on a swirl of delicious and mysterious sauces. The spinach ricotta tortelloni with a stilton, pistachio, and cognac sauce and the roast fillet of salmon with a saffron vermouth sauce were perfectly prepared and elegant to behold. It was a struggle to decide between the lemon crème brûlée with hazelnut biscuit, the steamed date pudding with butterscotch, and the Italian ice cream. While the service is especially attentive, there is no appreciable separation of smokers and nonsmokers, who are potentially at arm's length from each other. Nonsmokers may want to arrive early and ask for whatever isolation is possible.

✪ **P.D.'s Woodhouse.** 1 Coliemore Rd., Dalkey center, County Dublin. ☎ **01/284-9399.** Reservations recommended. Main courses £7.95–£15.95 ($11.15–$23.35). Service charge 10%. AE, CB, DC, MC, V. Mon–Sat 6–11pm; Sun 4–9:30pm. DART: Dalkey. IRISH/ MEDITERRANEAN.

This restaurant is brought to you by Hurricane Charlie, the worst tropical storm to hit Ireland in recent memory. The first and only oak-wood barbecue bistro in Ireland, P.D.'s Woodhouse depends on oaks ripped up by Charlie and stored in Wicklow. Like Charlie, the wild Irish salmon in caper and herb butter is devastating, as is the white sole. But whatever you do, don't miss the Halumi cheese kebabs—conversation-stopping grilled Greek goat cheese. On the other hand, the nut kebabs, one of several vegetarian entrees, are unnecessarily austere.

✪ **The Queens Bar and Restaurant.** 12 Castle St., Dalkey, County Dublin. ☎ **01/ 285-4569.** Reservations not accepted. Dinner main courses £7.85–£13.95 ($11–$19.55); bar menu £1.90–£7.25 ($2.65–$10.15). AE, DC, MC, V. Bar daily noon–midnight; bar food Mon–Sat noon–5pm, Sun 12:30–5pm. Restaurant Mon–Sat 6–11pm, Sun 6–10pm. DART: Dalkey. Bus: 8. INTERNATIONAL.

One of Ireland's oldest inns, this historic establishment has won a pocketful of awards, including Dublin's best pub in 1992. It has great atmosphere and food to match. In the center of town, the informal trattoria has an open kitchen—a contrast to the usual pub grub. The low end of the menu leans toward pastas and pizzas, while the high end includes spicy Jamaican jerk chicken, T-bone steak, roast half crispy duck, and the catch of the day. In addition, there are daily specials and an interesting selection of antipasti. Upstairs, a recent development, the Vico Restaurant and Piano Bar, adds new flavors and style to this revered and flourishing establishment.

PUBS

P. McCormack and Sons. 67 Lower Mounttown Rd. (off York Rd.), Dun Laoghaire, County Dublin. ☎ **01/284-2634.**

If you rent a car and head toward the city's southern seaside suburbs, this is a great place to stop for refreshment. Park in the lot and step into the atmosphere of your choice. The main section has an old-world feel, with globe lamps, stained-glass windows, books and jugs on the shelves, and lots of nooks and crannies for a quiet drink. In the skylit, plant-filled conservatory area, classical music fills the air, and out-doors you'll find a festive courtyard beer garden. The pub grub here is top-notch, with a varied buffet table of lunchtime salads and meats.

The Purty Kitchen. Old Dunleary Rd., Dun Laoghaire, County Dublin. ☎ **01/284-3576.** No cover for traditional music; cover £5–£6 ($7–$8.40) for blues and rock in the Loft.

Housed in a building that dates from 1728, this old pub has a homey atmosphere, with an open brick fireplace, cozy alcoves, a large fish mural, and pub poster art on the walls. There's often free Irish traditional music in the main bar area (the schedule varies, so call ahead). Blues and rock musicians play upstairs in the Loft on Thursday and Sunday at 9pm, and there's dance music with a DJ on Friday and Saturday at 9pm.

DUBLIN'S NORTHERN SUBURBS

Dublin's northern suburbs are best known as the home of **Dublin International Airport,** but they're also home to a delightful assortment of castles, historic buildings, gardens, and other attractions. In addition, the residential suburbs of **Drumcondra** and **Glasnevin** offer many good lodgings.

Just north of Dublin, the picturesque suburb of **Howth** offers panoramic views of Dublin Bay, beautiful hillside gardens, and many fine seafood restaurants. Best of all, it is easily reached on the DART. Farther north along the coast, but only 20 minutes from Dublin Airport, lies the bustling and attractive seaside town of **Skerries.** Skerries is a convenient and appealing spot to spend your first or last night in Ireland; or stay longer and explore all this area has to offer, including a resident colony of grey seals and the lowest annual rainfall in Ireland.

ATTRACTIONS

Ardgillan Castle and Park. Balbriggan, County Dublin. ☎ **01/849-2212.** Admission to house £3 ($4.20) adults, £2 ($2.80) seniors and students, £6.50 ($9.10) family. Castle open Oct–Dec and Feb–Mar Tues–Sun 11am–4:30pm; Apr–June Tues–Sun 11am–6pm; July–Aug daily 11am–6pm; Sept Tues–Sun 11am–6pm. Park open daily dawn to dusk. Closed Jan. Free parking year-round. Signposted off N1. Bus: 33.

Between Balbriggan and Skerries, north of Malahide, this recently restored 18th-century castellated country house sits right on the coastline. The house, home of the Taylour family until 1962, was built in 1738. It contains some fine period furnishings and antiques, as well as a public tearoom. But the real draw is the setting, right on the edge of the Irish Sea, with miles of walking paths and coastal views as well as a rose garden and an herb garden.

Casino Marino. Malahide Rd., Marino, Dublin 3. ☎ **01/833-1618.** Admission £2 ($2.80) adults, £1.50 ($2.10) seniors and group members, £1 ($1.40) students and children, £5 ($7) family. Feb–Apr and Nov Sun and Thurs noon–4pm; May and Oct daily 10am–5pm; June–Sept daily 9:30am–6:30pm. Closed Dec–Jan. Bus: 20A, 20B, 27, 27A, 27B, 42, 42B, or 42C.

Standing on a gentle rise 3 miles (4.8km) north of the city center, this 18th-century building is considered one of the finest garden temples in Europe. Designed in the Franco-Roman neoclassical style by Scottish architect Sir William Chambers, it was constructed in the garden of Lord Charlemont's house by the English sculptor Simon Vierpyl. Work commenced in 1762 and was completed 15 years later. It is particularly noteworthy for its elaborate stone carvings and compact structure, which make it appear to be a single story (it is actually two stories tall).

The Fry Model Railway. Malahide, County Dublin. ☎ **01/846-3779.** Admission £2.90 ($4.05) adults, £2.20 ($3.10) seniors and students, £1.70 ($2.40) children, £7.95 ($11.15) family. Apr–Oct Mon–Sat 10am–5pm, Sun 2–6pm; Nov–Mar Sun 2–5pm. Closed for tours 1–2pm year-round. Suburban Rail to Malahide. Bus: 42.

On the grounds of Malahide Castle (see listing below), this is an exhibit of rare hand-made models of more than 300 Irish trains, from the introduction of rail to the present. The trains were built in the 1920s and 1930s by Cyril Fry, a railway engineer and draftsman. The complex includes items of Irish railway history dating from 1834, and models of stations, bridges, trams, buses, barges, boats, the River Liffey, and the Hill of Howth.

Howth Castle Rhododendron Gardens. Howth, County Dublin. ☎ **01/832-2624.** Free admission. Apr–June daily 8am–sunset. DART: Howth. Bus: 31.

On a steep slope about 8 miles (13km) north of downtown, this 30-acre garden was first planted in 1875 and is best known for its 2,000 varieties of rhododendrons. Peak bloom time is in May and June. *Note:* The castle and its private gardens are not open to the public.

✪ Malahide Castle. Malahide, County Dublin. ☎ **01/846-2184.** E-mail: malahidecastle@ dublintourism.ie. Admission £3.15 ($4.40) adults, £2.65 ($3.70) students and seniors, £1.75 ($2.45) children under 12, £8.75 ($12.90) family; gardens free. AE, MC, V. Combination tickets with Fry Model Railway and Newbridge House available. Apr–Oct Mon–Sat 10am–5pm, Sun 11am–6pm; Nov–Mar Mon–Fri 10am–5pm, Sat–Sun 2–5pm; gardens May–Sept daily 2–5pm. Closed for tours 12:45–2pm (restaurant remains open). Suburban Rail to Malahide. Bus: 42.

About 8 miles (13km) north of Dublin, Malahide is one of Ireland's most historic castles. Founded in the 12th century by Richard Talbot, it was occupied by his descendants until 1973. The fully restored interior is the setting for a comprehensive collection of Irish furniture, dating from the 17th to the 19th centuries. One-of-a-kind Irish historical portraits and tableaux on loan from the National Gallery line the walls. The furnishings and art reflect life in and near the house over the past 8 centuries.

After touring the house, you can explore the 250-acre estate, which includes 20 acres of prized **gardens** with more than 5,000 species of plants and flowers. The Malahide grounds also contain the **Fry Model Railway** museum (see above) and **Tara's Palace,** an antique dollhouse and toy collection.

✪ National Botanic Gardens. Botanic Rd., Glasnevin, Dublin 9. ☎ **01/837-7596.** Free admission. Guided tour £1.50 ($2.25). Apr–Oct Mon–Sat 9am–6pm and Sun 11am–6pm; Nov–Mar Mon–Sat 10am–4:30pm and Sun 11am–4:30pm. Bus: 13, 19, or 134.

Established by the Royal Dublin Society in 1795 on a rolling 50-acre expanse of land north of the city center, this is Dublin's horticultural showcase. The attractions include more than 20,000 different plants and cultivars, a Great Yew Walk, a bog garden, a water garden, a rose garden, and an herb garden. A variety of Victorian-style glass houses are filled with tropical plants and exotic species. Remember this spot when you suddenly crave refuge from the bustle of the city. It's a quiet, lovely haven, within a short walk of Glasnevin Cemetery. All but the rose garden is wheelchair accessible. Parking is free for now, but a fee is being considered for later in 2000 or 2001.

Newbridge House and Park. Donabate, County Dublin. ☎ **01/843-6534.** Admission £3 ($4.20) adults, £2.60 ($3.65) seniors and students, £1.65 ($2.30) children, £8.25 ($11.55) family. Apr–Sept Tues–Sat 10am–1pm and 2–5pm, Sun 2–6pm; Oct–Mar Sat–Sun 2–5pm. Suburban rail to Donabate. Bus: 33B.

This country mansion 12 miles (19km) north of Dublin dates from 1740 and was once the home of Dr. Charles Cobbe, an archbishop of Dublin. Occupied by the Cobbe family until 1984, the house is a showcase of family memorabilia such as hand-carved furniture, portraits, daybooks, and dolls, as well as a museum of objects collected on world travels. The Great Drawing Room, in its original state, is reputed to be one of the finest Georgian interiors in Ireland. The house sits on 350 acres, laid out with picnic areas and walking trails. The grounds also include a 20-acre working Victorian farm stocked with animals, as well as a craft shop and a coffee shop. The coffee shop remains open during the lunch hour (1 to 2pm).

Skerries Mills. Skerries, County Dublin. ☎ **01/849-5208.** http://indigo.ie/~skerries. Admission £3 ($4.20) adults; £2.25 (3.15) seniors, students, and children; £7.50 ($10.50) family. Apr–Sept daily 10:30am–6pm; Oct–Mar daily 10:30am–4:30pm. Closed Dec 20–Jan 1. Suburban Rail. Bus: 33. Skerries town and the Mills signposted North of Dublin off the N1.

This fascinating new 45-acre historical complex has been open for only a year and is already becoming a major attraction. Why? Well, for one thing, what's more basic than bread? And this site has provided it on and off since the 12th century. Originally part of an Augustinian Priory, the mill has had many lives (and deaths). Last known as the Old Mill Bakery, providing loaves to the local north coast, it suffered a devastating fire in 1986 and lay in ruins until it was reborn as Skerries Mills in 1999. An ambitious restoration project has brought two restored windmills and a watermill, complete with grinding, winnowing, and threshing wheels, back into operation. And there's even an adjoining field of grains—barley, oats, and wheat, all that's needed for the traditional brown loaf—sown, harvested, and threshed using traditional implements and machinery. The result is not only the sweet smell of fresh bread but an intriguing glimpse into the past, brought to life not only by guided tours but also by the opportunity to put your own hand to the stone and to grind your own flour on rotary or saddle querns. Then, if you've worked up an appetite, there's a lovely tearoom, often hosting live music, Irish dancing, and other events. Besides all this, there are rotating special exhibits and a fine gift shop of Irish crafts.

ACCOMMODATIONS

Moderate

Doyle Skylon. Upper Drumcondra Rd., Dublin 9. ☎ **800/42-DOYLE** from the U.S., or 01/837-9121. Fax 01/837-2778. www.doylehotels.com. 88 units. TV TEL. £94–£128 ($131.60–$179.20) double. Rates include full Irish breakfast and service charge. AE, DC, MC, V. Bus: 3, 11, 16, 41, 41A, or 41B.

With a modern five-story facade of glass and concrete, this hotel stands out on the city's north side, situated midway between downtown and the airport. Set on its own grounds in a residential neighborhood next to a college, it is just 10 minutes from the heart of the city. Several major bus routes stop outside the door. Guest rooms contain all the latest amenities and colorful, Irish-made furnishings. For full-service dining, the Rendezvous Room is a modern, plant-filled restaurant with an Irish and Continental menu. For drinks, try the Joycean pub. The hotel has a concierge, room service, laundry service, and a gift shop.

Posthouse. Dublin Airport, County Dublin. ☎ **800/225-5843** from U.S., or 01/808-0500. Fax 01/844-6002. 249 units. TV TEL. £90–£180 ($126–$252) double. Rates include service charge and full breakfast. AE, DC, MC, V. Bus: 41 or 41C.

This is the only hotel on the airport grounds, 7 miles (11km) north of the city center. Behind a modern three-story brick facade, it has a sunken skylit lobby with a central courtyard surrounded by guest rooms. The rooms are contemporary and functional, with windows looking out into the courtyard or toward distant mountain vistas. Each room is equipped with standard furnishings plus a full-length mirror, a hair dryer, tea/coffee-making facilities, and a trouser press. Nonsmoking rooms and rooms for travelers with disabilities may be requested. The hotel has a concierge, 24-hour room service, valet laundry service, and a courtesy coach to and from the airport. There's a gift shop on the premises. Dining choices include the Garden Room restaurant for Irish cuisine, and Sampans for Chinese food (at dinner only). The Bodhrán Bar is a traditional Irish bar with live music on weekends.

Inexpensive

Egan's House. 7/9 Iona Park (between Botanic and Lower Drumcondra Rds.), Glasnevin, Dublin 9. ☎ **800/937-9767** from the U.S., or 01/830-3611. Fax 01/830-3312. www.holiday/ireland.com. 23 units. TV TEL. £56–£62 ($78.40–$86.80) double. Continental breakfast £4.20 ($5.90); full Irish breakfast £6 ($8.40). Children under 12 stay for 50% off in parents' room. MC, V. Limited free parking available. Bus: 3, 11, 13, 13A, 16, 19, 19A, 41, 41A, or 41B.

This two-story redbrick Victorian guest house is in the center of a pleasant residential neighborhood. It's within walking distance of the Botanic Gardens and a variety of sports facilities, including tennis, swimming, and a gym. Operated by John and Betty Egan, it offers newly redecorated rooms in a variety of sizes and styles, including ground-floor rooms. All offer such conveniences as hair dryers and tea/coffeemakers. Rooms for smokers and nonsmokers are available. The comfortable public rooms have an assortment of traditional dark woods, brass fixtures, and antiques.

Forte Travelodge. N1 Dublin-Belfast road, Swords, County Dublin. ☎ **800/CALL-THF** from the U.S., or 1800/709-709 in Ireland. Fax 01/840-9235. 100 units. TV. £49.95–£59.95 ($69.95–$83.95) double. No service charge. AE, DC, MC, V. Bus: 41 or 43.

About 8 miles (13km) north of downtown and 1½ miles (2.4km) north of Dublin airport, this recently expanded two-story motel offers large no-frills accommodations at reasonable prices. Each of the basic rooms, with a double bed and sofa bed, can sleep up to four people. The redbrick exterior blends nicely with the countryside, and the interior is clean and modern. Public areas are limited to a modest reception area, public pay phone, and adjacent budget-priced Little Chef chain restaurant and lounge.

Iona House. 5 Iona Park, Glasnevin, Dublin 9. ☎ **01/830-6217.** Fax 01/830-6732. 10 units. TV TEL. £68 ($95.20) double. No service charge. Rates include full breakfast. MC, V. Closed Dec–Jan. Parking available on street. Bus: 19 or 19A.

A sitting room with a glowing open fireplace, chiming clocks, brass fixtures, and dark wood furnishings sets a welcoming tone for guests at this two-story redbrick Victorian home. Built around the turn of the century, it has been operated as a guesthouse by John and Karen Shouldice since 1963. Iona House is in a residential neighborhood 15 minutes from the city center, between Lower Drumcondra and Botanic Roads, within walking distance of the Botanic Gardens. The newly refurbished rooms offer modern hotel-style appointments, orthopedic beds, and contemporary Irish-made furnishings. There are a lounge and a small patio. Seven nonsmoking rooms are available.

Redbank Guesthouse and Lodge. 7 Church St. and Convent Lane, Skerries, County Dublin. ☎ **01/849-1005** or 01/849-0439. Fax 01/849-1598. www.guesthouseireland.com. 12 units (several with shower only). TV TEL. Guesthouse £70 ($98) double; Lodge £54 ($75.60) double. Rates include service and full Irish breakfast. Guesthouse B&B and dinner for 2 £120 ($168); Lodge B&B and dinner for 2 £110 ($154). AE, DC, MC, V. Parking on street and lane. Suburban rail. Bus: 33.

Within a leap of each other, these two comfortable nooks in the heart of Skerries town are only 20 to 30 minutes by car from Dublin Airport, and so provide a convenient first or last night's lodging for your Ireland holiday. Better yet, they virtually abut the deservedly touted Redbank Restaurant (see under "Dining" below), so you can be guaranteed a memorable introductory or farewell meal in the country. The seven rooms in the guesthouse are generally a bit more spacious than the five in the lodge. Beige or yellow walls, dark wood furnishings, blue carpets, traditional white bedspreads, and floral drapes compose the unassuming and inviting country style of the rooms, all of which have hair dryers and tea/coffeemakers. The showers are excellent, just what you need after or before a long journey! And whatever you do, if you spend the night at the Redbank, be sure to dine here as well.

DINING

Expense

✪ **King Sitric.** East Pier, Howth, County Dublin. ☎ **01/832-5235.** Reservations required. Dinner main courses £16–£25 ($22.40–$35); fixed-price dinner £32 ($44.80). AE, DC, MC, V. May–Sept Mon–Sat noon–3pm; year-round Mon–Sat 6:30–10:30pm. DART: Howth. Bus: 31 or 31A. SEAFOOD.

Right on the bay, 9 miles (15km) north of Dublin, this long-established restaurant is in a 150-year-old former harbormaster's building. On a fine summer evening, it is well worth a trip out here to savor the finest of local fish and crustaceans, creatively prepared and presented. Entrees include poached ray with capers and black butter, fillet of sole with lobster mousse, roast pheasant, grilled monkfish, sirloin steak with red-wine sauce, and Howth fish ragout, a signature combination of the best of the day's catch. King Sitric also offers an award-winning wine list.

✪ **Redbank Restaurant.** 7 Church St., Skerries, County Dublin. ☎ **01/849-1005.** Reservations recommended. Dinner main courses £11–£19 ($15.40–$26.60); fixed-price dinners £28–£30 ($39.20–$42). AE, DC, MC, V. Mon–Sat 7–9:45pm; Sun 12:30–2:15pm. Suburban rail. Bus: 33. SEAFOOD/CONTEMPORARY IRISH.

Founded in 1983 by Terry and Margaret McCoy, the Redbank has been winning friends, influencing people, and garnering awards for nearly 20 years. The Redbank was literally a bank (The Munster & Leinster Ltd.) before it was a restaurant and uses the old vault as its wine cellar (that is, for its liquid assets). The lounge/bar where you order and await your meal as it is being cooked to order is particularly appealing, with a sure touch of elegance, and the larger of the two dining rooms is entirely nonsmoking.

Terry McCoy is an exuberant and inspired chef, who draws his inspiration first from the waters off Skerries harbor. The seafood selection *Paddy Attley* offers a platter of three fish of the day landed in the Skerries Harbor, each served in a uniquely enhancing sauce. Equally indescribable is the mound of char-grilled Dublin Bay prawns which arrive with a flattering red bib to protect and adorn the diner. The truth is that a dinner here is a both a spectacle and feast, and not to be missed. And, if full bliss has somehow eluded you by the time the dessert trolley is wheeled in, utter your last words of the night and succumb to the chocolate mocha. Just remember this—while restaurants are taken over by banks on a regular basis, it is the rare restaurant that takes over a bank. And this is just such a rare restaurant.

MODERATE

✪ **Abbey Tavern.** Abbey St., Howth, County Dublin. ☎ **01/839-0307.** Reservations recommended. Main courses £11–£22 ($15.40–$30.80). MC, V. Mon–Sat 7–11pm. DART: Howth. Bus: 31. SEAFOOD/INTERNATIONAL.

Well known for its nightly traditional music ballad sessions, this 16th-century tavern also has a full-service restaurant upstairs. Although the menu changes by season, entrees often include such dishes as scallops *Ty Ar Mor* (with mushrooms, prawns, and cream sauce), crêpes fruits de mer, poached salmon, duck with orange and Curaçao sauce, and veal à la crème. After a meal, you might want to join the audience downstairs for some lively Irish music.

Dee Gee's Wine and Steak Bar. Harbour Rd., Howth, County Dublin. ☎ **01/839-2641.** Reservations recommended on weekends. Dinner main courses £7–£13 ($9.80–$18.20). MC, V. Oct–Apr daily 7am–7pm; May–Sept daily 7am–9pm. DART: Howth. Bus: 31. IRISH.

If you plan a day's outing to Howth, don't miss this place. Facing Howth Harbour and Dublin Bay, this informal seaside spot opposite the DART station is ideal for a cup of coffee, a snack, or a full meal. A self-service snackery by day and a more formal, table-service restaurant at night, it offers indoor and outdoor seating. Dinner entrees range from steaks and burgers to shrimp scampi and vegetable lasagna. At lunchtime, soups, salads, and sandwiches are featured. Sit, relax, and watch all the activities of Howth from a front-row seat.

5 Out from Dublin

The scope of this chapter is more or less defined by what the distinguished Trinity geographer J. H. Andrews has labeled "the eastern triangle"—a wedge of Ireland's east coast extending north to south from County Wicklow to County Louth, and west to County Westmeath. Like a stage, compact and prominent, this relatively small space has witnessed and preserved more of the Irish drama than perhaps any other comparable part of the country.

The stretch of level coast from Dundalk to the Wicklows marks the greatest breach in Ireland's natural defenses, made worse—or better, depending on your perspective—by the inviting estuaries of the Liffey and the Boyne. These "opportunities" were not lost on explorers, settlers, and invaders across the millennia. Once taken, whether by Celts, Danes, Normans, or English, this area's strategic importance was soon recognized as the most likely command and control center for the whole of Ireland. Here lay Tara, the hill of kings; Dublin, the greatest of the Viking city-states; and the Pale, the English colonial fist holding the rest of Ireland in its grip. Here too are Newgrange and Knowth, marking one of the most profound prehistoric sites in the world; Kells, where Ireland's greatest treasure was fished from a bog; Mellifont, where the Irish Cistercian movement made its beginning; and the Valley of the Boyne, where the Irish finally lost their country to the English.

Rimmed by the Irish Sea, this eastern triangle—every point of which is an easy distance from Dublin City—has less rain, less bog, and more history than any other region of comparable concentration on the island. To the south, County Wicklow presents a panorama of gardens, lakes, mountains, and seascapes. To the east sit the flat plains of County Kildare, Ireland's prime horse country. In the north are the counties of Meath and Louth, packed with historic sites. Pair all of this with the region's central location, and you have an area that is both a great hub from which to explore and a historical and geographic microcosm for those who don't have time to hit the four corners of the land.

1 County Wicklow: The Garden of Ireland

County Wicklow extends from Bray, 12 miles (19km) S of Dublin, to Arklow, 40 miles (64km) S of Dublin

The borders of County Wicklow start just a dozen or so miles south of downtown Dublin, and within this county you'll find some of

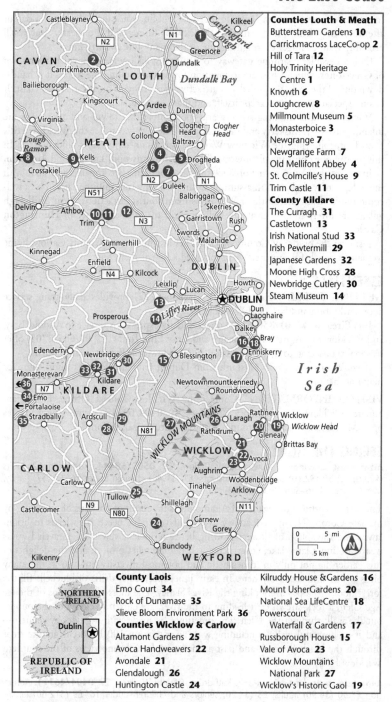

The East Coast

Counties Louth & Meath
Butterstream Gardens **10**
Carrickmacross LaceCo-op **2**
Hill of Tara **12**
Holy Trinity Heritage
  Centre **1**
Knowth **6**
Loughcrew **8**
Millmount Museum **5**
Monasterboice **3**
Newgrange **7**
Newgrange Farm **7**
Old Mellifont Abbey **4**
St. Colmcille's House **9**
Trim Castle **11**
County Kildare
The Curragh **31**
Castletown **13**
Irish National Stud **33**
Irish Pewtermill **29**
Japanese Gardens **32**
Moone High Cross **28**
Newbridge Cutlery **30**
Steam Museum **14**

County Laois
Emo Court **34**
Rock of Dunamase **35**
Slieve Bloom Environment Park **36**
Counties Wicklow & Carlow
Altamont Gardens **25**
Avoca Handweavers **22**
Avondale **21**
Glendalough **26**
Huntington Castle **24**

Kilruddy House &Gardens **16**
Mount UsherGardens **20**
National Sea LifeCentre **18**
Powerscourt
  Waterfall & Gardens **17**
Russborough House **15**
Vale of Avoca **23**
Wicklow Mountains
  National Park **27**
Wicklow's Historic Gaol **19**

Ireland's best rural scenery. If you're based in Dublin, you can easily spend a day or afternoon in Wicklow and return to the city for dinner and the theater. But you'll probably want to linger overnight at one of the many fine country inns.

One accessible, charming gateway to County Wicklow is the small harbor town of **Greystones,** which I hesitate to mention for fear of spoiling the secret. It is hands-down one of the most unspoiled and attractive harbor towns on Ireland's east coast. It has no special attractions except itself, and that's enough.

Wicklow's most stunning scenery and most interesting towns and attractions are inland, between Enniskerry and Glendalough. The best way to see the **Wicklow Hills** is on foot, following the **Wicklow Way** past mountain tarns and secluded glens. In this region, don't miss the picturesque villages of **Roundwood, Laragh,** and **Aughrim.**

In the southernmost corner of Wicklow, the mountains become hills and share with the villages they shelter an unassuming beauty, a sleepy tranquillity that can be a welcome respite from the bustle of Wicklow's main tourist attractions. Near **Shillelagh** village are lovely forests, great hill walking, and the curious edifice of **Huntington Castle.**

Just over the border of County Wicklow lies less-frequented County Carlow, home to many a delightful surprise. We've included a few of them here.

ESSENTIALS

GETTING THERE   Irish Rail (☎ 01/836-6222) provides daily train service between Dublin and Bray and Wicklow.

Bus Eireann (☎ 01/836-6111) operates daily express bus service to Arklow, Bray, and Wicklow towns. Both Bus Eireann and **Gray Line Tours** (☎ 01/605-7705) offer seasonal sightseeing tours to Glendalough, Wicklow, and Powerscourt Gardens.

If you're driving, take N11 south from Dublin City and follow turnoff signs for major attractions.

VISITOR INFORMATION   Contact the **Wicklow Tourist Office,** Fitzwilliam Square, Wicklow Town, County Wicklow (☎ 0404/69117; www.wicklow.ie). It's open Monday to Friday year-round, Saturday during peak season.

SEEING THE SIGHTS

Altamount Gardens. Tullow, County Carlow. ☎ **0503/59444.** Admission £2 adults ($2.80), £1.50 ($2.10) seniors and students, £1 ($1.40) children under 16, £5 ($7) family. Mar 17–Sept Thurs–Sun 10:30am–6:30pm.

The lush, colorful extravagance of Altamount is the result of 55 years of nurturing by the late Corona North. A shadowy avenue of venerable beech trees leads to bright lawns and the splash of flowers growing beneath ancient yew trees. Graveled walks weave around a large lake, constructed as a famine relief project, and the delights of this garden lie not only in its aesthetic and botanical diversity but also in the many birds which find sanctuary here. In early June, spectacular drifts of bluebells fill the forest floor on slopes overlooking the River Slaney. The moss-green depths of the Ice Age Glen, a rock-strewn cleft leading to the river, are currently closed to the public, but the walk through the Glen can sometimes be made with a guide, by request— and it's a beautiful walk, concluding with an ascent up 100 hand-cut granite steps through the bluebell wood, and past a small temple with fine views of the southern Wicklow Hills.

Avondale House & Forest Park. Rathdrum, County Wicklow. ☎ **0404/46111.** Admission £3.50 ($4.90) adults, £3 ($4.20) seniors and children under 16, £9 ($12.60) family. Daily mid-March to end Oct 11am–5pm. Parking £3 ($4.20). Entrance to park and house signposted off R752.

In a fertile valley between Glendalough and the Vale of Avoca, this is the former home of Charles Stewart Parnell (1846–91), one of Ireland's great political leaders. Built in 1779, the house is now a museum dedicated to his memory. Set in the surrounding 523-acre estate and boasting signposted nature trails alongside the Avondale River, Avondale Forest Park is considered the cradle of modern Irish forestry. A new exhibition area commemorates the American side of the Parnell family, most notably Admiral Charles Stewart of U.S.S. *Constitution*. The coffee shop serves teas and light lunches, featuring homemade breads and pastries.

✪ **Glendalough.** County Wicklow. ☎ **0404/45325** or 0404/45352. Free admission to site; £2 ($2.80) adults, £1.50 ($2.10) seniors, £1 ($1.40) children and students under 16, £5 ($7) family for exhibits and audiovisual presentation. Daily mid-Oct to mid-Mar 9:30am–5pm; mid-Mar to May and Sept to mid-Oct 9:30am–6pm; June–Aug 9am–6:30pm. Head 7 miles (11km) east of Wicklow on T7 via Rathdrum.

In the 6th century, St. Kevin chose this idyllically secluded setting—whose name derived from the Irish phrase *Gleann Da Locha,* meaning "The Glen of the Two Lakes"—for a monastery. Over the centuries, it became a leading center of learning, with thousands of students from Ireland, Britain, and all over Europe. In the 12th century, St. Lawrence O'Toole was among the many abbots who followed St. Kevin and spread the influence of Glendalough. But like so many early Irish religious sites, Glendalough fell into the hands of plundering Anglo-Norman invaders, and its glories came to an end by the 15th century.

Today, visitors can stroll from the upper lake to the lower lake and walk through the remains of the monastery complex, long since converted to a burial place. Although much of the monastic city is in ruins, the remains do include a nearly perfect round tower, 103 feet high and 52 feet around the base, as well as hundreds of timeworn Celtic crosses and a variety of churches. One of these is St. Kevin's chapel, often called St. Kevin's Kitchen, a fine specimen of an early Irish barrel-vaulted oratory with a miniature round belfry rising from a stone roof. A striking new visitor center at the entrance to the site provides helpful orientation, with exhibits on the archaeology, history, folklore, and wildlife of the area.

The main entrance to the monastic complex has been spoiled by a sprawling hotel and hawkers of various sorts, so you may want to cross the river at the visitor center and walk along the banks. You can cross back again at the monastic site, bypassing the trappings of commerce that St. Kevin once fled.

For a Gray Line bus tour to Glendalough, contact Gray Line Desk, Dublin Tourism Centre, Suffolk Street, Dublin 2 (☎ **01/605-7705;** e-mail: grayline@tlp.ie).

Huntington Castle. Clonegal, County Carlow (off N80, 4 miles/6.5km from Bunclody). ☎ **054/77552.** Guided tour £3.50 ($4.90) adults, £1.50 ($2.10) children. Jun–Aug daily 2–6pm; May and Sept Sun 2–6pm; other times by appointment.

At the confluence of the rivers Derry and Slaney, this castle was of great strategic importance from the time it was built, in the early 17th century. It was at the center of conflicts in the area until the early 20th century, when the IRA briefly used it as a headquarters. The castle is unlike many others you'll visit, since it has a lived-in feel. The magnificent decrepitude derives in part from the sometimes-overwhelming assortment of debris left by previous generations. The house has many stories to tell, and young Alexander Durdin-Robertson, whose ancestors built the place, seems to know them all; he gives a great tour. Don't forget to visit the garden, where waist-high weeds hide a lovely yew walk and one of the first hydroelectric facilities in Ireland. The castle's basement is home to a temple of the Fellowship of Isis, a religion founded here in 1976.

Killruddery House & Gardens. Off the main Dublin–Wicklow road (N11), Killruddery, Bray, County Wicklow. ☎ **01/286-2777.** House and garden tour £4.50 ($6.30) adults, £3 ($4.20) seniors and students over 12, £1 ($1.40) children; gardens only £3 ($4.20) adults, £2 ($2.80) seniors and students over 12, 50p (70¢) children. House May–June and Sept daily 1–5pm; gardens Apr–Sept daily 1–5pm.

This estate has been the seat of the earl of Meath since 1618. The original part of its mansion, dating from 1820, features a Victorian conservatory modeled on the Crystal Palace in London. The gardens are a highlight, with a lime avenue, a sylvan theater, foreign trees, exotic shrubs, twin canals, and a round pond with fountains that's edged with beech hedges. They are the only surviving 17th-century French-style gardens in Ireland.

Mount Usher Gardens. On the main Dublin–Wicklow road (N11), Ashford, County Wicklow. ☎ **0404/40116.** Admission £4 ($5.60) adults; £3 ($4.20) seniors, students, and children 5–12. Guided tours £20 ($28); call for reservation. Mar 17–Oct 31 daily 10:30am–6pm.

Encompassing 20 acres along the River Vartry, this sylvan site was once home to an ancient lake and more recently laid out in the informal, free-range "Robinsonian" style. It contains more than 5,000 tree and plant species from all parts of the world, including spindle trees from China, North American swamp cypress, and Burmese juniper trees. Fiery rhododendrons, fragrant eucalyptus trees, giant Tibetan lilies, and snowy camellias also compete for your eye. Informal and responsive to their natural setting, these gardens have an almost untended feel—a floral woodland, without pretense yet with considerable charm. A spacious tearoom overlooks the river and gardens. The courtyard at the entrance to the gardens contains an interesting assortment of shops, which are open year-round.

National Sea Life Centre. Strand Rd., Bray, County Wicklow. ☎ **01/286-6939.** www. sealife.ie. Admission £5.50 ($7.70) adults, £4.50 ($6.30) seniors, £4 ($5.60) students, £3.95 ($5.53) children, £17 ($23.80) family. Open year-round daily 10am–5pm.

When seen and enjoyed for what it is, Sea Life is surely worth a visit. The hyperbole of its title, however, reflects more closely the enthusiasm of its staff than the scale of the edifice. And more power to them, as Sea Life offers good family fun, even if it's a tad overpriced. Situated at water's edge, the center provides a family-focused introduction to the denizens of the nearby deep.

The labyrinthine path through the aquarium begins with a rock tunnel carved by a winding freshwater stream; from there, you follow the water's course toward the open sea, from freshwater river to tidal estuary to storm-pounded harbor and finally to the briny deep. Along the way, kids are quizzed on what they're learning, as they use "magic" glasses to read coded questions and find the answers on special scratch pads they've been given. One remarkable feature here is the close access visitors have to the sea life. It's possible (though not encouraged) to reach down and put your hand into many of the tanks; and, when you bend over and eyeball the fish, they as often as not return the favor, surfacing and staring back only inches from your face. Such keen alertness and interpersonal rapport coming from a ray or plaice was a surprise. Once you reach "the Deep" the emphasis is on scary critters, the ones with the sharpest teeth or the deadliest venom, like sharks (of course) and the dreaded blue-ringed octopus, whose bite carries enough poison to kill 10 people. The terror is sweeter than chocolate to children. You won't spend all day here, more like an hour or less; but you may come away on first-name terms with a Goby and that's more than okay.

⊗ **Powerscourt Gardens, House Exhibition, and Waterfall.** Off the main Dublin–Wicklow road (N11), Enniskerry, County Wicklow. ☎ **01/204-6000.** Gardens and house exhibition £5 ($7) adults, £4.50 ($6.30) seniors and students, £3 ($4.20) children 5–16, free for children under 5; gardens only £4 ($5.60) adults, £3.50 ($4.90) seniors and students, £2 ($2.80) children 5–16, free for children under 5; waterfall £2 ($2.80) adults, £1.50 ($2.10) seniors and students, £1 ($1.40) children 5–16, free for children under 5. AE, MC, V. Gardens and house exhibition daily Mar–Oct 9:30am–5:30pm, Nov–Feb 9:30am–dusk; waterfall daily Mar–Oct 9:30am–7pm, Nov–Feb 10:30am–dusk.

On a 1,000-acre estate less than a dozen miles south of Dublin city sits one of the finest gardens in Europe, designed and laid out by Daniel Robertson between 1745 and 1767. This property is filled with splendid Greek- and Italian-inspired statuary, decorative ironwork, a petrified-moss grotto, lovely herbaceous borders, a Japanese garden, a circular pond and fountain with statues of winged horses, and the occasional herd of deer. Stories have it that Robertson, afflicted with gout, was pushed around the grounds in a wheelbarrow to oversee the work. This service is no longer offered, but I doubt you'll mind the walk.

An 18th-century manor house designed by Richard Cassels, the architect of Russborough House (see below) and the man credited with the design of Dublin's Parliament house, stood proudly on the site until it was gutted by fire in 1974. The partially restored house contains a variety of high-quality gift shops and an exhibition, complete with video presentation, on the history of Powerscourt. The additional entrance fee to "the house" is actually for entrance to this exhibition, primarily the video, which is mediocre.

The pleasant cafeteria serves delicious, reasonably priced lunches with a view that's not to be believed. The adjacent garden center and pavilion is staffed with highly knowledgeable green thumbs who can answer all the questions you've collected while exploring the magnificent gardens. If the children deserve a treat by now, there is a nearby park. In my opinion, the waterfall is too little too far away at too high a price. After all, if you want to see water pouring down in Ireland, most days you can just look up.

Russborough House. Off N81, Blessington, County Wicklow. ☎ **045/865239.** Admission to main rooms £4 ($5.60) adults, £3 ($4.20) seniors and students, £2 ($2.80) children under 12. May–Sept daily 10:30am–5:30pm; Oct Sun 10:30am–5:30pm. Closed Nov–Apr.

Ensconced in this 18th-century Palladian house is the world-famous Beit Art Collection, with paintings by Vernet, Guardi, Bellotto, Gainsborough, Rubens, and Reynolds. The house is furnished with European pieces and decorated with bronzes, tapestries, and some fine Francini plasterwork. To visit the maze and rhododendron garden, call for an appointment. On the premises are a restaurant, shop, and playground.

St. Mullin's Monastery. On the scenic Barrow Dr., 7½ miles (12km) north of New Ross, St. Mullins, County Carlow. Admission free at any time to site; Heritage Centre open at the discretion of Seamus Fitzgerald.

This little gem is a well-kept secret. On a sunny day its idyllic setting—in a sleepy hamlet beside the River Barrow, ringed by soft carpeted hills—is cause enough for a visit. Besides that, this is a fascinating spot, an outdoor minimuseum of sorts, spanning Irish history from the early Christian period to the present, all in no more than several acres. There are the ruins of a monastery founded here at Ross-Broc (Badger Wood) by St. Moling (Mullin) in roughly A.D. 614. Plundered again and again by the Vikings in the 9th and 10 centuries, it was annexed in the 12th century by a nearby Augustinian abbey. Here, too, is a steep grassy motte and the outline of its accompanying bailey constructed by the Normans in the 12th century. In the Middle Ages, the monastery ruins were a popular destination, especially in the grip of the Black Death in 1348, when pilgrims would cross the river barefoot, circle the burial spot of St. Mullin nine times in prayer, adding small stones to the cairn marking the spot, and drink from the healing waters of the saint's well. The truth is that these ruins and waters are still the site of an annual "pattern" or pilgrimage near or on July 25.

Adjoining the monastery buildings is an ancient "working" cemetery still in use, where, contrary to common practice, Protestants and Catholics have long lain side by side. You'll also find the graves of 20 heroes from the 1798 Rebellion, including that of General Thomas Cloney. Be sure to find among the graveyard's stones the clandestine "penal altar" with a peephole from which the priest could see the top of the earthen motte or mound where a sentry stood lookout for British troops enforcing the ban on Catholic worship. If it's open at the time of your visit, the modest Heritage Centre in the adjoining 19th-century church contains some informative exhibitions and booklets and the ever-helpful local docent Seamus Fitzgerald. Even if the Heritage Centre is closed, there's a helpful site map and history mounted at the entrance to the cemetery.

Remarkably, the ferry across the River Barrow, instituted by St. Mullin in the 7th century, went out of use only in this century, and the bell in the founder's chapel still rings for burials in the abbey cemetery.

Vale of Avoca. Rte. 755, Avoca, County Wicklow.

Basically a peaceful riverbank, the Vale of Avoca was immortalized in the writings of 19th-century poet Thomas Moore. It's here at the "Meeting of the Waters" that the Avonmore and Avonbeg Rivers join to form the Avoca River. It's said that the poet sat under "Tom Moore's Tree" looking for inspiration and penned the lines, "There is not in the wide world a valley so sweet / as the vale in whose bosom the bright waters meet. . . ." The tree is a sorry sight—it's been picked almost bare by souvenir hunters—but the place is still worth a visit.

✪ **Wicklow Mountains National Park.** Glendalough, County Wicklow. ☎ **0404/ 45425.** Visitor Centre May–Aug daily 10am–6pm; Apr and Sept Sat–Sun 10am–6pm; closed other months.

Nearly 50,000 acres of County Wicklow make up this new national park. The core area surrounds Glendalough, including the Glendalough Valley and Glendalough Wood Nature Reserves. You'll find an information station at the Upper Lake at Glendalough. Information is available here on hiking in the Glendalough Valley and surrounding hills, including maps and descriptions of routes. (See "Sports & Outdoor Pursuits," below, for suggestions.) Free guided nature walks begin from the center on Tuesdays (departing 11am and returning 1:30pm) and Thursdays (departing 3pm and returning 4pm). The closest parking is at Upper Lake, where you'll pay £1.50 ($2.10) per car; my advice is to walk up from the Glendalough Visitor Centre, where the parking's free.

Wicklow's Historic Gaol. Kilmantin Hill, Wicklow Town, County Wicklow. ☎ **0404/ 61599.** www.wicklow.ie/gaol. Tour £4.20 ($5.90) adults; £3.30 ($4.60) senior and students, £2.60 ($3.65) children, £12 ($16.80) family with up to 3 children. Apr 17–Sept daily 10am–6pm (last admission at 4:50pm).

Once you learn what took place within these walls, you'll find it hard to believe that Wicklow Gaol closed its doors only as recently as 1924, after more than 2 centuries of terror. After passing under the hanging beam, visitors are lined up against the wall of the "day room" and confronted with some dark facts of prison life in 1799, when more than 400 prisoners, most of them rebels, occupied the gaol's 42 cells. Fed once every

4 days and allowed to walk in the prison yard for 15 minutes every four weeks, they must have found the hanging rope looking less and less hideous. Within the main cell-block, visitors are allowed to roam the gaol's individual cells and to discover their stories through a series of exhibitions and audio-visual presentations. The impact of these stories is immediate and powerful, for children as well as for adults, because this gaol once held both. And, as many prisoners were sent off to penal colonies in Australia and Tasmania, that story, too, is told here, with the help of a stage-set wharf and prison ship. There's an in-house cafe when you're all done, but its appeal is likely to be undercut by the less-than-appetizing experience you've just been through. Who can recommend jail, and yet I left informed and moved.

SHOPPING

County Wicklow offers a wide array of wonderful craft centers and workshops. Here is a small sampling.

✪ **Avoca Handweavers.** Avoca, County Wicklow. ☎ **0402/35105.** www.avoca.ie. Weaving shed daily May–Oct 9:30am–5:30pm.

Dating from 1723, this cluster of whitewashed stone buildings and a mill houses the oldest surviving hand-weaving company in Ireland. It produces a wide range of tweed clothing, knitwear, and accessories. The dominant tones of mauve, aqua, teal, and heather reflect the local landscape. You're welcome to watch as craftspeople weave strands of yarn spun from the wool of local sheep. The complex has a retail outlet and a tea shop (see "Dining" below). A second outlet shop, on the main N11 road at Kilmacanogue, Bray, County Wicklow (☎ **01/286-7466**), is open daily 9:30am to 5:30pm.

Bergin Clarke Studio. The Old Schoolhouse, Ballinaclash, Rathdrum, County Wicklow. ☎ **0404/46385.**

In this little workshop, Brian Clarke hand-fashions silver jewelry and giftware, and Yvonne Bergin knits stylish, colorful apparel using yarns from County Wicklow. Open May to September daily 10am to 8pm; October to April Monday to Saturday 10am to 5:30pm.

Fisher's of Newtownmountkennedy. The Old Schoolhouse, Newtownmountkennedy, County Wicklow. ☎ **01/281-9404.**

This shop, in a converted schoolhouse, stocks a wide array of men's and women's sporting clothes—quilted jackets, raincoats, footwear, blazers, and accessories. There's also a new tearoom. Open Monday to Saturday 9:30am to 5:30pm, Sunday 2 to 6pm.

The Woolen Mills Glendalough. Laragh, County Wicklow. ☎ **0404/45156.**

This long-established crafts shop in a converted farmhouse offers handcrafts from all over Ireland, such as Bantry Pottery and Penrose Glass from Waterford. Books, jewelry, and a large selection of hand-knits from the area are also sold. Open daily 10am to 6:30pm.

SPORTS & OUTDOOR PURSUITS

AN ADVENTURE CENTRE   Less than an hour's drive from Dublin center, and signposted on N81, the **Blessington Adventure Centre,** Blessington (☎ **045/865092**), offers outdoor activities for adults and children. Canoeing, kayaking, sailing, and windsurfing lessons and rentals on the Blessington lakes are available; on land, there are archery, orienteering, tennis, pony trekking, and riding lessons for all levels. Some representative prices per hour for adults are £6 ($8.40) for canoeing and kayaking,

£10 ($14) for sailing and windsurfing, and £12 ($16.80) for pony trekking. Full- and half-day multi-activity prices are also available.

CANOEING & KAYAKING   There are weekend courses on white-water and flat-water streams at the **National Adventure Center,** Ashford (☎ 0404/40169), a state-funded facility that provides training in a variety of outdoor activities. Basic equipment is provided; fees for 1- to 5-day courses range from £35 to £225 ($49 to $315). The center caters to a young clientele, and lodging is in hostels unless you arrange otherwise.

FISHING   The streams in Wicklow are not renowned fishing waters, although brown trout and river trout can be found in such rivers as the Avoca and the Augh-rim. Sea angling is popular all along the coast, but there are not any opportunities in Wicklow to rent boats or fishing equipment.

GOLF   County Wicklow's verdant hills and dales offer numerous opportunities for golfing. The new **Rathsallagh Golf Club** (☎ 045/403316) is an 18-hole, par-72 championship course at Dunlavin. Greens fees are £40 ($56) weekdays and £50 ($70) weekends. The seaside **European Club,** Brittas Bay (☎ 0404/47415), is a championship links with greens fees of £45 ($63) year-round. At the parkland **Glenmalure Golf Club,** Greenane, Rathdrum (☎ 0404/46679), greens fees start at £15 ($21) weekdays and £20 ($28) weekends. The **Arklow Golf Club** (☎ 0402/32492), a seaside par-68 course, charges greens fees of £18 ($25.20).

HORSEBACK RIDING   With its valleys, glens, secluded paths, and nature trails, County Wicklow is perfect for horseback riding. More than a dozen stables and equestrian centers offer horses for hire and instructional programs. Rates for horse hire average £10 to £20 ($14 to $28) per hour. Among the leading venues are **Broomfield Riding School,** Broomfield, Tinahely (☎ 0402/38117), and **Brennanstown Riding School,** Hollybrook, Kilmacanogue (☎ 01/286-3778). At the **Paulbeg Riding School,** Shillelagh (☎ 055/29100), experienced riders can explore the beautiful surrounding hills, and beginners can receive expert instruction from Sally Duffy, a friendly woman who gives an enthusiastic introduction to the sport.

   Devil's Glen Holiday and Equestrian Village, Ashford (☎ 0404/40013 or 40637; www.devilsglen.ie), splendidly situated at the edge of Devil's Glen, offers a full range of equestrian opportunities, from lessons to jumping to trekking to cross-country, as well as spotless, spacious, fully-equipped self-catering apartments, cottages, and bungalows, each with two or three bedrooms. The accommodations make a great base from which to explore the Wicklow Mountains and coastline, whether or not you ever climb into a saddle. Weekly rates run from £260 to £585 ($364 to $819), depending on season and size of unit. Weekend (Fri to Sun) and mid-week (Mon to Thurs) rates are also available. Most lessons and rides cost £15 ($21) per hour for adults and £12 ($16.80) per hour for children under 12. Both the equestrian center and the self-catering village are open year-round.

HUNTING   The **Broomfield Riding School,** Broomfield, Tinahely (☎ 0402/38117), offers access to the hunt for those who can demonstrate adequate equestrian skills, including jumping. The riding school is open year-round for lessons and trail rides.

WALKING   The **Wicklow Way** is a signposted walking path that follows forest trails, sheep paths, and country roads from the hills south of Dublin to the trail's terminus in Clonegal. It takes about 5 to 7 days to walk its entirety, with overnight stops at B&Bs and hostels along the route. Most people choose to walk sections as day trips; I've highlighted some of my favorites below.

You can pick up information and maps at the Wicklow National Park center in Glendalough or at any local tourist office. Information on less strenuous walks can be found in a number of local publications. Check out the *Wicklow Trail Sheets* available at tourist offices. They provide a map and route description for several short walks. Guests at the **Ballyknocken House B&B** (see "Walking," in chapter 3) have access to a list of walks beginning and ending at the house.

The most spectacular walks in Wicklow are in the north and central parts of the county, an area traversed by the Wicklow Way and numerous short trails. One lovely walk on the Way begins at the **Deerpark parking lot** near the Dargle River and continues to Luggala, passing Djouce Mountain; the next section, between Luggala and Laragh, traverses some wild country around Lough Dan.

You won't want to miss **the southern section of the Wicklow Way,** through Tinahely, Shillelagh, and Clonegal. Although not as rugged as the terrain in central Wicklow, the hills here are voluptuously round, with delightful woods and glens hidden in their folds. Through much of this section the path follows country roads that have been well chosen for their lack of vehicular traffic. Consider treating yourself to a night at **Park Lodge B&B,** Clonegal, Shillelagh (☎ **055/29140**), near the trail's terminus; double rooms run £72 to £80 ($100.80 to $112). If you're on foot, the exceedingly hospitable Osborne family can arrange to pick you up at one of several points along the trail between Shillelagh and Clonegal.

ACCOMMODATIONS
VERY EXPENSIVE

✪ **Tinakilly House Hotel.** On R750, off the Dublin–Wexford road (N11), Rathnew, County Wicklow. ☎ **800/525-4800** from the U.S., or 0404/69274. Fax 0404/67806. www.tinakilly.ie. 53 units. TV TEL. £130–£190 ($182–$266) double; £190 ($266) junior suite; £240 ($336) captain's suite with sea view. No service charge. Rates include full breakfast. AE, DC, MC, V.

Dating from the 1870s, this was the home of Capt. Robert Charles Halpin, commander of the *Great Eastern,* who laid the first successful cable connecting Europe with America. With a sweeping central staircase said to be the twin of the one on the ship, Tinakilly is full of seafaring memorabilia, paintings, and Victorian antiques. Many of the individually furnished rooms have views of the Irish Sea. Opened as a hotel by the Power family in 1983, it is adjacent to the Broadlough Bird Sanctuary and a 7-acre garden of beech, evergreen, eucalyptus, palm, and American redwood trees. Most of the rooms recently underwent a full renovation very much in keeping with the Victorian style. Don't be daunted by the wide selection of rooms here, because you really can't go wrong. While the Captain's Suites and the full suites are quite grand, even the standard attic rooms are cozy and truly charming.

In the mere 17 years since opening, Tinakilly House has garnered a wall of well-deserved prestigious awards, including recently being ranked no. 75 in the "Top 100 Hotels of the World" by the London *Times.*

Dining: The Brunel Restaurant, in the new east wing, is well known for fresh fish and local game. The kitchen blends country-house cooking with a nouvelle cuisine influence. Vegetables, fruits, and herbs come from the house gardens, and all breads are baked fresh daily on the premises (see listing below under "Dining").

Amenities: For rainy days or simply to regain your waist after you've succumbed to a feast, there's a small yet useful fitness suite with a treadmill and several other exercise machines.

EXPENSIVE

Glenview Hotel. Glen o' the Downs, Delgany, Dublin–Wexford road (N11), County Wicklow. ☎ **800/528-1234** in the U.S., or 01/287-3399. Fax 01/287-7511. E-mail: glenview@iol.ie. 74 units. TV TEL. £116–£170 ($162.40–$238) double. Rates include full Irish breakfast and service charge. AE, DC, MC, V.

With the Sugarloaf Mountain in the background, this hotel has been a popular stopping-off place on the main road for more than 50 years. It occupies an idyllic setting overlooking the Glen of the Downs. Totally refurbished and enlarged in 1998, it has a striking yellow facade and a bright, airy contemporary interior. The guest rooms and public areas maintain much of their traditional charm.

Dining/Diversions: The Woodlands Restaurant provides splendid views of the glens as well as fine cuisine. The Lodge Bar and Library Lounge also enjoy panoramic views of the countryside, including the hotel's 30 acres of gardens and woodlands.

Amenities: A luxurious health and leisure club was recently added.

✪ **Rathsallagh House.** Dunlavin, County Wicklow. ☎ **800/323-5463** from the U.S., or 045/403112. Fax 045/403343. www.rathsallagh.com. 29 units. TV TEL. £110–£210 ($154–$294) double. No service charge. Rates include full breakfast. AE, DC, MC, V. Closed Dec 23–31. No children under 12 accepted.

On the western edge of County Wicklow, this rambling, ivy-covered country house sits amid 530 acres of parks, woods, and farmland. The original house on the property was built between 1702 and 1704 and owned by a horse-breeding family named Moody. It was burned down in the 1798 Rebellion, and the Moodys moved into the Queen Anne–style stables, which were converted into a residence and served as a private home until the 1950s. Joe and Kay O'Flynn bought the property in 1978 and opened it as a country-house hotel 10 years later. Each room is individually decorated and named accordingly. Most rooms have a sitting area, a huge walk-in closet, and window seats, and some have Jacuzzis. All have hair dryer, tea/coffeemaker, vanity desk, good reading lamps over the bed, and antique furnishings. A recent recipient of the American Express Best-Loved Hotels of the World award, this much-touted guesthouse has a particularly warm, welcoming, unpretentious feel to it, a splendid home away from home.

Dining: The dining room, under the personal supervision of Kay O'Flynn, is widely noted for its excellent food, using local ingredients and vegetables and herbs from the garden.

Amenities: 18-hole championship golf course, modest-sized indoor heated swimming pool, sauna, hard tennis court, archery, croquet, billiards.

MODERATE

Glendalough Hotel. Glendalough, County Wicklow. ☎ **800/365-3346** from the U.S., or 0404/45135. Fax 0404/45142. www.glendaloughhotel.ie. 44 units. TV TEL. £86–£116 ($120.40–$162.40) double. Rates include full breakfast. AE, DC, MC, V. Closed Jan.

Without spending the night in a round tower, you can't get any closer to St. Kevin's digs than this seasoned veteran inn situated in a wooded glen at the very entrance to Glendalough, beside the Glendasan River. Dating from the 1800s, it was refurbished and updated in the mid-1990s with traditional Irish furnishings and standard modern comforts. Public rooms include the Glendasan Restaurant, overlooking the river, and the Glendalough Tavern. While this was once a sleepy and idyllic spot, it is now rather overrun, with tourists and their buses and all that caters to them.

✪ **Kilgraney Country House.** Just off the R705 (L18), 3½ miles (5.6km) from Bagenalstown on the Borris road, Bagenalstown, County Carlow. ☎ **0503/75283.** Fax 0503/75595. www.kilgraneyhouse.com. 6 units, all with private bathroom (4 with shower only). £70–£110

($98–$154) double. Rates include full breakfast. Dinner £28 ($39.20). MC, V. Closed Nov–Feb.

Kilgrany House harbors the unexpected. Once you pass through its late Georgian front door, the eclectic taste of the proprietors, Martin Marley and Bryan Leech, takes over. High ceilings and richly colored walls complement the bold lines of 20th-century drawings and hammered metal furniture of Asian influence. Rooms are soothing and simple and demonstrate a careful consideration of the tactile as well as the visual, but even here the unexpected slips in: perhaps the light pull is a horn-headed cane, or a Thai puppet waves from a bedside table. Such attention to detail invites a slow, lingering sojourn.

Dinner, served on a long table of Kilkenny black marble, is also a fusion of old and new, of the exotic and the traditionally Irish—wild salmon is wrapped with a band of Japanese seaweed, and a creamy potato soup is laced with curry. The ritual of dinner and the conversation it inspires mean that the meal can last well into the night. Our breakfast included raisin and orange pancakes as a first course, a truly superlative soda bread, and more standard second-course offerings of scrambled eggs with salmon or bacon and sausage.

✪ **Lorum Old Rectory.** Just off the R705 (L18), 4⅓ miles (7km) from Bagenalstown on the Borris road, Bagenalstown, County Carlow. ☎ **0503/75282.** Fax 0503/75455. www.lorum. com. 5 units, all with private bathroom (with shower only). TEL. £70–£75 ($98–$105) double. Rates include full breakfast. Dinner £25 ($35). AE, MC, V.

Set well back from the road and surrounded by cultivated fields, rolling pastures, and casual gardens in the serene Barrow Valley, the Old Rectory stands weathered and welcoming at the age of 138. Its hallmarks are hospitality and cuisine, both unforgettable. Upon arrival, I read through the guest book, as I often do, and found it full of extraordinary testimonials, including one to the effect that *on all our Ireland holidays, of all the places we've stayed, this is our favorite.* At that moment I found these to be big words for what appeared to be an appealing yet somewhat ordinary guesthouse. By the next morning, however, I could have written those words myself.

There is something contagious about the congeniality of this house. The Smiths are consummate hosts, perhaps because they love doing what they do. Bobbi Smith is a standout chef and the meals here match practically any you are likely to have anywhere in Ireland. The individual bedrooms, like siblings, are all of a piece, even as each holds its own. All are clean, comfortable, peaceful, and gifted with lovely views of the sensuous Carlow countryside. The half- or full-canopy beds are quite reasonably firm. Smoking is not permitted in bedrooms or in the dining room, though smokers are provided with their own cozy snug, complete with fireplace. There's a small gift shop just for guests, displaying the work of local artisans, of which Bobbi Smith is one. This is a place to which you will find yourself returning, either in happy memory or in fact.

The Old Rectory is also the base for **Celtic Cycling,** www.celticcycling.com (see chapter 6), which offers an array of 1- or 2-week cycling tours, or simply the gear you need to go it alone, with or without accommodation. The "sunny south" (not always but offering better odds than most), with its rolling hills and gentle breezes, is great cycling country; and Don Smith will help you make the most of it.

INEXPENSIVE

Derrybawn Mountain Lodge. Laragh, County Wicklow. ☎ **0404/45644.** Fax 0404/45645. E-mail: derrybawnlodge@eircom.net. 8 units. £50–£60 ($70–$84) double. No service charge. Rates include full breakfast. MC, V.

This elegant, comfortable fieldstone manor house in an idyllic parkland setting looks out over the surrounding hills. The rooms (all no-smoking) are spacious, bright, tastefully furnished, and outfitted with orthopedic beds. Public areas include a sitting room, dining room, and rec room with snooker table and facilities for making tea and coffee. Located just outside Laragh village, the place is convenient to fishing streams and hiking trails (including the Wicklow Way), and a great place from which to explore Wicklow's natural wonders.

✪ **Sherwood Park House.** Kilbride, Ballon, County Carlow. ☎ **0503/59117.** Fax 0503/ 59355. E-mail: info@sherwoodparkhouse.ie. 4 units. £50–£60 ($70–$84) double. 25% reduction for children. Dinner £20 ($28). AE, MC, V. Off the N80, 3km/1.8mi south of Ballon.

An 18th-century Georgian country house and working farm, Sherwood Park is a place of green fields, distant mountains, the promise of hot tea, and real sheep to count from the warmth of a canopy bed piled high with pillows. Rooms are comfortably large, and the two on the second floor even have smaller, adjoining rooms with a twin bed that are perfect for children. Guests are invited to use the sitting room, where peat fills the fireplace and an old piano sits in the corner, ready to command center stage when played by guests. Patrick and Maureen Owens are the genial hosts, and they help to create a festive occasion of even the rainiest evening. Maureen prepares the dinner, served in a high-ceilinged dining room. Conversation is encouraged as all are seated at a long, well-polished wood table, although it's difficult to get beyond contented murmurs over soup made from vegetables grown on the estate or delighted exclamations about the flavor of homemade strawberry ice cream.

Slievemore. The Harbour, Greystones (signposted on N11), County Wicklow. ☎ **01/ 287-4724.** 8 units (all with shower only). TV. £45 ($63) double. No service charge. Rates include full Irish breakfast. No credit cards. Free parking. Bus: 84.

This mid-19th-century harbor house offers white-glove cleanliness, spacious comfort, and (if you book early and request a seafront room) a commanding view of Greystones Harbor, Bray Head, and the Irish Sea. Proprietor Pippins Parkinson says that "people stumble on Greystones, find it by accident." Whether you're accident-prone or not, stay here, reserve a table for dinner at nearby Coopers (see "Dining," below), and you won't forget the day you stumbled on Greystones.

Tudor Lodge. Laragh, County Wicklow. ☎ and fax **0404/45554.** 6 units, all with private bathroom (shower only). TV. June–Sept £50 ($70) double; Sept–May £27 ($37.80) single, £45 ($63) double. MC, V.

The whitewashed walls of Tudor Lodge are fresh and inviting, recalling the rusticity of a country cottage. Bedrooms are spacious, and each has a small desk as well as both double and twin bed, tea/coffeemaker, and hair dryer. The dining room and living room are equally hospitable: large windows open to views of green meadows and the slopes of the Wicklow mountains. A brick fireplace and beamed ceilings make the living room a cozy retreat, and in 2000, a sunroom was added. A generous stone terrace lies just outside, and a riverside patio overlooks the Avonmore River at the end of the garden. Hosts Des and Liz Kennedy offer guests an appetizing array of breakfast choices, and will also prepare dinner for larger groups. Otherwise, the restaurants and pubs of Laragh are a short and scenic walk away. No smoking.

SELF-CATERING

Baltinglass. County Wicklow. ☎ **0508/81396.** Fax **0508/73510.** 3 cottages. TV TEL. £150–£395 ($210–$553) per week. No credit cards, but personal checks are accepted. From Baltinglass, drive 3 miles (4.8km) southeast on R747.

Fortgranite is—and has been for centuries—a working farm in the rolling foothills of the Wicklow Mountains. Its meadows and stately trees create a sublime retreat. Its

Readers Recommend

Keppel's Farmhouse, Ballanagh, Avoca, County Wicklow. ☎ **0402/35168**. £40 ($56) double with bathroom.
We had the good fortune to stay at Keppel's Farmhouse. Our room was very large and immaculate! Hair dryers, soap, and shampoos were welcome additions to the bathroom. There was a large, comfortable sitting room for guests, as well as a cozy sun porch. Joy's breakfast was delicious, and her tales of the filming of "Ballykissangel" were delightful! Charlie invited us to "tag along" as he went about his farming chores.
—Nancy Dowling, Chadds Ford, Penn.

unique stone cottages, formerly occupied by the estate's workers, are being restored and refurbished with appreciable care and charm by M. P. Dennis. Three are available to rent for a week or longer. The gate lodges—Doyle's and Lennon's—each have one double bedroom, sleeping two and fully equipped with all essentials. The third, Steward's Cottage, sleeps four and is furnished with lovely antiques. All have open fireplaces, and each has its own grounds and garden. Tranquillity, charm, and warmth are the operative concepts at Fortgranite, so those in search of something grand and luxurious will be disappointed. Think "cottage" and "character," and you will be delighted. Also, it's best to plan ahead, because word is out and availability is at a premium. Golf, fishing, hill walking, horse racing and riding, and clay-pigeon shooting can all be found nearby. Smoking is discouraged.

Manor Kilbride. N. Blessington, County Wicklow. ☎ **01/458-2105**. Fax 01/458-2607. 4 cottages. Cottages £280–£500($392–$700) per week year-round. AE, MC, V. 18 miles (29km) from Dublin. On N81, take Kilbride/Sally Gap turn 4 miles (6.5km) north of Blessington; after 1 mile (1.6km), left at sign for Sally Gap. Entrance gates 50 yd. (46m) ahead on right.

Gracefully situated amid 40 acres of mature gardens and wooded walks in the Wicklow Mountain foothills, Charles and Margaret Cully's Manor is a haven of charm and cordiality.

The grounds of the Manor include two small lakes and a stretch of the River Brittas. Four lovely stone self-catering cottages are available. The two courtyard cottages and the river lodge sleep four; the gate lodge is better suited to a couple. These are four-star cottages, with original beams and exposed stone walls and every amenity. The Cullys are rather lavish in their welcome baskets, so there's no need for an immediate trip to the market.

Tynte House. Dunlavin center, County Wicklow. ☎ **045/401561**. Fax 045/401586. www.iol.ie/~jclawler. 7 units, 4 homes, 4 apts, 4 cottages. TV TEL. £37 ($51.80) double; self-catering units £140–£310 ($196–$434) per week. Dinner £12.50 ($17.50). AE, MC, V.

Dunlavin is a drowsy three-pub town in western Wicklow, 30 miles (48km) southwest of Dublin. It's as convenient as it is peaceful. Tynte House, a lovingly preserved 19th-century family farm complex with new apartment units and holiday cottages, offers an attractive array of options for overnight and longer-term guests. The driving force is Mrs. Caroline Lawler, "brought up in the business" of divining visitors' needs and surpassing their expectations. In 2000 she was named one of the top 20 "landladies" in the U.K. and Ireland.

The guest rooms are warm and comfortable. The self-catering mews (renovated stables) houses have one to three bedrooms; the apartments hold one or two bedrooms; and the four new cottages range from two to four bedrooms and have working fireplaces. All are brilliantly designed and furnished with one eye on casual efficiency and the other on good taste. They have bold, bright color schemes, light pine furniture, spacious tiled bathrooms, cable TV, and open kitchens fully equipped with microwave, dishwasher, washer, and dryer. The no. 3 mews house and the open-plan apartment are our favorites, but none will disappoint. All mattresses are new, but some are firmer than others. This is a great anchorage for families, with a grassy play area and treehouse, an outdoor barbecue and picnic tables, a tennis court, and a game room with Ping-Pong and pool. Exact prices depend on the season and the size of the unit. Shorter stays and weekend discounts may be negotiated in the off-season.

DINING
EXPENSIVE
✪ **Brunel Restaurant.** In the Tinakilly House Hotel. On R750, off the Dublin–Wexford road (N11), Rathnew, County Wicklow. ☎ **0404/69274.** Fixed-price dinner £36 ($50.40). AE, DC, MC, V. Open year-round 12:30–2pm and 7:30–9pm. IRISH/FRENCH.

This extraordinary restaurant, which *Bon Appétit* magazine has called "a beacon to restore hope to the traveller's heart," has won as many accolades as the hotel to which it belongs (see above). The table d'hôte menu changes daily, which leaves us mostly with adjectives rather than nouns for its description. The cuisine is confidently balanced—sophisticated without being fussy; elegant without acrobatics. After all, chefs too are bound by the Hippocratic oath and must first do no harm, a duty taken deeply to heart in the Tinakilly kitchen. From then on, it's a matter of inspiration. The service, too, is precise and intuitive, letting the ritual follow its own course. All this makes for a meal you remember, like the char-grilled tiger prawns and lemongrass with fennel oil, the cream of roast chestnut and celery soup, the caramelized scallops on saffron potato mash, and the loin of Wicklow lamb, which I enjoyed. The wine list is vast and, while international, focuses on France. For an explosive finale, I recommend the warm fresh fruit salad served on an amaretto pâté bomb.

MODERATE
✪ **Coopers.** Above the Beach House, The Harbour, Greystones, County Wicklow. ☎ **01/287-3914.** Reservations recommended. Fixed-price early-bird 2-course dinner (Mon–Fri 5:30–7:30pm) £10 ($14); main courses £8.95–£15.95 ($12.55–$22.35). No service charge. AE, MC, V. Mon–Sat 5:30–11pm; Sun 12:30–4pm and 5:30–10pm. INTERNATIONAL/SEAFOOD.

Coopers is the perfect reward after making the cliff walk from Bray to Greystones. This is one of the most tasteful dining environments I've found in Ireland—vaulted beamed ceilings, exposed brick and stone walls, stained glass, three fireplaces, wrought-iron fixtures, and linen table settings. It's a warm, relaxed, comfortable place for couples and families of any age. The menu is a rarity in that it understates its offerings, with ordinary descriptions like "smoked lamb" for extraordinary fare. Roast duckling and steamed sea trout are specialties, and there's a fine wine list. There are spectacular views of the open sea on two sides, and a piano player on Friday and Saturday nights. Coopers is no secret, so book well ahead.

✪ **Danette's Feast.** 3¼ miles (5.2km) from Carlow town, immediately off the Hacketstown Rd., Urglin Glebe, Bennekerry, Carlow, County Carlow. ☎ **0503/40817.** Reservations required. Fixed-price dinner £28 ($39.20); Sun lunch £20 ($28). MC, V. Wed–Sat 7–9:30pm, Sun 1–2:30pm. INTERNATIONAL.

Should you arrive in Carlow on Monday or Tuesday, it's well worth changing your itinerary to stay over for at least one meal between Wednesday and Sunday in this superb little restaurant. Be sure, however, to book ahead—it seats only 30, and is very popular with locals as well as visitors. The restaurant is in the main Georgian section of the very large house, and an 18th-century two-story cottage is now the kitchen. Bright, strong colors are used throughout: drinks and "nibbles" or dips are served in the Red Room (which Danette likens to the color of Rioja wine). From there, you proceed to one of the two dining rooms. Partners Danette O'Connell and David Milne are both musicians, and if things are quiet enough you may find David at the piano.

The kitchen is Danette's domain, and her creations often combine ethnic flavors (like her chiles rellenos with goat cheese, Parma ham, and a puree of sun-dried tomatoes, or Mediterranean minced lamb with a red pepper sauce). The menu selection is quite varied and always includes a vegetarian dish, as well as organically grown vegetables whenever possible. Two things not to be missed: her tomato and fennel bread and, to finish off the meal, her caramelized lemon tart made from the eggs of their free-range hens. There is a separate nonsmoking room. Musical evenings are held once a month between September and May.

Roundwood Inn. Main St. (R755), Roundwood, County Wicklow. ☎ **01/281-8107.** Reservations recommended for dinner. Main courses £11–£16 ($15.40–$22.40). MC, V. Wed–Sat 1–2:30pm and 7:30–9:30pm. Pub food all day every day. IRISH/CONTINENTAL.

Dating from 1750, this old coaching inn is the focal point of an out-of-the-way spot in the mountains, Roundwood, that's said to be the highest village in Ireland. It has an old-world atmosphere, with open log fireplaces and antique furnishings. Menu choices range from steaks and sandwiches to traditional Irish stew, fresh lobster, smoked salmon, and seafood pancakes. In the bar, a déjà vu house specialty is chicken in the basket.

INEXPENSIVE

Avoca Handweavers Tea Shop. Avoca, County Wicklow. ☎ **0402/35105.** Lunch £2.35–£5.95 ($3.30–$8.35). Daily 9:30am–5pm. AE, DC, MC, V. TRADITIONAL/VEGETARIAN.

This innovative cafeteria is worth a visit for lunch, even if you're not interested in woolens. The wholesome meals are surprisingly imaginative for cafeteria fare. I had a delicate pea and mint soup, prepared with vegetable stock, accompanied by a deliciously hearty spinach tart. Other dishes on the often-changing menu might include sesame glazed chicken or locally smoked Wicklow trout. The tea shop has a regular local clientele, in addition to the busloads of visitors who come to shop.

The Opera House. Market Sq., Wicklow Town, County Wicklow. ☎ **0404/66422.** Reservations recommended Fri–Sun. Main courses £6.95–£14.95 ($9.75–$20.95). No service charge. MC, V. Daily Jun–Aug 11am–11pm, Sept–May 6–11pm. Occasionally closes on Tues in the winter. ITALIAN/SEAFOOD.

This Irish trattoria is a unique find in this traditional harbor town. The faux Mediterranean decor is warm and tasteful; outside, picnic tables provide streetside dining for nonsmokers. The smoked salmon and tagliatelle flamed in a cream-and-vodka sauce is a delicious bargain, and the house French table wine (£10.50/$14.70) suits both wallet and palate. The service is enthusiastic, if stretched a bit thin on weekends. For a delightful conclusion, treat yourself to the lemon brûlée.

Poppies Country Cooking. Enniskerry, County Wicklow. ☎ **01/282-8869.** All items 60p–£5.50 (84¢–$7.70). No credit cards. Daily 9am–7pm. IRISH.

This 10-table self-service eatery opposite the main square is popular for light meals and snacks all day. The menu ranges from homemade soups and salads to hominy pie, nut roast, baked salmon, vegetarian quiche, and lasagna.

Poppies Country Cooking. Trafalgar Rd., Greystones, County Wicklow. ☎ **01/287-4228.**
All items 60p–£5.50 (84¢–$7.70). No credit cards. Mon–Sat 10am–6pm, Sun 11:30am–7pm.
IRISH HOMESTYLE.

Poppies of Enniskerry has done it again, this time in Greystones, a short walk from the
bus or train. With the warm, familiar feel of a neighbor's kitchen—the neighbor who
can really cook—this is a local hangout. From fist-sized whole-grain scones to vegetarian nut roast, the portions are generous. Seating overflows the 10 tables into a lovely
flowered tea garden out back, if and when the sun appears, April to October. A note of
warning: The desserts are diet-breakers, so try not to even look unless you are prepared
to fall. Homemade jams, preserves, salad dressing, and even local artwork are on sale.

PUBS

Cartoon Inn. Main St., Rathdrum, County Wicklow. ☎ **0404/46774.**

With walls displaying the work of many famous cartoonists, this cottage-like pub claims
to be the country's only cartoon-themed pub. It's the headquarters for Ireland's Cartoon
Festival, held in late May or early June each year. Pub grub is available at lunchtime.

The Coach House. Main St., Roundwood, County Wicklow. ☎ **01/281-8157.**

Adorned with lots of colorful hanging flowerpots, this Tudor-style inn sits in the
mountains in the heart of Ireland's highest village. Dating from 1790, it is full of local
memorabilia, from old photos and agricultural posters to antique jugs and plates. It's
well worth a visit, whether to learn about the area or to get some light refreshment.

The Meetings. Avoca, County Wicklow. ☎ **0402/35226.**

This Tudor-style country-cottage pub stands idyllically at the "Meeting of the Waters"
associated with poet Thomas Moore. An 1889 edition of Moore's book of poems is on
display. Good pub grub is served every day, with traditional Irish music April to October every Sunday afternoon (from 4 to 6pm), and weekend nights all year.

2 County Kildare: Ireland's Horse Country

15 to 30 miles (24 to 48km) W of Dublin

County Kildare and horse racing go hand in hand—or should we say neck and neck?
It's home of the Curragh racetrack, where the Irish Derby is held in late June, and
smaller tracks at Naas and Punchestown. County Kildare is also the heartland of
Ireland's flourishing bloodstock industry. In this panorama of open grasslands and
limestone-enriched soil, you'll find many of Ireland's 300 stud farms.

Kildare is famed as the birthplace of Brigid, Ireland's second patron saint. Brigid
was a bit ahead of her time as an early exponent for women's equality—she founded a
coed monastery in Kildare in the 5th or 6th century.

ESSENTIALS

GETTING THERE **Irish Rail** (☎ **01/836-3333**) provides daily train service to
Kildare.

Bus Eireann (☎ **01/836-6111**) operates daily express bus service to Kildare.

By car, take the main Dublin–Limerick road (N7) west of Dublin from Kildare, or
the main Dublin–Galway road (N4) to Celbridge, turning off on local road R403.

VISITOR INFORMATION Contact the **Wicklow Tourist Office,** Wicklow Town
(☎ **0404/69117**). It's open year-round Monday to Friday, and Saturday during peak
season. There is also a seasonal (mid-May to Sept) information office in Kildare Town,
County Kildare (☎ **045/522696**).

SEEING THE SIGHTS

Castletown. R403, off main Dublin–Galway road (N4), Celbridge, County Kildare. ☎ **01/ 628-8252.** Admission £3 ($4.20) adults, £2 ($2.80) seniors, £1 ($1.40) children and students, £7.50 ($10.50) family. Easter day–Sept Mon–Fri 10am–6pm, Sat–Sun 1–6pm; Oct Mon–Fri 10am–5pm, Sun 1–5pm; Nov Sun 1–5pm. Closed Dec.

Castletown—designed by Italian architect Alessandro Galilei for William Connolly (1662–1729), then Speaker of the Irish House of Commons—is the grandest Palladian-style mansion in Ireland. In a 1722 letter to Bishop Berkeley, this architectural gem was touted as a "magnificent pile of a building . . . [destined to be] the finest Ireland ever saw." For all too long, "pile" came sadly close to the truth, as the once and future gem underwent extensive renovation in the hands of the Office of Public Works, its current overseer. Work continues, but Castletown was reopened to the public in 1999.

✪ **The Curragh.** Dublin–Limerick road (N7), Curragh, County Kildare. ☎ **045/441205.** www.curragh.ie. Admission £8–£12 ($11.20–$16.80) for most races; £15–£35 ($21–$49) for Derby. AE, DC, MC, V. Hours vary; first race usually 2pm.

Often referred to as the Churchill Downs of Ireland, this is the country's best-known racetrack, just 30 miles (48km) west of Dublin. Majestically placed at the edge of Ireland's central plain, it's home to the **Irish Derby,** held in late June. Horses race at least one Saturday a month from March to October. Recently, the main stand has been extensively renovated, a new betting hall has been added, and dining facilities (bars, restaurants, and food court) have been greatly expanded.

The track has rail links with all major towns. With Irish Rail, it offers a round-trip "Racing by Rail" package from Dublin (Heuston Station) for £12 ($16.80), including courtesy coach to the main entrance. There's also a "Racing Bus" leaving Dublin (Busaras) each race day. Call Bus Eireann for details (☎ **01/836-6111**).

✪ **Irish National Stud & Japanese Gardens & St. Fiachra's Garden.** Off the Dublin–Limerick road (N7), Tully, Kildare, County Kildare. ☎ **045/521617.** www.irish-national-stud.ie. Admission £6 ($8.40) adults; £4.50 ($6.30) seniors, students, and children over 12; £3 ($4.20) children under 12; £14 ($19.60) family. MC, V. Feb 12–Nov 12 daily 9:30am–6pm. Bus: From Busarus, Dublin, each morning, returning each evening.

Some of Ireland's most famous horses have been bred on the grounds of this government-sponsored stud farm. A prototype for other horse farms throughout Ireland, it has 288 stalls to accommodate mares, stallions, and foals. Visitors are welcome to walk around the 958-acre grounds and see the noble steeds being exercised and groomed.

A converted groom's house has exhibits on racing, steeplechasing, hunting, and show jumping, plus the skeleton of Arkle, one of Ireland's most famous horses.

The ✪ **Japanese garden** is among the finest Asian gardens in Europe. Laid out between 1906 and 1910, it's designed to symbolize the journey of the soul from oblivion to eternity. The Japanese-style visitor center has a restaurant and craft shop. The Commemorative Garden of St. Fiachra, in a natural setting of woods, wetlands, lakes, and islands, opened in 1999. The reconstructed hermitage houses a Waterford crystal garden of rocks, ferns, and delicate glass orchids.

Impressions

Pat: He was an Anglo-Irishman.
Meg: In the name of God what's that?
Pat: A Protestant with a horse.

—Brendan Behan (1923–64), *The Hostage*

The Irish Pewtermill. Timolin-Moone (signposted off N9 in Moone), County Kildare. ☎ **0507/24164.** www.kildare.ie/timolinpewter. Free admission. Year-round Mon–Fri 9:30am–4:30pm.

Ensconced in an 11th-century mill constructed for the nunnery of St. Moling—after whom the village of Timolin ("House of Moling") is named—Ireland's oldest pewter mill is a real find. Six skilled craftsmen cast traditional Irish silver-bright pewter in antique molds, some 300 years old. Casting takes place just about every day, usually in the morning. The showroom displays and sells a wide selection of high-quality hand-cast pewter gifts, from bowls to brooches. Prices are very reasonable. Custom-made gifts, such as tankards, engraved with family crests, may be commissioned. An additional attraction here is a set of excellent reproductions of the principal panels from Moone High Cross (see the listing below), with explanatory plaques. They're helpful in further understanding and appreciating the nearby treasure. If he is about, be sure to meet Sean Cleary, a veritable font of information on pewter casting, local history, and all things Irish, and a formidable storyteller besides.

Moone High Cross. Moone, County Kildare. Signposted off N9 on southern edge of Moone village.

This renowned high cross, recently restored on-site, stands in the ruins of Moone Abbey, the southernmost monastic settlement established by St. Columba in the 6th century. The formula of neglect and care that the ruins and grounds currently receive actually enhances them. The overgrown path to the site, for instance, is lined with bright annuals. The high cross, nearly 1,200 years old, is quite magnificent. A splendid example of Celtic stone carving, it contains finely crafted Celtic designs as well as numerous Biblical scenes, such as the temptation of Adam and Eve, the sacrifice of Isaac, and Daniel in the lions' den. The cross also holds several surprises, such as representations of a dolphin and a species of Near Eastern fish that reproduces when the male feeds the female her own eggs, which eventually hatch from her mouth. If you're nearby, you will be glad not to have passed by this exemplary co-creation of Celtic imagination and early Christian faith.

Newbridge Cutlery. Off Dublin–Limerick road (N7), Newbridge, County Kildare. ☎ **045/ 431301.** Free admission. Mon–Fri 9am–5pm, Sat 11am–5pm, Sun 2–5pm.

Look closely at the silverware when you sit down to eat at one of Ireland's fine hotels or restaurants—there's a good chance it was made by Newbridge, which for the past 60 years has been one of Ireland's leading manufacturers of fine silverware. In the visitor center, you can see a display of place settings, bowls, candelabras, trays, frames, and one-of-a-kind items. A video on silver making is also shown. Silver pieces are sold here, including "sale" items.

Steam Museum. Off Dublin–Limerick road (N7), Straffan, County Kildare. ☎ **01/627-3155.** Admission £3 ($4.20) adults; £2 ($2.80) seniors, children, and students; £10 ($14) family. Garden £2 ($2.80). Museum Apr–May and Sept Sun 2:30–5:30pm; June–Aug Tues–Sun 2–6pm. Walled garden June–July Tues–Fri and Sun 2–6pm; Aug Tues–Fri 2:30–5:30pm. Signposted off N7 at Kill Village.

Housed in a converted church, this museum is a must for steam-engine buffs. It contains two collections. The Richard Guinness Hall has more than 20 prototypical locomotive engines dating from the 18th century, and the Power Hall has rare industrial stationary engines. The steam and garden shop stocks a variety of recent books and videos on the Irish Railway, and serves as the sole outlet for National Trust Enterprises gifts, which can be excellent values. The 18th-century walled garden features several garden rooms extending to a delightful rosery. Call ahead for information on when the engines will be in operation.

SPORTS & OUTDOOR PURSUITS

GOLF   The flat plains of Kildare offer some lovely settings for parkland layouts, including two new 18-hole championship courses. The par-72 **Kildare Country Club,** Straffan (☎ **01/601-7300**), charges greens fees of £140 ($196). For a less costly game, the par-70 **Kilkea Castle Golf Club,** Castledermot (☎ **0503/45555**), charges £25 ($35) all week. Or try the par-72 championship course at the **Curragh Golf Club,** Curragh (☎ **045/441238**), with greens fees of £18 ($25.20) weekdays, £22 ($30.80) weekends.

HORSEBACK RIDING   Visitors can expect to pay an average of £10 to £15 ($14 to $21) per hour for trekking or trail riding in the Kildare countryside. To arrange a ride, contact the **Kill International Equestrian Centre,** Kill (☎ **045/877208**).

ACCOMMODATIONS
VERY EXPENSIVE

Kildare Hotel & Country Club. Straffan, County Kildare. ☎ **800/221-1074** from the U.S., or 01/601-7200. Fax 01/601-7299. www.kclub.ie. 45 units. MINIBAR TV TEL. £310–£380 ($434–$532) double; £550 ($770) 1-bedroom suite; £750 ($1,050) 2-bedroom suite; £1,000 ($1,400) Viceroy suite. No service charge. AE, CB, DC, DISC, MC, V.

Located 20 miles (32km) west of Dublin, this luxurious 330-acre five-star resort is a favorite of Ireland's sporting set. Straffan House, a 19th-century mansion, serves as the core of the hotel, with an adjacent new west wing that is a replica of the original building. An additional wing of 33 bedrooms is currently under construction. The guest rooms are spread out among the main hotel, courtyard suites, and a lodge. Hand-painted wall coverings and murals enhance the high ceilings, bow windows, wide staircases, antiques, and period pieces. The house overlooks a 1-mile (1.6km) stretch of the River Liffey.

Dining/Diversions: The main restaurant, the Bryerley Turk, features French food. The Gallery serves lighter fare, including afternoon tea; the Legends bar overlooks the golf course.

Amenities: 24-hour room service, nightly turndown, concierge, laundry and valet service, 18-hole Arnold Palmer–designed golf course, private access to salmon and trout fishing, two indoor and two outdoor tennis courts, two squash courts, gym, indoor swimming pool, sauna, solarium.

✪ **Kilkea Castle.** Castledermot, County Kildare. ☎ **0503/45156.** Fax 0503/45187. E-mail: kilkea@iol.ie. 36 units. TV TEL. £140–£240 ($196–$336) double. Rates include full Irish breakfast and service charge. AE, DC, MC, V. From Castledermot, follow signs approximately 2½ miles (4km).

Nestled beside the River Greese and surrounded by lovely formal gardens, this multi-turreted stone castle is a standout in the flat farmland of County Kildare. Considered the oldest inhabited castle in Ireland (1180), it was built by Hugh de Lacy, an early Irish governor, for Walter de Riddlesford, a great warrior. The castle later passed into the ownership of the legendary Geraldines, and it is supposedly haunted by the 11th Earl of Kildare. Every 7 years, the earl—dressed in full regalia and accompanied by his knights—is said to gallop around the castle walls.

Fully restored as a hotel in recent years, Kilkea is decorated with suits of armor and medieval banners, as well as a mix of Irish antiques and Asian tables, chests, and urns. About a third of the guest rooms are in the original castle building, with the rest in a newer courtyard addition; bathrooms throughout are modern tile and brass. Furnishings include dark woods, semicanopy beds, armoires, chandeliers, brass fixtures, gilt-framed paintings and mirrors, and floral designer fabrics.

Beyond the Pale in County Laois

Ireland is full of surprises and the Midlands are one of them. Not usually regarded as a tourist area, either by the Irish or by outsiders, Ireland's heartland is being rediscovered of late, to everyone's delight.

But where to begin? We suggest **Portlaoise** (pronounced "port-leash"). Only an hour southwest of Dublin's city center, Portlaoise makes a convenient stopover for those on their way to the Southwest or a congenial 2-night base for those eager to explore the hidden secrets of County Laois. In either case, we heartily recommend that you book a room in **Ivyleigh House,** Bank Place, Portlaoise, County Laois (☎ **0502/22081;** fax 0502/63343; e-mail: ivyleigh@gofree.indigo.ie). This gracious, historic Georgian home, a stone's throw from the heart of the town, is simply one of the finest guesthouses we have encountered anywhere in Ireland. It has been exquisitely restored, furnished with the finest of everything from antiques to table settings to linens, and dedicated to the principle that guests should enjoy their hosts' dream holiday. The breakfast here, a gourmet fete, is without peer in our experience. No wonder that in its first year of opening (1999), Ivyleigh House was awarded 5 diamonds (the highest rating) and the "little gem" award by the RAC (Royal Auto Club). The £70 ($98) it charges for a double room turns out to be a bargain. Now, to make a couple days of it, let us suggest the perfect agenda.

Once ensconced in Ivyleigh House, there are a handful of excellent restaurants within a 10-minute stroll, but we urge you to consider **Jim's Country Kitchen,** 27 Church St., Portlaoise (☎ **0502/62061**). Here you'll sample for yourself the full meaning of Ireland's "slow food" movement, the best of Irish produce and ingredients properly prepared, nothing rushed and nothing lost.

Then, early the next day, after the breakfast of your dreams, you can set out for the nearby ✪ **Slieve Bloom Environmental Park,** one of Ireland's natural

---

Dining/Diversions: The main dining room is de Lacy's, specializing in innovative Irish cuisine. The Geraldine Bar has a 12th-century atmosphere, with original stone walls, stained-glass windows, and huge fireplace crowned by a copper flue.

Amenities: Room service, concierge, baby-sitting, 18-hole golf course, indoor heated swimming pool, exercise room, saunas, spa pool, steam rooms, sun bed, toning table. Fishing for brown trout on the adjacent River Greese, two floodlit hard tennis courts, clay-pigeon shooting, bicycle rental, archery range.

EXPENSIVE

✪ **Barberstown Castle.** Straffan, County Kildare. ☎ **01/628-8157.** Fax 01/627-7027. E-mail: castleir@iol.ie. 22 units. TV TEL. £120–£140 ($168–$196) double; £175 ($245) suite. Service charge 10%. Rates include full Irish breakfast. AE, DC, MC, V. From Dublin city center or airport (30 min.), drive south on N7, take turn for Straffan at Kill; west on N4, take turn for Straffan at Maynooth.

Within easy reach of Dublin, this is a perfect country getaway with more than a touch of class. This exquisite hotel spans 750 years of Irish history within its walls. Its four segments—constructed in the 13th, 16th, 18th, and 20th centuries—somehow form a coherent and pleasing whole. Each luxurious guest room is named after one of the castle's former lords or proprietors. They begin with Nicholas Barby, who constructed the battlemented rectangular keep in the late 13th century, and include Eric Clapton,

wonders. But before you do so, be sure to pack a picnic provisioned at **Jim's Food Hall** (same Jim and same location as above) and to pick up (in **The Bookstore** just down the street from Ivyleigh House) a copy of Thomas P. Joyce's *Bladma: Walks of Discovery in Slieve Bloom,* the perfect pocket field guide, complete with ribbon bookmark. Joyce will both guide and enchant you step-by-step in your explorations.

On your drive back to Portlaoise, we would recommend a short detour to **Emo Court,** Emo, County Laois, a magnificently restored neoclassical mansion designed by the famed Georgian architect James Gandon; it's surrounded by 250 acres of formal geometric lawns and gardens, with meandering paths through a grove of trees so stately and sublime that you will think new thoughts.

Next, just 4 miles (6.5km) outside of Portlaoise (signposted SE off of N80), explore the ancient site called **The Rock of Dunamase,** an open site under excavation. It will require some modest climbing, but your reward will be quite stunning 360-degree panoramic views of the sensuously molded Laois landscape, all soft hillocks and quilted fields. All this from the battlements of a captivatingly ruined 12th-century castle.

Then, with your appetite intact, you can enjoy tea and coffee and provided treats in your room and decide whether to return to Jim's or to try one of the town's other fine eateries. Finally, as if your day hasn't had enough drama already, be sure to book (in advance) a seat at the spectacular new **Dunamaise Theatre** (☎ **0502/63355**), offering a year-round program of first-rate theater and music, only several doors down from Ivyleigh House!

There you have it, 2 memorable nights and a grand day beyond the pale, in a place you probably didn't even know existed!

---

who sold it to the present owners, Kenneth and Catherine Healy. The Barberstown story—from fortress to guesthouse—is a long one, with a happy ending for anyone deciding to stay here. The rooms are warm and elegant, with sitting area, four-poster bed, antique desk, chandelier, and spacious bathroom. Two-bedroom family accommodations are available, as is a room designed for guests with disabilities. Smoking is limited to the lounge.

Dining: The award-winning Castle Restaurant is open to nonguests by reservation.

Amenities: Golf can be arranged at a number of nearby courses, including the Kildare Country Club.

Hotel Keadeen. Off Dublin–Limerick road (N7), Newbridge, County Kildare. ☎ **045/431666.** Fax 045/434402. www.keadeenhotel.kildare.ie. 55 units. TV TEL. £120.75–£155.25 ($169.05–$217.35) double; £160 ($224) suite. No service charge. DC, MC, V.

Less than 2 miles (3.2km) east of the Curragh racetrack, this small country-style hotel is a favorite with the horse set. Just off the main road, it is well set back on 8 acres of grounds in a quiet garden setting. Equestrian art dominates the public rooms. The guest rooms are bright and spacious, with light woods, floral fabrics, and brass fixtures. The new executive rooms, each a double with a king-size bed and a comfortable alcove sitting area, are well worth the additional cost. All the common rooms and all but five of the guest rooms are on ground level, well suited to visitors with disabilities.

Dining/Diversions: On the premises is the Derby Room restaurant, and a casual lounge with many comfortable nooks.

Amenities: There's a beautifully designed, fully outfitted health and fitness center, complete with an 18m swimming pool.

DINING
EXPENSIVE

Moyglare Manor. Maynooth, County Kildare. ☎ **01/628-6351.** Reservations required. Fixed-price dinner £27.50 ($38.50). Service charge 12.5%. AE, DC, MC, V. Sun–Fri 12:30–2pm; daily 7–9:30pm. Closed Good Friday and Dec 25–27. FRENCH.

A half-hour's drive on the Dublin–Galway road (N4) delivers you to this grand Georgian mansion and inn, whose restaurant is surprisingly intimate. Elegance is the operative word here. Roast quail, baked plaice stuffed with shrimp, grilled sea trout, and steaks, all with fresh vegetables from the manor's own garden, are not known to disappoint.

MODERATE/INEXPENSIVE

Silken Thomas. The Square, Kildare, County Kildare. ☎ **045/521264.** Reservations recommended for dinner. Main courses £7–£14 ($9.80–$19.60). AE, MC, V. Mon–Sat 12:30–3pm and 6–10pm, Sun 12:30–3pm and 6–9pm. IRISH/INTERNATIONAL.

Formerly known as Leinster Lodge, this historic inn offers an old-world pub and restaurant with an open fire. It is named after a famous member of the Norman Fitzgerald family, whose stronghold was in Kildare. He led an unsuccessful rebellion against Henry VIII, and some of the decor recalls his efforts. The menu offers a good selection of soups, sandwiches, burgers, and salads, as well as steaks, roasts, mixed grills, and fresh seafood platters.

3 Counties Meath & Louth/The Boyne River Valley

30 to 50 miles (48km to 80km) N and W of Dublin

Less than 30 miles (48km) north of Dublin along Ireland's east coast runs the River Boyne, surrounded by the rich, fertile countryside of counties Meath and Louth. More than any other river in the country, this meandering body of water has been at the center of Irish history.

The banks of the Boyne hold reminders of almost every phase of Ireland's past, from the prehistoric passage tombs of Newgrange to the storied Hill of Tara, seat of the High Kings, to early Christian sites. This land was also the setting for the infamous Battle of the Boyne, when on July 1, 1690 (July 12 by modern calendars), King William III defeated the exiled King James II for the crown of England.

ESSENTIALS

GETTING THERE   Irish Rail (☎ 01/836-6222) provides daily train service between Dublin and Drogheda.

Bus Eireann (☎ 01/836-6111) operates daily express bus service to Slane and Navan in County Meath, and Collon and Drogheda in County Louth. Bus Eireann and **Gray Line Tours** (☎ 01/605-7705) offer seasonal sightseeing tours to Newgrange and the Boyne Valley.

By car, take N1 north from Dublin City to Drogheda, then N51 west to Boyne Valley; N2 northwest to Slane and east on N51 to Boyne Valley; or N3 northwest via Hill of Tara to Navan, and then east on N51 to Boyne Valley.

VISITOR INFORMATION   Contact the **Dundalk Tourist Office,** Jocelyn Street, County Louth (☎ **042/35484**); the **Drogheda Tourist Office,** Headfort Place (behind the town hall), Drogheda, County Meath (☎ **041/983-7070**); or the **Bru na Boinne Center,** Newgrange, Donore, County Meath (☎ **041/80305**).

COUNTY MEATH: THE ROYAL COUNTY

The southern portion of the Boyne belongs to County Meath, an area that consists almost entirely of a rich limestone plain, with verdant pasturelands and occasional low hills. Once a separate province that included neighboring County Westmeath, Meath was usually referred to as the "Royal County Meath," because it was ruled by the kings of pagan and early Christian Ireland, from the Hill of Tara near Navan. Centuries later, however, Ireland fell under Anglo-Norman clout, and Trim Castle was constructed in the 12th and 13th centuries to make certain that the fact of British rule was not lost on anyone.

The chief town of County Meath is Navan, but nearby Kells is better known to the traveler because of its association with the famous Book of Kells, the hand-illustrated gospel manuscript on display at Trinity College in Dublin (see chapter 4). The town of Kells, known in Gaelic as *Ceanannus Mor* ("Great Residence"), was originally the site of an important 6th-century monastic settlement founded by St. Columcille. Monks driven from Iona in the 9th century by the Vikings occupied it for a time. The monks may have brought with them at least an incomplete Book of Kells. The book was stolen in 1007, and recovered months later from a bog. The monastery was dissolved in 1551, and today only ruins and a number of crosses survive.

Less than 25 miles (40km) southeast of Kells, beside the River Boyne, stand the alluring ruins of Bective Abbey, a Cistercian monastery founded in 1147 and fortified in the 15th century. Today, the fortress aspect of the abbey prevails, and it feels more like a castle than a monastery. It is a great climbing ruin, with myriad staircases, passageways, and chambers—a favorite hide-and-seek venue for local children, and perfect for a family picnic.

A focal point of County Meath is **Slane,** a small crossroads village and gateway to prehistoric Newgrange. Nearby is the Hill of Slane, a lofty 500-foot mound overlooking one of the loveliest parts of the Boyne Valley. On this hill, tradition has it, Patrick lit the Christian paschal fire in direct defiance of the Irish King Laoghaire, throwing down the gauntlet for a confrontation between Ireland's old and new religious orders.

Even though Meath is primarily an inland county, it is also blessed with a 6-mile (9.7km) stretch of coastline and two fine sandy beaches, Bettystown and Laytown. History pops up everywhere in County Meath, even on the beach: the Tara Brooch was found at Bettystown in 1850. Often copied in modern jewelry designs, the brooch is one of Ireland's finest pieces of early Christian gold-filigree work, embellished with amber and glass. It's on view at the National Museum in Dublin.

SEEING THE SIGHTS

Butterstream Gardens. Trim, County Meath. ☎ **046/36017.** Admission £4 ($5.60). May–Sept daily 11am–6pm.

Butterstream is an idyllic orchestration of garden rooms, each holding the delights of spring and summer. Garden designer Jim Reynolds and his sole assistant meld the brilliant reds and yellows of a garden of hot colors with the gentle green foliage flanking a pond and the pale scepter of a white garden. Architectural notes resound throughout the garden; its vegetation is marked by a Doric folly or reshaped into topiary pyramids.

⭐ **Hill of Tara.** Off the main Dublin road (N3), Navan, County Meath. ☎ **046/25903.** Admission £1.50 ($2.10) adults, £1 ($1.40) seniors, 60p (84¢) children and students, £4 ($5.60) family. Early May to mid-June and mid-Sept to Oct daily 10am–5pm; mid-June to mid-Sept daily 9:30am–6:30pm. Closed Nov–Apr.

This glorious hill is best remembered as the royal seat of the high kings in the early centuries of the millennium. Every 3 years a *feis* (a banquet reaching the proportions of a great national assembly) was held. It's said that more than 1,000 people—princes, poets, athletes, priests, druids, musicians, and jesters—celebrated for a week in a single immense hall. The poet Thomas Moore wrote, "The harp that once through Tara's halls / the soul of music shed. . . ." A feis wasn't all fun and games, though: laws were passed, tribal disputes settled, and matters of peace and defense decided.

The last feis was held in A.D. 560, and thereafter Tara went into a decline associated with the rise of Christianity. If you rally to Tara's halls today, you won't see any turrets, towers, moats, or crown jewels—in fact, you won't even see any halls. All that remains of Tara's former glories are grassy mounds and some ancient pillar stones. There's no access to the interior. All the wooden halls rotted long ago, so you'll have to rely on your imagination. It's still a magnificent spot, with the hill rising 300 feet above the surrounding countryside, and the views surely as awesome as they were 1,500 years ago.

A new visitor center, with exhibits and a stirring audiovisual presentation, is in the old church beside the entrance to the archaeological area.

⭐ **Knowth.** Drogheda, County Meath. ☎ **041/988-0300.** Admission to Knowth and Bru na Boinne Centre £3 ($4.20) adults, £2 ($2.80) seniors, £1.25 ($1.75) students and children over 6, £7.50 ($10.50) family. No credit cards. Daily Nov–Feb 9:30am–5pm; Mar–Apr and Oct 9:30am–5:30pm; May 9am–6:30pm; June to mid-Sept 9am–7pm; mid- to late Sept 9am–6:30pm.

Dating from the Stone Age and under seemingly perpetual excavation, this great mound is believed to have been a burial site for the high kings of Ireland. Archaeological evidence points to occupation from 3000 B.C. to A.D. 1200. One mile (1.6km) northwest of Newgrange (see below), between Drogheda and Slane, Knowth is more complex than Newgrange, with two passage tombs surrounded by 17 smaller satellite tombs. The site has the greatest collection of passage tomb art ever uncovered in Western Europe. There is no access to the interior of the tombs at this time. All tickets are issued at the new visitor center. Combined tickets with Newgrange are available.

⭐ **Loughcrew.** Outside Oldcastle, County Meath. Admission £1 ($1.40) adults, 70p (98¢) seniors, 40p (56¢) children and students, £3 ($4.20) family. Mid-June to mid-Sept daily 10am–6pm. Other times: key is available (see below). From N3, take R195 through Oldcastle toward Mullingar. 1½ miles (2.4km) out of Oldcastle, look for a signposted left turn. The next left turn into Loughcrew is also signposted.

The 30 passage tombs of Loughcrew, also known as Slieve na Calliaghe or "the hill of the witch," crown three hilltops in western Meath. The views of the plains of Meath and of the lakelands of Cavan are spectacular on a clear day. Two of the cairns—ornamented with Neolithic carvings—can be entered with a key. Guided tours of the eastern cairn are offered from mid-June to mid-September, and a key is available at the office for the western tomb (in many ways the more interesting of the two). A £20 ($28) deposit is required for the key. From October to May the keys to both cairns can be gotten from Mrs. Basil Balfe (☎ **049/41256**), whose home is the first house on your right after turning into the Loughcrew drive.

⭐ **Newgrange.** Signposted off the N1 and N2, Drogheda, County Meath. ☎ **041/ 988-0300.** Guided tour and admission to Bru na Boinne Centre £4 ($5.60) adults, £3 ($4.20) seniors, £2 ($2.80) students and children over 6, £10 ($14) family. No credit cards.

Daily Nov–Feb 9:30am–5pm; Mar–Apr and Oct 9:30am–5:30pm; May 9am–6:30pm; June to mid-Sept 9am–7pm; mid- to late Sept 9am–6:30pm.

Newgrange is Ireland's best-known prehistoric monument, and one of the archaeological wonders of Western Europe. Built as a burial mound more than 5,000 years ago—long before the Great Pyramids and Stonehenge—it sits atop a hill near the Boyne, massive and impressive. The huge mound—36 feet tall and approximately 260 feet in diameter—consists of 200,000 tons of stone, a 6-ton capstone, and other stones weighing up to 16 tons each, many of which were hauled from as far away as County Wicklow and the Mountains of Mourne. Each stone fits perfectly in the overall pattern, and the result is a watertight structure, an amazing feat of engineering. Carved into the stones are myriad spirals, diamonds, and concentric circles. Inside, a passage 60 feet long leads to a central burial chamber with a 19-foot ceiling.

Fascination with Newgrange reaches a peak at the winter solstice, when at 8:58am, as the sun rises to the southeast, sunlight pierces the inner chamber with an orange-toned glow for about 17 minutes. This occurrence is so remarkable that, as of this writing, the waiting list for viewing extends through the year 2004. Admission to Newgrange is by guided tour only. It's 2 miles (3.2km) east of Slane.

Logistical tips: All tickets are issued at the visitor center, Bru na Boinne. Combined tickets with Knowth, another nearby megalithic passage tomb, are available. Because of the great numbers of visitors, especially in the summer, expect delays; access is not guaranteed.

Newgrange Farm. Off N51, 2 miles (3.2km) east of Slane (signposted off N51 and directly west of Newgrange monument), County Meath. ☎ **041/982-4119.** Admission £3 ($4.20) per person, £11 ($15.40) family. Daily 10am–5pm. Closed Sept–Easter.

A contrast to all the surrounding antiquity in the Boyne Valley, this busy 333-acre farm is very much a 20th-century attraction. Farmer Willie Redhouse and his family invite visitors on a 1½-hour tour of their farm, which grows wheat, oats, barley, rapeseed oil, corn, and linseed (flax). You can throw feed to the ducks, groom a calf, or bottle-feed the baby lambs or kid goats. Children can hold a newborn chick, pet a pony, or play with the pigs. In the aviaries are pheasants and rare birds. Horses, donkeys, and rare Jacob sheep romp in the fields. The high point of the week occurs at roughly 3pm every Sunday, when the sheep take to the track with Teddy Bear jockeys for the weekly Derby. This is especially engaging for children, who are given "part-owner" badges for the sheep of their choice so that they can shout their own ball of wool to victory. There is now a new Go-Karting and toy tractor play area for children.

Demonstrations of sheepdog working, threshing, and horseshoeing are given. The Redhouses spin and dye their own wool and have put together an exhibit of the fibers produced and the natural dyes used to color them. At the herb garden, visitors receive a lesson on picking edible plants and herbs. Many of the farm buildings are from the 17th century. There are a coffee shop (see "Dining," below) and indoor and outdoor picnic areas.

St. Colmcille's House. About 200 yd. NW of St. Columba's Church, Church Lane, Kells, County Meath. Free admission. Ask for key from caretaker Mrs. B. Carpenter on Church Lane.

St. Colmcille's Oratory, whose oldest parts date from the 9th century, sits in ancient glory amidst a row of modern terraced housing. The carefully placed stones of its curving roof and unusual two-story structure are enigmatic and prompt an immediate trip down the street for the key to unlock at least some of its secrets. Once an ancient church holding relics of St. Colmcille, the first-floor room still contains the traces of an ancient fireplace and entryway. But this isn't all: a narrow metal stair ascends 4.5m (15 ft.) to a dark vault just under the roof. The small two-chambered space has both a structural and a mythical dimension. It is thought to help reinforce the stone arch of the oratory roof and—though this is more conjectural—is also said to be the place where the Book of Kells was completed.

✪ **Trim Castle.** Trim, County Meath. ☎ **041/988-0300.** Admission to grounds and tour of keep £2.50 ($3.50) adults, £1.75 ($2.45) seniors, £1 ($1.40) children and students, £6 ($8.40) family. Admission to Grounds £1 ($1.40) adults, 70p (98¢) seniors, 40p (56¢) children and students, £3 ($4.20) family. June–Sept daily 10am–6pm (last admission at 5:15pm). Tours every 30 min.: 1st tour at 10:15am and last tour at 5:15pm. Closed Oct–May.

This is a magnificent sight for anyone still rapt by knights in armor and all things medieval. After years of being closed to the public for the sake of major restoration, Trim Castle (aka King John's Castle, and best known today as a central set for the film *Braveheart*) reopened to the public on July 12, 2000. Trim Castle's once and future repute rests with its being the most massive and important Anglo-Norman castle in Ireland. Norman lord Hugh de Lacy occupied the site in 1172 and completed the enclosed cruciform keep or great tower before the end of the century. In the 13th century, his son Walter enlarged the keep, circled it with a many-towered curtain wall, and added a Great Hall as an upgraded venue for courts, parliaments, and feasts. Later, the same son Walter, after losing control of his own castle to rebels, laid siege to Trim so as to regain it. This proved to be the one and only siege the castle endured until it was abandoned in 1641 and collapsed of its own weight sometime afterward. In fact, the castle never underwent any significant alteration during its 400-plus intact years.

The decision of the Heritage Service to restore it as a "preserved ruin" is a wise and effective one. What stands revealed now is the grand skeleton of the once-grand symbol of Anglo-Norman clout, just enough for visitors to reconstruct the flourishing whole in their imaginations. The guided tour of the keep is a must in this process. Be forewarned, however, that each tour is absolutely limited to 15 persons, so daily demand is likely to exceed capacity. Tours are on a first-come-first-served basis and cannot be booked in advance, so arrive early. The tour of the keep is not for everyone, however. The tour is unsuitable for children in arms, small unruly children, and anyone unable to tolerate steep climbs and formidable heights. It's perfectly safe but calls for the climbing of narrow stone steps and exact obedience to the guide's stated restrictions. All you need to enjoy it is a rich imagination, some modest stamina and tolerance of safe heights, and a willingness to do exactly as you're instructed.

SHOPPING

Mary McDonnell Craft Studio. Newgrange Mall Studio, Slane, County Meath. ☎ **041/982-4722.**

Textile artist Mary McDonnell welcomes visitors to watch as she creates beautiful leather items, ceramics, jewelry, quilts, cushions, and wall hangings. Her shop also stocks the work of other local artisans, with a wide selection of crafts inspired by ancient designs uncovered in the Boyne Valley. The studio also incorporates Slane Antiques, operated by Mark McKeever. It's worth a detour. Open Tuesday to Saturday 10:30am to 6pm, Sunday 3 to 6pm.

ACCOMMODATIONS

Conyngham Arms Hotel. Main St., Slane, County Meath. ☎ **800/44-UTELL** from the U.S., or 041/988-4444. Fax 041/982-4205. E-mail: conynghamarms@eircom.ie. 14 units. TV TEL. £55–£100 ($77–$140) double. No service charge. Rates include full breakfast. AE, DC, MC, V.

In the heart of one of the Boyne Valley's loveliest villages, this three-story stone-faced inn dates from 1850 and has been run by the same family for more than 60 years. The current proprietors, Kevin and Vonnie Macken, work hard to blend old-world charm and personal attention with 20th-century efficiency and innovative innkeeping. The guest rooms offer traditional dark wood furnishings, some with part-canopy beds, rich primary-color fabrics, and good reading lights. Other features include writing desks, towel warmers, mirrored closets, and hair dryers—but, in keeping with the building's character, no elevator. Exceptionally good bar food is available all day in the lounge. Dinner is served in the adjacent Flemings restaurant, two rooms with a lot of Irish memorabilia.

✪ **Lennoxbrook Country House.** Kells, County Meath. ☎ and fax **046/45902.** 4 units, 2 with private bathroom (shower only). £36 ($50.40) double without bathroom, £40 ($56) double with bathroom. 20% reduction for children. V.

A dense arch of ancient rhododendrons marks the entry to Lennoxbrook, the Mullan family home for 5 generations. Pauline Mullan and her three daughters are warm and informative hosts to those lucky enough to pull in the driveway. Tea is offered in the family's own kitchen or in the cozy sitting room. The house itself has been maintained and restored with thought and care.

Guest rooms are uncluttered and beautifully furnished—antique chairs are positioned beside bay windows, and high, old-fashioned beds have firm, new mattresses. The bathrooms within guest rooms have been recently redone; they're bright, pine paneled, and quite large. For those who prefer character over convenience, the rooms without their own bathrooms are particularly charming, and one of the two common bathrooms holds an enormous, intriguing old bathtub that promises adventure as well as luxury.

The attentiveness of the Mullan family is demonstrated in their willingness to provide for guests' needs in a way that is not done in more generic B&Bs. For example, laundry can be done for a reasonable fee and Pauline and her daughters will spend extra time at breakfast in helping guests plan the day's itinerary—especially useful, as the nearby area is an interesting one of gardens and historical sites. For those who want a longer stay, one of the upstairs rooms can be used as a self-catering apartment, with its own kitchen and sitting room on the ground floor.

DINING

Hudson's Bistro. Railway St., Navan, County Meath. ☎ **046/29231.** Reservations required Fri–Sat. Main courses £8–£15 ($11.20–$21). Early-bird (before 6pm) dinner £10 ($14). Service charge 10%. AE, MC, V. Mon–Sat 5:30–11pm, Sun 5:30–10pm. NOUVELLE INTERNATIONAL.

This snappy little bistro, decked out in sunny colors and bright pottery, is a treat for travelers passing through the Navan area, especially couples or small groups of friends who enjoy quiet talk, wine, and terrific food. Try the tender Greek lamb kebabs with saffron rice, ratatouille chutney, and crisp salad, or authentic, delicious spicy Thai curry with vegetables. Saffron fettuccine with prawns boasts perfectly cooked fresh pasta, although the sauce was too obscure for my taste. Daily soup and entree specials are offered. The desserts, such as "the Symphony," a house specialty that lives up to its name, are not to be missed. The staff is friendly and the chefs gladly accommodate vegetarian requests.

Newgrange Farm Coffee Shop. Off N51, Slane, County Meath. ☎ **041/982-4119.** All items £2–£6 ($2.80–$8.40). No credit cards. Easter–Aug daily 10am–5pm. IRISH.

On the premises of a working farm (see above), this self-service family-run restaurant is in a converted barn, now whitewashed and skylit. It has an open fireplace and local art on the walls. Ann Redhouse and her family oversee the baking and food preparation, using many ingredients grown on the farm or locally. The ever-changing blackboard menu ranges from homemade soups and hot scones or biscuits to sandwiches, with tempting desserts like apple tart and cream, carrot cake, and fruit pies. Food can also be enjoyed in an outdoor picnic area, and there is often live Irish traditional music in the summer.

COUNTY LOUTH/CUCHULAINN COUNTRY

To the north and east of Meath is Louth, the smallest of Ireland's counties, with a diversity of historic treasures and early Christian landmarks. **Carlingford,** one of Ireland's heritage towns, is on a spur of the Cooley Mountains, overlooking Carlingford Lough and the Irish Sea at the northernmost point of Ireland's east coast, south of Northern Ireland. Established by the Vikings, it is very much a medieval town dominated by a massive 13th-century castle. Legend has it that long before the Vikings came, Carlingford was part of the warriors' hunting grounds. On the heights above the town, folk hero Cuchulainn is said to have single-handedly defeated the armies of Ulster in an epic battle.

Louth is not a place of outstanding scenic beauty, and most visitors move on after exploring a few sites of historic interest.

SEEING THE SIGHTS

✪ **Holy Trinity Heritage Centre.** Carlingford, County Louth. ☎ **042/9373454.** Admission £1 ($1.40) adults, 50p (70¢) children under 16. Sept–May Sat–Sun noon–5pm; June–Aug daily 10am–7pm.

In a beautifully restored medieval church, this center has exhibits that detail the town's history from its Norman origins. If you book ahead, a visit can include a free guided walking tour of the town and a look at King John's Castle, the Mint, the Tholsel (the sole surviving, though altered, gate to the old medieval town), and a Dominican friary. The center overlooks the south shore of Carlington Lough, at the foot of Sliabh Foy, the highest peak of the Cooley Mountains.

Millmount Museum and Martello Tower. Duleek St., off the main Dublin road (N1), Drogheda, County Louth. ☎ **041/983-3097.** Admission £3.50 ($4.90) adults, £2.50 ($3.50) students, £2 ($2.80) children under 12, £9 ($12.60) family. Mon–Sat 10am–5:30pm, Sun 2:30–5pm.

In the courtyard of 18th-century Millmount Fort, this museum offers exhibits on the history of Drogheda and the Boyne Valley area. A Bronze Age oracle, medieval tiles, and a collection of 18th-century guild banners are on display. Also on display are domestic items, such as spinning, weaving, and brewing equipment; antique gramophones; mousetraps; and hot-water jars. A geological exhibit contains specimens of stone from every county in Ireland, every country in Europe, and beyond. In recent years, £1 million ($1.4 million) has been spent to restore a Martello Tower in the Millmount complex. The historic tower was opened to the public in summer 2000 and houses an exhibition on the military history of Drogheda.

Monasterboice. Off the main Dublin road (N1), 6 miles (9.7km) northwest of Drogheda, near Collon, County Louth. Free admission. Daily dawn–dusk.

Once a great monastery and now little more than a peaceful cemetery, this site is dominated by Muiredeach's High Cross. At 17 feet tall, it's one of the most perfect crosses in Ireland. Dating from the year 922, the cross is ornamented with sculptured panels of scenes from the Old and New Testaments. On the monastery grounds are the remains of a round tower, two churches, two early grave slabs, and a sundial.

Old Mellifont Abbey. On the banks of the Mattock River, 6 miles (9.7km) west of Drogheda, off T25, Collon, County Louth. ☎ **041/982-6459.** Admission £1.50 ($2.10) adults,

£1 ($1.40) seniors, 60p (84¢) students and children under 12, £4 ($5.60) family. Daily May to mid-June and mid-Sept to Oct 10am–5pm; mid-June to mid-Sept 9:30am–6:30pm.

"Old Mellifont" (distinct from "New Mellifont," a Cistercian monastery several miles away) was established in 1142 by St. Malachy of Armagh. Although little more than foundations survive, this tranquil spot is worth a visit for a few moments of quiet. Remnants of a 14th-century chapter house, an octagonal lavabo dating from around 1200, and several Romanesque arches remain. A new visitor center contains sculpted stones from the excavations.

ACCOMMODATIONS & DINING

Ballymascanlon House Hotel. Off the Dublin–Belfast road (N1), Dundalk, County Louth. ☎ **800/528-1234** from the U.S., or 042/93-71124. Fax 042/93-71598. 74 units. TV TEL. £104–£112 ($145.60–$156.80) double. No service charge. Rates include full breakfast. AE, DC, MC, V.

A stone-faced Victorian mansion dating from the early 1800s, Ballymascanlon was formerly the home of Baron Plunkett. The Quinn family converted it into a hotel in 1947, and has enlarged it several times. In fact, a new wing of guest rooms is in the works to be ready in summer 2001. The hotel stands on 130 acres of award-winning gardens and grounds, a peaceful oasis just 3 miles (4.8km) south of the Northern Ireland border. Rooms vary in size but are decorated in traditional style with antique touches.

The Dining Room specializes in local meats and seafood, using vegetables from the hotel gardens; the Cellar Bar offers light refreshment and (usually) traditional Irish music on weekends. The hotel has an indoor heated swimming pool, two lighted all-weather tennis courts, two squash courts, a sauna, a solarium, and a gym. An 18-hole parkland golf course surrounds the hotel.

McKevitts Village Inn. Market Sq., Carlingford, County Louth. ☎ **800/447-7462** from the U.S., or 042/9373116. Fax 042/9373144. 15 units. TV TEL. £50–£80 ($70–$112) double. No service charge. Rates include full breakfast. AE, DC, MC, V.

In the heart of a lovely medieval village, this is a great hotel for unwinding and taking long walks along the shores of Carlingford Lough. It's a vintage two-story property that has been updated and refurbished in recent years. Guest rooms vary in size and shape, but all have standard Irish furnishings and are very comfortable, with nice views of the town. There are an old-world bar and a very good restaurant that specializes in local seafood and produce. The hotel makes a great base for day trips into Northern Ireland and the Boyne Valley countryside.

AN EASY EXCURSION FROM COUNTY LOUTH

The town of **Carrickmacross** in County Monaghan has been famous for its tradition of lace making for more than 150 years. Five miles (8km) from County Louth's northwest border, the Lace Gallery of the **Carrickmacross Lace Co-op,** Main Street, Carrickmacross (☎ **042/966-2506**), is well worth a detour. On view are the beautiful, intricate handmade laces produced in the area. Demonstrations are given every once in a while; call to inquire.

The co-op is open April to October Wednesday and Saturday 9:30am to 12:30pm, and Monday, Tuesday, Thursday, and Friday 9:30am to 12:30pm and 1:30 to 5:30pm.

Accommodations & Dining

Nuremore Hotel. Ashbourne–Slane–Ardee road (N2), Carrickmacross, County Monaghan. ☎ **042/966-1438.** Fax 042/966-1853. www.nuremore-hotel.ie. 69 units. TV TEL. £130–£190 ($182–$266) double. No service charge. Rates include breakfast. AE, DC, MC, V.

In a town famous for its lace, this modern three-story hotel is equally well known for its hospitality and high standards. Set amid 100 acres of parkland and woods (including three lakes), it has been totally refurbished and expanded in recent years. The decor is traditional, with dark woods, marble fireplaces, and antique framed prints of the area. Most of the guest rooms feature bright colors, reproduction furniture, and semi-canopy beds; some have light woods and more contemporary styling. All afford lake or garden views.

Amenities: The hotel has a restaurant and lounge bar, an 18-hole championship golf course, and a heated indoor swimming pool. Guests have access to the squash court, two tennis courts, sauna, steam room, gym, whirlpool, and trout fishing on the privately stocked lake.

The Southeast 6

Wexford, Waterford, South Tipperary, and Kilkenny are often referred to as Ireland's "sunny southeast" because these counties usually enjoy more hours of sunshine than the rest of the country. No matter what the weather, they also provide a varied touring experience, from the world-famous Waterford Crystal Factory to the Viking streets of Wexford, from the majestic Rock of Cashel to Kilkenny's medieval splendor.

The Web site for all Southeast Tourism is **www.southeastireland. travel.ie**.

1 County Wexford

Wexford Town is 88 miles (142km) S of Dublin, 39 miles (63km) E of Waterford, 56 miles (90km) S of Wicklow, 116 miles (187km) E of Cork, 133 miles (214km) SE of Shannon Airport

County Wexford is most remarkable for the long stretches of pristine beach that line its coast, and for the evocative historic monuments in Wexford Town and on the Hook Peninsula. The Blackstairs Mountains dominate the western border of the county, and provide excellent hill walking. Bird-watchers can find an abundance of great sites, including Wexford Wildfowl Reserve and Great Saltee Island.

The modern English name of Wexford evolved from *Waesfjord,* which is what the Viking sea-rovers called it when they settled here in the 9th century. It means "the harbor of the mud-flats." Like the rest of Ireland, Wexford was under Norman control by the 12th century, and some reminders in stone of their dominance in this region survive.

Wexford is a hard-working Irish town without pretense or frills. Despite the number of tourists who navigate its streets, Wexford never slows down for them. This has its appeal, especially if you have been eating, sleeping, and exploring for days with mostly tourists on every side.

WEXFORD TOWN ESSENTIALS

GETTING THERE   Irish Rail provides daily train service to Wexford and Rosslare Pier. It serves **O'Hanrahan Station,** Redmond Place, Wexford (☎ **053/22522**).

Bus Eireann operates daily bus service to Wexford and Rosslare, into O'Hanrahan Station and Bus Depot, Redmond Place, Wexford (☎ **053/22522**).

The Southeast

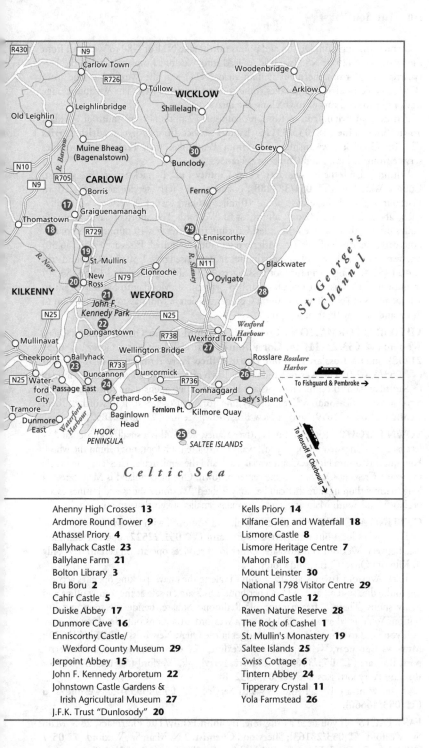

If you're driving from Dublin and points north, take N11 or N80 to Wexford; from the west, take N25 or N8. Two bridges lead into Wexford from the north—the Ferrycarrig Bridge from the main Dublin road (N11) and the Wexford Bridge from R741. The Ferrycarrig Bridge takes you into town from the west. The Wexford Bridge leads right to the heart of town along the quays.

Ferries from Britain run to Rosslare Harbour, 12 miles (19km) south of Wexford Town. **Stena Line** (☎ 053/33115) handles service from Fishguard, **Irish Ferries** (☎ 053/33158; www.irishferries.ie) from Pembroke. Irish Ferries also provides service from Le Havre and Cherbourg, France.

Within Ireland, the **Passage East Ferry County Ltd.,** Barrack Street, Passage East, County Waterford (☎ 051/382488), operates a car ferry service across Waterford Harbour. It links Passage East, about 10 miles (16km) east of Waterford, with Ballyhack, about 20 miles (32km) southwest of Wexford. The shortcut saves about an hour's driving time between the cities. Crossing time averages 10 minutes. It's continuous drive-on, drive-off service, with no reservations required. Fares are £4.50 ($6.30) one-way and £6.50 ($9.10) round-trip for car and passengers, 1.50 ($2.10) round-trip and £1 ($1.40) single trip for foot passengers, £2 ($2.80) one-way and £2.50 ($3.50) round-trip for cyclists. It operates April to September, Monday to Saturday 7am to 10pm, and Sunday 9:30am to 10pm; October to March, Monday to Saturday 7am to 8pm, and Sunday 9:30am to 8pm.

VISITOR INFORMATION   Contact the **Wexford Tourist Office,** Crescent Quay, Wexford (☎ 053/23111); the **Gorey Tourist Office,** Town Centre, Gorey (☎ 055/21248); and the **Rosslare Harbour Tourist Office,** Ferry Terminal, Rosslare Harbour (☎ 053/33622). The Wexford and Gorey Town offices are open year-round Monday to Saturday 9am to 6pm. The Rosslare Harbour office opens daily to coincide with ferry arrivals. **Seasonal offices,** open June to August, are at Enniscorthy, Town Centre (☎ 054/34699), and at New Ross, Town Centre (☎ 051/21857).

TOWN LAYOUT   Rimmed by the River Slaney, Wexford is a small, compact, and—let's face it—congested town; so you'll want to explore it on foot, not behind the wheel. Four quays (Custom House, Commercial, Paul, and the semicircular Crescent) run beside the water. Crescent Quay marks the center of town. One block inland is Main Street, a long, narrow thoroughfare that can be easily walked. Wexford's shops and businesses are on North and South Main Street and the many smaller streets that fan out from it.

GETTING AROUND   Wexford is small and compact, with narrow streets.

There is no local bus transport. **Bus Eireann** (☎ 051/22522) operates daily service between Wexford and Rosslare. Other local services operate on certain days only to Kilmore Quay, Carne, and Gorey.

To see Wexford Town, walk. Park your car along the quays; parking operates according to the disc system, at 30p (42¢) per hour. Discs are on sale at the tourist office and many shops. There is free parking off Redmond Square, beside the train and bus station. You'll need a car to reach County Wexford attractions outside of town.

If you need to rent a car, contact **Budget** at the Quay, New Ross (☎ 051/421670); **Murrays Europcar,** Wellington Place, Wexford (☎ 053/33634), or Rosslare Ferryport, Rosslare (☎ 053/33634); or **Hertz,** Ferrybank, Wexford (☎ 053/23511), or Rosslare Ferryport, Rosslare (☎ 053/33238).

If you want a cab, call Andrew's Taxi Service (☎ 053/45933) or Wexford Taxi (☎ 053/46666).

FAST FACTS   If you need a drugstore, try **John Fehily/The Pharmacy,** 28 S. Main St., Wexford (☎ 053/23163); **Sherwood Chemist,** 2 N. Main St., Wexford (☎ 053/22875); or **Fortune's Pharmacy,** 82 N. Main St., Wexford (☎ 053/42354).

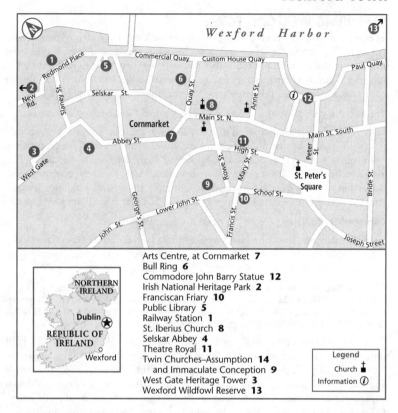

Arts Centre, at Cornmarket **7**
Bull Ring **6**
Commodore John Barry Statue **12**
Irish National Heritage Park **2**
Franciscan Friary **10**
Public Library **5**
Railway Station **1**
St. Iberius Church **8**
Selskar Abbey **4**
Theatre Royal **11**
Twin Churches–Assumption **14**
  and Immaculate Conception **9**
West Gate Heritage Tower **3**
Wexford Wildfowl Reserve **13**

NORTHERN
IRELAND

Dublin

REPUBLIC OF
IRELAND

Wexford

Legend

Church ✝
Information ⓘ

Two good places to do laundry are **My Beautiful Launderette,** St. Peter's Square, Wexford (☎ **053/24317**); and **Marlowe Cleaners,** 7 S. Main St., Wexford (☎ **053/ 22172**).

In an emergency, dial ☎ **999.** The **Garda Station** is on Roches Road, Wexford (☎ **053/22333**). In an emergency, **Wexford General Hospital** is on Richmond Terrace, Wexford (☎ **053/42233**).

Like most towns in Ireland today, Wexford offers free Internet access in its **Public Library** (☎ **053/21637**), which is in Selskar House, off Redmond Square just in from Commercial Quay. Its hours are Tuesday 1 to 5:30pm, Wednesday 10am to 4:30pm and 6 to 8pm, Thursday and Friday 10am to 5:30pm, and Saturday 10am to 1pm. The demand is so great, however, that it's usually necessary to call in advance to reserve a time. Otherwise, every day but Sunday between 9am and 5pm you can go to the **Westgate Computer Centre,** Westgate (☎ **053/46291**), next to the Heritage Tower. As a public service, the center offers Internet access for £2 ($2.80) per each 30 minutes online.

The weekly *Wexford People* covers town and county events and entertainment.

For photographic needs, try **Spectra Photo,** 6 N. Main St., Wexford (☎ **053/ 45502**).

The **General Post Office** on Anne Street, Wexford (☎ **053/22587**), is open Monday to Saturday 9am to 5:30pm.

EXPLORING WEXFORD TOWN

The best way to see the town is by walking the entire length of North and South Main Street, taking time to detour up and down the alleys and lanes that cross the street. The tourist office can supply you with a free map. You may want to start out by visiting the Westgate Heritage Tower (see below), which will provide you with valuable context and background information before you explore the rest of the city.

The Bull Ring. Off N. Main St., Wexford, County Wexford. Free admission.

In 1798, the first declaration of an Irish Republic was made here, and a statue memorializes the Irish pikemen who fought for the cause. Earlier, in the 17th century, the town square was a venue for bull baiting, a sport introduced by the butcher's guild. Tradition has it that, after a match, the hide of the ill-fated bull was presented to the mayor and the meat used to feed the poor. Currently, the activity at the ring is much tamer: a weekly outdoor market, open Friday and Saturday from 10am to 4:30pm.

Cornmarket. Off Upper George's St., Wexford, County Wexford.

Until a century ago, this central marketplace buzzed with the activity of cobblers, publicans, and more than 20 other businesses. Today it's just a wide street. The Wexford Arts Centre, in a structure dating from 1775, dominates the street.

✪ Irish National Heritage Park. Off Dublin–Wexford road (N11), Ferrycarrig, County Wexford. ☎ **053/20733.** www.inhp.com. Admission £5 ($7) adults, £4.50 ($6.30) seniors, £4 ($5.60) students, £3 ($4.20) youths 13–16, £2.50 ($3.50) children 4–12, £12.50 ($17.50) family. Mar–Oct daily 9:30am–6:30pm. Last admission 5pm.

This 36-acre living history park on the banks of the River Slaney provides an ideal introduction for visitors of all ages to life in ancient Ireland, from the Stone Age to the Norman invasion. Each reconstructed glimpse into Irish history is beautifully crafted and has its own natural setting and wildlife. The 20-minute orientation video is engaging and informative, but nothing can match a guided tour by head guide Jimmy O'Rourke. He is an utter master in bringing each site to life, captivating children and intriguing adults. The park's nature trail and interpretive center, complete with gift shop and cafe, add to its appeal and argue for allowing several hours for your visit here.

John Barry Monument. Crescent Quay, Wexford, County Wexford.

This bronze statue, a gift from the American people in 1956, faces out to the sea as a tribute to John Barry, a favorite son who became the father of the American Navy. Born at Ballysampson, Tacumshane, 10 miles (16km) southeast of Wexford Town, Barry emigrated to the colonies while in his teens and volunteered for the cause of the American Revolution. One of the U.S. Navy's first commissioned officers, he became captain of the *Lexington*. In 1797, George Washington appointed him commander-in-chief of the U.S. Navy.

St. Iberius Church. N. Main St., Wexford, County Wexford. ☎ **053/43013.** Free admission; donations welcome. May–Sept daily 10am–5pm; Oct–Apr Tues–Sat 10am–3pm.

Erected in 1660, St. Iberius was built on hallowed ground—the land had been used for houses of worship dating from Norse times. The church has a lovely Georgian facade and an interior known for its superb acoustics. Free guided tours are given according to demand.

Selskar Abbey. Off Temperance Row at Westgate St., Wexford, County Wexford. Open site (except when it's locked).

Said to be one of the oldest sites of religious worship in Wexford, this abbey dates from at least the 12th century. It was often the scene of synods and parliaments. The first

Anglo-Irish treaty was signed here in 1169, and it's said that Henry II spent the Lent of 1172 at the abbey doing penance for having Thomas à Becket beheaded. Although the abbey is mostly in ruins, its choir is part of a Church of Ireland edifice, and a portion of the original tower is a vesting room. The adjoining graveyard has suffered a disturbing amount of vandalism over the years. The entrance most likely to be open is to the left of Westgate.

✪ **The Twin Churches: Church of the Assumption and Church of the Immaculate Conception.** Bride and Rowe sts., Wexford, County Wexford. ☎ **053/22055.** Free admission; donations welcome. Daily 8am–6pm.

These twin Gothic structures (1851–58) were designed by architect Robert Pierce, a pupil of Augustus Pugin. Their 230-foot spires dominate Wexford's skyline. Cobbled on the main door of both churches are mosaics showing relevant names and dates.

Westgate Heritage Tower. Westgate St., Wexford, County Wexford. ☎ **053/46506.** Admission £1.50 ($2.10) adults, 50p (70¢) children and students, £4 ($5.60) family. May–Aug Mon–Fri 9am–4:30pm, Sat–Sun noon–5pm; Sept–Apr Mon–Fri 9:30am–4:30pm.

Westgate once guarded the western entrance of Wexford Town. Sir Stephen Devereux built it in the 13th century, on instructions of King Henry. Like other town gates, it consisted of a toll-taking area, cells for offenders, and accommodations for guards. Fully restored and reopened in 1992 as a heritage center, it presents artifacts, displays, and a 27-minute audiovisual display, titled *In Selskar's Shadow,* which provides an informative introduction to Wexford's complex and turbulent history. If you see this presentation prior to exploring the city, your ambles will likely be a good deal more meaningful to you.

✪ **Wexford Wildfowl Reserve.** North Slob, Wexford, County Wexford. ☎ **053/23129.** E-mail: cjwilson@esatclear.ie. Free admission. Apr 16–Sept daily 9am–6pm; Oct–Apr 15 daily 10am–5pm.

This national nature reserve is part of the North Slob, adjacent to Wexford Harbour, 3 miles (4.8km) east of Wexford Town. About 10,000 Greenland white-fronted geese—more than one-third of the world's population—spend the winter here, as do brent geese, Bewick's swans, and wigeons. The area is immensely attractive to other wildfowl and birds, and more than 240 species have been seen here. The reserve has a visitor center, an audiovisual program, a new exhibition hall, and an observation tower and blinds.

SIGHTSEEING TOURS

✪ **Walking Tours of Wexford.** c/o Seamus Molloy, "Carmeleen," William St., Wexford, County Wexford. ☎ **053/22663.** £3 ($4.20) adults, £1 ($1.40) children. Individual times scheduled when you call.

Proud of their town's ancient streets and vintage buildings, the people of Wexford spontaneously started to give tours to visitors more than 30 years ago. Eventually organized as the Old Wexford Society, the local folk have developed a real expertise over the years, and continue to give tours on a regular basis. All tours depart from Westgate Heritage Tower. Give Mr. Molloy a ring; if he's free, he'll be glad to show you around the city he loves!

SHOPPING

Shops in Wexford are open Monday to Thursday 9am to 5:30pm, Friday and Saturday 9am to 6pm; some shops stay open until 8pm on Friday.

Barkers. 36–40 S. Main St., Wexford, County Wexford. ☎ **053/23159.**

Established in 1848, this shop has long been a mainstay in Wexford. It stocks a large selection of Waterford crystal, Belleek china, and Royal Irish Tara china, as well as Irish linens and bronze and international products such as Aynsley, Wedgwood, and Lladró.

Faller Sweater Shop. 39 N. Main St., Wexford, County Wexford. ☎ **053/24659.**

As its name implies, this shop specializes in Aran hand-knit sweaters (of which it carries a large selection) and mohair, cotton, and linen knits. To warm and accessorize other parts of your body, you'll also find ties, scarves, wool socks, and tweed caps.

The Wexford Bookshop. 31 N. Main St., Wexford, County Wexford. ☎ **053/22223.**

This extensive and bustling emporium, spread out on three levels, has in fact much more than books. There's a long wall-full of magazines and newspapers, a selection of stationery, arts and crafts and supplies, and a slew of toys.

✪ **Wexford Silver.** 115 N. Main St., Wexford, County Wexford. ☎ **053/21933.**

Pat Dolan, one of Ireland's leading silversmiths, plies his craft at this shop. He and his sons create gold, silver, and bronze pieces by hand using traditional tools and techniques. They are members of a long line of Dolans who trace their silversmithing connections back to 1647. Open 10am to 5:30pm. A second workshop is in Kinsale (see Kinsale Silver in chapter 8).

The Wool Shop. 39 S. Main St., Wexford, County Wexford. ☎ **053/22247.**

In the heart of the town's main thoroughfare, this is Wexford's long-established best source for hand-knit items. The selection runs from caps and tams to sweaters and jackets, as well as tweeds, linens, mohairs, and knitting yarns.

ATTRACTIONS FARTHER AFIELD IN COUNTY WEXFORD

The rounded granite form of **Mount Leinster,** the highest in Wexford, is a landmark throughout the region. One of the most popular hang-gliding spots in Ireland, the summit is always windy, and often shrouded in clouds. If you can get to the top on a clear day, however, it will be an experience you won't soon forget. To get there, follow signs for the Mount Leinster Scenic Drive from the sleepy town of **Kiltealy** on the eastern slopes of the mountain. Soon you will begin climbing the exposed slopes; don't be distracted by the dazzling views, because the road is twisting and quite narrow in places. There's a parking area at the highest point of the auto road, and a paved access road (closed to cars) continues approximately 1.5 miles (2.4km) to the summit. From the top you can scramble along the ridge to the east, known as Black Rock Mountain. To return, continue along the Scenic Drive, which ends a few miles outside the town of Bunclody.

Ballyhack Castle. Off R733, Ballyhack, County Wexford. ☎ **051/389468.** Admission £1 ($1.40) adults, 70p (98¢) seniors, 40p (56¢) students and children, £3 ($4.20) family. June–Sept daily 9:30am–6:30pm. Closed Oct–May.

On a steep slope overlooking the Waterford estuary, about 20 miles (32km) west of Wexford, this large tower house is considered a Crusader castle. It's thought to have been built around 1450 by the Knights Hospitallers of St. John, one of the two great military orders founded at the beginning of the 12th century during the Crusades. The castle is open to the public while it is restored and turned into a heritage information center, with displays on the Crusader knights, medieval monks, and Norman nobles.

Ballylane Visitor Farm. Signposted off New Ross–Wexford road (N25), 27 miles (44km) west of Wexford Town and 3 miles (4.8km) east of New Ross, County Wexford. ☎ **051/ 425666.** Admission £3.50 ($4.90) adults; £2.50 ($3.50) seniors, students, and children; £11 ($15.40) family. Mar 17–Apr Sat–Sun and holidays noon–5pm; May–Oct daily 10am–6pm. Closed Nov–Feb.

In the heart of County Wexford's verdant countryside, this 200-acre farm is owned by the Hickey family. They invite visitors to get a firsthand look at their farm life, which includes such activities as tillage, sheep raising, and deer and pheasant husbandry. Guided tours, lasting about an hour, follow a set route covering fields of crops, woodlands, bog lands, ponds, and farm buildings. A tearoom, shop, and picnic area have been added in addition to a fully equipped caravan/RV park.

Enniscorthy Castle/Wexford County Museum. Castle Hill, Enniscorthy, County Wexford. ☎ **054/35926.** Admission £3 ($4.20) adults, £2 ($2.80) seniors and students, 50p (70¢) children. June–Sept daily 10am–6pm; Oct–Nov and Feb–May daily 2–5:30pm; Dec–Jan Sun 2–5pm.

Overlooking the River Slaney at Enniscorthy, 15 miles (24km) north of Wexford Town, this castle was built by the Prendergast family in the 13th century. It's said that the poet Edmund Spenser once owned it briefly. Remarkably well preserved and restored, it's now home to the Wexford County Museum, which focuses on the area's ecclesiastical, maritime, folk, agricultural, industrial, and military traditions. Displays include an old Irish farm kitchen, early modes of travel, nautical memorabilia, and items connected with Wexford's role in Ireland's struggle for independence, especially the 1798 and 1916 risings.

Irish Agricultural Museum and Famine Exhibition. Johnstown Castle. Bridgetown Rd., off Wexford–Rosslare road (N25), Wexford, County Wexford. ☎ **053/42888.** Admission to museum £2.50 ($3.50) adults, £1.50 ($2.10) students and children, £8 ($11.20) family; gardens £1.50 ($2.10) adults, 50p (70¢) children and students, or £3 ($4.20) by the car. No credit cards. Museum June–Aug Mon–Fri 9am–5pm, Sat–Sun 11am–5pm; Apr–May and Sept–Nov Mon–Fri 9am–12:30pm and 1:30–5pm, Sat–Sun 2–5pm; Dec–Mar Mon–Fri 9am–12:30pm and 1:30–5pm. Gardens year-round daily 9am–5:30pm.

The importance of farming in Wexford's history is the focus of this museum, on the Johnstown Castle Demesne 4 miles (6.5km) southwest of Wexford Town. In historic farm buildings, the museum contains exhibits on rural transport, planting, and the diverse activities of the farm household. There are also extensive displays on dairying, crafts, and Irish country furniture. Large-scale replicas illustrate the workshops of the blacksmith, cooper, wheelwright, harness maker, and basket maker. The 19th-century Gothic Revival castle on the grounds is not open to the public except for its entrance hall, where tourist information is available. Visitors can enjoy the 50 acres of ornamental gardens, which contain more than 200 kinds of trees and shrubs, three lakes, a tower house, hothouses, a statue walk, and a picnic area.

✪ **John F. Kennedy Arboretum.** Off Duncannon road (R733), New Ross, County Wexford. ☎ **051/388171.** Admission £2 ($2.80) adults, £1.50 ($2.10) seniors, £1 ($1.40) students and children, £5 ($7) family. Apr and Sept daily 10am–6:30pm; May–Aug daily 10am–8pm; Oct–Mar daily 10am–5pm.

Dedicated to the memory of the 35th U.S. president, this 600-acre arboretum is near a hill known as Slieve Coilte, about 20 miles (32km) west of Wexford. The arboretum overlooks the simple thatched cottage where JFK's great-grandfather was born. Opened in 1968, the arboretum was initiated with financial help from a group of Irish Americans; the Irish government funds its development and maintenance. More than 4,500 species of plants and trees from five continents grow here. There are an information center, play and picnic areas, and a small miniature railway. A hilltop observation point (at 888 ft.) presents a sweeping view of County Wexford and five neighboring counties, the Saltee Islands, the Comeragh Mountains, and parts of the rivers Suir, Nore, and Barrow.

A Trip Through History: Exploring the Ring of Hook

The **Hook Peninsula** in southwest County Wexford is a place of rocky headlands and secluded beaches. It sits between Bannow Bay and Waterford Harbor, two of the most significant inlets in medieval times for travelers from Britain to Ireland, and the abundance of archaeological remains reflects the area's strategic importance. The end of the peninsula is popular with birders as a site for watching the spring and fall passerine migration, and holds a lighthouse reputed to be one of the oldest in Europe. The route described below will guide you through a driving or biking tour, and hikers can see most of the places listed from the Wexford Coastal Pathway.

Start your exploration of the peninsula at the town of **Wellington Bridge.** Just west of town on R733 is a roadside stop on the left by a cemetery; from here you can look across Bannow Bay to the ruins of **Clonmines,** a Norman village established in the 13th century. This is one of the finest examples of a walled medieval settlement in Ireland, with remains of two churches, three tower houses, and an Augustinian priory. You can drive to the ruins if you wish—just follow R733 another mile west to a left turn posted for the Wicklow Coastal Pathway, and continue straight on this road where the Coastal Pathway turns right. The ruins are on private land, so you should ask permission at the farmhouse at the end of the road.

Continuing west on R733, turn left on R734 at the sign for the Ring of Hook, and turn right at the sign for **Tintern Abbey** (see below). The abbey was founded by the monks of Tintern in South Wales in the 13th century, and it has been much altered. The grounds are beautiful and contain a restored stone bridge that spans a narrow sea inlet.

J.F.K. Trust Dunbrody. The Quay, New Ross, County Wexford. ☎ **051/425239.** Fax 051/ 425240. www.dunbrody.com. Admission £3 ($4.20) adults; £1.50 ($2.10) seniors, students, and children; £8 ($11.20) family. Sept–June Mon–Fri 10am–5pm, Sat–Sun noon–5pm; July–Aug daily 10am–7pm.

Housed in twin 18th-century grain mills, the center tells the story of the Irish Diaspora: their lives and achievements abroad, beginning with the monks who went to Europe in the 6th century and continuing to the present day. A computerized data bank for tracing County Wexford roots is being developed with the Ellis Island Immigration Museum in New York and other immigration centers as far away as Australia and Argentina, and will contain more than four million names. A section of the center is devoted to John F. Kennedy, who was descended from a County Wexford family.

The *Dunbrody,* the largest tall ship ever built in the Republic of Ireland—458 tons and 176 feet long—is due to be launched in the spring of 2001. Thereafter, for at least several years, it will be moored on the New Ross quays as a floating exhibition center.

The National 1798 Visitor Centre. Millpark Rd., Enniscorthy, County Wexford. ☎ **054/ 37596.** Admission £4 ($5.60) adults, £2.50 ($3.50) seniors and students, £12 ($16.80) family. Mon–Sat 9:30am–6pm, Sun 11am–6pm.

Just south of Enniscorthy Castle, this visitor center, dedicated to the 1798 Rebellion and its aftermath, gives visitors insight into the birth of modern democracy in Ireland. Interactive computers, an audiovisual presentation, and an array of artifacts are on

At **Baginbun Head** is a fine beach nestled against the cliffs, from which you can see the outline of the Norman earthwork fortifications on the head. Here the Norman presence in Ireland was first established with the victory of Norman forces over the Irish at the Battle of Baginbun.

The **tip of the peninsula,** with its line of low cliffs, eroded in places to form blowholes, has been famous for shipwrecks since Norman times. There has long been a **lighthouse** on this site; the present structure consists of a massive base, built in the early 13th century, and a narrower top dating from the 19th century.

The Ring of Hook road returns along the western side of the peninsula, passing the beaches at **Booley Bay** and **Dollar Bay.** On a promontory overlooking the town of Duncannon is a **fort** built in 1588 to protect Waterford Harbour from the threat of attack by the Spanish Armada. Just north of Duncannon, along the coast, is the village of **Ballyhack,** where a ferry operates to Passage East in County Waterford, and a Knights Hospitallers castle (see "Ballyhack Castle," above) stands on a hill over the harbor.

A visit to the Hook Peninsula wouldn't be complete without a stop at **Dunbrody Abbey,** in a field beside the road about 4 miles (6.5km) north of Duncannon. The abbey, founded in 1170, is a magnificent ruin, and one of the largest Cistercian abbeys in Ireland. Despite its grand size, it bears remarkably little ornamentation. Tours are sometimes available; inquire at the visitor's center across the road.

At the eastern end of Enniscorthy is Vinegar Hill (390 ft.), where the Wexford men of 1798 made their last stand. Now a scenic viewing point, it offers panoramas of Wexford from its summit.

display to help dramatize the events in an interesting and exciting way. The center also incorporates a pleasant tearoom and gift shop.

✪ **Tintern Abbey.** Saltmills, New Ross, County Wexford. (☎ **051/562650**). Admission £1.50 ($2.10) adults, £1 ($1.40) seniors, 60p (84¢) students and children, £4 ($5.60) family. Mid-June to Sept daily 9:30am–6:30pm. Signposted 12 miles (19km) south of New Ross off of R733.

In a lovely rural setting overlooking Bannow bay, Tintern Abbey was founded under the patronage of William, the Earl of Marshall, by the Cistercian monks of Tintern in South Wales. The parts that remain—nave, chancel, tower, chapel, and cloister— date back to the early 13th century, though they have been much altered since then. The grounds are quite beautiful, and include a restored stone bridge spanning a narrow sea inlet.

Yola Farmstead. 10 miles (16km) south of Wexford Town, 1½ miles (2.4km) from Rosslare Ferry-port, Wexford–Rosslare road (N25), Tagoat, County Wexford. ☎ **053/32610.** E-mail: yolafst@iol.ie. Admission £3.50 ($4.90) adults, £2.50 ($3.50) seniors and students, £1 ($1.40) children, £8 ($11.20) family. June–Sept daily 9:30am–5pm; Mar–Apr and Nov Mon–Fri 9:30am–4:30pm. Closed other months.

A voluntary community project, this theme park depicts a Wexford farming community as it would have been 200 or more years ago. Thatched-roof buildings have been constructed, including barns housing farm animals. Bread and butter making are demonstrated, and craftspeople can be seen at work blowing and hand-cutting crystal at Wexford Heritage Crystal, a glass-production enterprise. A small area is devoted to endangered species. The **Genealogy Center** (☎ 053/31177; fax 053/32612; wexgen@iol.ie) is open May to October daily 9:30am to 5pm; January to April and November Monday to Friday 9:30am to 4:30pm. Closed in December. Consultation or one name search costs £20 ($28). The general Web site which includes this center is www.mayo-ireland.ie/Geneal/Frm.

SPORTS & OUTDOOR PURSUITS

BEACHES   County Wexford's beaches at **Courtown, Curracloe, Duncannon,** and **Rosslare** are ideal for walking, jogging, or swimming.

BICYCLING   You can rent a mountain bike at **Black's Cycle Center,** Arklow, County Wicklow (☎ **0402/31898**). The rate of £10 ($14) per day, £50 ($70) per week, includes helmet and panniers. This is a good starting point for excursions along the Wexford coastal roads, although for a short while you'll be riding on very busy N11 before reaching the coast road, so use extreme caution. There are also two Raleigh Rent-a-Bike locations in Wexford Town itself: **Hayes Cycle Shop,** 108 S. Main St. (☎ **053/22462**); and the **Bike Shop,** 9 Selskar St. (☎ **053/22514**), which allows one-way rentals. From Wexford, the road north up the coast through Curracloe to Blackwater is a scenic day trip. For complete 1- or 2-week cycling holidays in the Southeast, contact Don Smith at **Celtic Cycling,** Lorum Old Rectory, Bagenalstown (☎ **0503/75282;** www.celticcycling.com).

BIRD WATCHING   A good starting place for bird watching in the region is the **Wexford Wildfowl Reserve** (see above); warden Chris Wilson can direct you to other places of interest.

The ✪ **Great Saltee Island** is one of the best places in Ireland to watch seabirds, especially during May, June, and July, when the place is mobbed with nesting parents and their young. Like something out of a Hitchcock feature, the cliffs on the island's southernmost point are packed to overflowing with raucous avian residents, and the combined sound of their screeching, squawking, and chortling is nearly deafening at times. This is a place to get up close and personal with puffins, which nest in underground burrows, or graceful guillemots. Other species include cormorants, kittiwakes, gannets, and Manx shearwaters. The island is privately owned, but visitors are welcome on the condition that they do nothing to disturb the bird habitat and the island's natural beauty. From April to September, weather permitting, **Declan Bates** (☎ 053/29684) provides boat rides to the island and back from the town of Kilmore Quay (about 10 miles/16km south of Wexford Town). He charges £60 ($84) minimum for the boat, or £12 ($16.80) per person when there are at least five people.

Hook Head is a good spot for watching the spring and autumn passerine migration—the lack of sizable cliffs means that it isn't popular with summer nesting seabirds. In addition to swallows, swifts, and warblers, look out for the less common cuckoos, turtle doves, redstarts, and blackcaps.

While driving south from Gorey toward Ballycanew on R741, keep an eye out for a reddish **cliff** on the left, about 1.5 miles (2.4km) out of Gorey; this is a well-known peregrine aerie, with birds nesting until the early summer. The land is private, but it is possible to watch the birds from the roadside.

Other places of interest are **Lady's Island Lake** near Carnsore Point, an important tern colony, and neighboring **Tacumshin Lake.**

DIVING   The Kilmore Quay area, south of Wexford Town, offers some of the most spectacular diving in Ireland. For answers to all your questions and needs, consult **Wexford Diving Centre and Dive Charters,** Riverstown Farm, Murrintown, County Wexford (☎ **053/39373**).

FISHING   One center for sea angling in Wexford is the town of **Kilmore Quay,** south of Wexford Town on R739. Several people offer boats for hire, with all the necessary equipment; Dick Hayes runs **Kilmore Quay Boat Charters** (☎ **053/29704**) and is skipper of the *Cottage Lady.* The most popular rivers for fishing are the Barrow and the Slaney, where the sea trout travel upstream from mid-June to the end of August.

GOLF   In recent years, Wexford has blossomed as a golfing venue. The newest development is an 18-hole championship seaside par-72 course at **St. Helens Bay Golf Club,** Kilrane (☎ **053/33669**). Greens fees are £22 ($30.80) on weekdays and £25 ($35) on weekends. Tennis courts, sauna, and luxury cottages are available. The **Enniscorthy Golf Club,** Knockmarshall, Enniscorthy (☎ **054/33191**), an inland par-70 course with greens fees of £20 ($28) on weekdays, £22 ($30.80) on weekends, also welcomes visitors.

HORSEBACK RIDING   ✪ **Horetown House,** Foulksmills (☎ **051/565771**), offers riding lessons by the hour or in a variety of packages that include meals and lodging. One of the better residential equestrian centers in Ireland, it caters particularly to families and children. For more experienced riders, lessons in jumping and dressage are available, as is a game called polocross, which combines polo and lacrosse. Training in hunting and admission to the hunt can also be arranged. Riding is £12.50 ($17.50) per hour; bed-and-breakfast runs £45 to £53.50 ($63 to $75.32) for a double.

WALKING   The entire coastline is posted with brown signs indicating a man with a backpack walking on water: This is the **Wexford Coastal Path,** which theoretically allows you to walk the whole coast on beaches and country roads. In reality, the roads are often too full of traffic, so I wouldn't recommend walking the whole route, especially the bypass around Wexford Town. The markers are handy, however, for shorter walks along and between Wexford's beaches.

In the northern part of the county, the section of beach from Clogga Head (County Wicklow) to Tara Hill is especially lovely, as is the walk to the top of Tara Hill, which offers many viewpoints over sloping pastures to the sea. A good base for both these walks is **Carrigeen B&B,** Tara Hill, Gorey, County Wexford (☎ **055/21732**). It offers basic accommodations, a spectacular view of the sea, and a welcoming family (the Leonards) who are quite familiar with the local walks. Double rooms with private bath are £40 ($56). Farther south, the path veers off the roads and sticks to the beach from Cahore Point south to Raven Point and from Rosslare Harbour to Kilmore Quay.

There's a lovely coastal walk near the town of Wexford in the **Raven Nature Reserve,** an area of forested dunes and uncrowded beaches. To get there, take R741 north out of Wexford, turn right on R742 to Curracloe just out of town, and in the village of Curracloe, turn right and continue 1 mile (1.6km) to the beach parking lot. The nature reserve is to your right. You can get there by car, driving another half mile south, or walk the distance along the beach. The beach extends another 3 miles (4.8km) to Raven Point, where at low tide you can see the remains of a shipwreck, half-buried in the sand. The point is also a great place to watch migratory birds in winter and spring—the flight of the white-fronted geese at dusk is an experience you shouldn't miss.

On the border between Counties Wexford and Carlow is a long, rounded ridge of peaks known as the **Blackstairs Mountains,** which offer a number of beautiful walks in an area remarkably unspoiled by tourism. A good guide is *Walking the Blackstairs,* by Joss Lynam, which includes trail descriptions and information on local plants and wildlife. It's available at Wexford tourist offices. There is a road to the top of Mount Leinster; for information, see the description above under "Attractions Farther Afield in County Wexford."

ACCOMMODATIONS
EXPENSIVE

Ferrycarrig Hotel. P.O. Box 11, Wexford–Enniscorthy road (N11), Wexford, County Wexford. ☎ **053/20999.** Fax 053/20982. www.griffingroup.ie. 103 units. TV TEL. £100–£300 ($140–$420) double. No service charge. Rates include full breakfast. AE, DC, MC, V.

Situated next to the Ferrycarrig Bridge and opposite the Irish National Heritage Park about 2 miles (3.2km) north of town, this contemporary four-story hotel overlooks the River Slaney estuary and fertile Wexford countryside. Completely refurbished in 2000, the rooms are furnished in bright tones with light woods and modern art, and have picture windows that look out onto the river and well-cultivated gardens.

Dining/Diversions: On the premises are the Conservatory restaurant, noted for its seafood; the Boathouse Bistro (light fare); and the Dry Dock Bar.

Amenities: The hotel has tennis courts and a river walk, as well as a new leisure center with a pool, and two new waterside restaurants.

✪ Marlfield House. Courtown Rd., Gorey, County Wexford. ☎ **800/323-5463** from the U.S., or 055/21124. Fax 055/21572. www.marlfieldhouse.ie. 20 units. TV TEL. £157–£168 ($219.80–$235.20) double; state rooms from £275 ($385). Rates include full breakfast and service charge. AF, CB, DC, MC, V. Closed Dec 15–Jan.

Originally a dower house, then the principal residence of the Earl of Courtown, this splendid Regency manor home, 40 miles (65km) north of Wexford Town in the northernmost part of the county, was built around 1850. Thanks to the current owners, Ray and Mary Bowe, it has been masterfully transformed into a top-notch country inn with award-winning gardens. Although the individually decorated rooms have every modern convenience (including fully carpeted bathrooms), they retain their old-world charm. Many have four-poster or canopied beds, hand-carved armoires, and one-of-a-kind antiques. Guests are asked not to smoke in their rooms. The public rooms and lounge have comfortable, inviting furnishings, plus gilt-edge mirrors, crystal chandeliers, and marble fireplaces.

Dining: Marlfield has earned many plaudits for its cuisine, which incorporates organically grown fruits and vegetables from the garden. It's served in the main dining area or in a fanciful skylit Victorian-style conservatory room.

Amenities: Tennis court, croquet lawn.

MODERATE

✪ Ballinkeele House. Signposted off the N11 north of Wexford at Oylgate, Ballymurn, Enniscorthy, County Wexford. ☎ **053/38105.** Fax 053/38468. www.ballinkeele.com. 5 units. £100–£130 ($140–$182) double. Dinner £26 ($36.40). MC, V. Rates include full breakfast. Closed mid-Nov to Feb.

This grand Irish manor house, built in 1840 and in the Maher family for four generations now, is the perfect place to recover from the rigors of travel. You'll think you've stepped into another world as you walk into the majestic entrance hall. John and Margaret Maher are exemplary hosts, and see to it that you feel immediately at home; despite the grandeur of the accommodations, they create a cordial, relaxed atmosphere.

Dinner (book before noon) is served by candlelight in a chandeliered dining room. The food is excellent: starters might include avocado pâté or carrot and parsnip soup, while main courses range from trout with fennel to steak with whiskey sauce to pheasant in cream-and-brandy sauce; vegetarian options are also available.

Some 350 acres of fields and woodlands surround the house, with gardens in the process of being created around a pond—you'll have numerous options for short walks on which you may well encounter pheasants, foxes, black rabbits, all manner of birds, and if you're lucky the resident hedgehog. The cozy elegance of this house and the warmth of the Mahers make it one of the best places in the southeast to forget about budgeting and to live it up for a few days.

Riverside Park Hotel. At the junction of N11 and N30 on the south edge of town, The Promenade, Enniscorthy, County Wexford. ☎ **054/37800.** Fax 054/37900. www. riversideparkhotel.com. 60 units. TV TEL. £90 ($126) double; £120–£140 ($168–$196) suite. Rates include full Irish breakfast. AE, DC, MC, V.

Set on the green banks of the River Suir, the Riverside Park Hotel is a striking new (1998) addition to the town of Enniscorthy. The contemporary design of the hotel attracts the eye with a rich color scheme of terra-cotta and nautical blue, lots of glass, and a bold stone tower centerpiece. A flower-fringed terrace allows for dining and relaxing with a view of the River Slaney and its promenade. Guest rooms have a warm, bright feel to them, with bold print fabrics. They are thoughtfully designed, providing all the cubbies and counter space you have ever longed for. Front-facing rooms enjoy a fine view of the river from their own small balconies.

The hotel is home to the Promenade Bar, a stylish spot, and the more publike Mill House Bar. There are also The Moorings Restaurant with its tempting international menu, and the Alamo Bar and Grill with Mexican tastes to match its name. The hotel offers guest discounts at a fully equipped leisure center only minutes away on foot, as well as at the nearby Enniscorthy Golf Course. The Riverside Park Hotel makes a great base from which to explore the Blackstair Mountains, Wexford Town, the Wexford coast, and local attractions; and it's only a short walk from the town center of Enniscorthy.

Rosslare Great Southern. Wexford–Rosslare Harbour road (N25), about 12 miles (19km) south of Wexford Town, Rosslare Harbour, County Wexford. ☎ **800/44-UTELL** from the U.S., or 053/33233. Fax 053/33543. E-mail: res@rosslare.gsh.ie. 100 units. TV TEL. £108–£196 ($151.20–$274.40) double. AE, DC, MC, V.

For travelers taking the ferry to or from Britain or France, or for anyone fond of sea views, this modern three-story hotel is an appealing overnight stop. It's on a clifftop overlooking the harbor, and less than a mile from the ferry terminals. The decor is bright and airy, with lots of wide floor-to-ceiling windows and colorful contemporary furnishings in the guest rooms and public areas. Only 10 nonsmoking rooms are available; if this is your preference, reserve one early. The Norman Room Restaurant, serving meals throughout the day, offers sea views. There are also a lounge (with evening entertainment in the summer), a conservatory, an indoor heated swimming pool, a sauna, a gym, and a tennis court.

The Talbot. Trinity St., Wexford, County Wexford. ☎ **800/223-6764** from the U.S., or 053/22566. Fax 053/23377. www.talbothotel.ie. 100 units. TV TEL. £90–£102 ($126–$142.80) double. No service charge. Rates include full breakfast. AE, MC, V. Free parking.

On the western end of the quays, this modern six-story hotel has the advantage of overlooking the harbor while being within a block of the town's main shopping street. The recently refurbished guest rooms are outfitted with light woods and bright floral fabrics; many have river views, and all have orthopedic beds, hair dryers, and tea/coffeemakers. Nonsmoking rooms are available. Room service, concierge, and valet and laundry services are available, and there is a hairdressing salon on the premises. The Slancy Restaurant offers formal dining for lunch or dinner, and lighter fare is available all day at the Pike Grill. For drinks with traditional music, try the Tavern; for jazz or sixties music, the Trinity Lounge. Exercise facilities include a gym, saunas, a squash court, a solarium, table tennis, and an indoor heated swimming pool.

White's. George and Main Sts., Wexford, County Wexford. ☎ **800/528-1234** from the U.S., or 053/22311. Fax 053/45000. 82 units. TV TEL. £70–£90 ($98–$126) double. No service charge. Rates include full breakfast. AE, DC, MC, V.

Dating from 1779, this vintage hotel is right in the middle of town, with its older section facing North Main Street. Over the years it has been expanded and updated, resulting in lots of connecting corridors and guest rooms of varying size and standards. Some have four-poster or canopy beds, others modern light-wood furnishings. For the most part, the public rooms reflect the aura of an old coaching inn. Twenty-four-hour room service, 1-day dry cleaning, and concierge services are available, and exercise facilities include a Jacuzzi, gym, sauna, steam room, and solarium. White's is a member of Best Western Hotels Worldwide.

The main restaurant, Captain White's, serves top-class meals, and lighter fare is available all day in the Country Kitchen. There are two bars: the Shelmalier, where jazz and folk music often plays on weekends, and Speakers, a contemporary watering hole.

INEXPENSIVE

Clone House. Ferns, Enniscorthy, County Wexford. ☎ **054/66113.** Fax 054/66225. 5 units, 4 with bathroom. £40–£50 ($56–$70) double. No service charge. Rates include full breakfast. No credit cards. Closed Nov–Feb.

You're sure to receive a gracious welcome at this 300-acre working farm, the home of Tom and Betty Breen. The guest rooms are furnished with handsome antiques, as is the rest of the 250-year-old farmhouse. Three units have television sets. A courtyard opens onto a garden in back, and you can walk through the fields to the bank of the River Bann. Tom prides himself on his knowledge of the area (both the local region and Ireland as a whole), and will be glad to assist you in making plans for touring or outdoor activities. Only three rooms are designated nonsmoking; if this is important to you, book well in advance.

✪ **McMenamin's Townhouse.** 3 Auburn Terrace, Redmond Rd., Wexford, County Wexford. ☎ **053/46442.** Fax 053/46442. E-mail: mcmem@indigo.ie. 6 units. TEL. £44 ($61.60) double. No service charge. Rates include full breakfast. MC, V. Free parking.

At the west end of town, opposite the railroad station, this lovely Victorian-style town house offers up-to-date accommodations at an affordable price. Guest rooms are individually furnished with local antiques, including brass beds and caned chairs, and all have tea/coffee-making facilities. The guest rooms are nonsmoking and have orthopedic beds. Not all of them have televisions, so if this is important to you, ask. McMenamin's is operated by Seamus and Kay McMenamin, who formerly ran the Bohemian Girl pub and restaurant, so your stomach is in luck: Kay puts her culinary skills to work by providing gourmet breakfasts for guests in the nonsmoking dining room.

DINING
MODERATE

Lobster Pot. Carne, County Wexford. ☎ **053/31110.** Reservations recommended for dinner. Main courses £9.95–£16.95 ($13.95–$23.75); lobster £23–£25 ($32.20–$35). AE, MC, V. June–Aug daily noon–2pm and 6–9pm; Sept–Dec and Feb–May Tues–Sat noon–2pm and 6–9pm. SEAFOOD.

About 10 miles (16km) south of Wexford Town near the sea, this thatched-roof cottage restaurant is a popular spot for indoor and outdoor dining. The atmosphere is rustic, and the decor features local memorabilia such as crocks and kettles, framed newspaper clippings and pictures, and seafaring equipment. The menu, which is the same all day, features wild fresh salmon, panfried Dover sole, grilled trout, and baked crab. The house special is Lobster Pot Pourri (lobster and seafood in creamy white wine sauce). For non–seafood eaters, there are steaks, chicken Kiev, and roast duckling. Lighter items, popular at lunchtime, include seafood salads and chowders.

✪ **Mange2.** 100 S. Main St., Wexford, County Wexford. ☎ **053/44033.** Reservations recommended. Main courses £9.95–£13.50 ($13.95–$18.90). AE, MC, V. Daily 6–10:30pm. FRENCH FUSION.

In the Viking tradition, Wexford town has not been synonymous with fine dining not until the arrival of Mange2. Shortly after it opened in the summer of 1999, the word was out. This is French cooking *en famille* at its best—inventive without any wild antics, and quite eclectic, while retaining the subtlety and attention to detail that seem to be part of the French genetic code. The contrast of textures and delicate balance of flavors in our meals were remarkable. The roast red pepper and fennel samosa with baby beets and yogurt dressing was delicately crisp, as was the pine-nut fritter which accompanied the fillets of sole, while the roast breast of chicken found a perfect foil in thin strips of panfried chorizo and savory cabbage. The vegetable side dishes began with ingredients at the peak of freshness and arrived crisp and steaming, wrapped in parchment packets. The wine list is modest and judicious, with a quite decent house wine for roughly £10 ($14). The dessert menu is devastating. Try not to miss the baked passion-fruit ricotta cake with orange ice cream. Portions are generous, so you may want to pace yourself, sharing starters and desserts. Regrettably, no provision is made for nonsmokers, as this is an intimate space with a ceiling of only average height.

✪ **The Neptune.** Ballyhack Harbor, Ballyhack, County Wexford. ☎ **051/389284.** Reservations required. Main courses £12.50–£14 ($17.50–$19.60); lobster averages £20 ($28). AE, DC, MC, V. High season Mon–Sat 7–9pm; low season Thurs–Sat 7–9pm. (The parameters of high and low season are unpredictable and simply reflect demand.) Closed Dec–Jan. INTERNATIONAL/SEAFOOD.

On the western edge of County Wexford, about 20 miles (32km) from Wexford Town, this little gem is in an old house on the waterfront of a sheltered harbor town. The interior has an airy modern motif, with paintings and pottery by Irish artisans; tables are also set up outside on sunny days. Dinner options might include scallops in orange and ginger sauce, fillet of hake in citrus sauce, hot buttered lobster, Ballyhack wild salmon baked in cream, or the signature dish, hot crab Brehat (sautéed in port and baked with mushrooms, béchamel sauce, and cheese). The restaurant is easily accessible from Waterford (on the Ballyhack–Passage East car ferry) or Wexford, and worth the trip from any direction.

The Neptune is also home to the **Ballyhack Cookery Centre** (☎ 051/389284), which offers classes by prior arrangement in the summer months.

MODERATE/INEXPENSIVE

Bohemian Girl. 2 Selskar St., Wexford, County Wexford. ☎ **053/24419.** All items £1.50–£8 ($2.10–$11.20). MC, V. June–Aug 10:30am–11:30pm; Sept–May 10:30am–11pm; pub lunches year-round 12:30–3pm. PUB GRUB.

Named for an opera written by one-time Wexford resident William Balfe, this is a Tudor-style pub, with lantern lights, barrel-shaped tables, and matchbook covers on the ceiling. Its excellent pub lunches include fresh oysters, pâtés, combination sandwiches, and homemade soups.

Cellar Bistro. Cornmarket, at Abbey St., Wexford, County Wexford. ☎ **053/23764.** Reservations not accepted. All items £1.60–£8 ($2.25–$11.20). No credit cards. Daily 10am–6pm. IRISH/VEGETARIAN.

Housed in the Wexford Arts Centre, this charming eatery has a country-kitchen atmosphere, with stone walls, pine furnishings, and home cooking prepared by Chef Caroline. Selections include salads, soups, quiches, pizzas, and chili, with an emphasis on vegetarian items.

WEXFORD AFTER DARK
THE PERFORMING ARTS

Famed for its **Opera Festival** each October, Wexford is a town synonymous with music and the arts. Year-round performances are given at the **Theatre Royal,** High Street, Wexford (☎ **053/22144**), a beautiful theater dating from 1832. Booking for the opera festival (www.wexfordopera.com) opens in early May for the following October! Tickets range from £7 to £55 ($9.80 to $77).

There's usually something going on at the **Wexford Arts Centre,** Cornmarket, Wexford (☎ **053/23764**). Built as the market house in 1775, this building has served as a dance venue, concert hall, and municipal office. It has provided a focal point for all the arts in Wexford since 1974, and now houses three exhibition rooms and showcases a range of theatrical and artistic events. The staff is eager to meet visiting artists in all fields, with a view toward developing ongoing links with artists worldwide. Open year-round from 10am to 6pm daily.

To see traditional Irish music and dancing, head 10 miles (16km) south of Wexford to the **Yola Farmstead,** Wexford–Rosslare road (N25), Tagoat, County Wexford (☎ **053/32610**). For groups, by prior arrangement, the Farmstead stages traditional Irish banquets and ceili evenings of Irish music, song, dance, and recitations. If you're not a group and a banquet is planned, you might be able to join in. The average cost is £25 ($35) per person.

PUBS

Antique Tavern. 14 Slaney St., Enniscorthy, County Wexford. ☎ **054/33428.**

It's worth a 15-mile (24km) trip from Wexford City to Enniscorthy to see this unique Tudor-style pub, located off the main Dublin–Wexford road (N11). True to the name, the walls are lined with memorabilia from the Wexford area—old daggers, pikes, farming implements, lanterns, pictures, and prints. You'll also see mounted elk heads, an antique wooden birdcage, and a glass case full of paper money from around the world.

Con Macken's, The Cape of Good Hope. The Bull Ring, off N. Main St., Wexford, County Wexford. ☎ **053/22949.**

Long a favorite with photographers, this pub is unique for the trio of services it offers, aptly described by the sign outside the door: BAR–UNDERTAKER–GROCERIES. Hardly any visitor passes by without a second look at the windows; one displays beer and spirit bottles, the other plastic funeral wreaths. An alehouse for centuries, the Cape has always been at the center of Wexford political events, and rebel souvenirs, old weapons, and plaques line the bar walls.

The Crown Bar. Monck St., Wexford, County Wexford. ☎ **053/21133.**

Once a stagecoach inn, this tiny pub in the center of town has been in the Kelly family since 1841. Besides its historical overtones, it is well known for its museum-like collection of antique weapons. You'll see 18th-century dueling pistols, pikes from the

1798 Rebellion, powder horns, and blunderbusses, as well as vintage prints, military artifacts, and swords. Unlike most pubs, it may not always be open during the day, so it's best to visit in the evening.

Oak Tavern. Wexford–Enniscorthy road (N11), Ferrycarrig, County Wexford. ☎ **053/20945.**

Dating back over 150 years, this pub—originally a tollhouse—is 2 miles (3.2km) north of town, overlooking the River Slaney near the Ferrycarrig Bridge. Bar lunch choices are of the beef and vegetable hot pot and shepherd's pie variety. There is a riverside patio for outside seating on fine days, and traditional music sessions are held most evenings in the front bar.

The Wren's Nest. Custom House Quay, Wexford, County Wexford. ☎ **053/22359.**

Near the John Barry Memorial on the harbor, 5 minutes from the bus and train station, this pub has redesigned its front bar to include an old-style wood floor and ceiling, and attractive pine tables and chairs. The varied pub grub includes Wexford mussel platters, house pâtés, soups, salads, and vegetarian entrees. There is free traditional Irish music on Tuesday and Thursday nights.

2 County Waterford

Waterford City is 40 miles (65km) W of Wexford, 33 miles (53km) W of Rosslare Harbour, 98 miles (158km) SW of Dublin, 78 miles (126km) E of Cork, and 95 miles (153km) SE of Shannon Airport

Waterford City (pop. 42,500) is the main seaport of the southeast. Only 7 miles (11km) from the Atlantic, it is one of Ireland's windiest cities, boasting gale-force winds an average of 180 days every year. More significantly, this is Ireland's oldest city, founded by Viking invaders in the 9th century. In fact, Waterford is older than any of the major Nordic capitals of modern Europe, including Oslo, Stockholm, and Copenhagen. In recent years, a major archaeological endeavor has excavated nearly a fourth of the ancient Viking city, and some of the more striking finds from these excavations can be seen in the new Waterford Museum of Treasures at the Granary.

Although the historic district around Reginald's Tower is quite intriguing, the city is primarily a commercial center, dominated by its busy port. Because the rest of County Waterford is so beautiful, many travelers don't linger long in the capital city, though it is currently enjoying a fresh wave of renewal and development, some of which is aimed directly at visitors. Truth is, there's a good deal to see and to do here.

Coastal highlights south of Waterford include **Dunmore East,** a picturesque fishing village; **Dungarvan,** a major town with a fine harbor; **Ardmore,** an idyllic beach resort; and **Passage East,** a tiny seaport from which you can catch a ferry across the harbor and cut your driving time from Waterford to Wexford in half. Of all the coastal towns in County Waterford, Ardmore stands out as the perfect getaway. It has a beautiful and important early Christian site, a pristine Blue Flag beach, a stunning cliff walk, a fine craft shop, an excellent restaurant, comfortable seaside accommodations, and a quaint town recently named Ireland's tidiest. (Litter here and they'll cut your hands off, and rightfully so.) **Portally Cove,** near Dunmore East, is the home of Ireland's only Amish-Mennonite community.

In northwest County Waterford, the **Comeragh Mountains** provide many opportunities for beautiful walks, including the short trek to Mahon Falls. These mountains also have highly scenic roads for biking. Farther west, there's great fishing and bird watching on the **Blackwater estuary.**

WATERFORD CITY ESSENTIALS

GETTING THERE   Air service from Britain operates into **Waterford Airport,** off R675, Waterford (☎ **051/75589**). Carriers include **Suckling Airlines** from Luton, and **British Airways** (operated by British Regional) from London (Stansted) and Manchester.

    Irish Rail offers daily service from Dublin and other points into Plunkett Station, at Ignatius Rice Bridge, Waterford (☎ **051/873401**).

    Bus Eireann operates daily service into Plunkett Station Depot, Waterford (☎ **051/879000**), from Dublin, Limerick, and other major cities throughout Ireland.

    These major roads lead into Waterford: N25 from Cork and the south, N24 from the west, N19 from Kilkenny and points north, and N25 from Wexford.

    The Passage East Ferry County Ltd., Barrack Street, Passage East, County Waterford (☎ **051/382480** or 051/382488), operates car ferry service across Waterford Harbour. It links Passage East, about 10 miles (16km) east of Waterford, with Ballyhack, about 20 miles (32km) southwest of Wexford. This shortcut saves about an hour's driving time. Crossing time averages 10 minutes. It's continuous drive-on, drive-off service, with no reservations required. The fares are £4.50 ($6.30) one-way and £6.50 ($9.10) round-trip for car and passengers, 1.50 ($2.10) round-trip and £1 ($1.40) single trip for foot passengers, £2 ($2.80) one-way and £2.50 ($3.50) round-trip for cyclists. It operates April to September, Monday to Saturday 7am to 10pm, and Sunday 9:30am to 10pm; October to March, Monday to Saturday 7am to 8pm, and Sunday 9:30am to 8pm.

VISITOR INFORMATION   The **Waterford Tourist Office** is at 41 The Quay, Waterford (☎ **051/875788**). It's open April to June and September, Monday to Saturday 9am to 6pm; July and August, Monday to Saturday 9am to 6pm, Sunday 11am to 5pm; October, Monday to Saturday 9am to 5pm; November to March, Monday to Friday 9am to 5pm. The year-round office on the Square in Dungarvan (☎ **058/41741**) keeps comparable hours. The seasonal tourist office on the Square at Tramore (☎ **051/381572**) is open from mid-June to August, Monday to Saturday 10am to 6pm. Additionally, here are a couple of Web sites that will keep you up on Waterford goings-on: **www.waterford-online.ie** and **www.waterford-today.ie**. The Web site for all Southeast Tourism is **www.southeastireland.travel.ie**.

CITY LAYOUT   Rimmed by the River Suir, Waterford is a commercial city focused from the start on its quays. The city center sits on the south bank of the Suir. Traffic from the north, west, and east enters from the north bank over the Ignatius Rice Bridge and onto a series of four quays (Grattan, Merchants, Meagher, and Parade), but most addresses simply say "The Quay." Most shops and attractions are concentrated near the quay area or on two thoroughfares that intersect the quays: The Mall and Barronstrand Street (changing their names to Broad, Michael, and John Streets). Both of these streets were once rivers flowing into the Suir; and, in fact, the original waterways continue to flow roughly 50 feet beneath today's pavement.

GETTING AROUND   Bus Eireann operates daily **bus service** within Waterford and its environs. The flat fare is 70p (98¢). **Taxi** ranks are outside Plunkett Rail Station and along the Quay opposite the Granville Hotel. If you need to call a taxi, try **City Cabs** (☎ **051/852222**), **Metro Cabs** (☎ **051/857157**), or **Parnell Cabs** (☎ **051/853791**).

    To see most of Waterford's sights (except Waterford Glass), it's best to walk. Park along the quays; parking is operated by machines or by the disc system. Discs are on

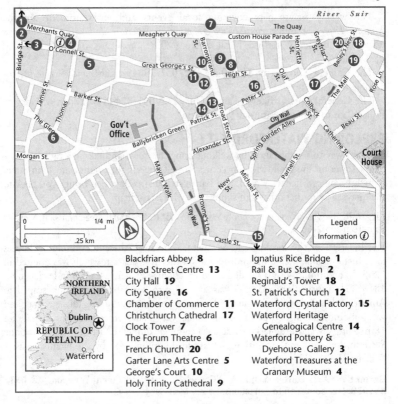

Blackfriars Abbey **8**
Broad Street Centre **13**
City Hall **19**
City Square **16**
Chamber of Commerce **11**
Christchurch Cathedral **17**
Clock Tower **7**
The Forum Theatre **6**
French Church **20**
Garter Lane Arts Centre **5**
George's Court **10**
Holy Trinity Cathedral **9**

Ignatius Rice Bridge **1**
Rail & Bus Station **2**
Reginald's Tower **18**
St. Patrick's Church **12**
Waterford Crystal Factory **15**
Waterford Heritage
Genealogical Centre **14**
Waterford Pottery &
Dyehouse Gallery **3**
Waterford Treasures at the
Granary Museum **4**

sale at the tourist office and in many shops. It will cost you under 1£ ($1.40) for 3 hours, or £2 ($2.80) for a full day. You'll need a car to reach the Waterford Glass Factory and Waterford County attractions outside of town.

To rent a car, contact **Hertz,** Dublin Road, Waterford (☎ **051/878737**), or **Murrays Europcar,** Cork Road, Waterford (☎ **051/373144**).

FAST FACTS   If you need a drugstore, try **Gallagher's Pharmacy,** 29 Barronstrand St. (☎ **051/878103**); and **Mulligan's Chemists,** 40–41 Barronstrand St. (☎ **051/ 875211**), and City Square Shopping Centre, Unit 12A (☎ **051/853247**).

Several good spots to do your laundry are **Eddies Dry Cleaners,** 82 The Quay (☎ **051/877677**); **Boston Cleaners,** 6 Michael St. (☎ **051/874487**); and **Dud 'n Suds,** Parnell Street (☎ **051/841168**), a self-service laundry offering full folding, ironing, and pressing services.

In an emergency, dial ☎ **999. Garda Headquarters** (☎ **051/874888**) is the local police station. **Holy Ghost Hospital** is on Cork Road (☎ **051/374397**), and **Waterford Regional Hospital** is on Dunmore Road (☎ **051/873321**).

Among the resources for gay travelers is the **Gay and Lesbian Line Southeast** (☎ **051/879907**). The **Waterford Gay and Lesbian Resource Centre** is at the Youth Resources Centre, St. John's Park (☎ **087/638-7931**).

The **Voyager Internet Cafe,** Parnell Court, off Parnell Street (☎ **051/843843**) is not in fact a cafe; but it does provide high-speed access with all the peripherals for £1.50 ($2.10) per 15 minutes. Open Monday to Saturday 11am to 11pm, Sunday 3 to 11pm.

The weekly newspapers covering local events and entertainment are the *Munster Express,* the *Waterford News & Star* and *Waterford Today,* online at www. waterford-today.ie. Waterford Local Radio (WLR) broadcasts on 97.5 FM and 95.1 FM.

The **Camera Shop,** 109 The Quay (☎ 051/75049), can handle your photographic needs.

The **General Post Office** on Parade Quay (☎ 051/874444) is open Monday to Friday 9am to 5:30pm, Saturday 9am to 1pm.

EXPLORING WATERFORD CITY

The best way to see the city is by walking along the quays and taking a right at Reginald's Tower on the Mall (which becomes Parnell Street). Turn right onto John Street (which becomes Michael, Broad, and Barronstrand street), which brings you back to the quays. The tourist office can supply you with a free map.

City Hall. The Mall, Waterford, County Waterford. ☎ **051/73501.** Free admission. Mon–Fri 9am–1pm and 2–5pm.

Headquarters of the local city government, this late-18th-century building houses local memorabilia, including information on the city's charter, which was granted in 1205. In addition, a display is dedicated to Thomas Francis Meagher, a leader in an 1848 Irish insurrection. Meagher was sentenced to death but eventually escaped to America, where he fought in the Civil War, earned the rank of brigadier general, and was appointed acting governor of Montana. City Hall's other treasures include an 18th-century Waterford glass chandelier, a complete dinner service of priceless antique Waterford glasses, and a painting of Waterford City in 1736 by the Flemish master William Van der Hagen.

Garter Lane Arts Centre. 5 and 22a O'Connell St., Waterford, County Waterford. ☎ **051/ 855038.** Free admission to exhibitions. Gallery Mon–Sat 10am–6pm.

One of Ireland's largest arts centers, the Garter Lane occupies two buildings on O'Connell Street. No. 5, the site of the former Waterford Library, holds exhibition rooms and artists' studios, and No. 22a, the former Friends Meeting House, is home of the Garter Lane Theatre, with an art gallery and outdoor courtyard. The gallery showcases works by contemporary and local artists.

Holy Trinity Cathedrals. Barronstrand and Henrietta sts., Waterford, County Waterford.

Waterford has two impressive cathedrals, one Catholic and the other Protestant, both built by the same architect, John Roberts, who lived 82 years (1714–96), fathered 22 children with the same beloved partner (in business and in bed), and built nearly every significant 18th-century building in and around Waterford. Holy Trinity on Barronstrand is the oldest Catholic and the only baroque Cathedral in Ireland and boasts 10 unique Waterford Crystal chandeliers. It's open daily 7:30am to 7pm. The Anglican or Church of Ireland Holy Trinity Cathedral (conveniently nicknamed Christ Church) on Henrietta Street has a most peculiar spire and only clear glass, because its first bishop and rector had a firm aversion to stained glass. Currently closed (except for services) for major conservation work, it is well worth a visit once it reopens.

Reginald's Tower. The Quay, Waterford, County Waterford. ☎ **051/73501.** Admission £1.50 ($2.10) adults, £1 ($1.40) seniors, 60p (84¢) children. Combined ticket with Waterford Treasures available. June–Aug daily 9:30am–9pm, May and Sept daily 9:30am–6pm, Oct–Apr daily 10am–5pm.

Circular, topped with a conical roof, and with walls 10 feet thick, this mighty tower stands at the eastern end of the Quay beside the river. It's said to have been built in

1003 by a Viking governor named Reginald and has never fallen into ruin, which makes it Ireland's oldest standing building in continuous use. Still dominating the Waterford skyline, it's particularly striking at night when fully floodlit. Over the centuries, it's been a fortress, a prison, a military depot, a mint, an air-raid shelter, and now a museum.

✪ **Waterford Crystal Factory and Gallery.** Cork Rd., Waterford, County Waterford. ☎ **051/373311.** Tour £3.50 ($4.90) adults, £1.75 ($2.45) students, free for children under 12. Free admission to audiovisual presentation and gallery. Tours Apr–Oct daily 8:30am–4pm; Nov–Mar Mon–Fri 9am–3:15pm. Showrooms Apr–Oct daily 8:30am–6pm; Nov–Mar Mon–Fri 9am–5pm.

Without a doubt, this is Waterford's number one attraction. Founded in 1783, the glass-making enterprise thrived, and Waterford became the crystal of connoisseurs. The devastating effects of the Irish famine forced the factory to close in 1851. Happily, it was revived in 1947, and Waterford has since regained its prominence among prized glassware. With more than 2,000 employees, Waterford is the largest crystal factory in the world and the major industry in Waterford.

Visitors are welcome to watch a 17-minute audiovisual presentation on the glass-making process and then take a 35-minute tour of the factory to see it firsthand, from mouth-blowing and shaping of molten glass to delicate hand-cutting. *Note:* Children under 10 are not permitted on the factory tour. Reservations are not required.

You can also stroll around the Waterford Crystal Gallery. The bilevel showroom contains the most comprehensive display of Waterford Crystal in the world, from all the glassware patterns to elaborate pieces like trophies, globes, and chandeliers. Crystal is on sale in the gallery. (But don't look for any discounts at the factory; there are no seconds to be had. The main advantage in shopping here is simply the wide selection.)

Waterford Heritage Genealogical Centre. St. Patrick's Church, Jenkins Lane, Waterford, County Waterford. ☎ **051/876123.** Fax 051/850645. www.waterford-heritage.ie. Free admission; basic search fee £30 ($42). Mon–Thurs 9am–5pm; Fri 9am–2pm.

Did your ancestors come from Waterford? Then follow the small lane between George's and Patrick's Streets to this historic building adjoining St. Patrick's, one of Ireland's oldest churches. The center specializes in tracing County Waterford ancestry. Church registers dating from 1655 and other surveys, rolls, and census lists are used as resources. An audiovisual presentation examines the heritage of the local people.

Waterford Pottery and The Dyehouse Gallery. Dyehouse Lane, Waterford, County Waterford. Pottery ☎ **051/878166,** www.waterfordpottery.com; Gallery ☎ **051/850399,** www.dyehouse-gallery.com. Free admission to exhibitions. Shop and gallery open Mon–Sat 10:30am–5:30pm, or phone for appointment.

Liz McCay is both the resident potter and the gallery director of this combined venue, where you'll find not only her own unique "Waterford Ware" inspired by a black ceramic style discovered in local Viking excavations, but also contemporary paintings and prints by many of Ireland's leading visual artists. The gallery hosts seven or eight exhibitions per year.

Waterford Treasures at the Granary Museum. Merchant's Quay, Waterford, County Waterford. ☎ **051/304500.** www.waterfordtreasures.com. Admission £4 ($5.60) adults, £3 ($4.20) seniors and students, £2 ($2.80) children, £12 ($16.80) family. Combined ticket with Reginald's Tower available. June–Aug daily 9:30am–9pm; May and Sept daily 9:30am–6pm; Oct–Apr daily 10am–5pm.

A short walk from Reginald's Tower along the quays, this impressive new heritage center and museum, housed in a restored and reconceived granary, unfolds Waterford's history, from its earliest Viking origins to the present. An exceptional collection of

Viking and medieval artifacts recovered from Waterford's lower levels is on display. The Granary, however, is no ordinary museum of artifacts under glass and walls of small print. It's also an ambitious state-of-the-art multimedia experience aimed at all ages, and launched with a three-dimensional audiovisual sea voyage viewed from the hull of a Viking boat actually rolling with the waves you're watching. But despite its ambitions, I felt that the museum's myriad exhibitions fail to cohere. The entire experience seems like a circus with too many rings, more chaotic than exciting. Attempts to accommodate supposed short attention spans can be self-fulfilling. (The salt with which my remarks are to be taken is the fact that the Granary was named the Irish Museum of the Year in 1999–2000.) If you make your own way at your own pace, however, there's a lot to see and to learn here; and the building itself, overhead and all around you, is truly beautiful. There's also a gift shop and cafe.

TOURS & CRUISES

At the Quay (☎ 051/421723), the **Galley Cruising Restaurants** (see the listing under "Dining," later in this section) also take passengers who are just along for the ride. Cruise-only prices from Waterford range from £6 to £12 ($8.40 to $16.80).

✪ **Waterford City Walking Tours.** Waterford Tourist Services, Jenkins Lane, Waterford, County Waterford. ☎ 051/873711. Tours Mar–Oct daily at noon and 2pm. £4 ($5.60) adults, free for accompanied small children.

Jack Burtchaell, well versed in the history, folklore, and wit of the city, conducts an engaging and informative 1-hour tour of the old city, leaving daily from the reception area of the Granville Hotel on the Quay. This is the very best way to begin your own explorations of Waterford.

SHOPPING

Most people come to Waterford for the crystal, but there are many other fine products in the shops and in the three multilevel enclosed shopping centers: **George's Court,** off Barronstrand Street, **Broad Street Centre** on Broad Street, and **City Square** off Broad Street. Hours are usually Monday to Saturday from 9 or 9:30am to 6 or 6:30pm. Some shops are open until 9pm on Thursday and Friday.

Aisling. 61 The Quay, Waterford, County Waterford. ☎ 051/873262.

Beside the Granville Hotel, this interesting shop (the name means "dream" in Gaelic) offers an assortment of unique crafts, from quilts, tartans, and kilts to floral art, miniature paintings, and watercolors of Irish scenes and subjects.

The Book Centre. Barronstrand St., Waterford, County Waterford. ☎ 051/873823.

This huge, four-level bookstore sells all types of books, newspapers, and magazines, as well as posters, maps, and music tapes and CDs. You can also make a photocopy or zap off a fax.

Joseph Knox. 3 Barronstrand St., Waterford, County Waterford. ☎ 051/875307.

For visitors, this store has long been a focal point. It carries a large selection of Waterford crystal, particularly specialty items like chandeliers.

Kelly's. 75/76 The Quay, Waterford, County Waterford. ☎ 051/873557.

Dating from 1847, this store offers a wide selection of Waterford crystal, Aran knitwear, Belleek and Royal Tara china, Irish linens, and other souvenirs.

Penrose Crystal. 32A Johns St., Waterford, County Waterford. ☎ 051/876537.

Established in 1786 and revived in 1978, this is Waterford's other glass company, which turns out delicate hand-cut and engraved glassware. The craftspeople practice the stipple engraving process, the highest art form in glass. A retail sales outlet is at Unit 8 of the City Square Shopping Centre. Both are open the usual hours, but the factory is also open Sunday from June to August, 2 to 5:30pm.

Woolcraft. 11 Michael St., Waterford, County Waterford. ☎ **051/874082.**

For more than 100 years, the Fitzpatrick family has operated this midcity shop, a reliable source for quality Irish knitwear. The focus is on hand-loomed and hand-knit Aran sweaters—2,000 square feet of 'em—at exceptionally low prices.

ATTRACTIONS FARTHER AFIELD IN COUNTY WATERFORD

✪ **Ardmore High Cross.** Ardmore, County Waterford. Open site.

Ardmore (Irish for "the great height") may well be the oldest Christian settlement in Ireland. St. Declan, its founder, is said to have been a bishop in Munster as early as the mid–4th century, well before Patrick came to Ireland. Tradition has it that the small stone Oratory, situated in a cemetery high above the town, marks his burial site. St. Declan's Oratory is one of several stone structures here composing the ancient monastic settlement, which you can explore freely on your own. The most striking is the perfectly intact 30-meter (97 ft.) high round tower, arguably the finest of all round towers in Ireland. There are also the ruins of a medieval cathedral and, nearby, St. Declan's well and church. To inform and enrich your explorations, you would do well to pick up a copy of "The Pilgrim's Round of Ardmore, County Waterford" at the local newsagent for £2 ($2.80), or join the local walking tour of ancient Ardmore led by Mary Murray, which leaves twice daily (11am and 3pm), Monday to Saturday, from the Tourist Information Office in the harbor.

✪ **Lismore Castle.** Lismore, County Waterford. ☎ **058/54424.** Admission to gardens £3 ($4.20) adults, £1.50 ($2.10) children under 16. Mid-Apr to mid-Oct daily 1:45–4:45pm. From Cappoquin, take N72 4 miles (6.5km) west.

Perched high on a cliff above the River Blackwater, this turreted castle has a long history. It dates to 1185, when Prince John of England built a similar fortress on this site. Local lore says that Lismore Castle was once granted to Sir Walter Raleigh for £12 ($16.80) a year, although he never occupied it. One man who did live here was Richard Boyle, the first Earl of Cork. He rebuilt the castle, including the thick defensive walls that still surround the garden, in 1626. Richard's son Robert, who was born at the castle in 1627, was the celebrated chemist whose name lives on in Boyle's Law. Most of the present castle was added in the mid–19th century. Today the 8,000-acre estate of gardens, forests, and farmland is the Irish seat of the Duke and Duchess of Devonshire, whose primary home is at Chatsworth, in England. Although the castle itself is not open for tours, the public is welcome in the splendid walled and woodland gardens.

The castle can be rented, complete with the duke's personal staff, to private groups for a minimum of £1,200 ($1,680) per day, which includes dinner, afternoon tea, breakfast, and staff. Contact Elegant Ireland (☎ **01/475-1632;** www.elegant.ie).

Lismore Heritage Centre. Lismore, County Waterford. ☎ **058/54975.** Admission £3 ($4.20) adults, £2.50 ($3.50) seniors, £2 ($2.80) children, £6 ($8.40) family. Apr–Oct daily 9:30am–5:30pm; Nov–Mar Mon–Fri 9:30am–5:30pm.

Where is the only Hindu Gothic bridge in Ireland? Step inside this building and find out. This new interpretive center, in the town's Old Courthouse, will not only answer that question, but also tell the history of Lismore, a charming town founded by St. Carthage in the year 636. "The Lismore Experience" is an exceptional award-winning multimedia presentation on the town's unique treasures, including the Book of Lismore, which dates back 1,000 years, and the Lismore Crozier (1116). Both were

---

A Walk to Mahon Falls

Located in the Comeragh Mountains, on R676 between Carrick-on-Suir and Dungarvan. At the tiny village of Mahon Bridge, 16 miles (26km) south of Carrick-on-Suir, turn west on the road marked for Mahon Falls, and continue to follow signs for the falls and the "Comeragh Drive." In about 3 miles (4.8km), you reach a parking lot along the Mahon River (which is, in fact, a tiny stream). The trail, indicated by two boulders, begins across the road from the parking lot. Follow the stream along the floor of the valley to the base of the falls. From here you can see the fields of Waterford spread out below you, and the sea a glittering mirror beyond. Walking time is about 30 minutes round-trip.

---

discovered hidden in the walls of Lismore Castle in 1814. The presentation also provides an excellent introduction to the surrounding area and its attractions. In addition, the center offers tours of the Lismore town and cathedral. Be sure to stop in the gift shop adjacent to the heritage center.

SPORTS & OUTDOOR PURSUITS

BEACHES   For walking, jogging, or swimming, visit one of County Waterford's wide sandy beaches at **Tramore, Ardmore, Clonea,** or **Dunmore East.**

BICYCLING   Wright's Cycle Depot Ltd., Henrietta Street, Waterford (☎ 051/874411), offers bikes only. At **Altitude Cycle and Outdoor,** 22 Ballybricken, Waterford (☎ 051/870356; e-mail: Altitude@indigo.ie), prices start at £10 ($14) daily, £60 ($84) weekly. Altitude Cycle offers helmets but few panniers. They also offer emergency repair service for travelers, and can complete just about any repair on the same day you bring the bike in.

From Waterford City, you can ride 8 miles (13km) to Passage East and take the ferry (£2/$2.80 with a bicycle) to Wexford and the beautiful Hook Peninsula. Or continue on from Passage East to Dunmore East, a picturesque seaside village with a small beach hemmed in by cliffs. The road from there to Tramore and Dungarvan is quite scenic. For a complete 1- or 2-week biking vacation in the Southeast, contact Don Smith at **Celtic Cycling,** Lorum Old Rectory, Bagenalstown, County Carlow (☎ and fax **0503/75282;** www.celticcycling.com).

FISHING   For sea angling, there are a number of licensed charter-boat companies operating out of Kilmore Quay, roughly 15 miles (24km) southwest of Wexford. One such is **Kilmore Quay Boat Charters;** contact Dick Hayes (☎ 053/29704). For landlubbers, the River Slaney, brimming with salmon and sea trout, can be fished from the old bridge in Enniscorthy.

GOLF   County Waterford's golf venues include three 18-hole championship courses. **Faithlegg Golf Club,** Faithlegg House (☎ 051/382241), a par-72 parkland course beside the River Suir, charges greens fees of £22 ($30.80) Monday to Thursday, £27 ($37.80) Friday to Sunday. **Dungarvan Golf Club,** Knocknagranagh, Dungarvan (☎ 058/43310), a par-72 parkland course, has greens fees of £20 ($28) on weekdays, £25 ($35) on weekends. **Waterford Castle Golf and Country Club,** The Island, Ballinakill, Waterford (☎ 051/871633), is a par-72 parkland course; greens fees are £27 ($37.80) on weekdays, £30 ($42) on weekends. In addition, the 18-hole par-71 inland course at **Waterford Golf Club,** Newrath, Waterford (☎ 051/876748), is a mile from the center of the city. Its greens fees are £22 ($30.80) on weekdays, £25 ($35) on weekends.

HORSEBACK RIDING   County Waterford is filled with trails. You can arrange to ride at **Killotteran Equitation Centre,** Killotteran, Waterford (☎ 051/384158); or **Nire Valley Equestrian Trail-Riding and Trekking,** Ballmacarberry (☎ 052/36147). Fees average £12 ($16.80) per hour.

SAILING, WINDSURFING & SEA KAYAKING   From May to September, the **Dunmore East Adventure Centre,** Dunmore East (☎ 051/383783), offers courses. Courses last 1 to 4 days and cost £18 to £30 ($25.20 to $42) per day, including equipment rental. Summer programs for children are also available. This is a great spot for an introductory experience, but there isn't much wave action for thrill-seeking windsurfers.

ACCOMMODATIONS
VERY EXPENSIVE
✪ **Waterford Castle.** The Island, Ballinakill, Waterford, County Waterford. ☎ 051/878203. Fax 051/879316. www.waterfordcastle.com. 19 units. TV TEL. £160–£250 ($224–$350) double; £290–£395 ($406–$553) suite. AE, MC, V.

As the pace of Ireland accelerates and even holidays become hectic, there's something simply magical and immediately relaxing about taking a boat to your room for the night. Islands are natural oases, and Waterford Castle is no exception. Dating back 800 years, this is the most secluded of Ireland's castles, on a private 310-acre island in the River Suir. It's only 2 miles (3.2km) south of Waterford and yet accessible only by the Castle's private car ferry. Comprising an original Norman keep and two Elizabethan-style wings, it is built entirely of stone, with leaded roofs, mullioned windows, granite archways, ancient gargoyles, and fairy-tale turrets, towers, and battlements.

Fully restored and refurbished in 1988, the Castle is luxuriantly maintained at a very high standard, and new amenities are always being thought of and added for your comfort here. The Castle's interior is full of oak-paneled walls, ornate plaster ceilings, colorful tapestries, spacious sitting areas with huge stone fireplaces, original paintings, and elegant antiques. Four of the five suites are furnished with four-poster or canopied beds, and all have hand-carved armoires, designer fabrics, and other regal accessories. All of the Castle's 19 rooms have orthopedic beds, antique free-standing bathtubs (with shower attached), splendid views, and tape/tuner/CD systems. In sum, the rooms display exquisite taste and offer the tranquillity of a pristine retreat. And, of course, once you've explored the wonders of your room, there's the rest of the island. The atmosphere is warm and graciously informal; the staff is excellent and members work together as a congenial team.

Dining/Diversions: There's the Munster Room restaurant, with a dazzling menu, and the Fitzgerald Room bar serving predinner drinks.

Amenities: 24-hour room service, concierge, laundry and valet service, 18-hole championship golf course, indoor heated pool, tennis courts, and local arrangements for horseback riding, fishing, and water sports.

EXPENSIVE
Jurys. Ferrybank, Waterford, County Waterford. ☎ 800/843-3311 from the U.S., or 051/832111. Fax 051/832863. www.jurys.com. 98 units. TV TEL. £118–£150 ($165.20–$210) double. Rates include full breakfast and service charge. AE, DC, MC, V. Closed Dec 24–26.

Set amid 38 acres of gardens and lawns, this modern six-story hotel is perched on a hill along the River Suir's northern banks. From this commanding position, each room enjoys a sweeping view of Waterford City. Recently refurbished, the rooms offer a Victorian-style decor of frilly floral fabrics, dark woods, and brass trim. Each room contains a hair dryer and luggage rack.

Dining/Diversions: Bardens Restaurant and the Conor Bar face the river and city.

Amenities: 24-hour room service, concierge, tea/coffee-making facilities, same-day dry cleaning and laundry, baby-sitting service. Indoor heated swimming pool, Jacuzzi, two saunas, steam room, gymnasium, two flood-lit outdoor tennis courts, hairdressing salon.

MODERATE

The Bridge. 1 The Quay, Waterford, County Waterford. ☎ **800/221-2222** from the U.S., or 051/877222. Fax 051/877229. www.treacyhotelsgroup.com. 123 units. TV TEL. £90–£120 ($126–$168) double. Rates include full Irish breakfast and service charge. MC, V. Parking lot £1.10 ($1.55).

Taking its name from its location, on the waterfront at the foot of the Ignatius Rice Bridge, this three-story vintage hotel is one of the city's oldest. The public rooms have retained their warm, old-world character, while the individual guest rooms have been renovated, trading old character for contemporary convenience. The rooms have light-wood furnishings and bright floral fabrics and are surprisingly quiet, despite the hotel's harried location. Beds are firm, and all rooms have tea- and coffee-making facilities. The Ignatius Rice Restaurant offers formal dining, the Kitchen serves light meals in a country-kitchen setting, and Crokers Bar and Timbertoes Bar provide liquid refreshment.

Granville. Meagher Quay, Waterford, County Waterford. ☎ **800/538-1234** from the U.S., or 051/305555. Fax 051/305566. www.granville-hotel.ie. 100 units. TV TEL. £90–£120 ($126–$168) double. No service charge. Rates include full breakfast. AE, DC, MC, V. Closed Dec 24–27. Parking available in nearby public lots.

Along the quayside strip of Waterford's main business district, this historic hotel looks out onto the south side of the River Suir. The Granville was originally a coaching inn, and an adjacent section was the home of Irish patriot Thomas Francis Meagher and a meeting place for Irish freedom fighters. The Cusack family bought it in 1980, and totally restored and enlarged it. Today the Granville is a member of Best Western International. The chain's 1998 refurbishment of the hotel preserved its architectural blend while providing handsome individually styled rooms with orthopedic beds, as well as a new floor of penthouse suites. Many of the front rooms look out onto the river. The hotel is home to the Bianconi Restaurant, and the Thomas Francis Meagher Bar, which is popular with a local clientele. Other amenities include room service, concierge, laundry, and valet.

Tower Hotel. The Mall, Waterford, County Waterford. ☎ **051/875801.** Fax 051/70129. www.towerhotelgroup.ie. 141 units. TV TEL. £100–£140 ($140–$196) double. Rates include full Irish breakfast and service charge. AE, DC, MC, V.

In a historic section of the city, this contemporary four-story hotel is named after Reginald's Tower, across the street. It's within walking distance of all major downtown attractions. A popular base for bus tours, it was completely refurbished and enlarged in 1991. The guest rooms are standard but comfortable, with an eclectic mix of colors and furnishings. The public rooms were recently extended, with emphasis on lovely wide-windowed views of the harbor. There are a full-service restaurant, a lounge overlooking the river, and a leisure center with an indoor swimming pool, a whirlpool, a steam room, saunas, and an exercise room.

INEXPENSIVE

Aglish House. Aglish, Cappoquin, County Waterford. ☎ **024/96191.** Fax 024/96482. E-mail: aglishhouse@tinet.ie. 4 units, 3 with private bathroom. TV TEL. £50 ($70) double. No service charge. Rates include full breakfast. MC, V.

Readers Recommend

St. Anthony's, Ballinaneesagh, Cork Road, Waterford. ☎ **051/375877;** fax 051/ 353063. £38 ($53.20) double with bathroom.

The accommodations were about the best of our entire trip. Each bedroom appears to have been decorated by an interior decorator; the lounge area was spacious and better appointed than many hotel lounges. A separate but complete kitchenette area allowed tea, coffee, and snacks whenever the spirit moved us. We cannot say enough about the kindness of Mrs. O'Keeffe; she provided us with much information about the area and suggested places that were enjoyable and not too touristy. Besides all this, she is a tremendous cook!

—Linda J. Brackbill, Royal Palm Beach, Fla.

This corner of the Waterford countryside possesses a mix of pastoral charm and wild beauty, and Aglish House is a perfect base from which to explore the area. The breakfast is especially good, and dinner is served with advance reservation. All the guest rooms are nonsmoking, and the orthopedic beds ensure a good night's sleep. The Moores are generous hosts, and their 300-year-old home is comfortable and spacious. As numerous photos and trophies attest, this is a family of avid cyclists, and they are well versed in the local bicycling routes. A short walk from the house are the Kiltera Ogham stones, inscribed pillars dating from pre-Christian times; also nearby is the lovely Blackwater estuary. A short drive brings you to the coast or the Knockmeal-down Mountains.

Brown's Townhouse. 29 S. Parade (at the southwest end of People's Park after Catherine St.), Waterford, County Waterford. ☎ **051/870594.** Fax 051/871923. www.brownstownhouse. com. 6 units, 3 with shower only. TV TEL. £50–£60 ($70–$84) double; £60–£85 ($84–$119) suites. Rates include full breakfast. MC, V. Free parking on street.

Les and Barbara Brown's convenient, comfortable bed-and-breakfast is only a 10-minute walk from the city quays and kitty-corner to the spacious and calming People's Park. The house has a cozy lived-in feeling to it. The guest rooms are individually decorated with firm beds and bright decor. All the rooms have hair dryers, coffee- and tea-making facilities, and superior showers. There are one double-bed suite, one double room with its own second-story outdoor deck, an attic family room, and three standard bedrooms. Breakfast options include buttermilk pancakes, lean Irish bacon, and fresh fruit salad. The resident retriever, Charlie (Brown), is a sweet fellow and an instant favorite with guests.

The Browns also rent a two-bedroom ground-level apartment in a newly built development a mile southeast of town. The apartment sleeps five and has all of the modern conveniences. It's available for £100 ($140) per night, £80 ($112) for each additional night, or £500 ($700) per week.

Cliff House Hotel. Ardmore, County Waterford. ☎ **024/94106.** Fax 024/94496. E-mail: cmv@indigo.ie. 13 units. TEL. £65–£84 ($91–$117.60) double. No service charge. Rates include full breakfast. AE, DC, MC, V. Closed Nov–Feb.

Perched above the breakers, this hotel has spectacular views of the bay at Ardmore and a long stretch of rocky coast. The rooms are modern and bright, and all but one are on the sea side of the building. There are a restaurant and pub on the lower level, and a terrace for outdoor dining. A beautiful walk around the point begins at the edge of the parking lot, taking in the Ardmore chapel and round tower, as well as the majestic sea cliffs; a leaflet published by the hotel describes this and other local walks.

There are also two bikes for hire at the hotel, and good cycling roads run from here along the coast.

✪ **Foxmount Farm and Country House.** Passage East Rd., Waterford, County Waterford. ☎ **051/874308.** Fax 051/854906. E-mail: foxmount@iol.ie. 5 units. £60 ($84) double. 25% discount for children under 12. No service charge. Rates include full breakfast. No credit cards. Closed Nov–Feb.

This elegant, secluded, 17th-century country home is the perfect place to relax and collect yourself after a busy day of sightseeing. Margaret and David Kent are superlative hosts and do all they can to ensure that your stay will be a memorable one. Two adjacent guest rooms share a separate alcove, perfect for a family, and four double rooms have private bathrooms. All have views of the fields around the house. A guide to walks in the area is available. Dinner is offered for £20 ($28), with tea following in the spacious, comfortable sitting room. The Jack Meades pub (see listing below) is within walking distance.

Three Rivers Guesthouse. Cheekpoint, County Waterford. ☎ **051/382520.** Fax 051/382542. E-mail: 3rivers@iol.ie. 14 units. £50–£70.60 ($70–$98.85) double. 3- and 5-night specials available. No service charge. Rates include full breakfast. AE, MC, V. Free parking.

This relatively new guesthouse enjoys a serene waterfront setting, yet it's just 7 miles (11km) from downtown Waterford. Aptly named, it sits on the harbor at the point where the rivers Suir, Nore, and Barrow meet. The rooms are bright and contemporary, with pastel tones, rattan furnishings, framed prints, and floral fabrics and comforters atop orthopedic beds. Most rooms have lovely views of the water, and all are non-smoking. Award-winning breakfasts are served in the bright dining room overlooking the rivers, and there's a large, plant-filled, conservatory-style TV and reading room. Proprietors Stan and Mailo Power enthusiastically provide local sightseeing guidance.

DINING
MODERATE

Dwyer's. 8 Mary St., Waterford, County Waterford. ☎ 051/877478 or 051/871183. Reservations recommended. Main courses £12.50–£16.50 ($17.50–$23.10); early-bird (6–7pm) 3-course fixed-price dinner £15 ($21). AE, DC, MC, V. Mon–Sat 6–10pm. IRISH/INTERNATIONAL.

On a quiet back street near the northern entrance to the city at Ignatius Rice Bridge, this small restaurant is owned and operated by Martin and Sile Dwyer, who cook everything to order in a homey 30-seat setting. The menu changes often, but choices often include wild salmon in filo pastry with cucumbers and fennel, roast squab pigeon with port wine sauce, roast marinated brill with gremolata sauce, and honey-glazed breast of duck with lemon sauce.

Jade Palace. 3 The Mall, Waterford, County Waterford. ☎ **051/855611.** Reservations recommended. Fixed-price lunch Mon–Sat £6.50 ($9.10), Sun £9.95 ($13.95); dinner main courses £8–£14 ($11.20–$19.60). MC, V. Mon–Sat noon–2:30pm and 5:30pm–midnight; Sun 1–3pm and 6–11:30pm. CHINESE.

Some of Waterford's better cuisine is served at this reliable restaurant, on the upstairs level above a Victorian-style bar. The menu, which has garnered several awards, is attentively served in a setting of pink linens, red velvet seats, Asian statuary, library books, gilt-framed paintings, fresh flowers, and silver cutlery (or chopsticks, if you prefer). Dishes include king prawns, duck Cantonese, fillet steak cooked at the table, lemon chicken, sweet-and-sour pork, baked lobster, and steamed fish with ginger.

O'Grady's. Cork Rd., Waterford, County Waterford. ☎ **051/378851.** Reservations recommended. Fixed-price lunch £10.95 ($15.35) for 2 courses, £14.95 ($20.95) for 3 courses; dinner main courses £10.50–£15 ($15.35–$21). AE, DC, MC, V. Mon–Sun 12:30–2:15pm and 6:30–9:30pm. Closed holidays. IRISH/INTERNATIONAL.

Midway between downtown and the Waterford Crystal Factory, this restaurant is in a 19th-century Gothic-style stone gate lodge. Modern Irish art enhances the light, airy interior, and the menu blends innovative cuisine and fresh local ingredients, with an emphasis on seafood. It offers dishes such as seafood ravioli with brunoise of black olives, peppers, and saffron cream; and rack of lamb with red currants and Madeira. The O'Gradys offer accommodation as well.

The Olde Stand. Michael St. (at Lady Lane), Waterford, County Waterford. ☎ **051/ 879488.** Reservations recommended. Dinner main courses £8–£14 ($11.20–$19.60); bar food £2–£8 ($2.80–$11.20). AE, DC, MC, V. Daily 10:30am–11pm. IRISH/SEAFOOD.

Overlooking the busy center of the city, this upstairs restaurant is part of a Victorian-style pub with a decor of old paintings and maps of Waterford. The restaurant features steaks and seafood, with choices including surf-and-turf, salmon in pastry, and seafood pan-cakes. The lower-level pub also offers morning coffee, a self-service carvery lunch, and snacks throughout the day. Open hours are subject to unpredictable seasonal variations.

The Reginald. 2/3 The Mall, Waterford, County Waterford. ☎ **051/855087.** Reservations recommended for dinner. Bar food £2–£7 ($2.80–$9.80); early-bird (before 7pm) 3-course dinner £10.95 ($15.35); dinner main courses £10.95–£16.95 ($15.35–$23.75). MC, V. Daily 9:30am–10:30pm. INTERNATIONAL/IRISH.

One of the city's original walls (ca. A.D. 850) is part of the decor at this pub and restaurant next to Reginald's Tower. In keeping with its Viking-inspired foundations, the Reginald is laid out in a pattern of caverns, alcoves, and arches. The restaurant offers innovative choices using local ingredients, such as fillet steak Aoife topped with avocado, chives, tomatoes, and green peppercorn sauce; and fillet of pink trout with vermouth sauce. There's live music midweek to Sunday.

After hours Thursday to Saturday, the Reginald becomes the Excalibur "Knight Club" (named after the film and housing a number of its props), with live music and dancing. There's no cover charge before 10pm. This is reputedly where Strongbow met Aoife. Who knows who you'll meet?

✪ **The Strand Seafood Restaurant.** In the Strand Inn, Dunmore East, County Waterford. ☎ **051/383174.** Reservations recommended. Main courses £12–£14 ($16.80–$19.60). No service charge. AE, MC, V. Mar–Oct daily 6:30–10pm; Nov–Dec and Feb Wed–Sun 6:30–10pm. Closed Jan. SEAFOOD.

This intimate restaurant, attached to two pubs, has an independent reputation for outstanding cuisine. If you manage to look up from your plate, the views of Water-ford Harbour and the Celtic Sea are stunning. Four or five daily seafood specials aug-ment the excellent menu. Grilled wild salmon with green gooseberry sauce sounds risky but generously rewards all takers, and fresh lemon sole stuffed with seafood mousse is gorgeous. A vegetarian choice is provided each evening; and plates of crisp sautéed vegetables are liable to appear all by themselves, so be forewarned. An alluring dessert cart lies in wait at the end of your meal.

✪ **The Tannery.** 10 Quay St., Dungarvan, County Waterford. ☎ **058/45420.** www. tannery.ie. Early-bird 3-course dinner (Tues–Fri 6:30–7:30pm) £16.50 ($23.10); dinner main courses £12.95–£16.95 ($18.15–£23.75); Sun 3-course lunch £16 ($22.40). No service charge. AE, DC, MC, V. Tues–Thurs 12:30–2:30pm, 6:30–9:30pm; Fri–Sat 12:30–2:30pm, 6:30–10pm; Sun 12:15–2:15pm (and 6–9pm July–Aug). CONTEMPORARY IRISH.

Until 1995 this impressive stone monument of a building on the quays was an oper-ating tannery; then 2 years later it reappeared as a stylish contemporary restaurant rec-ommended far and wide throughout the Southeast. Once gutted, this seasoned structure bequeathed its fine lines, vaulted ceiling, and ironwork beams to a fresh Nordic vision of light woods, polished metal, strategic mirrors, and bold contemporary art; and it all worked.

But on to the food. Life is brief and uncertain, so eat dessert first. Not really, but I am going to talk about it first, as the poached pears with toasted almonds and cocoa sorbet was visually the most exquisite finish I have ever witnessed to a meal. It was a still-life masterpiece, and it summed up the understated excellence we found here. This is what you would imagine a fine chef to prepare at home for treasured friends, contemporary Irish home-cooking in your dreams. The carrot soup with yogurt and almonds led the way to grilled sea bream with spicy pepperonata and roast rack of lamb with saffron, carrot, and date risotto. The wine list is modest and discerning, all you need to make the right choice. Children's menus are on hand for Sunday lunches and evenings until 8:30. And there's an entirely separate dining room for nonsmokers, available on request. The Tannery is, in sum, an exemplar of the new Irish cuisine and a measure of just how good it gets in even informal Irish eateries these days.

✪ **The Wine Vault.** High St., Waterford, County Waterford. ☎ **051/853444.** www.waterfordwinevault.com. Reservations recommended. Main courses £8.95–£18.95 ($12.55–$26.55). No service charge. AE, DC, MC, V. Mon–Sat 12:30–2:30pm and 5:30–10:30pm. CONTINENTAL/SEAFOOD.

Everyone knows you can't eat the scenery, but you can drink the history, or at least you can here at Waterford's Wine Vault. Waterford's famed wine merchants have been popping corks for 800 years, and David Dennison is the city's current winemaster. An International Sommelier and a member of the Chevalier du Taste du Vin, David is peerless in providing fine wines and the food with which to best appreciate them; and he does all this from a building steeped in the history of Waterford's wine trade. In recent excavations, a 13th-century Bordeaux wine jar was found on his premises, which gives you some idea of the vintages with which he delights his guests.

For unpretentious and inspired dining in Waterford town, this informal bistro whose waters and wines run deep is simply the place to be. Portions are mighty, but we guarantee you'll find room. The menu is judiciously selective, with several daily specials, often focused on the most alluring catch of the day. The herb-crusted salmon with peppered cucumber and cabernet sauvignon dressing was among the finest salmon dishes I've ever encountered, disarmingly simple and perfect. The homemade rocket pasta and the monkfish fillets with wild mushroom risotto were more rich and ambitious, with equal achievement. Here, the wines are for the sake of the food and the food for the sake of the wines. Nothing suffers, least of all the diners. I was staggered by one of the "Bordeaux High Flyers" in the wine menu, listed at £720 ($1,008), which went unopened. Bliss is available for less here. We passed on the Chocolate Nemesis and the Cassato Poncho and settled for the homemade lemon curd ice cream, which provided the perfect finish. The service here is exceptional—attentiveness without fuss, sophistication with warmth and humor. All that and heated plates! Smoking is permitted on the main floor, while nonsmokers have the romantic wine vault to themselves.

INEXPENSIVE

Bewley's. Broad St., Waterford, County Waterford. ☎ **051/870506.** All items 80p–£7.95 ($1.10–$11.15). Mon–Sat 8am–6pm. IRISH.

On the second level of the Broad Street Shopping Centre, this self-service spot is a branch of the famous Dublin coffeehouse of the same name. It serves breakfast, lunch, and coffee and tea all day. Homemade scones, fresh pastries, and soups are specialties.

A RESTAURANT AFLOAT

✪ **Galley Cruising Restaurants.** New Ross Quay, New Ross, County Wexford. ☎ **051/421723.** Reservations required. Lunch £14 ($19.60); afternoon tea £7 ($9.80); dinner £22–£26 ($30.80–$36.40). MC, V. Daily Apr–Oct from New Ross 12:30pm (lunch), 3pm (tea), 6 or 7pm (dinner); June–Aug from Waterford 3pm (tea). IRISH.

Capt. Dick Fletcher welcomes guests aboard the Galley Restaurants to enjoy full bar service and a meal while cruising the scenic waters of the Rivers Suir, Nore, or Barrow. The menu is limited, but the food is fresh and the views can't be equaled. Cruises last 2 to 3 hours. Boats normally leave from New Ross; during the summer months, trips also depart from Waterford.

WATERFORD AFTER DARK

Waterford has two main entertainment centers. Housed in one of Ireland's largest arts centers, the **Garter Lane Theatre,** 22a O'Connell St. (☎ 051/855038), presents the work of local production companies such as the Red Kettle and Waterford Youth Drama. Visiting troupes from all over Ireland also perform contemporary and traditional works at the 170-seat theater. Performances are usually Tuesday to Saturday, and tickets average £6 to £10 ($8.40 to $14) for most events. The box office is open Monday to Saturday 10am to 6pm, and accepts MasterCard and Visa.

When big-name Irish or international talents come to Waterford, they usually perform at the **Forum Theatre** at the Glen (☎ 051/871111), a 1,000-seat house off Bridge Street. Tickets average £10 to £16 ($14 to $22.40), depending on the event. The box office is open Monday to Friday, 11am to 1pm and 2 to 4pm. The Forum presents a late-night bar, Deja Vu, every Friday and Saturday. There's no cover, and the patrons are mostly in their mid- to late 30s.

From May to September, on Tuesday, Thursday, and Saturday (and Wed in July and Aug) at 8:45pm, the historic Waterford City Hall is home to the **Waterford Show,** a festive evening of music, storytelling, song, and dance. In high season, be sure to reserve a place in advance. Credit-card bookings (☎ 051/875823, or 051/381020 after 5pm) are accepted. Admission is £7 ($9.80), which includes a preshow drink and a glass of wine during the show.

There's also a new **Waterford Viking Show,** a 90-minute celebration of Waterford's Viking Heritage through music, dance, storytelling, and humor at the Granary, Merchants Quay. It happens in July and August at 8pm on Monday, Wednesday, and Friday. The cost is £10 ($14) per person. Call the Granary (☎ 051/304500) to reserve in advance.

Otherwise, Waterford's nightlife is centered in the hotel lounges and in the city's interesting assortment of pubs.

PUBS

Egans. 36/37 Barronstrand St., Waterford, County Waterford. ☎ 051/875619.

In the heart of the city center, this friendly pub is a showcase of Tudor style and decor, from its neat black-and-white facade to its cozy interior.

✪ **Jack Meades.** Cheekpoint Rd., Halfway House, County Waterford. ☎ 051/873187.

Waterford's most unusual pub is not in the city, but nestled beneath an old stone bridge in an area known as Halfway House, 4 miles (6.5km) south of town. Dating from 1705, the pub is widely known by the locals as Meades Under the Bridge, or "Ireland's only fly-over pub." As a public house with a forge, it was a stopping-off point for travelers between Waterford and Passage East in the old days. The facade and interior—wooden beams, historical paintings, antiques, and open, crackling fireplaces—haven't changed much in the intervening years. In July and August, there's music with sing-along sessions on Wednesday night, and all year, impromptu evening sessions can occur. The grounds include an icehouse, a corn mill, lime kilns, a viaduct, and a beer garden and barbecue area. On Sundays in summer, barbecues with outdoor music start at 2pm and run until roughly 7:30pm. From May to September, bar food is served daily.

The Kings. 8 Lombard St., Waterford, County Waterford. ☎ **051/874495.**

This pub just off the Mall dates from 1776, when it was called the Packet Hotel because of its proximity to the Waterford docks and the packet ships sailing to England. It was often a send-off point for emigrants from Ireland. Today it retains its original Georgian-style facade, and the interior reflects old-world charm, particularly in the cozy 20-seat front bar. Check out the mid-19th-century bar counter—it has panels that used to hold sandpaper for customers to strike a match.

The Munster. Bailey's New St., Waterford, County Waterford. ☎ **051/874656.**

The flavor of old Waterford prevails in this 300-year-old building, which also can be entered from the Mall. Often referred to as Fitzgerald's (the name of the family who owns it), this pub is rich in etched mirrors, antique Waterford glass sconces, and dark wood walls, some of which are fashioned out of timber from the old Waterford Toll Bridge. Among the many rooms are an original "Men's Bar" and a lively modern lounge, which often features traditional Irish music on weekends.

T. & H. Doolan. 32 George's St., Waterford, County Waterford. ☎ **051/841504.**

Once a stagecoach stop, this 170-year-old pub in the center of town claims to be Waterford's oldest public house. It is a favorite venue for evening sessions of ballad, folk, and traditional music. Lanterns light the whitewashed stone walls and a collection of old farm implements, crocks, mugs, and jugs.

3 South Tipperary

South Tipperary is one of Ireland's best-kept secrets. Here, far from the tour buses and the clicking of camera shutters, you may just find the Ireland everyone is looking for: lush, welcoming, unspoiled, and splendidly beautiful.

VISITOR INFORMATION　The **Clonmel Tourist Office** is on Sarsfield Street, Clonmel (☎ 052/22960). **Seasonal offices,** open June to August, are at Castle Street, Cahir (☎ 052/41453), and at the Town Hall, Cashel (☎ 062/61333). The Web site for all Southeast Tourism is www.southeastireland.travel.ie. To get the latest on news, listings, and events in Clonmel and the surrounding area, buy a copy of the local **Nationalist,** which hits the stands every Saturday. Among other things, it will tell you what's on at the Regal Theatre or the White Memorial Theatre, Clonmel's principal venues for the arts.

EXPLORING THE AREA

Clonmel, the capital of Tipperary and the largest inland town in Ireland, is the unassuming gateway to the region. A working town, as yet undistorted or distracted by massive tourism, Clonmel has everything you need to establish a strategic, pleasant base of operations in the southeast. Poised on the banks of the Suir, Clonmel once had the distinction of withstanding a Cromwellian siege for 3 months. More recently, the town has successfully resisted the lure of rapid, unplanned tourism, preserving its own landscape and character and so making itself all the more attractive to visitors. Its 5-mile (8km) riverfront walkway, bustling vitality, and prime location all make it a perfect base for exploring one of the most pristine and stunningly beautiful regions of Ireland.

Whether you're staying in Clonmel or just passing through, several marvelously scenic drives converge here: the **Comeragh or Nire Valley Drive** deep into the Comeragh Mountains, which rise from the south banks of the Suir; the **Knockmealdown Drive,** through the historic village of Ardfinnan and the Vee (see below); and the **Suir Scenic Drive.** All are signposted from Clonmel.

North of Clonmel and deep in the Tipperary countryside, **Cashel** is not to be missed. Because it's on the main N8 road, most people pass through en route from Dublin to Cork. If your travels don't take you to Cashel, a side trip from Waterford is worth the drive. In particular, two scenic routes are well worth a detour:

At Cahir, head north through the ✪ **Galty Mountains,** Ireland's highest inland mountain range, to the Glen of Aherlow. Often called "Ireland's Greenest Valley," the 7-mile (11km) Glen of Aherlow is a secluded and scenic area that was an important pass between the plains of counties Tipperary and Limerick.

If you're driving south into Waterford, head for the **"Vee."** This 11-mile (18km) long road winds through the Knockmealdown Mountains from Clogheen to Lismore and Cappoquin in County Waterford. It's one of the most dramatic drives in the southeast or, for that matter, anywhere in Ireland. The high point of the Vee is at the Tipperary-Waterford border, where the two slopes of the pass converge to frame the patchwork fields of the Galty Valley far below. At this point, numerous walking trails lead to the nearby peaks and down to the mountain lake of Petticoat Loose—named after a, shall we say, less-than-exemplary lady. A more edifying local character was Samuel Grubb, of Castle Grace, who so loved these slopes that he left instructions that he should be buried upright overlooking them. And so he is. The rounded stone cairn you might notice off the road between Clogheen and the Vee is where he stands in place, entombed, facing the Golden Vale of Tipperary.

Ahenny High Crosses. Kil Crispeen Churchyard, Ahenny, County Tipperary. 5 miles (8km) north of Carrick-on-Suir, signposted off R697. Open site. Box for donations.

You're likely to have this little-known and rarely visited site to yourself, except for the cows whose pasture you will cross to reach it. The setting is idyllic and, on a bright day, gorgeous. The remarkably well-preserved Ahenny high crosses are among the oldest in Ireland, dating from the 8th or 9th century. Tradition associates them with seven saintly bishops, all brothers, who are said to have been waylaid and murdered. Their unusual stone "caps," thought by some to be bishops' miters, more likely suggest the transition from wood crosses, which would have had small roofs to shelter them from the rain. Note too their intricate spiral and cable ornamentation in remarkably high relief, which may well have been inspired by earlier Celtic metalwork. Irish high crosses compose some of the most striking monuments of early Christianity in Ireland, and these are among the finest and most important examples of the form.

Athassel Priory. 2 miles (3.2km) South of Golden, County Tipperary. Open site.

This is the largest medieval priory in Ireland, spread out over 4 acres, and although it is in ruins, many delightful details from the original structure remain. Take the signposted road from the town of Golden, which is between Tipperary and Cashel on N74; the priory is in a field just east of the road, and its many pinnacles offer a strikingly picturesque scene. This was an Augustinian priory, founded in the late 12th century; the remaining structures date from that time until the mid–15th century. The main approach is over a low stone bridge and through a gatehouse that was the focal point of the outer fortifications. The church entrance is a beautifully carved doorway at its west end. To the south of the church is the cloister, whose graceful arches have been largely eroded by time. Don't miss the carved face protruding from the southwest corner of the chapel tower, about 30 feet above ground level.

The Bolton Library. On the grounds of St. John the Baptist Church, John St., Cashel, County Tipperary. ☎ **062/61944.** Admission £1.50 ($2.10) adults, £1 ($1.40) seniors and students, 50p (70¢) children. Mon–Fri 9:30am–5:30pm; Sun 2:30–5:30pm. Closed Mon Mar–Sept.

In this library, you'll see the smallest book in the world, as well as other rare, antiquarian, and unusual books dating from the 12th century. Ensconced here are works by Dante, Swift, Calvin, Newton, Erasmus, and Machiavelli. Also on display are some silver altar pieces from the original cathedral on the Rock of Cashel.

Brú Ború. Rock Lane, Cashel, County Tipperary. ☎ **062/61122.** Free admission to center; show £8 ($11.20); show and dinner £25 ($35). Daily Oct–Apr 9am–5:30pm; May–Sept 9am–6pm. Shows mid-June to mid-Sept Tues–Sat 9pm.

At the foot of the Rock of Cashel, this modern complex adds a musical element to the historic Cashel area. Operated by Comhaltas Ceoltoiri Eireann, Ireland's foremost traditional music organization, Brú Ború presents daily performances of authentic Irish traditional music at an indoor theater. Many summer evenings bring concerts to the open-air amphitheater. A heritage center, gift shop, restaurant, and self-service snack bar are also on hand.

✪ **Cahir Castle.** Cahir, County Tipperary. ☎ **052/41011.** Admission £2 ($2.80) adults, £1.50 ($2.10) seniors, £1 ($1.40) students and children, £5 ($7) family. Daily mid-Mar to mid-June and mid-Sept to mid-Oct 9:30am–5:30pm; daily mid-June to mid-Sept 9am–7:30pm; daily mid-Oct to mid-Mar 9:30am–4:30pm.

On a rock in the middle of the River Suir, this is one of Ireland's largest medieval fortresses. Its origins can be traced from the 3rd century, when a fort was built on the rock—hence the town's original name, City of the Fishing Fort. The present structure, which belonged to the Butler family from 1375 to 1961, is Norman and dates to the 13th and 15th centuries. It has a massive keep, high walls, spacious courtyards, and a great hall, all fully restored. The interpretive center offers an engaging 20-minute video introduction to the region's major historic sites, as well as guided tours of the castle grounds. Be sure to find your own way through the castle buildings, which are not included in the tour.

Ormond Castle. Signposted from the center of Carrick-on-Suir, Carrick-on-Suir, County Tipperary. ☎ **051/640787.** Admission £2 ($2.80) adults, £1.50 ($2.10) seniors, £1 ($1.40) students and children, £5 ($7) family. June–Sept daily 9:30am–6:30pm. Closed Oct–May.

The mid-15th-century castle built by Sir Edward MacRichard Butler on this strategic bend of the River Suir has lain in ruins for centuries. What still stands, attached to the ancient battlements, is the last surviving Tudor manor house in Ireland. Trusting that "if he built it, she would come," Thomas Butler, "Black Tom," constructed an extensive manor in honor of his most successful relation, Queen Elizabeth I—whose mother, Anne Boleyn, is rumored to have been born in Ormond Castle. She never came, but many others have, especially since the Heritage Service partially restored this impressive piece of Irish history. Current plans include an elaborate furnishing of the Earl's Room in period style. The manor's plasterwork, carvings, period furniture, and startling collection of original 17th- and 18th-century royal charters will make you glad you bothered to visit and wonder why Queen Elizabeth didn't.

✪ **The Rock of Cashel.** Cashel, County Tipperary. ☎ **062/61437.** Admission £3.50 ($4.90) adults, £2.50 ($3.50) seniors, £1.50 ($2.10) students and children, £8 ($11.20) family. Daily mid-June to mid-Sept 9am–7:30pm; daily mid-Sept to mid-Mar 9am–4:30pm; mid-Mar to mid-June daily 9am–5:30pm. Last admission 45 min. before closing.

When you reach the town of Cashel, look for signs to the Rock of Cashel, which dominates the Tipperary countryside for miles. An outcrop of limestone reaching 200 feet into the sky, "the Rock" tells the tales of 16 centuries. It was the castled seat of the kings of Munster at least as far back as A.D. 360, and it remained a royal fortress until 1101, when King Murtagh O'Brien granted it to the church. Among Cashel's many great moments was the legendary baptism of King Aengus by St. Patrick in 448. Remaining on the rock are the ruins of a two-towered chapel, a cruciform cathedral, a 92-foot round tower, and a cluster of other medieval monuments. The views of and from the Rock are spectacular. Forty-five–minute guided tours are available on request.

Swiss Cottage. Off Dublin–Cork road (N8), Cahir, County Tipperary. ☎ **052/41144.** Guided tour £2 ($2.80) adults, £1.50 ($2.10) seniors, £1 ($1.40) students and children, £5 ($7) family. Late Mar and mid-Oct to Nov Tues–Sun 10am–1pm and 2–4:30pm; Apr Tues–Sun 10am–1pm and 2–6pm; May to mid-Oct daily 10am–6pm.

The earls of Glengall used the Swiss Cottage as a hunting and fishing lodge as far back as 1812. It's a superb example of "cottage orné": a rustic house embodying the ideal of simplicity that so appealed to the Romantics of the early 19th century. The thatched-roof cottage has extensive timberwork, usually not seen in Ireland, and is believed to have been designed by John Nash, a royal architect. The interior has some of the first wallpaper commercially produced in Paris. The guided tour (the only way to see the building) lasts approximately 40 minutes.

✪ **Tipperary Crystal.** Waterford–Limerick road (N24), Ballynoran, Carrick-on-Suir, County Tipperary. ☎ **051/641188.** Free admission. Tours Mon–Fri 10am–3:30pm; shop and restaurant Mon–Fri 9am–5:30pm, Sun 11am–5pm.

If you're nearby, try not to miss this crystal factory, laid out in the style of traditional Irish cottages, complete with a thatched roof. Visitors are welcome to watch master craftspeople as they mouth-blow and hand-cut crystal. Unlike other crystal factories, Tipperary imposes no restriction on photographs and video recorders. The facility includes a showroom and restaurant.

SPORTS & OUTDOOR PURSUITS

BIRD WATCHING   As many as 15 species of Irish waterbirds—including mute swans, coots, wigeons, gadwalls, teals, grey herons, and moorhens—can be seen at the **Marlfield Lake Wildfowl Refuge,** several miles west of Clonmel in Marlfield. This is a little lake with an astonishing number of birds. On your way, you will likely pass signposts for **St. Patrick's Well,** less than a mile away, a tranquil spot with an effervescent pool of reputedly healing crystalline water. In the middle of the pool rises a seriously ancient Celtic cross. The legend that Patrick visited here seems more solidly rooted than most such claims. Even saints get thirsty.

BICYCLING   For complete 1- or 2-week cycling holidays in the Southeast, contact Don Smith at **Celtic Cycling,** Lorum Old Rectory, Bagenalstown, County Carlow (☎ and fax **0503/75282;** www.celticcycling.com).

FISHING   The **River Suir,** from Carrick-on-Suir to Thurles, was once one of the finest salmon rivers in Europe, but recent excessive trawling at its mouth has threatened its stock. It's still a decent salmon river, especially in the February run and from June to September. Trout (brown and rainbow) are in abundance here in the summer. Here you'll find some of the least expensive game fishing in Ireland; single weekday permits cost £15 to £25 ($21 to $35) for salmon, £5 ($7) for trout. They are available from **Kavanagh Sports,** Westgate, Clonmel, County Tipperary (☎ and fax **052/21279**), as is everything else you'll need. Manager Declan Byrne can outfit you with the all essentials and more. To orient yourself and to consider your options, pick up a copy of *Angling on the Suir,* a quite helpful pamphlet available at the Tourist Office. The **River Nore** and the nearby **River Barrow** are also known for good salmon and trout fishing.

For sea fishing, picturesque Dunmore East, 8 miles (13km) south of Waterford, is a good bet. Contact **John O'Connor** (☎ 051/383397) to charter a boat for reef, wreck, and shark fishing. Boat charter rates are £150 to £225 ($210 to $315) per day; rod and reel can also be rented. The species you're likely to encounter in this area during the summer include blue shark, cod, bass, whiting, conger, and ling.

✪ **HORSEBACK RIDING** **Hillcrest Riding Centre,** Glenbally, Tipperary (☎ 062/37915), is a registered riding stable based in the Galty Mountains offering trail rides, a cross-country course, and instruction in show jumping. Trail rides range from £10 ($14) an hour to £40 ($56) for a full day's ride. Hillcrest is a keen hunting stable, and for those anxious for the chase, horses and participation in local and neighboring hunts can be arranged. Hillcrest also offers longer trekking holidays, up to a week in duration. For trekking and trail riding on the slopes of the Comeragh Mountains, you can't do better than **Melodys Nire Valley Equestrian Centre,** Nire View, Ballycarbry, Clonmel (☎ 052/36147).

SWIMMING If you're staying in the area, you're welcome to swim at the **Clonmel civic swimming pool** (☎ 052/21972), near the Market Place. It's open Monday to Friday 10am to 10pm, Saturday and Sunday 10am to 8pm. Call for specific public swim hours.

TENNIS The courts of the **Hillview Sports Club,** Mountain Road, Clonmel (☎ 052/21805), may be used by visitors.

WALKING **R668** between Clogheen and Lismore is one of the most scenic stretches of road in the southeast, and some great walks begin at the **Vee Gap,** a dramatic notch in the Knockmealdown Mountains. About 1.5 miles (2.4km) north of R669 and R668, you reach the highest point in the gap; there is a parking lot, as well as a dirt road continuing down to a lake nestled into the slope below. This is Bay Lough, and the dirt road used to be the main thoroughfare over the gap; it now offers a fine walk to the shores of the lake, with outstanding views of the valley to the north. For a panoramic perspective on the region, start walking due east from the gap parking lot to the summit of Sugarloaf Hill; the hike is extremely steep, but well worth the effort—the views from the ridge are superb.

In the Clonmel area, there are a number of excellent river and hill walks, some more challenging than others. The most spectacular is the ascent of famed **Slievenamon,** a mountain rich in myth and lore. Detailed trail maps for at least a half a dozen walks are available for 50p (70¢) at the Clonmel Tourist Office on Sarsfield Street, Clonmel. Also available is a free leaflet guide to the birds, butterflies, and flora of nearby **Wilderness Gorge.**

The **Galty Mountains,** northwest of the Knockmealdowns, offer some great long and short walks. One beautiful route on a well-defined trail is the circuit of **Lake Muskry,** on the north side of the range. To get there, take R663 west out of Bansha, and follow signs for the town of Rossadrehid. To get to the trail, ask for directions in Rossadrehid; there are several turns, and the landmarks change frequently because of logging in the region. The trail leads you up a glaciated valley to the base of a ring of cliffs, where the crystalline waters of Lake Muskry lie; from here you can walk around the lake, take in the tremendous views of the valley, and return the way you came. Walking time to the lake and back is 3 hours.

Another option on this walk is to continue up past the lake to the top of the ridge, and from there along the ridgetop to Galtymore, a prominent dome-shaped peak about 3 miles (4.8km) west of Lake Muskry. It is a beautiful but extremely demanding walk, about 6 hours to Galtymore and back. This is only one of many extraordinary walks in the Glen of Aherlow. Trail maps and all the information and assistance you could think of asking for are available at the **Glen of Aherlow Failte Centre,** Coach Road, Newtown (☎ **062/56331**), ably directed by Helen Morrissey. It's open year-round, Monday to Friday 10am to 4pm, and daily June to October from 9am to 6pm. Guided 2-hour walks are best booked in advance. Or drop in, and one might be leaving shortly.

ACCOMMODATIONS
VERY EXPENSIVE
Cashel Palace. Main St., Cashel, County Tipperary. ☎ **800/221-1074,** 800/223-6510 from the U.S., or 062/62707. Fax 062/61521. www.iol.ie/tipp/cashel-palace.htm. 23 units. TV TEL. £100–£225 ($140–$315) double. Rates include full Irish breakfast and service charge. AE, DC, MC, V.

Originally built in 1730 as a residence for Church of Ireland archbishops, this stately red-brick Palladian mansion has been a hotel for 30 years. It has an ideal location, right in the middle of Cashel town yet within its own walled grounds, and recent owners have thoroughly updated the property and filled it with antiques and designer-coordinated fabrics. Its well-tended back garden holds mulberry bushes planted in 1702 to commemorate the coronation of Queen Anne, and a private pathway known as the Bishop's Walk that runs up a hill to the Rock of Cashel. The house itself is a proud display of Corinthian pillars, mantelpieces of Kilkenny marble, and a paneled early Georgian staircase of red pine. A 1999 addition of 10 rooms in the charming Mews House gives visitors a cozy nook next to the hotel.

Dining/Diversions: The Four Seasons restaurant offers splendid views of the revered Rock, especially at night when it is flood-lit. Other choices include the lower-level coffee shop-pub, the Buttery, and the Cellar Bar.

EXPENSIVE/MODERATE
Kilcoran Lodge Hotel. Dublin–Cork road (N8), Cahir, County Tipperary. ☎ **800/447-7462** from the U.S., or 052/41288. Fax 052/41994. 25 units. TV TEL. £78–£170 ($109.20–$238) double. Rates include full breakfast and service charge. AE, DC, MC, V.

A former hunting lodge nestled on 20 acres of wooded grounds, this old Victorian treasure is on a hillside set back from the main road a few miles west of Cahir. It was totally renovated and refurbished in 1998. The public areas retain their old-world charm, with open fireplaces, grandfather clocks, antique tables and chairs, brass fixtures, and tall windows that frame expansive views of the Suir Valley and Knockmealdown Mountains. Guest rooms have traditional furnishings and modern conveniences such as hair dryers, tea/coffeemakers, and garment presses.

Dining/Diversions: Dining choices include a formal restaurant with lovely views of the countryside, and a bar and lounge noted for its daytime pub grub, which includes Irish stew, traditional boiled bacon and cabbage, homemade soups, and hot scones.

Amenities: Indoor swimming pool, Jacuzzi, sauna, and solarium.

Hotel Minella. 1 mile (1.6km) east of Clonmel center on the south bank of the River Suir, Coleville Rd., Clonmel, County Tipperary. ☎ **052/22388.** Fax 052/24381. www.hotelminella.ie. 70 units. TV TEL. £100 ($140) double; £140–£150 ($196–$210) suite. Rates include full breakfast and service charge. AE, DC, MC, V.

The attractive centerpiece of this sprawling hotel complex along the River Suir was built in 1863. Its many additions have made it not only a haven for tourists but also a haunt for locals, whether they're celebrating a wedding or merely a Friday night out. Its riverbank location and attractive landscaping give it an appeal beyond its somewhat-incongruous mix of architectural styles. Once you're inside, its warm, welcoming, and utterly comfortable atmosphere take over.

The eye that seems to have overlooked the exterior of the hotel was quite attentive to its interior. The standard rooms are furnished in dark woods and paisley prints and have tea- and coffee-making facilities, irons and pants presses, and tiled bathtubs with rubber ducks. The steam-room suites are especially spacious and luxuriant, with rich colors, four-poster canopy beds, and private steam rooms with showers. The Jacuzzi suites have more standard beds and (of course) Jacuzzis. All the rooms have desks, ample well-designed shelf and wardrobe space, and views either of the river or of the nearby mountains. Nonsmoking rooms and rooms adapted for guests with disabilities are available upon request.

Dining/Diversions: Two spacious lounges and a bar serve drinks, lunches, and snacks. Snacks and drinks are also available in the outside riverfront garden when the weather permits. The main restaurant is quite appealing and has a large nonsmoking area.

Amenities: Room service, laundry/dry cleaning, currency exchange, baby-sitting. Perhaps the chief appeal of this hotel is its new fully equipped state-of-the-art health and fitness club to which hotel guests have free and full access. You could easily spend your days here. It's got everything, including gym, swimming pool, aerobic studio, outdoor hot tub, indoor Jacuzzi, sauna, aromatherapy steam room, therapy rooms, aquacruisers, all-season tennis court, fitness testing, and massage.

MODERATE

Dundrum House. Dundrum, County Tipperary. ☎ **800/447-7462** from the U.S., or 062/71116. Fax 062/71366. E-mail: dundrum@iol.ie. 60 units. TV TEL. £110–£121 ($154–$169.40) double. Service charge 10%. Rates include full Irish breakfast. Weekend discounts available. AE, DC, MC, V.

Six miles (9.7km) northwest of Cashel, this impressive Georgian country manor is nestled in the fertile Tipperary countryside, surrounded by 100 acres of grounds and gardens. The River Multeen runs through the property. Originally built as a residence in 1730 by the Earl of Montalt, then used as a convent school, it was renovated, updated, and turned into a hotel in 1978 by local residents Austin and Mary Crowe. It is furnished with assorted heirlooms, vintage curios, Victorian pieces, and reproductions. Each room is individually decorated, some with four-poster beds or hand-carved headboards, armoires, vanities, and other traditional furnishings. The exceptional weekend specials (such as £95/$124.50 double for 2 nights from May to Sept) are available throughout the year.

Dining choices include the elegant high-ceiling dining room and a unique bar and lounge in a former chapel with stained-glass windows. Exercise facilities include a championship 18-hole golf course, two tennis courts, riding stables, and trout-fishing privileges (although in recent years the river has been stocked with more golf balls than trout). A leisure center with a pool, sauna, and gym opened in 1998.

Lismacue House. Bansha, County Tipperary. ☎ **062/54106.** Fax 062/54126. http://indigo.ie/~lismac/. 5 units, 3 with private bathroom. TEL. £80 ($112) double without bathroom, £96 ($134.40) double with bathroom. Rates include full breakfast. Dinner from £25 ($37.50). AE, MC, V. Closed Dec 22–Jan 2.

On a low hill with fine views of the Galtee Mountains, this spacious country house is part rustic retreat and part elegant estate. A long, straight drive lined with ancient lime trees announces the house, which looks rather imposing with its crenellated roofline and carved limestone porch. Jim and Kate Nicholson are the hosts in this house, home to Kate's family since the early 18th century, and they've succeeded in creating the relaxed atmosphere of a comfortable summer lodge without underplaying the grandeur of the place. The guest rooms are all located in a grand 19th-century addition, now the main house, where ceilings are lofty and vast windows look out over fields and hills. The bedrooms are simply and somewhat sparsely furnished, though always in accord with the languorous elegance of the house; bathrooms are adequately spacious.

Jim, who's a great storyteller, presides over the dinner table, and Kate prepares memorable meals with the best of ingredients from home and abroad: seafood from West Cork; local lamb, beef, and vegetables; free-range eggs; and wines personally collected in France.

INEXPENSIVE

Ballyowen House. Dualla, Cashel, County Tipperary. ☎ **062/61265.** 3 units, 2 with private bathroom. £50 ($70) double. No service charge. Rates include full breakfast. No credit cards; personal checks accepted. Closed Oct–Apr.

This is a secluded retreat from which to explore Cashel, Cahir, and the immediate area. The imposing manor house, dating from 1750, is both elegant and charmingly antiquated. Surrounding the house are vast fields dotted with sheep and beautiful old trees. The rooms are extravagantly large and furnished with handsome antiques. The guest rooms are nonsmoking. Tea is available upon arrival, and breakfast is served in the spacious dining room. The McCan family offers a warm welcome and knowledgeable advice on walks and nearby sightseeing.

Bansha House. Bansha, County Tipperary. ☎ **062/54194.** Fax 062/54215. www.iol.ie/_tipp/banshahs.htm. 8 units, 5 with private bathroom. £46–£50 ($64.40–$70) double. No service charge. Rates include full breakfast. MC, V. Closed Dec 20–Jan 1.

The Marnanes have won many well-deserved awards during 25 years of offering accommodations in their elegant, comfortable Georgian manor farmhouse. The town of Bansha sits at the base of the magnificent Galty Mountains, which dominate the skyline on a clear day and make this house a great base for walking and bicycling or just taking in the scenery. The Primrose Cottage is available for guests who want to do their own cooking. Mary and John Marnane can also direct you to walks, ✪ **horseback riding,** bike rides, and drives in the area.

✪ **Kilmaneen Farmhouse.** Newcastle, County Tipperary. ☎ and fax **052/36231.** www.dirl.com/tipperary/kilmaneen.htm. 3 units, 2 with shower only. £40 ($56) double. No service charge. Rates include full breakfast. £15 ($21) dinner. MC, V. Open year-round.

This small gem of a B&B has recently been recognized as such, winning both national and regional top accommodation honors in 1999, and a national landscape award in 2000. The rooms are spotless and beautifully appointed. Even more, the location is breathtaking. As you drive to Kilmaneen, you will be pinching yourself to guarantee you're not dreaming the mountain vistas before your eyes. What isn't immediately visible is the great fishing available on the farm. You can cast for trout here, into either the Suir or the Tar, without any permit required, and you will be provided with a fisherman's hut for tying flies, storing equipment, and drying waders. If the mountains hold more allure for you, your host, Ken O'Donnell is trained in mountaineering and leads trekking and walking tours into the nearby ranges. Take your pick; there are three: the Knockmealdowns, the Comeraghs, and the Galtees. The bottom line here is that you will want to stay a week and not a night; so you may want to consider from the outset the O'Donnells' fully equipped four-star guest cottage, cozy enough for two and spacious enough for five. It rents for anywhere from £100 to £300 ($140 to $420), depending on the season and the number of occupants. Finding your way here can be tricky, so call ahead and ask for detailed directions.

Mr. Bumbles. Richmond House, Kickham St., Clonmel, County Tipperary. ☎ **052/29380.** Fax 052/29007. 4 units, all with shower only. TV. £40 ($56) double; £45 ($63) family room. No service charge. Rates include full breakfast. MC, V. At top of Clonmel Market Place.

Located above Mr. Bumbles restaurant (see "Dining," below), with their own exterior staircase, these four rooms are bright and simple. They are meticulously clean and have firm beds. The family room sleeps three. If you crave a night off from the social rituals of the standard B&B and want an excellent breakfast, this is the place. Better yet, it's possible to negotiate a B&B-and-dinner combination, which all but guarantees sweet dreams.

SELF-CATERING

✪ **Ballyknockane Estate.** 1.5 miles (2.4km) west of Ballypatrick off N76, Ballypatrick, Clonmel, County Tipperary. ☎ **052/33234.** Fax 052/33255. E-mail: robinmc@gofree.indigo.ie. 3 cottages, 1 coach house. TV TEL. Cottages £500 ($700) per week; coach house £800 ($1,120) per week. No credit cards.

Once the hunting lodge and grounds of the Marquess of Ormonde, this 5,000-acre estate is the ultimate retreat and wooded wonderland. Composing a large part of Slievenamon ("the Mountain of Women"), a hauntingly beautiful peak steeped in Irish legend, the estate has 50 miles (81km) of private roads and paths, a paradise for hikers, climbers, and birders. The cottages (each with three bedrooms, sleeping six) and the coach house (which has four bedrooms and sleeps eight) are situated within a beautifully maintained 52-acre arboretum, boasting many rare and exotic species of trees and shrubs. The fully equipped and cozy cottages are meticulously maintained and tastefully landscaped. The coach house, with its own walled enclosure, is far grander though a bit fraying here and there. Whichever you choose, you will be warmly welcomed and well attended during your stay here.

✪ **Coopers Cottage.** 1 mile (1.6km) off N24 at Bansha, Raheen, Bansha, County Tipperary. ☎ **062/54027.** Fax 062/54027. www.dirl.com/tipperary/coopers.htm. 1 cottage. TV TEL. £195–£350 ($273–$490) per week. No credit cards; personal checks accepted.

Stella and Eamonn Long have lovingly restored and renovated this 19th-century cooper's cottage, once Eamonn's family home, into an extraordinarily comfortable and tasteful country hideaway. While retaining the original cozy proportions and traditional lines, the Longs have created a house full of light, with generous skylights and windows opening to spectacular views of the Galty Mountains. The furnishings have a bright, contemporary feel. The house, which has three bedrooms and sleeps six, comes with absolutely everything, including a barbecue and a lovely modest fenced-in garden, with a patio area for sunny days. This is an ideal base for exploring the beautiful southeastern counties of Tipperary, Waterford, and Kilkenny. The town of Bansha is 2 miles (3.2km) down the lane.

Knocklofty Country House. 3 miles (4.8km) west of Clonmel (signposted from R665), Clonmel, County Tipperary. ☎ **052/38222** (hotel). Fax 052/38300. Self-catering ☎ **052/25444.** Fax 052/26444. www.tipp.ie/knocklof.htm. 17 hotel units, 4 with shower only. TV TEL. £80–£100 ($112–$140) double. Rates include full Irish breakfast and service charge. 17 self-catering units. TV TEL. £180–£410 ($252–$574) per week. AE, MC, V.

Knocklofty House is a grand, sprawling country house with both a distinguished past and big plans for the future. Its torso dates from the 17th century, with various extremities added in the 18th and 19th centuries. The fine bones are all there, and its deserved adornment is nearing completion. Work on restoring and redecorating all of its guest rooms was completed in April 2000. The setting, 105 acres of rolling park and pastureland along the River Suir, is exquisite. The river views are serene. Each guest room has its own character, but all share high ceilings, great wide windows, and orthopedic beds (all but several are king-sized). The elegant oak-paneled dining room (see "Dining," below) serves extraordinary cuisine, which guests await over a drink in the grand two-story Georgian library.

The well-appointed self-catering units offer an appealing array of options. There are hotel apartments, mews town houses, and cottages, some freestanding and some in a row. You won't believe what your cottage used to be—for example, a stable, a barn, or a shed. Our favorites are the garden lodge, a cozy one-bedroom stone cottage; "Mrs. Phelan's House," a stone three-bedroom cottage that once belonged to the longstanding (literally) housekeeper of Lady Dunoughmore; and the mews houses with one, two, three, or four bedrooms, circling a courtyard adjoining the great house. For inclement days, there's a small in-house health club with an exercise and weight room, a 16-meter pool, and a Jacuzzi. The sun bed, massage, and beauty treatments require advance booking. There are many memorable walks and drives nearby. Fishing is free (no permits required) for guests on this stretch of the Suir, known for brown and rainbow trout.

DINING
EXPENSIVE

Chez Hans. Rockside, Cashel, County Tipperary. ☎ **062/61177.** Reservations required. Main courses £14–£23.50 ($19.60–$32.90). MC, V. Tues–Sat 6:30–10pm. Closed Jan and Sept 5–12. FRENCH/IRISH.

It's not surprising that the Rock of Cashel, a landmark in Irish royal and ecclesiastical history, would inspire a great restaurant within its shadow. It's entirely appropriate, too, that the restaurant be housed in a former Gothic chapel at the foot of the path that leads to the mighty rock. The cathedral-style ceiling, original stone walls, lyrical background music, and candlelight atmosphere create the perfect setting for the cooking of chef-owner Hans Pieter Mataier. His repertoire includes such dishes as cassoulette of seafood, roast sea scallops, succulent herb-crusted roast lamb, and free-range duckling with honey and thyme.

MODERATE

Knocklofty House Restaurant. In Knocklofty Country House, 3 miles (4.8km) west of Clonmel (signposted from R665), Clonmel, County Tipperary. ☎ **052/38222** (hotel). Reservations recommended. Fixed-price lunch £13.95 ($19.55); fixed-price dinner £26 ($36.40); dinner main courses £12–£18 ($16.80–$25.20). AE, MC, V. Daily 7:30–10:30am and 12:30–2:30pm; Mon–Sat 7–9:30pm; Sun 6:30–8pm. IRISH/INTERNATIONAL.

A special spot frequented by locals for a treat and by lucky visitors, this boasts excellent cuisine served in a warm oak-paneled dining room overlooking the Suir River. Perusal of the menu over drinks in the library is the ritual; you are called when your meal is ready. The fixed-price lunch menu offers a range of international dishes, from chicken with mozzarella and sweet jalapeño chili, to roast beef with Yorkshire pudding. At dinner, we found the tender rack of lamb with sun-dried tomato and basil-scented *jus* and the whole panfried back sole meunière truly delicious. Fresh ingredients, inventive sauces, and generous portions are the hallmarks of this most pleasant restaurant. Of course, the menu changes weekly, so you'll discover for yourself what the chef has in mind for you.

Mr. Bumbles. Richmond House, Kickham St., Clonmel, County Tipperary. ☎ **052/29188.** Reservations recommended. Fixed-price 4-course dinner £23 ($32.20); main courses £10.95–£15.95 ($15.35–$23.35). No service charge. MC, V. Daily noon–3pm and 6–10pm. INTERNATIONAL.

For a newcomer to Clonmel, Mr. Bumbles has already created quite a buzz. With its natural woods, bright colors, and bistro feel, you almost expect a waterfront view—instead, there's a parking lot. But the restaurant is very inviting and the food simply first-rate. Many dishes are grilled or pan-seared with a Mediterranean slant to the spicing, and all are brilliantly fresh. Wild sea trout, Tipperary sirloin, and Mediterranean vegetables are representative entrees. The presentation is gorgeous, and portions are generous. The French house wines are quite fine and reasonable at roughly £10 ($14), and the French and Australian entries on the international wine list are particularly strong.

The Spearman Restaurant. 97 Main St., Cashel, County Tipperary. ☎ **062/61143.** Reservations recommended. Dinner main courses £7–£15 ($9.80–$22.35). AE, MC, V. May–Sept daily 12:30–3pm and 6–9:30pm; Oct and Dec–Apr Tues–Sun 12:30–3pm, Tues–Sat 6–9:30pm. Closed Nov and holidays. IRISH/INTERNATIONAL.

Once a grocery store, this attractive restaurant in the center of Cashel, behind the tourist office, offers an excellent, sophisticated menu at a very reasonable price; by combining the freshest local produce and some culinary imagination, it has gained a fine reputation. The menu includes such entrees as baked chicken with Gruyère cheese and Dijon mustard, poached salmon in creamy tarragon sauce, and steak with red-pepper and mushroom sauce.

INEXPENSIVE

Angela's Wholefood Restaurant. 14 Abbey St., Clonmel, County Tipperary. ☎ **052/ 26899.** Breakfast menu £2–£4 ($2.80–$5.60); lunch menu £1.60–£5.50 ($2.25–$7.70). No service charge. No credit cards. Mon–Fri 9am–5:30pm, Sat noon–5pm. INTERNATIONAL.

Angela's Wholefood Restaurant offers scrumptious, substantial fare at remarkable value. The blackboard menu might include custom-made breakfast omelets, spicy Moroccan lamb stew, savory tomato-and-spinach flan Provençal, homemade soups, sandwiches made to order, and an array of delicious salads. The food is vibrant, fresh, and appreciated by the bustling patrons who line up with trays in hand, from barristers (in garb) to baby-sitters.

PUBS

Gerry Chawkes. 3 Gladstone St. Upper, Clonmel, County Tipperary. ☎ **052/21149.**

Chawkes is a Clonmel landmark, a shrine not so much to stout as to sport. A fanatic fan of hurling and racing (dogs and horses), Gerry Chawke has made his pub a cult place, lined with fascinating memorabilia. Sports teams and clubs from throughout Ireland make a point of stopping here, as do local politicians in recovery from council meetings. You too will be quickly at home—Gerry will see to that.

Railway Bar. Clonmel, County Tipperary. No phone.

You'll need on-the-ground directions to find Kitty's, which is what locals call this pub. Roughly, it's in a cul-de-sac behind the train station. Any effort you make to find your way will not be wasted, especially on weekends, when a traditional music session is likely to break out anytime. This is the mother of all Irish music pubs in Clonmel. No one is paid or even invited to play here; they just do. Often, there are so many musicians and so many wanting to hear them that the music spills outside, down the lane. No frills here—just the best Irish music around, and a pub out of the who-knows-when past. Sadly, Kitty has now passed away, but her two daughters and son are carrying on admirably in her name and tradition.

The Ronald Reagan. Main St., Ballyporeen, County Tipperary. ☎ **052/67133.**

Yes, there really is a pub named after the former U.S. president, right in the middle of the town that was home to his great-grandfather, Michael Reagan. Filled with pictures and mementos of the president's June 3, 1984, visit to Ballyporeen, with a mural of the original Reagan homestead cottage on the back wall, the bar is part of the pub and gift-shop complex of local entrepreneur John O'Farrell. Partisan politics aside, it's worth a stop for a toast or at least a picture.

Sean Tierney. 13 O'Connell St., Clonmel, County Tipperary. ☎ **052/24467.**

This is truly a show pub, with all of the ribbons to prove it. To cite a few, in 7 of the past 10 years, it was named Tipperary Pub of the Year and twice the Munster Pub of the Year. First of all, it's remarkably classy, with lots of dark carved wood, shiny brass railings and fitments, and stained glass. It goes on and on from one level to another, with all manner of separate lounges, dining rooms, nooks, and snugs. Upstairs, there are a full-service restaurant with several distinct dining rooms, each with its own character, and a walled floral beer garden for outside drinks and meals when the weather is gracious.

4 County Kilkenny

Kilkenny City is 30 miles (48km) N of Waterford, 50 miles (81km) NW of Wexford, 75 miles (121km) SW of Dublin, 85 miles (137km) SE of Shannon Airport, 92 miles (148km) NE of Cork, and 38 miles (61km) NE of Cashel

✪ **Kilkenny City,** the centerpiece of County Kilkenny and the southeast's prime inland city, is considered the medieval capital of Ireland because of its remarkable collection of well-preserved castles, churches, public buildings, streets, and lanes.

Situated along the banks of the River Nore, Kilkenny (pop. 11,000) takes its name from a church founded in the 6th century by St. Canice. In the Irish language, *Cill Choinnigh* means "Canice's Church."

Like most Irish cities, Kilkenny had fallen into Norman hands by the 12th century. Thanks to its central location, it became a prosperous walled city and served as the venue for many parliaments during the 14th century. Fortunately, much of Kilkenny's great medieval architecture has been preserved and restored, and the basic town plan has not changed with the passing of the centuries. It's still a very walkable community of narrow streets and arched lanes.

The oldest house in town is purported to be **Kyteler's Inn** on St. Kieran Street. It was once the home of Dame Alice Kyteler, a lady of great wealth who was accused of witchcraft in 1324. She escaped and forever disappeared, but her maid, Petronilla, was burned at the stake. Now restored, the inn is currently used as a pub and restaurant, but it retains an eerie air, with appropriately placed effigies of witches and other memorabilia and decorations.

One building that stands out on the streetscape is the **Tholsel,** on High Street, with its curious clock tower and front arcade. Otherwise known as the town hall or city hall, it was erected in 1761 and served originally as the tollhouse or exchange. Milk and sugar candy were sold at the Tholsel, and dances, bazaars, and political meetings were held here. Today, completely restored after a fire in 1987, it houses the city's municipal archives.

Kilkenny is often referred to as the Marble City. Fine black marble used to be quarried on the outskirts of town. Until 1929, some of the city streets also had marble pavements.

Primarily a farming area, the surrounding County Kilkenny countryside is dotted with rich river valleys, rolling pasturelands, gentle mountains, and picture-postcard towns. Don't miss **Jerpoint Abbey,** on the River Nore just southwest of Thomaston on N9, one of the finest of Ireland's Cistercian ruins. Also on the Nore is the village of ✪ **Inistioge,** about 15 miles (24km) southeast of Kilkenny City. Inistioge has an attractive tree-lined square and an 18th-century bridge of nine arches spanning the river.

The town of Graiguenamanagh—its name means "village of the monks"—is home to **Duiske Abbey.** Surrounded by vistas of Brandon Hill and the Blackstairs Mountains, Graiguenamanagh is at a bend of the River Barrow, about 20 miles (32km) southeast of Kilkenny City.

Kells, about 6 miles (9.7km) south of Kilkenny City, is the only completely walled medieval town in Ireland. The extensive curtain walls, seven towers, and some of the monastic buildings have been well preserved.

KILKENNY CITY ESSENTIALS

GETTING THERE　**Irish Rail** provides daily service from Dublin into the Irish Rail McDonagh Station, Dublin Road, Kilkenny (☎ **056/22024**).

Bus Eireann, McDonagh Station, Dublin Road, Kilkenny (☎ **056/64933**), operates daily service from Dublin and all parts of Ireland.

Many roads lead to inland Kilkenny, including N9/N10 from Waterford and Wexford, N8 and N76 from Cork and the southwest, N7 and N77 from Limerick and the west, and N9 and N78 from Dublin and points north and east.

VISITOR INFORMATION　For information, maps, and brochures about Kilkenny and the surrounding area, contact the **Kilkenny Tourist Office,** Shee Alms House, Rose Inn Street, Kilkenny (☎ **056/51500;** www.southeastireland.travel.ie). It's open May to September, Monday to Saturday 9am to 6pm, Sunday 11am to 1pm and 2 to 6pm; April and October, Monday to Saturday 9am to 6pm; November to March, Monday to Saturday 9am to 1pm and 2 to 5pm.

CITY LAYOUT　The main business district sits on the west banks of the River Nore. A mile-long north-south thoroughfare, High Street, runs the length of the city, changing its name to Parliament Street at midpoint. It starts at the Parade, on the south end near Kilkenny Castle, and continues through the city to St. Canice's Cathedral at the northern end. Most of the city's attractions are along this route or on offshoot streets such as Patrick, Rose Inn, Kieran, and John. The tourist office can supply you with a good street map.

GETTING AROUND　There is no downtown bus service in Kilkenny. Local buses run to nearby towns on a limited basis, departing from the Parade. Check with **Bus Eireann** (☎ **056/64933**) for details.

If you need a taxi, call **Nicky Power Taxi** (☎ 056/63000), **Billy Delaney Cabs** (☎ 056/22457), **David Nagle** (☎ 056/63300), or **Phonecab** (☎ 056/63017).

Don't even try to drive in town—Kilkenny's narrow medieval streets make for extremely slow-moving traffic, and you'll almost certainly get stuck. If you have a car, park it at one of the designated parking areas at the Parade, the rail station, or one of the shopping centers. Some parking is free, and other spaces have coin-operated machines, usually for 20p (28¢) per hour. There's also a new central multistory car

Kilkenny City

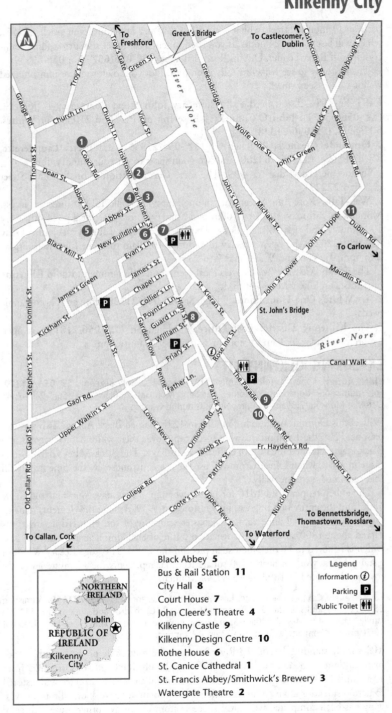

Black Abbey **5**
Bus & Rail Station **11**
City Hall **8**
Court House **7**
John Cleere's Theatre **4**
Kilkenny Castle **9**
Kilkenny Design Centre **10**
Rothe House **6**
St. Canice Cathedral **1**
St. Francis Abbey/Smithwick's Brewery **3**
Watergate Theatre **2**

Legend
Information (i)
Parking P
Public Toilet

NORTHERN
IRELAND

Dublin

REPUBLIC OF
IRELAND

Kilkenny
City

park on Ormonde Street, which costs 50p (70¢) per hour until you reach £5 ($7), which will last you for 24 hours. If you need to rent a car to see the surrounding countryside, call Barry Pender, Dublin Road, Kilkenny (☎ 056/65777 or 056/63839).

The best way to see Kilkenny City is on foot. Plot your own route or join a guided walking tour (see below).

FAST FACTS   If you need a drugstore, try **John Street Pharmacy,** 47 John St. (☎ 056/65971); **John O'Connell,** 4 Rose Inn St. (☎ 056/21033); or **Whites,** 5 High St. (☎ 056/21328).

Ormonde Cleaners, 29 High St. (☎ 056/21949), and **Bretts Launderette,** Michael Street (☎ 056/63200), are two good spots to get your laundry done.

In an emergency, dial ☎ 999. The local **Garda Station** is on Dominic Street (☎ 056/22222).

Web-Talk, Rose Inn Street (no phone), provides 64k ISDN Internet access, Monday to Saturday 10am to 10pm and Sunday 2 to 8pm, for £1 ($1.40) every 10 minutes and £5 ($7) an hour. There's a **Carnegie Library** at John's Quay (☎ 056/22021). It's open Tuesday to Saturday 10:30am to 1pm; Tuesday to Friday 2 to 5pm; Tuesday and Wednesday 7 to 9pm.

The weekly *Kilkenny People* covers local events and entertainment. **Radio Kilkenny** broadcasts on 96.6 FM and 96 FM.

Try **White's One-Hour Photo,** 5 High St. (☎ 056/21328), for your photographic needs.

The **Kilkenny District Post Office,** 73 High St. (☎ 056/21813), is open Monday to Friday 9:30am to 5:30pm, Saturday 9:30am to 1pm.

EXPLORING KILKENNY CITY

Black Abbey. Abbey St. (off Parliament St.), Kilkenny, County Kilkenny. ☎ 056/21279. Free admission; donations welcome. Apr–Sept Mon–Sat 7:30am–7pm, Sun 9am–7pm; Oct–Mar Mon–Sat 7:30am–5:30pm. No visits during worship.

Why is this Dominican church, founded in 1225, named Black Abbey? Two possible reasons: First, the Dominicans wore black capes over their white habits; second, the Black Plague claimed the lives of eight priests in 1348. The Black Abbey's darkest days came in 1650, when Oliver Cromwell used it as a courthouse; by the time he left, all that remained were the walls.

The abbey reopened in 1816 for public worship, a new nave was constructed by 1866, and the entire building was fully restored in 1979. Among the elements remaining from the original abbey are an alabaster sculpture of the Holy Trinity that was carved about 1400, and a pre-Reformation statue of St. Dominic carved in Irish oak, which is believed to be the oldest such piece in the world. The huge Rosary Window, a stained-glass work of nearly 500 square feet that represents the 15 mysteries of the rosary, was created in 1892 by Mayers of Munich.

✪ **Kilkenny Castle.** The Parade, Kilkenny, County Kilkenny. ☎ 056/21450. Admission £3.50 ($4.90) adults, £2.50 ($3.50) seniors, £1.50 ($2.10) children and students, £8 ($11.20) family. Daily Apr–May 10:30am–5pm; daily June–Sept 10am–7pm; Oct–Mar Tues–Sat 10:30am–12:45pm and 2–5pm, Sun 11am–12:45pm and 2–5pm.

Majestically standing beside the River Nore on the south side of the city, this landmark castle remained in the hands of the Butler family, the Dukes of Ormonde, from 1391 until 1967. It was given to the Irish government to be reconstructed and restored to period splendor as an enduring national monument. The work on all but the west wing has been completed with great success. From its sturdy corner towers (three of which are original and date to the 13th c.) to its battlements, Kilkenny Castle retains the lines of an authentic medieval fortress and sets the tone for the entire city. The

Ireland, the geographers tell us, is an island 300 miles long and 50 miles thick.
—Niall Tóibín (b. 1929)

exquisitely restored interior includes a fine collection of Butler family portraits, some from as far back as the 14th century. The 50-acre grounds include a riverside walk, extensive gardens and parkland, and a well-equipped children's play area. Access to the main body of the castle is by guided tour only, prefaced by an informative video introduction to the rise, demise, and restoration of the splendid structure. This is a very busy site, so get there early to avoid waiting.

✪ **Rothe House.** Parliament St., Kilkenny, County Kilkenny. ☎ **056/22893.** Admission £2 ($2.80) adults, £1.50 ($2.10) seniors and students, £1 ($1.40) children. Jan–Mar and Nov–Dec Mon–Sat 1–5pm, Sun 3–5pm; Apr–Jun and Sept–Oct Mon–Sat 10:30am–5pm, Sun 3–5pm; July–Aug Mon–Sat 10am–6pm, Sun 3–5pm.

This fine Tudor-style merchant's home, built in 1594, consists of three stone buildings divided by three cobbled courtyards. It has an arcaded front and a remarkable timber ceiling. Purchased in 1961 by the Kilkenny Archeological Society, it was restored and opened to the public in 1966. Inside are a museum of Kilkenny artifacts and a collection of period costumes. A family history research service for Kilkenny city and county has its offices here.

St. Canice Cathedral. Coach Rd., Irishtown, Kilkenny, County Kilkenny. ☎ **056/64971.** Free admission; donation (£1/$1.40 adults, 75p/$1.05 students) requested. Easter–Sept Mon–Sat 9am–1pm, daily 2–6pm; Oct–Easter Mon–Sat 10am–1pm, daily 2–4pm.

At the northern end of the city, this is the church that gave Kilkenny its name. The St. Canice's Cathedral that stands today is a relative newcomer, built in the 13th century on the site of the 6th-century church of St. Canice. The cathedral has benefited from much restoration work in recent years. It is noteworthy for its interior timber and stone carvings, its colorful glasswork, and the structure itself. Its roof dates from 1863; its marble floor is composed of the four marbles of Ireland; and its massive round tower, 100 feet high and 46 feet in circumference, is believed to be a relic of the ancient church (although its original conical top has been replaced by a slightly domed roof). If you want to climb to the tip of the tower, it will cost you £1 ($1.40) and more calories than you can count. The steps that lead to the cathedral were constructed in 1614. The library contains 3,000 volumes from the 16th and 17th centuries.

St. Francis Abbey Brewery. Parliament St., Kilkenny, County Kilkenny. ☎ **056/21014.** Free admission. June–Aug Mon–Fri at 3pm.

Established in 1710 by John Smithwick, the brewery occupies a site that originally belonged to the 12th-century Abbey of St. Francis. A local beer called Smithwick's (pronounced *Smith*-icks) is produced here, as are Budweiser and Land Kilkenny Irish beer. A video presentation and free samples are offered in the summer.

Organized Tours

Kilkenny Panoramic. Grayline/Guide Friday Irish City Tours, Kilkenny, County Kilkenny. ☎ **01/670-8822.** Apr–Oct daily (hours change seasonally according to demand). £6 ($8.40) adults, £3 ($4.20) children.

Hop aboard these open top-buses and explore the highlights of medieval Kilkenny. They run all day in a loop; so when you see something you want to explore, just hop off. Or just stay on all day and memorize everything you see and hear. Further details are available from the Kilkenny Tourist Office.

Tynan's Walking Tours. 10 Maple Dr., Kilkenny, County Kilkenny. ☎ **056/65929.** Tickets £3 ($4.20) adults, £2 ($2.80) seniors and students, £1 ($1.40) children. Mar–Oct Mon–Sat 9:15 and 10:30am, 12:15, 1:30, 3, and 4:30pm; Sun 11am, 12:15, 2, and 3pm. Nov–Feb Tues–Sat 10:30am, 12:15, and 3pm.

Walk the streets and lanes of medieval Kilkenny, accompanied by local historian Pat Tynan. Tours depart from the tourist office, Rose Inn Street.

SHOPPING

A haven for artisans, Kilkenny City and its surrounding area are known for good shopping. To assist visitors in discovering smaller workshops, the local tourist office provides a free **Craft Trail map** and information on local craft workers.

Kilkenny shopping hours are normally Monday to Saturday 9am to 6pm; many shops stay open until 9pm on Thursday and Friday.

The newest major addition to the shopping scene is **Market Cross,** a new shopping center off High/Parliament Street (☎ **056/65534**), with its own multistory parking lot.

The Book Centre. 10 High St., Kilkenny, County Kilkenny. ☎ **056/62117.**

This shop offers a fine selection of books about Kilkenny and the area, as well as books of Irish interest. Current bestsellers, maps, stationery, cards, and posters are sold. You can grab a quick daytime snack at the Pennefeather Cafe, upstairs.

Jerpoint Glass Studio. Signposted from the N9 just south of Jerpoint Abbey, Stoneyford, County Kilkenny. ☎ **056/24350.**

Last stop on the "Craft Trail" from Kilkenny to Stoneyford, this is the motherhouse of Jerpoint Glass, which you've probably been admiring in shops all across Ireland. The lines of their goblets, candlesticks, pitchers, vases, and much more are simple and fluid, often highlighted or infused with swirls of color. You can watch the glass being blown and then gladly blow your own budget next door at the factory shop, which includes an entire room of discounted seconds. Open Monday to Friday 9am to 6pm and Saturday 11am to 6pm.

Kilkenny Crystal. 19 Rose Inn St., Kilkenny, County Kilkenny. ☎ **056/21090.**

Established in 1969, this is the retail shop for Kilkenny's hand-cut crystal enterprise. It specializes in footed vases, rose bowls, bells, ring holders, wineglasses, carafes, and decanters. The factory is on Callan Road (☎ **056/25132**), 10 miles (16km) outside of town, and also welcomes visitors.

♻ Kilkenny Design Centre. Castle Yard, The Parade, Kilkenny, County Kilkenny. ☎ **056/ 22118.**

The 18th-century stables of Kilkenny Castle have been converted into an assembly of shops and workshops for craftspeople from all over Ireland. The Kilkenny Design Centre is in the original coach house, with an arched gateway and a copper-domed clock tower. The center and the smaller shops collected nearby provide a showcase for many of the country's top hand-crafted products—jewelry, glassware, pottery, clothing, candles, linens, books, leatherwork, and furniture. An excellent coffee shop and restaurant is on the upstairs level of the Design Centre. Open Monday to Saturday 9am to 6pm, Sunday 10am to 6pm.

Liam Costigan. Colliers Lane, off High St., Kilkenny, County Kilkenny. ☎ **056/62408.**

A fellow named Liam, an alumnus of the Kilkenny Design Centre, produces fine hand-crafted jewelry in this tiny shop; as you browse, you can watch him work.

Nicholas Mosse Pottery. Bennettsbridge, County Kilkenny. ☎ **056/27505.** www.NicholasMosse.com.

In a former flour mill on the banks of the River Nore, this enterprise is the brainchild of Nicholas Mosse, a potter since age 7. Using water power from the river to fire the kilns, he produces colorful earthenware from Irish clay, including jugs, mugs, bowls, and plates. All are hand-slipped and hand-turned, then decorated by hand with cut sponges and brushes. An on-site museum displays antique Irish earthenware made with this process. Pottery firsts and seconds are available. The shop expanded greatly in 1999 to included tasteful housewares. Open year-round Monday to Saturday 9am to 6pm, and Sunday 1:30 to 5pm in July and August.

P. T. Murphy. 85 High St., Kilkenny, County Kilkenny. ☎ **056/21127.**

The sign above the entrance says it all: watchmaker, jeweler, optician, and silversmith. This is Kilkenny's master jeweler. The shop is a very good source for Irish Claddagh and heraldic jewelry.

Yesterdays. 30 Patrick St., Kilkenny, County Kilkenny. ☎ **056/65557.**

Porcelain dolls and miniatures, lace, teddy bears, miniframes, perfume bottles, jewelry, and dollhouse furniture are found at this curiosity shop. It's definitely worth a browse.

ATTRACTIONS FARTHER AFIELD IN COUNTY KILKENNY

Duiske Abbey. Graiguenamanagh, County Kilkenny. ☎ **0503/24238.** Free admission; donations welcome. Daily 8am–7:30pm.

Duiske Abbey (1207) has a long and colorful history. It was suppressed in 1536, but its monks continued to occupy the site for many years. In 1774 the tower of the ruined abbey church collapsed. In 1813 the roof was replaced and religious services returned to the church; but the abbey didn't approach its former glory until the 1970s, when a group of local people mounted a major reconstruction effort. Now, with its fine lancet windows and a large effigy of a Norman knight, the abbey is the pride of Graiguenamanagh. The adjacent visitor center has an exhibit of Christian art and artifacts.

Dunmore Cave. Off Castlecomer road (N78), Ballyfoyle, County Kilkenny. ☎ **056/67726.** Admission £2 ($2.80) adults, £1.50 ($2.10) seniors, £1 ($1.40) students and children, £5 ($7) family. Mid-Mar to mid-June and mid-Sept to Oct daily 10am–5pm; mid-June to mid-Sept daily 10am–7pm; winter Sat–Sun and holidays 10am–5pm.

Known as one of the darkest places in Ireland, this series of chambers, formed over millions of years, contains some of the finest calcite formations found in any Irish cave. Known to humans for many centuries, the cave may have been the site of a Viking massacre in A.D. 928. Exhibits at the visitor center tell the story of the cave. It's about 7 miles (11km) from Kilkenny City.

✪ **Jerpoint Abbey.** On Waterford road (N9), 1½ miles (2.4km) south of Thomastown, Thomastown, County Kilkenny. ☎ **056/24623.** Admission £2 ($2.80) adults, £1.50 ($2.10) seniors, £1 ($1.40) students and children, £5 ($7) family. Mar–May and mid-Sept to mid-Nov daily 10am–5pm; June to mid-Sept daily 9:30am–6:30pm; late Nov Wed–Mon 10am–4pm.

About 11 miles (18km) southeast of Kilkenny, the impressive ruins of this 12th-century Benedictine (and later Cistercian) monastery, preserved in a peaceful country setting, offer a splendid array of artifacts from medieval times—from unique stone carvings on walls and tombs to a 14th- or 15th-century tower and cloister, as well as Irish Romanesque details of a late-12th-century abbey church. A tasteful interpretive center with an adjoining picnic garden makes this a perfect midday stop. Ms. Sheila Walsh is quite knowledgeable and articulate about the abbey, its art, and its history.

✪ **Kells Priory.** Kells, County Kilkenny. Off N76 or N10. From N76 south of Kilkenny, follow signs for R699/Callan and stay on R699 until you see signs for Kells.

The first time I set eyes on the Kells Priory, I wondered why no one had ever shouted, much less mentioned, it to me. With its encompassing fortification walls and towers, as well as complex monastic ruins, enfolded into the sloping south bank of the Kings River in unspoiled countryside, Kells is one of the most spectacular ruins in Ireland. It's a must for anyone entranced or intrigued with the medieval world. It's my favorite kind of oxymoron, an intact ruin, a feast for the eyes and the imagination. Like a perfect skeleton, it seems almost alive.

In 1193 Baron Geoffrey FitzRobert founded the priory and established a Norman-style town beside it. The current ruins date from the 13th to 15th centuries. Like every other stack of stones in Ireland, these could dictate volumes, and for them, like so many others, Cromwell was the last straw. Because you have to be your own guide here, you'll want to stop by the village pub, Shirley/Burgess Court, and buy *A Brief History of Kells, County Kilkenny,* by Albert Smith, Jr., for £2 ($2.80). Better yet, pick up the new self-guided tour to the site, *The Augustinian Priory of Kells, County Kilkenny,* by Daniel Tietzsch-Tyler, available at the Kilkenny Tourist Information office for £3.50 ($4.90).

The priory is less than a half mile from the village of Kells. Be sure to find the new footbridge behind the priory, which takes you across the river and intersects a riverside walk leading to an old mill. Also, before leaving Kells, drop a mile down the road to **Kilree Abbey,** whose small church and virtually intact round tower are well worth a slight detour.

If you'd rather go fishing, no license seems to be required; permits are available at Delaney's in the village. Finally, before you leave, drop a mile down the road to Kilree Abbey, whose small church and virtually intact round tower are well worth a slight detour.

Kilfane Glen and Waterfall. Thomastown, County Kilkenny. ☎ **056/24558.** Admission £3 ($4.20) adults, £2.50 ($3.50) seniors, £2 ($2.80) students and children. Apr–June and Sept Sun 2–6pm, July–Aug daily 11am–6pm. Closed Oct–Mar. Other times by appointment.

The main place of interest in this small garden is the glen, created in true picturesque style, with an artificial waterfall and a rustic cottage. The paths have been strategically placed to enhance one's sense of the place's grandeur. Views of cottage and waterfall have been carefully composed, and the sound of water creates a counterpoint to the visual delights of the garden. An installation by the American artist James Turrell, "Air Mass," is open to visitors, although the time of day when it was intended to be seen—dusk—unfortunately doesn't correspond with the garden hours in summer.

SPORTS & OUTDOOR PURSUITS

BICYCLING   Rent a bike to ride around the outskirts of Kilkenny, especially along the shores of the River Nore. Consult the Kilkenny Tourist Office, or contact **J. J. Wall,** 88 Maudlin St. (☎ **056/21236**), or **Kilkenny Cycles,** Lower Michael St. (☎ **056/64374**). Rates average £8 ($11.20) per day. For complete 1- or 2-week cycling holidays in the Southeast, contact Don Smith at **Celtic Cycling,** Lorum Old Rectory, Bagenalstown, County Carlow (☎ and fax **0503/75282;** www.celticcycling.com).

FISHING   The **River Nore,** southeast of Kilkenny, is known for salmon and trout. For advice, permits, and supplies, visit the **Sports Shop,** 82 High St., Kilkenny (☎ **056/21517**).

GOLF   The annual Irish Open Golf Tournament, the pinnacle of the Irish golfing year, took place in 1993 and 1994 at the **Mount Juliet Golf and Country Club,**

Thomastown, County Kilkenny (☎ 056/73000), 10 miles (16km) south of Kilkenny City. The 18-hole, par-72 championship course, designed by Jack Nicklaus, charges greens fees from £45 ($63) on weekdays, and from £55 ($77) on weekends. The price drops for Mount Juliet guests, and reduced early-bird and "sunsetter" rates are also available. Alternatively, try the 18-hole championship course at the **Kilkenny Golf Club,** Glendine, County Kilkenny (☎ 056/65400), an inland par-71 layout 1 mile (1.6km) from the city. Greens fees are £40 ($56) on weekdays, £50 ($70) on weekends.

ACCOMMODATIONS
VERY EXPENSIVE

✪ Mount Juliet Estate. Thomastown, County Kilkenny. ☎ **800/525-4800** from the U.S., or 056/73000. Fax 056/73019. www.mountjuliet.ie. 56 units. TV TEL. £115–£275 ($161–$385) double; £210–£340 ($294–$476) suite; £285–£390 ($399–$546) 2-bedroom garden lodge. No service charge. AE, DC, MC, V.

Kilkenny's top lodging facility is not in Kilkenny City, but 10 miles (16km) south in a little country village. A winding 2-mile (3.2km) path wends its way beside the pastures of the Ballylinch Stud Farm to this hotel, an 18th-century manor house set on a hillside overlooking the River Nore and surrounded by 1,500 acres of formal gardens, lawns, woodlands, and parkland. The trees alone are reason to spend time here. They are astounding. One magnificent ancient oak in particular is surely a church. Built in the 1760s, the house was named after Juliana (also known as Juliet), wife of the 8th Viscount Ikerrin, the first Earl of Carrick. The McCalmont family, leaders in the Irish horse-breeding industry, later owned it. Mount Juliet is also the home of Ireland's oldest cricket club. Guests can choose between the manor house, the Hunters Yard, and the Rose Garden lodges. Rooms are individually decorated, with traditional dark woods, designer fabrics, and antiques, and public areas are full of antiques, period pieces, and original art.

The **Paddocks,** a cluster of 12 **self-catering luxury lodges** lying between the 10th and 16th fairways, are also available. Each has a fully equipped kitchen, an elegantly furnished lounge/dining room, and en suite bedrooms. They rent for £1,750 ($2,450) weekly for two bedrooms and £2,625 ($3,675) weekly for three bedrooms.

Dining/Diversions: The Lady Helen McCalmont Room offers formal dining overlooking the river; lighter fare is served in the Old Kitchen, a basement-level bistro, and in the Loft, a chalet-style lodge in the sporting complex. The bar has an equestrian theme.

Amenities: 24-hour room service, concierge, valet and laundry service; 18-hole championship golf course designed by Jack Nicklaus; golf clubhouse with indoor swimming pool, indoor and outdoor tennis courts, badminton, squash, gym, sauna, and Jacuzzi; golf and fishing academies for on-site sports instruction; riding stables and 10 miles (16km) of bridle paths; salmon and trout fishing on exclusive 1½-mile (2.4km) stretch of River Nore; pheasant shooting. Fox hunting with the Kilkenny Hunt, which is headquartered on the estate.

EXPENSIVE

✪ Kilkenny Ormonde Hotel. Ormonde St., Kilkenny, County Kilkenny. ☎ **056/23900.** Fax 056/23977. www.kilkennyormonde.com. 118 units. MINIBAR TV TEL. £125–£180 ($175–$252) double; £225–£300 ($315–$420) suite. Rates include full breakfast and VAT, as well as Leisure Club fees and cover charge to Venue Bar. Service charge at the discretion of guests. AE, DC, MC, V. Free valet parking.

When this chic new hotel opened in the heart of Kilkenny town in May 2000, it became at once the city's premier guest address. Its dead-center location left it without scenic views, but its exceptional design and decor provide some striking scenery of its own. The emphasis is on bright open spaces with insightful use of natural materials— woods, stone, glass, metals, and fabric—to create tones and textures. The halls are wide and full of light, from windows and light shafts. Kilkenny is a particularly hectic town, and the soft, restful color palate of the guest rooms provides a welcome interior antidote to the day. A further antidote lies next door at the spectacular new Ormonde Leisure Club, connected by an underground walkway to the hotel. Here you'll find everything provided for the ultimate workout—all you need to contribute is the willpower. The spacious deluxe room, with a queen-size bed and a single bed, already has every expected comfort and amenity, including robes. With that as the standard, the ascending order of executive rooms, superior rooms, and suites extends the size of the beds and of the guest quarters, culminating in the five-room presidential suite. In our opinion, the superior rooms offer the best value of all. There are two floors of nonsmoking rooms, including all of the suites.

Dining/Diversions: Your options include the Ormonde Lounge, a cafe bar serving drinks and light meals from 10am to 9pm daily; and the Earls Bar and Bistro, a spacious informal bar and eatery serving lunch, dinner, and drinks daily. The menu here has a Mediterranean bent. Then for more formal fine dining Tuesday to Saturday there's Frederick's Restaurant, already winning awards for its international cuisine. Finally, if you like to stretch one day into the next, you're invited to the Venue Bar, which specializes Wednesday to Sunday in "live gigs" and doesn't call it a day until 2am.

Amenities: Concierge, room service, overnight laundry/dry cleaning, overnight shoeshine, currency exchange, business center (with use of computer and peripherals and Internet access). There's also a fabulous new leisure club with every instrument of torture and aerobic fitness you could dream of, as well as commensurate rewards, including a 20-meter pool, kiddie pool, volcano (a Jacuzzi-style tub that builds up and blows streams of water all at once, rather than continuously), Jacuzzi, steam room, sauna, massage, sun bed, and cafe.

MODERATE

Berryhill. Inistioge, County Kilkenny. ☎ and fax **056/58434.** 3 units. £90 ($126) double. Rates include full breakfast. MC, V. Closed Nov–Apr.

The ivy-clad gables of this eccentric country house overlook the River Nore, just outside the picturesque village of Inistioge. George and Belinda Dyer have created a uniquely pleasant retreat of this rambling house, built by the Dyer family in 1780. Each of the three spacious bedrooms is attached to a private sitting room, and each is decorated with a particular, unmistakable animal theme. The Elephant Room's distinctive feature is a cozy bathroom with a red bathtub, a small sofa, and fireplace, where you can bathe before a blazing fire while watching elephants cavort along the walls; the disadvantage here is the ground-floor location, adjacent to the carpark. In the Frog Room (on the second floor), an abundance of ivy makes a private nook of the veranda (there's a great view of the river). The animal theme is completed with a Pig Suite, on the west side of the house, with views toward the river from the front sitting room. There are walks to be had on the hill behind the house, and a path provides a short walking route to Inistioge village. Breakfast here is a memorable occasion, and options include fresh trout from the river. No smoking in the guest rooms.

Butler House. 16 Patrick St., Kilkenny, County Kilkenny. ☎ **056/65707.** Fax 056/65626. www.butler.ie. 13 units. TV TEL. £89–£149 ($124.60–$208.60) double; £179 ($250.60) suite. No service charge. Rates include full breakfast. AE, DC, MC, V. Free parking.

Built in 1770 by the 16th Earl of Ormonde as a dower house for Kilkenny Castle, this elegant three-story building has a front door facing busy Patrick Street and a backyard overlooking lovely, secluded 17th-century-style gardens, the Kilkenny Castle stables, and a craft center. Converted into a guesthouse in the late 1980s, it offers guest rooms of various sizes with eclectic furnishings. Amenities include VCRs and video rental. The house is only a 15-minute walk from the bus and train station.

Hotel Kilkenny. College Rd., Kilkenny, County Kilkenny. ☎ **056/62000.** Fax 056/65984. www.griffingroup.ie. 103 units. TV TEL. £90–£120 ($126–$168) double. No service charge. Rates include full breakfast. AE, MC, V.

In a residential neighborhood on the southwest edge of the city, this hotel combines a gracious 1830 country house with a block of modern rooms. The main house was once the home of Sir William Robertson, the architect who rebuilt Kilkenny Castle. Today it holds Gingers restaurant and the Rose Inn Bar, which was recently refurbished along with the guest rooms. The modern wing lacks the charm of the main building, but the rooms are comfortable and close to a new health complex with indoor swimming pool, sauna, hot tub, sun beds, gym, and two tennis courts.

✪ **The Newpark.** Castlecomer Rd., Kilkenny, County Kilkenny. ☎ **800/528-1234** from the U.S., or 056/22122. Fax 056/61111. www.newparkhotel.com. 111 units. TV TEL. £77–£100 ($107.80–$140) double. No service charge. DC, MC, V. Free parking.

A warm, friendly atmosphere pervades this lovely hotel about a mile north of the city center. Set amid 50 acres of gardens and parkland, it was opened as a small Victorian-style country hotel more than 35 years ago, and it has grown in size and gained in reputation ever since. The rooms are decorated in light woods with colorful Irish furnishings, and the recently refurbished public areas have a stylish, contemporary flair. The hotel has an indoor heated swimming pool, a sun lounge, a Jacuzzi, a gym, a steam room, saunas, and two tennis courts.

INEXPENSIVE

Abbey House. Thomastown, County Kilkenny. ☎ **056/24166.** Fax 056/24192. 6 units. TV TEL. £44–£60 ($61.60–$84) double. Includes full Irish breakfast and service charge. V. On Waterford road (N9), 1½ miles (2.4km) south of Thomastown, directly across from Jerpoint Abbey.

This attractive period residence—alongside the Little Arrigle River and across from Jerpoint Abbey—occupies an appealing setting. (It will soon be more so, when construction routing the highway around the Abbey is complete.) The front garden with sitting area is a perfect spot to relax, and the house's spacious living room, complete with piano and stacks of books, suits both quiet reading and a round of songs. Mrs. Helen Blanchfield has done a fine job of maintaining the period character of her Georgian (ca. 1750) home. She serves guests complimentary tea and scones on arrival. The comfortable, pleasant rooms vary in size; all have orthopedic beds. The nearby town of Thomastown and the grand abbey across the way are well worth a good look. Dinner (£15/$21) is served on request; bring your own wine.

✪ **Cullintra House.** The Rower, Inistioge, County Kilkenny. ☎ **051/423614.** E-mail: cullhse@indigo.ie. 6 units, 3 with bathroom. £40–£50 ($56–$70) double. No service charge. Rates include full breakfast. No credit cards.

Atmosphere is of primary importance at this quaint country farmhouse, presided over by the energetic Mrs. Cantlon and her several cats. As you would expect in a 200-year-old farmhouse, each rustic, charming guest room is unique. Dinner (£16/$22.40) begins between 9 and 9:30pm, announced by the sound of a gong, and guests sometimes don't depart from the candlelit dining room until the wee hours. A lovely art studio and conservatory has tea-making facilities and a piano; food is set here for the neighborhood foxes in the evening. Morning brings a relaxed breakfast schedule (served between 9am and noon), and perhaps a walk to Mount Brandon or the nearby *cairn* (prehistoric burial mound); a trail departs from the back gate. Mrs. Cantlon is an enthusiastic hostess, and clearly enjoys entertaining her guests and making them feel at home. If you enjoy candles, cats, and good food, this place is for you.

Lacken House. Dublin–Carlow road, Kilkenny, County Kilkenny. ☎ **056/61085.** Fax 056/62435. 8 units. TV TEL. £70 ($98) double. No service charge. Rates include full breakfast. MC, V.

A husband and wife duo, Eugene and Breda McSweeney, has made this restored Georgian home into one of the area's best guesthouses. Breda supervises the lodging and keeps the rooms—some nonsmoking and all with orthopedic beds—in tiptop shape. Eugene, an award-winning chef, oversees the restaurant (see listing below). The guest rooms are small but comfortable, with colorful furnishings. Lacken is on its own grounds with gardens, in the northeast corner of the city, about 10 minutes' walking distance from High Street and within a long block of the rail and bus station.

DINING
EXPENSIVE

✪ **Lacken House.** Dublin–Carlow road, Kilkenny, County Kilkenny. ☎ **056/61085.** Reservations required. Fixed-price dinner £25 ($35). MC, V. Tues–Sat 7–10:30pm. IRISH/INTERNATIONAL.

A stately Georgian house is the setting for this restaurant, on the northeast edge of the city. Chef Eugene McSweeney, who earned international laurels as chef of the Berkeley Court Hotel in Dublin during its early years, has carved out his own niche in this lovely setting. Breda McSweeney was named Sommelier of the Year in 1999. The menu changes daily but often includes dishes such as breast of pigeon with lentils and smoked bacon, baked crab au gratin, and fillet of Nore salmon with galette of potato and celeriac and sage-butter sauce. And if you want to learn the kitchen's secrets, the talented McSweeneys have started a cooking school where guests may attend morning classes.

MODERATE

Cafe Sol. 6 William St., Kilkenny, County Kilkenny. ☎ **056/64987.** Reservations recommended. Dinner main courses £8–£15 ($11.20–$21). MC, V. Mon–Sat 10am–5pm; Wed–Sat also 7–10pm. INTERNATIONAL.

The Cafe Sol is just that, a cafe of bright colors with lots of light streaming in from its floor-to-ceiling windows. Its diminutive size and unassuming informality are, however, largely a disguise—this is a touted eatery where you can enjoy some of the finest fare in Kilkenny. Four nights a week, the more ordinary lunch menu featuring homemade soups, salads, sandwiches, and hot plates gives way to a dinner menu with few frills but not without a few flourishes, such as celeriac and roasted hazelnut soup, followed by chicken and filo with tarragon or medallions of pork with Dijon mustard. As is the case with most restaurants in Ireland, especially small ones like this, the line dividing smoking and nonsmoking here is imaginary.

The Italian Connection. 38 Parliament St., Kilkenny, County Kilkenny. ☎ **056/64225.** Reservations recommended. Dinner main courses £7–£15 ($9.80–$21). MC, V. Daily noon–midnight. ITALIAN/INTERNATIONAL.

Just half a block from the Watergate Theatre, this small shop-front restaurant is popular for pre- and post-theater dining. The decor is appealing, with dark woods, wine casks, and crisp pink linens, and the menu is noted for pasta and pizza dishes. In addition, there are steaks, five variations of veal, seafood, and curries.

The Maltings. Bridge House, Inistioge, County Kilkenny. ☎ **056/58484.** Reservations required. Early-bird (6–8:30pm) fixed-price menu £7.50–£10.95 ($10.50–$15.35); dinner main courses £10.95–£14.50 ($15.35–$20.30). MC, V. Tues–Sun noon–3pm and 7–9:30pm. IRISH/CONTINENTAL.

Overlooking the River Nore about 10 miles (16km) southeast of Kilkenny City, this venerable restaurant offers simple, well-prepared food in an idyllic, romantic county-house setting. The menu includes chicken Kiev, roast half duck, fillet steak, and grilled salmon. No provisions are made for nonsmokers other than prohibiting pipes and cigars.

✪ **The Motte.** Plas Newydd Lodge, Inistioge, County Kilkenny. ☎ **056/58655.** Reservations recommended. 3-course set menu £23.50 ($32.90). Tues–Sat 7–9:30pm. MC, V. NEW IRISH.

In both cuisine and ambience, The Motte is fresh and exuberant. Guests are welcomed with a menu that takes advantage of locally available ingredients, and each table is crowned with a fantastic bouquet of Irish field flowers. The Motte dining room glows dimly with traces of gilt and candlelight; its space is intimate and the hosts are expansive.

For starters, the broccoli and cilantro soup was vigorously seasoned, a creamy, steaming concoction. Equally good but more daring were profiteroles filled with Cashel Blue and laced with chile chocolate sauce, airy pastry pockets dissolved in a sharp bite of cheese chased by a smooth thread of slightly bitter chocolate. Main courses range from sirloin in burgundy butter sauce to a selection of fish. Fillets of plaice were combined with a delicately flavored lemon butter, and the fish itself was cooked to tongue-tantalizing perfection. Sorbet preceded an excellent choice of rich desserts, and the chocolate cardomon truffle cake was especially notable, combining a velvety dense cake with custard and a drizzle of raspberry sauce. Final orders are at 9:30pm, although diners often remain until late in the evening; just book a table well in advance and surrender your evening to conversation and good food.

Parliament House Restaurant. Parliament St., Kilkenny, County Kilkenny. ☎ **056/63666.** Reservations recommended. Dinner main courses £12–£17 ($16.80–$23.80). AE, MC, V. Daily noon–3pm and 6–10:30pm. IRISH/CONTINENTAL.

Overlooking busy Parliament Street, this upstairs restaurant has a distinctive Edwardian decor, with high ceilings, chandeliers, and floral wallpaper. The menu offers a fine selection of local beef, veal, and lamb, as well as tasty combination dishes, such as prawns and mussels with hazelnuts, Nore salmon in pastry with lobster sauce, duckling in wine and garlic butter, and chicken Parliament (stuffed with seafood mousse and lobster sauce).

Ristorante Rinuccini. 1 The Parade, Kilkenny, County Kilkenny. ☎ **056/61575.** Reservations recommended. Lunch main courses £4.95–£7.95 ($6.95–$11.15); dinner main courses £7.95–£14.95 ($11.15–$20.95). AE, DISC, MC, V. Daily 12:30–2:30pm; Mon–Sat 6–10:30pm. Closed holidays. ITALIAN/IRISH.

Opposite Kilkenny Castle, this romantic candlelit restaurant specializes in the best of Irish seafood and locally produced beef. Dishes include steak Diane with brandy, and prawns Rinuccini (with cream sauce, mushrooms, and brandy). Chef Antonio Cavaliere also presents a full range of homemade Italian pastas and specialties, including spaghetti, fettuccine Alfredo, ravioli al pomodoro, lasagne al forno, and chicken cacciatore. Accommodation is also available.

INEXPENSIVE

Kilkenny Design Restaurant. The Parade, Kilkenny, County Kilkenny. ☎ **056/22118.** Reservations not accepted. All items £1.25–£7.95 ($1.75–$11.15). AE, DC, MC, V. Year-round Mon–Sat 9am–5pm, Sun 10am–5pm. IRISH.

Above the Kilkenny Design shop, this spacious self-service restaurant is an attraction in itself, with whitewashed walls, circular windows, beamed ceilings, framed art prints, and fresh, delicious food. The ever-changing menu often includes local salmon, chicken and ham platters, salads, and homemade soups. Pastries and breads offer some unique choices, such as cheese and garlic scones.

The Water Garden. Thomastown, County Kilkenny. ☎ **056/24690.** Reservations accepted. Lunch £4–£5 ($5.60–$7). No credit cards. Tues–Fri 10am–5pm; Sun 12:30–5pm. Closed Sun from Christmas to Easter. TEA/IRISH.

Just outside Thomastown on the road to Kilkenny, you'll find this cafe and small garden, operated by a local Camphill community for mentally and physically disabled children and adults. The cafe serves lunch, tea, and baked goods; meals are prepared with organic vegetables and meats raised on the community farm. Lunches include sandwiches made with home-baked bread, soups, and a vegetable or meat pâté. The garden (admission is £1/$1.40 adults, 50p/70¢ children) takes the form of a stroll along a small stream, with numerous aquatic plants on display; there's also a garden shop.

KILKENNY AFTER DARK

Kilkenny is home to one of Ireland's newest theaters (opened in 1993), the **Watergate Theatre,** Parliament Street (☎ **056/61674**). The 328-seat showplace presents both local talent and visiting professional troupes performing a variety of classic and contemporary plays, concerts, opera, ballet, one-person shows, and choral evenings. Ticket prices average £4 to £10 ($5.60 to $14). Most evening shows start at 8 or 8:30pm, matinees at 2 or 3pm.

Across the street is **John Cleere's,** 28 Parliament St. (☎ **056/62573**), a small pub theater that presents a variety of local productions, including the "Cat Laughs" comedy fest. It is also a venue for the Kilkenny Arts Week. Tickets average £3 to £6 ($4.20 to $8.40), and most shows start at 8:15 or 9:30pm.

PUBS

Caislean Ui Cuain (The Castle Inn). The Parade, Kilkenny, County Kilkenny. ☎ **056/65406.**

A striking facade with a mural of Old Kilkenny welcomes guests to this pub, founded in 1734 as a stagecoach inn. The interior is equally inviting, with dark wood furnishings, globe-style lights, a paneled ceiling, and local memorabilia. Scheduled and spontaneous traditional music often plays, and patrons and staff speak Irish.

Kytelers Inn. St. Kieran St., Kilkenny, County Kilkenny. ☎ **056/21064.**

If you are in a medieval mood, try this stone-walled tavern in the center of town. An inn since 1324, it was once the home of Dame Alice Kyteler, a colorful character who was accused of being a witch. The decor suggests caverns and arches, and the art and memorabilia have a witchcraft theme.

✪ **Langton House.** 69 John St., Kilkenny, County Kilkenny. ☎ **056/65133.**

This place is a frequent "Pub of the Year" winner. Enthusiasts delight in Edward Langton's rich wood tones, etched mirrors, stained-glass windows, brass globe lamps, and green velour banquettes. On cool evenings, the hand-carved limestone fireplace is warming, and for summer days there's a conservatory and garden area backed by the old city walls. Pub meals are a specialty.

Marble City Bar. 66 High St., Kilkenny, County Kilkenny. ☎ **056/62091.**

One of the best shop-front facades in Ireland belongs to this pub in the middle of the city. Its exterior is a showcase of carved wood, wrought iron, polished brass, and globe lamps, with flower boxes overhead—and the interior is equally inviting. Even if you don't stop for a drink here, you'll certainly want to take a picture.

✪ **Tynan's Bridge House.** 2 Horseleap Slip, Kilkenny, County Kilkenny. ☎ **056/21291.**

James and Cait Coady cheerfully welcome all comers to this award-winning 225-year-old pub, along the River Nore next to St. John's Bridge, on a street that was once used as an exercise run for horses. It holds a horseshoe-shaped marble bar, gas lamps, shiny brass fixtures, and silver tankards. Side drawers marked "mace," "citron," and "sago" are not filled with exotic cocktail ingredients, but remain from the years when the pub also served as a grocery and pharmacy. Shelves display 17th-century scales, shaving mugs, and teapots; there is even a tattered copy of Chaucer's *Canterbury Tales* for rainy days.

7

Cork City

It's been said that Cork City (pop. 180,000) is the Irish version of Manhattan. It's also been said that the earth is flat. True, both cities are built on islands, but that's about where the similarity ends. That said, Cork is not exactly a backwater burg, either. Stuck in the middle, neither as cosmopolitan as Dublin nor as scenic and historic as West Cork, it's the sporting, brewing, and university center of the southwest, and definitely a spot to consider visiting.

St. Finbarr is credited with laying the foundation of the city by starting a church and school in the 6th century. The area was a wetland, and St. Finbarr, flush with imagination, identified it as Corcaigh, or "the marshy place." In time, the school flourished and a considerable town grew.

Because of its relatively remote location and its citizens' spunky attitude, Cork asserted remarkable independence from outside authority, gradually earning the title "Rebel Cork." The name carried through to the 1919–21 Irish War of Independence, in which Cork men figured prominently.

Today, as the Republic's second-largest city, Cork is a busy commercial hub for the south of Ireland. Be warned that the traffic moves fast and the people talk faster, even with their almost-singsong accent. Be sure to taste the local brews, Beamish and Murphy's, and if you care for tea, ask for Barry's, blended in Cork since 1901.

And oh, yeah, this is where they keep the Blarney Stone, the rock that launched a thousand kisses (and a heck of a lot of tourist revenue). To kiss or not to kiss is a deeply personal decision that no guidebook could hope to help with. Look deep within yourself.

1 Orientation

Cork is 160 miles (258km) SW of Dublin, 128 miles (206km) SE of Galway, 63 miles (101km) S of Limerick, 76 miles (122km) S of Shannon Airport, 78 miles (126km) W of Waterford, and 54 miles (87km) E of Killarney

ARRIVING

GETTING THERE   Aer Lingus (☎ 021/432-7155; www.aerlingus. ie) flights from Dublin regularly serve Cork Airport, Kinsale Road (☎ 021/313131), 8 miles (13km) south of the city. In addition, there are direct flights from Amsterdam, Bristol, Exeter, Glasgow, Guernsey, Isle of Man, London, Manchester, Paris, Plymouth, and Rennes. The

Cork City

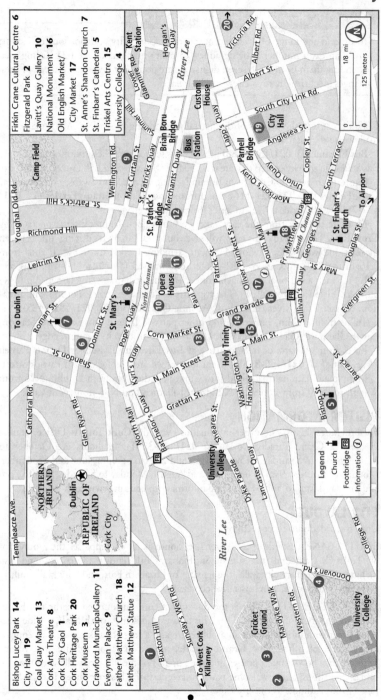

Firkin Crane Cultural Centre **6**
Fitzgerald Park **2**
Lavitt's Quay Gallery **10**
National Monument **16**
Old English Market/
City Market **17**
St. Anne's Shandon Church **7**
St. Finbarr's Cathedral **5**
Triskel Arts Centre **15**
University College **4**

Bishop Lucey Park **14**
City Hall **19**
Coal Quay Market **13**
Cork Arts Theatre **8**
Cork City Gaol **1**
Cork Heritage Park **20**
Cork Museum **3**
Crawford MunicipalGallery **11**
Everyman Palace **9**
Father Matthew Church **18**
Father Matthew Statue **12**

Legend
Church ✝ ■
Footbridge FB
Information *i*

NORTHERN
IRELAND

Dublin

REPUBLIC OF
IRELAND

Cork City

A Note on Phone Numbers in the Region

To expand the range of available numbers in Cork City and portions of County Cork, an extra number is being added to many numbers in the 021 dialing area, extending them from six to seven digits. We are doing our best to stay ahead of these changes, occurring here as elsewhere in Ireland.

Cork airport is in the process of dramatically expanding its services, and it may eventually handle transatlantic flights.

Bus Eireann (☎ 021/450-8188) provides bus service from the airport to Parnell Place Bus Station in the city center; the fare is £2.50 ($3.50) one-way, £3.50 ($4.90) round-trip.

Car ferry routes into Cork from Britain include service from Swansea on **Swansea/ Cork Ferries** (☎ 021/427-1166), and from Roscoff on **Brittany Ferries** (☎ 021/ 427-7801). All ferries arrive at Cork's Ringaskiddy Ferryport.

En route to Cork from the east, take the Carrigaloe-Glenbrook ferry, operated by **Cross River Ferries Ltd.** This ferry will save you at least an hour's driving time between the east and west sides of Cork Harbour, avoiding Cork City traffic. It runs from 7:15am to 12:30am. Cars cost £2 ($2.80) one-way, £3 ($4.20) round-trip, plus 50p (70¢) for each additional passenger. For cyclists and pedestrians, the fare is 60p (84¢) one-way, £1 ($1.40) round-trip. The trip lasts less than 5 minutes. For more information, contact Cross River Ferries Ltd., Atlantic Quay, Cobh (☎ 021/481-1485).

Trains from Dublin, Limerick, and other parts of Ireland arrive at **Kent Station,** Lower Glanmire Road, Cork (☎ 021/450-4777), on the city's eastern edge.

Buses from all parts of Ireland arrive at **Bus Eireann's Passenger Depot,** Parnell Place, Cork (☎ 021/450-8188), in the downtown area, 3 blocks from Patrick Street.

Many main national roads lead into Cork, including N8 from Dublin, N25 from Waterford, N20 from Limerick, N22 from Killarney, and N71 from West Cork.

VISITOR INFORMATION

For brochures, maps, and other information, visit the **Cork Tourist Office,** Tourist House, 42 Grand Parade, Cork (☎ 021/427-3251). Its hours are October to May, Monday to Saturday 9:15am to 1pm and 2:15 to 5:30pm; June and September, Monday to Saturday 9am to 6pm; July and August, Monday to Saturday 9am to 7pm and Sunday 10am to 5pm. For online information, consult **www.cork-guide.ie**.

CITY LAYOUT

Cork is divided into three sections:

SOUTH BANK   South of the River Lee, South Bank encompasses the grounds of St. Finbarr's Cathedral, the site of St. Finbarr's 6th-century monastery, and also includes 17th-century city walls, the remains of Elizabeth Fort, and City Hall, built in 1936 and Cork's chief administrative center.

FLAT OF THE CITY   This is the downtown core, surrounded on the north and south by channels of the River Lee. This area includes the **South Mall,** a wide tree-lined street with mostly Georgian architecture and a row of banks, insurance companies, and legal offices; the **Grand Parade,** a spacious thoroughfare that blends 18th-century bow-fronted houses and the remains of the old city walls with modern offices and shops; and a welcome patch of greenery, the **Bishop Lucey Park,** a fairly new (1986) addition to the cityscape.

Extending from the northern tip of the Grand Parade is the city's main thoroughfare, **St. Patrick Street.** Referred to simply as Patrick Street by Corkonians, this broad avenue was formed in 1789 by filling in an open channel in the river. It is primarily a street for shopping, but it is also a place for folks to stroll, be seen, and greet friends. Patrick Street is also the site of one of the city's best-known meeting places: the statue of 19th-century priest Fr. Theobald Matthew, a crusader against drink who is fondly called the "apostle of temperance." The statue—or "the stacha," as the locals call it— stands at the point where Patrick Street reaches St. Patrick's Bridge, and is the city's central point of reference.

NORTH BANK   St. Patrick's Bridge (or Patrick's Bridge), opened in 1859, leads over the river to the north side of the city, a hilly, terraced section where Patrick Street becomes **St. Patrick's Hill.** And is it ever a hill, with an incline so steep that it is nearly San Franciscan. If you climb the stepped sidewalks of St. Patrick's Hill, you will be rewarded with a sweeping view of the Cork skyline.

East of St. Patrick's Hill is **MacCurtain Street,** a commercial thoroughfare that runs east, leading to Summerhill Road and up into the Cork hills to the residential districts of St. Luke's and Montenotte. West of St. Patrick's Hill is one of the city's oldest neighborhoods, **St. Ann's Shandon Church,** and the city's original Butter Market building.

2 Getting Around

BY PUBLIC TRANSPORTATION   Bus Eireann operates bus service from Parnell Place Bus Station (☎ **021/450-8188**) to all parts of the city and its suburbs, including Blarney and Kinsale. The flat fare is 70p (98¢). Buses run frequently from 7am to 11pm Monday to Saturday, with slightly shorter hours on Sunday.

BY TAXI   Taxis are readily available throughout Cork. The main taxi ranks are along St. Patrick's Street, along the South Mall, and outside major hotels. To call for a taxi, try **ABC Cabs** (☎ **021/496-1961**), **Shandon Cabs** (☎ **021/450-2255**), **Supercabs** (☎ **021/450-0511**), or **Tele-Cabs** (☎ **021/450-5050**).

BY CAR   Most hotels have parking lots or garages; if you drive into Cork, it's best to park and explore the city on foot or by public transport. If you have to park in public areas, it costs 50p (70¢) per hour, whether you park in one of the city's two multistory parking lots, at Lavitt's Quay and Merchant's Quay, or on the street, where the disc system is in use. Parking discs, sold singly or in books of 10 for £5 ($7), are available at many shops and newsstands. There are also at least a dozen ground-level parking lots throughout the city.

Many international car-rental firms maintain rental desks at Cork Airport, including **Avis** (☎ **021/428-1169**), **Budget** (☎ **021/431-4000**), **Hertz** (☎ **021/496-5849**), and **Europcar** (☎ **021/496-6736**). **Avis** also has a large depot in Cork City at Emmet Place (☎ **021/428-1100**).

ON FOOT   The best way to see Cork is on foot, but don't try to do it all in 1 day. The South Bank and the central part, or flat, of the city can easily take a day to explore; save the Cork Hills and the North Bank for another day. You might want to follow the signposted Tourist Trail to guide you to all the major sights.

Fast Facts: Cork City

Drugstores   Try **Duffy's Dispensing Chemists,** 96 Patrick St. (☎ **021/ 427-2566**); **Hayes Conyngham and Robinson,** Wilton Shopping Centre (☎ **021/454-6500**); or **Murphy's Pharmacy,** 48 N. Main St. (☎ **021/ 427-4121**).

Emergencies   For emergencies, dial ☎ **999.**

Gay & Lesbian Resources   For information and aid, call the **Lesbian and Gay Resource Group and Community Centre,** 8 S. Main St. (☎ **021/427-8470**). The **Gay Information** line (☎ **021/427-1087**) is open Wednesday 7 to 9pm and Saturday 3 to 5pm. The **Lesbian Line** (also ☎ **021/427-1087**) is open Thursdays 8 to 10pm.

Hospitals   Try **Cork University Hospital,** Wilton Road (☎ **021/454-6400**); **Bon Secours Hospital,** College Road (☎ **021/454-2807**); or **City General Hospital,** Infirmary Road (☎ **021/431-1656**).

Information   See "Visitor Information," under "Orientation," earlier in this chapter.

Internet Access   Walk your mouse to the **Cyber Café,** Internet Center, Thompson House, MacCurtain Street (☎ **021/450-3511**).

Laundry & Dry Cleaning   Nasty Guinness stain on your Armani? Try **Castle Cleaners,** 90 N. Main St. (☎ **021/427-7603**), or **Winthrop Cleaners,** 18 Winthrop St. (☎ **021/427-6383**).

Library   **Cork Central Library,** Grand Parade (☎ **021/427-7110**), is a good bet.

Local Newspapers & Media   The *Irish Examiner* (www.examiner.ie) is Cork's daily morning newspaper; the *Evening Echo* is a daily afternoon paper. Local radio stations are Radio Cork, 89 FM, 96 FM, and 103 FM.

Photographic Needs   For film and other supplies, try **Cork Camera Services,** 80 Oliver Plunkett St. (☎ **021/427-0937**), or **John Roche Ltd.,** 55A Patrick St. (☎ **021/427-4935**).

Police   The local **Garda Headquarters** is on Barrack Street (☎ **021/431-6020**).

Post Office   The **General Post Office,** on Oliver Plunkett Street (☎ **021/ 427-2000**), is open Monday to Saturday 9am to 5:30pm.

3 Accommodations

VERY EXPENSIVE

✪ **Hayfield Manor.** Perrott Ave., College Rd., Cork, County Cork. ☎ **021/431-5600.** Fax 021/431-6839. www.hayfieldmanor.ie. U.S. reservations through Small Luxury Hotels of the World, ☎ **800/525-4800.** 87 units. A/C TV TEL. £210 ($294) double; £245 ($343) junior suite; £350 ($490) executive suite; £700 ($980) master suite. Rates include full Irish breakfast and service charge. AE, DC, MC, V.

Cork, Ireland's second city, has never been willing to take a second seat, and the same may be said of Hayfield Manor, the city's only five-star hotel. What an argument it is for starting from the ground up! Despite its period appearance and feel, Hayfield Manor was built in 1997 and expanded in 1999. Spend 1 night and you'll note how its designers thought of everything and did it right the first time. The guest rooms are especially spacious, with large windows, elegant furnishings, and bright marble bathrooms. Four guest rooms are fully accessible, and two are especially adapted for guests with disabilities. This place provides the range of amenities, level of comfort, and attention to detail you expect from a great privately owned hotel in the Irish tradition of unpretentious, all-embracing hospitality.

Although less than a mile from the city center and beside Cork's University College, Hayfield Manor is genuinely secluded. Its modest 3 acres of mature trees, orchard, and formal garden give the feeling of a grand estate, providing lovely views from virtually every window. The fully equipped conservatory leisure center—reserved exclusively for hotel guests—is singularly inviting and offers a pool, a gym, a steam room, an outdoor Jacuzzi, and a massage and beauty treatment room. The Hayfield Manor is not only a place to stay in Cork but also a reason to go there in the first place.

Dining/Diversions: The hotel bar offers a range of substantial food, including an early-bird menu daily from 6 to 7:30pm. The superb restaurant is open for breakfast, lunch, and dinner daily. The dinner menu includes fixed-price and à la carte options. The extensive wine list features a number of fine selections from the "Wine Geese," Ireland's distinguished vintners worldwide. Be sure to note the "end of bin" specials on the last page.

Amenities: You name it and Hayfield Manor offers it.

EXPENSIVE

Clarion Hotel & Suites, Morrisons Island. Morrison's Quay, Cork, County Cork. ☎ **800/44-UTELL** from the U.S., or 021/427-5858. Fax 021/427-5833. 40 units. TV TEL. £120 ($168) double; £140 ($196) 1-bedroom suite; £180 ($252) 2-bedroom suite; £170 ($238) 1-bedroom penthouse suite; £220 ($308) 2-bedroom penthouse suite. No service charge. AE, CB, DC, MC, V. Free parking.

Overlooking the River Lee just off the South Mall, this six-story downtown property is centrally located and is ideal for families or small groups, as most of the units are suites. The rooms, decorated with contemporary furniture and modern art, have views of the river, cityscape, and nearby bridges. Each suite contains a hallway, a sitting room, a dining area, a kitchen, a bathroom, and one or two bedrooms. Connecting rooms easily accommodate large parties or families. Nonsmoking suites are available on request. The public area includes the River Bank restaurant and lounge.

Jurys. Western road (N22), Cork, County Cork. ☎ **800/44-UTELL** from the U.S., or 021/427-6622. Fax 021/427-4477. www.jurys.com. 185 units. TV TEL. £152–£184 ($212.80–$257.60) double. Rates include full breakfast and service charge. AE, DC, MC, V. Free parking.

On the western edge of town, Jurys is well positioned, next to University College of Cork and along the banks of the River Lee, yet just a 5-minute walk from the city center. The modern two-story multiwinged structure was recently refurbished. The light-filled public areas include a skylit atrium, and there's a wall-length mural of Cork characters in the lobby. Guest rooms are furnished in traditional dark woods with designer fabrics, and have views of either the central courtyard gardens or the river and city. Nonsmoking rooms are available.

Dining/Diversions: There's the Fastnet, a seafood restaurant that serves dinner; the Glandore for meals throughout the day; the skylit Pavilion piano bar; and Corks Bar, a pub with river views, and free music most nights.

Amenities: Concierge, 24-hour room service, laundry and dry cleaning, indoor-outdoor heated swimming pool, sauna, gym, and squash court.

MODERATE

✪ **Arbutus Lodge.** St. Luke's Hill, Montenotte, Cork, County Cork. ☎ **021/450-1237.** Fax 021/450-2893. 20 units, 16 with private bathroom. TV TEL. £90 ($126) standard double; £125 ($175) superior double; £140–£200 ($196–$280) luxury suite. No service charge. Rates include full breakfast. AE, DC, MC, V.

Once the home of the Lord Mayor of Cork, Arbutus Lodge is a Cork institution, part of the fabric of the city. Perched high on St. Lukes Hill in fashionable Montenotte, it affords extraordinary views of the city from the dining room (and quite possibly from your room), yet the city center is an easy walk away. Each room is distinct, designed to have its own character. The Oriental Room and the Tivoli Room are especially elegant and spacious, and have city views. The standard is high, and all rooms were refurbished in 1999 or 2000. Many of the new suites border on grandeur (the Pine Suite is cozy and modest). The first guest in the presidential suite was Andrew Lloyd Webber, and the second was Mary Robinson, the president of Ireland. All suites have queen sofa beds in the living rooms, kitchenettes, VCRs, and fax/modems. Expect every amenity at Arbutus Lodge; and whatever you do, eat here (see "Dining," below). For lighter meals, there's the Gallery bar and patio.

Imperial Hotel. South Mall, Cork, County Cork. ☎ **800/44-UTELL** from the U.S., or 021/427-4040. Fax 021/427-5375. E-mail: imperial@iol.ie. 98 units. TV TEL. £80–£130 ($112–$182) double. Rates include full breakfast and service charge. AE, CB, DC, MC, V.

Within easy walking distance of Cork's major attractions and shops, this vintage four-story hotel is conveniently situated in the heart of the city's business district. With Waterford crystal chandeliers, marble floors, and brass fittings, the reception area and public rooms exude an aura of 19th-century grandeur, while the guest rooms are a mix of contemporary and traditional. Some have light woods and striped pastel tones; others, dark woods, antique fixtures, and semicanopy beds. Each room has a tea/coffeemaker, garment press, and VCR. This venerable hotel has been in need of attention, which it has been receiving of late. Dining options include the Orangery coffee shop, Clouds Restaurant and bar, and nautical Captains Bar.

Silver Springs Moran Hotel. Dublin Rd., Tivoli, Cork, County Cork. ☎ **021/450-7533.** Fax 021/450-7641. 109 units. TV TEL. £105–£115 ($147–$161) double. Rates include full breakfast and service charge. AE, DC, MC, V.

On a hillside overlooking the River Lee, surrounded by 42 acres of gardens and grounds, this modern seven-story hotel is 2 miles (3.2km) east of the main business district. A glass-walled elevator that offers views of the surrounding countryside connects the lobby and guest rooms. Each room, outfitted with hand-crafted Irish furniture and designer fabrics, has lovely views of the river, city, or gardens, plus little extras such as hair dryers and tea/coffeemakers.

There's Truffles Restaurant for gourmet fare; the Waterfront Grill for meals or snacks all day; the Flyover Bar; and Thady Quill's, a pub that offers live music Thursday to Saturday nights and a jazz brunch on Sunday mornings. Additional amenities include concierge, room service, laundry and dry cleaning, courtesy minibus service, indoor heated Olympic swimming pool, Jacuzzi, sauna, steam room, gym, aerobics room, indoor and outdoor tennis courts, squash court, nine-hole golf course, and heliport.

INEXPENSIVE

Jurys Cork Inn. Anderson's Quay, Cork, County Cork. ☎ **800/44-UTELL** from the U.S., or 021/427-6444. Fax 021/427-6144. www.jurys.com. 133 units. TV TEL. £55–£60 ($77–$84) per room. No service charge. Public car park. AE, DC, MC, V.

Open since 1994, this five-story hotel is in the busy heart of the city overlooking the River Lee, next to the bus station and 3 blocks from Patrick Street. The brick facade and mansard-style roof blend in with Cork's older architecture, yet the interior is bright and modern, with contemporary light-wood furnishings. The flat-rate room price covers one or two adults and two children—an amazingly good value for a city-center hotel. Nonsmoking rooms are available. Dining options include Arches Restaurant and the Inn Pub.

✪ **Lotamore House.** Dublin–Waterford road (N8/N25), Tivoli, County Cork. ☎ **021/ 482-2344.** Fax 021/482-2219. E-mail: lotamore@iol.ie. 20 units. TV TEL. £58–£64 ($81.20–$89.60) double. No service charge. Rates include full breakfast. AE, MC, V.

Overlooking the River Lee on 4 acres of wooded grounds and gardens 2 miles (3.2km) east of Cork City, this Georgian manor is one of the county's best guesthouses. Owned by two doctors, Mareaid and Leonard Harty, it is an exceedingly well-run facility, furnished with antiques, crystal chandeliers, and a fireplace dating from 1791. Extra comforts such as orthopedic beds, garment presses, and hair dryers have been provided in the rooms. Breakfast is the only meal served, but it's exceptional, with freshly squeezed juices and fruit on the menu every day. Nonsmoking rooms are available.

✪ **Maranatha Country House.** Tower, Blarney, County Cork. ☎ and fax **021/438-5102.** E-mail: douglasvenn@eircom.net. 6 units, all with private bathroom (5 with shower only, 1 with Jacuzzi). £38–£50 ($53.20–$75) double; £70 ($98) suite. 50% reduction for children. Rates include full breakfast. MC, V. Closed mid-Nov to Mar.

Olwen Venn is the energetic host at this 19th-century manor house, situated on 27 acres of fine woodland. Olwen's keen aesthetic sense is observable throughout the house, and she has gone to extraordinary lengths to make each room a unique and sumptuous experience. If the lacy frills and elaborate constructions in velvet of one bedroom aren't to your taste, you can be assured that the next room will offer another experience altogether. In all the rooms, the traditional rules of decorating have been discarded in favor of thoughtful (and often whimsical) effusiveness. The most luxurious is the ground-floor suite, which contains a canopy bed and a large Jacuzzi within its ample floor plan. The breakfast conservatory houses an abundance of fresh blossoms, and the breakfast itself is plentiful and delicious. No smoking.

4 Dining

EXPENSIVE

✪ **Arbutus Lodge.** St. Luke's Hill, Montenotte, Cork, County Cork. ☎ 021/450-1237. Reservations required. Fixed-price lunch £15.50 ($21.70); fixed-price dinner £25 ($35); dinner main courses £16–£19 ($22.40–$26.60). AE, DC, MC, V. Daily 1–2:30pm and 7–10pm. INTERNATIONAL.

Overlooking the city skyline from a hilltop, this lovely Georgian town-house restaurant has long been synonymous with gourmet cuisine in Cork—and, for that matter, in Ireland. It has long ranked among a handful of restaurants setting the standard toward which everyone else strives; and now, with a new chef, it too must strive to maintain its place. To even a jaded palate, a meal here can be startling. The one thing about the menu that's predictable is its excellence. On many evenings, the chef prepares an eight-course tasting menu encompassing the best of many dishes. The wine list has won more decorations than Patton and offers a more delicate finish. It provides marvelous reading, even before a cork is lifted. The skilled, gracious service staff adds to the rare pleasure of a dinner at Arbutus Lodge.

MODERATE

✪ **Cafe Paradiso.** 16 Lancaster Quay, Western Rd., Cork, County Cork. (across from the Jurys hotel). ☎ 021/427-7939. Reservations recommended. Dinner main courses £11–£13 ($15.40–$18.20). MC, V. Tues–Sat 12:30–3pm and 6:30–10:30pm. Tea, coffee, and cake from 10:30am. Closed Christmas week, Easter, last 2 weeks of Aug. VEGETARIAN.

If you still think of vegetarians as either deprived or demented, one meal here will turn you around. Widely recognized as the finest vegetarian restaurant in Ireland, Cafe

Paradiso casts the vegetable in "the starring role," as co-founder and chief chef Denis Cotter puts it. The menu features the freshest local produce, organic whenever possible, often supported by the finest Irish cheeses. Imagine starting with balsamic-roasted beetroot with organic salad leaves and sugar snaps, pesto dressing and Knoackalara sheep's cheese, or grilled potato gnocchi in fresh tomato-basil-olive oil sauce with Parmesan. Then move on to mangetout, rocket and red-onion risotto with Parmesan shavings and balsamic-roasted cherry tomatoes, or goat's cheese, pine nut, and roasted tomato charlotte on grilled eggplant and spinach polenta croutons and puy lentils with basil oil. Paradise will indeed come to mind as you feast on these subtle, complex creations. Dark chocolate tart or strawberry baked Alaska will complete the conversion of even the most hardened palate. The wine list is solid and selective, varied without being vast, with a number of choices by the glass or half-bottle. Cotter and his partner-in-perfection Bridget Healy have spilled their culinary secrets in *The Cafe Paradiso Cookbook,* on sale here and in bookstores for £20 ($28).

✪ **Jacques.** 9 Phoenix St., Cork, County Cork. ☎ **021/427-7387.** Reservations recommended. Fixed-price lunch £10.90 ($15.26); early-bird dinner (6–7pm) £11.90 ($16.65); fixed-price dinner £21.90 ($30.65); à la carte £12.90–£17.90 ($18.05–$25.05). AE, MC, V. Mon–Fri noon–3pm; Mon–Sat 6–10:30pm. IRISH/INTERNATIONAL.

Decorated with modern art on cheery lemon, tangerine, and green walls, this small, stylish bistro is the creation of sisters Eithne and Jacqueline Barry. It's on a side street in the heart of town, near the South Mall and General Post Office. Imaginative cuisine is the keynote, with featured dishes such as roast brace of quail, served Asian style on thread noodles; Tuscan chicken with polenta and Parmesan cheese with roast vegetables; and tagliatelle with wild mushroom in a garlic cream sauce.

Ristorante Rossini. 34/35 Princes St., Cork, County Cork. ☎ **021/427-5818.** Reservations recommended. Dinner main courses £4–£9.50 ($5.60–$13.30). AE, MC, V. Daily noon–midnight. ITALIAN.

If you're in Ireland and suddenly want to be in Italy, this shop-front restaurant is the place for you. Vaulted ceiling, dark wood furnishings, an open fireplace, fresh flowers, and pictures on the walls transport your mind, while the menu does the same for your stomach. Featured dishes include steaks and lamb chops, a variety of pasta dishes, *pollo Regina* (chicken with asparagus, artichokes, and butter sauce), tender pasta with fresh sage and Parma ham, and the house special, *sirloin Rossini* (steak prepared with prawns, cream, white wine, and peppercorns). There is also live Italian music Thursday to Saturday nights. The management promised to give diners who mention that Frommer's sent them a 10% discount.

INEXPENSIVE

Bullys Restaurant and Wine Bar. 40 Paul St., Cork, County Cork. ☎ **021/427-3555.** Reservations recommended. Main courses £4–£12 ($5.60–$16.80). MC, V. Mon–Sat noon–11:30pm; Sun 1–11pm. IRISH/ITALIAN.

On one of Cork's best shopping streets, near antique row, this small shop-front eatery has modern black-and-white furnishings enhanced by colorful plants. It offers pizza, pasta, and burgers, as well as seafood omelets and charcoal-grilled steaks. Bullys has two other Cork locations, at Bishopstown and Douglas.

✪ **Crawford Gallery Cafe.** Emmet Place, Cork, County Cork. ☎ **021/427-4415.** Reservations recommended for parties of 6 or more. All items £2.50–£8.50 ($3.50–$11.90). MC, V. Mon–Sat 10am–5pm. IRISH.

In a ground-floor room at the Crawford Art Gallery, this restaurant decorated with oil paintings and statuary is run by the Allen family of Ballymaloe House fame (see "East

Cork" in chapter 8). It serves breakfast, lunch, and afternoon tea. The menu includes such traditional dishes as lamb braised with vegetables and rosemary and served with champ (which is a traditional dish of buttery mashed potatoes with chopped green onions, and sometimes with chopped parsley, chives, and young nettle tops), and more contemporary open-faced sandwiches such as a wonderful smoked salmon, cheese, and pickle combination. All fish are brought in fresh daily from Ballycotton Bay, and breads and baked goods are from Ballymaloe kitchens.

✪ **Isaac's.** 48 MacCurtain St., Cork, County Cork. ☎ **021/450-3805.** Reservations recommended for dinner. Dinner main courses £6.95–£12.95 ($9.75–$18.15). AE, CB, MC, V. Mon–Sat 10am–10:30pm; Sun 6:30–9:30pm. Closed Christmas week. IRISH.

This restaurant on the city's north side is in a vintage warehouse-style building with stone arches, brick walls, big globe lights, tall ceilings supported by columns, and modern art. It can be noisy when busy, but the din never disturbs the enthusiastic patrons who come for the trendy food. The menu offers choices ranging from freshly prepared salads, burgers, steaks, and seafood chowders to international dishes such as beef bourguignon, gratin of smoked salmon and potato, and spinach tagliatelle with salmon, fennel, and cream. Daily blackboard specials add to the variety. Isaac's was the winner of the Year 2000 Bord Bia New Irish Cuisine Award.

Quay Co-op. 24 Sullivan's Quay, Cork, County Cork. ☎ **021/431-7026.** Dinner main courses £4.50–£5.50 ($6.30–$7.70). Daily 9:30am–10:30pm. Self-service. MC, V. VEGETARIAN/ VEGAN.

The ground floor of this renowned establishment is a whole-foods store that also sells delicious breads and cakes. The main attraction, however, is on the second floor. Reached by a narrow, steep, winding staircase, the restaurant far surpasses its rather-inauspicious street-front image. An array of delicious hot and cold dishes spreads out before you, including spinach and sun-dried tomato roulade, spanakopita, and lentil and coconut soup. Breads and cakes are especially good here. Be aware that some vegan offerings can seem bland if you're not used to this diet; don't let that keep you away, because they make up a relatively small proportion of the menu. The clientele includes much of Cork's countercultural community, both young and old.

5 Attractions

IN TOWN

Coal Quay Market. Cornmarket St., Cork, County Cork. Free admission. Mon–Sat 9am–5pm.

This is Cork's open-air flea market, a treasure trove of secondhand clothes, old china, used books, and memorabilia. It all happens on a street, now a little ragged, that was once Cork's original outdoor market.

Cork City Gaol. Convent Ave., Sunday's Well, Cork, County Cork. ☎ **021/430-5022.** Admission to gaol or exhibition £4 ($5.60) adult; £3 ($4.20) seniors, students, and children; £10 ($14) family. Mar–Oct daily 9:30am–6pm; Nov–Feb Sat–Sun 10am–5pm. Last admission 1 hour before closing.

About a mile west of the city center, this restored prison was infamous in the 19th century, when it housed many of Ireland's great patriots. Sound effects and lifelike characters inhabiting the cells re-create the social history of Cork. The "Radio Museum Experience," an exhibition drawn from the RTE Museum Collection, presents an "unforgettable journey down the wavelengths of time"—or, more simply, a restored 6CK Radio Studio and an array of antique radio equipment and memorabilia.

Cork Heritage Park. Bessboro Rd., Blackrock, Cork, County Cork. ☎ **021/435-8854.** Admission £3.50 ($4.90) adults, £2.50 ($3.50) seniors and students, £1.50 ($2.10) children, £7.50 ($10.50) family. Apr Sun noon–5:30pm; May–Sept Mon–Fri 10:30am–5:30pm, weekends noon–5:30pm. Closed Oct–Mar.

Two miles (3.2km) south of the city center, this new park is in a 19th-century courtyard on lovely grounds beside an estuary of Cork Harbour. The site was originally part of the estate of the Pike family, Quakers who were prominent in banking and shipping in Cork in the 1800s. The exhibits trace the maritime and shipping routes of Cork as well as the history of the Pike family, in a series of colorful tableaux. There is also an environmental center, an archaeology room, a small museum dedicated to the history of Cork fire fighting from 1450 to 1945, and stables that house models of a saddler and blacksmith.

Cork Public Museum. Fitzgerald Park, Cork, County Cork. ☎ **021/427-0679.** Admission Sun £1 ($1.40), £2 ($2.80) family; Mon–Fri free. Mon–Fri 11am–1pm and 2:15–5pm; Sun 3–5pm (until 6pm July–Aug). Bus: 8.

This museum occupies a magnificent Georgian building in a park on the western edge of the city. Exhibits include models depicting early medieval times; artifacts recovered from excavations in the city, some dating as far back as 4,000 years; and a working model of an early flour mill with an unusual horizontal water wheel. There's an archive of photographs and documents relating to Cork-born Irish patriots Terence McSwiney, Thomas MacCurtain, and Michael Collins. Antique Cork silver, glass, and lace are on display. An extension to the museum has recently been completed.

✪ **Crawford Municipal Gallery.** Emmet Place, Cork, County Cork. ☎ **021/4273377.** www.synergy.ie/crawford. Free admission. Mon–Sat 10am–5pm.

Works by such well-known Irish painters as Jack Yeats, Nathaniel Grogan, William Orpen, John Lavery, James Barry, and Daniel Maclise are the focal point of this excellent gallery in Cork's 18th-century former Customs house. Also on display are sculptures and hand-crafted silver and glass pieces. A fine restaurant and bookstore are on the premises. In 2000 the Gallery received a dramatic facelift, with a major futuristic extension.

Lavitts Quay Gallery. 5 Father Matthew St., Cork, County Cork. ☎ **021/427-7749.** Free admission. Mon–Sat 10am–6pm.

Operated by the Cork Arts Society, this gallery promotes the area's contemporary visual arts. It's in an early 18th-century Georgian house that overlooks the River Lee. The ground floor presents a variety of work by established artists, and the upper floor showcases up-and-coming talent.

✪ **Old English Market/City Market.** Grand Parade; enter from Patrick St., Grand Parade, Oliver Plunkett St., or Princes St., Cork, County Cork. Free admission. Mon–Sat 9am–6pm.

A Cork tradition since 1610, this marketplace unfolds in a building dating from 1786. Stands brim with meats, fish, vegetables, and fruit, and you'll also see such traditional Cork foods as *tripe* (animal stomach), *crubeens* (pigs' feet), and *drisheens* (local blood sausage). The market's name is a holdover from the days of English rule.

✪ **St. Anne's Shandon Church.** Church St., Cork, County Cork. ☎ **021/450-5906.** Church, tower, and bells £3.50 ($4.90) adults, £3 ($4.20) seniors and students, £7 ($9.80) family. Mon–Sat 8:30am–6pm.

Famous for its giant pepperpot steeple and its eight melodious bells, this is Cork's prime landmark. No matter where you stand in the downtown area, you can usually see the 1722 church's stone tower, crowned with a gilt ball and a fish weathervane.

Visitors are often encouraged to climb to the belfry and play a tune, so you might hear the bells of Shandon ringing at all times of the day.

✪ **St. Finbarr's Cathedral.** Bishop St., Cork, County Cork. ☎ **021/496-3387.** Free admission; donations welcome. Apr–Sept Mon–Sat 10am–5:30pm and Oct–Mar Mon–Sat 2–5:30pm.

This Church of Ireland cathedral sits on the spot St. Finbarr chose in A.D. 600 for his church and school. The current building dates from 1880 and is a fine example of early French Gothic style; its three giant spires dominate the skyline. The interior is highly ornamented with unique mosaic work. The bells were inherited from the 1735 church that previously stood on this site.

✪ **University College, Cork (U.C.C.).** Western Rd., Cork, County Cork. ☎ **021/490-2371.** Tours by arrangement.

A component of Ireland's National University, with about 7,000 students, this center of learning is housed in a quadrangle of Gothic Revival–style buildings. Lovely gardens and wooded grounds grace the campus. Tours include the Crawford Observatory, the lovely Harry Clarke stained-glass windows in the Honan Chapel, and the Stone Corridor, a collection of stones inscribed with the ancient Irish Ogham style of writing.

BUS TOURS

In July and August, **Bus Eireann,** Parnell Place Bus Station (☎ **021/450-8188**), offers narrated tours to all of Cork's major landmarks and buildings, including nearby Blarney. Fares start at £6 ($8.40).

Cork Panoramic. Grayline/Guide Friday Irish City Tours, Cork, County Cork. ☎ **01/ 670-8822.** Apr–Oct daily, with hours and number of tours reflecting seasonal demand. £8 ($11.20) adults, £7 ($9.80) students, £2.50 ($3.50) children.

Hop aboard these open top-buses and explore the sights of Ireland's second city. They run all day in a loop; so when you see something you want to explore, just hop off. Or just stay on all day and memorize everything you see and hear. Tour highlights include the Cork City Gaol, St. Ann's Church, and UCC (University College, Cork). Further details are available from the Cork Tourist Office.

NEARBY: BLARNEY CASTLE & MORE

Ballincollig Gunpowder Mills. About 5 miles (8km) west of Cork City on the main Cork–Killarney road (N22), Ballincollig, County Cork. ☎ **021/487-4430.** Admission £3 ($4.20) adults, £2.50 ($3.50) seniors and students, £1.80 ($2.50) children, £8 ($11.20) family. Apr–Sept daily 10am–6pm.

This industrial complex beside the River Lee was a hub for the manufacture of gunpowder from 1794 to 1903, a time of wars between Britain and France. In its heyday as Cork's prime industry, it employed about 500 men as coopers, millwrights, and carpenters. You can tour the restored buildings, and there are exhibits and an audiovisual presentation that tell the story of gunpowder production in the Cork area.

✪ **Blarney Castle and Stone.** R617, 5 miles (8km) northwest of Cork City, Blarney, County Cork. ☎ **021/438-5252.** Castle £3.50 ($4.90) adults, £2.50 ($3.50) seniors and students, £1 ($1.50) children, £7.50 ($10.50) family (2 adults and 2 children 8–14). May and Sept Mon–Sat 9am–6:30pm, Sun 9:30am–5:30pm; June–Aug Mon–Sat 9am–7pm, Sun 9:30am–5:30pm; Oct–Apr Mon–Sat 9am–sundown, Sun 9:30am–5:30pm. Bus: 154 from bus station on Parnell Place, Cork City.

While aspects of Blarney Castle are tacky and touristy, it remains one of the most haunting and striking castles in Ireland. What remains of this impressive castle is a massive square tower, with a parapet rising 83 feet. The infamous Blarney Stone is wedged far enough underneath the battlements to make it uncomfortable to reach, but not far enough that countless tourists don't, for reasons inexplicable, abandon all concern for health to kiss it.

After bypassing the stone, you should stroll through the gardens and a nearby dell beside Blarney Lake. The Badger Cave and adjacent dungeons, penetrating the rock at the base of the castle, can be explored by all but claustrophobes with the aid of a flashlight. Blarney House is closed until further notice.

6 Spectator Sports & Outdoor Pursuits

SPECTATOR SPORTS

GAELIC GAMES   Hurling and Gaelic football are both played on summer Sunday afternoons at Cork's **Pairc Ui Chaoimh Stadium,** Marina Walk (☎ **021/496-3311**). Check the local newspapers for details.

GREYHOUND RACING   Go to the dogs, as they say in Cork, at **Cork Greyhound Track,** Western Road, Cork (☎ **021/454-3013**), on Wednesday, Thursday, and Saturday at 8pm. Admission is £5 ($7).

HORSE RACING   The nearest racetrack is **Mallow Race Track,** Killarney Road, Mallow (☎ **022/50207**), approximately 20 miles (32km) north of Cork. Races are scheduled in mid-May, early August, and early October.

OUTDOOR PURSUITS

The **Tent Shop & Outside World,** 7 Parnell Place (☎ **021/278833**), is a one-stop source for outdoor needs, from canoe and tent rentals to surfing and mountaineering gear. Express repairs are offered for tourists in distress.

BICYCLING   Although walking is probably the ideal way to get around Cork, you can rent a bike at **Cyclescene,** 396 Blarney St. (☎ **021/430-1183**). It costs £10 ($14) per day or £40 ($56) per week. Open Monday to Saturday, 8:30am to 6pm.

FISHING   The **River Lee,** which runs through Cork, the nearby **Blackwater River,** and the many area lakes present fine opportunities. Salmon licenses, lake fishing permits, tackle, and equipment can be obtained from **T. W. Murray,** 87 Patrick St. (☎ **021/427-1089**), and the **Tackle Shop,** Lavitt's Quay (☎ **021/427-2842**).

GOLF   Corkonians welcome visitors to play on the following 18-hole courses, all within a 5-mile (8km) radius of the city: **Cork Golf Club,** Little Island (☎ **021/435-3451**), 5 miles (8km) east of Cork, with greens fees of £45 ($63) weekdays, £50 ($70) weekends; **Douglas Golf Club,** Maryboro Hill, Douglas (☎ **021/489-5297**), 3 miles (4.8km) south of Cork, with greens fees of £35 ($49) weekdays, £42 ($58.80) weekends; and **Harbour Point,** Little Island (☎ **021/435-3094**), 4 miles (6.5km) east of Cork, with greens fees of £23 ($32.20) weekdays, £26 ($36.40) weekends.

7 Shopping

Patrick Street is the main shopping thoroughfare, and many stores are scattered throughout the city on side streets and in lanes. In general, shops are open Monday to Saturday 9:30am to 6pm, unless indicated otherwise. In the summer, many shops remain open until 9:30pm on Thursday and Friday, and some are open on Sunday.

The city's antiques row is **Paul's Lane,** an offshoot of Paul Street, between Patrick Street and the Quays in the Huguenot Quarter. There are three shops along this lane, each brimming with old Cork memorabilia and furnishings: **Anne McCarthy,** 2 Paul's

Lane (☎ 021/427-3755); **Mills,** 3 Paul's Lane (☎ 021/427-3528); and **O'Regan's,** 4 Paul's Lane (☎ 021/427-2902). All are open Monday to Saturday 10am to 6pm.

The main mall is **Merchant's Quay Shopping Centre,** Merchant's Quay and Patrick Street. This enclosed complex houses large department stores, such as **Marks and Spencer** (☎ 021/427-5555), as well as small specialty shops, such as **Laura Ashley** (☎ 021/427-4070).

Cork's legendary department store is **Cashs,** 18 St. Patrick St. (☎ 021/427-6771). Dating to 1830, it offers three floors of wares and gift items, including Waterford crystal, Irish linen, and all types of knitwear and tweeds.

BOOKS & MUSIC

HMV. 81 Patrick St., Cork, County Cork. ☎ **021/427-0947.**

HMVs are a fixture throughout Ireland, a major source for CDs and cassettes across the full spectrum of music at competitive prices. Open daily 9:30am to 6pm, until 8pm Friday.

✪ **The Living Tradition.** 40 MacCurtain St., Cork, County Cork. ☎ **021/450-2040.** www.ossian.ie.

This small shop on the North Bank specializes in Irish traditional music—CDs, cassettes, books, videos, sheet music, and song books—as well as instruments such as *bodhrans* (Irish frame drums) and tin whistles. In addition, it stocks a good selection of recordings of musicians from around the world, along with hand-crafted goods.

Mainly Murder. 2A Paul St., Cork, County Cork. ☎ **021/427-2413.**

Tucked between French Church and Academy streets, this tiny bookshop is a huge treasure trove of whodunits for amateur sleuths or anyone looking for a good read. It stocks volumes on murder, mystery, and mayhem from Ireland, England, and many other English-speaking lands. It's well worth a visit to stock up for a rainy day. Open Monday to Saturday 10am to 5:30pm.

✪ **Mercier Press and Bookshop.** 5 French Church St., Cork, County Cork. ☎ **021/ 427-5040.**

Long a part of Cork's literary tradition, this shop stocks a variety of books, including those published by Cork-based Mercier Press, founded in 1944 and now Ireland's oldest independent publishing house. It has an extensive Irish-interest section, including volumes on history, literature, folklore, music, art, humor, drama, politics, current affairs, law, and religion.

Waterstone's Booksellers. 69 Patrick St. and 12 Paul St., Cork, County Cork. ☎ **021/ 427-6522.**

With entrances on two streets, this large British-owned shop is always busy. It has a good selection of books about Cork and of Irish interest, as well as sections on art, antiques, biography, religion, and travel. Mailing service is available. Open Monday to Thursday 9am to 8pm, Friday 9am to 9pm, Saturday 9am to 7pm, Sunday noon to 7pm.

CRAFTS

✪ **Crafts of Ireland.** 11 Winthrop St., Cork, County Cork. ☎ **021/427-5864.**

Just a block off Patrick Street, this well-stocked shop presents an array of local crafts, including weavings, wrought iron, batik hangings, candles, glass, graphics, leather work, pottery, toys, Irish wildlife mobiles, and Irish floral stationery. Open Monday to Saturday 9:30am to 5:30pm.

Meadows and Byrne. Academy St., Cork, County Cork. ☎ 021/427-2324.

Meadows and Byrne—also located in Galway and Bunratty, County Clare—claims to be the finest Irish home store, and unquestionably offers a wide and attractive array of contemporary furniture, furnishings, and household items. In this multilevel center, you'll find some of the finest in contemporary Irish design and crafts, including Jerpoint glass, Shanagarry pottery, and wrought-iron works by John Forkin.

✪ **Shandon Craft Centre.** Cork Exchange, John Redmond St., Cork, County Cork. ☎ 021/450-8881.

Cork's original Butter Market, a commercial exchange begun in 1730, is the site of this unique sightseeing and shopping experience: an enclosed emporium where 20th-century artisans practice a range of traditional trades and display their wares for sale. The crafts include porcelain dolls, jewelry, clothing, crystal, pottery, and handmade violins, cellos, and violas. From June to August, folk, traditional, jazz, and classical musicians offer free concerts from 1 to 2pm.

TWEEDS & WOOLENS

Blarney Woollen Mills. Blarney, County Cork. ☎ 021/438-5280.

About 6 miles (9.7km) northwest of Cork City, near the famous castle of the same name, this Kelleher family enterprise is housed in an 1824 mill. It's a one-stop source for Irish products, from cashmeres to crystal glassware, hats to heraldry, and tweeds to T-shirts, as well as the distinctive Kelly green Blarney Castle–design wool sweaters, made on the premises. Best of all, it's open until 10pm every night in summer.

House of Donegal. 6 Paul St. (1 block north of St. Patrick St., off the Grand Parade), Cork, County Cork. ☎ 021/427-2447.

"Tailoring to please" is the theme of this showroom and workshop. You can buy ready-made or specially tailored raincoats, classic trench coats, jackets, suits, and sportswear for men and women. The handsome rainwear, with Donegal tweed linings, is a special find.

Quills. 107 Patrick St., Cork, County Cork. ☎ 021/427-1717.

For tweeds, woolens, and knits at the best prices, don't miss this family-run enterprise on Cork's busy main thoroughfare. It's a branch of a shop that started small more than 20 years ago at Ballingeary, in the heart of the West Cork Gaeltacht. It now has similar shops in Killarney, Kenmare, and Sneem.

8 Cork After Dark

PUBS

✪ **An Bodhran Bar.** 42 Oliver Plunkett St., Cork, County Cork. ☎ 021/427-4544.

There's Irish traditional music at this friendly pub Monday to Thursday at 9pm. The old-world decor includes stone walls, dark woods, and a huge stained-glass window with Book of Kells–inspired designs depicting Irish monks playing traditional Irish instruments.

✪ **An Spailpin Fanac (The Loft).** 28–29 S. Main St., Cork, County Cork. ☎ 021/427-7949.

This is one of the city's choice spots for traditional Irish music, Sunday to Friday starting at 9:30pm. Opposite Beamish's Brewery, it was established in 1779, making it one of Cork's oldest pubs. It retains many of the furnishings of yesteryear, including brick walls, flagstone floors, open fireplaces, and an authentic snug.

Impressions

An Irishman is just a machine for turning Guinness into urine, which as any
Murphy's drinker will tell you is a superfluous exercise.

—Niall Tóibín (b. 1929)

John Henchy & Sons. 40 St. Luke's, Cork, County Cork. ☎ **021/450-7833.**

It's worth a walk up steep Summerhill Road, a northeast continuation of busy MacCurtain Street, to reach this classic pub near the Arbutus Lodge hotel. Established by John Henchy in 1884, it looks just the same as it did then, with lots of polished brass fittings, leaded-glass windows, silver tankards, thick red curtains, and a small snug. The original Henchy family grocery store still operates adjacent to the pub.

Le Chateau. 93 Patrick St., Cork, County Cork. ☎ **021/427-0370.**

Established in 1793, this is one of Cork's oldest pubs of great character, located right in the middle of the city's main thoroughfare. As pubs go, it's a large specimen, with a choice of rooms and alcoves filled with Cork memorabilia. Irish coffee is a specialty.

Maguire's Warehouse Bar. Daunt Sq., Grand Parade, Cork, County Cork. ☎ **021/427-7825.**

Just off Patrick Street in the heart of town, this Edwardian-style pub has a conversation-piece interior, with vintage bicycles, unicycles, and lots of old brass fixtures.

✪ Mutton Lane Inn. 3 Mutton Lane, off Patrick St., Cork, County Cork. ☎ **021/427-3471.**

Old Cork is alive and well at this tiny pub down an alley that was first trod as a pathway for sheep going to market. It was opened in 1787 as a public house by the Ring family, who used to make their own whiskey. It's now the domain of Maeva and Vincent McLoughlin, who have preserved the old-world aura, which incorporates lantern lights, dark wood-paneled walls, exposed-beam ceilings, and an antique cash register.

BARS & CLUBS

You're likely to have the last laugh at the **City Limits,** every Friday and Saturday night at The Comedy Club, 2 Coburg St. (☎ 450-1206).

Half Moon. Cork Opera House, Emmet Place, Cork, County Cork. ☎ **021/427-0022.** Cover £5–£10 ($7–$14). Thurs–Sun 11:30pm–3am.

After the main stage empties, the Cork Opera House Bar, the Half Moon, swings into action. It schedules an ever-changing program of contemporary music, from blues and ragtime to pop and rock, with comedy gigs on occasion.

The Lobby Bar. 1 Union Quay, Cork, County Cork. ☎ **021/431-9307.** Cover £3–£7 ($4.20–$9.80). Most music performances at 9pm.

This bar opposite City Hall presents a variety of musical entertainment, from folk, traditional, bluegrass, and blues to jazz, gypsy, rock, classical, and New Age.

THE PERFORMING ARTS

Cork Opera House. Emmet Place, Cork, County Cork. ☎ **021/427-0022.** Tickets £6–£30 ($8.40–$42); average £15 ($21). Box office 9am–7pm; curtain usually 8pm; matinees 1:30 or 3pm.

Just off Lavitt's Quay along the River Lee, this is southwest Ireland's major venue for opera, drama, musicals, comedies, dance, concerts, and variety nights.

Firkin Crane Cultural Centre. John Redmond St., Shandon, Cork, County Cork. ☎ **021/ 450-7487.** Tickets £8–£10 ($11.20–$14). Curtain usually 8pm.

Dating from the 1840s, this unique rotunda was part of Cork's original Butter Market, and the building's name derives from Danish words pertaining to measures of butter. Although destroyed by fire in 1980, the site was completely rebuilt and opened as a cultural center in 1992. Today, Firkin Crane is singularly dedicated to the under-standing and development of contemporary dance throughout Ireland. It serves as both a producing venue for new dance works and a presenting venue for touring national and international dance companies.

Triskel Arts Centre. Tobin St., off S. Main St., Cork, County Cork. ☎ **021/427-2022.** Tickets £1–£8 ($1.40–$11.20). Box office Mon–Sat 10am–5:30pm; curtain usually 8pm; some Sat–Sun matinees at 1:15 or 1:30pm.

This ever-growing arts center presents a variety of entertainment, including drama, poetry readings, musical recitals, opera, and popular Irish and traditional music con-certs. There is also a full program of daytime art workshops and gallery talks. The restaurant with bar is open for day and evening events.

THEATERS

Cork Arts Theatre. Knapp's Sq., Cork, County Cork. ☎ **021/450-8398.** Tickets £8 ($11.20) adults, £5 ($7) seniors and students. Shows Tues–Sat 8pm.

Across the river from the Opera House, this busy theater presents a wide variety of contemporary dramas, comedies, and musical comedies, to full houses. A multistory parking garage and the city center main street are a 10-minute walk away.

Everyman Palace. 17 MacCurtain St., Cork, County Cork. ☎ **021/450-1673.** Tickets £5–£8 ($7–$11.20). Box office Mon–Fri 10am–7pm; curtain 8pm.

This lovely, refurbished historic theater 2 minutes from the bus and train station is well known as a showcase for new plays, both Irish and international. The Irish National Ballet also performs here regularly.

Out from Cork

Once the haunt of outlaws, Cork long had a reputation as an inaccessible and unruly corner of the country. Aside from a drastic decrease in the number of outlaws, not much has changed—it's still adamantly unconventional and countercultural, and its populace continues to make waves. The landscape has hardly been tamed, either, and West Cork holds some of Ireland's most remote and wild coastal regions.

There's no better place to start a tour of County Cork than in Kinsale, a small harbor town directly south of Cork City.

1 Kinsale

18 miles (29km) S of Cork, 54 miles (87km) SE of Killarney, 97 miles (156km) SE of Shannon Airport, 177 miles (285km) SW of Dublin, and 20 miles (32km) E of Clonakilty

Less than 20 miles (32km) south of Cork City, ✪ **Kinsale** is a small fishing village with a sheltered semicircular harbor rimmed by hilly terrain. Considered the gateway to the western Cork seacoast, this compact town of 2,000 residents has also made a big name for itself as the "gourmet capital of Ireland." Home to more than a dozen award-winning restaurants and pubs, Kinsale draws food lovers year-round, particularly in October during the 3-day **Gourmet Festival.**

Kinsale fits the picture-postcard image of what a charming Irish seaport should look like—narrow, winding streets; well-kept 18th-century houses; imaginatively painted shop fronts; window boxes and street stanchions brimming with colorful flowers; and a harbor full of sailboats. Consequently, it has become a tourist mecca, so add traffic jams and tour buses to the list of the city's sights.

In 1601, the town was the scene of the Battle of Kinsale, a turning point in Irish history. The defeat of the Irish helped to establish English domination. After the battle, a new governor representing the British crown was appointed—a fella named William Penn. For a time, Penn's son William served in Kinsale as clerk of the admiralty court, but Penn Jr. did not stay long; he was soon off to the New World to found the state of Pennsylvania.

Just off the coast of the Old Head of Kinsale—about 5 miles (8km) west of the town—a German submarine sank the *Lusitania* in 1915. More than 1,500 people were killed, and many are buried in a local cemetery.

ESSENTIALS

GETTING THERE   **Bus Eireann** (☎ **021/450-8188**) operates regular daily service from Cork City to Kinsale. The arrival and departure point is at the Esso Garage on Pier Road, opposite the tourist office.

Kinsale is 18 miles (29km) south of Cork City on the Airport Road; if you're coming by car from the west, use N71. From East Cork, Cross River Ferries Ltd. provides regular service across Cork Harbour (see "East Cork," below).

VISITOR INFORMATION   The **Kinsale Tourist Office,** Pier Road, Kinsale (☎ **021/477-2234**), is open March through October.

GETTING AROUND   Kinsale's streets are so narrow that walking is the best way to get around. There is no local transport; if you need a taxi to outlying areas, call **O'Dea & Sons** (☎ **021/477-4900**) or **Allied Cabs** (☎ **021/477-3600**).

EXPLORING THE TOWN

✪ **Charles Fort.** Off the Scilly Rd., Summer Cove, County Cork. ☎ **021/477-2263.** Admission £2.50 ($3.50) adults, £1.75 ($2.45) seniors, £1 ($1.40) students, £6 ($8.40) family. Tours available on request. Mid-Mar to Oct daily 10am–6pm; Nov to mid-Mar weekends 10am–5pm; last admission 45 min. before closing.

Southeast of Kinsale, at the head of the harbor, this coastal landmark dates to the late 17th century. A classic star-shaped fort, it was constructed to prevent foreign naval forces from entering the harbor of Kinsale, then an important trading town. Additions and improvements were made throughout the 18th and 19th centuries, and the fort remained garrisoned until 1921. Across the river is James Fort (1602). An exhibition center and cafe were in the works in 2000.

Desmond Castle. Cork St., Kinsale, County Cork. ☎ **021/477-4855.** Admission £2 ($2.80) adults, £1.50 ($2.10) seniors and students, £1 ($1.40) children, £5 ($7) family. Mid-Apr to mid-June Tues–Sun 10am–6pm; mid-June to early Oct daily 10am–6pm. Last admission 45 min. before closing. Closed mid-Oct to mid-Apr.

A custom house built by the Earl of Desmond around 1500, this tower house has had a colorful history. The Spanish occupied it in 1601, and it was used as a prison for captured American sailors during the War of Independence. Locally, it's known as "French Prison" because 54 French seamen prisoners died here in a 1747 fire. During the Great Famine, the castle became a workhouse for the starving populace. At various times, the castle vaults have also been used as a wine storage depot. The castle recently underwent considerable restoration and now houses the **International Museum of Wine,** celebrating the vinicultural contributions of the Irish diaspora.

Kinsale Crystal. Market St., Kinsale, County Cork. ☎ **021/477-4493.** www.kinsalecrystal.ie. Free admission. Mon–Sat 9:30am–1:30pm.

Started in 1991 by a former Waterford Crystal master craftsman, this small workshop produces traditional full-lead, mouth-blown, and hand-cut crystal, with personalized engraving. Visitors are welcome to watch the entire fascinating process and admire the sparkling results.

Kinsale Regional Museum. Market Sq., Kinsale, County Cork. ☎ **021/477-2044.** Admission £2 ($2.80) adults, £1 ($1.40) students, 50p (70¢) children. Apr–Sept daily 10am–6pm; Oct–Mar Mon–Fri 11am–1pm and 3–5pm. Closed Jan.

This museum tells the town's story from its earliest days, with exhibits, photos, and memorabilia, highlighting such events as the Battle of Kinsale in 1601 and the sinking of the *Lusitania* in 1915, and featuring extensive traditional craft exhibits. It's in

County Cork

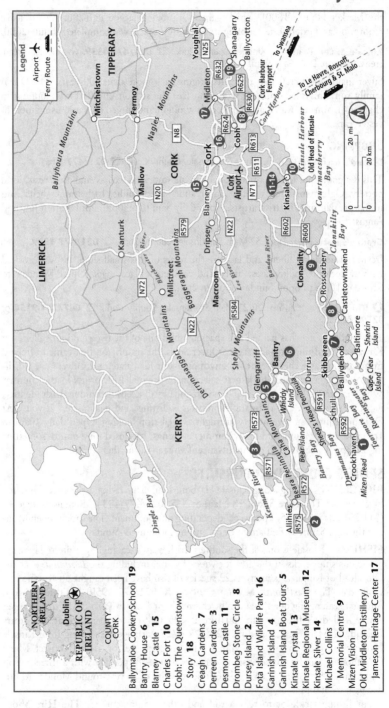

NORTHERN
IRELAND

Dublin ★

REPUBLIC OF
IRELAND

COUNTY
CORK

the Market House (1600), which gained an arched facade in 1706. An extensive renovation and extension, doubling its exhibition space, was completed in July 2000.

Kinsale Silver. Pearse St., Kinsale, County Cork. ☎ **021/477-4359.** www.iol.ie/~dolan. Free admission. Daily 9am–9pm.

Silver making is a craft that traces its origins back more than 300 years. The Dolan family runs this silversmithing workshop (see the section on Wexford shopping in chapter 6). You can watch as each piece is wrought and forged by hand, using tools of yesteryear.

SHOPPING

Boland's Irish Craft Shop. Pearse St., Kinsale, County Cork. ☎ **021/477-2161.**

This is a good spot to buy a traditional Kinsale smock, as well as Aran knit vests, local pottery, Ogham plaques, woolly and ceramic sheep, quilts, Irish leather belts, and miniature paintings by Irish artists. Open daily 8am to 6:30pm, until 9pm in July and August.

Granny's Bottom Drawer. 53 Main St., Kinsale, County Cork. ☎ **021/477-4839.**

Ireland's traditional linens and lace are the focus of this small shop. It's well stocked with tablecloths, pillowcases, and hand-crocheted place mats. Open Monday to Saturday 10am to 6pm, Sunday noon to 2pm.

✪ **The Irish Print Shop.** 20/21 Main St., Kinsale, County Cork. ☎ **087/261-9154** or 021/477-2565.

The London *Times* has named this spacious shop one of the two standout galleries in Kinsale's flourishing fine-arts scene. Oliver Sears, the proprietor, first came to Ireland from London as a chef. I can't say anything about his palate, but Oliver's eye is brilliant. He has assembled the largest selection of original Irish prints in the country. Why Irish art? Oliver's response: "Irish art today still keeps its unique, Irish identity; its pure, searching, and dramatic expression is distinct and passionate." If you can't find something you love here, you might as well stop looking. Open daily 10am to 1pm and 2 to 5:30pm, and many summer evenings. It's closed for a month sometime in January or February, so call in advance if you're visiting then.

SPORTS & OUTDOOR PURSUITS

BICYCLING   Biking along Kinsale Harbour is an exhilarating experience. To rent a bike, contact **The Hire Shop,** 18 Main St. (☎ **021/477-4884**). Rentals average £8 ($11.20) a day, £40 ($56) per week, depending on equipment. The shop is open Monday through Saturday 8:30am to 6pm, and many summer Sundays.

FISHING   Kinsale is one of the southern Irish coast's sea-angling centers. There are numerous shipwrecks in the area for wreck fishing, including the *Lusitania,* near the Old Head of Kinsale. As many as 22 species of fish have been caught off Kinsale in a single day. The **Castlepark Marina Centre** (☎ **021/477-4959**) has three 43-foot Aquastar sea-angling boats that can be chartered for £225 to £275 ($315 to $385) per day. A full day's fishing with rod hire is £35 ($49) per person. **Sporting Tours Ireland,** 71 Main St. (☎ and fax **021/477-4727**), arranges sea fishing from Kinsale Harbour or game fishing for salmon and trout in nearby rivers (contact Maria O'Mahony). The fee for sea fishing averages £20 ($28) per day with a three-person minimum; river fishing is £39 ($54.60) per day. It's open year-round Monday to Friday 9am to 5:30pm.

For fishing tackle or to rent a rod and other equipment, try **The Hire Shop,** 18 Main St. (☎ **021/477-4884**). It's open Monday to Saturday 8:30am to 6pm, and many summer Sundays. They offer a bicycle/fishing-tackle rental package of £15 ($21) for the day.

GOLF   Embraced by the sea on three sides, the new and spectacular ✪ **Old Head Golf Links** (☎ 021/477-4722; www.oldheadgolflinks.com) is a legend in the making. It seems destined to become one of the world's premier courses. It is hauntingly beautiful, rain or shine. Old Head has long been home to many species of wildlife, including rare migratory birds. The course retains a resident environmentalist to ensure that crucial habitats are not disturbed. The greens fees are currently £120 ($168) for 8 holes and £200 ($280) for 16 holes. Caddy fees run £20 ($28) for a junior caddy, £25 ($35) for a senior caddy.

Kinsale also boasts an 18-hole, par-71 golf course at **Farrangalway,** 3 miles (4.8km) north of town. Greens fees are £27 ($37.80) on weekends, £22 ($30.80) Monday through Friday. It's open daily 9am to 9pm. For information, contact the **Kinsale Golf Club,** Kinsale (☎ 021/477-4722).

SAILING   Yacht charters are available from **Sail Ireland Charters,** Trident Hotel, County Cork (☎ 021/477-2927; www.sailireland.com). From Kinsale it is possible to sail to Bantry Bay and back on a 1-week charter, or to the Dingle Peninsula on a 2-week charter. Prices for a six-berth, 35-foot yacht run £800 to £1,200 ($1,120 to $1,680) per week, not including outboard or skipper. A 10-berth 51-footer runs £1,500 to £1,900 ($2,100 to $2,660) per week.

SCUBA DIVING   The **Castlepark Marina Centre,** Kinsale (☎ 021/477-4959), can provide suits, tank fills, and skipper services to sites for experienced and qualified divers. See also Sporting Tours Ireland, under "Water Sports," below.

TENNIS   Courts are available at the **Oysterhaven Activity Centre** (☎ 021/477-0738), 5 miles (8km) from Kinsale, for £5 ($7) per hour. Racket rental is an additional £1 ($1.40). It's open Monday to Thursday 4:30 to 9pm, Friday to Sunday 10am to 6pm.

WALKING   A pedestrian path along the sea in Scilly, the community across the harbor from Kinsale, continues almost all the way to Charles Fort; it is signposted as the **Scilly Walk.** If you continue to walk south along the sea from Charles Fort, you'll find another path that follows the headland to the tip of **Frower Point,** which offers great views across the harbor to the Old Head of Kinsale. The complete walk from Kinsale to Frower Point is 5 miles (8km) each way, and any part of it is quite rewarding.

WATER SPORTS   Boaters favor Kinsale Harbour. At **Sporting Tours Ireland,** 71 Main St. (☎ and fax 021/477-4727), prices for scuba diving start at £30 ($42) per dive, minimum three persons. Canoeing, windsurfing, and dinghy sailing cost at least £12 ($16.80) per hour. Pleasure yacht hire prices are at a minimum of £100 ($140) per half day. Hours are daily 9am to 5:30pm. The **Oysterhaven Activity Centre** (☎ 021/477-0738), 5 miles (8km) from Kinsale, rents windsurfers, dinghies, and kayaks. It's open Monday to Thursday 10am to 9pm, Friday to Sunday 10am to 7pm.

ACCOMMODATIONS
MODERATE

✪ **The Blue Haven.** 3 Pearse St., Kinsale, County Cork. ☎ **021/477-2209.** Fax 021/477-4268. 17 units. TV TEL. £80–£150 ($112–$210) double. No service charge. Rates include full breakfast. AE, MC, V.

In the heart of town on the old Fish Market, the Blue Haven is an old-world inn with a history of hospitality. In 1999, Avril Greene purchased the inn from Brian and Anne Cronin, and he continues the tradition. All the rooms are individually furnished in bright, contemporary style, with local crafts and artwork, and views of either the town or the back gardens. Rooms in the new wing are named for the Irish exiles who left Kinsale and established wineries in Europe, such as Chateau McCarthy and Chateau Dillon. The new rooms have more traditional decor, with canopy beds, window seats, armoires, and brass fixtures. Besides the top-notch Blue Haven seafood restaurant (see "Dining," below), there are a pub with a nautical theme, and a wine and cheese shop.

The Moorings. Scilly, Kinsale, County Cork. ☎ **021/477-2376.** Fax 021/477-2675. 8 units. TV TEL. £100–£120 ($140–$168) double. No service charge. Rates include full breakfast. AE, DC, MC, V. Closed early Nov to Dec 27. Free parking.

Overlooking the harbor and marina, this newer two-story guesthouse has a bright, contemporary decor with lots of wide-windowed views of the water. The rooms are all nonsmoking, and are individually furnished with brass beds, pastel-colored quilts, light woods, and modern art. Each has over-the-bed reading lamps and a tea/coffeemaker. Five rooms with balconies face the harbor—three of which sleep three and the rest of which overlook the garden. Guests enjoy use of a cozy traditional parlor and a large sunlit conservatory with wraparound views of the water. Pat and Irene Jones are the innkeepers.

O'Connor's. Scilly, Kinsale, County Cork. ☎ **021/477-3222.** Fax 021/477-3224. www. kinsale.ie/oconnor.htm. 4 units, 2 with shower only. TV TEL. £90–£130 ($126–$182) double. Rates include full Irish breakfast and service charge. AE, MC, V.

At O'Connor's luxury B&B, you'll find an extraordinary standard of comfort and attention to detail. Perched above Kinsale Harbor, with uncompromised views of the town and seascape below, this spacious stone house offers lovely guest rooms, two with semicircular sunrooms, and two with large picture windows, all facing the harbor. The impeccably clean rooms are decorated in peaceful shades of fern green or rose and offer many thoughtful amenities. A several-course breakfast is served on request in your room, and it's no ordinary breakfast: fresh fruit salad, fresh squeezed juices in chilled goblets, smoked salmon, and so forth. Your only disappointment here will be if you've booked only 1 night. Both Kinsale and O'Connor's warrant a little lingering.

Trident. World's End, Kinsale, County Cork. ☎ **021/477-2301.** Fax 021/477-4173. www.tridenthotel.com. 58 units. TV TEL. £80–£130 ($112–$182) double. No service charge. Double room rates include full breakfast. AE, DC, MC, V.

On the harbor at the west end of the marina, this modern three-story hotel has been updated and refurbished in recent years. The rooms feature wide-windowed views of the harbor, with modern light-wood furnishings, floral fabrics, and art deco–style fixtures. Two luxurious suites with views of Kinsale Harbour are available. The Savannah Restaurant overlooks the water; also on the premises is the Fisherman's Wharf Bar. The hotel has a health center with sauna, steam room, gym, and Jacuzzi.

INEXPENSIVE

Castlepark Marina Centre. Castlepark, Kinsale, County Cork. ☎ **021/477-4959.** Fax 021/477-4958. www.activeireland.com. £10–£20 ($14–$28) private double with shower. MC, V.

This is no ordinary hostel; it's a full base of operations for those wanting to spend time on or under the nearby sea. Poised on the southern shore of Kinsale Harbour, and housed in a striking 200-year-old stone-and-slate boatyard, Castlepark Marina is a complex of facilities. It contains a B&B, restaurant, marina, and sea fishing outfitter. It's ideal for those wanting modest, clean, comfortable lodging and excellent no-frills dining at the water's edge. Hostel rooms are available for 2, 4, 6, 8, or 10 persons, all with bunk beds. The flat rate includes linens, duvets, showers, and use of the open

Danabel, Sleaveen, Kinsale, County Cork. ☎ **021/477-4087.** £40–£46 ($56–$64.40) double with private bathroom.

While we stayed in many very nice B&Bs, our favorite, beyond a doubt, was the Danabel. . . . Danabel sits high above the town of Kinsale with a commanding view of the harbor. It is about a 3-minute walk into the center of the town. The house itself is very quaint, with beautiful flowers growing all around, and delightfully decorated both outside and inside. The rooms were very ample in space, very clean, and nicely furnished, and the beds were very comfortable to weary travelers.

—Elizabeth Murphy

kitchen. In cleanliness and taste, this place far surpasses many B&Bs. The dining room serves excellent meals, including the day's catch from the marina's own boats. The center is wheelchair accessible. Ferry service is available from the marina to the center of Kinsale every hour for £1 ($1.40). Eddie and Ann McCarthy have done everything right here. This is a hostel to measure others by.

SELF-CATERING
✪ **Summer Cove Apartment.** Contact Elegant Ireland, ☎ **01/475-1632.** Fax 01/475-1012. www.elegant.ie. 1 apt. TV TEL. £1,000–£1,400 ($1,400–$1,960) per week, including utilities. MC, V.

If you want to enjoy Kinsale and the West Cork coast on your own terms, this luxurious holiday retreat is the perfect home away from home. Based in Summer Cove—a short 20-minute coastal walk from Kinsale—you're both in the midst and secluded, with spectacular views of Kinsale Harbour from the balcony. Every need has been anticipated, so you won't mind holing up here for as long as it takes the sun to return. The self-catering apartment here, much in demand, is often rented out for long stretches of time and may not be readily available. It has two bedrooms, one single and one double with a Jacuzzi bath.

DINING
EXPENSIVE
✪ **The Blue Haven.** 3 Pearse St., Kinsale, County Cork. ☎ **021/477-2209.** Reservations recommended. Main courses at dinner in the bar £5–£14 ($7–$19.60). Restaurant, 3-course dinner from £31 ($43.40); dinner main courses £18–£19.50 ($25.20–$27.30), £35 ($49) for lobster. AE, MC, V. Bar daily 12:15–3pm and 5:30–9:30pm; restaurant daily 7–10pm. SEAFOOD/IRISH.

Of all the restaurants in Kinsale, this one is the benchmark, and it has a huge following. To suit every budget and appetite, there are two menus, one for the top-of-the-line pub food in the atmospheric bar, and a full à la carte menu for the lovely skylit restaurant. The bar food includes smoked seafood quiches, seafood pancakes, oak-smoked salmon, steaks, pastas, and a lamb stew that's to die for. The restaurant offers a wide array of fresh seafood, including a house special of salmon slowly cooked over oak chips. Other specialties include brill and scallop bake, farmyard duck with sage-and-onion stuffing, and local venison (in season). The wines have Irish connections—they come from many of the French wineries that were started by Irish exiles, such as Chateau Dillon, McCarthy, Barton, Kirwan, Lynch, and Phelan. The wines are also on sale in the Blue Haven's wine and cheese shop.

✪ **The Vintage.** 50/51 Main St., Kinsale, County Cork. ☎ **021/477-2502.** Reservations recommended. Main courses £16–£22 ($22.40–$30.80). AE, MC, V. Mar–Apr and mid-Oct to Dec Tues–Sat 6:45–10pm; May to mid-Oct daily 6:45–10:30pm, Sun lunch. CONTINENTAL/ IRISH.

In a charming 200-year-old house in the heart of Kinsale, this landmark restaurant recently changed hands. Raoul and Seiko de Gendre, the new proprietors, have thoroughly redecorated, retaining the restaurant's charm and enhancing its elegance. House specialties include Irish salmon baked in a pastry crust, whole black sole meunière, oven-roasted Barbary duck, and grilled whole lobster. There is also a gourmet daily specials menu enhanced by the expanded new wine list of more than 160 vintages.

MODERATE

Cottage Loft. 6 Main St., Kinsale, County Cork. ☎ **021/477-2803.** Reservations recommended. Main courses £6.50–£18 ($9.10–$25.20); fixed-price dinner £17.50 ($24.50). AE, MC, V. May–Oct daily 5:30–10:30pm; Nov–Apr Tues–Sun 6:30–10:30pm. IRISH/INTERNATIONAL.

In a 200-year-old building in the heart of town, this shop-front restaurant has cottage-style decor with pink linens, antiques, caned chairs, leafy hanging plants, and wooden ceiling beams. The eclectic menu includes such items as delicious rack of lamb, farmyard duck in apple brandy sauce, fillet of lemon sole rolled in smoked salmon, and prawns with lobster sauce. A house specialty is seafood Danielle—salmon stuffed with crab, prawns, and peppers with prawn or nettle sauce.

✪ **Jim Edwards.** Market Quay, off Emmet Place, Kinsale, County Cork. ☎ **021/477-2541.** Reservations recommended for dinner. Dinner main courses £8.95–£16.95 ($12.55–$23.75). AE, MC, V. Daily 10:30am–11pm for bar food. Lunch 12:30–3pm; dinner 6–10:30pm. IRISH.

A classy nautical theme prevails at this pub and restaurant, with colored-glass windows, ships' wheels, sailing-ship art, plush red cushioned seating, and a clock over the door that tells time by letters instead of numbers. In a lane between the Methodist Church and the Temperance Hall, it is known for its good food. Dishes include boneless duck with cassis and red-currant sauce, rack of lamb, king prawns in light basil cream sauce, medallions of monkfish with fresh herbs, a variety of steaks, and a range of vegetarian dishes.

Max's Wine Bar Restaurant. Main St., Kinsale, County Cork. ☎ **021/477-2443.** Reservations recommended. Fixed-price early-bird 3-course dinner £12.50 ($17.50); dinner main courses £10–£16 ($14–$22.40). MC, V. Daily 12:30–3pm and 6:30–10:30pm. Closed Nov–Feb. INTERNATIONAL.

For more than 20 years, this old-world town house with an outdoor patio has been a local favorite for a light snack or a full meal. Now in the hands of Anne Marie Galvin, it promises even better fare. Grilled mussels remain a specialty. Other dishes include goat's-cheese pastas, fresh soups, and roast lamb with lavender sauce. Nonsmoking conservatory seating is available.

PUBS

The Dock. Castlepark, Kinsale, County Cork. ☎ **021/477-2522.**

On the outskirts of town, this pub overlooks the inner harbor. Fishing-themed posters and equipment line the walls, and the windows give views of the water. If the weather is nice, you can step out onto the front deck, with its row of inviting tables and chairs.

The Greyhound. Market Sq., Kinsale, County Cork. ☎ **021/477-2889.**

Photographers are enchanted with the exterior of this pub, with its neat flower boxes, rows of stout barrels, and handmade signs depicting its namesake, the swift Irish racing dog. The interior rooms are cozy and known for hearty pub grub, such as farm-house soups, seafood pancakes, shepherd's pie, and Irish stew.

Lord Kingsale. Main St. and Market Quay, Kinsale, County Cork. ☎ **021/477-2371.**

A touch of elegance prevails at this handsome pub, decorated with lots of polished horse brass and black-and-white Tudor-style trappings. It takes its name (and ancient spelling) from the first Anglo-Norman baron who took charge of this Irish port in 1223. You'll often find evening sing-alongs here, and the soup-and-sandwich pub grub is very good. There is nightly live entertainment in the summer.

The Shanakee. 6 Market St., Kinsale, County Cork. ☎ **021/477-7077.**

With an Anglicized name (derived from the Irish word *seanachie*, which means "storyteller"), this vintage pub is known for its music—traditional tunes and ballads nightly—and recently added a full restaurant.

The Spaniard. Scilly, Kinsale, County Cork. ☎ **021/477-2436.**

Named for Don Juan de Aguila, who rallied his fleet with the Irish in a historic but unsuccessful attempt to defeat the British in 1601, this old pub is full of local sea-faring memorabilia. It has a much-photographed facade, a great location in the hills overlooking Kinsale, and tables outside for snacks on sunny days. It draws large crowds for live music nightly in the summer, and on weekends at other times of the year. On Sunday year-round, there is a jazz-blues session at 5pm.

The White House. End of Pearse St., Kinsale, County Cork. ☎ **021/477-2125.**

With its Georgian facade and distinctive name over the front entrance, this is one pub that tempts many an American visitor to take a photograph. Inside, you will find a popular new bistro, the Antibes Room, with bright decor and a comfortable bar.

2 East Cork

The east end of County Cork is notably more tame than the west. What the region lacks in rugged splendor, it makes up in sophisticated amenities: Ballymaloe House is famed throughout Ireland for its fine cuisine, and Crosshaven holds the world's most venerable yacht club.

Lying 15 miles (24km) east from Cork City is the harbor town of **Cobh** (pro-nounced *Cove* and meaning "haven" in Irish). In the days before airline travel, Cobh was Ireland's chief port of entry, with three or four transatlantic liners calling each week. For thousands of Irish emigrants, particularly during the famine years and in the early part of this century, Cobh was the last sight of Ireland they ever saw. Cobh is still an important, heavily industrialized port. The new visitor attraction, Cobh: The Queenstown Story (see below), tells the city's history, which includes the construction of a magnificent Gothic Revival cathedral, completed in 1915.

The county's major coastal town is **Youghal** (pronounced *Yawl*), 30 miles (48km) east of Cork City, near the Waterford border. A leading beach resort and fishing port, Youghal is loosely associated with Sir Walter Raleigh, who was once the mayor and is said to have planted Ireland's first potatoes here. From a tourist's-eye view, present-day Youghal is a moderately attractive, congested town with a grand stretch of beach just beyond the center.

ESSENTIALS

GETTING THERE   If you're driving from Cork City, take the main Waterford road (N25) east. Exit at R624 for Fota and Cobh, or R632 for Shanagarry and Bally-cotton. Midleton and Youghal have their own signposted exits. To bypass Cork City (a capital idea during rush hour), take the car ferry operated by **Cross River Ferries Ltd.,** Atlantic Quay, Cobh (☎ 021/481-1485). It links Carrigaloe, near Cobh, with Glenbrook, south of Cork City. Ferries run daily from 7:15am to 12:45am; average crossing time is 5 minutes. No reservations are necessary. Fares are payable on the ferry. Cars cost £2 ($2.80) one-way, £3 ($4.20) round-trip, plus 50p (70¢) for each additional passenger.

Irish Rail (☎ 021/450-64777) operates daily train service between Cork City and Cobh via Fota Island. **Bus Eireann** (☎ 021/450-8188) also provides daily service from Cork City to Cobh and other points in East Cork.

VISITOR INFORMATION The **tourist office** is open daily 9:30am to 5:30pm at the Old Yacht Club in the lower harbor at Cobh (☎ 021/481-3301). **Seasonal tourist offices** operate at 4 Main St., Midleton (☎ 021/461-3702), and Market Square, Youghal (☎ 024/92390), from May or June through September.

SEEING THE SIGHTS

Ballymaloe Cookery School. Kinoith, Shanagarry, County Cork. ☎ 021/464-6785. Fax 021/464-6909. www.ballymaloe-cookery-school.ie. 1- to 5-day courses £195–£495 ($273–$693); 12-week certificate courses £4,275–£4,575 ($5,985–$6,405). Accommodations £15.50–£19.50 ($21.70–$27.30) per night extra, or (for the certificate course) £42–£55 ($58.80–$77) per week. Year-round; schedule varies.

Come to Ireland and learn to cook? Yes, if you head to this mecca of fine food, which offers more than 35 different courses a year. The success of the Ballymaloe House restaurant (see "Accommodations & Dining," below) led to the founding of this cooking school more than a dozen years ago. Courses, which range from 1 day to 12 weeks, appeal to all types of amateur and professional chefs, with topics such as bread making, weekend entertaining, hors d'oeuvres, seafood, vegetarian cuisine, family food, barbecue, mushrooms, and Christmas cooking. There are also courses for absolute beginners, on new trends in cooking, and for chef certificates.

The beautiful, extensive **gardens** on the grounds are open to visitors from April to October. New half-day gardening courses are available. Admission to the gardens is £4 ($5.60) adults, family discounts available. The Garden Café, open Wednesday to Sunday 11am to 6pm, serves memorable morning coffee, light lunches, and afternoon tea.

✪ **Cobh: The Queenstown Story.** Cobh Railway Station, Cobh, County Cork. ☎ 021/481-3591. Admission £3.50 ($4.90) adults, £3 ($4.20) seniors and students, £2 ($2.80) children, £10 ($14) family. Feb–Dec daily 10am–6pm. Last admission 5pm. Closed Jan.

This new heritage center commemorates the days when Cobh (then known as Queenstown) was a vital link in transatlantic liner traffic, particularly in the years of high emigration. Because more than 2.5 million people from all over Ireland departed from Cobh for new lives in the United States, Canada, and Australia, the city became synonymous with emigration. In the former railway station, the heritage center tells the story of the city, its harbor, and the Irish exodus in a series of displays, with an audiovisual presentation. The center also offers exhibits that re-create the age of luxury-liner travel and events such as the sinking of the *Titanic* and the *Lusitania*. The center also has a restaurant, a shop, and a new genealogical referral service.

✪ **Fota Island Wildlife Park & Arboretum.** Fota Island, Carrigtwohill, County Cork. ☎ 021/481-2678. www.fotawildlife.ie. Admission £4.80 ($6.70) adults; £2.70 ($3.80) students, seniors, and children; £18 ($25.20) family. Mid-Mar to Sept daily 10am–5pm; Oct–early Mar weekends 11am–5pm. Rail: Cork-Cobh line from Cork City to Fota station.

Ten miles (16km) east of Cork on the Cobh Road, this wildlife park was established in 1983. It's home to rare and endangered types of giraffes, zebras, ostriches, antelopes, cheetahs, flamingos, penguins, and peafowl. The animals and birds roam in natural wildlife settings, with no obvious barriers. Monkeys swing through the trees, and kangaroos, macaws, and lemurs have the run of 40 acres of grassland. Only the cheetahs are behind conventional fencing. Admission includes entrance to the adjacent **Fota Arboretum.** First planted in the 1820s, it contains trees and shrubs from the world's temperate and subtropical regions, from China to South America and the Himalayas. A coffee shop, a tour train, picnic tables, and a gift shop are on the grounds.

The Old Midleton Distillery/Jameson Heritage Centre. Distillery Rd., off Main St., Midleton, County Cork. ☎ **021/461-3594.** Admission £3.95 ($5.55) adults, £1.50 ($2.10) children. Daily 10am–6pm. Tours on request; last tour at 4:45pm.

If you've always wanted to know what makes Irish whiskey different from Scotch, you can find out at this hub of whiskey making, the production center for John Jameson Whiskey and other leading Irish brands. On hand are the largest pot still in the world (it has a capacity of more than 30,000 gallons) and many of the original 1825 structures, which have been meticulously preserved. They include the mill building, maltings, corn stores, still houses, warehouses, kilns, water wheel, and last copper stills manufactured in Ireland.

The modern distillery uses high-tech methods, but the production areas are closed to visitors. If you'd like a taste (so to speak) of the whiskey-making process, the center offers an audiovisual presentation, photographs, working models, and a demonstration. If you'd like a *real* taste, a whiskey tasting follows a tour. The restaurant at the center serves traditional Irish fare for lunch only.

ACCOMMODATIONS & DINING

Aherne's. 163 N. Main St., Youghal, County Cork. ☎ **800/223-6510** from the U.S., or 024/92424. Fax 024/93633. www.ahernes.com. 12 units. TV TEL. £100–£160 ($140–$224) double; £180 ($252) with dinner for 2. No service charge. Rates include full breakfast. AE, DC, MC, V.

In the heart of a busy seaside resort 30 miles (48km) east of Cork City, this cozy inn has long been a landmark because of its first-rate seafood, served in both the restaurant and the nautical-theme pub. The FitzGibbon family, which has owned Aherne's for three generations, has added excellent, spacious guest rooms. Each unit is individually decorated in the finest hotel style, with traditional furnishings, including antiques and designer fabrics, oversized 6-foot-long beds, and extra amenities such as a hair dryer and garment press. Nonsmoking rooms are available.

Dining/Diversions: There are two bars and a library-style sitting room, but the main reason to stay here is to be close to the restaurant. It's known for concentrating on the best of the local catch, including Blackwater salmon, giant prawn tails, rock oysters, and lobsters from the tank. Even the daytime bar food is worth a detour—seafood pies, chowders, crab sandwiches, and crisp salads.

Impressions

Oh, well do I remember the black December day
The landlord and the sheriff came to drive us all away;
They set my roof on fire with their cursed English spleen,
And that's another reason why I left old Skibbereen.

—Anonymous (19th c.)

✪ **Ballymaloe House.** Shanagarry, County Cork. ☎ **800/323-5463** from the U.S., or 021/465-2531. Fax 021/465-2021. www.ballymaloe.ie. 32 units. TEL. £130–£170 ($182–$238) double. No service charge. Rates include full breakfast. AE, DC, MC, V.

Combining a Georgian farmhouse facade with the tower of a 14th-century castle, this ivy-covered enclave of hospitality run by the Allen family is on a 400-acre farm, complete with grazing sheep and cows. Ballymaloe is about 20 miles (23km) southeast of Cork City, less than 2 miles (3.2km) from Ballycotton Bay. The only road sign you'll see is one that alerts you to the importance of four-legged traffic: DRIVE SLOW—LAMBS CROSSING. The guest rooms are furnished in informal, comfortable style, and the inn has a heated outdoor swimming pool, hard tennis courts, a trout pond, a nine-hole golf course, and a craft shop emphasizing local wares. Make no mistake—the high cost of a room here reflects, in part, the mystique of Ballymaloe House, to which you may want to assign your own value.

Dining: The biggest draw is the dining room, a trendsetter for much of Ireland's imaginative cookery. It relies on local seafood and produce, accompanied by fresh vegetables from the garden. The kitchen's success has spawned Ireland's first year-round, country-inn cooking school (see "Attractions," above), and a shelf of Allen family cookbooks.

Bayview Hotel. Ballycotton, Midleton, County Cork. ☎ **800/44-UTELL** from the U.S., or 021/464-6746. Fax 021/464-6075. E-mail: bayhotel@iol.ie. 35 units. TV TEL. £106–£130 ($148.40–$182) double. No service charge. Rates include breakfast. AE, MC, V. Closed Nov–Mar.

If location is everything, this hotel has a lot to offer. Set high on a hillside overlooking Ballycotton Bay, the sprawling three-story property is an ideal waterside retreat, yet is within 25 miles (40km) of Cork City. The hotel offers a spacious lobby, restaurant, and lounge with wide-windowed views of the bay, traditional furnishings, and contemporary art. The rooms have modern light-wood furniture and pastel and sea-toned fabrics, and most have panoramic views.

SELF-CATERING

Myrtleville Oceanside Retreat. Contact ☎ **01/475-1632.** Fax 01/475-1012. www.elegant.ie. 1 self-catering apt, 3 double bedrooms (1 with king-size bed, 2 with queens). TEL. £850–£1,050 ($1,190–$1,470) per week, including utilities. MC, V.

This timbered oceanside retreat—a curiosity in Ireland—offers a touch of Cape Cod and a lot more. It's right on the sea, with stunning views from the expansive deck and living room. Convenient to Cork City, Kinsale, golfing, yachting, deep-sea fishing, and a sandy beach, it's on a small country road, facing the Atlantic at precisely the spot where Victor Hugo worked on *Les Misérables.* Although the house is 80 years old, its decor and furnishings are new and graciously inviting.

3 West Cork

For many, West Cork is Ireland's ultimate destination, not as touristed as Kerry, yet just as alluring. It shares with Kerry the craggy topography and jagged coastline that create many hidden corners and seldom-explored byways. Though amenities for travelers are not always as easily found here as elsewhere in the country, those willing to rough it a little are amply rewarded.

West Cork's most and least favorite son was General Michael Collins, who was both born and murdered here. A hero to some, a traitor to others, the "Big Fella" unquestionably attained greatness. The memory of Collins, widely hailed as "the man who made Ireland," is preserved, in particular, at the Michael Collins Memorial Center and the ambush site near Macroom.

Some of the most beautiful coastal scenery (and severe weather) is on the islands. ✪ **Cape Clear,** home to a bird-watching observatory, is a well-known *gaeltacht:* many schoolchildren come to work on their Gaelic each summer. **Dursey Island,** off the tip of the Beara Peninsula, is accessible by a rickety cable car. **Garinish Island** in Glengarriff is the site of Ilnacullen, an elaborate Italianate garden.

West Cork is known for its enticing towns. A cluster of artists gives **Ballydehob** a creative flair. At the local butcher, colorful drawings of cattle, pigs, and chickens indicate what's available, and a mural on the outside wall of a pub depicts a traditional music session. Other notable enclaves include the yachting town **Schull,** and **Barleycove,** a remote, windswept resort that's the last stop before Mizen Head and the sheer cliffs at the island's southernmost tip.

ESSENTIALS

GETTING THERE   N71 is the main road into West Cork from north and south; from Cork and points east, N22 also leads to West Cork.

Bus Eireann (☎ 021/450-8188) provides daily bus service to the principal towns in West Cork.

VISITOR INFORMATION   Contact the **Skibbereen Tourist Office,** North Street, Skibbereen, County Cork (☎ 028/21766). It is open year-round Monday to Friday 9:15am to 5:30pm, with weekend and extended hours May through September. There are **seasonal tourist offices** in the Square, Bantry (☎ 027/50229); Rossa Street, Clonakilty (☎ 023/33226); and Main Street, Glengarriff (☎ 027/63084), operating from May or June through August or September.

EXPLORING THE REGION

A number of local historians offer **personal and group tours** of archaeological and historical sites in West Cork. Each tour has its own specific focus. A range of tours is offered by Don Healy, Ardagh, Rosscarbery, West Cork (☎ 023/48726, mobile 086/818-2580); and Dolores and Timothy Crowley (☎ 023/46107). Call for details and bookings. The cost begins around £10 ($14) and diminishes as the group increases in size. Currently, on Saturday mornings at 11am in summer, there's a **Michael Collins Tour** at the ambush site (Béal na mBláth, near Macroom), focused on the assassination of Michael Collins. This tour is conducted and booked by Fachtna O'Callaghan, Barley Hill, Rosscarbery (☎ 023/33223, mobile 086/235-7343).

You may also want to explore **Dursey Island,** a barren promontory extending into the sea at the tip of the Beara Peninsula. It offers no amenities for tourists, but the adventuresome will find great seaside walks and a memorable passage from the mainland on Ireland's only operating cable car. To get there, take R571 past Cahermore to its terminus. As you sway wildly in the rickety wooden cable car, reading the text of Psalm 91 (which has kindly been posted to comfort the nervous), you might wonder whether a ferry might not have been a wiser option. It wouldn't. Apparently the channel between island and mainland is often too treacherous to permit regular crossing by boat. There is no lodging on the island, so be sure you know when the last cable car departs for the mainland; for more information on the schedule, call ☎ 027/73017.

✪ **Bantry House.** Bantry, County Cork. ☎ 027/50047. Admission to house and gardens £6 ($8.40) adults, £4.50 ($6.30) seniors, £4 ($5.60) students and children 12–16, free for children under 12. Mar 17–Oct daily 9am–6pm. Closed Nov–Mar 16.

On the edge of the town of Bantry, this house was built around 1750 for the earls of Bantry. It has a mostly Georgian facade with Victorian additions. Its interior contains many items of furniture and objets d'art from all over Europe, including four Aubusson and Gobelin tapestries said to have been made for Marie Antoinette. Bantry

House is the home of Mr. and Mrs. Egerton Shelswell-White, descendants of the third Earl of Bantry. The gardens, with original statuary, are beautifully kept and well worth a stroll. Climb the steps behind the building for a panoramic view of the house, gardens, and Bantry Bay.

In the east and west wings of Bantry House, **bed-and-breakfast rooms** are available, tastefully furnished with reproductions in keeping with the period and style of the house. Prices for bed and breakfast, including a tour of the house and gardens, run £130 to £150 ($182 to $210).

✪ **Creagh Gardens.** On R595, 3½ miles (5.6km) S of Skibbereen, Creagh, Skibbereen, County Cork. ☎ **028/22121.** Admission £3 ($4.20) adults, £2 ($2.80) children. Daily 10am–6pm.

This is one of the most beautifully situated gardens in Ireland, hemmed in by colorful meadows and the waters of an exquisitely picturesque estuary. Serpentine paths wind among magnificent old oaks, maples, and beeches, with occasional prospects through meadow and wood to the weathered facade of Creagh House. In the early summer, the garden is loud with the drone of bees and the blazing colors of the massive rhododendrons, fuchsia, and hydrangeas. A walled garden encloses a greenhouse, vegetable garden, and collection of domestic fowl. Despite its modest size (20-plus acres), this garden contains many surprises and hidden corners, and really shouldn't be missed. If you want to taste some of what you see, a tearoom offers light lunches that feature produce from the walled organic garden.

Derreen Gardens. Signposted 1 mile (1.6km) off R571 in Lauragh, County Kerry. ☎ **064/83588.** Admission £3 ($4.20). Apr–Oct daily 10am–6pm.

This subtropical informal garden is on a site of great natural beauty, a hilly promontory on the breathtaking north coast of the Beara Peninsula. In the late 19th century, the garden was planted with American species of conifer, many of which have become venerable giants. One path follows the sweep of the shoreline through tunnels of rhododendron, while others wind through the dense foliage of the promontory, opening occasionally to a view of the mountains or an entrancing rocky glen. The garden is home to several rarities, most notably the New Zealand tree ferns that flourish in a small glade, among giant blue gum and bamboo.

Drombeg Stone Circle. Off R597 between Rosscarbery and Glandore, County Cork.

This ring of 17 standing stones is the finest example of a stone circle in County Cork. Hills slope gently toward the sea, a short distance away, and the builders could hardly have chosen a more picturesque spot. The circle has been dated to sometime between 153 B.C. and A.D. 127, but little is known about its ritual purpose. Just west of the circle are the remains of two huts and a cooking place; it is thought that heated stones were placed in a water trough (which can be seen adjacent to the huts), and the hot water was used for cooking. The cooking place dates from between A.D. 368 and 608.

✪ **Ilnacullin (Garinish Island).** Glengarriff, County Cork. ☎ **027/63040.** Admission to island £2.50 ($3.50) adults, £1.75 ($2.45) seniors, £1 ($1.40) children and students, £6 ($8.40) family; boat trips £5 ($7) per person. Island Mar and Oct Mon–Sat 10am–4:30pm, Sun 1–5pm; Apr–June and Sept Mon–Sat 10am–6:30pm, Sun 1–7pm; July–Aug Mon–Sat 9:30am–6:30pm, Sun 11am–7pm. Closed Nov–Feb. Last landing 1 hr. before closing.

Officially known as Ilnacullin, but usually referred to as Garinish, this balmy island was once barren. In 1919 it was transformed into an elaborately planned Italianate garden, with classical pavilions and myriad unusual plants and flowers from many continents. It's said that George Bernard Shaw wrote parts of *St. Joan* under the shade of the palm trees.

The island can be reached on a covered ferry operated by **Blue Pool Ferry,** the Blue Pool, Glengarriff (☎ **027/63333**), or another local service. Boats operate every 30 minutes during the island's visiting hours.

Michael Collins Memorial Centre. Signposted off N71, 3½ miles (5.6km) west of Clonakilty, Woodfield, County Cork.

There is very little to see here, unless you bring along your own images of Collins and his childhood, gleaned from biographies such as those by Frank O'Connor and Tim Pat Coogan. The stone farmhouse in which Collins and all his siblings were born was later turned into outbuildings, which survive. The new, larger farmhouse into which his family moved when Michael was 10 was burned to the ground in 1921 by the Black and Tans to punish Britain's public enemy number 1. Only the foundation remains. More a shrine than an "attraction," this is a place for those who revere Collins or hold him in awe. The same is true for the ambush site, where he was assassinated, at Béal na mBláth, near Macroom.

✪ **Mizen Vision.** Mizen Head, County Cork. ☎ **028/35591,** or 028/35115 (Mar–Nov). Fax 028/35603. www.mizenvision.com. Admission £3 ($4.20) adults, £2.25 ($3.15) seniors and students, £1.50 ($2.10) children, free for children under 5, £8.50 ($11.90) family. Mid-Apr to May and Oct daily 10:30am–5pm; July–Sept daily 10am–6pm; Nov to mid-Mar Sat–Sun 11am–4pm. Closed mid-Mar to mid-Apr and June. Take R591 to Goleen, and follow signs for Mizen Head.

At the tip of the Mizen Head Peninsula, the land falls precipitously into the Atlantic breakers in a line of spectacular sea cliffs. A suspension bridge permits access to the Irish Lights signal station, now a visitor center, on a small rock promontory, the southernmost point on the Irish mainland. It affords pinch-yourself-it-can't-be-real views of the surrounding cliffs, open sea, and nearby Three Castle Head. Whales, seals, dolphins, porpoises, and daredevil seabirds contribute to the spectacle. Even on a foggy day, the excellent guided tour and exhibitions make the fascinating history of the Mizen come alive for visitors. On a clear day, this is an absolute must.

For a cliffside walk from the suspension-bridge parking lot, see "Walking" under "Sports & Outdoor Pursuits," below. On the way out to Mizen Head, you'll pass Barleycove Beach, one of the most beautiful beaches in southwest Ireland, and a great place to explore.

1796 Bantry French Armada Exhibition Centre. East Stables, Bantry House, Bantry, County Cork. ☎ **027/51796.** Currently closed until further notice. Details regarding eventual reopening are uncertain at the time of publication.

This center commemorates Bantry Bay's role in the battle of 1796, when a formidable French armada—inspired by Theobold Wolfe Tone and the United Irishmen—sailed from France to expel the British. Almost 50 warships carried nearly 15,000 soldiers to this corner of southwest Ireland. Thwarted by storms and a breakdown in communications, the invasion never came to pass. Ten ships were lost. Too storm-damaged to return to France, the frigate *Surveillante* was scuttled off Whiddy Island, and lay undisturbed for almost 200 years. The remains of that ship are the centerpiece here.

SHOPPING

The Bandon Pottery Shop. St. Finbarr's Place, Bandon, County Cork. ☎ **023/43525.**

Right in the town center, this attractive shop produces a colorful line of hand-thrown tableware, vases, bowls, and other accessories. Paintings, sculpture, and other works of art are on display and for sale. Open Monday to Saturday 9:30am to 1pm and 1:30 to 5:30pm.

Southern Exposure: An Excursion to Cape Clear Island

Cape Clear Island, 8 miles (13km) off the mainland, is the southernmost inhabited point in Ireland. The country's islands are part of its last frontier, the last bits of rugged untamed splendor. Even Cape Clear is struggling to preserve the balance of beauty and livelihood that allows remote settlements to remain both remote and settled. This place can be bleak, with a craggy coastline and no trees to break the rush of sea wind, but that very barrenness appeals to many for its stark beauty, rough and irregular, but not without solace and grace. In early summer, wildflowers brighten the landscape, and in October, passerine migrants, some on their way from North America and Siberia, fill the air. Seabirds are present in abundance during the nesting season, especially from July to September. At any time, Cape Clear is unforgettable.

The first step to enjoying the island is reaching it. The ***Naomh Ciarán II*** offers passenger-only ferry service year-round, seas permitting. In the highest season (July and Aug), the *Naomh Ciarán II* leaves Baltimore Monday to Saturday at 11am, 2:15pm, and 7pm, and Sunday at noon, 2:15pm, 5pm, and 7pm; return service from Cape Clear departs Monday to Saturday at 9am and 6pm, and Sunday at 11am, 1pm, 4pm, and 6pm. Service is always subject to the seas and is more limited off-season. The passage takes 45 minutes, and a round-trip ticket costs £8 ($11.20). For inquiries, contact Captain Conchúr O'Driscoll (☎ **028/39135**).

Summer service is also available aboard ***Karycraft*** from Schull, departing Schull daily in July and August at 10am, 2:30pm, and 4:30pm; and departing Cape Clear at 11am, 3:30pm, and 5:30pm. In June and September, service is limited to one crossing daily, departing Schull at 2:30pm and Cape Clear at 5:30pm. The passage takes 45 minutes. For inquiries, contact Captain Kieran Molloy (☎ **028/28138**).

Once you're on Cape Clear, there are a number of things to see, including birds galore, seals, dolphins, the occasional whale, ancient "marriage stones," and

Courtmacsherry Ceramics. Main St., Courtmacsherry, County Cork. ☎ **023/46239.**

Overlooking the sea, this studio and shop offers an array of porcelain animals, birds, butterflies, and tableware, all inspired by the flora and fauna of West Cork. Visitors are welcome to watch potter Peter Wolstenholme at work on new creations. Open mid-March to September Monday to Saturday 10am to 6pm.

Prince August Ltd. Kilnamartyra, Macroom, County Cork. ☎ **026/40222.** Jan–May Mon–Fri 9am–5pm; Jun–Sept Mon–Sat 9am–5:30pm; Oct–Dec Mon–Fri 9am–5pm.

Prince August is Ireland's only toy-soldier factory. The shop produces and displays a huge collection of metal miniatures based on J. R. R. Tolkien's classic books *The Hobbit* and *The Lord of the Rings.* Factory tours are available. It's off the main N22 road, northwest of Kinsale.

SPORTS & OUTDOOR PURSUITS

BEACHES   Barleycove Beach offers vast expanses of pristine sand and a fine view out toward the Mizen Head cliffs; despite the trailer park and holiday homes on the far side of the dunes, large parts of the beach never seem to get crowded. Take R591 to Goleen, and follow signs for Mizen Head. There is a public parking lot at the Barleycove Hotel.

a goat farm offering courses on everything you ever wanted to know (about goats). Don't miss the hauntingly spectacular castle ruins on the island's western shore.

There's also a lot to do apart from hiking and sightseeing. **Cléire Lasmuigh,** Cape Clear Island Adventure Center (☎ 028/39198; e-mail: lasmuigh@iol.ie), offers an array of outdoor programs, from snorkeling and sea kayaking to hill walking and orienteering. Instruction or accompanied sessions are available by the hour, day, or week. For example, prices for a 5-day sea-kayaking package (including meals, housing, instruction, and equipment rental) start at £179 ($250.60). Coastal cruises—for sea angling, scuba diving, or bird watching—are the specialty of **Ciarán O'Driscoll** (☎ and fax **028/39153**). There are no plans for a shopping mall, but you will enjoy the local art and crafts and books in Harpercraft and the Back Room in Cotter's Yard, North Harbour, as well as the nearby pottery shop. While you're at it, pick up a copy of Chuck Kruger's *Cape Clear Island Magic.* There's no better introduction to the wonder of this place.

Modest hostel, B&B, and self-catering accommodations are available by the day, week, or month. The island's **An Óige Youth Hostel** (☎ 028/39198) is open April through November. Most B&Bs are open year-round. They include **Fáilte** (contact Eleanór Uí Drisceoil, ☎ 028/39135); and **Ard na Gaoith** (contact Eileen Leonard, ☎ **028/39160**). For self-catering cottages by the day or week, contact **Ciarán O'Driscoll** (☎ **028/39135**). To drop anchor, the **Southernmost House** (see "Self-Catering," below) is without parallel. You can't miss the town's three pubs and two restaurants, which will keep you well fortified. (Off the record, the fruit scones baked and served at Cistin Chléire on North Harbour are the best I've had anywhere.)

Cape Clear has an extensive Web site (**www.oilean-chleire.ie**), which I recommend exploring.

✪ BICYCLING The **Mizen Head, Sheep's Head, and Beara peninsulas** offer fine roads for cycling, with great scenery and few cars. The Beara Peninsula is the most spectacular; the other two are less likely to be crowded with tourists during peak season. The loop around Mizen Head, starting in Skibbereen, is a good 2- to 3-day trip, and a loop around the Beara Peninsula from Bantry, Glengarriff, or Kenmare is at least 3 days at a casual pace.

In Skibbereen, 18- and 21-speed bicycles can be rented from **Roycroft's Stores** (☎ **028/21235;** e-mail: roycroft@iol.ie); prices start at £35 ($40) per week. If you call ahead, you can reserve a lightweight mountain bike with toe clips at no extra cost—an enormous advantage over the leaden, battleshiplike bicycles rented at most stores. One-way riding from Skibbereen to Killarney or Kenmare can be arranged for an additional £15 ($21).

✪ BIRD WATCHING Cape Clear Island is the prime birding spot in West Cork, and one of the best places in Europe to watch seabirds and passerine migrants (see the box earlier in this section). The best time for seabirds is July to September, and October is the busiest month for passerines (and for bird-watchers, who flock to the island). There is a bird observatory at the **North Harbour,** with a warden in residence from March to November, and accommodations for bird-watchers; to arrange a stay, write to **Kieran Grace,** 84 Dorney Court, Shankhill, County Dublin. **Ciarán O'Driscoll** (☎ 028/39153), who operates a B&B on the island, also runs boat trips for bird-watchers, and has a keen eye for vagrants and rarities.

DIVING The **Baltimore Diving & Watersports Centre,** Baltimore, County Cork (☎ 028/20300), provides equipment and boats to certified divers for exploring the many shipwrecks, reefs, and caves in this region. The cost is £30 ($42) per dive with equipment. Various 2-hour to 15-day certified PADI courses are available for all levels of experience. For example, beginners can take a 2- to 3-hour snorkeling course for £12 to £15 ($16.80 to $21), or a scuba-diving course for £20 to £30 ($28 to $42); experienced divers can take the 2-week PADI instructor course.

FISHING The West Cork Coast is known for its many shipwrecks, which are quickly taken over by all manner of marine life after they hit the ocean floor. Wreck fishing is popular all along the Irish coast, and this is one of the best places for it. **Mark and Patricia Gannon** of Woodpoint House, Courtmacsherry (☎ 023/46427), offer packages that include bed and breakfast in their idyllic stone farmhouse and a day's sea angling aboard one of their two new Aquastar purpose-built fishing boats. A day's fishing costs £30 ($42) per person. Boats holding up to 12 people can be chartered for £230 to £250 ($322 to $350) per day, including a qualified skipper. For sea angling in Baltimore, contact **Michael Walsh** (☎ 028/20352) or **Kieran Walsh** at the Algiers Inn (☎ 028/20145).

✪ **KAYAKING** With 100 islands in the vicinity of Baltimore, numerous inviting inlets, and a plethora of sea caves, the coast of West Cork is a sea kayaker's paradise. **Lough Ine** offers warm, still waters for beginners, a tidal rapid for the intrepid, and access to a nearby headland riddled with caves that demand exploration. ✪ **Jim Kennedy** (☎ 028/33002; e-mail: atlanticseakayaking@eircom.net) offers day trips year-round. Jim is a top competitor in flat-water racing and an expert sea kayaker. With his knowledgeable, friendly instruction, even children and rank beginners soon feel at ease in a sea kayak. He operates from Maria's Schoolhouse (see "Accommodations," below), near the seaside village of Union Hall; the charge is £18 ($25.20) for 2 hours, £40 ($56) for a full day. The Schoolhouse is a fabulous base from which to explore the nearby coast by sea kayak. Jim also offers a "Fool-moon Paddle" (on the full moon and the 3 days before and after) for £25 ($35) per person. He leads overnight camping trips for £65 ($91) per person, supplying everything but sleeping bags. There is a minimum of four campers for these trips, so be sure to call ahead.

SAILING The **Glenans Sailing Club** was founded in France and has two centers in Ireland, one of which is in Baltimore Harbour. The centers provide weeklong courses at all levels, using dinghies, cruisers, catamarans, or windsurfers; prices are £310 to £344 ($434 to $481.60). The living facilities are spartan, with dorm-style accommodations and meals cooked by participants. The clientele is mostly middle-aged and younger, from Ireland and the Continent. Day sailing is available in Baltimore on Saturdays in June, July, and August for £35 ($49) per person; call ☎ 028/20154 or fax 028/20312 for advance booking.

WALKING One of the most beautiful coastal walks in West Cork begins along the banks of **Lough Ine,** the largest saltwater lake in Europe. Connected to the sea by a narrow isthmus, the lake is in a lush valley of exceptional beauty. To get there, follow signs for Lough Ine along R595 between Skibbereen and Baltimore; there is a parking lot at the northwest corner of the lake. The wide trail proceeds gradually upward from the parking lot through the woods on the west slope of the valley, with several viewpoints toward the lake and the sea beyond. Once you reach the hilltop, there is a sweeping view of the coast from Mizen Head to Galley Head. Walking time to the top and back is about 1½ hours.

At the mesmerizingly high cliffs of **Mizen Head,** it was once possible, for the sure of foot and steady of spirit, to explore the surrounding heights. No more. Access to the cliffs is limited to the suspension bridge leading to the "Mizen Vision" lighthouse. No ticket or admission is required for access to the bridge.

Near Lauragh on the Beara Peninsula is the abandoned town of **Cummingeera,** at the base of a cliff in a wild, remote valley. The walk to the village gives you a taste for the rough beauty of the Caha Mountains, and a sense for the lengths to which people in pre-famine Ireland would go to find a patch of arable land. To get to the start of the walk, take the road posted for Glanmore Lake south from R571; the road is ⁸/₁₀ mile (1.3km) west of the turnoff for Healy Pass. Follow the Glanmore Lake road ⁶/₁₀ mile (1km), then turn right at the road posted for "stone circle"; continue 1⅓ miles (2.1km) to the point at which the road becomes dirt, and park on the roadside. From here, there is no trail—simply walk up the valley to its terminus, about 1¼ miles (2km) away, where the ruins of a village hug the cliff's base. Where the valley is blocked by a headland, take the route around to the left, which is less steep. Return the way you came; the whole walk is 2½ miles (4km), is moderately difficult, and takes about 2 hours.

An easy seaside walk on the **Beara Peninsula** begins at Dunboy Castle, just over a mile west of Castletownbere on R572; this stretch of trail is part of the O'Sullivan Beara trail, which may eventually extend from Castletownbere to Leitrim. You can park your car along the road, by the castellated gatehouse, or drive up to the castle; the entry fee is 50p (70¢) for pedestrians, £2 ($2.80) for a car. The castle is a ruined 19th-century manor house overlooking the bay, with some graceful marble arches spanning the grand central hall. Just down the road are the sparse ruins of a medieval fortress. Beyond, the trail continues to the tip of Fair Head through overarching rhododendrons, with fine views across to Bear Island. A walk from the gatehouse parking lot to the tip of Fair Head and back takes about 2 hours.

The **Sheep's Head Way** makes a 55-mile (89km) loop, and incorporates numerous day loops. I recommend buying the *Guide to the Sheep's Head Way,* available in most local stores and tourist offices, which combines history, poetry, and topography in a fantastic introduction to the region. In the 17th century, the Sheep's Head Peninsula was described as "being all rocky and frequented only by eagles and birds—never to be inhabited by reason of the rough incommodities." It still is a rough place, and you won't find many tourists in its more remote reaches. There are treasures to be found here, but you might have to work a little harder to unearth them here than in regions long since "discovered."

One of Ireland's most beautiful spots, **Gougane Barra** (which means "St. Finbar's Cleft") is a still, dark, romantic lake a little northeast of the Pass of Keimaneigh, 15 miles (24km) northeast of Bantry off T64 (also well signposted on the Macroom-Glengarriff road). The River Lee rises in these deeply wooded mountains, and St. Finbar founded a monastery here, supposedly on the small island connected by a causeway to the mainland. Nothing remains of the saint's 6th-century community. The island now holds a tiny chapel and eight small circular cells, dating to the early 1700s, as well as a modern chapel. Today Gougane Barra is a national forest park, and there are signposted walks and drives through the wooded hills. There's a small admission charge per car to enter the park.

WINDSURFING   Lessons and equipment rental are available at the **Courtmac-sherry Leisure Center** (☎ **023/46177**); rates are £8 ($11.20) per hour. There is a sheltered beach in town where beginners can get started, and another beach that's good for wave jumping nearby.

ACCOMMODATIONS

EXPENSIVE

Ballylickey Manor House. Bantry-Glengarriff Rd. (N71), Ballylickey, County Cork. ☎ **800/ 323-5463** from the U.S., or 027/50071. Fax 027/50124. 11 units. TV TEL. £100–£200 ($140–$280) double. Service charge 10%. Rates include full breakfast. AE, CB, DC, MC, V. Closed mid-Nov to mid-Mar. Free parking.

Overlooking Bantry Bay on 10 acres of lawns and gardens, this well-established retreat offers a choice of accommodations in a 300-year-old manor house or in modern wooden cottages that surround the swimming pool. The units in the main house have a separate sitting room. All are decorated with country-style furnishings. This inn has an international ambience, thanks to the influence of its owners, the French-Irish Graves family, and a largely European clientele.

✪ **Longueville House.** Killarney road (N72), Mallow, County Cork. ☎ **800/323-5463** from the U.S., or 022/47156. Fax 022/47459. www.longuevillehouse.ie. 22 units. TV TEL. £120–£225 ($168–$315) double. Rates include full breakfast. Dinner £33 ($46.20); 7-course tasting menu £46 ($64.40). Service charge 10%. AE, DC, MC, V. Closed mid-Dec to early Mar. Self/valet parking.

No discussion of the County Cork area would be complete without mentioning Longueville House. Geographically, it's hard to classify—it's not really in West Cork, but it's northwest of Cork City. Built about 1720 and situated on a 500-acre farmland estate with its own winery, this convivial country retreat is the pride and joy of the O'Callaghan family. It produces a fine white wine, unique in this land known for its beers and whiskies, and is a welcoming and homey place to stay, convenient to both Cork City and West Cork. Guest rooms are furnished in old-world style, with family heirlooms and period pieces, and most have bucolic views of the gardens, grazing pastures, or vineyards. Nonsmoking rooms are available, and all guest rooms have orthopedic beds.

Dining: Most of all, this house is distinguished by its award-winning restaurant, the Presidents' Room, adorned with portraits of Ireland's past heads of state. The menu offers produce and vegetables from the hotel's farm and gardens. In the summer, meals are also served in a festive, skylit Victorian conservatory.

MODERATE

Baltimore Harbour Hotel. Signposted off R595 in Baltimore, County Cork. ☎ **028/ 20361.** Fax 028/20466. www.bhrhotel.ie. 64 units. TV TEL. £72–£100 ($100.80–$140) double; suites available for an additional £20–£40 ($28–$56). Rates include full Irish breakfast and service charge. Packages available. AE, DC, MC, V. Free parking.

Nearly every room in this strategically placed harbor hotel has a lovely view. The common rooms—bar, garden room, and Clipper Restaurant—are fresh, bright, and inviting, with a modern nautical feel. The guest rooms are quite comfortable, with extraordinary views of the harbor and mountainous coastline. Rooms 216 and 217 are especially spacious, at no extra cost. A host of weekend, multiple-night, and B&B-and-dinner packages offer special rates. Some nonsmoking rooms are available. Pub food is available in the Bar and Garden Room, and the Clipper Restaurant serves full fixed-price and à la carte dinners daily. The hotel also features a new leisure center, 18 self-catering apartments, and a children's summer activities program.

Kilbrittain Castle. 6 miles (9.7km) from Bandon, 35 miles (56km) from Cork airport, Kilbrittain, County Cork. ☎ **023/49601.** Fax 023/49702. E-mail: timcob@iol.ie. 5 units. £90

($126) double. Rates include full Irish breakfast but not VAT. Family discounts available. No credit cards.

Kilbrittain Castle—built by the grandson of Brian Boru, High King of Ireland, in 1035—is the oldest habitable castle in Ireland. "Habitable" hardly says it, however. Kilbrittain is very much lived in by the Cahil-O'Briens, who followed a long line of Irish chieftains, Norman invaders, Cromwellian troops, and English planters and made this their family home. Tim and Sylvia Cahil-O'Brien insist that Kilbrittain is not a hotel, and indeed it is not. One climb up the steep, winding tower staircase to the great hallway above, and then another to your room, is enough to convince you that neither Disney nor Sheraton had anything to do with this. It's best to leave your suitcases and your expectations below. The history in these walls is the history of Ireland, and Tim's stories will soon make the stones speak. Spending the night here—in surprising comfort and absolute peace—is a unique experience. The rooms (all non-smoking) are spacious, the views enchanting, and the breakfast offerings generous. Tim will gladly book your dinner in one of many nearby restaurants. Follow his advice, and you won't be disappointed.

✪ **Sea View.** Bantry-Glengarriff road (N71), Ballylickey, County Cork. ☎ **800/447-7462** from the U.S., or 027/50073. Fax 027/51555. 17 units. TV TEL. £90–£110 ($126–$154) double. Service charge 10%. Rates include full breakfast. AE, MC, V. Closed mid-Nov to mid-Mar. Free parking.

This handsome, comfortable, aptly named hotel is homey and full of heirlooms, antiques, and lots of tall windows. The cheerily decorated rooms are individually furnished, with orthopedic beds, traditional dark woods, and designer fabrics. In 2000 new bedrooms and suites were in the works. The establishment is best known for proprietor Kathleen O'Sullivan's award-winning cuisine. Besides the restaurant, there are also a cozy lounge bar and an outdoor patio. Sea View is off the main road, 3 miles (4.8km) from Bantry.

The Westlodge Hotel. Off Bantry-Glengarriff road (N71), Bantry, County Cork. ☎ **027/ 50360.** Fax 027/50438. www.westlodgehotel.ie. 95 units. TV TEL. £76–£115 ($106.40–$161) double. Rates include full breakfast and service charge. AE, DC, MC, V.

On a hillside overlooking Bantry Bay, this modern three-story hotel is surrounded by gardens and woodlands. A new series of nature trails was established around the hotel in 1999. The public areas and guest rooms are bright and airy, enhanced by wide windows, light-wood furnishings, and colorful Irish fabrics. Nonsmoking rooms are available. The hotel has a restaurant, a tavern, an indoor heated swimming pool, tennis and squash courts, a sauna, and a gym. Westlodge specializes in family holidays and offers organized activities June through August.

INEXPENSIVE

✪ **Ballinatona Farm.** 3 miles (4.8km) out of Millstreet on the Macroom road, Millstreet, County Cork. ☎ **029/70213.** Fax 029/70940. 6 units. TV. £40 ($56) double. Rates include full breakfast. Self-catering cabins £18 ($25.20) 1 night; £45 ($63) 3 nights; £70 ($98) per week, 4 beds. 25% discount for children under 12 sharing B&B with parents. MC, V. Closed Dec 15–Jan 5. Free parking.

Like the region that surrounds it, this place is a little-known treasure, just far enough off the beaten track to be spared the crowds that congest much of the southwest during the summer. True, the landscape isn't wild and rugged like that of the West Cork coast; its beauty is gentler, and requires time to be discovered. The energetic host, Jytte Storm, knows the region well—her love for this land and excitement over its hidden delights are truly infectious. Even if you've chosen this as a base for exploring points farther west, you'll probably find yourself spending more time than expected within walking distance of the house. Just a 15-minute walk brings you to the stunning valley that holds Coomeenatrush waterfall at its head, while longer walks take you along the ridgeline of the surrounding hills. The house is tucked into the hillside, high above the valley floor, and commands magnificent views. A modern addition has been designed to take full advantage of the site, and all but one room command striking vistas. The second-floor front room, reached by a spiral staircase, offers a breathtaking view, with glass walls on three sides.

Dunauley House. Seskin, Bantry, County Cork. ☎ and fax **027/50290.** www.dunauley.com. 5 units. £44–£60 ($61.60–$84) double. Rates include full breakfast. No credit cards. Closed Oct–Apr.

Rosemary McAuley's home appeals to the senses—the feel of starched white linen sheets, the extraordinary view from the sitting room across Bantry Bay to the Beara Peninsula, and the taste of Rosemary's award-winning breakfast to look forward to in the morning. The modern bungalow occupies a spectacular hillside site, and from the sitting room you can calmly survey the whole region. All the bedrooms are meticulously maintained, and each is equipped with a double and a twin bed. The upstairs rooms are somewhat smaller than those below, and face the rear carpark. Downstairs rooms do have a view, obstructed only by the lower level of the carpark. A lower-level suite includes a well-stocked kitchen with washer/dryer, a small sitting room, and a spacious bedroom—this can be rented with breakfast by the night for £60 ($84), or on a weekly self-catering basis for £200 to £300 ($280 to $420), depending on season. No smoking.

Fortview House. On R591 from Durrus toward Goleen, Gurtyowen, Toormore, Goleen, County Cork. ☎ **028/35324.** 5 units. £50 ($70) double. Rates include full breakfast. No credit cards. Closed Nov–Feb. Free parking.

This winner of the 1996 Irish Agritourism Award for the best B&B in the south boasts pristine country-style rooms, with antique pine furniture, wood floors, iron beds, and fresh crisp linens. Beamed ceilings and a warm color palette add to the comfortable feeling, and the spacious, inviting sitting room, equipped with tea and coffee facilities and an honor-system bar, completes the welcome. Violet Connell's extensive breakfasts are legendary, with seven varieties of fresh-squeezed juices jostling for space on a menu that includes pancakes, kippers, smoked salmon, and eggs prepared any way. There is now a self-catering cottage for six available on the Fortview grounds.

Galley Cove House. 1½ miles (2.4km) west of Crookhaven, County Cork. ☎ and fax **028/35137.** 4 units, 3 with private bathroom. TV. £38–£45 ($53.20–$63) double. Rates include full breakfast. MC, V. Closed Jan–Feb.

Maureen Newman's sparkling new seafront B&B offers a quiet haven with grand views of the sea and Fastnet lighthouse. Floral patchwork quilts and fresh flowers from the garden accent the pine floors and simple country furniture. A 20-minute walk in one direction takes you to Crookhaven (where O'Sullivans pub offers some of the best chowder I've ever had), and a similar walk in the opposite direction leads to a stunningly beautiful white-sand beach. Maureen's friendly, gracious manner will make you feel right at home. Beds are firm, and there is a strict nonsmoking policy for the entire house.

Glebe Country House. Balinadee (off Balinadee center), Bandon, County Cork. ☎ **021/4778294.** Fax 021/4778456. http://indigo.ie/~glebehse/. 4 units, 2 with shower only. TEL. £50–£70 ($70–$98) double. Rates include full Irish breakfast and service charge. 3 self-catering units. TV TEL. £220–£440 ($308–$616) per week. MC, V.

Glebe Country House was built in 1690 as a rectory and is currently the gracious home of Jill Bracken. The charming rooms, each unique and comfortable, enjoy views of the rose and herb gardens that wreath the house. A fireplace and piano accent the peaceful living room. The enticing breakfast possibilities might include waffles, scrambled eggs with rosemary shortbread, or "cheesy French toast," a Glebe House first. The spacious dining room provides a lovely setting for candlelit five-course dinners partly drawn from the house's garden (£18.50/$25.90; book before noon). Bring your own wine.

Comfortable self-catering is also available in the Coach House apartments behind the main house. The ground-floor, two-bedroom garden apartment sleeps five, with a double and single bed in one room and twin beds in the other. It is equipped with all essentials, and the open living-dining-kitchen area is decorated in simple country-cottage style. The especially pleasing one-bedroom loft apartment sleeps five, with a double and single bed in one room and a pull-out sofa in the living room. A compact kitchen has all you need to prepare substantial meals. Both apartments have linens, and each has a private patio-garden. A new chalet in the garden, Beech Lodge, is available for up to six guests.

The Heron's Cove. Signposted in the center of Goleen, County Cork. ☎ **028/35225.** Fax 028/35422. www.westcorkweb.ie/heron/. E-mail: suehill@tinet.ie. 5 units. TV TEL. £38–£50 ($53.20–$70) double. Rates include full breakfast. AE, DC, MC, V. Children under 12 (except infants) not accepted.

Most locals know the Heron's Cove as a restaurant (see below), but it's also an inviting place to stay. Its three sea-view rooms, with balconies, have particular appeal; in no. 3, you can easily imagine at high tide that you're aboard a ship. The rooms are comfortably furnished with real furniture, and the atmosphere of the entire B&B is so friendly as to be almost familial. Satellite TV, coffee and tea facilities, and hair dryers are provided in every room. While you're here, be sure to enjoy the galley below and explore the adjacent antiques and curios shop, with more than its share of remarkable items.

✪ Lettercollum House. Timoleague, County Cork. ☎ **023/46251.** Fax 023/46270. www.lettercollum.ie. 9 units. TEL. £40–£60 ($56–$84) double. No service charge. AE, MC, V. Closed Jan–Feb. Free parking.

This elegant Victorian home offers comfortable, modest, inviting quarters. Some of the bright rooms have great views of the surrounding hills. A walled garden provides organic vegetables for the restaurant. The surroundings are idyllic, and the pervading atmosphere is one of tranquillity. No one should stay here without sampling the extraordinary food from the in-house restaurant (see "Dining," below). Lettercollum House is a real treasure.

✪ Maria's Schoolhouse. Cahergal, Union Hall, County Cork. ☎ **028/33002.** Fax 028/33002. E-mail: mariasschoolhouse@tinet.ie. 8 units. £24–£34 ($33.60–$47.60) double; dorm £8 ($11.20) per person. Dinner £15 ($21). No service charge. MC, V. Closed Jan to mid-Mar.

The austere, handsome fieldstone exterior of this renovated schoolhouse gives way to a nontraditional bright purple and pink interior. The rooms are very comfortable, and each has its own character. A sunny, spacious hall is the scene of innovative dinners that focus on ethnic and vegetarian cuisine, and elaborate breakfasts. Every other Saturday there is an acoustic music concert with dinner. These events feature top musicians and are well worth attending. Maria Hoare is an amiable and outgoing host, as is Jim Kennedy, who runs his excellent sea-kayaking program from here. You can also rent a bicycle for £7 ($9.80) a day.

Rock Cottage. Barnatonicane, Schull, County Cork. ☎ **028/35538.** 3 units. TV. £50 ($70) double. Rates include full breakfast. Dinner from £22 ($30.80). MC, V. 7 miles (11km) from Durrus on R591.

This new B&B offers a wonderfully secluded, relaxing retreat in what was once Lord Bandon's hunting lodge. The spacious guest rooms in the tastefully restored Georgian building combine ample shares of elegance and comfort. But we've saved the best news for last. Your host, Barbara Klötzer, used to be the head chef at Blair's Cove and is now able to focus her culinary wizardry on a mere handful of lucky guests.

✪ **Rolf's Holiday Hostel.** ⅓ mile (0.5km) off R595, signposted just outside Baltimore center, Baltimore, County Cork. ☎ and fax **028/20289.** £13 ($18.20) per person double room; £9.50 ($13.15) per person family room; £8.50 ($11.90) per person in dorm; £3.50 ($4.90) per person for camping. MC, V.

Rolf's is a long-established, award-winning, family-run hostel that simply sets the standard. Beautifully situated on Baltimore Hill overlooking the harbor and the Mizen peninsula, this appealing cut-stone complex of buildings—somehow alpine, with steep lofts and wide beams—offers an array of lodging and dining options. All guests have access to the open self-catering kitchen, which is unlikely to compete with Rolf's Cafe Art and Restaurant. The "Art" here is not only the art of cooking, but the rotating exhibits of contemporary Irish painting and sculpture selected by Frederika Haffner, Rolf's daughter, a fine sculptor. Both cafe and restaurant are open daily from 8am to 9:30pm, providing excellent value across their impressive menus and wine lists. Johannes Haffner, Rolf's son, grew up here and takes great pride in offering the finest in hostel hospitality.

SELF-CATERING

✪ **Ahakista.** Contact Elegant Ireland. ☎ **01/475-1632.** Fax 01/475-1012. www.elegant.ie. 1 cottage. TEL. £650 ($910) per week. MC, V.

Simplicity, charm, and an alluring location on the Sheepshead Peninsula (the least touristed of Cork's three peninsulas) make this recently restored cottage a magnificent getaway. It's a short walk to the two-pub farming and fishing village of Ahakista, which is not why you'd be here. The old-fashioned cottage enjoys fine views of Dunmanus Bay and is surrounded by 60 miles (97km) of marked walking paths along the wild coastline, which Seamus Heaney has described as "water and ground in their extremity." The cottage has two bedrooms, one double and one twin.

Baltimore Holiday Homes. Off R595 just before Baltimore center, Baltimore, County Cork. Contact Home From Home Holidays, 26/27 Rossa St., Clonakilty, County Cork. ☎ **023/33110.** Fax 023/333131. E-mail: homefromhome@wct.ie. 32 cottages. TV TEL. £200–£500 ($280–$700) per week. 2-day rates available in low and mid-season. MC, V.

These well-established holiday cottages form an attractive cluster safely set back from the road and overlooking a lovely inlet. They are best suited to families wanting to settle in for a week's self-contained seaside and island-hopping holiday. Tennis courts and pitch-and-putt are offered, and the new leisure center of the nearby Baltimore Harbour Hotel is accessible for a fee. The cottages are bright and inviting, with white walls and pine furniture, and each has an open fireplace and three bedrooms. They are fully equipped, including washer, dryer, and microwave. Baltimore's two small food shops are minutes away on foot, and there is bus service to Skibbereen.

✪ **Blair's Cove House.** Barley Cove Rd., Durrus, County Cork. ☎ **027/61127.** Fax 027/61487. E-mail: blairscove@eircom.net. 4 apts, 2 cottages. £165–£750 ($231–$1,050) per week. B&B £30–£70 ($42–$98) per person, per night. B&B rate includes breakfast. MC, V.

Blair's Cove House is a beautifully restored 250-year-old rectory and small farm at the head of Dunmanus Bay. The famed restaurant (see below) shares the same complex and exquisite setting with two seasoned though relatively recent cottages. Altogether there are four apartments and two cottages to choose from, accommodating couples, families, or groups of up to eight. All exhibit the same discerning fine taste. This is self-catering at its best—your host has not only anticipated every need, but considered many a whim—in immediate proximity to some of the finest cuisine in Ireland.

Casino Cottage. 10 miles (16km) from Kinsale on the coast road (R600), Coulmain Bay, Kilbrittain, County Cork. ☎ **023/49944.** Fax 023/49945. 1 2-room cottage, with shower only. £160–£260 ($224–$364) per week. MC, V. Closed Feb to mid-Mar.

Nearby Casino House Restaurant operates this snug getaway along a rural road in a rolling country landscape only a 15-minute walk from the ocean beach. It shares the restaurant's simple, stylish decor. White walls, high ceilings, and an open stone fireplace (in the living room) combine to provide both space and coziness.

✪ **The Southernmost House.** Glen West, Cape Clear, County Cork. ☎ and fax **028/39157.** http://indigo.ie/~ckstory/. E-mail: ckstory@indigo.ie. 1 cottage. TV. £150–£390 ($210–$546) per week. No credit cards; personal checks accepted. Discounts for long-term rentals.

This exquisitely situated cottage is the southernmost dwelling on the southernmost inhabited Irish island, Cape Clear. Quite simply, it defines the word *getaway.* Five years were devoted to the restoration of this centuries-old traditional island cottage, and it shows. Everything was done right. The exposed stone walls, pine ceilings and floors, multiple skylights, and simple, tasteful furnishings make it a most pleasing and comfortable nook, and the views from virtually every window are stunning. If Cape Clear had a king, this is where he would live. Instead, Christy Moore, among others, has made a point of dropping anchor here. It's cozy enough for a love nest, and spacious enough for a family of six (it has three bedrooms). If it rains—and this has been known to happen on the "Cape"—the massive stone fireplace is the perfect antidote.

DINING
EXPENSIVE

✪ **Blair's Cove.** Barley Cove Rd., Durrus, County Cork. ☎ **027/61127.** Fax 027/61487. Reservations required. Dinner with starter buffet £30 ($42); buffet and dessert £22 ($30.80). MC, V. April–June and Sept–Oct Tues–Sat 7–9:30pm; July–Aug Mon–Sat 7–9:30pm. INTERNATIONAL.

A grassy country lane leads you to this romantic restaurant overlooking Dunmanus Bay, less than 10 miles (16km) from Bantry. Owners Philip and Sabine de Mey have converted a stone barn with a 250-year-old Georgian courtyard and terrace into one of the best dining experiences in southwest Ireland. Amid high ceilings, stone walls, open fireplaces, and contemporary art, each meal starts with a buffet of appetizers (perhaps salmon fumé, prawns, oysters, or mousse), a display large enough to satisfy some dinner appetites. If you decide to have an entree, then rack of lamb, grilled rib of beef, or monkfish fillet flambéed in Pernod will appear. For dessert, step up to the grand piano that doubles as a sweets trolley.

Chez Youen. The Pier, Baltimore, County Cork. ☎ **028/20136.** Reservations required. Fixed-price dinner £21.50 ($30.10); dinner main courses £9.50–£32 ($13.30–$44.80). AE, DC, MC, V. Mar–Oct daily 6pm–midnight, Sun noon–4pm. BRETON/SEAFOOD.

Overlooking the marina of this small harbor town, Brittany-born Youen Jacob's restaurant has been drawing people to West Cork since 1978. The decor is relaxing, with beamed ceilings, candlelight, floral pottery, and an open copper fireplace. Lobster is the specialty, fresh from local waters; the steaks, poached wild salmon in fennel, and leg of lamb are also very good. The chef's signature dish (the one that commands the £32/$44.80 price tag) is a gourmet shellfish platter, piled high with rare specimens not usually seen on ordinary menus: galley head prawns, Baltimore shrimp, and velvet crab, as well as local lobster and oysters, all served in a shell. The owners also run the neighboring Baltimore Bay Guesthouse and the lower-priced bistro, La Jolie Brise.

MODERATE

The Altar. Toormore, Goleen, County Cork. ☎ **028/35254.** Reservations recommended. Fixed-price dinner £25 ($35); dinner main courses £10–£18 ($14–$25.20). AE, MC, V. Tues–Sat 6–9:15pm. Closed Nov–Feb. IRISH/SEAFOOD.

Nestled deep in the West Cork countryside, this rustic cottage seems to appear out of nowhere. It has all the trappings of a country retreat, including the requisite open fireplace and stone walls. The menu, which changes daily, emphasizes local seafood, with choices such as whole sea trout stuffed with crabmeat sauce, and the Altar hot seafood platter. No smoking.

Casey's of Baltimore. Baltimore, County Cork. ☎ **028/20197.** Fax 028/20509. Reservations recommended for dinner. Fixed-price dinners £25 ($35); dinner main courses £8.20–£29.95 ($11.50–$41.95). AE, DC, MC, V. Daily 12:30–2:30pm and 6:30–9pm. Bar snacks Mon–Sat noon–9:30pm. Closed Nov 5–18, Dec 21–27, Feb 19–25. SEAFOOD/IRISH.

Overlooking Church Strand Bay, this nautical pub and restaurant has lovely views of the water, a beer garden, and a cottagelike interior with open peat fires. It specializes in simple fare, such as fresh local seafood and steaks. Casey's also offers clean and comfortable bed-and-breakfast accommodations.

✪ **Casino House.** 10 miles (16km) from Kinsale on coast road (R600), Coulmain Bay, Kilbrittain, County Cork. ☎ **023/49944.** Reservations recommended. Main courses £10–£15 ($14–$21). MC, V. Mar 17–June and Sept–Oct Thurs–Tues 7–9pm, Sun 1–3pm; July–Aug daily 7–9pm, Sun 1–3pm; Nov–Jan Fri–Sun 7–9pm, Sun 1–3pm. Closed Feb–Mar 16. INTERNATIONAL.

Why drive out of Kinsale, the "gourmet capital of Ireland," in search of a meal? One good answer is Casino House. The setting discovered and the ambience created by Kerrin and Michael Relja are phenomenal. The views of Courtmacsherry Bay will make you gasp, and the decor—somewhere between Nantucket and Provence—will promote both calm and appetite. Casino House, stylish without pretense, has been selected as one of the 100 best restaurants in Ireland, an honor it well deserves. You can do no better in Kinsale, although you can easily pay a lot more. The menu, which changes every week, is invariably inventive, with such starters and entrees as panseared asparagus tips with mixed greens and Parmesan shavings, terrine of quail with pistachio nuts and shiitake mushrooms, and fillet steak with mushrooms and onion ragout and potato pancakes. An exceptional selection of German wines highlights the excellent international wine list. The house wines from Italy are well selected for value and quality.

The Heron's Cove. Signposted in the center of Goleen, County Cork. ☎ **028/35225.** Reservations recommended. Main courses £11.75–£19.50 ($16.45–$27.30). AE, DC, MC, V. May–Oct daily noon–10pm. INTERNATIONAL.

This is a regular port of call, and not just for the great grey heron who appears every evening as if he's on salary. Locals know they can count on the Heron's Cove for excellent dining free of formality and risk. The modest dining room enjoys a splendid view of the cove. The fine menu, while focused on local seafood, has ample selections for both dedicated vegetarians and carnivores. The fisherman's broth is exceptional, as are monkfish in red pepper cream sauce, and Dunmanus Bay scallops panfried with leek and smoked bacon cream sauce. For dessert, the Russian cheesecake is awe-inspiring. A unique feature is the open-for-browsing cellar of 50 to 60 international wines. Study the labels, discuss them with other diners, and make your selection. Sue Hill, your host, knows her wines and will offer informed counseling if you find yourself locked in indecision.

✪ **Lettercollum House.** Timoleague, County Cork. ☎ **023/46251.** Reservations required. Fixed-price 5-course dinner £24 ($33.60). AE, MC, V. Mid-Mar to Nov daily 7:30–9:30pm, Sun 1–3pm. Open same hours on weekends Dec–mid-Mar. INNOVATIVE CONTINENTAL.

Owner and chef Con McLoughlin creates simple, original dishes based on organic produce from the adjacent walled garden, pigs raised on the premises, and locally caught fish. The menu changes daily, and there is always at least one vegetarian entree. Choices might include grilled wild salmon with sorrel sauce, cannelloni of sea spinach and brie with tomato butter sauce, or organic lamb tahini. The dining room was once a chapel, and the stained-glass windows remain. The service is rather informal, but the food is so good that it's best to overlook such shortcomings. (See also "Accommodations," above.)

Mary Anns. Castletownshend, Skibbereen, County Cork. ☎ **028/36146.** Reservations recommended for dinner. Bar food £1.50–£14.50 ($2.10–$20.30); restaurant 5-course fixed-price dinner £23.95 ($33.55). MC, V. Daily 12:30–2pm and 6–9pm. Closed holidays. IRISH.

Dating to 1844, this rustic pub is decorated with ships' wheels, lanterns, and bells. The menu offers salads and West Cork cheese plates, as well as more ambitious dishes, such as scallops meunière, sirloin steak with garlic butter, chicken Kiev, and deep-fried prawns. Weather permitting, you can sit in the pleasant outside courtyard.

Wine Vaults. 73 Bridge St., Skibbereen, County Cork. ☎ **028/23112.** All items £1.60–£11.95 ($2.40–$14.25). No credit cards. Daily noon–9pm; music and drinks until 12:30pm. INTERNATIONAL.

In the heart of a busy market town, this restaurant has a classy winery-style decor. It is a handy place for lunch or a light meal in transit. The menu includes soups, sandwiches on pita bread, and pizzas (the house special version is topped with mushrooms, peppers, onions, ham, and salami). There is live traditional music or jazz and blues nightly.

INEXPENSIVE

✪ **Adele's.** Main St., Schull, County Cork. ☎ **028/28459.** Reservations recommended. Lunch and baked goods £5–£10 ($7–$14); dinner main courses £9–£15 ($12.60–$21). MC, V. Apr–June and Sept–Nov Wed–Sun 9:30am–10pm; July–Aug daily 9:30am–10pm. SEAFOOD/PASTA.

During the day, this tiny establishment serves delicious baked goods, teas, and sandwiches, the work of Adele Connor's prolific culinary imagination. Sandwiches include ciabatta with tomato and slabs of local Gubbeen cheese, a real treat. The magic truly begins in the evening, when the upstairs dining room opens, and her son prepares meals that are delightful in their creative use of basic, local ingredients. The menu changes daily, and each dish is so enticing that it's always a challenge to choose: perhaps fresh mussels with angel-hair pasta and leeks, monkfish in saffron butter sauce, or tagliatelle with rosemary and parsley pesto. Panzanella, a marinated salad with red peppers, capers, and soaked bread crumbs, is a delicious summer appetizer. The atmosphere is casual, and families are welcome. There's a separate nonsmoking dining room. This place is one of the few good restaurants in Cork that won't take a big bite out of your budget. B&B is also available, at budget rates.

9

The Southwest:
County Kerry

Kerry is a place of disorienting contrasts, where the tackiest tourist attractions coexist with some of Ireland's most spectacular scenic wonders. It's a rugged place for the most part, some of it so rugged that it's seldom visited and remains quite pristine; Ireland's two highest mountains, Carrantuohill and Mount Brandon, are examples of such places. You could be driving along—say, on the famous Ring of Kerry, which traces the shores of the Iveragh Peninsula—make one little detour from the main road, and be in wild, unfrequented territory. The transition can be startling.

Thanks to its remoteness, County Kerry has always been an outpost of Gaelic culture. Poetry and music are intrinsic to the lifestyle, as is a love of the outdoors and sports. Gaelic football is an obsession in this county, and Kerry wins more than their share of the national championships. You'll also find some of Ireland's best golf courses, and the fishing for salmon and trout is equally hard to resist.

1 The Iveragh Peninsula

For the majority of the literally millions of annual tourists to County Kerry, whose explorations follow the turn of a bus driver's wheel, the Iveragh Peninsula is all but synonymous with the Ring of Kerry. The Ring, however, is nothing but a two-lane strip of tarmac measuring just over 100 miles (161km), tracing the peninsula's shores and missing its tip altogether, while the Iveragh Peninsula itself is nearly 700 square miles of wild splendor, which you'll notice once you get off the tourist strip. Admittedly, most everyone who gets this far feels compelled to "do" the Ring of Kerry; so, once it's done, why not take an unplanned turn and get truly lost so that you might stumble on the unexpected and the unspoiled?

ESSENTIALS
GETTING THERE **Bus Eireann** (☎ 064/34777) provides limited daily service from Killarney to Caherciveen, Waterville, Kenmare, and other towns on the Ring of Kerry. The best way to get to the Ring is by car, on N70 and N71. Some Killarney-based companies offer daily sightseeing tours of the Ring (see section 2 of this chapter, "Killarney").

VISITOR INFORMATION Stop in at the **Killarney Tourist Office,** Aras Fáilte, at the Town Centre Car Park, Beech Road, Killarney (☎ 064/31633), before you explore the area. For hours, see

County Kerry

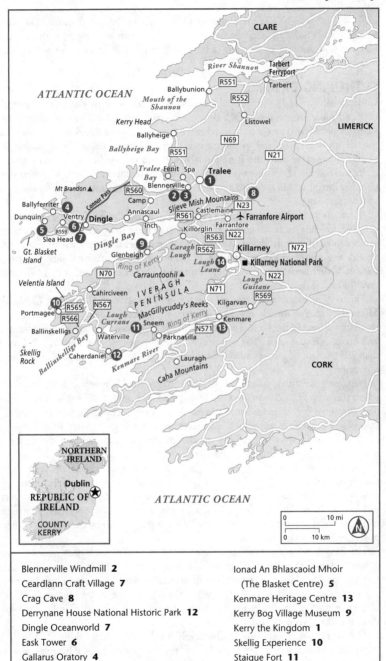

Blennerville Windmill **2**

Ceardlann Craft Village **7**

Crag Cave **8**

Derrynane House National Historic Park **12**

Dingle Oceanworld **7**

Eask Tower **6**

Gallarus Oratory **4**

Gap of Dunloe **14**

Ionad An Bhlascaoid Mhoir
(The Blasket Centre) **5**

Kenmare Heritage Centre **13**

Kerry Bog Village Museum **9**

Kerry the Kingdom **1**

Skellig Experience **10**

Staigue Fort **11**

Tralee Steam Railway **3**

section 2, below. The **Kenmare Tourist Office,** Market Square, Kenmare (☎ 064/ 41233), is open daily Easter through September, 9:15am to 5:30pm, with extended hours in July and August. The rest of the year (from Oct to Easter), it's open Monday to Saturday.

✪ THE RING OF KERRY

Undoubtedly Ireland's most popular scenic drive, the Ring of Kerry is a 110-mile (178km) route around the Iveragh Peninsula, a panorama of seacoast, mountain, and lakeland vistas. Bicyclists usually avoid this route, because the scores of tour buses that thunder through every day in the summer aren't always generous about sharing the road. For the most part, the Ring follows N70 and circles the Iveragh Peninsula; it starts and finishes at Killarney, but you can also use Kenmare as a base. The drive runs in either direction, but we strongly recommend a counterclockwise route for the most spectacular views.

Although it's possible to circle the peninsula in as little as 4 hours, the only way to get a feel for the area and the people is to leave the main road, get out of your car, and explore some of the inland and coastal towns. **Portmagee** is a lovely seaside town, connected by a bridge to **Valentia Island,** which houses the informative Skellig Heritage Centre. **Caherdaniel** has a museum devoted to Daniel O'Connell, one of Ireland's great historical figures.

The most memorable and magical site to visit on the Iveragh Peninsula is ✪ **Skellig Michael,** a rocky pinnacle towering over the sea, where medieval monks built their monastery in ascetic isolation. The crossing to the island can be rough, so you'll want to visit on as clear and calm a day as possible. Seabirds nest here in abundance, and more than 20,000 pairs of gannets inhabit neighboring Little Skellig during the summer nesting season.

Departing Killarney, follow the signs for **Killorglin.** When you reach this little town, you're on N70. You might want to stop and walk around Killorglin, a spot that's widely known for its annual mid-August horse, sheep, and cattle fair. It's officially called the **Puck Fair,** because local residents capture a wild goat (symbolizing the *puka* or *puki,* a mischievous sprite) from the mountains and enthrone it in the center of town as a sign of unrestricted merrymaking.

Continue on N70, and vistas of Dingle Bay will soon appear on your right. **Carrantuohill,** at 3,414 feet Ireland's tallest mountain, is to your left. The open bogland constantly comes into view. From it, the local residents dig pieces of peat, or turf, to burn in their fireplaces. Formed thousands of years ago, the boglands are mainly composed of decayed trees. They tend to be bumpy if you attempt to drive over them too speedily, so do be cautious.

The Ring winds around cliffs and the edges of mountains, with nothing but the sea below—another reason you will probably average only 30 mph (48kmph), at best. As you go along, you'll notice the remains of many abandoned cottages. They date from the famine years, in the mid-1840s, when the Irish potato crop failed and millions of people starved to death or were forced to emigrate. This peninsula alone lost three-fourths of its population.

The next town on the Ring is **Glenbeigh,** a palm tree–lined fishing resort with a lovely duned beach called Rossbeigh Strand. You might want to stop here or continue the sweep through the mountains and along the sea's edge to **Cahirciveen.** From Cahirciveen, you can make a slight detour to see **Valentia** (which you may also see spelled "Valencia"). The offshore island is 7 miles (11km) long and one of Europe's westernmost points. Connected to the mainland by a bridge at Portmagee, this was the site from which the first telegraph cable was laid across the Atlantic in 1866. In the 18th century, the Valentia harbor was famous as a refuge for smugglers and privateers; it's said that John Paul Jones, the Scottish-born American naval officer in the War of Independence, also anchored here quite often.

Head next for **Waterville,** an idyllic spot wedged between Lough Currane and Ballinskelligs Bay off the Atlantic. For years, it was known as the favorite retreat of Charlie Chaplin; today it's the home of the only Irish branch of Club Med.

If you follow the sea road north of town out to the Irish-speaking village of **Ballinskelligs,** at the mouth of the bay, you can also catch a glimpse of the two Skellig Rocks. Continuing on N70, the next point of interest is **Derrynane,** at **Caherdaniel,** the home of Daniel O'Connell, remembered as "the Liberator" who freed Irish Catholics from the last of the English Penal Laws in 1829. Derrynane is now a national monument and park, and a major center of Gaelic culture.

Watch for signs to **Staigue Fort,** about 2 miles (3.2km) off the main road. One of the best preserved of all ancient Irish structures, this circular fort is constructed of rough stones without mortar of any kind. The walls are 13 feet thick at the base, and the diameter is about 90 feet. Not much is known of its history, but experts think it probably dates from around 1000 B.C.

Sneem, the next village on the circuit, is a colorful little hamlet with twin parklets. Its houses are painted in vibrant shades of blue, pink, yellow, purple, and orange, like a little touch of the Mediterranean plunked down in Ireland.

As you continue on the Ring, the foliage becomes lusher, thanks to the warming waters and winds of the Gulf Stream. When you begin to see lots of palm trees and other subtropical vegetation, you'll know you are in **Parknasilla,** once a favorite haunt of George Bernard Shaw.

The final town on the Ring of Kerry route, **Kenmare,** is by far the most enchanting. Originally called Neidin ("little nest" in Irish), Kenmare is indeed a little nest of verdant foliage nestled between the River Roughty and Kenmare Bay. Well laid out and immaculately maintained by its proud residents (pop. 1,200), Kenmare easily rivals Killarney as an alternative base for County Kerry sightseeing.

On the return to Killarney, the final lap of the Ring road takes you through a scenic mountain stretch known as **Moll's Gap.**

Derrynane House National Historic Park. Caherdaniel, County Kerry. ☎ **066/ 947-5113.** Admission £2 ($2.80) adults, £1.50 ($2.10) seniors, £1 ($1.40) students and children, £5 ($7) family. Nov–Mar Sat–Sun 1–5pm; Apr and Oct Tues–Sun 1–5pm; May–Sept Mon–Sat 9am–6pm, Sun 11am–7pm.

On a 320-acre site along the Ring of Kerry coast between Waterville and Caherdaniel, this is where Ireland's Great Liberator, Daniel O'Connell, lived for most of his life. Ireland's Office of Public Works maintains the house as a museum. It's filled with documents, illustrations, and memorabilia related to O'Connell's life, including a 25-minute audiovisual display about him titled *Be You Perfectly Peaceable.*

Kenmare Heritage Centre. The Square, Kenmare, County Kerry. ☎ **064/41491.** Admission £2 ($2.80) adults, £1.50 ($2.10) seniors and students, £1 ($1.40) children under 12, £5 ($7) family. Mon–Sat 9:15am–5:30pm, with extended summer hours.

To learn more about the delightful town of Kenmare, the Ring of Kerry's "little nest," step inside this new visitor center. Exhibits recount Kenmare's history as a planned estate town that grew up around the mineworks founded in 1670 by Sir William Petty, ancestor of the Landsdownes, the local landlords. The center also displays locally made lace, and tells the story of the woman who originated the craft. A scripted walking trail around the town is also under development.

Kerry Bog Village Museum. Ring of Kerry road (N71), Ballycleave, Glenbeigh, County Kerry. ☎ **066/976-9184.** Admission £2.50 ($3.50) adults, £2 ($2.80) students, £8 ($11.20) family. AE, DC, MC, V. Mar–Nov daily 9am–6pm; Dec–Feb by appointment.

This little cluster of thatched-roof cottages shows what life was like in Kerry in the early 1800s. The museum village has a blacksmith's forge and house, turf-cutter's house, laborer's cottage, thatcher's dwelling, tradesman's house, and stable and dairy house. Stacks of newly cut turf sit piled high beside the road. There are also a football pitch and other recreational facilities. The interiors are furnished with authentic pieces gathered from all parts of Kerry.

Seafari Eco-nature Cruises and Seal-Watching Trips. Kenmare Pier, Kenmare, County Kerry. ☎ **064/83171.** www.seafariireland.com. Tickets £10 ($14) adults, £8 ($11.20) students, £5 ($7) children under 12, £25 ($35) family. May–Oct 4 cruises daily.

You'll see the sights of Kenmare Bay on board a 50-foot covered boat. The 2-hour cruises cover 10 miles (16km) and are narrated by well-versed guides who provide information on local history, geography, and geology. The guides point out sea otters, gray seals, herons, oyster catchers, and kingfishers. Boats depart from the pier next to the Kenmare suspension bridge. Reservations are recommended. Note no credit cards.

The Skellig Experience. Skellig Heritage Centre, Valentia Island, County Kerry. ☎ **066/947-6306.** Exhibition and audiovisual £3 ($4.20) adults, £2.70 ($3.80) seniors and students, £1.50 ($2.10) children under 12, £7 ($9.80) family of 2 adults and up to 4 children; exhibition, audiovisual, and sea cruise £15 ($21) adults, £13.50 ($18.90) seniors and students, £7.50 ($10.50) children under 12, £40 ($56) family. AE, MC, V. Apr–Oct 10am–6pm. Closed Nov–Mar.

Seven miles (11km) off the mainland Ring of Kerry route (R765) on Valentia Island, this new attraction blends right into the terrain, with a stark stone facade framed by grassy mounds. Inside, through a series of displays and audiovisual presentations, the center offers a detailed look at the area's birds and plant life. In particular, it tells the story of the Skellig Rocks, Skellig Michael, and Little Skellig. The sea cruise circuits the Skelligs.

✪ THE SKELLIG ISLANDS

A visit to these two crags rising precipitously from the sea, about 10 miles (16km) off the coast of the Iveragh Peninsula, is sure to be one of your more memorable experiences in Ireland. Seen from the mainland, the islands have a fantastic aspect, seeming impossibly steep and sharp-angled. Yet it was on the highest pinnacle of the larger island, **Skellig Michael,** that a community of monks chose to build a monastery in the 6th or 7th century. They carved steps out of the rock to provide access from the stormy waters below.

You'll start off by taking a 45-minute boat passage from the mainland. Upon disembarking, you'll begin a long ascent of the island using the same steps trodden by the monks for 6 centuries, until the monastery was abandoned in the 12th or 13th century. The monastic enclosure consists of six beehive-shaped huts of mortarless stone construction, two oratories, and a church; there is also a collection of carved stones that have been found on the island. The smaller of the Skellig Islands has no space for human habitation, but is home during nesting season to more than 20,000 pairs of gannets.

Ferries leave daily from Ballinskelligs, usually between 9am and noon; call **Joe Roddy** (☎ **066/947-4268**) or **Sean Feehan** (☎ **066/947-9182**). Ferries from Portmagee are run by **Murphy's** (☎ **066/947-7156**). The cost is £25 ($35) per person.

SHOPPING

Many good craft and souvenir shops lie along the Ring of Kerry, but those in **Kenmare** offer the most in terms of variety and quality. Kenmare shops are open year-round, usually Monday to Saturday 9am to 6pm. From May to September, many shops remain open till 9 or 10pm, and some open on Sunday from noon to 5 or 6pm.

Avoca Handweavers at Moll's Gap. Ring of Kerry road (N71), Moll's Gap, County Kerry. ☎ 064/34720.

In one of the most scenic settings, this shop is on a high mountain pass (960 ft. above sea level) between Killarney and Kenmare. It's a branch of the famous tweed makers of Avoca, County Wicklow, dating to 1723. The wares range from colorful hand-woven capes, jackets, throws, and knitwear to pottery and jewelry. Chefs trained at the Bally-maloe Cookery School staff the excellent coffee shop. Closed November to mid-March.

Cleo. 2 Shelbourne Rd., Kenmare, County Kerry. ☎ 064/41410.

A branch of the long-established Dublin store of the same name, this newly expanded trendy women's-wear shop is known for its beautiful, colorful tweed and linen fashions, as well as specialty items such as Kinsale cloaks.

Kenmare Bookshop. Shelbourne St., Kenmare, County Kerry. ☎ 064/41578.

This shop specializes in books on Ireland, particularly biographies and books by Irish writers, as well as maps and guides to the surrounding area. Offerings include ordinance survey maps, walking and specialist guides, and marine charts. There are also art cards and craft items relating to the Book of Kells. An upstairs room holds a display and audiovisual presentation on the Book of Kells, for those who can't get to Dublin to see the real thing. Admission to the upstairs exhibit is £2 ($3) adults, £1 ($1.50) children. The shop and exhibit are closed from January to March.

Nostalgia. 27 Henry St., Kenmare, County Kerry. ☎ 064/41389.

In a town known for its lace, it's a natural to stop into this shop. It carries new and antique lace, table and bed linens, traditional teddy bears, and accessories. Closed January to mid-March.

Quills Woolen Market. Market Sq. and Main St., Kenmare, County Kerry. ☎ 064/32277. North Sq., Sneem, County Kerry. ☎ 064/45277.

These are branches of the store of the same name in Killarney. They're known for Aran hand knits, Donegal tweed jackets, Irish linen, Celtic jewelry, and hand-loomed knitwear.

SPORTS & OUTDOOR PURSUITS

GOLF   Home to a myriad of seascapes and sand dunes, the Ring of Kerry is known for its great golf courses, particularly ✪ **Waterville Golf Links,** Waterville (☎ 066/947-4102; www.watervillegolf.com), on the edge of the Atlantic. On huge sand dunes, bounded on three sides by the sea, the 18-hole championship course is one of the longest in Ireland (7,234 yd.). Visitors are welcome. Greens fees are £75 ($105) weekdays.

Other challenging 18-hole courses on the Ring include **Dooks Golf Club,** Glenbeigh (☎ 066/976-8205), a seaside par-70 course on the Ring of Kerry road, with a fee of £25 ($35). The newly expanded **Kenmare Golf Club,** Kenmare (☎ 064/41291), is a parkland par-71 course; greens fees run £20 ($28) weekdays and £25 ($35) weekends.

WALKING   Ireland's longest low-level, long-distance path, the **Kerry Way,** traverses the Ring of Kerry. The first stage, from Killarney National Park to Glenbeigh, is inland, through wide and scenic countryside. The second stage is a circuit of the Iveragh Peninsula, linking Cahirciveen, Waterville, Caherdaniel, Sneem, and Kenmare, with a farther inland walk along the old Kenmare Road back to Killarney, for a total of 125 miles (202km). The route consists primarily of paths and "green" (unsurfaced) roads, such as old driving paths, butter roads, and routes between early Christian settlements. A leaflet outlining the route is available from the Killarney and Kenmare tourist offices.

ACCOMMODATIONS

VERY EXPENSIVE

✪ **The Park Hotel Kenmare.** Kenmare, County Kerry. ☎ **800/323-5463** from the U.S., or 064/41200. Fax 064/41402. www.parkkenmare.com. 48 units. TV TEL. £244–£484 ($341.60–$677.60) double. No service charge. Rates include full breakfast. AE, DC, MC, V. Closed Nov–Dec 23 and Jan 2 to mid-Apr. Free parking.

Dating from 1897, this Victorian-style château is a haven of impeccable service and luxurious living. Ensconced in palm tree–lined gardens beside Kenmare Bay, it originally served as a Great Southern Railway hotel, and was totally restored and refurbished about 20 years ago under the masterful ownership and management of Francis Brennan. The interior is rich in high-ceilinged sitting rooms and lounges, crackling open fireplaces, original oil paintings, tapestries, plush furnishings, and museum-worthy antiques (including an eye-catching cistern decorated with mythological figures and supported by gilded sea horses and dolphins).

The individually decorated guest rooms are decked out in a mix of Georgian and Victorian styles. Many have four-poster or canopy beds, hand-carved armoires, china lamps, curios, and little extra touches like telephones in the bathroom and towel warmers. Most have views of river and mountain vistas. Nonsmoking rooms are available. Amid all the elegance, this hotel exudes an intrinsically welcoming atmosphere.

Dining/Diversions: The elegant dining room, with romantic views of the water and gardens, is one of the most acclaimed hotel restaurants in Ireland, meriting a Michelin star. Other public areas include a hexagonal bar and a drawing room where a pianist plays each evening.

Amenities: Concierge, 24-hour room service, laundry and dry cleaning, nightly turn-down, 18-hole golf course, joggers' trail, tennis court, croquet lawn, salmon fishing.

Parknasilla Great Southern Hotel. Ring of Kerry road (N70), Parknasilla, Sneem, County Kerry. ☎ **064/45122.** Fax 064/45323. www.gsh.ie. 84 units. TV TEL. £200–£256 ($280–$358.40). Rates include full Irish breakfast and service charge. AE, MC, V. Valet parking.

Facing one of the loveliest seascape settings in Ireland, this château-style hotel sits amid 300 acres of lush, subtropical palm trees and flowering shrubs. George Bernard Shaw stayed here, and was inspired to write much of his play *Saint Joan.* Most of the individually furnished guest rooms look onto broad vistas of the Kenmare River and the Atlantic.

Dining/Diversions: For leisurely conversation and fine dining, the Parknasilla Great Southern offers its own Pygmalion Restaurant and cocktail bar.

Amenities: The hotel has a private nine-hole golf course (closed Nov to Mar), heated indoor saltwater swimming pool, steam room, sauna and Jacuzzi, outdoor hot tub, croquet, and tennis courts, and offers bicycle hire, riding, fishing, windsurfing, and boating. Room service, concierge, baby-sitting, valet and laundry/dry cleaning, secretarial services, video rentals.

Sheen Falls Lodge. Kenmare, County Kerry. ☎ **800/537-8483** from the U.S., or 064/41600. Fax 064/41386. www.sheenfallslodge.ie. 61 units. TV TEL. £168–£350 ($235.20–$490) double; £295–£520 ($413–$728) suite. No service charge. AE, DC, MC, V. Closed Dec 3–23.

Originally the 18th-century home of the Earl of Kerry, this relatively new resort sits beside a natural waterfall on 300 acres of lawns and semitropical gardens where the River Sheen meets the Kenmare Bay estuary. The public areas are spacious and graceful, with pillars and columns, open fireplaces, traditional furnishings, and original oil paintings. The guest rooms are large and spacious, decorated in elegant contemporary style; each overlooks the falls or bay. The hotel also maintains a vintage 1922 Buick to provide local excursions for guests.

Dining: La Cascade is a wide-windowed restaurant facing the falls, which are flood-lit at night; Oscar's Bar and Bistro offers less formal dining.

Amenities: 24-hour room service; concierge; laundry/dry cleaning; nightly turndown; leisure center with Jacuzzi, sauna, and steam room; billiards room; 1,000-volume library; 15-mile (24km) stretch of private salmon fishing; horseback riding; tennis; croquet; golf on nearby course; helicopter pad.

MODERATE

Butler Arms. Waterville, County Kerry. ☎ **066/947-4144.** Fax 800/447-7462 from the U.S., or 066/947-4520. E-mail: butarms@iol.ie. 30 units. TV TEL. £100–£145 ($140–$203) double. Rates include full Irish breakfast and service charge. AE, MC, V. Closed late Oct to Mar.

Once a favorite vacation retreat of Charlie Chaplin, this grand old inn is now run by the third generation of the Huggard family. Located on the edge of town and partially facing the sea, it has a sprawling, semiturreted white facade. The refurbished guest rooms are functional and pleasant, and many have views of the water or the palm tree–studded gardens. Most of the charming public rooms and bars have fireplaces. The inn has a full-service restaurant, nautically themed bar, sun lounge, and tennis court. There's free salmon and sea trout fishing on Lough Currane and private lakes.

Derrynane Hotel. Off Ring of Kerry road (N71), Caherdaniel, County Kerry. ☎ **800/528-1234** or 066/947-5136. Fax 066/947-5160. www.derrynane.com. 75 units. TV TEL. £77–£99 ($107.80–$138.60) double. Rates include full Irish breakfast and service charge. AE, DC, MC, V. Closed early Oct to mid-Apr. Free parking.

This contemporary three-story hotel, between Waterville and Sneem, is set amid beautiful beaches, hills, and the nearby Derrynane National Historic Park. The guest rooms are standard, but greatly enhanced by superb views from every window. The public areas include a restaurant and lounge and a heated outdoor swimming pool. A local guide is available to take guests on weekend walking trips.

Dromquinna Manor Hotel. Blackwater Bridge P.O., off Ring of Kerry road (N71), Kenmare, County Kerry. ☎ **064/41657.** Fax 064/41791. www.dromquinna.com. 46 units. TV TEL. £75–£116 ($105–$162.40) double; £360 ($504) treehouse suite. No service charge. Rates include full Irish breakfast. AE, MC, V. Free parking.

A bit over 2 miles (3.2km) west of Kenmare, this Victorian-style hotel was originally a private home dating from 1850. It is on 42 acres of woodland, with almost a mile of land facing the Kenmare River. Refurbished and expanded in recent years, it retains an old-world ambience, with log fireplaces, original oak paneling, ornate ceilings, and authentic bric-a-brac. Guest rooms are individually furnished, some with four-poster or Victorian-style beds, and some modern, with light woods and frilly floral fabrics; some face the water. Suites with two bedrooms and a large balcony are in the tree-house, said to be the only one in Ireland or Britain, situated 15 feet above ground. The hotel has a restaurant and boathouse-style bistro; sporting facilities include a tennis court, croquet, and rowboats for hire.

Towers. Ring of Kerry road (N70), Glenbeigh, County Kerry. ☎ **066/976-8212.** Fax 066/976-8260. E-mail: towershotel@eircom.net. 28 units. TV TEL. £78–£96 ($109.20–$134.40) double. Rates include full breakfast and service charge. AE, DC, MC, V. Closed Nov–Mar.

If you'd like to be in the heart of one of the Ring of Kerry's most delightful towns, this vintage brick-faced country inn is for you. Shaded by ancient palms, it sits in the middle of a small fishing village, yet is within a mile of the sandy Rossbeigh Strand and only 20 miles (32km) west of Killarney. Recently refurbished and updated, most of the rooms are in a contemporary new wing with lovely views of the nearby water. The inn has a lively old-fashioned pub and a good seafood restaurant.

MODERATE/INEXPENSIVE

Kenmare Bay. Sneem Rd., Kenmare, County Kerry. ☎ **064/41300.** Fax 064/41541. E-mail: kenmare@leehotels.ie. 136 units. TV TEL. £50–£80 ($70–$112) double. Rates include full breakfast and service charge. AE, DC, MC, V. Closed Nov–Mar.

On a hillside at the edge of town, just off the main road that winds around the Ring of Kerry, this modern hotel was recently expanded and refurbished. The guest rooms are furnished with light woods and tweedy or quilted fabrics, with large windows that look out onto the mountainous countryside. There's a full-service restaurant; the spacious lounge bar offers traditional Irish music sing-alongs on most evenings.

INEXPENSIVE

Hillcrest. Killarney Rd., ⅓ mile (0.5km) outside of Killorglin town, County Kerry. ☎ **066/976-1552.** Fax 066/976-1996. 5 units. TV. £36 ($50.40) double. Rates include full breakfast and service charge. MC, V. Closed Jan–Mar. Free parking.

The slightest of jogs off the Ring of Kerry road will take you to this comfortable haven, set well back from N70. The rooms of this Georgian-style bungalow are spacious and cheerful, with pastel walls offset by bright contemporary floral fabrics, painted white furniture, and dark-stained window frames. All rooms have firm beds, hair dryers, and tea/coffeemakers. The front rooms enjoy views of the nearby hills. This is a pleasant bargain that won't disappoint.

DINING
MODERATE

The Blue Bull. South Sq., Ring of Kerry Road (N70), Sneem, County Kerry. ☎ **064/45382.** Reservations recommended. Main courses £9–£16 ($12.60–$22.40). AE, MC, V. Bar food daily year-round 11am–8pm. Restaurant daily Mar–Oct 6–10pm. SEAFOOD/TRADITIONAL IRISH.

With a blue straw bull's head resting over the doorway, this old pub and restaurant has long been a favorite on the Ring of Kerry route, especially for Sir Andrew Lloyd Webber, who once called it the best bar restaurant in the world! There are three small rooms, each with an open fireplace and walls lined with old prints of County Kerry scenes and people, plus a skylit conservatory room in the back. Traditional Irish fare, like smoked salmon and Irish stew, shares the menu with such dishes as salmon stuffed with spinach, Valencia scallops in brandy, and chicken Kiev. There's traditional Irish entertainment most evenings.

D'Arcy's. Main St., Kenmare, County Kerry. ☎ **064/41589.** Reservations recommended. Main courses £11.50–£16.95 ($16.10–$23.75). MC, V. June–Aug 6–9:30pm; Sept–May 7–9pm (phone to confirm hours off-season). Closed Mon–Wed Jan 6 to mid-Feb and Dec 25. IRISH.

In a two-story stone house at the top end of Kenmare, this restaurant has a homey atmosphere with a big open fireplace. The chef-owner, Matt d'Arcy, who formerly presided at the kitchens of the nearby Park Hotel, has branched out to make his own culinary mark in this restaurant-rich town. Using fresh local ingredients, the creative menus include dishes such as baked sea trout in pastry with smoked salmon; fillet of beef in pastry with a stuffing of mushrooms, roast garlic, and shallots; and loin of Kerry lamb with eggplant, tomato, and garlic. B&B is also available.

The Huntsman. The Strand, Waterville, County Kerry. ☎ **066/947-4124.** Reservations recommended. Lunch and bar food items from £3 ($4.20); dinner main courses £10–£18.95 ($14–$26.55). AE, DC, MC, V. Daily Mar–Oct 10am–10pm; Nov–Feb Thurs–Sun 6–10pm. Closed Dec 23–27. INTERNATIONAL/SEAFOOD.

It's worth a trip to Waterville just to dine at this contemporary restaurant on the shores of Ballinskelligs Bay. Owner-chef Raymond Hunt takes the time to circulate and chat with diners, offering suggestions on the extensive menu, which uses only the freshest local catch and produce. Skellig lobster fresh from the tank and Kenmare Bay scampi are among the seafood dishes; meat dishes include rack of lamb, seasonal pheasant, rabbit, duck, and Irish stew.

✪ **Lime Tree.** Shelbourne Rd., Kenmare, County Kerry. ☎ **064/41225.** Reservations recommended. Main courses £12.75–£16.95 ($17.85–$23.75). MC, V. Apr–Nov daily 6:30–10pm. IRISH.

Innovative cuisine is the focus at this restaurant, in an 1821 landmark renovated schoolhouse next to the grounds of the Park Hotel. Paintings by local artists line the stone walls, and the menu offers such dishes as goat's-cheese potato cake with balsamic glaze, oak-planked wild salmon, fillet of Irish beef with colcannon, and oven-roasted Kerry lamb.

The Smuggler's Inn. Cliff Rd., Waterville, County Kerry. ☎ **066/947-4330.** Reservations recommended for dinner. Main courses £12–£27 ($16.80–$37.80); fixed-price dinner menu £25 ($35). AE, MC, V. Mar to mid-Nov daily 8:30am–11pm. SEAFOOD.

A mile north of the town along the Ballinskelligs Bay beach, this renovated farmhouse is on a sandy beach across the road from the entrance to the Waterville Golf Course. The decor is nautical, with fine sea views from the dining-room windows. The menu offers the freshest seafood, with dishes such as sea trout in capers and lemon butter, Ballinskelligs Bay black sole, sweet seafood curry, and steaks. Snacks and pub food are available all day. Accommodation is also available.

MODERATE/INEXPENSIVE

Packie's. Henry St., Kenmare, County Kerry. ☎ **064/41508.** Reservations recommended. Main courses £9.90–£18.90 ($13.85–$26.45). MC, V. Easter to mid-Nov Tues–Sat 5:30–10pm. IRISH.

With window boxes full of colorful seasonal plantings, this informal, bistro-style restaurant in the middle of town exudes a welcoming atmosphere. It has a slate floor, stone walls, and dark oak tables and chairs. On the walls is a collection of wonderful contemporary Irish art, and on the menu are tried-and-true favorites: Irish stew and rack of lamb. Also offered are creative combinations, such as gratin of crab and prawns, beef braised in Guinness with mushrooms, and blackboard fish specials. Chef-owner Maura Foley uses herbs from her own garden to enhance each dish.

Red Fox Inn. Ring of Kerry road (N71), Ballycleave, Glenbeigh, County Kerry. ☎ **066/ 976-9184.** Reservations recommended for dinner. Main courses £5.50–£14 ($7.70–$19.60). AE, DC, MC, V. Daily noon–9:30pm. IRISH.

Adjacent to the Kerry Bog Museum, this restaurant has an old Kerry cottage atmosphere, with open turf fireplaces, heirloom pictures on the walls, and local memorabilia. There are picnic tables outside. The menu includes hearty traditional dishes such as Irish stew, seafood pie, chicken and ham, leg of lamb, and steak. In the summer (May to Sept), there is Irish ceili band entertainment Wednesday through Sunday from 9:30 to 11:30pm. The bar serves snacks all day.

The Vestry. Ring of Kerry road (N71), on Kenmare Bay about 4 miles (6.5km) west of Kenmare, Templenoe, Kenmare, County Kerry. ☎ **064/41958.** Reservations recommended. Main courses £9.95–£17.95 ($13.95–$25.15). MC, V. Mar–Sept daily 6–9:30pm. MODERN IRISH/INTERNATIONAL.

As its name implies, this building is a former Church of Ireland edifice, constructed between 1790 and 1816, and in use for services until 1987. In 1993, it was tastefully converted into a restaurant, retaining many of its original decorations and fixtures. Recently, the modern Irish menu, highlighting fresh local seafood and vegetables, was expanded—"ecumenically," as it were—to include more exotic items such as kangaroo, ostrich, and wild boar. All are expertly prepared by award-winning chef Garrett OMahony.

INEXPENSIVE

Purple Heather. Henry St., Kenmare, County Kerry. ☎ **064/41016.** All items £2–£14 ($2.80–$19.60). No credit cards. Mon–Sat 11am–7pm. Closed Christmas week. IRISH.

This dependable pub and restaurant is in the heart of town. It's a great place to stop for a snack or a light meal with gourmet flair. The menu includes wild smoked salmon or prawn salad, smoked trout pâté, vegetarian omelets, and Irish cheese platters, as well as homemade soups.

2 Killarney

Killarney is 84 miles (135km) SW of Shannon, 192 miles (309km) SW of Dublin, 54 miles (87km) W of Cork, 69 miles (111km) SW of Limerick, and 120 miles (193km) SW of Galway

Killarney is the Grand Central Terminal of tourism in the southwest. If you've never seen a traffic jam of battling tour buses or been besieged by a bevy of pushy jaunting-car drivers, this is the place to seek out such curious and unusual spectacles of nature. If that's not your bag, it's easy enough to resist Killarney's gravitational pull and instead explore the incredibly scenic hinterlands that border the town on all sides. You might sneak into town at some point to sample the best of what this tourist megalopolis has to offer.

It's important to remember that the reason Killarney draws millions of visitors a year has nothing to do with the town. It's all about the lakes and mountains just beyond the town, and entering these wonders is ever so easy. Walk from the town car park toward the cathedral, and turn left into the National Park. In a matter of minutes, you'll see the reason for all the fuss. During the summer, the evenings are long, the light is often indescribable, and you needn't share the lanes. Apart from deer and locals, the park is all yours until dark.

The lakes are Killarney's main attraction. The first, the Lower Lake, is sometimes called "Lough Leane" or "Lough Lein," which means "the lake of learning." It's the largest, more than 4 miles (6.5km) long, and is dotted with 30 small islands. The second lake is aptly called the "Middle Lake" or "Muckross Lake," and the third simply "Upper Lake." Upper Lake, the smallest, is full of storybook islands covered with a variety of trees—evergreens, cedars of Lebanon, juniper, holly, and mountain ash.

The lakes and the surrounding woodlands are part of the 25-square-mile **Killarney National Park.** Found within its borders are two major estates, the Muckross and Knockreer demesnes, and the remains of major medieval abbeys and castles. A profusion of foliage, such as rhododendrons, azaleas, magnolias, camellias, hydrangeas, and tropical ferns, blossoms in season. At almost every turn, you'll see Killarney's own botanical wonder, the arbutus, or strawberry tree, plus eucalyptus, redwoods, and native oak.

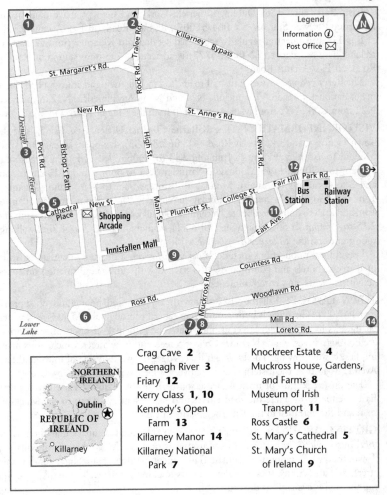

Crag Cave **2**
Deenagh River **3**
Friary **12**
Kerry Glass **1, 10**
Kennedy's Open
  Farm **13**
Killarney Manor **14**
Killarney National
  Park **7**

Knockreer Estate **4**
Muckross House, Gardens,
  and Farms **8**
Museum of Irish
  Transport **11**
Ross Castle **6**
St. Mary's Cathedral **5**
St. Mary's Church
  of Ireland **9**

The most noteworthy of Killarney's islands is **Innisfallen,** which seems to float peacefully in the Lower Lake. You can reach it by rowboat, available for rental at Ross Castle. St. Fallen founded a monastery here in the 7th century, and it flourished for 1,000 years. It's said that Brian Boru, the great Irish chieftain, and St. Brendan the Navigator were educated here. From 950 to 1320, the "Annals of Innisfallen," a chronicle of early Irish history, was written at the monastery; it's now in the Bodlein Library at Oxford University. Traces of an 11th-century church and a 12th-century priory can still be seen today.

ESSENTIALS
GETTING THERE   Aer Lingus offers flights from Dublin into Kerry County Airport, Farranfore, County Kerry (☎ **066/976-4644**), about 10 miles (16km) north of Killarney. **Ryanair** flies direct from London (Stansted) to Kerry, and Manx Airlines flies to Kerry from Luton and Manchester.

Irish Rail trains from Dublin, Limerick, Cork, and Galway arrive daily at the **Killarney Railway Station** (☎ 064/31067), Railway Road, off East Avenue Road.

Bus Eireann operates regularly scheduled service into Killarney from all parts of Ireland. The bus depot (☎ 064/34777) is adjacent to the train station at Railway Road, off East Avenue Road.

The Kerry people like to say that all roads lead to Killarney, and at least a half dozen major national roads do. They include N21 and N23 from Limerick, N22 from Tralee, N22 from Cork, N72 from Mallow, and N70 from the Ring of Kerry and West Cork.

VISITOR INFORMATION   The **Killarney Tourist Office,** Aras Fáilte, is at the Town Centre Car Park, Beech Road (☎ 064/31633). It's open January to April, Monday to Saturday 9:15am to 1pm and 2:15 to 5:30pm; May, Monday to Saturday 9:15am to 5:30pm; June, Monday to Saturday 9am to 6pm, Sunday 10am to 1pm and 2 to 6pm; July to August, Monday to Saturday 9am to 8pm, Sunday 10am to 1pm and 2 to 6pm; September, Monday to Saturday 9am to 6pm, Sunday 10am to 1pm and 2:15 to 6pm; October to December, Monday to Saturday 9:15am to 1pm and 2:15 to 5:30pm. It offers many helpful booklets, including the *Tourist Trail* walking-tour guide and the *Killarney Area Guide,* with maps.

Useful local publications include **Where: Killarney,** a quarterly magazine distributed free at hotels and guesthouses. It is packed with current information on tours, activities, events, and entertainment.

TOWN LAYOUT   Killarney is small, with a year-round population of approximately 7,000. The town is built around one central thoroughfare, Main Street, which changes its name to High Street at midpoint. The principal offshoots of Main Street are Plunkett Street, which becomes College Street, and New Street, which, as its name implies, is still growing. The Deenagh River edges the western side of town, and East Avenue Road rims the eastern side. It's all very walkable in an hour or two.

The busiest section of town is at the southern tip of Main Street, where it meets East Avenue Road. Here the road curves and heads southward out to the Muckross road and the entrance to the Killarney National Park.

GETTING AROUND   Killarney Town is so small and compact that there is no local bus service; the best way to get around is on foot. To see the best of Killarney Town, follow the signposted "Tourist Trail," encompassing the highlights of the main streets and attractions. It takes about 2 hours to complete the walk. A booklet outlining the trail is available at the tourist office.

Taxi cabs line up at the rank on **College Square** (☎ 064/31331). You can also phone for a taxi from **John Burke** (☎ 064/32448), **Dero's Taxi Service** (☎ 064/31251), or **O'Connell Taxi** (☎ 064/31654).

In Killarney Town, it's best to park your car and walk. Most hotels and guesthouses offer free guest parking. If you must park on the street, buy a parking disc and display it on your car; parking costs 30p (42¢) per hour, and hotels and shops sell discs. You'll need a car to drive from town to Killarney National Park on the Muckross and Kenmare road (N71).

If you need to rent a car in Killarney, contact **Avis,** the Glebe Arcade (☎ 064/36655); **Budget,** c/o International Hotel, Kenmare Place (☎ 064/34341); **Hertz,** 28 Plunkett St. (☎ 064/34126); or **Randles Bros.,** Muckross Road (☎ 064/31237).

Horse-drawn **jaunting cars** (light, two-wheeled vehicles) line up at Kenmare Place in Killarney Town. They offer rides to Killarney National Park sites and other scenic areas. Depending on the time and distance, prices range from £12 to £32 ($16.80 to $44.80) per jaunting car (up to four persons), based on four passengers. (For details, see "Organized Tours," below.)

FAST FACTS   If you need a drugstore, try **O'Sullivans Pharmacy,** 81 New St. (☎ **064/35866**), or **Donal Sheahan,** 34 Main St. (☎ **064/31113**).

In an **emergency,** dial ☎ **999.** The **Killarney District Hospital** is on St. Margaret's Road (☎ **064/31076**). The **Killarney Garda Station** is on New Road (☎ **064/31222**).

Full Internet access (over superfast ISDN lines), plus secretarial services, tea, coffee, and pastries, are available Monday through Saturday at **Café Internet,** 49 Lower New St. (☎ **064/36741;** www.cafe-internet.net). Facilities include scanners, color printers, and quik-cams. Internet fees run £3 ($4.20) for 30 minutes, £5 ($7) per hour. Open 9:30am to 7pm (10pm June through Sept).

If you need to do your laundry, head for the **Gleeson Launderette,** Brewery Lane, off College Square (☎ **064/33877**).

The **Killarney Public Library** is on Rock Road (☎ **064/32972**).

Local weekly newspapers include the **Kerryman** (www.kerryweb.ie) and the **Killarney Advertiser. Where: Killarney** (www.wherekillarney.com), a quarterly magazine, is chock-full of helpful, up-to-date information for visitors; it is distributed free at hotels and guesthouses. The local radio station is **Radio Kerry,** 97 FM.

For photographic needs, try **Eugene Ferris Photography,** 105 New St. (☎ **064/36118**), or **Killarney Photographic Centre,** 69 New St. (☎ **064/31225**).

The **Killarney Post Office,** New Street (☎ **064/31051**), is open Monday and Wednesday to Saturday 9am to 5:30pm, Tuesday 9:30am to 5:30pm.

For shoe repairs, try the **Cobbler,** Innisfallen Shopping Mall (no phone), or **M. K. O'Sullivan,** St. Anne's Road (☎ **064/31825**).

WHAT TO SEE & DO IN KILLARNEY
THE TOP ATTRACTIONS

The town of Killarney sits right on the doorstep of ✪ **Killarney National Park,** out Kenmare road (N71), 25,000 acres of natural beauty. You'll find three storied lakes—the **Lower Lake** (or Lough Leane), the **Middle Lake** (or Muckross Lake), and the **Upper Lake**—myriad waterfalls, rivers, islands, valleys, mountains, bogs, woodlands, and lush foliage and trees, including oak, arbutus, holly, and mountain ash. There's also a large variety of wildlife, including a rare herd of red deer. No cars are allowed in the park, so plan on hiking, biking, or hiring a horse-drawn jaunting car. The park offers four nature trails along the lakeshore.

There's access from several points along the Kenmare road (N71). The main entrance is at Muckross House, where a new visitor center features background exhibits on the park and a film titled *Mountain, Wood, Water.* A new restaurant is slated to open in 2000. Call ☎ **064/31440** for more information on the park. Admission is free, and it's open in all daylight hours year-round.

Amid mountains and lakelands, the winding, rocky ✪ **Gap of Dunloe** is about 6 miles (9.7km) west of Killarney. The route through the gap passes a kaleidoscope of craggy rocks, massive cliffs, meandering streams, and deep valleys. The road ends at Upper Lake. One of the best ways to explore the gap is by bicycle (see "Bicycling," under "Outdoor Pursuits," below). Horse fanciers may want to take one of the excursions offered by **Castlelough Tours,** 7 High St. (☎ **064/31115**); **Corcoran's Tours,** Kilcummin (☎ **064/36666**); **Dero's Tours,** 22 Main St. (☎ **064/31251** or 064/31567), or **Tangney Tours,** Kinvara House, Muckross Road (☎ **064/33358**). Combination coach/horse/boat tours cost £28 ($39.20). If you'd rather have someone else handle the horse, you can take a 7-mile (11km) jaunting-car tour. Excursions go from Kate Kearney's cottage through the Gap of Dunloe to Lord Brandon's Cottage and back.

Knockreer Estate. Cathedral Place, off New St., Killarney, County Kerry. ☎ **064/31440.** Free admission. Daily during daylight hours.

You'll enjoy lovely views of the Lower Lake from this setting, a part of the National Park grounds most recently opened to the public (1986). Once the home of Lord Kenmare, the estate has a turn-of-the-century house, a pathway along the River Deenagh, and gardens that mix 200-year-old trees with flowering cherries, magnolias, and azaleas. The house, not open to the public, is now a field study center for the National Park. Main access to Knockreer is through Deenagh Lodge Gate, opposite the cathedral, in town.

✪ **Muckross House & Gardens.** Kenmare road (N71), Killarney, County Kerry. ☎ **061/31440.** Admission £3.80 ($5.30) adults, £2.70 ($3.80) seniors, £1.60 ($2.25) students and children, £9 ($12.60) family. July–Aug daily 9am–7pm; mid-Mar to June and Sept–Oct daily 9am–6pm; Nov to mid-Mar daily 9am–5:30pm.

The focal point of the Middle Lake and, in many ways, of the entire national park, is the Muckross Estate, often called "the jewel of Killarney." It consists of a gracious ivy-covered Victorian mansion and its elegant surrounding gardens.

Dating from 1843, the 20-room Muckross House has been converted into a museum of County Kerry folk life, showcasing locally carved furniture, prints, maps, paintings, and needlework. Imported treasures like Oriental screens, Venetian mirrors, Chippendale chairs, Turkish carpets, and curtains woven in Brussels are on display.

In the cellars, now craft shops, local artisans demonstrate traditional trades such as bookbinding, weaving, and pottery. The adjacent mature gardens, known for their fine collection of rhododendrons and azaleas, are also worth exploring.

✪ **Muckross Traditional Farms.** Kenmare road (N71), Killarney, County Kerry. ☎ **064/31440.** Admission £3.80 ($5.30) adults, £2.70 ($3.80) seniors, £1.60 ($2.25) students and children, £9 ($12.60) family. Combination ticket with Muckross House available. Mid-Mar to Apr and Oct Sat–Sun 1–6pm; May daily 1–6pm; June–Sept daily 10am–7pm. Closed Nov to mid-Mar.

Located near the Muckross House estate, this 70-acre park is home to displays of traditional farm life and artisans' shops. The farmhouses and buildings are so authentically detailed that visitors feel they are dropping in on working farms and lived-in houses. The animals and household environments are equally fascinating for children and adults, making for a great family outing.

You'll be able to watch sowing and harvesting or potato picking and hay making, depending on the season. Farmhands work in the fields and tend the animals, while the blacksmith, carpenter, and wheelwright ply their trades in the old manner. Women draw water from the wells and cook meals in traditional kitchens with authentic utensils, crockery, and household items. *Note:* The combination ticket allows you to visit Muckross House for less than £2 ($2.80) extra per person.

Ross Castle. Ross Rd., off Kenmare road (N71), Killarney, County Kerry. ☎ **064/35851.** Admission £3 ($4.20) adults, £2 ($2.80) seniors, £1.25 ($1.75) students and children, £7.50 ($10.50) family. Apr daily 10am–5pm; May and Sept daily 10am–6pm; June–Aug daily 9am–6:30pm; Oct Tues–Sun 10am–5pm. Last admission 45 min. before closing. Closed Nov–Mar.

Newly restored, this 15th-century fortress sits on the edge of the Lower Lake, 2 miles (3.2km) outside Killarney Town. Built by the O'Donoghue chieftains, the castle distinguished itself in 1652 as the last stronghold in Munster to surrender to Cromwell's forces. All that remains today is a tower house, surrounded by a fortified bawn with rounded turrets. The tower has been furnished in the style of the late 16th and early 17th centuries, and offers a magnificent view of the lakes and islands from its top.

Access is by guided tour only. A lovely lakeshore walk stretches for 2 miles (3.2km) between Killarney and the castle.

St. Mary's Cathedral. Cathedral Place, off Port Rd., Killarney, County Kerry. ☎ **064/ 31014.** Free admission; donations welcome. Daily 10:30am–6pm.

Officially known as the Catholic Church of St. Mary of the Assumption, this limestone cathedral is the town's most impressive building. Designed in the Gothic Revival style by Augustus Pugin, it's cruciform in shape. Construction began in 1842, was interrupted by the famine years, and concluded in 1855. The magnificent central spire was added in 1912. The entire edifice was extensively renovated from 1972 to 1973. It's at the edge of town, on the far end of New Street.

MORE ATTRACTIONS

Crag Cave. Off Limerick road (N21), Castleisland, County Kerry. ☎ **066/41244.** Admission £4 ($5.60) adults, £3 ($4.20) seniors and students, £2 ($2.80) children over 6, £12 ($16.80) family (up to 4 children). Mid-Mar to June and Sept–Oct daily 10am–6pm; July–Aug 10am–7pm.

Believed to be more than a million years old, these limestone caves were discovered and first explored in 1983. Guides accompany you 12,510 feet into the passage on a well-lit tour revealing some of the largest stalactites in Europe. Exhibits, a craft shop, and a restaurant are on the premises, 15 miles (24km) north of Killarney.

Kennedy's Animal, Bird and Pet Farm. 6 miles (9.7km) east of Killarney, off the main Cork road (N22), Glenflesk, Killarney, County Kerry. ☎ **064/54054.** Admission £3 adults ($4.20), £2 ($2.80) children. May–Oct daily 10am–6pm. Closed Nov–Apr.

At this 75-acre dairy and sheep farm surrounded by mountain vistas, you'll see cows being milked, piglets being fed, and peacocks strutting their stuff. Horse-drawn machinery is on display.

✪ **Kerry Glass Studio & Visitor Centre.** Killorglin Rd., Fossa, Killarney, County Kerry. ☎ **064/44666.** Free admission. Daily 9am–4:30pm.

This studio produces Killarney's distinctive colored glass. Visitors are welcome to watch and photograph the artisans firing, blowing, and adding color to the glass as it is shaped into vases, paperweights, candleholders, and figurines. Free guided tours are conducted according to demand. The center includes a factory shop and snack bar. It's 4 miles (6.5km) west of the town.

Museum of Irish Transport. E. Avenue Rd., Killarney, County Kerry. ☎ **064/34677.** Admission £3 adults ($4.20); £2 ($2.80) seniors, students, and children; £6–£7 ($8.40–$9.80) family. Apr–Oct daily 10am–6pm. Closed Nov–Mar.

This museum presents a unique collection of vintage and classic cars, motorcycles, bicycles, carriages, and fire engines. It includes an 1825 hobby-horse bicycle; a 1907 Silver Stream, the only model ever built; a 1904 Germain, one of four remaining in the world; a 1910 Wolseley Siddeley once driven by William Butler Yeats; and an ill-fated De Lorean, a futuristic, stainless-steel car manufactured during its short life at a plant in Ireland. Lining the walls are early motoring and cycling periodicals, and license plates from all over the world.

St. Mary's Church. Church Place, Killarney, County Kerry. ☎ **064/31832.** Free admission; donations welcome. Daily 9:30am–5pm.

It's commonly believed that St. Mary's, an 1870 neo-Gothic church, stands on the site of the original "Church of the Sloe Woods" (in Irish, *Cill Airne*—the Anglicization of which is *Killarney*). It's in the heart of town, across from the tourist office.

ORGANIZED TOURS

A Private Tour

Corcoran's Chauffeur Tours. 8 College St., Killarney, County Kerry. ☎ **064/36666.** www.kerry-insight.com/corcorans. Day rates £165 ($231) for 7-, 8-, or 9-seat executive mini-coach to £260 ($364) for 33-seat Mercedes luxury coach.

From Mercedes sedans to limousines to 33-seat Mercedes luxury coaches, Corcoran's offers privately chauffeured tours, and golf and sightseeing tours throughout the Kingdom of Kerry.

Bus Tours

In addition to Killarney's main sights, some bus tours also venture into the two prime scenic areas nearby: the Ring of Kerry and Dingle Peninsula. From May to September, tours are offered daily; prices range from £8 to £14 ($11.20 to $19.60) per person. Check the following companies if that's the kind of tour for you: **Bus Eireann,** Bus Depot, Railway Road, off East Avenue Road (☎ **064/34777**); **Castlelough Tours,** 7 High St. (☎ **064/31115**); **Corcoran's Tours,** 10 College St. (☎ **064/36666**); and **Dero's Tours,** 22 Main St. (☎ **064/31251** or 064/31567). To get your bearings in Killarney, consider one of these sightseeing tours:

Dero's Tours. 7 Main St., Killarney, County Kerry. ☎ **064/31251** or 064/31567. www.derostours.com. Tour £8 ($11.20). May–Sept daily at 10:30am; schedules vary.

Besides showing off Killarney's lakes from the best vantage points, this 3-hour tour takes you to Aghadoe, the Gap of Dunloe, Ross Castle, Muckross House and Gardens, and Torc Waterfall. Frommer's readers who book directly with the Dero's office may receive a 5% discount.

Gap of Dunloe. Castlelough Tours, 7 High St., Killarney, County Kerry. ☎ **064/31115.** Tour £13 ($18.20). May–Sept; call for hours and reservations.

This tour takes you through the spectacularly scenic Gap of Dunloe and includes a boat tour of the Killarney lakes.

Jaunting Car Tours

If you enjoy walking or bicycling, just say no to the numerous drivers who will inevitably offer their services as you make your way around the Killarney lakes. The quaint horse-driven buggies are one of the main features of the landscape. If you decide to give them a try, keep in mind that jaunting-car rates are set and carefully monitored by the Killarney Urban District Council. Current rates, all based on four persons to a jaunting car, run roughly from £12 to £32 ($16.80 to $44.80) per jaunting car (up to four persons), based on four passengers. The price depends on the destinations, which include Ross Castle, Muckross House and Gardens, Torc Waterfall, Muckross Abbey, Dinis Island, and Kate Kearney's Cottage, gateway to the Gap of Dunloe. To arrange a tour in advance, contact **Tangney Tours,** Kinvara House, Muckross Road, Killarney (☎ **064/33358**).

Boat Tours

There is nothing quite like seeing the sights from a boat on the lakes of Killarney. Two companies operate regular boating excursions, with full commentary.

M.V. *Lily of Killarney* Tours. Old Weir Lodge, Muckross Rd., Killarney, County Kerry. ☎ **064/31068.** Tour £6 ($8.40) adults, £3 ($4.20) children, £15 ($21) family. Apr–Oct 10:30am, noon, 1:45pm, 3:15pm, and 4:30pm.

Departing from the pier at Ross Castle, this enclosed water bus cruises the lakes for just over an hour. Make reservations.

M.V. *Pride of the Lakes* Tours. Scotts Gardens, Killarney, County Kerry. ☎ **064/32638.** Tour £5 ($7) adults, £2.50 ($3.50) children, £12.50 ($17.50) family. Apr–Oct 11am, 12:30pm, 2:30pm, 4pm, and 5:15pm.

This enclosed boat offers daily sailings from the pier at Ross Castle. The trip lasts just over an hour, and reservations are suggested.

SHOPPING

Vying for tourist business, the shops of Killarney keep their prices competitive. Shopping hours are usually Monday to Saturday 9am to 6pm, but from May through September or October, most stores are open every day until 9 or 10pm. Almost all stores carry Kerry Glass products, a unique Killarney-made souvenir.

Although there are more souvenir and craft shops in Killarney than you can shake a shillelagh at, here are a few of the best.

Anu Design. 8 Main St., Killarney, County Kerry. ☎ **064/34799.**

This little shop specializes in jewelry, stationery, and clothing with Celtic design imprints and engravings inspired by the original art of Newgrange, the Book of Kells, and other historic symbols. The items range from T-shirts and art cards to stone, brass, ceramics, bronze, and silver jewelry.

Blarney Woollen Mills. 10 Main St., Killarney, County Kerry. ☎ **064/33222.**

A branch of the highly successful County Cork–based enterprise, this large store occupies a beautiful shop front on the corner of Plunkett Street in the center of town. The wares range from hand-knit or hand-loomed sweaters to tweeds, crystal, china, pottery, and souvenirs of all sizes, shapes, and prices.

Frank Lewis Gallery. 6 Bridewell Lane, Killarney, County Kerry. ☎ **064/31108.**

This gallery shows and sells a variety of contemporary and traditional paintings, sculptures, and photographic work of the highest quality by some of Ireland's most acclaimed emerging artists. It's in one of Killarney's enchanting lanes, in a restored artisan's dwelling near the post office.

Killarney Art Gallery. 3 Plunkett St., Killarney, County Kerry. ☎ **064/34628.**

This shop-front gallery features original paintings by leading Irish artists, from the Killarney area and elsewhere, as well as art supplies, Irish prints, and engravings.

Killarney Bookshop. 32 Main St., Killarney, County Kerry. ☎ **064/34108.** E-mail: killbook. iol.ie.

Stop into this shop for books and maps on the history, legends, and lore of Killarney and Kerry. It also stocks good maps of the area and other books of Irish and international interest. The mail-order catalog is available on request.

Quill's Woollen Market. 1 High St., Killarney, County Kerry. ☎ **064/32277.**

This is one of the best spots in town for hand-knit sweaters of all colors, sizes, and types, plus tweeds, mohair, and sheepskins. There are also branches in Sneem and Kenmare on the Ring of Kerry, in Cork City, and at Ballingeary, County Cork (the original shop).

Serendipity. 15 College St., Killarney, County Kerry. ☎ **064/31056.**

The shelves of this tidy shop feature a wide range of unusual crafts from local artisans, such as hand-thrown pottery, N. Mosse pottery, Stephen Pearce pottery, Jerpoint glass, and hand-crafted jewelry.

OUTDOOR PURSUITS

BICYCLING   **Killarney National Park,** with its many lakeside and forest pathways, trails, and byways, is a paradise for bikers. Various vehicles are available for rent, from 21-speed touring bikes and mountain bikes to tandems. Rental charges average £7 ($9.80) per day, £35 ($49) per week. Bicycles can be rented from **O'Neills Cycle Shop,** 6 Plunkett St. (☎ **064/35357**), and **David O'Sullivan's Cycles,** Bishop Lane, New Street (☎ **064/31282**). Most shops are open year-round daily 9am to 6pm, until 8 or 9pm in the summer.

One great ride beginning in Killarney takes you through the Gap of Dunloe along a dirt forest road, where you'll see some of the best mountain scenery in the area. It can be made into a 35-mile (56km) loop if you return on N71.

FISHING   Fishing for salmon and brown trout in Killarney's unpolluted lakes and rivers is a big attraction. Brown trout fishing is free on the lakes, but a permit is necessary for the rivers Flesk and Laune. A trout permit costs £3 to £10 ($4.20 to $14) per day.

Salmon fishing anywhere in Ireland requires a license; the cost is £3 ($4.20) per day, £10 ($14) for 21 days. In addition, some rivers also require a salmon permit, which costs £8 to £10 ($11.20 to $14) per day. Permits and licenses can be obtained at the Fishery Office at the **Knockreer Estate Office,** New Street (☎ **064/31246**).

For fishing tackle, bait, rod rental, and other fishing gear, as well as permits and licenses, try **O'Neill's,** 6 Plunkett St. (☎ **064/31970**). The shop also arranges the hire of boats and *ghillies* (fishing guides) for £60 ($84) per day on the Killarney Lakes, leaving from Ross Castle. Gear and tackle can also be purchased from Michael Collins at **Angler's Paradise,** Loreto Road (☎ **064/33818**).

GOLF   Visitors are always welcome at the twin 18-hole championship courses of the **Killarney Golf & Fishing Club,** Killorglin Road, Fossa (☎ **064/31034;** www.killarney-golf.com), 3 miles (4.8km) west of the town center. Widely praised as one of the most scenic golf settings in the world, these courses, known as "Killeen" and "Mahony's Point," are surrounded by lake and mountain vistas. Greens fees are £43 ($60.20).

HORSEBACK RIDING   Many trails in the Killarney area are suitable for horseback riding. Hiring a horse costs £14 to £16 ($19.60 to $22.40) per hour at **Killarney Riding Stables,** N72, Ballydowney (☎ **064/31686**), and **Rocklands Stables,** Rockfield, Tralee Road (☎ **064/32592**). Lessons and weeklong trail rides can also be arranged.

WALKING   Killarney is ideal for hiking. On the outskirts of town, the **Killarney National Park** offers four signposted nature trails. The **Mossy Woods Nature Trail** starts near Muckross House, by Muckross Lake, and rambles 1½ miles (2.4km) through yew woods along low cliffs. **Old Boat House Nature Trail** begins at the 19th-century boathouse below Muckross Gardens and leads half a mile around a small peninsula by Muckross Lake. **Arthur Young's Walk** (3 miles/4.8km) starts on the road to Dinis, traverses natural yew woods, and then follows a 200-year-old road on the Muckross Peninsula. The **Blue Pool Nature Trail** (1½ miles/2.4km) goes from Muckross village through woodlands and past a small lake known as the Blue Pool. Leaflets with maps of the four trails are available at the park visitor center.

Rising steeply from the south shore of Muckross Lake, **Torc Mountain** provides spectacular views of the Killarney Lakes and nearby ✪ **MacGillycuddy's Reeks.** Start at the Torc Waterfall parking lot, about 4 miles (6.5km) south of Killarney, and follow the trail to the top of the falls. At a T intersection, turn left toward the top parking lot, and almost immediately turn right on the Old Kenmare Road, which follows a small stream along the south slopes of Torc Mountain. After leaving the woods, you will see Torc Mountain on your right. Look for a crescent-shaped gouge in the side of the road, about 30 feet across, with a small cairn at its far edge. This is the beginning of the path to the ridge top, marked somewhat erratically by cairns along the way. Return the way you came; the whole trip is 6 miles (9.7km), takes about 4 hours, and is moderate in difficulty.

In addition to walking independently, visitors to the Killarney area can use a range of guided walks varying in grade and duration (from 1 day to a weekend to a full week). These walks and full guided walking holidays are offered by **SouthWest Walks Ireland Ltd.,** 40 Ashe St., Tralee, County Kerry (☎ **066/712-8733;** e-mail: swwi@ iol.ie). Or you can arrange in advance to meet up with the **Wayfarers,** an international organization of passionate pedestrians, who schedule 5-week-long footloose circuits of the Ring of Kerry each spring, summer, and fall. To receive a schedule and reserve your place, contact the **Wayfarers,** 172 Bellevue Ave., Newport, RI 02840 (☎ **800/ 249-4620;** www.thewayfarers.com).

For long-distance walkers, the 125-mile (202km) **"Kerry Way"** is a signposted walking route that extends from Killarney around the Ring of Kerry (see "Sports & Outdoor Pursuits," in section 1 of this chapter).

SPECTATOR SPORTS

GAELIC GAMES   The people of Killarney are passionately devoted to the national sports of hurling and Gaelic football. Games are played almost every Sunday afternoon during the summer at **Fitzgerald Stadium,** Lewis Road (☎ **064/31700**). For complete details, consult the local *Kerryman* newspaper or the Killarney Tourist Office.

HORSE RACING   Killarney has two annual horse-racing events, in early May and mid-July. Each event lasts for 3 or 4 days and draws large crowds. For more information, contact the **Killarney Racecourse,** Ross Road (☎ **064/31125**), or the tourist office.

ACCOMMODATIONS
VERY EXPENSIVE

✪ **Killarney Park Hotel.** Kenmare Place, Killarney, County Kerry. ☎ **064/35555.** Fax 064/35266. www.killarneyparkhotel.ie. 75 units. TV TEL. £150–£220 ($210–$308) double; £250–£500 ($350–$700) suite. No service charge. Rates include full breakfast. AE, DC, MC, V.

With a striking yellow neo-Georgian facade, this new four-story property is on the eastern edge of town, between the railway station and the tourist office. Public rooms are posh and spacious, with brass fixtures, oil paintings, wainscot paneling, deep-cushioned seating, open fireplaces, and a sunlit conservatory-style lounge overlooking the gardens. The rooms are decorated in contemporary style, with dark and light wood furnishings, quilted designer fabrics, and marble-finished bathrooms.

Dining/Diversions: Restaurant and piano bar.

Amenities: Indoor heated swimming pool, gym, steam room.

EXPENSIVE

Hotel Dunloe Castle. Off Killorglin Rd., Beaufort, Killarney, County Kerry. ☎ **800/ 221-1074** from the U.S., or 064/44111. Fax 064/44583. www.iol.ie/khl. 100 units. TV TEL. £134–£172 ($187.60–$240.80) double. No service charge. Rates include full breakfast. AE, DC, MC, V. Closed Oct to mid-Apr.

On extensive tropical grounds about 6 miles (9.7km) west of town, near the entrance to the Gap of Dunloe, this is not really a castle in the medieval sense. Instead, it's a contemporary-style five-story hotel that takes its name from a ruined 15th-century fortress nearby. Entirely renovated in 1993, it has traditional furnishings, with many valuable antiques. Surrounded by broad mountain vistas, the Dunloe has an agrarian ambience, with horses, ponies, and cows grazing in the adjacent fields. It's a good place to unwind for a few days; you'll need a car to get to town or to sightsee in the area.

Dining/Diversions: Restaurant and cocktail bar.

Amenities: Heated indoor swimming pool, sauna, tennis courts, horseback riding, fishing, putting green, fitness track.

Hotel Europe. Off Killorglin Rd., Fossa, Killarney, County Kerry. ☎ **800/537-8483** from the U.S., or 064/31900. Fax 064/32118. www.iol.ie/khl. 205 units. TV TEL. £116–£158 ($162.40–$221.20) double. No service charge. Rates include full breakfast. V. Closed Nov to mid-Mar. Free parking.

One of the most picturesque settings in Killarney belongs to this modern five-story property. It sits right on the shores of the Lower Lake, 3 miles (4.8km) west of town, adjacent to Killarney's two 18-hole championship golf courses, and surrounded by dozens of mountain peaks. The hotel's public areas are spacious, open, and filled with antiques, while guest rooms offer contemporary furnishings, all enhanced by spectacular lakeside vistas; most have private balconies.

Dining/Diversions: Choices include the aptly named Panorama Restaurant, an alpine-themed Lakeside Cafe, and two lounges for light refreshment.

Amenities: Olympic-size indoor pool, saunas, gym, tennis, boating, fishing, bicycling, hairdressing salon. The hotel also has its own stables with Haflinger horses.

✪ **Killarney Great Southern.** Railway Rd., off E. Avenue Rd., Killarney, County Kerry. ☎ **800/44-UTELL** from the U.S., or 064/31262. Fax 064/31642. www.gsh.ie. 180 units. TV TEL. £150–£166 ($210–$232.40) double. Rates include full breakfast. Service charge 12.5%. AE, DC, MC, V. Free parking.

Set amid 36 acres of gardens and lush foliage on the eastern edge of town, this four-story, ivy-covered landmark is the grande dame of Killarney hotels. Dating from 1854, it was built around the time of Queen Victoria's visit to Killarney and has since been host to presidents, princes, and personalities from all over the world, as well as many a modern-day tour group. The guest rooms offer every modern convenience, including a garment press and hair dryer, and sometimes a minibar. The public areas retain the charm of yesteryear, with high ceilings rimmed by ornate plasterwork, tall windows looking onto nearby mountain vistas, glowing fireplaces, and Waterford crystal chandeliers. The lobby and all guest rooms have been recently renovated. Train and bus terminals are opposite the hotel.

Dining/Diversions: The classic main dining room overlooks the gardens; the smaller Malton Room provides à la carte service in a clubby setting (dinner only). Light refreshments and snacks are available in the Lounge and the Punch Bowl Bar.

Amenities: Concierge, room service, laundry, dry cleaning, indoor heated swimming pool, sauna, J+acuzzi, steam room, gym, two tennis courts, hairdressing salon, gift shop.

Randles Court. Muckross road (N71), Killarney, County Kerry. ☎ **800/4-CHOICE** from the U.S., or 064/35333. Fax 064/35206. www.randleshotels.com. 49 units. TV TEL. £80–£160 ($112–$224) double. Rates include full breakfast and service charge. AE, DC, MC, V. Free parking.

A former rectory dating from the turn of the century, this gabled four-story house sits on a raised site off the main road outside Killarney Town on the road to Muckross House. Totally restored, enlarged, and refurbished, it opened as a hotel in 1992. Since then, the Randles, juniors and seniors, have worked together to enhance their new hotel venture with much success. The public areas of Randles Court hark back to earlier days, with marble floors, fireplaces, chandeliers, gilt mirrors, tapestries, and old prints. Three guest rooms are in the original building and the rest in a new wing. All have distinctive furnishings, including armoires, antique desks, or vanities, plus conveniences like hair dryers.

Dining/Diversions: The hotel has a new restaurant called Checkers, an outdoor patio, and, as of fall 2000, a new lounge bar.

Amenities: 24-hour room service, laundry, fitness center.

MODERATE

Cahernane House Hotel. Muckross road (N71), Killarney, County Kerry. ☎ **800/ 44-UTELL** from the U.S., or 064/31895. Fax 064/34340. www.cahernane.com. 44 units. TEL. £110–£135 ($154–$189) double. No service charge. Rates include full breakfast. AE, DC, MC, V. Closed Nov–Mar.

Originally built in 1877 as a manor home for the Herbert family (the earls of Pembroke), this country-house hotel is less than a mile from town. It lies on the shores of the Lower Lake, in a sylvan setting of ancient trees and well-tended rose gardens. As befits its Victorian heritage, it is furnished with antiques and period furniture, both in its public areas and in most of its rooms. Dining options include the Herbert, a gracious old-world main dining room, and the Pembroke, for lighter fare. Cahemane House also offers two tennis courts, pitch and putt, croquet, and salmon and trout fishing privileges.

Castlerosse Hotel and Leisure Centre. Killorglin Rd., Killarney, County Kerry. ☎ **800/ 528-1234** from the U.S., or 064/31114. Fax 064/31031. www.towerhotelgroup.ie. 110 units. TV TEL. £70–£100 ($98–$140) double. Rates include full Irish breakfast and service charge. AE, DC, MC, V. Closed Nov–early Mar.

Set on its own parklands between the Lower Lake and surrounding mountains, this modern, rambling, ranch-style inn is 2 miles (3.2km) from the heart of town and next to Killarney's two golf courses. The recently refurbished rooms offer bright, contemporary furnishings and views of the lake. Nonsmoking rooms are available. The inn has a restaurant, a lounge, a new leisure and fitness center, two tennis courts, walking paths, and jogging trails. A 9-hole golf course opened in April 2000. New self-catering two-bedroom suites are available for £195 to £625 ($273 to $875) per week, depending on the season. Special rates are often exclusively available on the hotel's Web site, so be sure to click your way to www.towerhotelgroup.ie/castlerosse/rates.htm.

Earls Court Guesthouse. Signposted off N71, Woodlawn Junction, Muckross road, Killarney, County Kerry. ☎ **064/34009.** Fax 064/34366. www.killarney-earlscourt.ie. 11 units, 1 single with shower only. TV TEL. £65–£95 ($91–$133) double. Rates include full Irish breakfast and service charge. MC, V. Closed Nov 6–Feb. Free private parking.

Award-winning Earls Court, a 5-minute walk from the town center, is among Killarney's most attractive quality guesthouses. On arrival, guests are greeted with tea and scones in a lovely lounge. The rooms are spacious and furnished with exceptional style and taste, with a range of Irish antiques. They are immaculately clean and immediately peaceful and pleasing, blending modern and classic decor. Some have sitting areas, and nearly all have balconies. The second-floor rooms, in particular, have clear views of the mountains. All beds are orthopedically firm, and all rooms are nonsmoking and offer dataports. The breakfast menu offers a range of selections, from apple crêpes to kippers and tomatoes; you can eat in the gracious, formal dining room or, by request, in your room.

✪ Kathleen's Country House. Madam's Height, Tralee road (N22), Killarney, County Kerry. ☎ **064/32810.** Fax 064/32340. www.kathleens.net. 16 units. TV TEL. £60–£83 ($84–$116.20) double. No service charge. Rates include full breakfast. AE, MC, V. Free parking. Closed mid-Nov to early Mar.

Of the many guesthouses in the area, this one stands out. About a mile north of town on 3 acres of gardens next to a dairy farm, it's a two-story contemporary house with a modern mansard-style roof and many picture windows. Enthusiastic, efficient hostess Kathleen O'Regan-Sheppard has outfitted the guest rooms with orthopedic beds, hair dryers, trouser presses, and tea/coffeemakers. Quite recently, all rooms were totally refurbished with antique pine furniture and light floral paisley fabrics, complemented by Kathleen's collection of contemporary pastels and paintings. A cozy new library–drawing room has been added and there's a sunroom. Smoking is permitted only in the enclosed front foyer.

✪ **Killeen House.** Aghadoe, Killarney, County Kerry. ☎ **064/31711.** Fax 064/31811. www.killeenhousehotel.com. 23 units. TV TEL. £80–£160 ($112–$224) double. Service charge 10%. Rates include full breakfast. AE, DC, MC, V. Free parking.

Dating from 1838 and set on high ground overlooking Killarney's lakes and golf courses, this rambling country manor house is surrounded by mature gardens in a quiet residential area about 2 miles (3.2km) northwest of town. Completely refurbished and opened for guests in 1992, it has a relaxed, homey feel, with all the comforts of a hotel. The guest rooms, which vary in size and decor, feature orthopedic beds and standard furniture. The public areas include a restaurant, fireside lounge, and golf-themed bar—the only pub in the world that accepts golf balls as legal tender.

✪ **Muckross Park Hotel.** Muckross road (N71), Killarney, County Kerry. ☎ **064/31938.** Fax 064/31965. www.muckrosspark.com. 27 units. TV TEL. £90–£130 ($126–$182) double. No service charge. Rates include full breakfast. AE, DC, MC, V. Closed Nov–Feb. Free parking.

Just off the main road about 2 miles (3.2km) outside of town, this hotel takes its name from the fact that it sits across the road from Muckross House and Killarney National Park. Although fairly new, it incorporates parts of the oldest hotel in Killarney, dating from 1795. It's furnished in country-house style, with paneled walls, open fireplaces, and equestrian-theme oil paintings. The rooms, which vary in size and decor, have period furniture, including some semicanopy beds, quilted fabrics, frilly draperies, and Victorian-style ceiling fixtures, plus modern amenities such as garment presses and hair dryers. Facilities include a traditional restaurant and Molly Darcy's, a traditional thatched-roof pub (see "Pubs," below).

INEXPENSIVE

✪ **Gleann Fia Country House.** Deerpark, Killarney, County Kerry. ☎ **064/35035.** Fax 064/35000. E-mail: glenfia@iol.ie. 17 units. TV TEL. £48–£60 ($67.20–$84) double. Rates include full breakfast. AE, MC, V. Closed Dec–Feb. Free parking.

Although it's just a mile from town, this modern guesthouse feels pleasantly secluded, tucked away in 26 acres of lawns and woodlands. Jerry and Nora Galvin are thoughtful hosts whose presence makes it a highly personable place. The house has an airy conservatory with tea-making facilities, a guest lounge, and an unusually extensive breakfast menu. The attractive guest rooms are all nonsmoking. Although all the house is modern, it has been thoughtfully and tastefully constructed, and definitely isn't your average purpose-built guesthouse. There is a nature walk along the stream by one side of the house.

Killarney Town House. 31 New St., Killarney, County Kerry. ☎ **064/35388.** Fax 064/35259. 11 units. TV TEL. £50–£55 ($70–$77) double. No service charge. Rates include full breakfast. MC, V. Free public parking.

This appealing three-story guesthouse is on one of the busiest streets in the heart of town. It's ideal for those who want a good, clean room and don't need a bar or restaurant on the premises. The guest rooms, identified by Killarney flowers rather than by numbers, offer all the basic comforts. There are three designated nonsmoking rooms. Breakfast is served in a bright, airy ground-floor dining room. It's a 10-minute walk from the bus and train station.

DINING
EXPENSIVE

✪ **Gaby's Seafood Restaurant.** 27 High St., Killarney, County Kerry. ☎ **064/32519.** Reservations recommended. Main courses £12.90–£28 ($18.05–$39.20). AE, DC, MC, V. Mon–Sat 6–10pm. Closed late Feb to mid-Mar and Christmas week. SEAFOOD.

One of Killarney's longest established restaurants, this nautically themed place is a mecca for seafood lovers. It's known for its succulent lobster, served grilled or in a house sauce of cognac, wine, cream, and spices. Other choices include turbot, haddock in wine, local salmon, and a giant Kerry shellfish platter—a veritable feast of prawns, scallops, mussels, lobster, and oysters.

MODERATE

✪ **Bricín.** 26 High St., Killarney, County Kerry. ☎ **064/34902.** Reservations recommended for dinner. Snacks £1.60–£5 ($2.25–$7); dinner main courses £8.50–£13.50 ($11.90–$18.90). AE, DC, MC, V. Year-round Tues–Sat 10am–4:30pm; Easter–Oct Mon–Sat 6–9:30pm. IRISH.

Traditional Kerry boxty dishes (potato pancakes with various fillings, such as chicken, seafood, curried lamb, or vegetables) are the trademark of this restaurant above a very good craft and bookshop. The menu also offers a variety of fresh seafood, pastas, and Irish stew. Specials might include fillet of pork with sage and apricot stuffing, and chicken Bricín (breast of chicken in red-currant and raspberry sauce). Bricín is in one of Killarney's oldest buildings, dating from the 1830s. It sports original stone walls, pine furniture, turf fireplaces, and—very rare in Ireland—a completely nonsmoking room that seats 40. Snacks and light fare are served during the day. In addition to the shop downstairs, the building houses the Bricín Art Gallery, which displays oils and watercolors by local artists.

✪ **Coopers Café and Restaurant.** Old Market Lane, off High St. (at New St.), Killarney, County Kerry. ☎ **064/37716.** Reservations recommended. Main courses £8.95–£14.95 ($12.55–$20.95). MC, V. Mon–Sat 12:30–3pm; Mon–Thurs 6:30–9:30pm; Fri–Sat 6:30–10pm; Sun 4–9:30pm. IRISH/CONTINENTAL.

This new (1999) creation of "Martin and Mo," two of Ireland's most touted restaurateurs, is already creating quite a buzz among both locals and tourists. Coopers has clearly broken the mold here in Killarney, with its chic, urban, nightclub decor, making the most of glass, stone, aluminum, and sharp black/white contrasts. Overhead, the many-tendrilled wire-sculpture chandeliers with flower-cup lights cast a magical fairylike illumination. The total effect is as captivating as the inventive and varied menu, which focuses on local Irish seafood and wild game. The skillfully rendered options include wild pheasant cooked in Irish cream liqueur, escalope of venison, fillet of wild pigeon, grilled swordfish and salmon, wild fillet of sea trout, and baked cod Provençale. For vegetarians, the warm goat-cheese salad with two pestos is but one fully satisfying selection. The alluring array of desserts includes crumbles, tarts, homemade ice creams, meringues, and crème brûlées, although it requires rare strength of character to get past the duo of dark chocolate and pistacio mousse. Martin and Mo appear well on their way to another triumph here at Coopers.

Foley's. 23 High St., Killarney, County Kerry. ☎ **064/31217.** Reservations recommended for dinner. Main courses £9.95–£16.95 ($13.95–$23.75). AE, DC, MC, V. Daily 12:30–3pm and 5–10pm. Closed Nov–Mar. IRISH.

A Georgian country-home atmosphere prevails at this restaurant in the heart of town. The ever-changing menu features such items as Dingle Bay scallops mornay, rainbow trout, and fresh salmon, as well as breast of pheasant in port wine, duck in black-currant sauce, steak, and Kerry mountain lamb. Don't pass up the home-baked brown-bread scones that accompany each meal.

Green's. 4 Bridewell Lane, off New St. across from Dunnes Stores, Killarney, County Kerry. ☎ **064/33083.** Reservations recommended. Dinner main courses £8.95–£11.95 ($12.55–$16.75). MC, V. Tues–Sun 12:30–3pm and 6:30–9:30pm. VEGETARIAN.

Everyone knows that big surprises often come in small parcels, and so it is with this uncommonly good, fanciful nook of a restaurant tucked away in one of Killarney's many back lanes. A little persistent looking will turn it up, and the reward is a tranquil, fresh, delicious meal seemingly far from the madding crowd. The menu changes with the season and with what's best in the markets, but you can expect the likes of carrot and coriander loaf with crème fraiche, whole-wheat spinach crepe filled with organic avocado and brazil nuts and three cheeses, or baked aubergine gateau. The modest selection of house wines, by bottle or glass, suits the cuisine well. An assortment of puddings, tarts, and other sweet whims awaits you at the finish line. This new contender in the Killarney cuisine scene is well worth one of your noons or nights out.

Robertino's. 9 High St., Killarney, County Kerry. ☎ **064/34966.** Reservations recommended. Main courses £6.95–£15.95 ($9.75–$22.35). AE, DC, MC, V. Daily 4–10:30pm (in summer, also open for lunch 12:30–3pm). ITALIAN.

Step through the wrought-iron gates of this restaurant to find the ambience of Italy—operatic arias playing in the background and Mediterranean-style decor of statues, murals, marble columns, palms, and hanging plants. There are five dining areas, including a "green zone" for nonsmokers. The menu offers dishes such as veal saltimbocca, roast rib of lamb flamed in Marsala wine sauce, steaks, and a variety of local seafood and homemade pastas.

Swiss Barn. 17 High St., Killarney, County Kerry. ☎ **064/36044.** Reservations recommended. Main courses £9.50–£21 ($13.30–$29.40); 4-course early-bird (until 7pm) special £11.50 ($16.10); 5-course tourist menu £16.50 ($23.10). AE, DC, MC, V. Mid-Mar to June daily 6–9:15pm; July–Sept daily 5:45–9:45pm; Oct–Dec Thurs–Mon 6–9pm. SWISS/CONTINENTAL.

With its rustic alpine decor, this restaurant aims to bring the taste of Switzerland and the Continent to Killarney. The menu offers Swiss favorites such as éminceé of veal Zurichoise, pork fillet in morel sauce, and fondue bourguignon, as well as veal cordon bleu, beef stroganoff, steaks, seafood, and vegetarian platters.

KILLARNEY AFTER DARK

At the **Killarney Manor Banquet,** Loreto Road (☎ 064/31551), you can have a five-course dinner in 19th-century style with a complete program of songs, ballads, and dance. It's held in a stately 1840s stone-faced mansion that was built as a hotel and later served as a convent and school. Of course, it's in the nature of these shows to be touristy, which doesn't mean even the Irish don't enjoy them every now and then. The performers know exactly what they're doing and really get into it, and people have a good time. The mansion is on a hillside 2 miles (3.2km) south of town overlooking the Killarney panorama. From April through October, the banquet is staged 6 nights a week (usually closed on Sun) starting at 7:45pm. The price is £29 ($40.60) per person for complete banquet and dinner. The entertainment segment only costs £11 ($15.40) and runs from 9 to 10:30pm. Reservations are required. AE, DC, MC, and V accepted.

   Dero's Tours, 22 Main St. (☎ 064/31251), offers a special bus and theater ticket to **Siamsa Tire,** the National Folk Theatre of Ireland, at Town Park, Tralee, 20 miles (32km) northwest of Killarney. (See "Tralee After Dark," in section 4 of this chapter.)

Pubs

Dunloe Lodge. Plunkett St., Killarney, County Kerry. ☎ **064/33503.**

This simple pub in the heart of town has a friendly, comfortable atmosphere. Don't be surprised if a local patron spontaneously pulls out a harmonica, an accordion, a banjo, or a fiddle and starts to play. Most nights you'll hear anything from Irish ballads to folk or rock music.

Kate Kearney's Cottage. Gap of Dunloe, Killarney, County Kerry. ☎ **064/44146.**

Almost everyone who ventures through the famous Gap first visits this former coaching inn, which is named for a woman who was believed to be a witch. Today this outpost 9 miles (15km) west of town is a refreshment stop with souvenirs on sale. From May through September, traditional music is performed on Sunday, Tuesday, and Wednesday from 9 to 11:30pm.

The Laurels. Main St., Killarney, County Kerry. ☎ **064/31149.**

The rafters here ring to the lilt of Irish song each evening. Ballad singers are booked nightly from April through October, starting at 9pm.

Molly Darcy's. Muckross Village, Muckross Rd., Killarney, County Kerry. ☎ **064/34973.**

Across from Muckross House, this is one of Killarney's best traditional pubs, with a thatched roof, stone walls, an oak-beamed ceiling, open fireplaces, alcoves, snugs, and lots of Killarney memorabilia. There's dancing on Sunday evenings.

Scotts Bar and Beer Garden. College St., Killarney, County Kerry. ☎ **064/31060.**

On a warm summer night, this is the place to enjoy an outdoor drink. Music ranges from ballads to piano or jazz.

Tatler Jack. Plunkett St., Killarney, County Kerry. ☎ **064/32361.**

This traditional pub is a favorite gathering place for followers of Gaelic football and hurling. Traditional music or ballads are scheduled from June through September, nightly from 9:30pm.

3 The Dingle Peninsula

Dingle Town is 30 miles (48km) W of Tralee and 50 miles (80km) NW of Killarney

Like the Iveragh Peninsula, Dingle has a spectacularly scenic peripheral road, and a substantially tacky tourist trade has blossomed along it. But as soon as you veer off the main roads, or penetrate to such hinterlands of the peninsula as the Blasket Islands or Brandon Head, you'll discover extraordinary desolate beauty, seemingly worlds away from the tour buses and shamrock-filled shops. Dingle Town itself is definitely touristy, but it's smaller and less congested than Killarney and retains more traces of being a real, year-round town with an identity beyond the tourist trade.

ESSENTIALS

GETTING THERE **Bus Eireann** (☎ 066/712-3566) provides daily coach service to Dingle from all parts of Ireland. The boarding and drop-off point is on Upper Main Street.

If you're driving from Tralee to Dingle, follow R559, or take R561 from Castlemaine.

VISITOR INFORMATION **The Dingle Tourist Office** is on Main Street, Dingle (☎ 066/915-1188). It is open seasonally, usually mid-April through October. Regular hours are Monday to Saturday 10am to 1pm and 2:15 to 6pm. Extended and Sunday hours in peak summer season.

For extensive, detailed tourist information on the Dingle Peninsula, see **www. dingle-peninsula.ie**, **www.kerrygems.ie**, and **www.kerry.tourguide.ie**.

GETTING AROUND   Dingle Town has no local bus service. **Bus Eireann** (☎ **066/ 712-3566**) provides service from Dingle to other towns on the peninsula. For local taxi or minibus service, contact **John Sheehy** (☎ **066/915-1301**). The best way to get around Dingle Town, with its narrow, winding, hilly streets, is to walk. The town is small, compact, and easy to get to know.

To see the sights beyond the town, drive west along R559 or take one of the sight-seeing tours suggested below.

FAST FACTS   In an emergency, dial ☎ **999.** The **Dingle Hospital** is on Upper Main Street (☎ **066/915-1455** or 066/915-1172). The local **Garda Station** is at Holy Ground, Dingle (☎ **066/915-1522**).

The **Niallann and Daingean** (Dingle Laundry) is on Green Street (☎ **066/ 915-1837**).

The **Dingle District Library** is on Green Street, Dingle (☎ **066/915-1499**).

In & About Dingle Peninsula is a newspaper-style publication distributed free at hotels, restaurants, shops, and the tourist office. It lists events, attractions, activities, and more.

EXPLORING THE PENINSULA

Don't miss **Slea Head,** at the southwestern extremity of the peninsula. It's a place of pristine beaches, great walks, and fascinating archaeological remains. The village of **Dunquin,** stunningly situated between Slea Head and Clogher Head, is home to the Blasket Centre. **Dunbeg Fort** sits on a rocky promontory just south of Slea Head, its walls rising from the cliff edge. Although much of the fort has fallen into the sea, the place is well worth a visit at the bargain-basement rate of £1 ($1.40) per person. From Slea Head, the Dingle Way continues east to Dingle Town (15 miles/24km) or north along the coast toward Ballyferriter.

Just offshore from Dunquin are the seven **Blasket Islands;** a ferry (☎ **066/ 915-6455**) connects Great Blasket with the mainland when the weather permits. The islands were abandoned by the last permanent residents in 1953, and now are inhabited only by a few summer visitors who share the place with the seals and seabirds. A magnificent 8-mile (13km) walk goes to the west end of Great Blasket and back, passing sea cliffs and ivory beaches; you can stop along the way at the only cafe on the island, which serves lunch and dinner.

East of Ballyferriter is **Gallarus Oratory,** one of the best-preserved early Christian church buildings in Ireland. With a shape much like an overturned boat, it's constructed of unmortared stone, yet is still completely watertight after more than 1,000 years.

✪ **Ceardlann Craft Village.** The Wood, Dingle, County Kerry. ☎ **066/915-1778.** Free admission. Daily 10am–6pm.

Just west of the Dingle Marina, this cluster of traditional cottages is a circular craft village, set on a hillside above the town and harbor. A local craft worker who produces

Then I went to Ireland. The conversation of those rugged peasants, as soon as I learnt to follow it, electrified me. It was as though Homer had come alive. Its vitality was inexhaustible, yet it was rhythmical, alliterative, formal, artificial, always on the point of bursting into poetry.

—George Thomson (1903–87), *The Prehistoric Aegean*

and sells his or her craft staffs each workshop. Handmade felts, fun jewelry and mosaics, and traditional Irish musical instruments are offered, as well as silver jewelry and ceramic pictures. A cafe on the premises serves excellent homemade soups, salads, and hot dishes.

✪ **Dingle Oceanworld.** Dingle Harbour, Dingle, County Kerry. ☎ **066/915-2111.** www. dingle-oceanworld.ie. Admission £5 ($7) adults, £4 ($5.60) seniors and students, £3 ($4.20) children, £12 ($16.80) family. MC, V. Daily Sept and June 9:30am–7pm; July–Aug 9:30am–8:30pm; Oct–May 9:30am–6pm.

This new harborside aquarium is already a main attraction for families, local and from afar. Dedicated to the exploration and understanding of the ocean's depths, it's also committed to excitement and fun. Along with the sea critters behind glass in the aquarium's 29 tanks, young docents carry around live lobsters, crabs, starfish, and other "inner space" creatures, and introduce them up-close to visitors. During feeding time at 2, 3, and 4pm, children are allowed to hand out the grub. This is a compact, hands-on, interactive place of wonder and learning. It has plenty of special features, like the walk-through tunnel tank, the creepy creatures tank, and the nursery (for deep-sea babes born at Oceanworld). All but the sharks in the new shark tank are indigenous to local waters; this is your chance to view live the entrees at Dingle's great seafood restaurants, or to all but rub noses with some of the most exotic of Dingle's offshore inhabitants. In addition, there are exhibits on Brendan the Navigator and the Spanish Armada, a cafe, and a gift shop.

Eask Tower. Carhoo Hill, Dingle, County Kerry. ☎ **066/915-1850.** Admission £1 ($1.40). Daily 8am–10pm. From Dingle, follow Slea Head Rd. 2 miles (3.2km), turn left at road sign-posted for Coláiste Íde, and continue another 2 miles (3.2km).

Built in 1847 as a signal for Dingle Harbour, Eask Tower was a famine relief project. It is a remarkable edifice, a 40-foot tower built of solid stone some 15 feet thick, with a wooden arrow pointing to the mouth of the harbor. The main reason for making the 1-mile (1.6km) climb to the summit of Carhoo Hill is not the tower, but the incredible panoramic views of Dingle Harbour, Connor Pass, Slea Head, and, on the far side of Dingle Bay, the high peaks of the Iveragh Peninsula. This is a great place to get your bearings in the region—you can see most of the southern part of the Dingle Peninsula.

✪ **Ionad An Bhlascaoid Mhoir/The Blasket Centre.** Dunquin, County Kerry. ☎ **066/ 915-6371.** Admission £2.50 ($3.50) adults, £1.75 ($2.45) seniors, £1 ($1.40) children and students, £6 ($8.40) family. Apr–June and Sept–Oct daily 10am–6pm; July–Aug daily 10am–7pm. Closed Nov–Mar.

This newly opened heritage center is perched on the westerly tip of the Dingle Peninsula, overlooking the Atlantic and the distant vistas of the remote Blasket Islands. The Great Blasket was once an outpost of Irish civilization and a nurturing ground for a small group of great Irish-language writers, but its inhabitants abandoned the island in 1953. Through a series of displays, exhibits, and a video presentation, this center celebrates the cultural and literary traditions of the Blaskets and the history of Corca Dhuibhne, the Gaeltacht area. The center also has a research room, a bookshop specializing in local literature, and a wide-windowed restaurant with views of the Blaskets.

SIGHTSEEING TOURS

Fungie the Dolphin Tours. The Pier, Dingle, County Kerry. ☎ **066/915-1967** or 066/ 915-2626. Tour £6 ($8.40) adults, £3 ($4.20) children under 12. Year-round daily 10am–6pm.

Fishing boats ferry visitors out into the nearby waters to see the famous Dingle dolphin, Fungie. Trips last about 1 hour and depart regularly, roughly every 2 hours off-season and as frequently as every half-hour in high season. Go to the pier, and chances are a trip will be leaving soon. If you want to get up close and personal with Fungie, you can also arrange an early-morning dolphin swim (see "Swimming with a Dolphin," below).

Hidden Ireland Tours. Dingle, County Kerry. ☎ **066/915-1868;** mobile 087/550334. Tours average £10–£35 ($14–$49). May–Sept daily.

Con Moriarty, a local exponent of active travel, conducts a variety of custom walking tours (half day and full day) around the cliff walks, hills, mountains, woods, and lakelands of Dingle, interspersing commentaries on local history, archaeology, folklore, and culture along the way. Participants are advised to bring sturdy footwear and rain- and windproof clothing. Tours can be custom-designed for those who prefer to travel by bike or car. Reservations are necessary.

Sciuird Archaeological Adventures. Holy Ground, Dingle, County Kerry. ☎ **066/ 915-1937.** Tour £8 ($11.20) per person. May–Sept daily 10:30am and 2pm.

A local expert leads these archaeological tours, which last 2 to 3 hours. They involve a short bus journey and some easy walking. Four or five monuments, from the Stone Age to medieval times, are on the route. All tours, limited to 8 to 10 people, start from the top of the pier. Reservations are required.

SHOPPING

Annascaul Pottery. Green St. Courtyard, off Green St., Dingle, County Kerry. ☎ **066/ 915-7186.**

Colorful locally made pottery and ceramics, with wildflower designs, are on sale here. The wares come in all sizes and shapes, including jewelry. Open daily Easter through October 10am to 6pm. The factory at nearby Annascaul is open year-round.

Brian De Staic. The Wood, Dingle, County Kerry. ☎ **066/915-1298.** www.brian-de-staic.ie.

Considered Ireland's leading goldsmith by many, Brian de Staic plies his trade in his workshop, located just west of the Dingle Pier. He specializes in unusual Irish jewelry, hand-crafted and engraved with the letters of the Ogham alphabet, an ancient Irish form of writing dating from the 3rd century. His collection includes pendants, bracelets, earrings, cuff links, brooches, and tie clips.

There are two other retail shops: Green Street, Dingle (☎ **066/915-1298**), and 18 High St., Killarney (☎ **064/33822**). Shop hours are November to May, Monday to Saturday 9am to 6pm, and June to October, daily 9am to 9pm.

Greenlane Gallery. Green St., Dingle, County Kerry. ☎ **066/915-2018.** http://homepage.eircom.net/~irish/art.

This gallery and shop offers a wide selection of contemporary Irish paintings, watercolors, sculpture, and ceramics. Works by leading Irish artists are always available, and private viewings can be arranged. Images are available by e-mail on request. Open daily 10am to 9pm in the summer, 11am to 5pm in the winter.

✪ Holden Dingle. The Old School House, signposted 3 miles (4.8km) west of town on the Ventry road (R559), off the Slea Head Dr., Burnham, Dingle, County Kerry. ☎ **066/ 915-1796.**

Jackie and Conor Holden offer beautiful hand-crafted suede and silk-lined leather handbags, suede and leather pouches, and duffel and travel bags, as well as briefcases, belts, wallets, and key cases. Their workshop is in a converted schoolhouse. Open summer Monday to Saturday 8:30am to 6:30pm, Sunday 10:30am to 5pm; winter Monday to Friday 9am to 5pm.

Louis Mulcahy Pottery. Clogher, Ballyferriter, County Kerry. ☎ **066/915-6229.** www.louismulcahy.com.

Located north of Dunquin, this is a large working pottery studio. It produces a range of pottery made from local clay and glazes devised at the shop. The finished products include giant vases, teapots, platters, and huge lamps. Complementary furniture and hand-decorated silk and cotton lampshades are available, as is a selection of Lisbeth Mulcahy's tapestries and weavings. Open daily 10am to 6pm. The Mulcahys have opened a new shop and cafe in Ballyferriter Village, just down the road. The shop specializes in distinctive painted lampshades and housewares.

✪ **The Weavers' Shop.** Green St., Dingle, County Kerry. ☎ **066/915-1688.**

One of Ireland's leading weavers, Lisbeth Mulcahy creates fabrics and tapestries inspired by seasonal changes in the landscape and seascape. She uses pure wool, Irish linen-cotton, and alpaca in weaving scarves, shawls, knee rugs, wall hangings, tapestries, table mats, and napkins. Open October to May Monday to Saturday 9am to 6pm; June to September Monday to Saturday 9am to 9pm, Sunday 10am to 6pm.

SPORTS & OUTDOOR PURSUITS

BEACHES   Some of the best (read: calmest) beaches in this area for swimming are east of Castlegregory, on the west side of Tralee Bay. The beaches of **Brandon Bay** are exceptionally scenic, and good for walking and swimming. There's beach access in Stradbally and Kilcummin, off the Connor Pass Road.

BICYCLING   Mountain bikes can be rented at the **Mountain Man,** Strand Street, Dingle (☎ **066/915-1868**), for £6 ($8.40) per day or £30 ($42) per week; rear panniers are included. Mike Shea knows the area well, and can suggest a number of 1-day or overnight touring options on the Dingle Peninsula. A great day trip is the road out to the tip of the peninsula past Slea Head and Clogher Head, which is outrageously beautiful and not too hilly. Touring and mountain bikes are also available year-round from **Foxy John Moriarty,** Main Street, Dingle (☎ **066/915-1316**). High-season prices start at £6 ($8.40) per day, £25 ($35) per week.

BIRD WATCHING   **Great Blasket Island** is of some interest for the fall passerine migration. In summer, the small, uninhabited islands surrounding Great Blasket attract an abundance of nesting seabirds, including more than 20,000 pairs of storm petrels. From Clogher Head north of Dunquin at the western extremity of the Dingle Peninsula, rare autumn migrants can sometimes be seen. Inch Peninsula, extending into Castlemaine Harbour south of Inch town, is a wintering ground for brent geese, which arrive in late August and move on in April; there is also a large wigeon population during the fall.

DIVING   The **Dingle Marina Centre,** on the marina, Dingle (☎ **066/915-2422;** e-mail: divedingle@tinet.ie), offers a full range of PADI lessons and certification courses for beginners and experienced divers, as well as day-trip dives. A 1-hour Discover Skuba lesson followed by an ocean dive is £45 ($63). A day trip to the Blasket Islands, including two dives, gear hire, and cylinders, also runs £45 ($63). On the North Dingle Peninsula, **Harbour House,** The Maharees, Castlegregory, County Kerry (☎ **066/713-9292**), is a diving center that offers packages including diving, room, and board at remarkable rates. The house is yards from the Scraggane Pier, and a 5- to 15-minute boat ride from most of the diving sites. All members of the Fitzgibbon family are active divers, and they offer a great vacation for people who share their passion. Classes for beginners are also available.

GOLF Ten miles (16km) west of Dingle Town, on the western edge of the Dingle Peninsula, overlooking the Atlantic, the **Dingle Golf Club** (Ceann Sibéal), Ballyferriter (☎ **066/915-6255**), welcomes visitors to play its 18-hole, par-72 course. Greens fees are £25 ($35).

HORSEBACK RIDING At **Dingle Horse Riding,** Ballinaboula House, Dingle (☎ **066/915-2018**), rides are available along nearby beaches or through the mountains. A 1½-hour mountain ride costs £16 ($22.40). Half-day, full-day, and 3- to 5-day packages including accommodations, meals, and riding can be arranged.

SAILING The **Dingle Sailing Club,** c/o The Wood, Dingle (☎ **066/915-1984;** e-mail: lfarrell@eircom.net), offers an array of courses taught by experienced, certified instructors. Summer courses run £90 to£110 ($126 to $154). To charter a yacht, contact **Dingle Sea Ventures,** Dingle (☎ **066/915-2244;** www.charterireland.com). Yachts that sleep 6 to 10 are available; prices run £865 to £2,084 ($1,211 to $2917.60) per week. Skippers' fees are £50 ($70) per day.

SEA ANGLING For packages and day trips, contact Nicholas O'Connor at **Angler's Rest,** Ventry (☎ **066/915-9947**); or Seán O'Conchúir (☎ **066/915-5429**), representing the **Kerry Angling Association.**

SWIMMING WITH A DOLPHIN A unique water sport in Dingle Bay is swimming with the resident dolphin, known as Fungie. Although Fungie can swim about 25 mph, he enjoys human company and is usually willing to slow down and swim with his new acquaintances. He's free and lives in the wild, but regularly comes by to interact with people. To arrange a dolphin encounter, contact Bridgit Flannery (☎ **066/915-1967**), almost any day from 8am to 8pm. You book a swim the day before, when you rent your gear (semi-dry suit, mask, snorkel, boots, and fins, all in one duffel). The full overnight outfitting cost is £14 ($19.60) per person. Then you show up in your gear early the next morning to be brought out by boat to your aquatic rendezvous. The 2-hour escorted swim costs an additional £10 ($14). If you prefer, you can use your rented outfit and swim out on your own. Fungie also welcomes drop-ins. This outing is for teenagers on up, although smaller children will certainly enjoy watching.

WALKING The **Dingle Way** begins in Tralee and circles the peninsula, covering 95 miles (153km) of gorgeous mountain and coastal landscape. The most rugged section is along Brandon Head, where the trail passes between Mount Brandon and the ocean. The views are tremendous, but the walk is long (about 15 miles/24km, averaging 9 hrs.) and strenuous, and should be attempted only when the sky is clear. The section between Dunquin and Ballyferriter (also 15 miles/24km) follows an especially lovely stretch of coast. For more information, see *The Dingle Way Map Guide,* available in local tourist offices and shops.

The best walk in the region, and one of the best in Ireland, is the ascent to ✪ **Brandon's summit.** The approach from the west is a more gradual climb, but the walk from the eastern, Cloghane side is far more interesting and includes the beautiful Paternoster Lakes. The road to the trailhead is signposted just past Cloghane on the road to Brandon town; drive about 3 miles (4.8km) on this road to a small parking lot and the Lopsided Tea House. Be sure to bring plenty of water and food, gear for wind and rain, and a good map. The trail climbs through fields, past an elaborate grotto, and along the slope of an open hillside where flashy red and white poles mark the way. As you round the corner of the high open hillside, the Paternoster Lakes and Brandon come into view. The walk through this glacial valley toward the base of the mountain is the most beautiful part of the trail; when the weather's bad, you won't have wasted your time if you turn around before reaching the summit. The only seriously strenuous leg of the journey is the climb out of this valley to the ridge, a short but intense scramble over boulders and around ledges. Once you reach the ridgetop, turn left and follow the trail another quarter mile or so to the summit. You can return the way you came or continue south along the ridge, returning to Cloghane on the Pilgrim's Route, an old track that circumnavigates the Dingle Peninsula. Although this is a day hike (about 4 hr. to the summit and back), and very well marked, it shouldn't be taken too lightly—bring all necessary supplies, and let someone know when you expect to return. Information on climbing routes and weather conditions is available at the Cloghane visitor's center.

WINDSURFING The beaches around Castlegregory offer a variety of conditions for windsurfing. Those on the eastern side of the peninsula are generally calmer than those to the west. Equipment can be hired from **Jamie Knox Adventure Watersports,** Maharees, Castlegregory, County Kerry (☎ **066/713-9411;** www.jamieknox.com), on the road between Castlegregory and Fahamore. Kayaks can also be rented by the hour.

ACCOMMODATIONS
EXPENSIVE/MODERATE
Dingle Skellig Hotel. Annascaul Rd., Dingle, County Kerry. ☎ **066/9151144.** Fax 066/9151501. www.dingleskellig.com. 116 units. TV TEL. £85–£176 ($119–$246.40) double. Rates include full breakfast. AE, MC, V. Closed Jan–Feb.

Named for the fabled Sceilig (or Skellig) Rocks off the coast, this modern three-story hotel enjoys an idyllic location next to Dingle Bay on the eastern edge of town. Expanded and totally refurbished in recent years by the Cluskey family, the public areas are decorated with Irish pine and brass touches. The guest rooms, with lovely views of the bay and countryside, are modern, with light woods and pastel-toned fabrics and wall coverings.

The Coastguard Conservatory Restaurant and Gallarus Lounge offer good views of Dingle Bay, and the Blaskets Bar serves bar food all day. Throughout the summer season, the Dingle Bay Cabaret provides a 3-hour spectacle, including audience participation in the Irish dancing. A range of children's entertainment is also available, and the new heated pool and health club awaits those who find the waters of Dingle Bay a bit too chilling.

MODERATE
Benners Hotel. Main St., Dingle, County Kerry. ☎ **066/915-1638.** Fax 066/915-1412. E-mail: benners@tinet.ie. 52 units. TV TEL. £60–£120 ($84–$168) double. Rates include full Irish breakfast and service charge. AE, DC, MC, V.

One of the few hotels open year-round, Benners is in the heart of town. The lovely Georgian doorway with a fanlight at the front entrance sets the tone. Dating from more than 250 years ago, the hotel, recently refurbished and expanded, blends old-world charm and modern comforts. It's furnished with Irish antique pine furniture, including four-poster beds and armoires in the guest rooms. All rooms have hair dryers and tea/coffeemakers. There are a restaurant that overlooks a walled garden, and two bars, including the Boston Bar.

INEXPENSIVE
✪ **An Benagh.** Cloghan, County Kerry. ☎ **066/713-8142.** www.kerryweb.ie. 4 units. £32–£36 ($44.80–$50.40) double. Rates include full breakfast. Dinner for guests £15–£17 ($21–$23.80). V.

Benagh is on the west side of Brandon Bay, where Mount Brandon gently slopes away into the sea. The area is breathtakingly beautiful, and from the house, the view across the bay toward the Magharee Islands and the inland mountains is one you won't soon forget. The guest rooms (all nonsmoking) are in a second-floor addition, and each has a window facing the bay. The decor is refreshingly simple, with wooden floors and white walls. The McMowran family is actively involved in local tourism, and can give you expert guidance on local walks and archaeological sites.

Barnagh Bridge Country Guesthouse. Cappalough, Camp, Dingle, County Kerry. ☎ **066/ 713-0145.** Fax 066/713-0299. E-mail: bbguest@eircom.net. 5 units. TV TEL. £36–£52 ($50.40–$72.80) double. No service charge. Rates include full breakfast. AE, MC, V. Closed Dec.

Opened in 1993 on a hillside overlooking Tralee Bay, almost equidistant between Tralee and Dingle, this stunning two-story modern house was built as a guesthouse by the Williams family. It makes an ideal touring base for those who prefer a country setting to a town. Each guest room takes its theme from a flower in the surrounding gardens, such as Fuchsia, Bluebell, and Rose. The newly redecorated rooms have modern light-wood furnishings and orthopedic beds, and most have views of the mountains and sea. Smoking is limited to the guest lounge.

✪ **Doyle's Townhouse.** 5 John St., Dingle, County Kerry. ☎ **800/223-6510** from the U.S., or 066/915-1174. Fax 066/915-1816. www.doylesofdingle.com. 16 units. TV TEL. £68 ($95.20) double. Service charge 10%. Rates include full breakfast. DC, MC, V. Closed mid-Nov to mid-Mar.

An outgrowth of the successful Doyle's Seafood Restaurant next door, this three-story guesthouse is a favorite Dingle hideaway. It has a lovely Victorian fireplace in the main sitting-room area, and many of the antique fixtures date from 250 years ago or more. Period pieces and country pine predominate in the guest rooms, although they're totally up-to-date with firm beds, bathrooms of Italian marble, towel warmers, and hair dryers. Front rooms look out onto the town, and back rooms have a balcony or patio and face a garden, with mountain vistas in the background.

✪ **Greenmount House.** John St., Dingle, County Kerry. ☎ **066/915-1414.** Fax 066/ 915-1974. E-mail: mary@greenmounthouse.com. 12 units. TV TEL. £45–£80 ($63–$112) double. No service charge. Rates include full breakfast. MC, V. Closed Dec 20–26.

Perched on a hill overlooking Dingle Bay and the town, this modern bungalow-style bed-and-breakfast home is a standout in its category. It was named RAC (Royal Automobile Club—the British equivalent of AAA) 1997 "Small Hotel of the Year" for Ireland. It has all the comforts of a hotel at bargain prices, including guest rooms decorated with contemporary furnishings, a public sitting room with an open fireplace, and a sunlit conservatory. The breakfasts alone, ranging from smoked salmon omelets to ham-and-pineapple toasties, have won awards for proprietors Mary and John Curran. No smoking in the guest rooms or dining room.

✪ **Milltown House.** Dingle, County Kerry. ☎ **066/915-1372.** Fax 066/915-1095. http://indigo.ie/~milltown/. 10 units. TV TEL. £50–£75 ($70–$105). Rates include full breakfast. MC, V.

You couldn't wish for a more picturesque setting than this bayside haven. Tucked away on the bank of a tidal inlet, Milltown House enjoys a privileged location just minutes from Dingle Town, providing both easy access and serene remove. The simple white-and-black 19th-century exterior conceals the exceptional class and comfort of a fine family-run guesthouse. It incorporates the amenities of a hotel with the informal warmth of a B&B. The spacious guest rooms—each uniquely designed—have sitting areas, orthopedic beds, tea/coffee-making facilities, and hair dryers. Half have sea views and nearly all have patios. Two are wheelchair accessible. The nonsmoking sitting room is elegant, and the conservatory breakfast room (where you'll enjoy a lavish breakfast menu) looks out on Dingle Bay. Robert Mitchum personally leased this country house while filming *Ryan's Daughter.*

SELF-CATERING

✪ **Illauntannig Island Cottage.** Contact Bob Goodwin, Maharees, Castlegregory, County Kerry. ☎ and fax **066/713-9443.** 1 cottage. Apr–May and Sept–Oct £280 ($392) per week; June–Aug £330 ($462) per week. Rates include transport to and from the island, bedding, and all utilities. No credit cards. Closed Nov–Mar.

For those who really want to get away from it all, in a stunningly beautiful place, this cottage presents a unique opportunity. Illauntannig is one of the seven Maharees Islands, about 1 mile (1.6km) offshore from Scraggane Bay, on the north shore of the Dingle Peninsula. The island covers an area of about 36 acres, and has been inhabited at least since the 6th century, when St. Seanach founded a monastery here. The remains of this monastic site, now a national monument, are a short walk from the house; perched on the water's edge are several beehive huts, an oratory, some beautiful stone crosses, and an enclosing wall. There is only one cottage on the island. The small stone structure has four bedrooms (sleeps eight), one bathroom, a sitting room with fireplace, and a sunny kitchen with dining alcove. Make no mistake—you're roughing it, with oil lamps substituting for electric, and precious drinking water brought over from the mainland. Still, the basic necessities are provided, with gas-powered refrigeration, a hot-water heater, and a toilet with shower. Your only companions for the week will be seabirds (many species nest on the island) and cows, the island's only year-round residents. Bob Goodwin, a venerable seaman with a wealth of knowledge on local birds and history, will check in on you every day by two-way radio, and can take you to the mainland as often as necessary for supplies. Although some might balk at the isolation or the austerity, for the right person, this place is a dream come true.

Kerry Cottages. Castlegregory, Dingle Peninsula, County Kerry (1 mile/1.6km from Castlegregory). ☎ **01/284-4000.** Fax 01/284-4333. www.kerrycottages.com. Book through Ray, Christine, and Jasmine Marshall, Kerry Cottages, 3 Royal Terrace West, Dun Laoghaire, County Dublin. 10 cottages. TV. £215–£795 ($301–$1,113) per week for a 2- or 3-bedroom cottage; £388–£1,465 ($543.20–$2,051) per week for a 4- or 5-bedroom cottage. MC, V.

These 10 cottages are off a quiet back road, just a few minutes on foot to the beach and another 20 minutes or so to Castlegregory village. The smallest cottage is a cozy two-bedroom retreat with a small private garden; six cottages have three bedrooms and semiprivate backyards. The largest is a palatial construction with five bedrooms, each with a private bathroom, and two others have four to five bedrooms. Second-story bedrooms in the larger cottages have great sea views. Each place is equipped with a washer-dryer and dishwasher, and the kitchens are well stocked. There's a fireplace in the front room, as well as an electric heating system with outlets throughout the house. A small playground area for kids, with swing set and slide, is part of the complex. Special rates are available for couples. Rates vary seasonally; the cottages are an especially good value during the off-season (Sept to May).

DINING
EXPENSIVE

✪ **Doyle's Seafood Bar.** 4 John St., Dingle, County Kerry. ☎ **066/915-1174.** Reservations required. Main courses £12–£20 ($16.80–$28). MC, V. Mon–Sat 6–10pm. Closed mid-Dec to mid-Feb. SEAFOOD.

This restaurant sets the standard in Dingle. It's been almost 25 years since John and Stella Doyle left Dublin to open the town's first seafood bar. John meets the fishing boats each morning and brings in the best of the day's catch, and Stella perfects her culinary skills—a combination that has achieved international acclaim. The atmosphere is homey, with stone walls and floors, sugan (a kind of straw) chairs, tweedy place mats, and old Dingle sketches. All the ingredients come from the sea, the Doyles' gardens, or nearby farms—and the Doyles even smoke their own salmon. Specialties include baked fillet of lemon sole with prawn sauce, salmon fillet in puff pastry with sorrel sauce, rack of lamb, and a signature platter of seafood (sole, salmon, lobster, oysters, and crab claws).

The Half Door. 3 John St., Dingle, County Kerry. ☎ **066/915-1600.** Reservations recommended. Dinner main courses £12–£30 ($16.80–$42). AE, MC, V. Easter–Oct Wed–Mon 12:30–2:30pm and 6–10pm. Closed Nov–Easter. SEAFOOD/INTERNATIONAL.

Aptly named, with a traditional half door at the entrance, this restaurant exudes country-cottage atmosphere. It has exposed-brick walls, low ceilings, and vintage furnishings, yet there is also a bright, airy conservatory at the back. The menu combines old and new, with dishes such as lobster thermidor, salmon en croûte, fillet of plaice in savory crust with mustard sauce, and roast farm duck with honey and lime sauce.

✪ **Lord Bakers.** Main St., Dingle, County Kerry. ☎ **066/915-1277.** Reservations recommended for dinner. Bar food £2–£10 ($2.80–$14); dinner main courses £10–£20 ($14–$28). AE, MC, V. Fri–Wed 12:30–2pm and 6–10pm. IRISH/SEAFOOD.

Named after a 19th-century Dingle poet, politician, and publican, this restaurant is part of a building that is reputedly the oldest pub in Dingle. The decor blends an old-world stone fireplace and cozy alcoves with a sunlit conservatory and art deco touches. The menu offers standard bar food, as well as crab claws or prawns in garlic butter, fried scampi, Kerry oysters, seafood Mornay, and steaks. Dinner specialties include sole stuffed with smoked salmon and spinach in cheese sauce, lobster thermidor, and rack of lamb.

MODERATE

✪ **Beginish.** Green St., Dingle, County Kerry. ☎ **066/915-1321.** Reservations recommended. Dinner main courses £11.80–£21 ($16.50–$29.40). MC, V. Tues–Sun noon–2pm and 6–10pm. Closed Jan. SEAFOOD.

If you're looking for the best seafood in Dingle, this is the place to go. Mrs. Pat Moore runs this delightful small restaurant, and she's managed to achieve an atmosphere of quiet elegance, unassuming and comfortable. There's a lovely conservatory overlooking the garden in back, with room for outdoor tables in summer. Although there are lamb and beef dishes, and a vegetarian special each night, the emphasis is on fish—the cooking is simple, traditional, and always delightful. Among the starters, the smoked salmon with shallots, capers, and horseradish cream is exquisite—nothing fancy, just excellent ingredients combined in the perfect proportions. Also delicious is the tomato and goat's-cheese mousse with fennel. You can't go wrong with any of the fish courses, such as the Monkfish with Provençal sauce or Cod on thyme-scented potatoes and sweet red peppers. For dessert, chef Pat Moore's hot rhubarb soufflé tart is legendary in these parts.

Fenton's. Green St., Dingle, County Kerry. ☎ **066/915-2172.** Reservations recommended. Lunch main courses £3–£7 ($4.20–$9.80); early-bird 6–7pm £14.95 ($20.95); fixed-price dinner £21.95 ($30.70). MC, V. Tues–Sun noon–2:30pm and 6–10pm. Closed Dec–Feb. INTERNATIONAL.

This restaurant in the heart of town combines a country-cottage interior with a garden courtyard patio. The diverse menu offers dishes such as hot buttered lobster, mussels in garlic with white wine sauce, and medallions of fillet steak on a garlic croûte topped with Cashel blue cheese.

The Waterside. Strand St., Dingle, County Kerry. ☎ **066/915-1458.** Reservations recommended for dinner. Cafe items £2–£10 ($2.80–$14); restaurant main courses £7–£12.95 ($9.80–$18.15). MC, V. Easter–Dec daily 2:30–10pm. INTERNATIONAL.

For a daytime snack with a Dingle ambience, this restaurant offers a setting opposite the busy town marina. It's a bright and airy place with a decor of blue and white, enhanced by seasonal flowers and plants. There is seating in a sunlit conservatory-style room as well as on an outdoor patio. It operates as a cafe by day and as a full-service restaurant on summer nights. The cafe (open afternoons from 2:30 to 6pm) features an array of specialty coffees, salads, soups, and pastries; from 6 to 10pm, the cafe becomes a full-service restaurant offering an array of dinners, including multiple pastas, rack of lamb, barbary duck, and a seafood platter.

INEXPENSIVE

✪ **An Cafe Liteartha.** Dykegate St., Dingle, County Kerry. ☎ **066/915-2204.** All items £1.50–£6 ($2.10–$8.40). No credit cards. Mon–Sat 9am–6pm, later in summer. IRISH.

A combination bookstore and self-service cafe, this is a treasure trove of books and maps of Irish interest, with a focus on life in this corner of County Kerry. The cafe section features soups, salads, seafood, and freshly baked scones and cakes, as well as traditional dishes such as Irish stew. It's an ideal spot to browse and to enjoy a quick lunch or snack in the middle of town.

PUBS

An Driochead/The Small Bridge. Lower Main St., Dingle, County Kerry. ☎ **066/915-1723.**

With its old-Dingle decor and a friendly atmosphere, this pub in the heart of town draws crowds throughout the year for spontaneous sessions of traditional Irish music, usually starting at 9:30pm. Be sure to arrive early if you want even standing room!

Dick Macks. Green St., Dingle, County Kerry. ☎ **066/915-1070.**

Although Richard "Dick" Mack died a few years ago, his family carries on the traditions of this unique pub where Dick hand-crafted leather boots, belts, and other items between his pub chores. The small leather shop is still on the left, opposite a tiny bar. Old pictures, books, and mugs, all part of the Dick Mack legend, line the walls. It's a favorite among locals, as it has been for celebrities such as Robert Mitchum, Timothy Dalton, and Paul Simon, whose names are commemorated with stars on the sidewalk just outside.

Kruger's Guest House and Bar. Ballinaraha, Dunquin, County Kerry. ☎ **066/915-6127.**

In the outer reaches of the Dingle Peninsula, this pub is a social center of the Irish-speaking district. The unusual name is attributed to its former owner, Muiris "Kruger" Kavanagh, a local man who was known as a fighter at school, and nicknamed after Paulus Kruger, a famous Boer leader. The local Kruger eventually emigrated to the United States, where he worked as a bodyguard, truck driver, nurse, journalist, and PR man for the Schubert Theater Company in New York City. After 16 years, he returned to Dunquin and opened this pub, to which he then drew his great circle of friends from the entertainment field. Although Kruger is gone, his pub is still an entertainment hub, with nightly performances of the "sean-nos" Irish singing (an old, unaccompanied style) plus traditional music and step dancing on weekends.

O'Flaherty's. Bridge St., Dingle, County Kerry. ☎ **066/915-1983.**

This rustic pub reflects the true flavor of the Dingle Peninsula. Old posters, prints, clippings, and photos of Irish literary figures line the walls. You'll also see poems on the Dingle area by local authors, and favorite Gaelic phrases. In the evenings, you'll usually find traditional music sessions.

4 Tralee

20 miles (32km) NW of Killarney

Tralee is the commercial center of County Kerry; with its population of 22,000, it's three times the size of Killarney. This is more a functioning town than a tourist center, and locals outnumber visitors, except during the ever-popular ✪ **Rose of Tralee festival** in August. The town is the permanent home of the National Folk Theatre of Ireland, Siamsa Tíre, which operates year-round but is most active during July and August.

The harbor of Tralee is 4 miles (6.5km) northwest of the town, at Fenit. A major sailing center, Fenit is where St. Brendan the Navigator was born in 484, or so it's said. Brendan is credited with sailing the Atlantic in a small leather boat known as a *coracle,* and discovering America long before Columbus.

ESSENTIALS

GETTING THERE **Aer Lingus** operates daily nonstop flights from Dublin into **Kerry County Airport,** Farranfore, County Kerry (☎ **066/976-4644**), about 15 miles (24km) south of Tralee.

Buses from all parts of Ireland arrive daily at the **Bus Eireann Depot,** John Joe Sheehy Road (☎ **066/712-3566**).

Trains from major cities arrive at the **Irish Rail Station,** John Joe Sheehy Road (☎ **066/712-3522**).

Four major national roads converge on Tralee: N69 and N21 from Limerick and the north, N70 from the Ring of Kerry and points south, and N22 from Killarney, Cork, and the east.

VISITOR INFORMATION The **Tralee Tourist Office,** Ashe Memorial Hall, Denny Street (☎ **066/712-1288**), offers information on Tralee and the Dingle Peninsula. It is open weekdays 9am to 1pm and 2 to 5pm, with weekend and extended hours in the spring and summer. There is also a first-rate cafe on the premises. For Tralee tourist information on the Web, explore **www.tralee-insight.com.**

GETTING AROUND The best way to get around Tralee's downtown area is to walk. If you prefer to take a taxi, call the **Taxi Rank** (8am to midnight), The Mall (☎ **066/718-1888**); **Kingdom Cabs,** Boherbee (☎ **066/712-7828**); or **Tralee Radio Cabs,** Monavelley (☎ **066/712-5451**).

FAST FACTS If you need a drugstore, try **Kelly's Pharmacy,** 9 The Mall (☎ **066/712-1302**), or **Cahill Sharon Chemist,** 37 Upper Castle St. (☎ **066/712-1205**).

The Laundry, Pembroke Street (☎ **066/712-3214**), and **Tru-Care Dry Cleaners,** 3 High St. (☎ **066/712-3245**), are good bets for sprucing up your clothes.

In an emergency, dial ☎ **999. Bon Secours Hospital** is on Strand Street (☎ **066/712-1966**). **Tralee General Hospital** is on Killarney road (N22; ☎ **066/712-6222**). The local **Garda Station** is off High Street (☎ **066/712-2022**).

The **Kerry County Library** is on Moydewell Road (☎ **066/712-1200**).

The weekly newspaper, the *Kerryman,* covers local events. The local radio station, Radio Kerry/97 FM, broadcasts from Park View (☎ **066/712-3666**).

Kennelly's Photocentre, Ltd., 6 Castle St. (☎ **066/712-3966**), can help with your photographic needs.

SEEING THE SIGHTS

During July and August, **Tralee Tourism,** Ostendia, Oakpark (☎ **066/712-5364**), sponsors guided walks that take in the local churches, the Square, Market Lane,

Ashe Hall, Siamsa Tíre, the Town Park, and principal streets. Departures are at 10am and 4 and 9pm. After the 9pm walks, participants are taken to the local pubs to enjoy folk and traditional music. Prices start at £2 ($2.80).

Blennerville Windmill. R559, Blennerville, County Kerry. ☎ **066/712-1064.** Admission £3 ($4.20) adults, £2.50 ($3.50) seniors and students, £1.50 ($2.10) children over 5, $7.50 ($10.50) family. Apr–Oct daily 10am–6pm. Closed Nov–Mar.

Just 3 miles (4.8km) west of Tralee and reaching 65 feet into the sky, this landmark is the largest working windmill in Ireland or Britain. Built in 1800 by Sir Rowland Blennerhasset, it flourished until 1850. After decades of neglect, it was restored in the early 1990s and is now fully operational, producing 5 tons of ground whole-meal flour per week. The visitor complex has an emigration exhibition center, an audio-visual theater, craft workshops, and a cafe.

Crag Cave. Off Limerick road (N21), Castleisland, County Kerry. ☎ **066/41244.** Admission £4 ($5.60) adults, £3 ($4.20) seniors and students, £2 ($2.80) children over 6, £12 ($16.80) family (up to 4 children). Daily mid-Mar to June and Sept–Oct 10am–6pm; July–Aug 10am–7pm.

Believed to be more than a million years old, these limestone caves were discovered and first explored in 1983. Guides accompany you 12,510 feet into the passage on a well-lit tour revealing some of the largest stalactites in Europe. Exhibits, a craft shop, and a restaurant are on the premises, 15 miles (24km) north of Killarney.

Kerry the Kingdom. Ashe Memorial Hall, Denny St., Tralee, County Kerry. ☎ **066/712-7777.** Admission £5.50 ($7.70) adults, £4.75 ($6.65) students, £3 ($4.20) children, £17 ($23.80) family. Mar–Oct daily 10am–6pm; Nov–Dec 2–5pm. Closed Jan–Feb.

One of Ireland's largest indoor heritage centers, the Kingdom offers three attractions that give an in-depth look at 7,000 years of life in County Kerry. A 10-minute video, *Kerry in Colour,* presents seascapes and landscapes; the Kerry County Museum chronologically examines the county's music, history, legends, and archaeology through interactive and hands-on exhibits; and the exhibit on Gaelic football is unique. Many items of local origin that were previously on view at the National Museum in Dublin are now here. Complete with lighting effects and aromas, a theme park–style ride, "Geraldine Tralee," takes you through a re-creation of Tralee's streets and houses during the Middle Ages. The gift shop was recently expanded to include many unique items.

✪ **Tralee Steam Railway.** Ballyard, Tralee, County Kerry. ☎ **066/712-1064.** Round-trip fare £3 ($4.20) adults, £2.50 ($3.50) students and seniors, £1.50 ($2.10) children, £7 ($9.80) family. Daily May–Oct. Trains depart Blennerville on the ½ hour (1st departure 10:30am) and depart Tralee on the hour (last departure 5pm). Note: Near the end of every month, the trains are off-track and serviced for a day or two.

Europe's westernmost railway, this restored steam train offers narrated, scenic 2-mile (3.2km) trips from Tralee's Ballyard Station to Blennerville. It uses equipment that was once part of the Tralee and Dingle Light Railway (1891 to 1953), one of the world's most famous narrow-gauge railways.

SPECTATOR SPORTS

DOG RACING   Greyhounds race year-round on Tuesday and Friday starting at 8pm at the **Kingdom Greyhound Racing Track,** Oakview, Brewery Road (☎ **066/712-4033**). Admission is £4 ($5.60) per person, including program.

HORSE RACING   Horse racing takes place twice a year (in early June and late Aug) at **Tralee Racecourse,** Ballybeggan Park (☎ **066/713-6148** and, on race days,

066/712-6188). Post time is usually 2:30pm. Admission starts at £8 ($11.20) adults, £4 ($5.60) seniors and students, and is free for children under 14.

OUTDOOR PURSUITS

GOLF   Like its neighbor Killarney, Tralee is great golfing turf. The **Tralee Golf Club,** Fenit/Churchill Road, West Barrow, Ardfert (☎ **066/713-6379**), overlooking the Atlantic 8 miles (13km) northwest of town, was the first Arnold Palmer–designed course in Europe. One of Ireland's newer courses, it's expected in time to rank among the best in the world. Greens fees are £60 ($84).

About 25 miles (40km) north of Tralee in the northwest corner of County Kerry is the famous ✪ **Ballybunion Golf Club,** Ballybunion, County Kerry (☎ **068/27146**). This facility offers visitors a new clubhouse and the chance to play on two challenging 18-hole seaside links, both on the cliffs overlooking the Shannon River estuary and the Atlantic. Tom Watson has rated the "old" course one of the finest in the world; the "new" one was designed by Robert Trent Jones. Greens fees are £60 ($84) for the "old" course and £35 ($49) for the "new" one.

HORSEBACK RIDING   If you'd like to see the Tralee sights from horseback, you can't do better than to hire a horse from **El Rancho Farmhouse and Riding Stables,** Ballyard (☎ **066/712-1840;** www.dingleweb.com/elrancho; e-mail: elrancho@iol.ie). Prices start at £12.50 ($17.50) per hour for 1- or 2-hour rides on the Slieve Mish Mountains and Queen Scotia's Glen. El Rancho also offers 3- or 6-day trail rides along the Dingle Peninsula.

ACCOMMODATIONS
EXPENSIVE

Ballyseede Castle Hotel. Tralee-Killarney road, Tralee, County Kerry. ☎ **066/712-5799.** Fax 066/712-5287. 12 units. TV TEL. £135–£190 ($189–$264.60) double. Service charge 12.5%. DC, MC, V. Free parking.

Ballyseede Castle, a 15th-century castle complete with live-in ghost, was once the chief garrison of the legendary Fitzgeralds, the earls of Desmond. The Blennerhassett family occupied it until 1966 and, in 1985, turned it into a hotel. The lobby has Doric columns and a hand-carved oak staircase. Decorated with cornices of ornamental plasterwork, two drawing rooms are warmed by marble fireplaces. You'll feel like royalty in the elegant guest rooms and in the Regency Restaurant, with its huge oil paintings and fabric-lined walls. A library and piano lounge are open to guests. The castle is 2 miles (3.2km) east of Tralee, on 30 acres of parkland.

Brandon Hotel. Princes St., Tralee, County Kerry. ☎ **800/44-UTELL** from the U.S., or 066/712-3333. Fax 066/712-5019. 182 units. TV TEL. £70–£160 ($98–$224) double. No service charge. Rates include full breakfast. AE, DC, MC, V. Closed Dec 24–28.

Named for nearby Mount Brandon, this is a modern, dependable five-story hotel at the west edge of town, with vistas of the Dingle Peninsula in the distance. The rooms are functional and well kept. On the premises are the Galleon restaurant, a coffee shop, two bars, and a leisure center with indoor heated swimming pool, sauna, steam room, and gym. Best of all, the hotel is just a block from the National Folk Theatre and tourist office, and within easy strolling distance of shops and downtown restaurants. "Convenience" is the word here.

MODERATE

Abbey Gate Hotel. Maine St., Tralee, County Kerry. ☎ **066/712-9888.** Fax 066/712-9821. 100 units. TV TEL. £76–£100 ($106.40–$140) double. No service charge. AE, CB, DC, MC, V. Limited parking.

Ashdale, Fenit Road, Tralee, County Kerry. ☎ and fax **066/712-8927.** £38–£44 ($53.20–$61.60) double with bathroom.

We were both absolutely delighted with Ashdale, and stayed there for several days because we enjoyed it so much. The home is newly built and beautifully furnished, and really does fulfill the description of "luxury accommodation." The rooms are extremely comfortable, light and airy and serene in atmosphere, spotlessly clean, with excellent facilities en suite. The foods offered at breakfast each morning were very high quality. The location was wonderful for us: it did not demand too long a drive from Shannon for our first day getting accustomed to driving in Ireland, and there were two excellent restaurants a very short distance away. The house itself overlooks a beautiful view of the Slieve Mish mountains and is so close to the sea that we were able to drive just a few minutes . . . to enjoy the view of the sun setting over the sea.

—Claudia Koshinsky Clipsham, Ontario, Canada, and Ruthalee Koshinsky, Greenburg, Penn.

This new three-story hotel brings much-needed quality accommodation and a broader dimension of social activity to the center of Tralee town. The hotel is ideally located within walking distance of Tralee's prime attractions, shops, and pubs. Guest rooms, like the public areas, are furnished with new reproductions, and fabrics, art, and accessories convey an air of Georgian and Victorian Tralee. Nonsmoking rooms are available. The Bistro Marche offers light fare, the Vineyard Restaurant has a decorative theme that matches its name, and the Old Market Place Bar is a nice place to have a Guinness.

Ballygarry House Hotel. Tralee-Killarney road, Leebrook, Tralee, County Kerry. ☎ **066/712-1233.** Fax 066/712-7630. 30 units. TV TEL. £70–£110 ($98–$154) double. Rates include full Irish breakfast and service charge. AE, MC, V. Closed Dec 20–28.

A mile south of town, this country inn is on the edge of a residential neighborhood, surrounded by well-tended gardens and sheltering trees. The recently updated guest rooms vary in size; each is individually furnished and decorated to reflect different aspects of County Kerry. Each has a name to match, such as Arbutus, Muckross, Valentia, and Slea Head. The public areas have a horsey theme, with pictures of prize-winning thoroughbreds, brass accessories, and other equestrian touches. The Monarchs restaurant and lounge bar are in the hotel.

INEXPENSIVE

The Shores. ½ mile (0.8km) west of Stradbally on the Conor Pass Rd., Cappatigue, Castlegregory, County Kerry. ☎ **066/713-9196.** 6 units. TV. £36–£44 ($50.40–$61.60) double. Rates include full breakfast. MC, V. Closed Dec–Jan.

The Shores is a modern house, tastefully extended in 1999, on the south side of Brandon Bay. It commands wonderful views of Tralee Bay and Mount Brandon. Annette O'Mahoney is an avid interior decorator; in her most recent reworking of the Shores, she extended a Victorian theme and a feeling of luxury throughout the house. Furnishings are lavish, with a canopy bed in one room and writing desks in three rooms. A downstairs room has a private entrance and a fireplace. All rooms have orthopedic beds, with crisp white cotton and cream lace linen, and tea/coffee-making facilities. Two rooms are adapted for guests with disabilities. There's a sundeck and a beach for when the heavens are kind, and a guest library and video rentals for when they are not. Breakfast options are particularly extensive, with smoked salmon and waffles as alternatives to the standard fry. The latest addition is a new self-catering cottage. No smoking.

DINING
MODERATE

✪ **Larkins.** Princes St., Tralee, County Kerry. ☎ **066/976-7217.** Reservations recommended. Main courses £7.90–£16 ($11.05–$22.40); set-price menu £13.90 ($19.45). DC, MC, V. Mon–Fri 12:30–2pm and 6:30–9:30pm; Sat 6:30–9:30pm (Sun hours June–Sept). IRISH/SEAFOOD/VEGETARIAN.

This bright, welcoming Irish-country restaurant with antique pine furnishings is conveniently located and widely acclaimed for its catch of the day and its roast rack of Irish lamb. Modestly priced and immodestly tasty, the offerings are well worth a stop. As a bonus, proprietor Michael Fitzgibbon greets guests personally and generously provides information on the area.

The Tankard. 6 miles (9.7km) northwest of Tralee, Kilfenora, Fenit, County Kerry. ☎ **066/713-6164.** Reservations recommended. Main courses £8–£15 ($11.20–$21). AE, DC, MC, V. Daily bar food 12:30–10pm; restaurant 6–10pm. SEAFOOD/IRISH.

This is one of the few restaurants in the area that capitalizes on sweeping views of Tralee Bay. Situated on the water's edge, it has wide picture windows and sleek contemporary decor. The straightforward menu primarily features local shellfish and seafood, such as lobster, scallops, prawns, and black sole. It also includes rack of lamb, duck, quail, and a variety of steaks. Bar food is available all day, but this restaurant is at its best in the early evening, especially at sunset.

TRALEE AFTER DARK

Siamsa Tire, the National Folk Theatre of Ireland, is at Town Park (☎ **066/712-3055**). Founded in 1974, Siamsa (pronounced *Sheem*-sha) offers a mixture of music, dance, and mime. Its programs focus on three themes: Fado Fado/The Long Ago; Sean Agus Nua/Myth and Motion; and Ding Dong Dedero/Forging the Dance. The scenes depict old folk tales and farmyard activities, such as thatching a cottage roof, flailing sheaves of corn, and twisting a *sugan* (straw) rope.

In addition to folk theater entertainment, Siamsa presents a full program of drama and musical concerts (from traditional to classical) performed by visiting amateur and professional companies. Admission is £12 ($16.80) for adults, £10 ($14) for seniors, students, and children. Performances take place Monday, Tuesday, Thursday, and Saturday in May and from September to mid-October; Monday to Thursday and Saturday in June; and Monday to Saturday in July and August. Curtain time is 8:30pm. Call ahead for reservations.

PUBS

An Blascaod (The Blasket Inn). Castle St., Tralee, County Kerry. ☎ **066/712-3313.**

Named for the Blasket Islands, this pub has a lovely modern facade and interior, and a stark red-and-black color scheme. Inside, there's a two-story atrium with an open fireplace, plus shelves lined with old books and plates.

Harty's Lounge Bar. 30 Lower Castle St., Tralee, County Kerry. ☎ **066/712-5385.**

This pub is celebrated as the original meeting house where the Rose of Tralee festival was born. It is also known for its traditional pub grub, such as steak and kidney pie, shepherd's pie, and Irish stew.

Kirby's Olde Brogue Inn. Rock St., Tralee, County Kerry. ☎ **066/712-3357.**

This pub has a barnlike layout, with an interior that incorporates agricultural instruments, farming memorabilia, and rush-work tables and chairs. There's excellent pub grub, specializing in steaks, as well as traditional music and folk ballads when the right people show up.

Oyster Tavern. Fenit Rd., The Spa, Tralee, County Kerry. ☎ **066/713-6102.**

The nicest location of any pub in the Tralee area belongs to this tavern, just 3 miles (4.8km) west of downtown, overlooking Tralee Bay. The pub grub available includes seafood soups and platters.

10 The West

In the west of Ireland, between almost-tropical Kerry and the rugged austerity of the northwest, lie four counties: Limerick, Clare, Galway, and Mayo. Unlike Galway (the county and the town), Limerick, Clare, and Mayo, for all that they have to offer, are not principal tourist destinations—but neither are they well-kept secrets. For instance, Westport, in County Mayo, is justifiably one of the most popular resort towns in Ireland, while the Burren in County Clare is a unique spectacle, with seldom a tour bus in sight.

We'll leave Galway aside for now (we'll get to it in chapters 11 and 12). This chapter focuses on its surprising western neighbors in the hope of encouraging and guiding you to explore beyond the bus-beaten track.

1 Limerick City & Environs

Limerick is 15 miles (24km) E of Shannon Airport, 123 miles (198km) SW of Dublin, 65 miles (105km) N of Cork, 69 miles (111km) NE of Killarney, and 65 miles (105km) S of Galway

Situated along the midwest coast of Ireland, Limerick is the third-largest city in the Republic, with a population approaching 80,000. As a port on the River Shannon, Limerick has long been a city of strategic and commercial importance. During the years that transatlantic flights were required to land at Shannon Airport, the city profited mightily from its proximity.

Very little of Limerick's ancient past will strike your eye, apart from its 12th-century cathedral, its 13th-century castle, the restored Customs House, and remnants of Norman fortifications. It's a sprawling, struggling, hard-working city with limited resources, yet it's mustered some residual energy to expend on polishing and preening itself for visitors. Limerick's recently developed riverside cultural and historic area, the "Heritage Precinct," has considerable appeal and is well worth a day's visit. This may mark the beginning of a renaissance for this proud city, which has known such a turbulent past.

The countryside around Limerick has a number of interesting sights. Southwest of Limerick, the village of Adare is worth a visit, as are Glin Castle, Lough Gur, and Rathkeale. See "Side Trips from Limerick City," at the end of this section, for suggestions.

Limerick City

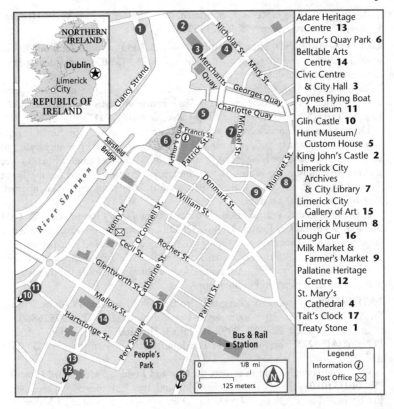

Adare Heritage Centre **13**
Arthur's Quay Park **6**
Belltable Arts Centre **14**
Civic Centre & City Hall **3**
Foynes Flying Boat Museum **11**
Glin Castle **10**
Hunt Museum/ Custom House **5**
King John's Castle **2**
Limerick City Archives & City Library **7**
Limerick City Gallery of Art **15**
Limerick Museum **8**
Lough Gur **16**
Milk Market & Farmer's Market **9**
Pallatine Heritage Centre **12**
St. Mary's Cathedral **4**
Tait's Clock **17**
Treaty Stone **1**

Legend
Information *(i)*
Post Office ✉

ESSENTIALS

GETTING THERE From the United States, Aer Lingus, Continental, and Delta Airlines operate regularly scheduled flights into **Shannon Airport,** off the Limerick-Ennis road (N18), County Clare (☎ **061/471444**), 15 miles (24km) west of Limerick. Domestic flights from Dublin and overseas flights from Britain and the Continent are available from a range of carriers. (See "Getting There," in chapter 2, for all the airlines' toll-free numbers and Web sites.) **Bus Eireann** (☎ **061/313333**) provides bus service from Shannon Airport to Limerick's Railway Station. The fare is £3.50 ($4.90). A taxi costs about £15 ($21).

Irish Rail operates direct trains from Dublin, Cork, and Killarney, with connections from other parts of Ireland. They arrive at Limerick's Colbert Station, Parnell Street (☎ **061/315555**).

Bus Eireann provides bus services from all parts of Ireland into Limerick's Colbert Station, Parnell Street (☎ **061/313333**).

Limerick City can be reached on N7 from the east and north; N20, N21, N24, and N69 from the south; and N18 from the west and north.

VISITOR INFORMATION The **Limerick Tourism Centre** is on Arthur's Quay, Limerick (☎ **061/317522**). It is open Monday to Friday 9:30am to 5:30pm, Saturday 9:30am to 1pm, with expanded and weekend hours in summer. Ask for a free copy of the *Shannon Region Visitors Guide,* which is packed with helpful information about activities and events in Limerick and the surrounding areas.

A seasonal tourist office is open March to November in the **Adare Heritage Centre,** Main Street, Adare (☎ 061/396255).

GETTING AROUND　Bus Eireann (☎ 061/313333) operates local bus service around Limerick and its environs; the flat fare is 75p ($1.05). Buses depart from Colbert Station, Parnell Street.

Taxis line up outside Colbert Station, at hotels, and along Thomas and Cecil streets, off O'Connell Street. To reserve a taxi, call **Economy Taxis** (☎ 061/411422), **Express Taxis** (☎ 061/417777), or **Top Cabs** (☎ 061/417417).

Driving around Limerick can be a little confusing because of the profusion of one-way streets—it's best to park your car and walk to see the sights. You might want to drive to King's Island for King John's Castle and the other historic sights (there's a free parking lot opposite the castle). If you must park downtown, head for the lot at Arthur's Quay, which is convenient to sightseeing and shopping, and well signposted. Parking is £1 ($1.40) per hour.

If you need to rent a car in Limerick, contact **Alamo/Treaty Rent-A-Car** (☎ 061/363663) or **Payless Car Rental** (☎ 061/328328). Most major international car-rental firms maintain desks at Shannon Airport (see the "County Clare" section, below).

The best way to get around Limerick is to walk. Follow the signposted "Tourist Trail" to see most of the city's main attractions; a booklet outlining the trail is available at the tourist office and in bookshops.

FAST FACTS　If you need a drugstore, try **Hogan's Pharmacy,** 45 Upper William St. (☎ 061/415195). After-hours service is available by calling ☎ 088/526800.

In an emergency, dial ☎ **999. St. John's Hospital** is on St. John's Square (☎ 061/415822). The local **Garda Headquarters** is on Henry Street (☎ 061/414222).

Gay travelers might want to contact the **Gay and Lesbian Switchboard Limerick** (☎ 061/310101; the gay line operates Mon and Tues 7:30 to 9:30pm; the lesbian line operates Thurs 7:30 to 9:30pm). The Drop In Centre, located at 29 Mallow St., is open Saturdays 2 to 4pm.

Take your dirty clothes to **Gaeltacht Cleaners,** 58 Thomas St. (☎ 061/415124), or **Speediwash Laundrette & Dry Cleaners,** 11 St. Gerard St. (☎ 061/319380).

The **Limerick County Library** is at 58 O'Connell St. (☎ 061/318477).

Local papers include the *Limerick Leader* (www.limerick-leader.ie), published four times a week, and the weekly *Limerick Chronicle.* The weekly *Clare Champion,* published in Ennis, is also widely read in Limerick. The *Limerick Events Guide,* issued free every 2 weeks, carries entertainment news. Radio Limerick broadcasts on 95 FM.

For photographic needs, try **Whelans Cameras,** 30 O'Connell St. (☎ 061/415246), or **Photo World,** 3 William St. (☎ 061/417515).

The **General Post Office** is on Post Office Lane, off Lower Cecil Street (☎ 061/314636). There is a branch of the post office at Arthur's Quay Centre, Patrick Street (☎ 061/415261).

SEEING THE SIGHTS

✪ **Hunt Museum.** The Custom House, Rutland St., Limerick, County Limerick. ☎ 061/312833. www.ul.ie/~hunt/. Admission £3.90 ($5.45) adults; £2.50 ($3.50) students, seniors, and children; £9 ($12.60) family. Tues–Sat 10am–5pm; Sun 2–5pm.

The Hunt Museum is happily ensconced in its new permanent home, the tastefully restored Old Custom House, the finest 18th-century building in Limerick. The facade is a reduced copy of the Petit Trianon at Versailles. The museum's collection of ancient, medieval, and modern treasures—reputed to be the finest in Ireland outside of Dublin's National Museum—includes antiquities and art objects from Europe and Ireland, ancient Irish metalwork, and medieval bronzes, ivories, and enamels. The late John and Gertrude Hunt, antiquarians and art historians, presented the collection to the Irish nation. The new museum has a shop and a most attractive restaurant that serves snacks and full meals.

✪ **King John's Castle.** Nicholas St., Limerick, County Limerick. ☎ **061/411201.** Admission £4.40 ($6.15) adults, £3.50 ($4.90) seniors and students, £2.70 ($3.80) children, £11.55 ($16.15) family. Apr–Oct daily 9:30am–5:30pm (last admission 4:30pm). Closed Nov–Mar.

Strategically built on the banks of the Shannon River, this royal fortress is the centerpiece of Limerick's historic area. It is said to date from 1210, when King John of England visited and was so taken with the site that he ordered a "strong castle" to be built here. It survives today as one of the oldest examples of medieval architecture in Ireland, with rounded gate towers and curtain walls. Thanks to a recent $7 million restoration, the interior includes an authentic archaeological excavation dating back to Hiberno-Norse times, as well as gallery displays and an audiovisual presentation portraying Limerick's 800 years of history. On the outside, the impressive facade has battlement walkways along the castle's walls and towers, offering sweeping views of the city.

Limerick City Gallery of Art. Pery Sq., Limerick, County Limerick. ☎ **061/310633.** Free admission. Mon–Fri 10am–6pm; Thurs 10am–7pm; Sat 10am–1pm; Sun 2–5pm.

Expanded and renovated in 1998 to occupy the whole neo-Romanesque Carnegie Building (1903), this gallery is in the People's Park, on the corner of Mallow Street. It houses a permanent collection of 18th-, 19th-, and 20th-century art, and also plays host to a wide range of traveling contemporary art exhibitions, including touring exhibitions from the Irish Museum of Modern Art. On some evenings, the gallery holds literary readings or traditional or classical music concerts at 8pm.

Limerick Museum. Castle Lane, at Nicholas St., Limerick, County Limerick. ☎ **061/417826.** Free admission. Tues–Sat 10am–1pm and 2:15–5pm.

This museum provides an insight into the history of Limerick. It contains displays on Limerick's archaeology, natural history, civic treasures, and traditional crafts of lace, silver, furniture, and printing. Also on view are historical paintings, maps, prints, and photographs. Of particular interest are the city's original charters from Oliver Cromwell and King Charles II, and the civic sword presented by Queen Elizabeth I.

✪ **St. Mary's Cathedral.** Bridge St., Limerick, County Limerick. ☎ **061/416238.** Donation £1 ($1.40). June–Sept Mon–Sat 9am–5pm; Oct–May Mon–Sat 9am–1pm.

Founded in the 12th century on a hill on King's Island, this site originally held a palace belonging to one of the kings of Munster, Donal Mor O'Brien. In 1172, he donated it for use as a church. The building contains many fine antiquities, including a Romanesque doorway, a pre-Reformation stone altar, and a huge stone coffin lid said to be that of Donal Mor O'Brien himself. Features added in later years include 15th-century *misericords* (supports for standing worshippers) with carvings in black oak, and a *reredos* (ornamental partition) on the high altar carved by the father of Irish patriot Patrick Pearse. St. Mary's is now a Church of Ireland property.

SHOPPING

Shopping hours in Limerick are Monday to Saturday 9:30am to 5:30pm. Many stores also stay open until 9pm on Thursday and Friday.

At the corner of Ellen Street and Wickham Street, in the heart of Limerick's old Irishtown, you'll find the **Milk Market,** a venue that hosts a memorable **Farmer's**

Market every Saturday morning from 8am to noon or 1pm. On Fridays, from roughly 11am to 4pm, this becomes an **Arts and Crafts Market.** Monday to Saturday in the Milk Market you'll find an informal bazaar of booths and stands selling everything from pottery to potato chips.

✪ **Arthur's Quay Centre.** Arthur's Quay, Limerick, County Limerick. ☎ **061/419888.**

With a striking four-story brick facade, this shopping complex overlooks Arthur's Quay Park and the Shannon River. It houses more than three dozen shops and services, ranging from Irish handcrafts to fashions, casual wear, shoes, music recordings, and books. Open Monday to Wednesday 9am to 7pm, Thursday and Friday 9am to 9pm, Saturday 9am to 6pm.

✪ **Cruises Street Shopping Centre.** Cruises St. (off Patrick St.), Limerick, County Limerick. No central phone.

This is the centerpiece of Limerick's downtown shopping district. Taking an original city street, the developers spent £18 million ($25.2 million) and turned it into an old-world village-style mall, with a total of 55 retail outlets and 20 residential apartments and offices.

Heirlooms. 32A Cruises St., Limerick, County Limerick. ☎ **061/419111.**

Long established in downtown Limerick, this shop moved to a larger space in the new Cruises Street Shopping Centre. Come here for a vast stock of local collectibles, including old books and maps, dolls, puppets, and biscuit tins, as well as frames, wood carvings, pottery, clocks, sculptures, jewelry, and candles.

Irish Handcrafts. 26 Patrick St., Limerick, County Limerick. ☎ **061/415504.**

Dating back more than 100 years, this family-run business specializes in products made by people from the Limerick area. The particular emphasis is on women's hand-knit and hand-loomed sweaters of all types, colors, and styles. There are also linen and lace garments. Open daily 9am to 6pm.

Leonards. 23 O'Connell St., Limerick, County Limerick. ☎ **061/415721.**

This long-established shop is a good source of men's tweed jackets, hats, caps, ties, and cravats, as well as silk ties, and cashmere and lambswool knitwear.

Todd William & Co. O'Connell St., Limerick, County Limerick. ☎ **061/417222.**

For more than 100 years, this has been Limerick's leading department store. It sells an array of Waterford crystal, Aran knitwear, Donegal tweeds, and ready-to-wear clothing.

White and Gold. 34 O'Connell St. (at Roches St.), Limerick, County Limerick. ☎ **061/419977.**

Irish Dresden figurines, the delicate porcelain pieces made at nearby Drumcollogher, are the special attraction of this chic gift shop. Other wares include fanciful European Christmas ornaments, intricate wind chimes, and Hummels.

SPECTATOR SPORTS & OUTDOOR PURSUITS

FISHING   Visitors are welcome to cast a line in the River Shannon for trout and other freshwater fish. For information and equipment, contact **Steves Fishing and Shooting Store,** 7 Denmark St. (☎ 061/413484).

GOLF   The Limerick area has three 18-hole golf courses, including a championship par-72 parkland layout at the **Limerick County Golf & Country Club,** Ballyneety (☎ **061/351881**), 5 miles (8km) east of Limerick. It charges greens fees of £20 ($28) weekdays, £15 ($21) weekends. The par-72 inland course at the **Limerick Golf Club,**

Ballyclough (☎ 061/415146), 3 miles (4.8km) south of Limerick, has greens fees of £22.50 ($31.50). The par-69 inland course at **Castletroy Golf Club,** Castletroy, County Limerick (☎ 061/335753), 3 miles (4.8km) east of Limerick, charges greens fees of £24 ($33.60) weekdays, £30 ($42) weekends.

GREYHOUND RACING Watch greyhounds race at the **Limerick Greyhound Track,** Market's Field, Mulgrave Street (☎ 061/415170). Races are on Monday, Thursday, and Saturday at 8pm. Admission is £3 ($4.20) on Monday and Thursday, £4 ($5.60) Saturday, including program.

HORSEBACK RIDING County Limerick's fertile fields provide good turf for horseback riding and pony trekking. Rates start at about £25 ($35) per hour. The **Clonshire Equestrian Centre,** Adare, County Limerick (☎ 061/396770), offers riding for all levels of ability, horsemanship classes, and instruction for cross-country riding, dressage, and jumping. Clonshire is also home to the Limerick Foxhounds; in the winter it's a center for hunting in the area. Per-hour rates average £20 ($28) adults, £12 ($16.80) students and children. Riding and board packages are available.

HORSE RACING Limerick has two racetracks nearby: the **Greenpark Race Course,** South Circular Road, Dooradoyle, Limerick (☎ 061/229377), and **Tipperary Race Course,** Limerick Junction (☎ 062/51357), about 20 miles (32km) southeast, near Tipperary. There is racing throughout the year; check the local newspapers for details. Admission averages £5 to £6 ($7 to $8.40) for most events.

ACCOMMODATIONS
EXPENSIVE

Jurys. Ennis Rd. (N18), Limerick, County Limerick. ☎ 800/44-UTELL from the U.S., or 061/327777. Fax 061/326400. www.jurys.com. 95 units. TV TEL. £128–£168 ($179.20–$235.20) double. Rates include full Irish breakfast and service charge. AE, DC, MC, V.

On the banks of the Shannon across the Sarsfield Bridge in a residential section, this contemporary-style hotel is just a 3-minute walk from O'Connell Street. Recently renovated, it's laid out in a bright and airy style, with a skylit, atrium-style foyer. The up-to-date guest rooms are spacious and practical, with traditional dark wood furniture and brass fixtures, and wide-windowed views of the gardens and river.

   Dining/Diversions: Choices include the Copper Room, a gourmet restaurant open only for dinner; an all-day coffee shop; and Limericks Bar, a pub with walls full of quotable and lyrical limericks.

   Amenities: Indoor heated swimming pool, sauna, steam room, Jacuzzi, tennis court.

MODERATE

Castle Oaks House. 6 miles (9.7km) east of Limerick City, off Dublin Rd. (N7), Castleconnell, County Limerick. ☎ 800/223-6510 from the U.S., or 061/377666. Fax 061/377717. www.castle-oaks.com. 20 units. TV TEL. £80–£104 ($112–$145.60) double. Suites also available. Service charge 10%. Rates include full breakfast. Free parking. AE, DC, MC, V.

Set on 25 acres of mature oak woodlands along the Shannon River, this two-story Georgian manor house is more than 150 years old. It has been a private residence, a convent, and, since 1987, a hotel. Among the original fittings are classic bow windows, a decorative staircase, and a skylit central dome, and left over from its convent days are stained-glass windows and a chapel (now used as a banquet room). The comfortable guest rooms are furnished with crown-canopy beds, soft pastel fabrics, and choice antiques from the area. The hotel has a restaurant, lounge bar, tennis court, and health club with indoor pool.

Limerick Inn. Ennis Rd. (N18), Limerick, County Limerick. ☎ **800/223-0888** from the U.S., or 061/326666. Fax 061/326281. www.limerick-inn.ie. 153 units. TV TEL. £100–£141 ($140–$197.40) double. No service charge. Rates include full breakfast. AE, DC, MC, V.

A country-club atmosphere permeates this rambling modern hotel, in a pastoral setting 3 miles (4.8km) west of the city. It is handsomely decorated with bright-toned designer furnishings and fabric-textured wall coverings. Public areas include spacious drawing rooms with views of the nearby grassy hills. There are a full-service restaurant (the Burgundy Room), a coffee shop, a piano lounge, a leisure center with a swimming pool and fitness equipment, a hairdressing salon, and a billiards room.

Limerick Ryan Hotel. Ardhu House, Ennis Rd. (N18), Limerick, County Limerick. ☎ **800/ 44-UTELL** from the U.S., or 061/453922. Fax 061/326333. www.ryan-hotels.com. 181 units. TV TEL. £70–£130 ($98–$182) double. No service charge. Rates include full breakfast. AE, DC, MC, V.

On the main road a mile west of the city center, this hotel combines one of Limerick's oldest buildings, the 1780 Ardhu House, with a modern wing of guest rooms. The public areas, part of the original house, are decorated in classic Georgian style. On the premises are the Ardhu Restaurant, the Ardhu Bar, and a sports bar with a giant screen.

INEXPENSIVE

Jurys Inn Limerick. Lower Mallow St., Limerick, County Limerick. ☎ **800/843-3311** from the U.S., or 061/207000. Fax 061/400966. www.jurys.com. 151 units. TV TEL. £49–£55 ($68.60–$77) double, triple, or family room. No service charge. AE, DC, MC, V. Discounted parking available at adjoining facility.

This is another new Jurys inn aimed at providing centrally situated, attractive, affordable accommodation in Ireland's major cities. The riverfront location is particularly appealing. The river-facing rooms, especially on the upper floors, have splendid views of the Shannon and the city's historic area. If you can get a corner room, you'll feel positively spoiled. Rooms are tastefully contemporary and eminently functional, with firm beds, tea/coffee-making facilities, large bathtubs, desks, and ample shelf and wardrobe space—everything you need, and very little you don't. Nonsmoking rooms are available. The hotel has a moderately priced and more than moderately good restaurant, the Arches, and the Inn Pub.

Shannon Grove. Athlunkard, Killaloe Rd. (R463), Limerick, County Limerick. ☎ **061/ 345756.** Fax 061/343838. 9 units. TV TEL. £50–£60 ($70–$84) double. Rates include full Irish breakfast. MC, V. Closed Dec 15–Jan 6.

In a quiet residential area a mile north of the city center, this modern two-story guesthouse, surrounded by lovely gardens, is just a quarter-mile walk from a curve of the Shannon River. The newly redecorated rooms have contemporary furnishings and firm beds. There are a TV lounge with a tea/coffeemaker, and two cheery breakfast rooms. There are also tables and chairs for outdoor seating in fine weather. Proprietor Noreen Marsh provides a particularly warm welcome and can help you plan an insider's tour of Limerick. If you don't have a car, you can take the local bus service that stops nearby.

DINING

Some of the best meals in Limerick are to be found in hotel dining rooms and in local pubs, so be sure to look above under "Accommodations" and below under "Pubs."

MODERATE

✪ **Patrick Punch's.** O'Connell Ave. (N20), Punchs Cross, Limerick, County Limerick. ☎ **061/229588.** Reservations recommended for dinner. Main courses £8.50–£14.50 ($11.90–$20.30). MC, V. Daily 10:30am–11:30pm. IRISH/INTERNATIONAL.

This popular pub-restaurant is on the main road on the southern edge of town, surrounded by gardens, ancient trees, and lots of parking. It has a three-tier lounge area, a glass-enclosed conservatory overlooking the gardens, and a clubby main room decorated with Tiffany-style lamps, dark woods, an open turf fireplace, and old photos of movie stars. The menu is equally varied, with dishes such as fillet of beef Wellington, chicken *Cleopatra* (with lemon and prawn sauce), and vegetable lasagna.

INEXPENSIVE

Piccola Italia. 55 O'Connell St., Limerick, County Limerick. ☎ **061/315844.** Reservations recommended. Main courses £5–£12 ($7–$16.80). Daily 6–11pm. ITALIAN.

With a name that means "Little Italy," this basement ristorante brings a touch of the Mediterranean to the heart of Limerick. The tables have red-and-white–checked tablecloths, and Chianti baskets hang from the ceiling. The menu is unmistakably Italian, from mushroom soup, cannelloni, lasagna, and fettuccine to scampi, salmon alla griglia, and steak pizzaiola.

LIMERICK CITY AFTER DARK
PUBS

The Locke Bar and Restaurant. 2A/3 Georges Quay, Limerick, County Limerick. ☎ **061/413733.**

Established in 1724, this is one of Limerick's oldest pubs, situated beside the east bank of the Shannon, just off Bridge Street. Although it started as a haven for sea captains visiting the port, today it's known for its traditional Irish music—played on Sunday and Tuesday year-round—and for its outdoor riverside seating. It has recently added a comfortable restaurant that offers seafood specialties.

Matt the Thrasher. Dublin Rd. (N7), Birdhill, County Tipperary. ☎ **061/379227.**

About 15 miles (24km) northeast of Limerick—and well worth the drive—this roadside tavern is a replica of a 19th-century farmers' pub. A rustic, cottagelike atmosphere prevails, with antique furnishings, agricultural memorabilia, traditional snugs (private rooms), and lots of cozy alcoves. A new patio and small restaurant have been added recently, and there's music on many evenings.

✪ **M. J. Finnegans.** Dublin Rd. (N7), about 5 miles (8km) east of Limerick City, Annacotty, County Limerick. ☎ **061/337338.**

Dating from 1776, this wonderfully restored and newly renovated alehouse takes its name from James Joyce's *Finnegans Wake,* and the decor reflects a Joycean theme, albeit with appropriate Limerick overtones. Special features include Irish ceili music on weekends, picnic tables for sitting by the rose garden on warm summer days, and excellent fare. A recent winner of many prestigious awards, including Black and White Pub of the Year, the International Dining Club Gold Award, and 1998 Pub of Distinction, Finnegans is rapidly expanding into a full-service inn and restaurant.

Nancy Blakes. 19 Upper Denmark St., just off Patrick St., Limerick, County Limerick. ☎ **061/416443.**

Situated downtown, this cozy old-world pub is known for its free traditional music sessions, year-round Sunday to Wednesday at 9pm. An added attraction, weather permitting, is the outdoor beer garden.

Vintage Club. 9 Ellen St., Limerick, County Limerick. ☎ **061/410694.**

In one of Limerick's older sections near the quays, this pub used to be a wine cellar, and the decor reflects it: barrel seats and tables, oak casks, and dark-paneled walls. A new attractive feature is the indoor/outdoor beer garden.

THE PERFORMING ARTS

Belltable Arts Centre. 69 O'Connell St., Limerick, County Limerick. ☎ **061/319709.** Tickets £5–£15 ($7–$21). Most shows Mon–Sat 8pm; call ahead.

Dramas, musicals, and concerts are staged year-round at this midcity theater and entertainment center. The summer program includes a season of professional Irish theater. By day, the building is open for gallery exhibits, showing the works of modern Irish artists as well as local crafts. There are a bar and a coffee shop. It's a 5-minute walk from the bus and train station.

University Concert Hall. University of Limerick, Plassey, County Limerick. ☎ **061/331549.** Tickets £10–£15 ($14–$21). Most performances 8pm.

On the grounds of the University of Limerick, this hall offers a broad program of national and international solo stars, variety shows, and ballet. It also books the Irish Chamber Orchestra, RTE Concert Orchestra, University of Limerick Chamber Orchestra, Limerick Singers, and European Community Orchestra. The monthly list of events is available from the tourist office.

GAY & LESBIAN CLUBS

Bubblicious, a long-established gay and lesbian nightclub on the top floor of the Savoy Complex, Bedford Row, is open Friday and Saturday nights. **Club Wilde** happens in the basement of the Glentworth Hotel, Glentworth Street, from 11pm on the first Saturday of the month.

SIDE TRIPS FROM LIMERICK CITY

Dotted about the County Limerick countryside, within a 25-mile (40km) radius of Limerick City, are many historic and cultural attractions. Here are a few suggestions:

✪ **Adare Heritage Centre.** Main St., Adare, County Limerick. ☎ **061/396666.** Admission £3 ($4.20) adults, £2 ($2.80) children, £6 ($8.40) family. Daily 9am–6pm.

Adare is one of County Limerick's special places. Its thatched-roof and Tudor-style houses, beautiful gardens, and ivy-covered medieval churches occupy wooded surroundings on both sides of the street beside the River Maigue. Those who want to linger and learn more should drop in on this heritage center. Housed in a stone building with a traditional courtyard, it offers a walk-through display on Adare's colorful history, along with a model of the town as it looked in medieval times. There is also a 20-minute audiovisual presentation illustrating the many facets of Adare today. The center also houses a cafe, craft shop, knitwear shop, and library.

Foynes Flying Boat Museum. Foynes, County Limerick. ☎ **069/65416.** Admission £3.50 ($4.90) adults, £3 ($4.20) seniors and students, £2 ($2.80) children, £9 ($12.60) family. MC, V. Apr–Oct daily 10am–6pm. Closed Nov–Mar. 23 miles (37km) east of Limerick on N69.

For aviation buffs, this museum is a must. This is the "first" Shannon Airport, the predecessor to the modern jetways of Shannon Airport in County Clare, restored and reopened as an attraction. It commemorates an era begun on July 9, 1939, when Pan Am's luxury flying boat *Yankee Clipper* landed at Foynes, marking the first commercial passenger flight on the direct route between the United States and Europe. On June 22, 1942, Foynes was the departure point for the first nonstop commercial flight from Europe to New York. This is also where bartender Joe Sheridan invented Irish coffee in 1942. At a festival each August, there's a contest to select the world Irish-coffee-making champion! The complex includes a 1940s-style cinema and cafe, the original terminal building, and the radio and weather rooms with original transmitters, receivers, and Morse code equipment.

✪ **Glin Castle.** Limerick-Tarbert Rd. (N69), County Limerick. ☎ **068/34173.** www. glincastle.com. Admission (for nonguests) to house and gardens £3 ($4.20) adults, £1 ($1.40) students. May–June daily 10am–noon, 2–4pm, and by appointment. Approximately 25 miles (40km) east of Limerick City.

Lilies of the valley and ivy-covered ash, oak, and beech trees line the driveway leading to this gleaming-white castle, home to the knights of Glin for the past 700 years. On the south bank of the Shannon Estuary, the sprawling estate contains 400 acres of gardens, farmlands, and forests. Although there were earlier residences on the site, the present home was built in 1785. It is more of a Georgian house than a castle, with added crenellations and gothic details. The current (29th) knight of Glin, Desmond FitzGerald, a noted historian and preservationist, maintains a fine collection of 18th-century Irish furniture and memorabilia. The house features elaborate plasterwork, Corinthian columns, and a unique double-ramp flying staircase. It's protected by three sets of toy fort lodges, one of which houses a craft shop and cafe. In addition, quite noble accommodation can be arranged for £170 to £270 ($238 to $378) double, with an additional £31 ($43.40) per person for dinner.

Irish Palatine Heritage Centre. Limerick-Killarney Rd. (N21), Rathkeale, County Limerick. ☎ **069/63511.** Admission £2 ($2.80) adults, £1.50 ($2.10) seniors, £1 ($1.40) students, £5 ($7) family. June–Aug Mon–Sat 10am–noon, daily 2–5pm, and by appointment.

Ireland's unique links with Germany are the focus of this new museum, 18 miles (29km) south of Limerick off the main road. Reflecting on the history of the several hundred Palatine families who emigrated from Germany and settled in this part of Ireland in 1709, it includes an extensive display of artifacts, photographs, and graphics. In addition, the museum seeks to illustrate the Palatines' innovative contributions to Irish farming life and their formative role in the development of world Methodism.

✪ **Lough Gur Visitor Centre.** 7 miles (11km) SE of Limerick City on R512, Lough Gur, County Limerick. ☎ **061/361511.** Museum and audiovisual presentation £2.20 ($3.10) adults, £1.70 ($2.40) seniors and students, £1.25 ($1.75) children, £6.05 ($8.45) family. Visitor Centre mid-May to Sept daily 10am–6pm (last admission 5:30pm); site open year-round.

Lough Gur is one of Ireland's principal archaeological sites. Excavations have shown that it was occupied continuously from the Neolithic period to late medieval times, and the natural caves nearby have yielded the remains of extinct animals, such as reindeer, giant Irish deer, and bear. The current site includes the foundations of a small farmstead built circa A.D. 900, a lake island dwelling built between A.D. 500 and 1000, a wedge-shaped tomb that was a communal grave around 2500 B.C., and the Grange Stone Circle, the largest and finest of its kind in Ireland. The lake and its shores, access to which is free, make a great place to explore and maybe set out a picnic.

The museum and audiovisual program, however, are worth neither the time nor the fee; they missed their opportunity to bring this important site alive for the visitor. It's better to explore on your own and use your imagination. If you're really keen on prehistoric Ireland and want to study the site, it's best to read up in advance or to bring along a guide that provides a map. Peter Harbison's *Guide to National and Historic Monuments of Ireland* is helpful here and throughout Ireland. For the average visitor, though, the interpretive signs are enough, and it's an enchanting spot.

ACCOMMODATIONS AROUND COUNTY LIMERICK
Very Expensive
✪ **Adare Manor.** Adare, County Limerick. ☎ **800/462-3273** from the U.S., or 061/396566. Fax 061/396124, or 201/425-0332 from the U.S. www.adaremanor.com. 63 units. TV TEL. £145–£395 ($203–$553) double. Service charge 15%. AE, DC, MC, V.

Most people wouldn't expect to find a five-star hotel in a village as tiny and secluded as Adare, 10 miles (16km) south of Limerick, but Ireland is surprising, with little gems tucked in all corners. This one is a 19th-century Tudor Gothic mansion, nestled on the banks of the River Maigue on an 840-acre estate. The former home of the earls of Dunraven, it has been masterfully restored and refurbished as a deluxe resort, with original barrel-vaulted ceilings, 15th-century carved doors, Waterford crystal chandeliers, ornate fireplaces, and antique-filled guest rooms (all nonsmoking). New two- to four-bedroom garden town houses for families and larger groups are also available.

Dining: Oak-paneled restaurant with views of the river and gardens.

Amenities: Heated indoor swimming pool, gym, sauna, riding stables, salmon and trout fishing, horseback riding, fox hunting, clay-pigeon shooting, a variety of nature trails for jogging and walking, 18-hole golf course designed by Robert Trent Jones.

Expensive

✪ **Dunraven Arms.** Main St. (N21), Adare, County Limerick. ☎ **800/447-7462** from the U.S., or 061/396633. Fax 061/396541. www.dunravenhotel.com. 76 units. TV TEL. £137.50–£171 ($192.50–$239.40) double. Service charge 12.5%. AE, DC, MC, V.

Nestled on the banks of the River Maigue, this 19th-century inn is a charming country retreat just 10 miles (16km) south of Limerick City. The public areas have an old-world ambience, with open fireplaces and antiques. Half of the rooms are in the original house, half in a new wing, and all are furnished in traditional style, with Victorian accents and period pieces.

Dining: The hotel's gardens supply fruit and vegetables for its award-winning restaurant.

Amenities: An extensive leisure center offers a pool, gym, and steam room.

Inexpensive

Abbey Villa. Kildimo Rd., Adare, County Limerick. ☎ **061/396113.** Fax 061/396969. 6 units. TV. £40–£50 ($56–$70) double. 33% discount for children. Rates include full breakfast. MC, V.

Mrs. May Haskett's home is a modern bungalow in a scenic setting, and she greets each guest warmly. Like the best of hosts, she will invite you to sit and chat while working out the best travel routes, yet she also recognizes the need to retire to your own room. The comfortable rooms are tastefully decorated, and all have satellite TV, electric blankets, and hair dryers. There are laundry facilities and private parking.

DINING AROUND COUNTY LIMERICK

Expensive

✪ **The Mustard Seed at Echo Lodge.** 8 miles (13km) from Adare, off the Newcastle West road from the center of Ballingarry, County Limerick. ☎ **069/68508.** Reservations recommended. Fixed-price 4-course dinner £32 ($44.80). AE, MC, V. Daily 7–9:30pm. Closed Feb, and Sun off-season. IRISH.

Creativity is the keynote at this lovely country-house restaurant set on 7 acres of gardens. The menu presents a creative mix of dishes, such as roulade of spinach encasing a pepper and tomato filling on warm salad of tomato and spinach, or maybe chicken coated in honey, garlic, and green peppercorns with scallion cream sauce. Organic produce and cheeses are included in the food preparation, and the atmosphere is peaceful and lovely. There is also a bed-and-breakfast at Echo Lodge.

Moderate

Inn Between. Main St., Adare, County Limerick. ☎ **061/396633.** Reservations recommended. Main courses £8.95–£14.95 ($12.55–$20.95). AE, DC, MC, V. Summer Thurs–Mon 12:30–2:30pm; year-round Thurs–Mon 6:45–9:30pm. IRISH.

Tucked in a row of houses and shops, this thatched-roof brasserie-style restaurant has a surprisingly airy skylit interior dominated by bright red and yellow tones, and a back courtyard for outdoor seating. Choices range from homemade soups and traditional dishes to innovative concoctions, such as medallions of beef fillet with green peppercorn sauce, wild salmon on leek fondue with tomato-and-chive butter sauce, and the classic Inn Between Burger, with homemade relish and french fries.

2 County Clare

Clares's chief town (Ennis) is 42 miles (67km) S of Galway, 17mi (27km) NW of Shannon Airport, 23mi (37km) NW of Limerick, 147 miles (235km) SW of Dublin, and 83 miles (133km) NW of Cork

After stepping off the plane at Shannon, your first sight of Ireland will be the vistas of County Clare: rich green fields and rolling hills joined by the meandering Shannon River. If you turn left off the main road, the barren, rocky Atlantic coast awaits you; if you continue north, you'll be heading into the historic town of **Ennis** and then to the rocky outpost known as **the Burren.**

Among the counties of Ireland, Clare is not a major celebrity. It is less dramatic and less touristed than its neighbors, Kerry and Galway. Clare can, however, boast some dazzling sites, such as the **Cliffs of Moher** and the Burren. It's the proud heir to a number of impressive ancient sites and monuments, from the Poulnabrone Dolmen to Bunratty Castle, with its a-lot-better-than-you-would-think folk park. The Burren's wildflowers and butterflies, the birds of the cliffs from Hags Head to Loop Head, the silent dolmens, and the pounding bodhrans of Doolin all contribute to Clare's appeal.

COUNTY CLARE ESSENTIALS

GETTING THERE   From the United States, Aer Lingus, Aeroflot, Continental, and Delta Airlines operate regularly scheduled flights into **Shannon Airport,** off the Limerick-Ennis road (N18), County Clare (☎ 061/471444), 15 miles (24km) west of Limerick. Domestic flights from Dublin and overseas flights from Britain and the Continent are available from a range of carriers. See "Getting There," in chapter 2, for the airline's phone numbers and Web sites.

Irish Rail provides service to Ennis Rail Station, Station Road (☎ 065/684-0444), and Limerick's **Colbert Station,** Parnell Street (☎ 061/315555), 15 miles (24km) from Shannon.

Bus Eireann provides bus services from all parts of Ireland into **Ennis Bus Station,** Station Road (☎ 065/682-4177), and other towns in County Clare.

By car, County Clare can be reached on N18. Shannon Airport has offices of the following international firms: **Alamo** (☎ 061/472342), **Avis** (☎ 061/471094), **Budget** (☎ 061/471361), and **Hertz** (☎ 061/471739). Several local firms also maintain desks at the airport; among the most reliable is **Dan Dooley Rent-A-Car** (☎ 061/471098).

From points south, County Clare can be reached directly, bypassing Limerick, on the **Tarbert-Killimer Car Ferry.** It crosses the Shannon River from Tarbert, County Kerry, to Killimer, County Clare. Trip time for the drive-on/drive-off service is 20 minutes; no reservations are needed. Ferries operate April to September, Monday to Saturday 7 or 7:30am to 9 or 9:30pm, Sunday 9 or 9:30am to 9 or 9:30pm; October to March, Monday to Saturday 7 or 7:30am to 7 or 7:30pm, Sunday 10 or 10:30am to 7 or 7:30pm. Crossings from Tarbert are on the half hour; from Killimer, on the hour. Summer fares for cars with passengers are £8 ($11.20) one-way, £12 ($16.80) round-trip. For more information, contact **Shannon Ferry Ltd.,** Killimer/Kilrush,

County Clare (☎ **065/905-3124;** e-mail: sferry@iol.ie). The Killimer Ferry terminal has a new gift shop and restaurant. Open daily 9am to 9pm.

VISITOR INFORMATION   A **tourist office** is in the Arrivals Hall of Shannon Airport (☎ **061/471644**). Hours coincide with flight arrivals and departures.

The **Ennis Tourist Office,** Clare Road, Ennis, County Clare (☎ **065/682-8366**), is about 1 mile (1.6km) south of town on the main N18 road. Open year-round Monday to Friday 9:30am to 5:15pm, with weekend and extended hours April to October.

Seasonal tourist offices in County Clare are at the Cliffs of Moher (☎ **065/ 708-1171**); O'Connell Street, Kilkee (☎ **065/905-6112**); and Town Hall, Kilrush (☎ **065/905-1577**). These offices are usually open May or June to early September.

FROM SHANNON AIRPORT TO ENNIS

The 15-mile (24km) road from Shannon Airport to Ennis, a well-signposted section of the main Limerick–Galway road (N18), is one of the most traveled routes in Ireland. It has the feel of a superhighway—a feel you won't often encounter in Ireland, and a misleading introduction to the land of *boreens* (country lanes). The whole point in Ireland, unless you know exactly where you must arrive in a hurry, is to turn off the straight-and-wide and get lost.

Now that you're on N18, turn right and proceed for 5 miles (8km). The village of **Bunratty** is before you, with its 15th-century medieval castle and theme park. Turn left, heading toward Ennis, and you pass through the charming river town of **Newmarket-on-Fergus,** home of **Dromoland Castle.**

The main town of County Clare, **Ennis** (pop. 18,000) is a compact enclave of winding, narrow streets on the banks of the River Fergus. The original site was an island on the river—hence the name *Ennis,* an Anglicized form of the Gaelic word *inis,* meaning "island." Easily explored on foot, Ennis offers a walking trail developed by the Ennis Urban District Council. A leaflet outlining the route is available free throughout the town.

ATTRACTIONS

Ballycasey Craft & Design Centre. Airport Rd. (N19), Shannon Airport, County Clare. ☎ **061/362105.** Free admission. Mon–Sat 9:30am–6pm.

Signposted within the airport complex, 3 miles (4.8km) from the main terminal, en route to the main road, this craft center is located in the courtyard of a restored Georgian manor house. The workshops feature hand-crafted items ranging from pottery, jewelry, and metalwork to knitwear and fashions. Watch the artisans as they work, and learn more about their trades.

✪ **Bunratty Castle and Folk Park.** Limerick–Ennis Rd. (N18), Bunratty, County Clare. ☎ **061/360788.** Admission £5.50 ($7.70) adults, £4 ($5.60) students and seniors, £3.10 ($4.35) children, £13.20 ($18.50) family. Daily 9:30am–5:30pm.

Long before you reach the village of Bunratty, vistas of this striking 15th-century fortress stand out along the main road from the airport. Nestled beside the O'Garney River, Bunratty Castle (1425) is Ireland's most complete medieval castle. The ancient stronghold has been carefully restored, with authentic furniture, armorial stained glass, tapestries, and works of art. By day, the building's inner chambers and grounds are open for public tours; at night, the castle's Great Hall serves as a candlelit setting for medieval banquets and entertainment (see "Dining," below).

Bunratty Castle is the focal point of a 20-acre theme park, Bunratty Folk Park. The re-creation of a typical 19th-century Irish village includes thatched cottages, farmhouses, and an entire village street, with school, post office, pub, grocery store, print shop, and hotel—all open for browsing and shopping. Fresh scones are baked in the

County Clare

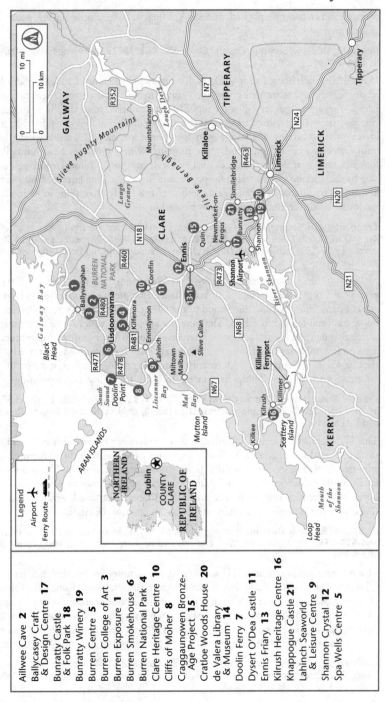

Legend

✈ Airport

- - - Ferry Route

10 mi

10 km

GALWAY

R352

Slieve Aughty Mountains

Mountshannon

Lough Derg

TIPPERARY

N7

Tipperary

Killaloe

Lough Graney

Slieve Bernagh

Limerick

R463

Sixmilebridge

LIMERICK

N24

CLARE

BURREN NATIONAL PARK

N18

Corofin

Quin

Newmarket-on-Fergus

Bunratty

21

18 20 19

Shannon

N20

Ballyvaughan

1

3 2

R480

Lisdoonvarna

5 4

Kilfenora

R481

Ennistymon

10

11

Ennis

12

13-14

Shannon Airport

R473

N21

Black Head

Galway Bay

R477

6

R478

7

Doolin Point

8

9

Lahinch

Miltown Malbay

Liscannor Bay

Slieve Callan

Mal Bay

N68

N67

Killimer Ferryport

Kilrush

16

Killimer

South Sound

ARAN ISLANDS

Mutton Island

Kilkee

Scattery Island

KERRY

River Shannon

Mouth of the Shannon

Loop Head

NORTHERN IRELAND

★ Dublin

COUNTY CLARE

REPUBLIC OF IRELAND

15

R460

R352

N18

Newmarket-on-Fergus

17

Sixmilebridge

cottages, and craftspeople ply such trades as knitting, weaving, candle making, pottery, and photography.

Bunratty Winery. Bunratty, County Clare. ☎ **061/362222.** Free admission. Daily 9:30am–5:30pm.

Housed in a coach house dating to 1816, this winery produces mead, a medieval drink made from honey, fermented grape juice, water, matured spirits, and a selection of herbs. Long ago, it was served by the jugful at regal gatherings and weddings. In fact, custom required that a bride and groom continue to drink mead for one full moon to increase the probability of a happy marriage. (Some speculate that this is where the term *honeymoon* came from.) Today, the Bunratty Winery produces mead primarily for consumption at Bunratty Castle's medieval-style banquets. Visitors are welcome to stop by the working winery, watch the production in progress, and taste the brew. Also available is traditional Irish potcheen, the first of this heady moonshine to be legally made and bottled in Ireland since it was banned in 1661.

Craggaunowen Bronze-Age Project. About 10 miles (16km) of Ennis, signposted off R469, Quin, County Clare. ☎ **061/367178.** Admission £4.40 ($6.15) adults, £3.50 ($4.90) seniors, £2.70 ($3.80) children. AE, DC, MC, V. Sat–Sun mid-Mar to end Oct 10am–6pm. Last admission 5pm.

Making use of an actual castle, *crannóg* (fortified island), and ring fort, the Craggaunowen Project has attempted to reconstruct and present glimpses of Ireland's ancient past, from the Neolithic period to the Christian Middle Ages. A special glass house has been created to exhibit Tim Severin's sea-proven replica of the curragh in which Brendan and his brother monks may have sailed to America in the 5th century. This project must have been launched with great vision and enthusiasm, but much of the original wind seems to have left its sails. As a "living history" project, it is currently on life support. The possibilities here are exciting, but the reality is disappointing.

Cratloe Woods House. Cratloe, County Clare. ☎ **061/327028.** Admission £2.50 ($3.50) adults, £1.75 ($2.45) seniors and students, £1.50 ($2.10) children. Mon–Sat 2–6pm. Closed mid-Sept to May.

This 17th-century house is a fine example of a longhouse, a type of Irish architecture that's almost obsolete. Steeped in history and long associated with the O'Brien clan, who trace their ancestry back to Brian Boru, the house is still lived in. It's filled with family portraits, works of art, and curios, and the grounds feature a collection of horse-drawn farming machinery. The primeval Garranon Oak Wood, which provided timbers for the Westminster Hall in London, is also part of the estate.

de Valera Library & Museum. Harmony Row, off Abbey St., Ennis, County Clare. ☎ **065/ 684-6353.** Free admission. Mon, Wed, and Thurs 10am–5pm; Tues and Fri 10am–8pm; Sat 10am–2pm.

This museum and library housed in a renovated 19th-century Presbyterian church pays tribute to Ireland's American-born freedom fighter and president, Eamon de Valera (1882–1975). It contains many of de Valera's personal possessions, including his car. There is also an art collection, and interesting area relics, such as a door from a Spanish Armada galleon that sank off the Clare coast in 1588 at a place now known as Spanish Point. A bronze statue of de Valera stands several blocks away at the Ennis Courthouse.

Ennis Friary. Abbey St., Ennis, County Clare. ☎ **065/682-9100.** Admission £1 ($1.40) adults, 70p (98¢) seniors, 40p (56¢) children and students, £3 ($4.20) family. Daily 9:30am–6:30pm. Closed Oct to mid-May.

Founded in 1241 and a famous seat of learning in medieval times, this Franciscan abbey made Ennis a focal point of western Europe for many years. Records show that

Knowing Your Castles

Ireland, as even the most casual visitor will notice, has no shortage of stones. When the first Irish farmers began to turn over the soil, the stones merely got in their way. Eventually, they put the stones to use, to build walls. The first walls were built to keep out animals and the elements. Eventually, however, what had to be kept out were other humans. In the world of walls, you can't miss the difference between walls raised to deter wolves and those raised to deter warriors.

The earliest stone fortifications in Ireland—round forts, often on hilltops—date from the Iron Age, sometime after 500 B.C. Dún Aengus on the Aran Islands, Staigue Fort in County Kerry, and the newly restored Lisnagun Ring Fort are among the survivors of as many as 30,000 stone forts that once protected the Irish from each other. On a smaller scale, individual families seem to have fortified their homes with mud and stone bulwarks. Another form of fortification was the *crannóg*, a stone and mud island, complete with palisades.

Later, in the early Christian period, the centers of Irish civilization—the monastic communities—came under attack from Vikings. Round towers that often climbed to nearly 100 feet in height were constructed to lift life, limb, and everything else precious out of harm's reach. This strategy, however, depended on the enemy's going away, like a dog that becomes tired of waiting for a treed cat to come down. Vikings, however, preferred to stay, and smoke or burn or starve the monks down from their towers.

With the Normans came the first Irish castles constructed with massive rectangular keeps. Trim Castle in County Meath and Carrickfergus Castle in County Antrim are impressive reminders of Norman clout. Cahir Castle in County Tipperary—with eight towers in its encircling battlements—has no equal in Ireland for sheer scale. Next came the tower house, a fortified residence. Needless to say, these were residences worthy of and requiring fortification. Bunratty Castle in County Clare and Dunguaire Castle in County Galway are splendidly restored examples of this kind of "safe house," which remained in vogue for several centuries. Wealthy merchants and others with less to protect built semifortified mansions, of which a well-preserved example is Rothe House in Kilkenny.

Nearly all of the above might loosely be called "castles." After all, a man's (or woman's) house is reputedly his or her castle—a point made then, as now, by walls, towers, dead bolts, motion detectors, and alarm systems.

---

in 1375 it buzzed with the activity of no fewer than 350 friars and 600 students. Although it was finally forced to close in 1692, and thereafter fell into ruin, the abbey still contains many interesting sculpted tombs, decorative fragments, and carvings, including the famous McMahon tomb. The nave and chancel are the oldest parts of the friary, but other structures, such as the 15th-century tower, transept, and sacristy, are also rich in architectural detail.

✪ **Knappogue Castle.** Quin, County Clare. ☎ **061/360788.** Admission £2.90 ($4.05) adults, £2 ($2.80) seniors and students, £1.50 ($2.10) children, £7.15 ($10) family. Daily 9:30am–5:30pm. Last admission 4:30pm. Closed Nov–Mar.

Approximately midway between Bunratty and Ennis, this castle was built in 1467 and was the home of the McNamara clan, who dominated the area for more than 1,000 years. The original Norman structure includes elaborate late-Georgian and Regency wings that were added in the mid–19th century. Now fully restored, it is furnished with authentic 15th-century pieces. Like Bunratty Castle, it serves as a venue for nightly medieval banquets in the summer (see "Dining," below).

Shannon Crystal. Sandfield Rd., Ennis, County Clare. ☎ **065/682-1250.** Free admission. Daily 9am–6pm.

In the north end of town (on the way to Galway road), this is the Shannon area's own crystal-making enterprise, producing original hand-cut glassware on the premises. The showroom is open to visitors, who can watch demonstrations by the master cutter.

SHOPPING

Avoca. Limerick-Ennis Rd. (N18), Bunratty, County Clare. ☎ **061/364029.**

This pink, thatched-roof cottage shop is a branch of the legendary County Wicklow–based Avoca Handweavers, the oldest company of its kind in Ireland, dating from 1723. Like its sister shops, this one carries the colorful tweeds and mohairs that have made the Avoca line famous, plus linen-cotton fashions, stylish sweaters, tweed totes, and a wide array of hats. A coffee shop, serving lunch and snacks, is on the premises. Open daily 9:30am to 5:30pm.

Belleek Shop. 36 Abbey St., Ennis, County Clare. ☎ **065/682-9607.** www.belleekshop.com.

In the heart of Ennis, overlooking the 16th-century Franciscan Abbey, this newly expanded shop is more than 90 years old. It was the first Belleek china outlet in southern Ireland. The shop is renowned for its extensive range of Waterford, Galway, and Tipperary crystals, fine china, tableware, and figurines. In recent years, it has expanded to include other Irish products, such as handmade character dolls, turf crafts, pewter, jewelry, and fashionable tweeds. Open Monday to Saturday 9am to 7pm.

Custy's Traditional Music Shop. 2 Francis St., Ennis, County Clare. ☎ **065/682-1727.**

If you'd like to bring back the melodious sounds of County Clare, this is the place to shop. The selection includes a full range of traditional and folk music tapes and CDs, as well as books, photos, paintings, and crafts pertaining to traditional music. You can also buy a fiddle, a tin whistle, a banjo, a concertina, an accordion, or a flute. Open Monday to Saturday 9:30am to 6pm.

Shannon Duty Free Shops. Shannon Airport, County Clare. ☎ **061/475047** or 061/471777.

Founded in 1947, this airport complex is known throughout the world as the mother of all duty-free shops. It offers tax-free bargains to shoppers passing through the airport. Most of the products are Irish, such as Waterford crystal, Belleek china, Donegal tweeds, Aran knitwear, Connemara marble, ceramic leprechauns, shillelaghs, and smoked salmon. You'll also find names like Wedgwood, Bing and Grondahl, Lladró, Anri, Limoges, Orrefors, and Pringle. Open daily 9:30am to 5:30pm.

HITTING THE LINKS

Where else but in Ireland can you step off a plane and step up to the first tee? The 18-hole, par-72 championship course at the **Shannon Golf Club,** Shannon Airport (☎ **061/471020**), welcomes visitors. Greens fees are £25 to £30 ($35 to $42). Within a half mile of the main terminal, it is surrounded by scenic vistas of County Clare, the Shannon River, and the busy jetways.

Other choices in the area include the par-71 **Dromoland Golf Club,** Newmarket-on-Fergus, County Clare (☎ **061/368444**), with greens fees of £30 to £35 ($42 to $49), or £20 ($28) for guests at the castle hotel. The par-69 parkland course at the

Ennis Golf Club, Drumbiggle, Ennis, County Clare (☎ 065/682-4074), charges greens fees of £18 ($25.20).

ACCOMMODATIONS
Very Expensive
○ **Dromoland Castle.** Limerick-Ennis Rd. (N18), Newmarket-on-Fergus, County Clare. ☎ **800/346-7007** from the U.S., or 061/368144. Fax 061/363355. www.dromoland.ie. 100 units. TV TEL. £140–£336 ($196–$470.40) double; £295–£810 ($413–$1,134) suite, depending on room and season. Full Irish breakfast £14 ($19.60). No service charge. AE, DC, MC, V.

You can vacation like royalty in this fairy-tale setting of turrets and towers (and every 20th-century luxury) at this impressive castle hotel just 8 miles (13km) from Shannon Airport. The castle was built in 1686 by the O'Briens, the high kings of Ireland, and was restored and refurbished 30 years ago as a hotel. It's nestled beside the River Rine, amid 400 acres of parklands and gardens that are home to varied species of wildlife, including a deer herd. As befits its royal exterior, the castle's drawing rooms and stately halls are full of splendid wood and stone carvings, medieval suits of armor, rich oak paneling, and original oil paintings. The rooms are individually decorated with designer fabrics and reproduction furniture; many look out onto the water or the romantic walled gardens.

Dining/Diversions: The Earl of Thomond restaurant is known for French cuisine served in a regal setting overlooking the lake. There is also a relaxing bar and lounge, and the Fig Tree restaurant in the golf and country club.

Amenities: Concierge, 24-hour room service, laundry/dry cleaning, 18-hole golf course, tennis courts, walking/jogging trails, fishing and boating equipment.

Expensive
Fitzpatrick Bunratty Shamrock Inn. Limerick-Ennis Rd. (N18), Bunratty, County Clare. ☎ **800/367-7701** from the U.S., or 061/361177. Fax 061/471252. www.fitzpatrickhotels. com. 115 units. TV TEL. £105–£159 ($147–$222.60) double. No service charge. Rates include full breakfast. AE, DC, MC, V.

Just 5 miles (8km) from Shannon Airport, this rambling two-story ranch-style hotel sits back from the main road next to Bunratty Castle and Folk Park. Rooms are contemporary, with beamed ceilings, light woods, Irish fabrics and furnishings, and tall windows offering views of the gardens and Bunratty Castle. In-room extras include hair dryers, irons, and luggage racks; some units have Jacuzzis. The public areas include a plant-filled sunlit conservatory and a spacious lobby-lounge.

Dining/Diversions: Seafood and game are the specialties of Truffles Restaurant, where there's also an efficient breakfast buffet each morning. An Bruion Bar is a lively lounge with musical entertainment most evenings.

Amenities: Concierge, valet and laundry service, room service, minibus service to and from the airport, leisure center with indoor heated swimming pool and sauna.

Moderate
Bunratty Castle Hotel. Bunratty, County Clare. ☎ **061/364116.** Fax 061/364891. E-mail: info@bunrattycastlehotel.iol.ie. 60 units. AC TV TEL. £80–£96 ($112–$134.40) double. Executive suites also available. Rates include full breakfast. AE, DC, MC, V.

The newly refurbished, greatly expanded Bunratty Castle Hotel, which adjoins Bunratty Castle, opened its doors to appreciative guests in 1998. It is heir to a long tradition of hospitality, beginning with a wooden fortress 700 years back, and extended to an inn and nightclub housed in an 18th-century stone structure. Add a tasteful extension, and you have a gracious hotel offering every comfort and convenience with a touch of elegance. The common rooms are both interesting and appealing, with an antique marble altar as a reception desk and a number of fine antiques. The spacious guest rooms are furnished in dark woods, floral fabrics, and brass fixtures, and have tea/coffee-making facilities, hair dryers, and custom climate control. Double rooms have orthopedic king-sized beds. With advance notice, baby-sitting is available.

Kathleen's Irish Pub and Restaurant is open every day for lunch and dinner. It serves pub grub and full meals, and stages traditional Irish music sessions every night in the summer and on weekends year-round. The highlight of the hotel is **Kathleen's Irish Nights,** every summer evening at 7pm. More like a family party than a stage show, this is a great way to celebrate your arrival or to console yourself before departure. The 2½-hour gala dinner costs £26 ($36.40) for adults and £13 ($18.20) for children. Make your reservations early—it often sells out in advance.

The hotel's 10-acre complex includes the **Bunratty Village Mills,** with nearly a dozen fine shops, sought out by locals as well as tourists.

Clare Inn Golf and Leisure Hotel. Limerick-Ennis Rd. (N18), Newmarket-on-Fergus, County Clare. ☎ **800/473-8954** from the U.S., or 065/682-3000. Fax 065/682-3759. www.lynchotels.com. 183 units. TV TEL. £50–£110 ($70–$154) double. No service charge. Rates include full breakfast. AE, DC, MC, V.

Panoramic views of the River Shannon and the Clare hills are part of the scene at this contemporary Tudor-style hotel. It sits within 8 miles (13km) of Shannon Airport, surrounded by the Dromoland Castle golf course. The public areas are bright and airy, with large picture windows. The rooms are recently renovated. Dining and entertainment choices include Deerfields restaurant, the Coffee Dock cafe, and the new Poacher's Pub. There's an 18-hole championship golf course, an indoor heated swimming pool, a Jacuzzi, a gym, a sauna, a solarium, two tennis courts, a jogging track, pitch and putt, and a games room.

Old Ground Hotel. O'Connell St., Ennis, County Clare. ☎ **065/682-8127.** Fax 065/682-8112. E-mail: oghotel@iol.ie. 83 units. TV TEL. £88–£120 ($123.20–$168) double. No service charge. Rates include full breakfast. AE, DC, MC, V.

Long a focal point in the busy market town of Ennis, this ivy-covered hotel dates to 1749. According to a citation at the front entrance, it has been known variously as the Great Inn of Jayl Street and the Kings Arms; part of the hotel was once used as the Town Hall and the Town Jail. Many of the furnishings are antiques—you'll find vintage tea chests in the halls, and there's even a 1553 fireplace that once warmed the interior of nearby Lemeneagh Castle. A complete upgrading and refurbishment was completed in 1997. There are a restaurant, a grill room, and a very atmospheric pub, the Poet's Corner. On many summer evenings, cabaret-style entertainment is offered.

Queens Hotel. Abbey St., Ennis, County Clare. ☎ **065/682-8963.** Fax 065/682-8628. www.irishcourthotel.com. 50 units. TV TEL. £60–£150 ($84–$210) double. No service charge. Rates include full breakfast. MC, V.

Only hardcore James Joyce fans will be familiar with the literary significance of this hotel, because Bloom makes but brief mention of it in *Ulysses*. All the same, the hotel understandably plays its literary connection to the hilt, with a Victorian-style restaurant named Joyce's and a bar called Bloom's. Nestled in the heart of Ennis next to the old friary, it is more than 100 years old, but was recently updated and expanded to contemporary standards, while preserving its old-world quality. The guest rooms are furnished in traditional style, with dark woods and frilly floral fabrics, along with the modern additions of garment presses, hair dryers, and tea/coffeemakers.

West County Conference and Leisure Hotel. Clare Rd. (N18), Ennis, County Clare. ☎ **065/682-3000.** Fax 065/682-3759. www.lynchotels.com. 152 units. TV TEL. £86–£120 ($120.40–$168) double. No service charge. Rates include full breakfast. AE, DC, MC, V.

This modern three-story hotel is on its own grounds on the southern edge of Ennis, 17 miles (27km) from Shannon. The decor incorporates wide-windowed facades and skylights in many of the public areas. The rooms are roomy and recently refurbished, and many have views of the nearby Clare hills. The health and leisure club offers three swimming pools plus a sauna, steam room, Jacuzzi, solarium, and gym. Dining and entertainment options include the Pine Room, a candlelit restaurant; the County Grill for a light meal; the Ivory Bar, a piano bar; and an Irish cabaret show in summer.

Inexpensive

Bunratty Woods Country House. Low Rd., Bunratty, County Clare. ☎ **061/369689.** Fax 061/369454. http://ireland.iol.ie/~bunratty. 15 units. TV TEL. £40–£45 ($56–$63) double; £45–£60 ($63–$84) minisuite. No service charge. Rates include full breakfast. MC, V.

A 10-minute walk from Bunratty Folk Park and only 6 miles (9.7km) from Shannon Airport, Bunratty Woods is an ideal spot to spend your first or last night in Ireland, or both. Just beyond the tourist thicket, you'll enjoy both convenience and tranquillity in this especially tasteful guesthouse, furnished in antique pine, with bare wood floors, handmade patchwork quilts, and firm beds. All rooms have hair dryers, tea/coffee-making facilities, and useful desks or tables. Most rooms have lovely views of the rolling Clare countryside. Smoking is permitted in the guest rooms, but not in the lounge or breakfast room. Be sure to ask the delightful hostess, Maureen O'Donovan, about local lore—she has some startling stories ready for the sharing. You won't go wrong here, which is precisely what you want as you inaugurate or conclude your visit to Ireland.

Cill Eoin House. Killadysert Cross, Clare Rd., Ennis, County Clare. ☎ **065/6841668.** Fax 065/6841669. E-mail: cilleoin@iol.ie. 14 units. TV TEL. £44–£48 ($61.60–$67.20) double. No service charge. Rates include full breakfast. AE, MC, V. Closed Dec 24–Jan 8. Free parking.

Just off the main N18 road at the Killadysert Cross, a half mile south of Ennis, this recently built two-story guesthouse is a real find. It offers bright, comfortable rooms with hotel-quality furnishings and firm beds at a very affordable price, capped by attentive service from the McGann family. During the summer, traditional Irish dinners are also available. Although it's within walking distance of Ennis, the rooms offer lovely views of the countryside. The house is named after the nearby medieval Killone Abbey ("Killone" is the Anglicization of *Cill Eoin*).

Self-Catering

Ballyhannan Castle. 3 miles (4.8km) from Quin, County Clare. Contact Elegant Ireland. ☎ **01/475-1632.** Fax 01/475-1012. www.elegant.ie. 1 unit. TV TEL. From £2,600 ($3,640) per week, including utilities and cleaning.

If money isn't an object, here is the fantasy splurge of a lifetime. This magnificently restored medieval Irish peel tower, entered through its own "barmkin," or walled courtyard, stands amid meadows and farmlands and enjoys panoramic views of the Shannon estuary. Amid authentic antiquity and splendor, including a minstrel's gallery and a medieval dining room, you'll find every modern comfort and convenience. The structure consists of a 15th-century keep, plus three bedrooms (two doubles with bathrooms, and one twin).

DINING

Medieval Banquets & Traditional Meals with Music

The medieval banquets at Bunratty and Knappogue castles and the traditional evening at Bunratty Folk Park can be booked in the United States through a travel agent or by calling ☎ **800/CIE-TOUR.** They're all slightly touristy, but visitors genuinely enjoy them, and even my Irish friends have been known to attend once in a while.

✪ **Bunratty.** Castle Limerick-Ennis Rd. (N18), Bunratty, County Clare. ☎ **061/360788.** Reservations required. Dinner and entertainment £32 ($44.80). AE, DC, MC, V. Daily year-round at 5:30 and 8:45pm. IRISH

Built in 1425, this splendid structure is the most complete and authentic example of a medieval castle in Ireland. Every evening, a full medieval banquet is re-created with music, song, and merriment. Seated at long tables in the castle's magnificent baronial hall, you'll feast on ancient recipes using modern Irish ingredients, all served in strictly medieval use-your-fingers style. For refreshment, there's mulled wine, claret, and mugs of mead (the traditional honey-based drink). To add to the fun, at each banquet a "lord and lady" are chosen from the participants to reign over the 3-hour proceedings, and someone else is thrown into the dungeon.

✪ **Knappogue Castle.** Quin, County Clare. ☎ **061/360788.** Reservations required. Dinner and entertainment £32 ($44.80). AE, DC, MC, V. May–Oct daily 5:30 and 8:45pm. IRISH

Once the stronghold of the McNamara clan, this castle was built in 1467. Now fully restored, it's the setting for authentic medieval banquets. This castle is smaller and more intimate than Bunratty, but you'll still feast on a medieval meal, followed by a colorful pageant of Irish history celebrating the influential role of women in Celtic Ireland. The program includes rhyme and mime, song, and dance.

✪ **Traditional Irish Night.** Bunratty Folk Park, off the Limerick-Ennis road (N18), Bunratty, County Clare. ☎ **061/360788.** Reservations required. Dinner and entertainment £27 ($37.80). AE, DC, MC, V. May–Sept daily 5:30 and 8:45pm. IRISH

Irish country life of yesteryear is the focus of this "at home" evening in a thatched farmhouse cottage. You'll dine on a traditional meal of Irish stew, homemade bread, and apple pie and fresh cream. Then the music begins: the flute and fiddle, accordion, bodhran, and spoons—all at a spirited, foot-tapping pace.

Moderate

Brogans. 24 O'Connell St., Ennis, County Clare. ☎ **065/682-9859.** Reservations recommended for dinner. Main courses £5–£12 ($7–$16.80). AE, DC, MC, V. Daily 10:30am–10:30pm. IRISH.

An old-timer in the center of town, this pub is known for its hearty meals, including Irish stew, beef stroganoff, and chicken curry. You might also try roast duck, Dover sole, or local salmon. The atmosphere is casual and the decor cozy, with brick walls, a copper-fluted fireplace, and ceiling fans. On Tuesday and Thursday night, ballad music is usually offered.

✪ **Cloister Restaurant and Bar.** Club Bridge, Abbey St., Ennis, County Clare. ☎ **065/682-9521.** Reservations recommended. Bar food £3–£10 ($4.20–$14); dinner main courses £11–£16.95 ($15.40–$23.75). AE, DC, MC, V. Daily bar 12:30pm–midnight; restaurant 12:30–3pm and 6–9:30pm. IRISH.

Next to the remains of a 13th-century abbey, this old-world gem offers innovative Irish cuisine. The decor is warmly elegant, with open turf fireplaces and stoves, beamed ceilings, and reproductions from the Book of Kells adorning the walls. The menu includes poached monkfish with red-pepper sauce, wild venison with juniper-and-Armagnac sauce, and suprême of chicken layered with Carrigline cheese and Irish Mist. A house specialty starter is Inagh goat cheese laced with port-wine sauce. Pub-style lunches are served in the skylit Friary Bar, adjacent to the old abbey walls.

Cruise's Pub Restaurant. Abbey St., Ennis, County Clare. ☎ **065/684-1800.** Reservations recommended. Main courses £6.50–£18.90 ($9.10–$20.25). MC, V. Daily 12.30–10pm. IRISH.

Housed in a 1658 building, this place has low beamed ceilings, timber fixtures and fittings, crackling fires in open hearths, lantern lighting, a rough flagstone floor strewn with sawdust, memorabilia from crockery to books, and a snug appropriately dubbed "The Safe Haven." On warm days, seating extends into an outdoor courtyard overlooking the friary. The menu offers a good selection of pub grub, including a specialty dish called Friars Irish Stew, as well as seafood, steaks, and vegetarian stir-fry. There are often impromptu music sessions.

AFTER-DARK FUN

In addition to the medieval banquets and traditional ceili evenings synonymous with this area, County Clare offers much to delight the visitor. A number of hotels present music or shows, particularly in the high season.

Cois na hAbhna. Gort Road, Ennis, County Clare. ☎ **065/682-0996.** Admission £2–£5 ($2.80–$7), depending on the event.

For pure traditional entertainment, try Cois na hAbhna (pronounced *Cush*-na *How*-na). This center stages sessions of music, song, and dance, followed by ceili dancing with audience participation. Tea and brown bread are served. Traditional dance sessions are run year-round by Dick O'Connell, Wednesdays from 8:30 to 11:30pm. Call for the most current schedule of ceilis and other events.

Durty Nelly's. Limerick–Ennis Rd. (N18), Bunratty, County Clare. ☎ **061/364861.**

This region has many pubs, but here's one you shouldn't miss: Established in 1620 next door to Bunratty Castle, the cottage tavern was originally a watering hole for the castle guards. Now, with a mustard-colored facade and palm trees at its entrance, it's a favorite before-and-after haunt of locals and of tourists who join the nightly medieval banquets at the castle. The decor—mounted elk heads and old lanterns on the walls, sawdust on the floors, and open turf fireplaces—hasn't changed much over the centuries. This is also a good spot for a substantial pub lunch or a full dinner in one of the two restaurants. Spontaneous Irish music sessions erupt here on most evenings.

✪ THE BURREN

Moving west from Ennis into the heart of County Clare, you'll come to an amazing district of 100 square miles called the Burren. The word *burren* derives from the Irish word *boirreann*, which means "a rocky place."

It is a strange, lunarlike region of bare carboniferous limestone, bordered by the towns of **Corofin, Ennistymon, Lahinch, Lisdoonvarna,** and **Ballyvaughan.** Massive sheets of rock, jagged boulders, caves, and potholes are visible for miles in a moonscape pattern, yet this is also a setting of little lakes and streams, and an amazing assemblage of flora. There is always something in bloom, even in winter, from fern and moss to orchids, rock roses, milkwort, wild thyme, geraniums, violets, and fuchsia. The Burren is also famous for its butterflies, which thrive on the rare flora. The pine marten, stoat, and badger, rare in the rest of Ireland, are common here.

The story of the Burren began more than 300 million years ago, when layers of shells and sediment were deposited under a tropical sea. Many millions of years later they were thrust above the surface and left open to the erosive power of Irish rain and weather, producing the limestone landscape that appears today. As early as 7,000 years ago, humans began to leave their mark on this landscape in the form of Stone Age burial monuments, such as the famed Poulnabrone Dolmen and Gleninsheen wedge tomb.

In addition to rock, the area has other unique attractions. Lisdoonvarna, on the western edge, is a town known for its spa of natural mineral springs. Each summer it draws thousands of people to bathe in its therapeutic waters of sulfur, chalybeate (iron), and iodine. Lisdoon, as the natives call it, is also known worldwide for playing host to an annual matchmaking festival (see the "Ireland Calendar of Events," in chapter 2, for details).

One of the most scenic Burren drives is along R480. The corkscrew-shaped road leads from Corofin to Ballyvaughan, a delightful little village overlooking Galway Bay.

EXPLORING THE REGION

Currently under development, ✪ **Burren National Park** will encompass the entire Burren area (100 square miles). It's a remarkable limestone plateau dotted with ruined castles, cliffs, rivers, lakes, valleys, green road walks, barren rock mountains, and plant life that defies all of nature's conventional rules. The area is particularly rich in archaeological remains from the Neolithic through the medieval periods—dolmens and wedge tombs (approximately 120), ring forts (500), round towers, ancient churches, high crosses, monasteries, and holy wells. In recent years, there has been considerable controversy about defining the park and placing a permanent visitor and interpretive center (along the lines of those at Connemara and Glenveagh national parks). Until the issues are resolved, the park remains without an official entrance point, with no admission charges or restrictions to access.

With its unique terrain and pathways, the Burren lends itself to **walking.** Visitors who want to amble through the hills and turloughs (dry lakes that sometimes take on water), limestone pavements and terraces, and shale uplands and inland lakes should follow the **Burren Way.** The 26-mile (42km) signposted route stretches from Ballyvaughan to Liscannor. An information sheet outlining the route is available from any tourist office. **Burren Walking Holidays,** in conjunction with the Carrigann Hotel (see "Accommodations," below), Lisdoonvarna (☎ **065/707-4036**), offers a wide selection of guided walks, from 1 day to a week or more.

✪ **Aillwee Cave.** Ballyvaughan, County Clare. ☎ **065/707-7036.** www.aillweecave.ie. Admission £4.75 ($6.65) adults, £3.75 ($5.25) seniors, £2.75 ($3.85) children, £15.50 ($21.70) family. V. Daily 10am–5:30pm. Closed mid-Nov to Feb.

One of Ireland's oldest underground sites, Aillwee was formed millions of years ago but remained hidden until local farmer Jacko McGann discovered it less than 50 years ago. The cave has more than 3,400 feet of passages and hollows running straight into the heart of a mountain. Its highlights are bridged chasms, deep caverns, a frozen waterfall, and the Bear Pits—hollows scraped out by the brown bear, one of the cave's original inhabitants. Guided tours, which last approximately half an hour, are conducted continuously. The site has a cafe and a craft-rock shop; a unique farmhouse cheese-making enterprise called Burren Gold Cheese, near the cave's entrance; and an apiary where honey is produced.

The Burren Centre. R476 to Kilfenora, County Clare. ☎ **065/708-8030.** Admission £2.50 ($3.50) adults, £2 ($2.80) students and children over age 8. MC, V. Oct and Mar–May daily 10am–5pm; June–Sept daily 9:30am–6pm. Closed Nov–Feb.

Established in 1975 in the heart of the Burren as a community development cooperative, this is a fine place to acquaint yourself with all facets of the area. The facility includes a new 25-minute audiovisual presentation, plus landscape models and interpretive displays that highlight the unique features of the region's geology, geography, flora, and fauna. Also here are tearooms, a shop stocked with locally made crafts and products, and picnic tables.

Burren College of Art. N67 to Ballyvaughan, Newtown Castle, Ballyvaughan, County Clare. ☎ **065/707-7200.** www.iol.ie/~burren/. Admission to castle or nature trail £2 ($2.80) adults, £1.25 ($1.75) children, £6 ($8.40) family; to both £3 ($4.20) adults, £2 ($2.80) children, £12 ($16.80) family.

If ever there were a great place for an artist to paint or a photographer to snap a picture, it's the Burren. Bearing that in mind, this new center of artistic learning has sprung up in the midst of the dramatic landscapes. On the grounds of a 16th-century castle, the newly constructed college opened in 1993. Although geared to 15-week semester programs and to granting full 4-year bachelor of fine arts degrees, it also offers a range of weekend and 1-week courses that are ideal for visitors. Fees vary according to the specifics of the course. The facilities include bright studios for sculpture, painting, photography, and drawing, plus a lecture theater, an exhibition area, a library, a cafeteria, and a shop. The restored castle and grounds are open to the public.

✪ Burren Exposure. Galway Rd. (N67), ¼ mile (0.4km) north of Ballyvaughan, County Clare. ☎ **065/707-7277.** Admission £3.50 ($4.90) adults, £2.75 ($3.85) seniors and students, £10 ($14) family. 1 week before Easter–Oct daily 10am–6pm (last admission 5:20pm).

This compact multimedia exhibition center provides an exciting and essential introduction to the extraordinary natural wonders and the rich historical legacy of the Burren. If you intend to explore the area at all, the 35 minutes you spend here will soon pay rich dividends—the center's beautifully crafted visuals and narratives will open and inform your eyes and ears. One of the staff members, a native of the Burren, told us that even he learned a great deal he had never known before, watching the center's three audiovisual presentations on the region's history and splendor. A stop here brings rewards on several fronts. Side by side with Burren Exposure is the Whitethorn Restaurant, one of the most tasteful, tastiest cafes in County Clare. It offers excellent seaside snacks and full lunches, as well as dazzling seascapes through slanted, floor-to-ceiling glass panels. Ask about the changing dinner schedule when you visit. Last but not least, the third component is a fine gift shop, containing a discerning selection of Irish clothing, crafts, jewelry, and books.

The Burren Smokehouse Ltd. Kincora Rd., Lisdoonvarna, County Clare. ☎ **065/ 707-4432.** www.burrensmokehouse.ie. Free admission. Daily 9am–7pm. Closed Dec–Feb.

Aficionados of smoked salmon flock here to see the fish-smoking process firsthand and to buy right from the source. Visitors are welcome to watch as fresh Atlantic salmon is sorted, hand-treated, salted, and then slowly smoked over Irish oak chips in the traditional way. Each side of salmon is then vacuum-sealed and chilled. Tours are given throughout the day. Smoked mackerel, eels, and trout are also produced here. The smokehouse provides a worldwide mail-order service. Yum.

Clare Heritage Centre. R476 to Corofin, County Clare. ☎ **065/683-7955.** Admission £2 ($2.80) adults, £1.50 ($2.10) seniors, students, and children. Apr–Sept Mon–Fri 9am–6pm, Sat–Sun 10am–5pm; Oct–Mar Mon–Fri 9am–5:30pm.

If you have Clare family roots, you'll be especially fascinated by this heritage museum and genealogical research center. Even if you don't, this center is worth a visit to learn about Irish history and emigration. Housed in a former Church of Ireland edifice built by a first cousin of Queen Anne in 1718, it has exhibits on Clare farming, industry, commerce, education, forestry, language, and music. All are designed to reflect life in County Clare during the past 300 years. There are also a tearoom and gift shop. The genealogical research facility is open year-round.

Dysert O'Dea Castle and Archaeology Centre. R476 to Corofin, County Clare. ☎ **065/683-7401.** Admission £3 ($4.20) adults, £2.50 ($3.50) seniors and students, £1.50 ($2.10) children, £7 ($9.80) family. Daily 10am–6pm. Closed mid-Oct to Apr.

Built in 1480 by Diarmaid O'Dea on a rocky outcrop of land, this castle was badly damaged during the Cromwellian years. It was restored and opened to the public in 1986 as an archaeology center and museum. Today, the castle offers exhibitions and an audiovisual show on the history of the area. It is also the starting point for a sign-posted trail that leads to 25 sites of historical and archaeological interest within a 2-mile (3.2km) radius. They include a church founded by St. Tola in the 8th century that contains a unique Romanesque doorway surrounded by a border of 12 heads carved in stone. The O'Deas, who were chieftains of the area, are buried under the church. Also at the center are a round tower from the 10th or 12th century, a 12th-century high cross, a holy well, a 14th-century battlefield, and a stone fort believed to date to the Iron Age. The castle bakery is currently under excavation.

Spa Wells Centre. Kincora Rd., Lisdoonvarna, County Clare. ☎ **065/707-4023.** Free admission. Daily 10am–6pm. Closed Nov–May.

Nestled in a shady park on the edge of town, this is Lisdoonvarna's famous Victorian-style spa complex, dating from the 18th century. The sulfur-laced mineral waters are served hot or cold in the pump room, drawn from an illuminated well. Sulfur baths can also be arranged. Videos of the Burren and the Shannon area are shown continuously in the visitor center.

ACCOMMODATIONS
Expensive
✪ **Gregans Castle Hotel.** Ballyvaughan–Lisdoonvarna Rd. (N67), Ballyvaughan, County Clare. ☎ **800/323-5463** from the U.S., or 065/707-7005. Fax 065/707-7111. www.gregans.ie. 22 units. TEL. £98–£136 ($137.20–$190.40) double. Suites available. No service charge. Rates include full breakfast. AE, MC, V. Closed Nov–Mar. Free parking.

If you want to spoil yourself utterly on your first night in Ireland as you recover from jet lag in tranquillity, this elegant haven is the place. Only an hour's drive from Shannon, just over 3 miles (4.8km) outside Ballyvaughan, it's nestled in the exotic floral moonscape of the Burren. The mid–19th-century country house is full of light and color, and offers lovely views from every window. Although not strictly a castle, it is on the site of the ancient family estates of the Martyn family and the O'Loughlens, princes of the Burren. Owned and managed by the Hayden family, Gregans embodies decades of attention to detail and gracious hospitality. The public areas, which include the newly renovated drawing room and library, contain heirlooms and period pieces, antique books, and Raymond Piper's mural paintings of Burren flora. Each unique guest room is individually decorated with designer fabrics, dark woods, and brass accents; some have four-poster or canopied beds. While the suites and superior rooms are especially spacious and luxuriant, none will disappoint.

Dining/Diversions: The attractive restaurant enjoys a well-deserved reputation for fine seafood and inspired cuisine. The Corkscrew Bar is a particular delight, with copper and brass hangings and an open turf fireplace.

Inexpensive
Carrigann Hotel. Lisdoonvarna, County Clare. ☎ **065/707-4036.** Fax 065/707-4567. www.gateway-to-the-burren.com. 20 units. TV TEL. £58–£74 ($81.20–$103.60) double. Rates include full breakfast. Dinner £19 ($26.60). MC, V. Closed Nov–Feb.

Rose bushes and flower-filled gardens surround this country-house hotel, on a hillside on the outskirts of town. Most of the rooms, which have standard furnishings and firm beds, enjoy garden views. There are a refurbished restaurant, lounge bar, and sun lounge. The Carrigann also offers Burren walking holidays (see "Exploring the Region," above). Horse riding, cycling, and fishing are arranged on request by the hotel.

✪ **Rusheen Lodge.** Knocknagrough, Ballyvaughan, County Clare. ☎ **065/707-7092.** Fax 065/707-7152. E-mail: rusheen@iol.ie. 8 units. TV TEL. £50–£60 double ($70–$84). No service charge. Rates include full breakfast. AE, MC, V. Closed Dec–Feb.

On the main road just south of Ballyvaughan village, this modern, bungalow-style guesthouse is completely surrounded by flowers. The innkeepers are Rita and John McGann, whose father, Jacko McGann, discovered the nearby Aillwee Caves, one of the area's most remarkable natural attractions. Rooms are furnished with light woods, semicanopied orthopedic beds, and floral fabrics, and include a tea/coffeemaker and hair dryer. Smoking is not permitted in the guest rooms or dining room. Breakfast, served in a cheery pastel-toned room overlooking the gardens, offers freshly caught local fish as an option. Burren flowers enhance the decor throughout the house. In addition to the consistent appreciation of its guests, Rusheen Lodge has won the RAC "Small Hotel and Guest House of the Year" award for Ireland.

DINING

Bofey Quinn's. Main St., Corofin, County Clare. ☎ **065/683-7321.** Main courses £5–£16 ($7–$22.40); lobster £25 ($35). MC, V. Jan–Mar and Oct–Dec daily noon–9pm; Apr–Sept daily 10:30am–10pm. IRISH.

An informal atmosphere prevails at this pub-restaurant in the center of town. Dinner specialties include fresh wild salmon and cod, as well as a variety of steaks, chops, mixed grills, and also pizza. Pub-grub lunches are available throughout the day. From May to mid-September, Mondays to Thursdays from 7:30 to 9:30pm, there's a harpist in the restaurant to pluck your appetite.

Tri na Cheile. Main St., Ballyvaughan, County Clare. ☎ **065/707-7029.** Reservations recommended. Main courses £9.95–£12.95 ($13.95–$18.15). MC, V. May–Sept Mon–Sat 6–10:45pm; Sun 12:30–3:30pm. IRISH.

Formerly Claire's, this homey, intimate restaurant in the middle of the village is now the common venture of Adele Laffan and Barry Richards, committed to offering the freshest and finest of Irish ingredients at reasonable prices. Sirloin; mussels and linguini; whole crab; beef curry; fillet of salmon; roast lamb with anchovies, garlic and rosemary; and roast chicken run the modest yet enticing gamut of current offerings. An additional vegetarian option, a vegetable curry, is also available.

THE CLARE COAST

One of Ireland's most photographed scenes, the ✪ **Cliffs of Moher** draw busloads and carloads of visitors to Clare's remote reaches every day of the year. Rising to heights over 700 feet above the Atlantic and extending about 5 miles (8km) along the coast, the cliffs are County Clare's foremost natural wonder.

The Cliffs are only the beginning, however. Another world-renowned highlight of the Clare Coast includes the golf resort at **Lahinch,** praised by ace golfers as the "St. Andrews of Ireland" and the paradigm of Irish links golf.

Farther up the coast is the secluded fishing village of **Doolin,** often referred to as the unofficial capital of Irish traditional music. Doolin, like Galway to the north, is also a departure point for the short boat trip to the Aran Islands.

The Clare Coast is dotted with a variety of **seaside resorts,** such as Kilrush, Kilkee, Miltown Malbay, and Ennistymon, that are particularly popular with Irish families. As you drive around this craggy coastline, you'll find many other off-the-beaten-path delights, with intriguing place names: Pink Cave, Puffing Hole, Intrinsic Bay, Chimney Hill, Elephant's Teeth, Mutton Island, Loop Head, and Lovers Leap.

ATTRACTIONS

✪ **Cliffs of Moher.** R478, 7 miles (11km) north of Lahinch, County Clare. ☎ **065/708-1171.** Free admission to cliffs; to O'Brien's Tower £1.05 ($1.45) adult, 60p (84¢) child. Cliffs visitor center daily 9:30am–5:30pm; O'Brien's Tower May–Sept daily 9:30am–5:30pm (weather permitting).

Hailed as one of Ireland's natural wonders, these 760-foot cliffs stretch for over 5 miles (8km) along Clare's Atlantic coast. They offer panoramic views, especially from the 19th-century O'Brien's Tower at the northern end. On a clear day you can see the Aran Islands, Galway Bay, and many distant vistas. The visitor center holds a tearoom, an information desk, and a craft and souvenir shop.

Kilrush Heritage Centre. Town Hall, Martyrs Sq., off Henry St., Kilrush, County Clare. ☎ **065/9051047.** Admission £2 ($2.80) adults, £1 ($1.40) children, £5 ($7) family. May–Sept Mon–Sat 10am–5pm.

Housed in the town's historic Market House, this center provides historic and cultural background on Kilrush—the "capital of West Clare"—and the south Clare coast. An audiovisual presentation, *Kilrush in Landlord Times*, tells of the struggles of the area's tenant farmers during the 18th and 19th centuries, particularly during the Great Famine. The museum is also the focal point of a signposted heritage walk around the town. The building, erected in 1808 by the Vandeleur family, the area's chief landlords, was burned to the ground in 1892 and rebuilt in its original style in 1931.

Lahinch Seaworld and Leisure Centre. The Promenade, Lahinch, County Clare. ☎ **065/708-1900.** www.lahinchseaworld.com. Admission to aquarium £4.50 ($6.30) adults, £3.50 ($4.90) seniors and students, £2.95 ($4.15) children, £13.50 ($18.90) family. Daily 10am–9pm.

After stretching your legs along the vast strand and exploring its countless tide pools, you can get a closer look at the denizens of the Clare Coast by visiting this compact, well-designed local aquarium. Among the sea creatures in residence are conger eels, sharks, and rays. In the "touch pool," you can tickle a starfish or surprise an anemone, and then admire the rays' efforts at water ballet. If you or your family are then inspired to take to the water yourselves, the leisure center next door charges very reasonable rates. For extra savings, combination tickets are available.

Scattery Island. Information Center, Merchants Quay, Kilrush, County Clare. ☎ **065/905-2144.** Free admission. Mid-June to mid-Sept daily 10:30am–6:30pm.

Scattery, a small, unspoiled island in the Shannon Estuary near Kilrush, is the site of a group of monastic ruins dating to the 6th century. A high round tower and several churches are all that remain of what was once an extensive settlement, founded by St. Sennan. Legends tell of a massive sea monster defeated by the saint on the island, from which the place derives its name in Gaelic. To visit the island, contact one of the boatmen who arrange ferries—frequency depends on demand, and even in summer there may be only one trip per day. Or ask at the Information Center on the mainland—in the village of Kilrush, just past the pier—when the next ferry departs. The Information Center also houses exhibits on the history and folklore of the island.

TRIPS TO THE ARAN ISLANDS

Doolin Ferry Co. The Pier, Doolin, County Clare. ☎ **065/707-4455.** Inisheer £15 ($21) round-trip, Inishmaan £18 ($25.20) round-trip, Inishmore £20 ($28) round-trip. Student, child, and family discounts available. Mid-Apr to Sept. Call for current schedule.

Although many people come to Doolin to see the sights and enjoy the music, they also come to board this ferry to the Aran Islands. The three fabled islands, sitting out in the Atlantic, are closer to Doolin than they are to Galway (roughly 5 miles/8km, or 30 min.). One-way tickets to Galway via the islands cost £20 ($28). Ferries operate at least daily during the season, with expanded service in the summer. (For more information about excursions to the Aran Islands, see "Side Trips from Galway City," in chapter 11.)

SHOPPING

Doolin Crafts Gallery. Ballyvoe, Doolin, County Clare. ☎ 065/707-4309.

Since 1982, this has been an oasis of fine craftsmanship in the heart of the Clare coast. Surrounded by gardens and next to the churchyard, this shop is the brainchild of two artisans—Matthew O'Connell, who creates batik work with Celtic designs on wall hangings, cushion covers, ties, and scarves; and Mary Gray, who hand-fashions contemporary gold and silver jewelry, inspired by the Burren's rocks, flora, and wildflowers. There are also products by other Irish craftspeople. There is a good coffee shop on the premises. Open daily 8:30am to 8pm.

Traditional Music Shop. Ballyreen, Doolin, County Clare. ☎ 065/707-4407.

In this town known for its traditional music, this small shop is a center of attention. It offers all types of Irish traditional music on cassette tape and compact disc, as well as books and instruments, including tin whistles and bodhrans. Open Easter to mid-October daily 10am to 6pm or later.

SPORTS & OUTDOOR PURSUITS

✪ **BIRD WATCHING**   The **Bridges of Ross,** on the north side of **Loop Head,** is one of the prime autumn bird-watching sites in Ireland, especially during northwest gales, when several rare species have been seen with some consistency. The **lighthouse** at the tip of the Head is also a popular spot for watching seabirds.

BOATING & FISHING   The waters of the lower Shannon estuary and the Atlantic coastline are known as a good place to fish for shark, skate, turbot, ray, conger eel, tope, pollock, and more. The new Kilrush Creek Marina, an attraction in itself, is the base for **Michael McLaughlin** (☎ and fax 065/905-5105; e-mail: m_mc_laughlin@ _hotmail.com), who offers boat charters for deep-sea angling. Prices are £30 ($42) per person for a day's fishing, £300 ($420) for an 8-hour boat charter for up to 12 persons. Rods and reels can be hired for £5 ($7) per day. Anne and Michael McLaughlin also provide comfortable accommodations, year-round, in their guesthouse, **San Esteban.** It is quite splendidly situated at the water's edge, just outside Doonbeg. The price of a double room with breakfast is £36 ($50.40).

Sea Angling is also available from **Kilrush Deep Sea Angling,** Cappa Road, Kilrush (☎ 065/905-1327; e-mail: shannondolphins@eircom.net). Fees run £30 ($42) per angler daily, £240 ($336) daily charter, £1,150 ($1,610) weekly charter.

DOLPHIN WATCHING   The Shannon Estuary is home to about 70 bottlenose dolphins, one of four such resident groups of dolphins in Europe. Cruises run by

---

Impressions

Being Irish, he had an abiding sense of tragedy which sustained him through temporary periods of joy.

—W. B. Yeats (1865–1939)

Dolphinwatch leave daily May to September from Carrigaholt. Advance booking is essential. During July and August, call ☎ **065/9058156;** otherwise, call 088/2584711. Fees are £10 ($14) for adults, £6 ($8.40) for children under 14.

GOLF   A day at **Lahinch Golf Club,** Lahinch (☎ **065/708-1003**), is not to be missed. There are two 18-hole courses, but the longer championship links course is the one that has given Lahinch its far-reaching reputation. This course's elevations, such as the 9th and 13th holes, reveal open vistas of sky, land, and sea; they also make the winds an integral part of the scoring. Watch out for the goats, Lahinch's legendary weather forecasters. If they huddle by the clubhouse, it means a storm is approaching. Visitors are welcome to play, especially on weekdays; greens fees range from £30 ($42) on weekdays to £48 ($67.20) on weekends.

ACCOMMODATIONS
Moderate

Aberdeen Arms. Main St., Lahinch, County Clare. ☎ **065/708-1100.** Fax 065/708-1228. www.aberdeenarms.ie. 55 units. TV TEL. £50–£98 ($70–$137.20) double. Rates include full Irish breakfast and service charge. AE, DC, MC, V.

In the heart of town, within view of the golf course that has made Lahinch famous, this hotel is over 140 years old. It's said to be the oldest golf links hotel in Ireland. It's ideal for golfers and vacationers touring the Clare coast. The guest rooms are contemporary and functional, and the public rooms have a country-inn atmosphere. On the premises are a restaurant, a coffee shop, and a golf-theme lounge where the chat usually centers on golf. For nongolfers, there are a tennis court, squash court, and gym.

Aran View House. Doolin, County Clare. ☎ **065/707-4061.** Fax 065/707-4540. 19 units. TV TEL. £70–£100 ($98–$140) double. Rates include full breakfast. AE, DC, MC, V. Closed Nov–Mar.

Dating from 1736, this three-story Georgian-style stone house stands on a hill on the main road. It offers panoramic views of the Clare coastline and, on a clear day, the Aran Islands. Innkeepers John and Theresa Linnane recently updated and refurbished it as a hotel in traditional Irish style. The guest rooms are decorated with dark woods, and some have four-poster beds and armoires. There are a restaurant and lounge. The hotel sits on 100 acres of farmland just north of town.

✪ **Ballinalacken Castle Country House.** Doolin, County Clare. ☎ and fax **065/74025.** http://homepage.tinet.ie/~ballinalackencastle. 12 units. £70–£88 ($98–$123.20) double. AE, DC, MC, V. Closed Oct–Mar.

The first thing to delight you about Ballinalacken is its location: situated just below the crest of a hill overlooking the Aran Islands, all rooms but three command fine sea views. The hotel is only a few minutes' drive from the traditional music sessions in Doolin, but is completely isolated from its touristic atmosphere, and it's only a few minutes' walk out onto the rocky drama of the Burren. The hotel itself, operated as a guest house by the O'Callaghan family for over 40 years, was built in the 1840s. Most of the guest rooms can be found in a new wing—we recommend asking for a room in the old house, where you'll find high ceilings, marble fireplaces, and, in room 16, a sweeping panorama of hill and sea. All rooms are traditionally furnished with hard wood furniture, and are quite spacious. Bathrooms are compact, white tiled, and modern, with strong showers and hair dryers (two of the rooms have showers only, no tubs).

But perhaps the best thing about Ballinalacken is not within the hotel itself—just behind the dining room, on the crest of the hill, is an exceptional ruined 15th century tower house open only to the hotel's guests. Before you leave, be sure to pick up the keys to the castle at reception, and climb its worn stair to scan the sea from crumbling battlements.

Inexpensive

Doolin House. Doolin, County Clare. ☎ **065/707-4259.** Fax 065/707-4474. 8 units. TEL. £30–£50 ($42–$70) double. No service charge. Rates include full breakfast. No credit cards. Closed Dec–Feb.

Built as a guesthouse in 1991, this two-story traditional stone house sits on the main road on the edge of Doolin, with views of the countryside and the sea. The guest rooms have traditional dark wood furnishings, with floral and pastel fabrics and accessories, and firm beds. Two rooms are on the ground floor. There are a TV lounge for guests and a private sauna.

Doonmacfelim House. Doolin, County Clare. ☎ **065/707-4503.** Fax 065/707-4129. www.kingsway.ie/doonmacfelim. 8 units. TEL. £36–£44 ($50.40–$61.60) double. No service charge. Rates include full breakfast. MC, V.

On the main street a few hundred feet from the famous Gus O'Connor's Pub (see below), this modern two-story guesthouse is a great value in the heart of Doolin. Although it's in the center of everything, the house is also surrounded by a dairy farm. The rooms have standard furnishings and nice views of the neighboring countryside and town. Guests have the use of a hard tennis court.

✪ **Knockerra House.** Kilrush, County Clare. ☎ **065/905-1054.** 3 units, 2 with private bathroom. £36–£40 ($50.40–$56) double with bathroom. Rates include full breakfast. 50% discount for children under 12. No credit cards. Signposted on the Ennis road, 4 miles (6.5km) north of Kilrush.

The Troy family house is set in the shelter of a beautiful grove of old trees, which is rare on Ireland's windswept west coast. The place defines serenity, with gardens tucked into a hillside and views over the neighboring fields. The house (built ca. 1875) has aged well, and bears the marks of time on its ivy-covered facade and the antiques that populate the spacious rooms. This is a good place for families—each room has a double and a twin bed, and the extensive grounds offer many places to explore. Fishing is free at Knockerra Lake, a 10-minute walk from the house. Knockerra House is a perfect first or last night in Ireland for those traveling through Shannon, and a good base for day trips in County Clare.

DINING

Barrtrá Seafood Restaurant. Barrtrá, Lahinch, County Clare. ☎ **065/708-1280.** Reservations recommended. Fixed-price dinners from £24 ($33.60); early-bird 5–6:30pm £15 ($21); main courses £14–£16 ($19.60–$22.40). AE, MC, V. Feb–Apr and Oct Thurs–Sun 5–10pm; May–June and Sept Tues–Sat 5–10pm; July–Aug daily 5–10pm. SEAFOOD/INTERNATIONAL.

In a country house overlooking Liscannor Bay, this wide-windowed restaurant is a good coastal eatery with ocean views. The menu changes daily. Dinner choices may include turbot with parsley pesto, shark steak with sun-dried tomatoes, haddock with lime and ginger sauce, and spinach pancake with pepper sauce. The menu also features house-smoked salmon and such local Clare cheeses as Kilshanny (in five flavors: garlic, pepper, herb, cumin, and plain), Poolcoin (Burren goat cheese), and Cratloe Hills Gold (sheep's cheese).

Bruach na hAille. Roadford, Doolin, County Clare. ☎ **065/707-4120.** Reservations recommended. Early-bird menu (6–7:30pm) £10 ($14); 5-course fixed-price dinner £18.50 ($25.90); main courses £8.50–£15.50 ($11.90–$21.70). AE. Mid-Mar to Oct daily 6–9:30pm. IRISH/SEAFOOD.

Beside the bridge over the River Aille, this restaurant's name means "bridge of the River Aille." It's a cozy, cottage-style place with a menu that emphasizes seafood, including lobster, crab, and local fish. Signature dishes include fillet of sole in cider with shellfish cream sauce, ragout of seasonal fish and shellfish, and baked seafood au gratin. In addition, there's a choice of steak, chicken, lamb, and veal dishes.

A PUB

✪ **Gus O'Connor's Pub.** Doolin, County Clare. ☎ **065/707-4168.**

No description of the Clare coast would be complete without mention of Gus O'Connor's. Situated in a row of thatched fishermen's cottages less than a mile from the roaring waters of the Atlantic, this simple pub beckons people from many miles around each evening. Besides its historic charm (it dates from 1832), its big draw is music: this is *the* spot in north County Clare for Irish traditional music sessions. If your hunger extends beyond music, the pub serves meals, specializing in seafood.

3 County Mayo

Mayo's chief town (Ballina) is 63 miles (101km) N of Galway, 120 miles (193km) N of Shannon Airport, 153 miles (246km) NW of Dublin, and 193 miles (311km) NW of Cork

Rimmed by Clew Bay and the Atlantic Ocean, County Mayo boasts many diverse attractions, although it has been widely identified as *The Quiet Man* country since that classic movie was filmed here in 1951. The setting for the film was **Cong,** a no-longer-so-quiet village wedged between Lough Mask and Lough Corrib and backed up against the County Galway border. Much of Mayo has resisted the pull of Hollywood, and still has remote bogs, beaches, cliffs, and crags where quiet splendor prevails.

Among Mayo's other attractions are the 5,000-year-old farmstead settlement at Ceide Fields, the Marian shrine at Knock, and some of Europe's best fishing waters at Lough Conn, Lough Mask, and the River Moy. **Ballina,** Mayo's largest town, calls itself the home of the Irish salmon.

COUNTY MAYO ESSENTIALS

GETTING THERE Aer Lingus provides daily service from Dublin into **Knock International Airport,** Charlestown, County Mayo (☎ **094/67222**). Charter flights from the United States operate in the summer. From Britain, there's service to Knock on **Aer Lingus** from Birmingham, **British Regional Airlines** from Manchester, and **Ryan Air** from London's Stansted. See "Getting There," in chapter 2, for the airlines' phone numbers and Web sites.

Irish Rail and **Bus Eireann** (☎ **096/21011**) provide daily service from Dublin and other cities into Ballina, Westport, and Castlebar, with bus connections into smaller towns. There is also express service from Galway into most Mayo towns.

From Dublin and points east, the main N5 road leads to many points in County Mayo; from Galway, take N84 or N17. From Sligo and points north, take N17 or N59. To get around County Mayo, it's best to rent a car. Two firms with outlets at Knock International Airport are **Casey Auto Rentals, Ltd.** (☎ **094/24618**), and **National Car Rental** (☎ **094/67252**).

VISITOR INFORMATION For year-round information, visit or contact the **Westport Tourist Office,** The Mall, Westport (☎ **098/25711;** e-mail: mmcgreal@_irelandwest.ie). It's open Monday to Friday 9am to 5:15pm, with weekend and extended hours in July and August.

The **Knock Airport Tourist Office** (☎ **094/67247**) is open June to September at times coinciding with flight arrivals.

Seasonal tourist offices, open from May or June to September or October, are the **Ballina Tourist Office,** Cathedral Road, Ballina, County Mayo (☎ **096/70848**);

County Mayo

The map of County Mayo with legend:

Ballintubber Abbey **10**	Foxford Woollen Mills **6**	National Shrine of
Ceide Fields **1**	Knock Folk Museum **11**	Our Lady of Knock **12**
Errew Abbey **5**	Mayo North	Rosserk Abbey **3**
Granuaile Centre **8**	Heritage Centre **4**	Salmon World **7**
	Moyne Abbey **2**	Westport House **9**

Castlebar Tourist Office, Linenhall Street, Castlebar, County Mayo (☎ 094/21207); **Knock Village Tourist Office,** Knock (☎ 094/88193); **Cong Village Tourist Office** (☎ 092/46542); **Achill Tourist Office,** Achill Sound (☎ 098/45384); and **Newport Tourist Office** (☎ 098/41895).

EXPLORING THE COUNTY

Unlike many other counties, County Mayo does not have one central city (although Westport is rapidly approaching that stature). It's a county of many towns, from large market and commercial centers, such as Castlebar, Claremorris, and Ballinrobe in the southern part of the county, to Ballina in the northern reaches. Most of the attractions of interest to visitors lie in the hinterlands, in smaller communities like Knock, Foxford, Ballycastle, Louisburgh, and Newport.

County Mayo's loveliest town, ✪ **Westport,** is nestled on the shores of Clew Bay. Once a major port, it is one of the country's few planned towns, designed by Richard Castle with a tree-lined mall, rows of Georgian buildings, and an octagonal central mall.

Southeast of Westport is ✪ **Croagh Patrick,** a 2,500-foot mountain dominating the vistas of western Mayo for many miles. St. Patrick is said to have prayed and spent the 40 days of Lent here in A.D. 441. To commemorate this belief, each year on the last Sunday of July, thousands of Irish people make a pilgrimage to the site, which has become known as St. Patrick's Holy Mountain.

The rugged, bog-filled, thinly populated coast of Mayo provides little industry for the locals, but offers scenic drives and secluded outposts to intrigue visitors. Leading the list is **Achill Island,** a heather-filled bogland with sandy beaches and cliffs dropping into the Atlantic. A bridge links it to the mainland. **Clare Island,** once the home of Mayo's amazing pirate queen, Grace O'Malley, sits south of Achill in Clew Bay.

The drive from Ballina along the edge of the northern coast to Downpatrick Head is particularly scenic. It includes a visit to **Killala,** a small, secluded harbor village that came close to changing the course of Ireland's history. In August 1798, France's General Humbert landed at Killala in an abortive attempt to lead the Irish in a full-scale rebellion against the British. For this reason, the phrase "The Year of the French" is part of the folk memory of Mayo. Novelist Thomas Flanagan used the incident as the basis for his best-selling novel of the same name.

You'll find two extraordinary ruined 15th-century Franciscan friaries signposted off the R314 between Killala and Ballina—Moyne and Rosserk are located about 2 miles (3.2km) apart, and both are dramatically situated on the shores of Killala Bay. The last friar at **Moyne Abbey** probably died in the 1800s, but processions of brown robed monks are easily imagined in the beautiful stone cloister. **Rosserk Abbey** is particularly fascinating: not only are its chapel windows well preserved, but visitors can climb a winding stone stair to see the domestic rooms of the friary and look out across the bay. The *piscina* of the church (a place for washing altar vessels) is carved with angels, and on its lower-lefthand column is a delightful detail: a tiny, elegant carving of a Round tower that recalls its 23-meter (75-ft.) tall counterpart in nearby Killala.

✪ **Ballintubber Abbey.** Off the main Galway-Castlebar road (N84), about 20 miles (32km) west of Knock, Ballintubber, County Mayo. ☎ **094/30934.** Free admission; £2 ($2.80) donation requested. Year-round daily 9am–midnight.

This abbey is known as the abbey that refused to die, because it is one of the few Irish churches that's been in continuous use for almost 800 years. Founded in 1216 by Cathal O'Connor, king of Connaught, it survived fires and other tragedies. Although the forces of Oliver Cromwell took off the church's roof in 1653 and attempted to suppress services, clerics persisted in discreetly conducting religious rites. Completely restored in 1966, the interior includes a video display and an interpretive center, and the grounds are landscaped to portray spiritual themes.

✪ **Ceide Fields.** On R314, the coastal road north of Ballina, between Ballycastle and Belderrig, Ballycastle, County Mayo. ☎ **096/43325.** Admission £2.50 ($3.50) adults, £1.75 ($2.45) seniors, £1 ($1.40) students and children, £6 ($8.40) family. Mid-Mar to May and Oct daily 10am–5pm; June–Sept daily 9:30am–6:30pm; Nov daily 10am–4:30pm.

Here, in a dramatic sea-edge setting, lies the oldest enclosed landscape in Europe, revealing a pattern of once-tilled fields as they were laid out and lived in 50 centuries ago. Preserved for millennia beneath the bog to which it had been lost, this Neolithic farming settlement, home to the builders of the nearby megalithic tombs, now shows its face again. Admittedly, it's a nearly inscrutable face, requiring all the resources of the interpretive center to make meaningful eye contact with the visitor. The visitor center offers a 20-minute video presentation and tours of the site.

Errew Abbey. Signposted about 2 miles (3.2km) south of Crossmolina on the Castlebar road, then 3 miles (5km) down a side road, County Mayo.

This ruined 13th-century Augustinian church sits on a tiny peninsula in Lough Conn and has great views of the lake. The cloister is well preserved, as is the chancel with altar and piscina (a basin for washing sacred vessels). An oratory with massive stone walls is in the field adjacent to the abbey—on the site of a church founded in the

6th century, and known locally as Templenagalliaghdoo, or "Church of the Black Nun." The site of the abbey is a remarkably tranquil place, and great for a picnic.

✪ **Foxford Woollen Mills Visitor Centre.** Off the Foxford-Ballina road (N57), 10 miles (16km) south of Ballina, St. Joseph's Place, Foxford, County Mayo. ☎ **094/56488.** Admission £3.75 ($5.25) adults; £3 ($4.20) seniors, students and children; £11.50 ($16.10) family. Apr–Sept Mon–Sat 10am–6pm and Sun 1:30–6pm; Oct–Feb Mon–Sat 10am–6pm. Last tour at 5:25pm.

Founded in 1892 by a local nun, Mother Agnes Morrogh-Bernard, to provide work for a community ravaged by the effects of the Irish famine, Foxford Woollen Mills brought prosperity to the area through the worldwide sales of beautiful tweeds, rugs, and blankets. Using a multimedia presentation, the center tells the story of this local industry, then offers an on-site tour of the working mills, which produce the famous Foxford woolen products. Tours run every 20 minutes and last approximately 45 minutes. A restaurant, a shop, an exhibition center, an art gallery, a heritage room, and other craft units (including a doll-making and doll-restoration workshop and a jewelry designer) are also part of the visit.

Granuaile Centre. Louisburgh, County Mayo. ☎ **098/66341.** Admission £2.50 ($3.50) adults, £1.50 ($2.10) seniors and students, £1.25 ($1.75) children. June to mid-Sept Mon–Sat 10am–6pm.

Using an audiovisual display and graphic exhibits, this center tells the story of one of Ireland's great female heroes, Granuaile (Grace) O'Malley (1530–1600). Known as the "pirate queen," Grace led battles against the English and ruled the baronies of Burrishoole and Murrisk, around Clew Bay. Her extraordinary exploits are recounted in Elizabethan state papers. The center also includes a craft shop and coffee shop.

Mayo North Heritage Centre. On Lough Conn, about 2 miles (3.2km) south of Crossmolina, off R315, Enniscoe, Castlehill, Ballina, County Mayo. ☎ **096/31809.** Fax 096/31885. http://mayo.irish-roots.net/. Admission to museum £3 ($4.20) adults, £1 ($1.40) child. Oct–Apr Mon–Fri 9am–4pm; June–Sept Mon–Fri 9am–6pm and Sat–Sun 2–6pm.

If your ancestors came from Mayo, this center will help you trace your family tree. The data bank includes indexes to church registers of all denominations, plus school roll

A Trip to Clare Island

Floating a mere 3½ miles (5.6km) off the Mayo coast, just beyond Clew Bay, Clare Island is roughly 40 square miles of unspoiled splendor. Inhabited for 5,000 years and once quite populous—with 1,700 prefamine residents—Clare is now home to 150 year-round islanders, plus perhaps as many sheep. Grace O'Malley's modest castle, and the partially restored Cistercian Abbey where she is buried, are among the island's few attractions. The rest is a matter of remote natural beauty, in which Clare abounds. The sea cliffs on the north side of the island are truly spectacular. Two ferry services, operating out of Roonagh Harbour, charge £10 ($14) per person, £25 ($35) family round-trip, for the 15-minute journey: O'Malley's Ferry Service, aboard the *Ocean Star* (☎ **098/25045**); and Clare Island Ferries, aboard the *Pirate Queen* (☎ **098/28288**).

Once you arrive on Clare, if you want the grand tour, look for Ludwig Timmerman's 1974 Land Rover. Ludwig offers cordial, informative tours from June to August. Otherwise, your transport options are mountain bikes or your own sturdy pinions. If you want to stay a while, a unique bed-and-breakfast opportunity awaits you at the island's decommissioned lighthouse (see "Accommodations," below).

books, leases, and wills. Even if you have no connections in Mayo, you'll enjoy the adjacent museum, with its displays of rural household items, farm machinery, and farm implements, including the *gowl-gob,* a spadelike implement exclusive to this locality. The center also offers a new 5- to 10-day blacksmithing course. The lovely Enniscoe Gardens adjoin the center; combined tickets to the center and gardens are available. A new tearoom opened in 1999.

Note: If your ancestors were from the southern part of Ireland, try the **South Mayo Family Research Centre,** Town Hall, Neale Road, Ballinrobe, County Mayo (☎ 092/41214). It's open Monday to Friday 9:30am to noon, 1:30 to 4pm.

National Shrine of Our Lady of Knock. On the N17 Galway road, Knock, County Mayo. ☎ 094/88100. Free admission to shrine; museum £2 ($3.20) adults, £1 ($1.40) seniors and children over age 5; free for children under 5. Shrine and grounds year-round daily 8am–6pm or later; museum May–Oct daily 10am–6pm.

It's said that here, in 1879, local townspeople witnessed an appearance of Mary, the mother of Jesus. Considered the Lourdes or Fatima of Ireland, Knock came to the world's attention in 1979, when Pope John Paul II visited the shrine. Knock's center-piece is a huge circular basilica seating 7,000 people and containing artifacts or fur-nishings from every county in Ireland. The grounds also hold a folk museum and a religious bookshop.

Salmon World. Farran Laboratory, Furnace, Newport, County Mayo. ☎ 098/41107.

In this county of great salmon fishing, it is only natural that a center would provide insight on the life cycle of the Atlantic salmon. Operated on the shores of Lough Furnace by the Salmon Research Agency of Ireland, it presents a video as well as fresh-water and marine aquariums, fish-feeding areas, and exhibits. A new research center is currently under construction; so Salmon World is currently closed, though it will likely reopen for the summer of 2001.

Westport House. Westport, County Mayo. ☎ 098/25430. Admission to house and chil-dren's animal and bird park £12 ($16.80) adults, £8.50 ($11.90) students, £7 ($9.80) seniors, £5 ($7) children; to house only £6 ($8.40) adults, £4 ($5.60) seniors and students, £7.50 ($10.50) children. Westport House only: May Sat–Sun 1:30–5:30pm and Sept daily 2–5pm. Westport House and children's animal and bird park: June daily 1:30–5:30pm, July–Aug Mon–Fri 11:30am–5:30pm and Sat–Sun 1:30–5:30pm, Sept daily 2–5pm.

At the edge of town you can visit Westport House, a late 18th-century residence that's home of Lord Altamont, the Marquis of Sligo, who is in residence with his family. The work of Richard Cassels and James Wyatt, the house is graced with a staircase of ornate white Sicilian marble, unusual art nouveau glass and carvings, family heirlooms, and silver. The grandeur of the residence is admittedly compromised by the commercial enterprises in its midst, including video games and a small amusement park.

SPORTS & OUTDOOR PURSUITS

FISHING   The waters of the River Moy and loughs Carrowmore and Conn offer some of the best fishing in Europe, and are some of Ireland's premier sources for salmon and trout. For general information about fishing in County Mayo, contact the **North Western Regional Fisheries Board,** Ardnaree House, Abbey Street, Ballina (☎ 096/22788).

To arrange a day's fishing, contact ✪ **Cloonamoyne Fishery,** Castlehill, near Crossmolina, Ballina (☎ 096/31851). Managed by an Irish-born former New Yorker, Barry Segrave, this professional angling service will advise and equip you to fish the local waters—for brown trout on loughs Conn and Cullin; for salmon on loughs Beltra, Furnace, and Feeagh; and for salmon and sea trout on the rivers Moy and Deel. The fishery rents fully equipped boats and tackle, teaches fly-casting, and provides transport to and from all fishing. Daily rates average £12.50 ($17.50) for a boat, £30 ($42) for a boat with engine, and £50 ($70) for a boat with engine and *ghillie* (guide).

County Mayo is also home to the **Pontoon Bridge Fly Fishing School,** Pontoon, County Mayo (☎ **094/56120**). This school offers 1- to 4-day courses in the art of fly-casting, as well as fly-tying, tackle design, and other information necessary for successful game fishing. Fees range from £30 to £100 ($42 to $140), depending on the duration of the course. Courses run daily from April to late September. The newly expanded Pontoon Bridge Hotel also runs painting and cooking classes.

Permits and state fishing licenses can be obtained at the **North Mayo Angling Advice Centre** (Tiernan Bros.), Upper Main Street, Foxford, County Mayo (☎ **094/ 56731**). It also offers a wide range of services, including boat hire and *ghillies* (guides).

For fishing tackle, try **Jones Ltd., General Merchants,** Main Street, Foxford, County Mayo (☎ **094/56121**), or **Walkins Fishing Tackle,** Tone Street, Ballina, County Mayo (☎ **096/22442**).

GOLF   County Mayo's 18-hole golf courses include a par-72 links course at **Belmullet Golf Course,** Carne, Belmullet, County Mayo (☎ **097/82292**), with greens fees of £25 ($35); and a par-71 inland course at **Castlebar Golf Club,** Rocklands, Castlebar, County Mayo (☎ **094/21649**), with greens fees of £20 ($28) weekdays, £25 ($35) weekends. The par-73 championship course at **Westport Golf Club,** County Mayo (☎ **098/28262**), charges greens fees of £20 ($28) weekdays, £25 ($35) weekends. Set on the shores of Clew Bay, the course winds around the precipitous slopes of Croagh Patrick Mountain. It's one of western Ireland's most challenging and scenic courses.

KAYAKING   Courses for adults and children are offered at the **Killala Bay Adventure and Education Centre,** operated with the Killala Youth Hostel, Killala, County Mayo (☎ **096/37172**). The kayaking is mostly in Killala Bay, a beautiful inlet north of Ballina, and very reasonable rates are available for packages including room, full board, and activities.

WALKING   The region to the east of the Mullet peninsula offers a spectacular array of sheer sea cliffs and craggy islands. The small, secluded beach at **Portacloy,** 8½ miles (14km) north of Glenamoy on the R314 is a good starting point for a dramatic walk. On a sunny day, its aquamarine waters and fine-grained white sand recall the Mediterranean more than the North Atlantic. At its western edge, there is a concrete quay. From here, head north up the steep green slopes of the nearest hill. Don't be too distracted by the fantastic view or adorable little sheep. The unassuming boggy slopes on which you are walking end precipitously at an unmarked cliff edge—the walk is not recommended for children. Exercise caution and resist the urge to try to get a better view of mysterious sea caves or to reach the outermost extents of the coast's promontories. Instead, use a farmer's fence as a guide and head west toward the striking profile of **Benwee Head,** about 1½ miles (2.4km) away. Return the same way to have a final swim in the chilly, tranquil waters of Portocloy.

ACCOMMODATIONS
VERY EXPENSIVE

✪ **Ashford Castle.** Cong, County Mayo. ☎ **800/346-7007** from the U.S., or 092/46003. Fax 092/46260. www.ashford.ie. 83 units. TV TEL. £280–£684 ($392–$957.60) double. Rates include tax and service charge. Christmas and New Year's packages available. AE, DC, MC, V.

From turrets and towers to drawbridge and battlements, this castle is indeed a fairy-tale resort. It dates from the 13th century, when it was first the home of the De Burgo

(Burke) family and later the country residence of the Guinnesses. A hotel since 1939, it has been enlarged and updated over the years. It drew worldwide media attention in 1984 when President Ronald Reagan stayed here during his visit to Ireland. On the shores of Lough Corrib amid 450 forested, flowering acres, it sits in the heart of the scenic territory that was the setting for the film classic *The Quiet Man*.

The interior is rich in baronial furniture, medieval armor, carved oak paneling and stairways, objets d'art, and masterpiece oil paintings. Guest rooms are decorated with designer fabrics and traditional furnishings, some with canopied or four-poster beds.

Dining/Diversions: The 130-seat main dining room serves contemporary Irish cuisine; the 40-seat Connaught Room is a French restaurant. Sip a cocktail in the vaulted basement-level dungeon bar. Jacket and tie are required for men after 7pm.

Amenities: Concierge, room service, laundry and dry cleaning, nine-hole golf course, tennis court, salmon and trout fishing, boating.

EXPENSIVE

✪ **Newport House Hotel.** Newport, County Mayo. ☎ **800/223-6510** from the U.S., or 098/41222. Fax 098/41613. E-mail: KJT1@anu.ie. 18 units. TEL. £156–£164 ($218.40–$229.60) double. No service charge. Rates include full breakfast. AE, DC, MC, V. Closed Oct to mid-Mar.

Close to the Clew Bay coast, this ivy-covered Georgian mansion sits at the edge of town along the Newport River, making it a favorite base for salmon anglers. Originally part of the estate of the O'Donnell family, ancient Irish chieftains, it has been a country-house hotel only in recent decades. The interior boasts splendid examples of ornate plasterwork and high ceilings, and a skylit dome crowns a curved central staircase. The public areas are filled with antique furnishings, oil paintings, and cases of fishing trophies. Rooms are spread among the main house and two smaller courtyard buildings. They're quite spacious and elegant, with Georgian sash windows and high ceilings. Each room is individually furnished with antiques and original paintings and prints.

Dining/Diversions: The restaurant is known for its fish dishes, including salmon smoked on the premises. If you catch a salmon, the chef will cook it for your dinner or smoke it for you to take home. There is also a small bar.

Amenities: Private salmon and sea-trout fishing on the Newport River and Lough Beltra.

MODERATE

Breaffy House. Claremorris Rd., Castlebar, County Mayo. ☎ **800/528-1234** from the U.S., or 094/22033. Fax 094/22276. www.breaffyhouse.ie. 62 units. TV TEL. £100–£130 ($140–$182) double. No service charge. AE, DC, MC, V. Free parking.

A long paved driveway leads to this sprawling three-story château-style hotel, picturesquely ensconced amid 100 acres of gardens and woodlands. The public areas are furnished with traditional and period pieces. Guest rooms vary in size and shape, each with individual furnishings and character. Facilities include the Garden restaurant and bar. A new leisure center and an addition of guest rooms are in the offing for 2001.

Clare Island Lighthouse. Clare Island, County Clare. ☎ and fax **098/45120.** http://homepage.eircom.net/~clareislandlighthous. 5 units. £100 ($140) double, reduced to £90 ($126) for stays beyond 1 night. No service charge. Rates include full breakfast. Optional evening meal £20 ($28). No credit cards.

Poised on the northern and remotest tip of Clare Island 387 feet above the Atlantic surf, this is (as far as we know) the only chance you'll have anywhere in Ireland to lodge within a lighthouse. Constructed in 1804 and decommissioned in 1965, the tastefully restored and renovated structure is an unforgettable getaway. The tower suite with a loft bedroom is a honeymoon fantasy; another room, with its own walled garden facing the open sea, is equally fantastic. Never mind the drop-off beyond the walls! This is not recommended for families with fearless, unruly children, or anyone who suffers from vertigo. Otherwise, Clare Island Lighthouse is, as it appropriately bills itself, "the last temptation."

The Downhill Hotel. Situated off Sligo Rd. (N59), Ballina, County Mayo. ☎ **800/221-1074** or 800/223-6510 from the U.S., or 096/21033. Fax 096/21338. E-mail: thedownhillhotel@ eircom.net. 50 units. TV TEL. £96–£116 ($134.40–$162.40) double. No service charge. Rates include full breakfast. AE, DC, MC, V. Closed Dec 22–27.

Incorporating a gracious 19th-century manor house with a modern new wing, this three-story hotel sits on 40 acres of wooded grounds on the banks of the Brosna River, a tributary of the River Moy, at the northern edge of town. The public areas exude traditional charm, while guest rooms vary from contemporary to traditional, with thoughtful extras like tea/coffeemakers and hair dryers.

For dining and entertainment, the Brosna restaurant overlooks Brosna Falls; a bilevel piano bar, Frogs Pavilion, has a unique brass dance floor. There is a newly renovated health and leisure center with an indoor heated swimming pool, two squash courts, sauna, Jacuzzi, gym, three all-weather tennis courts, hair salon, and game room.

✪ **Enniscoe House.** 2 miles (3.2km) south of Crossmollina, off R315, next to the North Mayo Heritage Centre, Castlehill, near Crossmolina, Ballina, County Mayo. ☎ **800/ 223-6510** from the U.S., or 096/31112. Fax 096/31773. www.enniscoe.com. 6 units. £106– £130 ($148.40–$182) double. No service charge. Rates include full breakfast. AE, MC, V. Closed mid-Oct to Mar. Free parking.

Overlooking Lough Conn and surrounded by a wooded estate with more than 3 miles (4.8km) of nature walks, this two-story Georgian country inn has been described as the last great house of North Mayo. Owned and managed by Susan Kellett, a descendant of the original family that settled on the lands in the 1660s, Enniscoe abounds with family portraits, antique furniture, early drawings and pictures of the house and surrounding area, and open fireplaces. Guest rooms are individually furnished, with huge hand-carved armoires and canopied or four-poster beds with firm mattresses, and have views of parkland or lake. Two guest rooms and the dining room are non-smoking. In the dining room, fish from local rivers, produce from the house's farm, and vegetables and herbs from the adjacent garden are daily pleasures. Enniscoe also has its own fishery (see Cloonamoyne Fishery under "Fishing" in "Sports & Outdoor Pursuits," above). Self-catering apartments are also available.

Mount Falcon Castle. Foxford Rd. (N57), Ballina, County Mayo. ☎ **800/223-6510** from the U.S., or 096/70811. Fax 096/71517. E-mail: mfsalmon@iol.ie. 9 units. £70–£120 ($98–$168) double. Rates include full breakfast. Dinner £25 ($35). AE, DC, MC, V. Closed Feb–Mar and Christmas week.

Built in 1876 by the same man who did much of the exterior work at Ashford Castle in Cong, this gabled Victorian-style structure has been owned and managed as a country-house inn by the Aldridge family since 1932. The decor in both the public areas and the guest rooms is an eclectic blend of comfortable old furniture with fluffy pillows, carved chests, and gilded mirrors. If you're fond of fishing, this is a real find— a stay here entitles you to salmon and trout fishing on Lough Conn and to fishing in a salmon preserve on the River Moy. The management enthusiastically caters to anglers' needs, and will prepare and serve you your day's catch for dinner. Set in a 100-acre wooded estate 4 miles (6.5km) south of Ballina, Mount Falcon has fine walking trails and an all-weather tennis court.

The Olde Railway Hotel. The Mall, Westport, County Mayo. ☎ **098/25166.** Fax 098/ 25090. www.anu.ie/railwayhotel. 27 units. TV TEL. £55–£90 ($77–$126) double. No service charge. Rates include full breakfast. AE, DC, MC, V.

William Thackeray's description of this hotel in 1834—"one of the prettiest, comfortablest inns in Ireland"—remains true. The Olde Railway Hotel, built in 1780 by Lord Sligo to accommodate his "overflow" house guests, has been tastefully restored by the Rosenkranz family. Its bright yellow facade is warm and welcoming; inside, it exudes charm and a touch of elegance. No two rooms are alike; each has been given a distinctive character. Twenty-two rooms face the tree-lined Carrowbeg River. The "superior" rooms are more spacious and include a sitting area with sofa. Most mattresses are new and back-friendly, but not all, so if it matters, ask for a firm one. In addition to the delightful glass conservatory-style dining room, there are a bar and a function room, both offering weekend entertainment. Bicycles are also available for guests who wish to take a pedal through town.

Westport Woods Hotel. Quay Rd., Westport, County Mayo. ☎ **098/25811.** Fax 098/ 26212. www.info@westportwoodshotel.ie. 111 units. TV TEL. £70–£120 ($98–$168) double. No service charge. Rates include full breakfast. AE, MC, V.

Nestled in a quiet woodland setting, this two-story chalet-style hotel is conveniently situated midway between the historic town center and the quay area, which overlooks Clew Bay. The public rooms are woody, bright, and airy, with contemporary furnishings. The well-maintained guest rooms offer standard comforts plus hair dryers and garment presses. The hotel has a full-service restaurant, a lounge, a tennis court, and a new leisure center.

INEXPENSIVE

Drom Caoin. Belmullet, County Mayo. ☎ and fax **097/81195.** E-mail: dromcaoin@ esatlink.com. 4 units, 2 with shower only, no tub. £38 ($53.20) double; £30 ($42) apt (without breakfast), £50 ($70) apt (with breakfast); £200 ($280) apt by the week (without breakfast). 33% reduction for children. MC, V.

The view of Blacksod Bay is terrific from Mairin Maguire-Murphy's comfortable home, a short walk from the center of Belmullet. Two of the guest rooms have recently been renovated into self-catering apartments that can be rented by the night or by the week, with or without breakfast. It's a great concept—you can actually settle in, cook some of your own meals, and enjoy the extra space of a suite for little more money than an average B&B room. The ground-floor apartment faces a carpark at the back of the house—not great in terms of view, but there's plenty of room for a family with a pull-out couch in the sitting room, a bedroom with double bed, and a loft-nook which is just the right size for a small child. The other apartment is on the upper floor of the house, and is very comfortable for a couple—the kitchen adjoins a small dining room/sitting room with a sloping ceiling, and a skylight view of the bay. It's not spacious, but very comfortable. The other two bedrooms are somewhat small, with compact bathrooms. Breakfast is something to look forward to here—omelets, fresh fish, and toasted cheese are offered periodically as alternatives to the standard fry, and the fresh scones are delicious.

Dun Maeve. Newport Rd., Westport, County Mayo. ☎ **098/26529.** Fax 098/25055. 6 units. £60 ($84) double. Rates include full breakfast. MC, V.

This beautifully restored and expanded 19th-century Georgian town house provides elegance, comfort, and extraordinary convenience—it is in the heart of Westport town, around the corner from the tourist office. It is clearly a cut above almost any

B&B you'll come across. Each room is unique and eminently tasteful; the range of accommodations will meet the needs of couples, families, and single travelers. The beds are firm, the bathrooms are spacious, and the breakfast-room conservatory is a real treat.

If you want to stay in the Westport area for a week or more, hostess Maria Hughes also offers two self-catering four-bedroom holiday homes. Each sleeps seven. They're less than a mile from the town, near the harbor, and come fully furnished with virtually everything you'll need. Rates range roughly from £300 to £500 ($420 to $700) per week.

✪ **Suantraí.** R314, at the east edge of town, Ballycastle, County Mayo. ☎ **096/43040.** 3 units. £34 ($47.60) double. No service charge. Rates include full Irish breakfast. No credit cards. Closed Aug 21–June 19.

Suantraí means "lullaby," and if you don't sleep soundly here, you'd best consult a physician. The rooms are spacious, bright, meticulously clean, and mercifully uncluttered, requiring only minutes to feel comfortably familiar. This modest, welcoming home sets a standard rarely met by B&Bs. The Chamberses (both teachers in the local school) and their family truly enjoy their guests—and the feeling's mutual.

DINING
MODERATE

✪ **Ardmore House.** The Quay, Westport Harbour, Westport, County Mayo. ☎ **098/ 25994.** Reservations recommended. Fixed-price dinner £25 ($35); main courses £11.95– £13.95 ($16.75–$19.55). AE, DC, MC, V. Daily 6:30–9pm. CONTINENTAL/IRISH.

On high ground at the edge of town overlooking the harbor, Ardmore House enjoys grand views of Clew Bay, source of the ingredients for the special Clew Bay seafood chowder. The varied entrees include fresh seafood crêpes and moist roast duck. In 1999, Ardmore House gained guest rooms.

The Asgard Tavern. The Quay, Westport, County Mayo. ☎ **098/25319.** Reservations recommended for dinner. Dinner main courses £7.95–£15.95 ($11.15–$23.35). AE, CB, DC, MC, V. Daily noon–3pm (bar food); restaurant Tues–Sun 7–11pm. INTERNATIONAL.

In the center of the harbor strip opposite Clew Bay, this nautical establishment consists of an informal ground-floor pub and a candlelit 50-seat restaurant upstairs. Bar food, available throughout the day in the pub, includes fresh fish, Irish stew, beef stroganoff, and steaks. In the evening, the restaurant offers a range of dishes, from creamy coquille St.-Jacques to medallions of beef in garlic sauce.

✪ **The Quay Cottage.** The Quay, Westport, County Mayo. ☎ **098/26412.** Reservations recommended. Main courses £10.50–£16.90 ($14.70–$23.65). AE, MC, V. Daily 6–10pm. Closed Dec 25. SEAFOOD/INTERNATIONAL.

Overlooking Westport Harbour, newly expanded Quay Cottage is awash with nautical bric-a-brac. The menu presents fresh, beautifully prepared seafood, such as lemon sole beurre blanc or wild local salmon, with an array of daily specials; a request for a plain steak can also be fulfilled. A separate nonsmoking room is available. You can take a waterside stroll after your meal.

INEXPENSIVE

The Continental Cafe. High St., Westport, County Mayo. ☎ **098/26679.** Main courses £2–£7 ($2.80–$9.80). No credit cards. Thurs–Tues noon–7pm. IRISH/VEGETARIAN.

Comforting, hearty food fills the simple tables of the Continental Cafe. The salad of the day, made with fresh, crisp greens and crunchy vegetables, accompanies hearty pita sandwiches, pasta casseroles, or quiche heavy with sharp cheddar. The menu is as eclectic as the decor; gado-gado from Thailand is served alongside the more prosaic stuffed baked potatoes and toasted sandwiches. Service is conscientious and friendly, and a whole floor is dedicated to nonsmoking. A selection of organic foods is for sale at the door.

The Old Mill. Foxford Woollen Mills, Foxford, County Mayo. ☎ **094/56756.** All items £1–£5.50 ($1.40–$7.70). MC, V. Mon–Sat 10am–5:30pm; Sun noon–5:30pm. IRISH.

On the grounds of the Foxford Woollen Mills (see "Exploring the County," above), the Old Mill serves an array of light meals and snacks in a historic setting that's bright and airy. On the menu: soups, salads, sandwiches, and cold meat plates, as well as quiche, lasagna, sausage rolls, scones, muffins, and desserts. There are also daily hot meal specials.

Galway City 11

Galway City is the focal point and gateway of County Galway and the west of Ireland. Located beside the River Corrib and at the mouth of Galway Bay off the Atlantic, it's a little over an hour's drive from Shannon Airport. With a population of 57,000, it is a major city by Irish standards, yet retains much of the accessibility and congeniality of a town.

In recent years, Galway has managed to grow and develop dramatically without losing any of its character. It's said to be one of the fastest-growing cities in Europe, but its "boom" has meant only more of the same, rather than uncontrolled expansion and disfigurement. Galway is perhaps the most prosperous city in Ireland, and arguably the most immediately appealing. It attracts droves of outsiders, either to visit or to settle, without alienating its long-standing population. The result is a city that feels lived-in, a real place that at the same time accommodates masses of visitors. Its university community and its well-rooted, lively arts scene contribute to its vitality and appeal.

Some say that Galway was named after the foreigners—*na Gall,* or the Galls—who had settled in the region. If so, then *Gaillimh,* or Galway, would mean "the place of the foreigners." The earliest historical references to the area date from A.D. 1124 and describe it as a "Gaelic hinterland."

Because of its position on the Atlantic, Galway emerged as a thriving seaport and developed a brisk trade with Spain. Close to the city docks, you can still see the area where Spanish merchants unloaded cargo from their galleons. The Spanish Arch was one of four arches built in 1594, and the Spanish Parade is a small open square where the visitors strolled in the evening.

Tradition has it that Christopher Columbus attended mass at Galway's St. Nicholas Collegiate Church before setting sail for the New World in 1477. Originally built in 1320, the church has been enlarged, rebuilt, and embellished over the years. It has also changed denominations at least four times.

From medieval times, Galway has been known as the "City of Tribes," thanks to 14 wealthy merchant families—the Athys, Blakes, Bodkins, Brownes, Darcys, Deanes, Fonts, Frenches, Joyces, Kirwans, Lynches, Martins, Morrises, and Skerrets—mostly of Welsh and Norman origin, who ruled the town for many years as an oligarchy.

By far the most important family was the Lynches, who gave the city not only its first mayor, in 1484, but 83 other mayors during the next 169 years. In the center of town, on Shop Street, is Lynch's Castle, dating from 1490 and renovated in the 19th century. It's the oldest Irish medieval town house used daily for commercial purposes (it's now a branch of the Allied Irish Bank). The exterior is full of carved gargoyles, impressive coats of arms, and other decorative stonework. If you walk northwest 1 block to Market Street, you'll see the Lynch Memorial Window embedded in a wall above a built-up gothic doorway. It commemorates the day in the 16th century when Mayor James Lynch FitzStephen—having condemned his son to death for the murder of a Spanish merchant but having found no one to carry out the deed—acted as executioner. He retreated into seclusion, brokenhearted.

In more recent centuries, two developments earned the city a place of prominence in the west: the founding of the Queens' College (now University College, Galway) in 1848, and the establishment of a rail link with Dublin in 1854.

Today, the activity of the city revolves around a pedestrian park at Eyre (pronounced *Air*) Square, originally a market area known as the Fair Green. It's officially called the John F. Kennedy Park in commemoration of his visit here in June 1963, and a bust of the president shares space in the park with a statue of a man sitting on a limestone wall—a depiction of Galway-born local hero Padraig O'Conaire, a pioneer in the Irish literary revival of the early 20th century and the epitome of a Galway Renaissance man.

Next to the downtown area, on the west bank of the River Corrib, is the Claddagh. Originally a fishing village, it once had its own fleet, laws, and king. Its name comes from the Irish *An Cladach,* which means "a flat stony shore." The people of Claddagh were descendants of early Gaelic families and spoke only Irish. Their stone streets were haphazardly arranged, with small squares rimmed by thatched mud-walled houses. This old-world scene came to an end in 1934 with the construction of a modern housing development.

One Claddagh tradition survives: the Claddagh ring, worn facing out for engagement and facing in for marriage. The ring's clasped hands, representing friendship, are a symbol dating from Roman times. The earliest known Claddagh ring, with the crown added for loyalty and the heart for love, was made in the 17th century by Galway goldsmith Richard Joyce. No longer widely worn as a wedding band, it is mostly either a souvenir or a token of friendship.

1 Orientation

Galway is 57 miles (92km) north of Shannon Airport, 136 miles (219km) west of Dublin, 65 miles (105km) northwest of Limerick, 130 miles (209km) northwest of Cork, and 120 miles (193km) north of Killarney

ARRIVING   **Aer Lingus** operates twice-daily service from Dublin into Galway Airport, Carnmore (☎ **091/755569**), about 10 miles (16km) east of the city. A taxi to the city center costs about £12 ($16.80); the occasional bus, if it coincides with your arrival, costs £2.50 ($3.50).

Irish Rail trains from Dublin and other points arrive daily at **Ceannt Station** (☎ **091/564222**), off Eyre Square, Galway.

Buses from all parts of Ireland arrive daily at **Bus Eireann Travel Centre,** Ceannt Station, Galway (☎ **091/562000**).

As the gateway to the west of Ireland, Galway is the terminus for many national roads. They lead in from all parts of Ireland, including N84 and N17 from the north points, N63 and N6 from the east, and N67 and N18 from the south.

Galway City

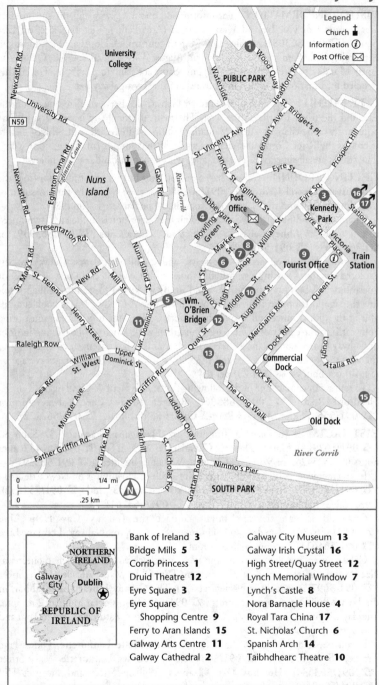

Legend
Church ✝
Information ⓘ
Post Office ✉

Bank of Ireland **3**
Bridge Mills **5**
Corrib Princess **1**
Druid Theatre **12**
Eyre Square **3**
Eyre Square
   Shopping Centre **9**
Ferry to Aran Islands **15**
Galway Arts Centre **11**
Galway Cathedral **2**

Galway City Museum **13**
Galway Irish Crystal **16**
High Street/Quay Street **12**
Lynch Memorial Window **7**
Lynch's Castle **8**
Nora Barnacle House **4**
Royal Tara China **17**
St. Nicholas' Church **6**
Spanish Arch **14**
Taibhdhearc Theatre **10**

VISITOR INFORMATION   For information about Galway and the surrounding areas, contact or visit **Ireland West Tourism** (Aras Fáilte), Victoria Place, off Eyre Square (☎ **091/563081;** e-mail: info@western-tourism.ie). Hours are May, June, and September daily 9am to 5:45pm; July and August daily 9am to 7:45pm; October to April Monday to Friday 9am to 5:45pm, Saturday 9am to 12:45pm. For further detailed information on events in Galway, consult **www.galway.net.**

CITY LAYOUT   The core of downtown Galway lies between Eyre Square on the east and the River Corrib on the west. The main thoroughfare begins west of Eyre Square. Its name changes—from William to Shop, Main Guard, and Bridge—before it crosses the River Corrib and changes again. If that sounds confusing, don't worry. The streets are all short, well marked, and, with a map in hand, easy to follow.

GETTING AROUND   Galway has excellent local bus service. Buses run from the **Bus Eireann Travel Centre** (☎ **091/562000**) or Eyre Square to various suburbs, including Salthill and the Galway Bay coastline. The flat fare is 70p (98¢).

There are taxi ranks at Eyre Square and all the major hotels in the city. If you need to call a cab, try **Abbey Cabs** (☎ **091/569369**), **Cara Cabs** (☎ **091/563939**), or **Galway Taxis** (☎ **091/561112**).

A town of medieval arches, alleyways, and cobblestone lanes, Galway is best explored on foot, wearing comfortable shoes. Once you check in at your hotel or guesthouse, it's best to leave your car and tour by walking. (To see the highlights, follow the signposts on the Tourist Trail of Old Galway. A handy 32-page booklet available at the tourist office and at most bookshops explains the tour.) If you must bring your car into the center of town, park it and then walk. There is free parking in front of Galway Cathedral, but most street parking uses the disc system. It costs 40p (56¢) for 1 hour; a book of 10 discs costs £4 ($5.60). Multistory parking garages average £1 ($1.40) per hour or £8 ($11.20) per day.

To rent a car, contact one of the following firms: **Avis Rent-A-Car,** Higgins Garage, Headford Road (☎ **091/568886**); **Budget Rent-A-Car,** Galway Airport (☎ **091/556376**); or **Murrays Rent-A-Car,** Headford Road (☎ **091/562222**).

FAST FACTS   If you need a drugstore, try **Flanagans Pharmacy,** 32 Shop St. (☎ **091/562924**); **Matt O'Flaherty Chemist,** 16 William St. (☎ **091/561442;** after hours 091/525426); or **Whelan's Chemist,** Williamsgate Street (☎ **091/562291**).

In an emergency, dial ☎ **999. University College Hospital** is on Newcastle Road (☎ **091/580580**). There's also **Merlin Park Regional Hospital** (☎ **091/757631**). The local **Garda Station** is on Mill Street (☎ **091/563161**).

Gay and lesbian travelers might contact the **Galway Gay Help Line** (☎ **091/566134**), Tuesday and Thursday 8 to 10pm; **Galway Lesbian Line** (☎ **091/564611**), Wednesday 8 to 10pm.

Galway offers places to log onto the Web and check your e-mail. The pioneer was **Net Access,** in the heart of the city in The Olde Malte Arcade, High Street (☎ **091/569772;** e-mail: info@netaccess.ie). The **Galway Library/An Leabhar,** in the Hynes Building, Augustine Street (☎ **091/561666**), is open Monday 2 to 5pm, Tuesday to Thursday 11am to 8pm, Friday 11am to 5pm, Saturday 11am to 1pm and 2 to 5pm.

If you need to do laundry, head for the **Olde Malte Laundrette,** Olde Malte Arcade, off High Street (☎ **091/564990**), or **Bubbles Laundrette,** Mary Street (☎ **091/563434**). **Heaslips Dry Cleaners,** William Street and Prospect Hill (☎ **091/568944**), can get your spots out for you.

The weekly *Connaught Tribune,* published in Galway, is the largest newspaper covering the west of Ireland. The other Galway weekly is the *Connaught Sentinel.*

Free weekly publications that cover the arts and entertainment include the *Galway Advertiser, Galway Observer,* and *Entertainment Weekly.* Local radio stations are Galway Bay FM 95.8 and FM 96.8, and Raidio na Gaeltachta, an Irish language and music station broadcasting on M. W. 556.

Try **Fahy Foto Camera Shop,** 13 High St. (☎ **091/562283**); **Galway Camera Shop,** 1 William St. (☎ **091/565678**); or **One Hour Photo,** Eglinton Street (☎ **091/562682**), for your photographic needs.

The **Post Office,** Eglinton Street (☎ **091/562051**), is open Monday to Saturday 9am to 5:30pm.

If you need a shoe repaired, head for **Mister Minit,** U4 Corbetts Court, Williamsgate Street (☎ **091/565055**).

2 Accommodations

VERY EXPENSIVE

✪ **Glenlo Abbey.** Bushy Park, Galway, County Galway. ☎ **091/526666.** Fax 091/527800. www.glenlo.com. 46 units. TV TEL. £280–£390 ($392–$546) double. No service charge. Rates include full breakfast. AE, DC, MC, V.

About 2 miles (3.2km) outside of Galway on the main Clifden road, this secluded five-star hotel overlooks Lough Corrib in a tranquil, sylvan setting, surrounded by a 9-hole golf course. Dating from 1740, it was originally the ancestral home of the French and Blake families, two of the 14 "tribes" that ruled the city for centuries. Totally restored and opened as a hotel in 1993, it has retained its grandeur in the public areas, which contain hand-carved wood furnishings, hand-loomed carpets, ornate plasterwork, and an extensive collection of Irish art and antiques. The guest rooms, which have lovely views of Lough Corrib and the countryside, are similarly decorated with traditional furnishings as well as marbled bathrooms; each room has a personal safe and garment press.

Dining/Diversions: Choices include the elegant River Room; the Kentfield Cocktail Lounge, decorated with a unique collection of pen-and-ink drawings of Irish writers; the Oak Cellar Bar; and the Pullman Restaurant, an antique restaurant car built in 1927 and once traversing the Monaco/Istanbul/St. Petersburg runs.

Amenities: Concierge, room service, laundry and dry cleaning, golf course, fishing in Lough Corrib.

EXPENSIVE/MODERATE

Ardilaun House. Taylor's Hill, Galway, County Galway. ☎ **800/44-UTELL** from the U.S., or 091/521433. Fax 091/521546. E-mail: ardilaun@iol.ie. 89 units. TV TEL. £88–£164 ($123.20–$229.60) double. Rates include full Irish breakfast and service charge. AE, DC, MC, V. Closed Dec 22–28. Free parking.

This Georgian-style country-house hotel takes its name from the Irish *Ard Oilean,* meaning "high island" and referring to a picturesque island nearby in Lough Corrib. Built in 1840 as a town house for a prominent Galway family, it became a hotel in 1962. With ancient trees and extensive gardens, it is in a hilly residential section about a mile west of the downtown area. It has been expanded and updated in recent years, and most of the rooms, in a modern three-story addition, are decorated with traditional furnishings, dark woods, and quilted fabrics.

Dining/Diversions: The atmosphere of an old mansion prevails in the public areas, especially in the Camilaun dining room and the Blazers, a hunting-theme bar that's a favorite local rendezvous.

Amenities: The hotel has a new, fully outfitted leisure center.

Corrib Great Southern Hotel. Dublin road (N6), Galway, County Galway. ☎ 800/
44-UTELL from the U.S., or 091/755281. Fax 091/751390. E-mail: res@corrib.gsh.ie.
180 units. TV TEL. £134–£144 ($187.60–$201.60) double. Rates include full Irish breakfast
and service charge. AE, DC, MC, V.

Set on high ground 2 miles (3.2km) east of the city, this modern five-story hotel offers
panoramic views of Galway Bay, from its skylit atrium-style lobby to the wraparound
windows in the public areas. Guest rooms are equally bright and airy, with lovely bay
views enhanced by contemporary furnishings, pastel fabrics, and modern art.

   Dining/Diversions: The Currach, the hotel's main restaurant, and O'Malley's Pub
offer views of Galway Bay.

   Amenities: Concierge, room service, laundry and dry cleaning, baby-sitting, children's program (July and Aug), indoor heated swimming pool, sauna, Jacuzzi, steam
room, table tennis.

✪ **Galway Great Southern Hotel.** 15 Eyre Sq., Galway, County Galway. ☎ 800/
44-UTELL from the U.S., or 091/564041. Fax 091/566704. www.gsh.ie. E-mail: res@galway.
gsh.ie. 115 units. TV TEL. £142–£158 ($198.80–$221.20) double. Rates include full Irish
breakfast and service charge. AE, DC, MC, V.

Dating from 1845, this handsome five-story hotel is the *grande dame* of the Galway
area. In the heart of the city, overlooking Eyre Square, it's next to the bus and rail station and within walking distance of all the major sights. The spacious public areas
have high ceilings, elaborate plasterwork, crystal chandeliers, and original Connemara
marble fireplaces. The recently refurbished guest rooms have traditional dark woods,
semicanopy beds, orthopedic mattresses, designer fabrics, and brass touches, with
extras such as hair dryers, garment presses, and tea/coffeemakers. Rooms overlooking
Eyre Square have views of the whole city.

   Dining/Diversions: Choices include the Oyster Room restaurant, for fine dining,
and O'Flaherty's Pub, an Old Galway bar that serves excellent pub grub.

   Amenities: Concierge, room service, dry cleaning and laundry, baby-sitting,
rooftop indoor heated swimming pool, sauna, steam room.

MODERATE

Brennan's Yard Hotel. Lower Merchant's Rd., Galway, County Galway. ☎ 800/44-UTELL
from the U.S., or 091/568166. Fax 091/568262. www.hotelbook.com. 45 units. TV TEL.
£70–£95 ($98–$133) double. No service charge. Rates include full breakfast. AE, DC, MC, V.
Free parking at nearby car park.

One of the cleverest restorations in Galway's historic area, this recently expanded four-
story stone building was formerly a warehouse. Opened as a hotel in 1992, it has compact, skylit public areas enhanced by modern Irish art. Guest rooms overlook the city's
Spanish Arch area and are decorated in contemporary style, with Irish pine furnishings, designer fabrics, and locally made pottery. In-room extras include a hair dryer
and tea/coffeemaker. The restaurant specializes in European and seafood dishes, and
the Spanish Bar offers bar food and snacks all day.

Victoria Hotel. Victoria Place, Eyre Sq., Galway, County Galway. ☎ 091/567433. Fax
091/565880. E-mail: bookings@victoriahotel.ie. 57 units. TV TEL. £75–£140 ($105–$196)
double. Rates include full Irish breakfast and service charge. AE, DC, MC, V.

Tucked in a peaceful corner of the city, opposite the tourist office and just a block
from Eyre Square, this new hotel has a great location. Plants and mirrors enhance
the modern art deco–style interior. Guest rooms are compact and contemporary,
with light-wood furnishings and pastel fabrics. In-room amenities include a tea/
coffeemaker, hair dryer, and garment press. The hotel has a restaurant-bar and
24-hour room service.

INEXPENSIVE

Adare Guest House. 9 Father Griffin Place, Galway, County Galway. ☎ **091/582638.** Fax 091/583963. E-mail: adare@iol.ie. 13 units. TV TEL. £40–£60 ($56–$84) double. No service charge. Rates include full breakfast. AE, MC, V. Free parking.

West of the River Corrib in a quiet residential area, this modern three-story guesthouse is within comfortable walking distance (2 blocks) of the Wolf Tone Bridge and the Spanish Arch area of the city. It offers modern accommodations with orthopedic beds and standard furnishings. Breakfast is served in a cheery dining room, using Royal Tara china and other Galway-produced accessories. Padraic and Grainne Conroym are the hosts.

Jurys Inn Galway. Quay St., Galway, County Galway. ☎ **800/44-UTELL** from the U.S., or 091/566444. Fax 091/568415. www.jurys.com. 128 units. TV TEL. £47–£69 ($65.80–$96.60) double or triple. No service charge. Prices may be higher at New Year's and in mid-July during the Arts Festival and Galway Races. DC, MC, V. Discounted parking available at adjoining facility.

This relatively new four-story hotel opposite the Spanish Arch was designed in keeping with the area's historic character. Geared to the cost-conscious traveler, it was the first of its kind in downtown Galway, providing quality hotel lodgings at guesthouse prices. The real draw is the central location, right in the heart of things yet bounded on one side by an almost-lulling canal. The guest rooms, with expansive views of the river or nearby Galway Bay, are simply decorated in contemporary "motel" style, with light-wood furniture, enhanced by pictures of Old Galway and Connemara. There are tea/coffeemakers in the rooms, and ice machines (once a rarity in Ireland) on the first and third floors. The beds are firm, and nonsmoking rooms are available. The hotel has a moderately priced restaurant, the Arches, and the Inn Pub.

Knockrea Guesthouse. Lower Salthill, Galway, County Galway. ☎ **091/520145.** Fax 091/529985. www.galway.net/pages/knockrea/. 9 units, 3 with shower only. TV TEL. £54 ($75.60) double. 25% reduction for children. Rates include full breakfast. MC, V. Private carpark.

In operation since the 1960s, Knockrea is situated on a commercial street in Salthill, a 15-minute walk from Galway city center and 5 minutes from the waters of Galway Bay. Eileen and Padraic Storan purchased the place in 1995, and since then, they've completely transformed the interior, bringing this cozy guesthouse up-to-date. The moderately spacious rooms are furnished in simple pine furniture, and the exposed floorboards are also pine. There are two family rooms, which offer more space and two twin beds in addition to the double bed found in most rooms. Bathrooms are somewhat more spacious than your average closet. Smoking is discouraged in the bedrooms, and one of the three sitting rooms is set aside for smokers. Eileen Storan is an able and sympathetic host—she knows the area well, and helps her guests to make the most of their time in Galway. A small kitchen is available for guests to make tea, and perishables can be stored in the fridge.

Roncalli House. 24 Whitestrand Ave., Lower Salthill, Galway, County Galway. ☎ and fax **091/584159.** 6 units, all with shower only. TV. £38 ($53.20) double. 20% reduction for children. Rates include full breakfast. MC, V.

The O'Halloran home is an exceptionally comfortable base for your explorations in Galway—Carmel and her husband Tim have been welcoming guests to their home for many years, and they're great hosts. A glowing fireplace takes the chill off cool evenings, and in good weather guests can relax on the outdoor patio or in an enclosed sun porch at the front of the house. There are two ground-floor bedrooms and four others upstairs, all with hair dryers and tea/coffeemakers; the rooms are exceptionally clean and moderate to small in size, while bathrooms are quite compact. The breakfast is admirably diverse—oatmeal, french toast, and pancakes are among the plentiful options. Galway city is a 12-minute walk from the house.

3 Dining

EXPENSIVE

deBurgos. 15/17 Augustine St., Galway, County Galway. ☎ **091/562188.** Reservations recommended. Main courses £11.95–£16.95 ($16.75–$23.75). AE, MC, V. Mon–Sat 6pm–midnight, Sun 7am–noon. INTERNATIONAL.

Named after one of Galway's most important Norman tribes, deBurgos is in what was originally the wine vault of a 16th-century merchant's house. It has an impressive interior—whitewashed walls, caverns, arches, turreted dividers, Oriental carpets, and medieval-style wall hangings—enhanced by flickering candles, fresh flowers, pink linens, and Irish music playing in the background. The imaginative menu offers dishes such as deBurgos three fillets (pork, veal, and beef) on a confit of shallots and chicken Nicole and stuffed with farci of chicken, shrimp, and chervil cream sauce. There's an array of seafood and vegetarian offerings. The chef will happily cater to special dietary requirements.

Kirwan's Lane. Kirwan's Lane, Galway, County Galway. ☎ **091/568266.** Reservations recommended. Main courses £14.95–£18.50 ($20.95–$25.90). AE, MC, V. Daily 12:30–2:30pm and 6–10:30pm. Closed Sun Sept–June. IRISH/CONTINENTAL.

The stylish contemporary decor and live piano music of Kirwan's Lane are immediately inviting. The promise of "creative cuisine" is kept, on the menu and on the plate, with often-surprising blends of herbs and spices. On the downside, in the emphasis on architectural presentation and what might be seen as a culinary costume party, sauce tends to overwhelm substance, masking the fish or fowl at the bottom of it all. That said, the menu is inventive and varied, the ambience pleasing, and the food rich and provocative.

Park Room Restaurant. Forster St., Eyre Sq., Galway, County Galway. ☎ **091/564924.** Reservations recommended. Main courses £12.95–£23.95 ($18.15–$33.55). AE, DC, MC, V. Daily 12:30–3pm and 6–10pm. INTERNATIONAL.

Just a half-block east of Eyre Square, this fine restaurant—sporting many awards, including the Galways Oyster Festival Best Seafood Award—at the back of the Park House Hotel, has old-world decor of stained glass, dark woods, oil paintings, and plants. The exquisite entrees include sirloin steak au poivre, roast duckling with peach and brandy sauce, fresh Carna scallops Mornay, and Dublin Bay prawns thermidor.

MODERATE

The House of Bards. 2 Market St., Galway, County Galway. ☎ **091/568414.** Reservations recommended. Main courses £8.95–£19.95 ($12.55–$27.95). MC, V. Daily 6:30–11pm. IRISH.

One of Galway's newer restaurants, the House is in one of the city's oldest buildings, with a fireplace oven dating from 1589. The crest over the fireplace is the marriage stone of Joyce and Skerret, two of Galway's 14 tribes. Whitewashed walls, arches, flagstone floors, candle wall sconces, medieval art, and the menu itself add to the 16th-century atmosphere. What choices! There are Lady Jane Darcy's Fancy (chicken with Irish cheese stuffing), the Chieftain's Choice (pork filled with cheese and apples in rosemary sauce), Knight's Armour (sirloin steak with Irish whiskey sauce), Jester's Leap (salmon stuffed with creamy dill sauce), and King's Ransom (baked scallops, mussels, and prawns in white-wine cheese sauce).

Picnic Fare Beyond Compare

Sheridans Cheesemongers, 1 Kirwan's Lane (☎ 091/564829; www.irishcheese. com), is headquarters for putting together a do-it-yourself movable feast. Myriad vats of gorgeous olives, mounds of fine Irish cheeses, baskets of crisp fresh loaves, savory arrays of sausages and sliced meats, and shelves of gourmet mustards, quince paste, eggplant caviar, and other delicacies all conspire to endanger the high chefs of Ireland. Open Monday to Saturday 9:30am to 6pm. If you're in town on Saturday morning, look for a Sheridans stand at the Galway Street Market, which forms around the walls of Saint Nicholas' Collegiate Church, a short walk away.

Tulsi. 3 Buttermilk Walk, Galway, County Galway. ☎ **091/564831.** Reservations recommended. Main courses £7.50–£15.50 ($10.50–$21.70) (with rice). MC, V. Mon–Sat noon–2:30pm and 6–10:30pm; Sun 1–5pm and 6–10:30pm. INDIAN.

Galway is becoming more cosmopolitan every week, as demonstrated by new ventures like Tulsi. It wasn't long ago that a decent Indian restaurant was impossible to find in Dublin, let alone Galway; the pace of change in Ireland is visible in the fact that this restaurant hasn't even made much of a splash in Galway's complex culinary waters. The food here isn't superlative, but the ingredients are fresh and the spicing is pleasurable. The menu doesn't offer any surprises, but old reliables like saag paneer won't disappoint. An extensive buffet lunch is available on Sunday afternoon. There are two restaurants under the same name and ownership in Dublin.

MODERATE/INEXPENSIVE

Conlon. Eglinton Court, Galway, County Galway. ☎ **091/562268.** Seafood bar items £2.95–£5.95 ($4.15–$8.35); main courses £4.45–£15.95 ($6.25–$22.35); lobster thermidor £18 ($25.20). DC, MC, V. Mon–Sat 11am–midnight; Sun 5pm–midnight. SEAFOOD.

If you have a craving for fish, go no further. Everything here is fresh, not frozen. Conlon boasts approximately 20 varieties of fresh fish and shellfish at any given time. The house specialties are wild salmon and oysters. Treasures of the deep await: grilled wild salmon, steamed Galway Bay mussels, and fishermen's platters (smoked salmon, mussels, prawns, smoked mackerel, oysters, and crab claws).

G.B.C. (Galway Bakery Company). 7 Williamsgate St., Galway, County Galway. ☎ **091/563087.** Coffee-shop items under £5 ($7); dinner main courses £6.25–£12.95 ($8.75–$18.15). AE, DC, MC, V. Coffee shop daily 8am–10pm; restaurant daily noon–10pm. INTERNATIONAL.

With a distinctive Old Galway shop-front facade, this building is two eateries in one: a ground-level self-service coffee shop and a full-service bistro upstairs. The restaurant menu lists a variety of dishes, priced to suit every budget, from steaks and seafood dishes to chicken Kiev or cordon bleu, as well as quiches, omelets, salads, and stir-fried vegetable platters. Baked goods, particularly the homemade brown bread, are an added attraction.

McDonagh's Seafood Bar. 22 Quay St., Galway, County Galway. ☎ **091/565001.** Reservations not accepted June–Aug. Main courses £5.75–£25 ($8.05–$35). AE, MC, V. Daily noon–10pm. SEAFOOD.

For fresh seafood in an authentic maritime atmosphere, Galway's best choice is this little shop front, divided into a fish market, a fish-and-chip shop, and a full-service restaurant. The McDonagh family, fishmongers for more than four generations, buys direct from local fishermen every day—and it shows, as crowds line up every night to get in. The choices usually include salmon, trout, lemon or black sole (or both), turbot, and silver hake, all cooked to order. In addition, you can crack your own prawns' tails and crab claws in the shell, or tackle a whole lobster.

The River God Cafe. Quay St. (at Cross St.), Galway, County Galway. ☎ **091/565811.** Reservations not accepted. Dinner main courses £7.50–£12.50 ($10.50–$17.50). AE, DC, MC, V. Mon–Sat noon–10pm; Sun 4–10pm. IRISH/CONTINENTAL.

This is a rewarding destination for those with hearty appetites and modest budgets. The casserole of cod and potatoes Connemara style, served in a wide, deep tureen, will put the color back into any hungry face. An equally lavish portion of wild mushroom tart with paprika potatoes will restore the vegetarian visitor. Other offerings include sheep-cheese Gouda with pesto, and loin of pork with Guinness mustard sauce. Neither the decor nor the cuisine is particularly refined or subtle, but both are satisfying. A full lunch special at roughly £5 ($7) is an especially savory bargain here.

INEXPENSIVE

Da Tang Noodle House. Middle St., Galway, County Galway. ☎ **091/561443.** Main courses £7–£10 ($9.80–$14). Daily noon–10pm. MC, V. Closed Sun off-season. CHINESE NOODLE HOUSE.

The noodles at Da Tang are superlative. Bowls of homemade soup noodles are large and result in more than a few appreciative slurps. The broth, seasoned with fresh coriander and chilies, has a pleasant bite. Vegetables abound: carrot, mushroom, bamboo shoots, and shreds of Chinese cabbage are all cooked to crunchy perfection. We particularly recommend the afternoon meal—the service is admirably fast, making this a great place to nourish your noodle along with a steady stream of Galwegians looking for a quick, healthy lunch.

✪ **Goya's.** Kirwan's Lane, Galway, County Galway. ☎ **091/567010.** All items under £6 ($8.40). No credit cards. Mon–Sat 10am–6pm. TEA HOUSE/BAKED GOODS.

Goya's recently burst its banks and moved from its tiny spot on Quay Street to this bright, much more spacious venue. Its reputation for seductive pastries has followed, and the new cafe is every bit as crowded as the old. You can't go wrong with the modest selection of baked goods. The emphasis is on simplicity. You probably won't find anything unexpected, but everything Emer Murray makes is delightful. Stop in for tea and a scone, or buy a loaf of exceptional soda bread for lunch.

4 Attractions

Some of Galway's top attractions are outdoors and free of charge. Leading the list is Galway Bay, and no one should miss a stroll around the Spanish Arch and Spanish Parade, through Eyre Square and the John F. Kennedy Park, or on the banks of the River Corrib.

For a change of pace, or if it rains, here are some indoor attractions:

Galway Arts Centre. 47 Dominick St. and 23 Nuns Island, Galway, County Galway. ☎ **091/565886.** Free admission to exhibits; concerts £2–£6 ($2.80–$8.40). Mon–Fri 10am–9:30pm; Sat 10am–5:30pm.

Originally the town house of W. B. Yeats's patron, Lady Augusta Gregory, this building was for many years the offices of the Galway Corporation. The center offers excellent concerts, readings, and exhibitions by Irish and international artists.

Galway Cathedral. University and Gaol rds., Galway, County Galway. ☎ **091/563577.** Free admission; donations welcome. Daily 8am–6pm.

Dominating the city's skyline, Galway Cathedral is officially known as the Cathedral of Our Lady Assumed into Heaven and St. Nicholas. Mainly in the Renaissance style, it's constructed of fine-cut limestone from local quarries, with Connemara marble floors. Completed in 1965, it took 8 years to build. Contemporary Irish artisans designed the statues, stained-glass windows, and mosaics. It's beside the Salmon Weir Bridge on the west bank of the River Corrib.

Galway City Museum. Off Spanish Arch, Galway, County Galway. ☎ **091/567641.** Admission £1 ($1.40) adults, 50p (70¢) students and children. Apr–Sept daily 10am–1pm and 2–5pm; Oct–Mar Tues–Thurs 10am–1pm and 2–5pm.

This little museum offers a fine collection of local documents, photographs, city memorabilia, examples of medieval stonework, and revolving exhibits.

✪ **Galway Irish Crystal Heritage Centre.** East of the city on the main Dublin road (N6), Merlin Park, Galway, County Galway. ☎ **091/757311.** www.galwaycrystal.ie. Free admission. Guided tour £2 ($2.80) adults, £1.50 ($2.10) seniors and students, £1 ($1.40) children, £5 ($7) family. June–Aug Mon–Fri 9am–7pm, Sat 9am–6pm, Sun 10am–6pm; Sept–May Mon–Sat 9am–5:30pm, Sun 10am–5:30pm.

Visitors to this distinctive crystal manufacturer are welcome to watch the craftsmen at work—blowing, shaping, and hand-cutting the glassware—as part of a great tour through the new heritage center. Demonstrations are continuous on weekdays. The shop and new restaurant are open daily.

Nora Barnacle House. Bowling Green, Galway, County Galway. ☎ **091/564743.** Admission £1 ($1.40). Mid-May to mid-Sept Mon–Sat 10am–5pm (closed for lunch), and by appointment.

Opposite the St. Nicholas church clock tower, this restored 19th-century terrace house was once the home of Nora Barnacle, wife of James Joyce. It contains letters, photographs, and other exhibits on the lives of the Joyces and their connections with Galway.

✪ **Royal Tara China Visitor Centre.** Tara Hall, Mervue, Galway, County Galway. ☎ **091/751301.** www.royal-tara.ie. Free admission and tours. Jan–June and Oct–Dec daily 9am–6pm; July–Sept daily 9am–9pm.

One of Galway's oldest enterprises, this company manufactures fine bone china gift and tableware, distinguished by delicate shamrock patterns and designs inspired by the Book of Kells, the Tara brooch, and the Claddagh ring. The showrooms are quite beautiful, and the tearooms are a congenial place to rest your legs. Look for the sign a mile east of Galway City, off the main Dublin road.

✪ **St. Nicholas' Collegiate Church.** Lombard St., Galway, County Galway. ☎ **091/564648.** Free admission to church; donations of £1.50 ($2.10) adults, £1 ($1.40) seniors and students requested. Tours £2 ($2.80); reservations required. Mid-Apr to Sept Mon–Sat 9am–5:45pm, Sun 1–5:45pm; Oct to mid-Apr Mon–Sat 10am–4pm, Sun 1–5pm.

It's said that Christopher Columbus prayed here in 1477 before setting out to discover the New World. Established about 1320, it has changed from Roman Catholic to Church of Ireland (Episcopal) at least four times, and is currently under the aegis of the latter denomination. Highlights include an authentic crusader's tomb dating from the 12th or 13th century, with a rare Norman inscription on the grave slab. In addition, there is a freestanding *benitier* (a holy-water holder) that's unique in Ireland, as well as a carved font from the 16th or 17th century, and a stone lectern with barley-sugar twist columns from the 15th or 16th century. The belfry contains 10 bells, some of which date from 1590. Guided tours, conducted by Declan O Mordha, a knowledgeable and enthusiastic church representative, depart from the south porch according to demand, except on Sunday morning.

TOURS & CRUISES

✪ *Corrib Princess.* Woodquay, Galway, County Galway. ☎ **091/592447.** Cruise £6 ($8.40) adults, £5 ($7) seniors and students, £2.50 ($3.50) children, £15 ($21) family. May, June, and Sept daily 2:30 and 4:30pm; July–Aug daily 12:30, 2:30, and 4:30pm.

This 157-passenger, two-deck boat cruises along the River Corrib, with commentary on all points of interest. The trip lasts 90 minutes, passing castles, sites of historical interest, and assorted wildlife. There is full bar and snack service. You can buy tickets at the dock or at the *Corrib Princess* desk at the tourist office.

Galway Panoramic. Grayline/Guide Friday Irish City Tours, Galway, County Galway. ☎ **01/670-8822.** Apr–Oct daily, with schedule varying according to demand. £6 ($8.40) adults, £5 ($7) students, £2 ($2.80) children.

Hop aboard these open-top buses and explore the highlights of Galway and its spectacular environs. They run all day in a loop, so when you see something you want to explore, just hop off. Or just stay on all day and memorize everything you see and hear. The tour includes vistas of the western coast of Ireland, Galway Bay, and distant views of the Arran Islands. Further details are available from the Galway Tourist Office.

5 Spectator Sports & Outdoor Pursuits

SPECTATOR SPORTS

GREYHOUND RACING   The hounds race year-round every Tuesday and Friday at 8:15pm at the **Galway Greyhound Track,** College Road, off Eyre Square (☎ **091/562273**). Admission is £3 ($4.20) and includes a racing card.

HORSE RACING   For 6 days at the end of July, thoroughbreds ply the track at the **Galway Racecourse,** Ballybrit (☎ **091/753870**), less than 2 miles (3.2km) east of town. Two-day race meetings are scheduled in early September and late October. Admission is £8 to £12 ($11.20 to $16.80), depending on the event and the day of the week.

OUTDOOR PURSUITS

BICYCLING   To rent a bike, contact **Celtic Cycles,** Queen Street (☎ **091/566606**), or **Richard Walsh Cycles,** Headford Road, Woodquay (☎ **091/565710**).

FISHING   Sitting beside the River Corrib, Galway City and nearby Connemara are popular fishing centers for salmon and sea trout. For the latest information on requirements for licenses and local permits, check with the **Western Regional Fisheries Board,** Weir Lodge, Earl's Island, Galway (☎ **091/563118;** e-mail: WRFB@iol.ie). The extraordinarily friendly WRFB also provides free consultation for overseas anglers on where to go at different times of the season for salmon or trout, where to find the best *ghillies* (guides), and which flies and gear to use. Maps and brochures are available on request. For gear and equipment, try **Duffys Fishing,** 5 Main Guard St. (☎ **091/562367**); **Freeney Sport Shop,** 19 High St. (☎ **091/568794**); or **Great Outdoors Sports Centre,** Eglinton Street (☎ **091/562869**).

GOLF   Less than 5 miles (8km) east of Galway is the 18-hole, par-72 championship **Galway Bay Golf & Country Club,** Renville, Oranmore, County Galway (☎ **091/790500**). It charges greens fees of £38 ($53.20) weekdays, £43 ($60.20) weekends. Less than 2 miles (3.2km) west of the city is the 18-hole, par-69 seaside course at **Galway Golf Club,** Blackrock, Galway (☎ **091/522033**), with greens fees of £20 ($28) weekdays, £25 ($35) weekends.

HORSEBACK RIDING   Riding enthusiasts head to **Aille Cross Equitation Cen-tre,** Aille Cross, Loughrea, County Galway (☎ **091/841216**), about 20 miles (32km) east of Galway. Run by personable Willy Leahy (who has appeared often on American television), this facility is one of the largest in Ireland, with 50 horses and 20 Con-nemara ponies. For about £12 ($16.80) an hour, you can ride through nearby farm-lands, woodlands, forest trails, and mountain lands. Weeklong trail rides in the scenic Connemara region are another specialty, as is hunting with the Galway Blazers in the winter.

6 Shopping

Galway offers malls of small shops clustered in some of the city's well-preserved and restored historic buildings. They include the **Cornstore** on Middle Street, the **Grain-store** on Lower Abbeygate Street, and the **Bridge Mills,** a 430-year-old mill building beside the River Corrib.

Eyre Square Centre, the downtown area's largest shopping mall with 50 shops, has incorporated a major section of Galway's medieval town wall into its complex.

Most shops are open Monday to Saturday 9 or 10am to 5:30 or 6pm. In July and August, many shops stay open late, usually until 9pm on weekdays, and some also open on Sunday from noon to 5pm.

Here's a sampling of some of Galway's best shops.

ANTIQUES & CURIOS

Cobwebs. 7 Quay Lane, Galway, County Galway. ☎ **091/564388.**

Established almost 25 years ago, this little shop is across from the Spanish Arch. It offers unique jewelry, antique toys, curios, and rarities from all parts of Ireland and beyond.

Curiosity Corner. Cross St., Galway, County Galway. No phone.

On a corner opposite the Spanish Arch, this shop carries a wide variety of unusual Irish-made gifts, including ceramics, scents, potpourri, and dried flowers.

BOOKS

Charlie Byrne's Bookshop. The Cornstore, Middle St., Galway, County Galway. ☎ **091/561766.** E-mail: chabyrne@iol.ie.

Prices are good in this mostly secondhand bookshop, specializing in paperback fiction and Irish-interest books. There are also some surprising finds to be had, with a fair selection of titles in archaeology, art history, the cinema, and music.

Hawkins House Bookshop. 14 Churchyard St. (off Shop St.), Galway, County Galway. ☎ **091/567507.**

This shop stocks new books concentrating on Irish poetry, drama, fiction, history, art, archaeology, genealogy, mythology, and music. It also has a great selection of children's books. It's beside St. Nicholas' Collegiate Church.

◐ **Kenny's Book Shop and Gallery.** Middle and High sts., Galway, County Galway. ☎ **091/562739.** www._kennys.ie.

A Galway fixture for more than 50 years, this shop is a sightseeing attraction unto itself. You'll find old maps, prints, and engravings. Books on all topics—many on local history, as well as whole sections on Yeats and Joyce—are wedged on shelves and win-dow ledges and piled in crates and turf baskets. Lining the walls are signed photos of more than 200 writers who have visited the shop over the years. In addition, Kenny's is famous for its antiquarian department, its book-binding workshop, and an ever-changing gallery of local watercolors, oils, and sculptures. Enough goes on here to keep eight members of the Kenny family busy.

CRYSTAL, CHINA & SOUVENIRS

Moons. William St. (at Eglinton St.), Galway, County Galway. ☎ **091/565254.**

This is Galway's long-established midcity department store, with crystal, china, linens, and gifts, as well as clothing and household items.

✪ **Treasure Chest.** 31–33 William St. and Castle St., Galway, County Galway. ☎ **091/ 563862.**

For more than 25 years, this attractive shop with a Wedgwood-style exterior has been a treasure trove of top-quality crafts, fashions, and gifts. You'll find everything from Waterford crystal chandeliers to Royal Tara and Royal Doulton china, Irish Dresden figurines, Lladró figures, and Belleek china. It also carries Irish designer clothing, Aran knitwear, lingerie, and swimwear, not to mention handmade leprechauns and Irish whiskey marmalade.

HANDCRAFTS

✪ **Design Ireland Plus.** The Cornstore, Middle St., Galway, County Galway. ☎ **091/ 567716.**

Ceramics, pottery, linen, lace, jewelry, leather bags, rainwear, blankets, stationery, candlesticks, multicolored sweaters and capes, and handcrafted batik ties and scarves—all designed and made in Ireland—are sold here and at a second location on Lower Abbeygate Street. Open Monday to Saturday 9am to 6pm; plus Sunday noon to 6pm in July and August.

Judy Greene Pottery. 11 Cross St. , Galway, County Galway. ☎ **091/561753.**

Don't miss this small shop for hand-thrown pottery painted by hand with Irish floral designs. Wares include goblets, vases, candleholders, dinner and tea services, garden pots, cut-work lamps, miniatures, and jewelry. Pieces can be specially commissioned.

Kevin McGuire & Son. 3 Lyndon Court, Rosemary Ave. , Galway, County Galway. ☎ **091/ 568733.**

Housed in a whitewashed cottage and a gray stone building 1 block from Eyre Square, this specialty leather shop offers Celtic and modern handbags, briefcases, music cases, wallets, watch straps, belts, pendants, and sheepskin rugs.

Meadows & Byrne. Castle St. , Galway, County Galway. ☎ **091/567776.**

Earthenware pottery and hand-blown glass have long been featured at this store, which also stocks wooden ware, textiles, tableware, scented beeswax candles, and Irish preserves and honey.

JEWELRY

✪ **Fallers of Galway.** Williamsgate St. , Galway, County Galway. ☎ **091/561226,** or 800/229-3892 from the U.S. (for catalogs).

Dating from 1879, Fallers has long been a prime source of Claddagh rings, many of which are made on the premises. It also sells Celtic crosses, some inlaid with Connemara marble, as well as gold and silver jewelry and crystal.

Hartmann's. 29 William St., Galway, County Galway. ☎ **091/562063.** www.hartmanns.ie.

The Hartmann family, which began in the jewelry business in the late 1800s in Germany, brought their skills and wares to Ireland in 1895, and opened this shop in 1942. They enjoy a far-reaching reputation as watchmakers, goldsmiths, and makers of Claddagh rings. The store also stocks Celtic crosses, writing instruments, crystal, silverware, and unusual clocks. It's in the heart of town, just off Eyre Square.

MUSIC & MUSICAL INSTRUMENTS
Mulligan. 5 Middle St. Court, Middle St. , Galway, County Galway. ☎ **091/564961.**

Mulligan's boasts of having the largest stock of Irish and Scottish traditional records, CDs, and cassettes in Ireland. There is also a good selection of folk music from all over the world, including Cajun, Latin American, and African, as well as country music, blues, and jazz. Open Monday to Thursday from 9:30am to 7pm, until 9pm Friday, until 6pm Saturday, and noon to 4pm Sunday.

✪ **P. Powell & Sons/The Music Shop.** The Four Corners, William St. , Galway, County Galway. ☎ **091/562295.**

Opposite Lynch's Castle, where William Street meets Abbeygate Street, this shop is known for Irish traditional music. In addition to cassettes and CDs, it sells tin whistles, flutes, bodhrans, accordions, and violins, as well as sheet music and a full range of music books. Open daily 9am to 5:30pm.

TWEEDS, WOOLENS & CLOTHING
Mac Eocagain/Galway Woollen Market. 21 High St. , Galway, County Galway. ☎ **091/562491.**

This shop brims with traditional Aran hand-knits and colorful hand-loomed sweaters and capes, as well as linens, lace, sheepskins, jewelry, and woolen accessories. Each item has two prices, one including value-added tax (VAT) and one tax-free for non–European Community (EC) residents. Open Monday to Saturday 9am to 6pm, Sunday noon to 5pm; in July and August, until 9pm Monday to Saturday, and Sunday 10am to 6pm.

✪ **O'Máille (O'Malley).** 16 High St. , Galway, County Galway. ☎ **091/562696.** www.iol.ie/omaille/.

Established in 1938, this shop draws customers from far and near for quality Irish clothing, including Irish-designed knitwear, traditional Aran knits, and tweeds for men and women. There is always a good selection of sweaters, jackets, coats, suits, capes, kilts, caps, and ties. Open Monday to Saturday 9am to 6pm.

7 Galway City After Dark
PUBS
An Pucan. 11 Forster St. , Galway, County Galway. ☎ **091/561528.**

A block east of Eyre Square, this old-fashioned nautical-theme pub is a great place to find some of the best Irish traditional music in Galway (daily from 9pm). It's also an Irish-language pub, where most of the patrons are native Irish speakers.

Busker Browns. Cross St. , Galway, County Galway. ☎ **091/563377.**

The relatively new pub and bistro has an Old Galway ambience, with alcoves and nooks and crannies, and offers a choice of bars. This is one of Galway's most mobbed spots, so secure your space early. Traditional music is performed throughout the week, and the place swings to Dixieland jazz on Sunday from noon to 2pm.

Crane Bar. 2 Sea Rd. , Galway, County Galway. ☎ **091/567419.**

In the southwestern part of Galway, at the corner of an open market area called "the Small Crane," this rustic pub is known for its nightly musical entertainment. It gives special rates to fiddlers, pipers, singers, and banjo and accordion players who pass the "efficiency" test. From 9pm every night, there is country and western downstairs and traditional Irish tunes upstairs.

Hole in the Wall. 9 Eyre St. , Galway, County Galway. ☎ **091/565593.**

Topped with a thatched roof, this old-world pub stands out on a busy shopping street 1 block from Eyre Square. It has a low beamed ceiling, open fireplaces, old sporting prints, and an old-fashioned jukebox. Cable TV screens show major sports events in this regular gathering spot for fans of Gaelic football and horse racing. Between the sports talk, traditional Irish music starts nightly in the summer at 9:30pm.

O'Malleys. 30 Prospect Hill, Galway, County Galway. ☎ **091/564595.**

Claiming to be Galway's oldest music pub, this informal watering hole has traditional Irish and folk music sessions with special guests on Fridays from October to March, and music with dancing in the summer.

The Quays. Quay St. and Chapel Lane, Galway, County Galway. ☎ **091/568347.**

You'll find this little treasure in the heart of the city, a half block from the Druid Theatre. In keeping with its churchly theme, it's full of tinted glass, carved wood, and even pews. The music is traditional but not ecclesiastical. Evening music ranges from traditional Irish to Dixieland, and usually starts at 9pm.

Rabbitt's. 23–25 Forster St. , Galway, County Galway. ☎ **091/566490.**

Dating from 1872, this pub is much the way it was a century ago. Old lanterns hang in the corners, skylights brighten the bar area, and pictures of Galway in horse-and-carriage days line the walls. A hefty bucket of ice sits on the counter, and a hearty Irish stew and Rabbitt's famous onion soup await in the kitchen. Run by the fourth generation of the Rabbitt family, it's a block east of Eyre Square.

Tigh Neachtain. 17 Cross St. , Galway, County Galway. ☎ **091/568820.**

This century-old pub in the heart of the medieval quarter was once the home of Richard Martin, a Galway politician and animal-rights activist known as "Humanity Dick." Now it's a pub known for traditional Irish music, kind not only to canine ears, but also to human ones.

CLUBS

Like a late relay, the clubs take up at 11:30pm when the pubs leave off. The place to see and be seen is **Central Park,** 36 Upper Abbeygate St. (☎ **091/565976**). Other hot spots are the **GPO,** Eglinton Street (☎ **091/563073**); **Baywatch** at the Hotel Monterey, Salthill (☎ **091/522715**), Ireland's only laser club; and **Club Cuba,** 1 Prospect Hill, Eyre Square (☎ **091/566135**).

   Zulu's Bar, Raven's Terrace (near Jury's Inn; ☎ **091/58124**), is Galway's first specifically gay bar. Fridays and Saturdays are gay nights at **The Attic @ Liquid,** Liquid, Salthill (☎ **091/522715**).

A MEDIEVAL BANQUET

On the shores of Galway Bay, **Dunguaire** is a splendid 16th-century castle that features a medieval banquet with a literary-themed show. In south County Galway on Ballyvaughan Road (N67), Kinvara, the castle is a nightlife option for people staying in Galway City, just a half-hour drive away (see "Side Trips from Galway City," below). The show features the work of Synge, Yeats, Gogarty, and other Irish writers who knew and loved this area. Banquets are staged in the summer months in keeping with demand and cost £30 ($42) per person. Reservations can be made at ☎ **061/361511.**

THEATERS

Druid Theatre. Chapel Lane, Galway, County Galway. ☎ **091/568617.** E-mail: druid@indigo.ie. Evening tickets £8–£14 ($11.20–$19.60). Box office Mon–Sat noon–8pm; evening shows 8pm.

Irish folk dramas, modern international dramas, and Anglo-Irish classics are the focus at this professional theater in the heart of Galway. Founded in 1975, the theatre is located in a converted grain warehouse and configured with 65 to 115 seats, depending on the production. Lunchtime performances are often staged during the summer. The Druid Theatre Company, of international repute, is much in demand and frequently on tour; so make your plans well in advance.

Siamsa, The Galway Folk Theatre. Claddagh Hall, Nimmos Pier, Galway, County Galway. ☎ **091/755479.** E-mail: siamsa@eircom.net. Tickets £10–£12 ($14–$16.80). Shows Jun–Aug Mon–Fri 8:45pm. Additional weekend shows depending on demand.

This delightful blend of traditional Irish music, dance, and folk drama will definitely put you in the Celtic swing of things. If you wished that Riverdance would never end, here you'll discover that it hasn't. It's just over the Wolfe Tone Bridge in Claddagh, a 10-minute walk at most from Jurys.

✪ **Taibhdhearc na Gaillimhe Theatre.** Middle St., Galway, County Galway. ☎ **091/ 563600.** E-mail: taibh@iol.ie. Tickets £10 ($14). Box office Mon–Sat 1–6pm and evening of shows until 8pm; shows 8pm; Spraci July–Aug Mon–Fri 8:45pm.

Pronounced *Thive*-yark and officially known as *An Taibhdhearc na Gaillimhe* (the Theater of Galway), this is Ireland's national stage of the Irish language. Founded in 1928, it is a 108-seat, year-round venue for Irish plays and visiting troupes (such as ballet). In the summer, the theater presents Spraci, a program of traditional music, song, dance, and folk drama.

8 Side Trips from Galway City

THE ARAN ISLANDS

West from the mouth of Galway Bay, 30 miles (48km) out at sea, the storied ✪ Aran Islands—**Inis Mór (Inishmore)**, **Inis Meain (Inishmaan)**, and **Inis Oirr (Inisheer)**—are outposts of Gaelic culture and language. Here the rugged islanders immortalized in John Millington Synge's play *Riders to the Sea* and Robert Flaherty's film *Man of Aran* maintain their hardscrabble traditional life, clinging like moss to the islands' harsh rocks and fishing from *currachs,* small craft made of tarred canvas stretched over a timber frame.

The island's 1,500 inhabitants live in stone cottages, often rely on pony-drawn transport, and speak Irish among themselves, breaking into English when necessary to converse with non-islanders. Inevitably, tourism has altered things somewhat, and many distinctively Aran traditions hang on more as curios than as everyday elements of life. Among them are *crios*—finger-braided belts made of colored wool that traditionally held up the islanders' heavy wool trousers, but are now more commonly made for the tourist trade. The classic hand-knit *bainin* sweaters that originated here are still worn, as there's nothing better for keeping out the chill. You'll see plenty of them, both on people's backs and in the islands' many woolen and craft shops.

Impressions

Some time ago, before the introduction of police, all the people of the islands were as innocent as the people here remain to this day. I have heard that at that time the ruling proprietor and magistrate of the north island used to give any man who had done wrong a letter to a jailer in Galway, and send him off by himself to serve a term of imprisonment.

—J. M. Synge (1871–1909), *The Aran Islands*

Most visitors debark from the ferries at Kilronan, Inishmore's main town and possibly the easiest place in the world in which to arrange or rent transportation. The mode is up to you: Jaunting cars can be hailed like taxis as you step off the boat, minivans stand at the ready, and bicycle rentals are within sight.

Among the attractions on the Arans is ✪ **Dún Aengus,** a stone cliff fortress on Inishmore that extends over more than 11 acres. Dating back 2,000 years, the fort is believed to have been of great significance. Less certain is what that significance was. Some think it was not a military structure at all, but rather a vast ceremonial theater. It's on the edge of a cliff that drops 300 feet to the sea, and offers a spectacular view of Galway Bay, the Burren, Connemara, and (with sharp eyes and clear skies) the Blasket Islands. A new Dún Aengus Interpretive Centre opened in 1999.

The new heritage center, **Ionad Arann,** Kilronan, Inishmore (☎ **099/61355**), explores the history and culture of the islands. Exhibits examine the harsh yet beautiful landscape, the Iron Age forts, and the churches of the first Christians. In addition, the 1932 film *Man of Aran,* directed by Robert Flaherty, is shown six times daily. The center is open March to October daily 11am to 5pm. Admission to the center is £2.50 ($3.50) adults, £2 ($2.80) students, £1.50 ($2.10) seniors and children, £6 ($8.40) family. Discounted combination tickets to the center and film are available. The cafe serves soups, sandwiches, and pastries throughout the day.

Here are the best ways to arrange an excursion to the Aran Islands:

Aer Arann. Connemara Airport, Inverin, County Galway. ☎ **091/593034.** Fax 091/593238. www.aerarann.ie. Fare £35 ($49) round-trip; £18 ($25.20) one-way. MC, V. Daily Apr–Sept 9am, 10:30am, 4pm, and 5pm; Oct–Mar 9am, 10:30am, and 3pm.

The fastest way to get from the mainland to the Aran Islands is on this local airline, which departs from a new airport approximately 18 miles (29km) west of Galway City. Flight time is 10 minutes, and bus service between Galway City and the airport is available. You can book your flight at the Galway Tourist Office and at Aer Arann Reservations. A range of specials is usually on offer, combining flights with bus/ferry/accommodation, and so forth.

Aran Island Ferries. Victoria Place, off Eyre Sq., Galway, County Galway. ☎ **091/568903.** Fax 091/568538. www.aranislandferries.com. Round-trip fare £15 ($21) adults, £12 ($16.80) seniors and students, £8 ($11.20) children; family and group rates on request. From Rossaveal Nov–Mar daily 10:30am and 5:30pm; Apr–Oct 10:30am, 1:30pm, and 6:30pm. Additional sailings July–Aug according to demand.

This company, with a number of offices in Galway center, offers extensive year-round daily service to all three Aran Islands. Most boats leave from Rossaveal in Connemara, 23 miles (37km) west of the city. Island Ferries provides coach connection service from its Victoria Place office 90 minutes before sailing time. During peak summer season, there are daily excursions from Galway Dock, which cost up to £5 ($7) more than tickets from Rossaveal. Inquire about times for the newest fast ferry in the fleet.

O'Brien Shipping. Galway Docks, Galway, County Galway. ☎ **091/567676.** Fare £14 ($19.60) per person round-trip, £12 ($16.80) students; £7 ($9.80) one-way interisland. From Galway Dock, June–Sept daily 10:30am; from Aran, June–Sept 5pm. Oct–May schedule varies.

The M.V. *Oileain Arann,* a 240-passenger, air-conditioned, three-deck ship launched in 1993, is the newest on the Galway–Aran Islands route. It has a full bar, snack bar, TV, and public telephone on board. Sailing time is 90 minutes. The booking office is at the Galway Tourist Office. Ask about discounts for seniors and children.

ACCOMMODATIONS ON INISHMORE

✪ **Kilmurvey House.** 5 miles (8km) from the ferry on the coast road, Kilmurvey, Kilronan, Aran Islands, County Galway. ☎ **099/61218.** Fax 099/61397. 12 units. TEL. £44 ($61.60) double. Rates include full breakfast. MC, V. Closed Nov–Easter.

This has been the place to stay on Inishmore since Dún Aengus fell into ruin. The 18th-century stone family home of the "Ferocious O'Flahertys" forms the core of this most hospitable and pleasant guesthouse, expanded to offer 12 diverse rooms, all quite comfortable and impeccably clean. Despite its origins, the spirit of the house could not be more gracious. An array of delights awaits you at breakfast, and an optional four-course dinner is served at 7pm with advance reservation. Kilmurvey House lies just below Dún Aengus, Inishmore's prime attraction. A handful of shops, cafes, and restaurants, as well as a "blue flag" (that is, pristine) white-sand beach, are within a short stroll.

DINING ON INISHMORE

Man of Aran. Kilmurvey, Kilronan, Aran Islands, County Galway. ☎ **099/61301.** Reservations required for dinner. Fixed-price dinners £17–£20 ($23.80–$28). No credit cards. Mon–Sat 1:30–3pm and 7:30–10pm. IRISH/CONTINENTAL.

If the Man of Aran restaurant looks familiar, it may be because you just saw it in the film at the Heritage Centre. It is the traditional thatched seaside cottage constructed in 1934 for the filming of *Man of Aran.* The resemblance stops there, however—the Man himself never for 1 day ate as well as you will here. After years of culinary training and experience in London, Maura Wolfe returned to Aran with her husband, Joe, and created one of the island's great surprises. It's a first-class restaurant drawing upon the organic vegetables and herbs grown with great toil in their garden. Maura conjures each day's menu on the spot, inspired by what is fresh and available from the sea and from the soil just beyond her front door. The result is exquisite home cooking, perfect, simple, and without pretense. Tables are limited, especially in the separate nonsmoking room. If you can't stay for dinner, at least stop by for lunch. B&B accommodation is also available.

OYSTER COUNTRY

South of Galway on the main road south (N18) are two small fishing villages, **Claren-bridge** and **Kilcolgan.** Each year at the end of September, the villages host the annual **Galway Oyster Festival.** Launched in 1954, the 5-day festival is packed with traditional music, song, dancing, sports, art exhibits, and, above all, oyster-tasting events and oyster-opening competitions. A Galway beauty is crowned "Oyster Pearl," and she reigns over the festival.

Even if you can't be there for the September festival, you can enjoy some of Ireland's best oysters during any other month with an "r" in it.

If you continue south on N18 for another 10 miles (16km), you'll see signs to **Coole Park** (☎ **091/631804**). Irish red deer, pine martens, red squirrels, and badgers inhabit this national forest. **Coole House** was once the home of Lady Augusta

Gregory, dramatist and folklorist. With W. B. Yeats and Edward Martyn, she founded the Abbey Theatre. Her house no longer stands, but an "autograph tree" bears initials carved by George Bernard Shaw, Sean O'Casey, John Masefield, Oliver St. John Gogarty, W. B. Yeats, and Douglas Hyde, the first president of Ireland. The restored courtyard has a visitor center, tearooms, picnic tables, and a garden with nature trails that run to the lake. Admission is £2 ($2.80) adults, £1.50 ($2.10) seniors, £1 ($1.40) students and children, £5 ($7) family. It's open mid-April to mid-June, Tuesday to Sunday 10am to 5pm; mid-June to August, daily 9:30am to 6:30pm; September, daily 10am to 5pm. Last admission 1 hour before closing.

In Gort on the N18 is **Thoor Ballylee** (☎ **091/631436**). The restored 16th-century Norman tower house was the summer home of the Nobel Prize–winning poet William Butler Yeats. Yeats described the house as "a tower set by a stream's edge"; it served as the inspiration for his poems "The Winding Stair" and "The Tower." In the interpretive center, an audiovisual presentation examines the poet's life. Also on the grounds are the original Ballylee Mill, partially restored, and a bookshop specializing in Anglo-Irish literature. Admission is £3.50 ($4.90) adults, £3 ($4.20) seniors and students, £1 ($1.40) children. It's open from Easter to September daily 10am to 6pm. There's a seasonal **Tourist Information Office** (☎ **091/631436**) located here, open May to September daily 10am to 6pm.

West off the main road, between Gort and Kilcolgan, is **Dunguaire Castle,** Kinvara (☎ **061/360788**). On N67 just east of Kinvara, this tower house and *bawn* (fortified enclosure) sits on the south shore of Galway Bay. It was erected in the 16th century by the O'Heynes family at the royal seat of the 7th-century King Guaire of Connaught. The castle was later the country retreat of Oliver St. John Gogarty, Irish surgeon, author, poet, and wit. The castle's greatest appeal is the view from its battlements of the nearby Burren and Galway Bay. Admission is £2.90 ($4.05) adults, £2 ($2.80) seniors and students, £1.70 ($2.40) children, £7.15 ($10) family. It's open daily from mid-April through September 9:30am to 5:30pm. Medieval banquets take place on summer evenings (see "Galway City After Dark," above).

WHERE TO EAT OYSTERS

✪ **Moran's Oyster Cottage.** The Weir, Kilcolgan, County Galway. ☎ **091/796113.** Main courses £3.50–£15.50 ($4.90–$21.70). AE, MC, V. Mon–Sat 10:30am–11:30pm, Sun noon–11:30pm. SEAFOOD.

If you miss the signpost for Moran's on N18, turn around and go back, because this is not a place to be missed. Presidents, prime ministers, movie stars, and locals who know their fish make a point of finding their way here. The food is simply legendary. Moran's won the B.I.M. Seafood Pub of the Year prize in 1999. For six generations, the Morans have been catching salmon and shucking oysters and preparing them to perfection here on the weir. In 1960, Willie Moran caught 105 wild salmon in 1 day on the Dun Killen River in front of the family pub, and went on to win the world title in oyster opening. Two of his staff members, Vincent Graham and Gerry Grealish, are also world champions. In short, they know their oysters. The wild smoked salmon is exquisite—sheer velvet. Willie Moran believes in a small menu, fresh and wild and with nothing in the way. Ambience? It's a thatched cottage with 36 swans and a blue heron outside the front door the night we were here. Renovations in 1999 were true to the spirit of the place.

Paddy Burkes. Ennis–Galway Rd. (N18), Clarenbridge, County Galway. ☎ **091/796226.** Reservations recommended for dinner. Main courses £8–£15 ($11.20–$21). AE, DC, MC, V. Mon–Sat 10:30am–10:30pm, Sun noon–9:30pm. SEAFOOD.

Platters of local oysters and mussels are served throughout the day at this homey tavern, with its lemon color and thatched roof. You can pick your favorite spot to relax in the half-dozen rooms and alcoves with original stone walls, open fireplaces, pot-bellied stoves, fishing nets on the walls, and traditional sugan chairs. In good weather, there is seating in a back garden beside a weir bridge. Lunch and snack items range from seafood soups and chowders to sandwiches, salads, and omelets. In the evening, you can also order full meals, with choices such as whole black sole, baked salmon, Atlantic plaice and crab with prawn sauce, honey roast duck with mead sauce, and medallions of beef with whiskey and mustard. The tavern is on the main road, 10 miles (16km) south of Galway City.

A SHOPPING STOP

Clarenbridge Crystal and Fashion Shop. N18, Clarenbridge, County Galway. ☎ **091/796178.** 10 miles (16km) south of Galway City.

This shop features all types and styles of Clarenbridge crystal, a local glass product hand-cut, engraved, and decorated at a factory a mile away. You'll also find a beautiful range of classic quality ladies' fashions and men's country clothing, framed prints, watercolors, and jewelry. Open Monday to Saturday 9:30am to 6pm, Sunday noon to 6pm.

12

Out from Galway

Along the rocky western coast, Galway is Ireland's second-largest county, forming (with Mayo; see chapter 10) the heart of the province of Connaught. "To hell or Connaught!" were the limited options Cromwell offered the Irish in the 17th century. Like a firestorm, Cromwell and his armies ravaged everything in their path, sending the native population running to the western edge of Ireland, where there was nothing much worth coveting or destroying. The displaced Irish were left here to eke out a living on minute, rock-infested farms. It was also here, where it seemed people had little left to lose, that the famine of 1845–49 took its greatest toll. Masses of people either starved or took off on ships sailing west, never to return.

History aside, this bleak outpost is stunningly beautiful—a fact you can appreciate if you don't have to eat the scenery to survive. It is indeed a feast, and, as it happens, the feast provides for everyone, because tourism is bringing prosperity to the west that the potato never did.

1 The Galway Bay Coast

It's certainly worth a trip to see Galway Bay's wide blue waters, with the Aran Islands sitting 30 miles (48km) off the coast like three giant whales at rest. With vistas of Galway Bay on your left, the drive along the coast from Galway City is quite spectacular.

GALWAY COAST ESSENTIALS

GETTING THERE & GETTING AROUND   The best way to see the sights along the Galway Bay coast is to drive. From Galway City, follow the coast road (R336). From Galway City to Inverin is 20 miles (32km).

VISITOR INFORMATION   Contact or visit the **Ireland West Tourist Office,** Aras Fáilte, Victoria Place, Galway, County Galway (☎ **091/563081**). It's open year-round; see chapter 11 for hours. Seasonal offices, open from late May to mid-September, are at Clifden (☎ **095/21163**) and Salthill (☎ **091/563081**).

EXPLORING THE COAST

Head west, following signs for the coast road (R336). Within 2 miles (3.2km) you'll be in **Salthill,** a modern beach resort that's somewhat along the lines of the New Jersey shore in the United States, and a

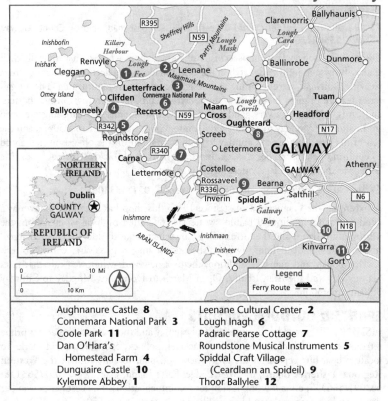

Aughnanure Castle **8**
Connemara National Park **3**
Coole Park **11**
Dan O'Hara's
    Homestead Farm **4**
Dunguaire Castle **10**
Kylemore Abbey **1**

Leenane Cultural Center **2**
Lough Inagh **6**
Padraic Pearse Cottage **7**
Roundstone Musical Instruments **5**
Spiddal Craft Village
    (Ceardlann an Spideil) **9**
Thoor Ballylee **12**

summer mecca for Irish families. It has a boardwalk and a fine beach, plus lots of bars, fast food, amusement rides, and game arcades. You will likely prefer to continue on this scenic road to the little towns like **Barna** and **Spiddal,** both of which are considered Irish-language towns. Spiddal, 12 miles (19km) west of Galway City, is also an ideal spot to shop for locally made Aran knit sweaters and other handcrafts produced by the people in the surrounding cottages.

The road continues as far as **Inverin,** then turns northward, with signposts for **Rossaveal.** From Rossaveal, you can make the shortest sea crossing from the Galway mainland to the Aran Islands (see "Side Trips from Galway City," in chapter 11). You might want to combine this coastal drive with a trip to the islands.

If you continue on R336, you'll leave the Galway Bay coast and travel past the rocky and remote scenery approaching the center of Connemara. **Casla (Costelloe)** is the home of Raidio na Gaeltachta, the Irish-language radio station, and **Rosmuc** is the site of the **Padraic Pearse Cottage.** The simple thatched-roof structure served as a retreat for Dublin-based Pearse (1879–1916), who was one of the leaders of Ireland's 1916 Rising. He used his time here to improve his knowledge of the Irish language. Now a national monument, the cottage contains documents, photographs, and other memorabilia. Admission is £1 ($1.40) for adults, 70p (98¢) for seniors, 40p (56¢) for students and children, £3 ($4.20) for families. It's open from mid-June to mid-September, daily 9:30am to 6:30pm (last admission 45 min. before closing).

At this point you can continue north into the heartland of Connemara or retrace your route back to Galway, setting out afresh the next day for Connemara.

SHOPPING

⊙ **Ceardlann an Spideil/Spiddal Craft Village.** Coast road, Spiddal, County Galway. ☎ **091/553041.**

Overlooking Galway Bay, this is a cluster of cottage shops where craftspeople ply their trades. Browse around and watch crafts being made. The selection includes pottery, weaving, knitwear, screenprinting and design, jewelry, and woodturning. The art galleries feature original hand-carved stone crafts, sculpture, paintings, prints, posters, and cards, and there's a very good coffee shop on the premises. Most shops are open in the summer Monday to Saturday 9:30am to 6:30pm, Sunday 2 to 5:30pm, and the rest of the year Monday to Saturday 9:30am to 5:30pm. In the off-season, call ahead to confirm open hours. For a snack, lunch, or light meal, **Jackie's Bistro,** in a rustic cottage at the Craft Village, offers highly recommended fare.

⊙ **Standun.** Coast road, Spiddal, County Galway. ☎ **091/553108.**

A fixture on the Connemara coast since 1946, this shop has long been known as a good source for traditional bainin sweaters, handcrafted by local women from the nearby Aran Islands and the surrounding Connemara countryside. Recently enlarged, it also offers colorful knits, tweeds, sheepskins, linens, glassware, china, pottery, jewelry, books, and maps. In addition, there's a new wide-windowed cafe that faces Galway Bay and the Aran Islands. Open March to December, Monday to Saturday 9:30am to 6:30pm.

SPORTS & OUTDOOR PURSUITS

FISHING   Rimmed by the waters of Galway Bay and the Atlantic, this area is prime territory for sea fishing, especially for mackerel, pollock, cod, turbot, and shark. To locate a boat-hire service in the area where you plan to stay, contact the **Western Regional Fisheries Board,** the Weir Lodge, Earl's Island, Galway (☎ **091/563118;** fax 091/566335; e-mail: wrfb@iol.ie), for recommendations. The cost per person per day, including rods, reels, and bait, is likely to average £40 to £50 ($56 to $70).

For those who prefer trout fishing, there's **Crumlin Fisheries,** Inverin, County Galway (☎ **091/593105**). This fishery has a lake stocked with sea-reared rainbow trout and allows two fish per person to be taken per day. Prices range from £10 ($14) for fishing from the bank to £25 ($35) for fishing with a boat; *ghillies* (guides) are available for £25 ($35) extra. Fishing starts at 9am daily; reservations must be made at least a day in advance.

SWIMMING   The Silver Strand at Barna and the beach at Spiddal are clean, sandy, and ideal for swimming.

ACCOMMODATIONS
EXPENSIVE

⊙ **Connemara Coast Hotel.** Coast road, Furbo, County Galway. ☎ **091/592108.** Fax 091/592065. E-mail: sinnott@iol.ie. 112 units. TV TEL. £118–£170 ($165.20–$238) double. Executive suites available. No service charge. Rates include full breakfast. AE, DC, MC, V. Free parking.

If you want to see the sun go down on Galway Bay, this is the place to stay. Six miles (9.7km) west of Galway City, it's along the shores of the famous bay, with unobstructed views of the coast and the Aran Islands. Recently refurbished and expanded, the guest rooms are decorated in colorful tweedy or floral style, and each has a picture-window view of the water. Beds are firm, and nonsmoking rooms are available. Some units have turf-burning fireplaces and private verandas.

Dining/Diversions: The bilevel Gallery restaurant has views of the bay. The pub and bar ("Sin Sceal Eile," or "That's Another Story")—named the 1998 Irish hotel bar of the year—offers traditional entertainment nightly in summer and on weekends the rest of the year.

Amenities: Award-winning leisure center, with indoor heated swimming pool, Jacuzzi, steam bath, gym, and two all-weather tennis courts.

INEXPENSIVE

Cloch na Scíth, Kellough Thatched Cottage. 9 miles (15km) from Galway center, just east of Spiddal, Coast road, Kellough, Spiddal, County Galway. ☎ **091/553364.** 3 units. £40 ($56) double. Rates include full breakfast. No credit cards. Free private parking.

If you want more than a touch of charm and authenticity on the shores of Galway Bay, look no further. The three guest rooms in Nancy Hopkins Naughton's centuries-old thatched farmhouse are bright, warm, and welcoming, with antique pine furniture, polished wood floors, and patterned quilts. All rooms are nonsmoking. The whole house is open to guests and is full of antiques and keepsakes from many generations of Naughtons. Tomas Naughton, Nancy's husband, is both a talented painter and an all-Ireland *sean-nos* singer; guests are often treated to traditional Irish sessions around the fire in the evening. As an afternoon snack, Nancy bakes a fresh corn cake in the open hearth each day and leaves it out for her guests, which have included an appreciative Julie Christie. A small sandy beach is minutes away by foot.

In addition, there is an inviting **self-catering thatched stone cottage,** built by Tomas's great-grandfather. It rents for £150 to £325 ($210 to $455) per week, depending on the season. It has two bedrooms, a kitchen-dining-living room with a wood stove, a spacious sunroom, and 1½ bathrooms.

DINING

♻ **Boluisce.** Coast road, Spiddal, County Galway. ☎ **091/553286.** Reservations recommended for dinner. Dinner main courses £6.50–£20 ($9.10–$28). AE, CB, DC, DISC, MC, V. Daily 12:30–10pm. SEAFOOD.

The name of this restaurant comes from an old Irish phrase meaning "patch of grazing by the water." If you're fond of seafood, this is one patch where you'll want to graze—on scallops, prawns, lobster, smoked salmon, or crab plate. The West Coast platter includes prawns, crab, lobster, mussels, and salmon. The house chowder is a meal in itself, brimming with salmon, prawns, monkfish, mussels, and more. Home-baked brown bread, made with whole meal, bran, and buttermilk, accompanies every meal; it's rich and nutty, and genial proprietor John Glanville will gladly share the recipe with you.

Twelve Pins. Coast road, Barna, County Galway. ☎ **091/592368.** Reservations recommended for dinner. Dinner main courses £6–£13.95 ($8.40–$19.55). AE, MC, V. Daily 12:30–3pm and 6:30–10pm. IRISH.

Named for the famous mountains of Connemara, this old-world roadside inn is a good place to come for fresh oysters or a seafood platter (oysters, mussels, smoked salmon, and prawns). Other creatively prepared seafood choices include scallops en croûte and trout *Oisin* (stuffed with almonds and seafood). For non-fish-eaters, the menu offers a traditional roast of the day, plus steaks, rack of lamb, duckling, vegetarian stir-fry, and lasagna.

2 Connemara

If you look at an average map or road sign, you won't usually see a marking or directional for Connemara. That's because it's not a city or town or county, but an area or region, like the Burren in County Clare. In general, Connemara constitutes the section west of Galway City, starting at Oughterard and continuing toward the Atlantic. It is an area of astounding barrenness and beauty.

CONNEMARA AREA ESSENTIALS
GETTING THERE & GETTING AROUND   From Galway City, **Bus Eireann** (☎ 091/562000) provides daily service to Clifden and other small towns en route. The best way to get around Connemara is to drive, following N59 from Moycullen and Oughterard. Or you can take a guided tour (see "Sightseeing Tours," below). Clifden is 40 miles (65km) west of Galway City.

VISITOR INFORMATION   Contact or visit the **Ireland West Tourist Office,** Aras Fáilte, Victoria Place, Galway, County Galway (☎ 091/563081; e-mail: info@western-tourism.ie). Open May, June, and September daily 9am to 5:45pm; July and August daily 9am to 7:45pm; October to April Monday to Friday 9am to 5:45pm, Saturday 9am to 12:45pm. The **Oughterard Tourist Office,** Main Street, Oughterard (☎ 091/552808), is open Monday to Friday 9am to 5:30pm, with extended hours in the summer. A **seasonal office,** open from May to September, is maintained at Clifden (☎ 095/21163).

EXPLORING THE AREA
The "capital," or largest town in Connemara, is **Clifden**—if you follow the signs for Clifden, you can't go wrong. The road marked N59 takes you around the heart of Connemara and then to County Mayo. You can also follow many of the smaller roads and wander around Connemara for days. Many people stay in this region for a week or so, usually basing themselves in one or more of the fine resorts and inns that dot the countryside, especially in places like **Cashel, Ballynahinch, Renvyle,** and Clifden.

In recent years, Clifden has exploded into a major tourist center, and it shows. B&Bs, pubs, and shops arm wrestle for space in the town center, which for the first time in its history experiences gridlock. Even so, it remains an attractive town, whose past and present can be seen on the two sides of its buildings—their backs gray and worn, their fronts bright and alluring.

Better yet, for a slower, more intact taste of Connemara town life, give the small, active fishing port of **Roundstone** a try. Roundstone is definitely on the move, and already has all of the essentials—glorious, pristine beaches, comfortable guesthouses, good restaurants, quality galleries and shops, and more than its share of natural charm. It's not exactly a secret, but for the time being it is blessedly just off the well-beaten track.

Another untrammeled Connemara treasure lies 7 miles (11km) offshore. A day spent on the island of **Inishbofin**—provided the weather is on your side—is one you'll not soon forget. (See "An Excursion to Inishbofin," later in this section.)

Little bays and inlets, small harbors, and beaches dot the coastline. At almost every turn are lakes, waterfalls, rivers, and creeks, while a dozen glorious mountains, known as the ✪ **Twelve Bens,** rise at the center. All of this is interspersed with rock-strewn

Impressions

Constantly the heart releases
Wild geese to the past
Look, how they circle poignant places.
—Thomas Kinsella (b. 1928): "A Lady of Quality"

land and flat fields of open bog, rimmed with gorse and heather, rhododendrons, and wildflowers. The tableau presents a dramatic panorama of sea and sky, land and bog.

Connemara's **boglands** began forming 2,500 years ago. During the Iron Age, the Celts preserved their butter in the bog. Today, with one-third of Connemara classified as bog, the turf (or peat) that's cut from the bog remains an important source of fuel. Cutting and drying turf is an integral part of the rhythm of the seasons in Connemara. Cutting requires a special tool, a spade called a *slane,* which slices the turf into bricks about 18 inches long. They are spread out to dry and stiffen so that they can be stacked in pyramids to permit air circulation for further drying. Finally they're piled up along the roadside for transport. You can always tell when a family is burning turf in a fireplace—the smoke coming out of the chimney is blue and sweet-scented.

As you drive around Connemara, you're sure to notice the absence of trees, felled and dragged off long ago for building English ships, houses, and furniture. (More of Cromwell's handiwork.) In recent years, however, the Irish government has undertaken an aggressive reforestation program, and vast areas of land have been set aside for planting trees, mostly pines, as a crop.

A trademark of this region is the **donkey,** still a worker on the farms. In some places you'll see a sturdy little horse known as the **Connemara pony,** the only horse breed native to Ireland (although it's had an infusion of Spanish blood over the centuries). Often raised in tiny fields with limestone pastures, these animals have great stamina and are invaluable for farming and pulling equipment. The Connemara pony is also noted for its gentle temperament, which makes it ideal for children's riding.

A major part of Connemara is designated as a **Gaeltacht,** or Irish-speaking area, so you may hear many of the people conversing in their native tongue. Traditional music thrives in this part of the countryside, as do handcrafts and cottage industries.

The much-imitated **Aran knit sweaters** are synonymous with this region. Made of oatmeal-colored wool from the native sheep, these semiwaterproof sweaters were first knit by the women of the nearby Aran Islands for their fishermen husbands and sons, and each family had a different stitch or pattern. Years ago, the patterns were not only a matter of aesthetics; they served as the chief way to identify men who had drowned in the treacherous waters off the coast. Today these sweaters are knit in the homes of Connemara and the nearby Aran Islands, then sold in the many craft shops throughout the region.

THE TOP ATTRACTIONS

Aughnanure Castle. 20 miles (32km) west of Galway City, signposted off N59, Clifden Rd., Oughterard, County Galway. ☎ **091/552214.** Admission £2 ($2.80) adults, £1.50 ($2.10) seniors, £1 ($1.40) students and children, £5 ($7) family. Mid-June to mid-Sept daily 9:30am–6:30pm.

Standing on a rocky island close to the shores of Lough Corrib, this castle is a well-preserved example of a six-story Irish tower house, with an unusual double bawn (a fortified enclosure) and a watchtower. It was built around A.D. 1500 as a stronghold of the O'Flaherty clan.

⭕ **Connemara National Park.** Clifden-Westport road (N59), Letterfrack, County Galway. ☎ **095/41054.** Admission £2 ($2.80) adults, £1.50 ($2.10) groups and seniors, £1 ($1.40) children and students, £5 ($7) family. Park year-round. Visitor center daily Apr–May and Sept to mid-Oct 10am–5:30pm; June 10am–6:30pm; July–Aug 9:30am–6:30pm. Visitor center closed late Oct–Mar.

This stunning national park incorporates 3,800 acres of Connemara's mountains, bogs, heaths, and grasslands. The grounds are home to herds of Connemara ponies and Irish red deer, as well as a variety of birds and smaller mammals. To orient and acquaint visitors with all the aspects of the park, the handsome exhibition center offers a series of displays and an informative 20-minute audiovisual presentation. Tea, coffee, soup, sandwiches, and freshly baked goods are on hand in the tearoom. If you're up to it, test your willpower against the cheesecake. During July and August, Tuesday and Thursday are "nature days" for children; on Monday, Wednesday, and Friday there are guided walks for the whole family. Call the center for information on these and other special programs.

Dan O'Hara's Homestead Farm. About 4 miles (6.5km) east of Clifden off the main N59 road, Lettershea, Clifden, County Galway. ☎ **095/21246.** Admission £3.50 ($4.90) adults, £3 ($4.20) seniors and students, £1.75 ($2.45) children, £10 ($14) family. Daily 10am–6pm. Closed Nov–Mar.

If you're wondering how Connemara farmers find soil to till on this rocky land, head to this small farm. It was once owned by Dan O'Hara, but the harsh conditions and high taxes of the time forced him to emigrate to the United States. Today, the newly expanded center incorporates an 8-acre prefamine farm and reflects daily life in the 1840s, with local people using traditional tilling and farming methods. The land also contains a reconstructed *crannóg* (fortified lake dwelling), an authentic megalithic tomb, and a dolmen. Attached to the farm and heritage center, farmhouse accommodations and some self-catering cottages are available.

Kylemore Abbey. Kylemore, County Galway. ☎ **095/41146.** Admission to Abbey Gate £3.30 ($4.60) adults, £2.30 ($3.20) seniors and students, £7 ($9.80) family; Garden Gate £3.30 ($4.60) adults, £2.30 ($3.20) seniors and students, £7 ($9.80) family; Abbey year-round daily 9am–5:30pm. Garden Easter–Sept daily 10:30am–4:30pm.

Originally a private residence (ca. 1868), this castellated house overlooking Kylemore Lake is a splendid example of neo-Gothic architecture. In 1920 it was turned over to the Benedictine nuns, who have since opened the grounds and part of the house to the public. The highlight is the recently restored gothic chapel, considered a miniature cathedral. The complex also includes a cafe, serving produce grown on the nuns' farm; a shop with a working pottery studio; and a visitor center where a video presentation gives you an overview of life at Kylemore, both past and present. The abbey is most atmospheric when the bells are rung for midday office or for vespers at 6pm. Admission to the Abbey is through two gates, each providing access to different attractions and facilities, and each requiring a separate fee! (It might help to think of it as a double collection.) The Abbey Gate offers access to the Abbey receptions rooms, the exhibition, the church, the lake walk, and the video; the Garden Gate opens to the walled garden, the exhibition, the tea house, the shop, and the wilderness walk. This was once a lovely site, but it has been increasingly commercialized in recent years and is on the brink of becoming a tourist trap.

Leenane Cultural Center. Clifden–Westport Rd. (N59), Leenane, County Galway. ☎ **095/42323.** Admission £2 ($2.80) adults; £1 ($1.40) seniors, students, and children over age 8; free for children under 8. Apr–Nov daily 9am–6pm.

An Excursion to Inishbofin

It has been said that Ireland's last unspoiled frontiers are its islands, and Inishbofin on its own makes a strong contribution to that claim. This small emerald-green gem lies 7 miles (11km) off the northwest coast of Connemara, and offers not only seclusion but spectacular beauty, provided the skies are clear enough to deliver the not-to-be-believed views of and from its shores. Once the domain of monks, then the lair of pirate queen Grace O'Malley, later Cromwell's infamous priest-prison, and currently home to a mere 180 year-round residents, Inishbofin is both steeped in history and oozing charm. It's well worth a day's expedition or a 1- or 2-day stay.

Numerous ferries to the island leave from and return to the sleepy port of Cleggan (8 miles/13km northwest of Clifden off N59) daily April through October. **Inishbofin Island Tours,** Kings of Cleggan, Cleggan, County Galway (☎ 095/44642), operates the largest, newest, and fastest boat, the *Island Discovery.* Tickets (£12/$16.80 per adult and £6/$8.40 per child, round-trip) are available at the offices in Clifden and Cleggan. *Note:* It's important, even necessary, to book in advance. The other option, which we prefer, is to ride with **Paddy O'Halloran** (☎ 095/45806) on the *Dun Aengus,* the island's worn and worthy mail boat. The *Dun Aengus* remains the vessel of choice for most locals. It has both more charm and more roll than its new rival, and skipper O'Halloran, after a half century at the wheel, definitely knows the way. Tickets (£10/$14 per person, round-trip) for *the Dun Aengus* are available at the **Spar Foodstore** in Cleggan (☎ 095/44750).

Overlooking Killary Harbour, this center focuses on the history of wool and the 20-some breeds of sheep in Ireland, and is well worth the price of admission. The sheep are on display in a field adjacent to the center, and inside you can peruse exhibits on the local wool industry. There are demonstrations of carding, spinning, and weaving, and visitors are invited to try their hand at it. A 13-minute audiovisual presentation provides background on local history and places of interest in the area. Demonstrations of sheep herding are given on request by a bored sheepdog who lives on the premises—ask for a demonstration and the dog will be eternally grateful. There's also an unexceptional gift shop and a cafe.

SIGHTSEEING TOURS

Several companies offer sightseeing tours of Connemara from Galway or Clifden.

Bus Eireann. Ceannt Station, Galway, County Galway. ☎ **091/562000.** Tour £12 ($16.80) adults, £10 ($14) seniors and students, £8 ($11.20) children, £35 ($49) family, with up to 3 children. Sun–Fri 10am.

Departing from the bus station in Galway, this 8-hour tour of Connemara takes in Maam Cross, Recess, Roundstone, and Clifden, as well as Kylemore Abbey, Leenane, and Oughterard.

Connemara Walking Centre. The Island House, Market St., Clifden, County Galway. ☎ **095/21379.** www.walkingireland.com. Tours £15 ($21). Mar–Oct; call for times and a detailed price list.

This company's expert local guides lead walking tours of Connemara, with an emphasis on history and archaeology as well as scenery. The walks cover different sections—from the Renvyle Peninsula and Roundstone Bog to the Kylemore Valley, Maumturk Mountains, and Sky Road. The tour to Inishbofin Island includes a 45-minute boat trip. Weeklong walking trips are based at Dun Gibbons, a new center dedicated to exploring Connemara's countryside. All walks assemble at Island House in Clifden and include bus transportation to the walking site. Advance reservations are required.

Corrib Cruises. Oughterard, County Galway. ☎ **092/46029** or 091/552808. www. corribcruises.com. 90-min. round-trip cruise to island £8 ($11.20) adults, £4 ($5.60) children, £20 ($28) family; Cong-Oughterard round-trip day cruise £12 ($16.80) adults, £4 ($5.60) children, £25 ($35) family. May–Sept daily. Be sure to book ahead and to confirm times.

Departing from the pier at Oughterard, this company's sightseeing boat cruises across Lough Corrib, Ireland's largest lake, measuring 68 square miles with 365 islands. The cruise stops at Inchagoill Island, home of a 12th-century monastery that was inhabited until the 1940s. One trip visits the island only, and the other goes to the island and to Cong in County Mayo, site of Ashford Castle and the area where the movie *The Quiet Man* was filmed. The Cong-Oughterard round-trip cruise can start at either place. In fact, there are currently four different day cruises on offer, as well as an evening Irish Hour (happy-hour) cruise.

SHOPPING

Avoca Handweavers. Clifden–Leenane Rd. (N59), Dooneen Haven, Letterfrack, County Galway. ☎ **095/41058.**

Six miles (9.7km) north of Clifden on an inlet of the bay, surrounded by colorful flower gardens, this shop has one of the loveliest and most photographed locations in Ireland. It features colorful tweeds, as well as all sorts of Connemara-made marble souvenirs, candles, jewelry, books, music, wood carvings, pottery, and knits. A snack shop is on the premises. Open April to October daily 9:30am to 6pm or later.

Celtic Shop. Main St., Clifden, County Galway. ☎ **095/21064.**

This shop offers a wide array of arts and crafts, including gold and silver Celtic jewelry, hand-woven Irish rugs, knitwear, hats, ceramics, and crystal. You'll also find a good selection of Irish and Celtic books. Open daily 9am to 9pm in July and August, 9am to 6pm September to June.

Connemara Marble Visitor Centre. Galway–Clifden Rd. (N59), Moycullen, County Galway. ☎ **091/555102.**

Connemara's unique green marble—diverse in color, marking, and veining—is quarried, cut, shaped, and polished here. Estimated by geologists to be about 500 million years old, the marble shows twists and interlocking bands of serpentine in various shades, ranging from light lime green to dark emerald. On weekdays, you'll see craftspeople at work hand-fashioning marble jewelry, paperweights, ashtrays, Celtic crosses, and other giftware. The shop and showroom, 8 miles (13km) west of Galway City on the main road (N59), are open daily 9am to 5:30pm.

✪ **Fuchsia Craft.** The Square, Oughterard, County Galway. ☎ **091/552644.**

Wedged in the center of Oughterard's main thoroughfare, this small shop is a treasure trove of unusual, hard-to-find crafts, produced by more than 100 craftspeople throughout Ireland. The items include handmade fishing flies, products made from pressed Irish peat, bronze sculptures, recycled art cards of Connemara scenes, decorative metal figurines fashioned from nails, and lithographs of early Ireland—as well as pottery, crystal, jewelry, knitwear, and much more. Open June to September daily 9am to 10pm; April, May, and October daily 9am to 7pm; November to March Monday to Saturday 9am to 6pm.

✪ **Millars Connemara Tweed Ltd.** Main St., Clifden, County Galway. ☎ **095/21038.**

This is the home of the colorful Connemara tweeds, an industry started in 1900 by Robert Millar as a small mill to process wool from local mountain sheep. Although most people travel to Clifden just to buy Millar's skeins of wool or hand-woven materials—plus ready-made ties, hats, caps, scarves, blankets, and bedspreads—today's shop is more than just an outlet for wool. You'll also find Irish patchwork, rush baskets, Aran crios belts, embroidery work, handmade miniature currachs, tin whistles, and blackthorn pipes, plus an art gallery of regional paintings. Open Monday to Saturday 9am to 6pm, with extended summer hours.

✪ **Roundstone Musical Instruments.** The Monastery, Michael Killeen Park, Roundstone, County Galway. ☎ 095/35875. www.bodhran.com.

Many of Ireland's most renowned musicians, including those who created the sounds of the immensely popular Riverdance show, play Malachy Kearns's instruments. A master craftsman, Malachy is one of the only full-time *bodhrán* makers in the world, and one of Ireland's most beloved celebrities. His contributions to Irish music recently earned him a place on the 32p stamp! The bodhran is an ancient one-sided frame drum; for the most resonant results, it is vital to have one of the quality goatskins Malachy seeks out from his many far-flung suppliers. While you wait, his artist wife, Anne, can decorate the skin with Celtic designs, initials, family crests, or any design you request in old Gaelic script. Malachy's workshop also makes wooden flutes (ebony), tin whistles, and Irish harps, and he has an excellent mail-order service. The newly expanded workshop-craftshop-cafe and Folk Instrument Museum, where you surely will want to linger, are open 9am to 6pm daily May to October, and 9:30am to 6pm Monday to Saturday November to April.

Sheepchandler Gallery. Roundstone Harbor, County Galway. ☎ 095/35040.

Recently ensconced in this attractive new location in the center of Roundstone, Katherine Parisot's fine gallery is a true delight. Her thoughtful selection of works by many of the finest contemporary artists in Ireland provides a focused glimpse into the country's art scene, as well as many temptations to bring home more than a sweater or a cap.

Síla Mag Aoide Designs (Shelagh Magee). The Monastery, Michael Killeen Park, Roundstone, County Galway. ☎ 095/35912.

Shelagh Magee is one of Ireland's most noteworthy artisans. Although inspired by ancient Celtic images and designs, her work is original and contemporary. In addition to a wide selection of her handmade silver jewelry, the shop offers a range of works, including watercolor prints and art cards of Connemara scenes, baskets, handmade wooden pencils, and miniature frames. It's open daily 9am to 9pm May to September, with shorter hours in the off-season.

SPORTS & OUTDOOR PURSUITS

For location, facilities, and quality of instruction, ✪ **Delphi Adventure Center,** Leenane, County Galway (☎ 095/42307), is one of the best of the many adventure centers in Ireland. Courses are available in a wide range of water sports, as well as in mountaineering, pony trekking, tennis, and archery. Accommodation is in bright, simply furnished single or dorm-style rooms. The food in the dining room is good and plentiful, and vegetarian meals can be arranged. Residential adventure holidays for children are offered. Weekend prices for room, full board, and activities begin at £125 ($175) for an adult. The nonresidential activities fee for 1 full day is £24 ($33.60). Waterskiing and horseback riding are available at additional cost. This place caters primarily to people in their 20s and 30s.

BICYCLING   Bicycles can be hired year-round from **John Mannion & Son,** Bridge Street, Clifden, County Galway (☎ 095/21160). The rate for a regular touring bike in high season is £6 ($8.40) per day. Mountain bikes can be hired from May through

Malachy Kearns, the Bodhrán Maker

I remember the first time I saw a bodhrán. I remember the first time I heard one. I was about 8 years old. I can remember the hair standing up on the back of my neck!

My father brought me to a family funeral in Donegal. It was away up in the north of Donegal somewhere near Crolly, and this would have been in the late Fifties.

We buried the man. I remember it was a cold afternoon too and afterwards the men adjourned to a pub in the village and, like a million boys of my age before and since, I was stuffed to the tonsils with orange squash and lemonade while the grown-ups drank fiery glasses of whiskey and big black pints of porter. There was a fireplace with an open fire and I remember sitting beside it, late in the evening, bored and stupefied with fizzy drinks and adult talking.

Then there was a bit of excitement at the door of the bar and who came in but the legendary fiddle player called Johnny Doherty, a man whose name is still spoken with near reverence by Irish musicians everywhere. He was thin and hardy and he had his fiddle, I think, in a green velvet sack instead of a timber case. He had small quick hands and a very quiet way about him. There was another man with him and he had a sack with him, too, a jute one this time, and when he left it down on the floor beside me, carefully, I heard it make a boomy kind of noise.

Johnny Doherty, still regarded as the prince of Donegal fiddlers, was a master musician who was also a semi-traveller. He moved all around Donegal at different times of the year staying and playing in selected houses for weeks and months at a time. It was a great honour to have him stay in your house and make his music under your roof. People came from everywhere just to hear him play.

Even as a child I knew there was something special about him when he began to play in that pub. He was sitting in the chair opposite me, swaying a bit in the gale of his own jigs and reels, his eyes empty and full in his face at the same time, as if they were seeing the music, in some strange way, and nothing else. The men that were standing listening, and sitting listening, were silent, except to say, "Good man, Johnny" now and again, and they even forgot that they had drinks in their hands. It was beautiful stuff.

But after a while it was even better because the other man that was with Johnny Doherty . . . and somebody told me he was a real traveller . . . he eventually took the first bodhrán I ever saw out of the jute bag. He warmed it to the fire, rubbing it now and again so that it muttered and grumbled almost, and then, without any beater, just like I am now this minute, he began to play.

And it was absolutely mighty.

I'm telling ye that the hair stood up on the back of my neck. I was mesmerised. That was certainly the occasion that determined, later in life, that I would become a bodhrán maker.

—From *Wallup!* by Malachy Kearns.
Printed with permission of the author. Available at bookstores and from Roundstone Musical Instruments (www.bodhran.com).

October at the **Little Killary Adventure Company,** Leenane, County Galway (☎ **095/43411**). They go for £15 ($21) per day, and road bikes for £10 ($14) per day.

DIVING   You can rent equipment and receive instruction at **Scubadive West,** Renvyle, County Galway (☎ 095/43922).

FISHING   Lough Corrib is renowned for brown-trout and salmon fishing. Brown-trout fishing is usually good from the middle of February, and salmon best from the end of May. The mayfly fishing commences around the middle of May and continues for up to 3 weeks.

Angling on Lough Corrib is free, but a state license is required for salmon. For expert advice and rental equipment, contact the **Cloonnabinnia Angling Centre,** Moycullen, County Galway (☎ 091/555555).

For salmon and sea trout, the **Ballynahinch Castle Fishery** at Ballynahinch, Recess (☎ 095/31006), is an angler's paradise. State fishing licenses, tackle hire and sales, maps, and great advice are available at the hotel.

At **Portarra Lodge,** Tullykyne, Moycullen, County Galway (☎ 091/555051; fax 091/555052), packages are available, including B&B accommodation in a modern guesthouse on the shores of Lough Corrib, dinners, and boats and tackle. Michael Canney is an avid angler and a great guide to this part of Galway. A double room with full breakfast is £45 to £50 ($63 to $70) per night. Weekly packages that include half-board, boat, and *ghillie* (guide) are also available.

GOLF   Visitors are welcome at the 18-hole, par-72 championship seaside course of the **Connemara Golf Club,** Ballyconneely, Clifden (☎ 095/23502), nestled in the heart of Connemara and overlooking the Atlantic. Greens fees from May to September are £35 ($49); October to April, £22 ($30.80).

The **Oughterard Golf Club,** Oughterard, County Galway (☎ 091/552131), is an 18-hole, par-70 inland course. The greens fees are £20 ($28).

HORSEBACK RIDING   Explore the stunningly beautiful Connemara Coast from May to September with **Connemara and Coast Trails,** Loughrea, County Galway (☎ 091/841216; e-mail: tct@eircom.net). For experienced and beginning riders alike. **Glen Valley Stables,** Glencroff, Leenane, County Galway (☎ 095/42269), has one of the best equestrian programs in Connemara. Treks of 1 to 3 hours take you into the hills surrounding beautiful Glen Valley, or along the shores of Killary Harbour. The program is run by Niall O'Neill, whose mother, Josephine O'Neill, has offered B&B accommodations at Glen Valley House and Stables for over a decade (see "Accommodations," below). Riding is £15 ($21) per person, per hour.

WALKING   Killary Harbour, a fjordlike inlet rimmed by mountains on both sides, is remote and wild at its western, seaward end. The green road, now a sheep track for much of its length, was once the primary route from the Rinvyle Peninsula to Leenane. The famine devastated this area; you'll pass an abandoned prefamine village on the far side of the harbor, the fields rising at a devilishly steep slope from the ruined cottages, clustered at the water's edge. This is a walk into Ireland's recent past, when many lived by subsistence farming and fishing, always perilously close to disaster.

The walk begins at the Killary Harbour Youth Hostel (where the German philosopher Ludwig Wittgenstein once stayed for a time, before it was a hostel). Heading away from the hostel on the local access road, take a left on a grassy path just before the first house on the left. This path continues all the way to Leenane, a distance of about 8 miles (13km), but the most beautiful part is the first 2 miles (3.2km) from the youth hostel. If you prefer not to return the way you came, look for the second of two roofed but abandoned houses on the right; it's right next to the trail, and partially obscured by rhododendrons. Just past this house is a path, scarcely discernible, that heads up the slope, veering back the way you came. If you can find this track, it's easy to follow as it climbs gradually to the ridge top, which it meets at a curious notch cut

Lough Inagh and the Walk to Maum Ean Oratory

Lough Inagh, nestled between the Maumturk and Twelve Pin Mountains in the heart of Connemara, is situated in one of the most spectacularly beautiful valleys in Ireland. The mountain slopes rise precipitously from the valley floor, and many small streams cascade into the lake in a series of sparkling waterfalls. The R344 cuts through the valley, linking Recess to the south and Kylemore Lake to the north.

The **Western Way,** a walking route that traverses the high country of Galway and Mayo, follows a quiet country road above the R344 through the Lough Inagh Valley. This short (2.5 miles/4km) walk follows the Western Way to the top of a mountain pass which has long been associated with St. Patrick, and which is now the site of a small oratory, a hollow in the rock known as **Patrick's Bed,** a life-size statue of the saint, and a series of cairns marking the Stations of the Cross. Together, these monuments make a striking ensemble, strangely eerie when the mists descend and conceal the far slopes in their shifting haze. On a clear day there are great views from here, with the Atlantic Ocean and Bertraghboy Bay to the southwest and another range of mountains to the northeast.

To reach the beginning of the walk, drive north on the R344, turning right on a side road—sign for Maum Ean—about 200m before the Lough Inagh Lodge Hotel. Continue on this side road for 4 miles (6.5km) to a large gravel parking lot on the left. Park here, and follow the well-worn trail 1¼ miles (2km) to the top of the pass, through glorious mountain scenery. The round-trip walking time is about 1 hour.

---

in the hillside—a local legend attributes this feature to the groove carved in the rock when the devil tried to pull a local saint into hell, using a long iron chain. Descending on the other side of the notch, make your way down to the hostel access road, which takes you back to the starting point. Total distance for the loop is about 5 miles (8km).

WATER SPORTS   Hobie Cat sailing and sail-boarding can be arranged at the **Little Killary Adventure Company,** Leenane, County Galway (☎ **095/43411**). Daily rates are £38 ($53.20) per day (two sessions), which entitles you to use the water-sports equipment and participate in all the center's supervised sporting activities, including kayaking, waterskiing, hill and coastal walking, rock climbing, archery, and more.

ACCOMMODATIONS
EXPENSIVE

Ballynahinch Castle. Ballynahinch, Recess, County Galway.   ☎ **095/31006.** Fax 095/31085. www.commerce.ie/ballynahinch. 40 units. £108–£134 ($151.20–$187.60) double. Rates include full breakfast. AE, DC, MC, V. Closed first 3 weeks in Feb. Free parking.

Set on a 350-acre estate at the base of Ben Lettery, one of the Twelve Bens mountains, this turreted, gabled manor house overlooks the Owenmore River. Dating to the 16th century, it has served over the years as a base for such diverse owners as the O'Flaherty chieftains and the sea pirate Grace O'Malley. It was also the sporting residence of the Maharajah Jans Sahib Newanagar, better known as Ranjitsinhgi, the famous cricketer. The guest rooms are individually named and decorated, and many have fireplaces and four-poster or canopy beds (all are orthopedic). A new wing of luxury rooms was added in the past 2 years. The restaurant, with its impressive Connemara marble fireplace, offers sweeping views of the countryside and the river. Most of all, this is a place for top-notch sea trout and salmon fishing. Each evening, the day's catch is weighed in and recorded at the Fishermen's Bar, usually making a cause for celebration. The castle has a tennis court and lovely gardens.

○ **Cashel House.** Cashel Bay, Cashel, County Galway. ☎ **800/323-5463** or 800/735-2478 from the U.S., or 095/31001. Fax 095/31077. www.cashel-house-hotel.com. 32 units. TV TEL. £118–£190 ($165.20–$266) double; £158–£220 ($221.20–$308) garden suite. Service charge 12.5%. Rates include full breakfast. AE, CB, DC, MC, V. Closed Jan 12–Feb 10. Free parking.

Set on 50 acres of exotic gardens and woodlands, this 100-year-old country house is nestled deep in the mountains and lakelands of Connemara. Established as a hotel in 1968 by enthusiastic innkeepers Dermot and Kay McEvilly, it has attracted a range of discerning guests over the years, including President and Madame de Gaulle, who spent 2 weeks here in 1969 and put Cashel House on the map. Among the public rooms are a lounge, a well-stocked library, and a conservatory-style restaurant that has won many awards for innovative cuisine. Rooms, which have wide-windowed views of the bay or the gardens, are decorated with Irish floral fabrics, European antiques, sheepskin rugs, rattan pieces, vintage paintings, and local heirlooms. Beds are firm, and nonsmoking rooms are available. The hotel has a private beach on the bay, a tennis court, fishing, boating, and signposted walking paths. The private stables offer riding lessons, dressage, and mountain trekking.

Renvyle House. Renvyle, County Galway. ☎ **095/43511.** Fax 095/43515. www.renvyle.com. 65 units. TV TEL. £50–£170 ($70–$238) double. Rates include full Irish breakfast and service charge. Packages available. AE, DC, MC, V. Closed Jan–Feb.

Originally the residence of the Blake family, this grand old house sits on a 200-acre estate along the Atlantic shoreline in the wilds of Connemara. It was purchased in 1917 by Oliver St. John Gogarty, a leading Irish poet, wit, surgeon, and politician, who fondly called this secluded seascape and mountain setting "the world's end." That's putting it mildly: It really is off the beaten track, not ideal for a quick overnight but perfect for a stay of a few days or longer. Updated and refurbished in recent years by current owner Hugh Coyle, it retains a turn-of-the-century ambience, particularly in its public areas. Guest rooms vary in size and decor, from rooms with balconies to attic rooms with dormer windows. There are a restaurant, a lounge bar, an outdoor heated swimming pool, horseback-riding stables, a 9-hole golf course, two all-weather tennis courts, fishing, and boating. The hotel also hosts a range of events, such as murder-mystery weekends, fly-fishing clinics, and painting weekends.

○ **Rosleague Manor.** Clifden–Leenane Rd. (N59), Letterfrack, County Galway. ☎ **800/223-6510** from the U.S., or 095/41101. Fax 095/41168. 16 units. TEL. £100–£150 ($140–$210) double. No service charge. Rates include full breakfast. AE, MC, V. Closed Nov–Easter.

Occupying a sheltered spot with views of Ballinakill Harbor and the Twelve Bens mountains, this two-story Regency house is surrounded by 30 acres of lush gardens and well-trimmed lawns. Brother and sister owners Paddy and Anne Foyle have decorated the interior with antiques, polished heirloom silver, Waterford crystal chandeliers, and paintings of local scenes. Many of the comfortably furnished guest rooms enjoy views of the bay. On the premises are a fine restaurant that uses produce from the garden, plus a tennis court and sauna. The manor is 7 miles (11km) north of Clifden, near the entrance to Connemara National Park.

Zetland Country House. Cashel Bay, Cashel, County Galway. ☎ **800/448-8355** from the U.S., or 095/31111. Fax 095/31117. www.connemara.net/zetland/. 19 units. TV TEL. £118–£188 ($165.20–$263.20) double. Rates include full breakfast and service charge. AE, CB, MC, V. Closed Nov–Mar. Free parking.

Built in 1850 as a sporting lodge, this three-story manor house was named for the earl of Zetland, a frequent visitor during the 19th century. Surrounded by lush gardens and ancient trees, Zetland became a hotel in the mid-1980s under its current owner, John Prendergast, a Paris-trained hotelier. The guest rooms, many of which look out onto the bay, have antique or reproduction furnishings. The dining room is known for its local seafood and lamb dishes, and its vegetables and fruit come from the inn's kitchen garden. If you enjoy fishing, note that the Zetland owns the Gowla Fishery, one of the best private sea-trout fisheries in Ireland. (It encompasses 14 lakes and 4 miles/6.5km of river.) The hotel staff is extraordinarily accommodating to anglers. The hotel has a tennis court, croquet, and a billiards room.

MODERATE

Abbeyglen Castle. Sky Rd., Clifden, County Galway. ☎ **800/447-7462** from the U.S., or 095/21201. Fax 095/21797. www.abbeyglen.ie. 29 units. TV TEL. £106–£130 ($148.40–$182) double. No service charge. Rates include full breakfast. AE, DC, MC, V. Closed early Jan–Feb. Free parking.

On a hilltop overlooking Clifden and the bay, this property dates from the 1820s, although it gained its castlelike facade only within the past 20 years. Happily, the turrets and battlements blend in well with the Connemara countryside. The recently refurbished public areas have brass candelabra chandeliers, arched windows, and vintage settees. There's a gothic-themed restaurant, and guest rooms have crown canopies. Twelve acres of gardens and parklands, a heated outdoor swimming pool, a sauna, a solarium, and a hard tennis court add to the enjoyment. Personable proprietor Paul Hughes can arrange fishing trips, packed lunches, and a host of other local activities.

Ardagh Hotel and Restaurant. Ballyconneely Rd., Clifden, County Galway. ☎ **095/21384.** Fax 095/21314. www.commerce.ie/ardaghhotel. 17 units. TV TEL. £95–£110 ($133–$154) double. No service charge. Rates include full breakfast. AE, DC, MC, V. Closed Nov–Mar.

Overlooking Ardbear Bay, about 2 miles (3.2km) south of Clifden, this modern two-story inn has a chalet atmosphere, with expansive windows. The rooms are spacious and individually decorated. Five guest rooms have individual balconies, and many face the sea. The award-winning second-floor restaurant specializes in lobster, salmon, oysters, and Connemara lamb. The hotel also has a solarium and lovely gardens.

✪ **Connemara Gateway.** Galway–Clifden Rd. (N59), Oughterard, County Galway. ☎ **091/552328.** Fax 091/552332. E-mail: sinnott@iol.ie. 62 units. TV TEL. £65–£130 ($91–$182) double. No service charge. Rates include full breakfast. AE, DC, MC, V. Closed Jan.

Less than a mile from the village of Oughterard and 16 miles (26km) west of Galway City, this contemporary two-story inn is well positioned. It sits on its own grounds, near the upper shores of Lough Corrib and across the road from an 18-hole golf course. Although it has a rambling modern exterior, a hearthside ambience permeates the interior, with leafy plants and homey bric-a-brac in the corridors. The rooms are warmly furnished with local tweed fabrics and hangings, oak dressers and headboards, and scenes of Connemara. Beds are firm, and nonsmoking rooms are available. A fine collection of original paintings by landscape artists John MacLeod and Kenneth Webb enhances the restaurant, and the lounge has a village-pub atmosphere. The inn has an indoor heated swimming pool, gym, sauna, sun lounge, tennis court, putting green, croquet lawn, and 10 acres of walking trails.

✪ **Delphi Lodge.** The Delphi Estate and Fishery, Leenane, County Galway. ☎ **095/42222.** Fax 095/42296. www.delphilodge.ie. 12 units, 5 cottages. £80–£120 ($112–$168) standard double; £120–£160 ($112–$224) lakeside double. No service charge. Rates include full Irish breakfast. £25 ($35) fixed-price dinner. 2- and 3-bedroom self-catering cottages £295–£695 ($413–$973) per week. AE, MC, V. Closed Christmas and New Year's holidays. Free parking.

At Delphi Lodge, you'll want to pinch yourself now and then to make sure you're not dreaming. Built in the early 19th century as a sportsman's hideaway for the Marquis of Sligo, it occupies a setting that almost defies description—crystalline lakes and rivers, hardwood forests, unspoiled ocean beaches, and luminous mountain slopes. All that, and salmon and sea trout out the front door, waiting to be caught! The rooms are luxuriously simple and spacious, furnished in antique and contemporary light pine and featuring orthopedic mattresses. Fishing permits and registration are available at the lodge for £80 ($112) in June and July, and equipment rental is £5 ($7). At dinner, the lodge can prepare your own catch of the day, or send it to you at home, smoked, after you return. Special 3-day weekend packages, including courses in fly-tying, watercolors, wine appreciation, and other diversions, are available in the off-season. If you're not going to spend October in Vermont, this is the place to be. All reservations must be made in writing or by fax.

Rock Glen Manor House. Ballyconneely Rd., Clifden, County Galway. ☎ **095/21035.** Fax 095/21737. www.connemara.net/rockglen-hotel. 27 units. TV TEL. £110–£130 ($154–$182) double. Rates include full breakfast and service charge. AE, DC, MC, V. Closed Nov to mid-Mar. Free private parking.

Originally an 18th-century hunting lodge, this rambling country house sits amid lovely gardens about 1½ miles (2.4km) south of Clifden. Expanded over the years and now in the hands of John and Evangeline Roche, Rock Glen is set back from the road, with views of Ardbear Bay and the Atlantic Ocean. It's a restful spot, with tastefully furnished rooms and public areas all refurbished in the last year. Most rooms, including the restaurant, face the sea, and half the guest rooms are on the ground floor. Guests have the use of a tennis court and putting green, and fishing privileges.

✪ **Sweeney's Oughterard House.** Galway–Clifden Rd. (N59), Oughterard, County Galway. ☎ **091/552207.** Fax 091/552161. wws.sweeneys-hotel.com. 20 units. TV TEL. £90–£130 ($126–$182) double. No service charge. Rates include full breakfast. AE, DC, MC, V. Closed late Dec to mid-Jan. Free parking.

A favorite with anglers, this ivy-covered, 200-year-old Georgian house has been run by the Sweeney-Higgins family since 1913. Across the road from the rushing, salmon-filled waters of the Owenriff River, the inn is surrounded by flowering gardens and ancient trees on the quiet western end of the village. The public rooms have an old-world charm, thanks to multipaned bow windows, comfortable original furnishings, and paintings by Irish artists. The guest rooms vary in size and decor, from antique-filled to modern light-wood styles. All include such extras as a hair dryer and tea/coffeemaker; some have four-poster or king-size beds. It's a great spot for fishing, taking long country walks, or catching up on your reading. There's a good dining room (book ahead) with an extensive wine cellar (more than 300 wines).

INEXPENSIVE

Doonmore Hotel. Inishbofin Island, County Galway. ☎ and fax **095/45804.** 25 units, 19 with private bathroom. TV TEL. £50–£58 ($70–$81.20) double with bathroom. Rates include full breakfast. AE, MC, V. Closed Nov–Mar.

This seasoned waterfront hotel enjoys the prime location on the island, with stunning views of the open sea and of nearby Inishshark and High Island. It even has its own seal colony just beyond its front doors. A range of room options is available,

including spacious family units with children's bunk beds. The appealing, unpretentious rooms in the new expansion are clean, full of light, and tastefully furnished with
simple pine furniture. The older rooms in the original hotel building are somewhat
worn but comfortable; some enjoy the hotel's finest sea views. All rooms have firm
beds and tea/coffee-making facilities. The hotel has a full-service dining room (wholly
nonsmoking) and a bar serving lunch and snacks. The hotel offers facilities for sea
angling and scuba diving. The immediate area is well known for both. The Doonmore
is a short walk from the ferry, and provides van service to and from the main harbor
on request.

✪ **Errisbeg Lodge.** Just over 1 mile (1.6km) outside of Roundstone on Clifden Rd., Roundstone, County Galway. ☎ and fax **095/35807.** www.connemara.net/errisbeg-lodge. 5 units.
£44 ($61.60) double. Rates include full breakfast. No credit cards. Free private parking.

Conveniently proximate to Roundstone yet blessedly ensconced between mountainside and sea, Errisbeg Lodge is a place where you may plan to spend a night and wind
up lingering for days. Jackie and Shirley King's family land, reaching high onto the
slopes of Errisbeg Mountain, is a sublime haven for innumerable rare species of wildflowers and birds, and Jackie loves nothing more than sharing these wonders with his
guests. Then there is the sea, spread out before you, with two glorious white-sand
beaches only minutes away on foot. Finally, when you return to your room, you'll find
it serenely spare, sparkling clean, with white textured walls, light pine furniture, and
pastel floral comforters, with either mountain or ocean view. It's all about tranquillity
here, and warm, gracious hospitality.

✪ **Glen Valley House and Stables.** Signposted 3½ miles (5.6km) west of Leenane on the
Clifden road, Glencroff, Leenane, County Galway. ☎ **095/42269.** Fax 095/42365. 4 units,
3 with private bathroom. £40 ($56) double. Closed Dec–Feb.

At the base of a remote glaciated valley, this farmhouse redefines "secluded." The
entrance drive follows the base of the valley for over a mile before you arrive at the
house, which has great views across to the far line of hills. The O'Neills are helpful yet
unobtrusive hosts, and their home attracts people looking for a serene, restful setting.
Don't miss the spectacular section of the Western Way walking trail that passes near
the house and follows the hills rimming Killary Harbour, with unforgettable views of
the harbor mouth—this is a great place to watch the sun set. The equestrian program
here is particularly good (see "Sports & Outdoor Pursuits," above); non-horse-lovers
will be glad to find the stables far enough from the house that the sound and smell of
horses doesn't overwhelm.

DINING
EXPENSIVE

✪ **Drimcong House.** Moycullen, County Galway. ☎ **091/555115.** Reservations required.
Fixed-price dinner £23.50–£29 ($32.90–$40.60); children's menu £11.50 ($16.10). AE, DC,
MC, V. Mon–Sat 7–11pm. Closed Dec 25–Mar. IRISH/INTERNATIONAL.

In a 300-year-old lakeside house on the main Clifden road, just under 10 miles
(16km) west of Galway City, this restaurant is the perfect setting for the quintessential Irish dining experience. As your order is taken, you'll relax in a book-filled drawing room and lounge with an open fireplace. Then you're escorted into one of two
elegant dining rooms (the back room looks out onto the lake; the front windows have
garden views). All the little touches await you at your table—fresh flowers, candlelight,
fine Irish silver and glassware, and hot brown scones. The three- to five-course dinners
live up to the setting. Entrees might include roast local lamb with ratatouille and herbs
or baked chicken breast with parsley mousse. *Bollito misto* is Drimcong's version of an

Italian dish with beef, or you can choose a vegetarian dinner, such as herb and vegetable soufflé or smoked-cheese-and-apple ravioli. Drimcong House employs a full-time organic gardener to tend the lush gardens. Chef Gerry Gavin and Drimcong House are the recipients of numerous awards, including the 1999 Irish Food Award for excellence.

MODERATE

Beola. Roundstone Harbor, Connemara, County Galway. ☎ **095/35933.** Reservations recommended. Main courses £9.95–£13.95 ($13.95–$19.55). AE, DC, MC, V. Easter to mid-Oct daily 6:30–9:30pm. SEAFOOD.

This attractive restaurant serves perhaps the finest and most inventive seafood dishes in Roundstone at near-budget prices. Beola, which belongs to the adjacent Eldon's Hotel, has an exceptionally welcoming staff to go with its exceptional cuisine. Smoked salmon parcels in filo pastry or hot avocado and prawns make a splendid first course. To follow, you can't miss with roast fillet of monkfish with lemon soy sauce, or grilled cod with nut dressing. For a memorable finish, try the Baileys and ginger cheesecake. The wine list offers a fine international selection at surprisingly affordable prices, and the South African house wine (Armiston Bay) is a high-quality surprise at £12 ($18) a bottle. The only drawback here is that no significant provision is made for non-smokers—the restaurant is a single unpartitioned space.

Burke's. Mount Gable House, Clonbur, County Galway. ☎ **092/46175.** Reservations recommended. Main courses £7.50–£14 ($10.50–$19.60). MC, V. Apr–Oct Mon–Sat 6–9pm. IRISH

The first thing you'll notice here is that everyone, from the barman to the waiters, is so friendly. The bright dining room is hidden beyond a long, dark barroom, where traditional music often starts at around 10pm. The meal begins well, with delicious home-baked breads. Vegetables that accompany the meal are locally grown and mostly organic. Main courses include honey roast duck breast with orange port sauce, and grilled lamb cutlets with red currant sauce. The vegetarian special changes daily, and shows a real consideration of how to eat well without meat. The food here is consistently simple in its conception and presentation, and consistently satisfying.

✪ High Moors. Off the Ballyconeely road, Dooneen, Clifden, County Galway. ☎ **095/21342.** Reservations recommended. Main courses £9.95–£13.95 ($13.95–$19.55). AE, CB, MC, V. Wed–Sun 6:30–10pm. Closed Nov–Easter. IRISH.

Less than a mile from Clifden, a narrow country road leads to this modern bungalow-style restaurant, set high on a hill with panoramic views of the Atlantic and the wild countryside. A homey ambience prevails—and well it should, because this is the home of Hugh and Eileen Griffin, host and chef, respectively. The food and menu are simple, based on what is fresh at the markets and what vegetables and herbs are in season in Hugh's organic gardens. Eileen's specialties include breast of chicken with basil and tomato; fillet of pork with three spices; wild salmon with sorrel butter sauce; ragout of salmon, sole, and scallops; and roast leg of Connemara lamb with red currant and rosemary. Try to book a table for sunset—if you can tear your attention away from the food, the views are incredible. Or you can enjoy the vistas with drinks or coffee from the new conservatory. About half of the tables are nonsmoking.

O'Grady's. Market St., Clifden, County Galway. ☎ **095/21450.** Reservations recommended for dinner. Dinner main courses £10–£20 ($14–$28). AE, MC, V. Apr–Oct Mon–Sat 12:30–2:30pm and 6:30–10pm. IRISH/SEAFOOD.

Since the mid-1960s, this restaurant has been drawing seekers of great seafood to Clifden. The menu features all that is freshest from the sea, with choices such as Clifden lobster with lemon or garlic butter, and fillet of Cleggan brill. For non-ish-eaters, there's fillet of beef with radish sauce, pork with peach stuffing in peppercorn cream sauce, and lamb with rosemary sauce.

INEXPENSIVE

Two Dog Cafe. Church St., Clifden, Connemara, County Galway. ☎ **095/22186.** www.twodogcafe.ie. All items 80p–£5.50 ($1.10–$7.70). V. June–Sept daily 9:30am–10pm; Oct–May Tues–Sun 10:30am–6:30pm. MEDITERRANEAN.

This bright, smoke-free cafe is a great place to relax and enjoy an array of homemade soups, Mediterranean sandwiches (constructed on baguettes, tortillas, and ciabatta), salads, fresh pastries, tea, and Italian coffee. The baguette with goat's cheese and grilled red peppers was particularly enticing. Wine is served by the glass or bottle.

This is also the place to connect with the Web. Full Internet access and services are available on the cafe's second floor. Dell PCs and Apple iMacs, loaded with the latest browsing software, are at the ready. You pay £1.50 ($2.10) for the first 15 minutes, 50p (70¢) for each additional 5 minutes, or £6 ($8.40) per hour, with discounts for students.

The Northwest 13

Above County Mayo on the Atlantic coast, extending the Republic like an index finger along the western border of the North, are counties Sligo, Donegal, and Leitrim.

If you're looking for a landscape of majestic wildness and splendor, Donegal is the place to go, although its austere beauty can become rather bleak when the weather turns gray and rainy. Several of Ireland's greatest natural wonders are here, such as the Slieve League cliffs and Horn Head. The most remote, pristine, and beautiful beaches in the country are tucked into the bays and inlets of Donegal's sharply indented coast.

The towns of Donegal are, for the most part, functional rather than beautiful—no doubt good places to live and work, but offering few amenities to the tourist. It isn't so easy to settle into this county, where the people aren't always accustomed to tourism and tend to be more reticent than folks in the tourist centers of the southeast and southwest. With some effort you'll find your way, but it might be hard work at times; in addition to dealing with the locals' ambivalence toward visitors, you have to contend with the road signs, which are cryptic or nonexistent on all but the national roads. In my experience, the political climate of Northern Ireland affects Donegal more directly than it does any other tourist destination in the Republic. The people's prevailing mood may have a lot to do with the status of the peace at the moment.

As in Donegal, the main appeal of County Sligo is not in its towns, but out in the countryside. The county does possess a wealth of historic sites, though, and fans of Yeats will enjoy visiting the plethora of sites associated with the poet and his writings.

There are a few sites in Leitrim—Glencar Waterfall, Dromahair, and Parke's Castle—that can most easily be visited from Sligo town, and for this reason we've included them in this chapter. You'll find more details on Leitrim in chapter 14.

1 Sligo & Yeats Country

136 miles (219km) NE of Shannon Airport, 135 miles (217km) NW of Dublin, 47 miles (76km) NE of Knock, 37 miles (60km) NE of Ballina, 87 miles (140km) NE of Galway, 73 miles (118km) N of Athlone, and 209 miles (337km) N of Cork

Sligo Town (pop. 18,000) is ideally located, nestled as it is in a valley between two mountains—Ben Bulben on the north and Knocknarea on the south. Although until recently it was more commercial center than tourist destination, that's been changing. Sligo is in the midst of a major renaissance. Between 1993 and 1999, roughly one-half to two-thirds of the town center was refurbished. From the visitor's perspective, the epicenter of this radical rejuvenation is on Sligo's new "Left Bank," where cafes and restaurants spill onto the waterfront promenade whenever the not-always-cooperative weather permits.

Be sure, however, to explore the surrounding countryside. As you'll quickly discover, this is Yeats country, and every hill, rill, cottage, vale, and lake seems to bear a plaque indicating its relation to the poet or his works.

SLIGO TOWN ESSENTIALS

GETTING THERE   Aer Lingus operates daily flights into **Sligo Airport,** Strandhill, County Sligo (☎ **071/68280**), 5 miles (8km) southwest of Sligo Town. The bus to Sligo town from the airport will cost you under £2 ($2.80), while you can expect a taxi to cost around £9 ($12.60).

Irish Rail, with its station on Lord Edward Street (☎ **071/69888**), operates daily service into Sligo from Dublin and other points.

Bus Eireann, also pulling into Lord Edward Street (☎ **071/60066**), operates daily bus service to Sligo from Dublin, Galway, and other points, including Derry in Northern Ireland.

Three major roads lead to Sligo: N4 from Dublin and the east, N17 from Galway and the south, and N16 from Northern Ireland.

VISITOR INFORMATION   For information about Sligo and the surrounding area, contact the **North West Regional Tourism Office,** Aras Reddan, Temple Street, Sligo (☎ **071/61201**). It's open year-round, weekdays 9am to 5pm, with weekend and extended hours April to August. The most comprehensive local Internet source for Sligo can be found at **www.sligo.ie.**

TOWN LAYOUT   Edged by Sligo Bay to the west, Sligo Town sits beside the Garavogue River. Most of the city's commercial district lies on the south bank of the river. **O'Connell Street** is the main north–south artery of the downtown district. The main east–west thoroughfare is **Stephen Street,** which becomes Wine Street and then Lord Edward Street. The **Tourist Office** is in the southwest corner of the town on Temple Street, 2 blocks south of O'Connell Street. Three bridges span the river; the **Douglas Hyde Bridge,** named for Ireland's first president, is the main link between the two sides.

GETTING AROUND   There is no public transport in the town of Sligo. During July and August, **Bus Eireann** (☎ 071/60066) runs from Sligo Town to Strandhill and Rosses Point.

Taxis line up at the taxi rank on Quay Street. If you prefer to call for a taxi, try **A Cabs** (☎ 071/45777), **ACE Cabs** (☎ 071/44444), **Greenline Hackney Cabs** (☎ 071/69000), or **Sligo Cabs** (☎ 071/71888).

You'll need a car to see the sights outside Sligo Town. If you need to hire a vehicle locally, contact **Budget Rent-A-Car,** Sligo Airport, Strandhill (☎ **0903/24614**); or **Murrays Europcar,** Sligo Airport (☎ **071/68400**).

The best way to see Sligo Town itself is on foot. Follow the signposted route of the Tourist Trail. The walk takes approximately 90 minutes. From mid-June to September, the **Tourist Office,** Temple Street, Sligo (☎ **071/61201**), offers guided tours; contact the office for details and reservations.

FAST FACTS   In an emergency, dial ☎ **999. St. John's Hospital** is at Ballytivan, Sligo (☎ **071/42606**), or you can try **Sligo County Hospital,** The Mall (☎ **071/42620**). The local **Garda Station** is on Pearse Road (☎ **071/42031**).

County Sligo

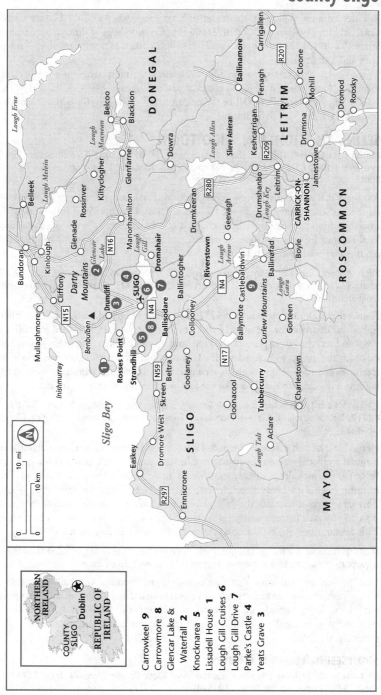

Carrowkeel **9**
Carrowmore **8**
Glencar Lake &
  Waterfall **2**
Knocknarea **5**
Lissadell House **1**
Lough Gill Cruises **6**
Lough Gill Drive **7**
Parke's Castle **4**
Yeats Grave **3**

Three minutes' walk from the center of Sligo Town, you'll find the **Galaxy Cyber Café,** Millbrook Riverside (☎ **071/40441**). **County Sligo Library,** on Stephen Street (☎ **071/42212**), is open Tuesday to Friday 10am to 5pm, Saturday 10am to 1pm and 2 to 5pm.

The weekly *Sligo Champion* and *Sligo Weekender* cover most area news and entertainment. The local North West Radio broadcasts from Sligo on FM 102.5 and FM 96.3.

The **Sligo General Post Office,** Wine Street (☎ **071/42646**), is open Monday through Saturday 9am to 5:30pm.

SEEING THE SIGHTS IN SLIGO TOWN

Model Arts Centre. The Mall, Sligo, County Sligo. ☎ **071/41405.** Free admission. Readings and lectures £3–£5 ($4.20–$7). No credit cards. Mon–Sat 11am–6pm; evening events 8pm.

Although this is a relatively new development in Sligo (it opened in 1991), it carries on the Yeatsean literary and artistic traditions. Housed in an 1850 Romanesque-style stone building that was originally a school, it offers nine rooms for touring shows and local exhibits by artists, sculptors, writers, and musicians. In the summer, there are often poetry readings or arts lectures.

Sligo Abbey. Abbey St., Sligo, County Sligo. ☎ **071/46406.** Admission £1.50 ($2.10) adults, £1 ($1.40) seniors, 60p (84¢) students and children, £4 ($5.60) family. No credit cards. Daily 9:30am–6:30pm. Closed Oct–May.

Founded as a Dominican house in 1252 by Maurice Fitzgerald, Earl of Kildare, Sligo Abbey was destroyed by fire in 1414 and rebuilt 2 years later. It flourished in medieval times and was the burial place of the kings and princes of Sligo. After many raids and sackings, the abbey was closed in 1641. Much restoration work has been done in recent years, and the cloisters are now considered outstanding examples of stone carving; the 15th-century altar is one of the few intact medieval altars in Ireland.

✪ Sligo County Museum & Niland Gallery. Stephen St. , Sligo, County Sligo. ☎ **071/42212.** E-mail: sligolib@iol.ie. Free admission. Tues–Sat 10am–noon and 2–4:50pm. Closed Oct–May.

Housed in a church manse of the mid–19th century, this museum exhibits material of national and local interest dating to pre-Christian times. One section, devoted to the Yeats family, includes a display of William Butler Yeats's complete works in first editions, poems on broadsheets, letters, and his Nobel Prize for literature (1923). This same section contains the Niland Gallery, a collection of oils, watercolors, and drawings by Jack B. Yeats and John B. Yeats. There is also a permanent collection of 20th-century Irish art, including works by Paul Henry and Evie Hone.

Yeats Memorial Building. Douglas Hyde Bridge, Sligo, County Sligo. ☎ **071/42693.** www.yeats-sligo.com. Free admission. Year-round Mon–Fri 9:30am–5pm.

In a 19th-century red-brick Victorian building, this memorial contains an extensive library with items of special interest to Yeats scholars. The building is also headquarters of the Yeats International Summer School and the Sligo Art Gallery, which exhibits works by local, national, and international artists. The latest addition to the memorial is a full cafe.

SIGHTSEEING TOURS & CRUISES

JH Transport. 57 Mountain Close, Carton View, Sligo, County Sligo. ☎ **071/42747** or 086/833-9084 (mobile). Bus tours £10 ($14) adults, £5 ($7) children 6–16. Waterbus return option £3.50 ($4.90) extra.

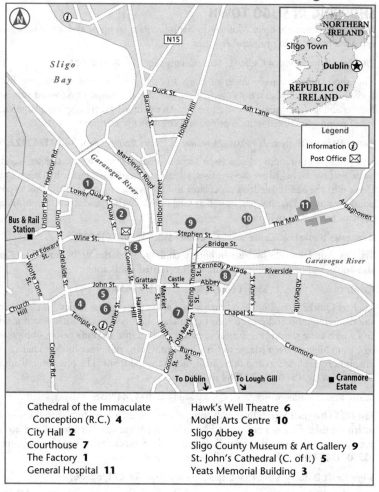

Cathedral of the Immaculate Conception (R.C.) **4**	Hawk's Well Theatre **6**
City Hall **2**	Model Arts Centre **10**
Courthouse **7**	Sligo Abbey **8**
The Factory **1**	Sligo County Museum & Art Gallery **9**
General Hospital **11**	St. John's Cathedral (C. of I.) **5**
	Yeats Memorial Building **3**

This fine family-operated company offers narrated minibus tours of the Sligo area, departing daily from the Sligo Tourist Office. The morning tour follows the Lough Gill Drive, and the afternoon tour visits Yeats's grave, Lissadell House, Glencar Lake and Waterfall, and—if time permits and the popular will is there—Carrowmore. Phone ahead to confirm schedules and booking. With the morning tour, you have the option of returning to Sligo on a waterbus via Innisfree Island.

Lough Gill Cruises. Blue Lagoon, Riverside, Sligo, County Sligo. ☎ **071/64266.** Lough Gill cruise £6 ($8.40) adults, £3 ($4.20) children over 10; Innisfree cruise £5 ($7) adults, £2.50 ($3.50) children over 10. June–Sept Lough Gill cruise daily 2:30 and 4:30pm; Innisfree tour daily 12:30, 3:30, and 6:30pm. Apr–May and Oct (Sun only) schedule subject to demand.

On this tour, you cruise on Lough Gill and the Garavogue River aboard the 72-passenger *Wild Rose* waterbus while listening to the poetry of Yeats. Trips to the Lake Isle of Innisfree are also scheduled. An on-board bar serves refreshments.

SHOPPING IN SLIGO TOWN

Most Sligo shops are open Monday to Saturday 9am to 6pm, and some may have extended hours during July and August.

The Cat & the Moon. 4 Castle St., Sligo, County Sligo. ☎ **071/43686.**

This shop offers uniquely designed crafts from throughout Ireland, ranging from beeswax candles and baskets to modern art, metal and ceramic work, wood turning, hand weaving, Celtic jewelry, and furniture. An expanded gallery displays a large variety of paintings, limited-edition prints, and occasionally sculpture.

Kates Kitchen/Hopper & Pettit. 24 Market St., Sligo, County Sligo. ☎ **071/43022.**

Kates has an outstanding delicatessen section, with gourmet meats, cheeses, salads, pâtés, and breads baked on the premises, all ideal makings for a picnic by Lough Gill. Don't miss the handmade Irish chocolates and preserves. Hopper & Pettit stocks potpourri, soaps, and natural oils, as well as Crabtree & Evelyn products. Open Monday to Saturday 9am to 6:30pm.

Keohanes Bookshop. Castle St., Sligo, County Sligo. ☎ **071/42597.**

Try this shop for works by Irish authors, including, of course, W. B. Yeats. There are also books and maps of Sligo and other Sligo-related publications.

✪ **M. Quirke.** Wine St., Sligo, County Sligo. ☎ **071/42624.**

Michael Quirke started out as a butcher, but a few years ago he traded his cleaver for wood-carving tools and transformed his butcher shop into a craft studio. Step inside and watch as he transforms chunks of native timbers into Ireland's heroes of mythology, from Sligo's Queen Maeve to Cu Chulainn, Oisin, and other folklore characters. He also carves chess sets and other Irish-themed wood items. The price of individual carvings averages £60 to £70 ($84 to $98).

Music Room. Harmony Hill, Sligo, County Sligo. ☎ **071/44765.**

Just off O'Connell Street, this small cottagelike store draws you to it with the sounds of Irish music. This is a great spot to purchase Irish musical instruments and accessories. A sister shop, the Record Room, a half block away on Grattan Street (☎ **071/43748**), offers cassettes, CDs, videos, and records.

Sligo Craft Pottery. Market Yard, Sligo, County Sligo. ☎ **071/62586.**

This shop features the work of one of Ireland's foremost ceramic artists, Michael Kennedy, who produces pottery and porcelain with layers of textured markings and drawings that form a maze of intricate patterns. He then applies glazes that reflect the strong tones and shades of the Irish countryside. The result is one-of-a-kind vases, jars, dishes, figurines, buttons, jewelry, and other pieces.

Sligo Crystal & Giftware Ltd. 2 Hyde Bridge House, Hyde Bridge, Sligo, County Sligo. ☎ **071/43440.**

This workshop, in new premises in Sligo Town, is noted for its personalized engraving of such items as family crests on mirrors or glassware. The craftspeople also produce hand-cut crystal candlesticks, glasses, and curio items like crystal bells and scent bottles. Crystal pieces can be cut to a pattern of your creation or choice. Weekdays, you'll see the craftspeople at work.

Wehrly Bros. Ltd. 3 O'Connell St. , Sligo, County Sligo. ☎ **071/42252.**

Established in 1875, this is one of Sligo's oldest shops, noted for a fine selection of jewelry and watches, as well as cold-cast bronze sculptures of Irish figures, silverware, Claddagh rings, Waterford crystal, Belleek china, and Galway crystal.

EXPLORING THE SURROUNDING COUNTRYSIDE

Sligo's great antiquity can be counted in the seemingly numberless grave mounds, standing stones, ring circles, and dolmens still marking its starkly stunning landscape. The county contains the greatest concentration of megalithic sites in all of Ireland.

A fitting place to begin exploring ancient Sligo is at **Carrowmore** (see listing below), a vast Neolithic cemetery that once contained perhaps as many as 200 passage tombs, some of which predate Newgrange by 500 years. From Carrowmore, the Neolithic mountaintop cemetery of **Carrowkeel** is visible in the distant south. Less than an hour's drive away (ask for detailed directions at the Carrowmore Visitors Centre), it offers an experience beyond any account: After a breathtaking ascent on foot, you'll find yourself alone with the past. The tombs, facing Carrowmore below and aligned with the summer solstice, are rarely visited. To this writer, even the memory of them brings chills of wonder.

To the west is **Knocknarea** (1,078 ft.), on whose summit sits a gigantic unexcavated *cairn* (grave mound). It's known as **Miscaun Meadhbh (Maeve's Mound)**, even though it predates Maeve—an early Celtic warrior queen who plays a central role in the Taín Bó Cuilnge, the Celtic epic—by millennia. Legend has it that she's buried standing, in full battle gear, spear in hand, facing her Ulster enemies even in death. This extraordinary tomb is 630 feet around at its base, 80 feet high, 100 feet in diameter, and visible for miles.

At the foot of Knocknarea is **Strandhill,** 5 miles (8km) from Sligo Town. This delightful resort area stretches into Sligo Bay, with a sand-duned beach and a patch of land nearby called Coney Island, which is usually credited with lending its name to the New York beach amusement area. Across the bay, about 4 miles (6.5km) north of Sligo Town, is another beach resort, Rosses Point.

Northwest of Sligo Bay, 4 miles (6.5km) offshore, lies the uninhabited island of ◒ **Inishmurray,** which contains the haunting ruins of one of Ireland's earliest monastic settlements. Founded in the 6th century and destroyed by the Vikings in 807, the monastery of St. Molaise contains in its circular walls the remains of several churches, beehive cells, altars, and an assemblage of "cursing stones" once used to bring down ruin on those who presumably deserved it. For transportation to the island, call **Joe McGowan** (☎ 071/66267) or **Brendan Merrifield** (☎ 071/41874).

Most of Sligo's attractions are associated in some way with the poet William Butler Yeats, as you'll note below.

✪ **Carrowmore Megalithic Cemetery.** Carrowmore Visitors Centre, County Sligo. ☎ **071/61534.** Admission £1.50 ($2.10) adults, £1 ($1.40) seniors, 60p (84¢) students and children, £4 ($5.60) family. No credit cards. Daily 9:30am–6:30pm. Both visitor center and site closed Oct–Apr. From Sligo, signposted on N15; from the south, signposted on N4.

Here, at the dead center of the Coolera Peninsula, sits the giant's tomb, a massive passage grave that once had a stone circle of its own. Circling it, and in nearly every instance facing it, were as many as 100 to 200 passage graves, each circled in stone. Tomb 52A, excavated in August 1998, is estimated to be 7,400 years old, making it the earliest known piece of freestanding stone architecture in the world. Circles within circles within circles describe a stone-and-spirit world of the dead whose power touches every visitor who stops to see and consider it—it's one of the great sacred landscapes of the ancient world. The cemetery's interpretive center offers informative exhibits and tours.

Glencar Lake. Off N16, Glencar, County Leitrim.

This Yeats Country attraction is not in Sligo, but just over the border in County Leitrim. Lovely Glencar Lake stretches east for 2 miles (3.2km) along a verdant valley, highlighted by two waterfalls, one of which rushes downward for 50 feet. Yeats's "The Stolen Child" speaks wondrously of this lake.

Lissadell House. Off the main Sligo–Donegal road (N15), 8 miles (13km) north of Sligo, Drumcliffe, County Sligo. ☎ **074/63150.** Admission £3 ($4.20) adults, £1 ($1.40) children. June to mid-Sept Mon–Sat 10:30am–12:30pm and 2–4:30pm.

On the shores of Sligo Bay, this large neoclassical building was another of Yeats's favorite haunts. Dating from 1830, it has long been the home of the Gore-Booth family, including Yeats's friends Eva Gore-Booth, a fellow poet, and her sister Constance, who became the Countess Markievicz after marrying a Polish count. She took part in the 1916 Irish Rising and was the first woman elected to the British House of Commons and the first woman cabinet member in the Irish Dáil. The house is full of such family memorabilia as the travel diaries of Sir Robert Gore-Booth, who mortgaged the estate to help the poor during the famine. At the core of the house is a dramatic two-story hallway lined with Doric columns leading to a double staircase of Kilkenny marble.

✪ The Lough Gill Drive. County Sligo and County Leitrim.

This 26-mile (42km) drive-yourself tour around Lough Gill is well signposted. Head 1 mile (1.6km) south of town and follow the signs for **Lough Gill,** the beautiful lake that figured so prominently in Yeats's writings. Within 2 miles (3.2km) you'll be on the lower edge of the shoreline. Among sites to see are **Dooney Rock,** with its own nature trail and lakeside walk (inspiration for the poem "Fiddler of Dooney"); the **Lake Isle of Innisfree,** made famous in Yeats's poetry and in song; and the **Hazelwood Sculpture Trail,** unique to Sligo, a forest walk along the shores of Lough Gill, with 13 wood sculptures.

The storied Lake Isle of Innisfree is only one of 22 islands in Lough Gill. You can drive the whole lakeside circuit in less than an hour, or you can stop at the east end and visit **Dromahair,** a delightful village on the River Bonet, technically part of County Leitrim.

The road along Lough Gill's upper shore brings you back to the northern end of Sligo Town. Continue north on the main road (N15), and you'll see the graceful profile of **Ben Bulben** (1,730 ft.), one of the Dartry Mountains, rising to the right.

✪ Parkes Castle. Lough Gill Dr., County Leitrim. ☎ **071/64149.** Admission £2 ($2.80) adults, £1.50 ($2.10) seniors, £1 ($1.40) students and children, £5 ($7) family. St. Patrick's weekend (near Mar 17) 10am–5pm; Apr–May Tues–Sun 10am–5pm; June–Sept daily 9:30am–6:30pm; Oct daily 10am–5pm.

On the north side of the Lough Gill Drive, within the County Leitrim border, Parke's Castle stands out as a lone outpost amid the natural tableau of lake view and woodland scenery. Named after an English family who gained possession of it during the 1620 plantation of Leitrim, this castle was originally the stronghold of the O'Rourke clan, rulers of the kingdom of Breffni. Beautifully restored using Irish oak and traditional craftsmanship, it exemplifies the 17th-century fortified manor house. In the visitor center, informative exhibits and a splendid audiovisual show illustrate the history of the castle and introduce visitors to the rich, diverse sites of interest in the surrounding area. This is an ideal place from which to launch your own local explorations. The tearoom offers fresh and exceptionally enticing pastries.

Yeats's Grave. Drumcliffe Churchyard, Drumcliffe, County Sligo. N15 to Drumcliffe.

Five miles (8km) north of Sligo Town is Drumcliffe, site of the Church of Ireland cemetery where W. B. Yeats is buried. It's well signposted, so you can easily find the poet's grave with the simple headstone bearing the dramatic epitaph he composed: "Cast a cold eye on life, on death; Horseman, pass by." This cemetery also contains the ruins of an early Christian monastery founded by St. Columba in A.D. 745.

SPORTS & OUTDOOR PURSUITS

BEACHES   For walking, jogging, or swimming, there are safe sandy beaches with promenades at **Strandhill, Rosses Point,** and **Enniscrone** on the Sligo Bay coast.

BICYCLING   With its lakes and woodlands, Yeats Country is particularly good biking territory. To rent a bike, contact **Gary's Cycles Shop,** Quay Street, Sligo (☎ **071/45418**), or **Conways Shop,** 6 Hugh St., Sligo (☎ **071/61370**).

FISHING   Boats, with or without *ghillies* (guides), are available at the **Blue Lagoon,** Riverside, Sligo (see "Pubs," below). Contact Peter Henry (☎ **071/45407** or 071/44040).

GOLF   With its seascapes, mountain valleys, and lakesides, County Sligo is known for challenging golf courses. Leading the list is ✪ **County Sligo Golf Club,** Rosses Point Road, Rosses Point (☎ **071/77134**), overlooking Sligo Bay under the shadow of Ben Bulben mountain. It's an 18-hole, par-71 championship seaside links famed for its wild, natural terrain and constant winds; greens fees are £35 ($49) weekdays, £45 ($63) weekends.

Five miles (8km) west of Sligo Town is **Strandhill Golf Club,** Strandhill (☎ **071/68188**), a seaside par-69 course with greens fees of £25 ($35) weekdays, £30 ($42) weekends.

In the southwestern corner of the county, about 25 miles (40km) from Sligo Town and overlooking Sligo Bay, the **Enniscrone Golf Club,** Enniscrone (☎ **096/36297**), is a seaside par-72 course. Greens fees are £26 ($36.40) weekdays, £35 ($49) weekends.

HORSEBACK RIDING   An hour's or a day's riding on the beach, in the countryside, or over mountain trails can be arranged at **Sligo Riding Centre,** Carrowmore (☎ **071/ 61353**), or at **Woodlands Equestrian Centre,** Loughill, Lavagh, Tubbercurry, County Sligo (☎ **071/84207**). Rates average £10 to £12 ($14 to $16.80) per hour.

ACCOMMODATIONS
EXPENSIVE

✪ **Cromleach Lodge.** Ballindoon, Castlebaldwin, County Sligo. ☎ **071/65155.** Fax 071/65455. E-mail: cromleac@iol.ie. 10 units. TV TEL. £138–£198 ($193.20–$277.20) mini-suite double. No service charge. Rates include full breakfast. AE, DC, MC, V. Closed Nov–Jan.

One of the best places to stay in Sligo is not in town, but 20 miles (32km) south. This lovely modern country-house hotel, nestled in the quiet hills above Lough Arrow, is run by Moira and Christy Tighe. You may never want to leave as you gaze out from the skylit bar and restaurant or your room at the panorama of lakeland and mountain scenery. The rooms are extra-large by Irish standards and have all the comforts of a top hotel, including oversized orthopedic beds, designer fabrics, and original oil paintings. Each room is named after a different part of the Sligo countryside (from Ben Bulben and Knocknarea to Moytura and Carrowkeel) and is decorated with colors reflecting its namesake. Half the rooms are nonsmoking, and there are separate smoking and non-smoking lounges. But the pièce de résistance is the dining room (see "Dining," below).

✪ **Markree Castle.** Collooney, County Sligo. ☎ **800/223-6510** or 800/44-UTELL from the U.S., or 071/67800. Fax 071/67840. E-mail: markree@iol.ie. 30 units. TV TEL. £128 ($179.20) double. No service charge. Rates include full breakfast. AE, CB, DC, MC, V. Closed several days at Christmas.

Located 8 miles (13km) south of Sligo off the main Dublin road, this is the county's oldest inhabited castle, having been the home of the Cooper family since 1640. The current owner, Charles Cooper, is the 10th generation of his family to live at Markree. The original house was altered and extended over the years, but the dramatic four-story turreted stone facade remains. Even the approach to the castle is impressive— a mile-long driveway, along pasturelands grazed by sheep and horses and past lovely gardens that stretch down to the Unsin River. The interior is equally regal, with a hand-carved oak staircase, ornate plasterwork, and a stained-glass window that traces the Cooper family tree back to the time of King John of England. The guest rooms, restored and equipped with modern facilities, have lovely views of the gardens, and the restaurant, known as Knockmuldowney (see "Dining," below), is a masterpiece of Louis Philippe–style plasterwork. The castle offers horseback riding, falconry, and salmon fishing on the Ballisodare River.

MODERATE

Ballincar House Hotel. 2 miles (3.2km) northwest of the Sligo Town center, Rosses Point Rd., Sligo, County Sligo. ☎ **800/447-7462** from the U.S., or 071/45361. Fax 071/44198. www.infowing.ie/ballincarhousehotel. 25 units. TV TEL. £74–£94 ($103.60–$131.60) double. Rates include full breakfast and service charge. AE, DC, MC, V.

Nestled on six tree-shaded pastoral acres overlooking Sligo Bay, this two-story hotel was built as a private residence in 1848, and extended and opened as a lodging in 1969. The public rooms preserve the house's charm, with open fireplaces, period furnishings, and original oil paintings of the area. Rooms are decorated in contemporary country style, and most look out onto the gardens or vistas of Sligo Bay. There's a full-service restaurant, bar, hard tennis court, sauna, and snooker table.

Sligo Park Hotel. Pearse Rd. (just over 1 mile/1.6km south of Sligo on the Dublin road/N4), Sligo, County Sligo. ☎ **071/60291.** Fax 071/69556. E-mail: sligopk@leehotels.ie. 110 units. TV TEL. £79–£109 ($110.60–$152.60) double. Rates include full breakfast and service charge. DC, MC, V. Free parking.

With a glass-fronted facade and skylit atrium lobby, this is Sligo's most contemporary hotel. It's back from the road on 7 acres of parkland, and surrounded by lovely gardens, with distant views of Ben Bulben to the north. Irish art enhances the modern public areas. Guest rooms are furnished in art deco style, with light woods, pastel-toned floral fabrics, quilted headboards, orthopedic beds, and framed scenes of the Sligo area. Nonsmoking rooms are available. The totally refurbished Hazelwood Restaurant, overlooking the gardens, the Rathanna Piano Bar, and a coffee shop are on the premises. The hotel has an indoor swimming pool, a whirlpool, a sauna, a steam room, a gym, and a tennis court.

✪ **Temple House.** Ballymote, County Sligo. ☎ **071/83329.** Fax 071/83808. www. templehouse.ie. 5 units, 4 with private bathroom. £84–£90 ($117.60–$126) double. Rates include full breakfast. Dinner £19 ($28.50). AE, MC, V. Closed Dec–Easter. Free private parking. No perfume, aftershave, or hair spray.

This vast Georgian mansion is beautifully situated in 1,000 acres of woods and parkland, overlooking a lake and the ruins of a Knights Templar castle, for which the place is named. The atmosphere of casual elegance and affable unpretentiousness is seductive, and chances are you'll want to spend more than 1 night. The house has seen better days and is a bit frayed at the edges, but still manages to impress with the sheer magnitude of its spaces and the antiquity of its eclectic furnishings. The Percivals have lived here since 1665, and many memorable events have transpired within these woods and walls. Sandy Percival brings life to the gallery of venerable family portraits

Every St. Patrick's Day every Irishman goes out to find another Irishman to make a speech to.

—Shane Leslie, *American Wonderland,* 1936

as he tells the stories of his ancestors. The two double rooms facing the front of the house are particularly spacious and stately; book them well in advance.

The walled garden is a short walk from the house and supplies vegetables for the excellent evening meals—with advance notice, vegetarians are well provided for. Dinner is served in the nonsmoking dining room.

One important note: Sandy Percival has an acute chemical sensitivity, so he asks guests to avoid the use of any cosmetic products, such as perfume, aftershave, or hair spray.

Yeats Country Hotel Golf and Leisure Club. Rosses Point Rd. (5 miles/8km northwest of Sligo Town), Rosses Point, County Sligo. ☎ **800/44-UTELL** from the U.S., or 071/77211. Fax 071/77203. 79 units. TV TEL. £60–£160 ($84–$224) double. Rates include full Irish breakfast and service charge. AE, DC, MC, V. Closed Jan.

Located next to an 18-hole golf course, this modern hilltop property overlooks several miles of sandy beach and the waters of Sligo Bay. The interior is furnished in bright contemporary style with wide windows looking out onto the neighboring attractions. All rooms have tea/coffee-making facilities and hair dryers. The hotel has a full-service restaurant and a lounge bar. There are tennis, basketball, and bowling facilities, and a new, fully equipped leisure center with an 18-meter swimming pool, sauna, gym, steam room, and Jacuzzi.

INEXPENSIVE

Dunfore Farmhouse. Ballinful, County Sligo. ☎ **071/63137.** Fax 071/63574. 4 units. £40 ($56) double. Rates include full breakfast. 50% discount for children under 12. MC, V. Closed Nov–Feb. Turn off N15 at Drumcliffe.

Ita Leyden, winner of two recent tourism awards, is an outgoing and energetic host who has done a great job of making this recently renovated farmhouse a pleasant base for exploring Sligo. Rooms have orthopedic beds, tea/coffee-making facilities, and fine views of the surrounding countryside (some across the bay to Rosses Point, others to Ben Bulben or the nearby Lissadell Wood). Breakfast is often enlivened by Ita's ardent recitation of her favorite Irish poetry, and you'll find literary touches throughout the house, from portraits of Irish writers to a painting by Yeats's brother Jack. When the weather is good, visitors can arrange a tour of the local coast in the Leydens' small motorboat, docked at nearby Raghly Harbor. If you'd like to rent the entire house by the week or month, inquire well in advance.

Glebe House. Coolaney Rd., Collooney, County Sligo. ☎ **071/67787.** Fax 071/30438. E-mail: glebehse@iol.ie TEL. 4 units, 2 with shower only. £46–£52 ($64.40–$72.80) double. Rates include full breakfast. AE, DC, MC, V.

A "glebe house" is an old rectory, and examples can be found throughout Ireland; this particularly fine specimen was built in the 1820s and restored by owners Brid and Marc Torrades in 1990, rescuing the house from years of neglect. The elegant ground-floor dining room is home to a much-acclaimed restaurant (see "Dining," below). The bedrooms are painted in strong, unusual colors and are moderately sized, with heavy, wooden beds. Bathrooms are extremely clean and quite small. Rooms overlook the tranquil grounds of the house and the nearby church steeple of the town of Collooney, and each is stocked with a selection of books and magazines.

SELF-CATERING

Beech Cottage. Lough Gill Dr., Dromahair, County Leitrim. ☎ **071/64110.** 1 house, 4 apts. House £500–£800 ($700–$1,120) per week; apt £140–£350 ($196–$490) per week. MC, V.

Beech Cottage, just outside Dromahair, focuses on its riding school and offers an array of packages that include horse riding, lessons, accommodations, and meals. They range from 1-day trekking trips to 7-day all-inclusive instructional holidays at all levels. Guests who love horses but prefer to watch are also warmly welcomed. If your interests combine horses, Yeats, and ancient Irish Neolithic sites, you will never want to leave. The tasteful, quiet 19th-century manor house sleeps seven, in excellent beds. The four self-catering apartments, attractively converted from old stone stables, have open-plan kitchen/dining and living rooms with fireplaces, and are equipped with all the essentials, including cable TV and washing machines. The stoves have *hobs* (burners), but no ovens. The deluxe three-person apartment is the gem of the four, with exposed stone walls, skylights, and a massive open stone fireplace. At this writing, there is an extension of the main house planned for 2001.

DINING

EXPENSIVE

✪ **Cromleach Lodge.** Ballindoon, Castlebaldwin, County Sligo. ☎ **071/65155.** Reservations required. Fixed-price 7-course tasting menu £40 ($56); main courses £18.75 ($26.25). AE, MC, V. Daily 6:30–9pm. Closed Nov–Jan. MODERN IRISH.

It's worth the drive 20 miles (32km) south of Sligo Town to dine at this lovely country house overlooking Lough Arrow. The panoramic views are secondary, however, to chef Moira Tighe's culinary creations, which have won a fistful of prestigious awards. The menu changes nightly, depending on what is freshest and best from the sea and garden. It may include such dishes as boned stuffed roast quail with a vintage port sauce, wild Atlantic salmon, and loin of lamb scented with garlic and Irish Mist. The pudding of white chocolate mousse can be counted on for perfect closure. The non-smoking dining room is a delight, with decorated plaster moldings and chair rails, curio cabinets with figurines and crystal, ruffled valances, potted palms, and place settings of Rosenthal china and fine Irish linens and silver.

✪ **Markree Castle Hotel and Restaurant.** Collooney, County Sligo. ☎ **071/67800.** Reservations required. Fixed-price dinners £23 and £28.95 ($32.20 and $40.55). AE, DC, MC, V. Daily 7–9:30pm; Sun 1–2:30pm. Closed several days at Christmas. INTERNATIONAL.

Long before Charles and Mary Cooper bought Markree Castle (see "Accommodations," above), they were winning culinary plaudits for Knockmuldowney restaurant, then in a small house at the base of Knocknarea Mountain on the shores of Ballisodare Bay. When they acquired the castle, they brought the restaurant's name with them and have now changed it to match the castle. Even though it's now in a more regal and spacious 60-seat setting, under 19th-century Louis Philippe–style plasterwork, the spotlight is still on the food. It includes such entrees as suprême of chicken with Cashel blue cheese, escallops of pork with Morvandelle cream sauce, and roast farmyard duckling with black-cherry-and-port sauce.

MODERATE

Austie's/The Elsinore. Rosses Point Rd. (4 miles/6.5km northwest of Sligo), Rosses Point, County Sligo. ☎ **071/77111.** Reservations recommended. Main courses £6–£16 ($8.40–$22.40). MC, V. Daily 6–10pm. SEAFOOD/INTERNATIONAL.

Set on a hill with lovely views of Sligo Bay, this pub-restaurant boasts nautical knick-knacks and fishnets, periscopes and corks, and paintings of sailing ships. Substantial pub grub is available during the day—open-faced "sandbank" sandwiches of crab, salmon, or smoked mackerel; crab claw, prawn, or mixed seafood salads; and hearty soups and chowders. The dinner menu offers such fresh seafood choices as panfried Dover sole, baked trout amandine, and crab au gratin, as well as steaks and chicken curry. Lobster is also available, at market prices. Outdoor seating on picnic tables is available in good weather.

✪ **Glebe House.** South of Sligo, off the main N4 road, Collooney, County Sligo. ☎ **071/67787.** Reservations recommended. Main courses £11.50–£16.95 ($16.10–$23.75). AE, MC, V. Apr–Sept daily 6:30–9:30pm; call for off-season hours. IRISH/FRENCH.

In a restored Georgian house near Collooney village and the Owenmore River, this homey restaurant is run by an Irish-French couple, Brid and Marc Torraden. They serve a sort of *cuisine bourgeoise,* and rely heavily on fresh herbs and vegetables picked from the gardens that surround the house. The menu changes daily, but often includes symphony of the sea (the day's best catch), noisettes of lamb with garlic, chicken breast filled with basil and mustard seed, panfried wild salmon with sorrel, roast beef and Yorkshire pudding, and pancake of vegetables in light mustard sauce. Bed-and-breakfast is available April through September.

INEXPENSIVE

✪ **The Cottage.** 4 Castle St., Sligo, County Sligo. ☎ **071/45319.** All items £1.50–£11.50 ($2.10–$16.10). No credit cards. Daily 9am–5:30pm; Fri–Sun 7:30–10:30pm. IRISH/VEGETARIAN.

For a light meal or snack, try this cottage-style vegetarian and whole-food restaurant in the heart of town. The emphasis is on fresh local ingredients, organic whenever possible. It's known for quiche, chili, pizza, baked potatoes with varied fillings, crab claws, seafood chowders, and hot open sandwiches on French bread topped with melted cheese. There is self-service and table service. The evening menu is eclectic, ranging from ethnic dishes to superb local seafood. All pastries and desserts are homemade, and you can tell.

The Winding Stair. Hyde Bridge House, Sligo, County Sligo. ☎ **071/41244.** All items £1.50–£5 ($2.10–$7). MC, V. Mon–Sat 10am–6pm. IRISH.

At the sister shop of the Winding Stair in Dublin, you'll find both food and food for thought. There's a wide selection of new, secondhand, and antiquarian books, along with self-service food that is simple and healthy—sandwiches made with additive-free meats or fruits (such as banana and honey), organic salads, homemade soups, confections, and natural juices.

SLIGO AFTER DARK
PUBS

The Blue Lagoon Tudor Room. Riverside, Sligo, County Sligo. ☎ **071/45407.**

Overlooking the Garavogue River, this pub is a 5-minute walk from the town center. It offers traditional Irish music sessions on Monday nights, ballads on Thursday, and a nightclub every Saturday. There is no cover charge.

Hargadon Brothers. 4 O'Connell St., Sligo, County Sligo. ☎ **071/70933.**

More than a century old, this is the most atmospheric bar in the center of the downtown area. Although it is strictly a pub now, it also used to be a grocery shop, as you'll see if you glance at the shelves on the right. The decor is a mélange of dark-wood walls, mahogany counters, stone floors, colored glass, old barrels and bottles, snugs (small private rooms), and alcoves lined with early prints of Sligo.

Stanford Village Inn. Main St., Dromahair, County Leitrim. ☎ **071/64140.**

If you're driving around Lough Gill from Sligo, this 160-year-old pub is a great mid-way stop for a drink or a snack. The decor is a delightful blend of old stone walls, vintage pictures and posters, oil lamps, and tweed-covered furnishings.

✪ **The Thatch.** Dublin–Sligo Rd. (N4), Ballisodare, County Sligo. ☎ **071/67288.**

Established in 1638 as a coaching inn, this pub is about 5 miles (8km) south of Sligo on the main road. It has a fully thatched roof and a whitewashed exterior, with a country-cottage motif inside. Irish traditional music usually starts at 9pm on Thursday and Sunday year-round, and Tuesday through Sunday in August.

Yeats Tavern. Donegal Rd. (N15), Drumcliffe, County Sligo. ☎ **071/63117.**

Four miles (6.5km) north of Sligo, across the road from the famous churchyard where William Butler Yeats is buried, this pub honors the poet's memory with quotations from his works, photos, prints, and murals. A modern tavern and restaurant with a copper-and-wood decor, it is a convenient place to stop for a snack or a full meal when touring Yeats Country.

THE PERFORMING ARTS

The Factory. Lower Quay St., Sligo, County Sligo. ☎ **071/70431.** Tickets £5–£7 ($7–$9.80). Curtain usually 8pm.

This is home to Sligo's award-winning Blue Raincoat Theatre Company. It is one of only three professional Irish acting companies (the Abbey in Dublin and the Druid in Galway are the others) that own their own theaters. The Factory was completely renovated in 1999. During July and August, the Blue Raincoat Theatre Company often presents lunchtime performances of Yeats's plays, as well as other Sligo-related productions.

Hawk's Well Theatre. Temple St., Sligo, County Sligo. ☎ **071/61518.** Tickets £6–£8 ($8.40–$11.20). Mon–Sat box office 10am–6pm; most shows 8pm.

The premier stage of Ireland's northwest region, this modern 350-seat theater presents a varied program of drama, comedy, ballet, opera, and concerts of modern and traditional music. It derives its name from *At the Hawk's Well,* a one-act play by Yeats. The theater occasionally produces shows, but mostly books visiting professional and local companies.

2 Donegal Town

138 miles (222km) NW of Dublin, 176 miles (283km) NE of Shannon Airport, 41 miles (66km) NE of Sligo, 43 miles (69km) SW of Derry, 112 miles (180km) W of Belfast, 127 miles (205km) NE of Galway, 250 miles (403km) N of Cork, and 253 miles (407km) NE of Killarney

Situated on the estuary of the River Eske on Donegal Bay, Donegal Town (pop. 3,000) is a very walkable little metropolis that's a pivotal gateway for touring the county. As recently as the 1940s, the town's central Diamond was used as a market for trading livestock and goods. Today, the marketing is more in the form of tweeds and tourist goods.

ESSENTIALS

GETTING THERE   **Aer Arann** operates regularly scheduled flights from Dublin to **Donegal Airport,** Carrickfinn, Kincasslagh, County Donegal (☎ **075/48284**), about 40 miles (65km) northwest of Donegal Town on the Atlantic coast.

Bus Eireann (☎ 074/21309) operates daily bus service to Donegal Town to and from Dublin, Derry, Sligo, Galway, and other points. All tickets are issued on the bus. The pickup and boarding point is in front of the Abbey Hotel on The Diamond.

There are also a small number of private bus companies serving the northwest region. For example, **McGeehan's Coaches** (☎ 075/46150) operates multiple daily buses between Donegal and Dublin. They leave from the Garda Station opposite the Donegal Tourist Office. Between Galway and Donegal (via Ballyshannon, Bundoran, and Sligo), **Feda O'Donnell** (☎ 075/48114 in Donegal, 091/761656 in Galway) operates at least one daily private coach. Other routes are also available.

If you're driving from the south, Donegal is reached on N15 from Sligo or A46 or A47 from Northern Ireland; from the east and north, it's N15 and N56; from the west, N56 leads to Donegal Town.

VISITOR INFORMATION   The **Donegal Tourist Office,** Quay Street (☎ 073/21148), is open Easter through September, Monday to Friday 9am to 5pm, Saturday 10am to 2pm, with extended hours in July and August.

TOWN LAYOUT   Donegal Town (pop. 3,000), which sits to the east of the River Eske, is laid out around a triangular central mall or market area called "The Diamond." **Main Street** and **Upper Main Street,** which form the prime commercial strip, extend northeast from The Diamond.

GETTING AROUND   Easily walkable, Donegal has no local bus service within the town. If you need a taxi, call **McGroary Cabs** (☎ 073/35240) or **Marley Taxis** (☎ 074/33013).

There is free parking along the Quay beside the tourist office and off Main Street.

Follow the signposted walking tour of Donegal Town; a booklet outlining the walk is available at the tourist office and most bookshops.

FAST FACTS   Two good local drugstores are **Begley's Pharmacy,** The Diamond (☎ 073/21232), and **Kelly's Pharmacy,** The Diamond (☎ 073/21031).

In an emergency, dial ☎ **999.** Donegal **District Hospital** is on Upper Main Street (☎ 073/21019). The local Garda Station is on Quay Street (☎ 073/21021).

Donegal Library, Mountcharles Road (☎ 073/21105), is open Monday, Wednesday, and Friday 3 to 6pm, Saturday 11am to 1pm and 2 to 6pm.

The **Donegal Post Office** on Tirconnail Street (☎ 073/21001) is open Monday, Tuesday, and Thursday to Saturday 9am to 5:30pm, Wednesday 9:30am to 5:30pm.

EXPLORING DONEGAL TOWN

The greatest attraction of Donegal Town is the town layout itself, a happy mix of medieval and modern buildings. Most of the structures of interest are there for you to enjoy at will, with no admission charges, no audiovisuals, no interpretive exhibits, and no crowds.

The Diamond is the triangular market area of town. It's dominated by a 25-foot-high obelisk erected as a memorial to four early17th-century Irish clerics from the local abbey who wrote *The Annals of Ireland,* the first recorded history of Gaelic Ireland.

Lough Derg, filled with many islands, lies about 10 miles (16km) east of Donegal. Legend has it that St. Patrick spent 40 days and 40 nights fasting in a cavern at this secluded spot, and since then it has been revered as a place of penance and pilgrimage. From June 1 to August 15, thousands of Irish people take turns coming to Lough Derg to do penance for 3 days at a time, remaining awake and eating nothing but tea and toast. It's considered one of the most rigorous pilgrimages in all of Christendom. To reach the lake, take R232 to Pettigo, then R233 for 5 miles (8km).

✪ Donegal Castle. Castle St., Donegal, County Donegal. ☎ 073/22405. Admission £3 ($4.20) adults, £1.50 ($2.10) seniors, £1 ($1.40) students and children, £5 ($7) family. Daily 9:30am–6:30pm. Closed Nov to mid-Mar.

Built in the 15th century beside the River Eske, this magnificent castle was once the chief stronghold for the O'Donnells, a powerful Donegal clan. In the 17th century, during the Plantation period, it came into the possession of Sir Basil Brook, who added an extension with 10 gables, a large bay window, and smaller mullioned windows in Jacobean style. The standing remains of the castle were beautifully restored and opened to the public in June 1996. Free 25-minute guided tours are available.

✪ The Friary of Donegal. The Quay, Donegal, County Donegal. Free admission.

Often mistakenly referred to as the Abbey, this Franciscan house was founded in 1474 by the first Red Hugh O'Donnell and his wife, Nuala O'Brien of Munster. Sitting in a peaceful spot where the River Eske meets Donegal Bay, it was generously endowed by the O'Donnell family and became an important center of religion and learning. Great gatherings of clergy and lay leaders assembled here in 1539. It was from this friary that some of the scholars undertook to salvage old Gaelic manuscripts and compile *The Annals of the Four Masters* (1632–36). Unfortunately, little remains of its glory days, except some impressive ruins of a church and a cloister.

Memorial Church of the Four Masters. Upper Main St., Donegal, County Donegal. ☎ 073/21026. Free admission; donations welcome. Mon–Fri 8am–6pm; Sat–Sun 7:30am–7:30pm.

Perched on a small hill overlooking the town, this Catholic church is officially known as St. Patrick's Church of the Four Masters. It is of fairly recent vintage, built in 1935 in Irish Romanesque style of red granite from nearby Barnesmore. It is dedicated to the four men who produced *The Annals of Ireland*. The church grounds are private.

South Donegal Railway Exhibition Centre. Anderson's Yard, off The Diamond, Donegal, County Donegal. No phone. Free admission. Mon–Sat 10am–5pm. Closed Oct–May.

This center houses displays dealing with County Donegal's narrow-gauge railway, which originally extended for 125 miles (202km), and ceased to operate by 1960. It's currently in the process of restoration; it is hoped that a section of the railway that runs through the scenic Barnesmore Gap will be restored. The displays include photographs, artifacts, posters, tickets, and equipment.

SHOPPING

Most Donegal shops are open Monday to Saturday 9am to 6pm, with extended hours in summer and slightly shorter hours in winter.

✪ Donegal Craft Village. Ballyshannon Rd., Donegal, County Donegal. ☎ 073/22015. E-mail: celticforest@eircom.net.

You'll find this cluster of individual craft-workers' shops in a rural setting about a mile south of town. This project provides a creative environment for an ever-changing group of artisans who practice a range of ancient and modern crafts: porcelain, ceramics, hand weaving, batik, jewelry, metalwork, visual art, and Irish musical instrument making. You can buy some one-of-a-kind treasures or just browse from shop to shop and watch the craftspeople at work. The coffee shop serves snacks and lunch in the summer only, and the grounds are a great place for a picnic. The craft studios are open January to Easter Monday to Friday 9:30am to 5:30pm; Easter through May and September to Christmas, Monday to Saturday 9:30am to 5:30pm; June to August, Monday to Saturday 9:30am to 5:30pm, Sunday 10:30am to 5:30pm.

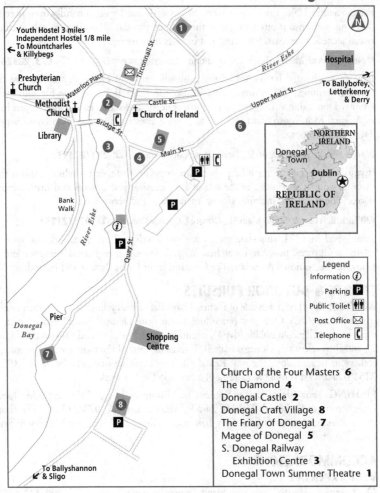

Legend
Information ⓘ
Parking 🅿
Public Toilet 🚻
Post Office ✉
Telephone ☏

Church of the Four Masters **6**
The Diamond **4**
Donegal Castle **2**
Donegal Craft Village **8**
The Friary of Donegal **7**
Magee of Donegal **5**
S. Donegal Railway
   Exhibition Centre **3**
Donegal Town Summer Theatre **1**

Forget-Me-Not/The Craft Shop. The Diamond, Donegal, County Donegal. ☎ **073/21168.**

This shop features a wide selection of gifts both usual and unusual. Items include handmade jewelry, Celtic art cards, Donegal County banners and hangings, woolly sheep mobiles, Irish traditional music figures, tweed paintings, bog oak sculptures, and beaten-copper art.

The Four Master Bookshop. The Diamond, Donegal, County Donegal. ☎ **073/21526.**

Facing the monument commemorating the Four Masters, this shop specializes in books of Irish and Donegal interest, plus Waterford crystal, Celtic-design watches, Masons ironstone figures, and souvenir jewelry.

✪ **Magee of Donegal Ltd.** The Diamond, Donegal, County Donegal. ☎ **073/22660.** www.mageeshop.com.

Established in 1866, this shop is synonymous with fine Donegal hand-woven tweeds. Weaving demonstrations take place throughout the day. Products on sale include tweed jackets, overcoats, hats, ties, and batches of material.

Melody Maker Music Shop. The Diamond, Donegal, County Donegal. ☎ **073/22326.**

If you're enchanted by the traditional and folk music of Donegal, stop in here for tapes, recordings, and posters. This is also the main ticket agency for southwest County Donegal, handling tickets for most concerts and sports nationwide. Open July to August, Monday to Saturday 9am to 7pm; September to June, Monday to Saturday 9:30am to 6pm.

Wards Music Shop. Castle St., Donegal, County Donegal. ☎ **073/21313.**

If you'd like to take home a harp, bodhran, bagpipe, flute, or tin whistle, this is the shop for you. It specializes in the sale of Irish musical instruments and instructional books. The stock also includes violins, mandolins, and accordions.

William Britton & Sons. Main St., Donegal, County Donegal. ☎ **071/21131.**

Established in 1874, this shop stocks antique jewelry, silver, crystal, clocks, sports-related sculptures, pens, and watches. W. J. Britton is a registered appraiser and a fellow of the National Association of Goldsmiths of Great Britain and Ireland.

SPORTS & OUTDOOR PURSUITS

BICYCLING   The north side of Donegal Bay offers great cycling roads—tremendously scenic and very hilly. One good but arduous route from Donegal Town follows the coast roads west to Glencolumbkille (day 1), continues north to Ardara and Dawros Head (day 2), and then returns to Donegal (day 3). It takes in some of the most spectacular coastal scenery in Ireland along the way. Rental bikes are available from **Pat Boyle** (☎ **073/22515**). The cost is roughly £7 ($9.80) a day, £45 ($63) a week.

FISHING   For advice and equipment for fishing in Lough Eske and other local waters, contact **Doherty's Fishing Tackle,** Main Street (☎ **073/21119**). The shop stocks a wide selection of flies, reels, bait, and fishing poles. It's open Monday to Saturday 9am to 6pm.

ACCOMMODATIONS
VERY EXPENSIVE

✪ **St. Ernan's House.** St. Ernan's Island, Donegal, County Donegal. ☎ **800/323-5463** from the U.S., or 073/21065. Fax 073/22098. www.sainternans.com. 12 units. TV TEL. £146–£250 ($204.40–$350) single or double. No service charge. Rates include full breakfast. MC, V. Closed Nov–Mar.

This is one of the area's most unusual lodgings—an 1826 country house that occupies an entire small island in Donegal Bay and is connected to the mainland by its own causeway. The island, named for a 7th-century Irish monk, is planted with hawthorn and holly bushes that have been blooming for almost 3 centuries. The public areas and the Georgian-theme dining room, which is acclaimed for its cuisine, have all been magnificently restored. They hold delicate plasterwork, high ceilings, crystal chandeliers, gilt-framed oil paintings, heirloom silver, antiques, and open log fireplaces. The guest rooms, all individually decorated by proprietors Brian and Carmel O'Dowd, have traditional furnishings, with dark woods, designer fabrics, floral art, and period pieces; most have views of the water. It's a delightful spot, almost like a kingdom unto itself, yet less than 2 miles (3.2km) south of Donegal Town.

MODERATE

The Abbey. The Diamond, Donegal, County Donegal. ☎ **073/21014.** Fax 073/23660. 49 units. TV TEL. £90–£110 ($126–$154) double. Rates include full breakfast and service charge. AE, DC, MC, V.

In the heart of town, with The Diamond at its front door and the River Eske at its back, this vintage three-story hotel has been updated and refurbished in recent years. The guest rooms, about half of which are in a new wing overlooking the river, have standard furnishings, bright floral fabrics, hair dryers, and garment presses. The Eske restaurant overlooks the back gardens; the modern bilevel Eas Dun Bar and Corabber Lounge has views of the River Eske; and an outdoor beer garden and patio offers great waterside views.

✪ **Harvey's Point Country Hotel.** Lough Eske, Donegal, County Donegal. ☎ **073/22208.** Fax 073/22352. E-mail: harveyspoint@eircom.ie. 20 units. MINIBAR TV TEL. £98–£110 ($137.20–$154) double. Rates include full breakfast. AE, DC, MC, V. Closed weekdays Nov–Mar. Free parking.

Four miles (6.5km) northwest of town, this modern, rambling, Swiss-style lodge occupies a 13-acre woodland setting on the shores of Lough Eske at the foot of the Blue Stack Mountains. The guest rooms, most of which feature views of Lough Eske and the hills of Donegal, have traditional furnishings, hair dryers, and tea/coffeemakers. Some have four-poster beds. There are a piano bar and lounge, and a first-rate coat-and-tie lakeside restaurant offering gourmet French cuisine from £14.50 to £17 ($20.30 to $23.80). The restaurant was recently expanded down to the edge of the Lough, so ask for a table by the window and enjoy the sunset on the water. For extra fees, there are two tennis courts, bicycle and boat hire, and trips on Harvey's Jarvey, a Clydesdale horse wagon.

Hyland Central. The Diamond, Donegal, County Donegal. ☎ **800/528-1234** from the U.S., or 073/21027. Fax 073/22295. 91 units. TV TEL. £70–£100 ($98–$140) double. Service charge 10%. Rates include full breakfast. AE, DC, MC, V. Closed Dec 24–27.

Owned and operated by the Hyland family since 1941, this four-story hotel faces Donegal's main thoroughfare; in back, a modern extension overlooks Lough Eske. Guest rooms are outfitted with traditional furnishings of dark woods, light florals, and quilted fabrics. Each room has a tea/coffeemaker and garment press; many rooms have views of the water. The new bistro-carvery overlooks Lough Eske, and there's an old-world pub lounge. The hotel has an indoor heated swimming pool, a Jacuzzi, a steam room, a sun bed, and a gym.

✪ **Rhu-Gorse.** Lough Eske Dr. (5 miles/8km outside of Donegal), Lough Eske, Donegal, County Donegal. ☎ and fax **073/21685.** E-mail: rhugorse@iol.ie. 3 units. £45–£55 ($63–$77) double. Rates include full breakfast. MC, V. Closed Nov–Mar. From Donegal, follow road to Killybegs; after ¼ miles (0.4km), turn right onto Lough Eske Dr. and follow signs.

This has to be one of the most simply satisfying B&Bs in Ireland. It's one of our hands-down favorites. Winding your way here is an effort well rewarded. A modern home of stature and character, Rhu-Gorse has a North Woods feel, with an ample stone fireplace, open beams, duvets, and lots of custom-fitted pine. Best of all are the panoramic views of Lough Eske and the encircling Blue Stack Mountains. Your traveler's stride might be broken by a sudden loss of all will to move on. Beds are firm, and smoking is not permitted in the rooms.

DINING

In addition to the dining rooms in the hotels listed above, try these restaurants for a snack or light meal.

Errigal. Upper Main St., Donegal, County Donegal. ☎ **073/21428.** Fish-and-chips £3–£5 ($4.20–$7). No credit cards. Oct–May Tues–Sat noon–11:30pm, Sun 4–11:30pm; June–Sept Mon, Tues, Thurs 12:30–11:30pm, Fri–Sun 4–11:30pm. FISH-AND-CHIPS.

Once a full-service restaurant, the family-run Errigal now focuses its culinary energies on a range of fresh fried fish-and-chips. Its current business is primarily takeout; there's limited seating. It's opposite the Church of the Four Masters.

The Weaver's Loft. In the Magee Shop, The Diamond, Donegal, County Donegal. ☎ **073/22660.** Main courses £3.50–£4.95 ($4.90–$6.95). AE, DC, MC, V. Mon–Sat 9:45am–5pm. IRISH.

Upstairs from Magee's tweed shop, this 60-seat self-service restaurant with its huge mural of Donegal on the wall conveys an aura of times past. The menu changes daily, but usually includes prawn, cheese, and fruit salads, as well as sandwiches, soups, cakes, and tarts.

DONEGAL AFTER DARK

If you're in Donegal during July and August, try to take in a performance of the Donegal Drama Circle at the **Donegal Town Summer Theatre,** O'Cleary Hall, Tirconnaill Street (no phone). Performances are held on Tuesday, Wednesday, and Thursday at 9pm, and feature works by Donegal-based playwrights. No reservations are necessary; admission prices start at £4 ($5.60) for adults, £2 ($2.80) for students.

PUBS

Biddys O'Barnes. Donegal–Lifford Rd. (N15), Barnesmore, County Donegal. ☎ **073/21402.**

It's worth a detour into the Blue Stack Mountains and the scenic Barnesmore Gap, 7 miles (11km) northeast of Donegal Town, to visit this pub, which has been in the same family for four generations. Stepping inside is like entering a country cottage, with blazing turf fires, stone floors, wooden stools and benches, and old hutches full of plates and bric-a-brac. A picture of Biddy, who once owned the house, hangs over the main fireplace. On most evenings there's a spontaneous music session.

Charlie's Star Bar. Main St., Donegal, County Donegal. ☎ **073/21158.**

The wins and losses of Donegal's hurling and Gaelic football teams are the topics of conversation at this bar, with its decor of team jerseys, pictures, and equipment. On some nights, there is spontaneous fiddle music.

The Olde Castle Bar. Castle St. Donegal, County Donegal. ☎ **073/21062.**

There is an old-Donegal aura at this little pub, which has a welcoming open fireplace, etched glass, whitewashed walls, and old jars and crocks.

The Schooner Inn. Upper Main St., Donegal, County Donegal. ☎ **073/21671.**

Model ships and seafaring memorabilia decorate this pub. There is music on most summer evenings, with traditional Irish music on Monday and Saturday, folk on Wednesday, and singing acts on Thursday, Friday, and Sunday.

3 The Donegal Bay Coast

The Donegal Bay coast extends for 50 miles (80km): from Bundoran, 20 miles (32km) S of Donegal Town, to Glencolumbkille, 30 miles (48km) W of Donegal Town

The Donegal Bay coast is composed of two almost equal parts: the area from Ballyshannon north to Donegal Town (Southern Donegal Bay) and the area west of Donegal Town, stretching to Glencolumbkille (Northern Donegal Bay). On a map, the coast looks like a lobster claw reaching out from Donegal Town to grasp the bay's beautiful waters. Beaches, water sports, and coastal scenery are definitely the main drawing cards, but the Donegal Bay coast holds many other attractions, from bustling seaport towns to folk museums and craft centers.

For scenic beauty, the two sides of the coast are far from equal. The southern side tends more toward the tourist (read tacky) seaside resort, with Bundoran as the litmus; Rossnowlagh is somewhat more appealing, however, and does have one of the finest beaches in the region. The northern Donegal Bay coast, on the other hand, is nothing short of spectacular. Once you travel west of Killybegs, the mountains reach right to the sea, creating the beautifully indented coastline around Kilcar and the incomparable Slieve League cliffs.

AREA ESSENTIALS

GETTING THERE & GETTING AROUND   **Ireland Airways** operates regularly scheduled flights from Dublin to Donegal Airport, Carrickfinn, Kincasslagh, County Donegal (☎ **075/48284**), about 40 miles (65km) north of Killybegs.

Bus Eireann (☎ **074/21309**) operates daily bus service to Killybegs and Glencolumbkille, on the northern half of the bay, and to Ballyshannon and Bundoran, on the southern half of the bay.

The best way to get to and around Donegal Bay is by car. Follow the N15 route on the southern half of the bay, the N56 route on the northern half of the bay.

VISITOR INFORMATION   Contact the **North West Tourism Office,** Aras Reddan, Temple Street, Sligo (☎ **071/61201**); the **Letterkenny Tourist Office,** Derry Road, Letterkenny (☎ **074/21160**); or **Bundoran Tourist Office,** Main Street, Bundoran, County Donegal (☎ **072/41350**). The first two are open year-round; the third is open from June through August.

SOUTHERN DONEGAL BAY

To reach the southern section of Donegal Bay from Sligo, take the N15 road up the Atlantic coast, and at about 20 miles (32km) north you'll come to **Bundoran,** the southern tip of County Donegal and a major beach resort.

Continuing up the coast, you'll pass **Ballyshannon,** dating back to the 15th century and one of the oldest inhabited towns in Ireland; it's another favorite with beachgoers, and boasts some 21 lively pubs, many offering traditional music in the evenings. In late July or early August there's the famous **Ballyshannon Folk Festival,** when music rings through the streets day and night.

Two kilometers (just over a mile) northwest of town, the once-famous Cistercian **Assaroe Abbey,** founded in 1184, now lies in ruins, although its mill wheel has been restored and is driven by water from the Abbey River just as in ancient days. Some 50 meters away, at the edge of the Abbey River, **Catsby Cave** is a grottolike setting where a rough-hewn altar reminds you that mass was celebrated here during the penal years when the ritual was prohibited by law.

At this point, leave the main road and head for the coastal resort of **Rossnowlagh,** one of the loveliest beaches in this part of Ireland. At over 2 miles (3.2km) long and as wide as the tides allow, it's a flat sandy stretch, shielded by flower-filled hills, and ideal for walking. You'll see horses racing on it occasionally. This spot is a splendid vantage point for watching sunsets over the churning foam-rimmed waters of the Atlantic.

Overlooking the beach from a hilltop is the **Franciscan Friary,** Rossnowlagh (☎ **072/51342**), which houses a small museum of local Donegal history. The complex also contains beautiful gardens and walks overlooking the sea, a tearoom with outdoor seating, and a shop with religious objects. Open daily from 10am to 8pm. There's no admission charge, but donations are welcome.

From Rossnowlagh, return to the main road via the **Donegal Golf Club** (see "Sports & Outdoor Pursuits," below) at Murvagh, a spectacular setting nestled on a rugged sandy peninsula of primeval duneland, surrounded by a wall of dense woodlands. From here, the road curves inland and it's less than 10 miles (16km) to Donegal town.

Shopping

Britton and Daughters. Off the Ballyshannon–Donegal road, Rossnowlagh, County Donegal. ☎ **072/52220.**

In a cottage opposite the Sand House Hotel, this workshop is a source of unusual artistic crafts. Its wares include mirrors or glass hand-etched with local scenes and Celtic, nautical, floral, and wildlife designs; prints of traditional musicians; carved rocks (heads, Celtic designs, dolphins, and so on); posters; and pottery with surfing and Irish music themes. Open Monday to Friday 10am to 6pm, plus Saturday in July and August.

Donegal Parian China. Bundoran Rd. (N15), Ballyshannon, County Donegal. ☎ **072/ 51826.**

Established in 1985, this pottery works produces wafer-thin Parian china gift items and tableware in patterns of the shamrock, rose, hawthorn, and other Irish flora. Free guided tours (every 20 min.) enable visitors to watch as vases, bells, spoons, thimbles, wall plaques, lamps, and eggshell coffee and tea sets are shaped, decorated, fired, and polished. There are an audiovisual room, an art gallery, a tearoom, and a showroom and shop. Open June through September daily 9am to 6pm.

Sports & Outdoor Pursuits

BEACHES   Donegal Bay's beaches are wide, sandy, clean, and flat—ideal for walking. The best are **Rossnowlagh** and **Bundoran.** At Rossnowlagh, surfing is a favorite pastime. When the surf is up, you can rent boards and wet suits locally for roughly £3 ($4.20) per hour per item.

GOLF   The Donegal Bay coast is home to two outstanding 18-hole championship seaside golf courses. **Donegal Golf Club,** Murvagh, Ballintra, County Donegal (☎ **073/34054**), is 3 miles (4.8km) north of Rossnowlagh and 7 miles (11km) south of Donegal Town. It's a par-73 course with greens fees of £25 ($35) weekdays, £30 ($42) weekends.

The Bundoran Golf Club, off the Sligo-Ballyshannon road (N15), Bundoran, County Donegal (☎ **072/41302**), is a par-69 course designed by the great Harry Vardon. The greens fees are £18 ($25.20) weekdays, £22 ($30.80) weekends.

HORSEBACK RIDING   **Stracomer Riding School Ltd.,** off the Sligo-Ballyshannon road (N15), Bundoran, County Donegal (☎ **072/41787**), specializes in trail riding on the surrounding farmlands, beaches, dunes, and mountain trails. An hour's ride averages £10 ($14).

Accommodations

Great Northern Hotel. Sligo–Donegal Rd. (N15), Bundoran, County Donegal. ☎ **072/ 41204.** Fax 072/41114. 98 units. TV TEL. £120–£130 ($168–$182) double. Rates include full Irish breakfast and service charge. AE, MC, V. Closed Jan.

Surrounded by 130 acres of parkland and sand dunes beside an 18-hole golf links, this sprawling multiwinged hotel is right on Donegal Bay. The hotel's interior was recently refurbished with a bright modern Irish motif, and the rooms were stylishly

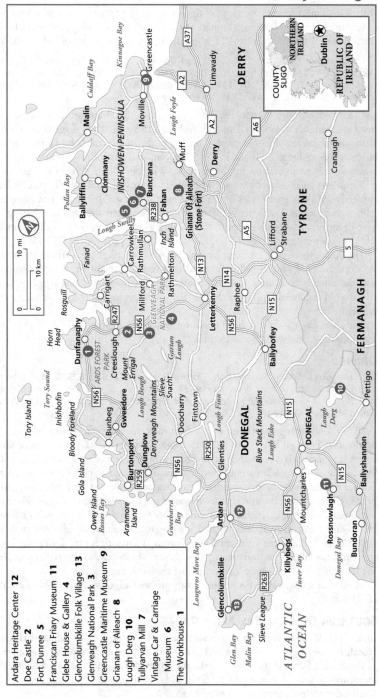

County Donegal

INISHOWEN PENINSULA

Kinnagoe Bay
Culdaff Bay
Greencastle **9**
Malin
Moville
Lough Foyle
Muff
Pollan Bay
Ballyliffin
Clonmany
Buncrana **6 7**
5
R238
Fahan
Grianan Of Aileach (Stone Fort) **8**
Lough Swilly
Fanad
Rosguill
Carrowkeel
Rathmullan
Carrigart
Inch Island
Rathmelton
Millford
2
R247
GLENVEAGH NATIONAL PARK
N56
3
4
Letterkenny
Raphoe
N56
N13
N14

Horn Head
Dunfanaghy **1**
ARDS FOREST PARK
Creeslough
Mount Errigal
N56
Ballybofey
N15

Tory Island
Tory Sound
Inishbofin
Bloody Foreland
Bunbeg
Gweedore
Lough Beagh
Slieve Snacht
Fintown
Doocharry
Gartan Lough
N56
R250
Lough Finn
Blue Stack Mountains
Lough Eske
DONEGAL
Donegal
N15

Gola Island
Owey Island
Rosses Bay
Aranmore Island
Burtonport
R259
Dunglow
Glenties
N56
Mountcharles
N56
Rossnowlagh **11**
N15
Ballyshannon

Gweebarra Bay
Ardara **12**
Killybegs
Inver Bay
Donegal Bay
Bundoran

Loughros More Bay
Glencolumbkille **13**
R263
Slieve League
Glen Bay
Malin Bay
ATLANTIC OCEAN

DERRY
Limavady
A37
A2
A2
Derry
A6
TYRONE
Cranaugh
Lifford
Strabane
A5
5
FERMANAGH
Pettigo **10**
Lough Derg

COUNTY SLIGO
NORTHERN IRELAND
REPUBLIC OF IRELAND
Dublin

10 mi
10 km

Ardara Heritage Center **12**
Doe Castle **2**
Fort Dunree **5**
Franciscan Friary Museum **11**
Glebe House & Gallery **4**
Glencolumbkille Folk Village **13**
Glenveagh National Park **3**
Greencastle Maritime Museum **9**
Grianan of Aileach **8**
Lough Derg **10**
Tullyarvan Mill **7**
Vintage Car & Carriage Museum **6**
The Workhouse **1**

redecorated; most rooms have views of the sea or the golf course. The hotel has a full-service restaurant, a grill room, a lounge, a heated outdoor swimming pool, and a lawn tennis court. A favorite with Irish families, it's on the northern edge of Bundoran.

✪ **Sand House Hotel.** Off the Ballyshannon–Donegal road (N15), Rossnowlagh, County Donegal. ☎ **800/44UTELL** from the U.S., or 072/51777. Fax 072/52100. www.sandhouse-hotel.ie. 45 units. TEL. £99–£130 ($138.60–$182) double. Rates include full Irish breakfast and service charge. AE, MC, V. Closed late Oct–early Apr.

On a crescent of beach overlooking the Atlantic coast, this award-winning three-story hotel is a standout in County Donegal. Although there are subtle suggestions of turreting on the roof, it does not pretend to be a castle. In fact, the Sand House started out as a fishing lodge in 1886. In 1949, Vincent and Mary Britton moved in and began their quest to create a top-notch hotel. With open log and turf fireplaces, the public rooms are decorated with antiques and local artwork, and a sunlit, plant-filled conservatory offers great views of the sea. Guest rooms are decorated with designer fabrics, antiques, and such period pieces as hand-carved armoires and vanities; some have canopied or four-poster beds. Wide picture windows with vistas of the Atlantic add the crowning touch.

The dining room—which, surprisingly, does not overlook the sea—is presided over by a creative chef who specializes in locally harvested Donegal Bay lobster, oysters, scallops, mussels, and other seafood. The lounge, cozy with an open fireplace, is a relaxing old-fashioned setting; the Surfers Bar is a larger gathering spot with a nautical decor.

The hotel has a 2-mile (3.2km) beach for walking, swimming, surfing, and other water sports; a tennis court; and croquet.

DINING

✪ **Smugglers Creek.** Rossnowlagh, County Donegal. ☎ **072/52366.** Reservations required for dinner. Dinner main courses £8–£16.75 ($11.20–$23.45); lobster £19.50 ($27.30). DC, MC, V. Daily 12:30–3pm and 6–9:30pm; evening sittings 6:30 and 8:30pm. Closed Mon–Tues Oct–Easter. SEAFOOD/IRISH.

For great food with grand sunset views, don't miss this little gem perched on a cliff overlooking Donegal Bay. It's in an 1845 stone building that has been restored and enlarged to include a conservatory-style dining area with open fireplaces, beamed ceilings, stone walls, wooden stools, porthole windows, crab traps, and lobster pots. Besides the views and homey, nautical decor, seafood is the star attraction, and proprietor Conor Britton even pulls his own oysters and mussels from local beds. The bar menu ranges from soups, salads, and sandwiches to buttered garlic mussels or fresh pâté. Dinner entrees include Smugglers sea casserole (scallops, salmon, and prawns with Mornay sauce), deep-fried squid with Provençal sauce, tiger prawns in garlic butter, wild Irish salmon hollandaise, steaks with whiskey sauce, and vegetarian pasta or stir-fry dishes. The restaurant is nonsmoking; the bar is not.

More than a dozen new B&B rooms with private bathroom are available for £55 ($77) double.

SOUTHERN DONEGAL BAY AFTER DARK

In summer, **Rossnowlagh** is a hub of social activity. People flock to the **Sand House Hotel,** Rossnowlagh, County Donegal (☎ 072/51777), for the nautical atmosphere of the Surfers Bar and the Slice of Ireland Cabaret. It's a 1-hour show of Donegal-theme music, song, dance, poetry, comedy, and drama, presented July and August on Wednesday at 9pm. Admission is roughly £5 ($7).

Farther south, **Dorrian's Thatch Bar,** Main Street, Ballyshannon, County Donegal (☎ 072/51147), holds nightly sessions of Irish traditional music in summer.

NORTHERN DONEGAL BAY

From Donegal Town, follow the main road (N56) for a slow, scenic drive along the northern coast of Donegal Bay. You'll encounter narrow roads, sheer cliffs, craggy rocks, boglands, and panoramic mountain and sea views. You'll also see the distinctive thatched-roof cottages that are typical of this area—with rounded roofs, because a network of ropes (*sugans*) ties down the thatch and fastens it to pins beneath the eaves, to protect it from the prevailing winds off the sea. It's only 30 miles (48km) to Glencolumbkille, but plan on at least several hours' drive.

Your first stop could be at **Killybegs**—where, if your timing is right, you can watch the fishing boats unloading the day's catch—or at Studio Donegal in Kilcar, if you're casting for tweed (see "Shopping," below). A must-stop is ✪ **Slieve League,** the highest sea cliffs in Europe. The turnoff for the Bunglas viewing point is at Carrick. Once at the cliffs, you must decide whether you want to merely gaze at their 1,000-foot splendor or to experience them up-up-up close and personal on the wind-buffeted walk along the ridge. This walk is for the fearless and fit.

Just before you come to Killybegs, the N56 road swings inland and northward. Continue on the coastal road west to **Glencolumbkille,** an Atlantic outpost dating back 5,000 years. It is said that St. Columba established a monastery here in the 6th century and gave his name to the glen. In the 1950s, this area was endangered by a 75% emigration rate, until the parish priest, James McDyer, focused the energies of the town not only on ensuring the community's future, but also on preserving its past. He helped accomplish both by founding the **Glencolumbkille Folk Park** (☎ **073/30017**). Built by the people of Glencolumbkille in the form of a tiny village, or *clachan,* this modest theme park of thatched cottages—each outfitted with period furniture and artifacts—reflects life in this remote corner of Ireland over the past several centuries. Two miniature playhouses are on hand for children. The tearoom serves a simple menu of traditional Irish dishes, such as stews and *brútin,* composed mainly of hot milk and potatoes. Don't miss the Guinness cake, a house specialty. In the *sheebeen,* a shop of traditional products, don't dismiss the admittedly bizarre-sounding local wines—fuchsia, heather, seaweed, and tea and raisin—until you've tried them all. They're surprisingly good. The medium-dry heather wine finishes first on my list. Recent additions to the folk park include a new visitors reception hall and a new interpretive center, housing a range of engaging exhibits. Admission and tour are £2 ($2.80) for adults, £1.50 ($2.10) for seniors and children, £7 ($9.80) for family. It's open from Easter through September, Monday to Saturday 10am to 6pm, Sunday noon to 6pm.

To continue touring from Glencolumbkille, follow the signs for Ardara over a mountainous inland road. Soon you'll come to **Glengesh Pass,** a narrow, scenic roadway that rises to a height of 900 feet before plunging into the valley below. The road leads eventually to **Ardara,** known for its tweed and woolen craft centers (see section 4, later in this chapter, on "The Atlantic Highlands").

SHOPPING

Studio Donegal. The Glebe Mill, Kilcar, County Donegal. ☎ **073/38194.**

Started in 1979, this hand-weaving enterprise is distinguished by its knobby tweed, subtly colored in tones of beige, oat, and ash. You can walk around both the craft shop and the mill and see the chunky-weave stoles, caps, jackets, and cloaks in the making. Other products fashioned of this unique tweed include tote bags, cushion covers, table mats, tapestries, and wall hangings. It's between Killybegs and Glencolumbkille, about 20 miles (32km) west of Donegal Town. Open Monday to Friday 9am to 5:30pm; plus Saturday 9:30am to 5pm in the summer.

SPORTS & OUTDOOR PURSUITS

BICYCLING   The north side of Donegal Bay offers great cycling roads—tremendously scenic though very hilly. One good but arduous route from Donegal Town follows the coast roads west to Glencolumbkille (day 1), continues north to Ardara and Dawros Head via Glengesh Pass (day 2), and then returns to Donegal (day 3). It takes in some of the most spectacular coastal scenery in Ireland along the way. Rental bikes are available in Donegal from Pat Boyle (☎ **073/22515**) for roughly £8 ($11.20) per day and £30 ($42) per week.

FISHING   Surrounded by waters that hold shark, skate, pollock, conger, cod, and mackerel, **Killybegs** is one of the most active centers on the northwest coast for commercial and sport sea-fishing. **Brian McGilloway** (☎ **073/32444**) operates full-day fishing expeditions on the 40-foot *Aquarius,* from Blackrock Pier. Prices average £25 ($35) per person per day, plus £5 ($7) for rods and tackle, or £200 ($280) for a party of 8 to 10 (eight is preferable for comfort). The daily schedule and departure times vary according to demand; reservations are required.

At **Mountcharles,** a coastal town midway between Donegal Town and Killybegs, **Michael O'Boyle,** Old Road (☎ **073/35257**), organizes deep-sea fishing trips. Outings are slated daily from 11am to 5pm and cost £15 ($21) per person. This company also offers guided boat trips and wildlife cruises on demand; prices start at £15 ($21) per person, with a 2-hour minimum booking.

WALKING   The peninsula that extends westward from Killybegs boasts some of the most spectacular coastal scenery in Ireland, and much of it is accessible only from the sea or on foot. The grandeur of the **Slieve League** cliffs is not to be missed. The best way to visit this natural monument is to hike from the Bunglass lookout point to Tramane Strand in Malin Beg, a few miles southwest of Glencolumbkille. This walk involves crossing the renowned "One Man's Pass," a narrow ridge with steep drops on both sides that should not be attempted by the acrophobic or by anyone wearing high heels. The distance from Bunglass to Trabane Strand is 9 miles (15km), and you will have to arrange a pickup at the end. The summits of the Slieve League, rising almost 2,000 feet above the sea, are often capped in clouds, and you should think twice about undertaking the walk if there is danger of losing visibility along the way.

Another lesser-known walk that is just as spectacular is the coastal walk between Glencolumbkille and the town of **Maghera** (which is not so much a town as a small cluster of houses). Glen Head, topped by a stone tower, dominates Glencolumbkille to the north. This walk begins with a climb to the tower and continues along the cliff face for 15 miles (24km), passing only one remote outpost of human habitation along the way, the tiny town of Port. For isolated sea splendor, this is one of the finest walks in Ireland, but it should be undertaken only in fine weather by experienced walkers with adequate provisions.

ACCOMMODATIONS

✪ **Bay View Hotel.** 1–2 Main St., Killybegs, County Donegal. ☎ **073/31950.** Fax 073/31856. www.bayviewhotel.ie. 40 units. TV TEL. £90–£114 ($126–$159.60) double. No service charge. Rates include full breakfast. AE, MC, V.

Right on the harbor in the middle of town, this four-story hotel was completely renovated and refurbished in 1992. Rooms are decorated in contemporary style with light pine furnishings, bright quilted fabrics, and brass accessories, all enhanced by wide-windowed views of the marina and fishing boats. Dining choices include the ground-floor Bay View Brasserie, for light meals all day and the traditional first-floor dining room, with lovely bay views and contemporary art. There are two bars, the ground-floor Fisherman's Wharf and the first-floor Upper Deck cocktail lounge. The hotel has an indoor heated swimming pool, a sauna, a steam room, a Jacuzzi, and a gym.

✪ **Bruckless House.** Signposted on N56, 12 miles (19km) west of Donegal, Bruckless, County Donegal. ☎ **073/37071.** Fax 073/37070. E-mail: bruc@iol.ie. 4 units, 1 with private bathroom. £60 ($84) double with bathroom, £50 ($70) double with shared bathroom. No service charge. Rates include full Irish breakfast. AE, MC, V. Closed Oct–Mar.

Clive and Joan Evans have restored their mid-18th-century farmhouse with such care and taste that every room is a pleasure to enter and enjoy. Furniture and art they brought back from their years in China add a special elegance. All the guest rooms are smoke-free, spacious, and bright. The sitting and dining rooms are gracious and comfortable, and Joan's gardens have taken first prize in County Donegal's country garden competition at least twice in recent years. Inside and out, Bruckless House is a gem. Be sure to ask Clive to introduce you to his fine Connemara ponies, which he raises and treasures.

✪ **Dún Ulún House.** R263 (1 mile/1.6km west of Kilcar), Kilcar, County Donegal. ☎ **073/38137.** 10 units, 9 with private bathroom. £30–£35 ($42–$49) double. Rates include full breakfast. MC, V.

Dún Ulún House, one of the best bargains in this part of the world, caters to a remarkably diverse clientele. First there's the B&B, in a modern, purpose-built guesthouse. The building is unremarkable, but remains in the memory long after you've left, thanks to the graciousness of the Lyons family and the extraordinary beauty of the seaside scene it overlooks. The newly redecorated rooms (with orthopedic beds) are pleasant and comfortable. Then there's the cottage, also overlooking the sea, with an open fire in the kitchen and basic, functional furnishings in the private guest rooms; rates are £7.50 to £13.50 ($10.50 to $18.90) per person per night. As of 2000, there's also a separate self-catering cottage across the street, which rents by the week for £200 ($280) plus whatever electricity you use. Finally, there's an in-house traditional music group made up of the Lyonses' daughter, two nieces, and two friends; these talented musicians often play for guests. Denis Lyons is a great source of information on the archaeology of the Kilcar region, and can direct you to many fascinating and little-known sites.

The Glencolumbkille Hotel. Glencolumbkille, County Donegal. ☎ **073/30003.** Fax 073/30222. 38 units. TV TEL. £60–£70 ($84–$98) double. No service charge. Rates include full breakfast. MC, V.

If you want to get away from it all, this hotel is the westernmost outpost in Donegal. Edged by Malin Bay and the Atlantic Ocean, encircled by craggy mountains that are populated mostly by meandering woolly sheep, it's a lovely spot, with turf fireplaces to warm you and a cottage atmosphere to cheer you. There's a good dining room, with panoramic views of the countryside. A renovation of the entire hotel, begun in 1996, was completed in 2000. Most rooms have views of the sea or the valley.

DINING

✪ **The Blue Haven.** Largymore, Kilcar, County Donegal. ☎ **073/38090.** Reservations recommended for dinner. Dinner main courses £5–£12 ($7–$16.80). MC, V. May–Sept daily 11am–11pm. IRISH.

On a broad, open sweep of Donegal Bay between Killybegs and Kilcar, this modern skylit restaurant offers 180-degree views of the bay from a semicircular bank of windows. It's an ideal stop for a meal or light refreshment while touring. The bar-food menu, available throughout the day, offers soups, sandwiches, and omelets with unusual fillings. The dinner menu includes fillet of rainbow trout, lemon sole bonne femme, T-bone and sirloin steaks, and savory mushroom pancakes.

In 2000, a new addition with 15 bedrooms sprouted here with views of Donegal Bay, offering bed and breakfast for £50 ($70).

PUBS

For good conversation and atmosphere at any time, step through the half door at the **Pipers Rest,** Kilcar, County Donegal (☎ 073/38205). The thatched-roof pub has original stone walls, arches, flagged floors, an open turf fire, and a unique stained-glass window depicting a piper. Music may erupt at any time, and usually does on summer nights; the pub also features a fine collection of pipes, many of which are likely to be in use.

4 The Atlantic Highlands

The Atlantic Highlands start at Ardara, 25 miles (40km) NW of Donegal Town, 10 miles (16km) N of Killybegs

Scenery is the keynote to the Atlantic Highlands of Donegal—vast stretches of coastal and mountain scenery, beaches and bays, rocks and ruins. It's sometimes lonely, but always breathtaking. Set far off the beaten track and deep amid the coastal scenery is Mount Errigal, the highest mountain in Donegal (2,466 ft.). It gently slopes down to one of Ireland's greatest visitor attractions, the **Glenveagh National Park.**

The best place to start a tour of Donegal's Atlantic Highlands is at **Ardara,** a small town on the coast about 25 miles (40km) northwest of Donegal Town. From here, it's easy to weave your way up the coast. This drive can take 4 hours or 4 days, depending on your schedule and interests.

The deeper you get into this countryside, the more you'll be immersed in a section known as the *Gaeltacht,* or Irish-speaking area. This should present no problems, except that most of the road signs are only in Irish. If you keep to the main road (N56), you should have no difficulties. If you follow little roads off to the seashore or down country paths, you might have a problem figuring out where you're going (unless you can read Irish). In many cases, the Irish word for a place bears no resemblance to the English equivalent (*An Clochan Liath* in Irish is *Dungloe* in English), so our best advice is to buy a map with place names in both languages or stick to the main road.

ATLANTIC HIGHLANDS ESSENTIALS

GETTING THERE & GETTING AROUND   **Ireland Airways** operates regularly scheduled flights from Dublin to **Donegal Airport,** Carrickfinn, Kincasslagh, County Donegal (☎ 075/48284), in the heart of the Atlantic coast.

Bus Eireann (☎ 074/21309) operates daily bus service to Ardara and Glenties.

The best way to get to and around Donegal's Atlantic Highlands is by car, following the main N56 route.

VISITOR INFORMATION   Contact the **North West Tourism Office,** Aras Reddan, Temple Street, Sligo (☎ 071/61201); the **Letterkenny Tourist Office,** Derry Road, Letterkenny (☎ 074/21160); or the **Donegal Tourist Office,** Quay Street, Donegal (☎ 073/21148). The first two are open year-round; the third is open from May through September.

EXPLORING THE REGION

Ardara, known for its local tweed and sweater industries, is worth a stop for shoppers (see the listings below in "Shopping"). North of Ardara, the route travels inland near

Gweebarra Bay and passes through Dungloe to an area known as the **Rosses,** extending from Gweebarra Bridge as far north as Crolly. This stretch presents a wealth of rock-strewn land, with many mountains, rivers, lakes, and beaches. Here you can visit **Burtonport** (otherwise known as *Ailt an Chorrain*), one of the country's premier fishing ports; it's said that more salmon and lobster are landed there than at any other port in Ireland or Britain.

North of the Rosses between Derrybeg and Gortahork is an area known as the **Bloody Foreland,** a stretch of land that derives its name from the fact that its rocks take on a warm ruddy color when lit by the setting sun. This is a sight that should not be missed.

By now, you'll be approaching the top rim of Donegal, which is dominated by a series of small peninsulas or fingers of land jutting out into the sea. Chief among these scenic areas are **Horn Head** and **Ards.** The latter contains a forest park with a wide diversity of terrain: woodlands, a salt marsh, sand dunes, seashore, freshwater lakes, and fenland.

In Tory Sound, 9 miles (15km) north of the mainland, lies treeless **Tory Island,** desolate and seemingly uninhabitable. The truth is that Tory Island, all of 2½ miles (4km) long and less than 1 mile (1.6km) wide, has been settled for thousands of years and currently boasts nearly 200 year-round inhabitants. Known for its painters and pirates, ruins and bird cliffs, Tory makes a great adventure. The crossing can be made daily, weather permitting, from Bunbeg or Magheraroarty with **Tory Island Ferries/ Donegal Coastal Cruises,** Strand Road, Middletown, Derrybeg, County Donegal (☎ 075/31320 or 075/31340). There are four daily sailings June through September, five sailings per week the rest of the year. Round-trip fares are £15 ($21) adults, £12 ($16.80) seniors and students, £7.50 ($10.50) children under 15, free for children under 5.

After Horn Head, the next spit of land to the east is **Rosguill.** The 10-mile (16km) route around this peninsula is called the Atlantic Drive. This leads you to yet another peninsula, the **Fanad,** with a 45-mile (73km) circuit between Mulroy Bay and Lough Swilly. The resort of **Rathmullan** is a favorite stopping point here.

After you drive to all these scenic peninsulas, it might come as a surprise that many of the greatest visitor attractions of the Atlantic Highlands are not along the coast, but inland, a few miles off the main N56 road near Kilmacrennan.

Ardara Heritage Centre. On N56 in the center of Ardara, County Donegal. ☎ **075/ 41704.** Admission £2 ($2.80) adults, £1 ($1.40) seniors and students, 50p (70¢) children under 14. Centre open Easter–Sept Mon–Sat 10–6pm, Sun 2–6pm.

Ardara has long been a center for weaving, and varied displays represent the history of tweed production in the region. The weaver in residence is sometimes present to demonstrate techniques. A video provides an outline of nearby places of interest. The center opened in 1995 and is building its collections and exhibits. A cafe serves inexpensive teas, soups, and simple meals.

Doe Castle. 3½ miles (5.6km) off N56; turnoff signposted just south of Creeslough, County Donegal. Free admission.

This tower house is surrounded on three sides by the waters of Sheep Haven Bay and on the fourth by a moat carved into the bedrock that forms its foundation. A battlemented wall with round towers at the corners encloses the central tower; the view from the battlements across the bay is superb. Built in the early 16th century, the castle was extensively restored in the 18th century and inhabited until 1843. If the entrance is locked, you can get the key from the house nearest the castle. With its remote seaside location and sweeping views of the nearby hills, this is one of the most beautifully situated castles in Ireland.

✪ The Glebe House and Gallery. 11 miles (18km) northwest of Letterkenny on the Churchill road (R251), Church Hill, County Donegal. ☎ **074/37071.** Admission £2 ($2.80) adults, £1.50 ($2.10) seniors, £1 ($1.40) students and children, £5 ($7) family. Mid-May to Sept Sat–Thurs 11am–6:30pm, last tour at 5:30pm.

Sitting in woodland gardens on the shores of Lough Gartan, about 4 miles (6.5km) southwest of Glenveagh, this Regency-style house was built as a rectory in the 1820s. It was owned until recently by English artist Derek Hill, who donated the house and his art collection to the Irish government for public use and as an enhancement to the area he loves. The house is decorated with Donegal folk art, Japanese and Islamic art, Victoriana, and William Morris papers and textiles. The adjacent stables have been converted into an art gallery housing the 300-item Hill Collection of works by Picasso, Bonnard, Kokoschka, Yeats, Annigoni, Pasmore, and Hill. It's more than surprising to find this first-rate 20th-century art collection in this remote part of Donegal, but then, this is a surprising place.

✪ Glenveagh National Park. Main entrance on R251, Church Hill, County Donegal. ☎ **074/37090.** Park admission or castle tour £2 ($2.80) adults, £1.50 ($2.10) seniors, £1 ($1.40) students and children, £5 ($7) family. No credit cards. Mid-Mar to first Sun in Nov daily 10am–6:30pm; closed Fri in Oct.

Deep in the heart of County Donegal, far off the coastal path, this 35,000-acre estate is considered by many to be Ireland's finest national park. The core of the park is the Glenveagh Estate, originally the home of the notorious landlord John George Adair, much despised for his eviction of Irish tenant farmers in 1861. He built the castle in the 1870s. From 1937 to 1983 the estate prospered under the stewardship of Henry McIlhenny, a distinguished Philadelphia art historian who restored the baronial castle and planted gardens full of exotic species of flowers and shrubs. McIlhenny subsequently gave Glenveagh to the Irish nation for use as a public park, and today the fairy-tale setting includes woodlands, herds of red deer, alpine gardens, a sylvan lake, and the highest mountain in Donegal, Mount Errigal. Visitors can tour the castle and gardens and explore the park on foot. The complex includes a visitor center with a continual audiovisual show; displays on the history, flora, and fauna of the area; and nature trails. There is a restaurant in the visitor center, and a tearoom in the castle.

The Workhouse. Just west of Dunfanaghy on N56, County Donegal. ☎ **074/36540.** Admission £2.50 ($3.50) adults, £2 ($2.80) seniors and students, £1.25 ($1.75) children. Mid-Mar to mid-Oct Mon–Fri 10am–5pm, Sat–Sun noon–5pm.

The imposing stone structure was constructed in 1844, just before the height of the famine, and it provided meals and a roof for more than 300 local people. Life in the workhouses was miserable, and they were places of last resort: Families were separated, inmates were subjected to harsh physical labor on a minimal food allowance, and once you entered you were forbidden to leave. Still, by 1846 most of the 100,000 places in workhouses throughout Ireland were filled. The newly expanded and enhanced exhibits portray the life of workhouse inmates, especially "Wee Hannah," and relate local famine history. There are also an exhibit on the history of Dunfanaghy and an audiovisual presentation on the natural history of the region. Occasionally, evening music, poetry, or drama events are offered. A cozy tea and gift shop with an open fire serves baked goods.

SHOPPING
Ardara is a hub of tweed and woolen production. Most shops are open Monday to Saturday 9am to 5:30pm, with extended hours in summer. These shops are all on the main street of the town (N56).

C. Bonner & Son. Front St., Ardara, County Donegal. ☎ **075/41303.**

With 500 hand-knitters throughout County Donegal and 50 weavers in its factory, C. Bonner & Son produces a wide selection of hand-knit and hand-loomed knitwear, including linen-cotton and colorful sheep-patterned lambswool sweaters, all for sale here in its factory outlet. Also for sale is a broad selection of crafts and gifts, including sheepskins, pottery, wildlife watercolors, wool hangings, linens, crystal, and china. Closed January and February.

C. Kennedy & Sons Ltd. Ardara, County Donegal. ☎ **075/41106.**

Established in 1904, this family-owned knitwear company employs about 500 home workers who hand-knit or hand-loom bainin sweaters, hats, scarves, and jackets in native Donegal patterns and colors. The shop also sells turf crafts, pottery, and dolls.

John Molloy. Ardara, County Donegal. ☎ **075/41133.**

In the heart of wool and weaving country, this factory shop is well stocked with hand-knits, homespun fashions, sports jackets, tweed scarves and rugs, and all types of caps, from kingfisher to ghillie styles. There's even a bargain bin. Factory tours and a shop weaving demonstration are available.

SPORTS & OUTDOOR PURSUITS

BEACHES   Some of the most pristine and secluded beaches in Ireland are along the northern and western coasts of Donegal. There are few such places anywhere else where you can be so alone on such magnificent expanses of sand. The only problem is finding a sunny day. There are several popular beaches on Dawros Head, including **Traighmore Strand** in Rossbeg, and extensive beaches in Portnoo and Navan. **Magheroarty** near Falcarragh on the northern coast has a breathtaking beach, unspoiled by crowds or commercial development. The same goes for **Tramore** beach on the west side of Horn Head near Dunfanaghy; you have to hike a short distance, but you are rewarded by miles of white sand and seclusion. Other secluded and sandy beaches ideal for walking and jogging include Carrigart, Downings, Marble Hill, and Port na Blagh.

BICYCLING   Raleigh mountain bikes can be rented with panniers and accessories from **Church Street Cycles,** Letterkenny, County Donegal (☎ **074/26204**). They cost £10 ($14) per day, £40 ($56) per week, with a £50 ($70) deposit. No credit cards. Letterkenny is a good starting point for exploring the coast of northern Donegal— Horn Head, Inishowen Peninsula, Tory Island, and Bloody Foreland Head are all within an easy day's ride. Cycles rented here can be returned in Sligo Town, Donegal Town, or Galway City for an additional fee of £15 ($21).

BIRD WATCHING   Horn Head, a nesting site for many species of seabirds, has the largest nesting population of razorbills in Ireland. **Malin Head,** at the end of the Inishowen Peninsula, is the northernmost point on the Irish mainland, and once was the site of a bird observatory; it's a good site for watching migrants in late autumn.

FISHING   The rivers and lakes in this area produce good catches of salmon, sea trout, and brown trout, and the coastal waters yield flounder, pollock, and cod. Fishing expeditions are offered by charter boats, fishing boats, and trawlers. For details, contact the **North Western Regional Fisheries Board,** Abbey Street, Ballina, County Mayo (☎ **096/22788;** fax 096/70543; e-mail: NWRFB@iol.ie).

GOLF   One of Ireland's most challenging golf courses is the **Rosapenna Golf Club,** Atlantic Drive, Downings, County Donegal (☎ **074/55301**), an 18-hole championship seaside par-70 links course. It was laid out in 1983 by Tom Morris of St. Andrews. Greens fees are £20 ($28) weekdays, £25 ($35) weekends.

Other 18-hole courses in this part of Donegal are **Dunfanaghy Golf Club,** Dunfanaghy, County Donegal (☎ 074/36335), a seaside par-68 course with greens fees of £14 ($19.60) weekdays, £17 ($23.80) weekends; **Narin & Portnoo Golf Club,** Narin-Portnoo, County Donegal (☎ 075/45107), a par-69 seaside course with greens fees of £15 ($21) weekdays, £18 ($25.20) weekends; and **Portsalon Golf Club,** Portsalon, County Donegal (☎ 074/59459), a seaside par-69 course with greens fees of £17 ($23.80) weekdays, £20 ($28) weekends.

HORSEBACK RIDING Dunfanaghy Stables, Arnolds Hotel, Dunfanaghy, County Donegal (☎ 074/36208), specializes in trail riding on the surrounding beaches, dunes, and mountain trails. An hour's ride averages £10 ($14).

WALKING   A section of the **Ulster Way** passes through Donegal between the towns of Falcarragh to the north and Pettigo to the south, on the border with Fermanagh. This trail traverses some remote and wild terrain, passing Errigal Mountain and Glenveagh Park before heading south into the Blue Stack Mountains.

There are some incredible walks on **Hook Head,** signposted off N56 just west of Dunfanaghy. Follow Hook Head Drive to the concrete lookout point. From here you can walk out to a ruined castle on the headland and continue south along a line of impressive quartzite sea cliffs that glitter in the sun as though covered with a sheet of ice. This is a moderately difficult walk.

The **Ards Forest Park** is on a peninsula jutting out into Sheep Haven Bay, about 3½ miles (5.6km) south of Dunfanaghy on N56. The park is mostly forested and includes an area of dunes along the water. There are signposted nature trails, and you can buy a guidebook as you enter the park.

ACCOMMODATIONS
EXPENSIVE

✪ **Rathmullan House.** Lough Swilly, Rathmullan, County Donegal. ☎ **800/223-6510** from the U.S., or 074/58188. Fax 074/58200. www.rathmullanhouse.com. 23 units. TEL. £100–£160 ($140–$224) double. Rates include full Irish breakfast and service charge. AE, DC, MC, V. Closed Jan to mid-Feb.

On the western shores of Lough Swilly about a half mile north of town, this secluded country mansion is surrounded by colorful rose gardens and mature trees. The mostly Georgian interior features intricate ceilings, crystal chandeliers, oil paintings, white marble log-burning fireplaces, and an assortment of antiques and heirlooms collected over the years by owners Bob and Robin Wheeler. Rooms vary in size and style of furnishings, but most have a comfortable Irish motif and overlook the lake and gardens. All have orthopedic beds, and two are equipped for travelers with disabilities.

Dining/Diversions: The nonsmoking restaurant, housed in a glass-enclosed pavilion crowned by a flowing silk Arabian-tent design, specializes in seafood. The atmospheric cellar bar serves light snacks and refreshment.

Amenities: New indoor heated saltwater swimming pool and steam room, drawing room, well-stocked library, private beach, and equipment for boating and trout fishing. The resident masseuse provides massage, reflexology, and aromatherapy.

MODERATE

Arnolds Hotel. Dunfanaghy, County Donegal. ☎ **800/44-UTELL** from the U.S., or 074/36208. Fax 074/36352. E-mail: arnoldshotel@eircom.net. 30 units. TV TEL. £80–£100 ($112–$140) double. No service charge. Rates include full breakfast. AE, DC, MC, V. Closed Nov–Mar 16.

In the Arnold family for three generations, this is a family-run business, with brothers Derek and William acting as desk clerks, porters, waiters, and whatever else needs doing. The Arnolds Hotel is an ideal base for touring northwest Donegal and for exploring Glenveagh National Park. Golf, fishing, and pony trekking can be arranged at the front desk. Or you may want to stay put—the hotel enjoys views of Sheephaven Bay and Horn Head, and serves great food. Renovated in 1997 and redecorated in 1999, Arnolds offers attractive and mostly spacious rooms, with beds of medium firmness. Nonsmoking rooms are not available.

Fort Royal Hotel. Rathmullan, County Donegal. ☎ **800/447-7462** from the U.S., or 074/58100. Fax 074/58103. E-mail: fortroyal@eircom.net. 15 units. TV TEL. £95–£115 ($133–$161) double. No service charge. Rates include full breakfast. AE, V. Closed Nov–Easter. Free parking.

Built in 1819, this rambling, three-story country house owned by the Fletcher family has been a hotel since 1948. It's set on 18 acres of gardens and woodlands, with a small sandy beach overlooking the water on the western shore of Lough Swilly, 1 mile (1.6km) north of the village. Both the public areas and the recently refurbished guest rooms are decorated with traditional furnishings, period pieces, and oil paintings showing scenes of Donegal. Facilities include a nonsmoking restaurant, lounge, tennis court, squash court, and golf course. The newly refurbished bar offers lovely views of the lough and an inviting terrace.

Ostan Na Rosann/Hotel of the Rosses. Dungloe, County Donegal. ☎ **075/22444.** Fax 075/22400. www.ostannarosann.ie. 48 units. TV TEL. £70–£80 ($98–$112) double. Rates include full breakfast. AE, DISC, MC, V. Free parking.

On a hill overlooking the Atlantic, this modern ranch-style hotel sits in the heart of the Rosses, a scenic Gaelic-speaking area. The guest rooms have wide-windowed sea views, standard furnishings, tea/coffee-making facilities, and hair dryers. Major refurbishment of the public areas was completed recently, and ongoing refurbishment continues throughout. The rooms, restaurant, and reception area are nonsmoking. A popular hotel with Irish families, it offers a dining room, a lounge, a nightclub/disco, an indoor heated swimming pool, a Jacuzzi, a steam room, a sauna, and a gym.

Rosapenna Golf Hotel. Atlantic Dr., Downings, County Donegal. ☎ **074/55301.** Fax 074/55128. www.rosapenna.ie. 53 units. TV TEL. £110–£120 ($154–$168) double. Rates include service charge and full breakfast. AE, DC, MC, V. Closed late Oct to mid-Mar.

Surrounded by Sheephaven Bay and the hills of Donegal, this contemporary two-story hotel is a favorite with golfers, who flock here to enjoy the hotel's 18-hole seaside course. Nongolfers come for the scenery, the seclusion (700 acres' worth), and the hotel's proximity to northern Donegal attractions. There are two all-weather tennis courts, and windsurfing. The guest rooms, dining area, and lounges are modern with an emphasis on panoramic views of land and sea. A new indoor pool with spa was opened in 2000.

SELF-CATERING

✪ **Donegal Thatched Cottages.** Cruit Island, c/o Conor and Mary Ward, Rosses Point, County Sligo. Signposted opposite Viking House Hotel on Kincasslagh Rd., 6 miles (9.5km) north of Dungloe, Cruit Island. ☎ **071/77197.** Fax 071/77500. Email: conorwar@ eircom.net. 10 cottages. £170–£670 ($238–$938) per cottage per week, plus £5 ($7) per person per week. Weekend discounts available. MC, V.

This cluster of cottages is on Cruit Island, an enchanting landscape of rock and sand just off the Donegal coast near Dungloe. Accessible by a small bridge, Cruit is a narrow spit of land reaching into the Atlantic, dwarfed by its nearby neighbors Aranmore and Owey Islands. The cottages are on the Atlantic side, which alternates rocky head-lands with unspoiled beaches; on the lee side is a lovely quiet beach that extends for miles. The view west toward Owey Island is captivating, and sunsets are notoriously glorious. There's a great seaside walk along the west side of the island, which takes in a series of lovely half-moon beaches.

Each cottage is built according to a traditional plan, resembling many of the rural homes you're sure to have seen while exploring the region. The interiors are simple and appealing, with wooden and tiled floors, high ceilings in the living/dining rooms, and a great loft bedroom on the second floor. The kitchen comes equipped with dish-washer and a washer and dryer for your laundry, and there's a master bedroom with its own private bathroom. Each cottage has three bedrooms, and can sleep up to seven guests. Although the location is somewhat remote, there are a number of pubs and restaurants within a short driving distance.

DINING

✪ **Waters Edge.** The Ballyboe, Rathmullan, County Donegal. ☎ **074/58182.** Reservations recommended for dinner. Dinner main courses £10.95–£15 ($15.35–$21). MC, V. Easter–Sept daily noon–10pm; Oct–Easter daily 6:30–10pm. IRISH/INTERNATIONAL.

As its name implies, this restaurant is on the edge of picturesque Lough Swilly, on the south end of town. Although the glassy facade on three sides gives the 70-seat dining area a modern look, the interior is quite traditional, with beamed ceilings, an open fireplace, nautical bric-a-brac, and watercolors of Donegal landscapes. The menu blends Irish dishes with such international favorites as wild salmon in brandy-bisque sauce, chicken Kiev, prawns Provençal, and steaks. Bar food, served all day, ranges from soups and sandwiches to pâtés, scampi, and fish-and-chips.

Rooms with a view and breakfast are available, for £40 ($56) double.

PUBS

Almost all the pubs in this Irish-speaking area provide spontaneous sessions of Irish traditional music in summer. Two places known for music are the **Lakeside Centre,** Dunlewey (☎ **075/31699**), and **Leo's Tavern,** Meenaleck, Crolly (☎ **075/48143**). The highly successful Irish group Clannad and the vocalist Enya got their starts at Leo's.

The don't-miss pub in Ardara is **Nancy's** (☎ **075/41187**) on Front Street, which has to be one of the smallest pubs in Ireland. What it lacks in size, it makes up for in character and charm.

The **Harbour Bar,** Main Street, Killybegs (☎ **073/31049**), holds an Irish music night on Tuesday during July and August.

5 The Inishowen Peninsula

Buncrana, the peninsula's chief town, is 70 miles (113km) NE of Donegal Airport, 52 miles (84km) NE of Donegal Town, 12 miles (19km) NW of Derry, 90 miles (145km) NE of Sligo, 223 miles (359km) NE of Shannon, and 161 miles (259km) NW of Dublin

This long, broad finger of land stretching north to the Atlantic between Lough Swilly to the west and Lough Foyle to the east is Ireland's northernmost point. Along the shores of both loughs and the Atlantic Ocean, long stretches of sandy beaches are backed by sheer cliffs. Inland are some of Ireland's most impressive mountains, with 615-meter (2,019-ft.) Slieve Snacht dominating the center of the peninsula. Its her-itage reaches back beyond recorded history, with relics of those distant days scattered across its face.

The Inishowen gets its name from Eoghain, a son of King Niall of the Nine Hostages, who lived at the time of St. Patrick in the 5th century. The king named this amazing finger of land for his son—Inis Eoghain means "the island of Owen."

To drive around the Inishowen is to traverse a ring of seascapes, mountains, valleys, and woodlands. It's been said that Donegal is a miniature Ireland; Donegal folk claim that Inishowen is a miniature Donegal.

Relatively undiscovered by most visitors to Ireland, Inishowen is a world apart, where present-day residents revere their ancient heritage, treasure the legends and antiquities of this remote region, and still observe many traditions of their ancestors. Traditional music and dance thrive here, and it's unlikely you'll face an evening when there's not a music session in a nearby pub.

INISHOWEN PENINSULA ESSENTIALS

GETTING THERE & GETTING AROUND   North West Busways (☎ 074/ 82619) offers service between Letterkenny and Moville, via Cardonagh and Buncrana, and there's daily Dublin–Inishowen service on offer by John McGinley (☎ 074/ 35201).

The best way to get to and around the Inishowen Peninsula is by car, following the signposted 100-mile (161km) Inishowen route.

VISITOR INFORMATION   Contact the **North West Tourism Office,** Aras Reddan, Temple Street, Sligo (☎ 071/61201); the **Letterkenny Tourist Office,** Derry Road, Letterkenny (☎ 074/21173); or the **Inishowen Tourism Society,** Chapel Street, Cardonagh, County Donegal (☎ 077/74933). All three are open year-round, Monday to Friday 9:30am to 5:30pm, with extended summer hours.

SEEING THE SIGHTS

In spite of its remote location, the Inishowen Peninsula circuit is one of the best-marked roads in Ireland, with all directions clearly printed in English and Irish, miles and kilometers. Among the many features of this 100-mile (161km) route (which runs from Letterkenny to Moville) is a string of beach resorts like Ballyliffin, Buncrana, Greencastle, and Moville. Natural wonders include the **Gap of Mamore,** 5 miles (8km) north of Buncrana, a pass rising to 800 feet and then slowly descending on a corkscrew path to sea level, and **Slieve Snacht,** a 2,019-foot mountain.

The peninsula's most impressive historic monument is the hilltop fort known as ✪ **Grianan of Aileach,** 10 miles (16km) south of Buncrana. One of the best examples of a ring fort in Ireland, it was built as a temple of the sun around 1700 B.C. From the mid–5th century to the early 12th, it was the royal residence of the O'Neills, the kings of this area.

After you've toured the Inishowen, or perhaps stayed a few days, head south through **Letterkenny** (pop. 5,000). The largest town in the county, it's on a hillside overlooking the River Swilly. There you can pick up N56, the main road, and drive to the twin towns of Ballybofey and Stranorlar. Change here to N15, which takes you to yet another scenic Donegal drive, the **Barnesmore Gap,** a vast open stretch through the Blue Stack Mountains, which leads you into Donegal Town and points south.

Greencastle Maritime Museum. Harbour, Greencastle, County Donegal. ☎ 077/81363. Admission £2 ($2.80) adults, £1 ($1.40) seniors and students, £5 ($7) family. June–Sept daily 10am–6pm; other times by appointment.

This compact maritime museum, in the harbor home of one of the busiest fishing fleets in Ireland, is housed in the old 1857 coast-guard station. Before you go in, be sure to take in the grand views of Lough Foyle, as well as the monument to those lost in nearby waters. The museum's modest, intriguing exhibits focus on the everyday struggles as well as the historic events beyond Greencastle Harbour, from Armada wrecks to famine-period emigration to the heroism of the Irish lifeboat rescue teams. In addition, there's a new Mesolithic exhibit with local 8,000-year-old finds. A small coffee, craft, and souvenir shop is also at hand. Best of all, Maire McCann's stories bring the museum's exhibits to life.

Guns of Dunree Military Museum. Signposted on the coast road north of Buncrana, County Donegal. ☎ **077/61817** or 077/21173. Admission £2 ($2.80) per car. June–Sept Tues–Sat 10:30am–6pm, Sun 12:30–8pm.

Perched on a cliff overlooking Lough Swilly, Fort Dunree is a military and naval museum incorporating a Napoleonic Martello tower at the site of World War I defenses on the north Irish coast. It features a wide range of exhibitions, an audio-visual center, and a cafeteria housed in a restored forge. Even if you have no interest in military history, it's worth a trip for the view. Dunree has one of the best vantage points in Donegal for unencumbered seascapes and broad mountain vistas.

Vintage Car & Carriage Museum. Buncrana, County Donegal. ☎ **077/61130.** Admission £2 ($2.80) adults, 50p (70¢) children. June–Sept daily 10am–8pm; Oct–May Sun noon–5pm.

Transportation of yesteryear is the theme of this museum, which houses a large collection of classic cars, horse-drawn carriages, Victorian bicycles, and vintage motorcycles, as well as model-car and railway exhibits.

SPORTS & OUTDOOR PURSUITS
BEACHES   Ballyliffin, Buncrana, Greencastle, and Moville have safe, sandy beaches that are ideal for swimming or walking.

GOLF   Donegal's northern coast is believed to be one of the first places where golf was played in Ireland, and it's been played on the Inishowen Peninsula for more than 100 years.

The Inishowen has three 18-hole golf courses. The **Ballyliffin Golf Club,** Ballyliffin, County Donegal (☎ 077/76119), the northernmost golf course in Ireland, is a par-71 links course with greens fees of £21 ($29.40) weekdays, £24 ($33.60) weekends. The **North West Golf Club,** Fahan, Buncrana, County Donegal (☎ 077/61027), founded in 1890, is a par-69 seaside course with greens fees of £15 ($21) weekdays, £20 ($28) weekends. **Greencastle Golf Course,** Greencastle, County Donegal (☎ 077/781013), is a par-69 parkland course with greens fees of £15 ($21) weekdays, £18 ($25.20) weekends.

WATER SPORTS   The Inishowen's long coastline, sandy beaches, and combination of open ocean and sheltered coves offer great opportunities for water sports. The northwest coast presents some of the most challenging surfing conditions in the world. For advice and specific information, contact the **Irish Surfing Association,** Tirchonaill Street, Donegal (☎ **073/21053;** www.indigo.ie/imagine/irish-surfing).

ACCOMMODATIONS
MODERATE
Mount Errigal. Derry Rd., Ballyraine, Letterkenny, County Donegal. ☎ **074/22700.** Fax 077/25085. www.mounterrigal.com. 82 units. TV TEL. £76–£108 ($106.40–$151.20) double. No service charge. Rates include full breakfast. AE, DC, MC, V.

South of Lough Swilly and less than a mile east of town, this contemporary two-story hotel is a handy place to stay. It's midway between the Inishowen Peninsula and Donegal Town, within 20 miles (32km) of Glenveagh National Park. Although it has a rather ordinary gray facade, the inside is bright and airy, with skylights, light woods, hanging plants, colored and etched glass, and brass fixtures. The guest rooms are outfitted in contemporary style, with cheerful colors and modern art, good reading lights over the beds, hair dryers, garment presses, and tea makers. On the premises are the full-service Glengesh Restaurant and the Buffet Counter coffee shop. The old-world lounge, Blue Stack Bar, offers piano music Monday through Thursday and live bands on the weekend. The hotel has an indoor heated swimming pool, a sauna, a steam room, and a gym.

Redcastle Hotel. Redcastle, Moville, County Donegal. ☎ **077/82073.** Fax 077/82214. 31 units. TV TEL. £70–£110 ($98–$154) double. No service charge. Rates include full breakfast. AE, DC, MC, V.

On the shores of Lough Foyle on the Inishowen's eastern coast, this country inn–style hotel offers a combination of old-world charms and modern comforts. The guest rooms are outfitted with designer fabrics, and each has a view of the lake or the adjacent golf course, a hair dryer, and a tea/coffeemaker. There are a coffee shop, a lounge, and the Art Gallery Restaurant, offering views and contemporary art. Guests have the use of a 9-hole golf course, two swimming pools, a Jacuzzi, a sauna, a steam room, a gym, and a tennis court.

INEXPENSIVE

Brooklyn Cottage. Greencastle, Inishowen, County Donegal. ☎ **077/81087.** 3 units, 2 with shower only, no tub. £36 ($50.40) double. No credit cards. Closed Jan–Feb.

Only tall panes of glass separate the living room of Brooklyn Cottage from the lapping waves of Lough Foyle. This modern bungalow is right on the brink of the Inishowen peninsula, and guests eat breakfast in a conservatory that takes advantage of a spectacular sea view (as do the living room and two of the bedrooms). A small coastal path skirts the rocky shore in front of the house, and it's possible to follow it to the neighboring town of Moville, about 2 miles (3.2km) away. The rooms themselves are small, but each has its own tea and coffee facilities and is meticulously kept. Peter Smith, who is your host here along with his wife, Gladys, is involved with the nearby Maritime museum and shares his knowledge of the area with guests. Brooklyn Cottage is within walking distance of the center of Greencastle yet occupies a seemingly remote site just beyond the port.

✪ The Strand. Ballyliffin, Clonmany, County Donegal. ☎ **077/76107.** Fax 077/76486. 21 units. TV TEL. £45–£60 ($63–$84) double. No service charge. Rates include full breakfast. MC, V.

On a hillside overlooking Pollan Strand, with views of nearby Malin Head, this small family-run hotel is on the edge of town, set apart in its own palm tree–lined rose gardens. The decor is modern Irish, with wide windows and traditional touches. Rooms have standard furnishings with such extras as tea/coffeemakers and hair dryers. There's a good restaurant, and the lounge bar is known for its local entertainment.

SELF-CATERING

Ballyliffin Self Catering. Rossaor House, Ballyliffin, County Donegal. ☎ and fax **077/76498.** 6 cottages. TV. July–Aug £450 ($630) per cottage per week; Apr–June and Sept £345 ($483) per cottage per week; Oct–Mar £245 ($343) per cottage per week. Rates include electric heat. MC, V.

Ballyliffin is a tiny seaside village on the west coast of Inishowen, with two golf courses in close proximity. This group of cottages is situated along the main road through town, a 10-minute walk from the fine sand and clear waters of Pollan Bay. The six connected cottages are all built in stone and pine, with lofty double-height living rooms and massive central fireplaces which the stairs circle on their way to the second floor. Each cottage has three bedrooms and two bathrooms—two of the bedrooms have a double bed and an attached bathroom, while the third bedroom has three single beds. In some cottages, second-floor bedrooms overlook the living room, where a foldout couch provides yet more sleeping space. The kitchen is well-equipped; appliances include a microwave, an electric stove, a dishwasher, and a washing machine and dryer.

DINING

✪ **The Corncrake.** Malin St, Carndonagh, County Donegal. ☎ **077/74534.** Reservations recommended. Dinner main courses £9–£12 ($12.60–$16.80). No credit cards. Easter–Sept daily 6–9pm; Oct–Dec weekends only. Closed Jan–Easter. IRISH/VEGETARIAN/CONTINENTAL.

A restaurant like the Corncrake is as rare as the endangered bird from which it takes its name. The freshest of ingredients are sought out by Brid McCartney and Noreen Lynch, and then transformed using a selection of herbs grown in their own gardens in a way that is nothing short of sublime. Starters include a prawn chowder where lemon and fresh coriander bring out the flavor of locally caught fish, and a cheese soufflé whose golden crown topples to reveal a velvet textured filling of egg, cream, and sharp cheddar. Hard acts to follow? Not for Brid McCartney. Meat and fish dishes are coupled with sauces and seasonings so masterful that they seem to give lamb a new tenderness and monkfish an unanticipated delicacy. And for vegetarians (you'll need to call a day in advance to request a vegetarian meal), there was goat cheese wrapped in red peppers, indisputably the most delectable pairing of vegetables and cheese ever. Yet even these dishes are upstaged by the desserts, prepared by Noreen. They range from a wholesome gooseberry fool to a blissful orange and Grand Marnier *panna cotta* (an Italian dessert of reduced cream and eggs). It's only the tranquil lighting and sedate setting of the Corncrake that keep diners from licking their plates.

✪ **Kealys Seafood Bar.** Greencastle, County Donegal. ☎ **077/81010.** Bar food £1.50–£7.50 ($2.10–$10.50); restaurant fixed-price menu $19.50 ($27.30); dinner main courses £14.50–£28 ($20.30–$39.20). Bar Wed–Sat 3–5pm and Sun 12:30–5pm; restaurant Wed–Sat 1–3pm and 7–9pm, Sun 7–8:30pm. SEAFOOD.

For a light meal, a snack, or a feast overlooking Lough Foyle and the fishing boats of the Foyle Fishermen's Co-op, try this little harborfront place. Bar and lunch items include Greencastle seafood chowder, local oysters, smoked-salmon salad, deep-fried plaice, southern fried chicken, sandwiches, lasagna, and burgers, while in the evening you'll find a full net of the day's catch: lobster, John Dory, monkfish, sole, and more. The locals claim that the fish is so fresh that it's reeled onto your plate. This is food of the people by the people for the people, and you can taste the difference.

St. John's Country House and Restaurant. Fahan, County Donegal. ☎ **077/60289.** Fax 077/60612. Reservations required. Fixed-price 6-course dinner £28 ($39.20). AE, DC, MC, V. Tues–Sat 6–10pm. IRISH.

On its own grounds overlooking Lough Swilly, this lovely Georgian house has two cozily elegant dining rooms. Open turf fireplaces, Waterford crystal, embroidered linens, and richly textured wallpaper add to the ambience. Best of all, the food is dependably good—baked Swilly salmon with lemon sauce, roast duck with port-and-orange sauce, spiced lamb en croûte with gooseberry-and-mint sauce, and John Dory with fennel.

B&B is available for £70 to £150 ($98 to $210) double.

Along the River Shannon's Shores

No matter where in the midlands you find yourself, you're never far from the Shannon. It is Ireland's fluid, winding spine, dividing east from west, flowing through lowland fields and bogs, and communing with countless lakes and lesser rivers. The Shannon is the constant by which you take your bearings in Ireland's heartland.

At 230 miles (371km), the Shannon is the longest river in Ireland or Great Britain. It influences and defines more of the Irish landscape than any other body of water. Rising in County Cavan, it flows south through the heartland of Ireland, touching nine other counties—Leitrim, Roscommon, Longford, Westmeath, Offaly, Galway, Tipperary, Clare, and Limerick—before reaching its mouth and separating counties Kerry and Clare as the Shannon estuary waters meet the Atlantic.

The Shannon takes many shapes and forms as it flows. At some points, it's almost 10 miles (16km) across; at others, it narrows to a few hundred yards. For centuries, the river was primarily a means of transportation and commerce, Ireland's most ancient highway; more recently, it's chiefly been a source of enjoyment and recreation.

The river can be divided into three segments: the **Lower Shannon and Lough Derg,** stretching from Killaloe to Portumna; the **Middle Shannon,** a narrow passage from the Birr/Banagher area to Athlone; and the **Upper Shannon,** from Lough Ree to Lough Allen and the river's source in County Cavan. In this chapter, we'll explore the river from south to north. This is not to imply that the river flows in that direction; rather, it's to help you start touring in the area that has the most to do and see.

While it's unlikely that you will follow the Shannon for all of its 214 navigable miles (345km), you'll encounter it in almost every cross-country route you take. So, whether you trace or cross its path, it makes sense here to point out some of the many delights to be found along and near the Shannon's shores.

1 Lower Shannon: The Lough Derg Drive

Killaloe is 16 miles (26km) NE of Limerick and 25 miles (40km) E of Ennis; Portumna is 40 miles (64.5km) SE of Galway and 27 miles (43.5km) E of Gort

The Lower Shannon, stretching from Killaloe, County Clare, north to Portumna, County Galway, encompasses one huge lake, Lough Derg. Often called an inland sea, **Lough Derg** was the main inland waterway trading route between Dublin and Limerick when canal and river commercial traffic was at its height in Ireland in the 18th and 19th centuries. It is the Shannon River's largest lake and widest point: 25 miles (40km) long and almost 10 miles (16km) wide, with more than 25,000 acres of water. Today Lough Derg can be described as Ireland's pleasure lake, because of all the recreational and sporting opportunities it provides.

AREA ESSENTIALS

GETTING THERE & GETTING AROUND   The best way to get to the Lough Derg area is by car or boat. Although there's limited public transportation, you'll need a car to get around the lake. Major roads that lead to Lough Derg are the main Limerick-Dublin road (N7) from points east and south, N6 and N65 from Galway and the west, and N52 from the north. The Lough Derg Drive, which is well signposted, is a combination of R352 on the west bank of the lake and R493, R494, and R495 on the east bank.

VISITOR INFORMATION   Because Lough Derg unites three counties (Clare, Galway, and Tipperary), there are several sources of information. They include the **Shannon Development Tourism Group,** Shannon, County Clare (☎ **061/361555,** www.shannon-dev.ie/tourism); **Ireland West Tourism,** Victoria Place, Eyre Square, Galway (☎ **091/563081**); and **Tipperary Lake Side & Development,** The Old Church, Borrisokane, County Tipperary (☎ **067/27155**). Seasonal information offices include the **Nenagh Tourist Office,** Connolly Street, Nenagh, County Tipperary (☎ **067/31610**), open early May to early September; and the **Killaloe Tourist Office,** The Bridge, County Clare (☎ **061/376866**), open May to September.

EXPLORING THE AREA

The road that rims the lake for 95 miles (153km), the **Lough Derg Drive,** is one of the most scenic routes in Ireland. It's a continuous natural setting where panoramas of hilly farmlands, gentle mountains, bucolic forests, and glistening waters are unspoiled by commercialization. Most of all, the drive is a collage of colorful shoreline towns, starting with Killaloe, County Clare, and Ballina, County Tipperary, on the south banks of the lake. They're called "twin towns" because they're usually treated as one community—only a splendid 13-arch bridge over the Shannon separates them.

Killaloe is home to Ireland's largest inland marina and a host of water-sports centers. Of historical note is a 9th-century oratory, said to have been founded by St. Lua—hence the name Killaloe, which comes from the Irish *Cill* ("church") of Lua.

Nearby is another oratory and cathedral, built in the 12th century and named for 6th-century St. Flannan; it boasts an exquisite Romanesque doorway. **Kincora,** on the highest ground at Killaloe, was the royal settlement of Brian Boru and the other O'Brien kings, but no trace of any building remains. Killaloe is a lovely town with lakeside views at almost every turn and many fine restaurants and pubs offering outdoor seating on the shore.

Five miles (8km) inland from Lough Derg's lower southeast shores is **Nenagh,** the chief town of north Tipperary. It lies in a fertile valley between the Silvermine and Arra Mountains.

On the north shore of the lake is **Portumna,** which means "the landing place of the oak tree." A major point of traffic across the Shannon, Portumna has a lovely forest park and a remarkable castle that's currently being restored.

Memorable little towns and harborside villages like **Mountshannon** and **Dromineer** dot the rest of the Lough Derg Drive. Some towns, like **Terryglass** and **Woodford,** are known for atmospheric old pubs where spontaneous sessions of traditional Irish music are likely to occur. Others, like **Puckane** and **Ballinderry,** offer unique crafts or locally made products.

The Lough Derg Drive is the Shannon River at its best.

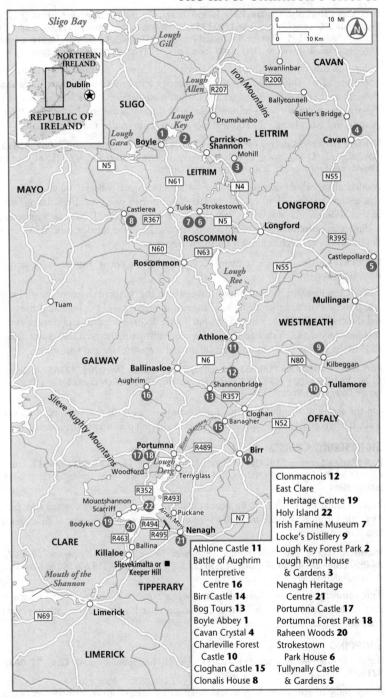

Clonmacnois **12**
East Clare
   Heritage Centre **19**
Holy Island **22**
Irish Famine Museum **7**
Locke's Distillery **9**
Lough Key Forest Park **2**
Lough Rynn House
   & Gardens **3**
Nenagh Heritage
   Centre **21**
Portumna Castle **17**
Portumna Forest Park **18**
Raheen Woods **20**
Strokestown
   Park House **6**
Tullynally Castle
   & Gardens **5**

Athlone Castle **11**
Battle of Aughrim
   Interpretive
   Centre **16**
Birr Castle **14**
Bog Tours **13**
Boyle Abbey **1**
Cavan Crystal **4**
Charleville Forest
   Castle **10**
Cloghan Castle **15**
Clonalis House **8**

East Clare Heritage Centre/Holy Island Tours. Off the Portumna–Ennis road (R352), Tuamgraney, County Clare. ☎ 061/921351. Admission to the center £2 ($2.80) adults, £1 ($1.40) children, £5 ($7) family; Holy Island Tours £5 ($7) adults, £2 ($2.80) children. Centre May–Sept daily 10am–6pm; Holy Island Tours Apr–Sept 11am–6pm, weather permitting.

Housed in the restored 10th-century church of St. Cronan (Ireland's oldest church in continuous use), this center explains the heritage and history of the East Clare area through a series of exhibits and an audiovisual presentation. A pier across the road is the starting point for a 15-minute boating excursion to nearby Inishcealtra (Holy Island), in Lough Derg. The trip includes a 45-minute guided tour of the island.

Nenagh Heritage Centre. Off Kickham St., Nenagh, County Tipperary. ☎ 067/32633. Admission £2 ($2.80) adults; £1 ($1.40) seniors, students, and children; £4 ($5.60) family. Mid-May to Sept Mon–Fri 9:30am–5pm, Sun 2–5pm.

Models of the whole Lough Derg area, with its main port villages, are on display at this center, 5 miles (8km) east of the lakeshore. In two stone buildings dating from about 1840, this site was once a jail, then a convent and school. Now, as a museum, it showcases collections of local arts, crafts, photography, and memorabilia. It's also the family history research center for northern Tipperary.

Portumna Castle. Off N65, Portumna, County Galway. No phone. Free admission to gardens. Daily 8am–4pm.

Built in 1609 by Earl Richard Burke, this castle on the northern shores of Lough Derg is said to have been one of the finest 17th-century manor houses in Ireland. A fire gutted the castle in 1826, but spared its Dutch-style decorative gables and rows of stone mullioned windows. Although the castle is currently being restored and is not accessible to the public, the surrounding gardens and lawns are open to visitors.

Portumna Forest Park. Off N65, Portumna, County Galway. ☎ 0905/42365. Admission £1.50 ($2.10) adults, £1 ($1.40) students and seniors, 60p (84¢) children over 5, £4 ($5.60) family. Daily dawn–9pm.

On the shores of Lough Derg, this 1,400-acre park is east of the town, off the main road. It offers trails and signposted walks, plus viewing points and picnic areas.

SIGHTSEEING CRUISES

R&B Marine Services Ltd. Killaloe Marina, Killaloe, County Clare. ☎ 061/375011. Cruise £5 ($7) adults, £3 ($4.20) children, £14 ($19.60) family. May–Sept Sunday 3:15pm or by arrangement.

Enjoy a cruise of Lough Derg on board the 48-seat *Derg Princess*, a covered river bus. Departing from Killaloe Marina, the 1-hour cruise travels past the fort of Brian Boru and into Lough Derg.

Shannon Sailing Ltd. New Harbor, Dromineer, Nenagh, County Tipperary. ☎ 067/24499. Cruise £4.50 ($6.30) adults, £2.50 ($3.50) children, £14 ($19.60) family. May–Sept daily; schedule varies.

This company operates a covered 53-seat water bus, the *Ku-ee-tu*. It sails from the southeastern shore of Lough Derg at Dromineer on a 1½-hour cruise with full commentary on local sights.

SHOPPING

Eugene & Anke McKernan. Handweavers, Main St., Tuamgraney, County Clare. ☎ 061/921527.

A husband-and-wife team, Eugene and Anke offer a colorful array of distinctive tweed scarves, jackets, vests, and blankets. The couple hand-weaves all items on the premises, which were formerly police barracks. Visitors are welcome to visit the workshop and see the weaving process. Open daily May to September 10am to 7pm; hours vary October to April.

Lakeshore Foods Factory Shop. Coolbawn, Ballinderry Village, Nenagh, County Tipperary. ☎ **067/22094.**

Originally the village forge, this old building was restored and converted into a small factory and shop for fine mustards, sauces, and dressings. It's on the Lough Derg Drive, between the villages of Puckane and Terryglass.

✪ **Old Church Craft Shop & Gallery.** The Old Church, R493, Terryglass, County Tipperary. ☎ **067/22209.**

Built on the site of the original abbey of St. Columba (A.D. 549), this stone-faced building dates from 1838. Transformed into a craft shop in 1984, it is a treasure trove of locally produced crafts and products. You might see Terryglass pottery, Rathbone traditional beeswax candles, Irish bonsai plants, bog oak pendants, wildlife mobiles, boxwood products from Birr Castle, Jerpoint glass, decorated horseshoes, miniature watercolors of Shannon River scenes, and books about the Shannon. The gallery has watercolors by artist-owner Jenny Boelens on permanent display. Open Easter to October daily 9am to 6pm.

Walsh Crafts. R493, Puckane, Nenagh, County Tipperary. ☎ **067/24229.** www.craftireland.com.

A rustic thatched-roof cottage, complete with traditional half-door, serves as the workshop for Paddy Walsh, a craftsman who carves and paints on natural wood. His works depict Ireland past and present, with Celtic and rural scenes and pieces with heraldic and religious themes. The items range from pendant-size figurines and symbols—such as St. Patrick, the harp, or a dove—to portrait-size scenes of Irish music sessions, pub facades and interiors, farmyards, cottages, castles, sporting events, and Christmas tableaux. The craft is ingenious and truly Irish, a great souvenir. Visitors are welcome to watch Paddy and his staff as they carve the wood and paint the colorful motifs. Open weekdays 9am to 5pm.

BOATING & OTHER WATER SPORTS

Water sports are the pièce de résistance of a visit to Lough Derg. If you enjoy boating, tubing, waterskiing, windsurfing, canoeing, or other water sports, this is the place for you.

Below we've listed a few of the businesses that specialize in these activities. In addition, the following companies also rent cabin cruisers along this section of the Shannon: **R&B Marine Services Ltd.,** Derg Marina, Killaloe, County Clare (☎ **061/375011**); **Emerald Star Line,** The Marina, Portumna, County Galway (☎ **0509/41120**); **Shannon Castle Line,** The Marina, Williamstown, County Clare (☎ **061/927042**); and **Shannon Sailing,** New Harbor, County Tipperary (☎ **067/24499**). The crafts range from two to eight berths; rates average £100 to £200 ($140 to $280) per person per week.

Lough Derg Sailing. Mountshannon Harbour, Mountshannon, County Clare. ☎ **061/927131.** Cruise £35 ($49) per day; hourly rates available. May–Sept daily by appointment.

With its nontidal waters and numerous bays, islands, and harbors, Lough Derg is ideal for sailing. This company offers daily sailing trips on the 29-foot yacht *Sangazure,* with instruction and training on board. The activities are especially geared toward beginners who want to learn the basics of sailing.

Watersports Lough Derg. Two Mile Gate, Killaloe, County Clare. ☎ **088/588430** (mobile). Waterskiing from £12 ($16.80); speedboat rides from £3 ($4.20) per person; tubing from £6 ($8.40); Jet-Skis from £12 ($16.80). May–Oct daily 11am–dusk.

This outdoor center offers waterskiing, speedboat rides, tubing, and jet skiing.

Whelan's Boat Hire. At the bridge, Killaloe, County Clare. ☎ **061/376159.** Boat rental £10 ($14) 1st hour, £5 ($7) each additional hour; £30 ($42) per day; £100 ($140) per week. Daily 9am–9pm.

Whelan's rents 19-foot lake boats with outboard engines for sightseeing or fishing in the waters of Lough Derg. Prices include fuel, fishing gear, life jackets, and rainwear. In the summer, Whelan's offers an hourly river tour that provides lots of local history and lore.

OTHER SPORTS & OUTDOOR PURSUITS

FISHING   An angler's paradise, Lough Derg has good stocks of brown trout, pike, bream, and perch. Fish weighing 36 to 90 pounds have been caught. Brown trout average 1 to 6 pounds. For tackle and guidance on local fishing, visit **Eddie Fahey,** Ballyminogue, Scariff, County Clare (☎ **061/921019**); or **Whelan's,** Summerhill, Nenagh, County Tipperary (☎ **067/31301**).

GOLF   Lovely parkland and woodland golfing in the Lough Derg area is offered at 18-hole clubs such as **Portumna Golf Club,** Portumna, County Galway (☎ **0509/41059**), with greens fees of £15 ($21); and **Nenagh Golf Club,** Beechwood, Nenagh (☎ **067/31476**), with greens fees of £10 ($14). The **East Clare Golf Club,** Scariff/Killaloe Road, Bodyke, County Clare (☎ **061/921322**), is an 18-hole championship course. Greens fees are £13 ($18.20) weekdays, £15 ($21) weekends.

SWIMMING   Lough Derg is known for clear, unpolluted water that's ideal for swimming, particularly at **Castle Lough, Dromineer,** and **Portumna Bay.** Portumna Bay has changing rooms and showers.

WALKING   There are some excellent walks in **Portumna Forest Park,** in **Raheen Woods,** and along the shoreline of **Lough Derg.** For a touch of scenic wilderness, walk a portion of the **Slieve Bloom Way,** a circular 21-mile (34km) signposted trail that begins and ends in Glenbarrow, County Laois.

ACCOMMODATIONS
MODERATE

Dromineer Bay Hotel. Dromineer Bay, Nenagh, County Tipperary. ☎ **067/24114.** Fax 067/24444. 24 units. £70–£130 ($98–$182) double. No service charge. Rates include full breakfast. AE, MC, V. Free parking.

Tucked along the shores of Lough Derg beside the Dromineer Yacht Club, this recently expanded two-story hotel, long a favorite with anglers, now also appeals to anyone looking for an informal riverside retreat. More than 100 years old, it was originally a coast-guard inn. The rooms are small and simply furnished, although some have four-poster beds and antiques. On the premises are the Moorings restaurant, open for dinner; the Boat House bar/coffee shop/delicatessen, for snacks and lunch; and the Captain's Deck Bar, with an open-air deck upstairs offering fine views of the water. For a little local color and history, look at the bar walls; they're decorated with photographs of the hotel and the village.

Lakeside Hotel. Killaloe, County Clare. ☎ **800/447-7462** from the U.S., or 061/376122. Fax 061/376431. E-mail: lakesidehotelkilaloe@eircom.net. 46 units. TV TEL. £65–£90 ($91–$126) double. No service charge. Rates include full breakfast. AE, MC, V.

Perched on the southern banks of Lough Derg and shaded by ancient trees, this two-story country house–style hotel has one of the loveliest settings of any property in the area. It was completely refurbished in 1994 in bright contemporary style. The guest rooms have standard furnishings, but are greatly enhanced by wide-windowed views of the lake or gardens. Ten nonsmoking rooms and nine superior family suites are available. The restaurant and bar lounge overlook the Shannon. There are an indoor heated swimming pool with water slide, Jacuzzi, sauna, gym, steam room, and tennis court. The hotel is on the Ballina side of the bridge, on the edge of town next to the marina.

✪ **Roundwood House.** 3 miles (4.8km) northwest of Mountrath, on R440 toward the Slieve Bloom Mountains, Mountrath, County Laois. ☎ **0502/32120.** Fax 0502/32711. 10 units. £86.65 ($121.30) double. No service charge. Rates include full Irish breakfast. Dinner (book by 2pm) £25.20 ($35.28). AE, DC, MC, V. Free parking.

Roundwood House offers a put-up-your-feet casual elegance equaled by few other guesthouses. A long-standing member of the select association of private homes known as "Hidden Ireland," Roundwood is very much lived in by Frank and Rosemarie Kennan and their children. The family's warmth and taste pervade the splendid 18th-century early Georgian Palladian country villa, set in 18 acres of secluded woods, pasture, and gardens. Roundwood breathes relaxation and leisure, although more active pursuits are close at hand—particularly the Slieve Bloom Way, a 50-kilometer hill walk through Ireland's most untrammeled range. The Kennans gladly launch or fetch serious hikers.

The six double rooms in the main house are spacious and decorated with a gifted eye for charm and simplicity. The two second-floor rooms share a large central play area that's ideal for families with children. The "Yellow House," across the herb garden and courtyard from the main building, dates from the 17th century and has been tastefully restored to offer four delightful double rooms. Roundwood's soft couches, firm beds, lovely views, myriad good books, large bathtubs, and exquisite meals may not inspire an active holiday, but they go a long way toward calming the soul. The nearest TV is a good walk away. For the restless, croquet and boule are the house sports.

INEXPENSIVE

Lantern House. 6 miles (9.7km) north of Killaloe on the main road, Ogonnelloe, Tuamgraney, County Clare. ☎ **061/923034.** Fax 061/923139. 9 units. TV TEL. £48 ($67.20) double. Rates include full breakfast. AE, DC, MC, V. Closed Dec to mid-Feb. Free parking.

This pleasant, unpretentious guesthouse enjoys wide vistas of Lough Derg. Palm trees grow on the well-tended hilltop grounds. All the public rooms overlook the Shannon, as do some of the guest rooms. Furnishings are homey and comfortable. The cozy lounge has a fireplace, and residents can enjoy a drink at a small bar. The restaurant (see "Dining," below) is quite popular among locals. There's no smoking in the guest rooms, and the beds are uneven. Some are soft enough to prove challenging for the dorsally afflicted.

RENT-A-COTTAGE

For an area of such amazing beauty and wide-open spaces, the Lough Derg region has surprisingly few hotels. In many ways, that's part of its allure—natural lakelands and forests unspoiled by condos, hotels, motels, and fast-food joints. This area, perhaps more than most other parts of Ireland, calls out for visitors to settle in and become part of the way of life. And that is why the "Rent an Irish Cottage" program was pioneered here almost 30 years ago.

The Shannon Development Company came up with the idea of building small rental cottages in rural areas where other satisfactory accommodations were scarce. The cottages were designed in traditional style, with exteriors of white stucco, thatched roofs, and half doors, but aside from the turf fireplaces, all of the furnishings, plumbing, heating, and kitchen appliances inside were totally up-to-date. The cottage idea was an instant success with people from Dublin and other large cities, and it's becoming equally popular with visitors from abroad who want to live like the locals.

The cottages, built in groups of 8 to 12, are on picturesque sites in remote villages such as Puckane, Terryglass, and Whitegate, overlooking or close to Lough Derg's shores. There are no restaurants or bars on-site, and guests are encouraged to shop in local grocery stores, cook their own meals, and congregate in the local pubs each evening. In other words, after a day or two, the visitors become part of the community. Rates range from £140 to £1,200 ($196 to $1,680) per cottage per week, depending on the size (one to six bedrooms) and time of year. Rental rates include bed linen and color TV; towels and metered electricity are extra. For more information, contact **Rent an Irish Cottage,** 85 O'Connell St., Limerick, County Limerick (☎ **061/411109;** fax 061/314821; www.rentacottage.ie).

In recent years, individual owners have built modern cottages with slate or tile roofs. One of the loveliest cottage settings belongs to the **Mountshannon Village Cottages,** Mountshannon, County Clare, a cluster of nine pastel-toned one- and two-story cottages perched on a hill overlooking Lough Derg at Mountshannon Harbour. Grouped like a private village around a garden courtyard, the cottages cost £140 to £450 ($196 to $630) per week, depending on the time of year and number of bedrooms. Some weekend rentals are also available. For more information, contact Bridie Cooke, Gortatleva, Bushypark, Galway, County Galway (☎ and fax 091/525295).

DINING
EXPENSIVE

Brocka-on-the-Water. Kilgarvan Quay, Nenagh, County Tipperary. ☎ **067/22038.** Reservations required. Fixed-price dinner £28 ($39.20); main courses £12–£18 ($16.80–$25.20). No credit cards. May–Oct Mon–Sat 7–9:30pm. INTERNATIONAL.

A small country lane, signposted off the Lough Derg Drive, leads to this country-house restaurant in a garden setting near the shores of Lough Derg. Rather than seeking waterside views, people flock here for the Byrne family's innovative cuisine and warm hospitality. You'll also delight in the antique furnishings. Each table is set with Waterford crystal lamps, Newbridge silver, hand-embroidered linens, and fresh flowers. The menu changes nightly, but specialties often include baked stuffed sole with a sauce of dill and lemon cream, panfried sirloin steak Gaelic-style (flamed in whiskey), ribbons of chicken breast with root ginger and honey, and pork medallions with herb bread crumbs and plum sauce. Many of the dishes are decorated with or incorporate fresh edible flowers from the garden. To finish, don't miss the carragin mousse or farmhouse cheeses from local farms.

MODERATE

Galloping Hogan's Restaurant. Ballina, County Clare. ☎ **061/376162.** Reservations recommended. Main courses £10.95–£16.50 ($15.35–$23.10); lobster £24.50 ($34.30). AE, MC, V. Daily 6:30–10pm. CONTINENTAL.

In a restored old railway station, this restaurant sits beside Lough Derg, overlooking the water on the Ballina side of the Killaloe bridge. The plant-filled conservatory-style room has a patio-terrace for fair-weather dining. The menu here includes rack of lamb and a variety of steaks. Seafood choices might be fresh lobster; grilled or poached scallop of salmon with chive butter sauce; panfried black sole on the bone with nut brown butter and chopped parsley; or baked cod with roasted peppers, tomatoes, fresh spinach, and chilie oil. Bar food is also available from noon to 10pm.

Goosers. Ballina, County Clare. ☎ **061/376791.** Reservations recommended for dinner. Bar food £2–£11 ($2.80–$15.40); dinner main courses £13.50–£23 ($18.90–$32.20). AE, MC, V. Daily 11am–11pm. IRISH.

With a thatched roof and bright mustard-colored exterior, this popular pub and restaurant sits on the Ballina side of the Shannon, looking out at the river and the broad vista of Killaloe. Its informal two rooms have open fireplaces, stone walls and floors, and beamed ceilings, and its pub area contains window seats, sugan chairs, and lots of nautical and fishing memorabilia. The restaurant has booth seating and windows that overlook an adjacent garden, and there's picnic-table seating outside in good weather. The bar-food menu lists the usual standards, including such traditional dishes as bacon and cabbage and Irish stew. The restaurant menu focuses on seafood—lobster, salmon, sole, and monkfish.

Lantern House. Ogonnelloe, County Clare. ☎ **061/923034.** Reservations recommended. Main courses £10–£15 ($14–$21). AE, MC, V. Mid-Feb to Oct daily 6–9pm. Closed Mon off-season. IRISH.

Perched high on a hillside amid palm tree–lined gardens just north of Killaloe, this country-house restaurant enjoys panoramic views of Lough Derg and the verdant hills of the surrounding countryside. Host Phil Hogan extends a warm welcome, and the candlelit dining room exudes old-world charm, with a beamed ceiling, wall lanterns, and lace tablecloths. Menu choices might be poached fresh local salmon, panfried sole, scallops Mornay, or sirloin steak.

INEXPENSIVE

Country Choice. 25 Kenyon St., Nenagh, County Tipperary. ☎ **067/32596.** Lunch main courses £2.50–£5 ($3.50–$7). Mon–Sat 9am–6pm; lunch served noon–6pm. IRISH.

Country Choice is just that: its shelves are brimming with the finest of Irish foodstuffs from an acclaimed local marmalade to farmhouse cheeses. Floury loaves of bread are heaped on the counter, and on the floor baskets glisten with the clear, green orbs of local gooseberries. This is the best place to fill up on picnic fixings before heading out to the shores of Lough Derg. A cafe at the back of the shop is the place to sit with a cup of good coffee and find out what's happening locally—it's a popular gathering place for locals and visitors. There's a reasonably priced lunch menu, and freshly baked goods are served in the morning.

Molly's Bar and Restaurant. Killaloe/Ballina, County Clare. ☎ **061/376632.** Reservations recommended for dinner. All items £2–£13 ($2.80–$18.20). AE, MC, V. Daily 12:30–11:30pm. IRISH.

Next to the Killaloe bridge, this brightly colored pub and restaurant offers views of Killaloe Harbour from most of its windows. The informal interior is like that of a comfortable cottage, with beamed ceilings, wall shelves lined with old plates, vintage clocks, pine and mahogany furnishings, period pictures and prints of the Shannon area, and a stove fireplace. The menu offers both light fare and full dinner selections, such as baked Limerick ham with Madeira sauce, Atlantic salmon Hibernian, and charcoal-grilled steaks. The open-faced fresh crab sandwich on brown bread is especially worth a stop. Outdoor seating is available on picnic-style tables. There's live music, traditional and modern, Thursday to Sunday, as well as a new disco and sports bar in the basement.

PUBS

There are public houses in every town around the Lough Derg route. The pubs of Terryglass, County Tipperary, on the east shore, and of Woodford, County Galway, on the west shore, are particularly well known for their lively sessions of Irish traditional music.

✪ **The Derg Inn,** Terryglass, County Tipperary (☎ 067/22037), with three cozy rooms, has a beer garden courtyard. It's worth a visit just to see this pub's decor of Tipperary horse pictures, old plates, books, beer posters, vintage bottles, hanging tankards, and lanterns. However, most people come for the free traditional music on Wednesday and Sunday.

Paddys Bar, Terryglass, County Tipperary (☎ 067/22147), is known for its fine display of antiques as well as traditional music nightly in summer.

Fiddler and tin-whistle player Anthony Coen was born in Woodford to a musical family that includes six traditional musicians out of nine children. He plays in his hometown, and is often accompanied by his talented daughters, Dearbhla, on the flute and tin whistle, and Eimer, on the concertina and bodhran. They can often be heard at **J. Walsh's Forest Bar** (☎ 0509/49012) or at **Moran's** (☎ 0509/49063), overlooking the Woodford River. The latter establishment is a curiosity—it's probably the only pub in Ireland where you'll find two clerics serving drinks at the bar during the summer. Both Carmelite Order priests, they are the owner's sons and spend their vacation time helping out in the family business. Only in Ireland!

2 Middle Shannon: From Birr to Athlone

Birr is 15 miles (24km) E of Portumna; Athlone is 60 miles (97km) E of Galway

The middle section of the Shannon River is where you'll find one of Ireland's greatest historic sites: the early Christian settlement of **Clonmacnois,** a spot that has been drawing visitors since the 6th century.

This region also includes vast stretches of boglands; the inland town of Birr, known for its magnificent and historic gardens; and **Banagher,** a river town with a picturesque harbor.

In addition, this stretch of the river curves into **Athlone,** the largest town on the Shannon and a leading inland marina for mooring and hiring boats. Athlone's other claim to fame is that it produced Ireland's most famous operatic tenor, the great John McCormack.

AREA ESSENTIALS

GETTING THERE & GETTING AROUND   The best way to get to the Middle Shannon area is by car or boat. Although there's public transportation, you'll need a car to get around the riverbanks. Major roads that lead to this area are the main Galway–Dublin road (N6) from points east and west, N62 from the south, and N55 and N61 from the north.

VISITOR INFORMATION   Information on this area can be obtained from the **Ireland West Tourism Office,** Victoria Place, Eyre Square, Galway (☎ 091/63081), and the **Midlands Tourism Office,** Clonard House, Dublin Road, Mullingar, County Westmeath (☎ 044/48650). Both are open Monday to Friday 9am to 6pm, plus Saturday during peak season.

Seasonal tourist information points are open from May or June to September at signposted sites in **Athlone** (☎ 0902/94630), **Ballinsloe** (☎ 0905/42131), **Birr** (☎ 0509/20110), and **Clonmacnois** (☎ 0905/74134).

EXPLORING THE AREA

Athlone Castle. Athlone, County Westmeath. ☎ **0902/92912.** Admission £3.50 ($4.90) adults, £1.80 ($2.50) seniors and students, £1 ($1.40) children under 13, £8 ($11.20) family. May to mid-Oct daily 10am–5pm. On the riverbank, signposted from all directions.

Built in 1210 for King John of England, this mighty stone fortress sits on the edge of the Shannon. It played an important part in Athlone's history, first as the seat of the presidents of Connaught and later as the headquarters of the governor of Athlone during the first Siege of Athlone in 1690 and the second in 1691. Declared a national monument in 1970, it was recently restored and adapted for use as a visitor center, museum, gallery, and tearoom. The exhibition area offers an audiovisual presentation on the Siege of Athlone. It also contains displays on the castle, the town, the flora and fauna of the Shannon region, and the great Irish tenor John McCormack, Athlone's most honored son. The castle's original medieval walls have been preserved, as have two large cannons dating from the reign of George II and a pair of 10-inch mortars that were cast in 1856.

Battle of Aughrim Interpretative Centre. Galway–Dublin road (N6), Aughrim, near Ballinasloe, County Galway. ☎ **0905/73939.** Admission £2.50 ($3.50) adults, £2 ($2.80) seniors and students, £5 ($7) family. June–Aug Tues–Sat 10am–6pm, Sun 2–6pm.

Using a high-tech three-dimensional audiovisual presentation, this center invites visitors to relive the Battle of Aughrim, on July 12, 1691. On that day, the army of James II of England confronted the forces of his son-in-law, William of Orange, and staged the bloodiest battle in Irish history. The confrontation involved 45,000 soldiers from eight European countries and cost 9,000 lives, changing the course of Irish and European history. The center, which also houses a bookshop, craft shop, and cafe, is in Aughrim village, adjacent to the actual Aughrim battlefield, which is signposted for visitors. Aughrim is on the main Dublin–Galway road, about 12 miles (19km) west of the Shannonbridge/Clonmacnois area.

Birr Castle Demesne. Birr, County Offaly. ☎ **0509/20336.** www.birrcastle.com. Admission £5 ($7) adults, £3.50 ($4.90) students and seniors, £2.50 ($3.50) children over 5, free for children under 6, £12 ($16.80) family. V. Year-round daily 9am–6pm. Take N52 23 miles (37km) southwest of Tullamore.

The main attraction of this inland estate 12 miles (19km) east of the river is its **100-acre garden.** The demesne (or estate) of the Parsons family, now the earls of Rosse, it's laid out around a lake and along the banks of the two adjacent rivers. It contains more than 1,000 species of trees and shrubs, including magnolias, cherry trees, chestnut, and weeping beech. The box hedges are featured in the *Guinness Book of Records* as the tallest in the world, and the hornbeam cloisters are a unique feature. Farther along the path you may combine a bit of stargazing with the garden stroll— the grounds also contain an astronomical exhibit, including an 1845 6-foot reflecting telescope, then the largest in the world, built by the third Earl of Rosse and recently restored to form as part of the new Historic Science Centre. The telescope operates twice daily, at noon and 3pm. During the summer, you can usually find additional rotating exhibits dealing with the history of Birr Castle and its residents. The 17th-century castle and residence is not open to the public.

✪ Bog Train Tours. Bord na Mona/The Irish Peat Board, Blackwater Works, Shannonbridge, County Offaly. ☎ **0905/74114.** Tours £4 ($5.60) adults, £3.30 ($4.60) seniors and students, £2.60 ($3.65) children, £10 ($14) family. Apr–Oct daily 10am–5pm; tours on the hour. Signposted from Shannonbridge.

Bogland discoveries are the focus of this tour in the heart of the Irish midlands, on the east bank of the Shannon. Visitors board the narrow-gauge Clonmacnois and West

Offaly Railway for a 5-mile (8km) circular ride around the Blackwater bog. The commentary explains how the bogland was formed and became a vital source of fuel. The route includes a firsthand look at turf cutting, stacking, and drying, and close-up views of bog plants and wildlife. Participants can even take a turn at digging the turf or picking some bog cotton. The ride lasts approximately 45 minutes. The visitor center also offers an audiovisual story about the bog. For groups who make advance arrangements, a 2- to 4-hour nature trail and field-study tour is available.

Charleville Forest Castle. Off N52/Birr road, Tullamore, County Offaly. ☎ **0506/21279.** Guided tour £3.50 ($4.90) adults, £2 ($2.80) children. Apr–May Sat–Sun 2–5pm; June–Sept Tues–Sun 11am–5pm.

Designed in 1798 by Francis Johnston, one of Ireland's foremost architects, this castle took 12 years to build and was the first of the great Gothic houses. Today it's considered one of the best of the early 19th-century castles remaining in Ireland. The castle has a fine limestone exterior, with fanciful towers, turrets, and battlements. The rooms have spectacular ceilings and plasterwork and great hand-carved stairways, as well as secret passageways and dungeons. Admission includes a guided tour.

✪ **Clonmacnois.** On R357, 4 miles (6.5km) north of Shannonbridge, County Offaly. ☎ **0905/74195.** Admission £3.50 ($4.90) adults, £2.50 ($3.50) seniors, £1.50 ($2.10) students and children, £8 ($11.20) family. Nov to mid-Mar daily 10am–5:30pm; mid-Mar to mid-May and mid-Sept–Oct daily 10am–6pm; mid-May to early Sept daily 9am–7pm.

Resting silently on the east bank of the Shannon, this is one of Ireland's most profound ancient sites. St. Ciaran founded the monastic community of Clonmacnois in 548 at the crucial intersection of the Shannon and the Dublin–Galway land route, and it soon became one of Europe's great centers of learning and culture. For nearly 1,000 years, Clonmacnois flourished under the patronage of numerous Irish kings. The last high king, Rory O'Conor, was buried here in 1198. In the course of time, Clonmacnois was raided repeatedly by native chiefs, Danes, and Anglo-Normans, until it was finally abandoned in 1552. Today you can see the remains of a cathedral, a castle, eight churches, two round towers, three sculpted high crosses, and more than 200 monumental slabs. The site includes an exemplary visitor center with a beautifully designed exhibition, a first-rate audiovisual program, and pleasant tearooms.

Locke's Distillery Museum. On N6, east of Athlone, Kilbeggan, County Westmeath. ☎ **0506/32134.** Admission £3.25 ($4.55) adults, £2.75 ($3.85) seniors and students, £8 ($11.20) family. Apr–Oct daily 9am–6pm; Nov–Mar daily 10am–4pm.

Established in 1757, this 18th- and 19th-century enterprise was one of the oldest licensed pot-still whiskey distilleries in the world. After producing whiskey for almost 200 years, it closed in 1953; over the past 15 years, a local group has restored it as a museum. In 1998 a major new exhibition space opened in the restored front grain loft to display a host of distilling artifacts. A 35-minute tour will not only tell you how whiskey was distilled using old techniques and machinery, but also inform you about the area's social history. It's almost midway between Dublin and Galway, making it a good stop-off point while you're on a cross-country journey or touring in the area. On the premises, you'll find a new restaurant, coffee shop, and craft shop.

SIGHTSEEING CRUISES

Rosanna Cruises. 15 Church St., Athlone, County Westmeath. ☎ **0902/73383.** Lough Ree trip £6 ($8.40) adults, £4 ($5.60) children; Clonmacnois trip £10 ($14) adults, £6 ($8.40) seniors, students, children. May–Sept, Lough Ree trip daily 2:30 and 4:30pm; Clonmacnois trip daily 9am.

This company offers cruises of the inner lakes of Lough Ree or to Clonmacnois on board the 71-passenger *Viking I.* Patrons hear live commentary on the 300-year Viking history on the Shannon and Lough Ree and refreshments. The Lough Ree trip takes 1½ hours; the 4-hour Clonmacnois trip includes a 1-hour stopover at the monastic site. The company furnishes children with Viking helmets, costumes, and plastic swords for the duration of the trip to add a touch of berserk authenticity. Buy tickets at the Strand Fishing Tackle Shop (☎ 0902/79277), where you'll also depart.

Shannon Holidays. Jolly Mariner Marina, Athlone, County Westmeath. ☎ **0902/72892.** www.iol.ie/wmeathtc/acl. Cruise £6 ($8.40) adults, £3.50 ($4.90) children. May–Sept, times vary.

This company operates cruises around Lough Ree on board the 60-passenger M.V. *Ross.* Average cruise time is 90 minutes, and the boat has a sundeck and a covered deck with a bar and coffee shop.

Silverline Cruisers Ltd. The Marina, Banagher, County Offaly. ☎ **0509/51112.** Cruise £4 ($5.60) adults, £2.50 ($3.50) children. June–Sept, times vary.

This company operates 90-minute cruises on the *River Queen,* a 54-seat enclosed river bus. The trip starts out by passing under the seven-arched Banagher Stone Bridge, then passes Martello towers and fortresses on its way downstream to Victoria Lock, the largest lock on the Shannon system. The taped commentary covers all the historical aspects of the route. There's a bar on board.

OUTDOOR PURSUITS & SPECTATOR SPORTS

BICYCLING   Bikes can be rented from **Shannon Holidays,** Jolly Mariner Marina, Athlone, County Westmeath (☎ 0902/72892), for £30 ($42) per week.

BOATING   The following companies rent cabin cruisers, usually for a minimum of 1 week, along this section of the Shannon: **Athlone Cruisers,** Jolly Mariner Marina, Athlone, County Westmeath (☎ 0902/72892; www.iol.ie/_wmeathtc/acl); **Carrick Craft Cruisers,** The Marina, Carrick-on-Shannon, County Leitrim (☎ 078/20236); **Silverline Cruisers,** The Marina, Banagher, County Offaly (☎ 0509/51112); and **Tara Cruiser Ltd.,** Kilfaughna, Knockvicar, County Roscommon (☎ 079/67777). Crafts range from three to eight berths; rates average £540 to £1,770 ($756 to $2,478) per week in high season.

GOLF   **Birr Golf Club,** Birr, County Offaly (☎ 0509/20082), is an 18-hole course on 112 acres of parkland countryside; the greens fees are £12 ($16.80) weekdays, £14 ($19.60) weekends.

In the Athlone area are the 18-hole **Athlone Golf Club,** Hodson Bay, Athlone, County Roscommon (☎ 0902/92073), with greens fees of £18 ($25.20) weekdays, £20 ($28) weekends; and the new 18-hole championship **Mount Temple Golf Club,** Moate, County Westmeath (☎ 0902/81841), 5 miles (8km) east of Athlone, with greens fees of £16 ($22.40) weekdays, £18 ($25.20) weekends.

HORSE RACING   Horse racing takes place in July, August, and September at the **Kilbeggan Racecourse,** Loughnagore, Kilbeggan, County Westmeath (☎ 0506/32176), off the main Mullingar road (N52), a mile from town. Admission is £5 ($7) for adults, £2.50 ($3.50) for students.

ACCOMMODATIONS & DINING
VERY EXPENSIVE

✪ **Hodson Bay Hotel.** Roscommon Rd., Athlone, County Westmeath. ☎ **0902/92444.** Fax 0902/80520. www.hodsonbayhotel.com. 133 units. TV TEL. £110–£200 ($154–$280) double. No service charge. Rates include full breakfast. AE, DC, MC, V.

On the shores of Lough Ree, this four-story hotel with a pale yellow facade stands out on the harborfront. Totally renovated and extended in 1992, it offers rooms with contemporary light-wood furnishings, pastel-toned quilted fabrics, and ortho-pedic beds. The public areas and most of the guest rooms overlook the marina and Hodson's Pillar, a stone monument on an island offshore that's reputed to mark the center of Ireland.

Dining: L'Escale Restaurant offers formal dining, and the Waterfront Bar & Buttery serves light fare.

Amenities: Indoor heated swimming pool, sauna, steam room, gym, and solarium. Adjacent 18-hole golf course.

MODERATE

✪ **Brosna Lodge Hotel.** Main St., Banagher, County Offaly. ☎ **0509/51350.** Fax 0509/51521. 14 units. TV TEL. £52 ($72.80) double. No service charge. Rates include full breakfast. DISC, MC, V. Free parking.

Although it sits on the main thoroughfare in a busy river town near Clonmacnois, this two-story hotel has a warm country atmosphere, thanks to a beautiful flower-filled front garden and enthusiastic innkeeper-owners Geraldine and Aidan Hoare. The pub-lic areas, which include Snipes Restaurant, a cozy bar, and a TV lounge, are furnished with traditional period pieces and local antiques. The rooms are bright and airy, and overlook the gardens or the town. Best of all, it's just a short walk to the riverfront.

Prince of Wales. Church St., Athlone, County Westmeath. ☎ **0902/72626.** Fax 0902/75658. 69 units. TV TEL. £80–£120 ($112–$168) double. No service charge. Rates include full breakfast. AE, DC, MC, V.

Dating from the 1780s and originally known as Rourke's Hotel, this three-story prop-erty is in the center of Athlone on a busy street. In spite of its age, it has a modern interior with tasteful brass touches and paneled walls. The rooms have contemporary Irish furnishings with light woods and multicolored fabrics, plus modern conve-niences, including tea/coffeemakers and garment presses. All have been recently refur-bished. On the premises are the Beech Tree restaurant, the Cherry Tree coffee shop, and the Hunters bar. A historical note: The hotel took its present name in 1863 to mark the marriage of the heir to the British throne.

INEXPENSIVE

Dooly's Hotel. Emmet Sq., Birr, County Offaly. ☎ **0509/20032.** Fax 0509/21332. www.doolyshotel.com. 18 units. TV TEL. £70–£74 ($98–$103.60) double. No service charge. Rates include full breakfast. AE, DC, MC, V. Free public parking.

Dating from 1747, this three-story Georgian hotel is in the center of town. Although one of Ireland's oldest former coaching inns, it's been thoroughly restored and refur-bished in recent years. The public areas retain their Georgian charm, while the guest rooms offer all the modern conveniences, such as tea/coffeemakers; rooms have views of the town or back garden. The Emmet Restaurant serves international fare, and the coffee shop is open 10am to 10pm—handy for travelers in search of a meal at odd hours. Also on the premises is the Coach House Bar.

PUBS

Of all the river towns in this section of the Shannon, Banagher is particularly well known for lively Irish traditional music sessions at two of its pubs. At **J. J. Hough's,** Main Street (no phone), there's music every night during the summer, and Friday to Sunday the rest of the year. The **Vine House,** West End (☎ **0902/51463**), offers music every night during the summer.

3 Upper Shannon: From Lough Ree to Lough Allen

Roscommon is 51 miles (82km) NE of Galway, 91 miles (147km) NW of Dublin; Longford is 80 miles (129km) NW of Dublin, 27 miles (44km) NE of Athlone; Carrick-on-Shannon is 35 miles (56km) SE of Sligo; Cavan is 65 miles (105km) NW of Dublin

The Upper Shannon River region is home to a remarkable assortment of castles, great houses, and museums. One of Ireland's newest and most significant collections, the **Irish Famine Museum,** Strokestown, County Roscommon, is of special importance as Ireland commemorates the 150th anniversary of the Great Hunger. This museum chronicles the great tragedy that changed the course of history in Ireland and the world, sending forth the Irish diaspora to England, the United States, Canada, and Australia.

In addition, the shores of the Upper Shannon encompass **Lough Ree,** the second largest of Shannon's lakes. Considered almost an inland sea, it's distinguished by long, flat vistas across the farming countryside of counties Roscommon, Westmeath, and Longford.

County Longford gives the river its literary associations. This eastern bank of the Shannon is often referred to as "Goldsmith country," because 18th-century dramatist, novelist, and poet Oliver Goldsmith was born at Pallas, near Ballymahon. Although Goldsmith did much of his writing in London, it's said that he drew on many of his Irish experiences for his works, including *She Stoops to Conquer.*

Above Lough Ree, the river is relatively narrow until it reaches the town of **Carrick-on-Shannon,** County Leitrim. It's situated on one of the great ancient crossing places of the Shannon. The town is particularly known as a center for boating, with a vast marina in the middle of the town where many companies rent cabin cruisers.

The whole county of **Leitrim** is uniquely affected by the Shannon's waters. It's divided into two parts, almost wholly separated by Lough Allen. A storage reservoir for a nearby hydroelectric plant, Lough Allen is the Shannon's third-largest lake, 7 miles (11km) long and 3 miles (4.8km) wide. North of Lough Allen, in County Cavan, is the source of the river: the **Shannon Pot,** on the southern slopes of the Cuilcagh Mountain.

The scope of the Shannon has been broadened in recent years, so it's now possible to travel from the Shannon River to Lough Erne, using a stretch of water known as the Ballinamore–Ballyconnell Canal. Following a painstaking restoration, it was reopened in the spring of 1994, after a lapse of 125 years. Because it provides a clear path from the Shannon in the Republic of Ireland to Lough Erne in Northern Ireland, the new passage is officially designated the Shannon–Erne Waterway. It's a symbol of cross-border cooperation and a touchstone in a new golden age of Irish waterway travel.

AREA ESSENTIALS

GETTING THERE & GETTING AROUND   The best way to get to the Upper Shannon area is by car or boat. Although there's public transportation, you'll need a car to get around the riverbanks and to the various attractions. Among major roads that lead to this area are the main Dublin–Sligo road (N4), the main Dublin–Cavan road (N3), N5 and N63 from Castlebar and the west, and N61 and N55 from the south.

VISITOR INFORMATION   Information on **County Roscommon** is available from the **Ireland West Tourism Office,** Victoria Place, Eyre Square, Galway (☎ 091/63081); on **County Longford** from the **Midlands East Tourism Office,** Clonard House, Dublin Road, Mullingar, County Westmeath (☎ 044/48761); on

County Cavan from the **Cavan Tourist Office,** Farnham Street, Cavan, County Cavan (☎ **049/4331942**); and on **County Leitrim** from the **North-West Tourism Office,** Aras Reddan, Temple Street, Sligo (☎ **071/61201**), and from the tourist office at Carrick-on-Shannon (☎ **078/20170**).

Seasonal information points, operating from June to August, are signposted in **Boyle** (☎ **079/62145**), **Longford** (☎ **043/46566**), and **Roscommon** (☎ **0903/26342**).

EXPLORING THE AREA

Boyle Abbey. N4, Boyle, County Roscommon. ☎ **079/62604.** Admission £1 ($1.40) adults, 70p (98¢) seniors, 40p (56¢) children and students, £3 ($4.20) family. Early Apr–Oct daily 9:30am–6:30pm.

Boyle Abbey was founded in 1161 as a daughter house of the Cistercian Abbey at Mellifont. Today it is the most impressive survivor of the early Irish Cistercian settlements of the late 12th and early 13th centuries. The Cistercian Order was founded in 11th-century France as a return to the uncompromised simplicity and tranquil austerity of the monastic calling. The abbey was to be a haven of otherworldliness, and yet the world's savagery descended on Boyle Abbey more than once. Its walls were torn down, and its monks murdered. What remains is a complex fossil clearly imprinted with both the serene and violent aspects of the abbey's history. The ruins of Boyle Abbey evoke in visitors a sense of what this place has seen, suffered, and enjoyed. The interpretive center, housed in the restored gatehouse, is informative and thoughtfully designed.

Cavan Crystal Visitor Centre. Dublin road (N3), Cavan, County Cavan. ☎ **049/433-1800.** Free admission. Mon–Fri 9:30am–6pm, Sat 10am–5pm, Sun noon–5pm.

One of the country's top three crystal companies, this establishment is known for its delicate glassware, mouth-blown and hand-cut by skilled craftspeople. Visitors are invited to watch as skilled master blowers fashion the molten crystal into intricate shapes and designs, followed by the precision work of the master cutters. The glassware is for sale in the extended craft and factory shop. The center also includes a restaurant.

✪ **Clonalis House.** On the N60 west of Castlerea, County Roscommon. ☎ **0907/20014.** Admission £3.50 ($4.90) adults, £2.50 ($3.50) seniors and students, £1.50 ($2.10) children over 7, free for children under 8. June–Sept 15 Mon–Sat 11am–5pm.

Standing on land that has belonged to the O'Conors for more than 1,500 years, this is one of Ireland's great houses. It's the ancestral home of the O'Conors, kings of Connaught, and the home of the O'Conor Don, the direct descendant of the last high king of Ireland.

The house, built in 1880, is a combination of Victorian, Italianate, and Queen Anne architecture, with mostly Louis XV–style furnishings, plus antique lace, horse-drawn farm machinery, and other memorabilia. It's primarily a museum of the O'Conor (O'Connor) family, with portraits, documents, and genealogical tracts dating back 2,000 years. Displays also include a rare ancient harp that's said to have belonged to Turlough O'Carolan (1670–1738), the blind Irish bard who composed songs that are still sung today. The grounds, with terraced and woodland gardens, also hold the O'Conor inauguration stone, similar to the Stone of Scone at Westminster Abbey.

Lough Key Forest Park. Enter from the main Dublin–Sligo road (N4), 2 miles (3.2km) east of Boyle, County Roscommon. ☎ **079/62363.** Admission to park £3 ($4.20) per car. Year-round daily dawn–dusk; admission charged Apr–Sept.

If you're driving cross-country and want to stop for a picnic and a walk, or if you're traveling with children and are in search of a perfect place to let them loose, look no further. Spanning 840 acres along the shores of Lough Key and made up of mixed woodlands, a lake, and more than a dozen islands, this is one of Ireland's foremost lakeside parks. The grounds include nature walks, ancient monuments, ring forts, a central viewing tower, picnic grounds, a cafe, and a shop. In addition to cypress groves and other diverse foliage, you'll find a unique display of bog gardens, where a wide selection of peat-loving plants and shrubs flourishes. Deer, otters, hedgehogs, birds, pheasants, and many other forms of wildlife roam the park. The lake is navigable from the Shannon on the Boyle River. Powerboats and rowboats are available to rent, and there are pony and cart rides through the park.

Lough Rynn House & Gardens. South of Carrick-on-Shannon, on the outskirts of Mohill, 3¼ miles (5.2km) from the main Dublin–Sligo road (N4), County Leitrim. ☎ **078/31427.** Admission £3.50 ($4.90) per car. Guided tour £1 ($1.40) adults, 50p (70¢) children. May–Aug daily 10am–7pm.

Seat of the Clements, the earls of Leitrim, this estate comprises 100 acres of woodland, ornamental gardens, open pastures, and lakes. Of particular interest is the 3-acre terraced walled garden dating from 1859. It's one of the largest of its kind in the country, laid out in the manner of a Victorian pleasure garden. The arboretum contains specimens of the tulip tree, California redwood, and other exotic species, including the oldest monkey puzzle tree in Ireland. Four thousand years of history can be seen at the rear of the house in one 180-degree sweep of the eye. The Neolithic burial tomb atop Druids Hill was constructed about 2000 B.C.; Reynolds Castle, a lonely sentinel by the lakeshore, dates from the 16th century; and Lough Rynn House was built in 1832.

✪ Strokestown Park House, Gardens & Famine Museum. On the main Dublin–Castlebar road (N5), Strokestown Park, Strokestown, County Roscommon. ☎ **078/33013.** www.strokestownpark.ie. Admission to gardens £3.25 ($4.55) adults, 50p (70¢) children, £7.50 ($10.50) family. Admission to house and museum £3.25 ($4.55) adults, £2.60 ($3.65) seniors and students, £1.50 ($2.10) children, £7.50 ($10.50) family. Apr–Oct daily 11am–5:30pm.

One of the defining events of Ireland's history, the Great Potato Famine of the 1840s, is the focus of this museum, which opened in 1994. Housed in the stable yards of Strokestown Park House, this museum illustrates how and why the famine started, how English colonial officials failed to prevent its spread, and how it reduced the Irish population of 8.1 million by nearly 3 million through death and mass emigration. The exhibits range from photographs, letters, documents, and satirical cartoons to farm implements and a huge cauldron that was used for soup to feed the people in a famine-relief program. This museum is particularly interesting for Irish Americans, tens of millions of whom trace their ancestry to those who left the country during and after the famine. The museum also seeks to relate the events of the Irish famine to con-temporary world hunger and poverty. A 4-acre pleasure garden was recently restored and opened to the public.

Strokestown Park House was the seat of the Pakenham–Mahon family from 1600 to 1979. The 45-room Palladian house, designed for Thomas Mahon by German architect Richard Castle in the 1730s, incorporates parts of an earlier tower house. The center block is fully furnished as it was in earlier days, surrounded by two wings. The north wing houses Ireland's last galleried kitchen (a kitchen gallery allowed the lady of the house to observe the culinary activity without being part of it). The south wing is an elaborate vaulted stable, often described as an equine cathedral.

Tullynally Castle and Gardens. About 20 miles (32km) east of Longford and 13 miles (21km) north of Mullingar, off the main Dublin–Sligo road (N4), Castlepollard, County Westmeath. ☎ **044/61159.** Admission to gardens £3 ($4.20) adults, £1 ($1.40) children; admission to both castle and gardens £5 ($7) adults, £2.50 ($3.50) children. Castle mid-June to July daily 2:30–6pm; gardens May–Aug daily 2–6pm. Closed in other months.

A turreted and towered Gothic Revival manor, this house has been the home of the Pakenham family, the earls of Longford, since 1655. The highlights include a great hall that rises through two stories, with a ceiling of plaster gothic vaulting, and a collection of family portraits, china, and furniture. There's also a collection of 19th-century gadgets. The 30-acre grounds are an attraction in themselves, with woodland walks, a linear water garden, a Victorian grotto, and an avenue of 200-year-old Irish yew trees. Tullynally is near Lough Derravaragh, an idyllic spot featured in the legendary Irish tale *The Children of Lir*. The tearoom is open daily May to August.

SPORTS & OUTDOOR PURSUITS

BOATING The following companies rent cabin cruisers along this part of the Shannon: **Athlone Cruisers,** Jolly Mariner Marina, Athlone, County Westmeath (☎ **0902/72892**); **Carrick Craft,** The Marina, Carrick-on-Shannon, County Leitrim (☎ **078/21248**); and **Emerald Star Line,** The Marina, Carrick-on-Shannon, County Leitrim (☎ **078/20234**).

GOLF There are two 18-hole championship golf courses in the area that should not be missed. Opened in 1993, the **Glasson Golf and Country Club,** Glasson, County Westmeath (☎ **0902/85120**), is on the shores of Lough Ree, 6 miles (9.7km) north of Athlone. Greens fees are £27 ($37.80) weekdays, £30 ($42) weekends. The **Slieve Russell Hotel Golf Club,** Cranaghan, Ballyconnell, County Cavan (☎ **049/26444**), charges greens fees of £32 ($44.80) weekdays, £40 ($56) weekends, for those not staying at the hotel.

Two other 18-hole courses in the area are **County Cavan Golf Club,** Arnmore House, Drumellis, County Cavan (☎ **049/433-1283**), with greens fees of £14 ($19.60) weekdays, £16 ($22.40) weekends; and **County Longford Golf Club,** Dublin Road, Longford (☎ **043/46310**), with greens fees of £12 ($16.80) weekdays, £15 ($21) weekends.

HORSEBACK RIDING **Moorlands Equestrian & Leisure Center,** Drumshanbo, County Leitrim (☎ **078/41095**), offers lessons, as well as trail rides along Lough Allen and the nearby hills. Children are welcome. During the off-season, B.H.S. certification courses in equestrian science are offered. Book lessons or trail rides at least 1 day in advance; ask for Karen or Neil McManus. Mountain walking, water sports, and accommodations are also offered.

ACCOMMODATIONS & DINING
EXPENSIVE

✪ **Slieve Russell Hotel.** Ballyconnell, County Cavan. ☎ **049/952-6444.** Fax 049/952-6474. www.quinn-group.com. 151 units. TV TEL. £140–£165 ($196–$231) double. No service charge. Rates include full breakfast. DC, MC, V. Free parking.

Set on 400 acres of parklands and gardens, including 50 acres of lakes and ponds, this impressive four-story hotel is named after a nearby mountain that's known in Irish as Slieve Rushen. Although relatively new, the hotel captures the opulence and charm of a bygone era, with public areas that boast marbled colonnades, huge open fireplaces, plush carpets, marble staircases, and wrought-iron trim. The conservatory-style Fountain Room exudes a country garden atmosphere, with its skylit glass dome and array of leafy plants. Guest rooms are modern and large, with light-wood furnishings, pastel-toned fabrics, and brass accessories. Each room has a garment press, tea/coffeemaker, and hair dryer. Situated near the Shannon-Erne Waterway, this hotel is a good base for touring not only the upper Shannon area, but also the attractions of Enniskillen and Northern Ireland.

Dining/Diversions: Choices include the Conall Cearnach Restaurant (gourmet cuisine); the brasserie-style Brackly Restaurant (light fare); the Kells Bar, with a stunning decor of illustrations from the Book of Kells; and the intimate Pike Bar for guests.

Amenities: Concierge, room service, baby-sitting, laundry and dry cleaning, 18-hole championship golf course, heated indoor swimming pool, sauna, steam room, Jacuzzi, exercise room, two squash courts, four all-weather tennis courts, hairdressing salon, gift shop, walking trails.

MODERATE

Hotel Kilmore. Dublin road (N3), Cavan, County Cavan. ☎ **049/433-2288.** Fax 049/4332458. www.quinn-group.com. 39 units. TV TEL. £80 ($112) double. No service charge. Rates include full breakfast. AE, DC, MC, V. Free private parking.

Located 2 miles (3.2km) south of Cavan Town, this modern hotel was built in the early 1980s and recently was totally refurbished and redecorated to provide a new level of comfort. The public areas are airy and bright, overlooking the garden with its trio of fountains. Guest rooms have hair dryers and tea/coffee-making facilities. Nonsmoking rooms available. The Annalee Restaurant specializes in fish and game dishes, and the Dome is a new state-of-the-art nightclub.

Park Hotel. Deer Park Lodge, Cavan–Dublin road (N3), Virginia, County Cavan. ☎ **049/854-7235.** Fax 049/854-7203. www.bihotels.com. 19 units, 16 with bathroom. TV TEL. £70–£100 ($98–$140) double. No service charge. Rates include full breakfast. AE, MC, V. Free parking.

Set on 100 acres of woodlands and gardens beside Lough Ramor, this hotel dates from 1751. Originally known as Deer Park Lodge, a sporting and summer residence of the Marquis of Headfort, it became a hotel in the 1930s. It has since had a number of renovations and extensions, making for lots of connecting corridors and varying standards of guest rooms. The public areas retain a definite 18th-century charm, with high ceilings, elaborate chandeliers, period furnishings, and original oil paintings. There are a restaurant, a lounge bar, a nine-hole golf course, a hard tennis court, fishing privileges, boating equipment, and forest walking trails. The hotel and its kitchen are used as the Irish campus for the Baltimore International (Culinary) College in the off-season.

INEXPENSIVE

✪ **Glencarne House.** Signposted on N4, between Carrick-on-Shannon and Boyle, Ardcarne, Carrick-on-Shannon, County Leitrim. ☎ **079/67013.** 6 units. £48 ($67.20) double. No service charge. Rates include full Irish breakfast. Fixed-price dinner £18 ($25.20). No credit cards. Closed mid-Oct to Feb.

Situated on a 100-acre working farm, Glencarne is a beautifully restored and recently redecorated late Georgian house with great charm and warmth. The two front rooms (nos. 1 and 2) enjoy a sweeping view of the valley below, and an especially spacious double with an adjoining twin combine to make an elegant family suite. Rooms feature brass poster beds, antique furnishings, and fresh flowers in abundance. Dinner is the high point of life at Glencarne; the Harringtons draw from their own produce and meats and present a fresh, sumptuous feast. Then, when there's nothing left to do but collapse, orthopedic beds are there to catch you.

✪ **Ross Castle and House.** Mount Nugent, County Cavan. Ross Castle. ☎ **049/854-0237.** Ross House ☎ and fax 049/854-0218. E-mail: rosshouse@eircom.net. 10 units. TEL. £50–£60 ($70–$84) double. No service charge. MC, V. House closed Dec–Feb. Signposted from Mount Nugent.

This 400-acre, family-run horse, cattle, and sheep farm on Lough Sheelin offers appealing options in accommodations and activities. It's a unique place, and one of the most affordable hideaways I have discovered in Ireland.

Ross Castle is a 16th-century fortified tower that's said to be haunted by a lovesick bride-to-be named Sabrina, whose lover, Orwin, drowned in Lough Sheelin en route to their elopement. They're buried together in a nearby field. Today, the place is restored, with central heating throughout (even in the tower rooms). It contains four guest rooms, including one family room, and is managed by Viola Harkort. Nearby Ross House, where the hosts are Peter and Ulla Harkort, is a spacious, comfortable manor house with seven guest rooms. Rooms in the house (unlike castle accommodations) have TV sets. The oldest portions of the building date from the mid–17th century.

Horseback riding, tennis courts, baby-sitting, sauna, and Jacuzzi are all on hand. Also available are fishing boats with or without motors—the place is noted for its brown trout and is stocked with pike and perch. One of the Harkorts' daughters, a physiotherapist at the regional hospital, offers guests massages in the evening, by appointment. On request, three-course dinners are served, with an excellent small selection of wines, modestly priced.

Whether you fish or not, for trout or ghosts, this is a most congenial spot.

A PUB

Although there are many good pubs in the area, don't miss the **Derragarra Inn,** Butlersbridge, County Cavan (☎ **049/433-1003**), for a drink or a meal. More than 200 years old, it's full of local farm implements and crafts, as well as exotic souvenirs collected by former owner John Clancy during his travels around the world. Relax by the old turf fireplace or on the garden patio. It's 4 miles (6.5km) north of Cavan Town.

Northern Ireland 15

John Hume, one of Northern Ireland's most distinguished statesmen and peacemakers, once said, "Anyone who isn't confused in Northern Ireland doesn't really understand what is going on." These are sobering words for anyone about to sketch, in a few paragraphs, this unique place and its remarkable people.

The north of Ireland (or "Ulster") has for thousands of years been a land apart. Bits of ancient walls, older than even the Irish memory, have been found, indicating the division and hostility reflected in the great Irish epic *The Tain*. Granted, there is no shortage of walls—or hostility, for that matter—in Ireland. But the North is different. Its walls and enmities have been drawn and redrawn, deepened and reinforced down to the present, as if the past were yesterday and today and tomorrow, without end.

Here is where it becomes confusing. "Northern Ireland," the title of this chapter, designates a political rather than a geographical destination. It is not simply a measure of latitude. Parts of the Republic, or "the South," lie farther north than "the North," whose boundaries follow historical, not topographical, contours and divisions. Think of the Mason-Dixon Line that once divided the American North and South, and then imagine that their Civil War had ended differently, with two Americas. Imagine that traveling from Philadelphia to Baltimore entailed showing your passport and changing currency. Then add to this image a peace that would not hold, a war that would not end.

To outsiders, the "Troubles"—mutually inflicted and endured by the people of Northern Ireland across several decades—are incomprehensible. Other people's prejudices and quarrels usually are. From a visitor's perspective, the violence has been remarkably contained. Like diplomats, foreigners have enjoyed a certain immunity. Derry and Belfast at their worst have been as safe for visitors as almost any comparable American city, and the Ulster countryside has been as idyllic and serene as Vermont. For the outsider, driving through Northern Ireland was and is no more cause for fear than driving to work. Not so for the people of Northern Ireland, whose wounds and grief run deep.

Fortunately, their resilience and resolve run even deeper. On May 22, 1998, Northerners and their fellow islanders in the Republic went to the polls and voted for a fresh future, one that would not be rutted or wrecked by the past. The agreement ratified that day dismantled the claims of both Ireland and Britain to the North and acknowledged the sovereign right of the people of Northern Ireland to envision and enact

Northern Ireland

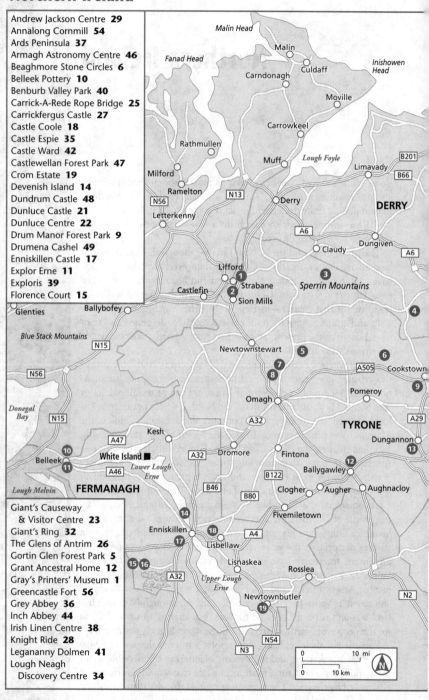

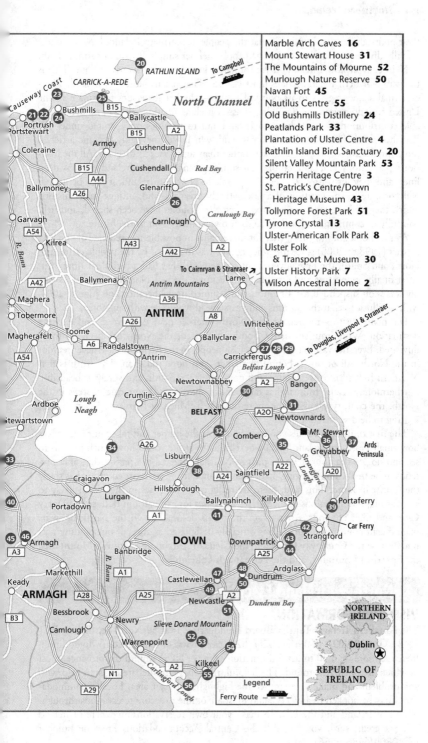

Marble Arch Caves **16**
Mount Stewart House **31**
The Mountains of Mourne **52**
Murlough Nature Reserve **50**
Navan Fort **45**
Nautilus Centre **55**
Old Bushmills Distillery **24**
Peatlands Park **33**
Plantation of Ulster Centre **4**
Rathlin Island Bird Sanctuary **20**
Silent Valley Mountain Park **53**
Sperrin Heritage Centre **3**
St. Patrick's Centre/Down
   Heritage Museum **43**
Tollymore Forest Park **51**
Tyrone Crystal **13**
Ulster-American Folk Park **8**
Ulster Folk
   & Transport Museum **30**
Ulster History Park **7**
Wilson Ancestral Home **2**

RATHLIN ISLAND   To Campbell

CARRICK-A-REDE

Causeway Coast

North Channel

Bushmills

B15

Ballycastle

Portrush
Portstewart

B15   A2

Coleraine

Armoy

Cushendun

B15

Cushendall   Red Bay

A44

Ballymoney

Glenariff

A26

Garvagh

Carnlough Bay

A54

Kilrea

Carnlough

R. Bann

A43

To Cairnryan & Stranraer

Ballymena

A2

A42

Antrim Mountains

Larne

Maghera

A36

Tobermore

ANTRIM

A8

Magherafelt

A26

Whitehead

A54

Toome

Randalstown

A6

To Douglas, Liverpool & Stranraer

Ballyclare

Ardboe

Lough
Neagh

Antrim

Carrickfergus

Belfast Lough

Stewartstown

Crumlin   A52

Newtownabbey   A2

Bangor

BELFAST   A20

Newtownards

A26

Comber

Mt. Stewart

Ards
Peninsula

Lisburn

Greyabbey

A22

Strangford
Lough

A20

Craigavon

Saintfield

A24

Lurgan

Hillsborough

Portaferry

A1

Ballynahinch

Killyleagh

Portadown

Car Ferry

DOWN

Strangford

Armagh

Downpatrick

Banbridge

A25

A3

Markethill

A1

Ardglass

Keady

Castlewellan

Dundrum

ARMAGH   A28

A25

Newcastle   A2

Bessbrook

Dundrum Bay

Camlough

Newry

Slieve Donard Mountain

B3

Warrenpoint

Kilkeel

N1   A2

Carlingford Lough

A29

Legend
Ferry Route

NORTHERN
IRELAND

Dublin

REPUBLIC OF
IRELAND

their political identity. Implied is that the people of Northern Ireland, however traditionally divided, are and must be one people, neither simply British nor simply Irish.

Neither Irish nor British, and yet somehow both. In other words, unique. This is the way Northern Ireland strikes most visitors. That means Northern Ireland, whatever final shape it gives to its political future—whether it decides to remain in the United Kingdom, join the Republic, or assert itself as a nation—has a unique, invaluable contribution to make both to Ireland and to the isles once united under the British Crown. The focus here is on Ireland, which will inevitably become a richer, more interesting island as it celebrates rather than suppresses its diversity. All the invasions, plantations, and conflicts of the past have given the face of Ireland its many deep lines, and they form its character. The people of Northern Ireland, it is to be hoped, will conspire in the creation of a fascinatingly diverse island, unique in its history, which they all have made and shared. Even the Troubles have been shared, and held painfully in common, and will make their own contribution to the future.

As this book goes to press, that future remains impossible to predict. For the past 2 years (1998 to 2000) since the peace accord was mandated by the people of Ireland, North and South, the new government of the North has had a turbulent time of it. After finally appointing and installing its executive, the new Northern Ireland Assembly was soon suspended for 4 months and resumed its deliberations on June 5, 2000, with no illusions that the months and years ahead would be without storm.

For many visitors to Ireland, the North offers a new, uncharted, and exciting destination. While tourism to the South has soared, the North has been relatively unvisited. Even the vast majority of the Irish people in the Republic have never set foot in the North. All of this is bound to change, and none too soon. The truth is that Northern Ireland is as welcoming and gracious as the South, and surely as beautiful. Furthermore, because tourism has taken much shorter and more careful steps in the North, the countryside is all the more unspoiled. Much of Northern Ireland is just waiting to be discovered.

The first thing that strikes you once you cross the border and take your bearings is how small Northern Ireland is. The next thing to strike you is how much there is to see and do. As the Tourist Board puts it, Northern Ireland is a nation that only pretends to be small. The divvying up of that nation, cutting across its counties, has solely the tourist in mind. This said, there are really only two cities in the North likely to serve as major destinations in themselves and bases for exploration: **Belfast** and **Derry City,** and their environs. After these, the major destinations in the North lie in its magnificent countryside, in regions officially designated as areas of outstanding natural beauty: the **Causeway Coast** and the **Glens of Antrim,** the **Mourne Mountains,** the **Sperrin Mountains,** and the **Fermanagh Lakelands.**

1 Northern Ireland Essentials

VISITOR INFORMATION

The **Northern Ireland Tourist Board** headquarters is at 59 North St., Belfast BT1 1NB (☎ **028/9024-6609;** fax 028/9024-0960; www.ni-tourism.com). In addition, there are more than 30 tourist information centers (TICs) around the province, most of which are open year-round. The helpful, friendly personnel are eager to help with any problem and make sure you see the highlights of their area. Local accommodations may be booked in any TIC, and most are online to secure reservations throughout all of Ireland and the UK. To make your own reservations anywhere in Ireland using a credit card, you can call the Central Accommodations Freefone number (☎ **0800/6686-6866**).

GETTING TO THE NORTH

BY AIR   Aer Lingus (☎ 800/474-7424; www.aerlingus.ie) offers scheduled flights from Boston and New York via Shannon to **Belfast International Airport** (☎ 028/94-422888). Other major carriers offer connecting flights from the United States and Canada via London/Heathrow, Glasgow, or Manchester. Charter service to Shannon, Dublin, and Belfast is offered by a range of operators, such as **Sceptre Charters** (☎ 800/221-0924) and **Irish Charters** (☎ 888/431-6688) in the U.S., and by **Air Transat Holidays** (☎ 800/587-2672) in Canada.

Direct flights into **Belfast International Airport** (www.bial.co.uk) include service by **British Airways** (☎ 0345/222111; www.british-airways.com) from Birmingham, Edinburgh, and London/Heathrow; and by **Virgin Express** (☎ 800/891199; www.fly.virgin.com) from London/Heathrow. In addition, there is service into **Belfast City Airport** (☎ 028/9045-7745; www.belfastcityairport.com) by a range of carriers, including **British Airways** flights from Edinburgh, Glasgow, Leeds, Liverpool, and Manchester, and by **Jersey European** (☎ 0990/676676) from Birmingham, Bristol, Exeter, London Stansted, and London Gatwick. Service to **Derry City Eglinton Airport** is provided by **British Airways** from Glasgow and Manchester, and by **Ryanair** (☎ 0541/569569 in Britain; www.ryanair.com) from London Stansted.

Most international flights into Ireland land in Dublin, with connecting flights to Belfast. Direct service into Belfast International includes **Sabena** (☎ 028/9448-4823) from Brussels and **Maersk Air** (☎ 0345/222111 in Britain) from Copenhagen.

BY FERRY   The quickest crossing from Britain to Northern Ireland is the 90-minute **SeaCat** (☎ 08705/523523; www.team-packet.com), a catamaran service from Stranraer, Scotland, to Belfast. Other ferry services into Belfast include **Norse Irish Ferries** (☎ 028/9077-9090; www.norse-irish-ferries.co.uk) from Liverpool, and the **Isle of Man Steam Packet Co.** (☎ 08705/523523) from Douglas, on the Isle of Man. In addition, **Stena Sealink** (☎ 08705/707070; www2.stenaline.com) operates from Stranraer, Scotland, to Belfast; **P&O European Ferries** (☎ 0870/242-4777; www.poef.com) from Cairnryan, Scotland, to Larne; and, in July and August, **SeaCat** from Campbell, Scotland, to Ballycastle, County Antrim.

BY CRUISE SHIP   Derry City is rapidly becoming a premier international cruise destination, with a reputation for friendliness and charm. Every year more cruise ships, including six-star luxury liners, call at the deep-water facilities at Lisahally or at the city center's newly refurbished Queen's Quay. For the latest information on cruises to Derry Port, contact the **Cruise Development Officer,** Derry City Council, 98 Strand Rd., Derry BT48 7NN (☎ 028/7136-5151; fax 028/7126-4858).

BY TRAIN   Trains on the **Irish Rail** (☎ 1850/366222; www.irishrail.ie) and **Northern Ireland Railways** (☎ 888/BRITRAIL or 028/9089-9411; www.raileurope.com) systems travel into Northern Ireland from Dublin's **Connolly Station** daily. They arrive at Belfast's Central Station, East Bridge Street (☎ 028/9089-9411). Monday to Saturday, eight trains a day connect Dublin and Belfast; on Sunday, five. The trip takes about 2 hours.

BY BUS   Ulsterbus operates buses between Belfast and all parts of Northern Ireland and the Republic. For schedules and prices, phone the **Ulsterbus Enquiries Hotline** (☎ 028/9033-3000). To purchase or reserve a ticket, call ☎ **028/9032-0011.** The express bus from Dublin to Belfast takes 3 hours and runs seven times daily Monday to Saturday, three times on Sunday.

BY CAR   Northern Ireland is directly accessible from the Republic of Ireland on many main roads and secondary roads. It is possible, but unlikely, that you will encounter checkpoints when crossing the border. Main roads leading to Northern Ireland from the Republic include N1 from Dublin, N16 from Sligo, N15 from Donegal, and N3 from Cavan. *Important note:* If you are renting a car and taking it across the border, make certain that all your insurance coverage is equally valid in the North and in the Republic. This holds for any coverage provided by your credit card.

GETTING AROUND IN THE NORTH

Northern Ireland has recently launched a major initiative called **Translink** (www. translink.co.uk) to coordinate rail, bus, and auto travel in the North, which will expand and enhance transportation services.

BY TRAIN   The hub of **Northern Ireland Railways** (☎ 028/9089-9411; www. raileurope.com) is Belfast, with two principal rail stations: **Great Victoria St. Station,** across from the Europa Bus Centre; and **Belfast Central Station,** East Bridge Street. Trains from Larne arrive at Yorkgate Station; otherwise, trains to and from all destinations depart from and arrive at Belfast Central. The three main routes in the North's rail system are north and west from Belfast to Derry via Ballymena; east to Bangor, tracing the shores of Belfast Lough; and south to Dublin via Newry. Be sure to refer to the box called "Money-Saving Rail & Bus Passes" in section 10 of chapter 2. For example, the **Irish Rover** is for use both in the Republic of Ireland and in the North.

BY BUS   **Ulsterbus** (☎ 028/9033-3000) runs daily scheduled service from Belfast to major cities and towns throughout Northern Ireland. From the **Laganside Buscentre,** Oxford Street, Belfast (☎ 028/9023-2356), buses leave for destinations in counties Antrim, Down (eastern), Derry (eastern), and Cookstown. Buses to most every other destination in the North, including Belfast International Airport and the Larne ferries, as well as the Republic, depart from the **Europa Bus Centre,** Glengall Street, Belfast (☎ 028/9032-0011). Bus service in the North is remarkably thorough and will get you to the most unlikely and remote destinations. For extra savings, be sure to investigate the bus and rail passes outlined in the above-mentioned box in section 10 of chapter 2, such as the **Freedom of Northern Ireland,** which offers 7 days' unlimited travel on bus and train in the North for £37 ($61.05), or 1 day for £10 ($16.50). It's available from **Northern Ireland Railways,** Central Station, East Bridge Street, Belfast (☎ 028/9089-9411), and **Europa Bus Centre,** 10 Glengall St., Belfast (☎ 028/9032-0011), as well as all major bus and train stations in Northern Ireland.

BY SIGHTSEEING TOUR   From June to August, **Ulsterbus** operates a wide variety of full- and half-day coach tours from the Europa Bus Centre, Glengall Street, Belfast. They run to places such as the Glens of Antrim, Causeway Coast, Fermanagh Lakelands, Sperrin Mountains, the Mountains of Mourne, and Armagh. There are also tours designed to take you to specific attractions, such as the Giant's Causeway, Old Bushmills Distillery in Bushmills, Navan Centre in Armagh, Ulster-American Folk Park in Omagh, and Tyrone Crystal Factory in Dungannon. For full information on the day tours and holiday packages, visit or phone the Ulsterbus tourism office at the Europa Bus Centre, Glengall Street (☎ 028/9033-3000). To consider in advance the range of tours available, take a look at **www.tourulster.com.**

BY CAR   The best way to travel around the Northern Ireland countryside is by car. The roads are in extremely good condition and are well signposted. Distances between major cities and towns are short. If you want to rent a car, **Avis** (☎ 028/9024-0404), **Budget** (☎ 028/9023-0700), **Europcar** (☎ 028/9031-3500), **Hertz** (☎ 028/9073-2451), and **McCausland** (☎ 028/9073-2451) have offices in Belfast city, in at least one of the Belfast airports, or both. If you rent a car in the Republic, you can drive it in the North as long as you arrange the proper insurance.

Fast Facts: Northern Ireland

Area Code   The new area code for all of Northern Ireland is **028.** Drop the "0" when dialing from within Northern Ireland.

Business Hours   Banks are generally open Monday to Friday 10am to 12:30pm and 1:30 to 3 or 4pm; they're closed on bank holidays. In Belfast and Derry City, banks tend not to close for lunch. Most shops are open Monday to Saturday 9 or 9:30am to 5 or 5:30pm, with one early-closing day a week, usually Wednesday or Thursday. Shops in tourist areas are likely to be open Sunday and to have extended hours, especially in the summer months.

Currency   Since Northern Ireland is part of the United Kingdom, it uses the pound sterling.

Electricity   The electrical current (220vAC) and outlets (requiring three-pin flat, fused plugs) are the same in the North as in the Republic. Note that they are not the two-pin round plugs standard throughout Europe.

Embassies & Consulates   The **U.S. Consulate General** is at Queen's House, 14 Queen's St., Belfast BT1 6EQ (☎ **028/9032-8239**). Other foreign offices include the **Australian High Commission,** Australia House, Strand, London WC2 B4L (☎ **020/7379-4344**); **Canadian High Commission,** Macdonald House, Grosvenor Square, London W1X 0AB (☎ **020/7499-9000**); **New Zealand High Commission,** New Zealand House, 80 Haymarket Sq., London SW1Y 4TQ (☎ **020/7930-8422**).

Emergencies   Dial ☎ **999** for fire, police, and ambulance.

Mail   United Kingdom postal rates apply, and mailboxes are painted red. Most post offices are open weekdays 9am to 5pm, Saturday 9am to 1pm.

Newspapers & Magazines   The morning national newspapers are the *News Letter* and the *Irish News;* the *Belfast Telegraph* is the only evening paper. All are published Monday to Saturday. On Sunday most Northern Irish depend on U.K. papers, which are readily available. For listings of upcoming cultural events throughout Northern Ireland, check the free bimonthly *Arts Link* brochure, published by the Arts Council of Northern Ireland and available at any Northern Ireland Tourist Board office.

Parking   Because of long-standing security concerns, parking regulations are more restrictive and more relentlessly enforced in the North than in the Republic.

Petrol (Gas)   The approximate price of 1 liter of unleaded gas is 71p ($1.17). There are 4 liters to the U.S. gallon, which makes the price of a gallon of unleaded gas £2.64 ($4.35)!

Police   The Northern Ireland police are known as the **Royal Ulster Constabulary (RUC).** Currently they share responsibility for security in the North with the British armed forces. Currently, the British military presence in Northern Ireland is at its lowest numbers since 1970, and further substantial reductions are planned. A thorough review and reconstitution of the North's security forces, mandated by the Good Friday Agreement, is under way.

Safety   It is important to follow all rules, and to cooperate with security personnel if the necessity arises. Whenever you are traveling in an unfamiliar city or country, stay alert. Be aware of your immediate surroundings.

Taxes   You pay a **VAT** (**value-added tax**) of 17.5% on almost everything, except B&B accommodations. The percentages vary with the category of the services and purchases. It is usually already included in the prices you're quoted by hotels and the prices you see marked on merchandise tags. VAT is already included in the hotel prices we've quoted in this guide. Many shops offer tax-free shopping schemes, such as "Cashback," and are pleased to explain the details. The refund procedure is essentially the same as for the Republic, outlined in "VAT Refunds" in chapter 2. Vouchers from the North can be presented at the Dublin or Shannon airports before departure from Ireland. For further information, contact HM Customs and Excise, Belfast International Airport (☎ **028/9441-3439** or 028/9442-3439).

Telephone   To reach Northern Ireland from anywhere but the Republic of Ireland or Great Britain, dial the country code (44) and then the area code minus the 0 (28) and finally the local eight-digit number. From the Republic of Ireland, omit the country code and simply dial 048 and then the local eight- digit number. From Great Britain, dial 028 and the eight-digit number. For local calls within Northern Ireland, simply dial the eight-digit local number.

2 Belfast

103 miles (166km) N of Dublin, 211 miles (340km) NE of Shannon, 125 miles (201km) E of Sligo, and 262 miles (422km) NE of Cork

Nestled beside the River Lagan and Belfast Lough and ringed by gentle hills, Belfast occupies a lovely setting, often called "the Hibernian Rio." The core of downtown Belfast sits beside the west bank of the River Lagan. The city revolves around a central point, Donegall Square, which holds the city hall; all roads radiate out from there. Donegall Place, which extends north from the square, leads to Royal Avenue, a prime shopping district. Bedford Street, which extends south from the square, becomes Dublin Road, which, in turn, leads to the Queen's University area.

Nearly half a million people, a third of Northern Ireland's population, reside within Belfast city limits.

With its large port, Belfast is an industrialized city, often referred to as the engine room that drove the whirring wheels of the industrial revolution in Ulster. Major industries range from linen production to rope making and shipbuilding. The *Titanic* was built in Belfast port, and today the world's largest dry dock is here.

The city's architecture is rich in Victorian and Edwardian buildings with elaborate sculptures over the doors and windows. Stone heads of gods, poets, scientists, kings, and queens peer down from the high ledges of banks and old linen warehouses. Some of Belfast's grandest buildings are on the banks of Waring Street. The Ulster Bank, dating from 1860, has an interior like a Venetian palace, and the Northern Bank, dating from 1769, was originally a market house.

The **Queen's University,** with its Tudor cloister, dominates the southern sector of the city. The original edifice was built in 1849 by Charles Lanyon, who designed more of Belfast's buildings than anyone else. The university was named for Queen Victoria, who visited Belfast in that year and had just about everything named in her honor for the occasion—dozens of streets, a hospital, a park, a man-made island, and the harbor's deepwater channel are all named after her. Today, the university enrolls 12,000 students and is the setting for the annual Belfast Festival at Queen's, one of the city's major annual arts events.

ESSENTIALS

GETTING THERE   For details, see "Getting to the North," in section 1 of this chapter. Belfast has two airports—Belfast International and Belfast City—and gets considerable sea traffic at Belfast Harbour and at Larne (30 min. from Belfast by train, bus, or car).

From Belfast International Airport, nearly 19 miles (31km) north of the city, it's best to take the **Airbus limousine** into the city center. It operates daily, leaves approximately twice an hour, and costs £5 ($8.25) per person. A taxi will run closer to £20 ($33). From Belfast City Airport, less than 4 miles (6.4km) from the city center, there are several options. I recommend taking a taxi, for roughly £6 ($9.90), until you familiarize yourself with the city. You can also take Citybus no. 21 from the airport terminal or the Sydenham Halt train from the station directly across from the airport, both for 80p ($1.30).

Belfast is the rail hub of the North and the point of origin for Northern Ireland's principal motorways, which link it to the Republic and to the major cities and towns of the North.

VISITOR INFORMATION   Brochures, maps, and other data about Belfast and the North are available from the **Northern Ireland Tourist Board,** 47 Donegall Place, near City Hall (☎ **028/9024-6609;** www.ni-tourism.com). It's open September to June, Monday to Saturday 9am to 5:15pm. In peak season, July and August, it's open at least Monday to Friday 9am to 6:30pm, Saturday 9am to 5:15pm, Sunday noon to 4pm. The tourist information desk at **Belfast City Airport** (☎ **028/9045-7745**) is open year-round Monday to Friday 5:30am to 10pm, Saturday 5:30am to 9pm, Sunday 5:30am to 10pm. The desk at **Belfast International Airport** (☎ **028/ 9442-2888**) is open March to September daily 24 hours, October to February daily 6:30am to 11pm.

GETTING AROUND   Citybus, Donegall Square West, Belfast (☎ **028/ 9024-6485**), provides local bus service within the city. Departures are from Donegall Square East, West, and North, plus Upper Queen Street, Wellington Place, Chichester Street, and Castle Street. There is an information kiosk on Donegall Square West. Fares are determined by the number of zones traversed. The average fare for city-center travel is 90p ($1.50). Multiple-trip tickets, day tickets, and 7-day passes offer significant savings.

If you've brought a **car** into Belfast, it's best to leave it parked at your hotel and take public transportation or walk around the city. If you must drive and want to park your car downtown, look for a blue P sign that shows a parking lot or a parking area. Belfast has a number of "control zones," indicated by a pink-and-yellow sign, where no parking is permitted. In general, on-street parking is limited to an area behind City Hall (south side), St. Anne's Cathedral (north side), and around Queen's University and Ulster Museum.

Taxis are available at all main rail stations, ports, and airports, and in front of City Hall. Most metered taxis are London-type black cabs with a yellow disc on the window. Other taxis may not have meters, so you should ask the fare to your destination in advance. Except for reasonably inexpensive service down the Shankill Road and the Falls Road, Belfast taxi fares are on the high side, with a £2 ($3.30) minimum and an additional £1 ($1.65) per mile.

Belfast is a good city for **walking.** To guide visitors on the best and safest areas for a stroll, the Belfast City Council has produced five self-guided walking-tour leaflets. They are city center south to Shaftesbury Square, city center north to the Irish News

Ulster: where every hill has its hero and every bog its bones.
—Sam Hanna Bell (b. 1909), "In Praise of Ulster"

office, Shaftesbury Square south to the university area, city center northeast to the port area, and Donegall Square south to Donegall Pass. Each walk is about a mile and lasts an hour. Ask for a leaflet for the walk or walks that interest you at the Northern Ireland Tourist Board.

FAST FACTS The **U.S. consulate general** is at Queen's House, 14 Queen's St., Belfast BT1 (☎ 028/9032-8239). For other embassies and consulates, see "Fast Facts: Northern Ireland," above.

In an emergency, dial ☎ **999** for fire, police, and ambulance. The most central hospital is **Shaftesbury Square Hospital,** 16–20 Great Victoria St. (☎ 028/9032-9808). Farther south, on Lisburn Road, is **Belfast City Hospital** (☎ 028/9032-9241). West of the city center on Grosvenor Road is the **Royal Victoria Hospital** (☎ 028/9024-0503).

The Belfast Gay and Lesbian Resource centers can be reached at **NIGRA/Northern Ireland Gay Rights Association,** Cathedral Buildings, Lower Donegall Street (☎ 028/9066-4111). Other helpful numbers are the **Lesbian Line Belfast** (☎ 028/9023-8688), Thursday 7:30 to 10pm; and **Cara-Friend** (☎ 028/9032-2023), Monday to Wednesday and Friday 7:30 to 10pm, for counsel on gay and lesbian matters. The Belfast number for **AIDS Helpline Northern Ireland** is ☎ 028/9024-9268. Or stop in at the Centre@Warehouse, 3rd floor, 7 James St. S., Belfast, Saturday 2 to 5pm.

You can log on at the **Revelations Café,** 27 Shaftesbury Sq. (☎ 028/9032-0337; www.revelations.co.uk). It's on Bradbury Place just south of Donegall Road.

Seek out **Duds 'n' Suds,** 37 Botanic Ave. (☎ 028/9024-3956), where you can have a snack while your clothes take a tumble, or **Agincourt Laundry,** 46 Agincourt Ave. (☎ 028/9033-1490).

The Belfast **GPO** (General Post Office) is at Castle Place, at the intersection of Royal Avenue and Donegall Place. It's open Monday to Friday 9am to 5:30pm, Saturday 9am to 7pm.

SEEING THE SIGHTS

For an overview of the city, **Citybus Tours** (☎ 028/9045-8484) offers a 3½-hour **Belfast City Tour.** It departs at 1pm Wednesday and Saturday from the GPO (main post office), late June to September. It costs £8 ($13.20) for adults, £5.50 ($9.10) seniors and children, £18 ($29.70) family. For roughly the same price, the **Black-taxi Tours** are also quite popular, and disturbing—they encompass local sites and stories of the barely historical Troubles. To arrange **Black-taxi Tours,** call Michael at ☎ 0800/052-3914 (toll-free) or 07860/127207 (mobile), or find all the details at **www.belfasttours.com.**

Themed walking tours are commonly offered during the summer, but they tend to be organized on a year-by-year basis; so as of this writing, I can't tell you what will be offered in the summer of 2001. Up-to-date information on current specialty tours is available from the Northern Ireland Tourist Board, 47 Donegall Place, near City Hall (☎ 028/9024-6609). For example, in 2000, there were **Historical Pub Tours of Belfast** (☎ 028/9268-3665), departing twice a week to pay visits to six pubs. Tours cost £5 ($8.25); drinks were extra.

Belfast

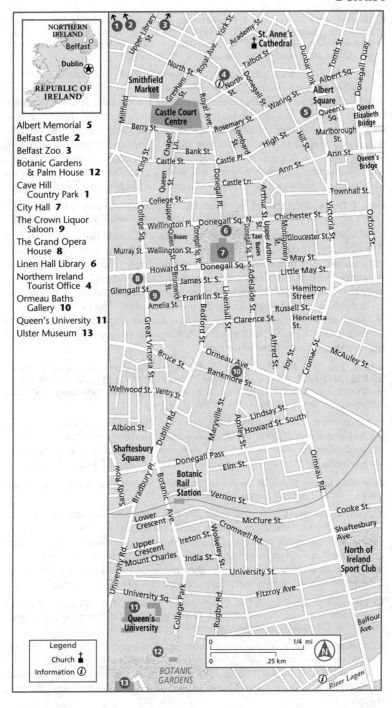

NORTHERN
IRELAND
Belfast
Dublin
REPUBLIC OF
IRELAND

Albert Memorial **5**
Belfast Castle **2**
Belfast Zoo **3**
Botanic Gardens
   & Palm House **12**
Cave Hill
   Country Park **1**
City Hall **7**
The Crown Liquor
   Saloon **9**
The Grand Opera
   House **8**
Linen Hall Library **6**
Northern Ireland
   Tourist Office **4**
Ormeau Baths
   Gallery **10**
Queen's University **11**
Ulster Museum **13**

Legend
Church ✝
Information ⓘ

St. Anne's
Cathedral

Smithfield
Market

Castle Court
Centre

Albert
Square

Queen's
Sq.

Queen
Elizabeth
Bridge

Queen's
Bridge

Shaftesbury
Square

Botanic
Rail
Station

North of
Ireland
Sport Club

Queen's
University

BOTANIC
GARDENS

River Lagan

0   1/4 mi
0   .25 km

⊙ **Belfast Botanic Gardens & Palm House.** Signposted from M1/M2 (Balmoral exit), Stranmillis Rd., County Antrim. ☎ **028/9032-4902.** Free admission. Palm House and Tropical Ravine Apr–Sept Mon–Fri 10am–noon, daily 1–5pm; Oct–Mar Mon–Fri 10am–noon, daily 1–4pm. Gardens daily 8am–sunset. Bus: 61, 71, 84, or 85.

Dating from 1828, these gardens were established by the Belfast Botanic and Horticultural Society. Ten years later they gained a glass house, or conservatory, designed by noted Belfast architect Charles Lanyon. Now known as the Palm House, this unique building is one of the earliest examples of curvilinear cast-iron glass-house construction. It contains many rare plant specimens, including such tropical plants as sugarcane, coffee, cinnamon, banana, aloe, ivory nut, rubber, bamboo, guava, and the striking bird of paradise flower. The Tropical Ravine, also known as the fernery, provides a setting for plants to grow in a sunken glen. Take time to stroll in the surrounding outdoor gardens of roses and herbaceous borders, established in 1927.

Belfast Castle. Signposted off the Antrim Rd., 2½ miles (4km) north of the city center, County Antrim. ☎ **028/9077-6925.** Free admission and parking. Castle daily 9am–6pm.

Northwest of downtown and 400 feet above sea level stands Belfast Castle, whose 200-acre estate spreads down the slopes of Cave Hill. The castle, which affords panoramic views of Belfast Lough and the city, was completed in 1870. It was the family residence of the third Marquis of Donegall, and was presented to the city of Belfast in 1934 and used for private functions. After extensive restoration, the castle reopened to the public in 1988; 2 years later, its cellars were transformed into a Victorian arcade, including an antiques and craft shop, a bar, and a bistro restaurant. The extensive grounds include a public park, which is ideal for walking, jogging, picnicking, and enjoying extraordinary views of the city.

Belfast Zoo. 5 miles (8km) north of the city on A6, Antrim Rd., County Antrim. ☎ **028/9077-6277.** Admission £5.50 ($9.10) adults, £2.75 ($4.55) children 4–16, free for seniors and children under 4. Apr–Sept daily 10am–5pm; Oct–Mar daily 10am–3:30pm (to 2:30pm on Fri). Bus: 9, 45, 46, 47, 48, 49, 50, or 51.

In a picturesque mountain park on the slopes of Cave Hill overlooking the city, this zoo was founded in 1920 as Bellevue Gardens. A completely new, modern zoo was designed in recent years. It emphasizes conservation, education, and breeding rare species, including Hawaiian geese, Indian lions, red lechwe, and golden lion tamarins.

Cave Hill Country Park. Off the Antrim Rd., 4 miles (6.5km) north of city center, County Antrim. Parking at Belfast Castle or Belfast Zoo (above).

This lovely park atop a 1,200-foot basalt cliff, said to resemble the profile of Napoleon (Mount Rushmore without the expense!), offers panoramic views, walking trails, and a number of interesting archaeological and historical sights. There are the Neolithic caves that gave the hill its name, and MacArt's Fort, an ancient earthwork built against the Vikings. In this fort, in 1795, Wolfe Tone and fellow United Irishmen planned the 1798 rebellion. On a lighter note, there's an adventure playground for the kids.

⊙ **City Hall.** Donegall Sq., Belfast, County Antrim. ☎ **028/9027-0456.** Free admission. Guided tours June–Sept Mon–Fri 10:30am, 11:30am, 2:30pm, Sat 2:30pm; Oct–May Mon–Sat 2:30pm. Otherwise by arrangement. Reservations required.

Completed in 1906, this magnificent public building is the core of Belfast, the axis around which the city radiates. It was built of Portland stone after Queen Victoria granted Belfast the status of a city in 1888. Similar to an American state capitol building (except for the big statue of Queen Victoria at the front), it dominates the main shopping area.

Tracing Your Roots

Contact the **Ulster Historical Foundation,** Balmoral Buildings, 12 College Sq. E., Belfast BTI 6DD (☎ **028/9033-2288;** fax 028/9023-9885; www.uhf.org.uk; e-mail: enquiry@uhf.dnet.co.uk), for help in tracking down Irish ancestors, particularly in Belfast, County Antrim, and County Down. The staff will furnish a list of helpful publications and help you find the appropriate genealogical source. See also "Tracing Your Irish Roots," in chapter 2.

Two private organizations that can also help are **Irish Genealogical Services,** 2 Lower Crescent, Belfast B17 1NR (☎ **028/9024-1412;** fax 028/9023-9972; contact David McElroy); and **Historical Research Associates,** Glen Cottage, Glenmachan Road, Belfast BT4 2NP (☎ **028/9076-1490;** contact Joan Phillipson or Jennifer Irwin). For a list of members and details of services for the **Association of Ulster Genealogists and Record Agents,** write **AUGRA,** Glen Cottage, Glenmachan Road, Belfast BT4 2NP.

✪ **Linen Hall Library.** 17 Donegall Sq. N, Belfast, County Antrim. ☎ **028/9032-1707.** Free admission. Mon–Fri 9:30am–5:30pm; Sat 9:30am–4pm.

Established in 1788 as an independent charitable institution, this is Belfast's oldest library. It is known for its collections of Irish books, local historical documents, Robert Burns's books, and volumes on heraldry.

Ormeau Baths Gallery. 18A Ormeau Ave., Belfast, County Antrim. ☎ **028/9032-1402.** Free admission. Tues–Sat 10am–6pm.

Occupying the site of, and partly incorporating, the old Victorian swimming baths designed by Robert Watt, Ormeau Baths Gallery opened in 1995 as the city's principal exhibition space for contemporary visual art. This striking and versatile facility can program multiple simultaneous exhibitions in a variety of media, and has become the premier showcase for the best of Northern Irish contemporary art.

✪ **Ulster Museum.** Signposted from M1/M2 (Balmoral exit); next to the Botanic Gardens, Stranmillis Rd., County Antrim. ☎ **028/9038-3000.** Free admission, except to major special exhibitions. Mon–Fri 10am–5pm; Sat 1–5pm; Sun 2–5pm. Bus: 61, 71, 84, or 85.

Built in the grand Classical Renaissance style, with an Italian marble interior, this museum summarizes 9,000 years of Irish history with exhibits on art, furniture, glass, ceramics, costume, industrial heritage, and a permanent display of products "Made in Belfast." One of the best-known exhibits is the collection of gold and silver jewelry recovered by divers in 1968 off the Antrim coast from the 1588 wreckage of the Armada treasure ship *Girona.* Other permanent collections focus on water wheels and steam engines, linen making, the post office, coins and medals, early Ireland, flora and fauna, and the living sea.

SHOPPING

Shops in Belfast city center are generally open Monday to Saturday 9:30am to 5:30pm, with many shops remaining open until 8 or 9pm on Thursday.

Before you set out, stop into the **Craftworks Gallery,** Bedford House, Bedford Street (☎ **028/9024-4465**), a display center and shop for the work of individual craftspeople from all over Northern Ireland. The gallery can supply a free copy of the brochure "Crafts in Northern Ireland," detailing local crafts and where to find them. It is just behind Belfast City Hall.

The **Castlecourt Shopping Centre** on Royal Avenue, Belfast's main downtown multistory shopping mall, is Northern Ireland's largest shopping complex, with more than 70 boutiques and shops.

Belfast's leading department stores are **Anderson & McAuley** and **Marks & Spencer,** both on Donegall Place, and **Debenham's** in the Castlecourt Shopping Centre on Royal Avenue. Other shops to look for include the following:

Smyth's Irish Linens. 65 Royal Ave., Belfast, County Antrim. ☎ **028/9024-2232.**

If you want to stock up on fine Irish linen damask tablecloths, napkins, and handkerchiefs, head for this shop in the heart of the city's prime shopping thoroughfare. It also stocks other traditional gift items and souvenirs, and offers VAT-free export. Open Monday to Saturday 10am to 5pm.

The Steensons. Bedford St. (behind Belfast City Hall), Belfast, County Antrim. ☎ **028/9024-8269.**

This is the main showroom of Bill and Christina Steenson, two of the most celebrated goldsmiths in Ireland. On display and for sale is the widest collection anywhere of the Steensons' unique gold and silver jewelry, as well as work by a select number of top designers from afar. Open Monday to Saturday 10am to 5:30pm.

Tom Caldwell Gallery. 40 Bradbury Place, Belfast, County Antrim. ☎ **028/9032-3226.**

Come here for a selection of paintings, sculptures, and ceramics by living artists, as well as handcrafted furnishings, rugs, and cast-iron candelabras. Open Monday to Friday 9:30am to 5pm, Saturday 10am to 1pm.

SPORTS & OUTDOOR PURSUITS

FISHING   The 5½-mile (8.9km) stretch of the Lagan River from Stranmillis weir to Shaw's Bridge offers decent coarse fishing, especially on summer evenings. From May to July, Lough Neagh has good shore and boat fishing. Contact Paddy Prunty at the **Kinnego Marina,** Oxford Island, Craigavon (☎ 028/3832-7573). For info, tackle, and bait, try the **Village Tackle Shop,** 55a Newtownbreda Rd., Belfast (☎ 028/9049-1916), or **Shankill Fishing Tackle,** 366 Shankill Rd., Belfast (☎ 028/ 9033-0949).

GOLF   The Belfast area offers four parkland 18-hole courses within 4 miles (6.5km) of the city center. Three miles (4.8km) southwest of the city, there's the **Balmoral Golf Club,** 518 Lisburn Rd., Belfast (☎ 028/9038-1514), with greens fees of £20 ($33) weekdays (except Wed), £30 ($49.50) weekends and Wednesday; 4 miles (6.5km) southwest of the city center, the **Dunmurry Golf Club,** 91 Dunmurry Lane, Dunmurry, Belfast (☎ 028/9061-0834), £17 ($28.05) weekdays, £26.50 ($43.75) weekends; 3 miles (4.8km) south of the city center, the **Belvoir Park Golf Club,** 73 Church Rd., Newtownbreda, Belfast (☎ 028/9049-1693), £33 ($54.45) weekdays, £38 ($62.70) weekends; and 3 miles (4.8km) north, the **Fortwilliam Golf Club,** Downview Avenue, Belfast (☎ 028/9037-0770), £22 ($36.30) weekdays, £29 ($47.85) weekends. Weekdays are usually better for visitors, and each club has preferred weekdays. Phone ahead. Club pros offer lessons, usually for about £25 ($41.25) per hour; book at least 2 days ahead.

HORSEBACK RIDING   Saddle up at the **Drumgooland House Equestrian Centre,** 29 Dunnanew Rd., Seaforde, Downpatrick, County Down (☎ 028/ 4481-1956). It offers 1- to 4-hour treks, beach rides, and lessons. Full equestrian holidays are available.

ACCOMMODATIONS
VERY EXPENSIVE

✪ **Culloden Hotel.** 142 Bangor Rd., County Down. ☎ **028/9042-5223.** Fax 028/9042-6777. www.hastingshotels.com. 75 units. TV TEL. £190 ($331.50) double. Rates include full breakfast. AE, DC, MC, V. Free valet parking.

The Belfast area's finest hotel is not in the city itself, but 5 miles (8km) east on the shore of Belfast Lough, in County Down. Set on 12 acres of secluded gardens and woodlands, this hotel incorporates a Gothic mansion built in 1876 of Scottish stone by William Auchinleck Robinson. A government official, he named it Culloden House in honor of his wife, the former Elizabeth Jane Culloden. On his death, the house passed to the Church of Ireland. After serving as a residence to a succession of bishops, it was sold and remained a private home until it opened as a hotel in 1963. The Hastings Hotel Group bought it in 1967 and has extended and refurbished it in luxurious style, outfitting it with many fine antiques and paintings, plasterwork ceilings, and Louis XV chandeliers. Guest rooms offer contemporary furnishings with a Victorian flair.

Dining/Diversions: Choices include the elegant Mitre Restaurant, overlooking the gardens; the Gothic Bar; and the Cultra Inn (☎ **028/9042-5840**), a casual pub-restaurant on the hotel grounds.

Amenities: Concierge, 24-hour room service, laundry/dry cleaning, baby-sitting, secretarial services, video rentals, bicycle rental, express checkout. The Elysium leisure complex includes an octagonal ozone pool, gym, Jacuzzi, steam room, all-weather tennis court, squash court, putting green, croquet lawn, and hairdressing salon.

Europa Hotel. Great Victoria St., Belfast, County Antrim. ☎ **028/9032-7000.** Fax 028/9032-7800. www.hastingshotels.com. 184 units. TV TEL. £166 ($273.90) double. Luxury suites available. AE, DC, MC, V. Discounted public car lot behind hotel; valet parking available; lots patrolled.

In the heart of the city beside the Grand Opera House, this is Belfast's largest and most modern hotel. Total renovation of this landmark hotel was completed in 1995, after damage from a 1993 bombing. The Europa was host to Bill Clinton, the first U.S. president to visit Northern Ireland, during his stay in Belfast. The rooms, refurbished recently, are stylish, gleaming, and comfortable, with such amenities as tea/coffeemakers and hair dryers. An extension of executive rooms is to be completed by 2001.

Dining/Diversions: Choices include the Gallery Restaurant for fine dining and the more informal Brasserie. The lobby bar offers drinks and light snacks. The Europa is also home to the Ulster Cabaret, a traditional evening of harp, fiddle, fife, Lambeg drum, dance, and Ulster humor, every weekend in July and August. Dinner (at 7pm) and cabaret (at 8:15pm) costs £32.50 ($53.65) per person.

Amenities: Concierge, room service, laundry/dry cleaning, baby-sitting, secretarial services, access to nearby health club.

✪ **The McCausland Hotel.** 34–38 Victoria St., Belfast, County Antrim. ☎ **800/525-4800** from the U.S., or 028/9022-0200. Fax 028/9022-0220. www.slh.com/Causland/. 60 units. MINIBAR TV TEL. £150–£170 ($247.50–$280.50) double; £200 ($330) junior suite. Rates include full Irish breakfast. AE, CB, DC, MC, V. Valet parking in carpark beside hotel. Charge 50p/hr. (83¢).

This sister hotel of the Hibernian in Dublin was recently created from two classically ornate Italianate warehouses designed by William Hastings in the mid-1850s. In their new incarnation, these two landmark structures, which once belonged to rival firms, house a fine new hotel conveniently situated in the heart of the city. Already listed among the "Small Luxury Hotels of the World," the McCausland offers a high standard of sophistication and comfort. The rooms are spacious and beautifully appointed, with hair dryers, tea/coffeemakers, and garment presses. Two of the four floors of guest rooms are nonsmoking, and all beds are orthopedic. Guest have access to a nearby health club.

Dining: The menu of the hotel's restaurant, Merchants, changes daily and offers an enticing array of gourmet seafood and meat dishes.

Amenities: 24-hour room service, twice-daily maid service, concierge, foreign currency exchange, secretarial services, fax/modem connections.

MODERATE

Dukes Hotel. 65–67 University St. (off Botanic Ave.), Belfast, County Antrim. ☎ **028/ 9023-6666.** Fax 028/9023-7177. www.dukes-hotel.com. 21 units. TV TEL. £110 ($181.50) double midweek; £72 ($118.80) double weekend. Rates include full breakfast. AE, DC, MC, V. On-street parking.

In a tree-lined residential area near the university, this hotel is in a former Victorian residence. The interior is bright and modern, with art deco furnishings, waterfalls, and plants. Rooms are contemporary, with double-glazed windows, light-wood furnishings, floral fabrics, modern art, and such amenities as a bathroom phone, mirrored closets, a hair dryer, a tea/coffeemaker, and a complimentary basket of fruit. Refurbishment of the guest rooms and public areas was completed in June 1996. Nonsmoking rooms are available, and there's 24-hour room service. On the premises are Dukes Restaurant, Dukes Bar, and a health club with gym and sauna. The hotel is within a half-mile walk of the center of the city.

INEXPENSIVE

Ashberry Cottage. 19 Rosepark Central, Belfast, County Antrim. ☎ **028/9028-6300.** 3 units, 1 with bathroom. TV. £38 ($62.70) double. Rates include full breakfast. No credit cards. Private parking. Take A20 to Rosepark, the second turn on the right past the Stormont Hotel.

"Cozy" is the word for Hilary and Sam Mitchell's modern bungalow, and you'll be completely spoiled from the moment they greet you with a welcome tray of tea and goodies. Not only do they both know the Belfast area well, but Hilary works for the Northern Ireland Tourist Board and is well qualified to help you plan your travels throughout the province. The attractive guest rooms have tea/coffee-making facilities. Sam is the morning cook, and his breakfast has been described as "the best breakfast in Europe." Evening meals also draw raves from guests. Sam will meet you at the airport or railway station with advance notice. No smoking.

Ash-Rowan Guest House. 12 Windsor Ave. (between Lisburn and Malone rds.), Belfast, County Antrim. ☎ **028/9066-1758.** Fax 028/9066-3227. 5 units. TV TEL. £79 ($130.35) double. £25 ($41.25) dinner. Rates include full breakfast. AE, MC, V. Private parking lot outside.

On a quiet, tree-lined street in a residential neighborhood, this four-story Victorian house sits near Queen's University. Proprietors Evelyn and Hazlett have outfitted it with country-style furnishings, family heirlooms, and antiques, along with bouquets of fresh flowers from the garden. The rates include a choice of 12 traditional breakfasts, including the Ulster fry or scrambled eggs with kippers or smoked salmon.

DINING
EXPENSIVE

✪ **Cayenne.** 7 Lesley House, Shaftesbury Sq., Belfast, County Antrim. ☎ **028/9033-1532.** Reservations required. Fixed-price dinner £9.50–£12.50 ($15.70–$20.65). AE, DC, MC, V. Mon–Fri noon–2:15pm; Mon–Sat 6–11:15pm. INTERNATIONAL.

Chef-owner Paul Rankin has a penchant for using the best of Ulster produce in creative combinations of taste and color. In yet another inspired creative urge, he has changed the name of his excellent restaurant from the well-recognized Roscoff to Cayenne. The decor and menu have been transformed as well to thrill the eye and palate. The menu offers dishes such as lemongrass-crusted salmon with Chinese greens and citrus butter, char-grilled sirloin with mushrooms and a smoked chili butter, and roast skate with capers and brown butter. If possible, save room for the lovingly prepared warm, soft chocolate cake with coconut ice cream.

MODERATE

La Belle Epoque. 61–63 Dublin Rd. (at the corner of Ventry Lane), Belfast, County Antrim. ☎ **028/9032-3244.** Reservations recommended. Fixed-price 3-course dinner £15 ($24.75). AE, CB, DC, MC, V. Mon–Fri noon–11:30pm, Sat 5:30–11:30pm. Closed July 12–13 and Christmas. FRENCH.

This brasserie-style spot is housed in a double shop front in a brick building. The menu offers a creative mixture of fruit- and vegetable-based sauces. It includes dishes such as chicken with almond crust and mushroom sauce, veal in creamy artichoke sauce, fillet of turbot with salmon trout mousse, and panfried salmon with broccoli and ginger sauce. All dishes are unusual and delicious, and vegetarian options are always available.

✪ **Nick's Warehouse.** 35 Hill St., Belfast, County Antrim. ☎ **028/9043-9690.** Reservations recommended. Main courses £6.95–£13.60 ($11.45–$22.45). AE, DC, MC, V. Mon–Fri noon–3pm; Tues–Sat 6–9:30pm (drinks until midnight). INTERNATIONAL.

In an old warehouse between St. Anne's Cathedral and the tourist office, Nick's offers a wine bar setting downstairs and a classy dining room upstairs, with brick walls and an open kitchen. There's a variety of international appetizers, from gazpacho to curly kale soup to a platter of Italian salami or gravlax (cured Norwegian salmon). Main courses include sirloin steaks, hot-and-sour beef with water chestnuts, lamb chops with honey and ginger sauce, and fillet of salmon with fennel hollandaise. There's always an interesting vegetarian offering. The menu, however, changes daily to take advantage of the season's freshest basics.

Skandia. 50 Howard St. , Belfast, County Antrim. ☎ **028/9024-0239.** Reservations recommended for dinner. Dinner main courses £5–£13 ($8.25–$21.45). AE, MC, V. Mon–Sat 11am–11pm. IRISH.

A block west of Donegall Square, this restaurant is a convenient, dependable place to dine at almost any time of day. It has a homey atmosphere, with banquette seating and a salad bar in the middle of the room. Dishes might include grilled salmon, scampi, or turbot steamed with celery, mushrooms, and nuts, as well as salads, pastas, vegetarian dishes, burgers, steaks, ribs, and omelets. Skandia is a favorite with families.

INEXPENSIVE

Planet Harveys. 95 Great Victoria St. , Belfast, County Antrim. ☎ **028/9023-3433.** Main courses £4.95–£7.95 ($8.15–$13.10). MC, V. Tues–Thurs and Sun 5–11:30pm; Fri–Sat 5–midnight. INTERNATIONAL.

An American atmosphere prevails here, with U.S. flag decor and a menu that offers choices such as steaks, burgers, salads, pizza, tacos, pasta, and a signature Frisco Bay platter (prawns, crab claws, scampi, mussels, and langoustines). Other options include beef Stroganoff, chicken Kiev, and smoky pork fillet stuffed with cheese and smoked bacon.

BELFAST AFTER DARK
PUBS

Pub hours are generally Monday to Saturday from 11:30am to 11pm, and Sunday from 12:30 to 2:30pm and from 7 to 10pm. Children are not permitted on licensed premises.

✪ **Crown Liquor Saloon.** Great Victoria St., Belfast, County Antrim. ☎ **028/9024-9476.**

Dating from 1826 and situated opposite the Grand Opera House, this gaslit pub, a feast of Victoriana, is a member of the National Trust. The pub boasts a marvelous array of 10 *snugs* (small private rooms) on the right, each with its own door and call bell. There are a tin ceiling, a tile floor, etched and smoked glass, a beveled mirror with floral and wildlife decorations, scalloped lamps, and a long bar with inlaid colored glass and marble trim.

Kelly's Cellars. 32 Bank St. (just off Royal Ave.), Belfast, County Antrim. ☎ **028/9032-4835.**

Recognized as Belfast's oldest tavern in continuous use, this pub dates to 1720 and has a storied history, including being a headquarters for leaders in the 1798 Insurrection. It's also been a favorite haunt for actors and novelists. The interior is festooned with such memorabilia as old ledgers, coins, china, prints, maps, and international soccer caps. There is often traditional music in the evenings.

Pat's Bar. 19 Prince's Dock St., Belfast, County Antrim. ☎ **028/9074-4524.**

For a taste of Belfast's harbor atmosphere, join the sailors, dockers, and local businesspeople at this pub at the gates of Prince's Dock. You'll see an antique hand-carved beech bar, pinewood furnishings, a red-tile floor, and black-and-white photos of the pub's earliest days. There's an interesting collection of memorabilia given to the bar's owner by sailors passing through the port—clogs, swords, tom-toms and maracas, a telescope, and a bayonet. There's traditional Irish music on Friday and Saturday night at 9pm.

White's Tavern. 2–4 Winecellar Entry (between High and Rosemary sts.), Belfast, County Antrim. ☎ **028/9024-3080.**

Tucked into a historic cobblestoned trading lane, this old tavern was established in 1630 as a wine and spirit shop. It's full of old barrels and hoists, ornate snugs, brick arches, large copper measures, framed newspaper clippings of 200-year-old vintage, quill pens, and other memorabilia. It's a good pub for conversation and browsing, and features jazz and traditional music, as well as quiz nights, darts, and theme nights.

THE PERFORMING ARTS

For up-to-date listings of shows and concerts, there are several sources. *That's Entertainment* is free and widely available at tourist offices and pubs, as is *The Big List*. *Artslink,* published monthly, is also free and useful. The *Buzz* is neither free nor particularly useful—it comes out only every 2 months. And there's always the *Belfast Daily Telegraph* and *The Irish News*. If you have your laptop with you, you'll find just about everything on **www.entertainment.ireland.ie**, keyword: belfast.

The latest, largest venue to appear on the arts scene is the **Belfast Waterfront Hall,** Oxford Street, Laganside (☎ **028/9033-4455** for credit card reservations; ☎ **028/9033-4400** for program information). The other leading concert and performance halls in Belfast are the **Grand Opera House,** Great Victoria Street (☎ **028/9024-1919;** www.gohbelfast.com), which presents a wide variety of entertainment; **Ulster Hall,** Bedford Street (☎ **028/9032-3900**), which stages major concerts from rock to large-scale choral and symphonic works by the Ulster Orches-tra and Northern Ireland Symphony Orchestra; and **Kings Hall Exhibition and Conference Centre,** Balmoral (☎ **028/9066-5225;** www.kingshall.co.uk), for super-star concerts and other musical events, as well as everything from sheep sales to bridal fairs.

Theaters include the **Belfast Civic Arts Theatre,** 41 Botanic Ave. (☎ **028/ 9031-6900**), for popular shows, musicals, and comedies; the **Lyric Theatre,** Ridgeway Street (☎ **028/9038-1081**), for new plays by Irish and international playwrights; and the **Group Theatre,** Bedford Street (☎ **028/9032-9685**), for performances by local drama societies.

For stand-up comedy, the Belfast epicenter is in the basement of the **Empire Music Hall,** 42 Botanic (☎ **028/9032-8110**). It's home every Tuesday at 9pm to *The Empire Laughs Back.* If you'd rather sit down than stand up, get there at least an hour early. Other occasional comedy venues include the **Factory,** 52 Hill St. (☎ **028/ 9024-4000**), and the **Old Museum Arts Centre,** College Square North (☎ **028/ 9023-5053**).

Tickets, which cost £7 to £30 ($11.55 to $49.50) for most events, can be purchased in advance from the **Virgin Ticket Shop,** Castle Court, Belfast (☎ **028/9032-3744**).

3 Side Trips from Belfast

CARRICKFERGUS
12 miles (19km) NE of Belfast

It's said that Carrickfergus, County Antrim, was a thriving town when Belfast was a sandbank. In 1180, John de Courcy, a Norman, built a massive keep at Carrickfergus, the first real Irish castle, to guard the approach to Belfast Lough.

Stop into the **Carrickfergus Tourist Information Office,** Heritage Plaza, Antrim Street, Carrickfergus, County Antrim (☎ **028/9336-6455**). It's open June to Sep-tember Monday to Friday 9am to 6pm, Saturday 10am to 6pm, Sunday noon to 6pm; October to May weekdays 9am to 5pm.

Andrew Jackson Centre. Boneybefore, Carrickfergus, County Antrim. ☎ **028/9336-6455.** Admission £1.20 ($2) adults, 60p ($1) seniors and children, £3 ($4.95) family. June–Sept Mon–Fri 10am–1pm, daily 2–6pm; reduced hours in Apr–May and Oct. Closed Nov–Mar.

This simple one-story cottage with earthen floor and open fireplace was the ancestral home of Andrew Jackson, seventh president of the United States. His parents emi-grated to the United States in 1765. The house now contains a display on the life and career of Andrew Jackson and Ulster's connections with America. On weekends in July and August, there are craft demonstrations reflecting rural folk life, such as sampler making, basket weaving, griddle making, quilting, and lace making.

✪ **Carrickfergus Castle.** Marine Highway, Antrim St., Carrickfergus, County Antrim. ☎ **028/9335-1273.** Admission £2.70 ($4.45) adults, £1.35 ($2.25) seniors and children, £7.30 ($12.05) family. Combination ticket with Knight Ride £4.85 ($8) adults, £2.40 ($3.95) seniors and children, £13.15 ($21.70) family. Apr–Sept Mon–Sat 10am–6pm, Sun 2–6pm; Oct–Mar Mon–Sat 10am–4pm, Sun 2–4pm.

This remarkably well-preserved and formidable castle, with Ireland's oldest Norman keep, strikes a menacing pose at the strategic entrance to Belfast Lough. The site's guides, audiovisual presentation, and exhibits help visitors imagine and consider the castle's turbulent past. In the summer, medieval banquets, a medieval fair, and a crafts market are held, adding a touch of play and pageantry. Gifts and refreshments are also available.

Knight Ride. The Heritage Plaza, Antrim St., Carrickfergus, County Antrim. ☎ **028/ 9336-6455.** www.carrickfergus.org. £2.70 ($4.45) adults, £1.35 ($2.25) seniors and children, £7.30 ($12.05) family. Combination ticket with Carrickfergus Castle £4.85 ($8) adults, £2.40 ($3.95) seniors and children, £13.50 ($22.30) family. Apr–Sept Mon–Sat 10am–6pm, Sun noon–6pm; Oct–Mar Mon–Sat 10am–5pm, Sun noon–5pm.

The Knight Ride is an action-packed monorail theme ride spanning 8 centuries of Carrickfergus history, from sailing ships to haunted houses to historic invasions. This is one way to fill the imaginations of the whole family with pictures of the past before you explore Carrickfergus Castle.

CULTRA
7 miles (11km) E of Belfast

✪ **Ulster Folk & Transport Museum.** 153 Bangor Rd. (7 miles/11km northeast of Belfast on the A2), Cultra, Holywood, County Down. ☎ **028/9042-8428,** or 028/9042-1444 for 24-hr. information. Day ticket to both museums £4 ($6.60) adults; £2.50 ($4.15) seniors, students, and children; £9 ($14.85) family. Apr–Jun and Sept, Mon–Fri 9:30am–5pm, Sat 10:30am–6pm, Sun noon–6pm; July–Aug Mon–Sat 10:30am–6pm, Sun noon–6pm; Oct–Mar Mon–Fri 9:30am–4pm, Sat–Sun 12:30–4:30pm.

This 176-acre site, which brings together many parts of Ulster's past, is deservedly one of the North's most popular attractions.

Sixty acres are devoted to a unique outdoor folk museum featuring a collection of 19th-century buildings, all saved from the bulldozer's path and moved intact from their original sites in various parts of Northern Ireland. You can walk among 19th-century farmhouses, mills, and churches; climb to the terraces of houses; and peruse rural schools, a forge, a bank, a print shop, and a small conical hut where a watchman would sit with his musket guarding the linen laid out on the green to bleach in the sun. There are demonstrations of people cooking over an open hearth, plowing the fields with horses, thatching roofs, and practicing traditional Ulster crafts such as textile making, spinning, quilting, lace making, printing, spade making, and shoemaking.

In the new transport museum, the collection ranges from donkey carts to De Loreans, and includes an exhibit on the Belfast-built *Titanic.* The exhibit on Irish railways is considered one of the top 10 of its kind in Europe. In 1996, the museum opened the "Car in Society" exhibit, further enhancing its already-impressive reputation.

THE ARDS PENINSULA
The Ards Peninsula, beginning about 10 miles (16km) east of Belfast, curls around the western shore of ✪ **Strangford Lough,** and at 18 miles (29km) long is one of the largest sea inlets in the British Isles. A place of great natural beauty, the peninsula boasts a wonderful bird sanctuary and wildlife reserve, and its shores are home to multifarious species of marine life. Two roads traverse the peninsula: A20 (the Lough road) and A2 (the coast road). The Lough road is the more scenic.

At the southern tip of the Lough, continuous car ferry service connects Portaferry with Strangford on the mainland side. It runs every half hour, weekdays 7:30am to 10:30pm, Saturday 8am to 11pm, Sunday 9:30am to 10:30pm. No reservations are needed. A one-way trip takes 5 minutes and costs £4 ($6.60) for a car and driver, 80p ($1.30) for each additional passenger.

The Portaferry **Tourist Information Office,** Shore Street, near the Strangford ferry departure point (☎ 028/4272-9882), is open Monday to Saturday 9am to 5pm, Sunday 2 to 6pm. There are two National Trust properties in this area, one on the Ards Peninsula and the other just across the lough at Portaferry.

Castle Espie. 78 Ballydrain Rd., Comber, County Down. ☎ **028/9187-4146.** castle. espie@wwwt.org.uk. Admission £3.25 ($5.35) adults, £2.25 ($3.70) seniors and students, £2 ($3.30) children, £8.50 ($14.05) family. Mar–Oct Mon–Sat 10:30am–5pm, Sun 11:30am–6pm; Nov–Feb Mon–Sat 11:30am–4pm, Sun 11:30am–5pm. 13 miles (21km) SE of Belfast, signposted from the A22 Comber–Killyleagh–Downpatrick road.

This marvelous center, owned and managed by the Wildlife and Wetlands Trust, is home to a virtual U.N. of geese, ducks, and swans, many of which are extraordinarily rare. Many are so accustomed to visitors that they will eat grain from your hand. Children will have the disarming experience of meeting Hooper swans eye-to-eye. Guided trails are specially designed for children and families, and the center sponsors a host of activities and events throughout the year.

The Castle Espie reserve, strategically situated on Strangford Lough, is also, in the words of center manager James Orr, a "honeypot" for serious bird-watchers. They come from far and wide for a world-class eyeful of waterfowl. From Brent Hide, for example, up to 3,000 pale-bellied brent can be seen in early winter. The shores of Strangford Lough are among the top bird sites in the world, and are of extraordinary beauty even when your bird of choice is hiding. The center's book and gift shop are enticing for naturalists of all ages, and the restaurant serves deliciously diverting lunches and home-baked sweets.

Castle Ward. Strangford, County Down. ☎ **028/4488-1204.** House admission £2.60 ($4.30) adults, £1.30 ($2.15) children, £6.50 ($10.75) family; estate admission £3.50 ($5.80) per car in high season, £1 ($1.65) per car off-season. House Apr–May and Sept–Oct Sat–Sun 1–6pm; June–Aug Fri–Wed 1–6pm. Castle tour at 5pm; estate open year-round dawn–dusk.

Situated 1½ miles (2.4km) west of Strangford village, this National Trust house dates from 1760 and is half classical and half Gothic in architectural style. It sits on a 700-acre country estate of formal gardens, woodlands, lakelands, and seashore. A restored 1830s corn mill and a Victorian-style laundry are on the grounds, and the theater in the stable yard is a venue for operatic performances in summer.

Exploris. Castle St., Portaferry, County Down. ☎ **028/4272-8062.** Admission £3.95 ($6.50) adults, £2.80 ($4.60) children, £12.30 ($20.30) family. Apr–Aug Mon–Fri 10am–6pm, Sat 11am–6pm, Sun 1–6pm; Sept–Mar Mon–Fri 10am–5pm, Sat 11am–5pm, Sun 1–5pm.

Northern Ireland's aquarium concentrates on the rich diversity of life found in Strangford Lough and the nearby Irish Sea. Displays include models of the saltwater environment found beneath the surface of Strangford Lough, as well as examples of thousands of species of local and regional sea life. The newest addition is the seal sanctuary. The aquarium complex contains a cafe and gift shop, a park, a picnic area, a children's playground, a bowling green, tennis courts, and woodlands.

The Giant's Ring. Ballynahatty, County Down. 5 miles (8km) SW of Belfast center, west off A24; or 1 mile (1.6km) S of Shaw's Bridge, off B23.

This massive prehistoric earthwork, 600 feet in diameter, has more or less at its center a megalithic chamber with a single capstone. It was doubtlessly a significant focus of local cults as long as 5,000 years ago. Today this 7-acre ritual enclosure is a place of wonder for the few and neglect for the many.

Grey Abbey. Greyabbey, County Down. Admission £1 ($1.65) adults, 50p (83¢) children. Apr–Sept Tues–Sat 10am–7pm, Sun 2–7pm. On the east side of Greyabbey, 2 miles (3.2km) southeast of Mt. Stewart.

The impressive ruins of Grey Abbey enjoy a beautifully landscaped setting, perfect for both reflection and a tasteful picnic. It was founded in 1193 for the Cistercians and contained one of the earliest Gothic churches in Ireland. True to Cistercian simplicity, there was and is very little embellishment here, but the Cistercians, like the Shakers, knew well that restraint is no impediment to beauty. All the same, amid the bare ruined choirs, there is a fragmented stone effigy of a knight in armor, possibly a likeness of John de Courcy, husband of the abbey's founder, Affrica of Cumbria. There's also a small visitor center.

Legananny Dolmen. Slieve Croob, County Down. Take A24 from Belfast to Ballynahinch, B7 to Dromara, then ask directions.

This renowned, impressive granite dolmen on the southern slope of Slieve Croob looks, in the words of archaeologist Peter Harbison, like "a coffin on stilts." This is one of the most photographed dolmens in Ireland, but you have to see it up close to admire it fully. The massive capstone seems almost weightlessly poised on its three supporting uprights.

✪ **Mount Stewart House.** On the east shore of Strangford Lough, southeast of Newtownards, 15 miles (24km) southeast of Belfast, on A20, Newtownards, County Down. ☎ **028/4278-8387.** House, garden, and temple admission £3.50 ($5.80) adults, £1.75 ($2.90) children. House Apr and Oct Sat–Sun 1–6pm; May–Sept Mon and Wed–Sun 1–6pm. Garden mid-Mar Sun 11am–6pm; Apr–Sept daily 11am–6pm; Oct Sat–Sun 11am–6pm. Temple Apr–Oct Sat–Sun 2–5pm. Bus: 9, 9A, or 10 from Laganside Bus Centre (Mon–Sat).

Once the home of Lord Castlereagh, this 18th-century house sits on the eastern shore of Strangford Lough. It has one of the greatest gardens in the care of the National Trust, with an unrivaled collection of rare and unusual plants. The house is noteworthy for its art works, including *Hambletonian* by George Stubbs, one of the finest paintings in Ireland, and family portraits by Batoni, Mengs, and Lazlo. The Temple of the Winds, a banqueting house built in 1785, is also on the estate. In 1999, Mount Stewart was one of 32 sites in the United Kingdom nominated as a potential World Heritage Site. Final selection would place it in the company of such sites as the Taj Mahal and the Great Wall of China.

SPORTS & OUTDOOR PURSUITS

BICYCLING   If you want to explore the area on your own two wheels, you can rent bicycles at the **Strangford Arms Hotel,** 92 Church St., Newtownards (☎ **028/9181-4141**), for roughly £8 ($13.20) a day. Cycle rental by the day or week, and delivery in the North Down/Ards area, are available from **Gary Harkness Cycle Hire,** 53 Frances St., Newtownards (☎ **028/9181-1311**). If you want some guidance and companionship, contact Tony Boyd at **The Emerald Trail Bicycle Tours,** 15 Ballyknocken Rd., Saintfield (☎ **028/9081-3200;** www.emeraldtrail.com).

BIRD WATCHING   See the listing for **Castle Espie,** above.

DIVING   The nearby loughs and offshore waters are a diver's dream—remarkably clear and littered with wrecks. To charter a diving expedition in Strangford Lough, contact **Des Rogers** (☎ **028/4272-8297**). **Norsemaid Sea Enterprises,** 152 Portaferry Rd., Newtownards, County Down (☎ **028/9181-2081**), caters 4- to 10-day diving parties along the Northern Irish coast, in Belfast Lough and Strangford Lough, amid the St. Kilda Isles and along the coast of Scotland. One of Europe's finest training centers, **DV Diving,** 138 Mountstewart Rd., Newtownards, County Down (☎ **028/9146-4671;** e-mail: rcf80@dial.pipex.com), offers a wide range of diving courses.

FISHING   For info, tackle, and bait, try the **Village Tackle Shop,** 55a Newtownbreda Rd., Belfast (☎ **028/9049-1916**), or **H.W. Kelly,** 54 Market St., Downpatrick, County Down (☎ **028/4461-2193**). Sea-fishing trips from Portaferry into the waters of Strangford Lough and along the County Down coast are organized by Peter Wright,

Norsemaid Sea Enterprises, 152 Portaferry Rd., Newtownards, County Down (☎ 028/9181-2081). Reservations are required. This company also offers diving charters, day cruises, hill walking, and wildlife cruises. To outfit yourself and fish for rainbow trout year-round, visit **Ballygrangee Fly Fishery,** Mountstewart Road, Carrowdore, County Down (☎ 028/4278-8883).

GOLF   There are several well-established courses a short drive from Belfast in north County Down. They include the **Bangor Golf Club,** Broadway, Bangor (☎ 028/9127-0922), with greens fees of £20 ($33) weekdays, £25 ($41.25) weekends; **Downpatrick Golf Club,** 43 Saul Rd., Downpatrick (☎ 028/4461-5947), with greens fees of £15 ($24.75) weekdays, £20 ($33) weekends; and the **Scrabo Golf Club,** 233 Scrabo Rd., Newtownards (☎ 028/9181-2355), with greens fees of £15 ($24.75) weekdays, £20 ($33) weekends.

SAILING   RYA sailing lessons and yacht charter are available from **Down Yachts,** 37 Bayview Rd., Killinchy, County Down (☎ 028/9754-2210).

ACCOMMODATIONS IN THE AREA
Moderate
Portaferry Hotel. The Strand, Portaferry (29 miles/47km from Belfast), County Down. ☎ **028/4272-8231.** Fax 028/4272-8999. www.portaferryhotel.com. 14 units. TV TEL. £90 ($148.50) double. Rates include full breakfast. Dinner £25 ($41.25). AE, CB, DC, MC, V. Free parking.

Set in a designated conservation area and incorporating a terrace dating from the mid–18th century, the Portaferry Hotel retains the charm of a seasoned waterside inn while offering all the amenities of a modern hotel. Guest rooms are individually designed in keeping with the hotel's traditional character, and many have excellent views of the lough. The award-winning restaurant specializes in fresh local seafood. Nonsmoking rooms are available.

Inexpensive
✪ **Ballycastle House.** 20 Mountstewart Rd. (5 miles/8km southeast of town on A20), Newtownards, County Down. ☎ and fax **028/4278-8357.** 3 units. £40 ($66) double. Children's and senior discounts available. Rates include full breakfast. No credit cards. Free parking.

Mrs. Margaret Deering's home is a beautiful 300-year-old farmhouse that has been elegantly refurbished. The guest rooms are nicely appointed and offer restful rural views. Washing and ironing facilities are available for guests' use. A self-catering cottage is also available. No smoking.

✪ **The Cottage.** 377 Comber Rd. (a 3-mile/4.8km drive east of Belfast on A20), Dundonald, County Down. ☎ **028/9187-8189.** 2 units. TEL. £42 ($69.30) double. Children's discount available. Rates include full breakfast. No credit cards.

Your enchantment with the Cottage is likely to begin as you arrive. The driveway brings you into full view of a lovely lawn and colorful flowerbeds that beckon the traveler to sit awhile. Mrs. Elizabeth Muldoon has realized every cottage lover's dream—she has lovingly retained the original charm of the house and installed every modern convenience. The living room is picture-pretty, as is the rustic dining area. Guest rooms are beautifully furnished, with many antiques scattered about. Guests are invited to enjoy the conservatory out back. The Cottage is one of the most inviting accommodations in the area.

Greenlea Farm. 48 Dunover Rd. (off A2), ½ mile/0.8km north of Ballywalter, County Down. ☎ and fax **028/4275-8218.** 5 units, none with bathroom. TV. £36 ($59.40) double. 50% discount for children under 12 (under 5 free). 10% senior discount. Rates include full breakfast. High tea £6.50–£10 ($10.75–$16.50); dinner £10–£12 ($16.50–$19.80). No credit cards. Free parking.

A comfortable old farmhouse that has been thoroughly modernized, Greenlea looks out from its hilltop to the Ards Peninsula and across to the coast of Scotland and the Isle of Man. The warm, friendly hostess, Mrs. Evelyn McIvor, teaches crafts and enjoys sharing her considerable knowledge of the area with guests. The lounge and dining room have picture windows that frame the spectacular view, and the dining room holds lovely antique pieces, with lots of silver and crystal. Recreational options include tennis and bowling. Mrs. McIvor has one large family room with bunk beds for two children and a double for parents, as well as accommodations for singles and doubles. Greenlea Farm is half a mile from Ballywalter, the first farm on the left on the Dunover road (about 23 miles/37km southeast of Belfast on A2, at the top of the Ards Peninsula).

DINING

Primrose Bar and Restaurant. 30 Main St., Ballynahinch, County Down. ☎ **028/ 9756-3177.** Dinner main courses £4.95–£12 ($8.15–$19.80). AE, MC. V. Daily 11am– 11:30pm. TRADITIONAL/SEAFOOD/SALADS.

The Primrose—a blacksmith shop in a former life—is known locally for its steak casseroles, open-faced prawn sandwiches, and fresh-baked wheaten bread. Other offerings include chicken dishes, pizza, and a variety of salads. There's always a nice fire blazing, and local opinion concurs that "the craic is always good." The adjacent Primrose Pop-In serves afternoon tea, quiche, and pies Monday to Saturday 9am to 4:30pm.

DOWNPATRICK

23 miles (37km) SE of Belfast

Downpatrick, one of the North's oldest cities, is closely identified with St. Patrick. Legend tells us that when Patrick came to Ireland in 432 to begin his missionary work, strong winds blew his boat into this area. He had meant to sail up the coast to County Antrim, where as a young slave he had tended flocks on Slemish Mountain. Instead, he settled here and converted the local chieftain Dichu and his followers to Christianity. Over the next 30 years, Patrick roamed to many other places in Ireland, carrying out his work, but he wound up back here to die. He is said to be buried in the graveyard of Downpatrick Cathedral. A large stone claims to mark the spot.

For information in the Down District, stop into the **Downpatrick Tourist Information Centre,** 74 Market St., Downpatrick, County Down (☎ **028/4461-2233**). It's open October to mid-June Monday to Friday 9am to 5pm, Saturday 9am to 1pm and 2 to 5pm; mid-June to September Monday to Saturday 9am to 6pm and Sunday 2 to 6pm. A "St. Patrick's Country" coach tour is offered according to demand and can be booked through this office.

Down Cathedral. The Mall, Downpatrick, County Down. ☎ **028/4461-4922.** Mon–Fri 9:30am–5pm; Sat–Sun 2–5pm.

As its name suggests, Downpatrick was once a *dún* or fort, as early as the Bronze Age. Eventually, here on the Hill of Down, ancient fortifications gave way to a line of churches, which have superseded each other for 1,800 years, like a stack of Russian matryoshkas. Today's cathedral represents an 18th- and 19th-century reconstruction of its 13th- and 16th-century predecessors. Just south of the cathedral stands a relatively recent monolith inscribed with the name *Patric.* By some accounts, it roughly marks the grave of the saint, who is said to have died at Saul, 2 miles (3.2km) northeast. The tradition identifying this site as Patrick's grave seems to go back no further than the 12th century, when John de Courcy reputedly transferred the bones of saints Bridgit and Columbanus here to lie beside those of St. Patrick.

Inch Abbey. Off A7, 2 miles (3.2km) NW of Downpatrick. Admission to abbey 75p ($1.25) adults, 40p (66¢) children. Abbey Apr–Sept Tues–Sat 10am–1pm and 1:30–7pm; Oct–Mar 10am–1pm and 1:30–4pm. Grounds daily dawn–dusk. From Downpatrick, take A7 1 mile (1.6km) and turn left.

John de Courcy founded Inch Abbey in the 1180s as an act of atonement for his destruction of the nearby abbey of Erenagh. It occupied a strategic site on an island in the Quoile Marshes, within sight of the Mound of Down and Downpatrick Cathedral. Its ruins, like those of so many Cistercian abbeys, having suffered terminal impoverishment, only age rather than expire.

St. Patrick Heritage Centre/Down County Museum. The Mall, Downpatrick, County Down. ☎ **028/4461-5218.** Free admission, except for some special events. June–Aug Mon–Fri 10am–5pm, Sat–Sun 2–5pm; Sept–May Tues–Fri 10am–5pm, Sat 2–5pm.

Next to the cathedral and sharing an extensive 18th-century jail complex, the St. Patrick Centre and the County Museum provide some intriguing glimpses into the rich history of this area. You'll also be introduced to some of the county's more notorious figures, from St. Patrick to a handful of prisoners sent off to Australia in the 19th century.

DINING

Down Arts Centre Café. Irish St., Downpatrick, County Down. ☎ **028/4461-5283.** All items £1–£7 ($1.65–$11.55). Mon–Wed and Fri–Sat 9am–5pm; Thurs 9am–9pm.

You won't have any difficulty finding this place. Look for the clock tower atop a Victorian redbrick building in the very center of Downpatrick, and enter below. Its soups, salads, sandwiches, and pastries provide a satisfying snack or lunch break on your day's outing from Belfast.

LISBURN

10 miles (16km) SE of Belfast

Irish Linen Centre and Lisburn Museum. Market Sq., Lisburn, County Antrim. ☎ **028/9266-3377.** Free admission. Mon–Sat 9:30am–5pm.

The focus of this new center and museum is the linen industry, long synonymous with Northern Ireland. Through the re-creation of factory scenes and multimedia presentations, visitors can trace the history of Irish linen production, from its earliest days in the 17th century to the high-tech industry of today. There are opportunities to see linen in all stages of production, and to watch skilled weavers at work on restored 19th-century looms in the workshop. There are also a cafe and a research library.

If you have a thing about linen and want to give over a whole day to its consideration, you can book a place in an **Irish Linen Tour** by calling the Banbridge Gateway Tourist Information Centre (☎ **028/4062-3322**). From May to September, there are tours every Wednesday and Saturday.

LOUGH NEAGH

10 miles (16km) W of Belfast

Lough Neagh, at 153 square miles, is the largest lake in the British Isles. Often called an inland sea, the lough is 20 miles (32km) long and 10 miles (16km) wide, with a 65-mile (105km) shore. It is famous for its eels, an Ulster delicacy. Hundreds of tons of eels from Lough Neagh are exported each year.

Boat trips on Lough Neagh depart regularly from the nearby **Kinnego Marina** (☎ **0374/811248,** mobile), signposted from the main road. They last about 45 minutes and cost £4 ($6.60) for adults, £2 ($3.30) for children.

Lough Neagh Discovery Centre. Oxford Island, Craigavon, County Armagh. ☎ **028/3832-2205.** Admission £3 ($4.95) adults, £2.30 ($3.80) seniors, £1.80 ($2.95) children, £6.70 ($11.05) family. Apr–Sept daily 10am–7pm; Oct–Mar Wed–Sun 10am–5pm.

Midway between Belfast and Armagh city, this center is on the southern shore of Lough Neagh at Oxford Island, a 270-acre nature reserve with a range of habitats such as reed beds, woodlands, and wildflower meadows. The center provides an excellent introduction to all that the lough has to offer. It contains historical and geographic exhibits, an interactive lab explaining the ecosystems of the lough, walking trails, bird-watching observation points, and picnic areas. For a closer look at everything in sight, the center has binoculars for hire.

ARMAGH

40 miles (65km) SW of Belfast

One of Ireland's most historic cities, Armagh takes its name from the Irish *Ard Macha,* or Macha's Height. The legendary pagan queen Macha is said to have built a fortress here in the middle of the first millennium B.C.

Most of Armagh's history, however, focuses on the 5th century, when St. Patrick chose this place as a base from which to spread Christianity; he called it "my sweet hill" and built a stone church here. Ever since, Armagh has been considered the ecclesiastical capital of Ireland. Today there are two St. Patrick's cathedrals, Catholic and Anglican, seats of the primates of both denominations.

Many of the public buildings and the Georgian town houses along the Mall are the work of Francis Johnston, a native of Armagh, who also left his mark on Georgian Dublin. Buildings, doorsteps, and pavements are made of warm-colored pink, yellow, and red local limestone that make the city glow even on a dull day.

In addition to being Ireland's spiritual capital, this area is known for its apple trees, earning Armagh the title "the Orchard of Ireland."

Stop into the **Armagh Tourist Information Office,** the Old Bank Building, 40 English St., Armagh (☎ **028/3752-1800**). It's open April to September, Monday to Saturday 9am to 5pm, Sunday 1 to 5:30pm; October to March, Monday to Saturday 9am to 5pm, Sunday 2 to 5pm. For a host of tourist information on County Armagh, take a look at **www.armagh-visit.com**.

Armagh Astronomy Centre and Planetarium. College Hill, Armagh, County Armagh. ☎ **028/3752-3689.** Admission to show and exhibition area £3.75 ($6.20) adults, £2.75 ($4.55) seniors and children, £11 ($18.15) family. Exhibition area only £1 ($1.65) adults, 50p (83¢) seniors and children. Mon–Fri 10am–4:45pm, Sat 1:15–4:45pm.

On your way up College Hill from the Mall, you'll pass the 200-year-old Armagh Observatory, still in service but closed to the public. Farther up the hill stands the Astronomy Centre and Planetarium complex, whose Astropark, Hall of Astronomy, Eartharium Gallery, and planetarium offer an engaging array of exhibits and shows, with lots of hands-on learning for the whole family.

Armagh County Museum. The Mall East, Armagh, County Armagh. ☎ **028/3752-3070.** Free admission. Mon–Fri 10am–5pm; Sat 10am–1pm and 2–5pm.

Housed in what appears to be a miniature Greek temple, this is the oldest county museum in Ireland. Its rather extensive collection, documenting local life across the millennia, ranges from prehistoric ax heads to wedding dresses. In addition to natural history specimens and folklore items, the museum has an extensive art collection, which includes works by George Russell and John Luke. There is also a rotating exhibition. The museum's maps, photographs, and research library can also be consulted.

Benburb Valley Park, Castle, and Heritage Centre. 89 Milltown Rd., Benburb, County Armagh. ☎ **01861/548170** or 028/3754-8170. Park: Free admission. Daily until dusk. Castle and heritage centre: Admission £1.50 ($2.50). Apr–Sept Mon–Sat 10am–5pm. 7 miles (11km) northwest of Armagh; take B128 off A29.

Begin in the town and explore the dramatic banks of the River Blackwater, a favorite for canoeists and anglers. The park follows the river and brings you to a tree-lined gorge with a partially restored 17th-century castle perched on a cliff high overhead. Another half mile brings you to the Benburb Valley Heritage Centre, a restored linen mill, and the Benburb Castle site, within the grounds of a Servite monastery.

✪ **Navan Fort.** The Navan Centre, 81 Killylea Rd., Armagh, County Armagh. ☎ **028/3752-5550.** Fax 028/3752-2323. www.navan.com. Admission £3.95 ($6.50) adults, £3 ($4.95) students and seniors, £2.25 ($3.70) children, £7–£10 ($11.55–$16.50) family. Open year-round Mon–Sat 10am–5pm, Sun 11am–5pm. 2 miles (3.2km) from Armagh on A28, signposted from Armagh center.

Navan Fort (in Irish, *Emain Macha*) was, in pre-Christian Ireland, a seat of power and a site of ritual. It was the royal and religious capital of Ulster. As at Tara, very little remains—only mounds, mute and unimpressive until their remarkable stories are told. The adjacent interpretive center does just this, quite strikingly. The Navan Centre is an artificial mound, barely visible until you're upon it. Inside, the magic begins. Through a series of exhibits and two multimedia presentations, the history and pre-history of Emain Macha, its mysteries and legends, unfold. A book and gift shop and cafe are also on hand. The center is also the focus of educational and artistic programs and events year-round.

Palace Stables Heritage Centre. Palace Desmesne, Armagh, County Armagh. ☎ **028/3752-9629.** Admission £3.50 ($5.80) adults, £2.75 ($4.55) seniors, £2 ($3.30) children, £9.50 ($15.70) family. Apr–Aug Mon–Sat 10am–5:30pm, Sun 1–6pm; Sept–Mar Mon–Sat 10am–5pm, Sun 2–5pm. 10-min. walk from town, off Friary Rd.

This center takes visitors back to a day in the life of the Irish primate's palace in 1776. It's in a restored Georgian stable block on what were once the palace grounds. The adjoining palace, icehouse, and primate's chapel are accessible only by guided tour, included in the admission price. There are a garden, a children's playroom and adventure area, a craft shop, and the Stables Restaurant.

Peatlands Park. 33 Derryhubbert Rd. (7 miles/11km southeast of Dungannon, at exit 13 off M1), The Birches, County Armagh. ☎ **028/3885-1102.** Free admission to park. Rail ride £1 ($1.65) adults, 50p (83¢) children. Vehicle access to park daily 9am–dusk. Railway June–Aug 2–6pm.

Once a part of the Churchill Estate, Peatlands Park consists of more than 600 acres of peat faces and small lakes in the southwest corner of the Lough Neagh basin, designated as a Natural Nature Reserve. To preserve the park's protected fauna and flora, you're asked to stay on the system of marked walking paths or to take a ride on a narrow-gauge railway. Nature walks and events are offered through the year.

St. Patrick's Trian Visitor Complex. 40 English St. (off Friary Rd, a 10-min. walk from town), Armagh, County Armagh. ☎ **028/3752-1801.** Admission (includes 3 multimedia exhibitions) £3.75 ($6.20) adults, £2.75 ($4.55) seniors and students, £2 ($3.30) children, £9.50 ($15.70) family. July–Aug Mon–Sat 10am–5:30pm, Sun 1–6pm; Sept–June Mon–Sat 10am–5pm, Sun 2–5pm.

Housed in the old Second Presbyterian Church in the heart of Armagh, this modern visitor complex provides an informative and engaging introduction to Armagh, the "motherhouse" of Irish Christianity. Its dramatic presentations, including the *Armagh*

Story and *The Land of Lilliput* (complete with a giant Gulliver beset by Lilliputians), are entertaining for the whole family. This is a good first stop to get your bearings in local history and culture. There are a craft courtyard and a cafe, as well as a visitor genealogical service, if you have local roots.

4 The Causeway Coast & the Glens of Antrim

66 miles (106km) from Larne to Portstewart on the coastal A2; Larne is 25 miles (40km) from Belfast

Over 9,000 years ago, the first visitors to Ireland made landfall on the Causeway Coast. It was accessible, attractive, and there—all that was needed then, or now, to invite the curious to these spectacular shores. Steeped in myth and legend, pounded by its own history, and graced with true grandeur, the North Antrim Coast is one of the most dramatic coastlines in Ireland.

Heralded in story and song, the Glens of Antrim consist of nine green valleys, sitting north of Belfast and stretching from south to north. The glens have individual names, each based on a local tale or legend. Although the meanings are not known for certain, the popular translations are as follows: Glenarm (glen of the army), Glencloy (glen of the hedges), Glenariff (ploughman's glen), Glenballyeamon (Edwardstown glen), Glenaan (glen of the rush lights), Glencorp (glen of the slaughter), Glendun (brown glen), Glenshesk (sedgy glen), and Glentaisie (Taisie's glen).

The people who live in the Glens of Antrim are descendants of the ancient Irish and the Hebridean Scots, so this area is one of the last places in Northern Ireland to let go of the Gaelic tongue. To this day, the glen people are known to be great storytellers.

Two of Ireland's foremost attractions are also here: the **Giant's Causeway** and **Old Bushmills Distillery.** For bird-watchers, the coastal moors and cliffs, and the offshore nature reserve on **Rathlin Island,** are prime destinations. There's plenty of exploring and outdoor adventuring. Each August, the seaside town of **Ballycastle** plays host to one of Ireland's oldest traditional gatherings, the Oul' Lammas Fair.

VISITOR INFORMATION The principal **tourist information centers** in North Antrim are at Narrow Guarge Road, **Larne** (☎ 028/2826-0088); Sheskburn House, 7 Mary St., **Ballycastle** (☎ 028/2076-2024); 44 Causeway Rd., **Bushmills** (☎ 028/2073-1855); and Dunluce Centre, Sandhill Drive, **Portrush** (☎ 028/ 7082-3333). All but the Dunluce Centre are open year-round; hours vary seasonally. Summer hours, at the minimum, are Monday to Friday 10am to 5pm, Saturday 10am to 4pm, Sunday 2 to 6pm.

EXPLORING THE COAST

The area identified as the Antrim coast is 60 miles (97km) long, stretching north of **Larne** and west past Bushmills and the Giant's Causeway to **Portrush.** The route takes in marine seascapes and chalky cliffs. It includes the National Trust village of **Cushendun,** with pretty Cornish-style cottages, as well as a string of beach resorts favored by Irish and English vacationers, such as **Portrush, Portstewart,** and **Portballintrae.** This coastal drive also meanders under bridges and arches, passing bays, sandy beaches, harbors, and huge rock formations.

Carrick-A-Rede Rope Bridge. Larrybane, County Antrim. ☎ 028/2073-1159. Free admission. Bridge, center, and tearoom Apr–June and early Sept daily 10am–6pm; July–Aug 10am–8pm. Parking £2 ($3.30).

Five miles (8km) west of Ballycastle off the A2 road, this open rope bridge spans a chasm 60 feet wide and 80 feet above the sea between the mainland and a small island. Local fishermen put up the bridge each spring to allow access to the island's salmon fishery, but visitors can use it for a thrilling walk and the chance to call out to each other, "Don't look down!" (This is good advice.) If you are acrophobic, stay clear; if you don't know whether you are, this is the place to find out.

Note: The 12-mile (19km) coastal cliff path from the Giant's Causeway to the rope bridge is always open and is well worth the exhaustion.

✪ **Dunluce Castle.** 87 Dunluce Rd. (3½ miles/5.6km east of Portrush off A2), Bushmills, County Antrim. ☎ **028/2073-1938.** Admission £1.50 ($2.50) adults, 75p ($1.25) seniors and children under 16. Apr–May and Sept Tues–Sat 10am–6pm, Sun 2–6pm; June–Aug Mon–Sat 10am–7pm, Sun noon–6pm; Oct–Mar Tues–Sat 10am–4pm, Sun 2–6pm. Last admission 30 min. before closing.

This site was once the main fort of the Irish MacDonnells, chiefs of Antrim. It's the largest and most sophisticated castle in the North, consisting of a series of fortifications built on rocky outcrops extending into the sea. The present castle incorporates two of the original Norman towers dating from 1305, and was the power base of the north coast for 400 years. The visitor center shows an audiovisual presentation with background on the site.

Dunluce Centre. 10 Sandhill Dr., Portrush, County Antrim. ☎ **028/7082-4444.** Turbo Tours £2.50 ($4.15); Earthquest £1.75 ($2.90); Myths & Legends £2.50 ($4.15); Tower 50p (83¢); all four £5 ($8.25), £15 ($24.75) family. Apr–June daily noon–5pm; July–Aug daily 10am–8pm; Sept and Mar Sat–Sun noon–5pm.

Opened in June 1993, this family-oriented entertainment complex provides a variety of indoor activities. It offers a multimedia show, Myths & Legends, that illustrates the folklore of the Antrim coast, as well as Turbo Tours, a thrill ride simulating a modern-day space ride, and Earthquest, an interactive display on the wonders of nature. There is also a viewing tower with panoramic views of the coast, a Victorian-style arcade of shops, a restaurant with a children's play area, and a fully equipped Tourist Information Center (☎ **028/7082-3333**).

✪ **Giant's Causeway.** Causeway Rd., Bushmills, County Antrim.

A World Heritage Site, this natural rock formation is often called the eighth wonder of the world. It consists of roughly 40,000 tightly packed basalt columns that extend for 3 miles (4.8km) along the coast. The tops of the columns form stepping stones that lead from the cliff foot and disappear under the sea. They're mostly hexagonal, and some are as tall as 40 feet. Scientists estimate that they were formed 60 or 70 million years ago by volcanic eruptions and cooling lava. The ancients, on the other hand, believed the rock formation to be the work of giants. Another legend has it that Finn MacCool, the Ulster warrior and commander of the king of Ulster's armies, built the causeway as a highway over the sea to bring his girlfriend from the Isle of Hebrides. (And you thought sending a limo was cool.) To reach the causeway, follow the walk from the parking area past amphitheaters of stone columns and formations with fanciful names like Honeycomb, Wishing Well, Giant's Granny, King and his Nobles, and Lover's Leap, and up a wooden staircase to Benbane Head and back along the cliff top.

Note: In the spring of 2000, the new Giant's Causeway Visitors Centre tragically burned to the ground. Plans for its replacement are currently under consideration.

✪ **Old Bushmills Distillery.** Main St., Bushmills, County Antrim. ☎ **028/2073-1521.** www.bushmills.com. Admission £3.50 ($5.80) adults, £3 ($4.95) seniors and students, £1.50 ($2.50) children, £9 ($14.85) family. Apr–Oct Mon–Sat 9:30am–5:30pm, Sun noon–5:30pm (last tour 4pm); Nov–Mar Mon–Fri 10:30am–3:30pm (last tour 3:30pm).

Licensed to distill spirits in 1608, but with historical references dating as far back as 1276, this is the oldest distillery in the world. Visitors are welcome to tour the facility and watch the whiskey-making process, starting with fresh water from the adjacent

River Bush and continuing through distilling, fermenting, and bottling. At the end of the tour, you can sample the wares in the Poststill Bar, where there are fascinating exhibits on the long history of the distillery. Twenty-five–minute tours depart regularly April to October; November to March, there are tours at 10:30am, 11:30am, noon, 1:30pm, 2:30pm, and 3:30pm. The Bushmills coffee shop serves tea, coffee, homemade snacks, and lunches.

Rathlin Island RSPB Seabird Viewpoint. Rathlin Island, off the coast of Ballycastle, County Antrim. ☎ **028/2076-3948;** www.island-trail.com. Free admission. Seabird-viewing facility by appointment Apr–Aug.

For peace and solitude, plan a trip to this boomerang-shaped island, 6 miles (9.7km) off the coast north of Ballycastle and 14 miles (23km) south of Scotland. It is almost 4 miles (6.5km) long, yet less than 1 mile (1.6km) wide at any point. Rathlin Island is almost completely treeless, with a rugged coast of 200-foot-high cliffs, a small beach, and a native population of 100. Don't worry—there are also a pub, a restaurant, and a guesthouse, in case you get stranded. This is a great bird-watching center, especially in spring and early to mid-summer.

Boat trips operate daily from Ballycastle pier; crossing time is 45 minutes. The round-trip fare is £7.80 ($12.85) for adults, £5.80 ($9.55) for seniors and students, and £3.90 ($6.45) for children 5–16. The number and schedule of crossings varies from season to season and from year to year, and are always subject to weather. There are usually at least several crossings a day. It's best to confirm departures by phoning the **Caledonian MacBrayne ticket office** (☎ 028/2076-9299) well in advance.

On the island, a **minibus** (summer only) will take you from Church Bay to the West Light Platform and the Kebble Nature Reserve for roughly £2.50 ($4.15) adults, £1.25 ($2.05) children, round-trip. There are also minibus tours offered by **McCurdy's Minibus Tours** (☎ 028/2076-3909) or **Irene's Minibus Tours**(☎ 028/ 2076-3949). Bicycles can be rented from **Soerneog View Hostel** (☎ 028/ 2076-3954).

A SHOPPING STOP

The Steensons. Toberwine St., Glenarm, County Antrim. ☎ and fax **028/2884-1445.**

This is the workshop-showroom of Bill and Christina Steenson, two of the most celebrated goldsmiths in Ireland. On display and for sale is a small, impressive selection of their pieces, as well as a sampling of the work of other distinguished Irish goldsmiths and silversmiths with a similar contemporary eye. Open Mon-day to Friday 9:15am to 5:15pm, plus Saturday and Sunday 1 to 5:30pm in the summer.

SPORTS & OUTDOOR PURSUITS

The **Ardclinis Activity Center,** High Street, Cushendall, County Antrim (☎ and fax 028/2177-1340; e-mail: Ardclinis@aol.com), offers a range of year-round outdoor programs and courses. They include everything from rock climbing and mountain biking to windsurfing and rafting. Half-day, full-day, and weeklong activities for ages 8 and older are offered, as well as 5- and 6-night scenic walking and cycling tours. You can show up and hope for a place, but it's better to book at least several weeks ahead. The center will arrange local B&B or hostel accommodations.

FISHING The best time to fish in the North Antrim Glens is July to October, both for salmon and for sea trout. The rivers of choice are the Margy, Glenshesk, Carey, and

Dun. The **Marine Hotel** (see "Accommodations," below) in Ballycastle offers an array of services to the game angler. For locally arranged game fishing, contact **Gillaroo Angles,** 7 Cooleen Park, Jordanstown, Newtownabbey, County Antrim (☎ **028/ 9086-2419**). For info, tackle, and bait, try **Red Bay Boats,** Coast Road, Cushendall (☎ **028/2177-1331**).

GOING SKY HIGH   If you have to have the bird's-eye view, you may want to contact the **Wild Geese Parachute Club** (☎ **028/2955-8609**); the **Ulster Gliding Club** (☎ **028/7775-0301**), weekends only; or **Microlight Flying** (☎ **028/7086-8002** or 028/7082-3793). While you're at it, keep your eyes peeled for a familiar sight—a monk from Dublin who hang-glides off the Causeway cliffs every month or so. He's known by locals only as "Flyer Tuck."

You can also book a spectacular helicopter ride over the North Antrim Coast through the **Helicopter Centre,** Belfast International Airport (☎ **028/9445-2663**).

GOLF   North Antrim boasts several notable courses in the short coastal stretch from Ballycastle to Portstewart, including the **Ballycastle Golf Club,** Cushendall Road, Ballycastle (☎ **028/2076-2536**), and the **Royal Portrush Golf Club,** Dunluce Road, Portrush (☎ **028/7082-2311**). Royal Portrush has three links courses, including the Dunluce Course, ranked no. 3 in the U.K. Just over the border in County Londonderry are two more courses to be reckoned with: the **Portstewart Golf Club** (with three links courses), 117 Strand Rd., Portstewart (☎ **028/7083-2015**); and the **Castlerock Golf Club** (with two links courses), 65 Circular Rd., Castlerock (☎ **028/7038-48314**). Some days and times are better than others for visitors, so it's advisable to call ahead for times and fees, which range from £20 to £60 ($33 to $99) for 18 holes, depending on the course and the day of the week.

PONY TREKKING   **Watertop Farm Family Activity Centre,** 188 Cushendall Rd., Ballycastle (☎ **028/2076-2576**), offers pony trekking and other outdoor family activities, daily in July and August and weekends in late June and early September. In the Portrush area, contact **Maddybenny Riding Centre** (☎ **028/7082-3394; www.maddybenny.freeserve.co.uk**), also offering accommodation which won "Farmhouse of the Year" award for all of Ireland in 1999. Also, in Castlerock, there's **Hillfarm Riding and Trekking Centre** (☎ **028/7084-8629**).

SAILING   The **Cushendall Sailing and Boating Club** offers dinghy sailing lessons to beginners for roughly £75 ($123.75) per week during July and August. Contact James Farrell (☎ **028/2177-1272**).

SCUBA DIVING   For organized dives off Rathlin Island, contact **Tommy Cecil** (☎ **028/2076-3915**).

WALKING   The **Ulster Way,** 560 miles (904km) of marked trail, follows the North Antrim Coast from Glenarm to Portstewart. The **Moyle Way** offers a spectacular detour from Ballycastle south to Glenariff. Maps and accommodations listings for both ways are in the free NITB booklet *The Ulster Way: Accommodation for Walkers.* Or pick up a copy of *Walking the Ulster Way,* by Alan Warner (Appletree Press, 1989). The NITB also offers *An Information Guide to Walking,* full of useful information for avid pedestrians.

Last but far from least is the newly upgraded (at the cost of $500,000) **Causeway Coast Path.** It stretches from Bushfoot Strand, near Bushmills, in the west to Ballintoy Harbour in the east. Short of sprouting wings, this is surely the way to take in the full splendor of the North Antrim coast.

ACCOMMODATIONS
MODERATE

✪ **Bushmills Inn.** 9 Dunluce Rd., Bushmills, County Antrim. ☎ **028/2073-2339.** Fax 028/2073-2048. www.bushmills-inn.com. 33 units, 26 with private bathroom. TV TEL. £98–£138 ($161.70–$227.70) double. Family rooms available. Rates include full breakfast. MC, V. Free private parking.

In the center of the famous whiskey-making village of the same name, this inn dates from the 17th century. The Coaching Inn section was totally restored and refurbished in 1987, and 22 new rooms in the Mill House were completed for 1998. The interior of the Coaching Inn has old-world charm, with open turf fireplaces, gas lamps, and antique furnishings. Guest rooms in this section are comfortable and contemporary in design, with country pine and caned furniture, floral wallpaper, brass fixtures, and vintage prints. The new Mill House rooms are considerably more spacious than the original Coaching Inn rooms and offer such extras as modem and fax connection, trouser press, iron, hair dryer, hospitality tray, and baby-listening facility. Some nonsmoking rooms are available. On the premises are a lounge bar, a gallery and drawing room, and the Barony restaurant, which features recipes using Bushmills whiskey.

Causeway Coast Hotel. 36 Ballyreagh Rd., Portrush, County Antrim. ☎ **028/7082-2435.** Fax 028/7082-4495. 21 units. TV TEL. £85 ($140.25) double. Rates include full breakfast. AE, MC, V.

Opposite the 9-hole Ballyreagh Golf Course and overlooking the Atlantic coastline, this rambling resort is between Portstewart and Portrush, but away from the bustle of both towns. Rooms have modern furnishings, garment presses, hair dryers, and tea/coffeemakers. Some rooms have sea views and private balconies. The property also includes self-catering apartments with kitchens. Dining options are the Dunluce restaurant, Tramways Steak Bar, and the Wine Bar.

Londonderry Arms. 20 Harbour Rd., Carnlough, County Antrim. ☎ **800/44-PRIMA** from the U.S., or 028/2888-5255. Fax 028/2888-5263. www.glensofantrim.com. 35 units. TV TEL. £85 ($140.25) double. Rates include full breakfast. High tea £10.95 ($18.10); dinner £19.95 ($32.90). AE, DC, MC, V.

At the foot of Glencloy, one of the nine Antrim glens, this ivy-covered former coaching inn dates to 1848; at one point Sir Winston Churchill owned it (through a family inheritance). It has been a hotel in the hands of the O'Neill family since 1947. It sits in the heart of a delightful coastal town with views of the harbor across the street. The hotel recently expanded, and a surprising degree of tasteful continuity was achieved between the original Georgian structure and the new wing. Elegant refurbishing of the older rooms is ongoing. Each room has its own character, yet is furnished with the same fine eye and excellent taste. The award-winning restaurant and the Arkle Bar are favorites for locals and attract a wider following. This is a family-run hotel, and it shows in the warmth of hospitality and careful attention to detail.

Magherabuoy House Hotel. 41 Magheraboy Rd., Portrush, County Antrim. ☎ **028/7082-3507.** Fax 028/7082-4687. 38 units. TV TEL. £100 ($165) double. Rates include full breakfast. AE, DC, MC, V.

Nestled amid gardens at the edge of Portrush, this country manor–style hotel enjoys panoramic views of the town and seacoast, yet is away from the resort hubbub. The traditional ambience—dark woods, gilded mirrors, and open fireplaces—contrasts with the guest rooms, which are contemporary and smart, with frilly fabrics, brass fittings, and floral wallpapers. On the premises are a restaurant, lounge, snack bar, and nightclub, and a leisure complex with Jacuzzi and gym.

Marine Hotel. 1 North St., Ballycastle, County Antrim. ☎ **012657/2076-2222.** Fax 028/7076-9507. 32 units. TV TEL. £75 ($123.75) double. Rates include full breakfast. Dinner £14 ($23.10). AE, DC, MC, V.

Sitting right on the harbor at Ballycastle, this refurbished three-story contemporary-style hotel is a favorite with Irish vacationers. The rooms offer lovely views of the sea and bright modern furnishings. Nonsmoking units are available. The hotel is home to the Glass Island restaurant, Marconi lounge bar, and Legends, a nightclub featuring a variety of music from disco to cabaret, country and western, jazz, and pop. The country club run by the hotel offers a pool, sauna, and fitness room.

The Marine Hotel and Country Club complex includes 27 **self-catering apartments** (☎ **028/9066-7110**). They are rented only by the week in high season. During the rest of the year, they're available by the night or for a weekend. Weekly rates range from £220 to £395 ($363 to $651.75).

INEXPENSIVE

Cushendall Youth Hostel. 42 Layde Rd., Cushendall, County Antrim. ☎ **028/2177-1344.** Fax 028/2177-2042. Sleeps 44–54. Dorm and family rooms £9 ($14.85) per person over 17, £6.50–£7.50 ($10.75–$12.40) per person under 18. MC, V. Daily 7:30–10:30am and 5–11:30pm. Closed Dec 23–Feb. Private parking in front of hostel. Signposted from Cushendall center.

Newly renovated, this superior hostel has been in service for 30 years; clearly, practice makes perfect. It is quite attractive and close to immaculate. The dining and guest rooms are all nonsmoking. A comfortable TV and reading lounge, complete with open fireplace, is also available. The commodious kitchen offers far more than most hostels, both in facilities (including ovens and microwave) and in spotlessness. On an old farm half a mile outside the village center, the hostel is accessible by bus and is near the Ulster Way. There's a locked bike shed.

The Meadows. 81 Coast Rd., Cushendall, County Antrim. ☎ **028/2177-2020.** 6 units, all with shower only. TV. £40 ($66) double. Family rates negotiable. Rates include full Irish breakfast and service charge. V.

This newly constructed guesthouse provides spacious, well-designed accommodations in a lovely coastal setting. The front-room views of the sea and, on a clear day, of Scotland are quite splendid. All rooms are nonsmoking and are simply spotless. All have their own tea and coffee facilities. There's one family room, and one unit is fully adapted for travelers with disabilities. A spacious lounge is reserved for guests, and the breakfast room is particularly inviting. A 10-minute walk from the center of Cushendall, the Meadows offers exceptional convenience, comfort, and good value. Anne Carey, your host, will gladly arrange for you to eat at the private boat club across the road.

Sanda. 29 Kilmore Rd., Glenariff, County Antrim. ☎ **028/2177-1785.** E-mail: sanda@antrim.net. 2 units, both with shower only. £30–£34 ($49.50–$56.10) double. Family rates negotiable. Rates include full Irish breakfast and service charge. No credit cards. Closed Dec–Feb.

Perched high at the mouth of Glenariff, the Queen of the Glens, Sanda affords truly spectacular views. The two guest rooms are modest and immaculate. The beds are very firm, and a pleasant lounge, complete with TV and a stack of intriguing books about the area, is available to guests. Smoking is not permitted in the rooms. Host Donnell O'Loan is quite knowledgeable and articulate about the area—its ancient sites as well as its current attractions.

SELF-CATERING

Bellair Cottage. Glenarm, County Antrim. Contact RCH, ☎ **028/9024-1100.** Fax 028/9024-1198. www.cottagesinireland.com. 1 cottage. TV TEL. £300–£430 ($495–$709.50) per week. Also available for 2- or 3-day stays. Additional charge for heat and electricity. MC, V.

This century-old farmhouse and attached barn have been beautifully converted into a gracious, inviting traditional home away from home for one or two families. It has three bedrooms, and sleeps six. It occupies a lovely secluded setting high on Glenarm Glen, with a stone-walled garden that's perfect for children. The exquisite master bedroom wins our private design award for bedroom of the year. For an extended working holiday or summer—or sabbatical year, for that matter—Bellair is a good size for two people, giving each a private workplace. The nearby North Antrim Coast is all the inspiration any writer, painter, photographer, or gazer could ask for.

✪ **Tully Cottage.** Glenarm, County Antrim. Contact RCH, ☎ **028/9024-1100.** Fax 028/9024-1198. www.cottagesinireland.com. 1 cottage. TV TEL. £275–£395 ($453.75–$651.75) per week. Also available for 2- to 3-day stays. Additional charge for heat and electricity. MC, V.

This is one of the loveliest self-catering cottages we've found. Although it has two bedrooms and is large enough to accommodate four quite comfortably, Tully is the perfect love nest or honeymoon nook. It is both elevated and secluded, affording spectacular views of Glenarm Glen and the North Channel down to the Mull of Galloway, plus total privacy. The old farm cottage has been lovingly restored and tastefully appointed to offer equal charm and comfort. The beds are firm, the tub is extra-long, the traditional fireplace is up to the task, and the kitchen is fully equipped. This is a perfect base for exploring the stunning North Antrim coast or for curling up. It will feel like home within hours, and a week will never seem enough. Horse riding, day boats, trekking, and rock climbing can be arranged in advance; bicycles can be waiting for you at the cottage, all through RCH.

DINING
MODERATE

✪ **Hillcrest Country House.** 306 Whitepark Rd., Giant's Causeway, County Antrim. ☎ **028/2073-1577.** Reservations required. Main courses £7.95–£11.95 ($13.10–$19.70). MC, V. Mon–Sat noon–9:30pm, Sun noon–9pm. IRISH.

Surrounded by lovely gardens and situated opposite the entrance to the Giant's Causeway, this restaurant offers lovely wide-windowed views of the coast, which are particularly beautiful at sunset. The menu emphasizes local ingredients and creative sauces: salmon baked with cucumbers, mushrooms, and fennel sauce; grilled venison with game mousse laced with Black Bush Irish whiskey; roast North Antrim duck with sage and onion stuffing and peach brandy; and noisettes of lamb with rosemary and garlic sauce.

Bed-and-breakfast accommodations are available, with special off-season weekend packages.

✪ **Ramore.** Ramore St., The Harbour, Portrush, County Antrim. ☎ **028/7082-4313.** Reservations required. Main courses £9.95–£14.95 ($16.40–$24.65). MC, V. Wine bar Mon–Sat noon–2pm and 5:30–9pm; restaurant Tues–Sat 6:30–10:30pm. INTERNATIONAL.

On the east end of the harbor overlooking boats and the sea, this restaurant is known for its international menu. Choices include chicken breast with fresh asparagus and vinaigrette of pine nuts, sun-dried tomatoes, Parmesan, and truffle oil; duck on a bed of shredded cabbage; and pork filled with Parma ham and Emmenthal cheese. You might also try paella, Thai chicken, tempura prawns, fish of the day, rack of lamb, or steak.

INEXPENSIVE

Sweeney's Wine Bar. 6b Seaport Ave., Portballintrae, County Antrim. ☎ **028/ 2073-2405.** Reservations recommended for dinner. Main courses £5–£8 ($8.25–$13.20). No credit cards. Mon–Sat 12:30–8pm, Sun 12:30–2:30pm and 7–9pm. IRISH.

This is a pubby, informal spot on the coast, with a conservatory-style extension and outdoor seating in good weather. The menu features pub grub—burgers, pasta, seafood plates (prawns, scampi, cod, and whitefish), seafood pie, steak and kidney pie, and stir-fry vegetables.

Victoriana Restaurant. Dunluce Ave., Portrush, County Antrim. ☎ **028/7082-4444.** Main courses £1.90–£5 ($3.15–$8.25). No credit cards. Apr–June and Sept daily noon–5pm; July–Aug daily 10am–8pm; Oct Sat–Sun noon–5pm. SELF-SERVICE.

In the new Dunluce Center, this Victorian-theme bilevel restaurant is a great place to stop for refreshment when touring the Antrim coast. The menu includes sandwiches, omelets, salads, pastas, and steaks, as well as sausage, beans, chips, and "Ulster fry" (a cheese and onion pie).

PUBS

Harbour Bar. The Wharf, Portrush, County Antrim. ☎ **028/7082-5047.**

This is a good place for a before- or after-dinner libation. It sits on the wharf overlooking the boat-filled harbor, and you'll find mostly locals in the plain, old-style bar. It's all so very Irish.

J. McCollam. Mill St., Cushendall, County Antrim. ☎ **028/2177-1992.**

Known to locals as Johnny Joes, J. McCollam has been for nearly a century the hottest scene in Cushendall for traditional music and Antrim atmosphere. You have to be willing to wedge yourself in, but you're not likely to have any regrets.

M. McBrides. 2 Main St., Cushendun Village, County Antrim. ☎ **028/2176-1511.**

Opened in 1840, Mary McBride's was the smallest pub or bar in Europe until, quite recently, it expanded to include a bistro and restaurant. The old Guinness record–holding pub is still intact, so squeeze in and partake of the legend for yourself. Live, traditional music tends to break out in the pub's conservatory on weekend evenings.

The Riverside Bistro serves light lunches and dinners (noon to 9pm). The Waterside Restaurant, specializing in seafood, serves a diverse menu of dinners (6 to 9pm), including Torr Head lobster and Cushendum salmon; main courses run £6.50 to £16.50 ($10.75 to $27.25).

5 The Mourne Mountains

30 miles (48km) SW of Belfast

South and west from Downpatrick lie the rolling foothills of the Mournes, the highest mountains in Northern Ireland. A dozen of their nearly 50 summits rise above 2,000 feet, all of which are dominated by the barren peak of **Slieve Donard** (2,796 ft.). Its breathtaking vista includes the full length of Strangford Lough, Lough Neagh, the Isle of Man, and, on a crystalline day, the west coasts of Wales and Scotland. (The recommended ascent of Slieve Donard is from Donard Park on the south side of Newcastle.)

Like giant drumlins, described by C. S. Lewis as "earth-covered potatoes," all but two of the Mournes's purple peaks are soft and rounded. Remote and veined by very few roads, the mountains are a rambler's dream. If you suddenly envisage barren windswept moors, you're on the right track. The ancestral home of the Brontës is here, in ruin. But all is not desolate here. There are forest parks, sandy beaches, lush gardens, and, of course, pubs.

Besides walking and climbing and sighing at the wuthering splendor of it all, there's **Newcastle,** a popular, lively seaside resort, complete with beach and one of the finest golf courses in Ireland. Several other coastal towns strung along A2—**Kilkeel, Rostrevor,** and **Warrenpoint**—have their own charms. But here the mountains are the thing, and naturally you can't have cliffs and the sea without birds and castles and the odd dolmen. Finally, if at the end of the day your idea of nightlife has mostly to do with the stars, the Mourne Mountains provide a luminous getaway.

ESSENTIALS

GETTING THERE   If you're driving up from Dublin, turn east off the Dublin–Belfast road at Newry and take A2, tracing the north shore of Carlingford Lough, between the mountains and the sea. It's a drive you won't soon forget.

VISITOR INFORMATION   For information in the Down District, stop into the **Downpatrick Tourist Information Centre,** 74 Market St., Downpatrick, County Down (☎ **028/4461-2233**), open October to mid-June Monday to Friday 9am to 5pm, Saturday 9am to 1pm and 2 to 5pm; mid-June to September Monday to Saturday 9am to 6pm and Sunday 2 to 6pm. (Downpatrick, covered in section 3 of this chapter, "Side Trips from Belfast," is a good gateway stop as you head into the Mourne Mountains from Belfast.)

There's also the **Newcastle Tourist Information Centre,** 10–14 Central Promenade, Newcastle, County Down (☎ **028/4372-2222;** fax 028/4372-2400). It's open Monday to Saturday 9am to 5pm and Sunday 2 to 6pm, with extended hours in the summer. A coach tour of the Mournes, offered according to demand, can be booked here. Or try the **Mourne Countryside Centre,** 91 Central Promenade, Newcastle, County Down (☎ **028/4372-4059**), open June to September Monday to Friday 9am to 7pm, weekends noon to 6pm. The center dispenses plenty of information and maps and sponsors guided mountain walks every Monday and Saturday.

SEEING THE SIGHTS

Annalong Cornmill. 7½ miles (12km) south of Newcastle, Annalong, County Down. ☎ **028/4376-8736.** Admission £1.50 ($2.50) adult, 75p ($1.25) children. Feb–Nov Tues–Sat 11am–5pm.

Overlooking the small fishing harbor of Annalong, this restored early 19th-century corn mill—powered by a water wheel and a 1920s 20hp engine—is still in operating condition. The mill complex, which remained in business until 1965, contains a kiln for drying the grain, several millstones, and an array of related machinery. This is not a site for thrill seekers, but it does have a certain interest for anyone wanting to imagine life long before the automatic bread machine. In fact, the guided tour by James Trainor is so spirited and informative that the mill suddenly returns to life and becomes quite fascinating.

✪ **Castlewellan Forest Park.** 4 miles (6.5km) northwest of Newcastle on A50, The Grange, Castlewellan Forest Park, Castlewellan, County Down. ☎ **028/4377-8664.** Free admission. Parking £3.80 ($6.25). Daily 10am–dusk.

Surrounding a fine trout lake and watched over by a magnificent private castle, this splendid forest park is well worth an outing. Woodland walks, a lakeside sculpture trail, formal walled gardens, and even excellent trout (brown and rainbow) fishing await. The real draw is the National Arboretum, begun in 1740 and now grown to

10 times its original size. The largest of its three greenhouses features aquatic plants and a collection of free-flying tropical birds. The summer coffee house is open from 10am to 5pm. The town of Castlewellan, elegantly laid out around two squares, is also worth a stroll.

Drumena Cashel (Stone Fort). 2 miles (3km) southwest of Castlewellan, off A25, County Down.

The walls of this irregularly shaped ancient stone-ring fort—a farmstead, dating from the early Christian period—were partially rebuilt in 1925–26 and measure 9 to 12 feet thick. The *souterrain* (underground stone tunnel) is T-shaped and was likely used in ordinary times for cold storage. In the extreme, it hopefully provided some protection from Viking raiders. There were once, it seems, tens of thousands of such fortifications in Ireland, and this is one of the better-preserved examples in this region.

Dundrum Castle. 4 miles (6.5km) east of Newcastle, off A2, Dundrum, County Down. No phone. Admission 75p ($1.25) adults, 40p (66¢) children. Apr–Sept Tues–Sat 10am–1pm and 1:30–7pm, Sun 2–7pm; Oct–Mar Tues–Sat 10am–1pm and 1:30–4pm, Sun 2–4pm.

This was the site of an early Irish fortification, of which nothing is visible now. The oldest portions of these striking and quite extensive ruins date from the late 12th century, and the most recent are from the 17th century. The hilltop setting is quite lovely, and the views from the keep's parapet are especially grand. This was once the mightiest of the Norman castles along the Down coast. It still commands the imagination, if nothing else.

Greencastle Fort. 4 miles (6.5km) southwest of Kilkeel, Greencastle, Cranfield Point, Mouth of Carlingford Lough, County Down. No phone. Admission 75p ($1.25) adult, 40p (66¢) children. Apr–Sept Tues–Sat 10am–1pm and 1:30–7pm, Sun 2–7pm; Oct–Mar Tues–Sat 10am–1pm and 1:30–4pm, Sun 2–4pm.

The first castle on this site, built in 1261, faced its companion, Carlingford Castle, across the lough. It was a two-story rectangular tower surrounded by a curtain wall with corner towers. Very little survives. Most of what you see is from the 14th century, a fortress that fell to Cromwell in 1652, never to rise again.

Murlough Nature Reserve. On the main Dundrum–Newcastle road (A2), southeast of Dundrum, County Down. ☎ **028/4375-1467.** Free admission. Parking £2 ($3.30).

Sand dunes, heathland, and forest, surrounded by estuary and sea, make for a lovely outing on a clear bright day, but you'll want to bring a windbreaker. Binoculars, too, because this is a prime habitat for a host of waders and sea birds. Bring a picnic, and you may find your dessert on the dunes, which are strewn with wild strawberries in the summertime.

Nautilus Centre. Rooney Rd., Kilkeel Harbour, Kilkeel, County Down. ☎ **028/4176-5555.** Free admission. Year-round Mon–Sat 10am–6pm, Sun noon–6pm.

Opened in the spring of 1998, this multipurpose center is an ideal place to begin your exploration of Kilkeel, Northern Ireland's premier fishing port. For a start, you can have a fisherman's breakfast in the center's Sea Breeze Diner (see "Dining," below). The Nautilus Heritage Centre features a compact exhibition with an interactive multimedia display, introducing visitors to the mission and development of Northern Ireland's modern fishing fleet. You'll also find, in the center's Harbour Store, fresh fish on ice, fishing gear and tackle, and a selection of gifts and souvenirs.

Silent Valley Mountain Park. 4 miles (6.5km) north of Kilkeel on Head Rd., Silent Valley, County Down. ☎ **028/9074-6580.** Admission £3 ($4.95) per car. Information Centre Easter–Sept daily 10am–6:30pm; Oct–Easter 10am–4:30pm.

More than 90 years ago, the 22-mile (36km) dry-stone Mourne Wall was built to enclose Silent Valley, which was dammed to create the Silent Valley Reservoir, to this day the major source of water for County Down. The 22-mile (36km) **Mourne Wall trek** threads together 15 of the range's main peaks—more than most hikers want to take on. A fine alternative is the more modest walk from the fishing port of Kilkeel to the Silent Valley and Lough Shannagh. An even less strenuous alternative is to drive to the Silent Valley Information Centre and take the shuttle bus to the top of nearby Ben Crom. The bus runs daily in July and August, weekends only in May, June, and September, and costs £1.10 ($1.80) round-trip, 55p (90¢) for children. There is also a restaurant, gift shop, children's playscape, and picnic area.

Tollymore Forest Park. Off B180, 2 miles (3.2km) northwest of Newcastle, Tullybrannigan Rd., Newcastle, County Down. ☎ **028/4372-2428.** Free admission. Parking £3 ($4.95). Daily 10am–dusk.

Tollymore House is no more. What remains is a delightful 1,200-acre wildlife and forest park, laid out in the 18th century by James Hamilton, an earl with an eye. The park offers a number of walks along the Shimna River, noted for its salmon, or up into the north slopes of the Mournes. The forest is a nature preserve inhabited by a host of local wildlife, including badgers, foxes, otters, and pine martens. Don't miss the trees for the forest—there are some exotic species here, including magnificent Himalayan cedars and a 100-foot-tall sequoia in the arboretum. For more strenuous activities, there's the Tollymore Outdoor Centre (see "Sports & Outdoor Pursuits," below).

SHOPPING

The Celtic Crafts Gallery. 45 Dromara Rd., Dundrum, County Down. ☎ **028/ 4375-1327.**

You'll find an impressive array of Celtic-design crafts here, as well as original gold and silver jewelry by Mary Doran. In addition, there are a pleasant cafe and panoramic views of the Mourne Mountains. Open April to September Monday to Saturday 10am to 5pm, Sunday 2 to 5pm; October to March Tuesday to Saturday 10am to 5pm.

The Mourne Grange Craft Shop and Tea Room. Camphill Village Community, 169 Newry Rd., Kilkeel, County Down. ☎ **028/4176-0103.**

This gift shop is a browser's paradise, full to the brim with unique quality handcrafted goods, from pottery and silk scarves to toys for young and old. There's also a fine selection of books of local interest and beyond. The cheerful, nonsmoking tearoom serves an array of freshly baked pastries to complement a cup of coffee or pot of tea. The proceeds of this shop help support the Rudolf Steiner–inspired Kilkeel Camphill Community for children and adults with special needs. Open Monday and Wednesday to Saturday 10am to 12:30pm and 2 to 5:30pm, Sunday 2 to 5:30pm. The tearoom closes a half hour before the shop.

SPORTS & OUTDOOR PURSUITS

BICYCLING The Mourne roads are narrow and often bordered by 5½-foot-high dry-stone walls. There is also precious little traffic, and the vistas are spectacular. The decision's yours; if you decide to pedal across the Mournes, you can rent touring and mountain bikes for £6.50 ($10.75) per day from **J. P. Quinn,** 4–6 Bridge St., Kilkeel (☎ **028/4176-2654**). Weekly rates are available.

The foothills of the Mournes around Castlewellan are ideal for cycling, with panoramic vistas and very little traffic. In these parts, the perfect year-round outfitter is **Ross Cycles,** 44 Clarkhill Rd., signposted from the Clough–Castlewellan road, one-half mile out of Castlewellan (☎ **028/4377-8029**), which has light-frame, highly geared mountain bikes for the whole family, with helmets and children's seats. All cycles are fully insured, as are their riders. You can park and ride, or request local delivery. Daily rates are £5 to £7.50 ($8.25 to $12.40). Family and weekly rates are available.

FISHING   The best time to fish for trout and salmon is August to October. Some sizable sea trout can be seen on the Whitewater River in the Mournes, and not all of them get away. The **Burrendale Hotel** in Newcastle (☎ 028/4372-2599) and the **Kilmorey Arms Hotel** in Kilkeel (☎ 028/4176-2220) offer special holiday breaks for game anglers. For further information, as well as tackle, bait, and outfitting needs, try **Four Seasons,** 47 Main St., Newcastle (☎ 028/4372-5078).

GOING SKY HIGH   You can book a 1-hour, guaranteed-to-render-you-speechless helicopter ride over the Mountains of Mourne by calling the **Helicopter Centre,** Belfast International Airport (☎ 028/9445-3663; fax 028/9442-3233).

GOLF   ✪ **Royal County Down,** Newcastle, County Down (☎ 028/4372-3314), is nestled in huge sand dunes with the Mountains of Mourne in the background. This 18-hole, par-71 championship course was created in 1889. Greens fees are £70 ($115.50) weekdays, £80 ($132) weekends. For a fraction of the cost, the **Kilkeel Golf Club,** Mourne Park, Ballyardle, Kilkeel (☎ 028/4176-5095), is a beautiful parkland course on the historic Kilmorey Estate. The best days for visitors are weekdays except Tuesday, and greens fees are £16 ($26.40) weekdays, £20 ($33) weekends.

HORSEBACK RIDING   The **Mount Pleasant Trekking and Horse Riding Centre** (☎ 028/4377-8651) offers group trekking tours into Castlewellan Forest Park for £8 ($13.20) an hour. For riding in the Tollymore Forest Park or on local trails, contact the **Mourne Trail Riding Centre,** 96 Castlewellan Rd., Newcastle (☎ 028/4372-4315). They have quality horses for experienced riders and offer beach rides for the highly skilled. The **Drumgooland House Equestrian Centre,** 29 Dunnanew Rd., Seaforde, Downpatrick, County Down (☎ 028/4481-1956), also offers trail riding in the Mournes, including 1½-hour trekking around Tollymore and Castlewellan Forest Parks from £20 ($33). Full equestrian holidays are also available.

OUTDOOR ACTIVITY CENTER   The **Tollymore Outdoor Centre** (☎ 028/4372-2158), on the grounds of Tollymore Forest Park (see "Seeing the Sights," above), but with its own entrance, offers courses on rock climbing, hill walking, orienteering, and canoeing.

SAILING   For leisure sailing cruises—from sightseeing to a meal afloat—contact Pamela or Aidan Reilly at **Leisure Sailing Cruises,** 5 Coastguard Villas, Newcastle (☎ 028/4372-2882).

ACCOMMODATIONS
EXPENSIVE

✪ **Glasdrumman Lodge Country House and Restaurant.** 85 Mill Rd., Annalong, County Down. ☎ **028/4376-8451.** Fax 028/43767041. 10 units. TV TEL. £135 ($222.75) double. £35 ($57.75) dinner in restaurant. Rates include full breakfast. MC, V.

"Simple elegance" is the mark Graeme and Joan Hall set in establishing this extraordinary place, and they have achieved just that. Poised between sea and mountains, with splendid views of each, Glasdrumman Lodge is encrusted with awards for fine dining and gracious accommodation, including the Irish "Most Romantic Hotel" award in 1997. Some of the light-filled rooms have working fireplaces, and No. 4, "Knockree," has an especially grand view of the sea. Note that the lodge is only 2 miles (3.2km) from the Silent Valley.

Dining: The intimate dining room is renowned for gourmet fare and charges accordingly. If you're up to a splurge, you won't be disappointed here.

✪ **The Slieve Donard Hotel.** Downs Rd., Newcastle, County Down. ☎ **028/4372-3681.** Fax 028/4372-4830. www.hastingshotels.com. 130 units. TV TEL. £130 ($214.50) double; £140–£225 ($231–$371.25) suite. Children's discount available. Rates include full breakfast. AE, CB, DC, MC, V.

From this turreted, redbrick Victorian hotel on the seafront, you look across Dundrum Bay to where the Mountains of Mourne sweep down to the sea. Outside, you can walk along the 4-mile (6.5km) curving sandy strand to their very feet. When the hotel was built, in 1897, there were coal fires in every bathroom. These days, the public areas and guest rooms incorporate every modern convenience. Front rooms overlooking the sea are especially appealing. Other rooms look out to the mountains or Royal County Down Golf Course.

Dining: The elegant Oak Restaurant, with its grand central fireplace, serves fine traditional Irish fare. At the entrance to the Slieve Donard's 6-acre grounds, the warm, oak-beamed Percy French Inn serves excellent pub lunches and dinners in a more informal setting.

Amenities: The Elysium, the Slieve Donard's exclusive private health spa, offers heated pool, gym, steam room, Jacuzzi, beauty salon, miniature-golf, and tennis courts. As a reward, or perhaps as an alternative, the club has its own bar.

MODERATE

✪ **Burrendale Hotel and Country Club.** 51 Castlewellan Rd., Newcastle, County Down. ☎ **028/4372-2599.** Fax 028/4372-2328. 69 units. TV TEL. £99 ($163.35) double. Rates include full buffet breakfast. AE, DC, MC, V.

This meticulously maintained contemporary hotel enjoys a fine location between the Mournes and the shore, and is a 15-minute walk from Newcastle Centre and the Royal County Down Golf Course. The gracious rooms are suitably spotless and spacious, and have all the amenities, including tea/coffeemakers and trouser presses. Beds are firm, and nonsmoking rooms are available. In addition, such attention has been paid to the needs of guests with disabilities that the Burrendale has recently won the British Airways award for disabled access and amenities, both in the hotel and in the country club.

The Vine Restaurant serves modern Irish cuisine, with a focus on seafood and an extensive array of vegetarian entrees. The nonsmoking, informal Cottage Kitchen emphasizes healthy, heart-conscious, and family meals. The Cottage Bar is an inviting pub. There are room service (10am to 10pm), baby-sitting and baby-listening monitors, and laundry and dry-cleaning service. In addition to a gym, a pool, saunas, Jacuzzis, and steam rooms, there's a health and beauty salon, offering aromatherapy massages, makeovers, manicures, and much more. Both water and landlubber aerobics classes are scheduled throughout the week.

✪ **Kilmorey Arms Hotel.** 41 Greencastle St., Kilkeel, County Down. ☎ **028/4176-2220.** Fax 028/4176-5399. 26 units. £75 ($123.75) double. High tea £10 ($16.50). Children's and senior discounts available. Rates include full breakfast. MC, V.

In this pleasant seaside resort, the Kilmorey Arms is a delightful small inn that dates back 200 years. Its homey atmosphere draws Irish families back year after year, and people in the town favor the attractive public rooms. There's a nonsmoking cocktail lounge, and the public bar is full of character—if you're just passing through Kilkeel, stop by this interesting bar for a pint. A number of guest rooms are reserved for nonsmokers.

INEXPENSIVE

Briers Country House. 39 Middle Tollymore Rd. (1½ miles/2.5km from the beach at Newcastle, off B180), Newcastle, County Down. ☎ **028/4372-4347.** Fax 028/4372-6633. 9 units. TV TEL. £50 ($82.50) double. High tea £8 ($13.20); dinner £12 ($19.80). Rates include full breakfast. 3-day and weekly rates available. MC, V. Free private parking.

Mary and David Bowater have lovingly converted this 200-year-old house, keeping its old-world charm. There are some 2 acres of gardens, with a trout pond, and the Bowaters grow most of their own fruit and vegetables and make their own breads and preserves. The dining room overlooks the pond and gardens, and the nicely appointed guest rooms (all nonsmoking) have good views. The house is at the foot of the Mountains of Mourne, beside the Tollymore Forest Park.

Grasmere. 16 Marguerite Park, Bryansford Rd., Newcastle, County Down. ☎ **028/4372-6801.** 3 units, 2 with private bathroom. TV. £36 ($59.40) double. Rates include full breakfast. No credit cards. Closed Dec 25. Private parking.

Mrs. McCormick presides over this pleasant modern bungalow on the edge of Newcastle, off the Bryansford–Newcastle road (B180), with views of the Mournes. Surrounded by green fields, Grasmere is only a 10-minute walk from the beach, and there are a golf course and some forest walks nearby.

✪ Slieve Croob Inn. Seeconnell Centre, 119 Clanvaraghan Rd. (signposted 1 mile/1.6km out of Castlewellan on the A25), Castlewellan–Clough Rd., Castlewellan, County Down. ☎ **028/4377-1412.** Fax 028/4377-1162. www.slievecroob@nireland.com. 7 units in the inn; 10 1- to 3-bedroom self-catering cottages. TV TEL. Inn £60 ($99) double; cottages £170–£350 ($280.50–$577.50) per week. AE, MC, V.

The setting for this small, exquisite resort complex—a patchwork of drumlin pastureland just shy of the Mournes's peaks—is not to be believed. The panoramic views of Slieve Croob, Newcastle Bay, and the Isle of Man are breathtaking. This is a rambler's fantasy, with 5 miles (8km) of trails on Slieve Croob and a plethora of lazy mountain lanes to explore. The spotless inn is tastefully designed and outfitted in crisp mountain-lodge style. There's simple pine furniture throughout. Tea/coffee-making facilities and trouser presses are standard, as are orthopedic beds. In addition to standard doubles, there is a fabulous three-bedroom family apartment with its own outer door. Laundry facilities and currency exchange are available. The full-service restaurant is open 9am to 9pm daily, and the Branny Bar features traditional music Tuesday to Sunday. A new conservatory-style function room with splendid views of the surrounding hills is in the works, with a new equestrian center and 18-hole golf course envisioned for the near future.

There are also 10 one- to three-bedroom **self-catering cottages**—the most appealing, even luxurious, we have encountered anywhere in Northern Ireland.

SELF-CATERING

Hannas Close. Aughnahoory Rd., Kilkeel, County Down. Contact RCH at ☎ **028/9024-1100.** Fax 028/9024-1198. www.cottagesinireland.com. 7 cottages. TV. £175–£400 ($288.75–$660) per week. Also available for 2- to 3-day stays. Additional charge for heat and electricity. V.

Hannas Close is a meticulously restored *clachan,* or medieval-style extended-family settlement, founded in 1640 and refurbished in 1997. On a low bluff over a lovely shallow stream, facing the spectacular Mountains of Mourne, this born-again *clachan* is so quiet that there's little to wake you other than birdsong. In the refurbishment of the cottages, every effort was made to re-create the past while attending to contemporary codes and standards of comfort. The cottages, which sleep from two to seven, have everything you'll need, including washing machines, microwaves, and central heating. All have an open fireplace or a wood stove. They are ideal for families or young couples, although the steep steps and rustic character of the cottages won't suit everyone. A small museum in the Close can help you imagine the former life of the rural mountainside world you'll enter here.

DINING

Most of the dining in the Mournes, with or without frills, gourmet or generic, happens in hotels, guesthouses, and pubs. When your stomach growls, be sure to also consider the accommodations listed above and the pubs listed below.

The Fisherman. 68 Greencastle St., Kilkeel, County Down. ☎ **028/4176-2130.** Reservations recommended. Dinner main courses £6.95–£16.95 ($11.45–$27.95). MC, V. Wed–Sat noon–2:30pm, Thurs–Fri 6–9:30pm, Sat 6–10:30pm, Sun 5–10:30pm. SEAFOOD.

Locals consider this recently refurbished restaurant the best in town. It emphasizes fresh fish and friendly service. Luscious seasonal lobster stuffed with prawns competes for attention with mixed seafood Creole, and grilled haddock with bacon and fine herbs. Diners preferring fare from terra firma will do well to try the lamb cooked in red wine sauce with a julienne of carrots and mange tout, or tarragon chicken. The Fisherman is on the main street, opposite the BP station.

Pavilion Bistro and Restaurant. 36 Downs Rd., Newcastle, County Down. ☎ **028/4372-6239.** Reservations recommended. Dinner main courses £3.95–£11.95 ($6.50–$19.70); daily specials £5.50 ($9.10); fixed-price dinner £19.50 ($32.20). MC, V. Daily noon–10pm. INTERNATIONAL.

On the north end of Newcastle's waterfront, facing the sea, you will find this gracious restaurant. Royal County Down golfers especially appreciate its mission of serving tasty fresh fare in generous portions, 7 days a week, all day. Gilded mirrors and tile fireplaces accent the tasteful Victorian dining rooms (smoking and nonsmoking). The bistro-style menu changes daily and includes such entrees as savory pork loin and fresh plaice with lemon herb sauce. The dinner menu includes such items as fillet of sole served with fresh salmon and dill mousse, and roast chestnut and apple duck. The tempting finales include shortbread with fruit coulis and brandy cream.

The Pavilion plans to open an adjoining 15-room inn, which should be altogether appealing.

Sea Breeze Diner. Nautilus Centre, Rooney Rd., Kilkeel Harbour, Kilkeel, County Down. ☎ **028/4176-4888.** No reservations. Dinner main courses £3.25–£12.95 ($5.35–$21.35). No credit cards. Mon–Sat 10am–7pm; also open Sun in summer. SEAFOOD.

This informal harborside spot in the new Kilkeel Nautilus Centre offers fresh home cooking with an emphasis on the catch of the day. From this harborside vantage point, you can see the catch coming in. Start with a salad of fresh prawns, then move on to something modest, such as fresh fish cakes, or go full sail with sole and prawns or the "land and sea" steak and prawns special. No spirits are served, but you can bring your own wine or beer (from the Kilkeel Wine Market, across from the Kilmorey Arms Hotel on Greencastle Street in Kilkeel center).

PUBS

Harbour Inn. 6 Harbour Dr., Annalong Harbour, Annalong, County Down. ☎ **028/4376-8678.**

You won't find a quainter "wee" harbor on the Down Coast than Annalong, and the Harbour Inn, as its name suggests, is poised right on the dock. The black guillemots tend to outnumber anyone else here, but they too welcome visitors. Awaiting a warm day, picnic tables sit out front for the perfect dockside happy hour. Otherwise, there's an inviting lounge and full restaurant serving lunch, high tea, dinner, and bar snacks. A live band, often of the Irish country-western persuasion, shows up every Saturday, and there's an unpredictable disco now and then.

Jacob Halls. Greencastle St., Kilkeel, County Down. ☎ **028/4176-4751.**

If there's a chill in the air, you'll leave it behind in Jacob Halls, with its three massive fires blazing at the least pretense. This well-worn pub is a hub of hospitality for all ages—all over 18, that is. Vintage local photographs line the walls. There's live music Wednesday to Sunday, and pub grub from lunch on.

The Percy French. Downs Rd., Newcastle, County Down. ☎ **028/4372-3175.**

The Percy French has stood watch over the gates of the Slieve Donard Hotel for a century. It's named after the famed Irish composer who died in 1920, leaving behind these words as an epitaph:

> Remember me is all I ask—and yet
> If remembrance proves a task—forget.

Forgetting is not a real option, however, as long as this fine old *faux*-Tudor pub pours the perfect pint and serves delicious fare. The same beamed roof encloses both the lounge and a full-service restaurant, with a traditional Irish menu. There's live traditional music on Saturday, and disco every Friday.

6 Derry City

73 miles (118km) NW of Belfast, 39 miles (63km) SW of Portrush, 70 miles (113km) NW of Armagh, 61 miles (98km) NE of Enniskillen, 144 miles (232km) NW of Dublin, and 220 miles (354km) NE of Shannon

Derry, also known as Londonderry, is the second-largest city of Northern Ireland (pop. 72,300) and the unofficial capital of the northwestern region of the province.

The city derives its name from the Irish words *Doire Calgach,* meaning "the oak grove of Calgach." Calgach was a warrior who set up a camp here in pre-Christian times. The name survived until the 10th century, when it became *Doire Colmcille* in honor of St. Columba, who founded his first monastery in Derry in A.D. 546. He is supposed to have written, "The angels of God sang in the glades of Derry and every leaf held its angel." Over the years, the name was anglicized to Derrie, or simply Derry.

Set on a hill on the banks of the Foyle estuary, strategically close to the open sea, Derry has often come under siege. At the time of the Plantation of Ulster in the 17th century, the City of London sent master builders and money to reconstruct the ruined medieval town, and the name became, for some of its inhabitants, Londonderry.

The city's great 17th-century walls, about a mile in circumference and 18 feet thick, are a legacy from that era. Although they were the focus of attacks (including sieges in 1641, 1649, and 1689), the walls withstood many tests of time and are unbroken. They make Derry one of the finest examples of a walled city in Europe.

The rest of the city's architecture is largely Georgian, with brick-fronted town houses and imposing public buildings. Basement-level pubs and shops are common.

The focal point of Derry is **the Diamond,** a square in the center of the city, just west of the banks of the Foyle River. Four streets radiate out from the Diamond: Bishop, Ferryquay, Shipquay, and Butcher. Each extends for several blocks and ends at a walled gateway of the same name (Bishop's Gate, Ferryquay Gate, Shipquay Gate, and Butcher's Gate). A massive wall that rings the inner city connects the gates.

Two bridges connect the east and west banks of the River Foyle. The Craigavon Bridge, built in 1933, is one of the few examples of a double-decker bridge in the British Isles. The Foyle Bridge, Ireland's longest bridge, opened in 1984 and provides a dual-lane carriageway about 2 miles (3.2km) north of the Craigavon Bridge. West of the river are two major areas: the walled inner city and, farther west, an area known as the Bogside. East of the Foyle is the area usually referred to as Waterside, where most of the fine hotels and many of the city's restaurants are located. Also in Waterside is a small grassy viewing point called the "Top of the Hill," where you can enjoy spectacular eagle's-eye views of the city and its splendid environs. You'll never find your own way there, so take a taxi and bring your map. Short of a helicopter tour, this is the best way to get your initial bearings.

About 12 miles (19km) east of the city is another Georgian enclave, the town of **Limavady** in the Roe Valley. It was here that Jane Ross wrote down the tune of a lovely air she heard, played by a fiddler as he passed through town. It became the famous "Londonderry Air," otherwise known as "Danny Boy."

For longer than anyone wants to remember, Derry was immersed in, and all but identified with, the Troubles. In the 1960s and 1970s, the North's civil rights movement was both born here and baptized in blood. The victims of Bloody Sunday are the symbols of the struggle for equality in the North, an effort for which this city and its people paid dearly. By 1980, nearly a third of the inner city was in ruins. But that was then, and this is now. In the years since, Derry has rebuilt some walls and dismantled others, and has become increasingly engaged in the struggle to build a new North. Today, Derry is one of the most vital and appealing centers of culture and commerce in Northern Ireland, and it's destined to become a major tourist mecca, once word gets out.

Another secret about Derry is how close it is to many of the major sights of Ireland's northwest corner. To cite a few highlights, the Inishowen Peninsula, the Giant's Causeway and the North Antrim Coast, the Northwest Passage and the Sperrins, and Glenveagh National Park in Donegal are all within an hour's drive. Derry is an ideal base of operations from which to explore one of Ireland's most unspoiled and dazzling regions.

ESSENTIALS

GETTING THERE   Service to **Derry City Eglinton Airport** (☎ 028/ 7181-0784) is provided by **British Airways** (☎ 0345/222111; www.british-airways.com) from Glasgow and Manchester, and by **Ryanair** (☎ 0541/569569 in Britain; www.ryanair.com) from London Stansted. The no. 43 Limavady **bus** stops at the airport. A **taxi** for the 8-mile (13km) journey to the city center costs about £10 ($16.50). If you're landing in either of the Belfast airports, without a connection to Derry, the **Airporter** coach can take you straight to Derry. Call Jennifer Smyth, 3 Lower Clarendon St. (☎ 028/7126-9996), for information and reservations.

Derry City is an important port of call for an increasing number of cruise ships, including six-star luxury liners, which call at the deep-water facilities at Lisahally or at the city center's newly refurbished Queen's Quay. For the latest information on cruises to Derry Port, contact the Cruise Development Officer, Derry City Council, 98 Strand Rd., Derry BT48 7NN (☎ 028/7136-5151).

Frequent trains from Belfast and Portrush arrive at the **Northern Ireland Railways Station** (☎ 028/7134-2228), on the east side of the Foyle River. A free Linkline bus brings passengers from the train station to the city center.

The fastest bus between Belfast and Derry, the no. 212 Maiden City Flyer, operated by **Ulsterbus** (☎ 028/9033-3000 in Belfast; 028/7126-2261 in Derry), is about twice as fast as the train; it takes a little over 90 minutes. **Ulsterbus** also has service from Portrush and Portstewart. From the Republic, **Bus Eireann** offers three buses a day from Galway's **Bus Eireann Travel Centre,** Ceannt Station, Galway

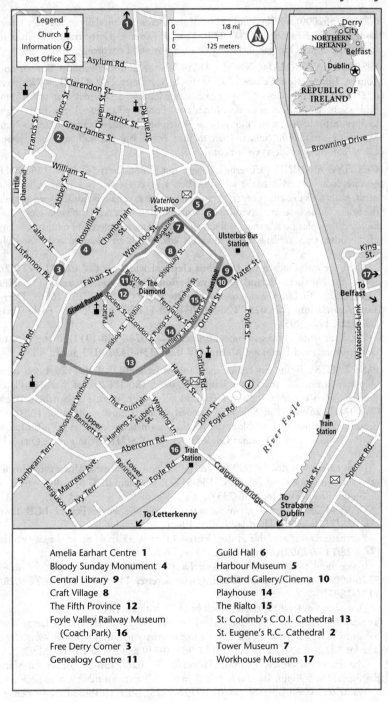

Derry City

Legend

✝ Church
ⓘ Information
✉ Post Office

0 — 1/8 mi
0 — 125 meters

NORTHERN IRELAND — Derry City, Belfast
Dublin
REPUBLIC OF IRELAND

Asylum Rd.
Clarendon St.
Francis St.
Prince St.
Queen St.
Patrick St.
Strand Rd.
Great James St.
William St.
Little Diamond
Abbey St.
Rossville St.
Chamberlain St.
Fahan St.
Lisfannon Pk.
Fahan St.
Waterloo St.
Magazine St.
Waterloo Square
Butcher St.
Shipquay St.
The Diamond
Society St.
Palace St.
Grand Parade
Bishop St. Within
London St.
Pump St.
Ferryquay St.
Linenhall St.
Market St.
Artillery St.
Orchard St.
Water St.
Foyle St.
East Wall
Ulsterbus Bus Station
Lecky Rd.
Carlisle Rd.
Hawkin St.
The Fountain
Bishop Street Without
Upper Bennett St.
Harding St.
Aubery St.
Wapping Ln.
John St.
Foyle Rd.
Abercorn Rd.
Lower Bennett St.
Sunbeam Terr.
Maureen Ave.
Ferguson St.
Ivy Terr.
Foyle Rd.
Train Station
Craigavon Bridge
River Foyle
Browning Drive
King St.
To Belfast
Waterside Link
Train Station
Duke St.
Spencer Rd.

To Letterkenny
To Strabane Dublin

(☎ **091/562000**), via Sligo and Donegal; and there's one bus daily to and from Cork. **Lough Swilly Bus Service** (☎ **028/7126-2017**) serves Derry from a number of towns in County Donegal, including Dunfanaghy and Letterkenny.

VISITOR INFORMATION   The **Derry Visitor and Convention Bureau and Tourist Information Centre** is at 44 Foyle St., Derry (☎ **028/7126-7284**; fax 028/7137-7992). It's open October to Easter, Monday to Thursday 9am to 5:15pm, Friday 9am to 5pm; Easter to May, Monday to Thursday 9am to 5:15pm, Friday 9am to 5pm, Saturday 10am to 5pm; June to September, Monday to Friday 9am to 7pm, Saturday 10am to 6pm, Sunday 10am to 5pm. For all you ever wanted to know about Derry, consult **www.derryvisitor.com**.

GETTING AROUND   Ulsterbus, Foyle Street Depot, Derry (☎ **028/7126-2261**), operates local bus service to the suburbs. There is no bus service within the walls of the small, easily walkable city. There is also no bus service to certain nationalist areas outside the walls. Those areas are served by the black London-style taxis known in Derry and Belfast as "people's taxis," which will not go to most areas of interest to tourists. Use any of the other taxis available throughout the city, which are plentiful and reasonably priced.

There are taxi stands at the **Ulsterbus Depot,** Foyle Street (☎ **028/7126-2262**), and at the **Northern Ireland Railways Station,** Duke Street, Waterside (☎ **028/ 7134-2228**). To call a cab, contact **Co-Op Taxis** (☎ **028/7137-1666**), **Derry Taxi Association** (☎ **028/7126-0247**; 0850-111755 mobile); or **Foyle Taxis** (☎ **028/7126-3905**).

Local car-rental offices include **Europcar** (☎ **028/7130-1312**) at the City of Derry Airport, and **Desmond Motors** (☎ **028/7136-0420**), 173 Strand Rd.

FAST FACTS   In the city center, the **Bank of Ireland** (☎ **028/7126-4992**) is on Shipquay Street, and the **Ulster Bank** (☎ **028/7126-1882**) is at Waterloo Place. Both are open weekdays 9:30am (10am on Wed) to 4:30pm. The **Northern Bank** (☎ **028/7126-5333**) at Shipquay Place is open Saturday 9:30am to 12:30pm. Bureaux de change are available at the Tourist Information Centre (see "Visitor Information," above), and at **Thomas Cook Travel** (☎ **028/7185-2500**) in the Quayside Centre.

In an emergency, dial ☎ **999** for fire, police, and ambulance. **Altnagevin Hospital** is on Glenshane Road (☎ **028/7134-5171**). The main **RUC or police station** is on Strand Road (☎ **028/7136-7337**).

Gay and lesbian travelers might want to call the **Foyle Friend LGB Line** (☎ **028/7126-4400**), Thursday 7:30 to 10pm.

Internet access is available at the **Central Library,** 35 Foyle St. in the city center (☎ **028/7127-2300**), for £2.50 ($4.15) per hour.

If you need to do laundry, seek out **Dud 'n' Suds,** 141 Strand Rd. (☎ **028/ 7126-6006**), or **Foyle Dry Cleaning/Launderette,** 147 Spencer Rd. (☎ **028/ 7131-1897**).

Derry has two local papers, and each has a "What's On" section: the *Derry Journal,* Tuesday and Friday; and the *Londonderry Sentinel,* every Wednesday. The Derry Visitor and Convention Bureau publishes a free quarterly publication called *What's On?.* The local Derry radio stations are **Q102** (FM 102.9) and **Radio Foyle** (FM 93.1).

The main **Post Office,** 3 Custom House St. (☎ **028/7136-2563**), is open Monday 8:30am to 5:30pm, Tuesday to Friday 9am to 5:30pm, Saturday 9am to 12:30pm.

Walkrite, 6 Great James St. (☎ **028/7126-9225**), offers reliable on-the-spot emergency shoe repairs.

SEEING THE SIGHTS

In July and August, **Ulsterbus** operates **Civic Bus Tours** of the Derry sights. Tours are Tuesday at 2pm and cost £3.20 ($5.30) adults, £2.20 ($3.65) seniors and children. Tours leave from the Ulsterbus Depot, Foyle Street. For further information, call the **Tourist Information Centre** (☎ 028/7126-7284).

The Derry Visitor and Convention Bureau sponsors **Inner City Walking Tours,** June to September Monday to Friday. They depart at 10:30am and 2:30pm from the Tourist Information Centre, 44 Foyle St. The price is £3.25 ($5.35) adults, £2 ($3.30) seniors and children. **McNamara Walking Tours** (☎ 028/7134-5335; 0788-9963858 mobile) offers an informative, entertaining walking tour of the city June to September, daily at 10am, noon, 2pm, and 4pm. The cost is £3.50 ($5.80) adults, £1.50 ($2.50) seniors and children.

Another fine option is the "Essential Walking Tour of Historic Derry," offered by **Northern Tours** (☎ 028/7128-9051). It leaves from the Tourist Information Centre, May to September, daily at 10:30am and 2:30pm. The cost is £3 ($4.95) adults, free for children.

Finally, if you're tired of foot and want to be conducted in regal fashion, Martin McGowan will take you by horse-drawn carriage through the old city and unravel its history as you go. Call **Charabanc Tours** (☎ 028 7127-1886 or 0780-8039533 mobile) for details and reservations from May to October.

Amelia Earhart Centre. Ballyarnett, County Derry. ☎ **028/7135-4040.** Free admission. Cottage Mon–Fri 10am–4pm; farm and sanctuary daily 10am–dusk.

Located 3 miles (4.8km) north of Derry off the A2 road, this cottage commemorates Amelia Earhart's landing here in 1932, as the first woman to fly the Atlantic solo. The grounds encompass the Ballyarnett Community Farm and Wildlife Centre, with a range of farmyard animals and wildlife.

✪ **Cathedral of St. Columb.** London St., Derry, County Derry. ☎ **028/7126-7313.** £1 ($1.65) donation requested. Mar–Oct Mon–Sat 9am–5pm; Nov–Feb Mon–Sat 9am–1pm and 2–4pm.

Within the city walls near the Bishop's Gate, this cathedral, built as a Church of Ireland edifice between 1628 and 1633, is a fine example of the Planters Gothic style of architecture. It was the first cathedral built in Europe after the Reformation. Several sections were added afterward, including the impressive spire and stained-glass windows that depict scenes from the great siege of 1688–89. The chapter house contains a display of city relics, including the four original keys to the city gates, and an audiovisual presentation that provides background on the history of the building and the city.

The Fifth Province. Calgach Centre, 4–22 Butcher St. , Derry, County Derry. ☎ **028/7137-3177.** Admission £3 ($4.95) adults, £1 ($1.65) seniors and children, £6 ($9.90) family. Mon–Fri 9:30am–4pm. Extended summer hours.

This ambitious multimedia experience was many years in the making. Drawing from remote legends of a fifth Irish province at the navel of ancient Ireland, the idea here is to imagine and experience a once and future Ireland centered and at one. This multistage high-tech tour through time—past, present, and future—is designed to be absorbing for adults and children alike.

Foyle Valley Railway Centre. Foyle Rd. , Derry, County Derry. ☎ **028/7137-3177.** Free admission. Train rides £2.50 ($4.15) adults, £1.25 ($2.05) seniors and children, £7 ($11.55) family. Centre Tues–Sat 10am–4:30pm; trains Mon–Fri 10am–4:30pm, Sat 11:30am–4:30pm.

Just outside the city walls near the Craigavon Bridge, where four railway lines once crossed paths, this center focuses on the local history of letting off steam. Besides viewing exhibits and retired trains, you can take a 20-minute narrow-gauge trip through the Foyle Riverside Park.

Genealogy Centre. Calgach Centre, 4–22 Butcher St., Derry, County Derry. ☎ **028/ 7137-3177.** Fax 028/7137-4818. £20 ($33) initial search fee. Mon–Fri 9am–5pm.

Did your ancestors come from Derry or nearby? If you're of Irish ancestry, it's possible, and maybe even likely. Derry served as the principal port for thousands of emigrants who left Ulster for the New World in the 18th and 19th centuries; records show that Ulster men and women became the second-most-numerous group in the colonial population, and played an important role in the American Revolution and the settlement of the West. This heritage library and Genealogy Centre, in the heart of the old walled city, can help you research your Derry roots.

Guildhall. Shipquay Place, Derry, County Derry. ☎ **028/7137-7335.** Free admission. Mon–Fri 9am–5pm; Sat–Sun by appointment. Free guided tours July–Aug.

Just outside the city walls, between Shipquay Gate and the River Foyle, this Tudor Gothic–style building looks much like its counterpart in London. The original structure on this site was built in 1890, but it was rebuilt after a fire in 1908 and after a series of bombs in 1972. The hall is distinguished by its huge four-faced clock and by its stained-glass windows, made by Ulster craftsmen, that illustrate almost every episode of note in the city's history. The hall is used as a civic and cultural center for concerts, plays, and exhibitions.

Harbour Museum. Harbour Sq. , Derry, County Derry. ☎ **028/7137-7331.** Free admission. Mon–Fri 10am–1pm and 2–5pm.

The full-sized replica of St. Columba's curragh, which occupies most of the floor space of the ground-floor exhibition room, immediately makes clear the maritime focus of this small, eclectic collection. It will take you only a few minutes to browse through the seemingly random yet often fascinating items on display. The building itself deserves some attention, too. If the door is closed, just ring the bell.

Orchard Gallery. Orchard St. , Derry, County Derry. ☎ **028/7126-9675.** Free admission. Tues–Sat 10am–6pm.

The Orchard Gallery, founded in 1978, is Derry's prime venue for contemporary visual art. Mounting 20 or more exhibitions and events each year, the gallery fosters and displays the work of a wide range of contemporary local, Irish, and international artists. Central to the gallery's mission, as well, is its innovative, multifaceted Education and Community Outreach Scheme. The art that originates here is meant to provoke a generously creative and collaborative response from the wider community, especially Derry's children and youth. Sharing the same building with the Orchard Gallery is the Orchard Cinema, where you're likely to find the latest international films.

✪ **St. Eugene's Cathedral.** Fransic St. , Derry, County Derry. Free admission. Mon–Sat 7am–9pm, Sun 7am–6:30pm.

Designed in the Gothic Revival style, this is Derry's Catholic cathedral, nestled in the heart of the Bogside district just beyond the city walls. The foundation stone was laid in 1851, but work continued until 1873. The spire was added in 1902. It's built of local sandstone and is known for its stained-glass windows depicting the Crucifixion, by Meyer of Munich.

✪ **Tower Museum.** Union Hall Place, Derry, County Derry. ☎ **028/7137-2411.** Admission £4 ($6.60) adults, £1.50 ($2.50) children, £8 ($13.20) family. July–Aug Mon–Sat 10am–5pm, Sun 2–5pm; Sept–June Tues–Sat 10am–5pm.

Housed in O'Doherty Tower, a medieval-style fort, this award-winning museum presents the history of the city, from its geological formation to the present day. Visitors are invited to walk through time, and a series of exhibits and audiovisual presentations provoke their imaginations along the way. The Tower's collection of historical artifacts includes items salvaged from the Spanish Armada, ravaged by storms off the Irish coast in 1588. The Tower Museum, a must for all visitors to Derry, is just inside the city walls next to Shipquay Gate, and will soon (in late 2000) be expanded to include a new Spanish Armada museum.

The Workhouse Museum and Library. 23 Glendermott Rd., Waterside, Derry, County Derry. ☎ **028/7131-8328.** Free admission. Sept–June Mon–Thurs 10am–4:30pm, Sat 10am–4:30pm; July–Aug Mon–Sat 10am–4:30pm, Sun 2–4pm.

This splendid, compact museum on the Waterside, only minutes from Derry Centre, opened in May 1998 and is still being developed. It occupies the central building—the inmates' dorms and the master's quarters—of a 19th-century workhouse complex. The story told here is both grim and moving. Built to employ and maintain the poor, the workhouse was little more than a concentration camp. A visit ensures that you will leave feeling deliriously fortunate.

This museum also presents intriguing multimedia exhibitions focused on two moments in Derry's history: the Great Famine, when between 1845 and 1849 roughly 12,000 people a year left Ireland forever from the port of Derry; and the Battle of the Atlantic, when Derry played a major role in the defeat of the Kriegsmarine. The German U-boat fleet surrendered at Derry in May 1945.

SHOPPING

The city center offers some fine shopping, including two modern multistory malls: the **Richmond Centre,** facing the Diamond at the corner of Shipquay and Ferryquay Streets; and the new **Foyleside Shopping Centre,** just outside the walls. **London Street,** beside St. Columb's Cathedral, is Derry's antique row, where most of the city's antique and curio shops cluster. Rather than mention each shop by name, I recommend strolling down London Street and discovering them for yourself.

In general, shops are open Monday to Saturday 9am to 5:30pm. Shops in the two large shopping centers are open Monday to Wednesday and Saturday 9am to 5:30pm, Thursday and Friday 9am to 9pm. In the summer, some shops are open on Sunday.

Austin & Co., Ltd. The Diamond, Derry, County Derry. ☎ **028/7126-1817.**

This is the city's landmark three-story Victorian-style department store, specializing in fashions, perfumes, china, crystal, and linens. It's Ireland's oldest department store, established in 1839. The coffee shop on the third floor looks out on a panorama of the city.

Bookworm Bookshop. 18–20 Bishop St. (at London St.), Derry, County Derry. ☎ **028/7128-2727.**

This shop specializes in books on Irish history, politics, poetry, art, and fiction, as well as maps, guides, and postcards. A coffee shop is in the works. Open Monday to Saturday 9:30am to 5:30pm.

✪ **Derry Craft Village.** Shipquay St. (enter on Shipquay or Magazine St.), Derry, County Derry. ☎ **028/7126-0329.**

In the heart of the inner city near the Tower, this unique shopping complex reflects Old Derry, with architecture of the 16th to 19th centuries. It houses retail shops, workshops, residential units, and a thatched-cottage pub offering an Irish Night (ceili and supper) almost every Thursday in July and August.

MTM. Richmond Centre, Derry, County Derry. ☎ **028/7137-1970.**

Whether you've left home without your favorite tapes or are looking for something more local on the Irish traditional scene, you're likely to find it here. You can book tickets for major concerts and plays throughout the island.

SPORTS & OUTDOOR PURSUITS

BICYCLING Whether you want to rent a bike and do your own exploring, or sign up for a cycling tour of County Derry and County Donegal, **An Mointean Rent-a-Bike and Cycle Tours,** 245 Lone Moor Rd., Derry (☎ 028/7128-7128), offers excellent service. Rental of mountain or touring bikes costs £9 ($14.85) a day, £35 ($57.75) a week. Package tours with bed and breakfast included are also available.

FISHING The Foyle System of rivers makes this a promising area for snagging brown and sea trout (Apr to early July and Sept) and a variety of salmon (Mar to Sept). In addition, there is a stocked lake at Glenowen. Call **Glenowen Fisheries Co-operative** (☎ 028/7137-1544) for bookings. You can outfit yourself and get useful information at **Rod and Line,** 1 Clarendon St., Derry (☎ 028/7126-2877). If you're looking for an experienced local *ghillie* (guide) or boatman, contact **Mark Stewart,** Salmon Anglers Northwest, c/o Glenowen Fisheries Co-operative (☎ 028/7137-1544), or **Lance Thompson,** Faughan Angler's Association, 26a Carlisle Rd., Derry (☎ 028/7126-7781). For a game-fishing rod license, contact the **Foyle and Carlingford Locks Agency,** 8 Victoria Rd., Derry (☎ 028/7134-2100).

GOLF Derry has two 18-hole parkland courses: the **City of Derry Golf Club,** 49 Victoria Rd. (☎ 028/7134-6369), with greens fees of £20 ($33) weekdays, £25 ($41.25) weekends; and the **Foyle International Golf Centre,** 12 Alder Rd., Derry (☎ 028/7135-2222), which charges greens fees of £11 ($18.15) weekdays, £14 ($23.10) weekends. It is always best to phone ahead. Weekdays are best for visitors at the City of Derry Golf Club; any day of the week should be fine at the Foyle Golf Centre.

HORSEBACK RIDING **Ardmore Stables,** 8 Rushall Rd., Ardmore (☎ 028/7134-5187), offers lessons, trail rides, and pony trekking. Across the border, only 4 miles (6.5km) from Derry in County Donegal, **Lenamore Stables,** Muff, Inishowen (☎ 077/84022), also offers lessons and trekking, and has guest accommodations.

LEISURE CENTERS The city leisure centers offering the fullest range of sports activities are **Templemore Sports Complex,** Buncrana Road (☎ 028/7126-5521), and the **Lisnagelvin Leisure Centre,** Richill Park (☎ 028/7134-7695). Guests are welcome at both, and pay a modest visitors' fee for the use of the pool, tennis courts, gym, and so on.

WALKING In Derry, walking the **city walls** is a must. Just outside the city, off the main Derry–Belfast road, you'll come across **Ness Woods,** where there are scenic walks and nature trails, as well as the North's highest waterfall.

ACCOMMODATIONS
MODERATE

✪ **Beech Hill Country House Hotel.** 32 Ardmore Rd., Derry, County Derry. ☎ **800/44-PRIMA** from the U.S., or 028/7134-9279. Fax 028/7134-5366. www.beech-hill.com. 27 units. TV TEL. £85 ($140.25) double. Rates include full breakfast. Dinner £26.95 ($44.45). AE, MC, V. Private parking at hotel.

In a residential area southeast of the city, this lovely country-house hotel dates from 1729. Antiques and marble fireplaces decorate the public areas, and some of the pleasant guest rooms have four-poster beds with frilly floral covers. The hotel's elegant Ardmore restaurant is, amazingly, all nonsmoking, and there's a comfortable lounge. A new minigym is now in place with sauna and steam and a Jacuzzi. The wooded grounds are lovely, and there's an arbor of beech trees for which the hotel is named.

Broomhill Hotel. Limavady Rd., Derry, County Derry. ☎ **028/7134-7995.** Fax 028/7134-9304. 42 units. TV TEL. £65 ($107.25) double. Rates include full breakfast. MC, V. Free private parking.

Lovely views of Lough Foyle are a feature of this modern hotel, on its own grounds in a residential area 1½ miles (2.4km) east of the city, on the main road near the Foyle Bridge. Rooms are modern, with standard furnishings, welcome trays, and garment presses. The Garden Restaurant offers views of the river and the city.

✪ **Everglades Hotel.** Prehen Rd., Derry, County Derry. ☎ **028/7134-6722.** Fax 028/7134-9200. 64 units. www.hastingshotels.com. TV TEL. £100 ($165) double. Rates include full breakfast. High tea £10 ($16.50); dinner £17 ($28.05). AE, DC, V. Free parking.

On a hill overlooking the east bank of Lough Foyle in the prosperous Waterside district, this newly refurbished three-story contemporary hotel takes its name from Florida's Everglades. Like much of Florida, the hotel is built on reclaimed waterfront land. Guest rooms have modern furnishings with light woods, floral designer fabrics, and rattan touches; extras include a garment press, hair dryer, and tea/coffeemaker. On the premises are Satchmo's Restaurant and the tasteful Library Bar, which features live jazz on weekends.

✪ **The Trinity Hotel.** 22–24 Strand Rd., Derry, County Derry. ☎ **028/7127-1271.** Fax 028/7127-1277. www.thetrinityhotel.com. 40 units. TV TEL. £85 ($140.25) double. Luxury suites available. Rates include Irish/continental breakfast and service charge. AE, DC, MC, V. Free parking.

New in 1996, this was the only hotel to open its doors in Derry's city center in over 20 years. The Trinity Hotel merges clean modern lines with more traditional design elements. Large windows overlooking the street echo the surrounding Georgian neighborhood. The spacious rooms are tastefully decorated in warm, restful tones, accented by modern furniture in attractive maple veneer. The overall effect is chic and fanciful without compromising comfort. The brilliant bathrooms with towel warmers softly whisper "bubble bath." A trouser press, tea/coffee-making facilities, and a hair dryer are standard in all rooms. Dining choices include the adjoining Nolan's Bistro, a convivial late-night spot that has a Wednesday quiz night; the popular Porter's Cafe Bar; and the casual Trinity Restaurant, which offers live music and dancing most nights. There's foreign-currency exchange, and guests have complimentary use of the nearby Xstress Fitness Center.

✪ **White Horse Hotel.** 68 Clooney Rd., Campsie, County Derry. ☎ **028/7186-0606.** Fax 028/7186-0371. E-mail: info@whitehorse.demon.co.uk. 43 units. TV TEL. £70 ($115.50) double. Rates include full breakfast. Weekly and weekend discounts available. AE, DC, MC, V.

This hotel stands out as one of the more appealing moderately priced hotels in the North. Its countryside setting 4 miles (6.5km) northeast of the city, on the Limavady

A Note on Prices

Derry prices for both accommodations and dining are exceptionally reasonable. The fact that Derry has barely any expensive hotels or restaurants does not mean that it lacks first-class lodging or dining. The city offers more for less and is, for the foreseeable future, a real bargain.

road, is restful, and there's good, frequent bus service into Derry. The owners have transformed an old inn into a modern, comfortable, attractive hostelry. Guest rooms are spacious and well appointed, with tea/coffeemakers, and there are washing and ironing facilities. The tasteful dining room serves three meals daily, with a lunch and dinner carvery, as well as à la carte menus. There is live music in the sophisticated bar and lounge on Friday and Saturday night.

INEXPENSIVE

Clarence House. 15 Northland Rd., Derry, County Derry. ☎ and fax **028/7126-5342.** 9 units, 7 with private bathroom. £50 ($82.50) double with bathroom. Children's discount available. Rates include full breakfast. High tea £10 ($16.50); dinner £14 ($23.10). MC, V with 60% charge. On-street parking.

Mrs. Eleonora Slevin offers singles, doubles, twin rooms, and family rooms in this well-kept brick guesthouse. Rooms are quite comfortable, and the house and its hostess have become favorites of BBC and RTE television crews, who come back again and again. The washing and ironing facilities are a bonus. Baby-sitting can be arranged, and there are restaurants within easy walking distance.

✪ The Saddlers House and the Old Rectory. Saddlers House, 36 Great James St., Derry, County Derry. ☎ **028/7126-9691.** Fax 028/7126-6913. E-mail: lucy@fdn.co.net. 7 units, 3 with private bathroom. TV. £40–£45 ($66–$74.25) double. Old Rectory, 16 Queen St., Derry. ☎ **028/7126-4223.** Fax 028/7126-6913. E-mail: lucy@sdn.co.net. 5 units, 1 with private bathroom. TV. £40–£45 ($66–$74.25) double. Both: Children's and senior discounts available. Rates include full breakfast. No credit cards.

Peter and Joan Pyne have beautifully restored these two 19th-century town houses. The Saddlers House is cozy Victorian. The more elegant Old Rectory is late Georgian and has been revived with such care that it won a Civic Trusts Ireland conservation award. It is among the last Georgian-style houses still in service as residences in Derry. These two noteworthy houses are several blocks from each other and are only minutes away by foot from Derry center. At the risk of runaway alliteration, they offer considerable comfort, convenience, character, and charm at budget rates.

DINING
EXPENSIVE

✪ Ardmore Room Restaurant. Beech Hill Country House Hotel, 32 Ardmore Rd., Derry, County Derry. ☎ **028/7134-9279.** Reservations recommended. Fixed-price 4-course dinner £25.95 ($42.80). MC, V. Daily 12:30–2:30pm and 6:30–9:30pm. CONTINENTAL/TRADITIONAL.

Lunch in this pretty dining room draws many business types, who can relax in what was once a billiard room overlooking gardens while enjoying a superb meal. In the evening, there's a soft, romantic ambience. Among the outstanding specialties are monkfish accompanied by vegetables with ginger and balsamic vinaigrette, and brill poached in champagne with dill butter sauce. There's an extensive international wine list, as well as an extraordinary selection of home-baked specialty breads.

MODERATE

Brown's Bar and Brasserie. 1–2 Bond's Hill, Waterside, Derry, County Derry. ☎ **028/7134-5180.** Reservations recommended. Main courses £6.95–£13.50 ($11.45–$22.30). MC, V. Tues–Fri noon–2:30pm; Tues–Sat 5–11pm. INTERNATIONAL.

Behind the unassuming exterior of this Waterside area row house, you will find some of the finest food in Derry. This lively spot has won a dedicated local clientele and attracted the attention of distant connoisseurs. The decor is warm, streamlined, and minimalist, with sculptural dried-flower arrangements. The inviting informality is conducive to quiet conversation or a gathering of friends. The innovative menu blends the best of modern Irish, Italian, and Thai influences with an emphasis on fresh and, when possible, organic ingredients. Seared loin of lamb with porcini cream and reduced pan juices atop a bacon and pea potato cake was perfectly prepared, and suprêmes of chicken with parsnip puree and tiger prawn–coconut sauce gave chicken another face. Our neighbor pronounced fresh monkfish on tagliatelle with tarragon and paprika cream "first rate." For a dramatic climax, go for the architecturally ambitious pineapple and toffee sponge with citrus fruit salad.

Da Vinci's Bar and Restaurant. 15 Culmore Rd., Derry, County Derry. ☎ 028/7137-2074. Reservations recommended. Dinner main courses £7.95–£13.95 ($13.10–$23). A range of fixed-price and early-bird specials, like the "Beat the Clock" special (Mon–Sat 5:30–7:30pm), "the time you arrive is the price you pay." AE, MC, V. Mon 5:30–9:30pm; Tues–Fri 5:30–10pm; Sat 5:30–10:30pm; Sun 5:30–9pm. INTERNATIONAL.

The glow of candlelight and rich Renaissance reds and blues romantically warm the rough stone walls, arched doorways, and dramatic wrought-iron fittings. It's more than enough to coax the informed diner to venture a short distance (5 min.) from Derry center. You can choose from delights such as grilled sea bass with tikka crust and lime-cherry relish; escalope of pork finished with roasted baby apples and blackberries; or pesto cream over tender chicken breast stuffed with sun-dried tomatoes. Stop in to see the magnificent mahogany central bar and its towering three-faced clock, which just might have sprung from Leonardo's imagination after a few pints.

✪ La Sosta. 45A Carlisle Rd., Derry, County Derry. ☎ 01504/374817 or 028/7137-4817. Reservations recommended. Main courses £7–£14 ($11.55–$23.10). AE, MC, V. Tues–Sat 6–10:30pm. ITALIAN.

An evening at La Sosta begins with surprise, and ends with contentment. The first and only surprise at La Sosta is the fact of finding such a fine Italian restaurant inconspicuously tucked away on a quiet side street in Derry. After this initial response, each course serves as a gradual confirmation of Claudio Antonucci's skill as a chef. Each dish is simple in conception, composed so that you can taste and enjoy each ingredient. Absent are the complicated, concealing sauces; everything here is on the surface, but this surface is varied and compelling and always delicious. Characteristic is the ravioli stuffed with spinach and ricotta with asparagus, frenchbeans, chives, and ginger—it's that subtle suggestion of ginger that brings all these fine ingredients together to make a memorable flavor. The wine list is good, and the house wine a particularly flavorful complement to the meal. Pure contentment is the only way to describe a selection of refreshing desserts.

Oysters. Spencer Rd., Waterside, Derry, County Derry. ☎ 028/7134-4875. Reservations recommended. Dinner main courses £5.95–£10.95 ($9.80–$18.05). MC, V. Mon–Sat 5:30–10pm; Sun 12:30–2:30pm and 5:30–9pm. INTERNATIONAL.

You'd never know from looking at it that Oysters is new to the Derry scene—it's already crowded with locals, even on weeknights. The nautical theme pervades every room to the point that you can almost convince yourself that you're below deck—eating, I might add, like a captain. The cuisine is first-rate, both in presentation and across the palate. The menu is vast, featuring Thai, Portuguese, Caribbean, Indian, and traditional Irish entrees. The modest wine list is well selected and most affordable. Coconut-crusted chicken with coriander and tiger prawns, and seared salmon with mango and chile sauce with fresh linguine were both admirable; sea bass with bacon and tarragon cream remains a tempting road not taken.

Reggie's Seafood Restaurant. 165 Strand Rd., Derry, County Derry. ☎ **028/7126-2050.** Dinner main courses £6.95–£9.95 ($11.45–$16.40). No credit cards. Mon–Fri noon–2:30pm and 5:30–10pm; Sat 5–10:30pm. SEAFOOD.

The freshest fish go into tasty seafood dishes in this bright, cheerful eatery that offers very good value. Assorted seafood in a pasta nest with creamy white-wine sauce is excellent, and fillet of turbot with hazelnut mousseline sauce is also very good. There is a good cheese board, a selection of teas, and freshly ground Bewley's coffee.

INEXPENSIVE

Badger's. 16–18 Orchard St. , Derry, County Derry. ☎ **028/7136-0763.** Reservations not accepted. Dinner main courses £3.95–£5.95 ($6.50–$9.80). MC, V. Mon noon–3pm; Tues–Thurs noon–7pm; Fri–Sat noon–9:30pm. IRISH/INTERNATIONAL.

This comfortable corner pub restaurant is just the place to enjoy a simple, satisfying dinner before the theater, or to settle into after your day's adventures for a drink and a chat. Tastefully decorated and graced with stained glass and wood paneling, the two levels have a Victorian feel but were designed with a more modern appreciation of light and openness. It's a popular meeting spot for locals who come for the friendly service and such well-prepared favorites as savory steak, vegetable and Guinness casserole with a crisp puff-pastry lid, or the flavorful hot sandwiches known as "damper melts."

Piemonte Pizzeria. 2 Clarendon St., Derry, County Derry. ☎ **028/7126-7313.** Dinner main courses £5–£7 ($8.25–$11.55). V. Daily 5pm–midnight.

If you're craving the thin, crispy crust and zesty toppings of a well-made pizza, then Piemonte may be what you're looking for. Eight-inch pizzas are served at reasonable prices, and toppings include usual favorites like salami and cheese or more startling options like "Pizza Yellow Pages," a mixture of cheese, tomato, tuna, and banana. Less commendable are the pasta choices—portions are generous but the bland sauce of a vegetarian cannelloni served double duty as a mediocre tomato and basil soup. Stick to the pizza and you should leave the dark, slightly smoky interior of Piemonte well satisfied.

Ramsey's Cafe. 10 William St. , Derry, County Derry. ☎ **028/7126-9236.** Main courses under £6 ($9.90). No credit cards. Mon–Sat 8am–midnight; Sun 6pm–midnight. LIGHT MEALS/PASTRIES/SALADS.

At this great drop-in eatery in the heart of the city, Anne Ramsey dishes up heaping plates of hot meals, fresh salads, fish-and-chips, and a variety of bakery items. It's self-service and very busy at almost any hour.

DERRY AFTER DARK

One thing to keep in mind as you're sketching out your after-dark plans is that Derry is one of Ireland's most youthful cities—roughly 40% of its population is under 30. This fact, coupled with an 18-year-old drinking age, means that the night scene is mostly driven by the young—few, if any, gray hairs appear in the hottest spots. On weekends, after 1 or 2 in the morning when the clubs empty, the city center can become a rather loud and volatile area.

THE PERFORMING ARTS

Derry has long been associated with the arts, especially theater, poetry, and music. While its financial resources have been modest, its commitment remains inventive and tenacious. Until the completion of the new **Millennium Complex** in 2001—which will be a grand venue for Derry's art scene—the principal venues for concerts, plays, and poetry readings are the **Guildhall,** Shipquay Place (☎ **028/7136-5151**); the **Foyle Arts Centre,** Lawrence Hill (☎ **028/7126-6657**); the **Playhouse,** 5–7 Artillery St. (☎ **028/7126-8027**); and the **Rialto,** 5 Market St. (☎ **028/ 7126-0516**). Ticket prices for most performances range from £12 to £15 ($19.80 to $24.75).

PUBS

Derry City pubs rarely resemble the small, cozy nooks you often find in the Republic. They tend to be rather grand by comparison and a bit theatrical, more like stage sets than parlors. In addition, Derry pubs are known for their music and communal quiz evenings, when teams compete in a free-range Irish form of Trivial Pursuit. There are even pub debating contests, in the midst of which you'll hear Irish eloquence at its well-lubricated best. Here's a small sampling of Derry's more-than-ample pub options.

Along **Waterloo Street,** just outside the city walls, are a handful of Derry's most traditional and popular pubs, known for their live music and simply as the place to be. The **Dungloe,** the **Gweedore,** and **Peador O'Donnells** are three well-established hot spots. Walk from one end of Waterloo to the other, which will take you all of 2 minutes, and you'll likely find the bar for you.

In addition to Sandinos (see below), gay and lesbian travelers might want to check out **Ascension,** at 64 Strand Rd. It's open until 1am most days and has free disco on Tuesdays and Thursdays and karaoke on Sundays.

The Clarendon. 48 Strand Rd., Derry, County Derry. ☎ **028/7126-3705.**

This inviting bar offers more quiet and calm than most of Derry's bars. It's a congenial pub for those who have broken 30 and are somewhere beyond the sonic boom. You can have a conversation here as well as a drink. Sundays and Tuesdays are quiz nights, when you can display whatever wisdom might have come with your years.

River Inn/Glue Pot. Shipquay St., Derry, County Derry. ☎ **028/7137-1965.**

These two adjoining bars make up the oldest pub in Derry. The downstairs River Inn inhabits cellars opened to the thirsty public in 1684—if you've already kissed the Blarney Stone, why not kiss these revered walls? The upstairs Glue Pot is a more modern cocktail bar, not as appealing as the cellars, but a good deal more appealing than its name.

Sandinos Cafe Bar. Water St., Derry, County Derry. ☎ **028/7130-9297.**

One of Derry's trendiest bars, this is where many of the city's gays and lesbians and literary folks prefer to settle in for the evening. Its "South of the Border" theme refers to the States' Mexican border, not to the North's border on the Republic. There are blues on Friday, jazz on Saturday, and an open mike for local poets every Sunday. In this intriguing shoebox of a bar, 30 is a quorum, so come early to secure a place for the evening. In 1999, the *Irish Times* named it one of the 100 top pubs in Ireland.

THE CLUB SCENE

Provided you're under 25 and have no ambitions to be a piano tuner, there are several places where you'll want to be seen if not heard. Two multi-entertainment complexes stand out. First, there's **Squires Night Club,** 33 Shipquay St. (☎ **028/7126-6017**), behind the Townsman bar. Once you pay the cover charge, usually £2 to £5 ($3.30 to $8.25), you can make your way up to the **VIP** or farther back to the 1,200-capacity voxbox. Second, there's **Earth** (possibly recognizable as such), 122–124 Strand Rd.

(☎ 028/7130-9372), where your club choices are **Café Roc** and **Coles Bar.** The **Strand,** 35–38 Strand Rd. (☎ 028/7126-0494), features a classy bar serving mostly pub grub, and downstairs, an open venue for live bands. On weekend nights, in the bar, the tables are moved aside and the Strand morphs into a nightclub for the 20-plus crowd.

The night scene in Derry, like anywhere else, is a movable feast, so be sure to check the current *What's On?* listings.

7 The Sperrin Mountains

40 miles (65km) E to W along the Londonderry–Tyrone border

Southeast of Derry, the Sperrin Mountains slowly rise up out of County Tyrone. They reach their highest point at Sawel, from which you can see as far as the Foyle Estuary and across the Northern Ireland countryside to Lough Neagh and the Mournes. This is splendid wide-open walking country that golden plover, red grouse, and thousands upon thousands of sheep call home.

In the Sperrins, you won't be likely to find the tallest, oldest, deepest, or most famous of anything in Ireland. Even the highest peak in the range—Sawel, at 2,204 feet—is an easy climb. This is Ireland in a minor key. It is a corner of Ireland largely unsung and unspoiled. You'll see mostly wildflowers here, rather than formal gardens, and cottages rather than castles. All the same, gold has been found in these mountains. Poetry, too. Seamus Heaney grew up on the edge of the Sperrins and found words to suit their subtle splendor.

Unless you come to farm, chances are you'll spend your time exploring the dark russet blanket bogs and purple heathland, the gorse-covered hillsides, and the lovely forest parks, whether on foot, cycle, or horseback. For the more acquisitive, there are salmon and trout on the Foyle System from Strabane to Omagh, as well as game on the moors. There is also a handful of first-rate historical museums and sights for the whole family. As for minor destinations for a morning walk or an afternoon drive, there's no shortage of standing stones (about 1,000 have been counted), high crosses, dolmens, and hill forts—more reminders that every last bit of bog on this island has its own slew of stories, if only we could hear them told.

VISITOR INFORMATION   There are four nationally networked tourist information centers in County Tyrone. The **Cookstown Centre,** 48 Molesworth St., Cookstown (☎ 028/8676-6727), is open weekdays 9am to 5pm, with weekend and extended hours Easter to September. The **Kilmaddy Centre,** Ballgawley Road (off A4), Dungannon (☎ 028/8776-7259), is open Monday to Thursday 9am to 5pm, with Friday and weekend hours in the spring and summer. The **Omagh Centre,** 1 Market St., Omagh (☎ 028/8224-7831), is open Easter to September Monday to Saturday 9am to 5pm; October to Easter Monday to Friday 9am to 5pm. The **Strabane Centre,** Abercorn Square, Strabane (☎ 028/7188-3735), is open April to October, Monday to Saturday 9:30am to 5pm.

SEEING THE SIGHTS

An Creagán Visitors' Centre. A505 (12½ miles/20km east of Omagh), Creggan, County Tyrone. ☎ 028/8076-1112. Admission £2 ($3.30) adults, £1 ($1.65) children. Apr–Sept daily 11am–6:30pm; Oct–Mar Mon–Fri 11am–4:30pm.

This is a helpful place to take your bearings in the Sperrins. Besides viewing interpretive exhibitions on the region, you can find out the best cycling and trekking routes, rent bicycles, and have a meal in the restaurant.

Impressions

Don't be surprised
If I demur, for, be advised
My passport's green.
No glass of ours was ever raised
To toast the Queen.

—Seamus Heaney (b. 1939), *An Open Letter*

Beaghmore Stone Circles. 10½ miles (17km) northwest of Cookstown, signposted from A505 to Omagh, County Tyrone.

In 1945, six stone circles and a complex assembly of cairns and alignments were uncovered here, in remote moorland north of Evishbrack Mountain and near Davagh Forest Park on the southern edge of the Sperrins. The precise function of this intriguing concentration of Bronze Age stonework is unknown, but it may have involved astronomical observation and calculation.

Drum Manor Forest Park. 2½ miles (4km) west of Cookstown on A505, County Tyrone. ☎ **028/8676-2774.** Admission £2.50 ($4.15) per car; pedestrians £1 ($1.65) adults, 50p (83¢) children. Daily 10am–dusk.

Once a private estate, this extensive park and woodland has numerous trails and three old walled gardens, one of which has been designed as a butterfly garden. There is also a pond that attracts a variety of wildfowl, a heronry, and a visitor center, with exhibits on butterflies and other local wildlife.

Gortin Glen Forest Park. B48 (7 miles/11km north of Omagh), Cullion, County Tyrone. ☎ **028/8164-8217.** Free admission. Parking £3 ($4.95). Daily 9am to 1 hr. before sunset.

Nearly a thousand acres of planted conifers make up this beautiful nature park, established in 1967. The woodlands are a habitat to a variety of wildlife, including a herd of Japanese silka deer. The park's 4½-mile (7.3km) forest drive offers some splendid vistas of the Sperrins. There is also a nature center, wildlife enclosures, trails, and a cafe. For those planning to arrive and leave on foot, the Ulster Way passes through the park.

Grant Ancestral Home. 20 miles (32km) southeast of Omagh off A4, Dergina, Ballygawley, County Tyrone. ☎ **028/7188-3735.** Admission £1 ($1.65) adults, 50p (83¢) seniors and children. Apr–Sept Mon–Sat noon–5pm, Sun 2–6pm.

This farm cottage was the home of the ancestors of Ulysses S. Grant, 18th president of the United States. Grant's maternal great-grandfather, John Simpson, was born here and emigrated to Pennsylvania in 1738 at the age of 22. The cottage has two rooms with mud floors and has been restored and furnished with period pieces, including a settle bed and dresser. The site includes a visitor center with an audiovisual presentation, a tearoom, and various exhibits, including a collection of typical 18th-century agricultural implements.

Gray's Printers' Museum. 49 Main St., Strabane, County Tyrone. ☎ **028/7188-4094.** Admission £1.80 ($2.95) adults, 90p ($1.50) children, £4.50 ($7.45) family. Museum Tues–Fri 11am–5pm, Sat 11:30am–5pm. Guided tours of printing press Apr–Sept Tues–Sat 2–5pm.

The museum and print shop housed together here are unrelated (apart from being "flatmates"). The print shop, maintained by the National Trust, dates from 1760. It has an attractive bow-front window and an exhibit of 19th-century hand-operated printing presses. John Dunlop, founder of the first daily newspaper in the United

States and printer of the American Declaration of Independence, learned his trade here. An audiovisual show provides insight into how the original presses operated and the part Dunlop played in America's early printing days. The museum, operated by the local district council, is a venue for changing exhibits germane to the history and culture of the region. Access to the printing press is through the museum.

Plantation of Ulster Visitor Centre. 50 High St., Draperstown, County Derry. ☎ **028/7922-7800.** Admission £3 ($4.95) adults, £2.50 ($4.15) seniors and students, £1.50 ($2.50) children, £7.50 ($12.40) family. Apr–Sept daily 10am–5pm; Oct–Mar daily 10am–4pm.

This new interpretive center tells the story of the Ulster Plantation of 1610, which marked the completion of the Elizabethan Conquest of Ireland. To do so, it uses an array of graphic images, audiovisual presentations, and interactive displays. Anyone wanting to understand the divisions that to this day define Irish geography and disrupt Irish life would do well to consider the center's informative and moving exhibits. The restaurant serves homemade meals, and the gift shop stocks a selection of local crafts.

Sperrin Heritage Centre. 274 Glenelly Rd. (east of Plumbridge off B47), Cranagh, County Tyrone. ☎ **028/8164-8142.** Admission £2 ($3.30) adults, £1 ($1.65) seniors and children. Apr–Sept Mon–Fri 11am–6pm, Sat 11:30am–6pm, Sun 2–7pm.

Here, in the heart of the Sperrins, is *the* place to get the local bearings and background. A range of computerized presentations and other exhibits introduce the history, culture, geology, and wildlife of the region. This is a gold-mining area, and for a small additional fee (65p/$1.05 adults, 35p/58¢ children) you'll have a chance to try your hand at panning for gold. A cafeteria, craft shop, and nature trail share the grounds.

Tyrone Crystal. Oaks Rd. (2 miles/3.2km east of town), Killybrackey, Dungannon, County Tyrone. ☎ **028/8772-5335.** Admission £2 ($3.30) adults; free for seniors and children. Craft shop Mon–Sat 9am–5pm. Tours every 30 min. Apr–Oct Mon–Thurs and Sat 9:30am–3:30pm, Fri 9:30am–noon; Nov–Mar Mon–Thurs 9:30am–3:30pm, Fri 9:30am–noon.

With a 200-year-old tradition, this crystal factory is one of Ireland's oldest and best known. Visitors are welcome to tour the operation and see glass being blown and crafted, carved, and engraved by hand. A 25-minute audiovisual presentation tells the story of the development of Tyrone Crystal, a showroom displays the finished products, and a very good cafe adds sustenance.

Ulster History Park. Cullion (on B48, 7 miles/11km north of Omagh), Omagh, County Tyrone. ☎ **028/8164-8188.** Admission £4 ($6.60) adults; £2.50 ($4.15) seniors, students, and children; £10 ($16.50) family. Apr–Sept Mon–Sat 10:30am–6:30pm, Sun 11:30am–7pm; Oct–Mar Mon–Fri 10:30am–5pm. Last admission 90 min. before closing. Bus: From Omagh.

Ireland's history from the Stone Age to the 17th-century Plantation period is the focus of this outdoor theme park. There are full-scale models of homes, castles, and monuments through the ages, including a Mesolithic encampment, Neolithic dwelling, crannóg lake dwelling, church settlement with round tower, and motte-and-bailery type of castle common. The park also contains an audiovisual theater, a gift shop, and a cafeteria.

✪ **Ulster-American Folk Park.** Mellon Rd. (3 miles/4.8km north of Omagh on A5), Castletown, Camphill, Omagh, County Tyrone. ☎ **028/8224-3292.** Admission £4 ($6.60) adults, £2.50 ($4.15) seniors and children 5–16, £10 ($16.50) family. Oct–Easter Mon–Fri 10:30am–5pm; Easter–Sept Mon–Sat 10:30am–6pm, Sun 11am–6:30pm. Last admission 1 hour before closing.

This outdoor museum seeks to present the story of emigration from this part of rural Ireland to America in the 18th and 19th centuries. There are reconstructions of the thatched cottages the emigrants left behind, and prototypes of the log cabins that became their homes on the American frontiers. The park developed around the homestead where Thomas Mellon was born in 1813. He went to Pittsburgh and prospered to the point where his son Andrew became one of the world's richest men. The Mellon family donated part of the funding to build this excellent park. Walk-through exhibits include a forge, weaver's cottage, smokehouse, schoolhouse, post office, Sperrin Mountain famine cabin, and full-scale replica of an emigrant ship in a dockside area that features original buildings from the ports of Derry, Belfast, and Newry. A self-guided tour of all the exhibits, which are staffed by interpreters in period costume, takes about 2 hours. Musical events that tie in with the Ulster-American theme, such as a bluegrass music festival in September, take place each year.

Wilson Ancestral Home. Off Plumbridge Rd., Dergalt, Strabane, County Tyrone. ☎ **028/8224-3292.** Admission £1 ($1.65) adults, 50p (83¢) children. Apr–Sept daily 2–6pm.

This small thatched, whitewashed cottage on the slopes of the Sperrin Mountains was the home of Judge James Wilson, grandfather of Woodrow Wilson, 28th president of the United States. James Wilson left the house in 1807 at the age of 20. It contains some of the family's original furniture, including a tiny out-shot bed (sleeping nook) in the kitchen close to the fire, larger curtained beds, and a portrait of the president's grandfather over the fireplace. Wilsons still occupy the modern farmhouse next door. *Note:* Opening hours are subject to change; phone in advance.

SPORTS & OUTDOOR PURSUITS

BICYCLING   The Sperrin countryside is ideal for cycling. Bicycles can be rented by the day or week from the **An Creagán Visitors' Centre** (see "Seeing the Sights," above), or from **Conway Cycles,** 1 Old Market Place, Omagh (☎ **028/8224-6195**). Bike rentals run roughly £7 ($11.55) a day, £30 ($49.50) a week.

BIRD WATCHING   The Sperrins are home to golden plovers, peregrines, ravens, grouse, and hen harriers. **Sawel Mountain,** the highest of the Sperrins, is a great place to take out your binoculars and twitcher book.

FISHING   The **Foyle System** of rivers, from Derry to Omagh and Limavady to Dungiven, makes this a promising area for snagging brown and sea trout (Apr to early July and Sept) and a variety of salmon (Mar to Sept). There's also some good coarse fishing available north and west of Omagh, on the Baronscourt Lakes and on the Strule and Fairy Water Rivers. The necessary permits, equipment, and good advice are available from **C. A. Anderson & Co.,** 64 Market St., Omagh (☎ **028/8224-2311**); **Mourne Valley Tackle,** 50 Main St., Newtownstewart (☎ **028/8166-1543**); and **Floyd's Fish and Tackle,** 28 Melmount Villas, Strabane (☎ **028/7188-3981**). In fact, if you're in the market for an experienced *ghillie* (guide), ask at the above for **Martin Floyd.**

GOLF   There are several 18-hole courses in County Tyrone within a modest drive from the heart of the Sperrins: **Strabane Golf Club,** 33 Ballycolman Rd., Strabane (☎ **028/7138-2007**), with greens fees of £15 ($24.75) weekdays, £17 ($28.05) on weekends; **Newtownstewart Golf Club,** 38 Golf Course Rd., Newtownstewart (☎ **028/8166-1466**), with greens fees of £12 ($19.80) weekdays, £17 ($28.05) weekends; **Omagh Golf Club,** 83a Dublin Rd., Omagh (☎ **028/8164-1442**), with greens fees of £12 ($19.80) weekdays, £17 ($28.05) weekends; and **Killymoon Golf Club,** 200 Killymoon Rd., Cookstown (☎ **028/8676-3762**), with greens fees of £18 ($29.70) weekdays, £22 ($36.30) weekends.

HORSEBACK RIDING   To rent by the hour or take a several-day trekking trip through the mountains, contact the **Edergole Riding Centre,** 7 Moneymore Rd., Cookstown (☎ **028/8676-2924**).

WALKING   Whether you're on foot or wheels or horseback, be sure to traverse the **Glenshane Pass** between Mullaghmore (1,818 ft.) and Carntogher (1,516 ft.), and the **Sawel Mountain Drive** along the east face of the mountain. The vistas along these routes through the Sperrins will remind you of why you've gone out of your way to spend time in Tyrone.

ACCOMMODATIONS
MODERATE

✪ **Grange Lodge.** 7 Grange Rd. (signposted 1 mile/1.6km south of M1, Junction 15), Moy, Dungannon, County Tyrone. ☎ **028/8778-4212.** Fax 028/8778-4313. 5 units. TV TEL. £69 ($113.85) double. Rates include full breakfast. Dinner £22 ($36.30). MC, V. Closed Jan. Free parking.

Norah and Ralph Brown are the gracious hosts of this lovely guesthouse, which began life as a 17th-century settler's hall. Set on a 20-acre estate, it's a tranquil retreat and a good base for day trips throughout County Tyrone. Guest rooms are attractive and comfortable, and the dining room looks out over green lawns backed by wooded parklands. Norah excels in the kitchen (she's won all sorts of culinary awards), and a breakfast specialty is porridge flavored with Bushmills Whiskey and cream. All guest rooms are nonsmoking.

INEXPENSIVE

✪ **The Grange.** 15 Grange Rd., Ballygawley, County Tyrone. ☎ **028/8556-8053.** 3 units. TV. £32 ($52.80) double. Children's discount available. Rates include full breakfast. No credit cards. Closed Dec.

There's loads of character in this charming little cottage near the Ballygawley roundabout and the Folk Park. It dates to 1720, but has been thoroughly modernized. Mrs. Lyttle is the hostess, and her rooms (two doubles and one single) are done up nicely. Washing and ironing facilities are on hand, and Mrs. Lyttle welcomes small children.

Greenmount Lodge. 58 Greenmount Rd. (8 miles/13km southeast of Omagh on A5), Gortaclare, Omagh, County Tyrone. ☎ **028/8284-1325.** Fax 028/8284-0019. 8 units. TV TEL. £38 ($62.70) double. Children's discount available. Rates include full breakfast. Dinner £12.50 ($20.65). MC, V.

On a 150-acre farm, this is a large first-rate guesthouse. Four of the nicely appointed rooms are family units. All the bedrooms have recently been refurbished. Mrs. Frances Reid, the friendly hostess, is a superb cook; both breakfasts and evening meals are a delight.

SELF-CATERING

Sperrin Clachan. Glenelly Valley, Cranagh, County Tyrone. Contact RCH at ☎ **028/9024-1100.** Fax 028/9024-1198. www.cottagesinireland.com. 8 cottages. TV. £110–£330 ($181.50–$544.50) per week. Also available for 2- or 3-day stays. No credit cards.

This restored *clachan,* or family cottage compound, sits beside the Sperrin Heritage Centre in the beautiful Glenelly Valley. It makes an ideal base for exploring the natural riches and cultural legacy of the Sperrin region, as well as the city of Derry, only 25 miles (40km) to the north. The cottages have everything you'll need to set up house, including washing machines, dishwashers, microwaves, and central heating. They sleep two, three, four, or five. All have an open fireplace.

In addition to these, Rural Cottage Holidays offers a wide array of other traditional cottages in the region, including the award-winning, four-star Glenelly Cottages.

DINING

✪ **Mellon Country Inn.** 134 Beltany Rd., Omagh, County Tyrone. ☎ **028/8166-1244.** Fax 028/8166-2245. Dinner main courses £6.95–£16.95 ($11.45–$27.95). AE, MC, V. Daily 10:30am–10pm. INTERNATIONAL.

Located 1 mile (1.6km) north of the Ulster-American Folk Park, this old-world country inn combines an Irish theme with a connection to the Mellons of Pennsylvania. The menu includes simple fare—burgers, soup, salads, and ploughman's platters—as well as elegant dishes such as lobster Newburg, beef Stroganoff, coquilles St.-Jacques, and sole bonne femme. The house specialty is Tyrone black steak, a locally bred hormone-free beef. Food is available all day, including late breakfast and afternoon tea.

For diners interested in lodging, a new addition of 15 rooms should now be completed.

8 The Fermanagh Lakelands

Enniskillen, in the heart of the Fermanagh Lakelands, is 83 miles (134km) SW of Belfast, 61 miles (98km) SW of Derry, 52 miles (84km) W of Armagh, 27 miles (44km) SW of Omagh, 108 miles (174km) NW of Dublin, and 168 miles (271km) NE of Shannon

Tucked in the extreme southwest corner of Northern Ireland, County Fermanagh is a premier resort area dominated by Lough Erne, a long lake dotted with 154 islands and rimmed by countless alcoves and inlets. It has 50 miles (81km) of cruising waters—the least congested in Europe—ranging from a shallow channel in some places to a 5-mile (8km) width in others. The total signposted driving circuit around the lake is 65 miles (105km).

The 1994 reopening of the Shannon-Erne Waterway, linking the lough to the Shannon system, greatly enhanced the lure of Lough Erne as a cruising destination. The 40-mile (65km) waterway between the cross-border village of Leitrim and Lough Erne consists of a series of 16 lochs, three lakes, and the Woodford River.

The hub of this lakeland paradise, wedged between the upper and lower branches of Lough Erne, is Enniskillen, a delightful resort town that was the medieval seat of the Maguire clan and a major crossroads between Ulster and Connaught. Both Oscar Wilde and Samuel Beckett were once students here, at the royal school.

At the northern tip of the lake is Belleek, sitting right on the border with the Republic of Ireland, and known the world over for delicate bone chinaware. At the southern end of the lake is County Cavan and another slice of border with the Irish Republic. The surrounding countryside holds diverse attractions, from stately homes at Florence Court and Castle Coole to the unique Marble Arch Caves. In the waters lie myriad islands, Devenish and Boa being two of the most interesting.

In medieval times, a chain of island monasteries stretched across the waters of Lough Erne, establishing it as a haven for contemplatives. Making certain allowances for less lofty minds, the Fermanagh Lakelands remain a great place to get away from it all and to gaze, in a phrase from Hopkins, at the "pied beauty" of it all.

VISITOR INFORMATION Contact the **Fermanagh Tourist Information Centre,** Wellington Road, Enniskillen, County Fermanagh (☎ **028/7032-3110**). It's open weekdays, year-round, from 9am to 5:30pm (7pm in July and Aug). From Easter to September it's also open on weekends, Saturday 10am to 6pm and Sunday 11am to 5pm. For an introduction to the Fermanagh Lakelands on the Web, take a look at **www.fermanagh-online.com**.

EXPLORING THE LAKELANDS

Erne Tours Ltd., Enniskillen (☎ 028/6632-2882), operates cruises on Lower Lough Erne. The M.V. *Kestrel,* a 63-seat cruiser, departs from the Round "O" Jetty, Brook Park, Enniskillen. Trips, including a stop at Devenish Island, last just under 2 hours. They operate daily in July and August at 10:30am, 2:15pm, and 4:15pm; in May and June on Sunday at 2:30pm; and in September on Tuesday, Saturday, and Sunday at 2:30pm. Call for reservations and to confirm times. The fare is £5 ($8.25) for adults, £2.50 ($4.15) for children under 14.

The **Share Holiday Village,** Smith's Strand, Lisnaskea (☎ 028/6772-2122), operates cruises on Upper Lough Erne. The 1½-hour trips are conducted on board the *Viking,* a 30-passenger canopied long ship. Sailings are April to August Saturday and Sunday 3pm. Ring for reservations and confirmation. The fare is £4 ($6.60) for adults, £3 ($4.95) for seniors and children under 18. Share Centre also offers other water-sports activities and self-catering chalets.

Independent boatmen offer ferry crossings to some of the many islands in Lough Erne. From April to September, a ferry runs to Devenish Island from Trory Point, 4 miles (6.5km) from Enniskillen on A32. From June to September, a ferry runs to White Island, departing from Castle Archdale Marina, 10 miles (16km) from Enniskillen on the Kesh road. For both, departures are Tuesday to Saturday 10am to 7pm, Sunday 2 to 7pm. The round-trip fare is £2.25 ($3.70) for adults, £1.20 ($2) for children. Be sure to visit Devenish, Boa, and White Islands. Bridges connect Boa Island to the shore.

Belleek Pottery. Belleek, County Fermanagh. ☎ 028/6865-8501. www.belleek.ie. Free admission; tours £2.50 ($4.15) adults and children over 12. Apr–June and Sept, Mon–Fri 9am–6pm, Sat 10am–6pm, Sun 2–6pm; July–Aug Mon–Fri 9am–6pm, Sat 10am–6pm, Sun 11am–6pm; Oct Mon–Fri 9am–5:30pm, Sat 10am–5:30pm, Sun 2–6pm; Nov Mon–Fri 9am–5:30pm, Sat 10am–5:30pm; Dec–Mar Mon–Fri 9am–5:30pm.

With the possible exception of Waterford crystal, Belleek china is the name most readily identified throughout the world as a symbol of the finest Irish craftsmanship. Established in 1857, this pottery enterprise produces distinctive, delicate porcelain china, made into tableware, vases, ornaments, and other pieces. The visitor center has a museum showing the product from earliest days to the present. Tours are conducted weekdays every 20 minutes, with the last tour at 3:30pm. The coffee shop serves tea, coffee, snacks, and a hot lunch.

✪ **Castle Coole.** 1½ miles (2.4km) southeast of Enniskillen on the main Belfast–Enniskillen road (A4), County Fermanagh. ☎ 028/6632-2690. House admission £3 ($4.95) adults, £1.50 ($2.50) children, £8 ($13.20) family; grounds £1.50 ($2.50) per car. Easter–May and Sept Sat–Sun 1–6pm; June–Aug Fri–Wed 1–6pm (last tour 5:15pm).

On the east bank of Lower Lough Erne, this quintessential neoclassical mansion was designed by James Wyatt for the earl of Belmore and completed in 1796. Its rooms include a lavish state bedroom hung with crimson silk, said to have been prepared for George IV. Other features include a Chinese-style sitting room, magnificent wood-work, fireplaces, and furniture dating to the 1830s. A nearly 1,500-acre woodland estate surrounds the house. A classical music series runs from May to October.

Crom Estate. Newtownbutler, County Fermanagh. ☎ 028/6773-8118. Admission £3 ($4.95) per car or boat. Apr–Sept Mon–Sat 10am–6pm, Sun noon–6pm. 21 miles (34km) south of Enniskillen. Take A4 and A34 from Enniskillen to Newtownbutler, then take the sign-posted right turn onto a minor road.

This nearly 2,000-acre nature reserve is a splendid National Trust property, with forest, parks, wetlands, fen meadows, and an award-winning lakeshore visitor center.

There are numerous trails, with hides for observing birds and wildlife, as well as a heronry and boat rental. The estate is also a great place to fish for bream and roach. Permits and day tickets are available at the gate lodge. During the summer, there are frequently special programs and guided nature walks on weekends.

✪ **Devenish Island.** 1½ miles (2.4km) downstream from Enniskillen. Admission 75p ($1.25). Ferry from Trory Point (4 miles/6.5km from Enniskillen on A32). Apr–Sept, every 20–30 min. Round-trip fare £2.25 ($3.70) adults, £1.20 ($2) children.

This is the most extensive of the ancient Christian sites in Lough Erne. In the 6th century, St. Molaise founded a monastic community here, to which the Augustinian Abbey of St. Mary was added in the 12th century. In other words, this is hallowed ground, hallowed all the more by the legend that the prophet Jeremiah is buried somewhere nearby (figure that out!). The intact 12th-century round tower was erected with Vikings in mind. The island is a marvelous mélange of remnants and ruins, providing a glimpse into the lake's mystical past. While you're at it and in the spirit, be sure to explore Boa and White Islands, with their extraordinary carved stone figures, and bring your camera (see the introduction to this section for details on island hopping).

✪ **Enniskillen Castle.** Castle Barracks, Enniskillen, County Fermanagh. ☎ **028/6632-5000.** Admission £2 ($3.30) adults, £1.50 ($2.50) seniors and students, £1 ($1.65) children, £5 ($8.25) family. May–June and Sept Mon 2–5pm, Tues–Fri 10am–5pm, Sat 2–5pm; July–Aug Tues–Fri 10am–5pm, Sat–Mon 2–5pm; Oct–Apr Mon 2–5pm, Tues–Fri 10am–5pm.

Dating from the 15th century, this magnificent stone fortress sits overlooking Lough Erne on the western edge of town. It incorporates three museums: the medieval castle, with its unique twin-turreted Watergate tower, once the seat of the Maguires, chieftains of Fermanagh; the county museum, with exhibits on the area's history, wildlife, and landscape; and the museum of the famous Royal Inniskilling Fusiliers, with a collection of uniforms, weapons, regimental memorabilia, and medals dating from the 17th century. New exhibits include life-size figurines and 3-D models of old-time castle life.

ExplorErne. Erne Gateway Centre, off main Enniskillen–Belleek road, Corry, Belleek, County Fermanagh. ☎ **028/6865-8866.** Admission £1 ($1.65) adults, 50p (83¢) seniors and children, £2.50 ($4.15) family. Mid-Mar to Oct daily 10am–6pm.

Just outside Belleek village, this new exhibition offers an engaging multimedia introduction to Lough Erne. It covers its geologic formation and the lives, ancient and modern, lived along its reedy banks. Science, myth, and history blend to tell the story of this legendary, alluring lake.

✪ **Florence Court.** Florence Court, off A32, County Fermanagh. ☎ **028/6634-8249.** Admission £3 ($4.95) adults, £1.50 ($2.50) children, £7.50 ($12.40) family. Apr and Sept Sat–Sun 1–6pm; May–Aug Wed–Mon 1–6pm.

One of the most beautifully situated houses in Northern Ireland, this 18th-century Palladian mansion is set among dramatic hills, 8 miles (13km) southwest of Upper Lough Erne and Enniskillen. Originally the seat of the earls of Enniskillen, its interior is rich in rococo plasterwork and antique Irish furniture, while its exterior has a fine walled garden, an icehouse, and a water wheel–driven sawmill. The forest park offers a number of trails, one leading to the top of Mount Cuilcagh (nearly 2,200 ft.). The tearoom serves coffee, tea, and snacks.

✪ **Marble Arch Caves.** Marlbank, Florence Court, off A32, County Fermanagh. ☎ **028/6634-8855.** Admission £6 ($9.90) adults, £4 ($6.60) seniors and students, £3 ($4.95) children under 18, £14 ($23.10) family. Reservations recommended. Late Mar–June and Sept, daily 10am–4:30pm (last tour at 4:30pm); July–Aug daily 10am–5pm (last tour at 5pm).

Arts & Crafts

If you'd rather sketch a trout than snag it, you might want to contact the **Ardess Craft Centre,** near Kesh (☎ **028/6863-1267**). It offers a range of courses, from drawing and painting to stone walling and weaving. Room and board are available and optional. For a complete guide to crafts in the Fermanagh region, go to **www.fermanaghcraft.com**.

Located west of Upper Lough Erne and 12 miles (19km) from Enniskillen near the Florence Court estate, these caves are among the finest in Europe for exploring underground rivers, waterfalls, winding passages, and hidden chambers. Electrically powered boat tours take visitors underground, and knowledgeable guides explain the origins of the amazing stalactites and stalagmites. Tours last 75 minutes and leave at 15-minute intervals. The caves are occasionally closed after heavy rains, so phone ahead before making a special trip.

SHOPPING

Enniskillen has fine shops along its main street, which changes its name six times (East Bridge, Townhall, High, Church, Darling, Ann) as it runs the length of the town. Most shops are open Monday to Saturday 9:30am to 5:30pm.

The largest shopping complex in Enniskillen is the **Erneside Shopping Center,** a modern bilevel mall on Shore Road, just off Wellington Road. It stays open until 9pm on Thursday and Friday. The other principal towns for shopping in the area are **Irvinestown** and **Lisnaskea.**

The town's former Butter Market offers a nifty shopping experience. Dating from 1835, it has been restored and transformed into **The Buttermarket, The Enniskillen Craft and Design Centre,** Down Street (☎ **028/6632-3837**). It offers craft workshops and retail outlets, with occasional traditional music, craft fairs, and street theater to enliven the atmosphere.

SPORTS & OUTDOOR PURSUITS

BICYCLING   Several of the water-sports and activity centers in the area, such as **Erne Tours** and **Lakeland Canoe Center** (see "Water Sports," below), also rent bicycles. Bicycles are also available from **Corralea Activity Centre,** Belcoo (☎ **028/6638-6668**); **Out & Out Activities,** 501 Rosscor, Belleek (☎ **028/ 6865-8105**); and **Marble Arch Cycle Hire,** 69 Marlbank Rd., Florencecourt (☎ **028/6634-8320**). Daily bike rental runs £7 to £10 ($11.55 to $16.50). For cycle tours with **Kingfisher Cycle Trail,** contact Pat Collum at the Tourist Information Centre, Wellington Road, Enniskillen (☎ **028/6632-0121;** www.cycleireland.com).

BIRD WATCHING   These lakelands are prime bird-watching territory. To mention a few, you'll find whooper swans, great-crested grebes, golden plovers, curlews, corncrakes, kingfishers, herons, merlins, peregrines, kestrels, and sparrow hawks. On Upper Lough Erne, the primary habitats are the reed swamps, flooded drumlins, and fen; on the lower lake, the habitats of choice are the less-visited islands and the hay meadows. Two important preserves are at the Crom Estate (see "Exploring the Lakelands," above) and the Castlecaldwell Forest and Islands.

BOATING   Lough Erne is an explorer's dream, and you can take that dream all the way to the Atlantic if you want. The price range for fully equipped two- to eight-berth cruisers is £400 to £1,300 ($660 to $2,145) per week, including VAT, depending on the season and the size of the boat. The many local cruiser-hire companies include

Belleek Charter Cruising, Belleek (☎ **028/6865-8027**); **Erne Marine,** Bellanaleck (☎ **028/6634-8267**); and **Erincurrach Cruising,** Blaney (☎ **028/6864-1737**). Erincurrach has a cruiser that's specially adapted for travelers with disabilities.

On Lower Lough Erne, north of town, you can hire motorboats from **Manor House Marine,** Killadeas (☎ **028/6862-8100**). Charges average £40 ($66) for a half day, and £60 ($99) for a full day.

FISHING The **Fermanagh Lakes** are an angler's heaven. If you can't catch a fish here, you must have been one in a past life. The best time for salmon is February to mid-June; for trout, mid-March to June or mid-August until late September. As for coarse fishing, about a dozen species await your line in the area's lakes and rivers. If you've left time for advance planning and consultation, contact the **Fisheries Conservancy Board,** 1 Mahon Rd., Portadown BT62 3EE (☎ **028/3833-4666**). For on-the-spot info, tackle, and bait, try **Trevor Kingston,** 18 Church St., Enniskillen (☎ **028/6632-2114**). For locally arranged game fishing, call or drop in on **Melvin Tackle,** Main Street, Garrison, County Fermanagh (☎ **028/6865-8194**). All necessary permits and licenses are available at the **Fermanagh Tourist Information Centre** (see "Visitor Information," above).

GOLF There are two 18-hole courses in the Lakelands, both in Enniskillen. The **Enniskillen Golf Club,** in the Castle Coole estate (☎ **028/6632-5250**), charges greens fees of £15 ($24.75) weekdays, £18 ($27.90) weekends. The **Castle Hume Golf Club,** Castle Hume (☎ **028/6632-7077**), is 3½ miles (5.6km) north of Enniskillen, with greens fees of £15 ($24.75) weekdays, £20 ($33) weekends.

HORSEBACK RIDING The **Ulster Lakeland Equestrian Centre,** Necarne Castle, Irvinestown (☎ **028/6862-1919**), is an international center that offers full equestrian holidays. Pony trekking and riding lessons are available from **Drumhoney Stables,** Lisnarick (☎ **028/6862-1892**), and **Lakeview Riding Centre,** Leggs, Belleek (☎ **028/6865-8163**).

WALKING The southwestern branch of the **Ulster Way** follows the western shores of Lough Erne, between the lake and the border. The area is full of great walks. One excellent 7-mile (11km, 3- to 7-hr.) hike is from a starting point near Florence Court and the Marble Arch Caves (see "Exploring the Lakelands," above) to the summit of **Mount Cuilagh** (2,188 ft.). A trail map is included in the Northern Ireland Tourist Board's *Information Guide to Walking.*

WATER SPORTS The **Lakeland Canoe Center,** Castle Island, Enniskillen (☎ **028/6632-4250**), is a water-sports center based on an island west of downtown. For a full day of canoeing and other sports, including archery, cycling, dinghy sailing, and windsurfing, prices start roughly at £12 ($19.80) per day. Camping and simple accommodations are also available at a modest cost. The **Share Holiday Village,** Smith's Strand, Lisnaskea (☎ **028/6772-2122**), offers sailing, canoeing, windsurfing, and banana skiing. A single 2½-hour session, including instruction and equipment, costs £5 ($7.45) per person. Other water-sports centers include the **Boa Island Activity Centre,** Tudor Farm, Kesh (☎ **028/6863-1943**); and the **Drumrush Watersports Centre,** Kesh (☎ **028/6863-1035**).

ACCOMMODATIONS
EXPENSIVE

✪ **Castle Leslie.** Glaslough, County Monaghan. ☎ **047/88109.** Fax 047/88256. www.castleleslie.com. 14 units, 4 with shower only. £130–£150 ($214.50–$247.50) double. Rates include full Irish breakfast and service charge. Packages available. MC, V. Drive through the center of Glaslough to castle gates.

What do W. B. Yeats, Winston Churchill, and Mick Jagger have in common? They've all loved Castle Leslie, just across the border in County Monaghan. A stay here is one of Ireland's unique surprises, an experience well worth whatever detour it takes. The 1,000-acre estate, with its three lakes (famous for pike) and ancient hardwood forests, casts a relaxing spell, and the great house—27,000 square feet of history—is as comfortable as an old slipper. Sammy Leslie and her remarkable family and staff provide the quintessential Victorian retreat. This is a place of astounding treasures—the bridle worn by Wellington's horse Copenhagen at Waterloo, Wordsworth's harp, the Bechstein grand on which Wagner composed *Tristan and Isolde,* and Winston Churchill's baby clothes, to mention only a few—all lying about as if they were the most ordinary of family hand-me-downs, which they are. The greatest treasures are the stories you will take away with you. The house, and especially each of its unique guest rooms, is indescribable, so walk through at your own pace on the extensive Web site. Whatever you do, stay more than 1 day, or you'll be kicking yourself all the way to Tipperary, which is a long way. The meals alone (see "Dining," below) are worth the drive. Seven-day golfing holidays, taking in five courses, are available, with equal attention paid to nongolfing companions.

MODERATE

✪ **Manor House Country Hotel.** Killadeas, Irvinestown, Enniskillen, County Fermanagh. ☎ **028/6862-1561.** Fax 028/6862-1545. 46 units. TV TEL. £110 ($181.50) double. Rates include full breakfast. Dinner £23 ($37.95). AE, MC, V.

Dating from 1860, this splendid three-story Victorian mansion has a varied history that includes its use by American forces as a base during World War II. The public areas are full of antiques and ornate plasterwork, and the windows look out to Lough Erne. Rooms are furnished in traditional style, with dark woods, frilly fabrics, and decorative wallpaper; some have four-posters or half-canopy beds, and each has a garment press and tea/coffeemaker. The hotel has an indoor heated swimming pool, as well as a gym, steam room, sauna, tennis court, marina, and beauty salon. It sits on the shores of Lower Lough Erne, 5½ miles (8.9km) north of Enniskillen.

INEXPENSIVE

Belmore Court Motel. Temp Rd., Enniskillen, County Fermanagh. ☎ **028/6632-6633.** Fax 028/6632-6362. www.motel.co.uk. 30 units. TV TEL. £40 ($66) double; £45 ($74.25) double with minikitchen. Continental breakfast £3 ($4.95). AE, MC, V. Free private parking.

One of the newer lodgings in the area, this three-story motel offers a variety of accommodations. Most have kitchenettes, and about a third of the units have two bedrooms or a bedroom and sitting room. All have contemporary furnishings, with light woods, floral fabrics, down comforters, and vanity area/desks, plus tea/coffeemakers. It is on the east edge of town, within walking distance of all the major sights and shops.

SELF-CATERING

Corraquil Luxury Cottages. Teemore, County Fermanagh. Contact RCH at ☎ **028/9024-1100.** Fax 028/9024-1198. www.cottagesinireland.com. 6 cottages. TV. £250–£385 ($412.50–$635.25) per week. Also available for 2- or 3-day stays. Additional charge for heat and electricity. MC, V.

These comfortable traditional cottages, on the banks of the Shannon-Erne Waterway, are ideal for couples or families wanting to take full advantage of the splendid fishing, walking, boating, bird watching, and exploring that the Lakelands offer. The cottages sleep three, four, five, and six. What's more, taking to the waterways could not be more convenient—a small fleet of day cruisers moors just beyond the front yard. You'll find everything you need, including washing machines. All cottages have an open fire as well as central heating.

In addition to these six cottages, Rural Cottage Holidays offers a surprisingly diverse and attractive selection of self-catering cottages, lodges, and estates throughout the Lakelands region.

DINING

✪ **Castle Leslie.** Glaslough, County Monaghan. ☎ **047/88109.** Reservations required. Fixed-price dinner £29.50 ($48.70); à la carte menu available. MC, V. Daily 7–9:30pm. Closed 2 weeks Jan. Drive through the center of Glaslough to castle gates. IRISH/INTERNATIONAL.

Dinner at Castle Leslie (see "Accommodations," above) offers all the relaxed graciousness of a prewar dinner party. The dining rooms in the great house look out on one of the estate's lovely lakes and on ancient hardwood forests. The view alone is a perfect appetizer. Sammy Leslie, trained at a fine Swiss culinary school, is largely responsible for the wizardry in the kitchen. The cuisine is excellent, with a well-chosen wine list. The menu changes to embrace what is freshest and most enticing to the chef; imagine starting with roast goat's-cheese salad with beetroot and hazelnuts, proceeding to honey roast quail, fillet of salmon, or grilled fillet of beef with Madeira sauce, and finishing with white chocolate crème brûlée.

✪ **Franco's.** Queen Elizabeth Rd., Enniskillen, County Fermanagh. ☎ **028/6632-4424.** Reservations not accepted. Dinner main courses £6.95–£18.95 ($11.45–$31.25). AE, MC, V. Daily noon–11pm. IRISH/ITALIAN.

Next to the Butter Market in three converted and restored buildings that were once part of Enniskillen's working waterfront, this restaurant blends old-world ambience and the legacy of the sea with contemporary recipes and fresh local ingredients. Choices might include fillet of beef en croûte, black sole and salmon with sorrel sauce, lobster thermidor, Lough Melvin salmon on a bed of spinach in pastry and saffron sauce, or duck breast in plum sauce. There's a variety of specialty pastas and pizzas too. Wednesday to Sunday, traditional music starts at 9pm.

Saddlers. 66 Belmore St., Enniskillen, County Fermanagh. ☎ **028/6632-6223.** Dinner main courses £5.95–£10.95 ($9.80–$18.05). MC, V. Mon–Sat 5–11pm; Sun 12:30–10pm. INTERNATIONAL.

An equestrian atmosphere prevails at this restaurant over the Horse Show Bar. Barbecued pork ribs, steaks, surf-and-turf, burgers, and mixed grills are the hearty choices, along with local seafood, salads, pizzas, and pastas. The house special is sirloin Sandeman, with bacon, shallots, peppercorns, and port-wine sauce.

ENNISKILLEN AFTER DARK

Many or even most of the pubs and hotels in the area offer live entertainment, especially in the summer and on weekends.

The area's outstanding public house is ✪ **Blakes of the Hollow,** 6 Church St., Enniskillen (☎ **028/6632-2143**). Opened in 1887, the pub has been in the Blake family ever since, retaining its original Victorian decor and ambience, with a long marble-topped mahogany bar and pine-wood alcoves.

Plan an evening at the **Ardhowen Theatre,** Dublin Road, Enniskillen (☎ **028/6632-5440**). Also known as the Theatre by the Lakes because of its enviable position overlooking Upper Lough Erne, this 300-seat theater presents a varied program of concerts, drama, cabarets, jazz, gospel, blues, and other modern music. Tickets run from £3 to £7 ($4.95 to $11.55) for most performances; curtain time is usually 8:30pm.

Appendix: Ireland in Depth

1 Ireland Today

The Irish landscape remains breathtaking, its natural beauty intact, its rivers and lakes still largely pollution free, and its people disarmingly gracious. These are the essential components of Irish tourism, according to a 1995 document issued by Ireland's Department of Foreign Affairs. According to the latest 1999 estimate, they now bring nearly six million visitors to Ireland each year, an ever-growing number that already far surpasses Ireland's population of 3.7 million. Irish hospitality is legendary, and deservedly so.

Included in that hospitality, however, can be a misleading sense of tranquillity, continuity, and cohesion. Like an overgrown family, Ireland is mostly inclined to keep its turmoil to itself and to offer its guests the vacation of their lives, which is what its guests are mostly looking for.

What is easy for any visitor to miss or to underestimate is the depth and pace of the change occurring in Ireland today. Ireland has long been a land of profound conflicts, and never more so than at present. To mention one, *Irish* and *Roman Catholic* are assumed by many to be synonymous. The truth is that they have never meant the same thing, nor made lasting peace with each other. The Roman Catholicism preached by Patrick was transformed as fast as it was embraced by the Celts of Ireland. The Vatican, like the British royalty, found the Irish unruly and bent on taking their own road. For all their faith and devotion, Irish Catholics have never finally decided whether to trust or mistrust their hierarchy, appointed from Rome. Recent public scandals in the Church, followed not by candor but by cover-up, have served only to widen ancient misgivings. The 1996 referendum to permit legal divorce—as well as the decriminalizing of homosexuality and the passing of the abortion information law— all urged and supported by Ireland's first female president, Mary Robinson, point to an Ireland where Rome's iron grip is being pried away a finger at a time.

The Ireland of today, which may present a traditional face to the tourist, is increasingly defined and determined by its youth, whose sheer numbers and unconventional ways are creating a generation gap of seismic proportions. For one thing, they aren't marrying and having children with anything approximating the regularity of their

> *There are no overall certitudes in Ireland any more. There's a lot of diversity of thinking, a lot of uncertainty, a lot of trying to assimilate other cultures. It's a time when we need to take stock, to look into our hearts, and find a sense of Irishness, to find pride in ourselves that will make us sure of what we are.*
> —Mary Robinson, former President of Ireland, during her 1990 presidential campaign

parents. Young people are taking their time before approaching the altar, and taking even longer before starting a family. Although it has since recovered somewhat, the Irish birthrate fell in 1993, for the first time in recorded history, below the minimum population replacement rate of 2.1 children per woman of child-bearing age. This is not to say that the Irish are endangered. What are endangered, however, are the stereotypes visitors might have of them.

Another gap dividing the Irish people is a product of Ireland's sudden and dramatic economic boom. In 1998 the economy ran in the black for the first time in 30 years, and the following year clocked in as the world's fourth-fastest-growing economy, beating out all of its European rivals. In fact, the current growth rate of the Irish economy (over 11%) is more than four times the EU average, and in 2000 Ireland surpassed the United States as the number one exporter of computer software. Nicknamed the Celtic or emerald tiger, Ireland has emerged as Europe's unlikely and unrivaled *wunderkind.* Partly, it's a matter of Ireland's having received more than $16 billion from the European Union over the past dozen years, but it's also a matter of Ireland's own policies and initiatives having paid off. The bottom line is that some people in Ireland are getting very rich, but most only work and watch. The paradoxical situation—wealth accompanied by rising crime, rural poverty, teen violence and suicide, and urban homelessness—is familiar to many nations, but new to Ireland.

Although Ireland today is increasingly prosperous, European, and committed to pluralistic human values, it is at the same time determined to preserve its rich legacy and distinct character. While Irish-speaking and -reading citizens represent a minority of the population, Irish writers, especially poets, continue to create new work. In fact, Ireland has an Irish-language television channel. Helping to fire the renaissance is the fact that the Irish, including some of their most talented artists and writers, are staying or coming home in large numbers. According to a 1999 statistic, net migration to Ireland is at a historic high, with "returnees" accounting for more than half of recent immigration figures.

Finally, it must be said that the cry for peace in and with the North has never been more desperate or determined. The peace process has been turbulent and uncertain, with negotiators hesitant to move forward, yet dreading any return to the chaos that preceded it. The majority of the Irish people, North and South, want peace above all else, but murderous factions on both sides—defying common sense and common decency—simply ignore them. One day a lasting peace will break out, as miraculous and inevitable as springtime, no matter how long and dark the winter has been.

2 History 101

Dateline

- **8000 B.C.** Earliest human immigration to Ireland.
- **3500 B.C.** Farmers and megalithic builders reach Ireland.
- **2000 B.C.** First metalworkers come to Ireland.
- **700 B.C.** Celtic settlement of Ireland begins.
- **A.D. 432** Traditional date of Patrick's return to Ireland.
- **500–800** Ireland's "Golden Age."
- **795** First Viking invasion.
- **841** The Norse build a sea fort on the River Liffey.
- **853** Danes take possession of the Norse settlement.
- **988** Dublin officially recognized as an Irish city.
- **1014** Battle of Clontarf. Brian Boru defeats the Vikings.
- **1167–69** Norman invasion of Ireland.
- **1171** Henry II visits Ireland and claims feudal lordship.
- **1204** Dublin Castle becomes base of British power.
- **1297** First parliamentary sessions in Dublin.
- **1541** Henry III proclaims himself king of Ireland.
- **1534–52** Henry VIII begins suppression of Catholic Church in Ireland.
- **1558–1603** Reign of Elizabeth I. Elizabeth conducts several Irish wars, initiates the "plantation" of Munster, divides Ireland into counties, and in 1591 founds Trinity College, Dublin.
- **1601** Mountjoy defeats combined Spanish and Irish forces at Kinsale.
- **1603** Articles of Confederation introduced. "Plantation" of Ulster commences.
- **1607** The flight of the Irish earls, marking the demise of the old Gaelic order.

continues

The Irish past, like that of every other people, may be divided into two parts: prehistory and history. This is a distinction we make, looking back at them. *History* here means written history: texts, not stories; words, not pictures. *Prehistoric* has a hunched-over, savage ring to it, but that's our problem. People who didn't write about themselves were still people, and they might have had better things to do.

So how do we know about the prehistoric past? Except for some monuments still staring us in the face, prehistoric Ireland has to be dug up like a grave rather than opened up like a book. Indeed, Ireland has richly rewarded the archaeologist's shovel, and the farmer's plow, for that matter. Many treasures have been unearthed by chance in the course of other chores. To be found underfoot or under bog are the remains of houses, forts, tombs, tools, weapons, ornaments—all the whatnots of earlier lives—offering wordless clues to the past. It's said that ancient stones speak. Actually, they mumble at best. It's up to archaeologists and prehistorians, using both science and intuition, to turn those mumblings into a confession.

The first Irish antiquaries, the earliest writings of the Irish about their own past, characterize that past as a series of "invasions" beginning before the deluge and continuing into the present. That, too, is mostly how modern historians tell the story of the Irish past, which I'll retell briefly here.

IRISH PREHISTORY

THE FIRST SETTLERS At the end of its last ice age, around the year 8000 B.C., Ireland warmed up to agreeable, even attractive, temperatures. With some degree of confidence, we can place the date of the first human habitation of the island somewhere between the late 8000s and the early 6000s B.C. Regardless of where in that span the date actually fell, Ireland seems to have been among the last lands in Europe to have felt the human footprint.

Ireland's first colonizers, Mesolithic Homo sapiens, walked, waded, or floated—depending on the status of the early land bridges—across the narrow strait from Britain in search of flint and, of course, food. They found both and stayed on, more or less uneventfully (from our perspective, at least), for a good 4,000 to 5,000 years. Their contribution to the future of Ireland may seem minimal, but most beginnings are. And they did, after all, begin the gene pool.

THE NEOLITHIC AGE The next momentous prehistoric event was the arrival of Neolithic farmers and herders, sometime around 3500 B.C. The Neolithic "revolution" was the first of many to come to Ireland a bit late, at least 5,000 years after its inception in the ancient Near East. The domestication of the human species—settled life, agriculture, animal husbandry—brought with it a radically increased population, enhanced skills, stability, and all the implications of leisure. Unlike Ireland's Mesolithic hunters, who barely left a trace, this second wave of colonizers began at once to transform the island. They came with stone axes fabricated in factories and widely traded, which could fell a good-sized elm in less than an hour. Ireland's hardwood forests, slashed and burned 1 hour at a time, began to recede to make room for tilled fields and pastureland. Villages sprang up, like those discovered and reconstructed at Lough Gur, County Limerick. Larger, more permanent homes, planked with split oak, appeared roughly at this time.

Far more startling, however, is the appearance of massive megalithic monuments, including court cairns, dolmens, passage tombs, and wedge tombs, only a small percentage of which have been excavated. The more than 1,000 megalithic monuments that have been unearthed mumble symphonically about beliefs, cults, and aspirations as profound as any we might imagine. A visit to Newgrange and Knowth in the Boyne Valley and to Carrowmore in County Sligo will both dazzle and deepen anyone's understanding of the human past. It certainly did so for the later Celtic inhabitants of the island, who wondered and told stories about the tremendous stones and mounds raised by what, they assumed, must have been giants—their ancestors, whom they imagined to inhabit them still. They called them the people of the *sí*, who eventually became the *Tuatha Dí Danann*, then the faeries. The once-great and now-little people lived a quite magical life, mostly underground, in the thousands of *raths*, or earthwork structures, coursing the island like giant mole works.

- **1641** Irish Catholic revolt in Ulster led by Sir Phelim O'Neill ends in defeat.
- **1649** Oliver Cromwell invades and begins the reconquest of Ireland.
- **1690** The forces of James II, a Catholic, are defeated at the Battle of the Boyne, assuring British control of Ireland.
- **1691** Patrick Sarsfield surrenders Limerick. He and some 14,000 Irish troops, the "Wild Geese," flee to the Continent.
- **1704** Enactment of first Penal Laws. Apartheid comes to Ireland.
- **1778** The Penal Laws are progressively repealed.
- **1782** The Irish Parliament is granted independence.
- **1791** Wolfe Tone founds the Society of the United Irishmen.
- **1796–97** Wolfe Tone launches an invasion from France, fails, is taken captive, and commits suicide.
- **1798** "The Year of the French." A French invasion force is defeated at Killala Bay. General Humbert surrenders to Cornwallis.
- **1800** The Irish Parliament is induced to dissolve itself.
- **1803** In Dublin, Robert Emmet leads a rising of less than 100 men and is hanged.
- **1829** Daniel O'Connell secures passage of the Catholic Emancipation Act.
- **1841** Daniel O'Connell is named lord mayor of Dublin.
- **1845–48** The Great Famine. Two million Irish die or emigrate.
- **1848** The revolt of the Young Irelanders ends in failure.
- **1858** The Irish Republican Brotherhood, a secret society known as the Fenians, is founded in New York.

continues

- **1867** A Fenian uprising is easily crushed.
- **1879** Michael Davitt founds the National Land League to support the claims of tenant farmers.
- **1879–82** The "land war" forces the enactment of reform. The tenant system unravels; land returns to those who work it.
- **1884** Gaelic Athletic Association is formed to preserve native sports.
- **1886 and 1894** Bills for Home Rule are defeated in Parliament.
- **1893** The Gaelic League is founded to revive the Irish language.
- **1904** Establishment of the Abbey Theatre.
- **1905–08** Founding of Sinn Fein, "we ourselves," with close links to the Irish Republican Brotherhood.
- **1912** Third Home Rule bill passes in the House of Commons and is defeated by the House of Lords.
- **1913** Founding of the Irish Citizens Army.
- **1916** Patrick Pearse and James Connolly lead an armed uprising on Easter Monday to proclaim the Irish Republic. Defeat is followed by the execution of 15 leaders of the revolt.
- **1918** Sinn Fein wins a landslide election victory against the Irish Parliamentary Party.
- **1919** Sinn Fein, led by Eamon de Valera, constitutes itself as the first Irish Dáil and declares independence.
- **1919–21** The Irish War of Independence. Michael Collins commands the Irish forces.
- **1921** Anglo-Irish Treaty. Ireland is partitioned. Twenty-six counties form

continues

In the ensuing millennia of the prehistoric period, the first farmers were followed by others, skilled in prospecting and metallurgy. Bronze implements and ornaments, and some jewelry wrought in gold, were now added to the pots and woven fabrics already being produced on the island. A still later wave of farmers and craftsmen moved their settlements from the edges of lakes to the center, where they constructed artificial islands surrounded by palisades. An example of these curious creations, called *crannógs,* has been reconstructed at the Craggaunowen Project, County Clare. A visit there—as well as to Lough Gur in County Limerick and to the Irish National Heritage Park at Ferrycarrig, County Wexford—would reward anyone interested in learning more about life in prehistoric Ireland. Although the Bronze Age Irish (like the Stone Age Irish who preceded them) left no written records, they did bequeath to their dead, and so to us, works of exquisite beauty. Examples may be seen in the National Museum in Dublin.

THE CELTS The first "invasion" of Ireland that can be traced with historical confidence is that of the Celts, cousins of the *Celtae* who sacked Rome and the *Keltoi* who did the same to Delphi. Indeed, Irish history before the modern period may be sketched in terms of four invasions: those of the Celts, the Vikings, the Normans, and the English. Each left an indelible imprint on the landscape and the psyche of the island. Ireland and the Irish people today are the heirs, culturally and genetically, of their prehistoric and historic invaders.

Of all of Ireland's uninvited guests, the Celts made the greatest impact. They came in waves, the first perhaps as early as the 6th century B.C. and continuing until the end of the millennium. In time, they controlled the island and absorbed into their culture everyone they found there. Their ways and their genes were, in a word, dominant. They brought iron weapons, war chariots, codes of combat and honor, cults and contests, poetic and artistic genius, music and mania, all of which took root and flourished in Irish soil as if they were native plants. The Celts, however, were dismally disorganized in comparison with the kingdoms and empires of Europe. They divided the island among as many as 150 tribes, or *tuatha,* grouped under alliances with allegiance to one of five provincial kings. The provinces of Munster, Leinster, Ulster, and Connaught date from this period. They fought among themselves, fiercely, over cattle (their "currency" and standard of wealth), land, and women. None among them ever achieved high kingship of the island, though not for lack of trying. One of the most impressive monuments from the time of the warring Celtic chiefs is the stone fortress of Dún Aengus on the Aran Islands.

IRISH HISTORY

THE COMING OF CHRISTIANITY The

Celtic powers-that-be neither warmly welcomed nor violently resisted the Christians who, beginning in the 5th century A.D., came ashore and walked the island with a new message. Although threatened to the core, the Celtic kings and bards settled for a bloodless rivalry and made no Christian martyrs.

Not the first, but eventually the most famous, of these Christian newcomers was Patrick, a young Roman citizen torn from his British homeland in a Celtic raid and brought to Ireland as a slave. In time, he escaped slavery but not Ireland, to which he felt called. Ordained a priest and consecrated a bishop, Patrick made his own raid on Ireland and took its people by storm. He abhorred slavery, which he had known firsthand, and he preached it off the island. Within 30 years, the Christian church, like a young forest, was well rooted and spreading in every direction. By the time of his death, around A.D. 461, the Roman Empire was in near collapse while Ireland was on the brink of its golden age.

The truth of Ireland's conversion to Christianity was that it was mutual. The church of Patrick was, like the man who brought it, Roman, something Ireland never was and never would be. Roman Catholicism didn't "take" in Ireland. Instead, it "went native" and became uniquely Celtic. Patrick's eminent successors, Columcille, Bridgit, and Columbanus, were Irish in a way that Patrick could never be—and so was their church. Although orthodox on most points of doctrine, the Irish church was Celtic in structure, tribal and unruly by Roman

the Free State. William Cosgrave becomes the first president. His party, Cumann na nGaedheal, later becomes Fine Gael.

- **1922** The Free State adopts its first constitution.
- **1922–23** The Irish civil war, between the government of the Free State and those who opposed the treaty. Michael Collins is assassinated.
- **1932** Eamon de Valera leads Fianna Fáil to victory and becomes head of government.
- **1932–38** Economic war with Britain brings great hardship.
- **1937** Ireland's 26 counties adopt a new constitution, abandoning membership in British Commonwealth.
- **1938** Douglas Hyde inaugurated as Eire's first president.
- **1939** Dublin is bombed by Germany at start of World War II, but Ireland remains neutral.
- **1948** The Republic of Ireland Act. Ireland severs its last constitutional links with Britain.
- **1955** Ireland is admitted into the United Nations.
- **1959** Eamon de Valera becomes president of Ireland.
- **1963** U.S. President John F. Kennedy visits Dublin.
- **1969** Violence breaks out in Northern Ireland. British troops are called in.
- **1972** In Derry, a peaceful rally turns into "Bloody Sunday." The Northern Irish Parliament is dissolved, and the North is ruled directly from Britain.
- **1973** Ireland joins the European Community.
- **1986** Ireland signs the Anglo-Irish Agreement.
- **1990** Ireland elects Mary Robinson, its first woman president.

continues

- **1992** Ireland approves the European Union.
- **1993** The Joint Declaration on Northern Ireland establishes the principles and framework for a peaceful, democratic resolution of issues regarding the political status of the North.
- **1994** The IRA announces a cease-fire, and the Protestant paramilitaries follow suit. Commencement of peace talks.
- **1995** The British and Irish governments issue "A New Framework for Agreement," and U.S. President Bill Clinton makes a historic visit to Ireland, speaking to large crowds in Belfast and Derry. Received with great enthusiasm in the Republic, he is made a "freeman" of the City of Dublin.
- **1996** The IRA resumes its campaign of violence. New disturbances in the North lead to the worst rioting in 15 years. The cease-fire is over, and the peace process is in tatters.
- **1997** The IRA declares a new cease-fire. On October 7, Sinn Fein enters inclusive all-party peace talks designed to bring about a comprehensive settlement in the North.
- **1998** The all-party peace talks conclude with the Good Friday Agreement, affirmed by all participating parties and strongly supported in referendums held on the same day in the Republic and in the North. The North elects its new assembly. The strength and resolve of the new government, however, is put to a bitter test in July by the standoff at Drumcree and the eruption of violence across the North, culminating in the unspeakable

continues

standards. To Ireland, an island without towns or cities, the Roman system of dioceses and archdioceses was beside the point. Instead, the Irish built monasteries with extended monastic families, each more or less autonomous and regional. The pope, like an Irish high king, was essentially a peer. He had to defend his title with every challenge, like a prizefighter. Besides, the pope reigned in "a place out of mind," a place currently in a shambles.

IRELAND OF THE SAINTED MISSIONARIES Meanwhile, Ireland flourished for several centuries as a land of saints and scholars. Its monasteries were centers of learning and culture—some of the few left in post-Roman Europe—where literacy itself was effectively kept alive through the voluminous and imaginative work of scholars and scribes. Moreover, some of these monasteries—Bridgit's own, for instance—were models of sexual equality, populated by both men and women and sometimes presided over by a woman, a high abbess, who was likely to have a handful of bishops under her jurisdiction.

Not only were monks and scholars drawn to Ireland in great numbers, but they were sent out in great numbers as well, to Britain and the Continent, bearing with them all the otherwise-forgotten knowledge of Europe. As historian Thomas Cahill wrote in his *How the Irish Saved Civilization,* "Wherever they went the Irish brought with them their books, many unseen in Europe for centuries and tied to their waists as signs of triumph, just as Irish heroes had once tied to their waists their enemies' heads." The influence of these monks cannot be underestimated. They went everywhere; it's likely that some of them even reached North America. And they worked with a fervor, so much so that the Irish penned more than half the biblical commentaries written between 650 and 850.

The prime legacy of these monks lies in knowledge perpetuated, but like their megalithic ancestors, they too left some enduring monuments to their profound spirituality. With any imagination, visits to the early monastic sites—Glendalough in County Wicklow, Clonmacnois in County Offaly, and Skellig Michael off the Kerry coast—together with a stop at Trinity College Dublin to see the Book of Kells, will help bring to life Ireland's lost age of splendor.

THE VIKING INVASIONS The monastic city-states of early medieval Ireland died no natural death. After several centuries of dazzling peace, the sea brought new invaders, this time the Vikings. The seagoing berserkers from Scandinavia, in assaulting Ireland's monasteries, went straight for the jugular of Irish civilization. Regardless of their Celtic blood, the monks were not warriors, and the round towers to which they retreated were neither high enough nor strong enough to protect them and their treasures from the Scandinavian pirates. The Vikings knew a soft touch when they saw one and just kept coming, from around 800 into the 10th century. The Vikings knew how to pillage and plunder, but, thankfully, they didn't know how to read. Therefore, they didn't much bother with the books they came across, allowing the monks some means besides their memories of preserving their knowledge and of passing their history down to us.

For better or worse, the Vikings did more than hit and run. They settled as well, securing every major harbor on Ireland's east coast with a fortified town. These were the first towns in Ireland: Dublin, Cork, Waterford, and the river city of Limerick. Eventually, the Irish, though disinclined to unite, did so anyway. This led to decisive Viking defeats by the armies of Brian Boru in 999 and 1014. When the Vikings left, they left their towns behind, forever altering the Irish way of life. The legacy of the Vikings in Ireland is complex, and a visit to Dublin's Wood Quay and the city walls of Waterford may put those interested on the scent.

With the Vikings gone, Ireland enjoyed something of a renaissance in the 11th and 12th centuries. Meanwhile, its towns grew, its regional kings made their bids for high kingship, and its church came under concerted pressure to conform with the Vatican. All of these, in fact, played their part in ripening Ireland for its next invasion. Prosperous and factionalized, Ireland made attractive prey, and it was, tragically, an Irish king who opened the door to the predator. Diarmait Mac Murchada, King of Leinster, whose ambition was to be king of all of Ireland, decided he needed outside help and called on a Welsh Norman, Richard de Clare, better known as Strongbow. Strongbow and his army, in turn, acted on behalf of Henry II of England, who had taken the pious and political precaution of securing a papal blessing for the invasion of

massacre at Omagh. The response across Ireland is horror, accompanied by a resonant appeal for a final end to all sectarian violence. John Hume and David Trimble are awarded the Nobel Peace Prize for their key roles in bringing about this agreement.

- **1999** The implementation of the Good Friday Agreement is blocked by the Unionist demand—"in the spirit" but contrary to the letter of the Good Friday Agreement— that IRA decommissioning precede the appointment of a New Northern Ireland executive. The peace process stalls and threatens to unravel, until late in November the deadlock is broken and the new power-sharing Northern Ireland Executive is established.

- **2000** Less than four months after they were up and running, Peter Mandelson, the Northern Ireland Secretary, suspends the Northern Ireland Executive and Assembly. Direct British rule is restored, and the peace process is in freefall. In spite of this, the British military presence in Northern Ireland continues to diminish, reaching only 14,000, the lowest level since 1970. Then in May, a bold initiative on the part of the Provisional IRA makes possible a return to devolution. On May 29, power is restored to the institutions established by the Belfast Agreement, and the cloud cover over the peace begins to break up.

Catholic Ireland. The accommodating pope was Adrian IV, who must have envisioned not only a more papal Ireland but also a more British one. After all, he was the first and only Briton ever to ascend to the papacy.

THE NORMAN INVASION   In successive expeditions from 1167 to 1169, the Normans crossed the Irish Sea with crushing force. When you see the massive Norman fortifications at Trim, you'll realize the clout the invaders brought with them. In 1171, Henry II of England made a royal visit to what was now one of his domains. Across the next century, the Normans settled in, consolidated their power, developed Irish towns and cities, and grew terribly fond of the island. They became as Irish as the Irish themselves.

In 1314, Scotland's Robert the Bruce defeated the English at Bannockburn and set out to fulfill his dream of a united Celtic kingdom. He installed his brother Edward on the Irish throne, but the constant state of war took a heavy toll. Within 2 years, famine and economic disorder had eroded any public support Edward might have enjoyed. By the time he was defeated and killed at Dundalk in 1317, few were prepared to mourn him. Over the next 2 centuries, attempts to rid Ireland of its Norman overlords were laudable but fell short. Independent Gaelic lords in the north and west continued to maintain their territories. By the close of the 15th century, British control of the island was effectively limited to the Pale, a walled and fortified cordon around what might have been called "greater Dublin." The Normans themselves became more and more Irish and less and less British in their loyalties. Ireland was becoming British in name only.

ENGLISH POWER & THE FLIGHT OF THE EARLS   In the 16th century, under the Tudors, the brutal reconquest of Ireland was set in motion. In mid-century, Henry VIII proclaimed himself king of Ireland, something his predecessors had never done. However, it wasn't until late in the century that the claim was backed up by force. Elizabeth I, Henry's daughter, declared that all Gaelic lords in Ireland must surrender their lands to her, with the altruistic pronouncement that she would immediately regrant them—a proposition met with no great joy, to say the least. The Irish, under Ulster's Hugh O'Neill and Red Hugh O'Donnell, struck out, defeating the Earl of Essex, whom Elizabeth had personally sent to subdue them. In 1600, a massive force commanded by Lord Mountjoy landed and set about subduing the country. By 1603 O'Neill was left with few allies and no option but to surrender, which he did on March 23, the day before Elizabeth died. Had he waited, who knows how history would have differed? As it was, O'Neill had his lands returned, but constant harassment by the English prompted him, along with many of Ireland's other Gaelic lords, to sail for the continent on September 14, 1607, abandoning their lands and their aspirations.

THE COMING OF CROMWELL   By the 1640s, Ireland was effectively an English plantation. Family estates had been seized and foreign (Scottish) labor brought in to work them. The persecution of Catholics, begun with Henry

---

Impressions

The great Gaels of Ireland
Are the men that God made mad,
For all their wars are merry,
And all their songs are sad.

> —G. K. Chesterton, "The Ballad of the White Horse," 1911

VIII's split from Rome, barred them from practicing their faith. Resentment led to uprisings in Ulster and Leinster in 1641, and by early 1642 most of Ireland was again under Irish control. Any hope of extending the victories was destroyed by internal disunion and by the eventual decision to support the Royalist side in the English civil war. In 1648, English King Charles I was beheaded, and the following year the Royalist forces in Ireland were defeated at Rathmines. The stage was set for disaster.

In 1649, Oliver Cromwell arrived in Dublin as commander in chief and lord lieutenant of Ireland, and set about destroying all opposition. One of the most brutal and effective butchers any empire has ever enlisted, Cromwell simply devastated Ireland, which still bears the scars of his savagery. To this day, some Irish spit when they say his name. Cromwell left no doubt about who was in charge. His campaign lasted only 7 months, but his brutal, bloodthirsty methods broke the back of all resistance. In his siege of the town of Drogheda alone, 3,552 Irish were killed, while Cromwell lost only 64 men. After subduing all but Galway and Waterford, Cromwell left Ireland and its administration in the care of his lieutenants and returned to England. His stamp lingered for centuries, and the memory of it still burns.

The Irish were offered a choice after the massacres: Anyone suspected of resisting the English forces could leave the country, give up their lands and resettle in Connaught or County Clare, or die. With this expropriation, the English gained control over most of the country's arable land, and cemented their power.

After the restoration of the British monarchy in 1660, and especially after the succession to the throne of the Catholic King James II in 1685, Irish Catholics began to sense hope in the air. By 1688, Protestant power in the country was seriously diminished, but William of Orange's seizure of the English throne in November of that year reversed the trend. James fled to France to regroup, then sailed to Ireland to launch his counterattack. He struck first at Londonderry, to which he laid siege for 15 weeks before being defeated by William's forces at the Battle of the Boyne. The battle effectively ended James's cause and the last Irish hope of freedom in Ireland. Soon after, the Treaty of Limerick sealed the defeat, and many Irish patriots sailed for America to fight the British Empire in a war that could be won.

THE PENAL LAWS After James's defeat, the boot of English power sat heavier than ever on Ireland's neck. Protestant lords were granted total political power and control of the land, and laws were enacted to effectively impoverish the Catholic population. Catholics could not purchase land; Catholic landholdings were split up unless the family who held them converted; Catholic schools and priests were banned; and Catholics were barred from professions or commissions in the army and were forced to pay a tax to the Anglican church. The laws had an unintended consequence, though. As happens whenever unjust laws are inflicted on a people, they institutionalized civil disobedience and inspired creative sedition.

Meanwhile, the new British lords and landlords of Ireland settled in, sunk their own roots, planted crops, made laws, and sowed their own seed. Inevitably, over time, the "Angles" became the Anglo-Irish. Hyphenated or not, they were Irish, and their loyalties were increasingly unpredictable. Colonialism only works effectively for one generation, after all—the very next generation is native to the new country, not the old. As this process played out in Ireland, history settled into one of its periodic states of inactivity, and little of note transpired. Prosperity remained on the Protestant side of the fence, and deprivation on the Catholic side. The Penal Laws remained in effect for a century. The first were relaxed in 1770, and the bulk of them repealed with England's 1783 acknowledgment of the Irish Parliament's right, along with the king, to determine the laws by which Ireland should be governed.

WOLFE TONE, THE UNITED IRISHMEN & THE 1798 REBELLION

England's difficulty is Ireland's opportunity, or so the saying goes, so when war broke out between the British and French in the 1790s, the United Irishmen—a nonviolent society formed to lobby for admission of Catholic and landless Irishmen to the Irish parliament—went underground to try to persuade the French to intervene on Ireland's behalf against the British. Their emissary in this venture was a Dublin lawyer named Wolfe Tone. In 1796, Tone sailed with a French invasion force bound for Ireland, but was turned back by storms.

Come 1798, Ireland was embroiled in insurrection. Wexford and Ulster teetered, with the United Irishmen proving to have united not enough of their countrymen to mount a credible, sustainable campaign. The nadir of the rebellion came when Wolfe Tone, having raised another French invasion force, sailed into Lough Swilley in Donegal and was promptly captured by the British. At his trial, wearing a French uniform, Tone requested that he be shot. When the request was refused, he slit his own throat. The rebellion was over. In the space of 3 weeks, more than 30,000 Irish had been killed. In the aftermath of "The Year of the French," as it came to be known, the British induced the Irish parliament to dissolve itself, and Ireland reverted to strict British rule.

DANIEL O'CONNELL In 1828, a Catholic lawyer named Daniel O'Connell, who had earlier formed the Catholic Association to represent the interests of tenant farmers, was elected to the British parliament to represent Ireland. Public opinion was so solidly behind him that he was able to persuade the Duke of Wellington, Britain's prime minister, that the only way to avoid an Irish civil war was to force the Catholic Emancipation Act through parliament. Once this was secured, O'Connell accepted the position as Ireland's MP (Member of Parliament). For 12 years he served in the post, winning concessions and fighting against unpopular leftovers of the Penal Laws. In 1841 he left parliament and was elected lord mayor of Dublin, and began his push for repeal of the Irish-British union imposed after the 1798 rebellion. Toward this end, he organized enormous meetings that often reached the hundreds of thousands, but succeeded in provoking an unresponsive conservative government to such an extent that it eventually arrested O'Connell on charges of seditious conspiracy. The charges were dropped, but the incident—coupled with dissension among the Irish, criticism by a group known as the Young Irelanders, and distress from the incipient famine—led to the breaking of his power base. "The Liberator," as he had been known, faded, his health failed, and he eventually died on a trip to Rome. The Young Irelanders, led by "Meagher of the Sword," went on to stage a pathetic revolt in 1848. The English authorities easily put it down.

THE GREAT HUNGER As the efforts of Ireland's hoped-for liberators failed, the Irish were faced with something they could barely imagine: a worse state of affairs.

In the years 1845 through 1848, famine struck. The majority of Ireland owned by the Irish was harsh, difficult land, unsuitable for most farming. For this reason the Irish had come to depend on the potato, one of the hardiest of crops, as the staple of their diet. When blight struck, they were left with nothing to keep body and soul together.

It has often been said that colonialism can succeed only when it's paired with genocide, and in the "Great Hunger," as it's called, that collusion nearly came to pass. Whether the famine was an act of God, the British, or bad farming practices on the part of the Irish peasantry remains unresolved. The fact stands that it claimed a million Irish lives and dispatched another million to the sea on death ships, most pointed toward the United States. Those who remained faced only continued hardship, and in the years ahead emigration reached flood level. Within a century, the population of Ireland was less than half of what it had been in 1841.

THE STRUGGLE FOR HOME RULE   Fewer Irish did not mean more manageable Irish, however. On multiple fronts, violent and nonviolent, the Irish people kept up the pressure on Britain. They won some partial concessions, but gratitude was minimal. The return of selected stolen goods appears generous only to thieves. What the Irish wanted back was Ireland, intact: land, religion, language, and law. In the 1870s and 1880s, Ireland's Member of Parliament, Charles Stewart Parnell, was able to unite various factions of Irish nationalists, including the Fenian Brotherhood in America and the Land League, to fight for home rule. In a tumultuous decade of legislation, he came close, but revelations about his long affair with Kitty O'Shea, wife of a former follower, brought about his downfall, and an end to the legislative quest for home rule.

THE EASTER REBELLION & THE WAR OF INDEPENDENCE Coming close counts for nothing in revolution, and near-misses on the negotiated front opened the way to violence. The 1912 defeat of the third Home Rule Bill in the House of Lords, after it had passed in the House of Commons, was followed in 1913 by the founding of the Irish Citizens Army and the Irish Volunteers. Revolution was imminent. The motive had been there for centuries, the ability was in development, and the opportunity was around the corner. In 1916, the Irish celebrated Easter, the feast of the Resurrection, in unique fashion.

On Easter Monday 1916, the Irish tricolor flag was raised over the General Post Office in the heart of Dublin. Inside were 1,500 fighters, led by the Gaelic League's Patrick Pearse and Socialist leader James Connolly. Pearse read the newly written Proclamation of the Irish Republic, and his men fought off the British for 6 days before being captured. Pearse, Connolly, and 12 other leaders were imprisoned, secretly tried, and speedily executed.

In looking back over Irish history for those turning points that cumulatively led to the violence of 1916, the War of Independence, and the Irish civil war, William Butler Yeats wrote of four bells that tolled for Ireland. One sounded at each of its irreversibly decisive moments: the Flight of the Earls, the Battle of the Boyne, the spread of French revolutionary ideas under the United Irishmen, and the fall of Parnell. However it is that we trace the path to violence, the 1916 rising, compounded by the savage stupidity of the British response, all but guaranteed that Ireland's future would be decided by the gun. Like the religious faith the people had strained for centuries to preserve, the Irish faith in revolution was seeded and nourished by the blood of martyrs—martyrs the British had been fools enough to provide.

The last straw for the British was Sinn Fein's landslide victory in the general election of 1918 and its subsequent proclamation of the first Dáil, or independent parliament. The declaration of independence issued 2 years earlier from the General Post Office now seemed a good deal more real. When the British attempted to smash the new parliament, the result was the War of

Independence, in which the Irish forces, led by Michael Collins, eventually forced the British to the negotiating table.

The Anglo-Irish Treaty of 1921 gave independence to only 26 of 32 Irish counties. The fate of the remaining six counties in Ulster was yet to be decided. Meanwhile, they would remain within the United Kingdom. Some of the Irish, weary of war, accepted compromise as close enough to victory and embraced the Free State of Ireland. Others, led by Eamon de Valera, shouted betrayal and declared the Free State their latest enemy. The ensuing civil war claimed many casualties, including Michael Collins and Cathal Brugha, two of the revolution's shining heroes.

Victory—if civil wars have winners—went to de Valera and those who opposed the treaty. They did not overturn it, though, and their successors have yet to do so. Instead, they reformed the government and led the new Free State of Ireland out of the ravages of war and into the rigors of peace. The Free State, in passing the Republic of Ireland Act in 1948, severed its last constitutional ties to Britain. Only 25 years later did it join the European Community, pursuing its ties to Europe where the Irish people had for centuries looked for friendship and support.

Ireland was the first colony acquired by the British Empire and nearly the last to be relinquished, but regrettably, this story still has no proper ending. The "troubles" spawned by the partitioning of Ireland in 1921 have lived on to the end of the century, a wound that until very recently has shown little promise of healing. There remain two Irelands, fewer than there have been in the past and yet, for some, still one too many.

3 Some Movers & Shapers of Ireland's 20th Century

SAMUEL BECKETT (1906–89)   Playwright and novelist, Beckett is one of four Irish winners of the Nobel Prize for Literature (1969). A native of Dublin, he taught French at Trinity College, Dublin. In 1938, he moved to France, where he served as a secretary to James Joyce, became involved with the Resistance, worked with the Irish Red Cross, and wrote. His most performed drama, *Waiting for Godot* (1952), remains one of the definitive plays of the 20th century. Beckett's brilliance was minimalist in style, paring words and gesture to the bone, creating more with less.

BRENDAN BEHAN (1923–64)   Playwright, travel writer, journalist, IRA activist, and raconteur, Behan is remembered for his boisterous ways as well as for his writings. His best works include his autobiography, *Borstal Boy* (1958), and the plays *The Quare Fellow* (1954) and *The Hostage* (1958), first written in Irish. The streets of his native Dublin are the setting for many of his works.

MICHAEL COLLINS (1890–1922)   Michael Collins was born and raised in West Cork, the son of a farmer. At age 15 he emigrated to London, where he joined Sinn Fein, the Irish Republican Brotherhood (IRB), and in 1914 the Irish Volunteers. Two years later, he returned to Ireland to avoid British conscription. Within several months, at age 26, Collins found himself in the General Post Office fighting a losing revolution, and subsequently returned to Britain in irons. Before the year was out, however, he was back in Dublin, on the supreme council of the IRB. In the war for independence, Collins was the legendary commander-in-chief of the IRA, everywhere and nowhere, striking and eluding the British like a phantom. Having brought the British to the negotiating table, he accepted the division of Ireland with great reluctance,

❓ Did You Know?

- The Irish per capita consumption of poetry surpasses that of any other English-speaking country. Not surprisingly, they also produce their fair share.

- For certain scenic areas in Ireland, mobile phone "masts," as they're known, have been designed in the shape of trees, to minimize the visual blight on the Irish landscape caused by the cellular revolution.

- On Irish coins, "heads" refers to the side bearing the harp, the national emblem. "Tails" is the side once occupied by the British monarchs, now replaced by animals, such as the cow, horse, and rooster.

- Katherine Kelly, one of Ireland's authenticated little people, was 34 inches tall and weighed 28 pounds when she died in 1735.

- The newt (*Triturus vulgaris*) is Ireland's only indigenous reptile.

- Robert Emmet is said to have been able to rattle off the English alphabet backward without taking a breath. This was not how or why he died.

- Little John, Robin Hood's "main man," met his end not in Sherwood Forest, but in Arbour Hill in Dublin, where he was hanged.

- Under Cromwell, it became law that the same bounty was offered for the head of a wolf and the head of a priest—£5.

- The longest formal debate on record anywhere in the world was conducted at University College Galway in 1995. The motion debated—for 28 days—read as follows: "This house has all the time in the world."

- In January 1997, the Irish government granted its first-ever divorce. The recipient was a terminally ill man, long separated from his wife, who sought to marry his current partner before he died. They did marry, and he died shortly afterward.

- When the Censorship of Films Act was passed in 1923, the first appointed censor was James Montgomery, who confessed to knowing little to nothing about films. He was quite clear, however, about his job, which, in his own words, was "to prevent the Californication of Ireland."

- In 2000, Ireland was ranked seventh among the world's most competitive nations, edging ahead of Germany, Britain, and Japan, and so giving new meaning to "the fighting Irish."

hoping to avoid further bloodshed and judging it to be the best deal the Irish would get. He knew and said, at the same time, that the treaty would prove to be his death warrant. He was right. On August 22, 5 days before he would have turned 31, he was ambushed and assassinated. In 1996, director Neil Jordan put his story on film, with Liam Neeson in the title role.

JAMES CONNOLLY (1868–1913) Born of poor Irish Catholic parents in Edinburgh, Connolly worked from age 11, and at 14 falsified his age to enlist in the British army. After being posted in Dublin, he deserted and returned to Scotland. He eventually made his way back to Ireland, where he founded the Irish Socialist Republican Party. Unable to support a family in Dublin, Connolly emigrated to America, where he was active in launching the

Industrial Workers of the World and founded the Irish Socialist Federation in New York City. Several years later, however, he was back at it in Ireland, closing the port of Dublin to bring about the release of James "Big Jim" Larkin (see below). In 1916, Connolly was appointed commandant-general of the Dublin forces and led the assault on the General Post Office. Wounded and unable to stand for his own execution, he was strapped to a chair when brought before the Kilmainham firing squad.

EAMON DE VALERA (1882–1975)   The Irish nationalist politician was born in New York of an Irish mother and a Spanish father. When his father died in 1885, de Valera's mother sent the boy to Ireland, and his grandmother raised him in County Limerick. He joined the Irish Volunteers in 1913 and commanded the Boland's Mills garrison in the 1916 Easter Rising, for which he received the death sentence. It was eventually commuted on account of his American citizenship. After fiercely opposing the Anglo-Irish Treaty and serving with the IRA in the Irish civil war, de Valera formed Fianna Fáil. He went on to become the first president of Dáil Eireann, the Irish Parliament, and the first Taoiseach (prime minister). From 1959 to 1973, he served as president of the Republic.

MAUD GONNE (1865–1953)   Born in England and educated on the French Riviera, Gonne spent several years in Ireland when her father, a colonel in the British army, was posted to Dublin Castle. Moved by the Irish cause, she pledged herself to the struggle. Although she turned down a proposal of marriage from W. B. Yeats, Gonne founded with him the Association Irlandaise in Paris and later played the title role in his momentous production of *Cathleen ní Houlihan*. She was a member of the secret Irish Republican Brotherhood and later established two organizations: *Inghinidhe Na héireann* (Daughters of Ireland) and the Women's Prisoner's Defense League. Imprisoned in 1923, she was released after beginning a hunger strike. Maud Gonne has been called Ireland's Joan of Arc.

SEAMUS HEANEY (b. 1938)   Born and educated in Derry, this celebrated contemporary poet has been called Ireland's Robert Frost and, perhaps more appropriately, a latter-day Yeats. Heaney's poems about his homeland in the North of Ireland appear in his collections *North* (1975), *Field Work* (1979), *Station Island* (1984), and *Seeing Things* (1991). In 1995 he was awarded the Nobel Prize for Literature, the fourth Irishman to be so honored.

JOHN HUME (b. 1937)   Nicknamed "St. John" for reasons apparent to anyone who considers his life, John Hume might be said to be the Martin Luther King of Northern Ireland. An ex-seminarian and former schoolteacher from Derry, Hume emerged in the 1960s as a leading figure in the North's Civil Rights Movement. He went on to commit his life to envisioning and securing equality and peace in the North. As a co-founder and head of the Social Democratic and Labour Party, and as the voice of conscience and creative nonviolence, Hume more than any other figure in the North has brought his homeland to the brink of a lasting peace. This was duly recognized in 1998, when he was awarded the Nobel Peace Prize. True to his nickname, in the spring of 1999, John Hume announced that he was donating his £300,000 Nobel award to the poor and to victims of violence in the North. It will be distributed impartially to those on either side of the divide that he has given his life's energies to bridging and eventually dissolving. Most deservedly, on May 1, 2000, John Hume was awarded "The Freedom of the City of Derry," making him only the 40th recipient of that honor in the history of the city.

JAMES JOYCE (1882–1941)   Born in Dublin, Joyce left the city at age 22 and spent most of his life abroad. Even so, he used Dublin as the setting for all his writings, including his masterwork, *Ulysses* (1922). Joyce's other writings include *Portrait of the Artist as a Young Man* (1916), *Dubliners* (1914), and *Finnegan's Wake* (1938). Although his imaginative stream-of-consciousness works were banned in Ireland (for indecency) when they were first published, he eventually gained his own people's recognition as a great 20th-century novelist.

JAMES LARKIN (1876–1947)   James Larkin, born into an impoverished Irish emigrant family in Liverpool, spent his first 8 years with his grandparents in County Down. At the age of 9, he returned to Liverpool and went to work. Larkin, a dockworker, eventually rose to foreman, but lost his job and became a union organizer after he supported his fellow workers in a strike. He became notorious for his militancy and eloquence. In Dublin in 1909, "Big Jim" founded the Irish Transport and General Workers' Union and served as its general secretary. In and out of prison in Ireland, he sailed to America to raise money for the struggle and wound up serving nearly 3 years in Sing Sing for "criminal anarchy." Returning to Ireland, he founded the Irish Workers' League, became a Dublin city councilor, and served in the Dáil (parliament) from 1937 to 1938 and 1943 to 1944.

SEAN O'CASEY (1880–1964)   Born into poverty as John Casey in Dublin, the Abbey Theatre playwright based three of his greatest works on his early life in Dublin tenements: *The Shadow of a Gunman* (1923), *Juno and the Paycock* (1924), and *The Plough and the Stars* (1926).

FRANK O'CONNOR (1882–1941)   Michael O'Donovan's mother, to whom he was greatly devoted, was an O'Connor, and as a writer he took her name. His father was a laborer and had served as a bandsman in the British Army. In his teens, O'Connor worked as a railway clerk and volunteered for the IRA. Later, in the civil war, he fought against the treaty and was imprisoned at age 20. After his release from prison, he became a librarian and began to publish the stories that would soon make him famous. In 1935 he directed the Abbey Theatre, a position he resigned from several years later. Throughout his life, O'Connor's voice and pen gave expression to a balance of wit, poignancy, integrity, and severe criticism, which made him both a delight and a challenge to his readers.

PATRICK PEARSE (1879–1916)   Trained as a lawyer in Dublin, Pearse was an educator and poet who worked, fought, and died in the cause of Irish freedom. As commander-in-chief of the Irish Republican Brotherhood and the Irish Volunteers, he led the 1916 Easter Rising, proclaimed the birth of the Irish Republic, and accepted unconditional surrender 5 days later. He was

Impressions

[Irish] has now gone underground. It is, so to speak, being forgotten consciously. It nevertheless beats like a great earth-throb in the subconsciousness of the race. The Irish language is thus become the runic language of modern Ireland. Even though only a dwindling few think overtly in it all of us can, through it, touch, however dimly, a buried part of ourselves of which we are normally unaware. Through Gaelic we remember ancestrally—are again made very old and very young.

—Sean O'Faolain (1900–91), The Irish

Not Just Boiled Potatoes Anymore

In the past 25 years, Irish cuisine has undergone a major makeover. Ireland once enjoyed a singular reputation for overcooked meats, waterlogged vegetables, piles of potatoes, and cream-on-cream desserts. Recently, however, healthful preparation and appealing presentation of fresh natural ingredients have become the norm, or at least the measure of success.

The transformation of Irish cuisine did not start from scratch. The raw materials had always been there—beef and lamb nurtured on Irish pastures, an abundance of freshwater fish and ocean seafood, a bounty of produce, and dairy goods straight from the local creamery. It seems that travel inspired Irish chefs to take the next step. Abroad, they learned the arts of French and Californian cuisine. At the same time, visitors came to Ireland in greater numbers and requested crisper, more recognizable vegetables and a wider selection of seafood. In kitchens from Dublin to Donegal, the "new Irish cuisine" now reigns. To prove it, Irish chefs regularly bring home dozens of gold medals from the International Food Olympics.

A note of caution: Although a new standard has been set, it is still quite common to find vegetables boiled into oblivion, and the once-rampant white sauce is far from endangered or extinct.

---

executed by a firing squad in Kilmainham Jail. His poems, such as "The Rebel" and "The Mother," found together in *Collected Works* (1917), have brought him further acclaim in recent years.

GEORGE BERNARD SHAW (1856–1950)   Author of *Man and Superman* (1903), *Major Barbara* (1905), *Pygmalion* (1912), *Candida* (1903), and *St. Joan* (1923), Shaw won the Nobel Prize for Literature in 1926. Although he left school at age 15, Shaw spent a great deal of time at the National Gallery in Dublin and later credited the institution with providing the best part of his early education. He bequeathed it one-third of his royalties. His birthplace, at 33 Synge St., is a museum in his honor.

JOHN MILLINGTON SYNGE (1871–1909)   Noted Abbey Theatre playwright and one of the founders of the Irish Literary Revival, Synge was born in Dublin but is best remembered for plays that reflect rural life in western Ireland. They include *The Shadow of the Glen* (1903), *Riders to the Sea* (1904), and *Playboy of the Western World* (1907).

JACK BUTLER YEATS (1871–1957)   Like that of his older brother the poet, Jack Yeats's imagination was profoundly influenced by the west of Ireland, specifically Sligo, where he spent much of his childhood. After studying art in London and settling in Devon, Yeats returned to Ireland in 1910. After illustrating works at the heart of the Irish Literary Revival, he began to establish an international reputation as a painter in oils. Yeats wrote a number of books, including memoirs, novels, and plays, but they garnered less recognition than his drawings and paintings.

WILLIAM BUTLER YEATS (1865–1939)   Poet and dramatist, Yeats was also a founding member of the Abbey Theatre. His poems and plays, which deal with mystic and Celtic legendary themes, won him the Nobel Prize for Literature in 1923. Yeats served in the Irish Senate but rejected a knighthood in 1915. He was born in Dublin and summered in the West, particularly in Sligo, where he is buried.

4 Language

Ireland has two official languages, Irish and English. Today, English is the first and most commonly spoken language for the vast majority of the Irish people, although Irish instruction is compulsory in the public schools. Every public school teacher must pass a proficiency examination in Irish in order to be certified. All Irish citizens are entitled by law to conduct any official business with the state (legal proceedings, university interviews, and filing taxes, for example) in the Irish language. According to a 1996 census, the Irish-speaking population of the Gaeltacht, in those scattered regions of the country where Irish is the first and, in some cases, only language spoken, was over 61,000. Irish speakers, however, are not confined to the Gaeltacht. Dublin, for instance, has a significant number of Irish-speaking individuals and families.

Irish, a Celtic language, belongs to the same Indo-European family as most European tongues. Modern Irish descends from Old Irish, the language of Ireland's Golden Age and the earliest variant of the Celtic languages. While the Irish-speaking population of Ireland was reckoned at four million in 1835, it stands now at slightly over a third of that figure. Even so, poets and playwrights continue to write in Ireland's mother tongue, and Irish programming holds its own on television and radio.

5 The Arts

VISUAL ARTS

Three-dimensional, geometric figures etched into prehistoric granite slabs and burial tombs in the Irish countryside are the earliest specimens of Irish art. The 6th century saw delicate enamel work and manuscript illumination produced at monasteries. The Tara Brooch, the Ardagh Chalice, the Cross of Cong, and the recently restored Derrynaflan chalice and paten are just some of the early Irish artistic gems displayed in the National Museum.

Without question, the **Book of Kells,** on view at Trinity College Dublin, is Ireland's greatest treasure. Dating from the late 8th or early 9th century, the Book of Kells (a rendering of the Gospels) predates the monastery of Kells in County Meath, where it was found. It may have been produced on the island of Iona.

The decorative arts flourished in Ireland in the 17th and 18th centuries. Exquisite silverware, plasterwork, cut glass, hand-carved furniture, and tapestries filled the great Georgian and Palladian-style homes built for the gentry who settled in Ireland from Great Britain.

The lush Irish countryside, with its varied colors and ever-changing skies, lends itself wonderfully to landscape painting. Among Ireland's great artists of this genre were James Arthur O'Connor and Paul Henry; the latter studied at Whistler's studio in Paris before settling down to paint in Connemara. Contemporary artists Brian Bourke and Camille Souter take a postmodern approach to landscapes. Patrick Hickey and Pauline Bewick are acclaimed for their distinctive graphic arts. North and South, Ireland boasts more than 100 art galleries. In Dublin, no fewer than 50 galleries are found, and more seem to spring up each day. The relatively new Irish Museum of Modern Art also showcases contemporary creativity.

ARCHITECTURE

The fortification walls surviving at least in part around many Irish towns and cities can be credited to the Normans, who also built great churches and

Some people don't like the Irish, but we're very popular among ourselves.
—Brendan Behan (1923–64)

cathedrals but are best remembered for their **castles.** Many Norman castles are still occupied today. Others recline, moss-covered, more or less as ruins, some with rectangular keeps, lichened towers, and timeworn turrets making mute gestures into the empty air above.

The British left their own unique architectural legacy, from the Georgian avenues, squares, and public buildings of Dublin, Limerick, and Armagh to the sprawling "big houses" of the countryside. Built by the Anglo-Irish aristocracy and absentee landlords, these **manor homes** date from the 17th and 18th centuries and reflect a spirit of "spare no expense." More than 40 of these great houses, originally occupied by the rich and powerful, are open to the public as museums. Others have been converted into hotels.

Also dotting the rural landscape are simple whitewashed, **thatched-roof stone cottages.** They're traditionally the homes of farming people, many of whom have traded in their cottages for modern bungalows and two-story stucco homes.

Modern Irish architecture tends toward glass-and-concrete construction, but many newer buildings are designed to blend harmoniously with nearby Georgian, Edwardian, and Victorian landmarks. In recent years, the work of contemporary Irish architects has gained increasing international notice and praise.

For an intriguing professional survey of contemporary architectural projects, real and virtual, throughout Ireland, visit www.archeire.com on the Web. Be sure to click on "Architectural Dublin," named Ireland's best noncommercial Web site in 1997, where you will find a historical introduction to Dublin architecture, from the earliest structures to the latest demolitions.

Index

Index

Index